the book of **books**

500 years of graphic innovation

the book of **books**

500 years of graphic innovation

Edited by Mathieu Lommen

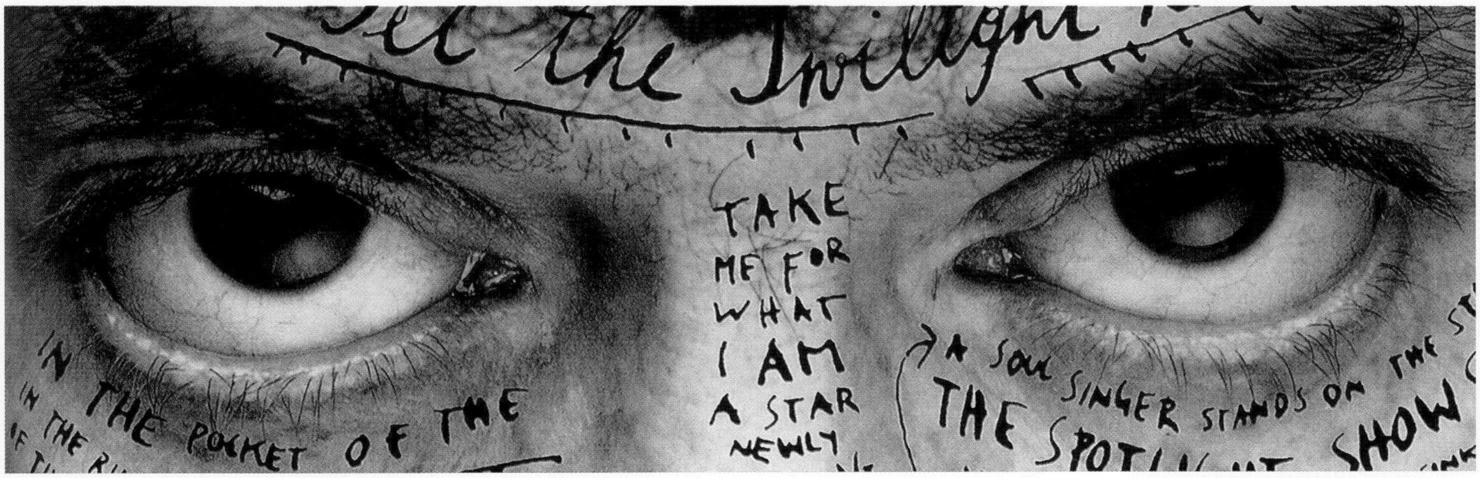

Thames & Hudson

Page 1: detail of *La fin du monde filmée par l'ange N.-D.*, designed by Fernard Léger (see p. 308)
Page 3: detail of *Sagmeister: Made You Look,* designed by Stefan Sagmeister (see p. 440)
Page 7: detail of *Mechanick Exercises*, printed by Joseph Moxon (see p. 168).

First published in the United Kingdom in 2012
by Thames & Hudson Ltd, 181A High Holborn,
London WC1V 7QX

www.thamesandhudson.com

First published in 2012 in hardcover in the
United States of America by Thames & Hudson Inc.,
500 Fifth Avenue, New York, New York 10110

thamesandhudsonusa.com

British Library Cataloguing-in-Publication Data
A catalogue record for this book is available from
the British Library

Library of Congress Catalog Card Number
2011922566

ISBN 978-0-500-51591-4

Printed in the Netherlands

Contents

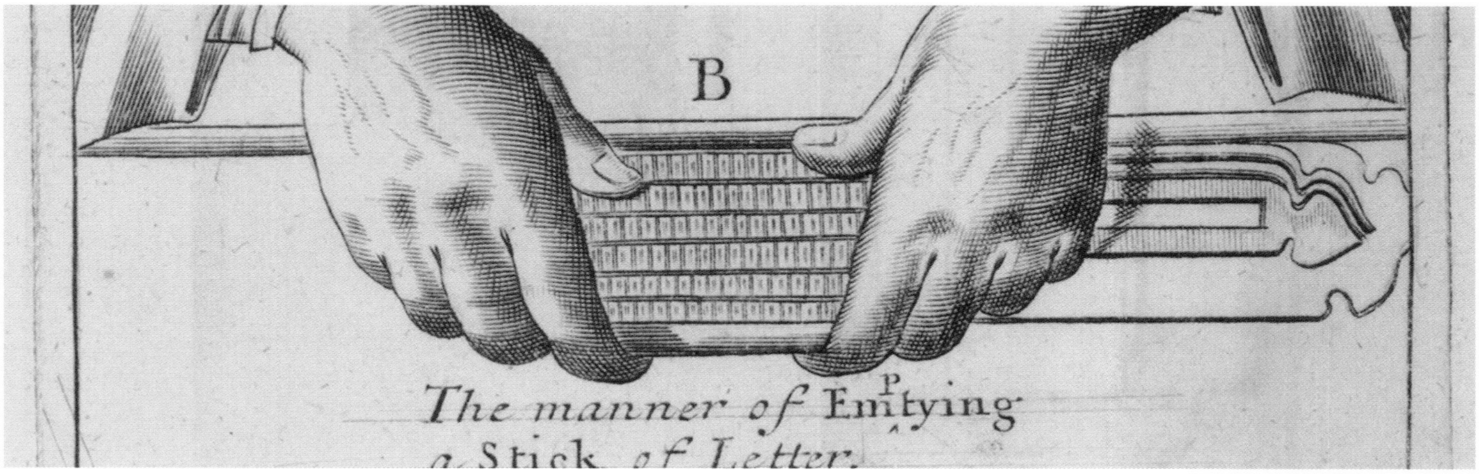
B
The manner of Emptying
a Stick of Letter.

Introduction

The Gutenberg Bible, printed *c.* 1455. Berlin State Library: Preussischer Kulturbesitz.

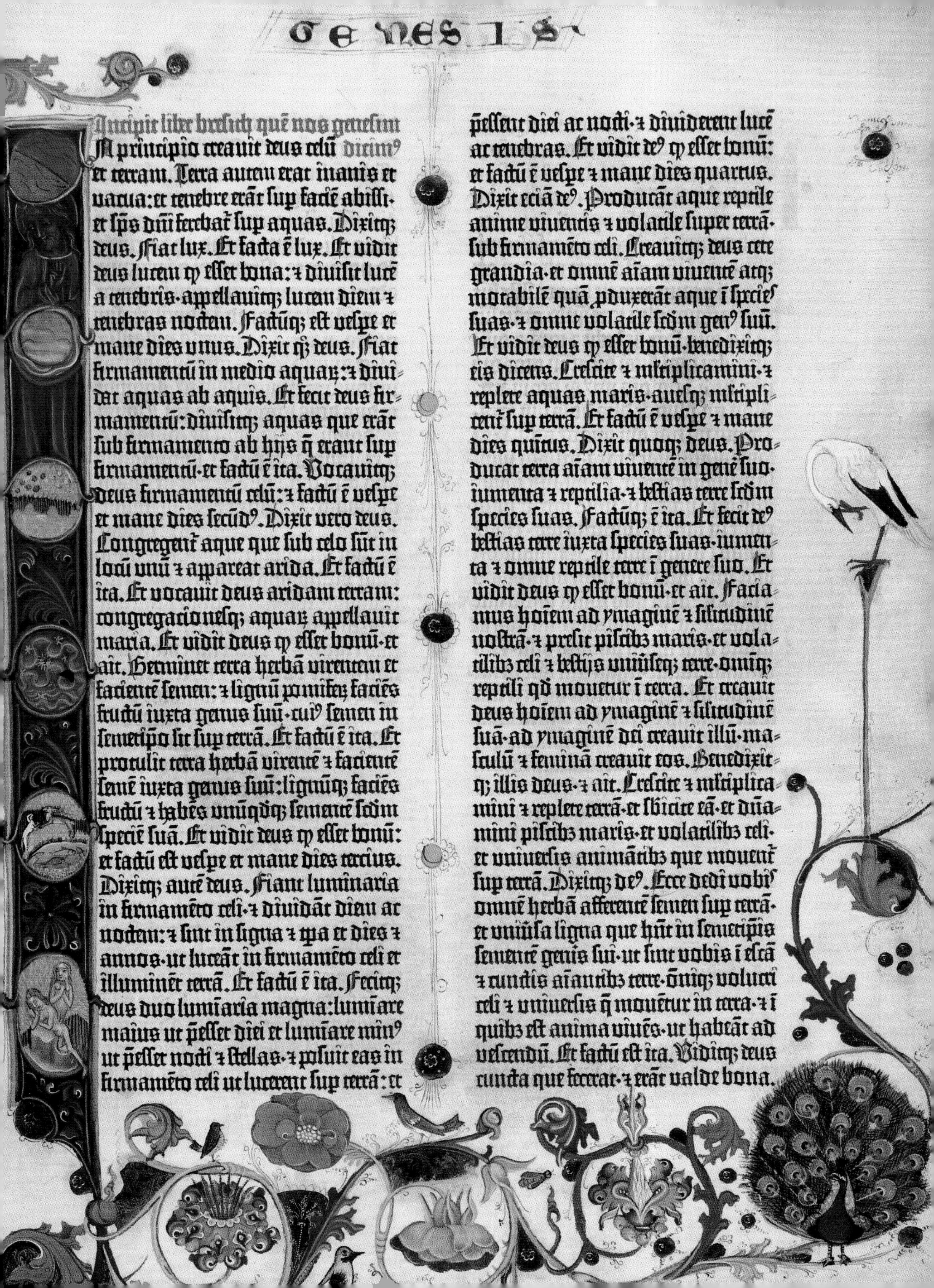

Incipit liber bresith quē nos genesim
In principio creauit deus celū dicim⁹
et terram. Terra autem erat inanis et
vacua: et tenebre erāt sup faciē abissi:
et spūs dñi ferebat̃ sup aquas. Dixitq;
deus. Fiat lux. Et facta ē lux. Et vidit
deus lucem q̄ esset bona: ⁊ diuisit lucē
a tenebris. appellauitq; lucem diem ⁊
tenebras noctem. Factūq; est vespe et
mane dies vnus. Dixit q; deus. Fiat
firmamentū in medio aquaꝝ: ⁊ diuidat aquas ab aquis. Et fecit deus firmamentū: diuisitq; aquas que erāt
sub firmamento ab hijs q̄ erant sup
firmamentū. et factū ē ita. Vocauitq;
deus firmamentū celū: ⁊ factū ē vespe
et mane dies secūd⁹. Dixit vero deus.
Congregent̃ aque que sub celo sūt in
locū vnū ⁊ appareat arida. Et factū ē
ita. Et vocauit deus aridam terram:
congregacionesq; aquaꝝ appellauit
maria. Et vidit deus q̄ esset bonū. et
ait. Germinet terra herbā virentem et
facientē semen: ⁊ lignū pomiferꝝ faciēs
fructū iuxta genus suū. cui⁹ semen in
semetipo sit sup terrā. Et factū ē ita. Et
protulit terra herbā virentē ⁊ facientē
semē iuxta genus suū: lignūq; faciēs
fructū ⁊ hābēs vnūqdq; sementē scdm
speciē suā. Et vidit deus q̄ esset bonū:
et factū est vespe et mane dies tercius.
Dixitq; autē deus. Fiant luminaria
in firmamēto celi. ⁊ diuidāt diem ac
noctem: ⁊ sint in signa ⁊ tpa et dies ⁊
annos. ut luceāt in firmamēto celi et
illuminēt terrā. Et factū ē ita. Fecitq;
deus duo lumīaria magna: lumīare
maius ut p̄esset diei et lumiare min⁹
ut p̄esset nocti ⁊ stellas. ⁊ posuit eas in
firmamēto celi ut lucerent sup terrā: et
p̄essent diei ac nocti. ⁊ diuiderent lucē
ac tenebras. Et vidit de⁹ q̄ esset bonū:
et factū ē vespe ⁊ mane dies quartus.
Dixit eciā de⁹. Producāt aque reptile
anime viuentis ⁊ volatile super terrā.
sub firmamēto celi. Creauitq; deus cete
grandia. et omnē aīam viuentē atq;
motabilē quā pduxerāt aque ī species
suas. ⁊ omne volatile scdm gen⁹ suū.
Et vidit deus q̄ esset bonū. benedixitq;
eis dicens. Crescite ⁊ mltiplicamini. ⁊
replete aquas maris. auesq; mltipli-
cent̃ sup terrā. Et factū ē vespe ⁊ mane
dies quītus. Dixit quoq; deus. Pro-
ducat terra aīam viuentē in genē suo.
iumenta ⁊ reptilia. ⁊ bestias terre scdm
species suas. Factūq; ē ita. Et fecit de⁹
bestias terre iuxta species suas. iumenta ⁊ omne reptile terre ī genere suo. Et
vidit deus q̄ esset bonū. et ait. Faciamus hoīem ad ymaginē ⁊ siltudinē
nostrā. ⁊ presit piscibꝫ maris. et volatilibꝫ celi ⁊ bestijs vniūsesq; terre. omiq;
reptili qd mouetur ī terra. Et creauit
deus hoīem ad ymaginē ⁊ siltudinē
suā. ad ymaginē dei creauit illū. masculū ⁊ feminā creauit eos. Benedixit-
q; illis deus. ⁊ ait. Crescite ⁊ mltiplicamini ⁊ replete terrā. et sbicite eā. et dñā-
mini piscibꝫ maris. et volatilibꝫ celi.
et vniuersis animātibꝫ que mouent̃
sup terrā. Dixitq; de⁹. Ecce dedi vob'
omnē herbā afferentē semen sup terrā.
et vniūsa ligna que hñt in semetipis
sementē genis sui. ut sint vobis ī escā
⁊ cunctis aīantibꝫ terre. oīq; volucri
celi ⁊ vniuersis q̄ mouentur in terra. ⁊ ī
quibꝫ est anima viuēs. ut habeāt ad
vescendū. Et factū est ita. Viditq; deus
cuncta que fecerat. ⁊ erāt valde bona.

Introduction **In the 1920s, organizations in several countries established design competitions for books. The impetus came from the United States with 'Fifty Books of the Year'. These exhibitions and catalogues were intended to promote 'the book' and raise it to a higher aesthetic level. Today, more than thirty countries hold competitions of this kind. This visual history brings together books to illustrate a canon of more than five hundred years of Western book design.**

For many years, it was printers who set the trends; the profession of graphic designer emerged only gradually at the beginning of the twentieth century. The aesthetic canon was developed primarily by designers and critics in the English-speaking world. One particular influence was Stanley Morison, whose *Four Centuries of Fine Printing* (1924) was reprinted several times, translated into German and French and revised under the title *The Typographic Book, 1450–1935* (1963). Morison, no great supporter of modernism, was primarily interested in highbrow text-centred books. Later overviews often follow this traditional typographic approach. The innovators are better represented in more recent general overviews of graphic design, but in these, the book tends to disappear from view after the early nineteenth century, when books had to compete with advertisements, commercial and cultural posters and illustrated magazines, which are often better suited to reproduction at a reduced scale.

This book showcases book design in all its forms: reference works and works of art, 'machines for reading' and picture books, prestigious collector's items and throw-away paperbacks. It includes work by famous printers of the hand-press period – Nicolas Jenson, Aldus Manutius, Christoffel Plantin, the Elzeviers, John Baskerville,

Giambattista Bodoni – and trendsetting designers of the modern era – William Morris, El Lissitzky, Jan Tschichold, Paul Rand, Massin, Irma Boom. It also includes remarkable illustrated works by architects and artists such as Giovanni Battista Piranesi and Maria Sibylla Merian. Special attention is devoted to printers' manuals, illuminating the printing process, and also to type specimens and writing masters' copybooks, placing letterforms in a broader context.

In the hand-press period, up to about 1830, most books were accessible only to the elite, although seventeenth-century Dutch publishers did begin introducing inexpensive editions of the most popular works. The nineteenth century saw affordable books with a luxurious appearance come on the market thanks to the mechanization of printing and a growing reading public. From this time onwards, a book's purchaser no longer needed to have it bound: the publisher had the entire print run (or a large portion of it) identically bound. These industrial bindings are what is largely illustrated here. For each book, the type or one of the typefaces used is also highlighted and briefly discussed. Although the particular copy illustrated may have an interesting or even an important history of its own – its provenance, binding or manuscript annotations – that is not discussed here.

These books have been selected from the Special Collections of the University of Amsterdam. The University Library has its origins in the former City Library, which was established in 1578, when Protestants took control of the Amsterdam city council and confiscated the property of the monastic libraries. Both scholarly citizens and students could gain access to the materials. In the nineteenth and twentieth centuries, the library received several large collections as donations or on permanent loan. Chief among these are the library of the Dutch Booktrade Association (founded 1845), on permanent loan since 1958, and in particular the Typographical Library (founded 1913) of Typefoundry Amsterdam, acquired in 1971. This prestigious collection, largely assembled by their in-house designer S. H. de Roos, documents and illustrates graphic technique and design in the broadest sense.

A number of the editions included here are now available in digital form. For new books, publishers consciously choose to produce an e-book, a printed book or both. Many designers and readers nevertheless still feel strongly attracted to the printed book: by its tactile qualities, by the varieties of paper and their effect on the illustrations, and by the various ways of finishing the book. The future of the printed book lies in its qualities as a physical object.

Special Collections

Within the Special Collections at the University of Amsterdam, one of the main areas of focus is graphic design, from poster design to book and type design.

Since its founding in 1578, the Amsterdam University Library has of course mainly collected its books for their content; later, however, it also began to choose books based on their production method or design. In the library of the Booktrade Association and the Typographical Library, there are in-house international collections in which design is heavily represented. Since the second half of the twentieth century, several design archives have been added. Meanwhile, the Special Collections cover more than 25 kilometres of shelves, constituting a rich and diverse heritage.

A recent development is the establishment of a Heritage Centre for Graphic Design, Typography and Advertising. There, a number of organizations work together to collect and preserve collections for educational and research purposes, as well as for a wider audience. Within the Special Collections at the University of Amsterdam, considerable work is being carried out on the heritage of graphic design, which is also evident in this visual history.

Steph Scholten, director UvA Heritage
Garrelt Verhoeven, chief curator of Special Collections

s Avenir Next (2
designed by Adri
Frutiger (born 19

The font used in this book is Avenir Next (2004), designed by Adrian Frutiger (born 1928). It is an adaptation of Frutiger's original 1988 design for Linotype, produced in collaboration with Akira Kobayashi. Avenir is a more humanist approach to the geometric-style sans serifs that emerged after the late 1920s, such as Futura.

The invention and spread of printing

Detail of *Van den proprieteyten der dinghen*, printed by Jacob Bellaert (see p. 40)

The invention and spread of printing **Johannes Gutenberg (c. 1394/99-1468) established the first known European printing office with movable type in the German free city of Mainz in around 1450. His books betray no influence from Chinese ceramic or Korean cast bronze type, although Chinese papermaking and woodblock printing had reached Europe via Islamic intermediaries. A clever mechanic with family ties to Mainz's mint, Gutenberg practised gem polishing and mass-produced pilgrims' mirrors, possibly stamping the metal parts in a press. His printing office issued some smaller works before completing his famous 42-line Bible in around 1455. His assistant Peter Schoeffer, a former scribe, may deserve credit for the form of their letters. Debts forced Gutenberg to cede his equipment and stock to Johann Fust, who continued printing with Schoeffer.**

Type manufacture borrowed techniques from goldsmithing, coin minting and pewter casting. Nicolas Jenson's 1480 will and surviving materials from the 1490s suggest type was cast in adjustable moulds using copper matrices struck with steel punches when he began in 1470. Some earlier types may also have been made this way, but many show evidence of more obscure techniques, abandoned soon after.

The earliest types followed gothic manuscript hands that were often associated with specific genres of text: formal Textura (for northern Bibles and liturgical texts), Rotunda (for legal texts) and the more cursive bastarda (for indulgences). The 1462 sack of Mainz scattered its workmen, and some brought printing to Italy (1465), where humanist and Rotunda manuscript hands predominated. After some provisional forms, they adapted the humanist hand to create roman type (used for humanist and classical

texts). Jenson in Venice produced the most influential books, the earliest classical and humanist texts using roman and Greek types, followed by canon law, Bibles and liturgical works using Rotunda (southern European printers rarely used Textura).

After 1469, printing rapidly spread from dozens of printing offices in Germany, Strasbourg, Italy and the Low Countries to hundreds throughout Europe. Typographical research suggests that trade in matrices from Cologne, Venice, Strasbourg and Basel supported this expansion. Koberger, Ratdolt and Leeu built internationally connected publishing houses on an industrial scale, producing hundreds of editions, some in print runs of more than a thousand. Aldus Manutius, specializing in classical and humanist texts, reasserted Venice's lead. His smaller format books, appealing to scholarly markets, and his Greek (1495) and italic (1501) types, were quickly copied internationally, while his seminal roman type (1495) exerted its influence in France in around 1530.

After 1470, an expanding range of type sizes and styles and woodcut initials and borders gradually reduced dependence on expensive colour printing or hand-drawn initials and decoration. Title pages became a standard component in the same period, promoting the names of the publishers who needed to recover their investment in large editions. After fifty years, the printed book had evolved many of its now familiar features. JAL

Nicolas Jenson (*c.* 1430?–80), apprenticed at the royal mint in Paris, became master of the royal mint at Tours. He probably learned die-cutting at the mints. In 1458 King Charles VII sent him to Mainz to secretly investigate and report on Johann Gutenberg's 'invention of printing with punches and curious characters'. They may not have known that Johann Fust and Peter Schoeffer had taken over Gutenberg's operation. King Charles died in 1461 and if Jenson returned to France, he did not stay long. It is tempting to suppose he worked for Fust and Schoeffer until the sack of Mainz in 1462, but he next appears in Venice in 1468. Some suggest that he cut the roman type introduced there by Johannes de Spira (1469), since it marks the first step towards the style and technical quality of the roman in Jenson's first books (1470).

One of the most prolific and influential of early printers, Jenson distributed his books, mostly in Latin, throughout Europe. Beginning with classical works set in roman type, he gradually shifted to devotional works, papal publications, bibles and canon law set in Rotunda type, a blackletter style used for the majority of books printed in southern Europe at the time. His roman type marks a crucial turning point in the history of printing. It served as a model for all that followed, establishing the form still used today, but his superb Greek (1471) and Rotunda (1474) also served as models for many others. JAL

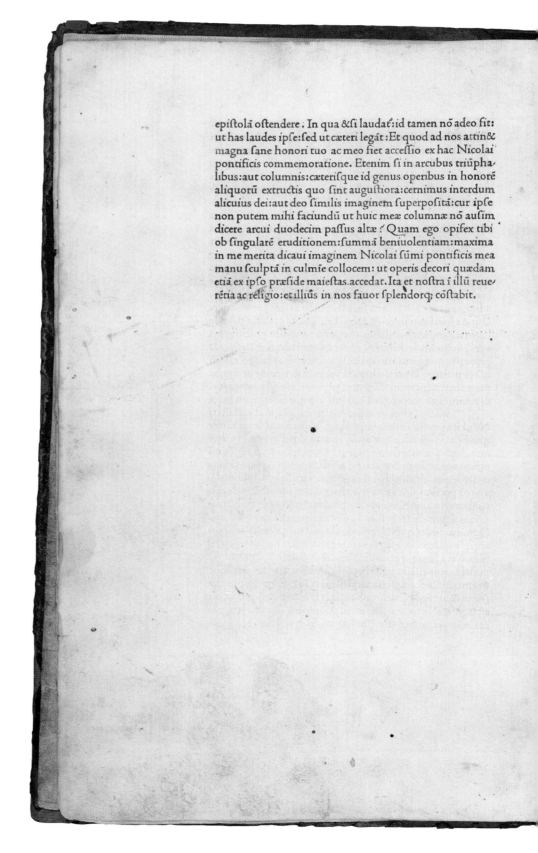
epiſtolã oſtendere. In qua &ſi laudat: id tamen nõ adeo fit: ut has laudes ipſe: ſed ut cæteri legãt: Et quod ad nos attin& magna ſane honori tuo ac meo fiet acceſſio ex hac Nicolai pontificis commemoratione. Etenim ſi in arcubus triũphalibus: aut columnis: cæteriſque id genus operibus in honorẽ aliquorũ extructis quo ſint auguſtiora: cernimus interdum alicuius dei: aut deo ſimilis imaginem ſuperpoſitã: cur ipſe non putem mihi faciundũ ut huic meæ columnæ nõ auſim dicere arcui duodecim paſſus altæ? Quam ego opifex tibi ob ſingularẽ eruditionem: ſummã beniuolentiam: maxima in me merita dicaui imaginem Nicolai ſũmi pontificis mea manu ſculptã in culmĩe collocem: ut operis decori quædam etiã ex ipſo præſide maieſtas accedat. Ita et noſtra ĩ illũ reuerẽtia ac religio: et illiũs in nos fauor ſplendorq; cõſtabit.

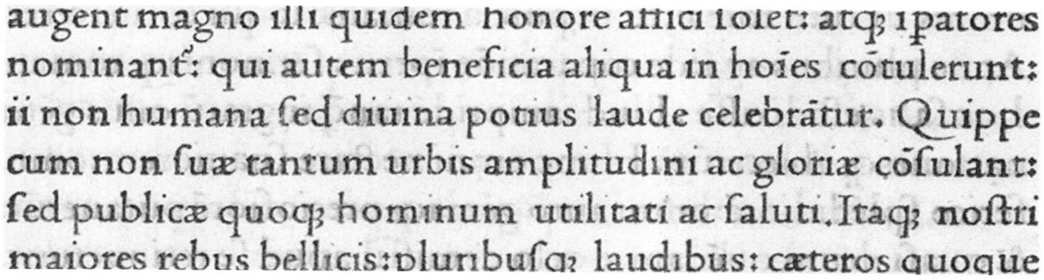
augent magno illi quidem honore affici ſolet: atq; īpatores
nominant: qui autem beneficia aliqua in hoĩes cõtulerunt:
ii non humana ſed diuina potius laude celebrãtur. Quippe
cum non ſuæ tantum urbis amplitudini ac gloriæ cõſulant:
ſed publicæ quoq; hominum utilitati ac ſaluti. Itaq; noſtri
maiores rebus bellicis: pluribuſq; laudibus: cæteros quoque

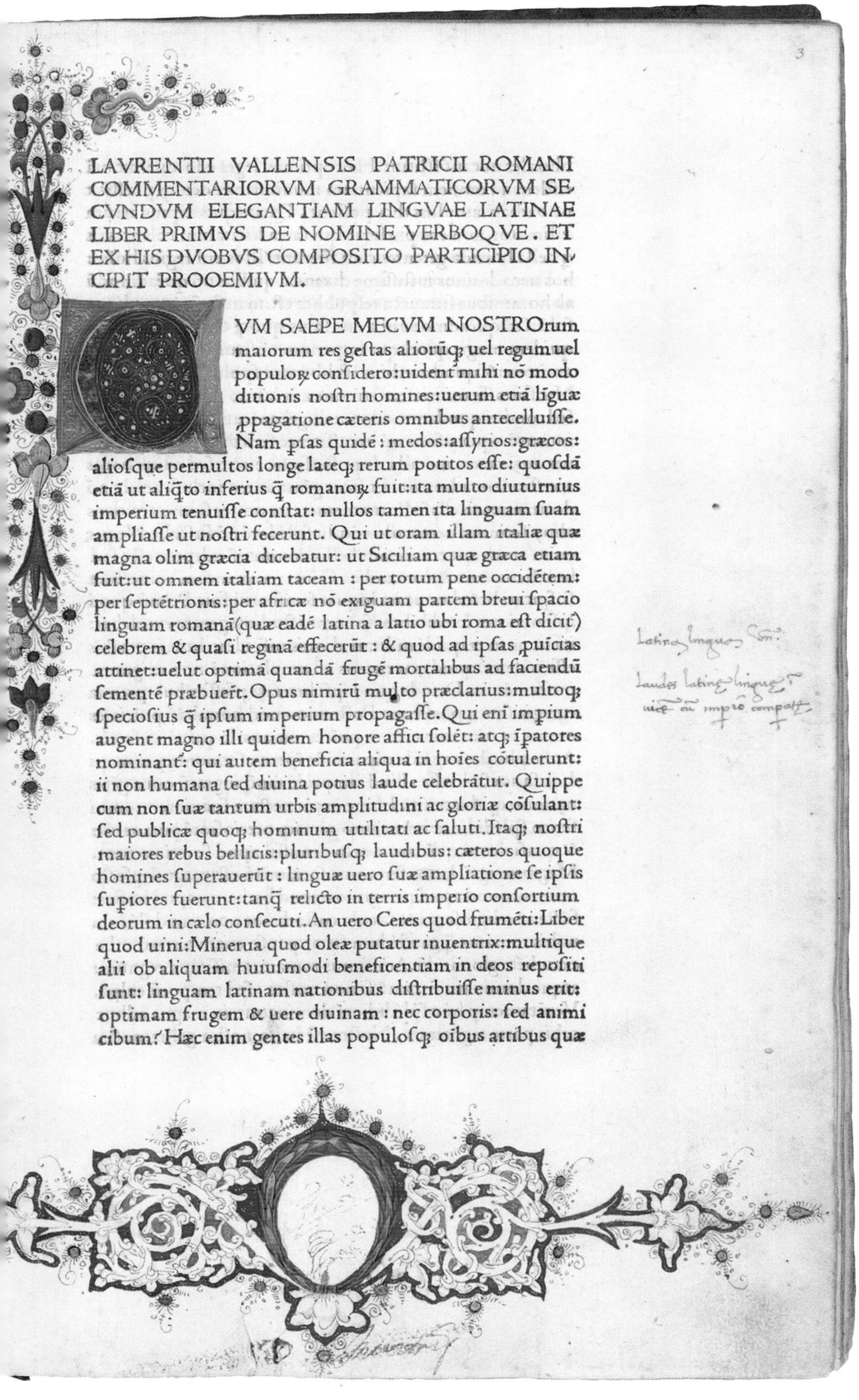
LAVRENTII VALLENSIS PATRICII ROMANI COMMENTARIORVM GRAMMATICORVM SECVNDVM ELEGANTIAM LINGVAE LATINAE LIBER PRIMVS DE NOMINE VERBOQVE. ET EX HIS DVOBVS COMPOSITO PARTICIPIO INCIPIT PROOEMIVM.

VM SAEPE MECVM NOSTROrum maiorum res geſtas aliorũq; uel regum uel populorum conſidero: uident mihi nõ modo ditionis noſtri homines: uerum etiã lĩguæ ꝓpagatione cæteris omnibus antecelluiſſe. Nam ꝑſas quidẽ: medos: aſſyrios: græcos: alioſque permultos longe lateq; rerum potitos eſſe: quoſdã etiã ut aliq̃to inferius q̃ romanorum fuit: ita multo diuturnius imperium tenuiſſe conſtat: nullos tamen ita linguam ſuam ampliaſſe ut noſtri fecerunt. Qui ut oram illam italiæ quæ magna olim græcia dicebatur: ut Siciliam quæ græca etiam fuit: ut omnem italiam taceam: per totum pene occidẽtem: per ſeptẽtrionis: per africæ nõ exiguam partem breui ſpacio linguam romanã (quæ eadẽ latina a latio ubi roma eſt dicit̃) celebrem & quaſi reginã effecerũt: & quod ad ipſas ꝓuĩcias attinet: uelut optimã quandã frugẽ mortalibus ad faciendũ ſementẽ præbuerĩt. Opus nimirũ multo præclarius: multoq; ſpecioſius q̃ ipſum imperium propagaſſe. Qui enĩ impium augent magno illi quidem honore affici ſolet: atq; īpatores nominant: qui autem beneficia aliqua in hoĩes cõtulerunt: ii non humana ſed diuina potius laude celebrãtur. Quippe cum non ſuæ tantum urbis amplitudini ac gloriæ cõſulant: ſed publicæ quoq; hominum utilitati ac ſaluti. Itaq; noſtri maiores rebus bellicis: pluribuſq; laudibus: cæteros quoque homines ſuperauerũt: linguæ uero ſuæ ampliatione ſe ipſis ſuꝑiores fuerunt: tanq̃ relicto in terris imperio conſortium deorum in cælo conſecuti. An uero Ceres quod frumẽti: Liber quod uini: Minerua quod oleæ putatur inuentrix: multique alii ob aliquam huiuſmodi beneficentiam in deos repoſiti ſunt: linguam latinam nationibus diſtribuiſſe minus erit: optimam frugem & uere diuinam: nec corporis: ſed animi cibum? Hæc enim gentes illas populoſq; oĩbus artibus quæ

Roman printing types derive their capitals (directly or indirectly) from ancient Roman inscriptions, but their lower case from humanist manuscript hands written with a broad-edged pen. Jenson's roman (1470) not only surpassed its predecessors in quality, but began to make the lower case – especially its serif structure – match the capitals.

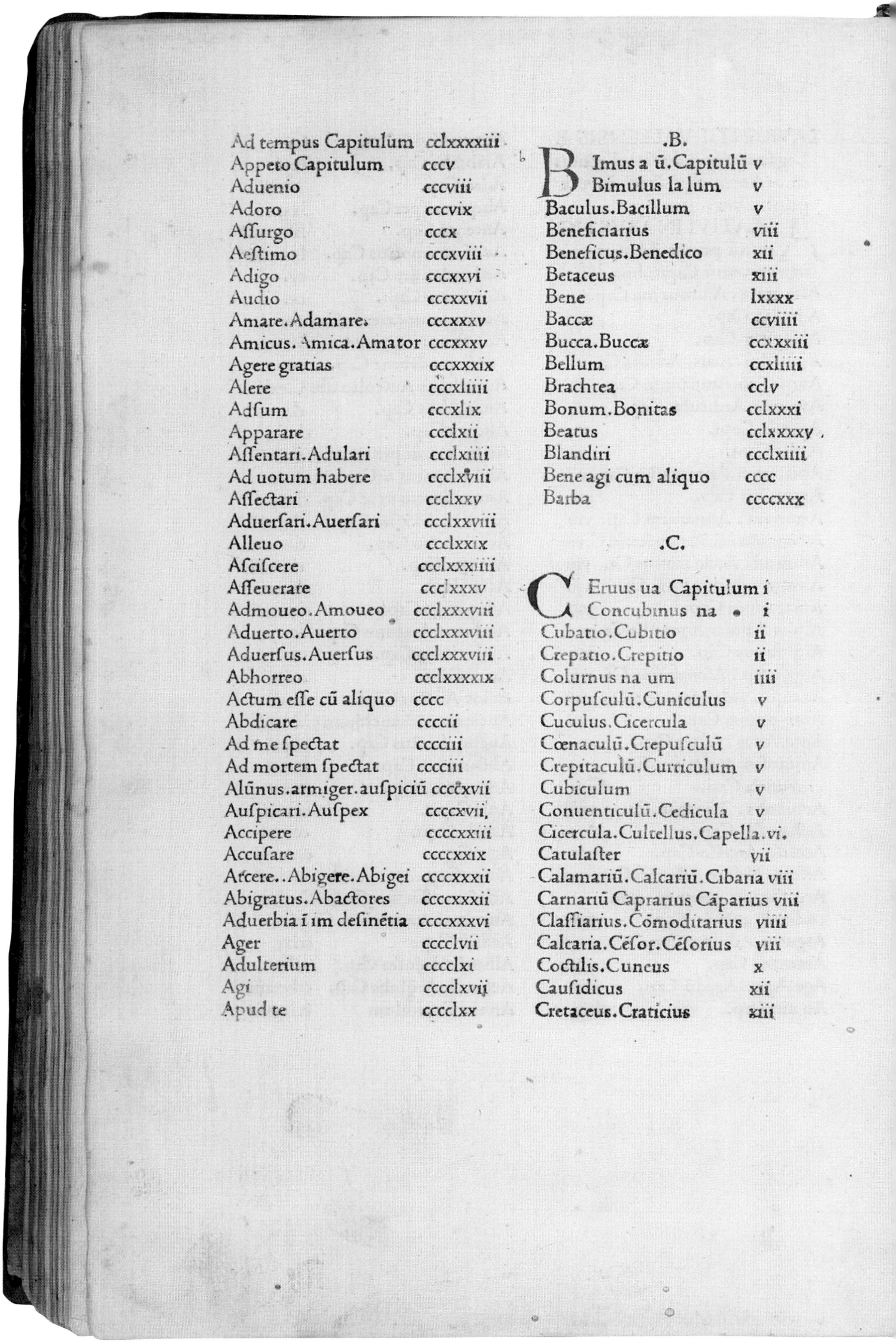

1480 **Gheraert Leeu** *Dialogus creaturarum moralisatus*. Gouda: Gheraert Leeu, 1480. 28.5 cm.

The successful printer Gheraert Leeu of Gouda produced this book of fables, partly based on Aesop's fables. Leeu, born between 1445 and 1450, later settled in Antwerp. In 1492, he was murdered by a punchcutter with whom he had a labour dispute. This book is celebrated primarily for its beautiful woodcuts, made by an anonymous engraver. The text was written in the north of Italy in the fourteenth century; the most probable author is Magninus Mediolanensis.

The *Dialogus creaturarum moralisatus* ('The Dialogues of the Creatures Moralized') contains 122 dialogues between various characters, including people, animals, plants, planets, rocks, mountains, water, and the wind. One character usually personifies virtue, and the other, vice. Each dialogue is followed by a distich (a rhyming couplet) summarizing the lesson. This is followed by a moralizing text containing further explanation. In some cases, these texts are also fables, based on various sources.

The dialogues are illustrated with woodcut illustrations, which are strikingly original and simple, drawn in pure lines, almost without any hatching. Printers in other Dutch cities soon started to imitate

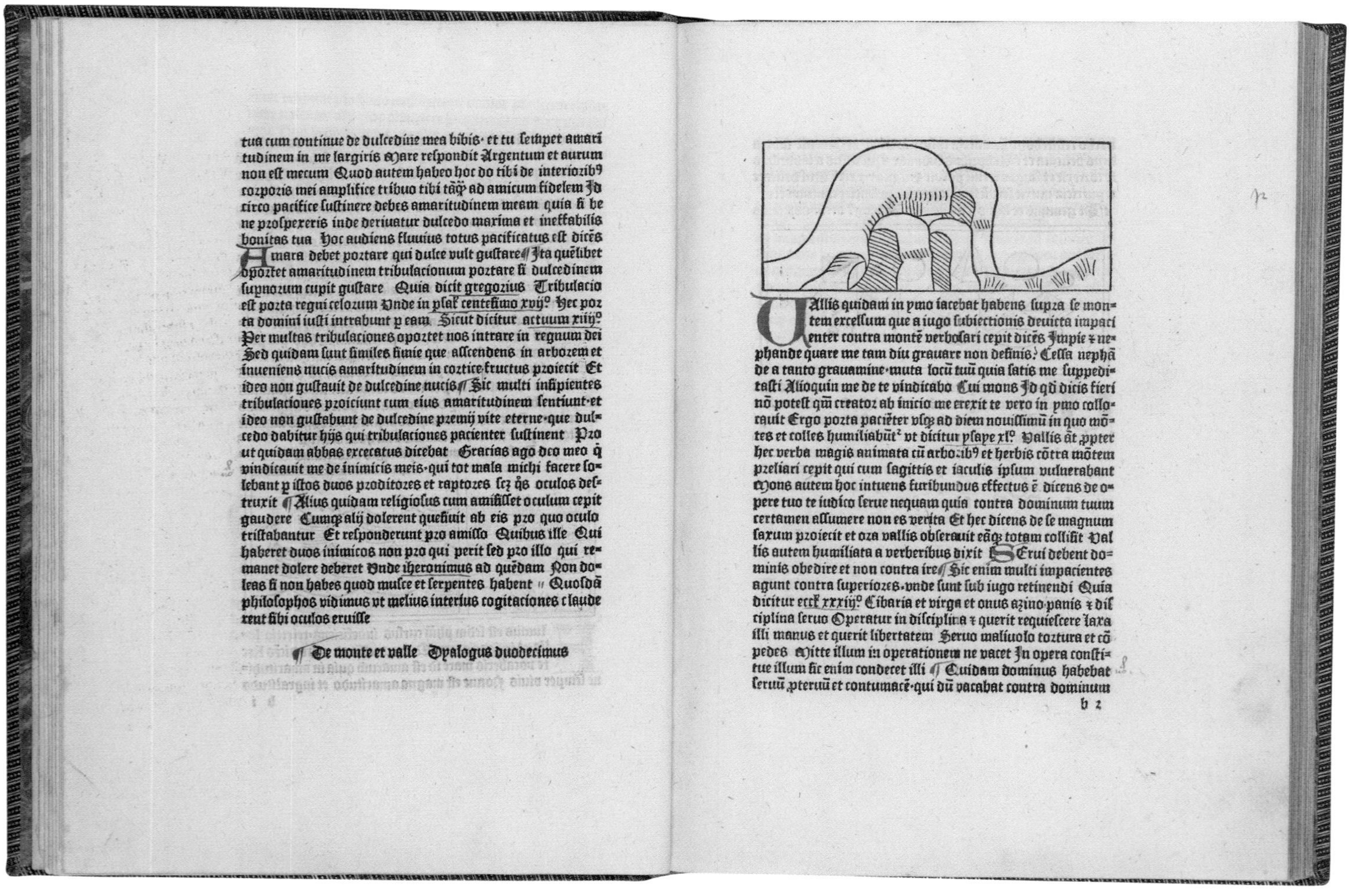

this style; these included the woodcutter in Haarlem who became known as the 'Master of Bellaert' (see page 40). Partly due to its attractive illustrations, *Dialogus creaturarum moralisatus* became a bestseller. Leeu printed six editions: three in Latin, two in Dutch, and one in French. In the sixteenth century, the woodcuts were still being used for Latin and Dutch editions. Copies of the original illustrations were used for reprints in Cologne and Stockholm. AP

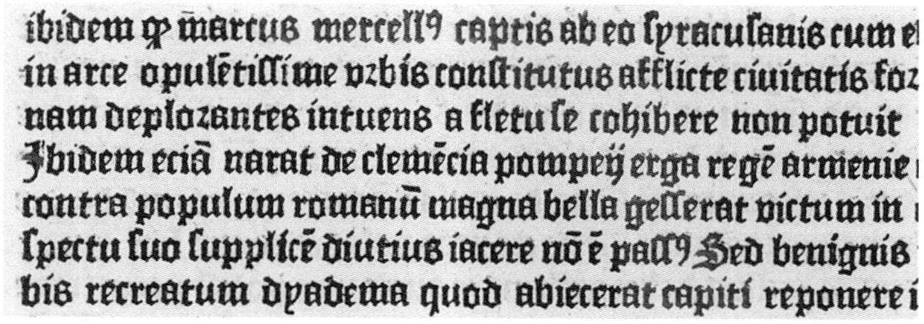
ibidem q marcus mercell9 captis ab eo syracusanis cum e
in arce opulẽtissime vrbis constitutus afflicte ciuitatis for
nam deplorantes intuens a fletu se cohibere non potuit
Ibidem eciã narat de clemẽcia pompeij erga regẽ armenie
contra populum romanũ magna bella gesserat victum in
spectu suo supplicẽ diutius iacere nõ ẽ pass9 Sed benignis
bis recreatum dyadema quod abiecerat capiti reponere i

Gheraert Leeu used his second printing type in several variant states from 1477 to 1483, primarily for Dutch texts. This excellent Textura type is said to be based on manuscript hands used in Holland and therefore was probably cut locally. In 1483, he imported a Textura from Venice, apparently for use in a major Latin work.

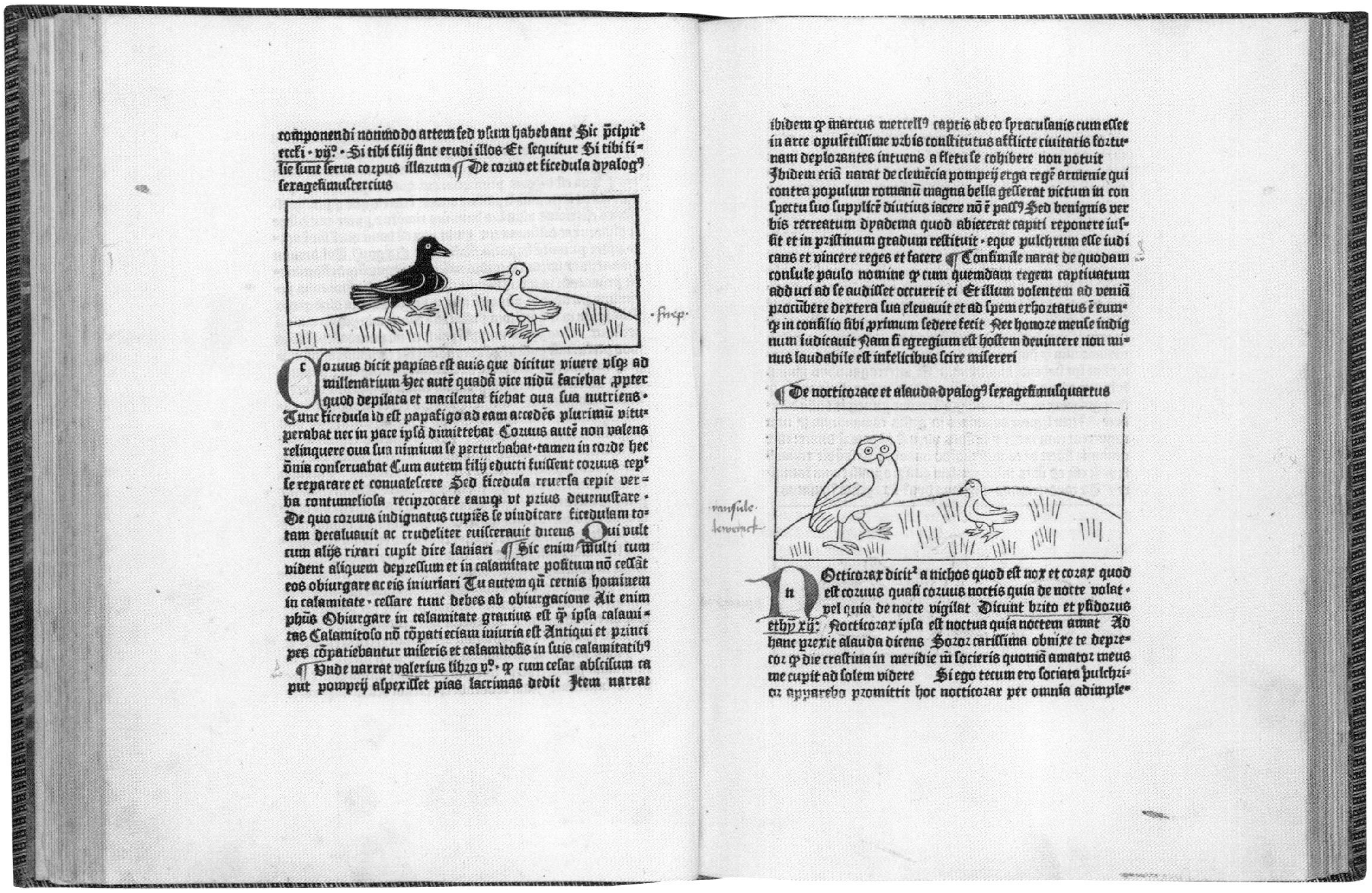

Lupus cū azello simul sarrabat sed azinus simpliciter
desup laborabat · lupus autē maliciose inferius trahe
bat cupiens occasionē īuenire ut azinū devoraret Vn=
de querimonias fecit versus azinū · quare mittis sarraturam
in oculis meis ? Azin9 respondit Ego hec tibi nō facio sed pu=
re sarrā guberno Si vis tu desup sarrare gaudeo · quia infe
rius operabor fideliter Cui lupus Nescio · si dirigis sarraturā
in oculis meis tuos eruā Sarrantibus autē illis lup9 fortiter
insufflare cepit sup sarraturam ut sarraturam in oculis socij
mandaret sed pter cōmissurā lingni saratura cecidit in o=
culos lupi Lupus autem pre dolore se retorsit et iuravit ut

vehiculum precipitaret · sed iudicio dei penetral cecidit et lu-
pum mactauit Azinus autem saliēs se incolumē cōseruauit di
cens Multi gladio necantur quo necare meditātur Sic eni
faciūt maliciosi qui expādūt rethe ante oculos sociorū vt eos
fraudulenter capiāt Sed sicut eccl · xxvij° Qui parat foueam
proximo suo incidet ī eā prout esopus volens ostendere q̄ q̄ vult
decipere alios deus eum decipit et damnat · introducit exem-
plum q̄ quidam furicus venit ad flumē et non audebat vltra
natare Hunc videns rana volens eum decipere dixit Bene ve
nias frater et amice Dicitur enī · frater in angustijs cōprobat[2] ·
Unde veni mecum quia valde bene natare scio Credēs h° furi-
c9 permisit se ligari cum filo ad pedem rane Cūq3 natassent in
fluctibus rana submergebat se et furicum necabat Interea
milu9 desup volabat et videns furicum rapuit · et simul cum
eo traxit ranā et vtrūq3 comedit Unde esopus Sic pereant q̄
se prodesse fatēt[2] et obsunt Ut discat in auctorē pena redire suū

De vrso et lupo Dyalog9 centesimusoctauus ·:· ·

Ursus clamitauit lupū ad se et ait Sum9 nos īter fe-
ras nominati · sed si simul prociem9 erimus magis
sublimati Placuit hic sermo lupo et cōiuraciones et
societatē statuerunt Ursus autē informauit lupū dicēs volo
tecum ī estate manere · tu vero de quo venatus eris me saciabis
ego autem in cella te refocillabo q̄a optime preparatus sum
in hyeme Nolo q̄ permaneas in pruina cum algore sed in cauer

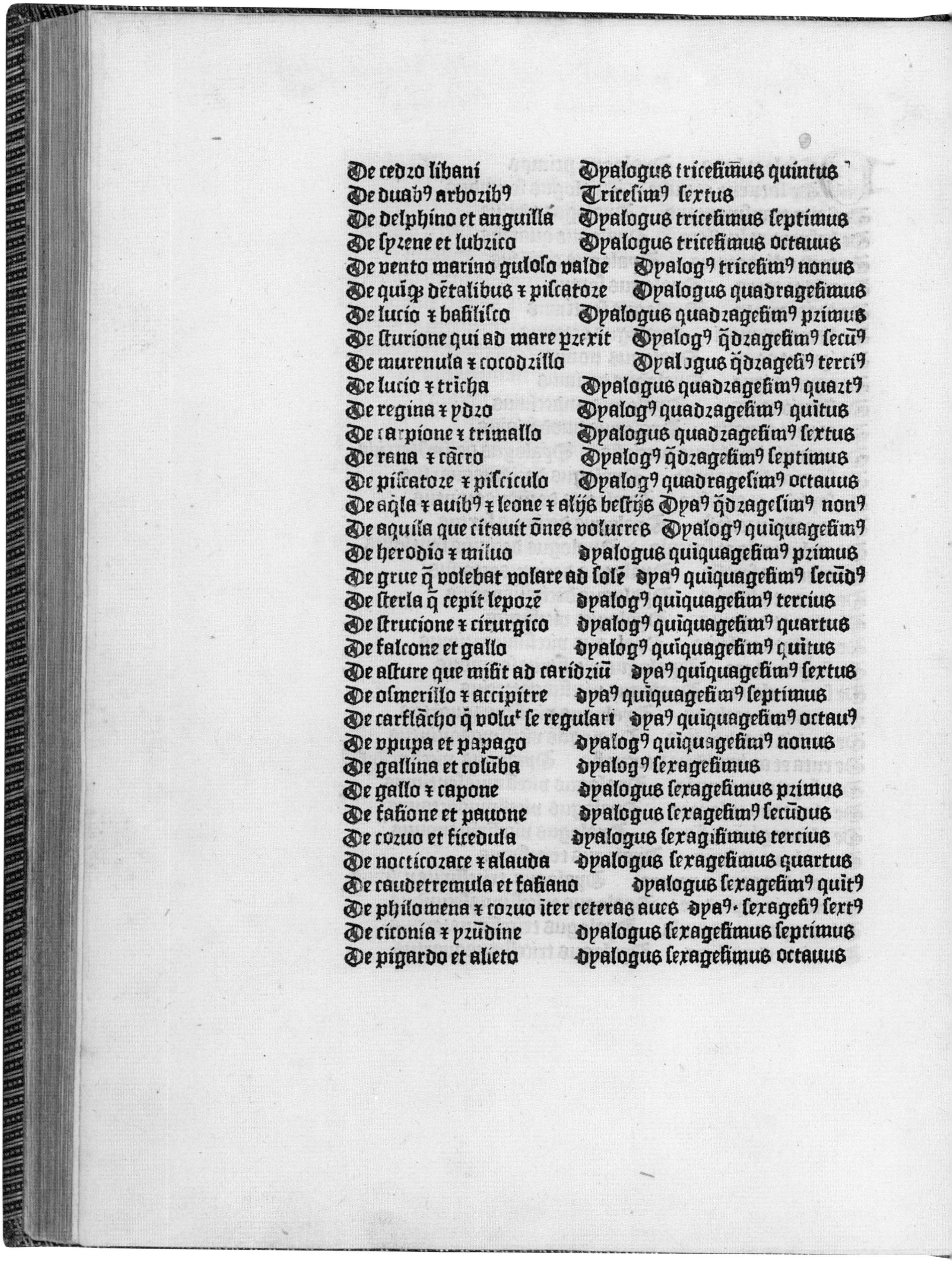

De cedro libani	Dyalogus tricesimus quintus
De duabꝰ arboribꝰ	Tricesimꝰ sextus
De delphino et anguilla	Dyalogus tricesimus septimus
De syrene et lubrico	Dyalogus tricesimus octauus
De vento marino guloso valde	Dyalogꝰ tricesimꝰ nonus
De quinq3 dētalibus ⁊ piscatore	Dyalogus quadragesimus
De lucio ⁊ basilisco	Dyalogus quadragesimꝰ primus
De sturione qui ad mare perexit	Dyalogꝰ q̄dragesimꝰ secūꝰ
De murenula ⁊ cocodrillo	Dyalogus q̄dragesi̅ terciꝰ
De lucio ⁊ tricha	Dyalogus quadragesimꝰ quartꝰ
De regina ⁊ ydro	Dyalogꝰ quadragesimꝰ quītus
De carpione ⁊ trimallo	Dyalogus quadragesimꝰ sextus
De rana ⁊ cācro	Dyalogꝰ q̄dragesimꝰ septimus
De piscatore ⁊ pisciculo	Dyalogꝰ quadragesimꝰ octauus
De aq̄la ⁊ auibꝰ ⁊ leone ⁊ aliis bestiis	Dyaꝰ q̄dragesimꝰ nonꝰ
De aquila que citauit ōnes volucres	Dyalogꝰ quīquagesimꝰ
De herodio ⁊ miluo	dyalogus quīquagesimꝰ primus
De grue q̄ volebat volare ad solē	dyaꝰ quīquagesimꝰ secūdꝰ
De sterla q̄ cepit leporē	dyalogꝰ quīquagesimꝰ tercius
De strucione ⁊ cirurgico	dyalogꝰ quīquagesimꝰ quartus
De falcone et gallo	dyalogꝰ quīquagesimꝰ quītus
De asture que misit ad caridriū	dyaꝰ quīquagesimꝰ sextus
De osmerillo ⁊ accipitre	dyaꝰ quīquagesimꝰ septimus
De carflācho q̄ voluᵗ se regulari	dyaꝰ quīquagesimꝰ octauꝰ
De vpupa et papago	dyalogꝰ quīquagesimꝰ nonus
De gallina et colūba	dyalogꝰ sexagesimus
De gallo ⁊ capone	dyalogus sexagesimus primus
De fasione et pauone	dyalogus sexagesimꝰ secūdus
De coruo et ficedula	dyalogus sexagisimus tercius
De nocticorace ⁊ alauda	dyalogus sexagesimus quartus
De caudetremula et fasiano	dyalogus sexagesimꝰ quītꝰ
De philomena ⁊ coruo iter ceteras aues	dyaꝰ sexagesiꝰ sextꝰ
De ciconia ⁊ prūdine	dyalogus sexagesimus septimus
De pigardo et alieto	dyalogus sexagesimus octauus

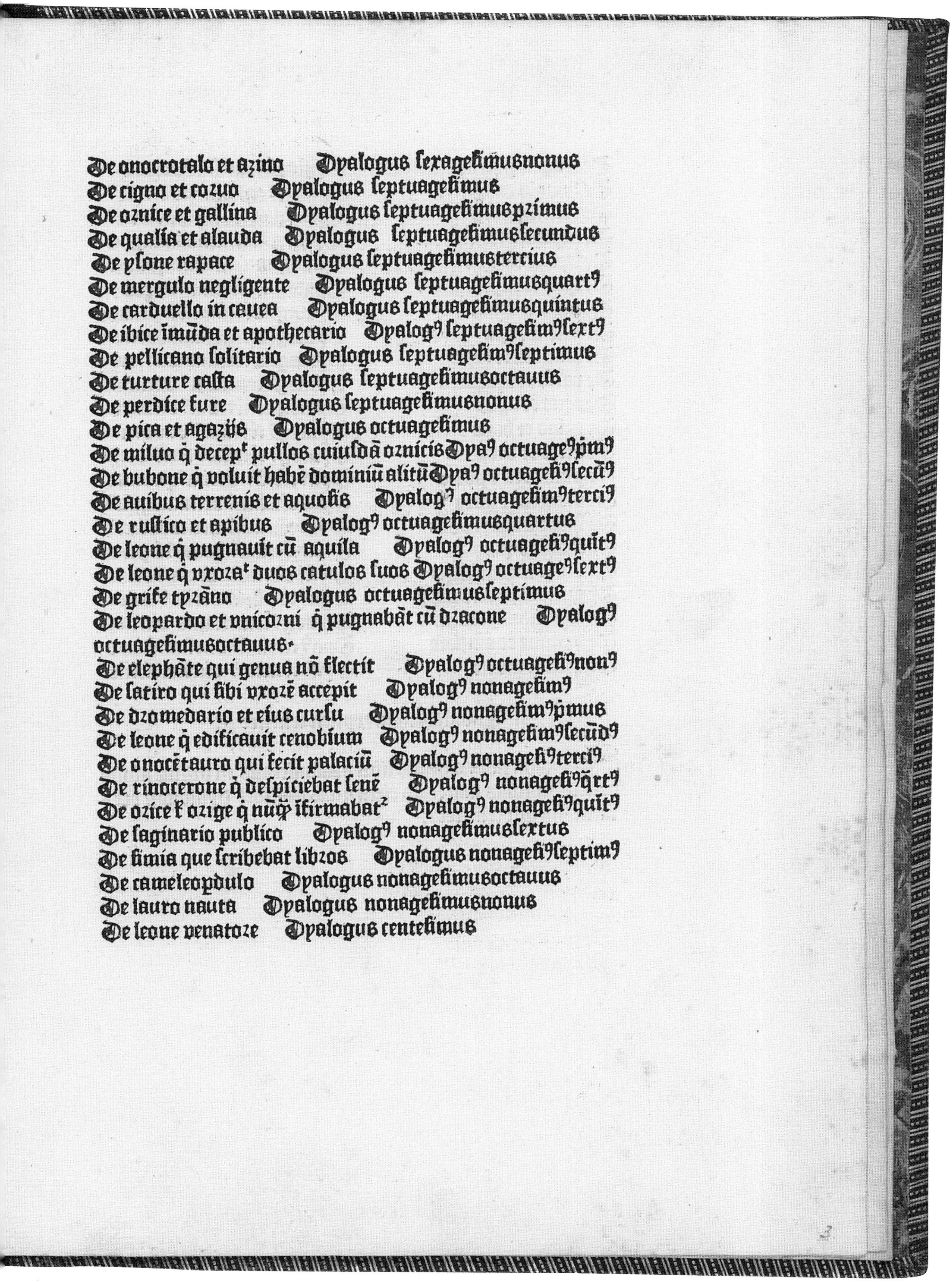

De onocrotalo et azino Dyalogus sexagesimusnonus
De cigno et coruo Dyalogus septuagesimus
De ornice et gallina Dyalogus septuagesimusprimus
De qualia et alauda Dyalogus septuagesimussecundus
De ysone rapace Dyalogus septuagesimustercius
De mergulo negligente Dyalogus septuagesimusquartꝰ
De carduello in cauea Dyalogus septuagesimusquintus
De ibice imūda et apothecario Dyalogꝰ septuagesimꝰsextꝰ
De pellicano solitario Dyalogus septuagesimꝰseptimus
De turture casta Dyalogus septuagesimusoctauus
De perdice fure Dyalogus septuagesimusnonus
De pica et agazīis Dyalogus octuagesimus
De miluo q̄ decepᵗ pullos cuiusdā ornicis Dyaꝰ octuagesꝰp̄mꝰ
De bubone q̄ voluit habē dominiū alitū Dyaꝰ octuagesīꝰsecūꝰ
De auibus terrenis et aquosis Dyalogꝰ octuagesimꝰterciꝰ
De rustico et apibus Dyalogꝰ octuagesimusquartus
De leone q̄ pugnauit cū aquila Dyalogꝰ octuagesīꝰquītꝰ
De leone q̄ vxoraᵗ duos catulos suos Dyalogꝰ octuagesꝰsextꝰ
De grife tyrāno Dyalogus octuagesimusseptimus
De leopardo et vnicorni q̄ pugnabāt cū dracone Dyalogꝰ
octuagesimusoctauus.
De elephāte qui genua nō flectit Dyalogꝰ octuagesīꝰnonꝰ
De satiro qui sibi vxorē accepit Dyalogꝰ nonagesimꝰ
De dromedario et eius cursu Dyalogꝰ nonagesimꝰp̄mus
De leone q̄ edificauit cenobium Dyalogꝰ nonagesimꝰsecūdꝰ
De onocētauro qui fecit palaciū Dyalogꝰ nonagesīꝰterciꝰ
De rinocerone q̄ despiciebat senē Dyalogꝰ nonagesīꝰq̄rtꝰ
De orice ꝁ orige q̄ nūq̄ īfirmabatᶻ Dyalogꝰ nonagesīꝰquītꝰ
De saginario publico Dyalogꝰ nonagesimussextus
De simia que scribebat libros Dyalogus nonagesīꝰseptimꝰ
De cameleopdulo Dyalogus nonagesimusoctauus
De lauro nauta Dyalogus nonagesimusnonus
De leone venatore Dyalogus centesimus

1482 **Erhard Ratdolt** Euclid, *Elementa geometriae*. Venice: Erhard Ratdolt, 1482. 32 cm.

This was the first printed edition of Euclid's *Elements of Geometry*, translated into Latin via Arabic. No edition in the original Greek appeared until 1533. The first large-scale printed scientific text and the first printed book to include such an extensive array of diagrams, it became essential reading for Renaissance scholars and went through many editions in the sixteenth century.

Erhard Ratdolt (1447–1527/28) came from the Bavarian city of Augsburg, where he first worked in his family's cabinetmaking and plaster-casting shop. He moved to Venice in 1474 and set up a printing office, issuing books with partners from 1476 to 1478 and alone from 1480. In 1486 the Bishop of Augsburg persuaded him to return home to set up a printing office there, where he remained to his death.

One of the most prolific of early printers, Ratdolt also took great care with the editorial and graphic quality of his books. Scholars and bibliophiles in his time and ours have admired this expensive and ambitious Euclid. It includes a woodcut border on the opening page, three sizes of Rotunda type (in a few copies, the dedication is printed in gold and includes a larger fourth Rotunda), hundreds of impressions of dozens of decorated woodcut initials in three sizes, and more than four hundred diagrams (some remarkably complex), apparently assembled from straight and curved metal rules. The scholar Curt Bühler called the clearly laid-out whole 'a masterpiece of early typographical ability and ingenuity'. Ratdolt reprinted leaves two to nine; the copy illustrated includes the second printing. JAL

This is a good Rotunda type, the most popular style in southern Europe. Bartholomeus of Cremona (1473) and Nicolas Jenson (1474), both in Venice, introduced the first well-made types in this style. Ratdolt included ten sizes in his 1486 type specimen, but by then he had replaced or revised the face shown here.

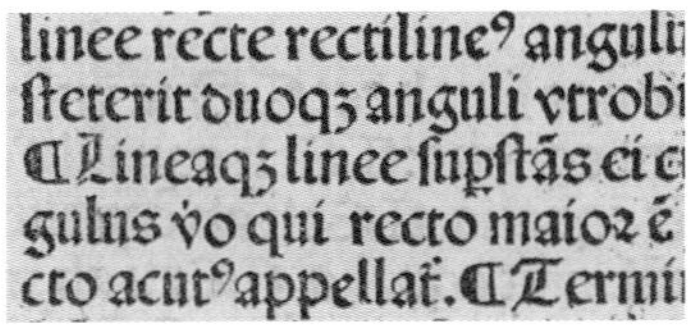

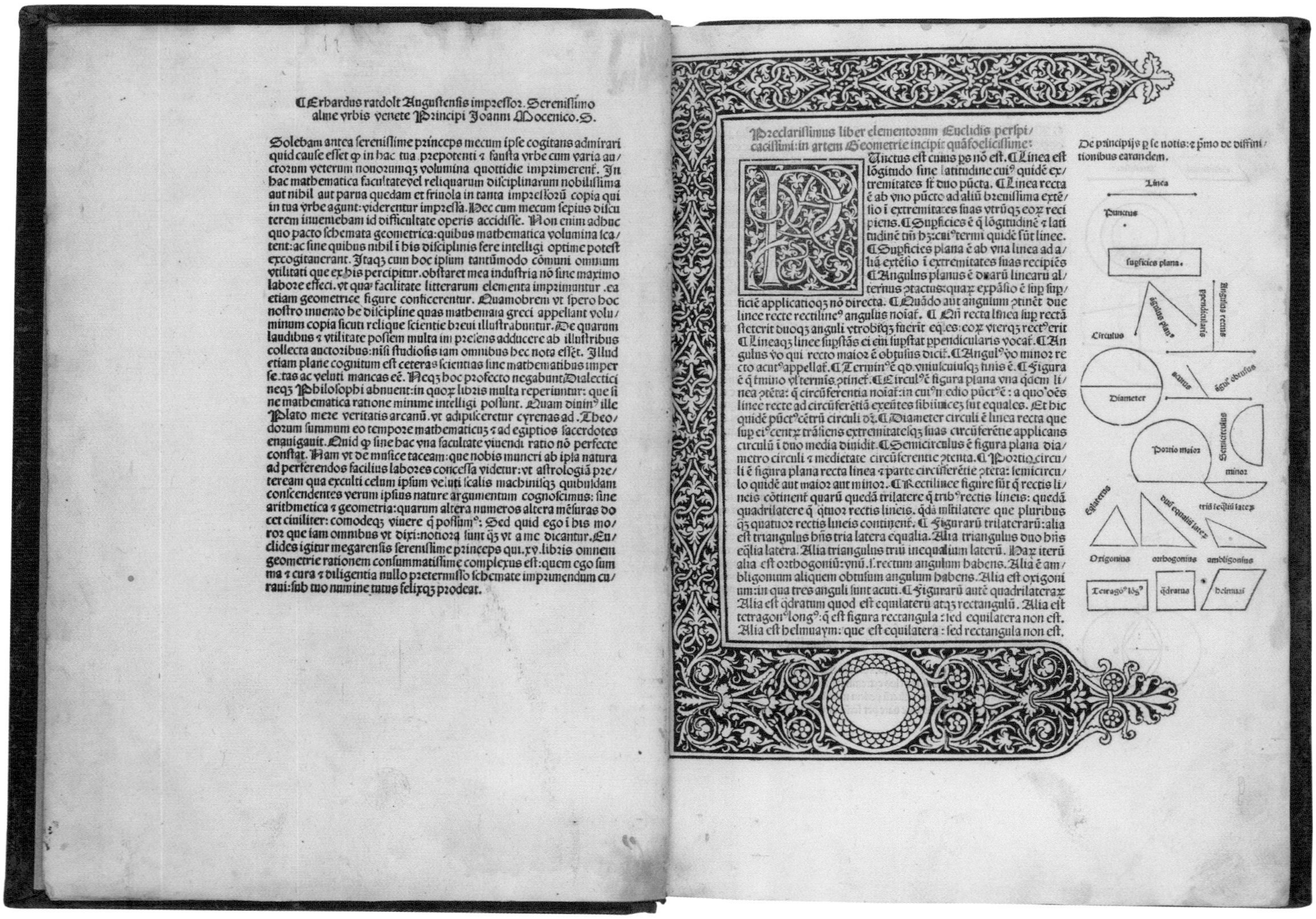

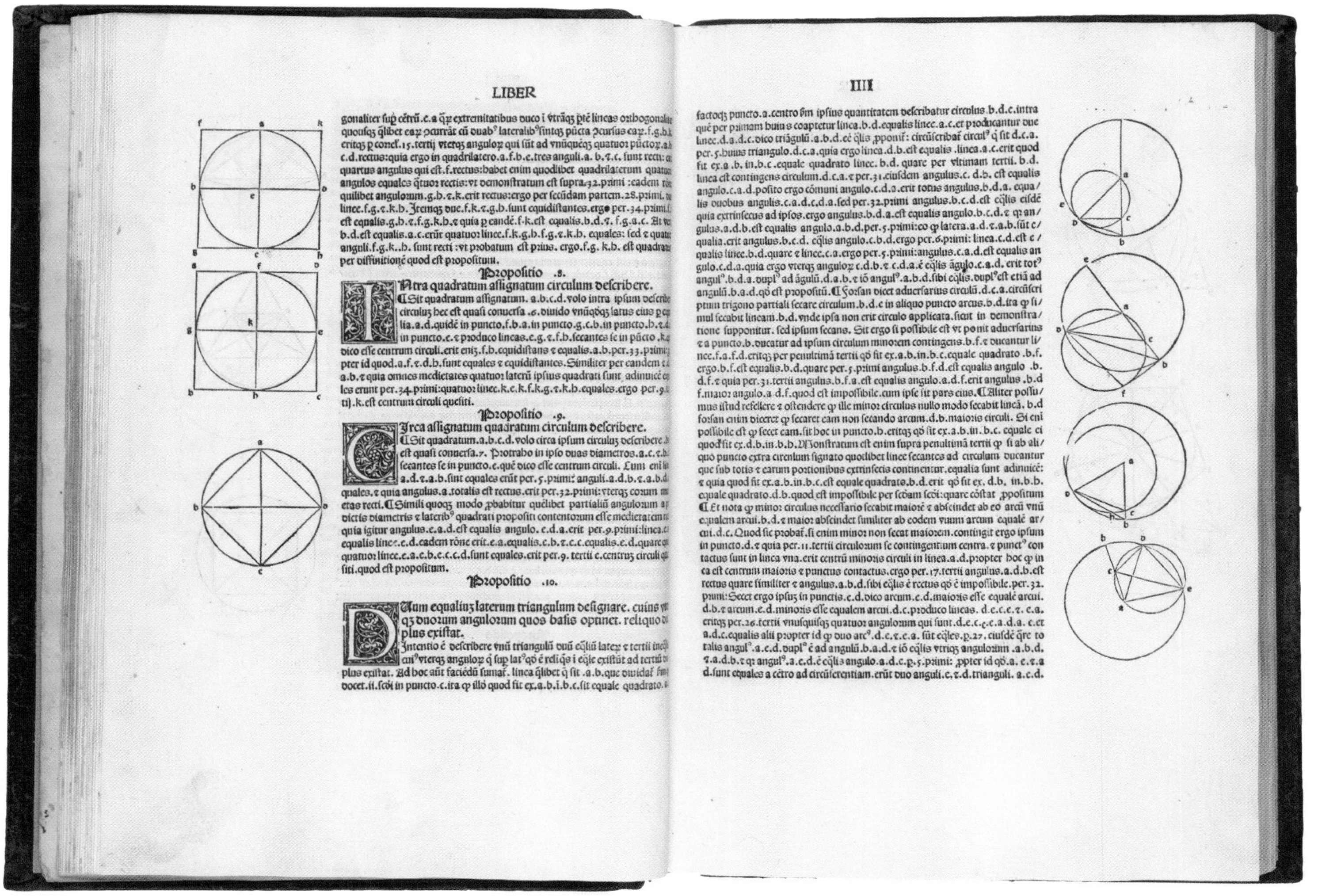
LIBER
IIII
Propositio .8.
Propositio .9.
Propositio .10.

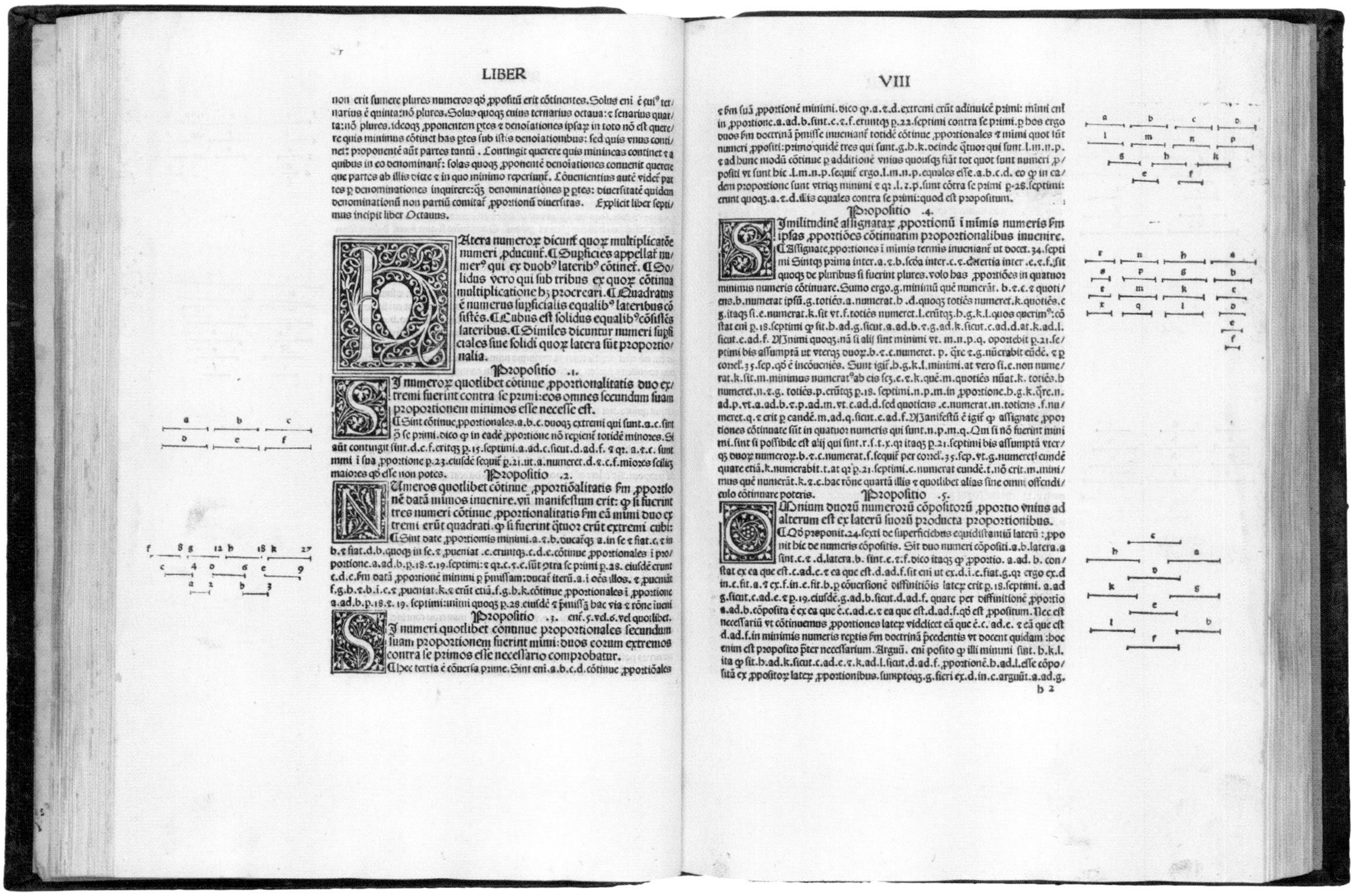
LIBER
VIII
Propositio .1.
Propositio .2.
Propositio .4.
Propositio .5.

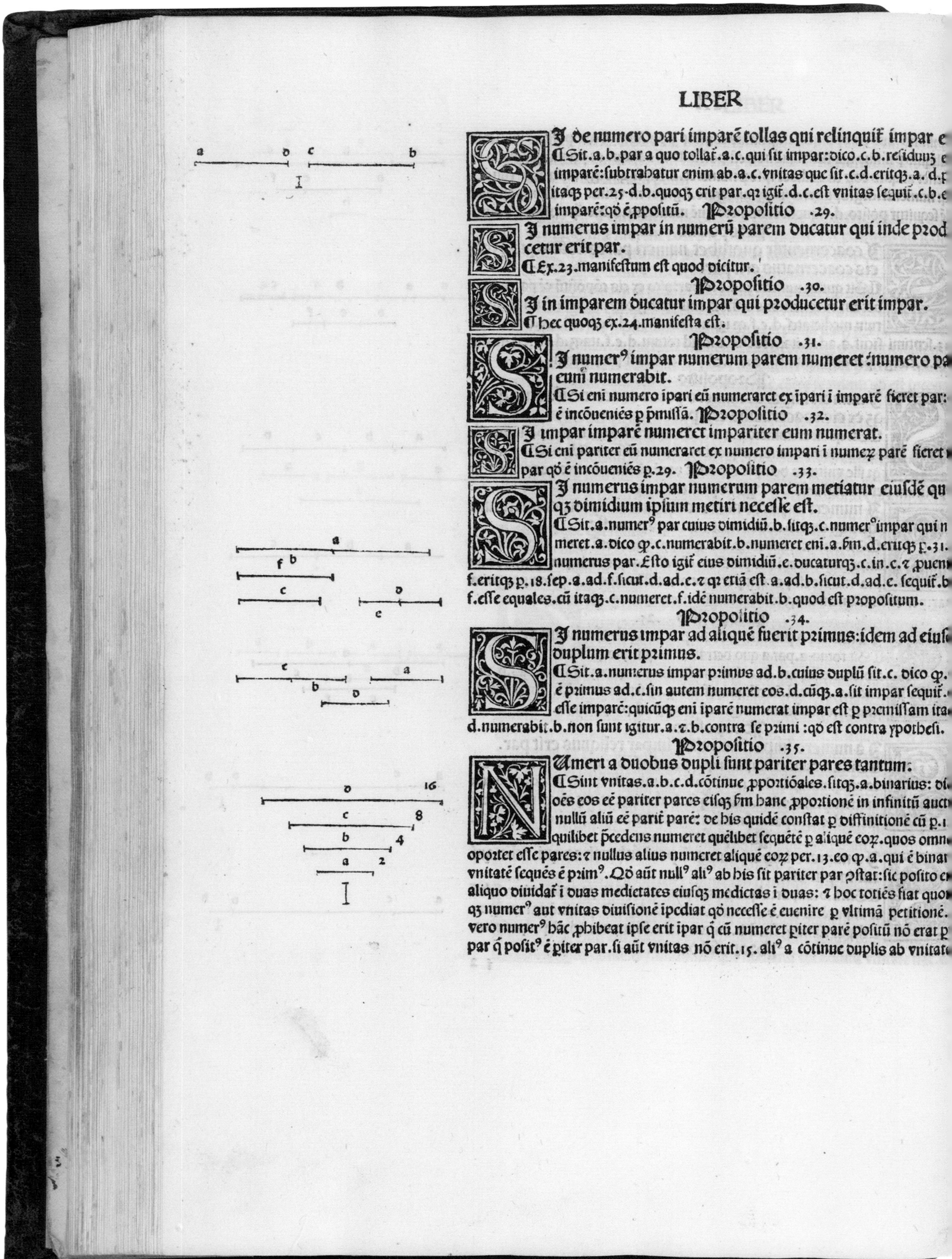

LIBER

SI de numero pari imparē tollas qui relinquit impar e
¶Sit.a.b.par a quo tollat.a.c.qui sit impar: dico.c.b.residuū e
imparē: subtrahatur enim ab.a.c.vnitas que sit.c.d.eritq3.a.d.p
itaq3 per.25.d.b.quoq3 erit par.q2 igit.d.c.est vnitas sequit.c.b.e
imparē: qd ē ppositū. Propositio .29.

SI numerus impar in numerū parem ducatur qui inde prod
cetur erit par.
¶Ex.23.manifestum est quod dicitur.

Propositio .30.

SI in imparem ducatur impar qui producetur erit impar.
¶Hec quoq3 ex.24.manifesta est.

Propositio .31.

SI numer9 impar numerum parem numeret: numero pa
eum numerabit.
¶Si eni numero ipari eū numeraret ex ipari i imparē fieret par:
ē incōueniēs p pmissā. Propositio .32.

SI impar imparē numeret impariter eum numerat.
¶Si eni pariter eū numeraret ex numero impari i numer2 parē fieret
par qd ē incōueniēs p.29. Propositio .33.

SI numerus impar numerum parem metiatur eiusdē qu
q3 dimidium ipsum metiri necesse est.
¶Sit.a.numer9 par cuius dimidiū.b.sitq3.c.numer9 impar qui n
meret.a.dico q2.c.numerabit.b.numeret eni.a.fm.d.eritq3 p.31.
numerus par. Esto igit eius dimidiū.e.ducaturq3.c.in.e.z pueni
f.eritq3 p.18.sep.a.ad.f.sicut.d.ad.e.z q2 etiā est.a.ad.b.sicut.d.ad.e.sequit.b
f.esse equales.cū itaq3.c.numeret.f.idē numerabit.b.quod est propositum.

Propositio .34.

SI numerus impar ad aliquē fuerit primus: idem ad eius
duplum erit primus.
¶Sit.a.numerus impar primus ad.b.cuius duplū sit.c.dico q2.
ē primus ad.c.sin autem numeret eos.d.cūq3.a.sit impar sequit.
esse imparē: quicūq3 eni iparē numerat impar est p premissam ita
d.numerabit.b.non sunt igitur.a.z.b.contra se primi: qd est contra ypothesi.

Propositio .35.

NUmeri a duobus dupli sunt pariter pares tantum:
¶Sint vnitas.a.b.c.d.cōtinue pportiōales.sitq3.a.binarius: di
oēs eos eē pariter pares eisq3 fm hanc pportionē in infinitū auct
nullū aliū eē parit parē: de his quidē constat p diffinitionē cū p.1
quilibet pcedens numeret quēlibet sequētē p aliquē eo2.quos omn
oportet esse pares: z nullus alius numeret aliquē eo2 per.13.eo q2.a.qui ē binar
vnitatē sequēs ē prim9. Qd aūt null9 ali9 ab his sit pariter par pstat: sic posito e
aliquo diuidat i duas medietates eiusq3 medietas i duas: z hoc totiēs fiat quo
q3 numer9 aut vnitas diuisionē ipediat qd necesse ē euenire p vltimā petitionē.
vero numer9 hāc phibeat ipse erit ipar q cū numeret piter parē positū nō erat p
par q posit9 ē piter par.si aūt vnitas nō erit.15.ali9 a cōtinue duplis ab vnitat

Propositio .36.

N Umerus cuiusmedietas est impar est pariter impar.

¶ Sit.a.numerus cuius medietas que sit .b .sit impar dico. a.esse pariter imparē.sit eni.c.binari⁹manifestū itaqꝫ qm̄ ex.c.in.b.fit.a. sit aūt.d.quilibet numerus par numerās.a. qui numeret eū scōm.e eritqꝫ p scōam ptē.20.septimi.e.ad.b .sicut.c.ad.d.igif.e .numerat b.nā qꝛ.c.numerat.d.erit itaqꝫ.e.numerus impar.erat eni ⁊.b.p diffinitionē igif a.est pariter impar.

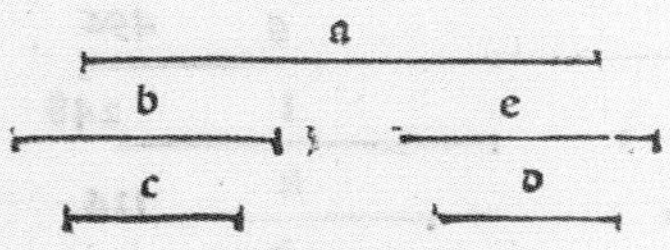

Propositio .37.

O Mnis numerus a duobus nō duplus cuius medietas est par est pariter par ⁊ impariter.

¶ Sit numer⁹.a. nō duplus a duobus cuius medietas que sit .b.ponatur par.dico ipsū esse pariter parē ⁊ ipariter.sit eni.c.binarius de quo manifestū ē ꝙ ipse numerat.a.ꝫm.b.qꝛ vero.a.nō est duplus a duobus:necesse ē si eius medietas que ē.b.in alias duas medietates diuidaf:medietatisqꝫ medietas in alias duas vt tandē occurrat numerus impediēs diuisionē qui ꝓpter hoc ꝙ diuisionē nō recipit erit impar.sitqꝫ is in quo sistit diuisio.d. in numero q̄ppe necesse ē stari qꝛ siusqꝫ ad vnitatē puenirect diuisio eēt.a de numeris duplis a binario de quibus nō ē:de.d.vero manifestū ē ꝙ ipse numerat.a.p hanc cōem sciam:ois numerus numerās aliū numerat omnē numeratū ab illo.Numeret ergo eū ꝫm.c.eritqꝫ.e.par.Alioquin.cū.d.sit maior impar sequeref p.30.a.eē imparē:qꝛ igif.b.numerus par numerat.a.ꝫm.c.qui quoqꝫ ē par est eni binarius At vero.e.numer⁹ par numerat eādē ꝫm.d.q̄ ē impar.ꝯstat ex diffinitiōe numerꝝ a.eē piter parē ⁊ impiter:qd̄ ē ꝓpositū.

Propositio .38.

S I de scōo atqꝫ vltimo numerorꝝ cōtinue ꝓportionalium equale primi dematur quantū ē reliquū scōi ad primum tm̄ eē reliquū vltimi ad coacervatum ex cūctis precedentibus necessario comprobatur.

¶ Sint ꝯtinue ꝓportionales.a.b.c.d.e.f.g.h.demafqꝫ.de.c.d.eq̄lis.a.b.qui sit.c.k.⁊ de.g.h.qui sit.g.l.dico tūc ꝙ ꝓportio.k.d.ad.a.b. ē sicut.l.h ad cōpositū ex.e.f.c.d.⁊.a.b.sumaf ex.g.h.equalis.e.f.qui sit.g.m. ⁊ eq̄lis.c.d.q̄ sit.g.n.eritqꝫ.l.n.eq̄lis.k.d.manifestū aūt ē p.12.sep.ꝙ cū sit.g.h.ad. g.m. sicut g.n.ad.g.n.erit.h.m. residuū ad .m.n.residuū sint.g.h.ad.g.m.ideoqꝫ sicut.e.f. ad.c.d.sili quoqꝫ mō erit.m.n.ad.l.n.sicut.c.d.ad.a.b.pmutatim igif erit. h.m. ad.e.f.⁊.m.n.ad.c.d.sicut.n.l.ad.a.b.itaqꝫ cōiuncti p.13.sep.erit.l.h. cōpositus ex.h.m.m.n.⁊.l.n.ad cōpositū ex.e.f.c.d.⁊.a.b.sicut.l.n.ad.a.b. ideoqꝫ sicut.k. d.ad.a.b.qd̄ est propositum.

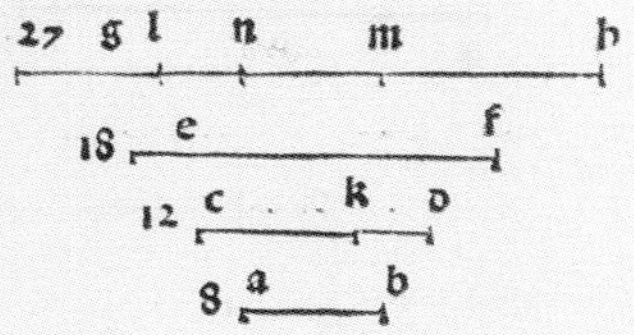

Propositio .39.

C Um coaptati fuerint numeri ab vnitate cōtinue dupli qui cōiuncti faciāt numerū primū extremus eorꝝ in aggregatum ex eis ductus producit numerum perfectum.

¶ Sint ab vnitate ꝯtinue dupli.a.b.c.d.ex eis aūt ⁊ vnitate coacervatus sit.e.qui ponaf eē numer⁹prim⁹in quē.c.multiplicef.d.⁊ proueniat.f.g.dico.f.g.eē numerꝝ pfectū. Sumāf igif.h.k.l.ꝯtinue dupli ad.e.ut tot sint.e.h.k.l.quot sint cōtinue dupli ad vnitatē sumpti.eritqꝫ p equā ꝓportionalitatē.l.ad.e.sicut.d.ad.a.quare p primā ptē.20.sep.ex.a. in.l.ꝓuenit.f.g. Nā ipse f.g.ꝓuenit ex.d.in.e.⁊ qꝛ.a.ē binari⁹ ē.f.g.duplus ad.l.sunt igif. e.h.k. l.⁊.f.g.

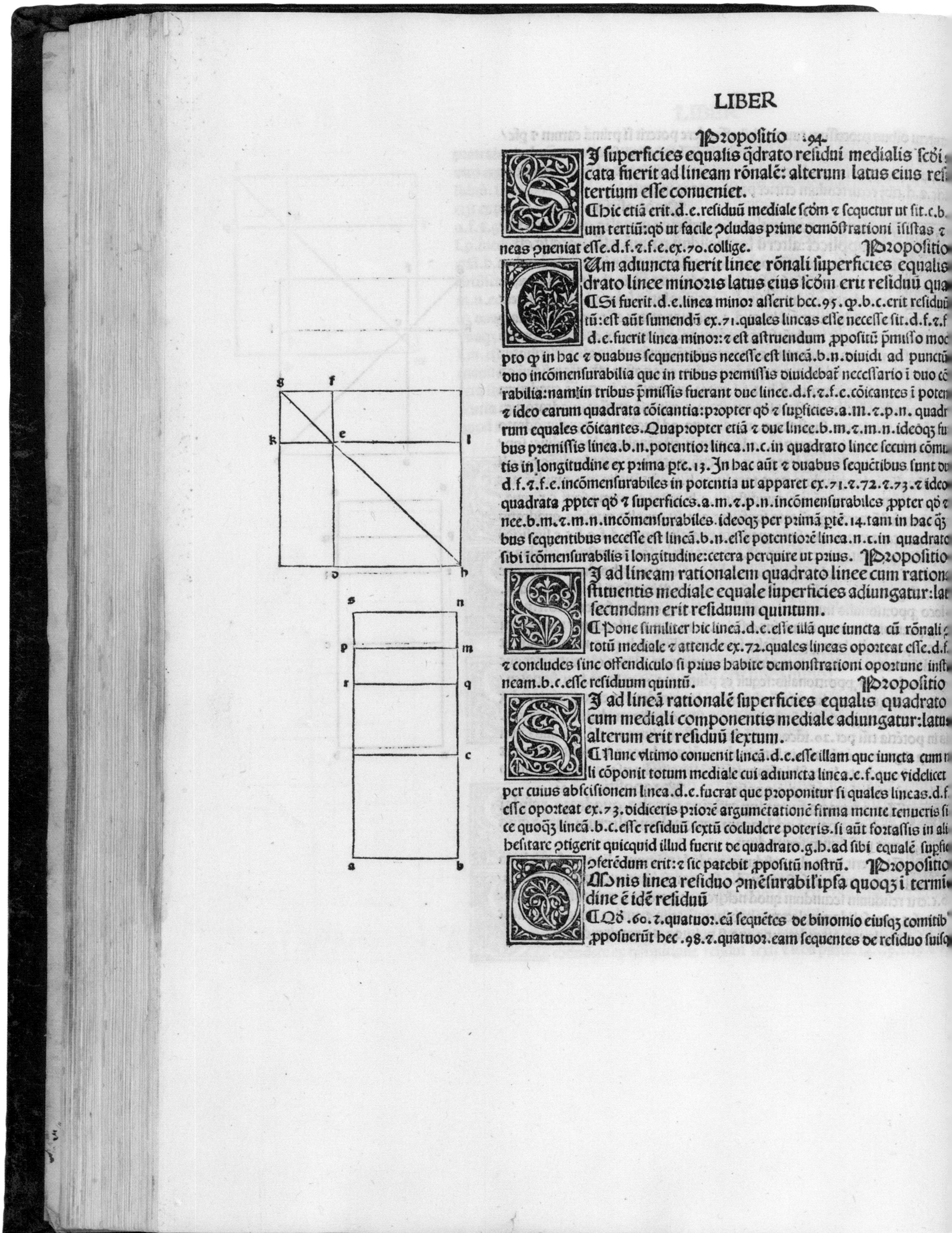

LIBER

Propositio .94.

SI superficies equalis q̃drato residui medialis scdi
cata fuerit ad lineam rõnalẽ: alterum latus eius resi
tertium esse conueniet.
¶ hic etiã erit.d.e.residuũ mediale scdm ꝛ sequetur ut sit.c.b.
um tertiũ: qd ut facile ↄcludas prime demõstrationi isistas ꝛ
neas ↄueniat esse.d.f.ꝛ.f.e.ex.70.collige. Propositio

CUm adiuncta fuerit linee rõnali superficies equalis
drato linee minoris latus eius scdm erit residuũ qua
¶ Si fuerit.d.e.linea minor asserit hec.95.q̃.b.c.erit residuũ
tũ: est aũt sumendũ ex.71.quales lineas esse necesse sit.d.f.ꝛ.f
d.e.fuerit linea minor: ꝛ est astruendum ꝑpositũ: p̃misso mod
pro q̃ in hac ꝛ duabus sequentibus necesse est lineã.b.n.diuidi ad punctũ
duo incõmensurabilia que in tribus premissis diuidebat̃ necessario i duo cõ
rabilia: nam in tribus p̃missis fuerant due linee.d.f.ꝛ.f.e.cõicantes i poten
ꝛ ideo earum quadrata cõicantia: propter qd ꝛ supficies.a.m.ꝛ.p.n. quadr
rum equales cõicantes. Quapropter etiã ꝛ due linee.b.m.ꝛ.m.n.ideoq3 fu
bus premissis linea.b.n.potentior linea.n.c.in quadrato linee secum cõmu
tis in longitudine ex prima pte.13. In hac aũt ꝛ duabus sequẽtibus sunt du
d.f.ꝛ.f.e.incõmensurabiles in potentia ut apparet ex.71.ꝛ.72.ꝛ.73.ꝛ ideo
quadrata ꝑpter qd ꝛ superficies.a.m.ꝛ.p.n.incõmensurabiles ꝑpter qd ꝛ
nee.b.m.ꝛ.m.n.incõmensurabiles.ideoq3 per primã ptẽ.14.tam in hac q̃3
bus sequentibus necesse est lineã.b.n.esse potentiorẽ linea.n.c.in quadrato
sibi icõmensurabilis i longitudine: cetera perquire ut prius. Propositio

SI ad lineam rationalem quadrato linee cum ration
stituentis mediale equale superficies adiungatur: lat
secundum erit residuum quintum.
¶ Pone similiter hic lineã.d.e.esse illã que iuncta cũ rõnali ↄ
totũ mediale ꝛ attende ex.72.quales lineas oporteat esse.d.f.
ꝛ concludes sine offendiculo si prius habite demonstrationi oportune insi
neam.b.c.esse residuum quintũ. Propositio

SI ad lineã rationalẽ superficies equalis quadrato
cum mediali componentis mediale adiungatur: latus
alterum erit residuũ sextum.
¶ Nunc vltimo conuenit lineã.d.e.esse illam que iuncta cum n
li cõponit totum mediale cui adiuncta linea.e.f.que videlicet
per cuius abscisionem linea.d.e.fuerat que proponitur si quales lineas.d.f
esse oporteat ex.73.vidiceris priorẽ argumẽtationẽ firma mente tenueris si
ce quoq̃3 lineã.b.c.esse residuũ sextũ cõcludere poteris. si aũt fortassis in ali
hesitare ↄtigerit quicquid illud fuerit de quadrato.g.h.ad sibi equalẽ supfic
ↄferẽdum erit: ꝛ sic patebit ꝑpositũ nostrũ. Propositio

OMnis linea residuo ↄmẽsurabil' ipsa quoq3 i termi
dine ẽ idẽ residuũ
¶ Qd.60.ꝛ.quatuor.eã sequẽtes de binomio eiusq3 comitib'
ꝑposuerũt hec.98.ꝛ.quatuor.eam sequentes de residuo suisq

omittibus verum esse proponunt: quibus qui vsqꝫ ad solitum habitum institerit
as ignorare non poterit. Quicquid autem in illis de cōicantia in longitudine et
otentia tantum dictum est: in his quoqꝫ idem oportet intelligi. nam omnis linea
siduo cōmunicans in longitudine siue in potentia tm̄ ipsa etiā est residuum. sed
communicat in longitudine: non solum est ipsa residuum. sed etiam eiusdē spēi
esiduum. Verbi gratia: linea cōmunicans in longitudine residuo primo est resi/
uū pmū: ⁊ secūdo cōicans est scōm. sic quoqꝫ in ceteris: Qd̄ aūt linea communi/
at residuo in potentia tantum: ipsam quoqꝫ necesse est esse residuum sed nō eius/
em speciei: imo īpossibile est vt linea cōmunicans in potentia tantū residuo pri/
o aut scōo aut tertio aut quarto aut quinto cadat simul cum eo sub eadem specie
d necesse est vt ābo cadāt simul sub trib⁹ primis speciebus aut ābo simul sub tri/
us postremis. Sit itaqꝫ exempli gratia. a. residuū cui cōmunicet. b. in longitudi/
e: dico q̄ .b. erit residuū eiusdē speciei cū. a. Adiungatur enim linea. c. ad lineā
. ⁊ cum illa sit per cuius abscisionē. a. fuit residuū: ⁊ ad. b. adiūgat̄ alia que sit. d.
d quā sic se habeat. b. sicut. a. ad. c. sitqꝫ composita ex. a. ⁊. c. e. composita vero ex
. ⁊. d. sit. f. eritqꝫ ex permutata ꝓportionalitate. a. ad. b. sicut. c. ad. d. ⁊ p. 13. quin
erit. c. ad. f. sicut. a. ad. b. vel sicut. c. ad. d. cum itaqꝫ. a. cōmunicet cum. b. erit per
. c. cōmunicans cum. d. ⁊. e. quoqꝫ cōmunicans cum. f. ⁊ quia etiam est necessa/
o ex permutata proportionalitate. e. ad. c. sicut. f ad. d. sequitur p. 12. vt si fuerit
potentior. c. in quadrato linee sibi cōicantis in longitudine vel si forte incōmen/
rabilis: sit similiter. f. potentior. d. at qm̄ omnis linea cōmunicans in longitudi
e linee rationali est similiter illi rationalis: similiter dico quia ambe erunt rationa
s in longitudine vel ambe in potentia tantum: sequitur ex diffinitionibus residu
um vt. b. sit residuum eiusdem speciei cum. a. Si autē. b. cōmunicat in potentia
ntū cum. a. ipsa quoqꝫ erit residuum non tamen eiusdem speciei necessario. sed
ēadmodū dictū est: cuius demōstratio ex his que in. 60. de binomijs dicta sunt
lligenda est.

Propositio .99.

Omnis linea vtrilibꝫ residuo mediali cōmunicans: est sub ipsius termio ⁊ ordine residuū mediale. ¶ Vez est qd̄ dicit̄ siue cōicet linea cum vtrolibet residuo mediali in longitudine siue in potentia. Sit enim. a. vtrūlibet residuū mediale cui. b. cōicet in lōgi/
tudine vl̄ potētia. dico q̄ .b. ē etiā residuū mediale q̄le fuerit. a. adiū
gat̄ eni linea. c. ad lineā. a. ⁊ sit. c. p c⁹ abscisionē. a. fuit residuū mediale: ⁊ ad. b.
adiūgat̄ alia q̄ sit. d. sitqꝫ. b. ad. d. sicut. a. ad. c. totaqꝫ ꝯposita ex. a. ⁊. c. sit. e. ⁊ ex.
. d. sit. f. describāt̄ igit̄ q̄drata. c. ⁊. d. q̄ sint. g. ⁊. h. ⁊ supficies. e. i. c. sit. k. ⁊. f. i. d. ⁊
it. l. Et q̄r ē vt pri⁹. e. ad. f. ⁊ c. ad. d. sicut. a. ad. b. sūt aūt. e. ⁊. c. mediales potentia
m̄ cōicātes ex. 69. ⁊. 70. sequit̄ ex. 21. vt. f. ⁊. d. eis cōicātes. sint etiā mediales po
tētia tm̄ cōicātes: ꝯstat aūt ex prima sexti q̄ sit. k. ad. g. sicut. e. ad. c. ⁊. l. ad. h. sicut
. ad. d. ⁊ q̄r ē. e. ad. c. sicut. f. ad. d. sequit̄ ut sit. k. ad. g. sicut. l. ad. h. Et pmutati. k.
d. l. sicut. g. ad. h. cū q̄. g. cōicet cū. h. sequit̄ vt. k. cōicet. cū. l. Si igit̄. k. ē rōnale qd̄
ē in residuo mediali primo erit etiā p diffinitionē. l. rōnalis q̄re p. 69. b. etiā ē resi/
duū mediale primū. si aūt. k. sit medial̄ qd̄ ē i residuo mediali scōo: erit p. 21. etiā. l
medialis: ideoqꝫ. b. p. 70. residuū mediale scōꝫ q̄re ꝯstat ꝓpositū. Idē aliter Si liēa
. cōicat cū liēa. a. q̄ ē vtrūlibet residuū mediale i lōgitudie l̄ i potētia sit supficies
. e. adiūcta ad lineā rōalē. c. d. eq̄lis q̄drato. a. ⁊. f. g. eq̄lis q̄drato. b. erūtqꝫ ob hoc

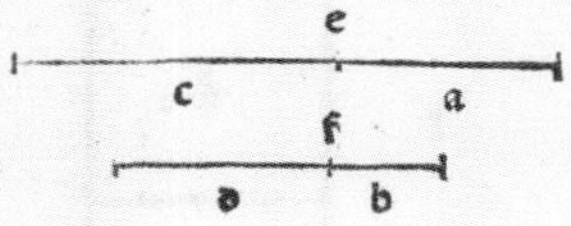

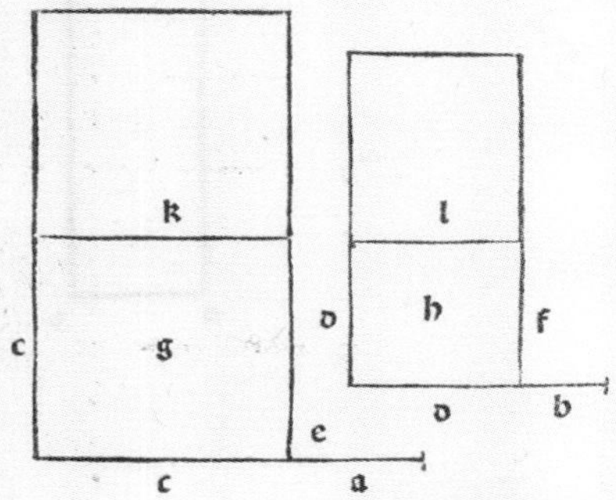

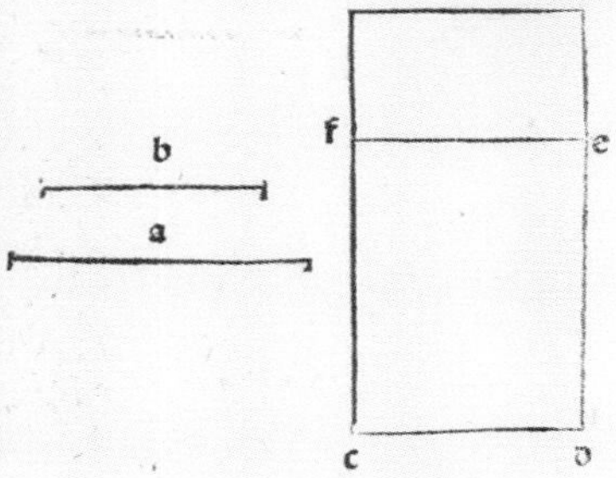

1483 **Bonino de Boninis** Robertus Valturius, *De re militari*. Verona: Bonino de Boninis, 1483. 30.5 cm.

Illustrator: Matteo de' Pasti.

In around 1455, Robertus Valturius wrote this book about the art of warfare. The illustrations are attributed to Matteo de' Pasti (*c.* 1420–67/68). Valturius worked in the service of Sigismondo Pandolfo Malatesta, army commander and lord of Rimini. Sigismondo ordered some (handwritten) copies of his manuscript to be presented to several famous leaders, including his father-in-law Francesco Sforza, Lorenzo de' Medici, Louis XI of France, and Ottoman sultan Mehmed II.

Valturius's text was for the most part based on the classics; the new weapons of warfare that made use of gunpowder are only dealt with in passing. The technical and scientific illustrations, however, paint a contemporary picture. In its time, *De re militari* was the ultimate handbook for military leaders: it deals with siege towers, catapults, various cannons (among them a revolving platform with eight cannons), a submarine, and the hand grenade invented by Sigismondo.

The illustrations from the first Veronese edition (1472) are reproduced by Boninis in 95 woodcuts; a woodcut of a military tent has been added. Leonardo da Vinci borrowed some of his designs from Boninis's edition. Boninis's real name was Dobrić Dobričević (*c.* 1454–1528). He had learned the trade in Venice and set up with Venetian printing materials in Verona in 1480. Immediately after finishing *De re militari* he must have relocated to Brescia, where he produced over forty books. In 1491, he left for Lyon. Some time later, he relocated to Treviso, where he was active as a publisher and occasionally as a printer. Boninis's popular edition of Valturius was republished in Paris in 1532, as a reprint and in a French translation. AP

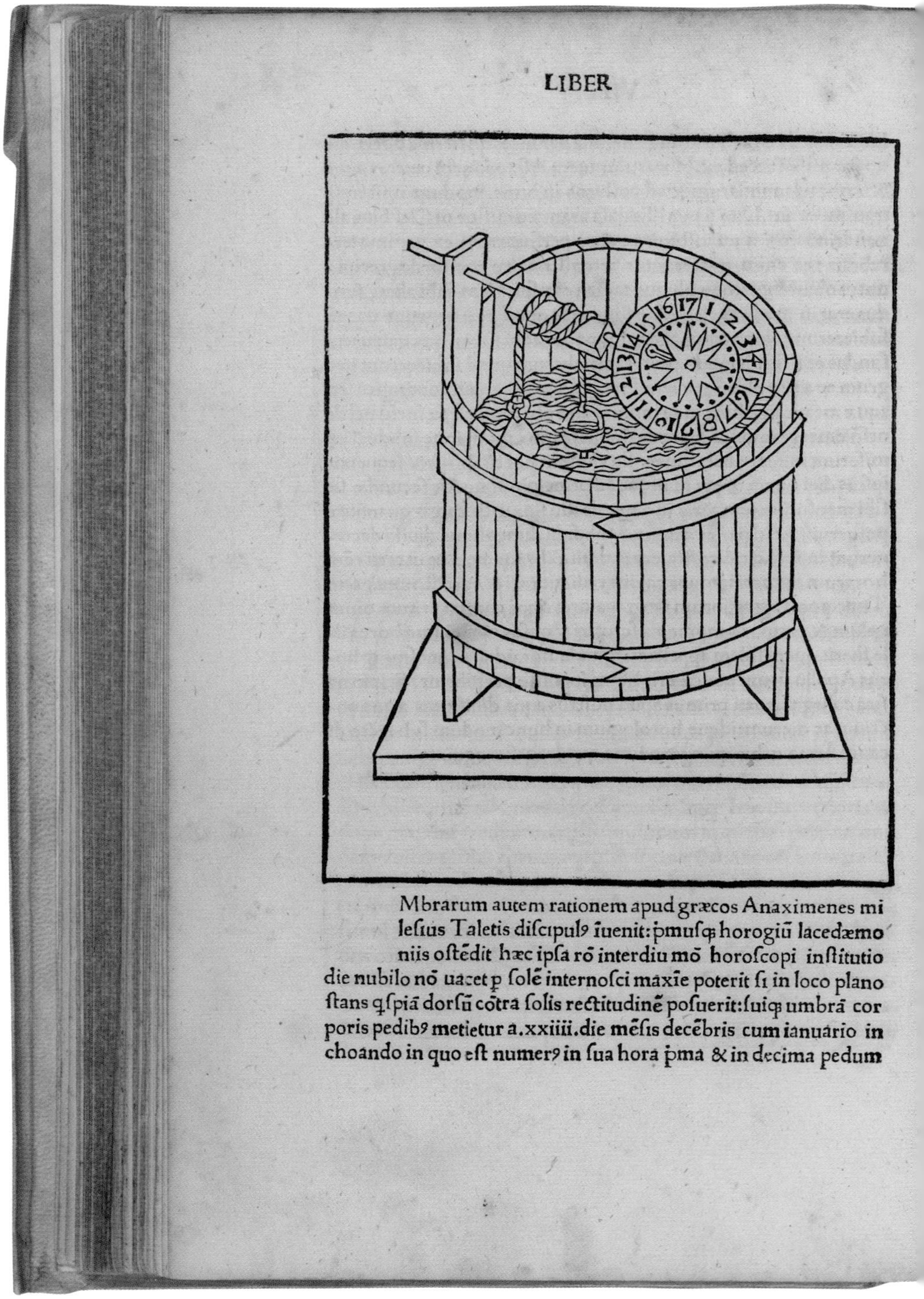

LIBER

Mbrarum autem rationem apud græcos Anaximenes mi
leſius Taletis diſcipul9 īuenit: ꝑmuſq; horogiū lacedæmo
niis oſtēdit hæc ipſa rō interdiu mō horoſcopi inſtitutio
die nubilo nō uacet ꝑ ſolē internoſci maxīe poterit ſi in loco plano
ſtans qſpiā dorſū cōtra ſolis rectitudinē poſuerit: ſuiq; umbrā cor
poris pedib9 metietur a.xxiiii.die mēſis decēbris cum ianuario in
choando in quo eſt numer9 in ſua hora ꝑma & in decima pedum

A roman following the general style of Nicolas Jenson's but inferior in cutting, alignment and printing. One can nevertheless see some more modern features, such as the larger and lower dot on the i, the tighter spacing and some narrower capitals.

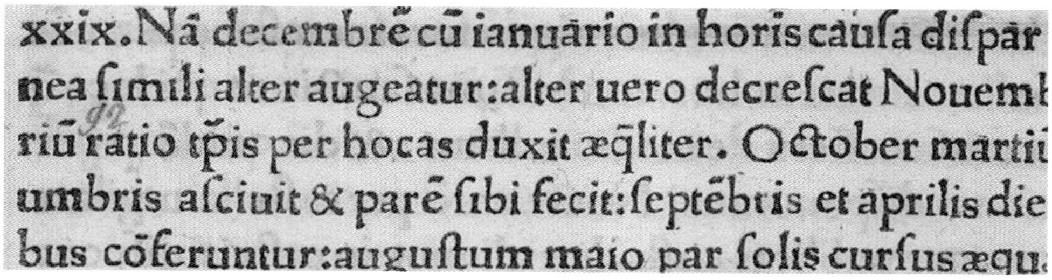
xxix. Nā decembrē cū ianuário in horis caúſa diſpar
nea ſimili alter augeatur:alter uero decreſcat Nouemb
riū ratio tp̄is per hocas duxit æq̄liter. October martii
umbris aſciuit & parē ſibi fecit:ſeptēbris et aprilis die
bus cōferuntur:auguſtum maio par ſolis curſus æqu

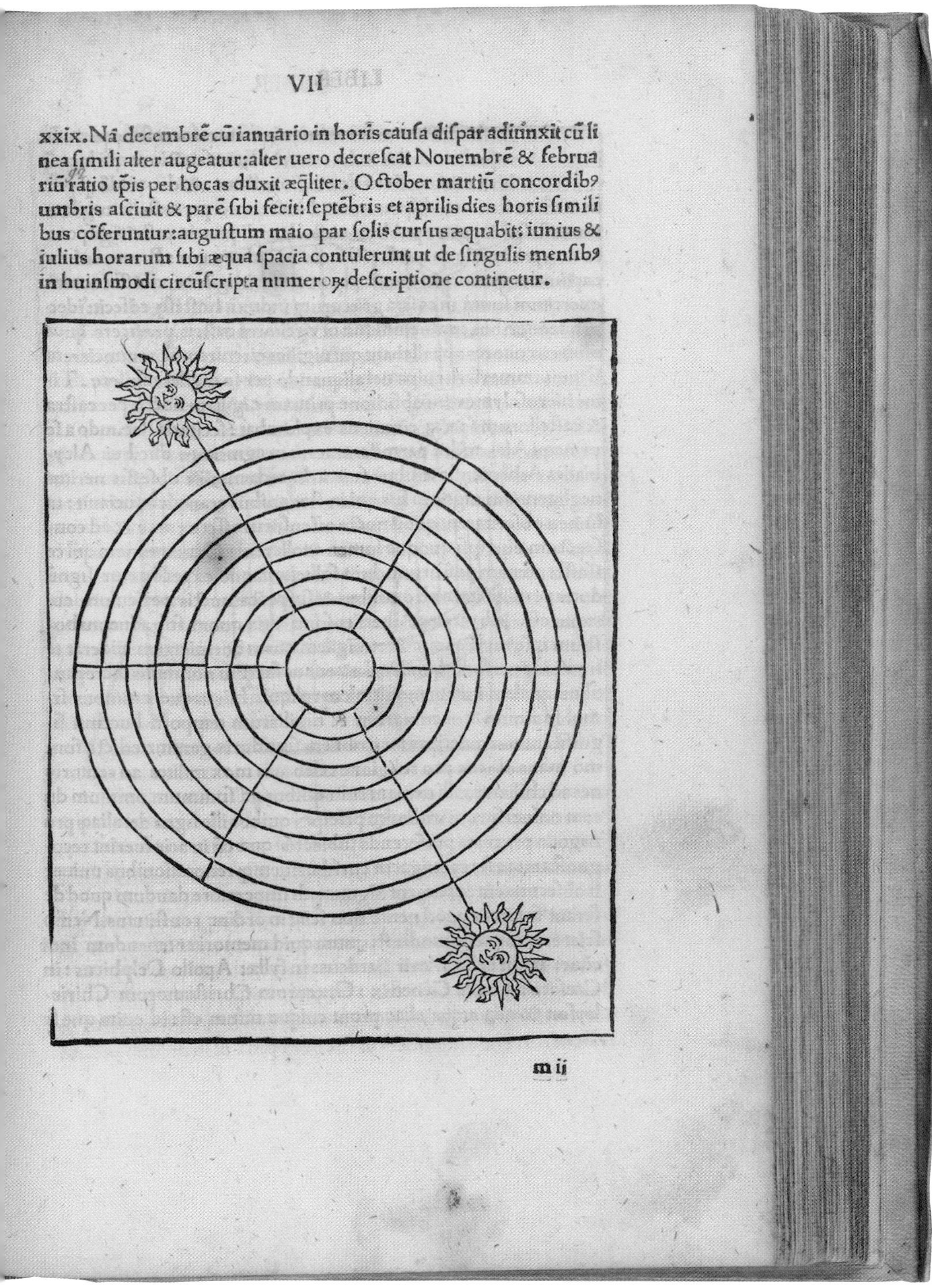
VII

xxix. Nā decembrē cū ianuário in horis caúſa diſpar adiūnxit cū li
nea ſimili alter augeatur:alter uero decreſcat Nouembrē & februa
riū ratio tp̄is per hocas duxit æq̄liter. October martiū concordibꝰ
umbris aſciuit & parē ſibi fecit:ſeptēbris et aprilis dies horis ſimili
bus cōferuntur:auguſtum maio par ſolis curſus æquabit: iunius &
iulius horarum ſibi æqua ſpacia contulerunt ut de ſingulis menſibꝰ
in huinſmodi circūſcripta numerorū deſcriptione continetur.

m ij

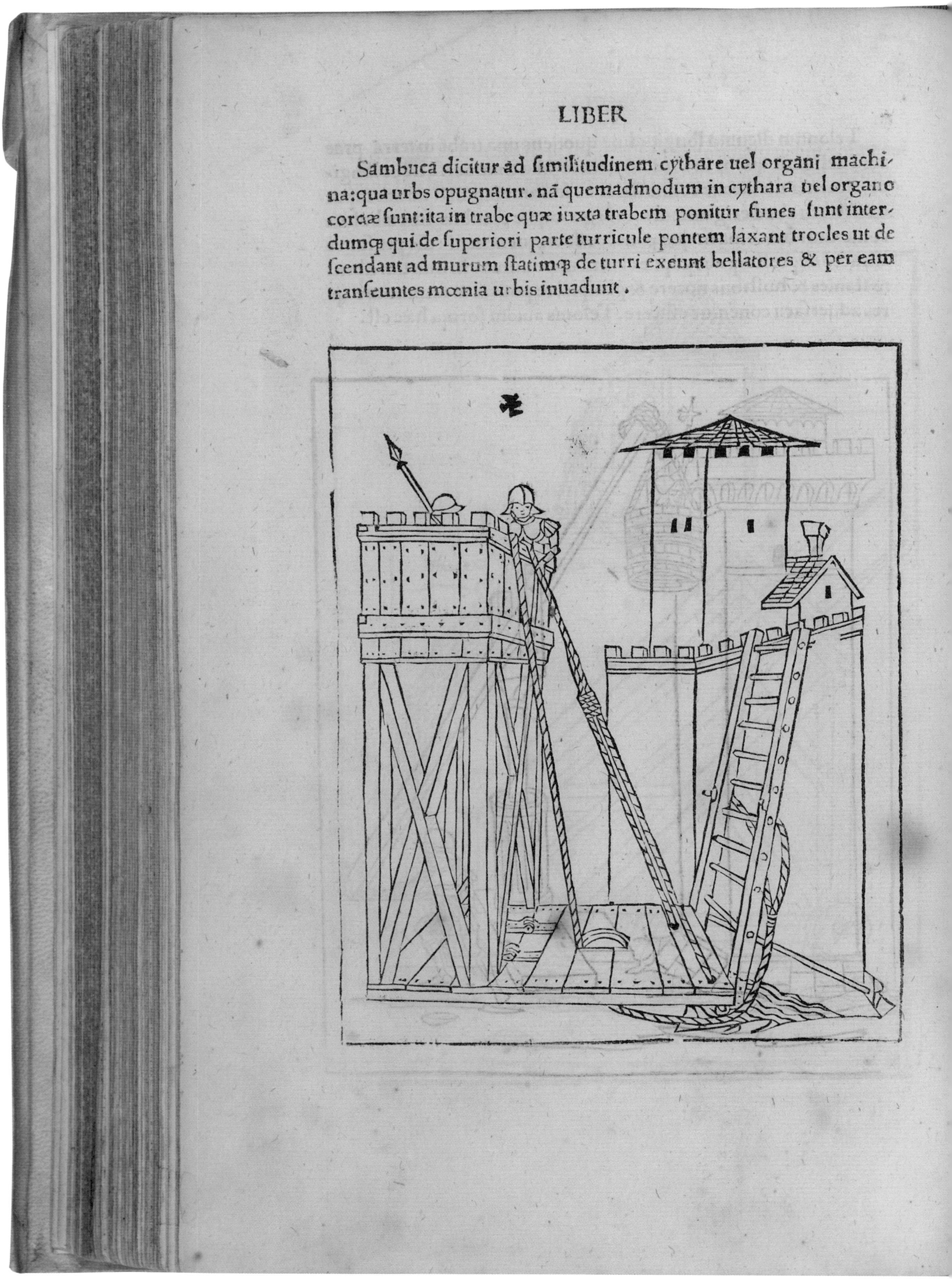

LIBER

Sambuca dicitur ad similitudinem cythare uel organi machina: qua urbs opugnatur. nā quemadmodum in cythara uel organo cordæ sunt: ita in trabe quæ iuxta trabem ponitur funes sunt interdumq; qui de superiori parte turricule pontem laxant trocles ut descendant ad murum statimq; de turri exeunt bellatores & per eam transeuntes mœnia urbis inuadunt.

X

Exostrã pons dicitur qui de turri lignea in murum repente pro ducitur: factus est duabus trabibus septusq3 uimine : quem subito p latum inter turrem murumq3 constituunt & per eã egredientes ma chinam bellatores in ciuitatem transeunt & muros occupant.

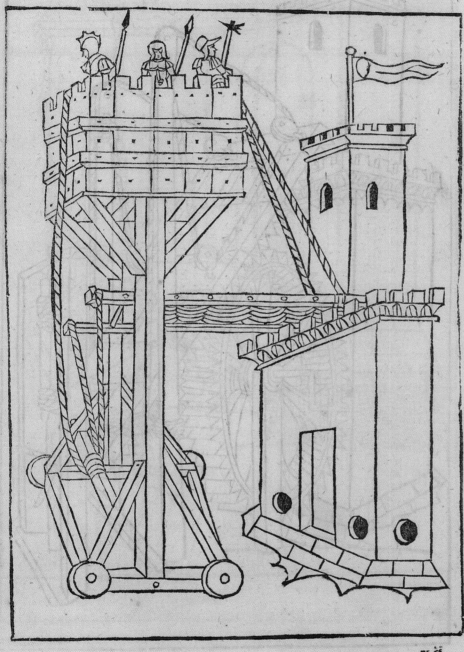

x ii

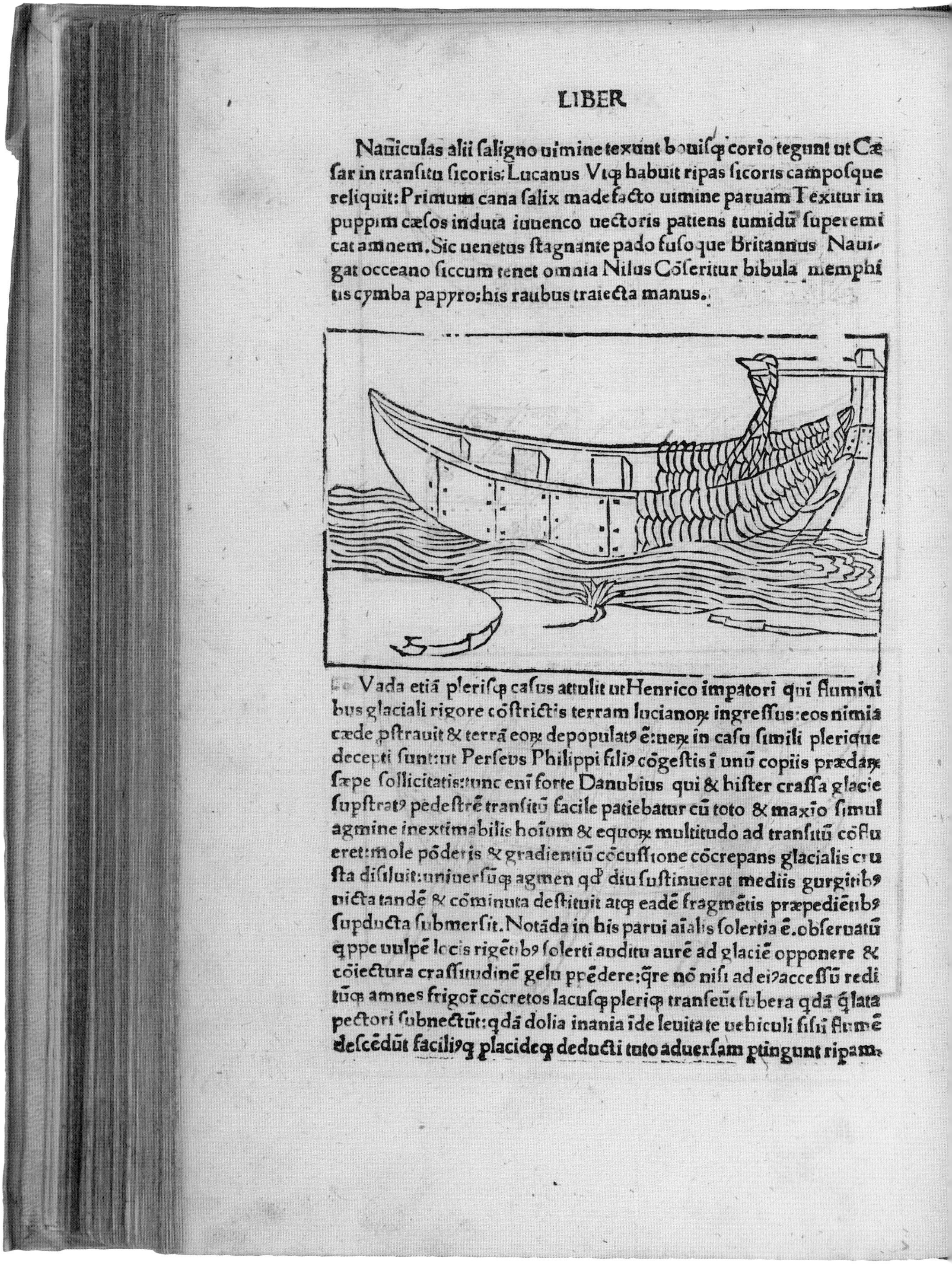

Naũiculas alii saligno uimine texunt bouisq; corio tegunt ut Cæsar in transitu sicoris; Lucanus Vtq; habuit ripas sicoris camposque reliquit: Primum cana salix madefacto uimine paruam Texitur in puppim cæsos induta iuuenco uectoris patiens tumidũ superemicat amnem. Sic uenetus stagnante pado fusoque Britannus Nauigat occeano siccum tenet omnia Nilus Cõseritur bibula memphitis cymba papyro; his raubus traiecta manus.

Vada etiã plerisq; casus attulit ut Henrico impatori qui fluminibus glaciali rigore cõstrictis terram lucianorũ ingressus: eos nimia cæde pstrauit & terrã eorũ depopulatus ẽ: uerũ in casu simili plerique decepti sunt: ut Perseus Philippi filius cõgestis ĩ unũ copiis prædarũ sæpe sollicitatis: tunc enĩ forte Danubius qui & hister crassa glacie supstratus pedestrẽ transitũ facile patiebatur cũ toto & maxĩo simul agmine inextimabilis hoĩum & equorũ multitudo ad transitũ cõflueret: mole põderis & gradientiũ cõcussione cõcrepans glacialis crusta dissiluit: uniuersũq; agmen qd diu sustinuerat mediis gurgitibus uicta tandẽ & cõminuta destituit atq; eadẽ fragmẽtis præpedientibus supducta submersit. Notãda in his parui aĩalis solertia ẽ. obseruatũ qppe uulpẽ locis rigẽtibus solerti auditu aurẽ ad glaciẽ opponere & cõiectura crassitudinẽ gelu ppẽdere; qre nõ nisi ad eius accessũ reditũq; amnes frigorẽ cõcretos lacusq; pleriq; transeũt subera qdã q̃ lata pectori subnectũt: qdã dolia inania ĩde leuitate uehiculi sisũ flumẽ descẽdũt faciliusq; placideq; deducti tuto aduersam ptingunt ripam.

1485 **Jacob Bellaert** Bartholomaeus Anglicus, *Van den proprieteyten der dinghen*. Haarlem: Jacob Bellaert, 1485. 26 cm.

Illustrator: Master of Bellaert.

Jacob Bellaert printed and published this popular medieval encyclopedia in Dutch. The period during which he was active in Haarlem was short (from late 1483 to the end of the summer of 1486) but productive. He may have been previously employed by Gheraert Leeu, printer in nearby Gouda. For the printing of *Van den proprieteyten der dinghen*, Bellaert used a new typeface and eleven specially made woodcuts. Among the eighteen editions that are known to have been published by Bellaert, this is the only one in which his name is printed.

This encyclopedia was originally completed in around 1245 by the Franciscan monk Bartholomaeus Anglicus, who hailed from England. Divided into nineteen books, which are each subdivided into chapters, *Van den proprieteyten der dinghen* ('Of the Properties of Things') describes the properties of all things 'both visible and invisible, corporeal and incorporeal', and presents the contemporary scientific knowledge required to interpret the Bible correctly. The hierarchical order in which God was believed to have arranged all of creation is reflected in the encyclopedia's arrangement.

Eleven of these nineteen books open with beautiful full-page woodcuts (20 x 14 cm), which have been coloured in this copy. The illustrations consist of multiple scenes that exemplify the contents of the book that they introduce. The anonymous artist also illustrated several other editions by Bellaert. Because of the innovative qualities of his extraordinary woodcuts, he is now known as the 'Master of Bellaert' (*fl.* 1484–86). AP

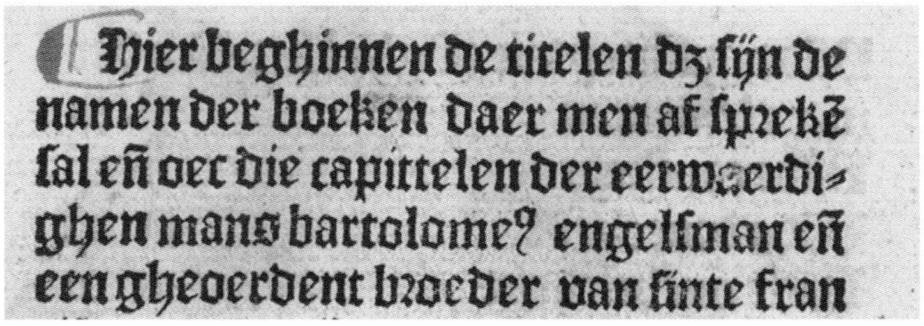

Hier beghinnen de titelen dz ſÿn de
namen der boeken daer men af ſprekē
ſal eñ oec die capittelen der eerwaerdi-
ghen mans bartolome? engelſman eñ
een gheoerdent broeder van ſinte fran

This Textura is first known from Bellaert's books, the earliest of which was published in 1483, but it was used a few months later by Gheraert Leeu. Bellaert used no other types and it has been suggested that this one originated with Leeu, fifty kilometres away, but the relationship between Leeu and Bellaert remains unclear.

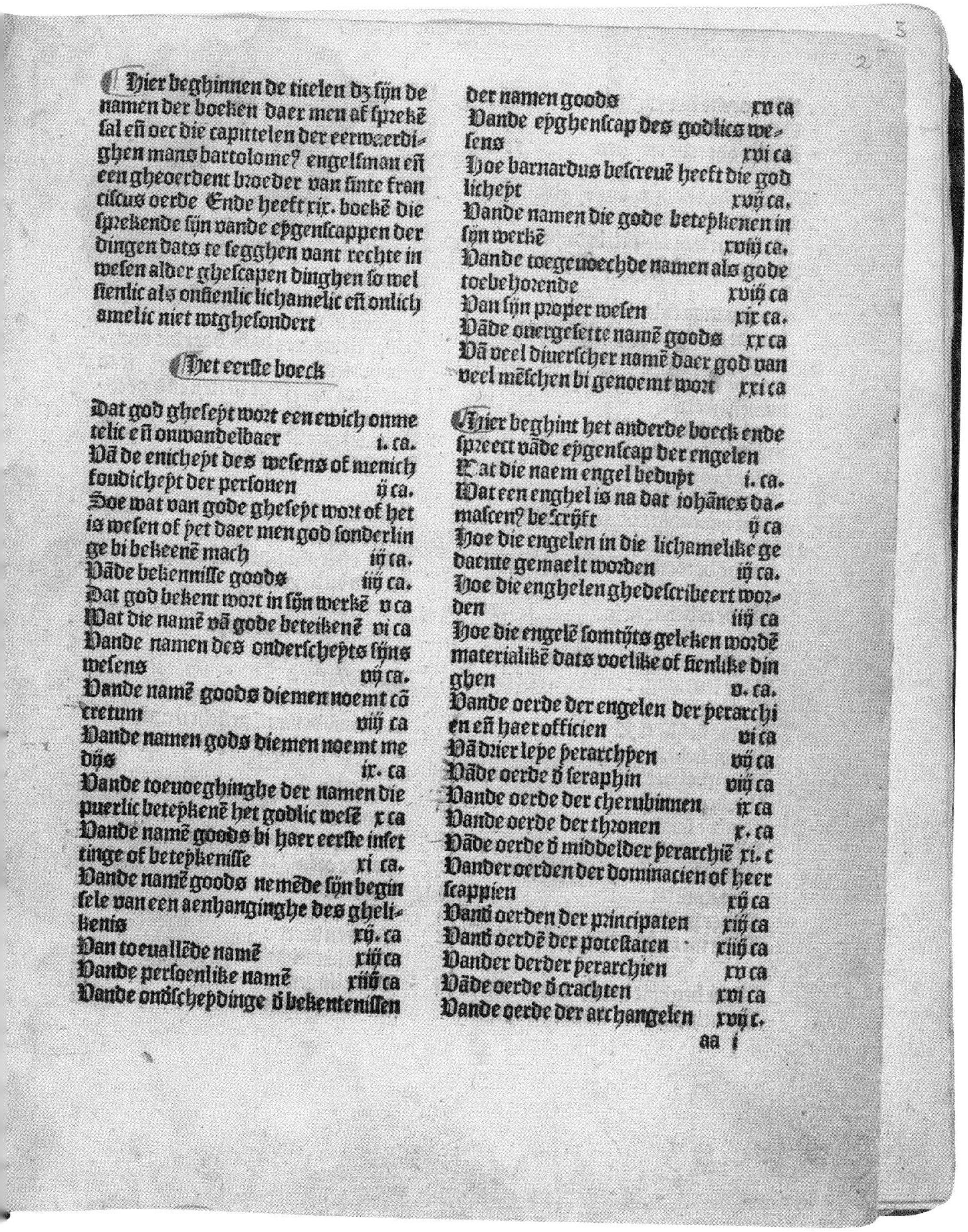

Hier beghinnen de titelen dz ſÿn de
namen der boeken daer men af ſprekē
ſal eñ oec die capittelen der eerwaerdi-
ghen mans bartolome? engelſman eñ
een gheoerdent broeder van ſinte fran
ciſcus oerde Ende heeft xix. boekē die
ſprekende ſÿn vande eygenſcappen der
dingen dats te ſegghen vant rechte in
weſen alder gheſcapen dinghen ſo wel
ſienlic als onſienlic lichamelic eñ onlich
amelic niet wtgheſondert

Het eerſte boeck

Dat god gheſeyt wort een ewich onme
telic eñ onwandelbaer i. ca.
Vā de enicheyt des weſens of menich
foudicheyt der perſonen ij ca.
Soe wat van gode gheſeyt wort of het
is weſen of yet daer men god ſonderlin
ge bi bekeenē mach iij ca.
Vāde bekenniſſe goods iiij ca.
Dat god bekent wort in ſÿn werkē v ca
Wat die namē vā gode beteikenē vi ca
Vande namen des onderſcheyts ſÿns
weſens vij ca.
Vande namē goods diemen noemt cō
cretum viij ca
Vande namen gods diemen noemt me
dÿs ix. ca
Vande toevoeghinghe der namen die
puerlic beteykenē het godlic weſē x ca
Vande namē goods bi haer eerſte inſet
tinge of beteykeniſſe xi ca.
Vande namē goods nemēde ſÿn begin
ſele van een aenhanginghe des gheli-
kenis xij. ca
Van toevallēde namē xiij ca
Vande perſoenlike namē xiiij ca
Vande onōſcheydinge ō bekenteniſſen
der namen goods xv ca
Vande eyghenſcap des godlics we-
ſens xvi ca
Hoe barnardus beſcreuē heeft die god
licheyt xvij ca.
Vande namen die gode beteykenen in
ſÿn werkē xviij ca.
Vande toegevoechde namen als gode
toebehorende xviij ca
Van ſÿn proper weſen xix ca.
Vāde overgeſette namē goods xx ca
Vā veel diverſcher namē daer god van
veel mēſchen bi genoemt wort xxi ca

Hier beghint het anderde boeck ende
ſpreect vāde eygenſcap der engelen
Wat die naem engel beduyt i. ca.
Wat een enghel is na dat iohānes da-
maſcen? beſcrÿft ij ca
Hoe die engelen in die lichamelike ge
daente gemaelt worden iij ca.
Hoe die enghelen ghedeſcribeert wor-
den iiij ca
Hoe die engelē ſomtÿts geleken wordē
materialikē dats voelike of ſienlike din
ghen v. ca.
Vande oerde der engelen der yerarchi
en eñ haer officien vi ca
Vā drier leye yerarchyen vij ca
Vāde oerde ō ſeraphin viij ca
Vande oerde der cherubinnen ix ca
Vande oerde der thronen x. ca
Vāde oerde ō middelder yerarchiē xi. c
Vander oerden der dominacien of heer
ſcappien xij ca
Vanō oerden der principaten xiij ca
Vanō oerdē der poteſtaten xiiij ca
Vander derder yerarchien xv ca
Vāde oerde ō crachten xvi ca
Vande oerde der archangelen xvij c.
aa i

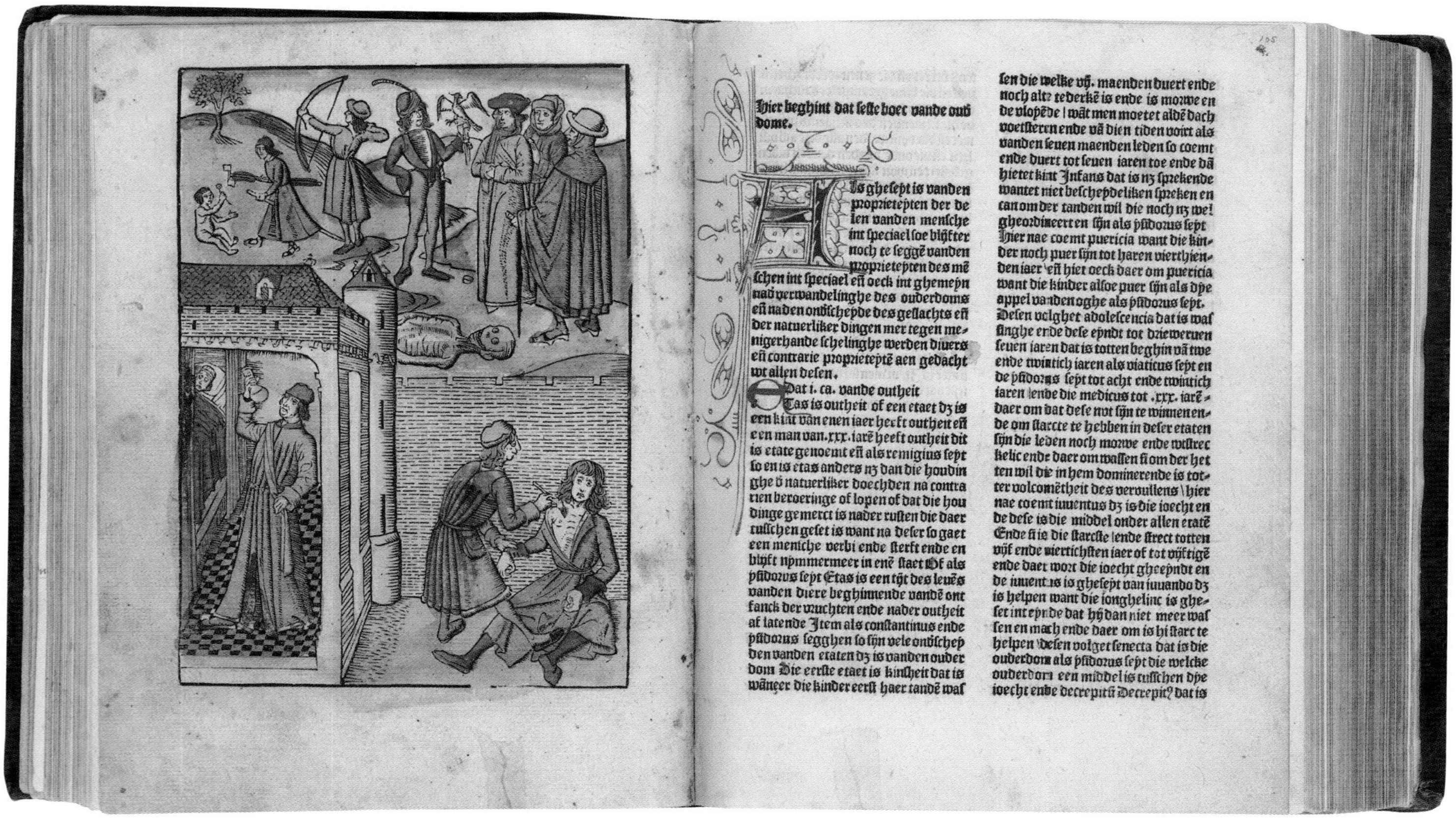

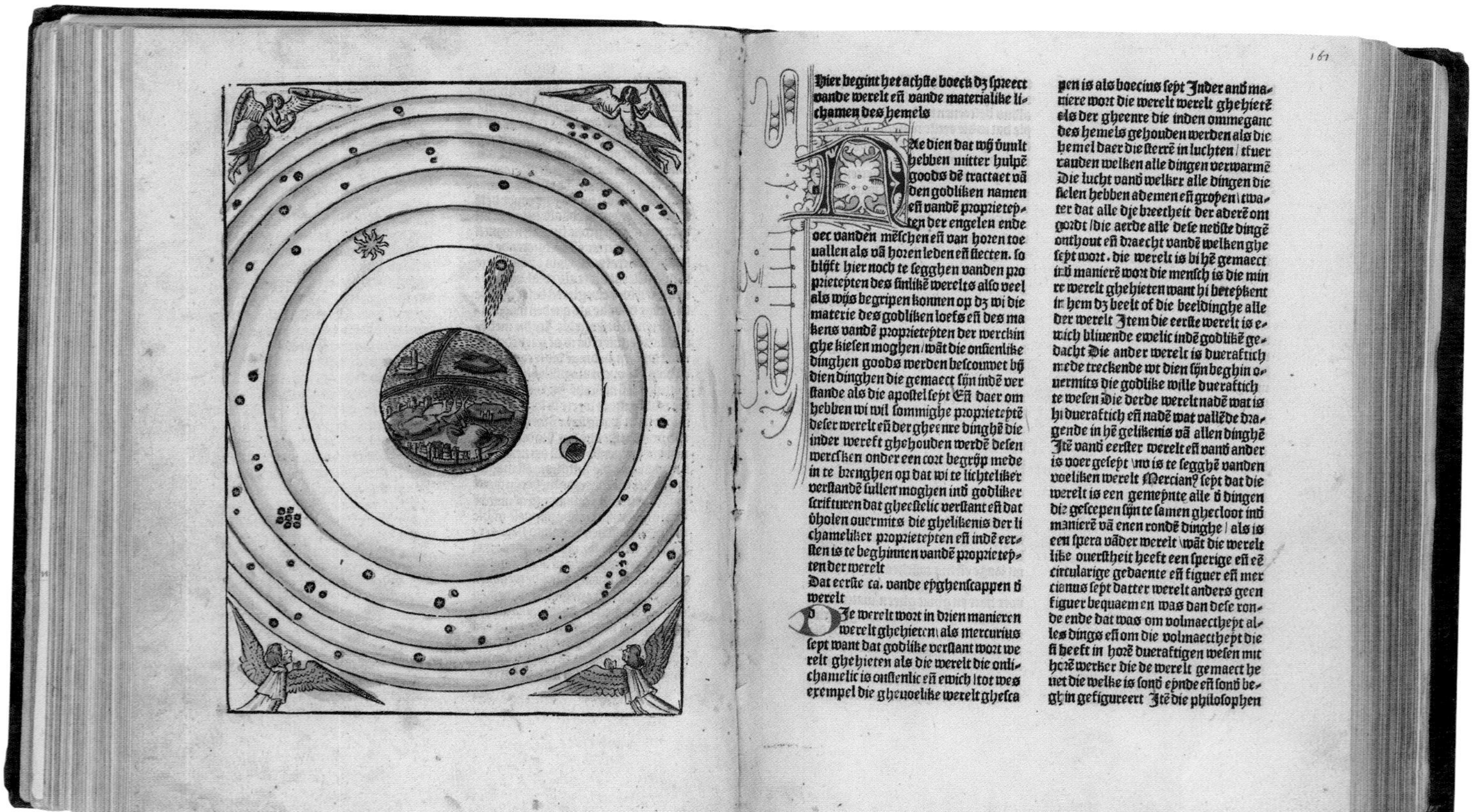

Hier beghint het xiiij. boec ende spreect vander aerden eñ haer deelē. ende ist eerste capittel
Dat ij. capittel vande aerde.

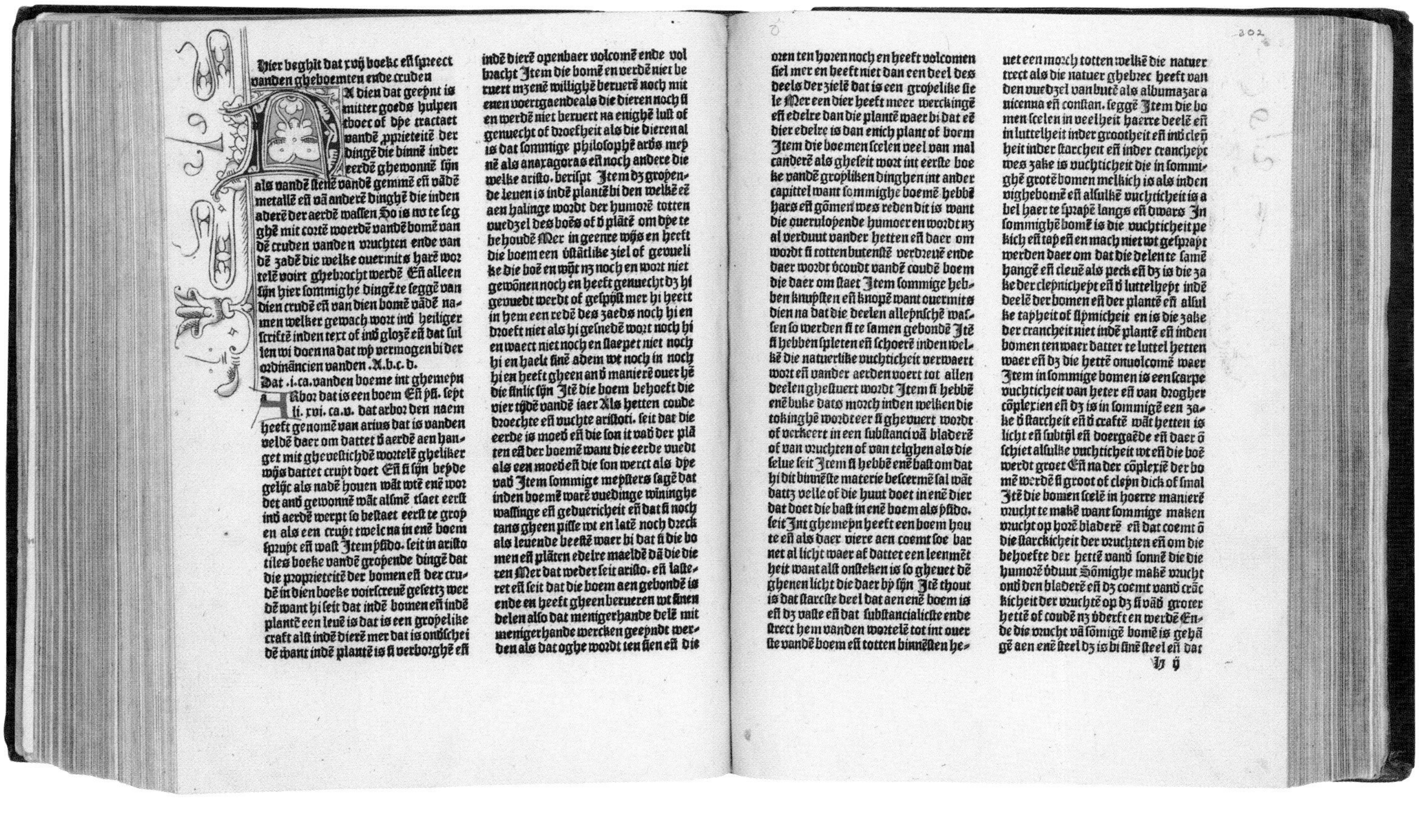
Hier beghint dat xvij boecke eñ spreect vanden gheboemten ende cruden

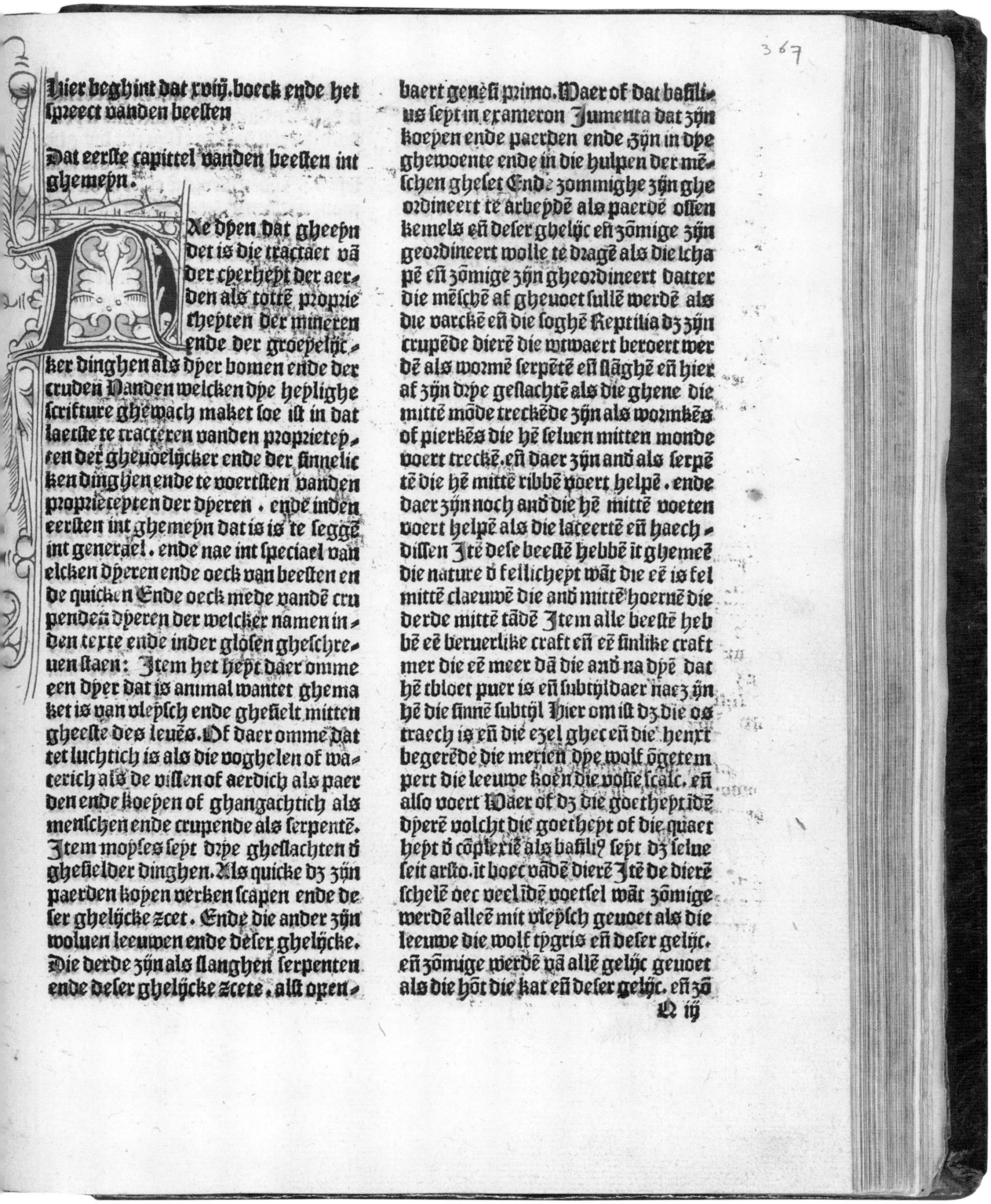

Hier beghint dat xviij. boeck ende het
spreect vanden beesten

Dat eerste capittel vanden beesten int
ghemeyn.

Ae dyen dat gheeyn
det is die tractaet vã
der cyerheyt der aer-
den als totte proprie
theyten der mineren
ende der groeyelyc-
ker dinghen als dyer bomen ende der
cruden Vanden welcken dye heylighe
scrifture ghewach maket soe ist in dat
laetste te tracteren vanden proprieteyten der gheuoelycker ende der sinnelic
ken dinghen ende te voertsten vanden
proprieteyten der dyeren . ende inden
eersten int ghemeyn dat is is te seggẽ
int generael . ende nae int speciael van
elcken dyeren ende oeck van beesten en
de quicken Ende oeck mede vandẽ cru
penden dyeren der welcker namen inden texte ende inder glosen gheschre-
uen staen: Item het heyt daer omme
een dyer dat is animal wantet ghema
ket is van vleysch ende ghesielt mitten
gheeste des leuẽs. Of daer omme dat
tet luchtich is als die voghelen of wa-
terich als de vissen of aerdich als paer
den ende koeyen of ghangachtich als
menschen ende crupende als serpentẽ.
Item moyses seyt drye ghestachten ṽ
ghesielder dinghen. Als quicke dz zyn
paerden koyen verken scapen ende de
ser ghelycke zcet. Ende die ander zyn
woluen leeuwen ende deser ghelycke.
Die derde zyn als slanghen serpenten
ende deser ghelycke zcete . alst open-
baert genesi primo. Waer of dat basili-
us seyt in exameron Jumenta dat zyn
koeyen ende paerden ende zyn in dye
ghewoente ende in die hulpen der mẽ-
schen gheset Ende zommighe zyn ghe
ordineert te arbeydẽ als paerdẽ ossen
kemels eñ deser ghelyc eñ zõmige zyn
geordineert wolle te dragẽ als die scha
pẽ eñ zõmige zyn gheordineert datter
die mẽschẽ af gheuoet sullẽ werdẽ als
die varckẽ eñ die soghẽ Reptilia dz zyn
crupẽde dierẽ die wtwaert beroert wer
dẽ als wormẽ serpẽtẽ eñ slãghẽ eñ hier
af zyn drye geslachtẽ als die ghene die
mittẽ mõde treckẽde zyn als wormkẽs
of pierkẽs die hẽ seluen mitten monde
voert treckẽ. eñ daer zyn anď als serpẽ
tẽ die hẽ mittẽ ribbẽ voert helpẽ . ende
daer zyn noch anď die hẽ mittẽ voeten
voert helpẽ als die laceertẽ eñ haech-
dissen Itẽ dese beestẽ hebbẽ it ghemeẽ
die nature ṽ fellicheyt wãt die eẽ is fel
mittẽ claeuwẽ die anď mittẽ hoernẽ die
derde mittẽ tãdẽ Item alle beestẽ heb
bẽ eẽ beruerlike craft eñ eẽ sinlike craft
mer die eẽ meer dã die anď na dyẽ dat
hẽ tbloet puer is eñ subtyl daer nae zyn
hẽ die sinnẽ subtyl Hier om ist dz die os
traech is eñ die ezel ghet eñ die henxt
begerẽde die merien dye wolf õgetem
pert die leeuwe koen die vosse scalc. eñ
also voert Waer of dz die goetheyt ĩdẽ
dyerẽ volcht die goetheyt of die quaet
heyt ṽ cõplexiẽ als basili9 seyt dz selue
seit aristo. it boec vãdẽ dierẽ Itẽ de dierẽ
schelẽ oec veel ĩdẽ voetsel wãt zõmige
werdẽ alleẽ mit vleysch geuoet als die
leeuwe die wolf tygris eñ deser gelyc.
eñ zõmige werdẽ vã allẽ gelyc geuoet
als die hõt die kat eñ deser gelyc. eñ zõ
Q iij

1493 **Nuremberg Chronicle** Hartmann Schedel, *Liber chronicarum*. Nuremberg: Sebald Schreyer & Sebastian Kammermaister, 1493. 46 cm. Illustrators: Michael Wolgemut, Wilhelm Pleydenwurff. Printer: Anton Koberger, Nuremberg.

The humanist Hartmann Schedel had the idea of producing a history of the world, from the first day of creation onwards, in two editions: Latin and German. For this enterprise, the physician from Nuremberg had his own library at his disposal, as well as notes he had taken as a student in Padua. In addition, he could make use of his financier Sebald Schreyer's large library. The idea for the publication took definite shape in 1478, when the financiers entered into a first contract with the engravers, Michael Wolgemut (1434/7–1519) and Wilhelm Pleydenwurff (*c.* 1460–94).

The realization of this monumental book can be reconstructed because contracts and the manuscript printer's copy have been preserved. Detailed drawings of the complicated layout of text and images were made before the typesetter went to work. Both artists were responsible for the correctness of the proceedings in the printing office of Anton Koberger (*fl. c.* 1471–1511), the biggest printer in Germany at the time. The production of the volume, generally known as the *Nuremberg Chronicle*, was a huge project.

The 53 woodcuts of townscapes were used for 101 different cities, while the 96 woodcuts of emperors, kings, and popes were used to depict 598 different persons; rewriting history in this way was not unusual at the time. With almost 2,000 illustrations – some of which were probably by the young Albrecht Dürer – this is the most abundantly illustrated book from the period of the incunabula. Of the approximately 1,400 printed copies of the *Nuremberg Chronicle*, more than 400 copies have been preserved worldwide. AP

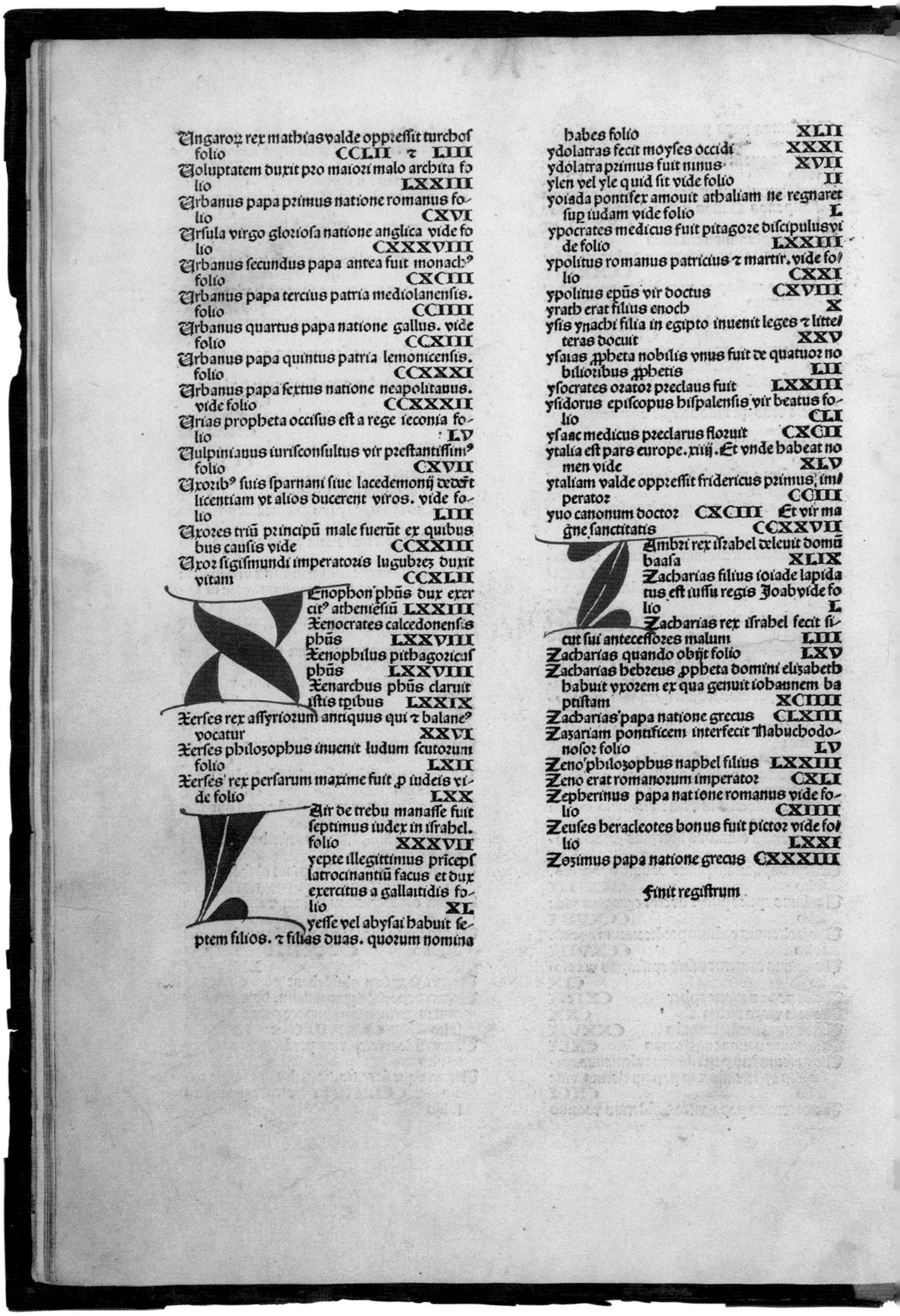
Ungarorum rex mathias valde oppressit turchos folio CCLII et LIII
Voluptatem duxit pro maiori malo archita folio LXXIII
Urbanus papa primus natione romanus folio CXVI
Ursula virgo gloriosa natione anglica vide folio CXXXVIII
Urbanus secundus papa antea fuit monachus folio CXCIII
Urbanus papa tercius patria mediolanensis. folio CCIIII
Urbanus quartus papa natione gallus. vide folio CCXIII
Urbanus papa quintus patria lemonicensis. folio CCXXXI
Urbanus papa sextus natione neapolitanus. vide folio CCXXXII
Urias propheta occisus est a rege ieconia folio LV
Vulpinianus iurisconsultus vir prestantissimus folio CXVII
Uxoribus suis spartani siue lacedemonii dederunt licentiam vt alios ducerent viros. vide folio LIII
Uxores trium principum male fuerunt ex quibus bus causis vide CCXXIII
Uxor sigismundi imperatoris lugubrez duxit vitam CCXLII
Xenophon phus dux exercitus atheniensium LXXIII
Xenocrates calcedonensis phus LXXVIII
Xenophilus pithagoricus phus LXXVIII
Xenarchus phus claruit istis tpibus LXXIX
Xerses rex assyriorum antiquus qui et balaneus vocatur XXVI
Xerses philozophus inuenit ludum scutorum folio LXII
Xerses rex persarum maxime fuit pro iudeis vide folio LXX
Yair de trebu manasse fuit septimus iudex in israhel. folio XXXVII
yepte illegittimus priceps latrocinantium facus et dux exercitus a gallaitidis folio XL
yesse vel abysai habuit septem filios. et filias duas. quorum nomina habes folio XLII
ydolatras fecit moyses occidi XXXI
ydolatra primus fuit ninus XVII
ylen vel yle quid sit vide folio II
yoiada pontifex amouit athaliam ne regnaret sup iudam vide folio L
ypocrates medicus fuit pitagore discipulus vide folio LXXIII
ypolitus romanus patricius et martir. vide folio CXXI
ypolitus epus vir doctus CXVIII
yrath erat filius enoch X
ysis ynachi filia in egipto inuenit leges et litteras docuit XXV
ysaias propheta nobilis vnus fuit de quatuor nobilioribus prophetis LII
ysocrates orator preclaus fuit LXXIII
ysidorus episcopus hispalensis vir beatus folio CLI
ysaac medicus preclarus floruit CXCII
ytalia est pars europe. xiiij. Et vnde habeat nomen vide XLV
ytaliam valde oppressit fridericus primus, imperator CCIII
yuo canonum doctor CXCIII Et vir magne sanctitatis CCXXVII
Zambri rex israhel deleuit domum baasa XLIX
Zacharias filius ioiade lapidatus est iussu regis Joab vide folio L
Zacharias rex israhel fecit sicut sui antecessores malum LIII
Zacharias quando obijt folio LXV
Zacharias hebreus propheta domini elizabeth habuit vxorem ex qua genuit iohannem baptistam XCIIII
Zacharias papa natione grecus CLXIII
Zazariam pontificem interfecit Nabuchodonosor folio LV
Zeno philozophus naphel filius LXXIII
Zeno erat romanorum imperator CXLI
Zepherinus papa natione romanus vide folio CXIIII
Zeuses heracleotes bonus fuit pictor vide folio LXXI
Zozimus papa natione grecus CXXXIII

Finit registrum

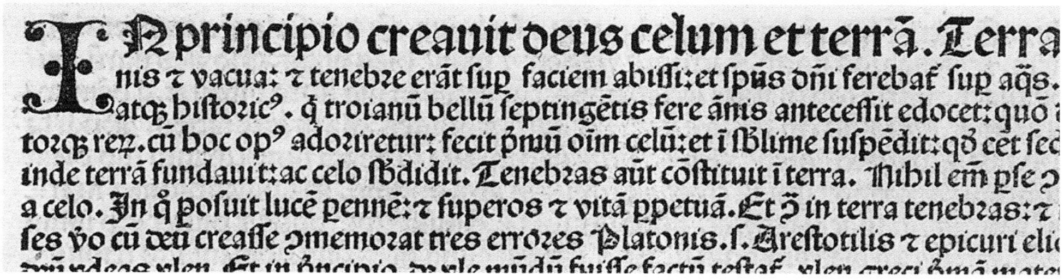
In principio creauit deus celum et terrã. Terra
nis ⁊ vacua: ⁊ tenebre erãt sup faciem abissi: et spũs dñi ferebat sup aqs.
atq; historic⁹. q troianũ bellũ septingẽtis fere ãnis antecessit edocet: quõ
torq; rex. cũ hoc op⁹ adoriretur: fecit p̃muũ oĩm celũ: et i sblime suspẽdit: qõ cet sec
inde terrã fundauit: ac celo sbdidit. Tenebras aũt cõstituit i terra. Nihil em̃ p se
a celo. In q̃ posuit lucẽ pennẽ: ⁊ superos ⁊ vitã ppetuã. Et 3 in terra tenebras: ⁊
ses vo cũ deũ creasse memorat tres errores Platonis. s. Arestotilis ⁊ epicuri eli

A contract obliged Koberger to use a good type that was acceptable to his patrons and to the artists who prepared the illustrations. He had used the larger type since 1482 but apparently had the smaller one specially cut: fine Rotundas were already a well-established style. Neither follows the less formal hands in the manuscript printer's copy.

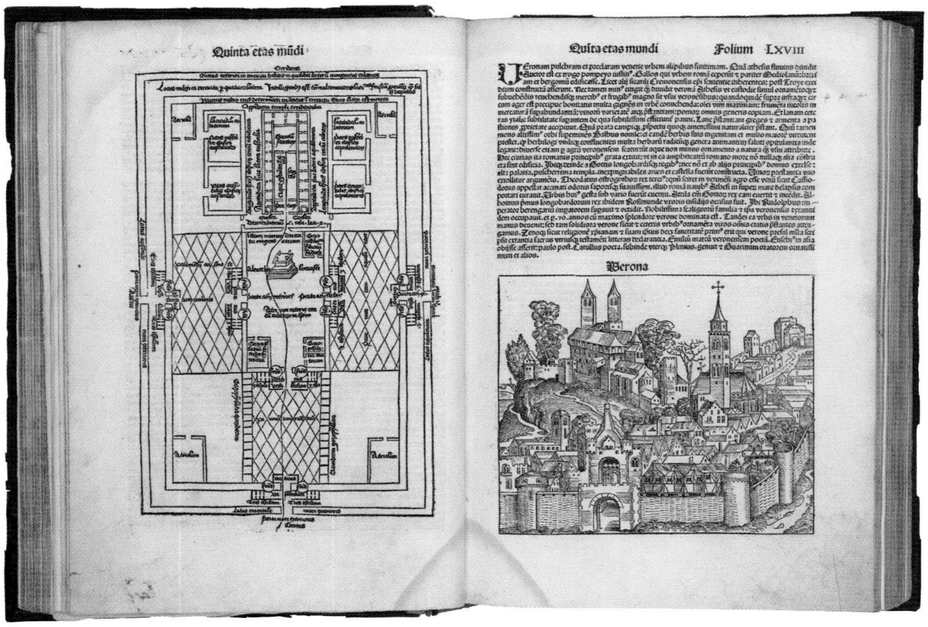
Quinta etas mūdi
Quĩta etas mundi
Folium LXVIII
Verona

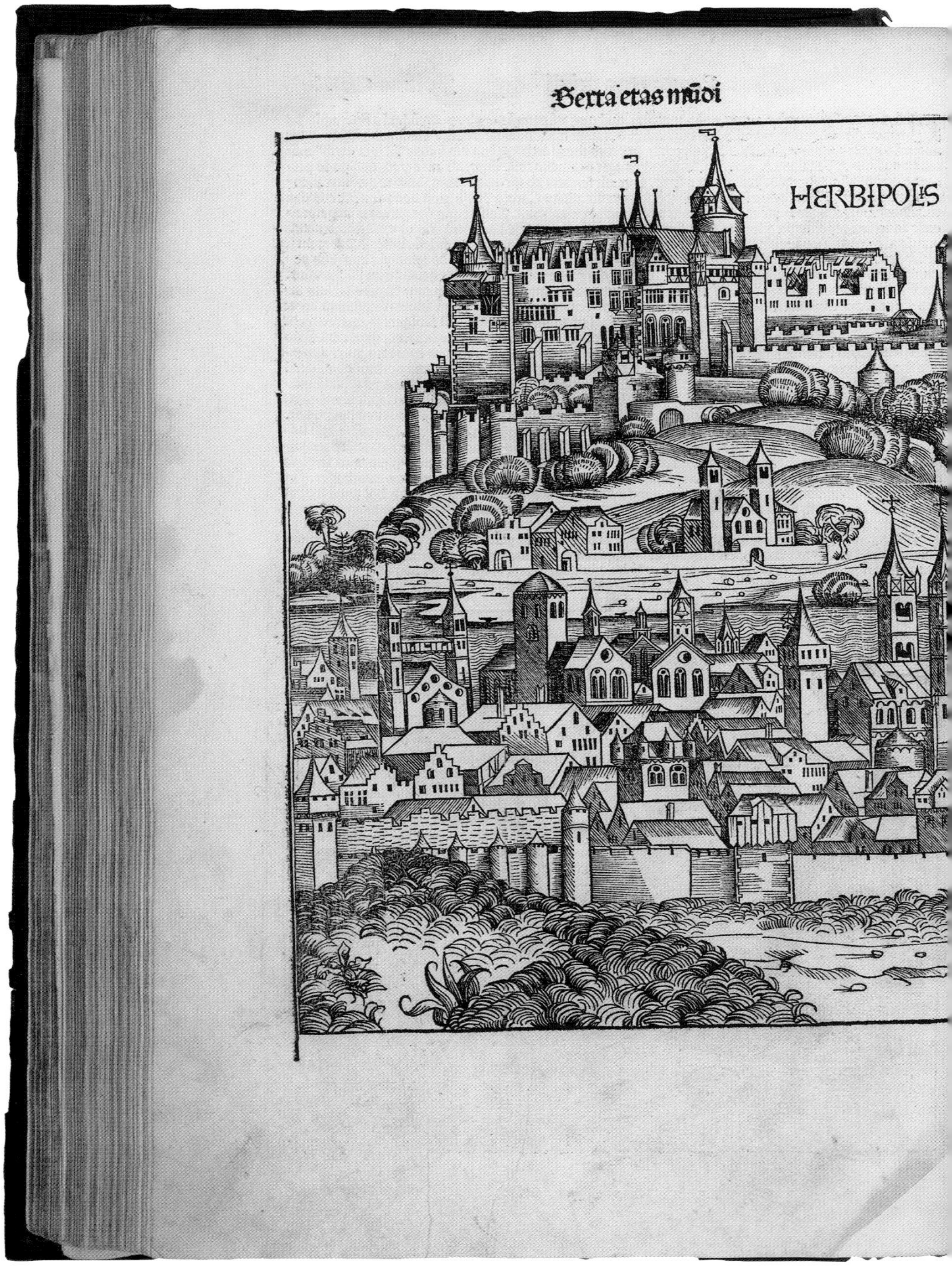
Sexta etas mūdi
HERBIPOLIS

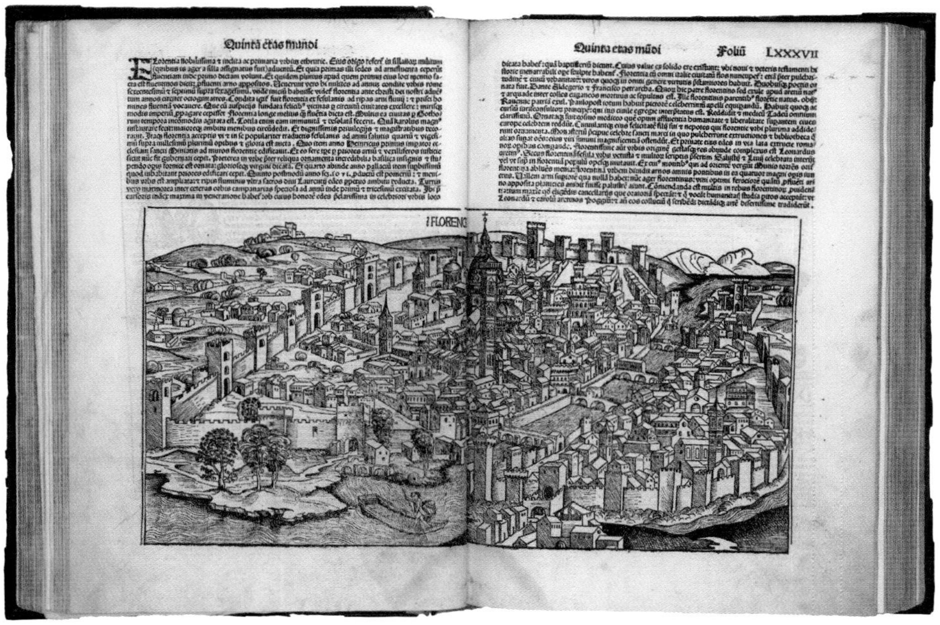

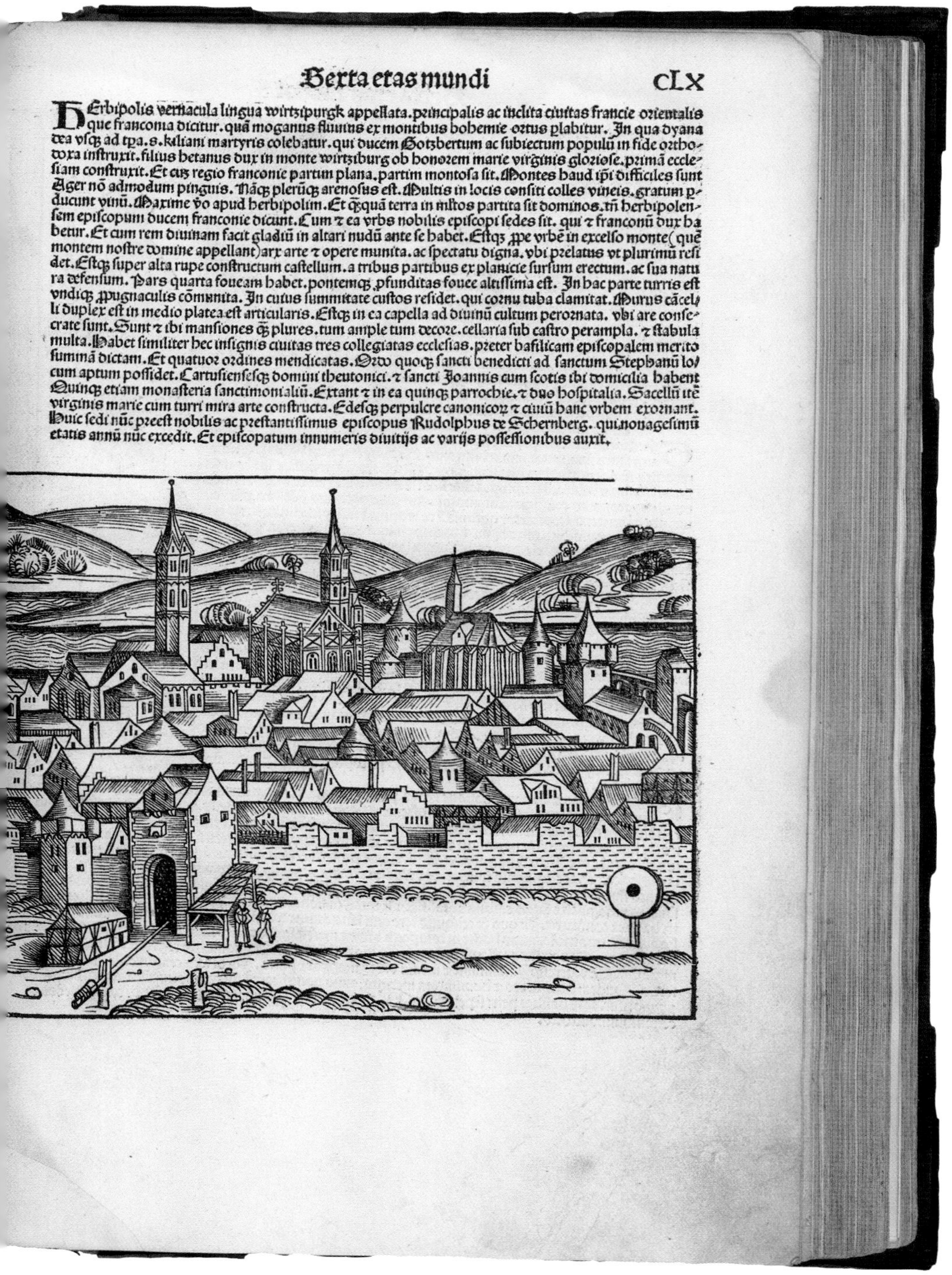

Sexta etas mundi CLX

Herbipolis vernacula lingua wirtzipurgk appellata. principalis ac inclita ciuitas francie orientalis que franconia dicitur. quã moganus fluuius ex montibus bohemie ortus plabitur. In qua dyana dea vsqꝫ ad tpa. s. kiliani martyris colebatur. qui ducem Gotzbertum ac subiectum populũ in fide orthodoxa instruxit. filius betanus dux in monte wirtziburg ob honorem marie virginis gloriose. primã ecclesiam construxit. Et cũ regio franconie partim plana. partim montosa sit. Montes haud ipi difficiles sunt Ager nõ admodum pinguis. Nãqꝫ plerũqꝫ arenosus est. Multis in locis consiti colles vineis. gratum pducunt vinũ. Maxime vo apud herbipolim. Et qꝫquã terra in mltos partita sit dominos. tñ herbipolensem episcopum ducem franconie dicunt. Cum ⁊ ea vrbs nobilis episcopi sedes sit. qui ⁊ franconũ dux habetur. Et cum rem diuinam facit gladiũ in altari nudũ ante se habet. Estqꝫ ppe vrbẽ in excelso monte (quẽ montem nostre domine appellant) arx arte ⁊ opere munita. ac spectatu digna. vbi prelatus vt plurimũ residet. Estqꝫ super alta rupe constructum castellum. a tribus partibus ex planicie sursum erectum. ac sua natura defensum. Pars quarta foueam habet. pontemqꝫ. pfunditas fouee altissima est. In hac parte turris est vndiqꝫ ppugnaculis cõmunita. In cuius summitate custos residet. qui cornu tuba clamitat. Murus cãcelli duplex est in medio platea est articularis. Estqꝫ in ea capella ad diuinũ cultum perornata. vbi are consecrate sunt. Sunt ⁊ ibi mansiones qꝫ plures. tum ample tum decore. cellaria sub castro perampla. ⁊ stabula multa. Habet similiter hec insignis ciuitas tres collegiatas ecclesias. preter basilicam episcopalem merito summã dictam. Et quatuor ordines mendicatas. Ordo quoqꝫ sancti benedicti ad sanctum Stephanũ locum aptum possidet. Cartusiensesqꝫ domini theutonici. ⁊ sancti Joannis cum scotis ibi domicilia habent Quinqꝫ etiam monasteria sanctimonialiũ. Extant ⁊ in ea quinqꝫ parrochie. ⁊ duo hospitalia. Sacellũ itẽ virginis marie cum turri mira arte constructa. Edesqꝫ perpulcre canonicorꝫ ⁊ ciuiũ hanc vrbem exornant. Huic sedi nũc preest nobilis ac prestantissimus episcopus Rudolphus de Schernberg. qui nonagesimũ etatis annũ nũc excedit. Et episcopatum innumeris diuitijs ac varijs possessionibus auxit.

1495 **Johannes & Gregorius de Gregoriis** **Johannes de Ketham, *Fasciculus medicinae*; ed. Petrus Andreas Morsianus. Venice: Johannes & Gregorius de Gregoriis, 1495. 32 cm. Illustrator: School of Andrea Mantegna.**

This collection of classical, Arab, and medieval medical treatises is traditionally attributed to the German physician Johannes de Ketham. However, it is questionable that he is the actual anthologist. *Fasciculus medicinae* was the first illustrated medical book ever to appear in print and the collection covers the entire spectrum of medieval medicine. The full-page woodcuts are probably from the school of the Italian painter Andrea Mantegna (1431–1506). On some of the pages, letterpress text is set within the woodcut. The woodcut illustrations consist of contours only; that is to say, thin lines, without any of the usual hatching. This 'white' style probably came into fashion in around 1480. Printing these woodcuts presented difficulties. The paper was pushed onto the woodblocks with enormous amounts of pressure, and the thin ridges could easily break off if the press had not been adjusted carefully.

Although the text is in Latin, the printer did not use the customary roman type. Around the time that the *Fasciculus* was published, roman type was temporarily out of fashion. In most contemporaneous editions, the initials and section marks are painted, but in the *Fasciculus* they are printed. The buyers were thus spared the expense of illuminators and rubricators.

The brothers De Gregoriis worked together in Venice from 1480 until 1505, and ranked amongst the largest publishers in that trading city. Internationally, Venice was the most important book producer of the era and attracted numerous printers and publishers to set up business there, the most famous of whom were Nicolas Jenson and Aldus Manutius. PD

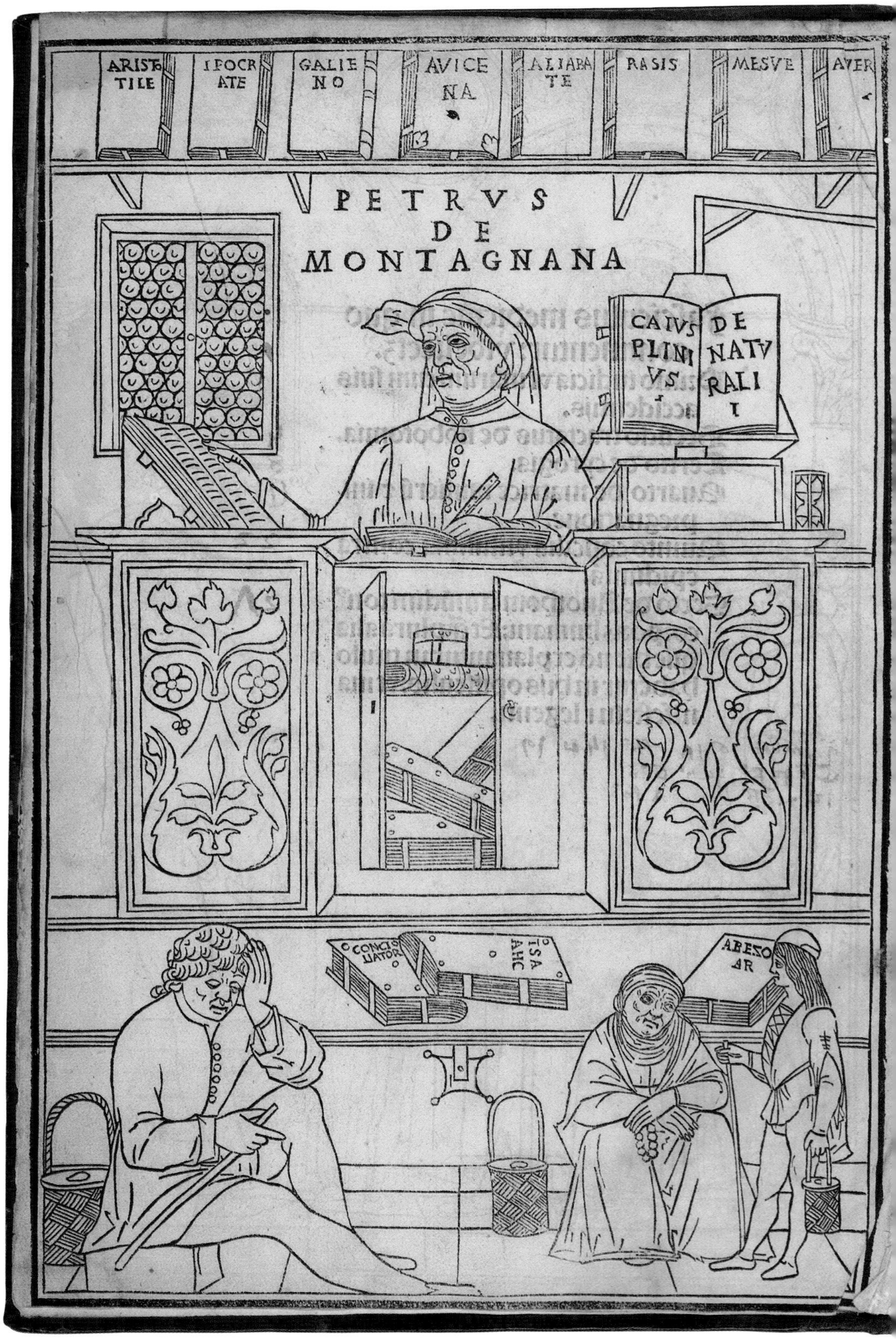

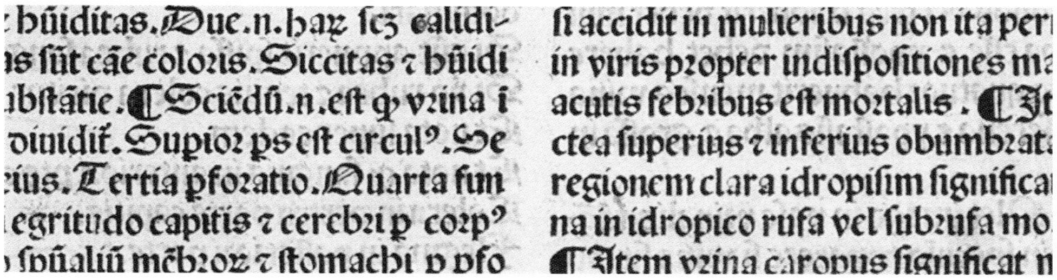
: hũiditas. Due.n.hãȝ ſcȝ calidi-
s ſũt cãe coloris. Siccitas ꝛ hũidi
bſtãtie. ¶ Sciẽdũ.n.eſt ꝗ vꝛina i
diuidit̃. Supioꝛ ps eſt circul⁹. Se
rius. Tertia pfoꝛatio. Quarta fun
egritudo capitis ꝛ cerebꝛi p coꝛp⁹
ſpũaliũ mẽbꝛoꝝ ꝛ ſtomachi v vſo

ſi accidit in mulieribus non ita per
in viris pꝛopter indiſpoſitiones m
acutis febꝛibus eſt moꝛtalis. ¶ It
ctea ſuperius ꝛ inferius obumbꝛat
regionem clara idropiſim ſignifica
na in idropico ruſa vel ſubꝛuſa mo
¶ Item vꝛina caropus ſignificat n

Rotunda types were the norm in Italy at this time. This one is probably a revision of one used by the same printing office in 1491. Rotunda is slightly less formal than Textura, which remained more popular in northern Europe.

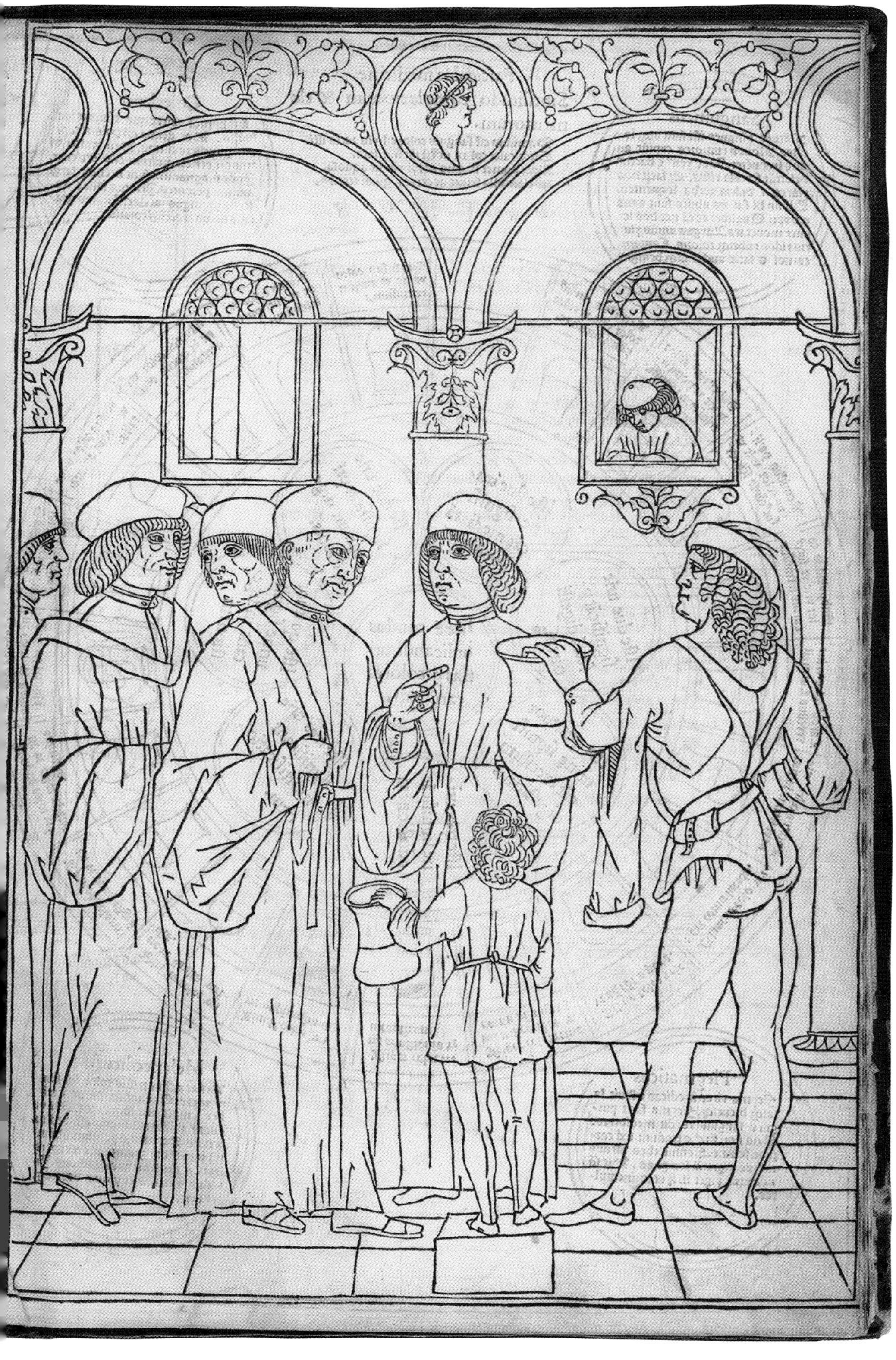

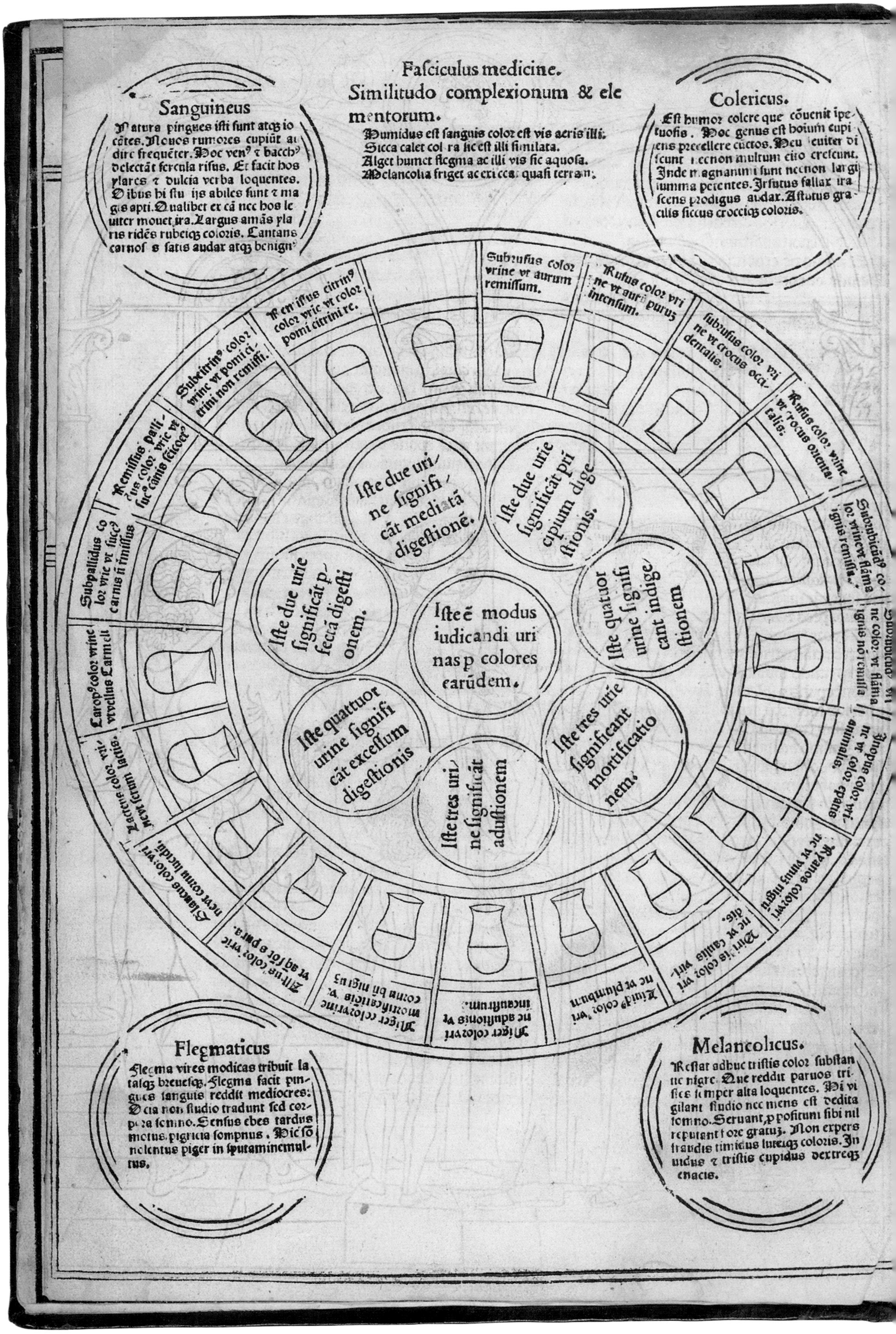
Fasciculus medicine.
Similitudo complexionum & ele mentorum.
Sanguineus
Colericus.
Flegmaticus
Melancolicus.
Iste e modus iudicandi urinas p colores earūdem.
Iste due urine significāt mediatā digestionē.
Iste due urine significāt principium digestionis.
Iste quatuor urine significant indigestionem
Iste tres urine significant mortificationem.
Iste tres urine significāt adustionem
Iste quatuor urine significāt excessum digestionis
Iste due urine significāt pfectā digestionem.

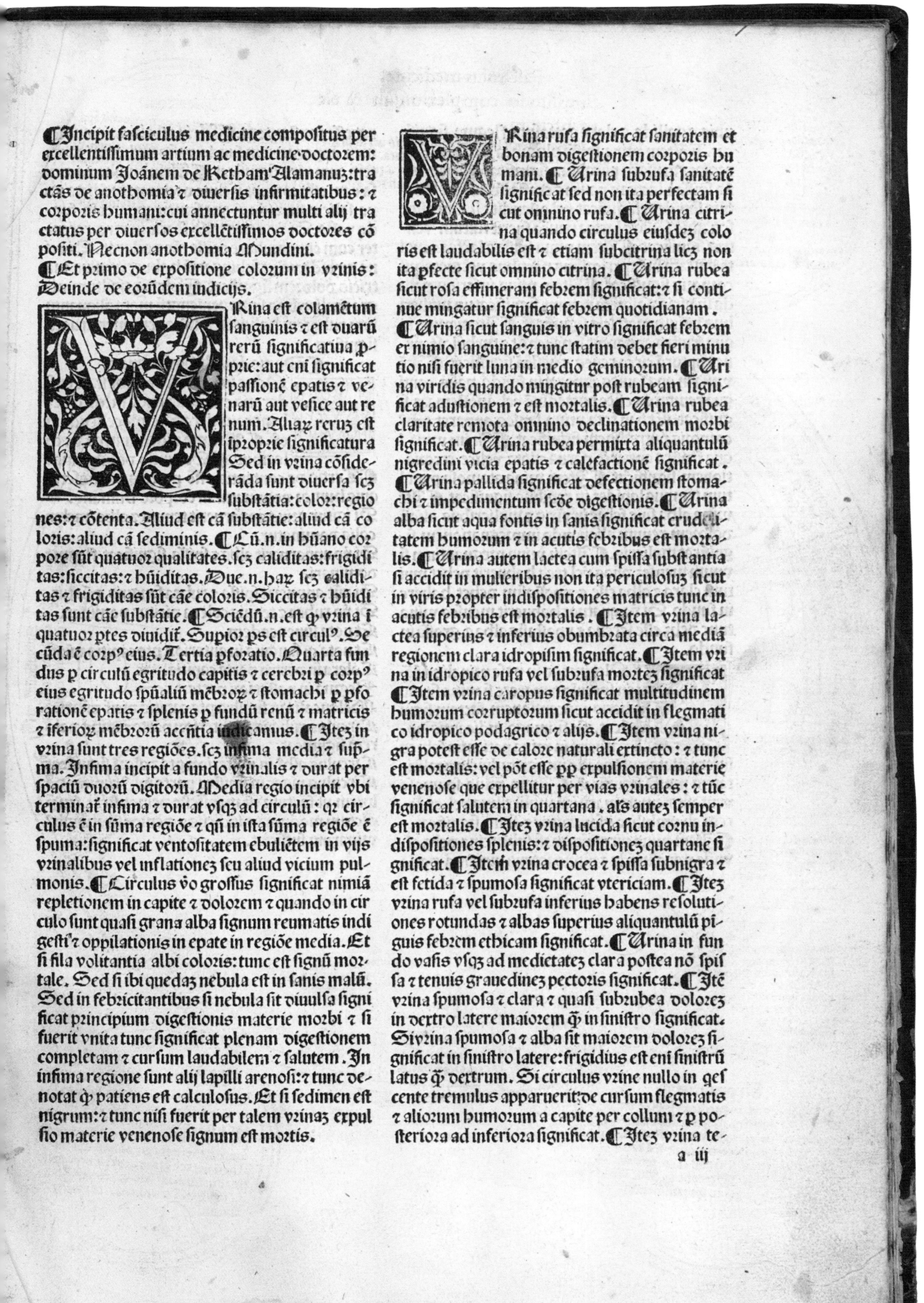

¶ Incipit fasciculus medicine compositus per excellentissimum artium ac medicine doctorem: dominum Joãnem de Ketham Alamanuz: tractãs de anothomia ⁊ diuersis infirmitatibus: ⁊ corporis humani: cui annectuntur multi alij tractatus per diuersos excellẽtissimos doctores cõpositi. Necnon anothomia Mundini.

¶ Et primo de expositione colorum in vrinis: Deinde de eorũdem indicijs.

VRina est colamẽtum sanguinis ⁊ est duarũ rerũ significatiua ꝓprie: aut eñi significat passionẽ epatis ⁊ venarũ aut vesice aut renum. Aliaꝝ reruz est īproprie significatura Sed in vrina cõsiderãda sunt diuersa scz substãtia: color: regiones: ⁊ cõtenta. Aliud est cã substãtie: aliud cã coloris: aliud cã sediminis. ¶ Cũ.n. in hũano corpore sũt quatuor qualitates. scz caliditas: frigiditas: siccitas: ⁊ hũiditas. Due.n. haꝝ scz caliditas ⁊ frigiditas sũt cãe coloris. Siccitas ⁊ hũiditas sunt cãe substãtie. ¶ Sciẽdũ.n. est ꝙ vrina ĩ quatuor ꝑtes diuidit᷑. Supior ꝑs est circulꝰ. Secũda ẽ corpꝰ eius. Tertia ꝑforatio. Quarta fundus ꝑ circulũ egritudo capitis ⁊ cerebri ꝑ corpꝰ eius egritudo spũaliũ mẽbroꝝ ⁊ stomachi ꝑ ꝑforationẽ epatis ⁊ splenis ꝑ fundũ renũ ⁊ matricis ⁊ iferioꝝ mẽbrorũ accñtia indicamus. ¶ Itez in vrina sunt tres regiões. scz infima media ⁊ supꝑma. Infima incipit a fundo vrinalis ⁊ durat per spaciũ duorũ digitorũ. Media regio incipit vbi terminat᷑ infima ⁊ durat vsqz ad circulũ: qr circulus ẽ in sũma regiõe ⁊ qñ in ista sũma regiõe ẽ spuma: significat ventositatem ebuliẽtem in vijs vrinalibus vel inflationez seu aliud vicium pulmonis. ¶ Circulus v̾o grossus significat nimiã repletionem in capite ⁊ dolorem ⁊ quando in circulo sunt quasi grana alba signum reumatis indigestiᷓ ⁊ oppilationis in epate in regiõe media. Et si fila volitantia albi coloris: tunc est signũ mortale. Sed si ibi quedaz nebula est in sanis malũ. Sed in febricitantibus si nebula sit diuulsa significat principium digestionis materie morbi ⁊ si fuerit vnita tunc significat plenam digestionem completam ⁊ cursum laudabilem ⁊ salutem. In infima regione sunt alij lapilli arenosi: ⁊ tunc denotat ꝙ patiens est calculosus. Et si sedimen est nigrum: ⁊ tunc nisi fuerit per talem vrinaz expulsio materie venenose signum est mortis.

VRina rufa significat sanitatem et bonam digestionem corporis humani. ¶ Urina subrufa sanitatẽ significat sed non ita perfectam sicut omnino rufa. ¶ Urina citrina quando circulus eiusdez coloris est laudabilis est ⁊ etiam subcitrina licz non ita ꝑfecte sicut omnino citrina. ¶ Urina rubea sicut rosa effimeram febrem significat: ⁊ si continue mingatur significat febrem quotidianam. ¶ Urina sicut sanguis in vitro significat febrem ex nimio sanguine: ⁊ tunc statim debet fieri minutio nisi fuerit luna in medio geminorum. ¶ Urina viridis quando mingitur post rubeam significat adustionem ⁊ est mortalis. ¶ Urina rubea claritate remota omnino declinationem morbi significat. ¶ Urina rubea permixta aliquantulũ nigredini vicia epatis ⁊ calefactionẽ significat. ¶ Urina pallida significat defectionem stomachi ⁊ impedimentum scẽe digestionis. ¶ Urina alba sicut aqua fontis in sanis significat crudelitatem humorum ⁊ in acutis febribus est mortalis. ¶ Urina autem lactea cum spissa substantia si accidit in mulieribus non ita periculosuz sicut in viris propter indispositiones matricis tunc in acutis febribus est mortalis. ¶ Item vrina lactea superius ⁊ inferius obumbrata circa mediã regionem clara idropisim significat. ¶ Item vrina in idropico rufa vel subrufa mortez significat ¶ Item vrina caropus significat multitudinem humorum corruptorum sicut accidit in flegmatico idropico podagrico ⁊ alijs. ¶ Item vrina nigra potest esse de calore naturali extincto: ⁊ tunc est mortalis: vel põt esse ꝑꝑ expulsionem materie venenose que expellitur per vias vrinales: ⁊ tũc significat salutem in quartana. alͥs autez semper est mortalis. ¶ Itez vrina lucida sicut cornu indispositiones splenis: ⁊ dispositionez quartane significat. ¶ Item vrina crocea ⁊ spissa subnigra ⁊ est fetida ⁊ spumosa significat ictericiam. ¶ Itez vrina rufa vel subrufa inferius habens resolutiones rotundas ⁊ albas superius aliquantulũ pinguis febrem ethicam significat. ¶ Urina in fundo vasis vsqz ad medietatez clara postea nõ spissa ⁊ tenuis grauedinez pectoris significat. ¶ Itẽ vrina spumosa ⁊ clara ⁊ quasi subrubea dolorez in dextro latere maiorem ꝙ in sinistro significat. Si vrina spumosa ⁊ alba sit maiorem dolorez significat in sinistro latere: frigidius est eñi sinistrũ latus ꝙ dextrum. Si circulus vrine nullo in quiescente tremulus apparuerit: de cursum flegmatis ⁊ aliorum humorum a capite per collum ⁊ ꝑ posteriora ad inferiora significat. ¶ Itez vrina te-

a iij

Johannes & Gregorius de Gregoriis

1499 **Hypnerotomachia Poliphili** Francesco Colonna, *Hypnerotomachia Poliphili*. Venice: Aldus Manutius, 1499. 29 cm. Illustrator: Benedetto Bordone.

The *Hypnerotomachia Poliphili* ('Poliphilo's Strife of Love in a Dream') was written by Francesco Colonna and printed by Aldus Manutius (*c.* 1451–1515) and is considered by some to be the most beautiful book ever produced. It is a typical Renaissance book in both form and content. An allegorical romance, the *Hypnerotomachia* is set in an antiquity imagined by a Renaissance audience: a world of architecture, gardens, and parades, all within a symbolic context. The hero, Poliphilo, travels towards the human soul, towards true love.

Even though the typesetting and the printing are imperfect by modern standards, the book's typographic design turned out to be epoch-making. Throughout the book, only one font was used (in one size). This roman type, the design of which was commissioned by Manutius, is a fine example of the new forms introduced during the Italian Renaissance. The large decorative initials, which are printed from woodcuts, clearly reflect the ideals of the new artistic movement, as do the famous woodcut illustrations, which were probably designed by Benedetto Bordone (d. 1530). Various forms are used within the layout, particularly the inverted triangle, which may be considered a kind of visual typography. The use of a blank space or indent to indicate the beginning of a new paragraph was a brand new feature in 1499.

This book has been highly influential in the arts, especially in iconography. Among book collectors, it is still a sought-after object. FAJ

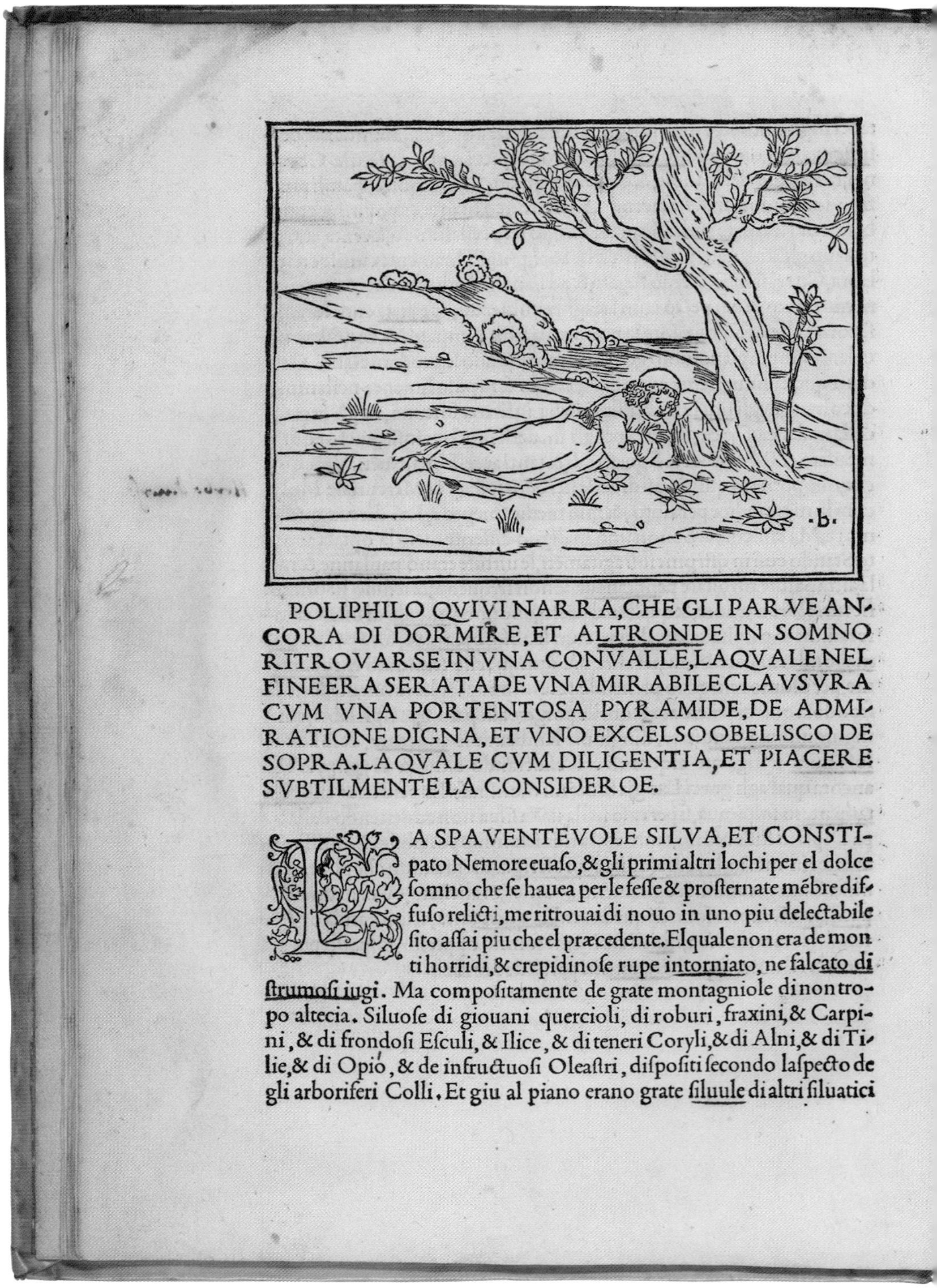

POLIPHILO QVIVI NARRA, CHE GLI PARVE ANCORA DI DORMIRE, ET ALTRONDE IN SOMNO RITROVARSE IN VNA CONVALLE, LAQVALE NEL FINE ERA SERATA DE VNA MIRABILE CLAVSVRA CVM VNA PORTENTOSA PYRAMIDE, DE ADMIRATIONE DIGNA, ET VNO EXCELSO OBELISCO DE SOPRA. LAQVALE CVM DILIGENTIA, ET PIACERE SVBTILMENTE LA CONSIDEROE.

LA SPAVENTEVOLE SILVA, ET CONSTIPATO Nemore euaſo, & gli primi altri lochi per el dolce ſomno che ſe hauea per le feſſe & proſternate mébre diffuſo relicti, me ritrouai di nouo in uno piu delectabile ſito aſſai piu che el præcedente. El quale non era de monti horridi, & crepidinoſe rupe intorniato, ne falcato di ſtrumoſi iugi. Ma compoſitamente de grate montagniole di non tropo altecia. Siluoſe di giouani quercioli, di roburi, fraxini, & Carpini, & di frondoſi Eſculi, & Ilice, & di teneri Coryli, & di Alni, & di Tilie, & di Opio, & de infructuoſi Oleaſtri, diſpoſiti ſecondo laſpecto de gli arboriferi Colli. Et giu al piano erano grate ſiluule di altri ſiluatici

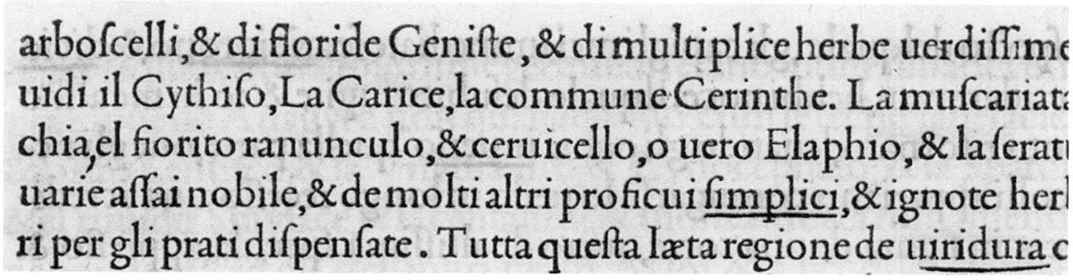
arboſcelli,& di floride Geniſte, & di multiplice herbe uerdiſſime
uidi il Cythiſo, La Carice, la commune Cerinthe. La muſcariata
chia,el fiorito ranunculo,& ceruicello, o uero Elaphio, & la ſerat
uarie aſſai nobile,& de molti altri proficui ſimplici,& ignote her
ri per gli prati diſpenſate. Tutta queſta læta regione de uiridura c

Francesco Griffo (*fl.* 1475?–1518) cut Aldus's roman types (1495 and 1499, the latter shown here). He went further than Jenson in assimilating the calligraphic lower case with the more formal inscriptional capitals. The style spread via copies cut in Paris in around 1530 by Claude Garamont, whose refined versions found an international market.

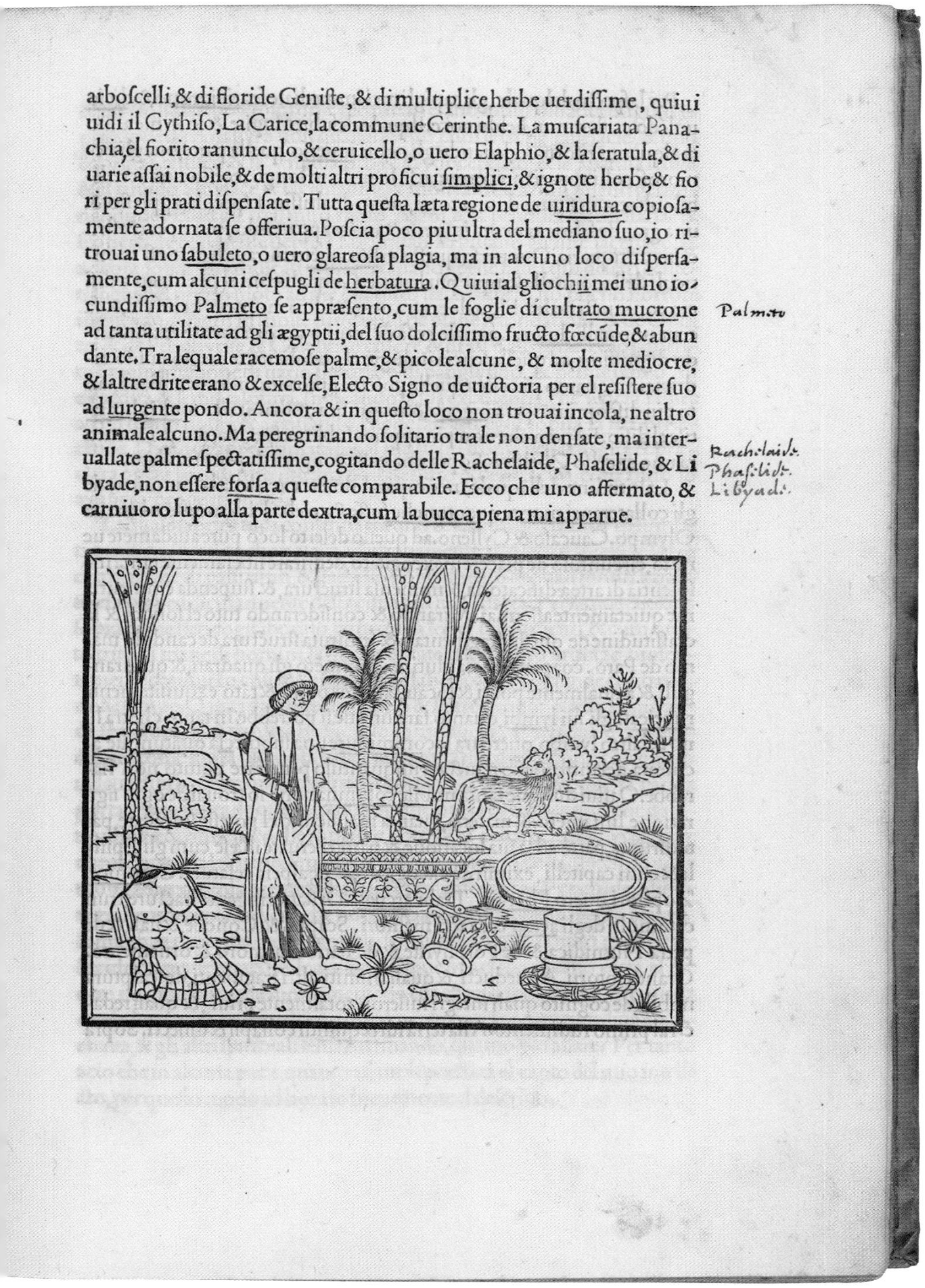
arboſcelli,& di floride Geniſte, & di multiplice herbe uerdiſſime, quiui uidi il Cythiſo, La Carice, la commune Cerinthe. La muſcariata Panachia,el fiorito ranunculo,& ceruicello, o uero Elaphio, & la ſeratula,& di uarie aſſai nobile,& de molti altri proficui ſimplici,& ignote herbe,& fiori per gli prati diſpenſate. Tutta queſta læta regione de uiridura copioſamente adornata ſe offeriua. Poſcia poco piu ultra del mediano ſuo, io ritrouai uno ſabuleto, o uero glareoſa plagia, ma in alcuno loco diſperſamente, cum alcuni ceſpugli de herbatura. Quiui al gliochii mei uno iocundiſſimo Palmeto ſe appræſento, cum le foglie di cultrato mucrone ad tanta utilitate ad gli ægyptii, del ſuo dolciſſimo fructo fœcūde,& abundante. Tra lequale racemoſe palme,& picole alcune, & molte mediocre, & laltre drite erano & excelſe, Electo Signo de uictoria per el reſiſtere ſuo ad lurgente pondo. Ancora & in queſto loco non trouai incola, ne altro animale alcuno. Ma peregrinando ſolitario tra le non denſate, ma interuallate palme ſpectatiſſime, cogitando delle Rachelaide, Phaſelide, & Libyade, non eſſere forſa a queſte comparabile. Ecco che uno affermato, & carniuoro lupo alla parte dextra, cum la bucca piena mi apparue.

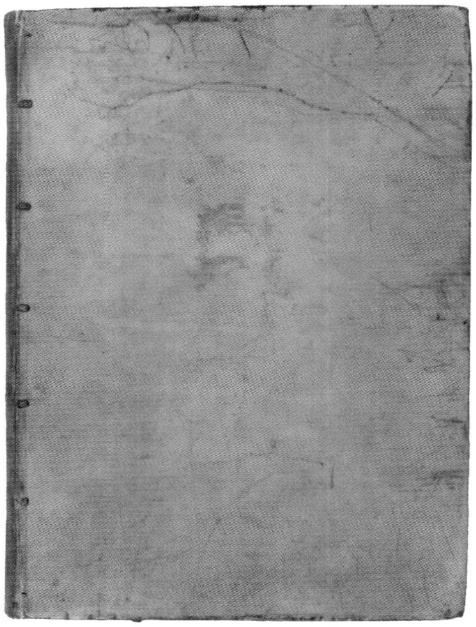

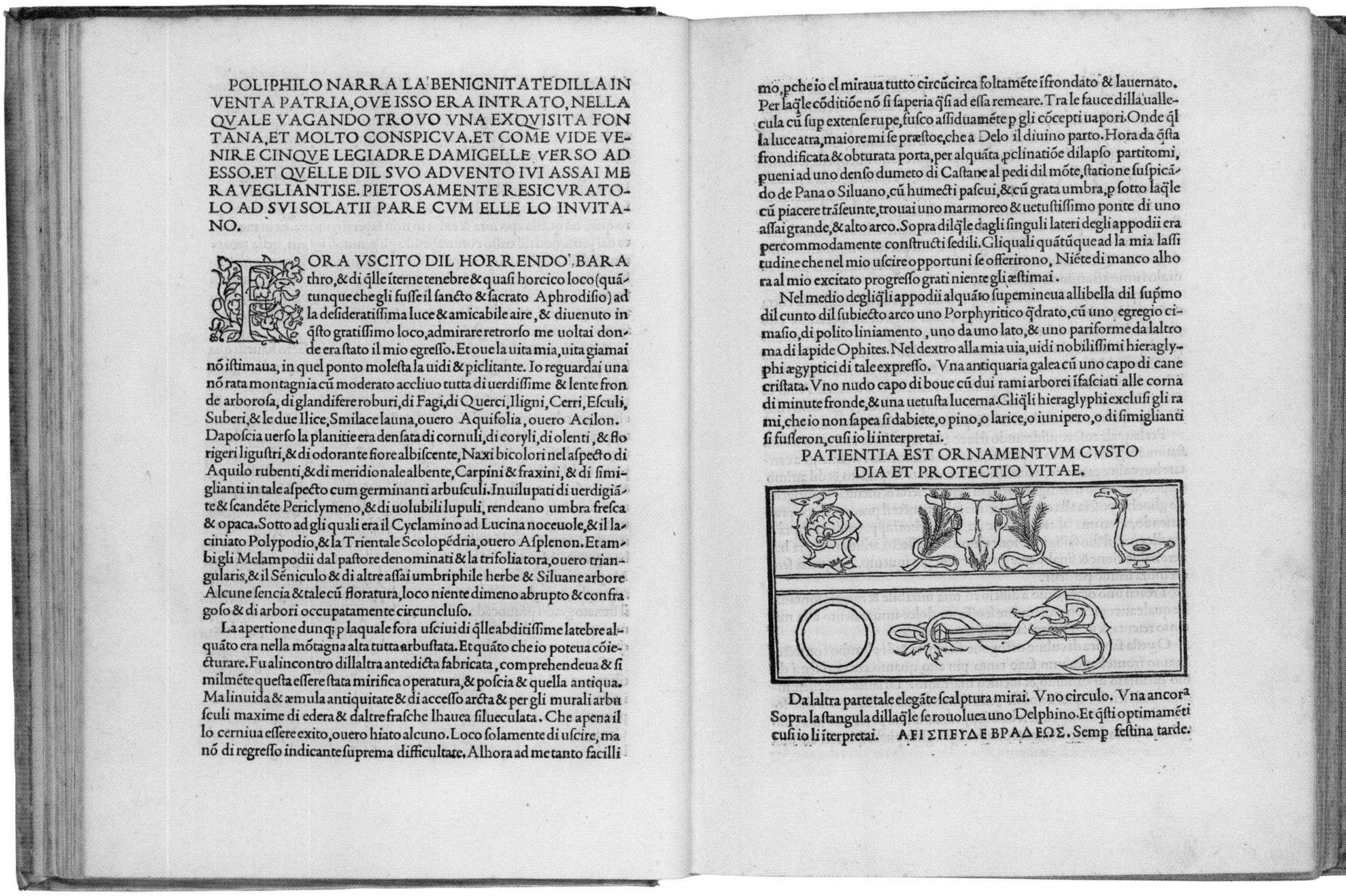
POLIPHILO NARRA LA BENIGNITATE DILLA INVENTA PATRIA, OVE ISSO ERA INTRATO, NELLA QVALE VAGANDO TROVO VNA EXQVISITA FONTANA, ET MOLTO CONSPICVA. ET COME VIDE VENIRE CINQVE LEGIADRE DAMIGELLE VERSO ADESSO. ET QVELLE DIL SVO ADVENTO IVI ASSAI MERAVEGLIANTISE. PIETOSAMENTE RESICVRATOLO AD SVI SOLATII PARE CVM ELLE LO INVITANO.
HORA VSCITO DIL HORRENDO BARATHRO, & di qlle iterne tenebre & quasi horcico loco (quãtunque che gli fusse il sancto & sacrato Aphrodisio) ad la desideratissima luce & amicabile aire, & diuenuto in qsto gratissimo loco, admirare retrorso me uoltai donde era stato il mio egresso. Et oue la uita mia, uita giamai nõ istimaua, in quel ponto molesta la uidi & piclitante. Io reguardai una nõ rata montagnia cũ moderato accliuo tutta di uerdissime & lente fronde arborosa, di glandifere roburi, di Fagi, di Querci, Iligni, Cerri, Esculi, Suberi, & le due Ilice, Smilace launa, ouero Aquifolia, ouero Acilon. Daposcia uerso la planitie era densata di cornuli, di coryli, di olenti, & florigeri ligustri, & di odorante fiore albiscente, Naxi bicolori nel aspecto di Aquilo rubenti, & di meridionale albente, Carpini & fraxini, & di simiglianti in tale aspecto cum germinanti arbusculi. Inuilupati di uerdigiãte & scandẽte Periclymeno, & di uolubili lupuli, rendeano umbra fresca & opaca. Sotto ad gli quali era il Cyclamino ad Lucina noceuole, & il laciniato Polypodio, & la Trientale Scolopẽdria, ouero Asplenon. Et ambi gli Melampodii dal pastore denominati & la trifolia tora, ouero triangularis, & il Sẽniculo & di altre assai umbriphile herbe & Siluane arbore Alcune sencia & tale cũ floratura, loco niente dimeno abrupto & confragoso & di arbori occupatamente circunclusо.
La apertione dunq; p laquale fora usciui di qlle abditissime latebre alquãto era nella mõtagna alta tutta arbustata. Et quãto che io poteua cõiecturare. Fu alincontro dillaltra antedicta fabricata, comprehendeua & similmẽte questa essere stata mirifica operatura, & poscia & quella antiqua. Ma linuida & æmula antiquitate & di accesso arcta & per gli murali arbusculi maxime di edera & daltre frasche lhauea silueculata. Che apena il lo cerniua essere exito, ouero hiato alcuno. Loco solamente di uscire, ma nõ di regresso indicante suprema difficultate. Alhora ad me tanto facilli
mo, pche io el miraua tutto circũcirca soltamẽte ĩfrondato & lauernato. Per laqle cõditiõe nõ si saperia qsi ad essa remeare. Tra le fauce dilla uallecula cũ sup extense rupe, fusco assiduamẽte p gli cõcepti uapori. Onde ql la luce atra, maiore mi se præstoe, che a Delo il diuino parto. Hora da qsta frondificata & obturata porta, per alquãta pclinatiõe dilapso partitomi, pueni ad uno denso dumeto di Castane al pedi dil mõte, statione suspicãdo de Pana o Siluano, cũ humecti pascui, & cũ grata umbra, p sotto laqle cũ piacere trãseunte, trouai uno marmoreo & uetustissimo ponte di uno assai grande, & alto arco. Sopra dilqle dagli singuli lateri degli appodii era percommodamente constructi sedili. Gliquali quãtũque ad la mia lassitudine che nel mio uscire opportuni se offerirono, Niẽte di manco alhora al mio excitato progresso grati niente gli æstimai.
Nel medio degliqli appodii alquãto supemineua allibella dil supmo dil cunto dil subiecto arco uno Porphyritico qdrato, cũ uno egregio cimasio, di polito liniamento, uno da uno lato, & uno pariforme da laltro ma di lapide Ophites. Nel dextro alla mia uia, uidi nobilissimi hieraglyphi ægyptici di tale expresso. Vna antiquaria galea cũ uno capo di cane cristata. Vno nudo capo di boue cũ dui rami arborei ĩfasciati alle corna di minute fronde, & una uetusta lucerna. Gliqli hieraglyphi exclusi gli rami, che io non sapea si dabiete, o pino, o larice, o iunipero, o di simiglianti si fusseron, cusi io li interpretai.
PATIENTIA EST ORNAMENTVM CVSTODIA ET PROTECTIO VITAE.
Da laltra parte tale elegãte scalptura mirai. Vno circulo. Vna ancora Sopra la stangula dillaqle se rouoluea uno Delphino. Et qsti optimamẽti cusi io li ĩterpretai. ΑΕΙ ΣΠΕΥΔΕ ΒΡΑΔΕΩΣ. Semp festina tarde.

TRIVMPHVS
SECVNDVS
Sopra de questo superbo & Triumphale uectabulo, uidi uno bianchissimo Cycno, negli amorosi amplexi duna inclyta Nympha filiola de Theseo, dincredibile bellecia formata, & cum el diuino rostro obsculantise, demisse le ale, tegeua le parte denudate della ĩgenua Hera, Et cũ diuini & uoluptici oblectamenti istauano delectabilmente iucundissimi ambi connexi, Et el diuino Olore tra le delicate & niuee coxe collocato. Laquale commodamente sedeua sopra dui Puluini di panno doro, exquisitamente di mollicula lanugine tomentati, cum tutti gli sumptuosi & ornanti correlarii opportuni. Et ella induta de uesta Nymphale subtile, de serico bianchissimo cum trama doro texto prælucente Agli loci competenti elegante ornato de petre pretiose. Sencia defecto de qualunque cosa che ad incremento di dilecto uenustamente concorre. Summamente agli intuenti conspicuo & delectabile. Cum tutte le parte che al primo fue descripto di laude & plauso.
*
EL TERTIO cæleste triumpho seguiua cum quatro uertibile rote di Chrysolitho æthiopico scintule doro flammigiante, Traiecta per el quale la seta del Asello gli maligni dæmonii fuga, Alla leua mano grato, cum tutto quello c di sopra di rote e dicto. Daposcia le assule sue in ambito per el modo compacte sopra narrato, erano di uirente Helitropia Cyprico, cum potere negli lumi cælesti, el suo gestãte cœla, & il diuinare dona, di sanguinee guttule punctulato.
Offeriua tale historiato insculpto la tabella dextra. Vno homo di regia maiestate ĩsigne, Oraua in uno sacro templo el diuo simulacro, quello che della formosissima fiola deueua seguire. Sentendo el patre la eiectione sua per ella del regno. Et ne per alcuno fusse pregna, Fece una munita structura di una excelsa torre, Et in quella cum solẽne custodia la fece inclaustrare. Nella quale ella cessabonda assedẽdo, cum excessiuo solatio, nel uirgineo sino gutte doro stillare uedeua.
*

HYEMI AEOLIAE.S.

Ad queſto nobile figmento el præſtante artifice, electo ſolertemente el marmoro hauea, che oltra la candidecia ſua era uenato (al requiſito loco) de nigro, ad exprimere el tenebroſo aere illumino, & nebuloſo cum cadente grandine. Sopra la plana della dicta ueneranda, Ara rigidamente rigoroſo ꝑmineua el rude ſimulachro del hortulano cuſtode, cum tutti gli ſui decenti & propriati inſignii. Laquale myſterioſa Ara tegeua uno cupulato umbraculo, ſopra quatro pali nel ſolo infixi affirmato & ſubſtentato. Gli quali pali diligétemente erano inueſtiti di fructea, & florea frondatura, Et el culmo tutto intecto de multiplici fiori, & tra ciaſcuno palo nel lymbo dellapertura, o uero hiato del umbraculo affixo pendeua una ardente lampada, & in circuito ornatamente bractee doro dalle freſche & uerifere aure inconſtante uexate, & cum metallei crepituli ſonante. nelquale ſimulachro, cum maxima religione & priſco rito rurale & paſtorale alcune amole, o uero ampulle uitree cum ſpumáte cruore del immolato Aſello, & cum caldo lacte & ſcintillante Mero ſpargendo rumpeuano, & cum fructi. fiori. fronde. feſta, & gioie libauano, Hora drieto a queſto glorioſo Triumpho, conduceuano, cum antiqua & ſiluatica cerimonia illaqueato el ſeniculo Iano, de reſte & trece intorte di multiplici fiori, cantanti carmini ruralméte Talaſſii, Hymænei, & Feſcennii, & iſtrumenti rureſtricum ſuprema lætitia & gloria, celebremente exultanti, & cum ſolenni plauſi ſaltanti, & uoce fœmelle altiſone, Per laquale coſa nó manco piacere & dilecto cum ſtupore quiui tali ſolenni riti & celebre feſte me inuaſe, che la admiratione degli præcedenti triumphi.

*

Et quiui le ualue doro reſerate, inſeme introrono. Ma io me affermai ſopra il ſancto & riuerendo limine. Er cum uigilanti ochii, nelamantiſſimo obiecto ímobilemente infixi reſpectante, uidi la monitrice iubente, che la mia polia uero myropolia ſe geniculaſſe ſopra il ſumptuoſo pauimento, & cum ſincera deuotione coricarſe.

Il quale pauimento era mirabile tuto di gemme lapidoſo, orbitaméte compoſito, cũ ſubtile factióe, cum multiplice & elegante innodatióe politamente diſtincto, opera officulataméte taſſelata, diſpoſita in uirente ſoglie, & fiori, & auicule, & altri animali, ſecúdo che opportuno era il grato colore delle ꝓtioſe petre ſplendido illucente, cũ perfecto coæquamento, dallequale geminato rimonſtraua quelli che erano intrati.

Sopra queſto dunque la mia audacula Polia, denudati religioſamente gli lactei genui, cum ſumma elegantia genuflexe. Piu belli che unque uedeſſe la Miſericordia ad ſe dedicati. Per laquale coſa iſteti ſoſpeſamente attento cũ gli ſilenti labri. Et per non uolere gli ſancti litamenti interrõpere & le ꝓpitiatione contaminare, & interrumpere le ſoléne ꝓce, & il myſterioſo miniſterio, & le arale cerimonie perturbare, gli íprobi ſoſpiri da ualido amore infiammati debitamente incarcerai.

Hora dinanti di una ſanctificata Ara, nella mediana dil ſacrulo operoſamente ſituata, di diuina fiamma lucente, geniculata humilmente ſe ſtaua.

La

La dimonſtratione dilla quale ara ſuccinctaméte dicendo, mirai uno conſpicuo excogitato di inſueta factura. Lo imo dilla dicta ſopra il gradato & marmoreo pedaméto era uno rotondo lataſtro. Sopra ilquale undulaua una foliatura auriculare, maxima cum politura laciniata, & eximiaméte cauliculata finiendo il mucronato aduna cordicella, ouero nextrulo, ouero regulo, contento ſopra il lataſtro. & ſimilmente nel naſciméto di lambiente foliamento, ſuperaſſideua unaltra cordicella, & tra queſta & unaltra era ſoppreſſa una troclea modificataméte alueata. & poſcia una coronicetta. Sopra la méſula ouero piano dilla dicta Troclea, ſupaſtaua unaltra rotonditate regulata, poſcia alquanto gululata ſe contraheua uerſo la ſuperficie plana & expedita. Nella parte mediana dillaquale promineua uno ſtriato ſtilo, piu porrecto nella inferiore parte ſopra la piana cum proportionata crepidine. Diuiſo dũque il diametro dilla inferna rotundatione di queſto ſtilo. partitione una era alla proiectura ambiente conſignata. Il ſuperno capo due portione hauea cum tornatile gulule & lo imo ancora debitamente riſeruatoſe. So pradicto ſtipite tegeua una inuerſa piana rotundata, tanto in proiecto gyrando, quãto lextremo exito degli labri dilla ſubiecta Troclea Ornata nella ſuperiore parte, nello extremo circuito in cliua dimonſtratione cum una ſima di ſpectanda folliatura da una egregia coronetta perpollitamente naſcendo. Nel circinato cõtento dunque dillaquale coronetta bellamente occupaua la apertura di uno elegãte fiore, in balauſtico liniamento deformato, cum gli calicei labri ſopra il piano lambenti, & quadripartito in periucũdo foliaméto acanthino fatiſcéte. Sotto il quale nella laciniata diſcrepantia ſubſideua unaltra foglia artificioſamente exſcalpta. Sopra il cacuminaro dilquale, doppo gli debiti liniamenti egregiaméte ritondaua uno nodo di exqſito expreſſo. Al q̃le infixa appoſita dilatatamente promineua, una antiquaria platina doro puriſſimo, cum gli labri largiuſculi, & paucolo lacunata. Nel piano orulo de gli labri alternatamente promineuano incomparabili adamanti & carbunculi cum ꝓſtante deformatione pyramidale, nella circuitione mirabilmente diſpoſiti di incredibile craſſitudine, Ceda quiui il Scypho dil fortiſſimo Hercule. Il Cantharo dil iucundo Baccho, Et il Carcheſio allimmortale Ioue dicato.

o iii

Hypnerotomachia Poliphili

The sixteenth century

Detail of *Theuerdank*, printed by Johann Schönsperger the Elder (see p. 78)

Wider über das erdtrich gan
Allererst stund auf der Tewr Man.

Wie der Ernhold die drey haubtlewt Fürwittig Unnfalo unnd Neydelhart vor der Künigin umb Jr poßhayt willen verklagt/unnd Rechtens wider Sy begert.

108

Als die sach alle was volbracht
Der Ernhold an die valschait dacht

The sixteenth century **Italy and especially Venice (home of Aldus Manutius) retained their leading role in the development of typographic design into the early sixteenth century. Roman typefaces, closely associated with the Renaissance and with humanism, gradually drove out blackletter type in those regions, whose printers and publishers also established the layout principles for several genres. In around 1520, cities north of the Alps began to take over this leading role, especially in France, with Henri and Robert Estienne, Simon de Colines and Michel de Vascosan in Paris and Jean de Tournes in Lyon. In Switzerland, Basel took the lead with Johann Froben and Johannes Oporinus. Beginning with the styles of type and layout established in Italy, they created the book as we know it today, with an informative title page and a clear articulation of the text.**

Printers in these northern regions also began using roman type more often, not only in scholarly works in Latin but also in texts in the national vernacular languages. At first, these romans were often imitations of Nicolas Jenson's type (*c.* 1470), but from around 1530 new French styles appeared. These were inspired by romans that the Italian punchcutter Francesco Griffo made for Aldus Manutius in the last years of the fifteenth century. The most important of these new types were the elegant romans of the Paris punchcutter Claude Garamont (or Garamond), which are still well known today. Aldus also introduced the first italic in 1501 as an independent type, but over the course of the century it gradually evolved into an auxiliary to the roman.

The title page displayed the name of the author and the title of the book, separated from the imprint by a large expanse of white space. The layout gave structure to the

body text through the use of different type styles and sizes, paragraph indicators, indentations, white space between text elements and other means of articulation. This gave the presentation a greater clarity. In addition, illustrations became more precise, in part thanks to the new technique of copperplate engraving. In the Low Countries after the middle of the century, Christoffel Plantin and others continued to develop these aspects of design.

During the sixteenth century, the advance of scholarship – in both the sciences and the humanities – and the rise of book collecting stimulated the development of printing. We can place the birth of the modern book in the sixteenth century, primarily in Paris.

Popular books, often religious in character, tended to retain older forms. FAJ

1503 **Wolfgang Hopyl & Henri Estienne I** Jacques Lefèvre d'Étaples et al., *In hoc libro contenta: epitome compendiosaque introductio in libros arithmeticos divi Severini Boetii* (and other works). Paris: Wolfgang Hopyl & Henri Estienne, 1503. 112 leaves. 27.5 cm.

Henri Estienne I (*c.* 1460–1520), who produced some hundred and fifty books between 1502 and his death, initially collaborated with Wolfgang Hopyl (*fl.* 1489–1522/3). The title page of this academic textbook functions as a table of contents ('The contents of this book: a summary of and introduction to the arithmetic books of Boethius…'). The book contains texts on mathematics, geometry, and astronomy by Jacques Lefèvre d'Étaples and two of his students, Josse Clichthove and Charles de Bovelles. In the Renaissance and in classical antiquity, these sciences were considered to be the foundation of the divine.

The layout, designed after Italian examples such as Aldus Manutius's 1497 Iamblichus edition, provides the complicated texts with a clear structure. Printed pilcrows indicate paragraphs and headings. Running heads and folio numbers are also printed, but initials were not available at this printing house. The printers left blank spaces for the initials, indicated by a small letter, the guide letter. The buyer of the book could then commission an illuminator to insert a decorative initial. In this volume, the spaces for the initials were left blank. Two romans were used, both Jenson adaptations; the smaller one was used for annotations. In Paris in around 1500, blackletter faces were still prevalent; the decision to set this book in roman type must therefore have been deliberate. FAJ

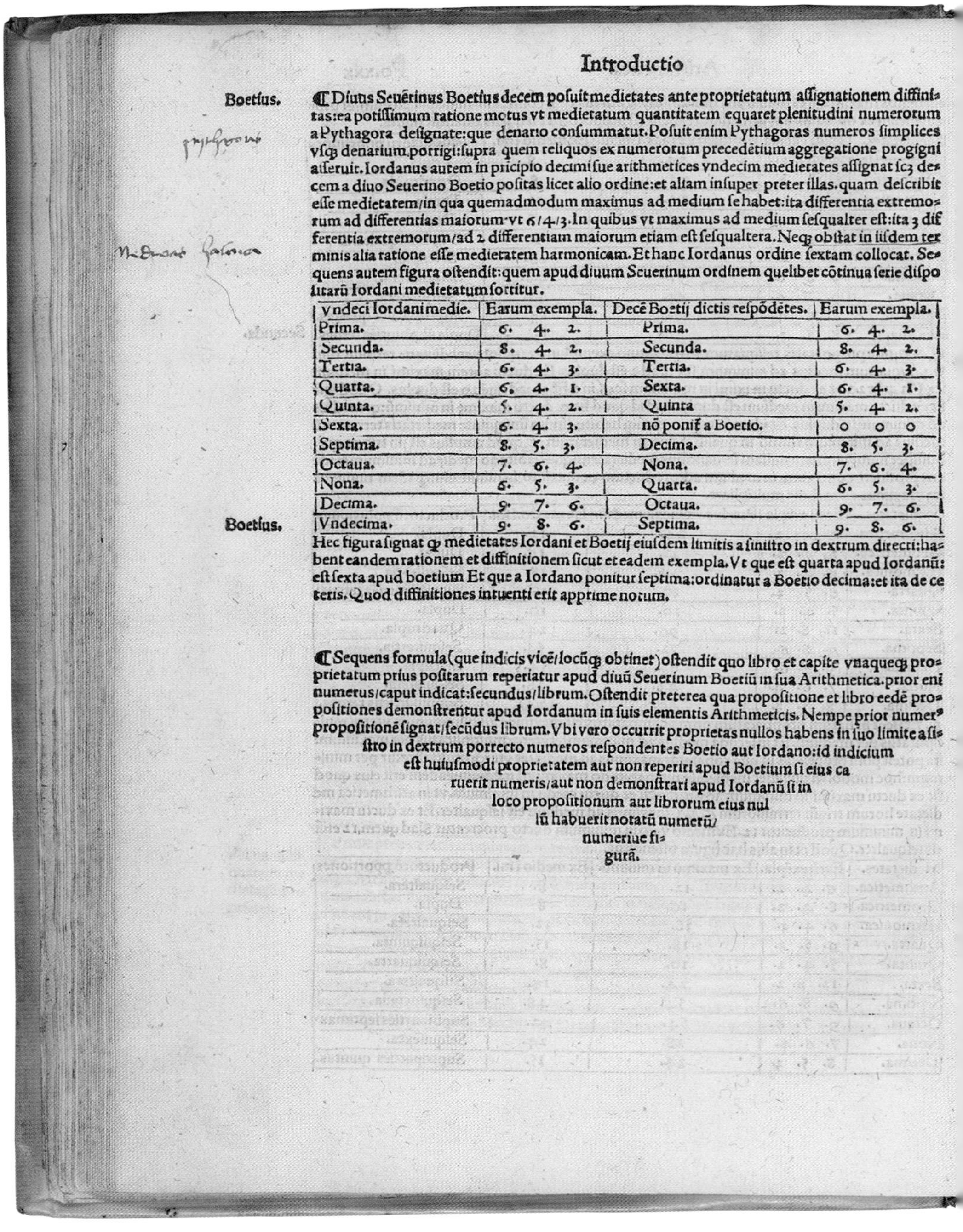

Introductio

Boetius.

¶ Diuus Seuerinus Boetius decem posuit medietates ante proprietatum assignationem diffinitas: ea potissimum ratione motus vt medietatum quantitatem equaret plenitudini numerorum a Pythagora designate: que denario consummatur. Posuit enim Pythagoras numeros simplices vsq3 denarium porrigi: supra quem reliquos ex numerorum precedētium aggregatione progigni asseruit. Iordanus autem in pricipio decimi sue arithmetices vndecim medietates assignat sc3 decem a diuo Seuerino Boetio positas licet alio ordine: et aliam insuper preter illas. quam describit esse medietatem/ in qua quemadmodum maximus ad medium se habet: ita differentia extremorum ad differentias maiorum· vt 6/4/3. In quibus vt maximus ad medium sesqualter est: ita 3 differentia extremorum/ ad 2 differentiam maiorum etiam est sesqualtera. Neq3 obstat in iisdem terminis alia ratione esse medietatem harmonicam. Et hanc Iordanus ordine sextam collocat. Sequens autem figura ostendit: quem apud diuum Seuerinum ordinem quelibet cōtinua serie dispositarū Iordani medietatum sortitur.

Vndeci Iordani medie.	Earum exempla.	Decē Boetij dictis respōdētes.	Earum exempla.
Prima.	6. 4. 2.	Prima.	6. 4. 2.
Secunda.	8. 4. 2.	Secunda.	8. 4. 2.
Tertia.	6. 4. 3.	Tertia.	6. 4. 3.
Quarta.	6. 4. 1.	Sexta.	6. 4. 1.
Quinta.	5. 4. 2.	Quinta	5. 4. 2.
Sexta.	6. 4. 3.	nō ponit a Boetio.	o o o
Septima.	8. 5. 3.	Decima.	8. 5. 3.
Octaua.	7. 6. 4.	Nona.	7. 6. 4.
Nona.	6. 5. 3.	Quarta.	6. 5. 3.
Decima.	9. 7. 6.	Octaua.	9. 7. 6.
Vndecima.	9. 8. 6.	Septima.	9. 8. 6.

Boetius.

Hec figura signat q medietates Iordani et Boetij eiusdem limitis a sinistro in dextrum directi: habent eandem rationem et diffinitionem sicut et eadem exempla. Vt que est quarta apud Iordanū: est sexta apud boetium Et que a Iordano ponitur septima: ordinatur a Boetio decima: et ita de ceteris. Quod diffinitiones intuenti erit apprime notum.

¶ Sequens formula (que indicis vicē/ locūq3 obtinet) ostendit quo libro et capite vnaqueq3 proprietatum prius positarum reperiatur apud diuū Seuerinum Boetiū in sua Arithmetica. prior eni numerus/ caput indicat: secundus/ librum. Ostendit preterea qua propositione et libro eedē propositiones demonstrentur apud Iordanum in suis elementis Arithmeticis. Nempe prior numerus propositionē signat/ secūdus librum. Vbi vero occurrit proprietas nullos habens in suo limite a sinistro in dextrum porrecto numeros respondentes Boetio aut Iordano: id indicium est huiusmodi proprietatem aut non reperiri apud Boetium si eius caruerit numeris/ aut non demonstrari apud Iordanū si in loco propositionum aut librorum eius nullū habuerit notatū numerū/ numeriue figurā.

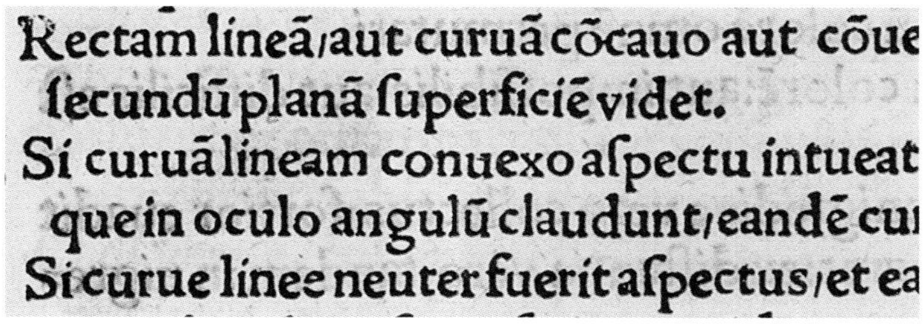

Rectam lineã/aut curuã cõcauo aut cõue
ſecundũ planã ſuperficiẽ videt.
Si curuã lineam conuexo aſpectu intueat
que in oculo angulũ claudunt/eandẽ cu
Si curue linee neuter fuerit aſpectus/et ea

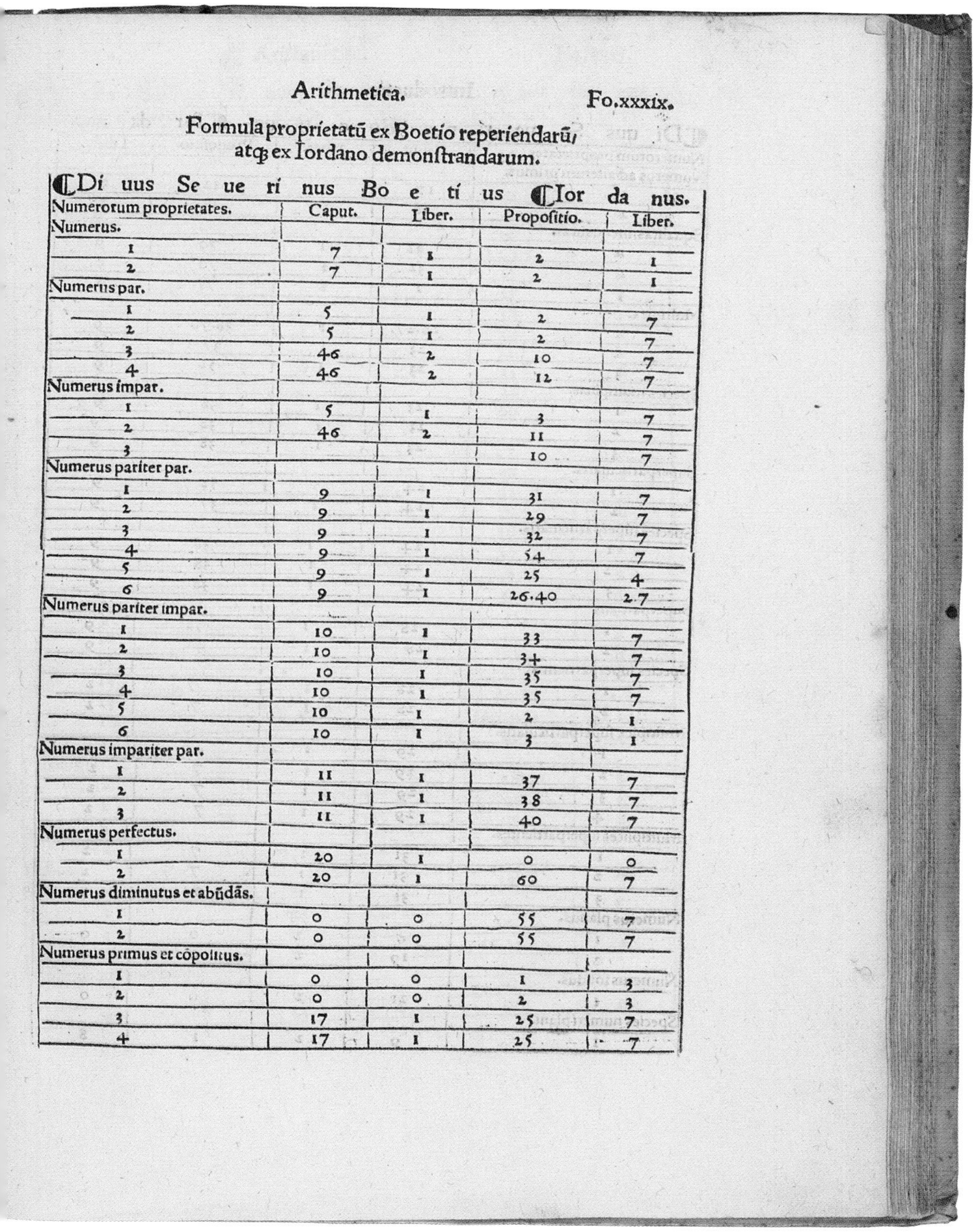

Arithmetica. Fo.xxxix.

Formula proprietatũ ex Boetio reperiendarũ/
atq; ex Iordano demonſtrandarum.

Diuus Seuerinus Boetius			Iordanus.	
Numerorum proprietates.	Caput.	Liber.	Propoſitio.	Liber.
Numerus.				
1	7	1	2	1
2	7	1	2	1
Numerus par.				
1	5	1	2	7
2	5	1	2	7
3	46	2	10	7
4	46	2	12	7
Numerus impar.				
1	5	1	3	7
2	46	2	11	7
3			10	7
Numerus pariter par.				
1	9	1	31	7
2	9	1	29	7
3	9	1	32	7
4	9	1	54	7
5	9	1	25	4
6	9	1	26.40	2.7
Numerus pariter impar.				
1	10	1	33	7
2	10	1	34	7
3	10	1	35	7
4	10	1	35	7
5	10	1	2	1
6	10	1	3	1
Numerus impariter par.				
1	11	1	37	7
2	11	1	38	7
3	11	1	40	7
Numerus perfectus.				
1	20	1	0	0
2	20	1	60	7
Numerus diminutus et abũdãs.				
1	0	0	55	7
2	0	0	55	7
Numerus primus et cõpoſitus.				
1	0	0	1	3
2	0	0	2	3
3	17	1	25	7
4	17	1	25	7

This Venetian-style roman, probably from Basel (1494), has large, awkward and sometimes misaligned capitals. In Paris (1498) it became the most popular roman of its day; it was still used in the 1530s, and spread to Kraków (1504), London (1508) and Antwerp (1519), with some variant letters.

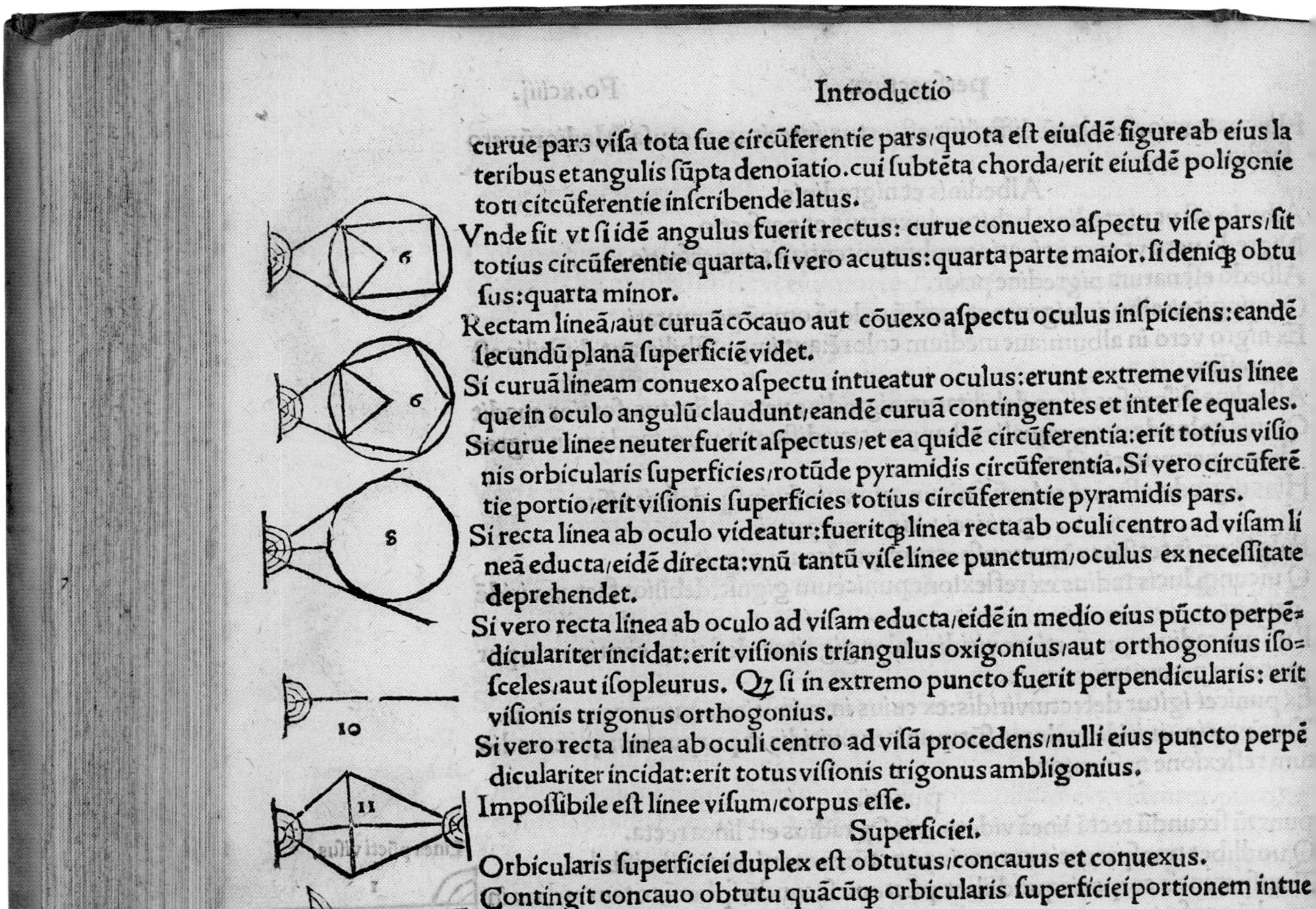

Introductio

curue pars visa tota sue circūferentie pars/quota est eiusdē figure ab eius la
teribus et angulis sūpta denoiatio.cui subtēta chorda/erit eiusdē poligonie
toti circūferentie inscribende latus.
Vnde fit vt si idē angulus fuerit rectus: curue conuexo aspectu vise pars/sit
totius circūferentie quarta.si vero acutus:quarta parte maior.si deniqꝫ obtu
sus:quarta minor.
Rectam lineā/aut curuā cōcauo aut cōuexo aspectu oculus inspiciens:eandē
secundū planā superficiē videt.
Si curuā lineam conuexo aspectu intueatur oculus:erunt extreme visus linee
que in oculo angulū claudunt/eandē curuā contingentes et inter se equales.
Si curue linee neuter fuerit aspectus/et ea quidē circūferentia:erit totius visio
nis orbicularis superficies/rotūde pyramidis circūferentia.Si vero circūferē
tie portio/erit visionis superficies totius circūferentie pyramidis pars.
Si recta linea ab oculo videatur:fueritqꝫ linea recta ab oculi centro ad visam li
neā educta/eidē directa:vnū tantū vise linee punctum/oculus ex necessitate
deprehendet.
Si vero recta linea ab oculo ad visam educta/eidē in medio eius pūcto perpē=
diculariter incidat:erit visionis triangulus oxigonius/aut orthogonius iso=
sceles/aut isopleurus. Qꝫ si in extremo puncto fuerit perpendicularis: erit
visionis trigonus orthogonius.
Si vero recta linea ab oculi centro ad visā procedens/nulli eius puncto perpē
diculariter incidat:erit totus visionis trigonus ambligonius.
Impossibile est linee visum/corpus esse.

Superficiei.

Orbicularis superficiei duplex est obtutus/concauus et conuexus.
Contingit concauo obtutu quācūqꝫ orbicularis superficiei portionem intue
ri:totā vero orbicularem non contingit.
Conuexus visus:orbicularis superficiei portionē neqꝫ maiorē/neqꝫ mediam/
at solam minorē ex necessitate deprehendit.
Orbiculariū superficierū concaui et conuexi visus:paribus curuarū linearum
intuitionibus proportionantur.
Vtriqꝫ sphericarū superficierū visus:sunt pyramides rotūde/quarū bases sūt
orbiculares superficies conspecte.
Circuli itē visus:est pyramis rotunda/cuius basis ipse est circulus.
Si recta linea ab oculi cētro/ad visam planā superficiem ducta fuerit eidem di
recta:extremas dūtaxat eius lineas oculus intuebitur.
Si vero ab oculo linea recta/ad visā superficiē planā ducta eidem ad angulos
occurrat:eandē totā superficiē oculus deprehendet.
Figure plane poligonie visus:est laterata pyramis/totidē laterū et angulorū

Corporis.

propriū corporis interuallū:est profunditas per se inuisibilis.
Vnde fit vt et corpus/propria dimensione sit inuisibile.

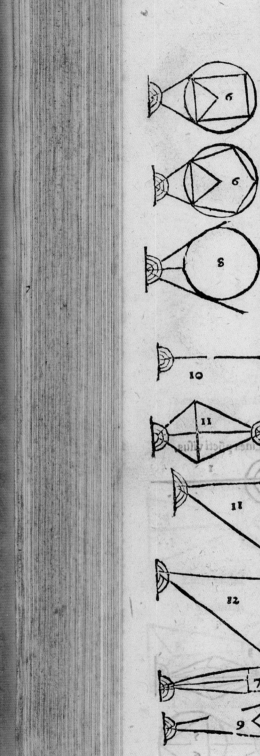

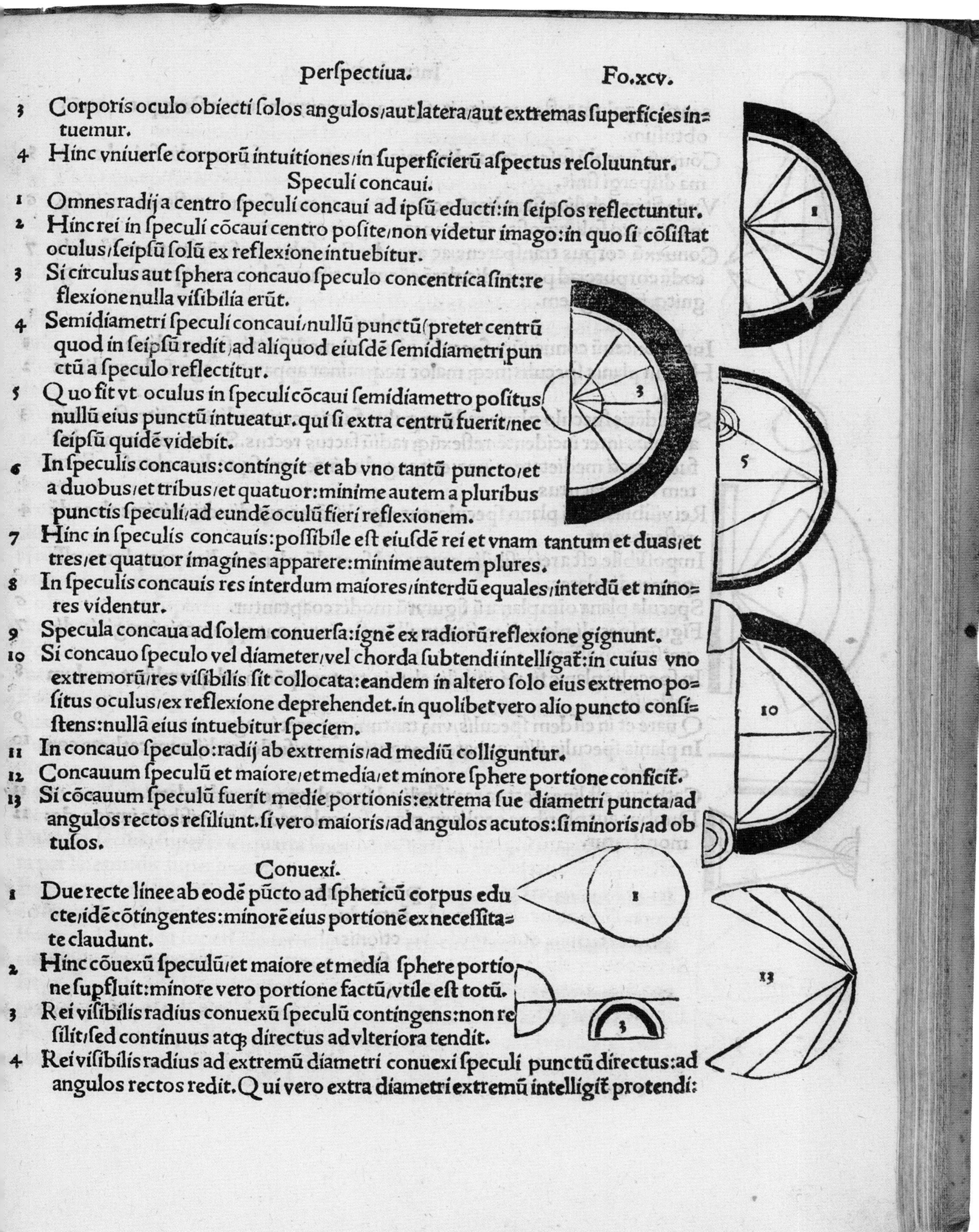

perſpectiua. Fo.xcv.

3 Corporis oculo obiecti ſolos angulos/aut latera/aut extremas ſuperficies intuemur.

4 Hinc vniuerſe corporũ intuitiones/in ſuperficierũ aſpectus reſoluuntur.

Speculi concaui.

1 Omnes radij a centro ſpeculi concaui ad ipſũ educti: in ſeipſos reflectuntur.

2 Hinc rei in ſpeculi cõcaui centro poſite/non videtur imago: in quo ſi cõſiſtat oculus/ſeipſũ ſolũ ex reflexione intuebitur.

3 Si circulus aut ſphera concauo ſpeculo concentrica ſint: reflexione nulla viſibilia erũt.

4 Semidiametri ſpeculi concaui/nullũ punctũ (preter centrũ quod in ſeipſũ redit) ad aliquod eiuſdẽ ſemidiametri punctũ a ſpeculo reflectitur.

5 Quo fit vt oculus in ſpeculi cõcaui ſemidiametro poſitus nullũ eius punctũ intueatur. qui ſi extra centrũ fuerit/nec ſeipſũ quidẽ videbit.

6 In ſpeculis concauis: contingit et ab vno tantũ puncto/et a duobus/et tribus/et quatuor: minime autem a pluribus punctis ſpeculi/ad eundẽ oculũ fieri reflexionem.

7 Hinc in ſpeculis concauis: poſſibile eſt eiuſdẽ rei et vnam tantum et duas/et tres/et quatuor imagines apparere: minime autem plures.

8 In ſpeculis concauis res interdum maiores/interdũ equales/interdũ et minores videntur.

9 Specula concaua ad ſolem conuerſa: ignẽ ex radiorũ reflexione gignunt.

10 Si concauo ſpeculo vel diameter/vel chorda ſubtendi intelligat̃: in cuius vno extremorũ/res viſibilis ſit collocata: eandem in altero ſolo eius extremo poſitus oculus/ex reflexione deprehendet. in quolibet vero alio puncto conſiſtens: nullã eius intuebitur ſpeciem.

11 In concauo ſpeculo: radij ab extremis/ad mediũ colliguntur.

12 Concauum ſpeculũ et maiore/et media/et minore ſphere portione conficit̃.

13 Si cõcauum ſpeculũ fuerit medie portionis: extrema ſue diametri puncta/ad angulos rectos reſiliunt. ſi vero maioris/ad angulos acutos: ſi minoris/ad obtuſos.

Conuexi.

1 Due recte linee ab eodẽ pũcto ad ſphericũ corpus educte/idẽ cõtingentes: minorẽ eius portionẽ ex neceſſitate claudunt.

2 Hinc cõuexũ ſpeculũ/et maiore et media ſphere portione ſupfluit: minore vero portione factũ/vtile eſt totũ.

3 Rei viſibilis radius conuexũ ſpeculũ contingens: non reſilit/ſed continuus atq; directus ad vlteriora tendit.

4 Rei viſibilis radius ad extremũ diametri conuexi ſpeculi punctũ directus: ad angulos rectos redit. Qui vero extra diametri extremũ intelligit̃ protendi:

1505 **Aldus Manutius** Johannes Aurelius Augurellus, [*Poemata*]. Venice: Aldus Manutius, 1505. 16.5 cm.

These poems by the humanist and alchemist Augurellus were published as part of a series of books designed by printer Aldus Manutius (*c.* 1451–1515); the series included texts by classical and later also contemporary writers, Augurellus among them. The works of Virgil, the classical poet par excellence, were the first to appear in 1501. The small octavo format of the volumes is notable. Portable pocket books had been made before – as had pocket-sized handwritten manuscripts – but Aldus published them as a series with a uniform layout. With these *libri portatiles*, Aldus was targeting the growing market of readers interested in humanism.

The Latin and Italian texts in the series are set in an italic that had recently been cut on the initiative of Aldus. This italic was a typographic representation of the humanist script and, like that script, it was not used to distinguish or highlight text, but rather for the body text – a typeface of equal standing to the roman. Erasmus preferred these small italics and thought them the most beautiful letters of all. In this edition, the initials are not printed but indicated by a guide letter. Italic capitals did not yet exist, so roman capitals were used instead.

Since 1502, Aldus used his now famous printer's device, a dolphin entwined around an anchor, signifying speed and calmness. His motto was '*festina lente*': make haste slowly. Aldus's emblem became a hallmark of typographic quality. FAJ

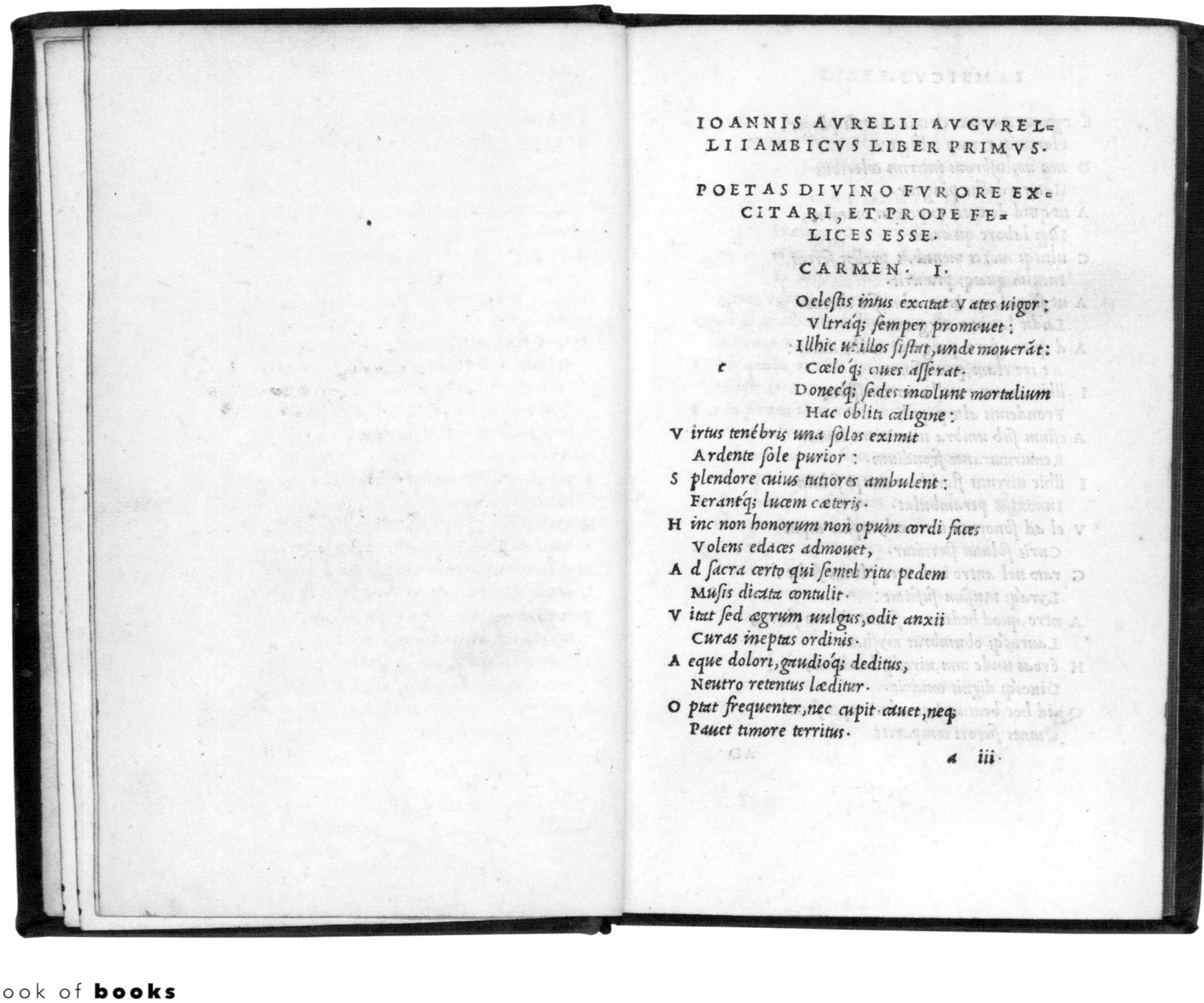

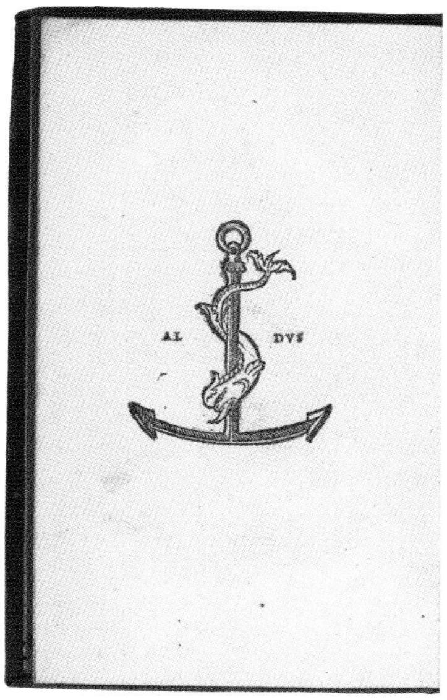

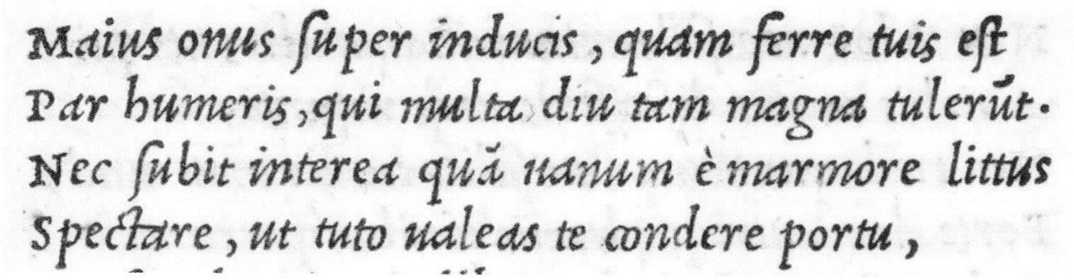
Maius onus ſuper inducis, quam ferre tuis eſt
Par humeris, qui multa diu tam magna tulerũt.
Nec ſubit interea quã uanum è marmore littus
Spectare, ut tuto ualeas te condere portu,

The first italic, cut by Francesco Griffo (*fl.* 1475?–1518) for Aldus Manutius, was used for a few words in 1500 and an extensive text in 1501. Immediately popular as an independent book type, copies spread to dozens of printers in several countries. Italic became an auxiliary to roman only gradually, from the late sixteenth century on.

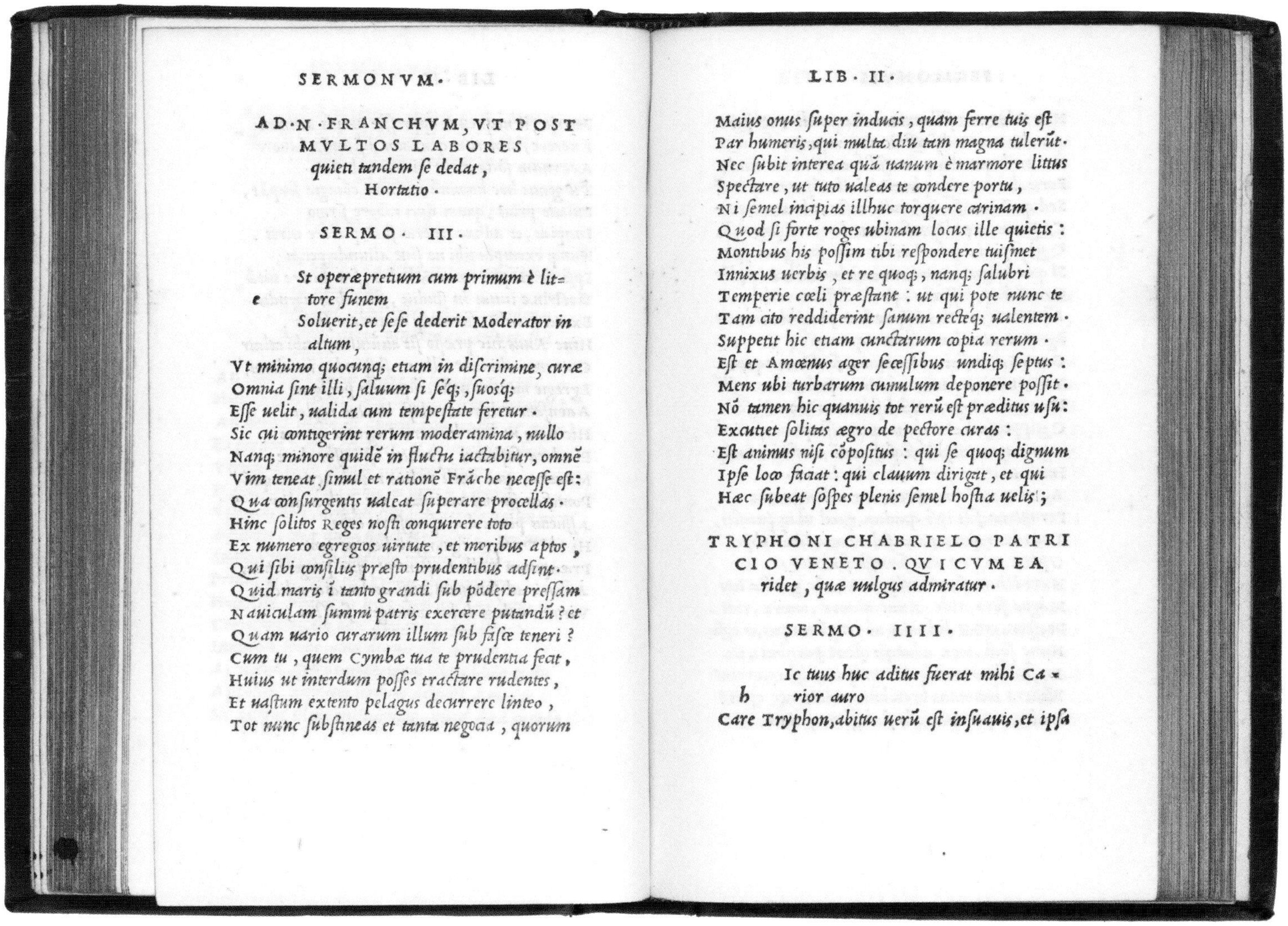
SERMONVM.

AD·N·FRANCHVM, VT POST
MVLTOS LABORES
quieti tandem ſe dedat,
Hortatio.

SERMO. III.

e St operæpretium cum primum è lit=
tore funem
Soluerit, et ſeſe dederit Moderator in
altum,
Vt minimo quocunq; etiam in diſcrimine, curæ
Omnia ſint illi, ſaluum ſi ſéq;, ſuoſq;
Eſſe uelit, ualida cum tempeſtate feretur.
Sic cui contigerint rerum moderamina, nullo
Nanq; minore quidẽ in fluctu iactabitur, omnẽ
Vim teneat ſimul et rationẽ Frãche neceſſe eſt:
Qua conſurgentis ualeat ſuperare procellas.
Hinc ſolitos Reges noſti conquirere toto
Ex numero egregios uirtute, et moribus aptos,
Qui ſibi conſilijs præſto prudentibus adſint.
Quid maris ĩ tanto grandi ſub põdere preſſam
Nauiculam ſummi patris exercere putandũ? et
Quam uario curarum illum ſub faſce teneri?
Cum tu, quem Cymbæ tua te prudentia fecit,
Huius ut interdum poſſes tractare rudentes,
Et uaſtum extento pelagus decurrere linteo,
Tot nunc ſubſtineas et tanta negocia, quorum

LIB. II.

Maius onus ſuper inducis, quam ferre tuis eſt
Par humeris, qui multa diu tam magna tulerũt.
Nec ſubit interea quã uanum è marmore littus
Spectare, ut tuto ualeas te condere portu,
Ni ſemel incipias illhuc torquere carinam.
Quod ſi forte roges ubinam locus ille quietis:
Montibus his poſſim tibi reſpondere tuiſmet
Innixus uerbis, et re quoq;, nanq; ſalubri
Temperie cœli præſtant: ut qui pote nunc te
Tam cito reddiderint ſanum recteq; ualentem.
Suppetit hic etiam cunctarum copia rerum.
Eſt et Amœnus ager ſeceſſibus undiq; ſeptus:
Mens ubi turbarum cumulum deponere poſſit.
Nõ tamen hic quanuis tot rerũ eſt præditus uſu:
Excutiet ſolitas ægro de pectore curas:
Eſt animus niſi cõpoſitus: qui ſe quoq; dignum
Ipſe loco faciat: qui clauum dirigat, et qui
Hæc ſubeat ſoſpes plenis ſemel hoſtia uelis;

TRYPHONI CHABRIELO PATRI
CIO VENETO. QVICVM EA
ridet, quæ uulgus admiratur.

SERMO. IIII.

h Ic tuus huc aditus fuerat mihi Ca=
rior auro
Care Tryphon, abitus uerũ eſt inſuauis, et ipſa

1509 Luca Pacioli **Luca Pacioli, *Divina proportione*; ed. Antonio Capella. Venice: Paganino de Paganini, 1509. 27.5 cm.**

Illustrators: Leonardo da Vinci (polyhedrons) and others.

De divina proportione ('About the Divine Proportions') is the first printed book to illustrate the construction of roman capitals. These woodcuts, however, showing the capitals in a geometric grid of square, triangle, and circle, are part of a larger framework: a series of texts in Italian about the 'divine' geometric principles that were considered to be the foundation of everything.

The compiler, the mathematician Luca Pacioli (1445–1514), begins his book with a discussion of these principles, which go back to Euclid and Plato. This discussion is followed by a text on architecture, based on the classical handbook by Vitruvius, and an Italian translation of a text by the painter Piero della Francesca on multisided solids, illustrated with woodcuts based on drawings by Leonardo da Vinci. These 'divine proportions' should not be confused with the golden section, which is a nineteenth-century concept. The book continues with an alphabet that demonstrates the Renaissance theory of the construction of roman capitals, with descriptions that can be taken as practical instructions. This part of the book is intended to provide examples for painters and sculptors – it has no direct connection to typography.

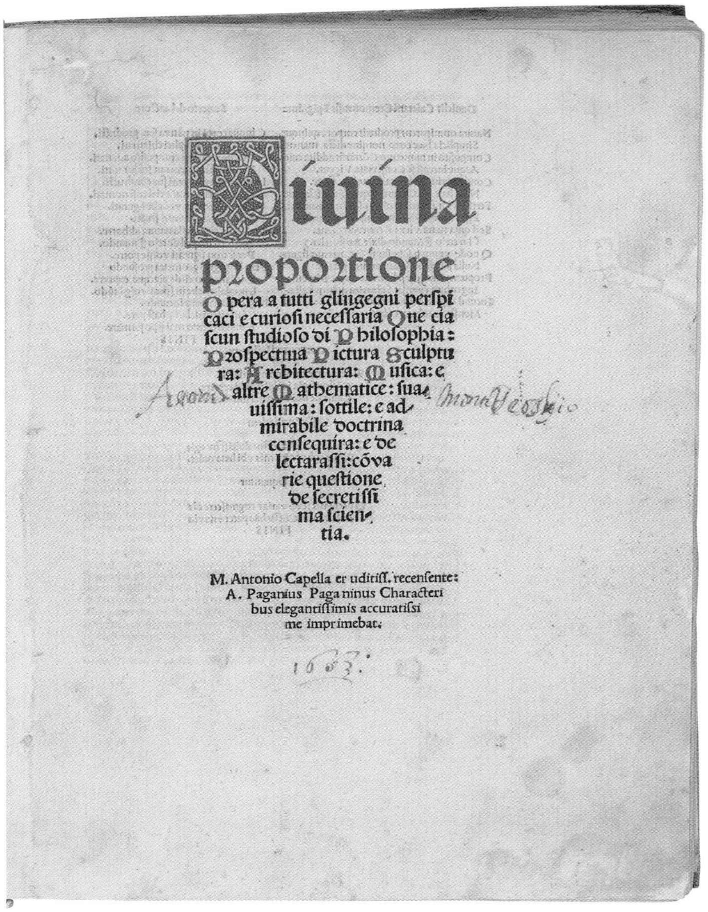
Diuina proportione
Opera a tutti glingegni perspicaci e curiosi necessaria Oue ciascun studioso di Philosophia: Prospectiua Pictura Sculptura: Architectura: Musica: e altre Mathematice: suauissima: sottile: e admirabile doctrina consequira: e delectarassi: cōvarie questione de secretissima scientia.
M. Antonio Capella eruditiss. recensente: A. Paganius Paganinus Characteribus elegantissimis accuratissime imprimebat.

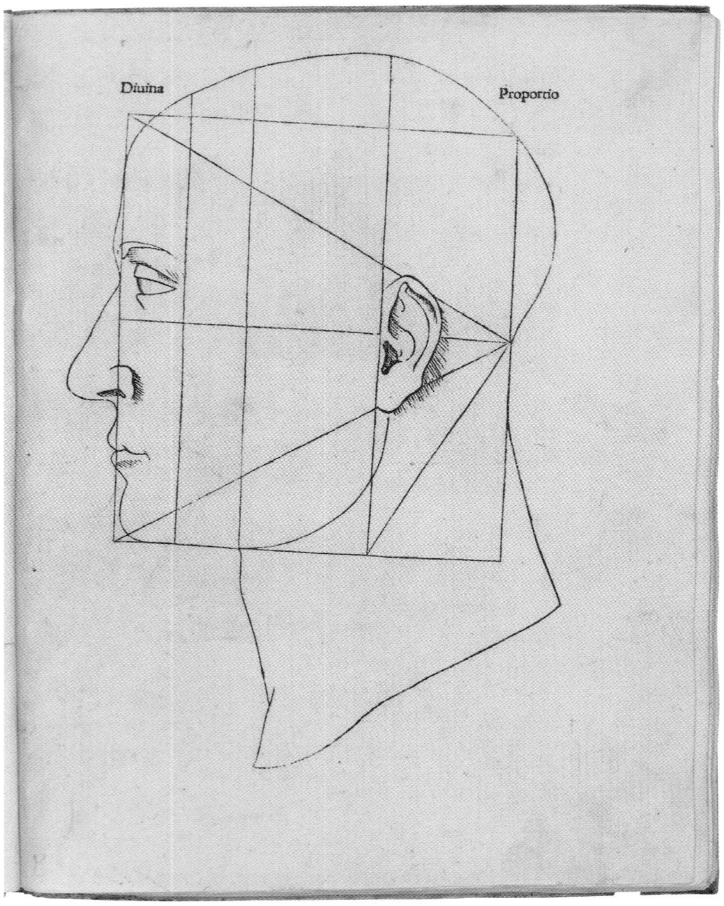

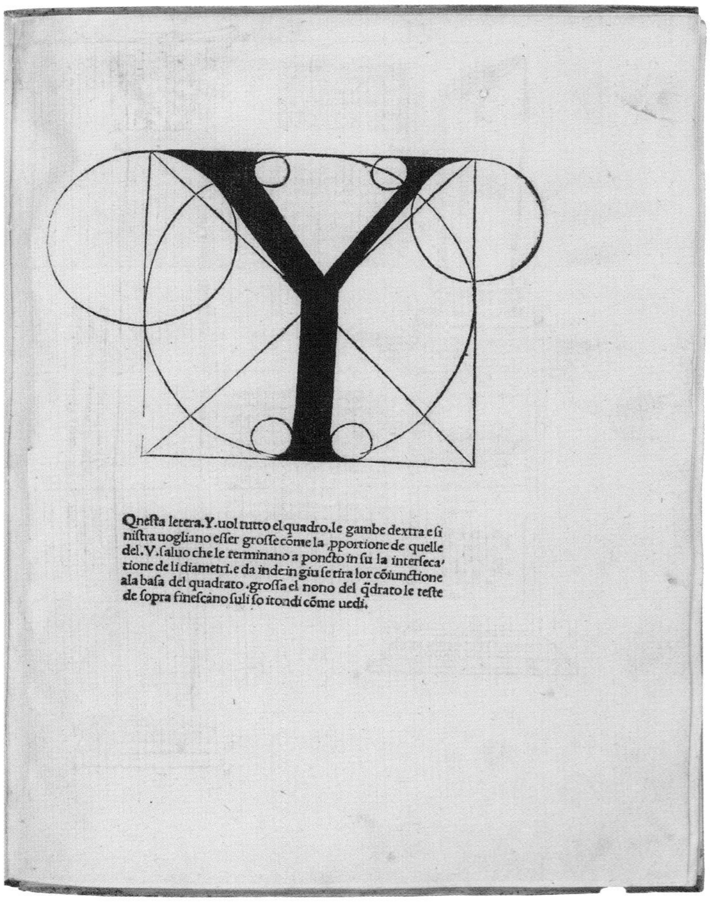
Qnesta letera. Y. uol tutto el quadro. le gambe dextra e sinistra uogliano esser grosse cōme la pportione de quelle del. V. saluo che le terminano a poncto in su la intersecatione de li diametri. e da inde in giu se tira lor cōiunctione ala basa del quadrato. grossa el nono del q̃drato le teste de sopra finescano suli so itondi cōme uedi.

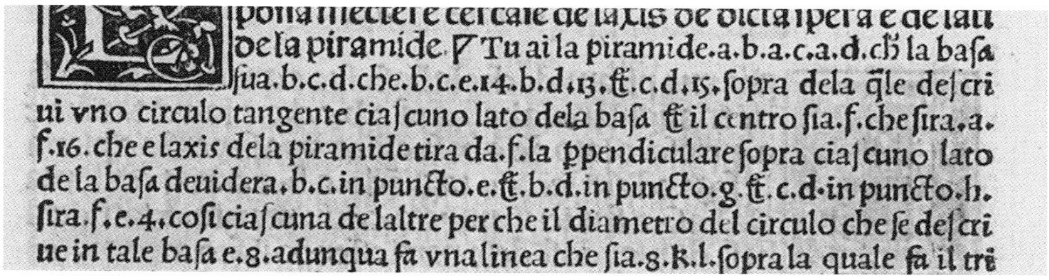
posta mectere e cercare de laxis de dicta spera e de lati
de la piramide. ¶ Tu ai la piramide.a.b.a.c.a.d.chā la basa
sua.b.c.d.che.b.c.e.14.b.d.13.&.c.d.15.sopra dela qle descri
ui vno circulo tangente ciascuno lato dela basa & il centro sia.f.che sira.a.
f.16.che e laxis dela piramide tira da.f.la ppendiculare sopra ciascuno lato
de la basa deuidera.b.c.in puncto.e.&.b.d.in puncto.g.&.c.d.in puncto.h.
sira.f.e.4.cosi ciascuna de laltre per che il diametro del circulo che se descri
ue in tale basa e.8.adunqua fa vna linea che sia.8.k.l.sopra la quale fa il tri

While the larger roman used below the letter constructions follows the traditional Venetian style, this smaller one includes angular forms, calligraphic foot-terminals, a descending f and long s, and several special alternative sorts, giving it a cursive flavour, even though it remains completely upright.

The body text typeface used by Paganino de Paganini (d. 1538) is an Italian variant of blackletter type, which is close to the roman; the initials are Italian-style woodcuts. FAJ

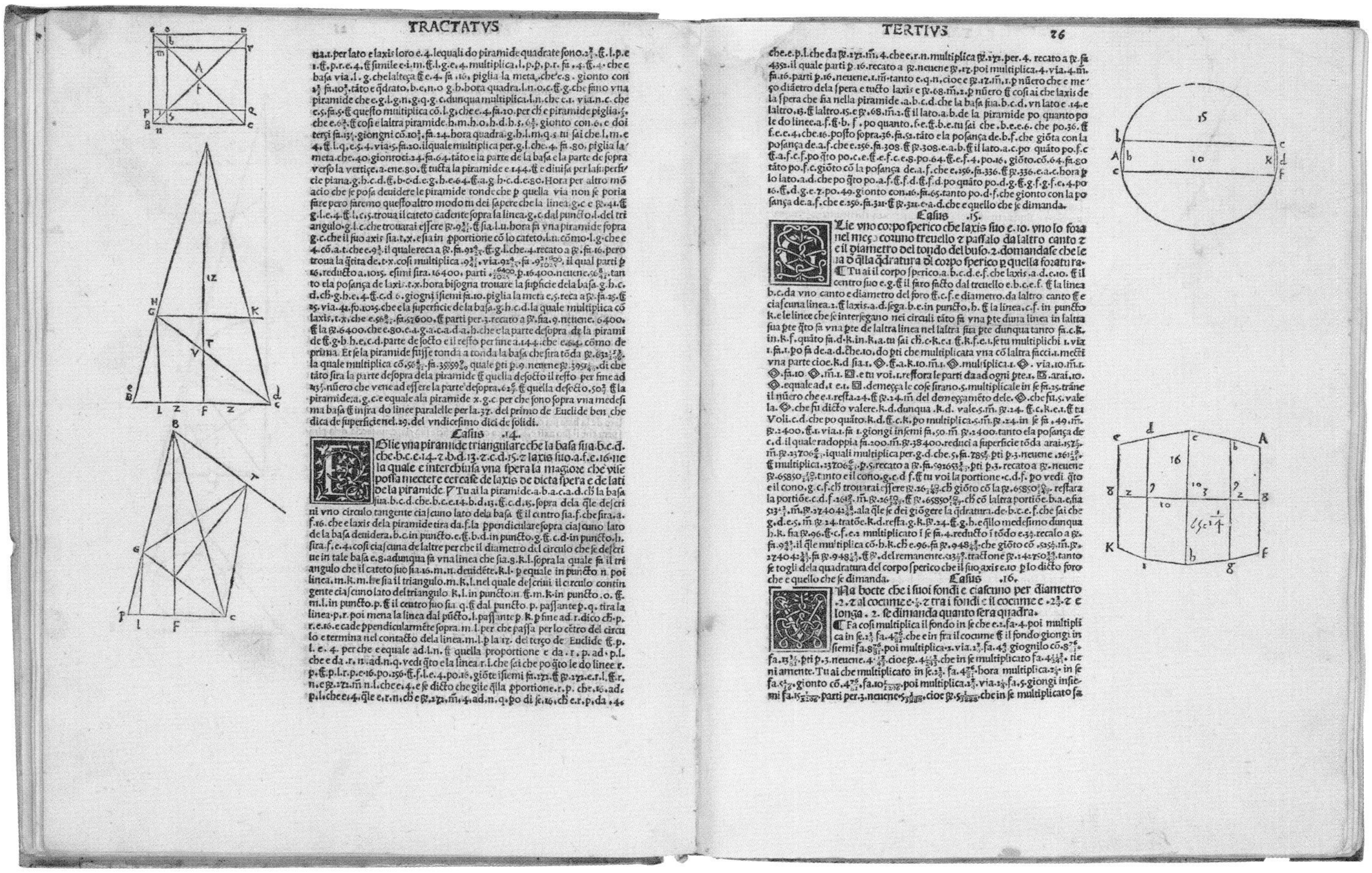
TRACTATVS
TERTIVS 26

1509 **Henri Estienne I** *Quincuplex psalterium*; ed. Jacques Lefévre d'Étaples. Paris: Henri Estienne, 1509.

292 leaves. 27 cm.

The *Quincuplex psalterium* (The Fivefold Psalter) is one of the highlights of sixteenth-century French printing, both in form and content. This book was the first printed scholarly edition that contained multiple Latin translations of the Book of Psalms.

The main body of the text consists of the three most important translations (all three by St Jerome), which are set in parallel, in three columns, in a large roman face. On the title page they are listed: the Gallic (used in France), the Roman (used in Rome), and the Hebrew (translated from the original Hebrew). The last section of the book contains two more translations, both set in a smaller type: the older Latin translation, which is based on the Septuagint, and Jacques Lefévre d'Étaples's own interpretation.

The printer is Henri Estienne I (*c.* 1460–1520), the progenitor of a family of famous publishers and printers. From 1502 until 1520, he worked in Paris on a series of scholarly books for academics. While the woodcut on the title page of the *Quincuplex psalterium* still looks medieval, the typographic design of the book exemplifies the new Italian Renaissance forms that had just arrived in France. Ample attention is paid to

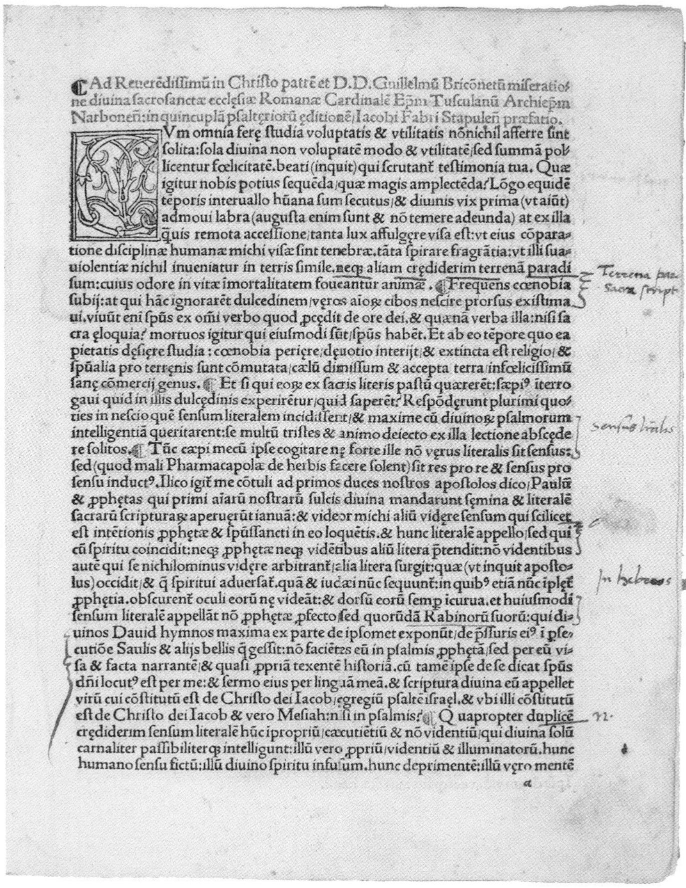

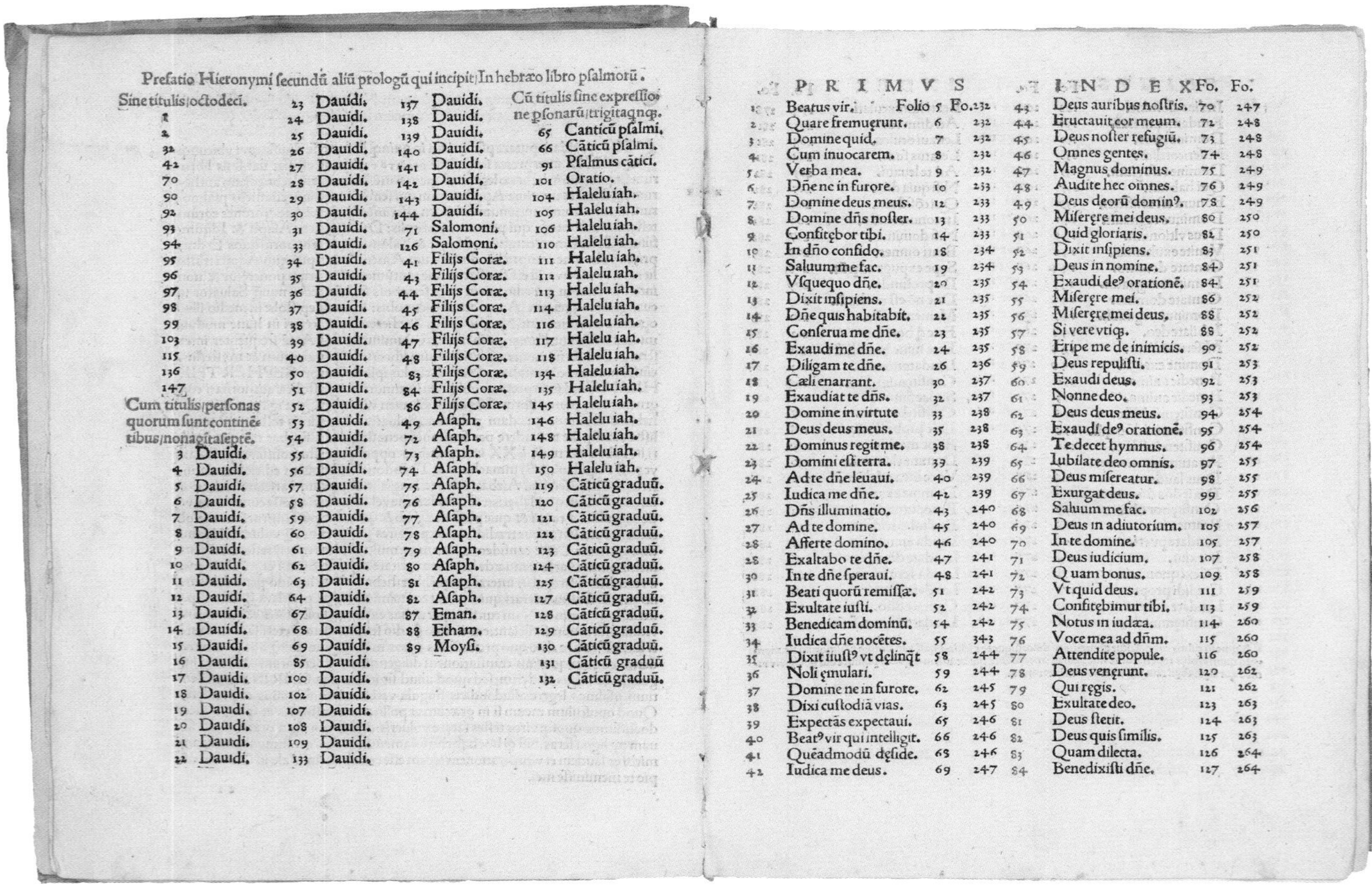

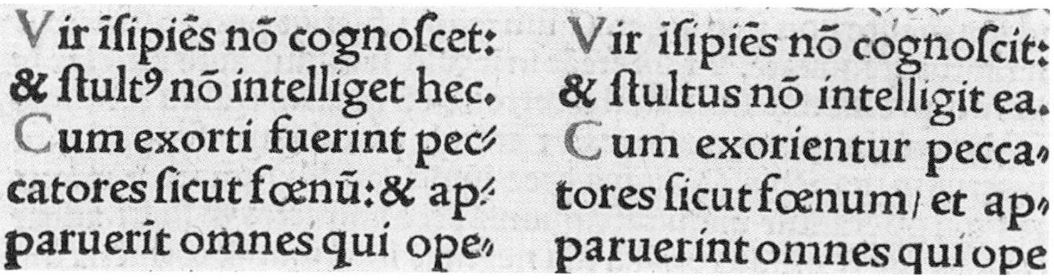

Vir iſipiēs nō cognoſcet: / & ſtultꝰ nō intelliget hec. / Cum exorti fuerint pec- / catores ſicut fœnū:& ap- / paruerit omnes qui ope-

Vir iſipiēs nō cognoſcit: / & ſtultus nō intelligit ea. / Cum exorientur pecca- / tores ſicut fœnum/ et ap- / paruerint omnes qui ope

This is the larger of two roman types that were used earlier by Hopyl and Estienne. The better alignment of the capitals of the larger size, and the better production generally, show off the type to better effect in this book by Henri Estienne alone. Many Paris printers used both of these typefaces, cut in the 1490s.

articulation: the text is articulated with paragraph marks, ornaments, and the use of a second colour (red). Only two romans are used, both in Venetian style, while the annotations are set in a smaller type. FAJ

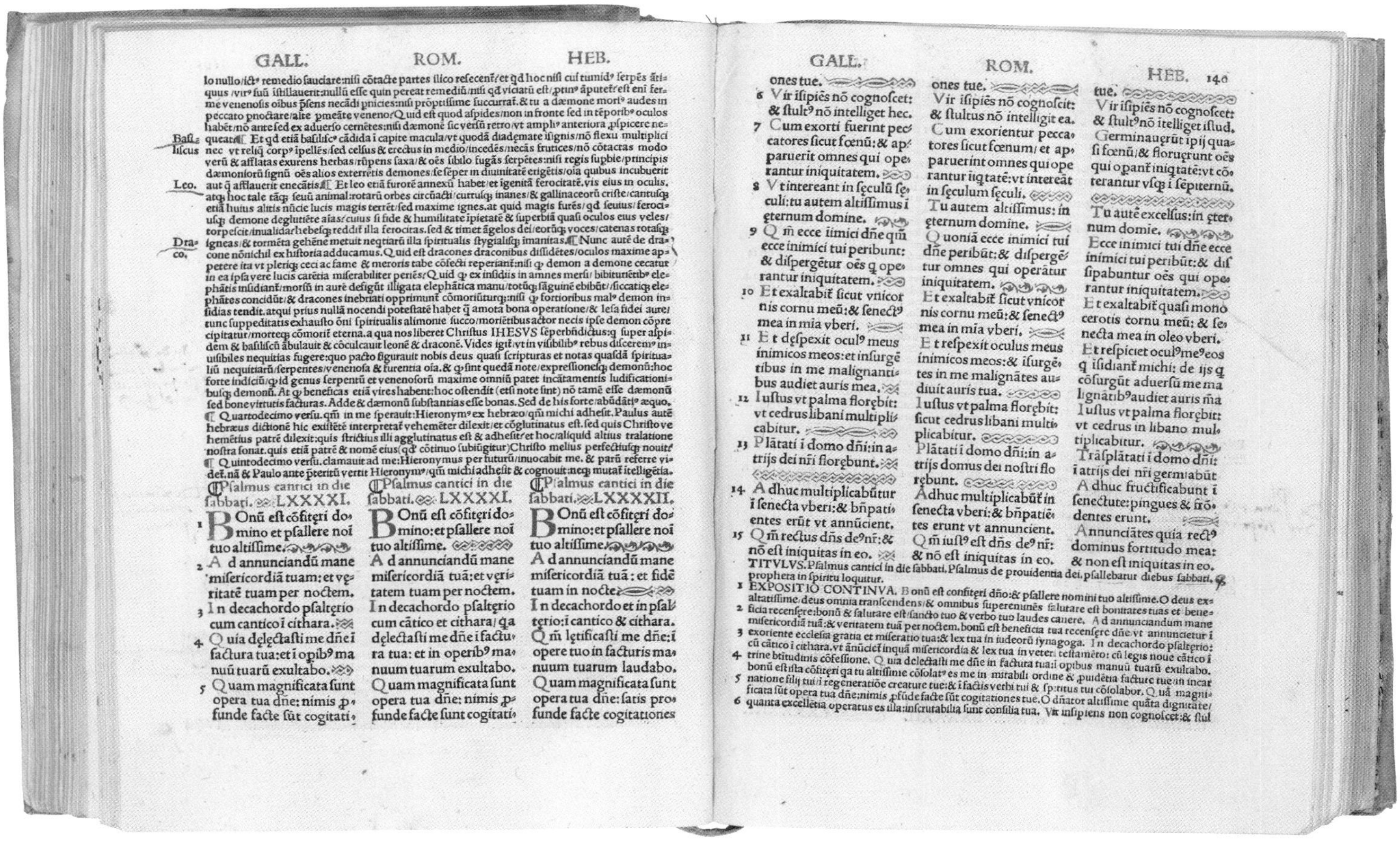

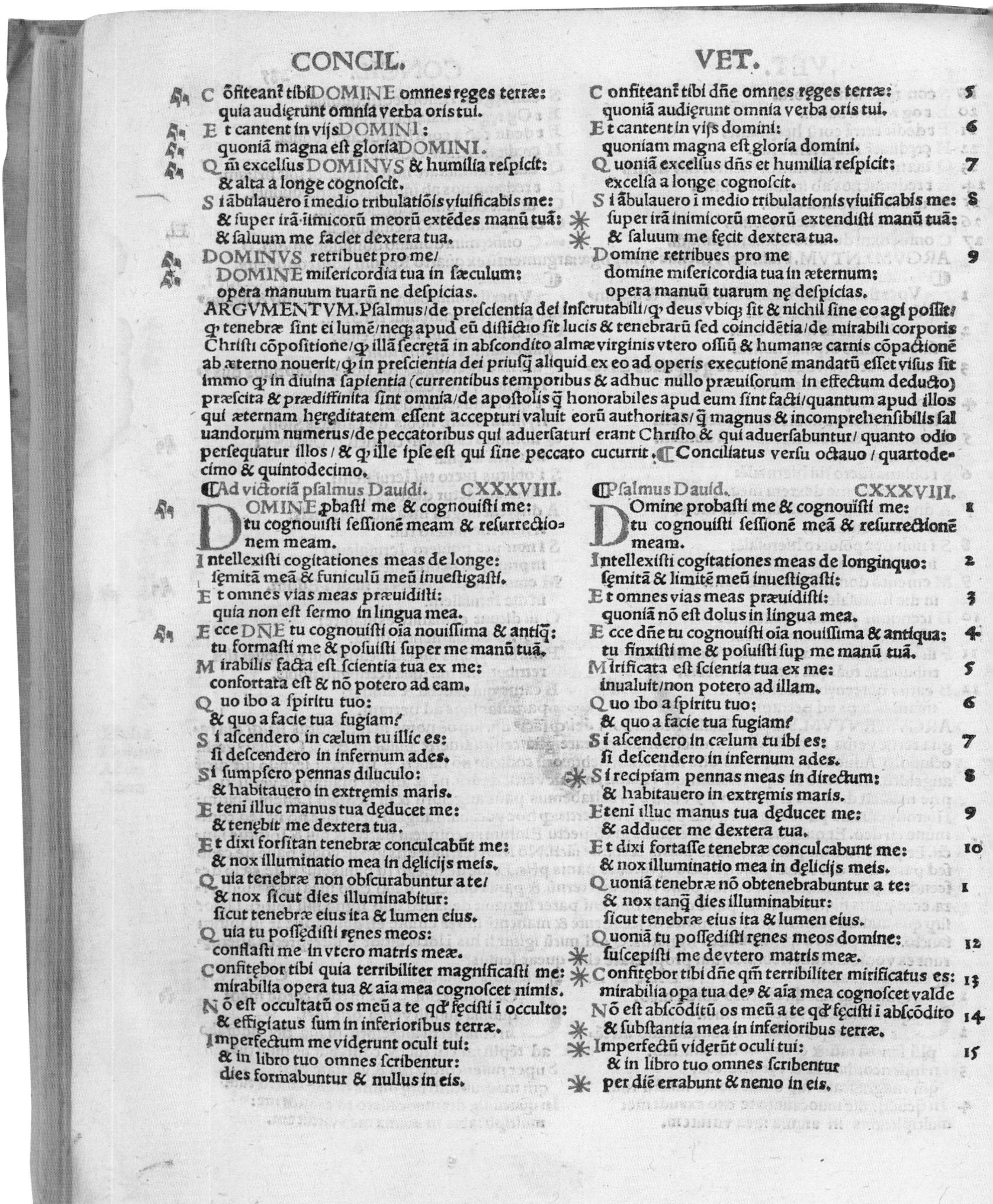

CONCIL.

Cõfiteanť tibi DOMINE omnes reges terræ:
quia audierunt omnia verba oris tui.
Et cantent in vijs DOMINI:
quoniã magna est gloria DOMINI.
Qm̃ excelsus DOMINVS & humilia respicit:
& alta a longe cognoscit.
Si ãbulauero ĩ medio tribulatiõis viuificabis me:
& super irã ĩimicorũ meorũ extẽdes manũ tuã:
& saluum me faciet dextera tua.
DOMINVS retribuet pro me/
DOMINE misericordia tua in sæculum:
opera manuum tuarũ ne despicias.

VET.

Confiteanť tibi dñe omnes reges terræ: 5
quoniã audierunt omnia verba oris tui.
Et cantent in vijs domini: 6
quoniam magna est gloria domini.
Quoniã excelsus dñs et humilia respicit: 7
excelsa a longe cognoscit.
Si ãbulauero ĩ medio tribulationis viuificabis me: 8
super irã inimicorũ meorũ extendisti manũ tuã:
& saluum me fecit dextera tua.
Domine retribues pro me 9
domine misericordia tua in æternum:
opera manuũ tuarum ne despicias.

ARGVMENTVM. Psalmus/de prescientia dei inscrutabili/q deus vbiq; sit & nichil sine eo agi possit/q tenebræ sint ei lumẽ/neq; apud eũ distictio sit lucis & tenebrarũ sed coincidẽtia/de mirabili corporis Christi cõpositione/q illã secretã in abscondito almæ virginis vtero ossiũ & humanæ carnis cõpactionẽ ab æterno nouerit/q in prescientia dei priusq̃ aliquid ex eo ad operis executionẽ mandatũ esset visus sit immo q in diuina sapientia (currentibus temporibus & adhuc nullo præuisorum in effectum deducto) præscita & prædiffinita sint omnia/de apostolis q̃ honorabiles apud eum sint facti/quantum apud illos qui æternam hereditatem essent accepturi valuit eorũ authoritas/q̃ magnus & incomprehensibilis saluandorum numerus/de peccatoribus qui aduersaturi erant Christo & qui aduersabuntur/quanto odio persequatur illos/& q ille ipse est qui sine peccato cucurrit. ¶ Conciliatus versu octauo/quartodecimo & quintodecimo.

¶ Ad victoriã psalmus Dauidi. CXXXVIII.

DOMINE ꝓbasti me & cognouisti me:
tu cognouisti sessionẽ meam & resurrectionem meam.
Intellexisti cogitationes meas de longe:
semitã meã & funiculũ meũ inuestigasti.
Et omnes vias meas præuidisti:
quia non est sermo in lingua mea.
Ecce DÑE tu cognouisti oĩa nouissima & antiq̃:
tu formasti me & posuisti super me manũ tuã.
Mirabilis facta est scientia tua ex me:
confortata est & nõ potero ad eam.
Quo ibo a spiritu tuo:
& quo a facie tua fugiam?
Si ascendero in cælum tu illic es:
si descendero in infernum ades.
Si sumpsero pennas diluculo:
& habitauero in extremis maris.
Eteni illuc manus tua deducet me:
& tenebit me dextera tua.
Et dixi forsitan tenebræ conculcabũt me:
& nox illuminatio mea in delicijs meis.
Quia tenebræ non obscurabuntur a te/
& nox sicut dies illuminabitur:
sicut tenebræ eius ita & lumen eius.
Quia tu possedisti renes meos:
conflasti me in vtero matris meæ.
Confitebor tibi quia terribiliter magnificasti me:
mirabilia opera tua & aĩa mea cognoscet nimis.
Nõ est occultatũ os meũ a te qđ fecisti ĩ occulto:
& effigiatus sum in inferioribus terræ.
Imperfectum me viderunt oculi tui:
& in libro tuo omnes scribentur:
dies formabuntur & nullus in eis.

¶ Psalmus Dauid. CXXXVIII.

Domine probasti me & cognouisti me: 1
tu cognouisti sessionẽ meã & resurrectionẽ meam.
Intellexisti cogitationes meas de longinquo: 2
semitã & limitẽ meũ inuestigasti:
Et omnes vias meas præuidisti: 3
quoniã nõ est dolus in lingua mea.
Ecce dñe tu cognouisti oĩa nouissima & antiqua: 4
tu finxisti me & posuisti sup me manũ tuã.
Mirificata est scientia tua ex me: 5
inualuit/non potero ad illam.
Quo ibo a spiritu tuo: 6
& quo a facie tua fugiam?
Si ascendero in cælum tu ibi es: 7
si descendero in infernum ades.
Si recipiam pennas meas in directum: 8
& habitauero in extremis maris.
Eteni illuc manus tua deducet me: 9
& adducet me dextera tua.
Et dixi fortasse tenebræ conculcabunt me: 10
& nox illuminatio mea in delicijs meis.
Quoniã tenebræ nõ obtenebrabuntur a te: 11
& nox tanq̃ dies illuminabitur:
sicut tenebræ eius ita & lumen eius.
Quoniã tu possedisti renes meos domine: 12
suscepisti me de vtero matris meæ.
Confitebor tibi dñe qm̃ terribiliter mirificatus es: 13
mirabilia opa tua deus & aĩa mea cognoscet valde
Nõ est abscõditũ os meũ a te qđ fecisti ĩ abscõdito 14
& substantia mea in inferioribus terræ.
Imperfectũ viderũt oculi tui: 15
& in libro tuo omnes scribentur
per diẽ errabunt & nemo in eis.

VET.

6 Michi autē valde honorificati sūt amici tui deus:
valde cōfortati sunt principatus eorū.
7 Dinumerabo eos & sup arenā multiplicabūtur:
exurrexi & adhuc sum tecum.
8 Si occideris deus peccatores:
viri sanguinum declinate a me.
9 Quoniā dices in cogitatione:
accipient in vanitate ciuitates suas.
0 Nonne eos qui oderant te odio habui:
& super inimicis tuis tabescebam:
1 Perfecto odio oderam illos:
inimici facti sunt michi.
2 Proba me deus & scito cor meū:
scrutare me & cognosce semitas meas.
3 Et vide si via iniquitatis in me est:
& deduc me in via æterna.

CONCIL.

Michi autē nimis honorificati sūt amici tui DEVS El.
nimis cōfortatus est principatus eorū.
Dinumerabo eos & sup arenā multiplicabuntur:
exurrexi & adhuc sum tecum.
Si occideris DEVS peccatores: Eloha.
viri sanguinū declinate a me.
Quia dicitis in cogitatione:
accipient in vanitate ciuitates suas.
Nōne qui oderūt te DOMINE oderā:
& super inimicos tuos tabescebam:
Perfecto odio oderam illos:
inimici facti sunt michi.
Proba me DEVS & scito cor meū: El.
interroga me & cognosce semitas meas.
Et vide si via iniquitatis in me est:
& deduc me in via æterna.

ARGVMENTVM. Psalmus/depcatio aduersus pestiferæ doctrinæ venena seminantes & scripturarū sanctarum intelligentias adulterantes. ¶ Conciliatus versu nono.

VET.

¶ Psalmus Dauid. CXXXVIIII.
1 EXime me domine ab homine maligno:
a viro iniusto erue me.
2 Qui cogitauerūt iniustitias in corde:
tota die constituebant bella.
3 Acuerunt linguas suas sicut serpentes:
venenum aspidū sub labijs eorum.
4 Conserua me dñe de manu peccatoris:
ab hominibus iniustis erue me.
5 Qui cogitauerunt supplantare gressus meos:
absconderunt superbi muscipulam michi.
6 Et restes extēderūt muscipulas pedibus meis:
iuxta semitas scandalū posuerunt michi.
7 Dixi domino deus meus es tu:
percipe domine vocē deprecationis meæ.
8 Dñe dñe virtus salutis meæ:
obumbrasti super caput meū in die belli.
9 Non tradas me dñe a desiderio meo peccatori:
cogitauerunt aduersum me ne derelinquas me:
ne forte exaltentur.
0 Caput circuitus eorū:
labor labiorum ipsorū teget eos.
1 Decident super eos carbones ignis & deijcies eos
in miserijs non subsistent.
2 Vir linguosus non dirigetur super terram:
virū iniustū mala venabunt in interitū.
3 Cognoui quia faciet dñs iudiciū egentis:
& causam pauperum.
4 Verūtamen iusti confitebuntur nomini tuo:
inhabitabunt recti cum vultu tuo.

CONCIL.

¶ Psalmus Dauid. CXXXVIIII.
* ERipe me DOMINE ab homine malo:
a viris iniquis eripe me.
Qui cogitauerūt iniquitates in corde:
tota die constituebant prælia.
Acuerunt linguas suas sicut serpentes:
venenū aspidū sub labijs eorum. Selah.
Custodi me DOMIÑE de manu peccatoris:
ab hominibus iniquis eripe me.
Qui cogitauerunt supplantare gressus meos:
absconderunt superbi laqueum michi.
Et funes extenderunt in laqueum:
iuxta iter scandalum posuerunt michi. Selah.
Dixi DOMINO DEVS meus es tu: El.
exaudi DOMINE vocē deprecationis meæ.
DOMINE DÑE virtus salutis meæ: Adonai
obumbrasti super caput meū in die belli.
* Non tradas DOMINE desideriū peccatori:
cogitauerunt contra me/ne derelinquas me:
ne forte exaltentur.
Caput circuitus eorum:
labor labiorū ipsorū operiet eos.
Cadēt sup eos carbones/in ignē deijcies eos:
in miserijs non subsistent.
Vir linguosus non dirigetur in terra:
virū iniustū mala capient in interitu.
Cognoui quia faciet DOMINVS iudiciū inopis:
& vindictam pauperum.
Verūtamen iusti confitebuntur nomini tuo:
& habitabunt recti cum vultu tuo.

ARGVMENTVM. Psalmus/oratio fidelium in spiritu/vt eos custodiat deus a peccato oris/a peccato cordis & prauis cogitationibus/a prauorū societatibus & communicatione operum eorum/optant a iustis corripi/precantur pro delinquentibus & opprimentibus eos/q peccatores in rete vltionis diuinæ casuri sunt ipsi vero euasuri. ¶ Conciliatus versu quinto/sexto & vndecimo.

VET.

¶ Psalmus Dauid. CXXXX.
1 DOmine clamaui ad te exaudi me: intende
voci depcatiōis meæ dū clamauero ad te.
2 Dirigat oro mea sicut incēsū i cōspectu tuo:

CONCIL.

¶ Psalmus Dauid. CXXXX.
DOMINE clamaui ad te exaudi me:
intēde voci meæ cū clamauero ad te.
Dirigat oro mea sicut incensū i cōspectu tuo:

1514 **Complutensian Polyglot** *Biblia polyglotta, hebraice, chaldaice, graece et latine*. Alcalá de Henares: **Arnao Guillén de Brocar, 1514–17. 6 volumes. 38 cm.**

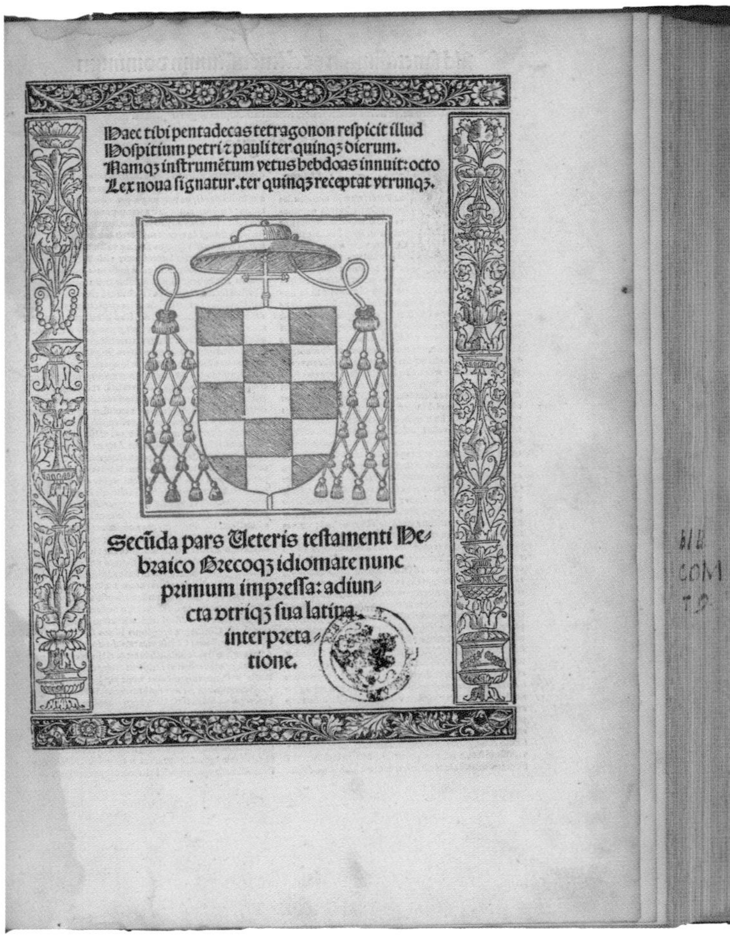

The Complutensian Polyglot Bible is the first complete edition of the Bible in more than one language; it also contains the first printed edition of the New Testament in Greek. In 1502, the Spanish statesman and cardinal Francisco Jiménez de Cisneros decided to publish this polyglot Bible in honour of the future emperor Charles V. He acquired some Hebrew manuscripts and he borrowed several others from the Vatican library in Rome. As the founder of the University of Alcalá de Henares (*Complutum* in Latin), Cisneros also managed to attract several scholars specializing in theology, Greek, and Hebrew, who prepared critical editions of the texts. He asked Arnao Guillén de Brocar (d. 1523) to print the Polyglot; Arnao settled in Alcalá in 1511.

The New Testament, in Greek and Latin, was printed in 1514. It took three more years to complete the four volumes containing the Old Testament in Hebrew, Latin, and Greek (the Septuagint), and the Aramaic text of the first five Bible books, parallel to a verbal Latin translation. The sixth volume contained, among other things, an elaborate Hebrew grammar and an Aramaic glossary.

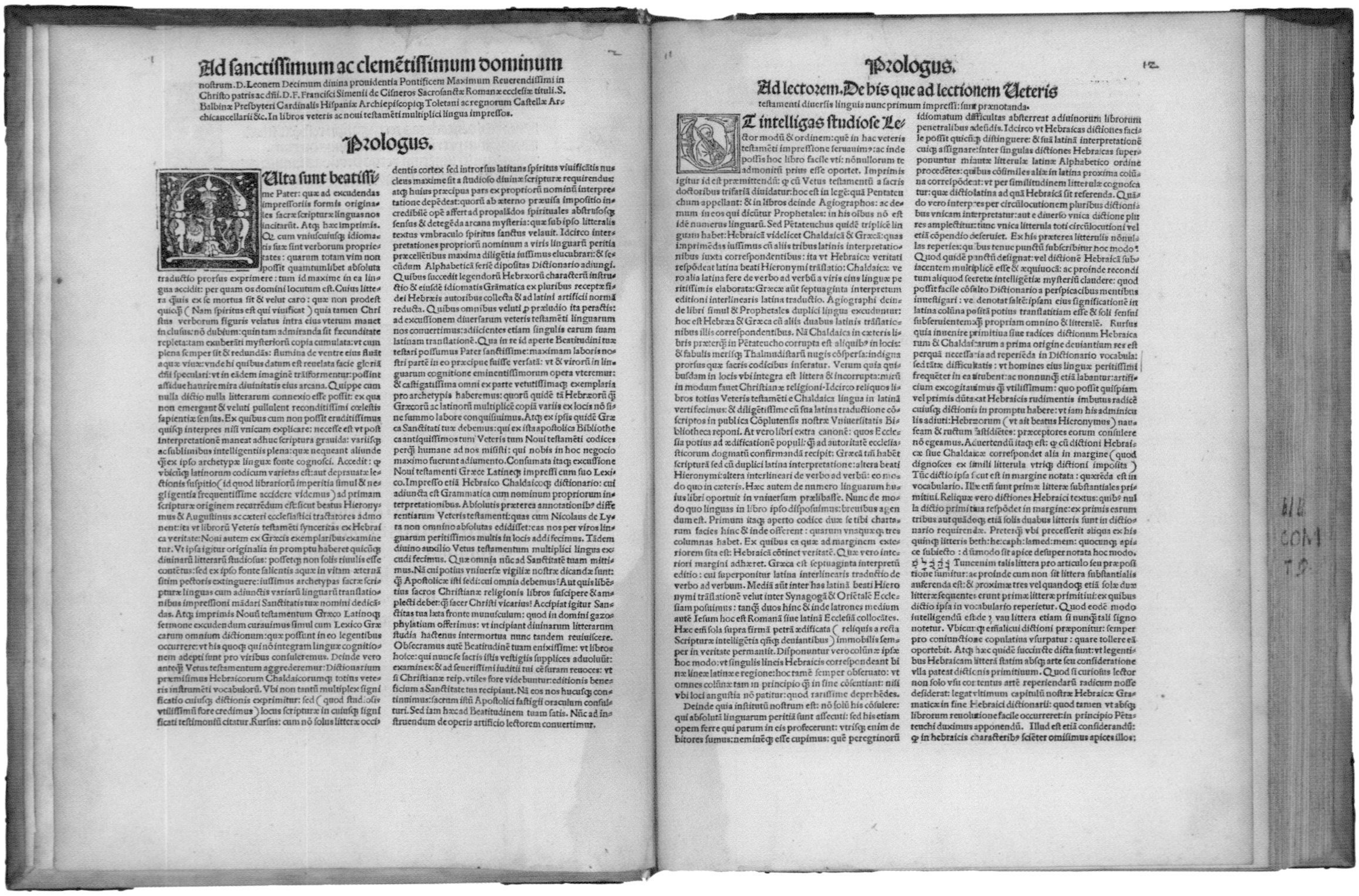

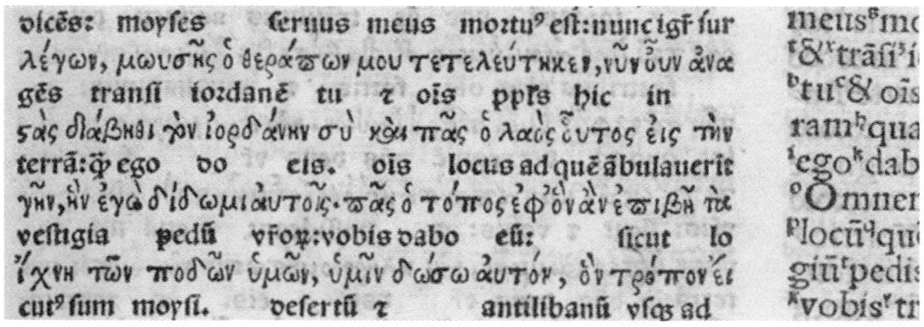
dicēs: moyses seruus meus mortu⁹ est: nunc igr sur
λέγων, μωυσῆς ὁ θεράπων μου τετελεύτηκε, νῦν οὖν ἀνα
gēs transi iordanē tu et ois ppls hic in
στὰς διάβηθι τὸν ἰορδάνην σὺ καὶ πᾶς ὁ λαὸς οὗτος εἰς τὴν
terrā: quā ego do eis. ois locus ad quē ābulauerit
γῆν, ἣν ἐγὼ δίδωμι αὐτοῖς. πᾶς ὁ τόπος ἐφ' ὃν ἂν ἐπιβῆτε
vestigia pedū vroꝝ: vobis dabo eū: sicut lo
ἴχνει τῶν ποδῶν ὑμῶν, ὑμῖν δώσω αὐτόν, ὃν τρόπον εἴ
cut⁹ sum moysi. desertū et antilibanū vsq ad

This small Greek type in the 1517 Old Testament, used at Venice in 1509, follows the style popularized by Aldus Manutius from 1495 on. Most modern scholars and bibliophiles have favoured the larger, more conservative Greek from the 1514 New Testament, skilfully cut in the style established by Nicolas Jenson in 1471.

Meanwhile, Erasmus had obtained an exclusive privilege for his 1516 Greek New Testament, which meant that the distribution of the Complutensian Polyglot had to be postponed. The copy in the Vatican library – printed on vellum and bound in red velvet – was inscribed in 1521. Cisneros died four months after the completion of this work, to which he had contributed over fifty thousand gold ducats from his private fortune. His coat of arms is printed on the title page. AP

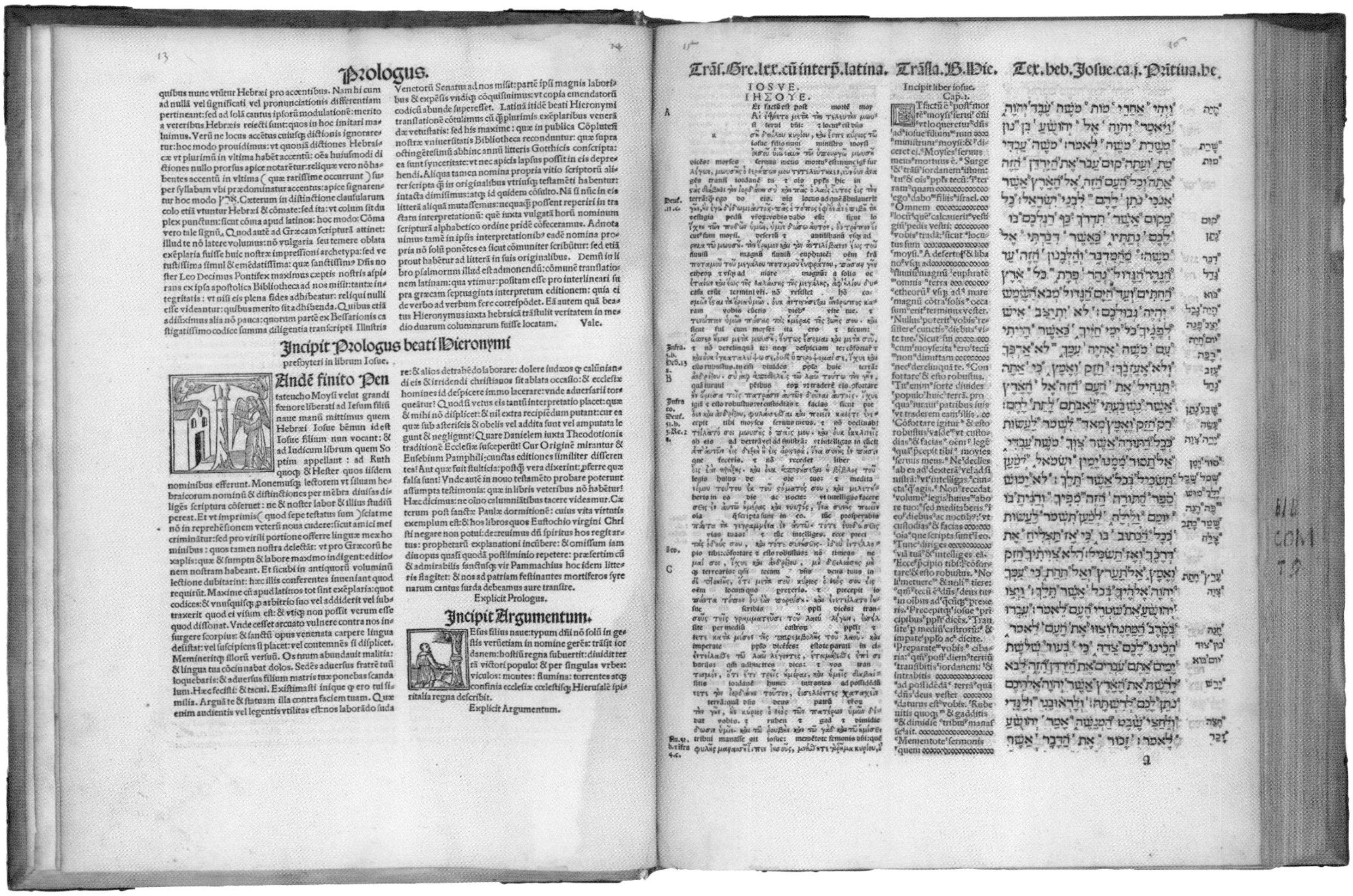

1516 **Johann Froben** *Novum instrumentum*; ed. Desiderius Erasmus. Basel: Johann Froben, 1516. 29.5 cm.

The *Novum instrumentum* ('New Instrument'), edited by Erasmus, was the first printed book to contain the original Greek text of the New Testament. Erasmus added a new Latin translation and extensive annotations. The subtitle on the title page, which is built up from geometric shapes, mentions that many manuscripts and commentaries by the Fathers of the Church were consulted for this corrected text. Erasmus proves himself not only a great philologist, but also a courageous man: he replaces Jerome's Latin translation (approved by Rome) with his own translation, which is printed parallel to the Greek text. It is the act of a self-consciously humanist scholar. Erasmus also was one of the first modern authors: in Basel, in the shop of his printer and publisher Johann Froben (*c.* 1460–1527), he personally saw to it that his text was reproduced correctly. This edition was a major influence on the Protestant Bible editions and Bible translations that were published shortly after the *Novum instrumentum*.

Froben printed an edition of 1,200 copies, which sold out quickly. The title page and the Renaissance borders on some of the pages show the influence of Italian and French Renaissance editions. Both of the typefaces used are influenced by Jenson's Venetian roman. FAJ

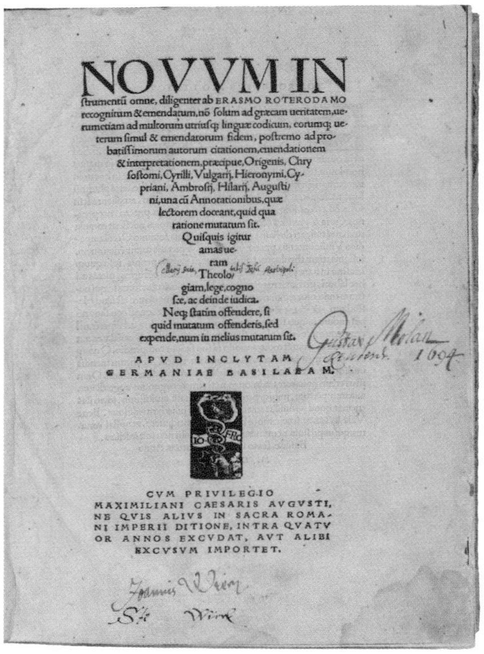

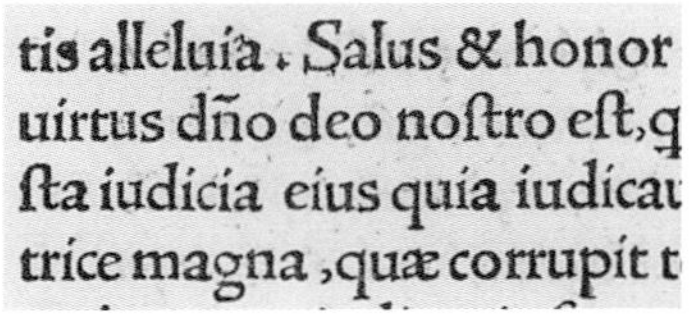

Peter Schoeffer II (*c.* 1475/80–1547) cut some of the first internationally distributed roman types, possibly including this one (introduced by Froben, 1513). Less elegant than Nicolas Jenson's but livelier and more angular, with a higher stroke contrast, its shorter ascenders and descenders and tighter spacing made it practical and successful.

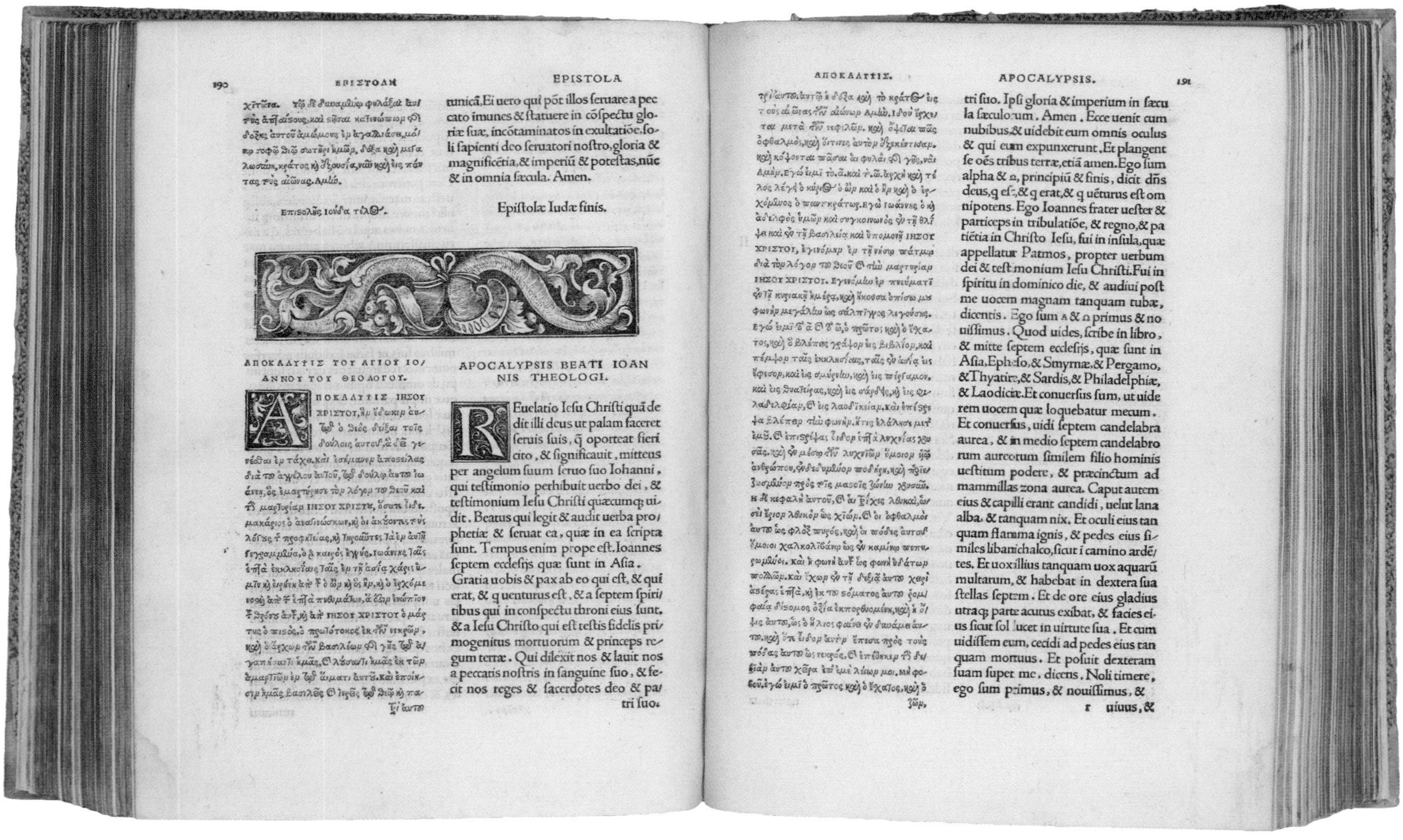

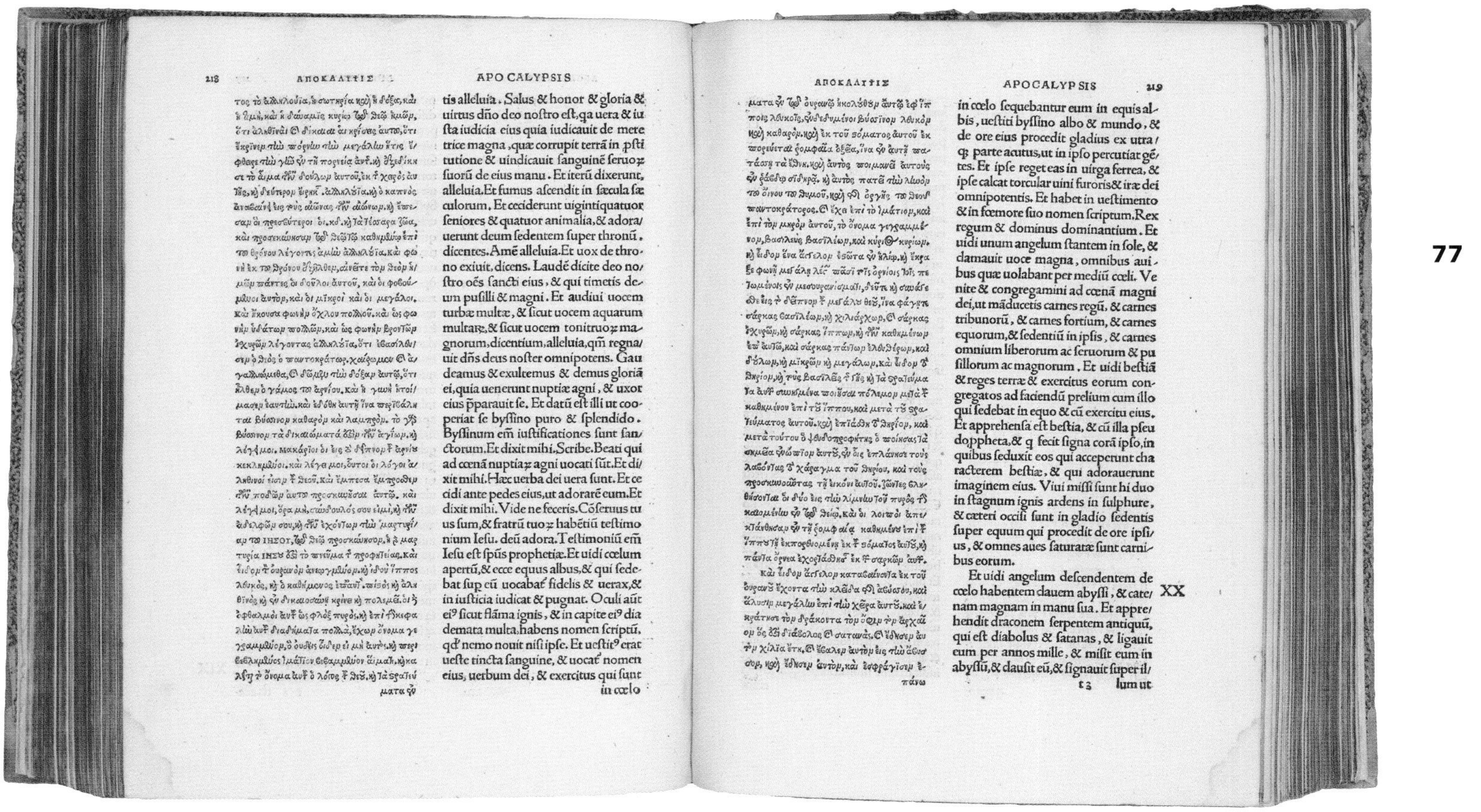
218
ΑΠΟΚΑΛΥΨΙΣ
APOCALYPSIS
ΑΠΟΚΑΛΥΨΙΣ
APOCALYPSIS 219
XX

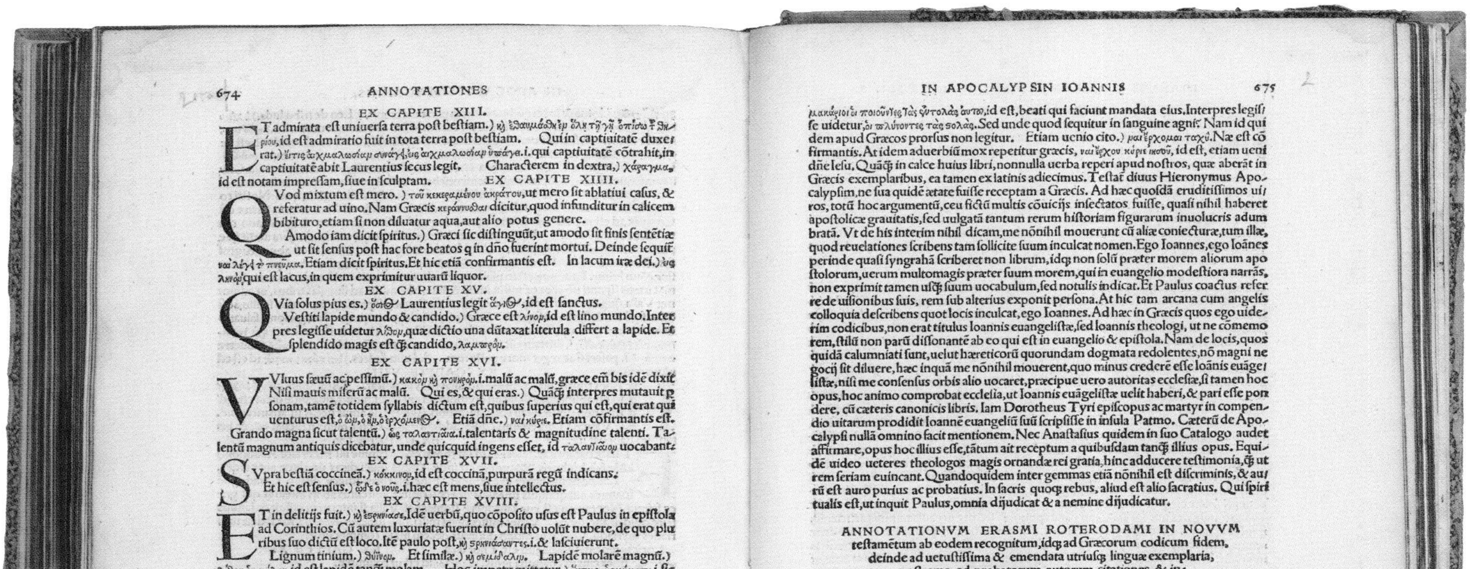
674 ANNOTATIONES
IN APOCALYPSIN IOANNIS 675
ANNOTATIONVM ERASMI ROTERODAMI IN NOVVM testamētum ab eodem recognitum, idq; ad Græcorum codicum fidem, deinde ad uetustissima & emendata utriusq; linguæ exemplaria, postremo, ad probatorum autorum citationes, & interpretationes, finis. Basileæ, Anno salutis hūanæ. M.D.XVI. Kalendis Martij.

1519 **Theuerdank** **Maximilian I, *Die geuerlichkeiten und eins teils der geschichten des loblichen streitbaren und hochberümbten helds und Ritters Tewrdannckhs*. Augsburg: Johann Schönsperger der Ältere, 1519. 580 pp. 36 cm.**

Illustrators: Hans Schäufelein, Hans Burgkmair, Leonhard Beck. Woodblock cutters: Jost de Negker, Heinrich Kupferwurm.

The *Theuerdank* is a veiled autobiography of the Roman Catholic German emperor Maximilian I in the form of a medieval chivalric romance. Maximilian (1493–1519), a patron of the arts, was closely involved with the design of his book. An Augsburg printer, Johann Schönsperger the Elder (*fl.* 1481–1524), did the printing. The production of the book took over five years. The emperor had stipulated that the distribution of the book was to take place after his death.

Apart from copies on paper, the first edition of the *Theuerdank* (1517) also included about forty copies on parchment. In a treaty with Archduke Ferdinand, Maximilian's grandson, it was stipulated how these luxury copies were to be divided among the gentry. Another edition, more typographically precise, appeared in the year of Maximilian's death. This second edition, shown here, is preceded by an imperial privilege that granted Schönsperger exclusive publishing rights to the book.

The *Theuerdank* acquired an almost mythical status due to its genesis, its rarity and, most of all, its exceptional design. For a long time it was thought that the text could not have been set with movable type, because of the variants of the individual letters and because of the enormous swashes. Until the nineteenth century it was thought that no movable type was used for the work, but in reality only the title page was completely cut in wood. In the beautiful illustrations, Albrecht Dürer's influence is evident. LM

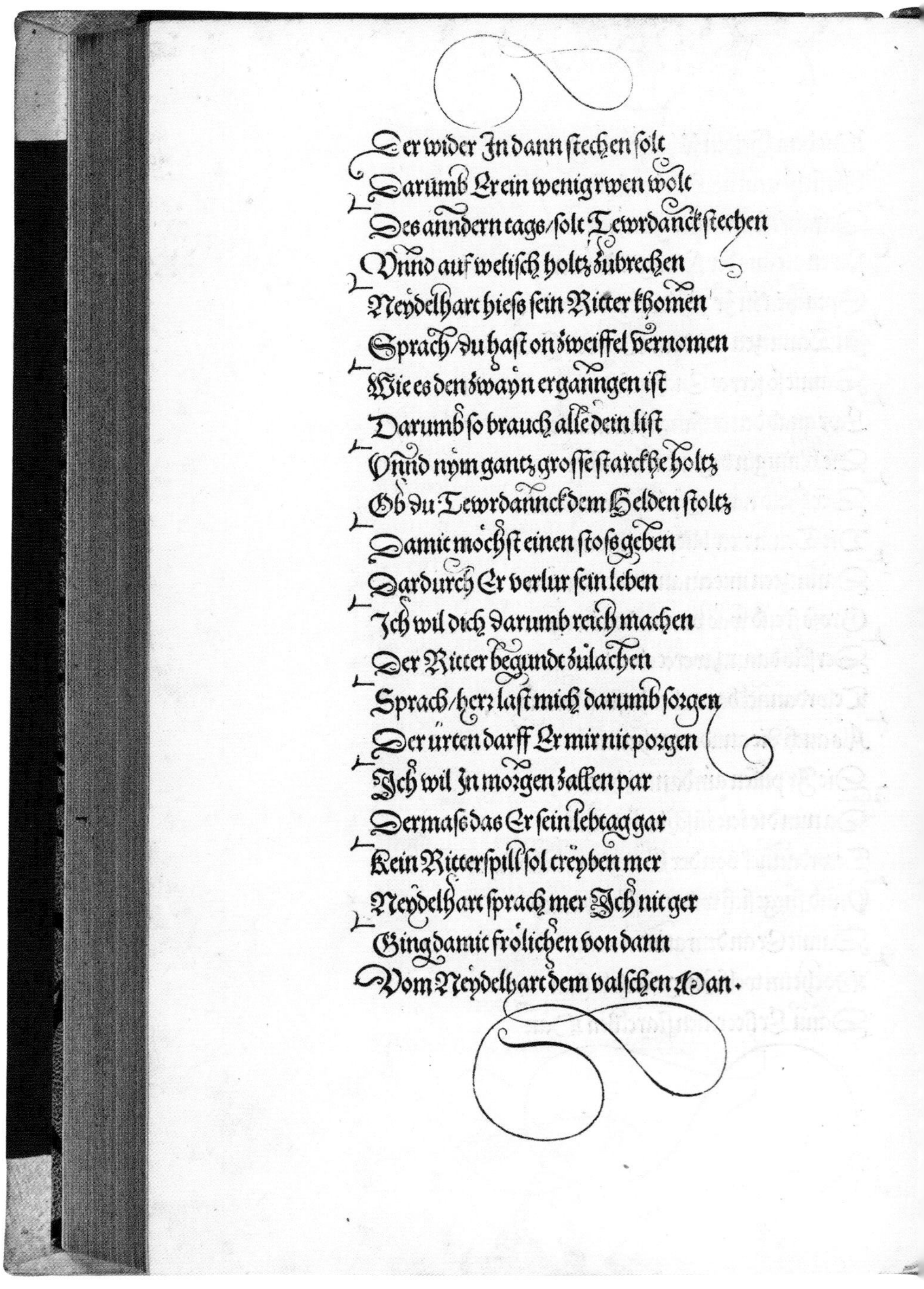

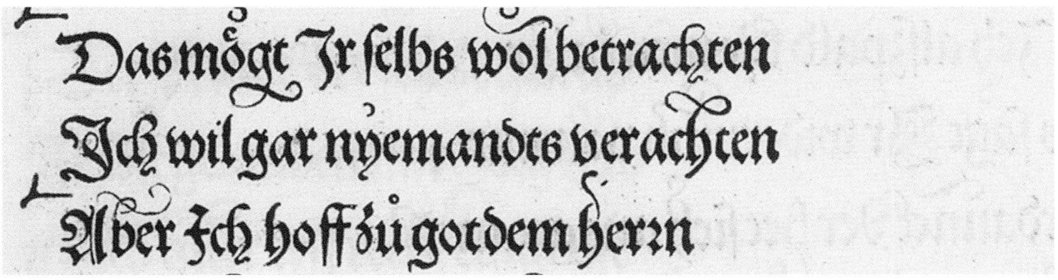
Das mögt Jr selbs wol betrachten
Ich wil gar nyemandts verachten
Aber Ich hoff zu got dem herrn

This spectacular early Fraktur blackletter type was introduced in the 1517 edition, after models by Vinzenz Rockner. Schönsperger introduced the first Fraktur in 1513 and secular German printing relegated the older Schwabacher type to auxiliary use from around 1560. Fraktur remained the norm for works in German until the Nazis banned it in 1941.

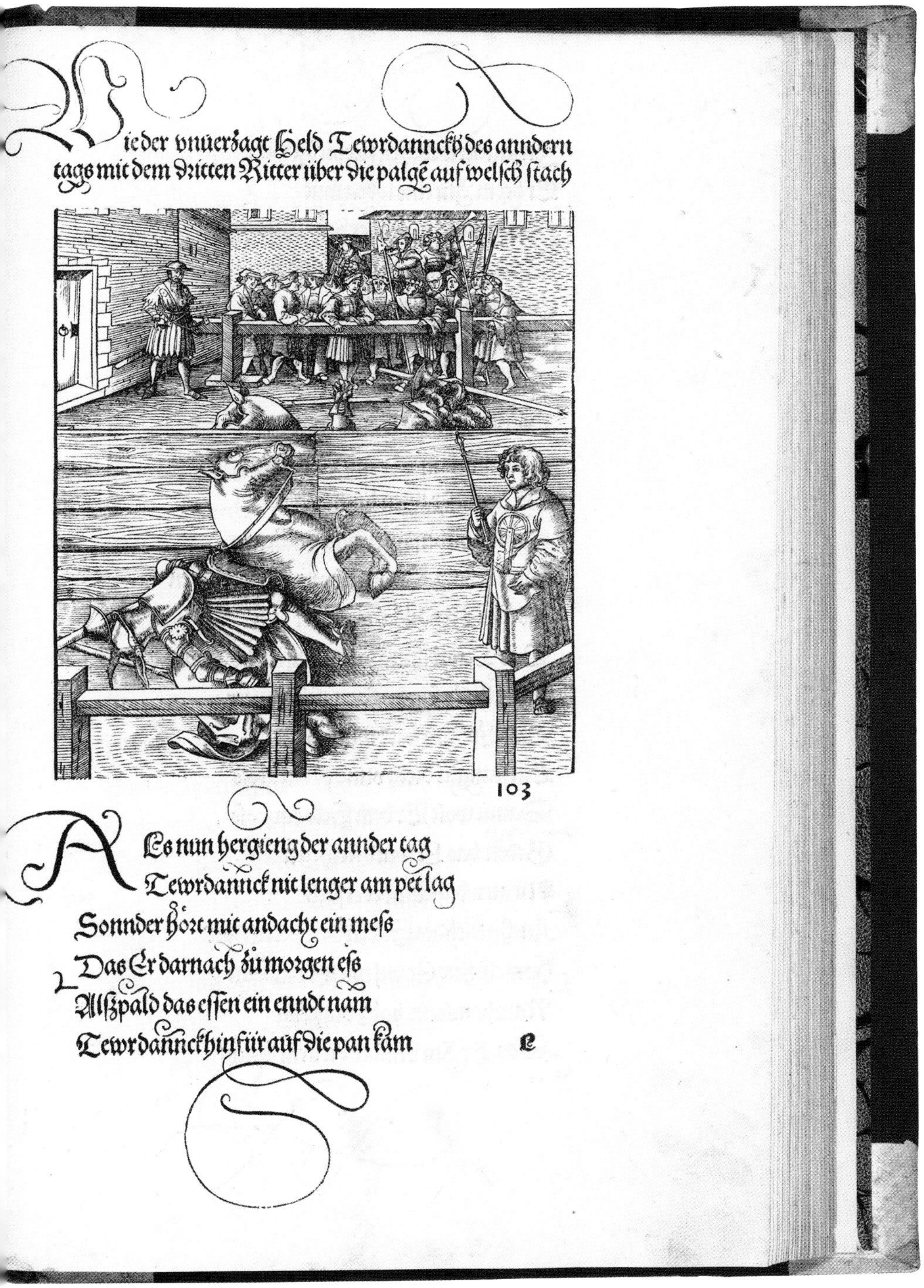
Wie der unverzagt Held Tewrdannckh des anndern tags mit dem dritten Ritter über die palgē auf welsch stach

103

Als nun hergieng der annder tag
Tewrdannck nit lenger am pet lag
Sonnder hört mit andacht ein mess
Das Er darnach zu morgen ess
Allßpald das essen ein enndt nam
Tewrdannck hinfür auf die pan kam
E

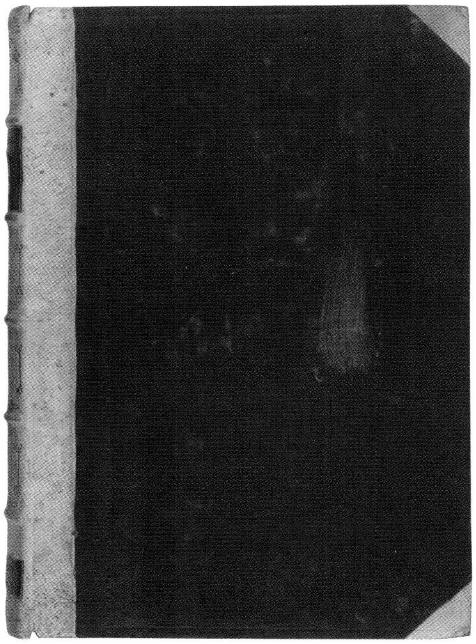

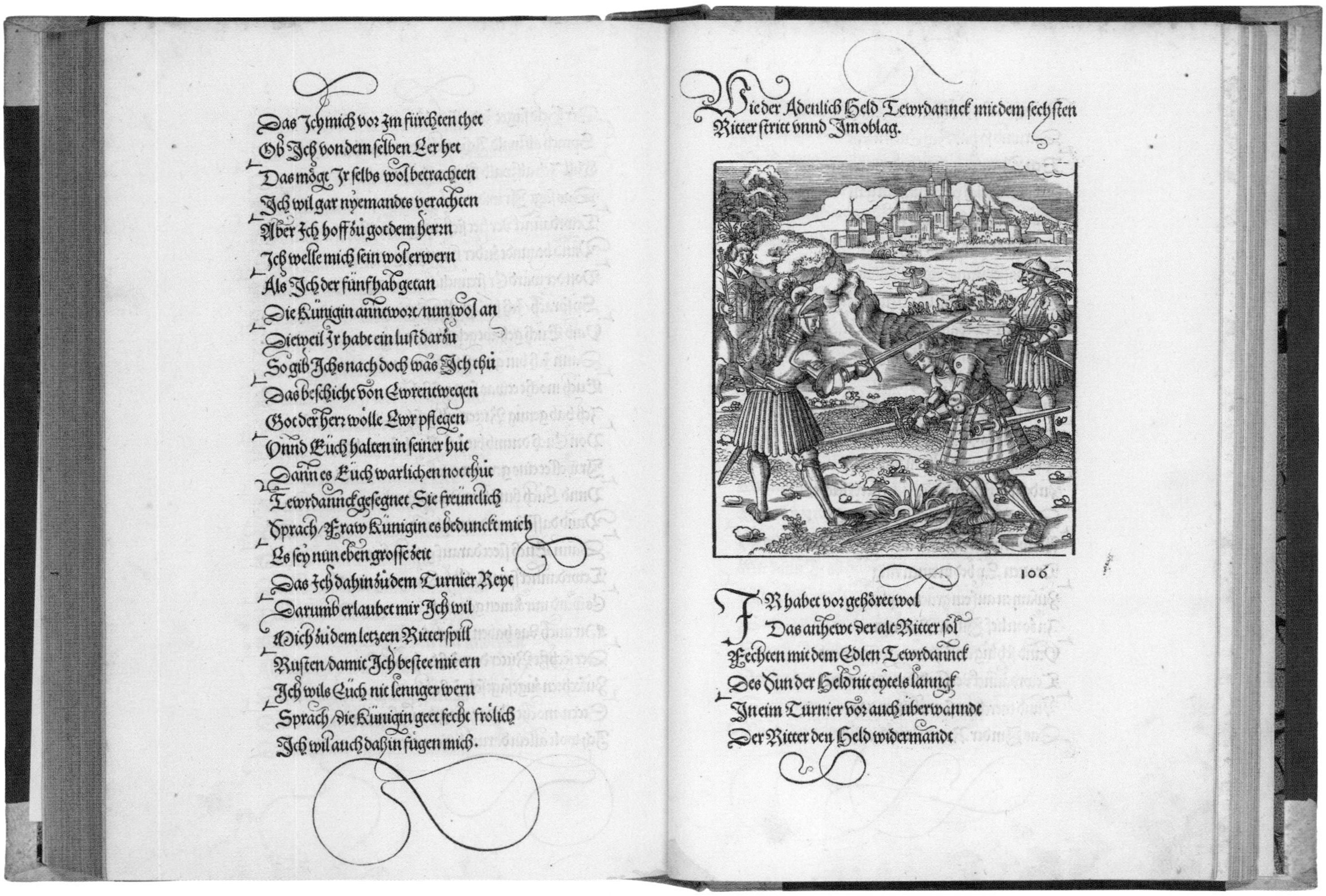
Das Ich mich vor Im fürchten thet
Ob Ich von dem selben Ler het
Das mögt Jr selbs wol betrachten
Ich wil gar nyemandes verachten
Aber Ich hoff zu got dem herrn
Ich welle mich sein wol erwern
Als Ich der fünf hab getan
Die Künigin anntwort/nun wol an
Dieweil Jr habt ein lust darzu
So gib Ichs nach doch was Ich thu
Das beschicht von Ewrentwegen
Got der herr wölle Ewr pflegen
Vnnd Euch halten in seiner hut
Dann es Euch warlichen not thut
Tewrdannck gesegnet Sie freündlich
Sprach/Fraw Künigin es bedunckt mich
Es sey nun eben grosse zeit
Das Ich dahin zu dem Turnier Reyt
Darumb erlaubet mir Ich wil
Mich zu dem letzten Ritterspill
Rusten/damit Ich beste mit ern
Ich wils Euch nit lennger wern
Sprach/die Künigin geet secht frölich
Ich wil auch dahin fügen mich.

Wie der Adenlich Held Tewrdannck mit dem sechsten Ritter stritt vnnd Im oblag.

106

Jr habet vor gehöret wol
Das anhewt der alt Ritter sol
Fechten mit dem Edlen Tewrdannck
Des thun der Held nit eytels lannck
In ein Turnier vor auch überwannde
Der Ritter den Held widermande

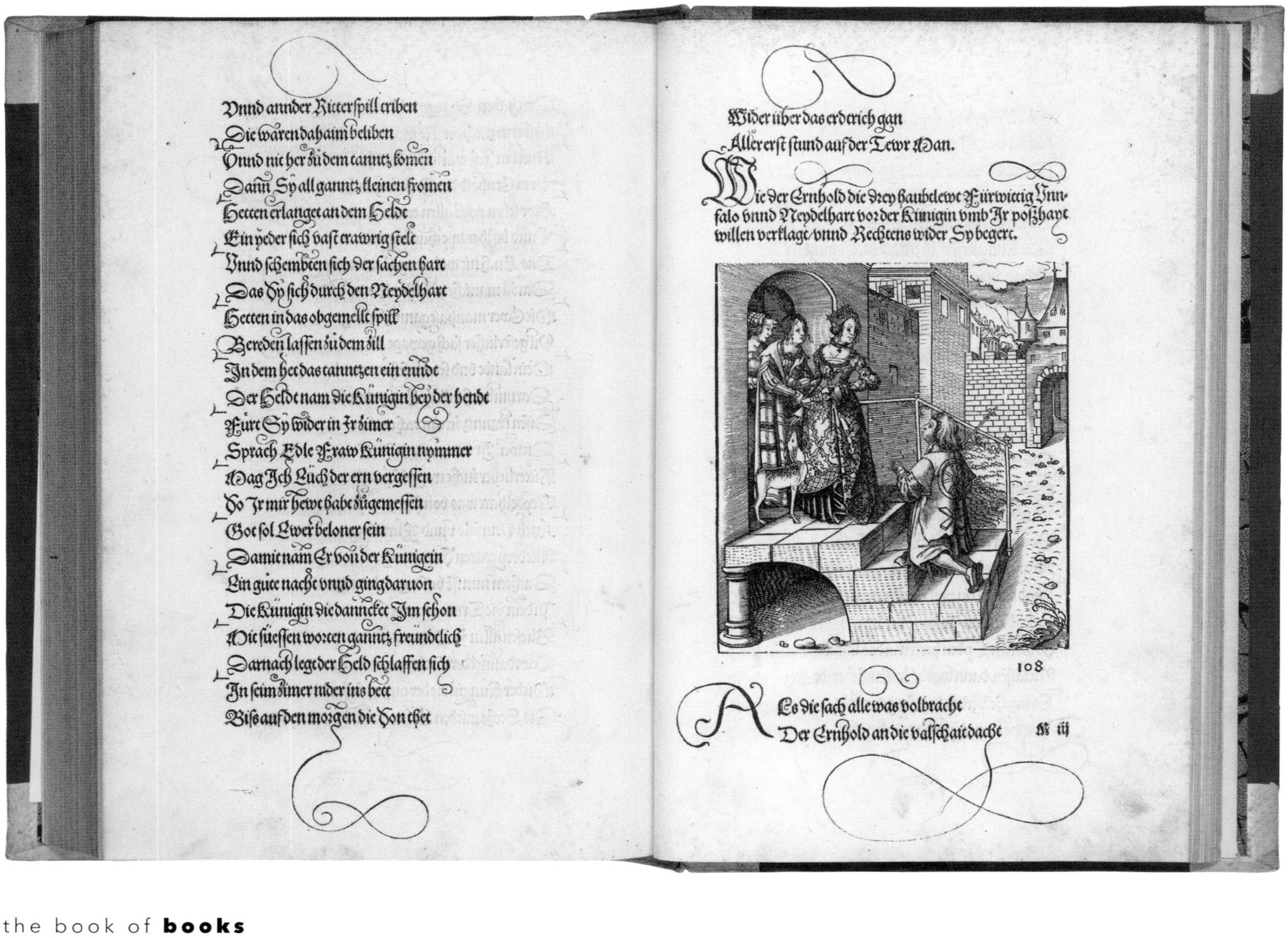
Vnnd annder Ritterspill triben
Die waren dahaim beliben
Vnnd nit her zu dem tanntz komen
Dann Sy all ganntz kleinen fromen
Hetten erlanget an dem Helde
Ein yeder sich vast trawrig stelt
Vnnd schemten sich der sachen hart
Das Sy sich durch den Neydelhart
Hetten in das obgemelt spill
Bereden lassen zu dem zill
In dem het das tanntzen ein ennde
Der Held nam die Künigin bey der hende
Fürt Sy wider in Jr zimer
Sprach Edle Fraw Künigin nymmer
Mag Ich Euch der ern vergessen
So Jr mir hewt habt zugemessen
Got sol Ewer beloner sein
Damit nam Er von der Künigein
Ein gute nacht vnnd ging daruon
Die Künigin die dannckt Im schon
Mit süessen worten ganntz freündlich
Darnach leget der Held schlaffen sich
In sein zimer nider ins bett
Biss auf den morgen die Son thet

Wider über das erdtrich gan
Allererst stund auf der Tewr Man.
Wie der Ernhold die drey haubtlewt Fürwittig Vnnfalo vnnd Neydelhart vor der Künigin vmb Jr posshayt willen verklagt/vnnd Rechtens wider Sy begert.

108

Als die sach alle was volbracht
Der Ernhold an die valschait dacht
K iij

Das furt aller neyd wurd abgestellt
In aller diser weyten welt
Ich sorg aber vil sein dermassen
Gesyt/das sys nit werden lassen
Jr hört das Ich Euch warn trewlich
Das ein yeder wöll hüeten sich
Vor solchem neydischem hertzen
Jr secht was gar hertten schmertzen
Ich yetzund darumb müss leyden
Jr solt auch valsch punde vermeyden
Dann die in die lenng nit mügen
Den herren bleiben verschwigen
Mit solhem will Ich beschliessen
Vnnd mein neyd mit dem todt püessen
Nach solcher red der nachrichter
Nam den armen Neydelhart her
Vnnd warff den aus über den ganng
Als das geschach Neydelhart nit lang
Lebet/sonnder gab auf sein geist
Der nachrichter sprach als außweist
Die vrtail/hab Ich gericht recht
Also nam das Neydisch geschlecht
Jr enndt vnnd sein letzte hinfart
Als nun solchs alles volbracht wardt.

Wie die Künigin Ernreich noch ein sach an den hochberümbten Held Tewrdannck die Er thun solt werben liess/ vnnd die potschafft dem Ernhold beuolhen ward.

113

Liess die Künigin samblen ein Rat
Darein Sy auch zukhomen gebot
Des Edlen Helden Ernhold
Der Jm in trewen het geuolgt

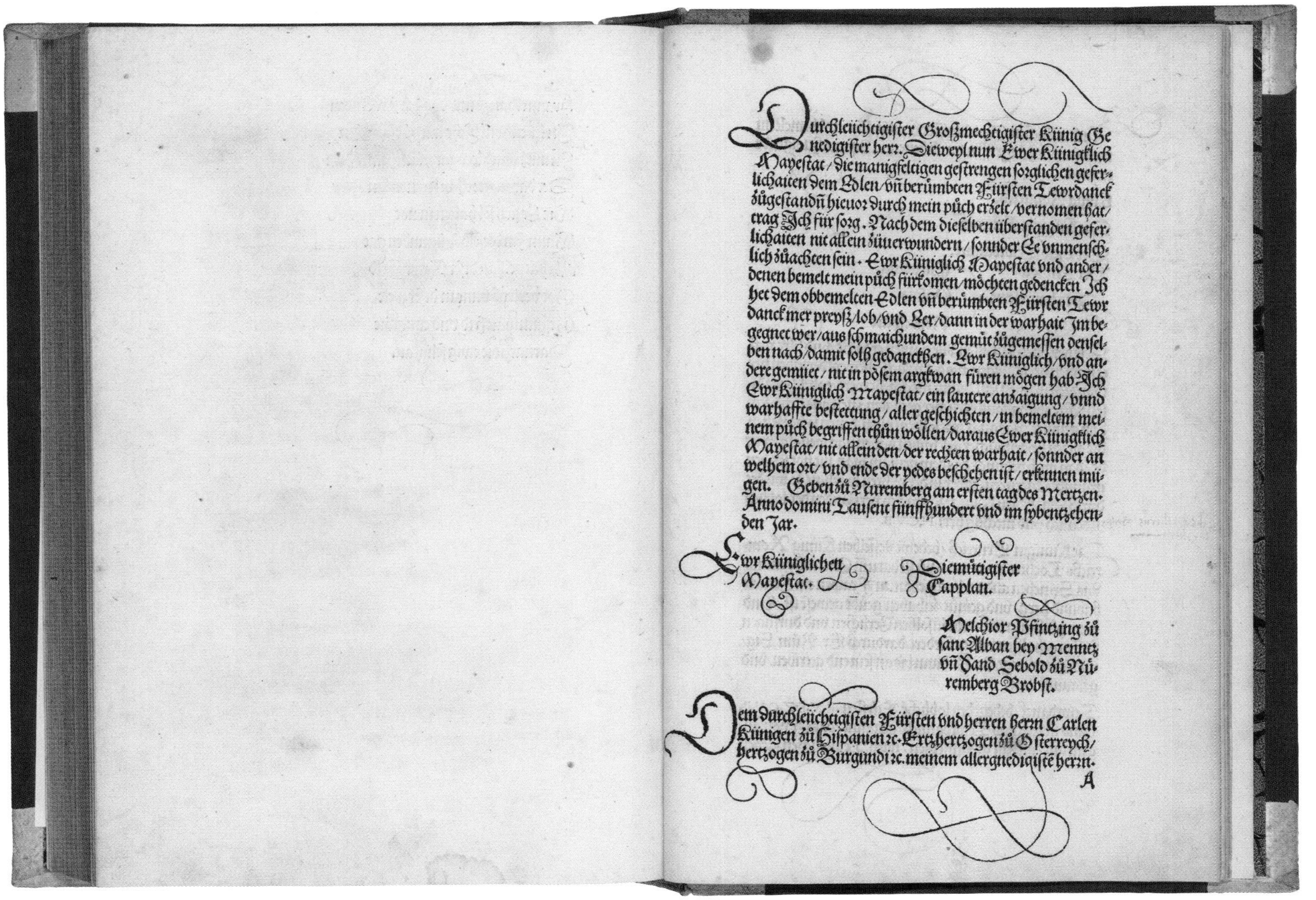

Durchleüchtigister Großmechtigister Künig Genedigister herr. Dieweyl nun Ewer Künigklich Mayestat/die manigfeltigen gestrengen sorglichen geferlichaiten dem Edlen/vñ berümbten Fürsten Tewrdanck zügestandñ hieuor durch mein püch erzelt/vernomen hat/trag Ich für sorg. Nach dem dieselben überstanden geferlichaiten nit allein züuerwundern/sonnder Er vnmenschlich zuachten sein. Ewr Küniglich Mayestat vnd ander/denen bemelt mein püch fürkomen/möchten gedencken Ich het dem obbemelten Edlen vñ berümbten Fürsten Tewrdanck mer preysz/lob/vnd Er/dann in der warhait Jm begegnet wer/aus schmaichundem gemüt zügemessen denselben nach/damit solh gedanckhen. Ewr Küniglich/vnd andere gemüet/nit in pösem argkwan füren mögen hab Ich Ewr Küniglich Mayestat/ein lautere anzaigung/vnnd warhaffte bestettung/aller geschichten/in bemeltem meinem püch begriffen thün wöllen/daraus Ewer Künigklich Mayestat/nit allein den/der rechten warhait/sonnder an welhem ort/vnd ende der yedes beschehen ist/erkennen mügen. Geben zü Nuremberg am ersten tag des Mertzen. Anno domini Tausent fünffhundert vnd im sybentzehenden Jar.

Ewr Küniglichen Mayestat.

Diemütigister Capplan.

Melchior Pfintzing zü sant Alban bey Menntz vñ Sand Sebold zü Nüremberg Brobst.

Dem durchleüchtigisten Fürsten vnd herren hern Carlen Künigen zü Hispanien 2c. Ertzhertzogen zü Osterreych/hertzogen zü Burgundi 2c. meinem allergnedigistë herrn.

A

1521 **Vitruvius** **Marcus Vitruvius Pollio, *De architectura libri dece*; ed. Cesare Cesariano. Como: Gottardo da Ponte, 1521.**

183 leaves. 40 cm. Illustrator: Cesare Cesariano and others.

Vitruvius's *De architectura* is the only classical text on the theory and practice of architecture that has been preserved. The first printed and illustrated edition (in Latin) dates from 1511, and was edited by Fra Giovanni Giocondo. The edition shown here is a careful Italian adaptation by Cesare Cesariano (1476/8–1543), a painter and architect who worked in Milan for most of his life. His detailed illustrations do not always follow the Fra Giocondo edition, and many of them are original and innovative. Cesariano's edition was finished by two of his collaborators, probably because the financiers of the book thought that the final corrections were taking too long.

As far as layout is concerned, *De architectura* is typical for its era: Vitruvius's texts are set in a larger font and are surrounded by annotations. In the late Middle Ages, the use of such designs was typically reserved for legal texts. The illustrations are woodcuts – engravings would only be used for book illustrations half a century later. Nonetheless, some of the crucial parts of the book have a remarkable layout. On the title page, for instance, the title takes the form of a triangle, positioned above the large printer's device as though it were a roof. Early in the sixteenth century, standard layouts for title pages did not exist and experiments abounded. The chapter titles take the shape of airy triangles, set within the larger and darker blocks of annotations. The first lines of text below the chapter titles are set in capitals. PD

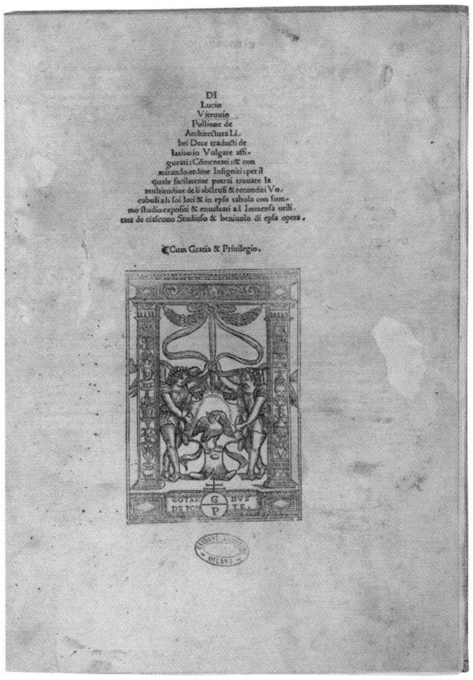

Half a century after Nicolas Jenson's Eusebius, many Italian types had hardly changed. This one ignores both the Aldine roman (1495) that was soon to change the form of roman type via Paris punchcutters, and the type introduced by Peter Schoeffer II and others (*c.* 1512), which was rapidly spreading through several countries.

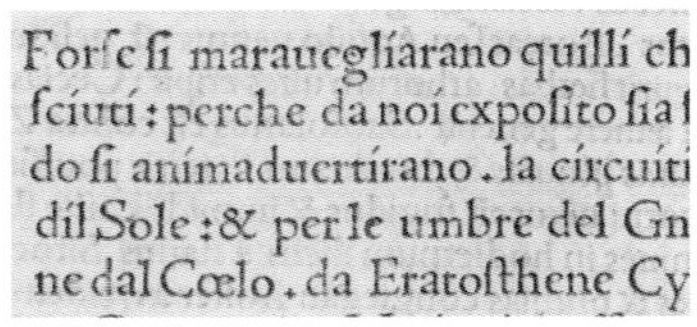

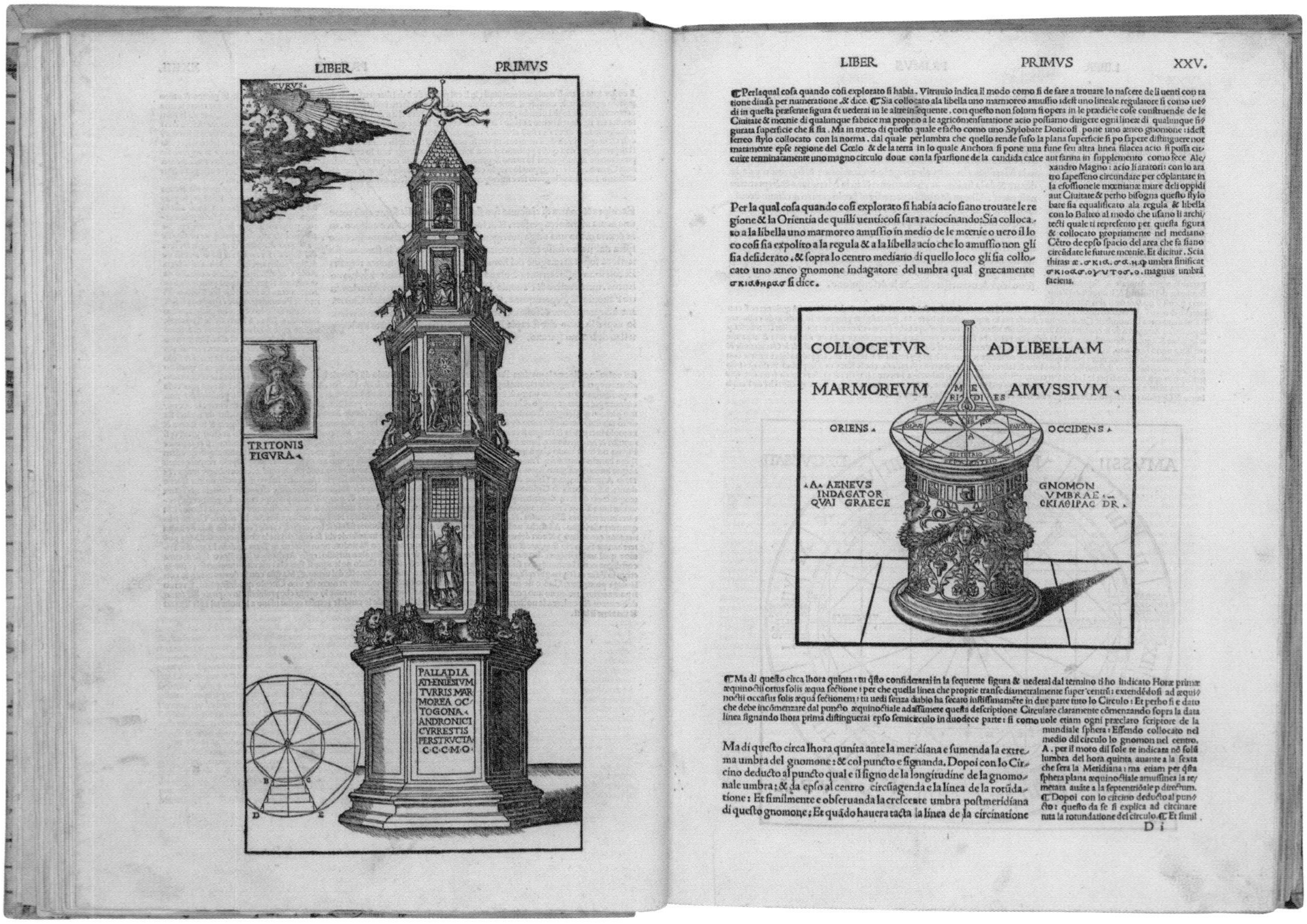

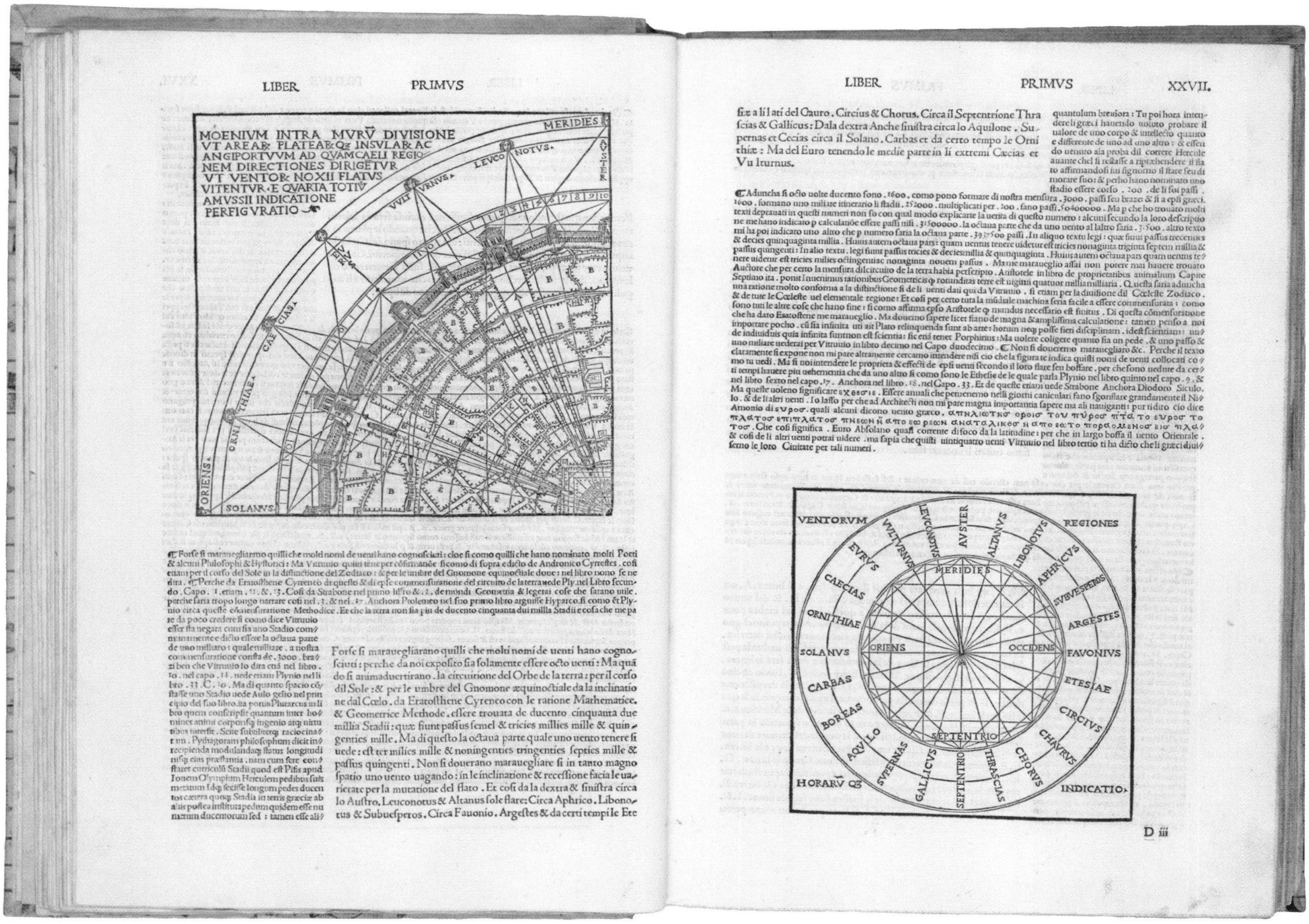
LIBER PRIMVS
LIBER PRIMVS XXVII.
MOENIVM INTRA MVRV DIVISIONE VT AREAE PLATEAE QZ INSVLAE AC ANGIPORTVVM AD QVAMCAELI REGIONEM DIRECTIONES DIRIGETVR VT VENTOR NOXII FLATVS VITENTVR E QVARTA TOTIV AMVSSII INDICATIONE PERFIGVRATIO
MERIDIES
AVSTER
LEVCONOTVS
SOLANVS
ORIENS
VENTORVM
REGIONES
HORARV QZ
INDICATIO
MERIDIES
ORIENS
OCCIDENS
SEPTENTRIO
D iii

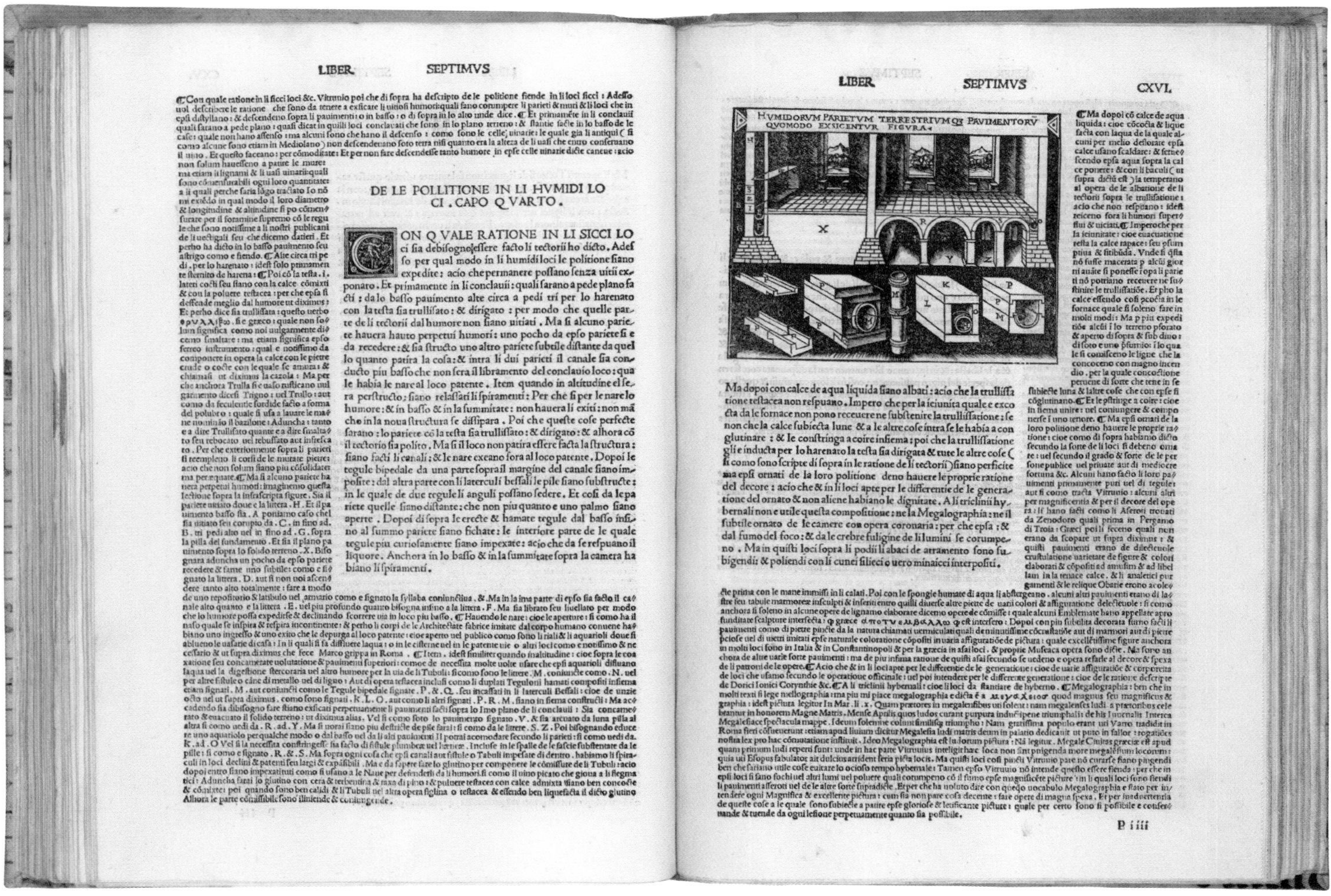
LIBER SEPTIMVS
LIBER SEPTIMVS CXVI.
DE LE POLLITIONE IN LI HVMIDI LO CI . CAPO QVARTO .
HVMIDORVM PARIETVM TERRESTRIVM QZ PAVIMENTORV QVOMODO EXSICENTVR FIGVRA
P iiii

1524 **Ludovico degli Arrighi** (Vincentino) **Ludovico degli Arrighi, *La operina di Ludovico Vicentino da imparare di scrivere littera cancellarescha*. Rome, text dated 1522 (first published 1523/24). 16 leaves. 21 cm. This may be a slightly later printing and lacks all but the first 4 leaves. Woodblock cutter: Ugo da Carpi.**

This was the first published writing manual to illustrate the formal chancery hand, printed entirely from woodblocks. Ludovico degli Arrighi (c. 1485?–1527) was born near Vicenza and is therefore also known as Vicentino. He is first recorded at Rome, where he published a book in 1510. He may therefore have been fifteen or twenty years younger than his greatest rival and possible master, Tagliente in Venice.

By 1514, Arrighi had established himself as a leading calligrapher working for private patrons. Soon after, he worked as a copyist in the Papal chancery, then set up his own printing office, setting books in the first chancery italic printing types in 1524; these had upright capitals, sometimes including decorative swashes like those in the woodcut version illustrated. He used a face of this kind when he added a second part (text dated 1523, published 1525?) to the manual shown here. His partner in the press, Lautizio Perugino de Bartolomeo dei Rotelli, cut these types for him. Though more elegant than the 1501 Aldine italic and copied by other Italian presses, Arrighi's italic types contributed to mainstream typographic developments primarily when Peter Schoeffer II, Robert Granjon and others blended them with the Aldine italic in the 1530s and 40s. This established what was to remain the standard form of italic type for two centuries.

In the early twentieth century, writing manuals by Arrighi and his contemporaries guided Edward Johnston and others who revived broad-edged pen calligraphy, and Arrighi's italic typefaces served as direct models for new ones in the 1920s. JAL

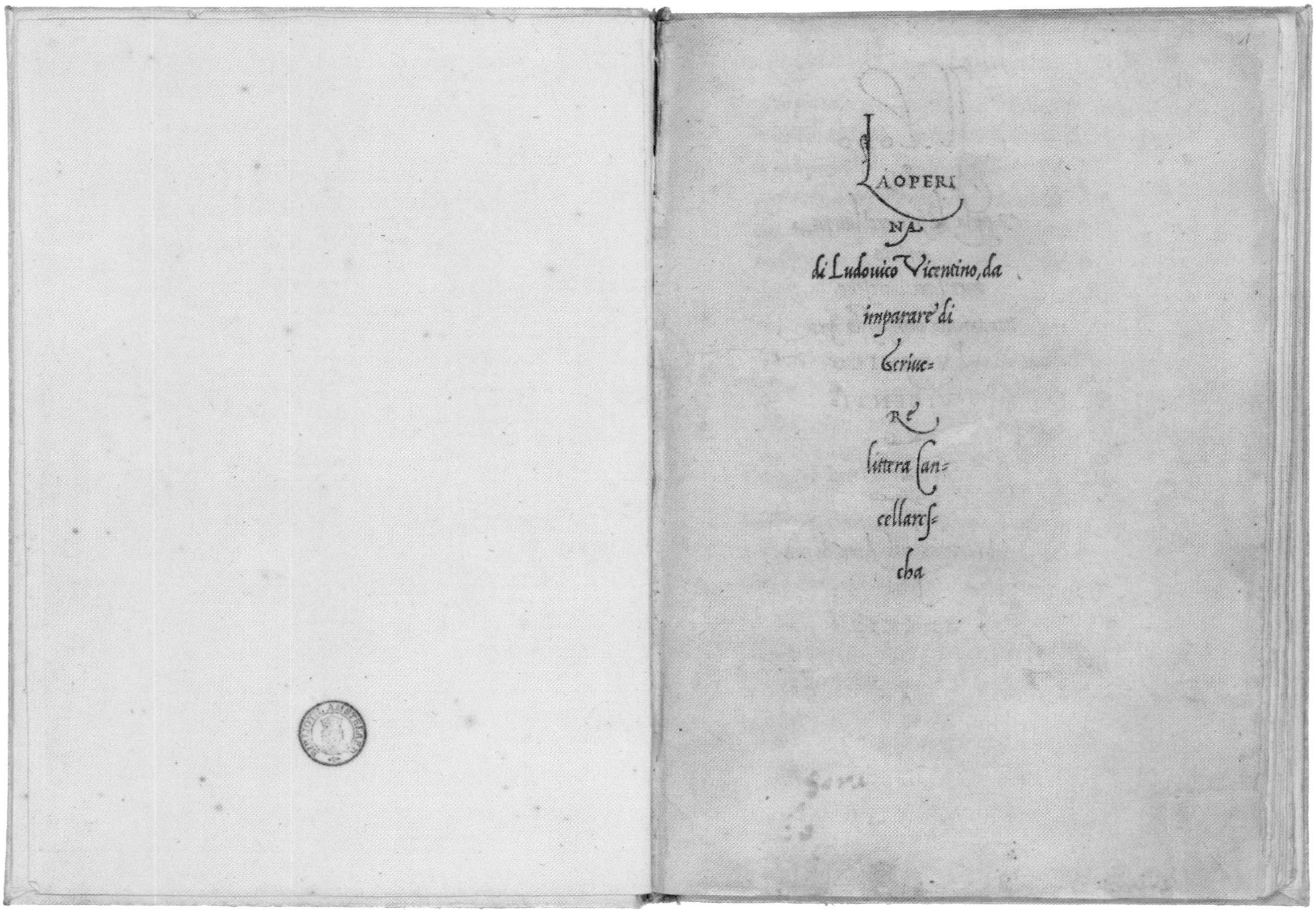

dar qualche essempio di scriuere, et regulata=
mente formare gli caratteri e note delle lre(
che cancellaresche hoggi di chiamano) uoletier

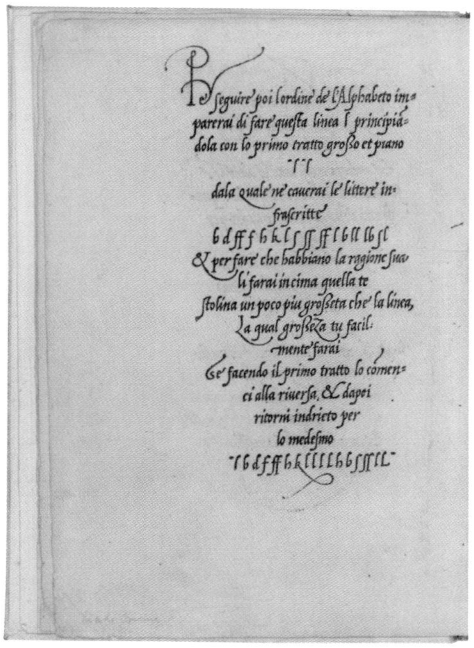
P er seguire poi l'ordine de l'Alphabeto im=
pararai di fare questa linea l principia=
dola con lo primo tratto grosso et piano
dala quale ne cauerai le littere in=
frascritte
& per fare che habbiano la ragione sua
li farai in cima quella te
stolina un poco piu grossetta che la linea,
La qual grossezza tu facil=
mente farai
Se facendo il primo tratto lo comen=
ci alla riuersa, & dapoi
ritorni indrieto per
lo medesimo

Arrighi's chancery italic, cut on woodblocks by Ugo da Carpi (1479/81–1532/33). Da Carpi's expert woodcutting contributed significantly to the book's success, but their collaboration proved short-lived, perhaps the impetus for Arrighi to have a chancery italic type cut for his later books.

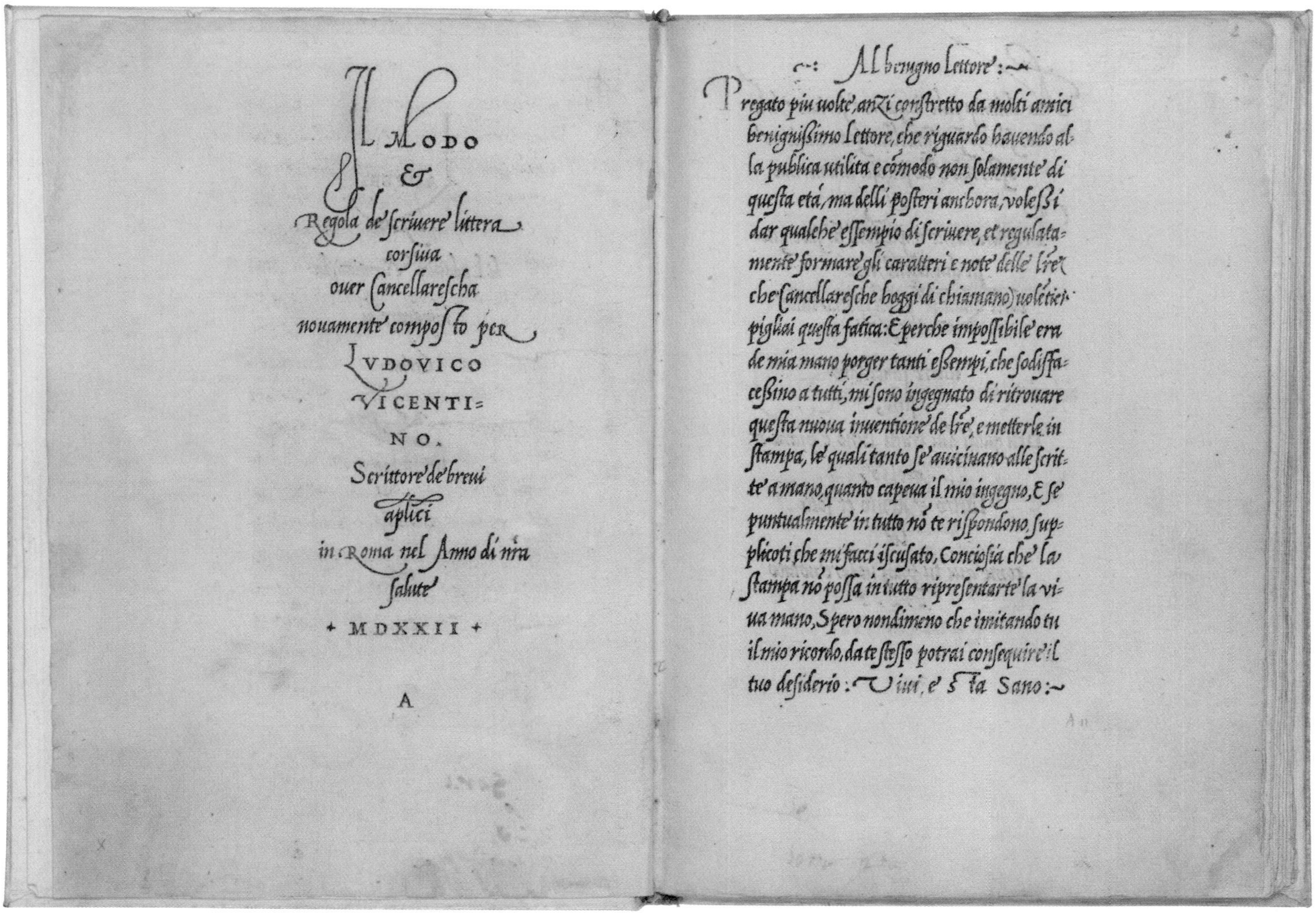
IL MODO
&
Regola de scriuere littera
corsiua
ouer Cancellarescha
nouamente composto per
LVDOVICO
VICENTI=
NO.
Scrittore de breui
aplici
in Roma nel Anno di nra
salute
+ MDXXII +
A

Al benigno Lettore:
Pregato piu uolte, anzi constretto da molti amici
benignissimo Lettore, che riguardo hauendo al
la publica utilita e cómodo non solamente di
questa età, ma delli posteri anchora, volessi
dar qualche essempio di scriuere, et regulata=
mente formare gli caratteri e note delle lre(
che Cancellaresche hoggi di chiamano) uolétier
pigliai questa fatica: E perche impossibile era
de mia mano porger tanti essempi, che sodisfa=
cessino a tutti, mi sono ingegnato di ritrouare
questa nuoua inuentione de lre, e metterle in
stampa, le quali tanto se auicinano alle scrit=
te a mano, quanto capeua il mio ingegno, E se
puntualmente in tutto nó te rispondono, sup=
plicoti che mi facci iscusato, Conciosia che la
Stampa nó possa in tutto ripresentarte la vi=
ua mano, Spero nondimeno che imitando tu
il mio ricordo, da te stesso potrai conseguire il
tuo desiderio: Viui, e Sta Sano:

1525 **Albrecht Dürer** Albrecht Dürer, *Underweysung der Messung, mit dem Zirckel und Richtscheyt, in Linien Ebnen unnd gantzen Corporen*. Nuremberg: Hieronymus Andreas Formschneider, 1525. 89 leaves and 2 folding slips. 28.5 cm.

This remarkably accurate, detailed and well-illustrated treatise on practical plane and solid geometry (with an emphasis on perspective) and constructed lettering was written in German for artists and artisans: 'A manual of measurement of lines, areas, and solids by means of compass and ruler'. It was one of very few German-language mathematics books and certainly the most substantial. Demand among scholars and foreigners led to a 1538 Paris edition in Latin.

Albrecht Dürer (1471–1528), from Nuremberg, learned goldsmith's work under his father and turned to woodcut book illustration as an apprentice painter. Returning from a visit to Venice in 1495, he began seriously studying mathematics and art theory, especially perspective. He set up his own workshop and in 1498 produced an illustrated *Apocalypse* with his godfather, the printer Anton Koberger, establishing himself as the greatest woodcut illustrator of the age. Hieronymus Andreae 'Formschneider' (block-cutter) produced the woodblocks for some of his drawings from about 1515 and set up a printing office in 1525.

Dürer's present greatest work as author helped spread Renaissance learning north of the Alps. The more than one hundred and fifty illustrations include two woodcuts showing artists at work with mechanical aids for perspective drawing; measuring instruments (including sundials); constructions of shadows and plain and solid figures (including logarithmic and other spirals, sine waves, cone sections, geometric solids and gores for a globe); polygons (to be applied to parquet floors and window panes); orthographic projections; architectural columns; classical roman capitals and gothic Textura minuscule letters. JAL

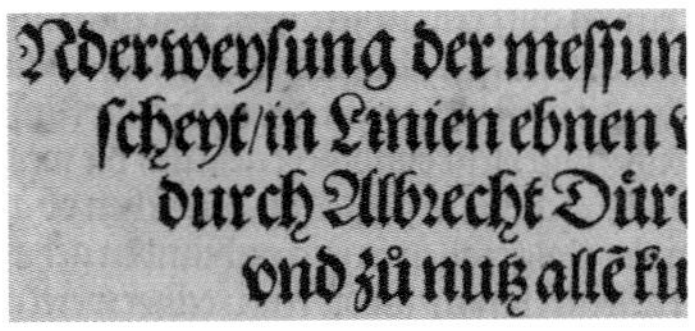

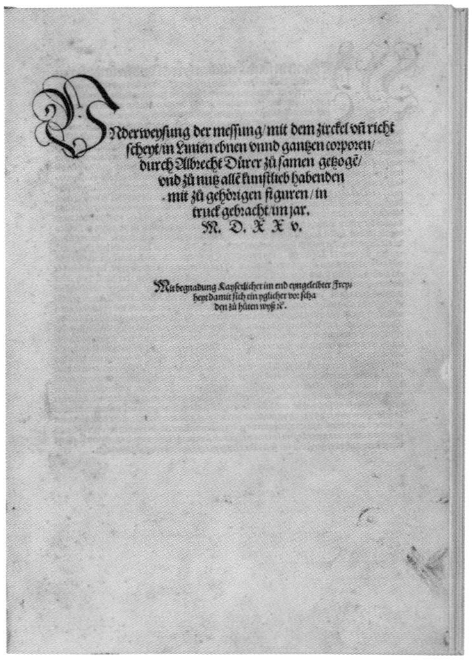

The definitive Fraktur type, copied for four centuries. Hieronymus Andreae (c. 1485?–1556), woodblock and metal die cutter, cut the first version (1522) for Dürer following a model by the writing master Johann Neudörffer (1497–1563) and developed the design further in several sizes for his own press, beginning in 1525.

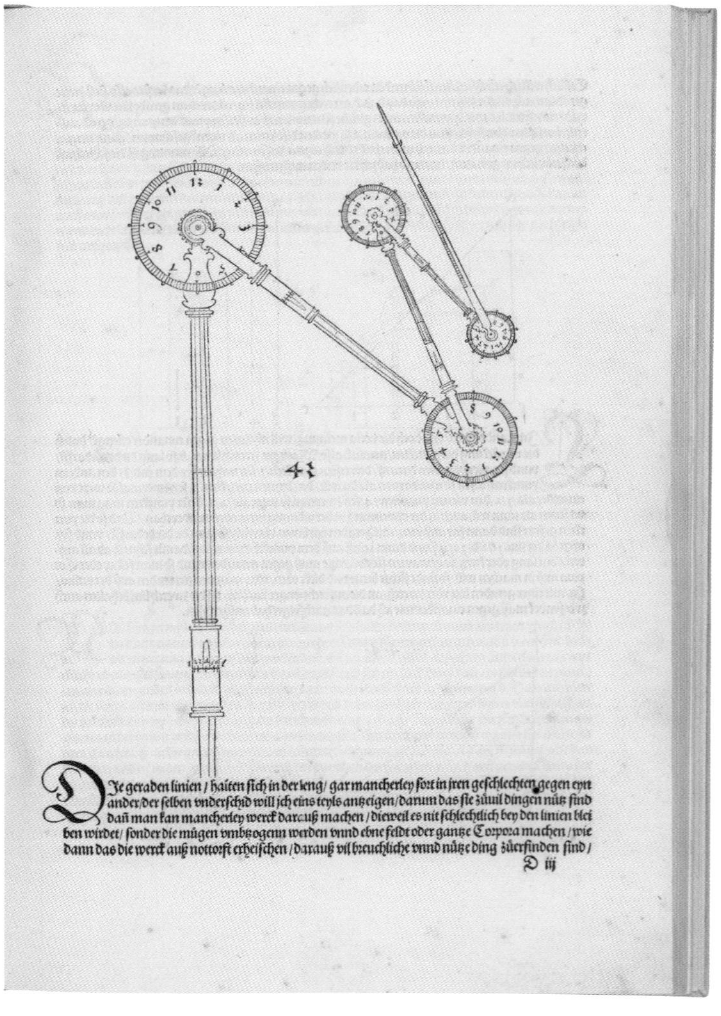

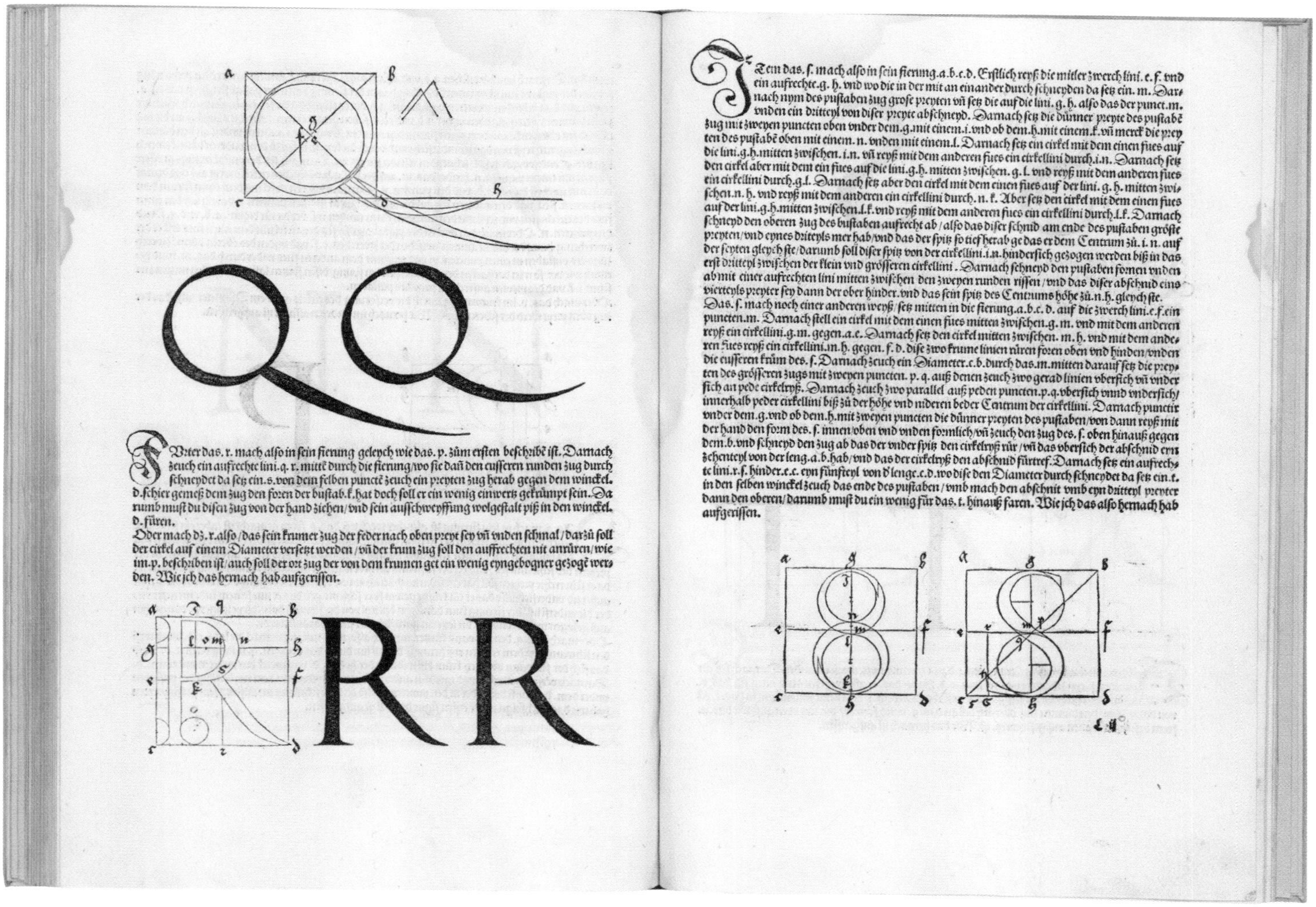

Vnter das. r. mach also in sein fierung geleych wie das. p. züm ersten beschribē ist. Darnach zeuch ein aufrechte lini. q. r. mittē durch die fierung/wo sie dann den eusseren runden zug durch schneydet da setz ein. s. von dem selben punctē zeuch ein preyten zug herab gegen dem winckel. d. schier gemeß dem zug den foren der bustab. k. hat doch soll er ein wenig einwertz gekrümpt sein. Darumb must du disen zug von der hand ziehen/vnd sein außschweyffung wolgestalt piß in den winckel. d. füren.
Oder mach dz. r. also/das sein krumer zug der feder nach oben preyt sey vnd vnden schmal/darzü soll der cirkel auf einem Diameter versetzt werden/vnd der krum zug soll den auffrechten nit anrüren/wie im. p. beschriben ist/auch soll der ort zug der von dem krumen get ein wenig eyngebogner gezogē werden. Wie jch das hernach hab aufgerissen.

Item das. s. mach also in sein fierung. a. b. c. d. Erstlich reyß die mitler zwerch lini. e. f. vnd ein aufrechte. g. h. vnd wo die in der mit an einander durch schneyden da setz ein. m. Darnach nym des pustaben zug grose preyten vnd setz die auf die lini. g. h. also das der punct. m. vnden ein dritteyl von diser preyte abschneyd. Darnach setz die dünner preyte des pustabē zug mit zweyen puncten oben vnder dem. g. mit einem. i. vnd ob dem. h. mit einem. k. vnd merck die preyten des pustabē oben mit einem. n. vnden mit einem. l. Darnach setz ein cirkel mit dem einen fues auf die lini. g. h. mitten zwischen. i. n. vnd reyß mit dem anderen fues ein cirkellini durch. i. n. Darnach setz den cirkel aber mit dem ein fues auf die lini. g. h. mitten zwischen. g. l. vnd reyß mit dem anderen fues ein cirkellini durch. g. l. Darnach setz aber den cirkel mit dem einen fues auf der lini. g. h. mitten zwischen. n. h. vnd reyß mit dem anderen ein cirkellini durch. n. k. Aber setz den cirkel mit dem einen fues auf der lini. g. h. mitten zwischen. l. k. vnd reyß mit dem anderen fues ein cirkellini durch. l. k. Darnach schneyd den oberen zug des bustaben aufrecht ab/also das diser schnid am ende des pustaben gröste preyten/vnd eynes driteyls mer hab/vnd das der spitz so tief herab ge das er dem Centrum zü. i. n. auf der seyten gleych ste/darumb soll diser spitz von der cirkellini. i. n. hindersich gezogen werden biß in das erst dritteyl zwischen der klein vnd grösseren cirkellini. Darnach schneyd den pustaben fornen vnden ab mit einer aufrechten lini mitten zwischen den zweyen runden rissen/vnd das diser abschnid eins vierteyls preyter sey dann der ober hinder. vnd das sein spitz des Centrums höhe zü. n. h. gleych ste.
Das. s. mach noch einer anderen weyß/setz mitten in die fierung. a. b. c. d. auf die zwerch lini. e. f. ein puncten. m. Darnach stell ein cirkel mit dem einen fues mitten zwischen. g. m. vnd mit dem anderen reyß ein cirkellini. g. m. gegen. a. c. Darnach setz den cirkel mitten zwischen. m. h. vnd mit dem anderen fues reyß ein cirkellini. m. h. gegen. f. d. dise zwo krume linien rüren foren oben vnd hinden/vnden die eusseren krüm des. s. Darnach zeuch ein Diameter. c. b. durch das. m. mitten darauf setz die preyten des grösseren zugs mit zweyen puncten. p. q. auß denen zeuch zwo gerad linien vbersich vnd vndersich an yede cirkelryß. Darnach zeuch zwo parallel auß yeden puncten. p. q. vbersich vnnd vndersich/innerhalb yeder cirkellini biß zü der höhe vnd nideren beder Centrum der cirkellini. Darnach punctir vnder dem. g. vnd ob dem. h. mit zweyen puncten die dünner preyten des pustaben/von dann reyß mit der hand den form des. s. innen/oben vnd vnden formlich/vnd zeuch den zug des. s. oben hinauß gegen dem. b. vnd schneyd den zug ab das der vnder spitz den cirkelryß rür/vnd das vbersich der abschnid ein zehenteyl von der leng. a. b. hab/vnd das der cirkelryß den abschnid fürtref. Darnach setz ein aufrechte lini. r. s. hinder. e. c. eyn fünfteyl von d'lenge. c. d. wo dise den Diameter durch schneydet da setz ein. t. in den selben winckel zeuch das ende des pustaben/vmb mach den abschnit vmb eyn dritteyl preyter dann den oberen/darumb must du ein wenig für das. t. hinauß faren. Wie jch das also hernach hab aufgerissen.

C iij

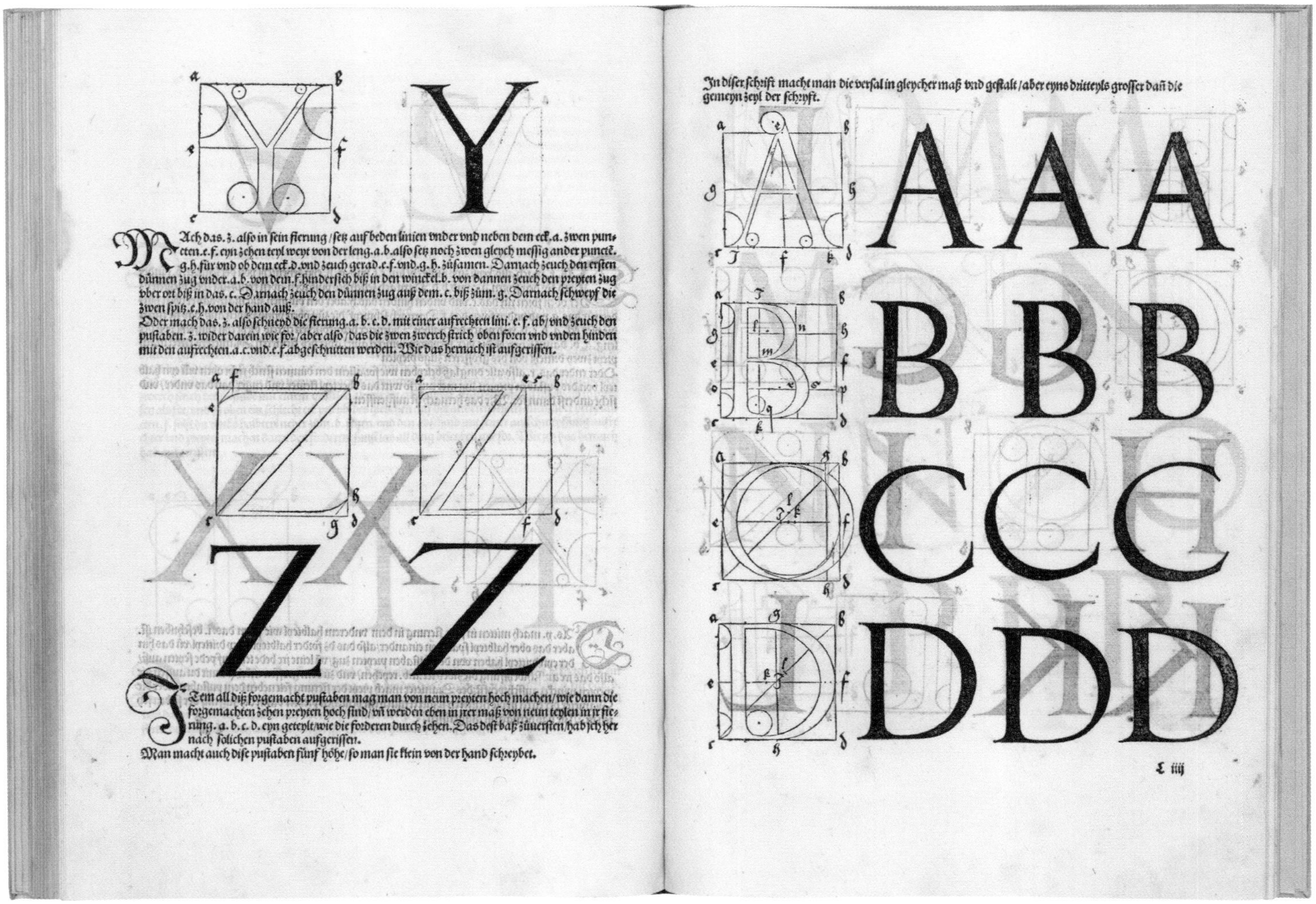

Nach das. z. also in sein fierung/setz auf beden linien vnder vnd neben dem eck. a. zwen puncten. e. f. eyn zehen teyl weyt von der leng. a. b. also setz noch zwen gleych messig ander punctē. g. h. für vnd ob dem eck. d. vnd zeuch gerad. e. f. vnd. g. h. züsamen. Darnach zeuch den ersten dünnen zug vnder. a. b. von dem. f. hindersich biß in den winckel. b. von dannen zeuch den preyten zug vber ort biß in das. c. Darnach zeuch den dünnen zug auß dem. c. biß züm. g. Darnach schweyf die zwen spitz. e. h. von der hand auß.
Oder mach das. z. also schneyd die fierung. a. b. c. d. mit einer aufrechten lini. e. f. ab/vnd zeuch den pustaben. z. wider darein wie for/aber also/das die zwen zwerch strich oben foren vnd vnden hinden mit den aufrechten. a. c. vnd. e. f. abgeschnitten werden. Wie das hernach ist aufgerissen.

Item all diß forgemacht pustaben mag man von neun preyten hoch machen/wie dann die forgemachten zehen preyten hoch sind/vnd werden eben in jrer maß von neun teylen in jr fierung. a. b. c. d. eyn geteylt/wie die forderen durch zehen. Das deßt baß züuersten/hab jch hernach solichen pustaben aufgerissen.
Man macht auch dise pustaben fünf höhe/so man sie klein von der hand schreybet.

In diser schrift macht man die versal in gleycher maß vnd gestalt/aber eyns dritteyls grosser dann die gemeyn zeyl der schryft.

C iiij

1529 **Geoffroy Tory** Geoffroy Tory, *Champ fleury, auquel est contenu l'art et science de la deue et vraye proportion des lettres attiques* ... Paris: Geoffroy Tory & Gilles de Gourmont, 1529. 80 leaves. 24.5 cm. Illustrator: Geoffroy Tory.

As suggested by the subtitle, *Champ fleury* (a name for paradise) is a treatise on the proportions of Roman capitals by the publisher, graphic designer, printer, and translator, Geoffroy Tory (*c*. 1480–1533). Underlying the book is a Renaissance idea that goes back to classical antiquity: everything is based on geometric principles. But *Champ fleury* also connects the capitals with the proportions of the human body, and in this aspect the book is different from a similar book by Pacioli, dated 1509. The book contains woodcuts in which a capital is combined with the human figure, within a grid. The book was intended for painters and lettercutters rather than typographers. Tory was only involved with the production of the book in the capacity of publisher. The technical quality of the printing is rather weak and the typeface used for the book is unremarkable. Here and there, however, the layout is reminiscent of Italian examples. As with most books before around 1530, no italics are used.

Champ fleury also includes a defence of the French language, which is characteristic of the French Renaissance. The subject is placed within a scarcely comprehensible context of platonic ideas, mythological representations, and allegories. There is a brief discussion of typography towards the end of the book, where several alphabets are printed. For the majority of these, however, woodcuts were used instead of movable type. FAJ

The first widely used Parisian roman, introduced in 1499, spread to the Low Countries (1513), London (1519) and Saxony (1524). Well cut in the style of Nicolas Jenson, it remained in use for a decade after Parisian romans in the Aldine style first appeared in 1530.

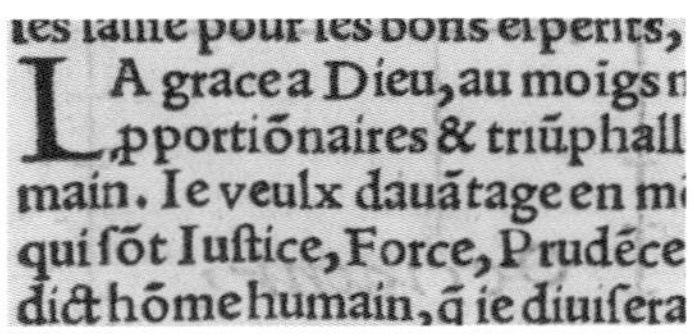

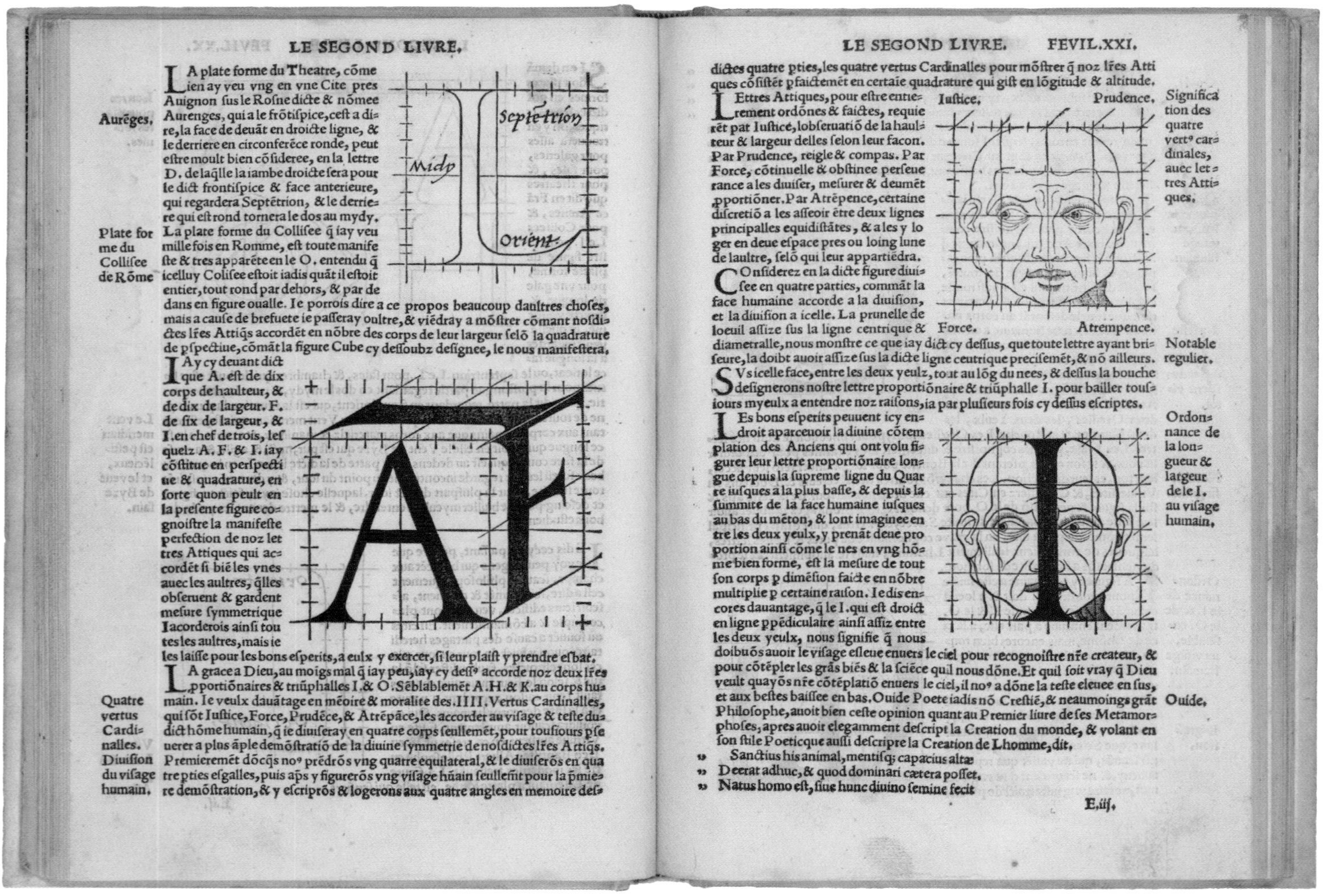

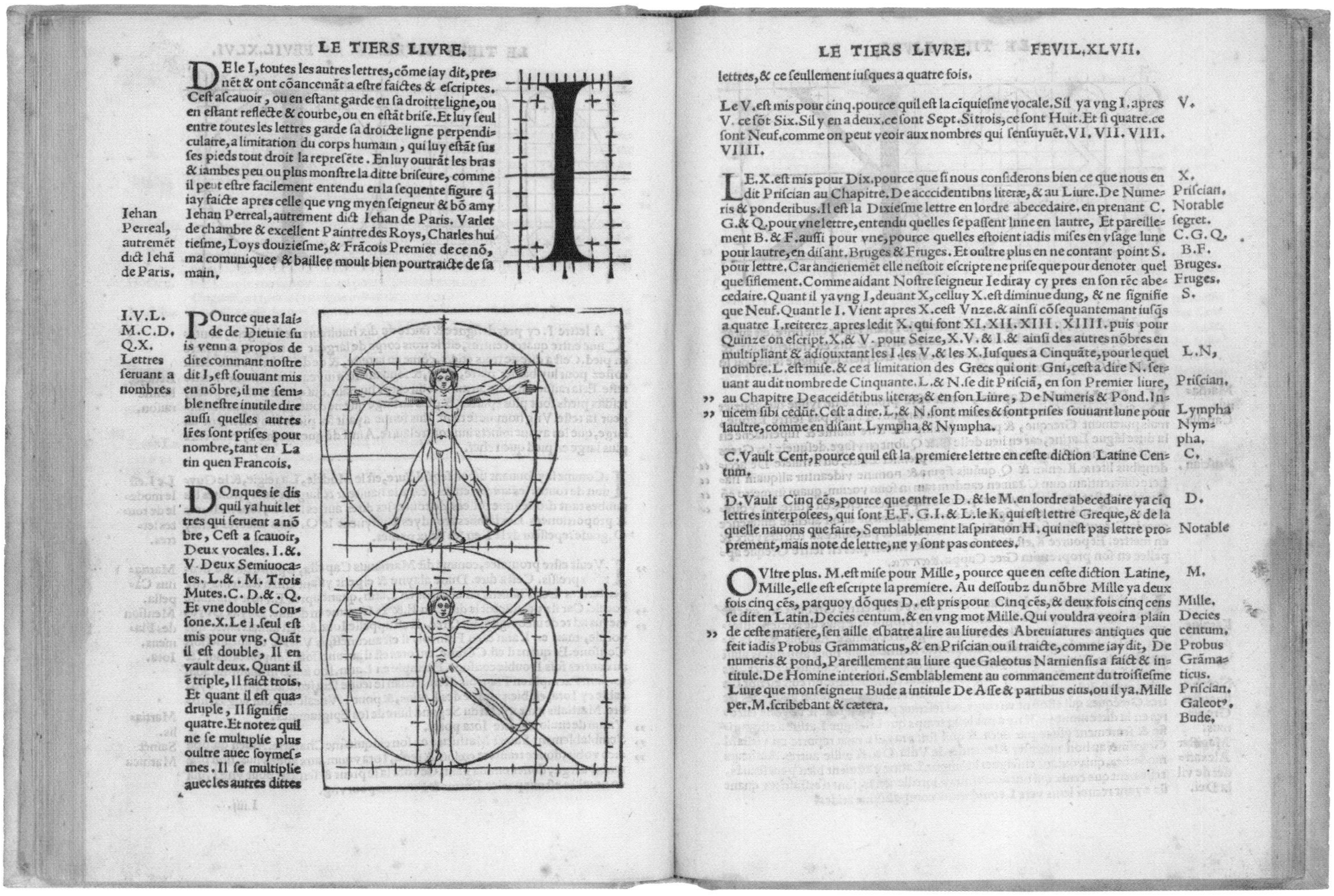

LE TIERS LIVRE.

DE le I, toutes les autres lettres, cōme iay dit, prenēt & ont cōancemāt a estre faictes & escriptes. Cest ascauoir, ou en estant garde en sa droitte ligne, ou en estant reflecte & courbe, ou en estāt brise. Et luy seul entre toutes les lettres garde sa droicte ligne perpendiculaire, a limitation du corps humain, qui luy estāt sus ses pieds tout droit la represēte. En luy ouurāt les bras & iambes peu ou plus monstre la ditte briseure, comme il peut estre facilement entendu en la sequente figure q̃ iay faicte apres celle que vng myen seigneur & bō amy Iehan Perreal, autrement dict Iehan de Paris. Varlet de chambre & excellent Paintre des Roys, Charles huitiesme, Loys douziesme, & Frācois Premier de ce nō, ma comuniquee & baillee moult bien pourtraicte de sa main,

Iehan Perreal, autremēt dict Iehā de Paris.

POurce que a laide de Dieu ie suis venu a propos de dire commant nostre dit I, est souuant mis en nōbre, il me semble nestre inutile dire aussi quelles autres lres sont prises pour nombre, tant en Latin quen Francois.

I.V.L. M.C.D. Q.X. Lettres seruant a nombres

DOnques ie dis quil ya huit lettres qui seruent a nōbre, Cest a scauoir, Deux vocales. I. & V Deux Semiuocales. L. & . M. Trois Mutes. C. D. & . Q. Et vne double Consone. X. Le I. seul est mis pour vng. Quāt il est double, Il en vault deux. Quant il ē triple, Il faict trois, Et quant il est quadruple, Il signifie quatre. Et notez quil ne se multiplie plus oultre auec soymesmes. Il se multiplie auec les autres dittes

LE TIERS LIVRE. FEVIL.XLVII.

lettres, & ce seullement iusques a quatre fois.

Le V. est mis pour cinq. pource quil est la ciquiesme vocale. Sil ya vng I. apres V. ce sōt Six. Sil y en a deux, ce sont Sept. Si trois, ce sont Huit. Et si quatre. ce sont Neuf, comme on peut veoir aux nombres qui sensuyuēt. VI. VII. VIII. VIIII. — V.

LE.X. est mis pour Dix. pource que si nous considerons bien ce que nous en dit Priscian au Chapitre. De accidentibus literæ, & au Liure. De Numeris & ponderibus. Il est la Dixiesme lettre en lordre abecedaire. en prenant C. G. & Q. pour vne lettre, entendu quelles se passent lune en lautre, Et pareillement B. & F. aussi pour vne, pource quelles estoient iadis mises en vsage lune pour lautre, en disant. Bruges & Fruges. Et oultre plus en ne contant point S. pour lettre. Car ancienemēt elle nestoit escripte ne prise que pour denoter quelque siflement. Comme aidant Nostre seigneur Ie diray cy pres en son rēc abecedaire. Quant il ya vng I, deuant X, celluy X. est diminue dung, & ne signifie que Neuf. Quant le I. Vient apres X. cest Vnze. & ainsi cōsequantemant iusq̃s a quatre I. reiterez apres ledit X. qui sont XI. XII. XIII. XIIII. puis pour Quinze on escript. X. & V. pour Seize, X. V. & I. & ainsi des autres nōbres en multipliant & adiouxtant les I. les V. & les X. Iusques a Cinquāte, pour le quel nombre. L. est mise. & ce a limitation des Grecs qui ont Gni, cest a dire N. seruant au dit nombre de Cinquante. L. & N. se dit Prisciā, en son Premier liure, » au Chapitre De accidētibus literæ, & en son Liure, De Numeris & Pond. In» uicem sibi cedūt. Cest a dire. L. & N. sont mises & sont prises souuant lune pour laultre, comme en disant Lympha & Nympha. — X. Priscian. Notable segret. C.G.Q. B.F. Bruges. Fruges. S. L.N, Priscian. Lympha Nympha.

C. Vault Cent, pource quil est la premiere lettre en ceste diction Latine Centum. — C.

D. Vault Cinq cēs, pource que entre le D. & le M. en lordre abecedaire ya ciq lettres interposees, qui sont E.F. G.I. & L. le K. qui est lettre Greque, & de laquelle nauons que faire, Semblablement laspiration H. qui nest pas lettre proprement, mais note de lettre, ne y sont pas contees. — D. Notable

OVltre plus. M. est mise pour Mille, pource que en ceste diction Latine, Mille, elle est escripte la premiere. Au dessoubz du nōbre Mille ya deux fois cinq cēs, parquoy dōques D. est pris pour Cinq cēs, & deux fois cinq cens se dit en Latin. Decies centum. & en vng mot Mille. Qui vouldra veoir a plain » de ceste matiere, sen aille esbatre a lire au liure des Abreuiatures antiques que feit iadis Probus Grammaticus, & en Priscian ou il traicte, comme iay dit, De numeris & pond, Pareillement au liure que Galeotus Narniensis a faict & intitule. De Homine interiori. Semblablement au commancement du troisiesme Liure que monseigneur Bude a intitule De Asse & partibus eius, ou il ya. Mille per. M. scribebant & cætera. — M. Mille. Decies centum. Probus Grāmaticus. Priscian. Galeot⁹. Bude.

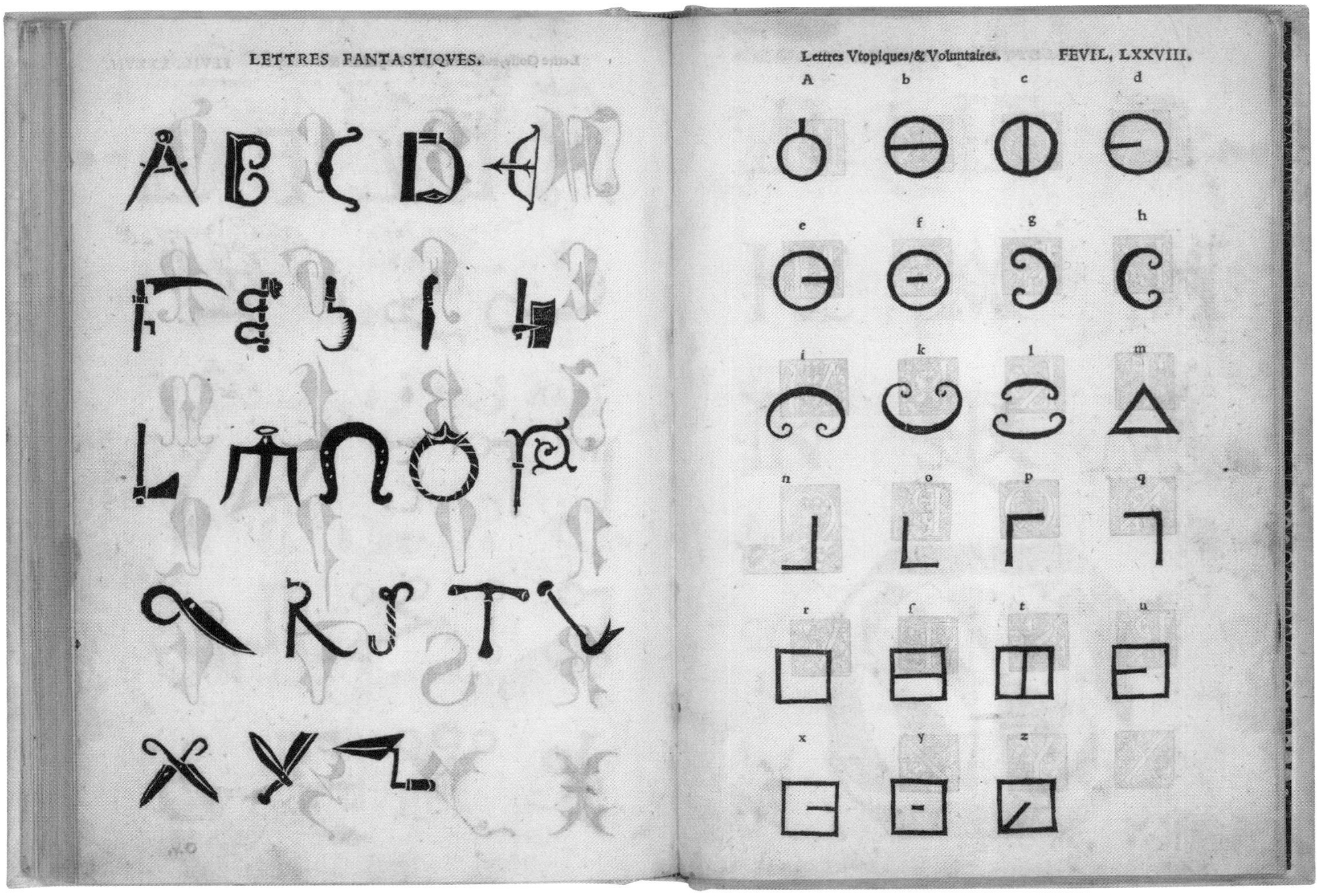

LETTRES FANTASTIQVES.

Lettres Vtopiques/& Voluntaires. FEVIL. LXXVIII.

Geoffroy Tory

1532 **Marco Fabio Calvo** Marco Fabio Calvo, *Antiquae urbis Romae cum regionibus simulachrum*. Rome: Valerio Dorico, 1532. 46 pp. 44 cm. Lettering: Ludovico degli Arrighi. Woodblock cutter: Tolomeo Egnazio (illustrations).

An 'archeological' study of classical Rome entitled *Antiquae urbis Romae* was published in 1527. The book was the result of a project, commissioned by the Pope, which painter and sculptor Raphael had initiated. After Raphael's early demise, the book was published by his friend, philologist and archaeologist Marco Fabio Calvo (*c.* 1450–1527). It remains unclear to what extent Calvo made use of Raphael's work.

Antiquae urbis Romae includes schematic and partly idealized reconstructions of the city during the times of Romulus, Servius Tullius, Augustus, and Pliny. The woodcut illustrations were cut by Tolomeo Egnazio da Fossombrone. Ludovico degli Arrighi (*c.* 1485?–1527), the calligrapher who printed the book, designed both the movable type and the woodblock lettering. This edition, in a large format, was subsidized by Cardinal Francesco Armellini and dedicated to Pope Clement VII, both members of the prominent Medici family.

Antiquae urbis Romae was published exactly one month before the bloody Sack of Rome, when the city was pillaged by the mutinous troops of Charles V. Both Calvo and Arrighi died that same year, and almost all copies of the book were lost. The reprint reproduced here appeared five years after the tragedy. The book is virtually a facsimile of the first edition: the original woodcuts were used and the typography is identical. PD

Ctaua autem Regio Forum
incipit, et in Septentrionem
quæ in eo fuerant, referuntur. Arcus Augu
s. Georgius dicitur Templum Deum Penat
mitium. Templum Iani. Domitiani Equus a

Arrighi (c. 1485?–1527) introduced the first italic type in the chancery style in 1524, more elegant than Aldus's but less practical. Even the more restrained second italic shown here (1526) failed to displace the Aldine until the two blended to establish a new standard style that dominated from the 1540s.

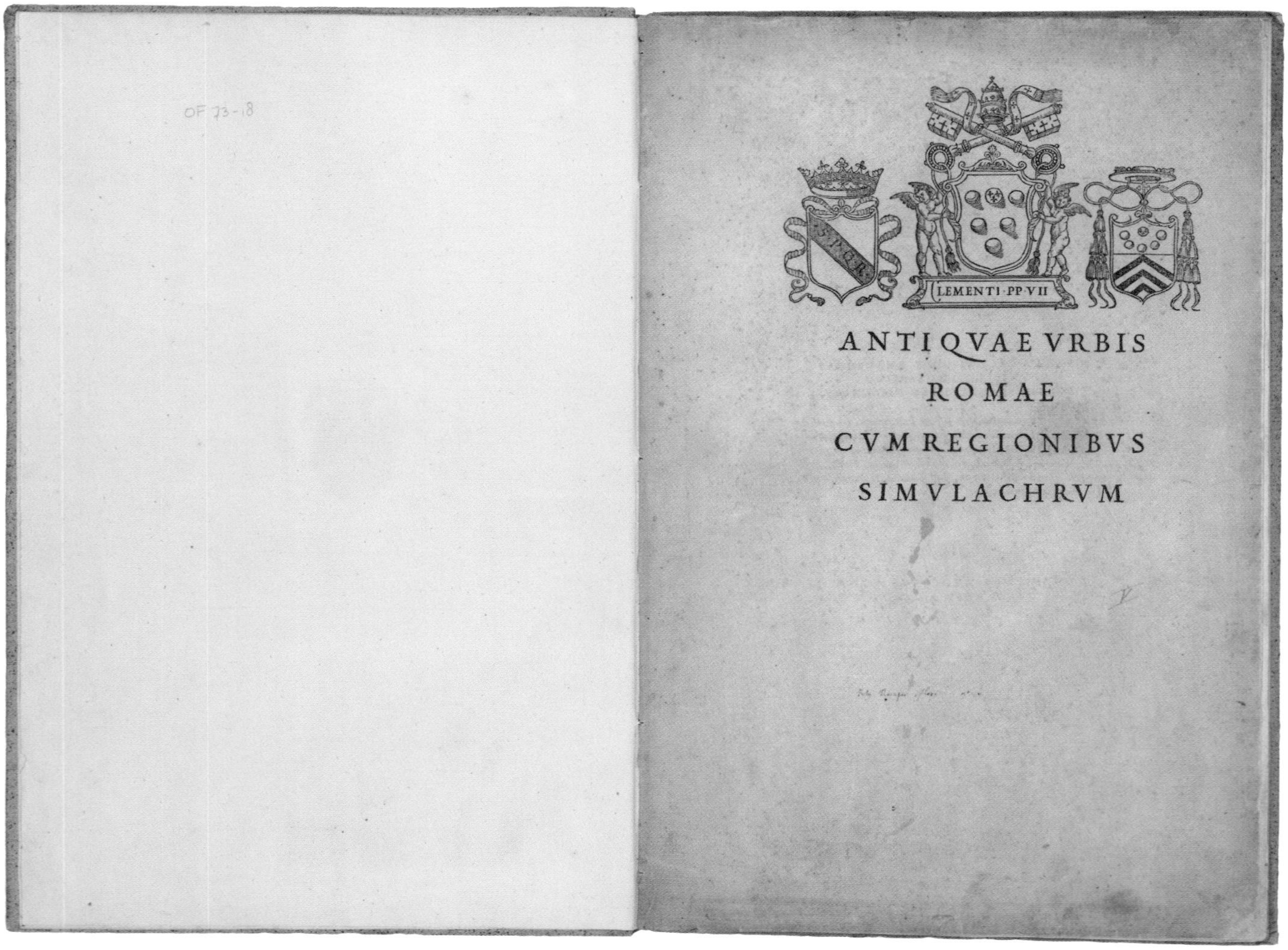

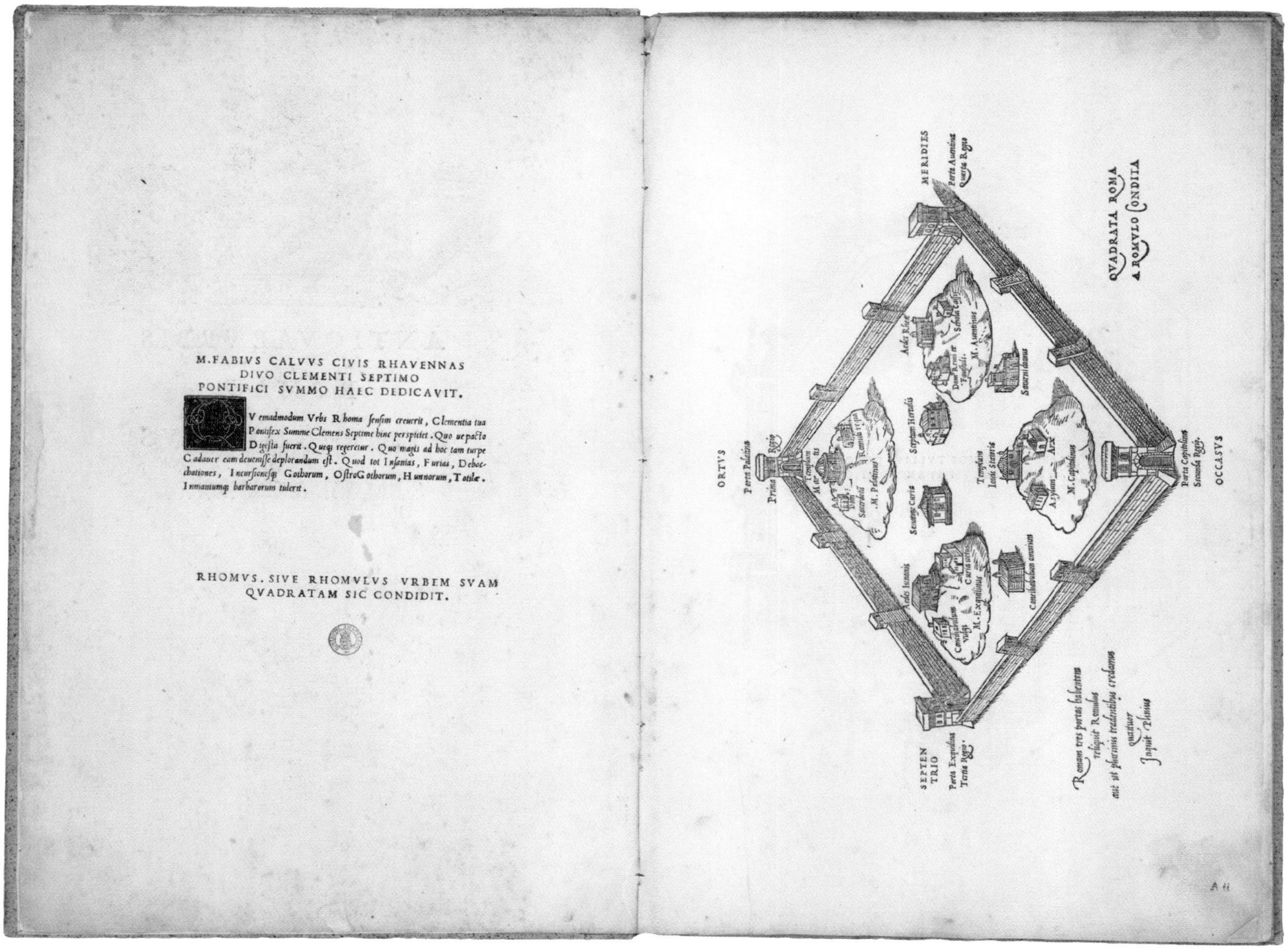

M.FABIVS CALVVS CIVIS RHAVENNAS
DIVO CLEMENTI SEPTIMO
PONTIFICI SVMMO HAEC DEDICAVIT.

Q Vemadmodum Vrbs Rhoma sensim creuerit, Clementia tua Pontifex Summe Clemens Septime hinc perspiciet. Quo uel pacto Digesta fuerit. Queq; regeretur. Quo magis ad hoc tam turpe Cadauer eam deuenisse deplorandum est. Quod tot Insanias, Furias, Debacchationes, Incursionesq; Gothorum, OstroGothorum, Hunnorum, Totilæ. Inmaniumq; barbarorum tulerit.

RHOMVS. SIVE RHOMVLVS VRBEM SVAM
QVADRATAM SIC CONDIDIT.

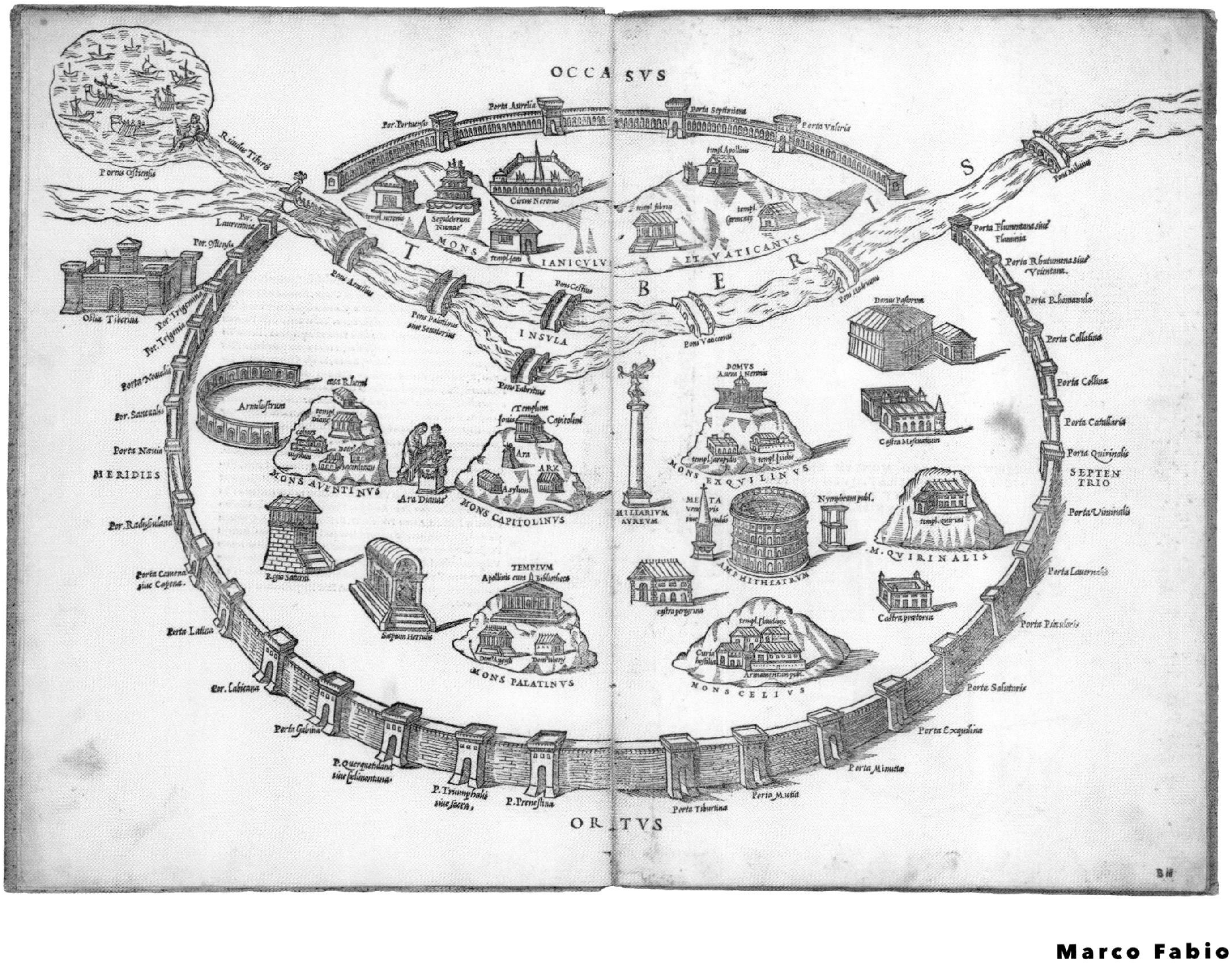

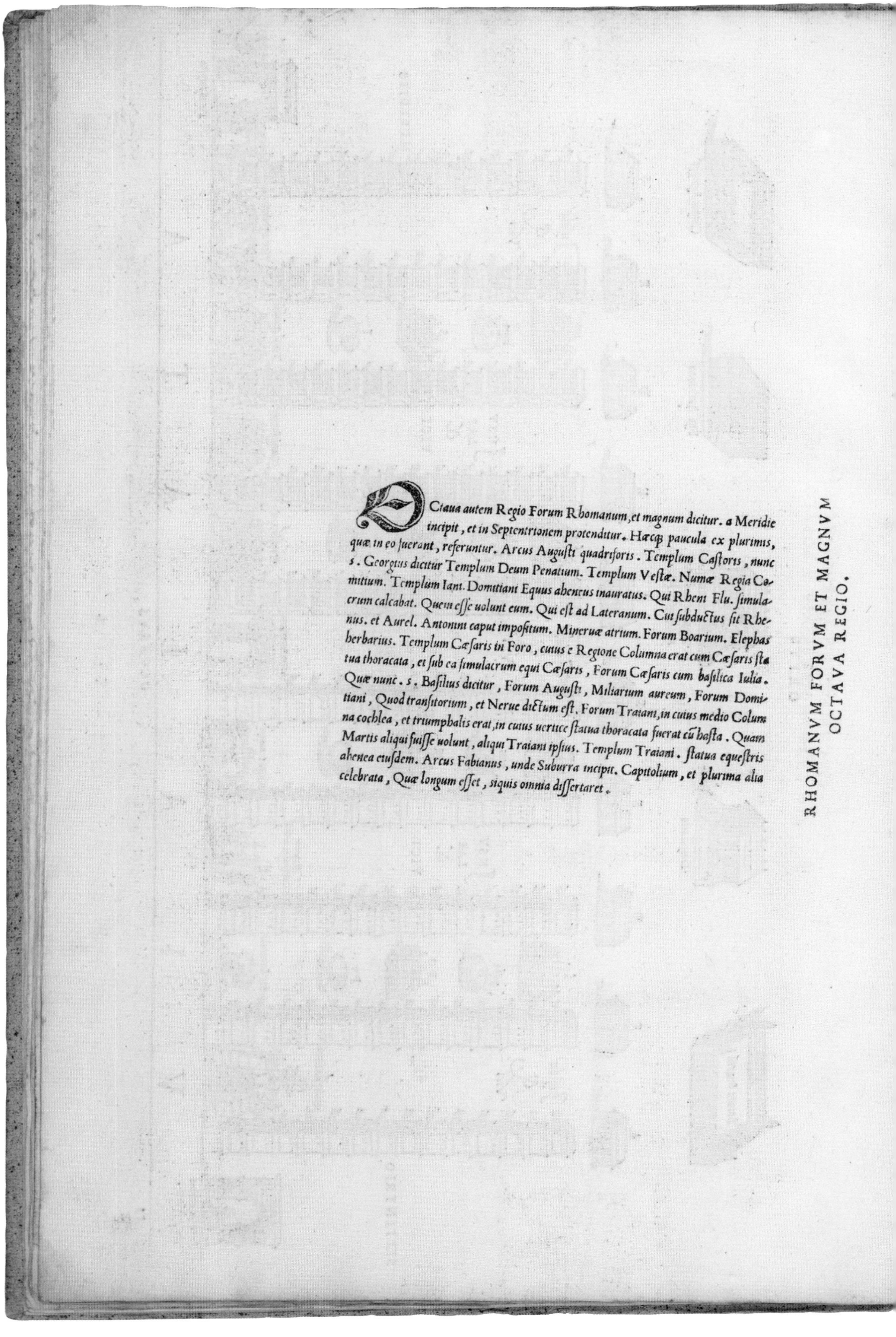

RHOMANVM FORVM ET MAGNVM OCTAVA REGIO.

Octaua autem Regio Forum Rhomanum, et magnum dicitur. a Meridie incipit, et in Septentrionem protenditur. Hæcq; paucula ex plurimis, quæ in eo fuerant, referuntur. Arcus Auguſti quadrifons. Templum Caſtoris, nunc s. Georgius dicitur Templum Deum Penatium. Templum Veſtæ. Numæ Regia Comitium. Templum Iani. Domitiani Equus ahenæus inauratus. Qui Rheni Flu. ſimulacrum calcabat. Quem eſſe uolunt eum. Qui eſt ad Lateranum. Cui ſubductus ſit Rhenus. et Aurel. Antonini caput impoſitum. Mineruæ atrium. Forum Boarium. Elephas herbarius. Templum Cæſaris in Foro, cuius e Regione Columna erat cum Cæſaris ſtatua thoracata, et ſub ea ſimulacrum equi Cæſaris, Forum Cæſaris cum baſilica Iulia. Quæ nunc. s. Baſilius dicitur, Forum Auguſti, Miliarium aureum, Forum Domitiani, Quod tranſitorium, et Nerue dictum eſt. Forum Traiani, in cuius medio Columna cochlea, et triumphalis erat, in cuius uertice ſtatua thoracata fuerat cū haſta. Quam Martis aliqui fuiſſe uolunt, aliqui Traiani ipſius. Templum Traiani. ſtatua equeſtris ahenea eiuſdem. Arcus Fabianus, unde Suburra incipit. Capitolium, et plurima alia celebrata, Quæ longum eſſet, ſiquis omnia diſſertaret.

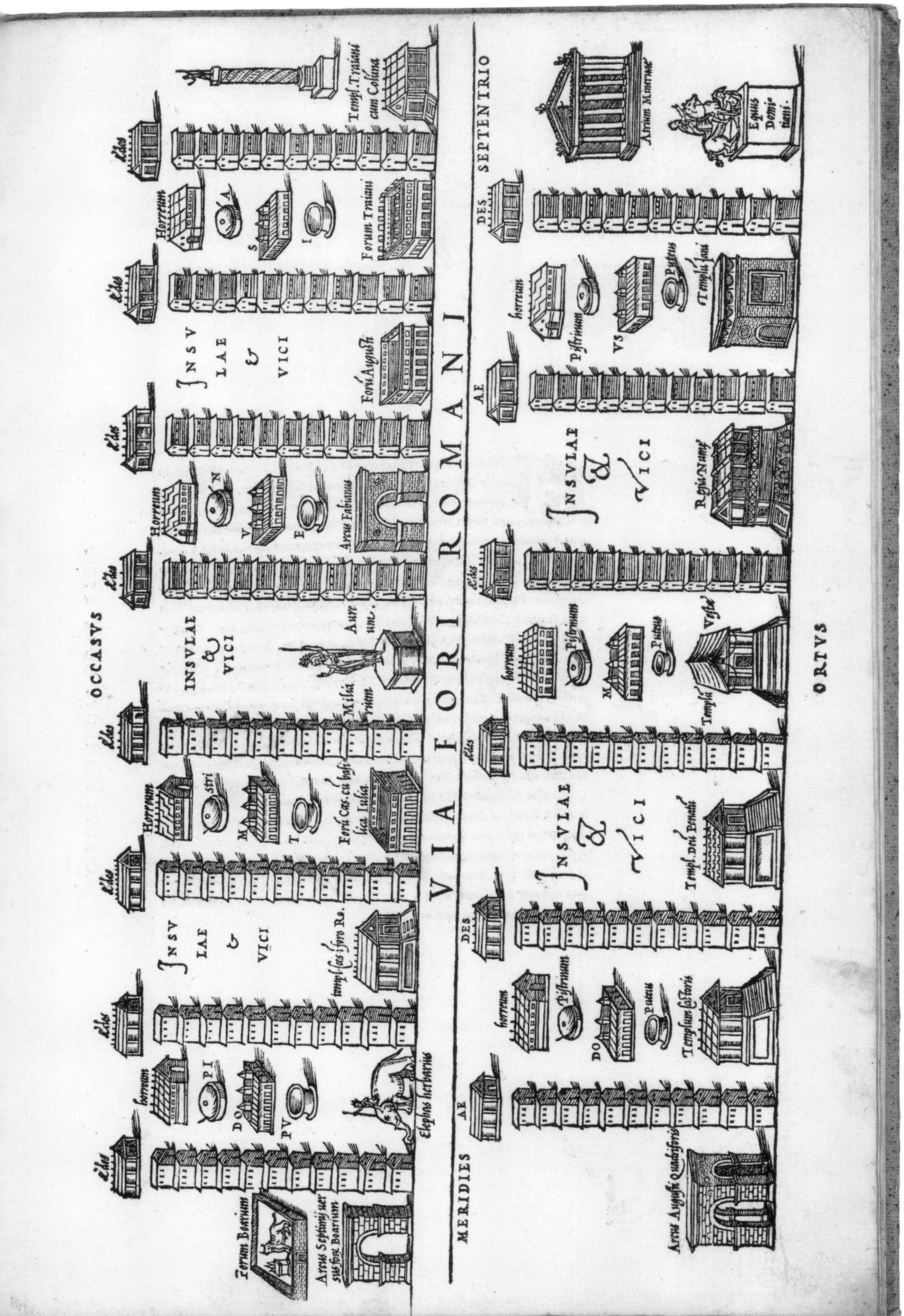
OCCASVS
VIA FORI ROMANI
ORTVS
MERIDIES
SEPTENTRIO

Decoration and illustration

Detail of *De humani corporis fabrica*, written by Andreas Vesalius (see p. 102)

ANDREAE VESALII
BRVXELLENSIS, SCHOLAE
medicorum Patauinæ professoris, de
Humani corporis fabrica
Libri ſeptem.
CVM CAESAREAE
Maiest. Galliarum Regis, ac Senatus Veneti gra
tia & priuilegio, ut in diplomatis eorundem continetur.

Decoration and illustration **Professional scribes producing manuscript books in around 1450 left spaces for any initials, illustrations and sometimes even words that required larger or red lettering. Their fellow scribes, rubricators, illuminators and miniaturists added these elements and further decoration separately. Most early printed books also had elements of this kind added by hand, commissioned by the owner.**

Gutenberg abandoned his attempt to print some red text in his 42-line Bible. Fust and Schoeffer's 1457 Psalter includes splendid colour-printed initials, a rare exceptional case. Long used for prints, woodcuts became common for book illustrations, decorated initials, borders and occasional words only gradually after 1480, sometimes cut by the illustrators themselves. They could be inked and printed with the type. Albrecht Dürer, in the decades around 1520, epitomized the great age of woodcut illustration.

Intaglio printing remained exceptional in book illustration until the 1560s. The engraved copperplate was inked and the smooth unengraved parts rubbed clean. The ink was transferred from plate to paper by pressing between rollers, requiring illustrations to be printed either as separate plates inserted in the book or by printing the sheets once with copperplates and once letterpress. This and the limited press runs made copperplate illustration expensive, but its finer detail and subtle tonal qualities attracted Christoffel Plantin and other leading printers. Engraving also proved ideal for writing masters' copybooks.

Images etched with acid deteriorated more quickly than engravings, so the large press runs of most book illustrations (unlike art prints) demanded at least some

engraving. Colour printing – by inking one plate or block in several colours or using multiple plates or blocks – could rarely compete with hand colouring.

Small pictorial or decorative elements could be cast like type. From the 1550s, sets of cast decorations (fleurons) were assembled to form large arabesques. This fashion gradually ebbed after 1620, while the 1730s brought new rococo fleurons.

Duplicating larger letters, blocks of text, pictures or decorations demanded other techniques. Woodcuts were duplicated from around 1475, perhaps by sandcasting, and Plantin acquired sandcasts of large woodcut letters in 1574. Type-metal matrices were struck from brass patterns by 1551. Both techniques continued into the eighteenth century, joined by casts in papier mâché (1696) and plaster (1715). Dutch typefounders made sandcasts from wooden, brass and type-metal patterns, and many Dutch printers used cast decorated initials after around 1615. 'Dabbing' (1740) rendered finer details: the pattern was dropped into solidifying type-metal and a duplicate similarly made from the resulting matrix. Typefounders in several countries used this technique extensively from the 1780s until electrotyping supplanted it in about 1840. JAL

1538 **Hans Holbein the Younger** *Les simulachres & historiees faces de la mort*. Lyon: Melchior & Gaspar Trechsel, 1538. 18 cm. Illustrator: Hans Holbein the Younger. Woodblock cutter: Hans Lützelburger.

In his hometown of Basel, painter and draughtsman Hans Holbein the Younger (1497–1543) designed hundreds of decorative initials for prominent publishers such as Johann Froben. In doing so, he left his individual mark on the visual style of sixteenth-century books. When the iconoclastic Protestants came to power in Basel, Holbein left for England, where he became a highly regarded portrait painter.

Holbein's *Les simulachres & historiees faces de la mort*, commonly called *The Dance of Death*, was published in Lyon in 1538. The theme of this series of woodcuts is death. They were made in the 1520s by the virtuoso Hans Lützelburger (*fl. c.* 1517–26?) who, from 1523 onwards, worked almost exclusively for Holbein. *Les simulachres* begins with the Book of Genesis. Each page consists of a biblical quote, an illustration, and a quatrain. The illustrations show figures from all walks of life, both rich and poor, thus indicating the universality of death.

The brothers Melchior and Gaspar Trechsel were well-known Lyon printers with international connections. *Les simulachres* seems slightly old-fashioned because of the typefaces the book is set in. The copy shown here reinforces this impression because lines have been drawn in pen to indicate the blocks of text, which gives the book the character of a medieval manuscript. PD

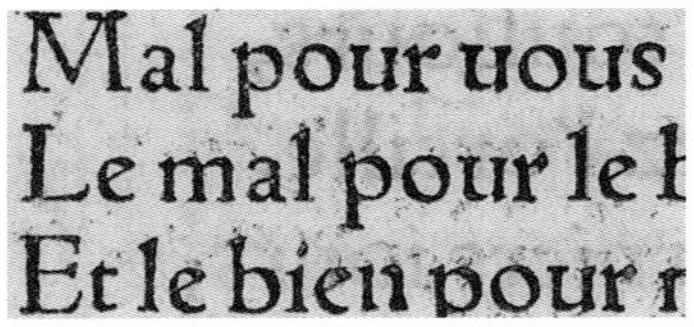

Although Parisian romans in the Aldine style appeared in 1530, only the largest size ('Canon', unknown among Venetian romans) saw extensive use elsewhere before 1550. The roman used here follows the popular style introduced in *c.* 1512, perhaps by the punchcutter Peter Schoeffer II, whose work awaits further study.

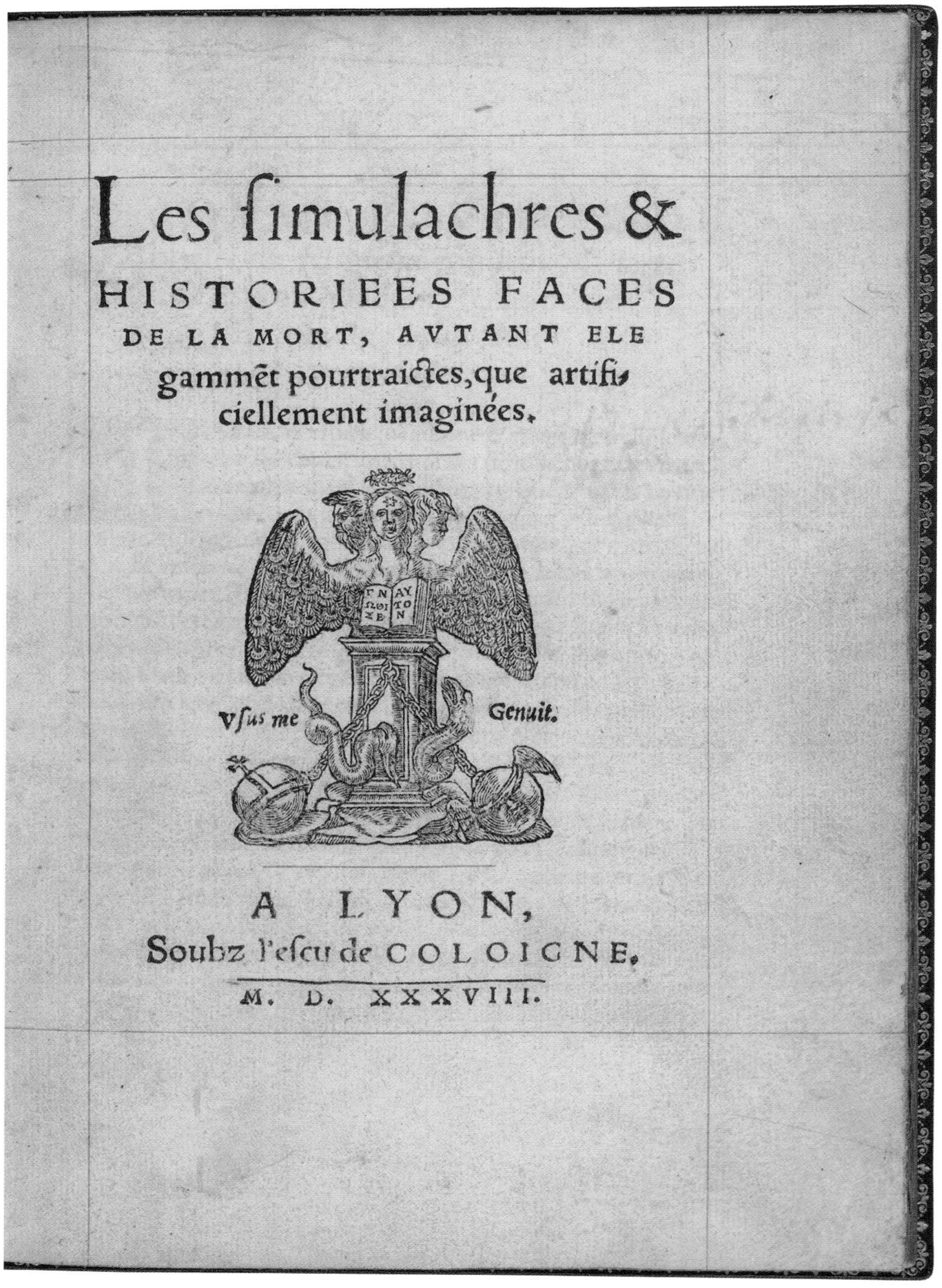

Les simulachres &
HISTORIEES FACES
DE LA MORT, AVTANT ELE
gammẽt pourtraictes, que artifi-
ciellement imaginées.

A LYON,
Soubz l'escu de COLOIGNE.
M. D. XXXVIII.

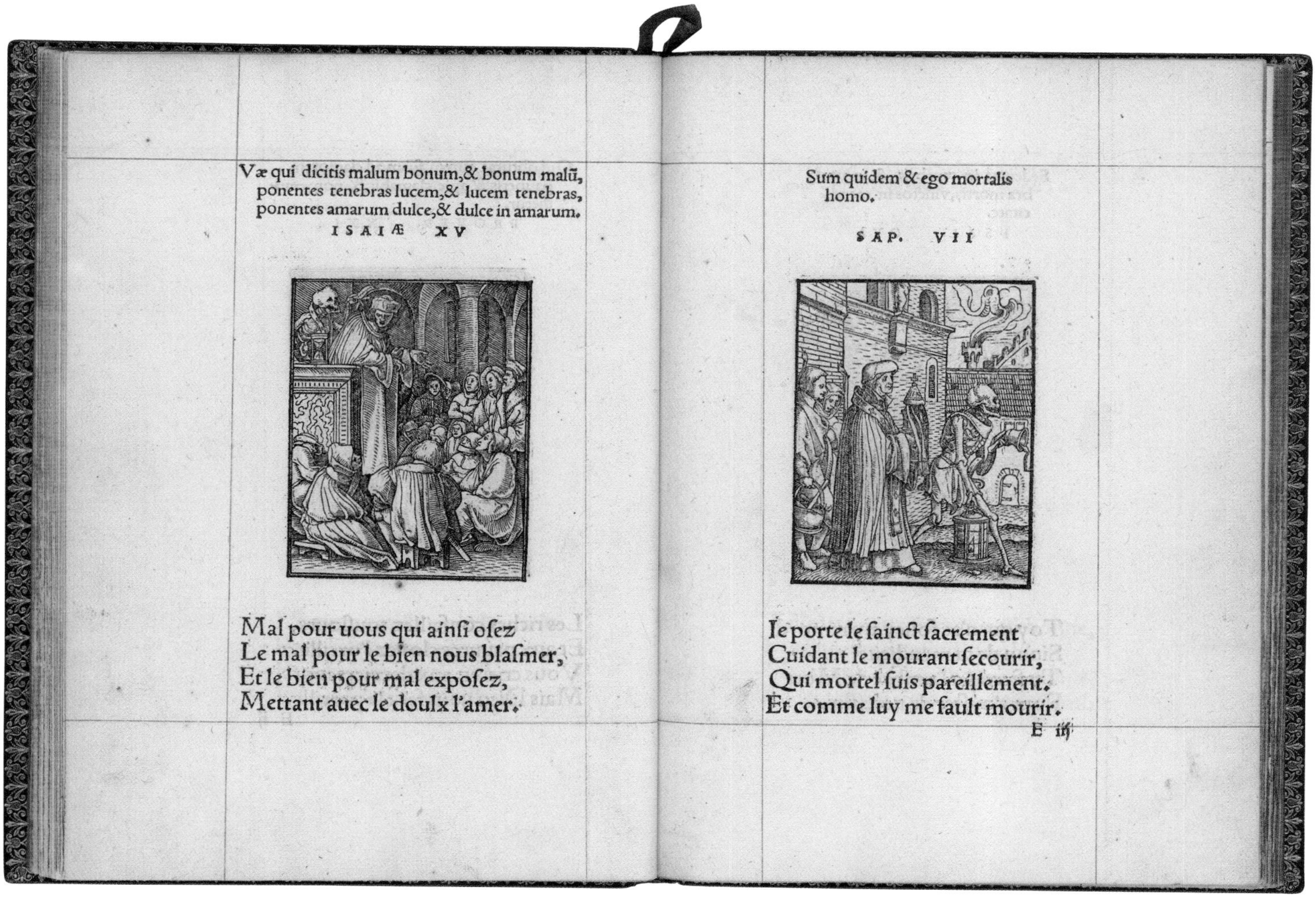

Væ qui dicitis malum bonum, & bonum malũ, ponentes tenebras lucem, & lucem tenebras, ponentes amarum dulce, & dulce in amarum.

ISAIÆ XV

Mal pour uous qui ainſi oſez
Le mal pour le bien nous blaſmer,
Et le bien pour mal expoſez,
Mettant auec le doulx l'amer.

Sum quidem & ego mortalis homo.

SAP. VII

Ie porte le ſainct ſacrement
Cuidant le mourant ſecourir,
Qui mortel ſuis pareillement.
Et comme luy me fault mourir.

E iij

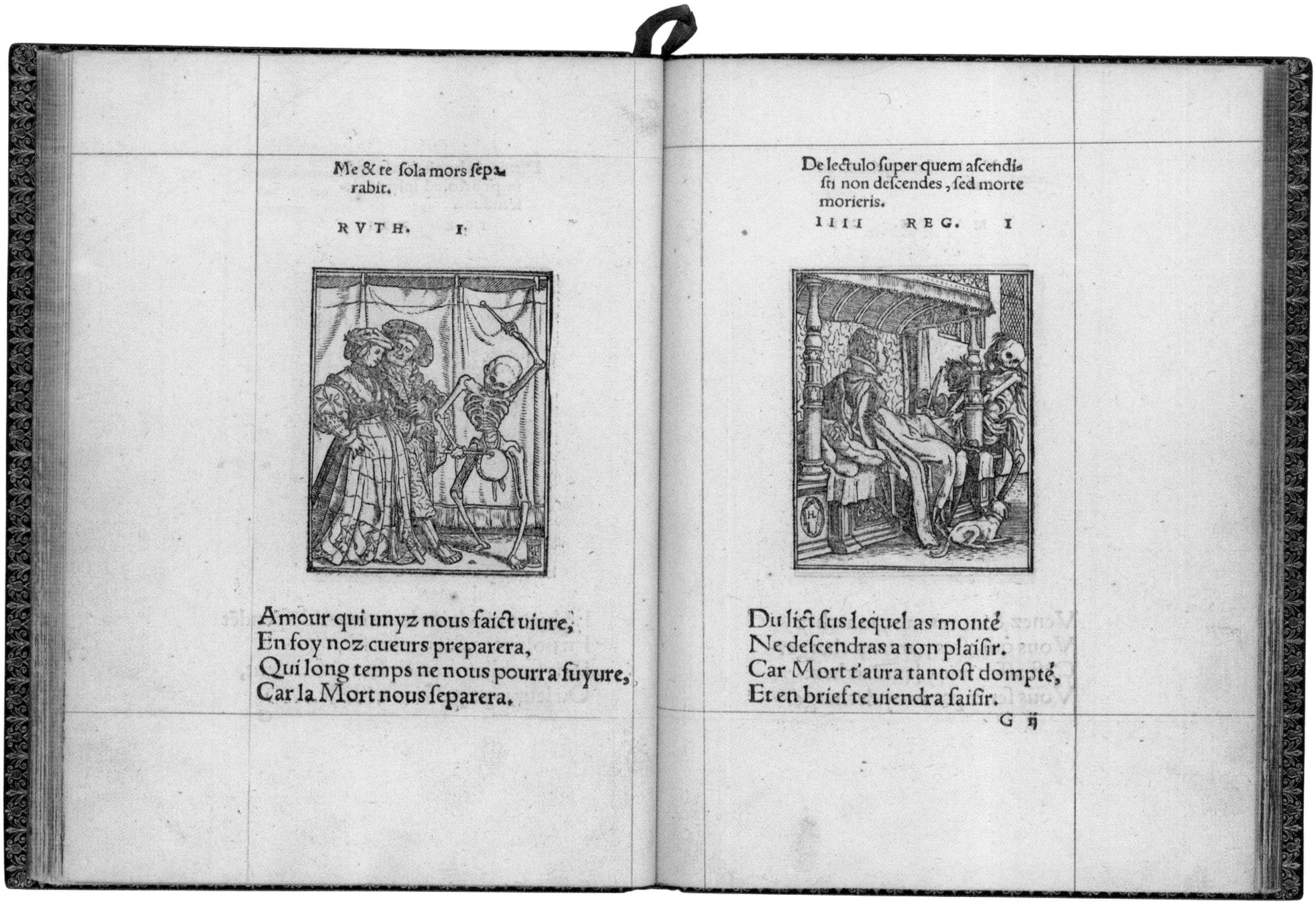

Me & te ſola mors ſeparabit.

RVTH. I

Amour qui unyz nous faict uiure,
En foy noz cueurs preparera,
Qui long temps ne nous pourra ſuyure,
Car la Mort nous ſeparera.

De lectulo ſuper quem aſcendiſti non deſcendes, ſed morte morieris.

IIII REG. I

Du lict ſus lequel as monté
Ne deſcendras a ton plaiſir.
Car Mort t'aura tantoſt dompté,
Et en brief te uiendra ſaiſir.

G ij

1538 **Robert Estienne** *Biblia*. Paris: Robert Estienne, 1538–40. 4 volumes. 47.5 cm.

Robert Estienne (1503–59), using the Latinized name of Robertus Stephanus, was the most important descendant of a family of scholarly French printers. His Bible editions provoked attacks from powerful conservatives at the Sorbonne, Paris's Catholic university. Eventually, Robert Estienne relocated to Geneva, where he became a Protestant. This Vulgate Bible is one of the finest editions he prepared and a good example of classical sixteenth-century French typography.

The type page has perfect proportions, with a traditional French running headline in a beautiful, large lower case, which was also used for the chapter titles. The notes are set in the fore-edge and back margins. There are also letters (a, b, c, etc.) in the margins, for ease of reference. In a later Bible edition, Estienne introduced the chapter and verse numbering which is still in use today. Paragraphs start with a drop cap: a large initial letter that drops down over several lines. The frequently used abbreviations had already fallen into disuse many years previously.

In the copy shown here, hand-drawn lines have been added to highlight the typographic structure of the page. These lines (and similar additions) are frequently found in sixteenth-century books. They usually date from the nineteenth century, and probably served to lend style to books, much like the medieval buildings were 'restored' by Viollet-le-Duc at that time. PD

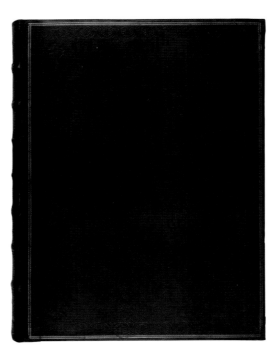

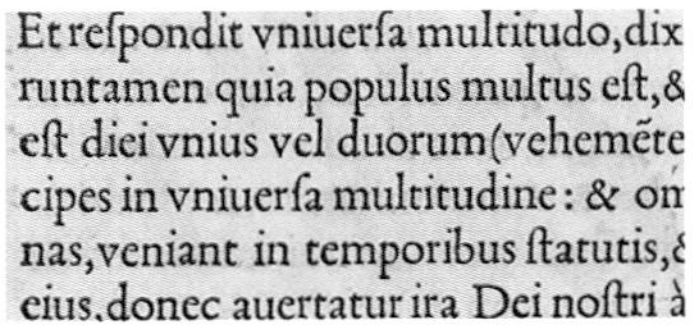

Et respondit vniuersa multitudo,dix
runtamen quia populus multus est,&
est diei vnius vel duorum(vehemẽte
cipes in vniuersa multitudine: & om
nas,veniant in temporibus statutis,&
eius.donec auertatur ira Dei nostri à

Seminal types of the highest quality, Estienne's exclusive roman and accompanying heading type (1530) brought Aldine-style romans to Paris and were the first to provide a full range of matching romans. Now attributed to 'Maitre Constantin' (d. c. 1533), they were formerly credited to Claude Garamont, who copied them for the open market and developed the style further.

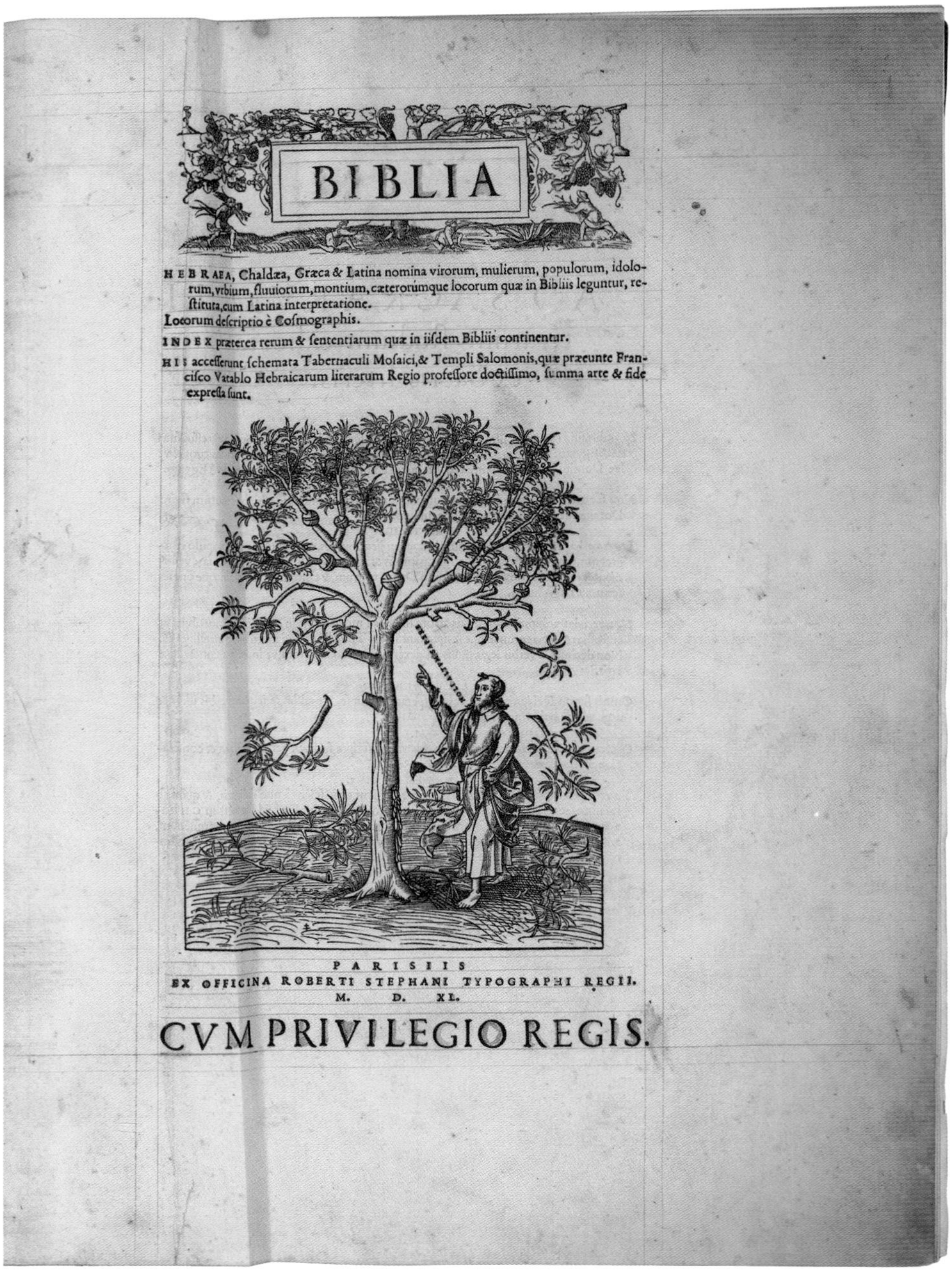

BIBLIA

HEBRAEA, Chaldæa, Græca & Latina nomina virorum, mulierum, populorum, idolorum, vrbium, fluuiorum, montium, cæterorúmque locorum quæ in Bibliis leguntur, restituta, cum Latina interpretatione.
Locorum descriptio è Cosmographis.
INDEX præterea rerum & sententiarum quæ in iisdem Bibliis continentur.
HII accesserunt schemata Tabernaculi Mosaici, & Templi Salomonis, quæ præeunte Francisco Vatablo Hebraicarum literarum Regio professore doctissimo, summa arte & fide expressa sunt.

PARISIIS
EX OFFICINA ROBERTI STEPHANI TYPOGRAPHI REGII.
M. D. XL.

CVM PRIVILEGIO REGIS.

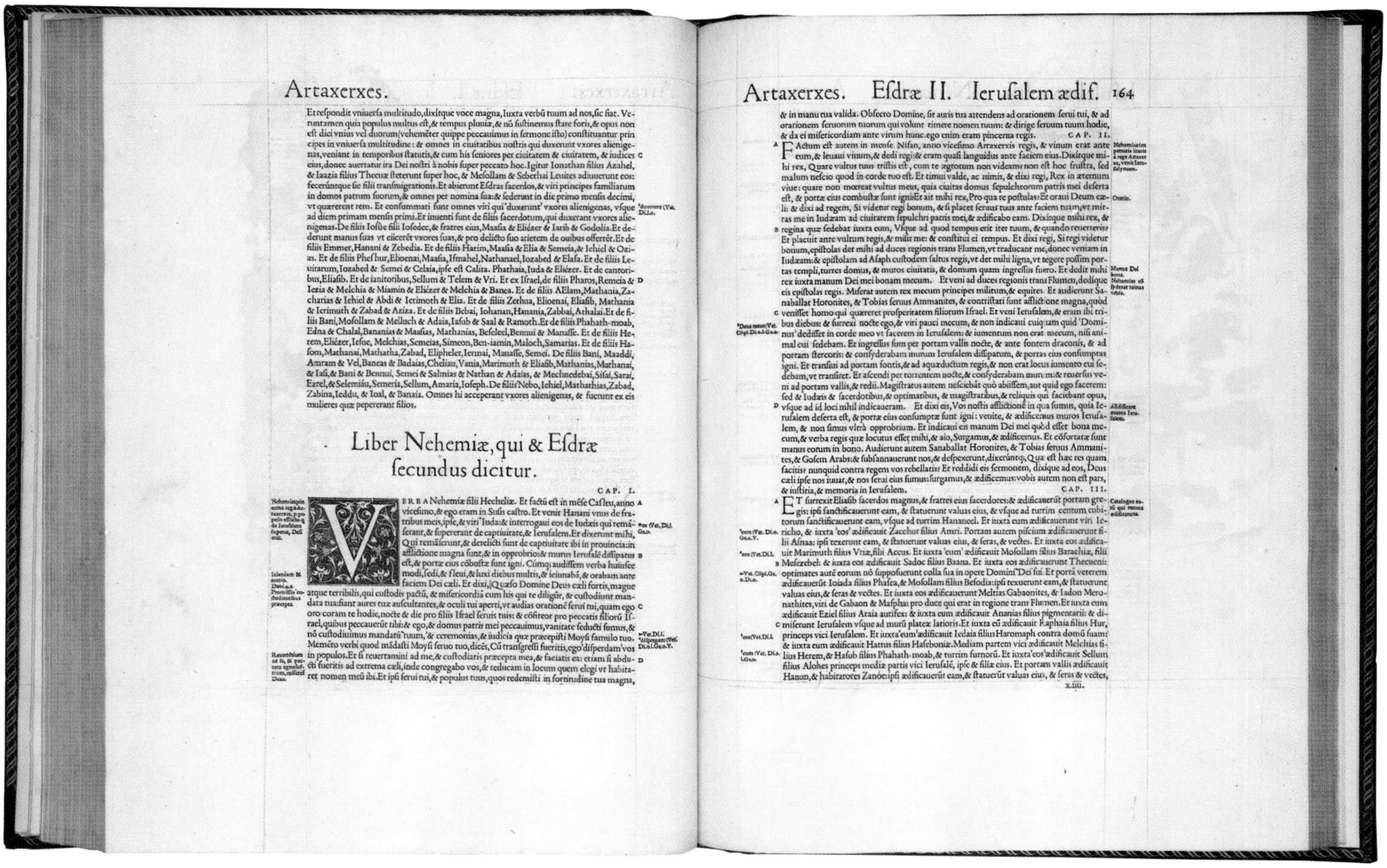

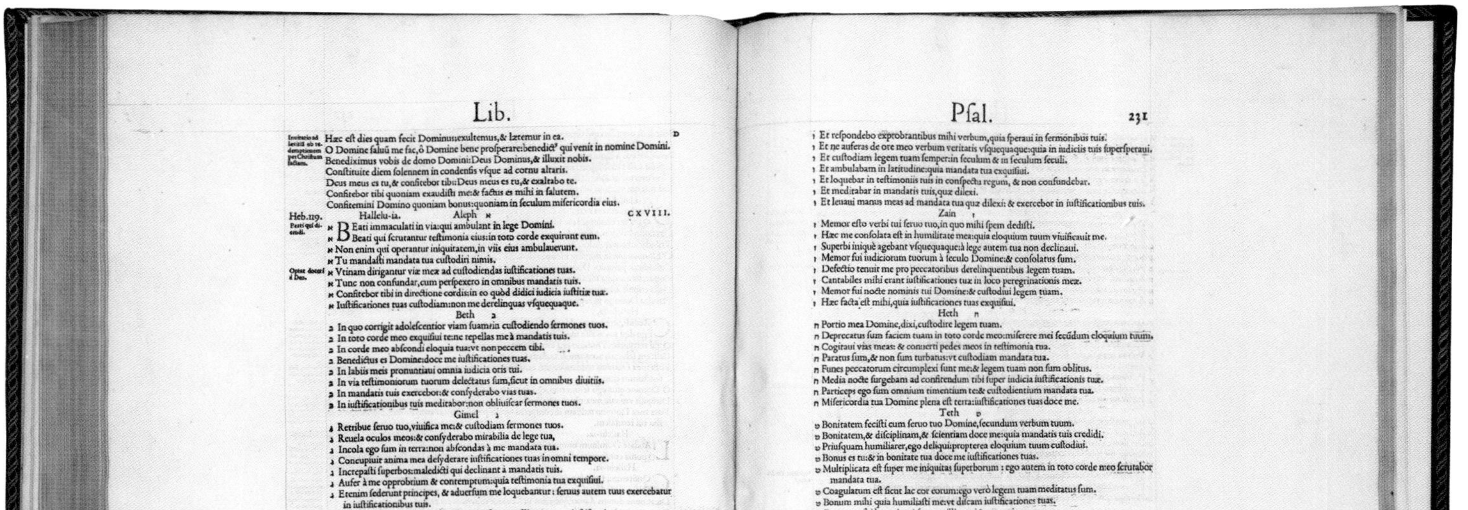

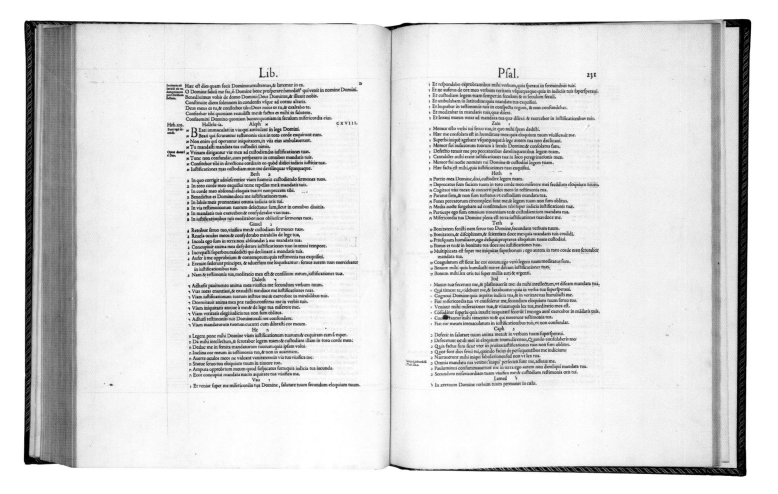

Robert Estienne

1543 **Andreas Vesalius** Andreas Vesalius, *De humani corporis fabrica*. Basel: Johannes Oporinus, 1543. 663 pp. 42 cm.

Illustrators: attributed to Jan Steven van Calcar and workshop of Titian.

De humani corporis fabrica ('On the fabric of the human body'), by the Brussels-born physician Andreas Vesalius (Andries van Wesel), marks the birth of human anatomy as a science. It contains an elaborate, accurate, clearly structured and illustrated account of dissections performed by the author. Empirical research replaces the customary reiteration of accepted views dating from classical antiquity, especially those of Galen. Vesalius, who was a lecturer at the University of Padua, commissioned Johannes Oporinus (1507–68), also a physician, to print and publish the book. Oporinus worked across the Alps in Basel, then an important centre of book production.

The introduction by Vesalius gives a clear insight into the relationship between the author and the printer, and shows Vesalius as not only a scientist but also a co-designer, who partly determines the typography. He also expresses his concern for the accuracy of the text and his fear of unauthorized reprints, which might lack this textual accuracy. A reference system connects the large woodcuts – now renowned – with the text.

The monumental volume is technically perfect. The roman typeface used has an old-fashioned flavour; it was not until the second edition in 1555 that new French typefaces in the Garamont style were utilized.

The book brought Vesalius lasting fame and also resulted in his appointment as imperial physician to the court of Charles V. It was frequently plagiarized. FAJ

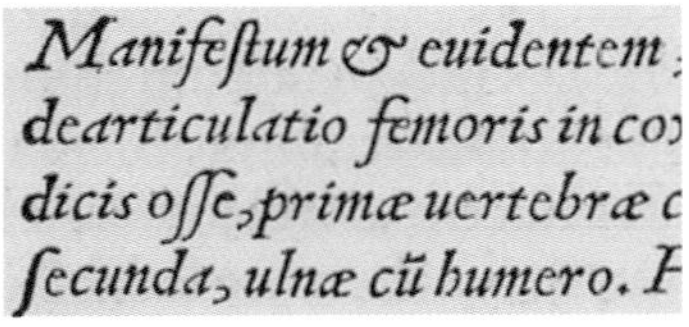
Manifeſtum & euidentem ;
dearticulatio femoris in co
dicis oſſe, primæ uertebræ c
ſecunda, ulnæ cū humero. F

The first successful italic with sloped capitals, attributed to Peter Schoeffer II, quickly spread from Lyon (1537) and Basel (1538) to the rest of Europe. Robert Granjon and others refined its combination of Aldine and chancery styles to establish a new style that reigned into the eighteenth century.

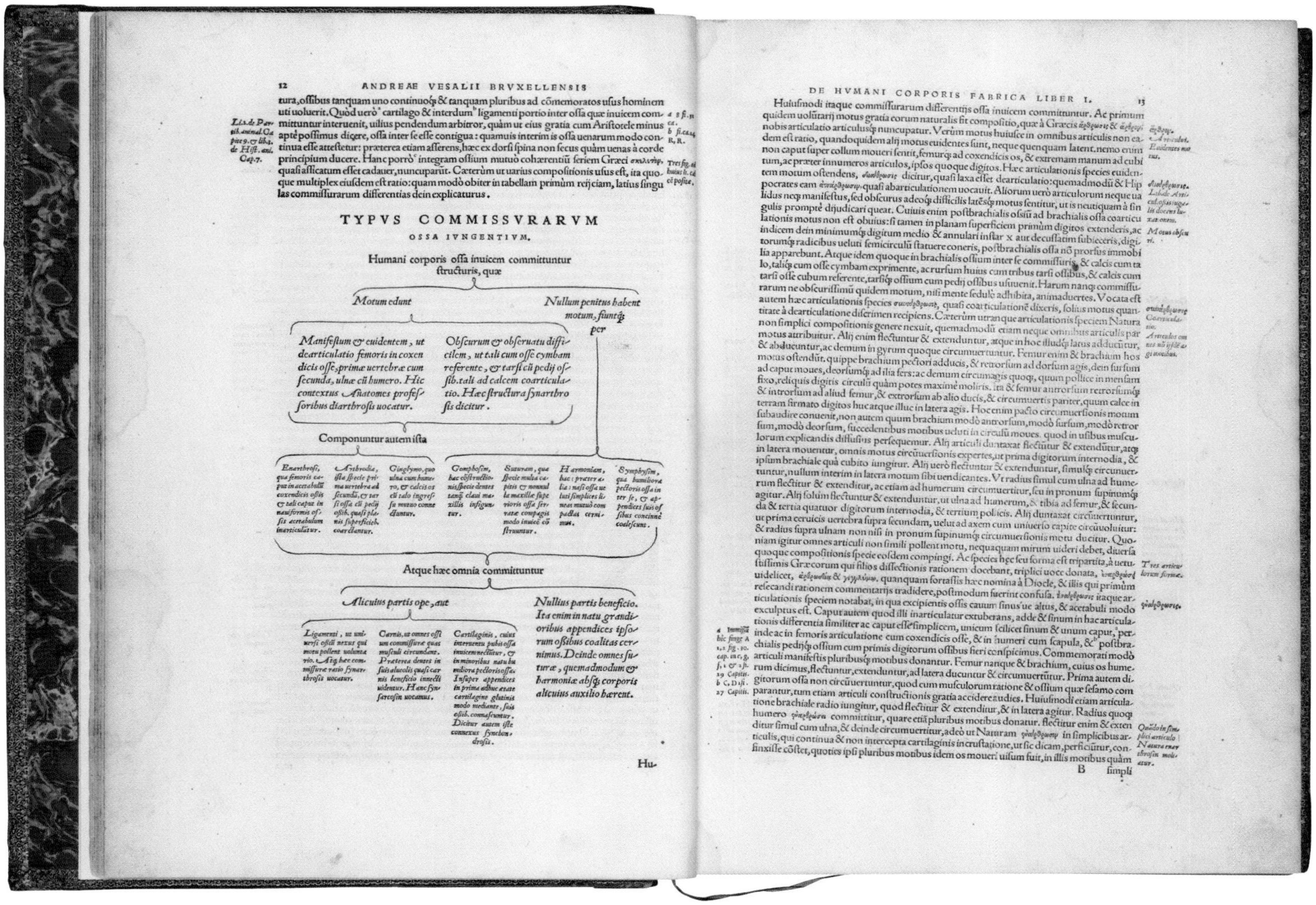
12 ANDREAE VESALII BRVXELLENSIS
TYPVS COMMISSVRARVM
OSSA IVNGENTIVM.
Humani corporis ossa inuicem committuntur structuris, quæ
Motum edunt
Nullum penitus habent motum, suntque per
Componuntur autem ista
Atque hæc omnia committuntur
Alicuius partis ope, aut
DE HVMANI CORPORIS FABRICA LIBER I. 13

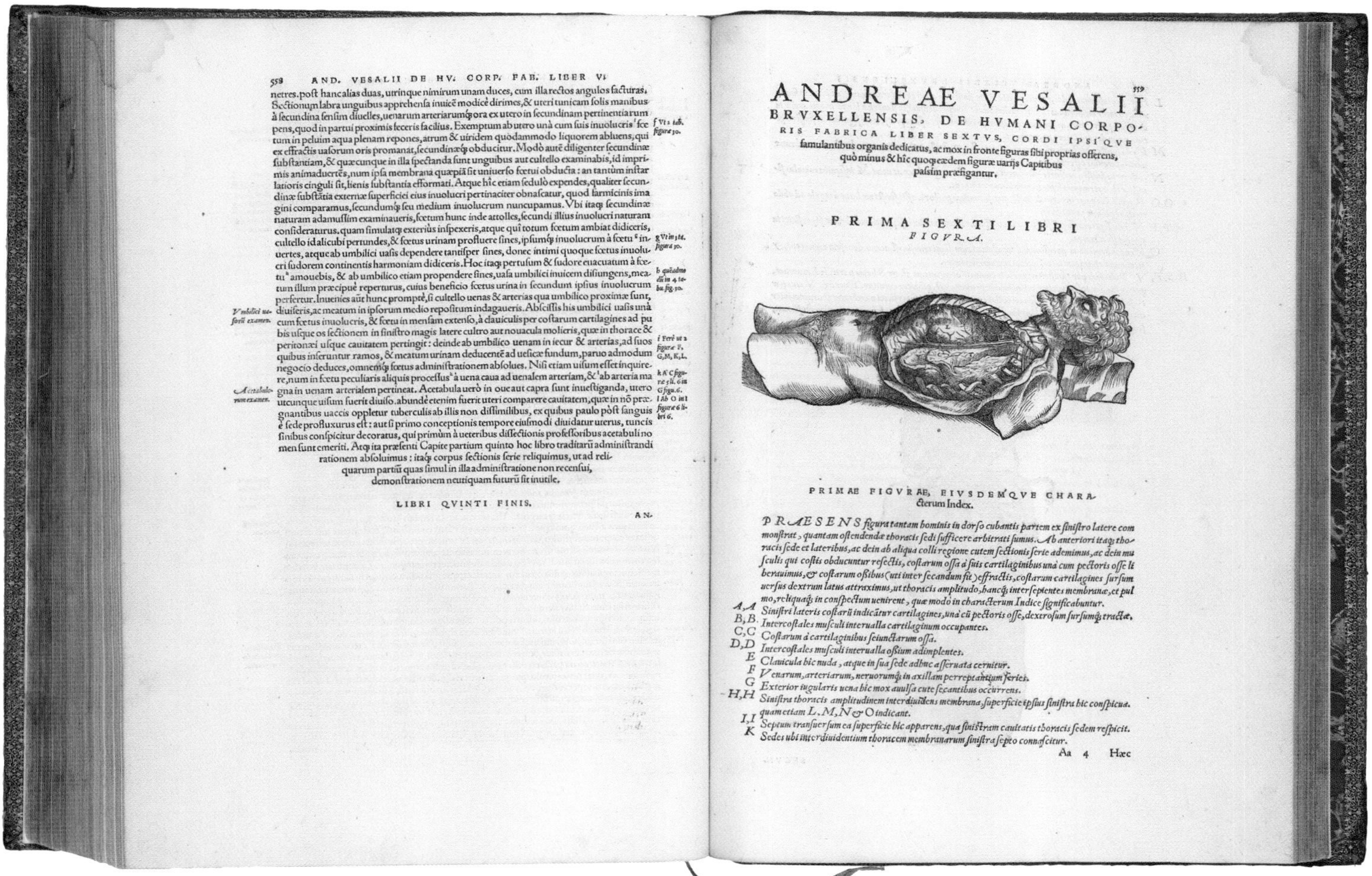
558 AND. VESALII DE HV. CORP. FAB. LIBER VI
LIBRI QVINTI FINIS.
ANDREAE VESALII
BRVXELLENSIS, DE HVMANI CORPORIS FABRICA LIBER SEXTVS, CORDI IPSIQVE
PRIMA SEXTI LIBRI
FIGVRA.
PRIMAE FIGVRAE, EIVSDEMQVE CHARACterum Index.

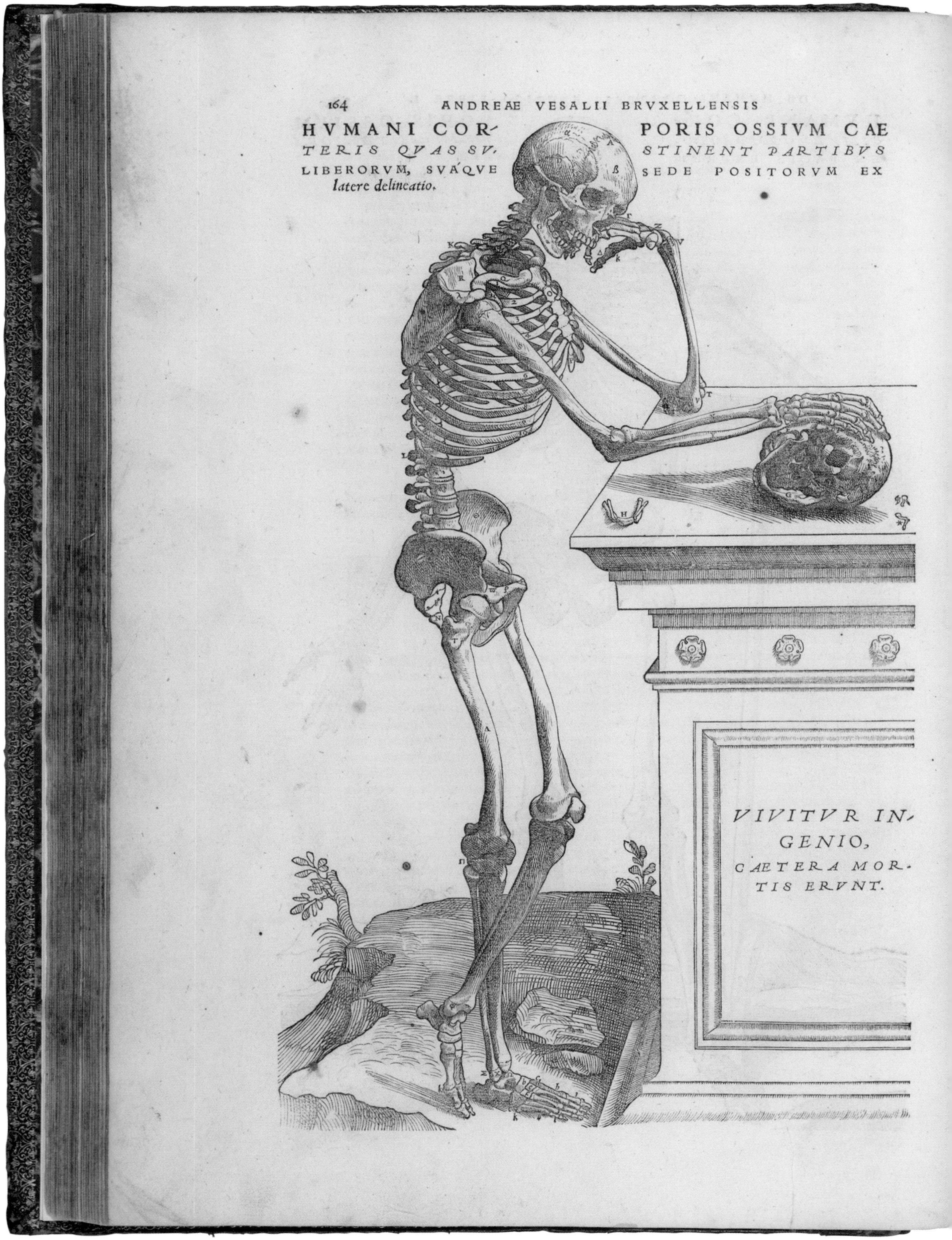
164 ANDREAE VESALII BRVXELLENSIS
HVMANI COR- PORIS OSSIVM CAE
TERIS QVAS SV- STINENT PARTIBVS
LIBERORVM, SVÁQVE SEDE POSITORVM EX
latere delineatio.
VIVITVR IN-
GENIO,
CAETERA MOR-
TIS ERVNT.

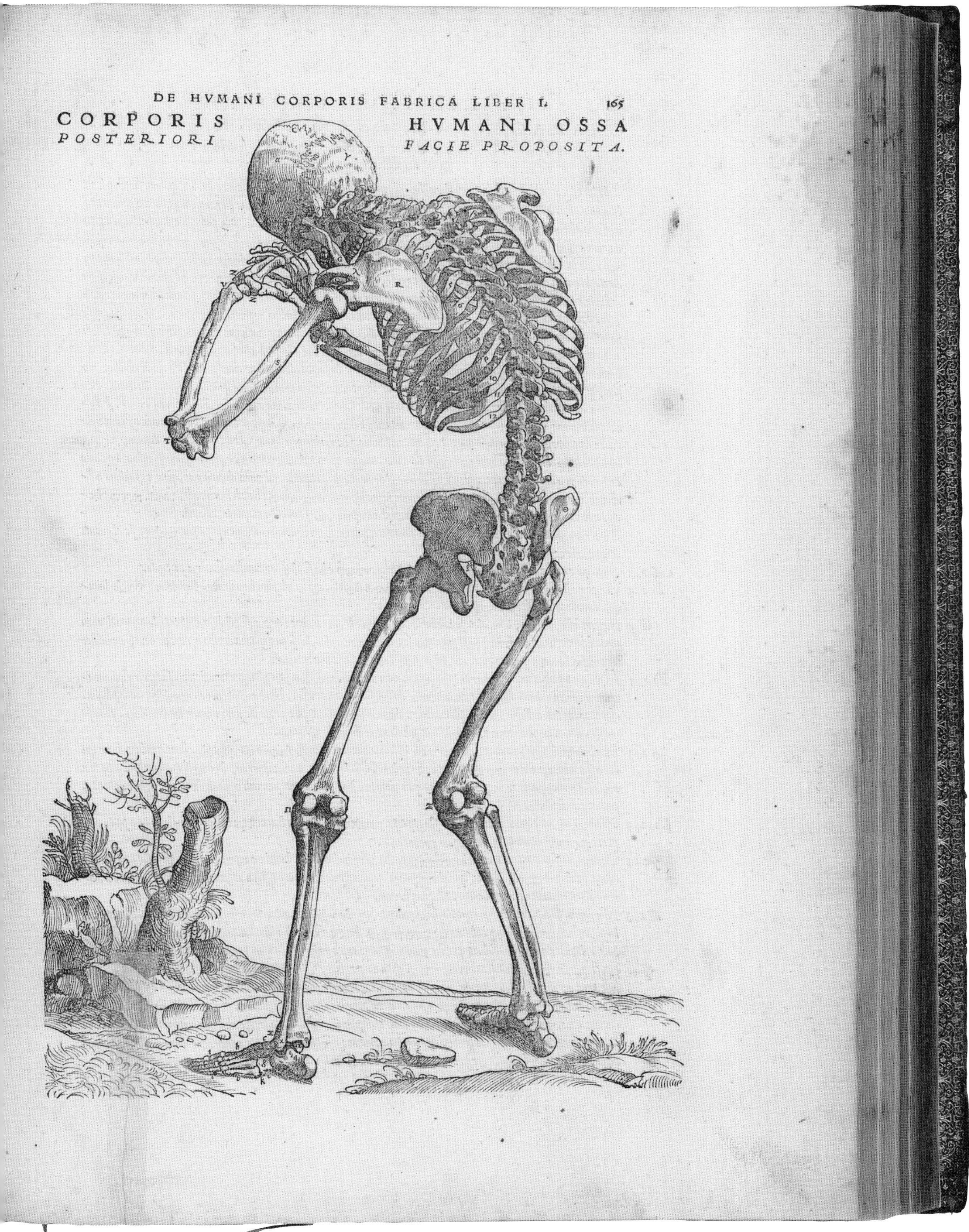
DE HVMANI CORPORIS FABRICA LIBER I. 165
CORPORIS HVMANI OSSA
POSTERIORI FACIE PROPOSITA.

1545 **Simon de Colines** Charles Estienne, *De dissectione partium corporis humani libri tres*. Paris: Simon de Colines, 1545.

375 pp. 38 cm. Illustrators: Jean 'Mercure' Jollat and others.

Charles Estienne (1505–64) was the son of the printer Henri Estienne I, and the stepson of Simon de Colines (d. 1546), the printer of the book shown here. Colines is considered to be the greatest typographic innovator of the French Renaissance. In little over a quarter of a century, he produced some eight hundred publications, which are admired for their typographic design.

Estienne started his career as a physician and academic. In 1550 he took over the family business and became a printer-publisher. The Estiennes were scholars first, and printers second. This is reflected in their publications. Technical quality was not always their first concern; their typesetting and printing, at times, lack the appropriate care. However, in content and subject matter, the books produced by the Estiennes tower high above those of their contemporaries.

The illustrations in Estienne's *De dissectione* date from the early 1530s, long before Vesalius's epoch-making 1543 edition. Because of a copyright conflict with the surgeon Étienne de La Rivière – who is mentioned for his contributions – *De dissectione* came out after the publication of Vesalius's book.

De dissectione is famous for its illustrations. The anatomical parts of the illustrations are placed within the whole as separate wooden blocks. The reason might be that the woodcuts are based on contemporary erotic prints. Men and women are shown sitting or reclining in languorous positions that have little to do with anatomy. The interior of the relevant body parts is shown, which creates an alienating effect. PD

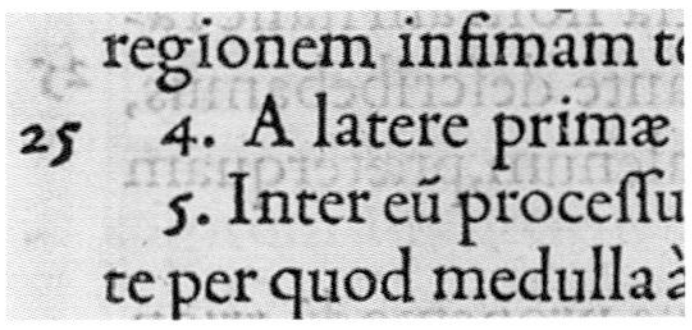

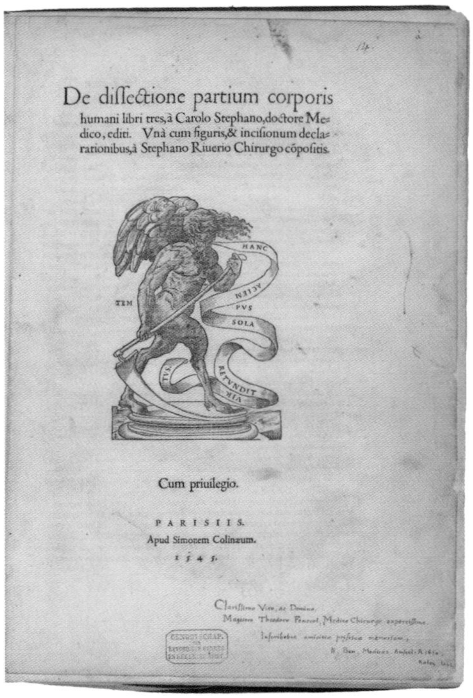

Colines foreshadowed the 'Aldine revolution' in Paris, introducing new romans (some of his own cutting) influenced by Italian models. After Estienne's punchcutter (Constantin?, 1530) and Augereau (1531) introduced full-fledged Aldine romans, Colines revised his types, this one from 1528 in 1533. Garamont soon became the style's greatest master.

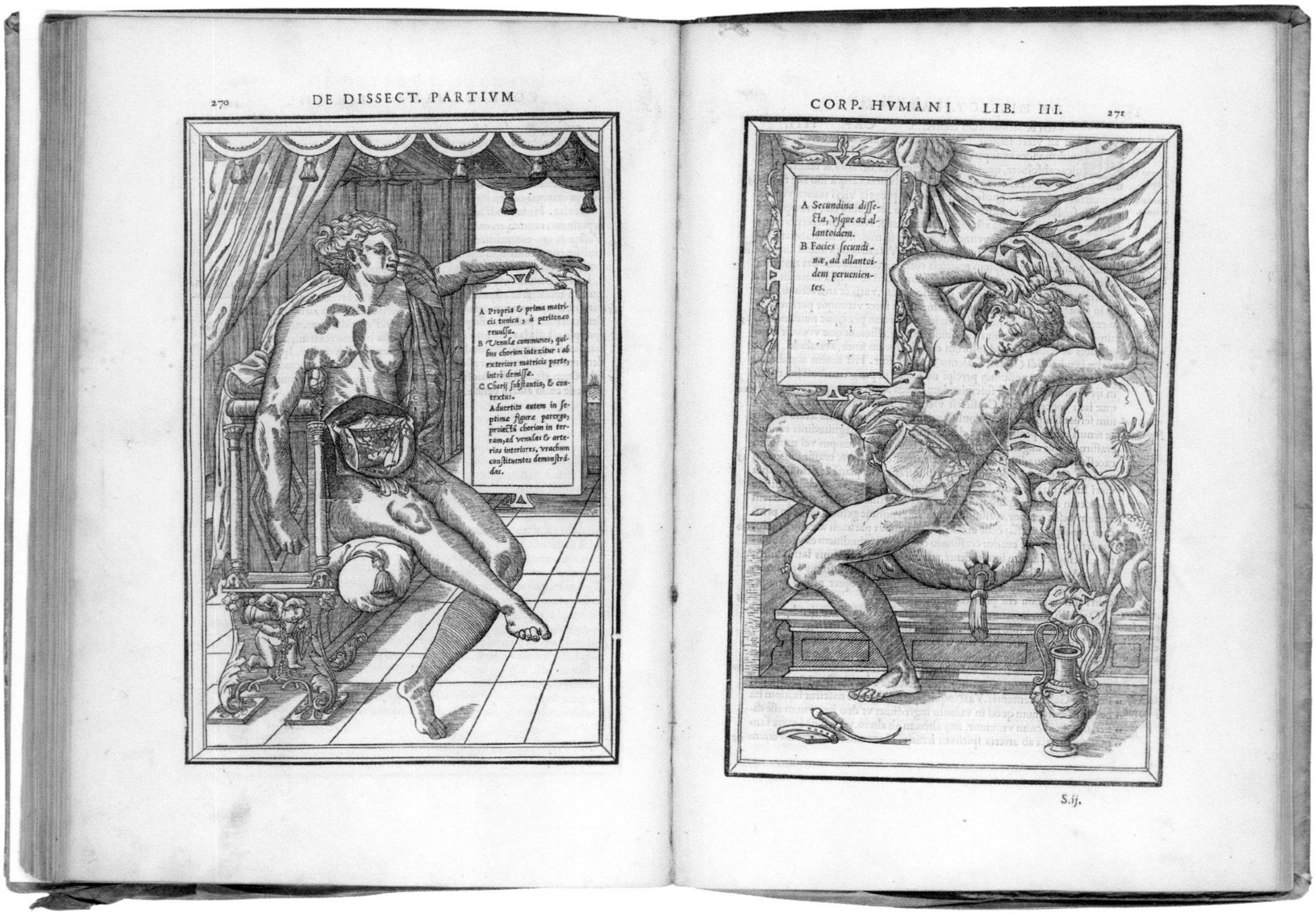

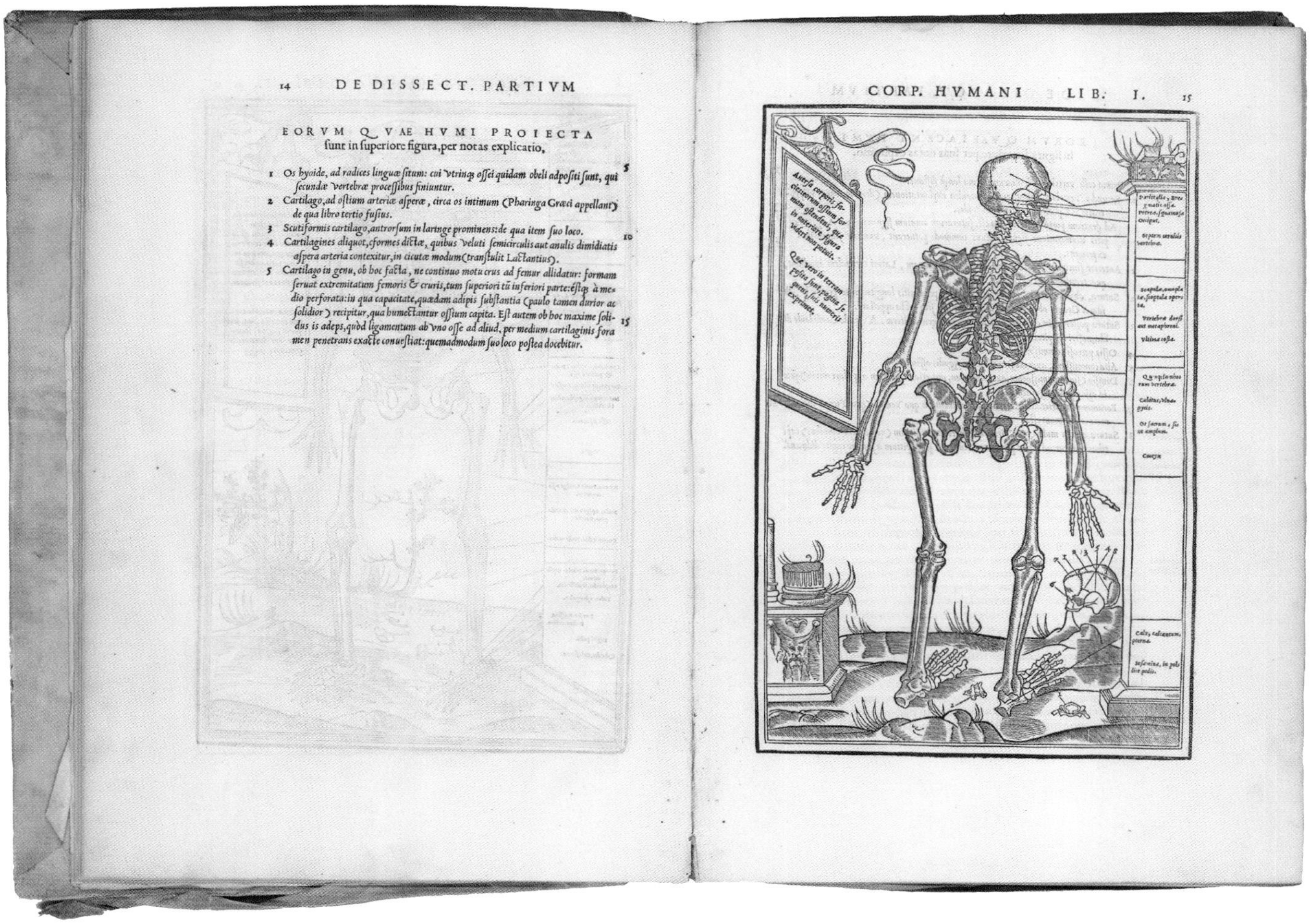

EORVM QVAE HVMI PROIECTA sunt in superiore figura, per notas explicatio,

1 Os hyoide, ad radices linguæ situm: cui vtrinque ossei quidam obeli adpositi sunt, qui secundæ vertebræ processibus finiuntur.
2 Cartilago, ad ostium arteriæ asperæ, circa os intimum (Pharinga Græci appellant) de qua libro tertio fusius.
3 Scutiformis cartilago, antrorsum in laringe prominens: de qua item suo loco.
4 Cartilagines aliquot, cformes dictæ, quibus veluti semicirculis aut anulis dimidiatis aspera arteria contexitur, in cicutæ modum (transtulit Lactantius).
5 Cartilago in genu, ob hoc facta, ne continuo motu crus ad femur allidatur: formam seruat extremitatum femoris & cruris, tum superiori tũ inferiori parte: éstque à medio perforata: in qua capacitate, quædam adipis substantia (paulo tamen durior ac solidior) recipitur, qua humectantur ossium capita. Est autem ob hoc maxime solidus is adeps, quòd ligamentum ab vno osse ad aliud, per medium cartilaginis foramen penetrans exacte conuestiat: quemadmodum suo loco postea docebitur.

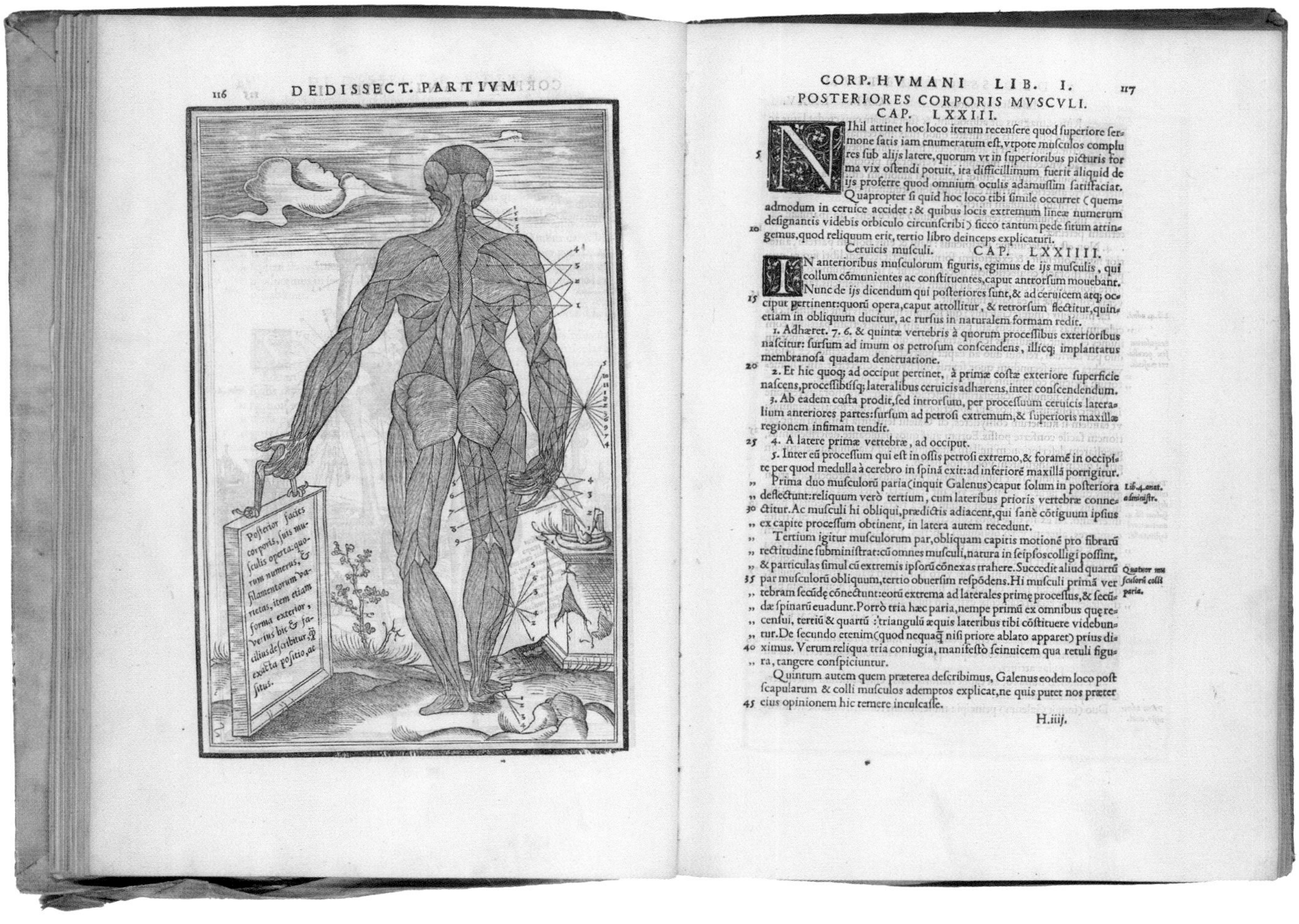

POSTERIORES CORPORIS MVSCVLI.
CAP. LXXIII.

Nihil attinet hoc loco iterum recensere quod superiore sermone satis iam enumeratum est, vtpote musculos complures sub alijs latere, quorum vt in superioribus picturis forma vix ostendi potuit, ita difficillimum fuerit aliquid de ijs proferre quod omnium oculis adamussim satisfaciat. Quapropter si quid hoc loco tibi simile occurret (quemadmodum in ceruice accidet: & quibus locis extremum lineæ numerum designantis videbis orbiculo circunscribi) sicco tantum pede situm attingemus, quod reliquum erit, tertio libro deinceps explicaturi.

Ceruicis musculi. CAP. LXXIIII.

In anterioribus musculorum figuris, egimus de ijs musculis, qui collum cõmunientes ac constituentes, caput antrorsum mouebant. Nunc de ijs dicendum qui posteriores sunt, & ad ceruicem atque occiput pertinent: quorũ opera, caput attollitur, & retrorsum flectitur, quinetiam in obliquum ducitur, ac rursus in naturalem formam redit.

1. Adhæret. 7. 6. & quintæ vertebris à quorum processibus exterioribus nascitur: sursum ad imum os petrosum conscendens, illícque implantatus membranosa quadam deneruatione.

2. Et hic quoque ad occiput pertinet, à primæ costæ exteriore superficie nascens, processibúsque lateralibus ceruicis adhærens, inter conscendendum.

3. Ab eadem costa prodit, sed introrsum, per processuum ceruicis lateralium anteriores partes: sursum ad petrosi extremum, & superioris maxillæ regionem infimam tendit.

4. A latere primæ vertebræ, ad occiput.

5. Inter eũ processum qui est in ossis petrosi extremo, & foramẽ in occipite per quod medulla à cerebro in spinã exit: ad inferiorẽ maxillã porrigitur.

Prima duo musculorũ paria (inquit Galenus) caput solum in posteriora deflectunt: reliquum verò tertium, cum lateribus prioris vertebræ connectitur. Ac musculi hi obliqui, prædictis adiacent, qui sanè cõtiguum ipsius ex capite processum obtinent, in latera autem recedunt. *Lib. 4. anat. administr.*

Tertium igitur musculorum par, obliquam capitis motionẽ pro fibrarũ rectitudine subministrat: cũ omnes musculi, natura in seipsos colligi possint, & particulas simul cũ extremis ipsorũ cõnexas trahere. Succedit aliud quartũ par musculorũ obliquum, tertio obuersim respõdens. Hi musculi primã vertebram secũdę cõnectunt: eorũ extrema ad laterales primę processus, & secũdæ spinarũ euadunt. Porrò tria hæc paria, nempe primũ ex omnibus quę recensui, tertiũ & quartũ triangulũ æquis lateribus tibi cõstituere videbuntur. De secundo etenim (quod nequaquam nisi priore ablato apparet) prius diximus. Verum reliqua tria coniugia, manifestò seinuicem qua retuli figura, tangere conspiciuntur. *Quatuor musculorũ colli paria.*

Quintum autem quem præterea describimus, Galenus eodem loco post scapularum & colli musculos ademptos explicat, ne quis putet nos præter eius opinionem hic temere inculcasse.

H.iiij.

1546 **Jacques Kerver** **Francesco Colonna, *Hypnerotomachie, ou discours du songe de Poliphile*. Paris: Jacques Kerver, 1546. 157 leaves. 32.5 cm. Illustrator: attributed to Jean Cousin and Jean Goujon. Printer: Louis Cyaneus.**

An anonymous translation of Francesco Colonna's *Hypnerotomachia* (see page 54) was published by the Parisian printer Jacques Kerver (d. 1583) in 1546, one year after the publication of the second edition by Aldus Manutius's son. The subtitle of the translation reads 'Discourse on the dream of Poliphilus'. On the title page, which has a woodcut border in the Fontainebleau style, Italian influences are abandoned in favour of French Renaissance typography; various romans are used, as well as italic capitals. Furthermore, romans, capitals, and italics are used in the chapter headings. The roman used for the main text is a French design; it is one of the many types cut in Paris in around 1540 that were based on Griffo roman, the roman used in the 1499 *Hypnerotomachia*. The woodcuts and typographic layout are modelled after the 1499 edition. In some places, although not consistently, paragraphs are indicated by indents.

This edition and its reprints (1554, 1561, and 1600) gave France the opportunity to acquaint itself thoroughly with the Renaissance perception of classical antiquity. FAJ

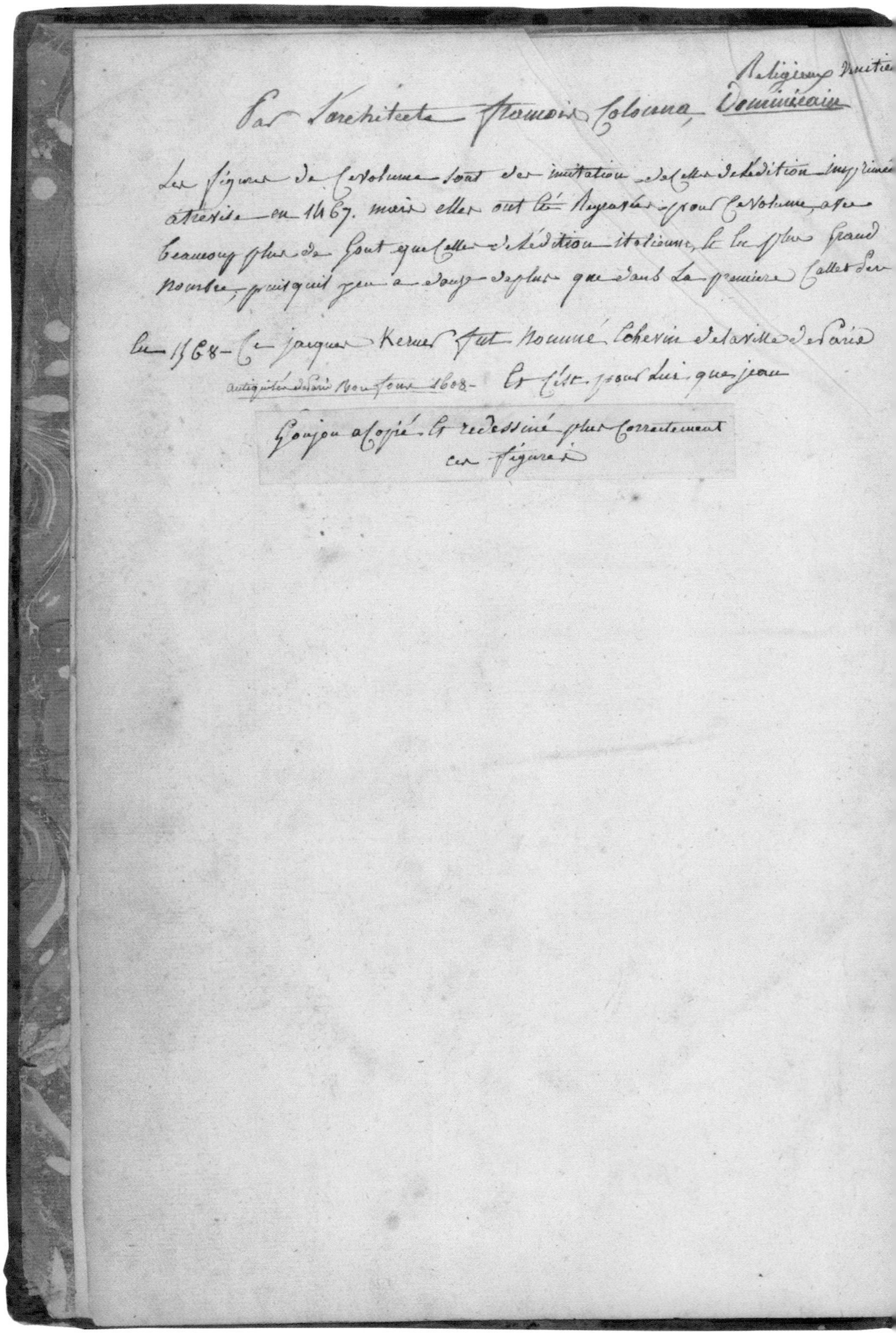

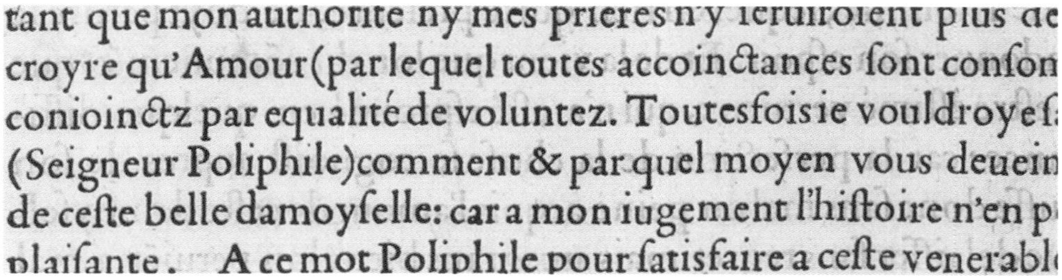
tant que mon authorite ny mes prieres n'y ſeruiroient plus de
croyre qu'Amour (par lequel toutes accoinctances ſont conſon
conioinctz par equalité de voluntez. Toutesfois ie vouldroye ſ
(Seigneur Poliphile) comment & par quel moyen vous deuein
de ceſte belle damoyſelle: car a mon iugement l'hiſtoire n'en p
plaiſante. A ce mot Poliphile pour ſatisfaire a ceſte venerabl

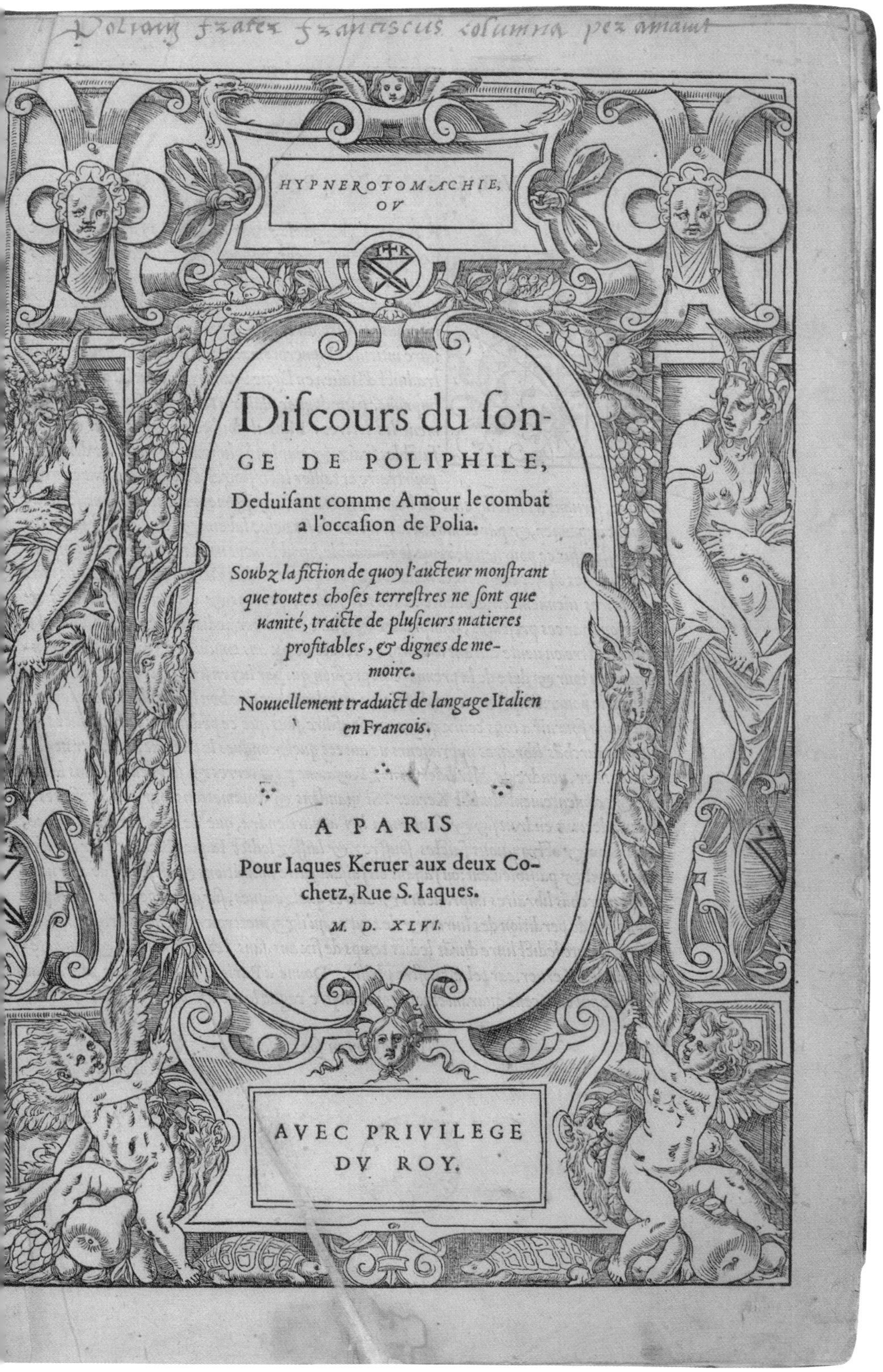
HYPNEROTOMACHIE, OV

Diſcours du ſonge de Poliphile,
Deduiſant comme Amour le combat a l'occaſion de Polia.

Soubz la fiction de quoy l'aucteur monſtrant que toutes choſes terreſtres ne ſont que uanité, traicte de pluſieurs matieres profitables, & dignes de memoire.

Nouuellement traduict de langage Italien en Francois.

A PARIS
Pour Iaques Keruer aux deux Cochetz, Rue S. Iaques.
M. D. XLVI.

AVEC PRIVILEGE DV ROY.

Claude Garamont (c. 1510–61) probably cut this roman (1539) and almost certainly the italic in the headings (1541, still with upright capitals). These are some of the earliest types to demonstrate the remarkable talent that he was to refine over the next two decades.

LIVRE PREMIER DE

Hercinia ſylua.

qui me feit doubter d'eſtre arriué en la foreſt noire, en laquelle ne repairent fors beſtes ſauuaiges & dangereuſes : pour crainte deſquelles ie m'efforceay a mõ poſſible de chercher vne brieue yſſue:et me mey de faict a courir ſans tenir voye ne ſentier, ny ſauoir quele part me deuoie adreſſer, ſouuent trebuchant parmy les troncz & eſtocz des arbres qui lá eſtoient a fleur de terre. I'alloie aucunesfois auãt, puis tout court tournoie en arriere, ores en vn coſté, tantoſt en l'autre, les mains & le viſage deſſirez de ronces, chardons, & eſpines. Et qui me faiſoit pis que tout, c'eſtoit qu'a chaſcun pas i'eſtoie retenu de ma robe, qui ſ'acrochoit aux buyſſons & haſliers. Le trauail que i'en eu, fut ſi grand & tant exceſſif, qu'en moy ny eut plus de conſeil: & ne ſceu bonnement que faire, ſinon me plaindre a haulte voix: mais tout cela eſtoit en vain, car ie n'eſtoie entẽdu de perſone, excepté de la belle Echo, qui me reſpõdoit du creux de la foreſt: ce qui me feit reclamer le ſecours de la piteuſe Ariadna, & deſirer le filet qu'elle bailla au deſloial Theſeus pour le guider parmy le Labyrinthe.

Poliphile

POLIPHILE. 2

Poliphile craignant le peril de la FOREST, FEIT SON ORAISON A IVPITER:

puis en trouua l'yſſue, tout alteré de ſoif. Et ainſi qu'il ſe uouloit rafraichir en une fontaine, il ouyt un chant melodieux, pour lequel ſuiure abandonna l'eau preſte: dont il ſe trouua puis apres en plus grande angoiſſe que deuant.

OBfuſqué de mon entendement, ſans pouuoir cognoiſtre quel party ie deuoie prendre, ou mourir en celle foreſt eſgarée, ou eſperer mon ſalut incertain, ie faiſoie tout mon effort d'en yſſir: mais tant plus alloie auãt, plus entroy ie en grãdes tenebres, fort foible, & trẽblant pour la peur que i'auoie: car ie n'attẽdoie ſinon que quelque beſte me vint afronter pour me deuorer: ou que heurtãt du pied a vn tronc ou racine, ie tumbaſſe dans quelque abyſme, & feuſſe englouti de la terre, cõme fut Amphiaraus. En ceſte maniere ſe troubloit mon entẽdement, ſans eſperance, & ſans raiſon, errant ſans voie ny ſentier. Parquoy voiant qu'en mon faict n'y auoit autre remede, ie me voys recommander a la diuine miſericorde, diſant, O Dieſpiter treſgrãd, treſbõ, treſpuiſſant, & treſſecourable, ſi p hũbles & deuotes prieres l'humanite peult meriter le ſecours des diuins ſuffrages, & doit eſtre de vous exaucee, ie apreſent repentãt & dolẽt de toutes mes fragilitez & offenſes paſſees, vous ſupplie & inuoque, ſouuerain pere eternel, recteur du ciel & de la terre, qu'il plaiſe a voſtre deité incõprehẽſible, me deliurer de ces perilz, ſi que ie puiſſe acheuer le cours de ma vie par quelque autre melieure fin. A peine eu ie finé mon oraiſon bien deuotemẽt proferée, & d'vn cueur tout humilié, les yeulx pleins de larmes, croiant fermemẽt q̃ les dieux ſecourent & ſauuent ceulx qui les inuoquent de pure volũté, que ie me trouuay hors de la foreſt: dont tout ainſi que ſi d'vne nuict froide & humide ie feuſſe paruenu en vn iour clair & ſerain, mes yeulx ſortans de telle obſcurité, ne pouuoient bien (pour quelque temps) ſouffrir la clairté du ſoleil. I'eſtoie haſlé, triſte, & angoiſſeux, tant qu'il ſembloit proprement que ie ſortiſſe d'une baſſe foſſe, preſque tout rõpu & briſé de chaines & de fers, changé de viſage, debile, & de cueur alenty, en ſorte que n'eſtimoie plus rien tout cela qui m'eſtoit preſent. Oultre ce i'auoie telle ſoif, que l'air fraiz & delicat ne me pouuoit aucunemẽt rafraichir, ny ſatiſfaire a la ſechereſſe de ma bouche. Mais apres auoir reprins vn petit de courage, par toutes manieres deliberay d'appaiſer ceſte ſoif: parquoy allay querant parmy celle contrée, tant que ie trouuay vne groſſe veine d'eau fraiche, ſourdant & bouillonnant en vne belle fontaine, qui couloit par vn petit ruyſſeau, lequel deuenoit vne riuiere bruyante atrauers les pierres & troncz des arbres tumbez & renuerſez en ſon canal, & contre leſquelz celle eau ſe regorgeoit comme courroucée & marrie de ce qu'ilz la cuidoient retarder, elle qui eſtoit augmentée de pluſieurs autres ruyſſeletz, auec aucuns torrens engendrez des neiges fondues, precipitees des montaignes, qui ne ſembloient eſtre gueres loing,

A ij

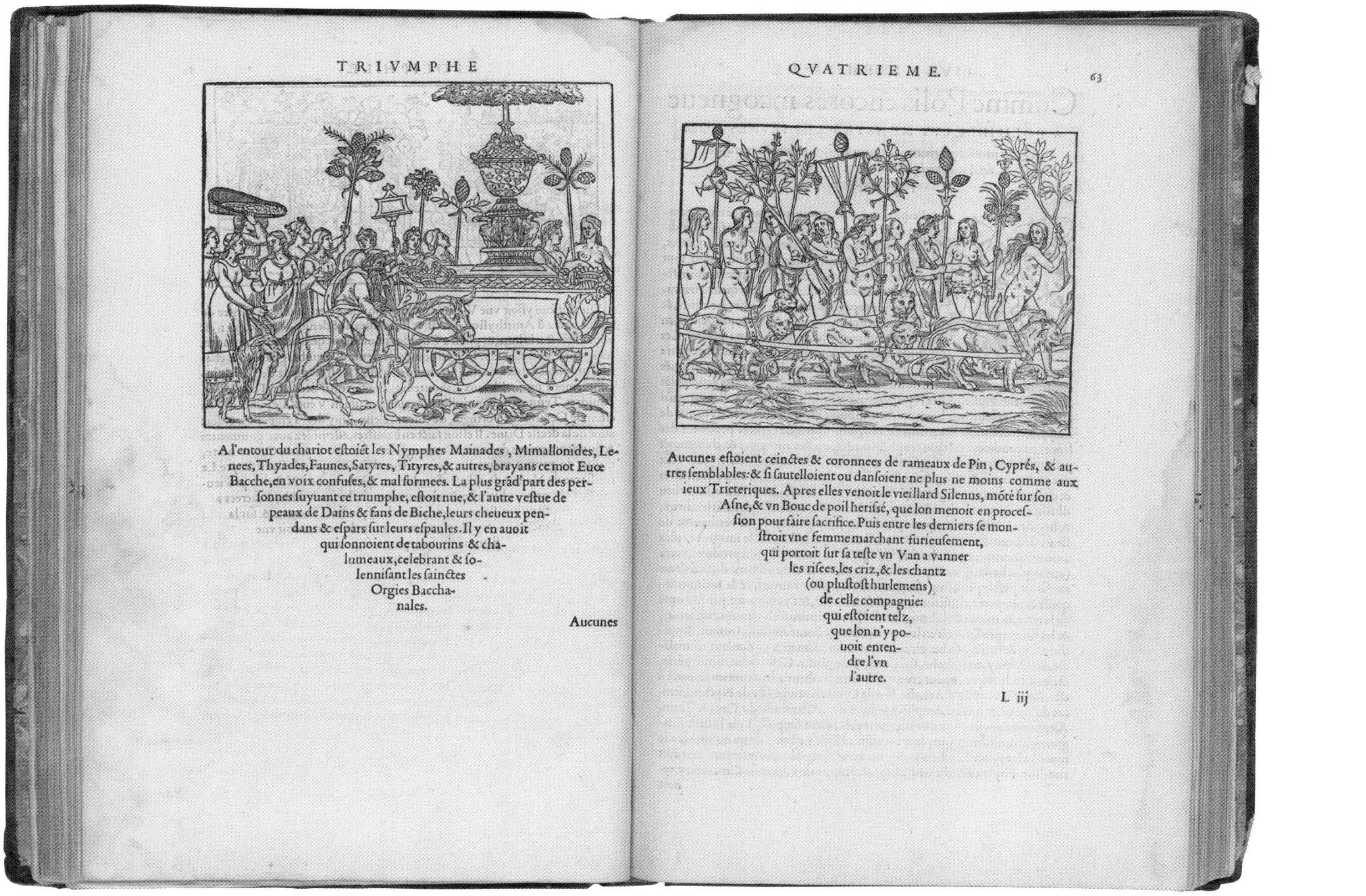
TRIVMPHE

A l'entour du chariot estoiét les Nymphes Mainades, Mimallonides, Lenees, Thyades, Faunes, Satyres, Tityres, & autres, brayans ce mot Euœ Bacche, en voix confuses, & mal formees. La plus grád'part des personnes suyuant ce triumphe, estoit nue, & l'autre vestue de peaux de Dains & fans de Biche, leurs cheueux pendans & espars sur leurs espaules. Il y en auoit qui sonnoient de tabourins & chalumeaux, celebrant & solennisant les sainctes Orgies Bacchanales.

Aucunes

QVATRIEME. 63

Aucunes estoient ceinctes & coronnees de rameaux de Pin, Cyprés, & autres semblables: & si sautelloient ou dansoient ne plus ne moins comme aux ieux Trieteriques. Apres elles venoit le vieillard Silenus, mõté sur son Asne, & vn Bouc de poil herissé, que lon menoit en procession pour faire sacrifice. Puis entre les derniers se monstroit vne femme marchant furieusement, qui portoit sur sa teste vn Van a vanner les risees, les criz, & les chantz (ou plustost hurlemens) de celle compagnie: qui estoient telz, que lon n'y pouoit entendre l'vn l'autre.

L iij

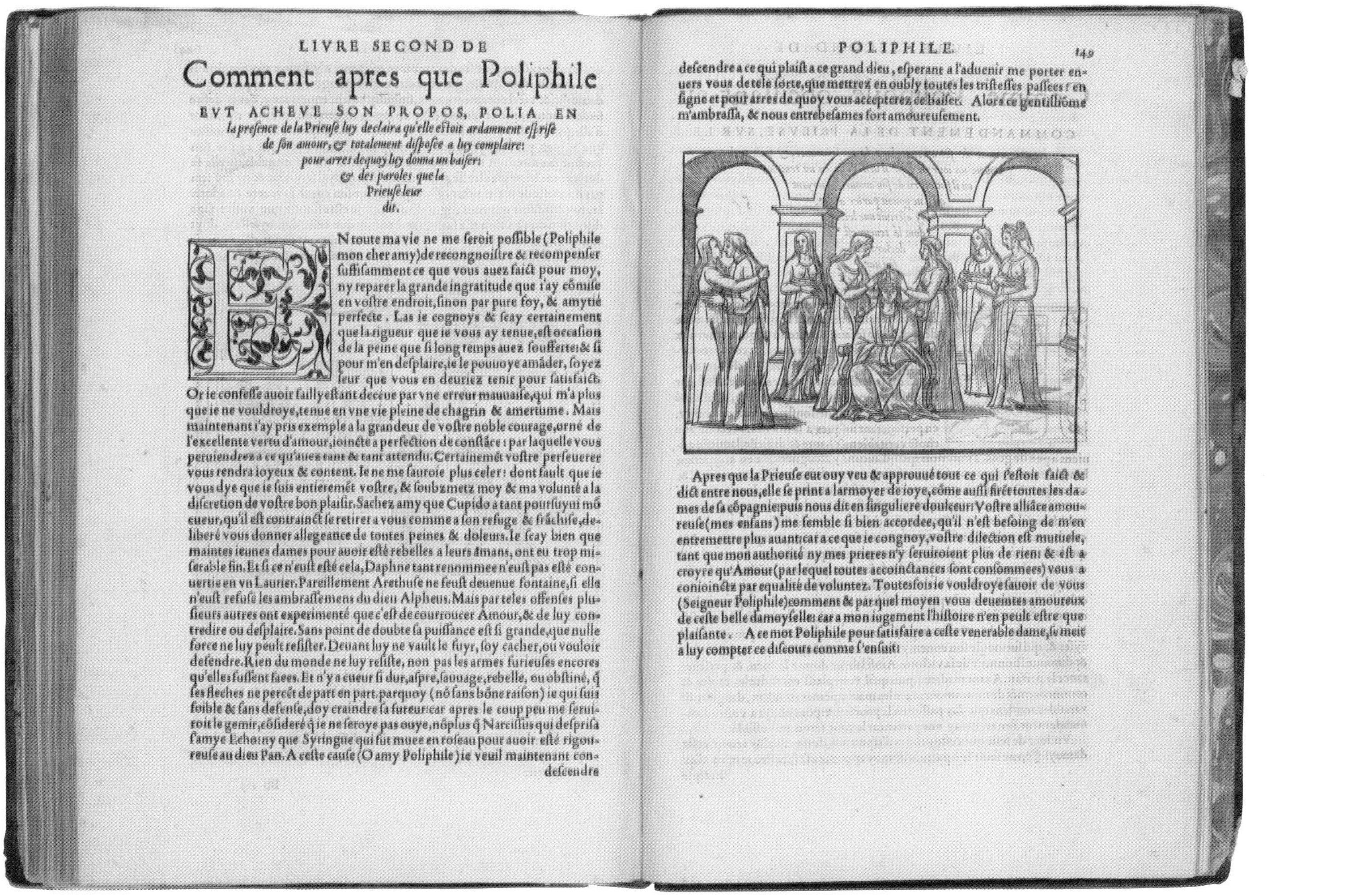
LIVRE SECOND DE

Comment apres que Poliphile EVT ACHEVE SON PROPOS, POLIA EN *la presence de la Prieuse luy declaira qu'elle estoit ardamment esprise de son amour, & totalement disposee a luy complaire: pour arres dequoy luy donna un baiser: & des paroles que la Prieuse leur dit.*

EN toute ma vie ne me seroit possible (Poliphile mon cher amy) de recongnoistre & recompenser suffisamment ce que vous auez faict pour moy, ny reparer la grande ingratitude que i'ay cõmise en vostre endroit, sinon par pure foy, & amytié perfecte. Las ie cognoys & scay certainement que la rigueur que ie vous ay tenue, est occasion de la peine que si long temps auez soufferte: & si pour m'en desplaire, ie le pouuoye amãder, soyez seur que vous en deuriez tenir pour satisfaict. Or ie confesse auoir failly estant deceue par vne erreur mauuaise, qui m'a plus que ie ne vouldroye, tenue en vne vie pleine de chagrin & amertume. Mais maintenant i'ay pris exemple a la grandeur de vostre noble courage, orné de l'excellente vertu d'amour, ioincte a perfection de constãce: par laquelle vous peruiendrez a ce qu'auez tant & tant attendu. Certainemét vostre perseuerer vous rendra ioyeux & content. Ie ne me sauroie plus celer: dont fault que ie vous dye que ie suis entieremét vostre, & soubzmetz moy & ma volunté a la discretion de vostre bon plaisir. Sachez amy que Cupido a tant poursuyui mõ cueur, qu'il est contrainct se retirer a vous comme a son refuge & frãchise, deliberé vous donner allegeance de toutes peines & doleurs. Ie scay bien que maintes ieunes dames pour auoir esté rebelles a leurs ãmans, ont eu trop miserable fin. Et si ce n'eust esté cela, Daphne tant renommee n'eust pas esté conuertie en vn Laurier. Pareillement Arethuse ne feust deuenue fontaine, si elle n'eust refusé les ambrassemens du dieu Alpheus. Mais par teles offenses plusieurs autres ont experimenté que c'est de courroucer Amour, & de luy contredire ou desplaire. Sans point de doubte sa puissance est si grande, que nulle force ne luy peult resister. Deuant luy ne vault le fuyr, soy cacher, ou vouloir defendre. Rien du monde ne luy resiste, non pas les armes furieuses encores qu'elles fussent faees. Et n'y a cueur si dur, aspre, sauuage, rebelle, ou obstiné, q̃ ses fleches ne percét de part en part. parquoy (nõ sans bõne raison) ie qui suis foible & sans defense, doy craindre sa fureur: car apres le coup peu me seruiroit le gemir, cõsideré q̃ ie ne seroye pas ouye, nõplus q̃ Narcissus qui desprisa s'amye Echo: ny que Syringue qui fut muee en roseau pour auoir esté rigoureuse au dieu Pan. A ceste cause (O amy Poliphile) ie veuil maintenant condescendre

POLIPHILE. 149

descendre a ce qui plaist a ce grand dieu, esperant a l'aduenir me porter enuers vous de tele sorte, que mettrez en oubly toutes les tristesses passees: en signe et pour arres de quoy vous accepterez ce baiser. Alors ce gentilhõme m'ambrassa, & nous entrebesames fort amoureusement.

Apres que la Prieuse eut ouy veu & approuué tout ce qui s'estoit faict & dict entre nous, elle se print a larmoyer de ioye, cõme aussi firét toutes les dames de sa cõpagnie: puis nous dit en singuliere douleur: Vostre alliãce amoureuse (mes enfans) me semble si bien accordee, qu'il n'est besoing de m'en entremettre plus auant: car a ce que ie congnoy, vostre dilection est mutuele, tant que mon authorité ny mes prieres n'y seruiroient plus de rien: & est a croyre qu'Amour (par lequel toutes accoinctances sont consommees) vous a conioinctz par equalité de voluntez. Toutesfois ie vouldroye sauoir de vous (Seigneur Poliphile) comment & par quel moyen vous deueintes amoureux de ceste belle damoyselle: car a mon iugement l'histoire n'en peult estre que plaisante. A ce mot Poliphile pour satisfaire a ceste venerable dame, se meit a luy compter ce discours comme s'ensuit:

1550 **Michael Isingrin** Leonhart Fuchs, *Den nieuwen herbarius, dat is, dboeck vanden cruyden*. Basel: Michael Isingrin, *c.* 1550. 33.5 cm.

In 1542, Michael Isingrin published a beautiful Latin edition of the herbal of Leonhart Fuchs (1501–66). A revised version in German appeared after one year. Fuchs had given the artists the instruction to make drawings (without the use of hatching) of the entire plant, including roots, stalks and stems, leaves, flowers, seeds, and fruits, so the plants could be identified in nature in each of their stages. In this, the book not only departed from earlier botanical publications, which often included unrecognizable depictions, but also from editions that depicted only one specimen.

Because of its royal format and the full-page illustrations, this edition was a prestigious possession rather than a book for everyday use. Only a select group of people could afford such costly volumes; therefore, Isingrin, active as printer from 1531 until 1557 in Basel, also produced a 'Kleine Fuchs' ('Small Fuchs'), for which he had all of the woodcuts remade in a smaller size, without losing detail. In 1545, he published both a German and a Latin pocket-sized edition containing only the woodcuts and an index to the illustrations. These were the first practical field guides.

For the Dutch edition shown here (partly coloured by hand), Isingrin reused the scaled-down illustrations, but he added descriptions and medicinal uses. This version set a standard for herbals in the Netherlands: simple, usable, and affordable. The author himself was immortalized by Charles Plumier, when he named the fuchsia after Fuchs. AP

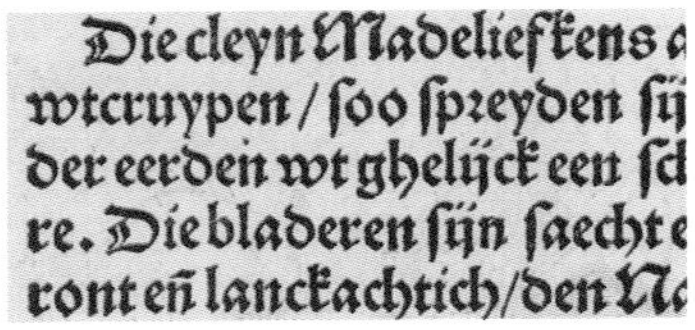

Luther's 1522 German New Testament promoted Schwabacher, a semi-cursive blackletter type introduced in *c.* 1483, stabilizing its form. The example shown here nearly matches the Mittel (14 point) Schwabacher sold by Bartholomeus Voskens in *c.* 1665 and by his successors until 1781. Fraktur, used for the headings, replaced Schwabacher as the norm for German secular works in around 1560.

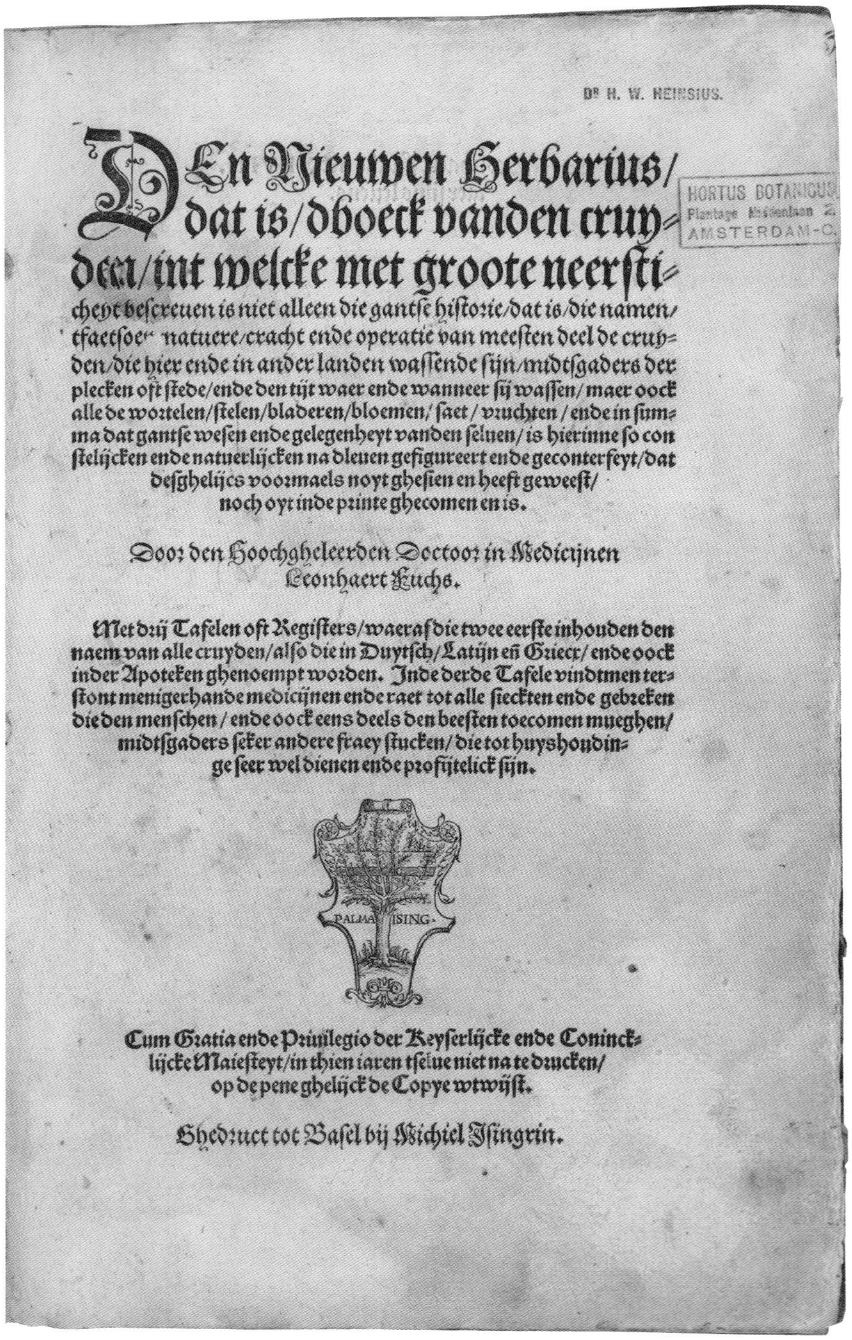

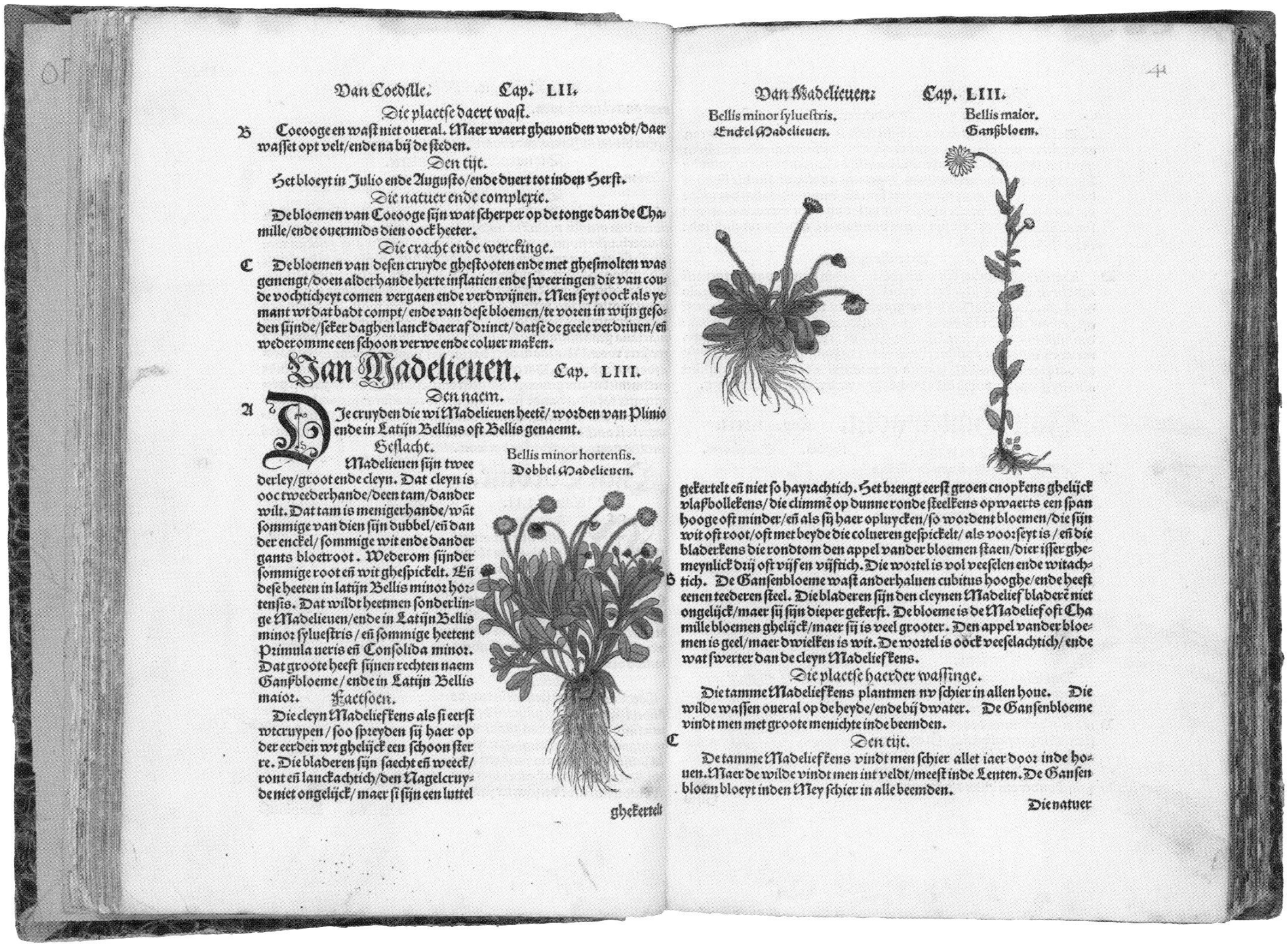

Van Coeölle. Cap. LII.
Die plaetse daert wast.
B Coeooge en wast niet oueral. Maer waert gheuonden wordt/daer wasset opt velt/ende na bij de steden.
Den tijt.
Het bloeyt in Julio ende Augusto/ende duert tot inden Herst.
Die natuer ende complexie.
De bloemen van Coeooge sijn wat scherper op de tonge dan de Chamille/ende ouermids dien oock heeter.
Die cracht ende werckinge.
C De bloemen van desen cruyde ghestooten ende met ghesmolten was gemengt/doen alderhande herte inflatien ende sweeringen die van coude vochticheyt comen vergaen ende verdwijnen. Men seyt oock als yemant wt badt compt/ende van dese bloemen/te voren in wijn gesoden sijnde/seker daghen lanck daeraf drinct/datse de geele verdriuen/en wederomme een schoon verwe ende coluer maken.
Van Madelieuen. Cap. LIII.
Den naem.
A Die cruyden die wi Madelieuen heete/worden van Plinio ende in Latijn Bellius oft Bellis genaemt.
Gheslacht.
Madelieuen sijn twee derley/groot ende cleyn. Dat cleyn is ooc tweederhande/deen tam/dander wilt. Dat tam is menigerhande/wāt sommige van dien sijn dubbel/eñ dander enckel/sommige wit ende dander gants bloetroot. Wederom sijnder sommige root eñ wit ghespickelt. Eñ dese heeten in latijn Bellis minor hortensis. Dat wildt heetmen sonderlinge Madelieuen/ende in Latijn Bellis minor syluestris/eñ sommige heetent Primula veris eñ Consolida minor. Dat groote heeft sijnen rechten naem Gansbloeme/ende in Latijn Bellis maior.
Facetsoen.
Die cleyn Madeliefkens als si eerst wtcruypen/soo spreyden sij haer op der eerden wt ghelijck een schoon sterre. Die bladeren sijn saecht eñ weeck/ront eñ lanckachtich/den Nagelcruyde niet ongelijck/maer si sijn een luttel ghekertelt

Bellis minor hortensis. Dobbel Madelieuen.

Van Madelieuen. Cap. LIII. 41

Bellis minor syluestris. Enckel Madelieuen.

Bellis maior. Gansbloem.

ghekertelt eñ niet so hayrachtich. Het brengt eerst groen cnopkens ghelijck vlasbollekens/die climmē op dunne ronde steelkens opwaerts een span hooge oft minder/eñ als sij haer oplugcken/so wordent bloemen/die sijn wit oft root/oft met beyde die coluren gespickelt/als voorseyt is/eñ die bladerkens die rondtom den appel vander bloemen staen/dier isser ghemeynlick drij oft vijf en vijftich. Die wortel is vol veeselen ende witachtich. B De Gansenbloeme wast anderhalven cubitus hooghe/ende heeft eenen teederen steel. Die bladeren sijn den cleynen Madelief bladerē niet ongelijck/maer sij sijn dieper gekerft. De bloeme is de Madelief oft Chamille bloemen ghelijck/maer sij is veel grooter. Den appel vander bloemen is geel/maer dwielcken is wit. De wortel is oock veeselachtich/ende wat swerter dan de cleyn Madeliefkens.
Die plaetse haerder wassinge.
Die tamme Madeliefkens plantmen nv schier in allen houe. Die wilde wassen oueral op de heyde/ende bij dwater. De Gansenbloeme vindt men met groote menichte inde beemden.
C Den tijt.
De tamme Madeliefkens vindt men schier allet iaer door inde houen. Maer de wilde vindt men int veldt/meest inde Lenten. De Gansen bloem bloeyt inden Mey schier in alle beemden.
Die natuer

Van Kersen. Cap. CLXI.
gesichte. Dese gomme in wijn gedroncken/is goet voor de ghene die den steen hebben. Met azijn gemengt sijnde/is sij goet voor de ionge kinderē om dat root ionck te verdriuen/alsment daer op strijct.
Van blaw Corenbloemen. Cap. CLXII.
Den naem.
A De blaw Corenbloeme die wort van Plinio geheeten Cyanus/om der coluer wille die dese bloemen hebben. Sommige heetense Baptisecula/oft beter Blaptisecula/also wi sulcx in onsen Latijnschen Herbario verclaert hebben.
Facetsoen.
De blaw Corenbloeme heeft eenen gecanten steel/eñ smal/scherpe/aschverwighe bladeren. De bloemen sijn schoon hemelblaw/ende wassen wt cleyn/rōde/rouwe/geschelferde knoppekens/ende na dat sij ghebloeyt hebben/so sijn sij binnē vol wits hayrachtichs saets. De wortel is lanck/houdtachtich ende veeselachtich.
B Plaetse haerder wassinghe.
Dit cruyt is gheneyn/ende wasset int coren.
Den tijt.
Het bloeyt meest in Junio ende Julio/ende is seer lieflick om aensien. En de hoewel dat dese bloeme gheen en rueck en geeft/nochtans so maect men daer oock cransen ende hoeyen af.
Natuer ende complexie.
Dit cruyt is cout van natuere/ende drijft achterwaerts/also men dat mercken mach aen sijnen smaeck.
C Cracht ende werckinge.
Dese blaw Corenbloeme is wtnemende goet tot hittige roode oogen/ende tot alle ander ontsteken inflammatien/alsmense stootet ende daer op leyt. Si is oock goet tot quade rottende gaten/wonden/ende vlceratien/alsmense stootet/ende dat sap daer wt perst/ende daerin doet. Oft datmen die droocht ende pulueriseert/ende dat poeder daerinne stroyt.
Van Ayeuyn.

Cyanus. Blaw Corenbloemen.

Van Ayeuyn. Cap. CLXIII. 119
Den naem.
A Ayeuyn heetmen in Griecx Crommyon/ende in Latijn Cepa/eñ also wordet noch op den dach van heden inde Apoteke ghenoempt.
Gheslacht.
Daer sijn veel manieren ende gheslechten van Ayeuyn/ghelijck als Theophrastus ende Plinius vertellen/ende noodeloos ware hier te verhalen. Maer den Ayeuyn die hier te lande wast/is som groot/som cleyn/ende sommighe van coluer root/sommighe wit/sommighe ront/ende dander lanck. Maer de beste dat sijn de ronde/ende die root sijn.
Facetsoen.
Ayeuyn heeft bladeren schier gelijck Loock/die sijn binnen hol/de stelen oft pijpen sijn rondt/ende die crijghen int sop ronde bollekens met dunne witte vellekens ouertrocken/die breken met der tijt op/ende daer B wt cruypen bleeckwitte/ghesterrede bloemkens veel bij een. De bloemkēs worden cleyne knoppekens oft bollekens/ende in elck van dien liggen twee oft drij swerte ghehoeckte greynkens besloten. Die wortel is rondt ghelijck een cleyn bolleken/ende dat sijn binnen veel dunne schelferingen oft vellekens/waeraf de buytenste dunne/teeder/en de rootachtich sijn. Aen dit bolleken hanghen int opperste cleyn witte veeselinghen ghelijck als hayr.
Plaetse sijnder wassinge.
Ayeuyn wast geerne in vet/morw/ende vocht eertdrijck. Ende men setten C oueral inde houen.
Den tijt.
Den Ayeuyn saeytmen inden Meerte/ende hij bloeyt meest in Julio. Ende daerna volget dat swert saet. Den rijpen Ayeuyn treckmen ghemeynlick wt der eerden ontrent S. Barthelmeus dach.
Natuer ende complexie.
Den Ayeuyn is werm inden vierden graedt/ende van groue substantie/ende sonderlinghe alsmen dat sap daer wt dowt oft perst.
Cracht

Crommyon. Ayeuyn.

Michael Isingrin

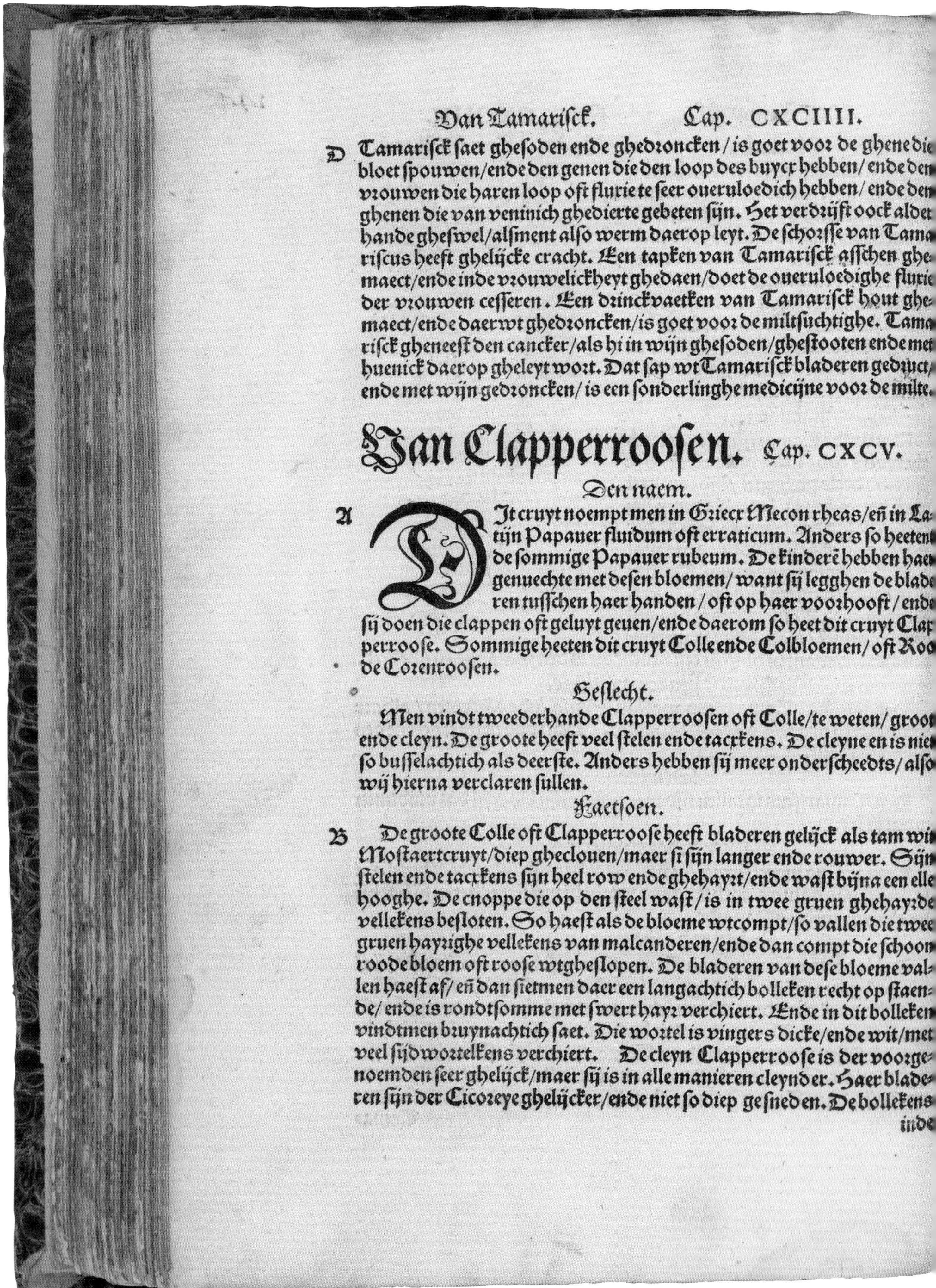

Van Tamarisck. Cap. CXCIIII.

D Tamarisck saet ghesoden ende ghedroncken/ is goet voor de ghene die bloet spouwen/ende den genen die den loop des buycx hebben/ ende den vrouwen die haren loop oft flurie te seer oueruloedich hebben/ ende den ghenen die van veninich ghedierte gebeten sijn. Het verdrijft oock alder hande gheswel/alsment also werm daerop leyt. De schorsse van Tama riscus heeft ghelijcke cracht. Een tapken van Tamarisck asschen ghe-maect/ende inde vrouwelickheyt ghedaen/doet de oueruloedighe flurie der vrouwen cesseren. Een drinckvaetken van Tamarisck hout ghe-maect/ende daerwt ghedroncken/is goet voor de miltsuchtighe. Tama risck gheneest den cancker/als hi in wijn ghesoden/ghestooten ende met huenick daerop gheleyt wort. Dat sap wt Tamarisck bladeren gedruct/ ende met wijn gedroncken/ is een sonderlinghe medicijne voor de milte.

Van Clapperroosen. Cap. CXCV.

Den naem.

A Dit cruyt noempt men in Griecx Mecon rheas/eñ in La-tijn Papauer fluidum oft erraticum. Anders so heeten de sommige Papauer rubeum. De kinderẽ hebben hae genuechte met desen bloemen/ want sij legghen de blade ren tusschen haer handen / oft op haer voorhooft / ende sij doen die clappen oft geluyt geuen/ende daerom so heet dit cruyt Clap perroose. Sommige heeten dit cruyt Colle ende Colbloemen/ oft Roo de Corenroosen.

Geslecht.

Men vindt tweederhande Clapperroosen oft Colle/te weten/ groot ende cleyn. De groote heeft veel stelen ende tacxkens. De cleyne en is nie so busselachtich als deerste. Anders hebben sij meer onderscheedts/ also wij hierna verclaren sullen.

Faetsoen.

B De groote Colle oft Clapperroose heeft bladeren gelijck als tam wi Mostaertcruyt/diep ghecloven/maer si sijn langer ende rouwer. Sijn stelen ende tacxkens sijn heel row ende ghehayrt/ende wast bijna een elle hooghe. De cnoppe die op den steel wast/is in twee gruen ghehayrde vellekens besloten. So haest als de bloeme wtcompt/so vallen die twee gruen hayrighe vellekens van malcanderen/ende dan compt die schoon roode bloem oft roose wtgheslopen. De bladeren van dese bloeme val-len haest af/ eñ dan sietmen daer een langachtich bolleken recht op staen-de/ ende is rondtsomme met swert hayr verchiert. Ende in dit bolleken vindtmen bruynachtich saet. Die wortel is vingers dicke/ende wit/met veel sijd wortelkens verchiert. De cleyn Clapperroose is der voorge-noemden seer ghelijck/maer sij is in alle manieren cleynder. Haer blade-ren sijn der Cicoreye ghelijcker/ende niet so diep gesneden. De bollekens inde

Van Clapperroosen. Cap. CXCV.

Mecon rhœas.
Clapperroosen.

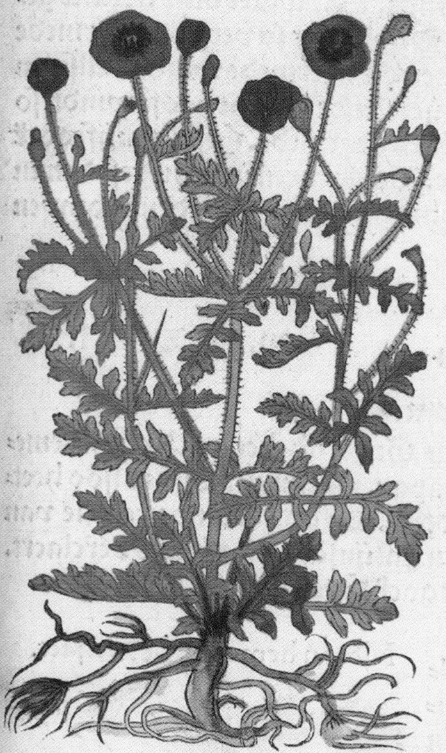

Papauer erraticum alterum.
Roode Corenroosen.

inde bloemen sien nederwaert. De wortel is langer ende geelder.

Plaetse haerder wassinghe.

De Clapperroosen wassen bijna in alle coren ende vruchten. Maer de groote Clapperroose en is niet so ghemeyn als de cleyne.

Den tijt.

De Clapperroosen bloeyen inde Lenten / ende den gantsen somer tot inden Oogst.

Natuer ende complexie.

De natuere van beyde de Clapperroosen is tot vercoelinge geneycht. Ende daeromme so vercoelen sij ghelijck als ander Papauer oft Huelcruyden.

Die cracht ende operatie.

Vijf oft ses bollekens tot ouer de helft in wijn ghesoden ende gedroncken / dat doet den mensch slapen. Dat saet ghestooten / ende met Meede ghedroncken / maect weeck inden buyck. Desgelijcx doetet oock alsment inde pepercoecken bact. De bladeren met de bollekens ghestooten / vercoelen alderhande hitte oft brandt / alsment daerop leyt. In water ghesoden / ende doecken daerin nat ghemaect / ende om thooft ghewonden / maken den mensch slapende. Dat voorseyde water blust de ontstekinge

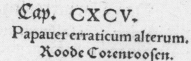

B ende

1551 **Michel de Vascosan** Euclid, *Elementorum liber decimus*; ed. Pierre Mondoré. Paris: Michel de Vascosan, 1551.

140 leaves. 22 cm.

Elementorum liber decimus ('Tenth Book of the Elements') is a Latin translation of an important geometry book from Greek antiquity. This is a 1551 edition by the humanist publisher-printer Michel de Vascosan (*c.* 1500–77). Vascosan, who is relatively obscure now, was a great French typographer of the sixteenth century. In his work, we see the pinnacle of the French style, which would still have followers in the twentieth century. The layout of the title page has become classic: author's name and title at the top of the page, imprint at the bottom, both elements centred and separated from each other by a large expanse of white. The Renaissance-style initials are printed from woodcuts. The roman is no longer a derivative of Jenson's type but is in the style of the new French types (Garamont). More unusual is the use of the two italics (still with roman capitals) for the annotations and several other parts of the text: italics are no longer used for the main text, but as a distinguishing type in contrast to the roman. Michel de Vascosan also served scholarship well with his attention to textual accuracy. FAJ

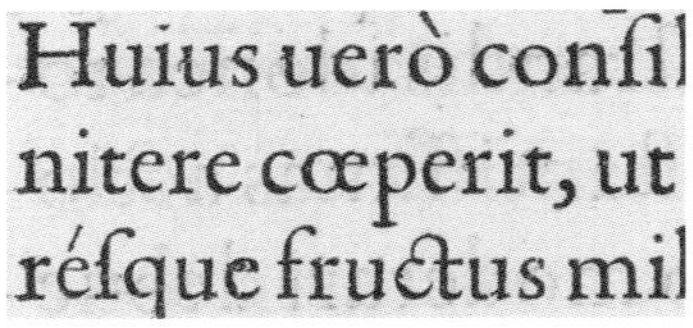
Huius uerò consil
nitere cœperit, ut
résque fructus mil

This is the last Gros Romain (17 point) roman by Claude Garamont (*c.* 1510–61), but with the older form of M (with no serif at the upper right): one of the best types by perhaps the most famous punchcutter of all time, freshly cast. One printer used it earlier, in 1549.

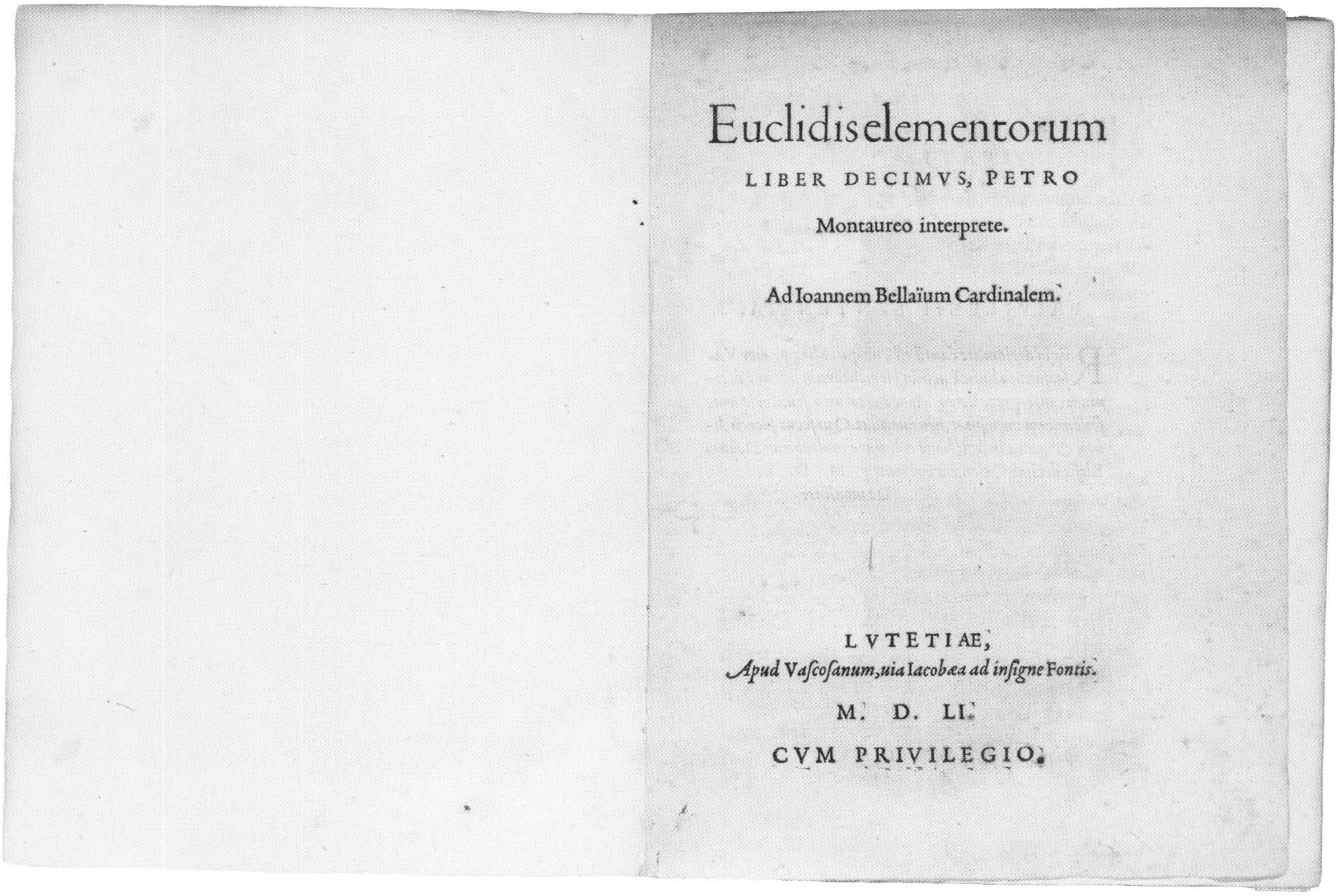
Euclidis elementorum
LIBER DECIMVS, PETRO
Montaureo interprete.

Ad Ioannem Bellaïum Cardinalem.

LVTETIAE,
Apud Vascosanum, uia Iacobæa ad insigne Fontis.
M. D. LI.
CVM PRIVILEGIO.

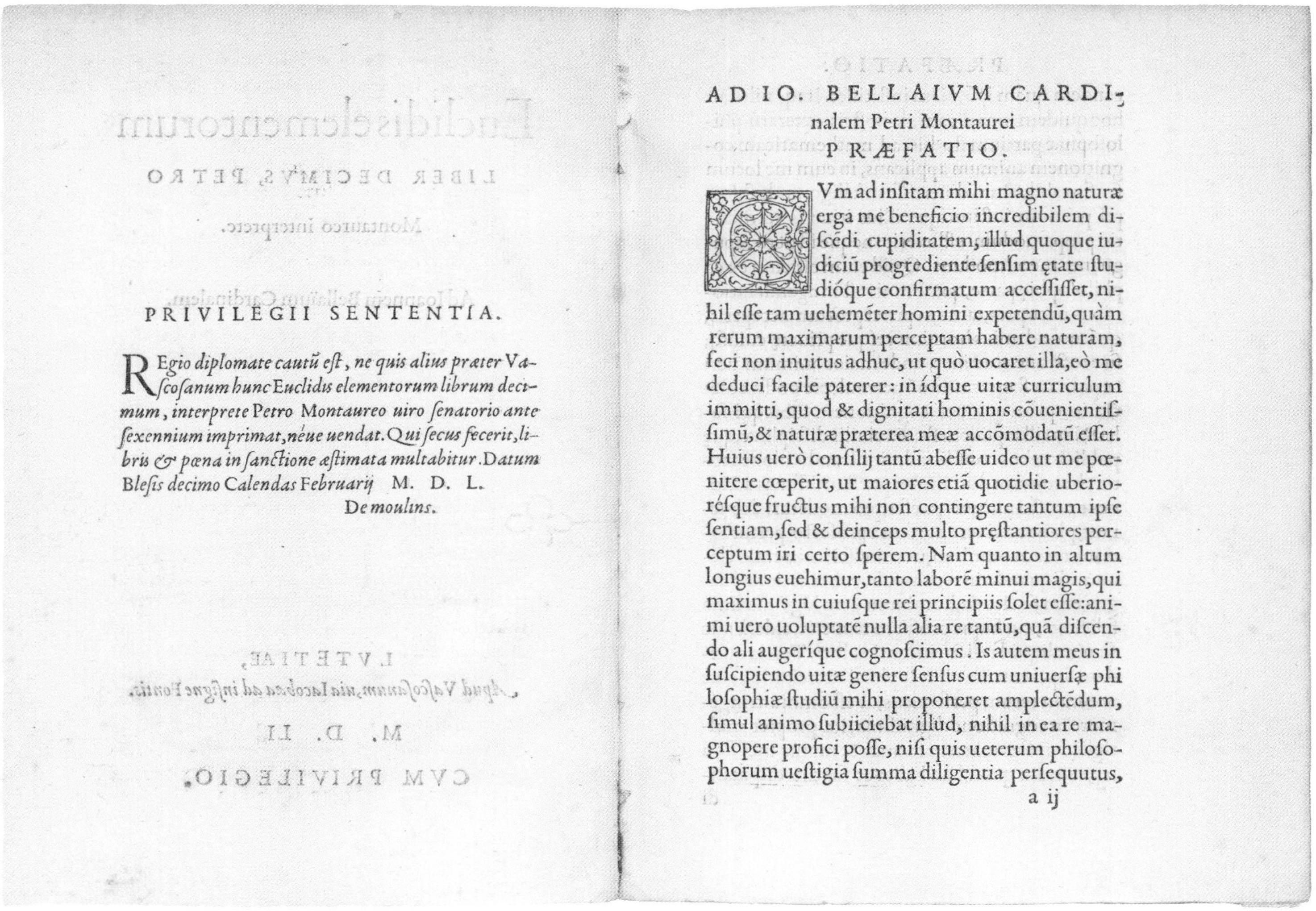

PRIVILEGII SENTENTIA.

Regio diplomate cautū est, ne quis alius præter Vascosanum hunc Euclidis *elementorum librum decimum, interprete* Petro Montaureo *uiro senatorio ante sexennium imprimat, néue uendat. Qui secus fecerit, libris & pœna in sanctione æstimata multabitur.* Datum Blesis *decimo* Calendas Februarij M. D. L.

De *moulins.*

AD IO. BELLAIVM CARDI-nalem Petri Montaurei PRÆFATIO.

Cum ad insitam mihi magno naturæ erga me beneficio incredibilem discẽdi cupiditatem, illud quoque iudiciū progrediente sensim ętate studióque confirmatum accessisset, nihil esse tam uehemẽter homini expetendū, quàm rerum maximarum perceptam habere naturam, feci non inuitus adhuc, ut quò uocaret illa, eò me deduci facile paterer: in ídque uitæ curriculum immitti, quod & dignitati hominis cōuenientissimū, & naturæ præterea meæ accõmodatū esset. Huius uerò consilij tantū abesse uideo ut me pœnitere cœperit, ut maiores etiã quotidie uberioresque fructus mihi non contingere tantum ipse sentiam, sed & deinceps multo pręstantiores perceptum iri certo sperem. Nam quanto in altum longius euehimur, tanto laborẽ minui magis, qui maximus in cuiusque rei principiis solet esse: animi uero uoluptatẽ nulla alia re tantū, quã discendo ali augeríque cognoscimus. Is autem meus in suscipiendo uitæ genere sensus cum uniuersæ philosophiæ studiū mihi proponeret amplectẽdum, simul animo subiiciebat illud, nihil in ea re magnopere profici posse, nisi quis ueterum philosophorum uestigia summa diligentia persequutus,

a ij

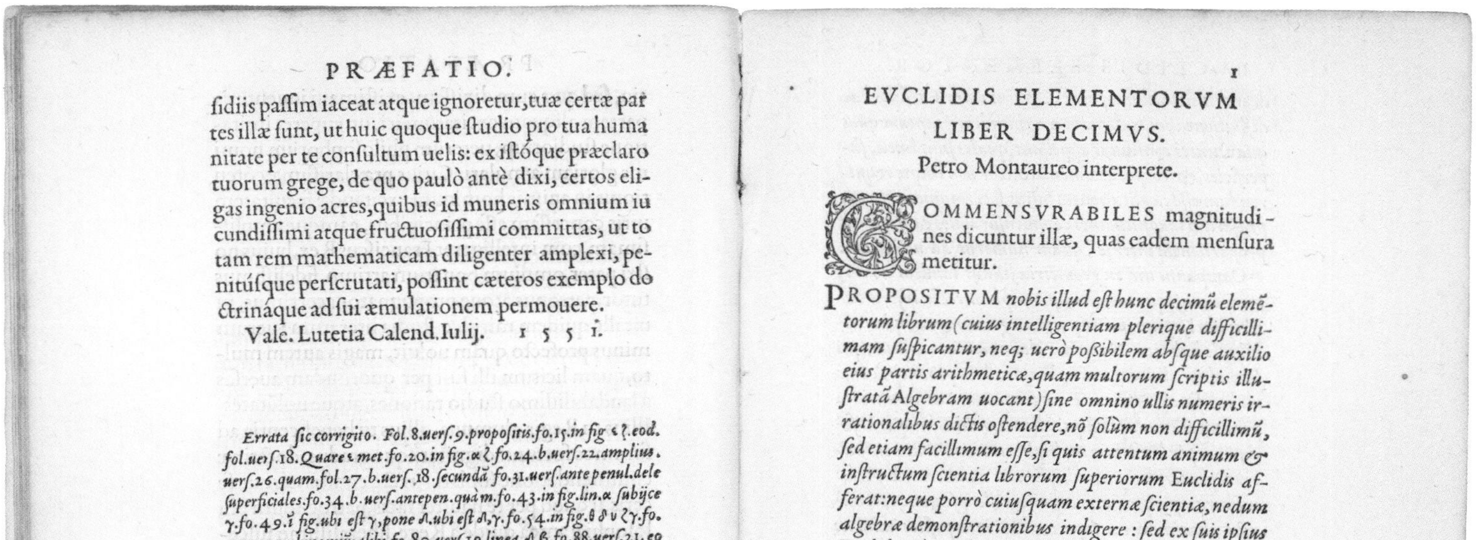

PRÆFATIO.

sidiis passim iaceat atque ignoretur, tuæ certæ partes illæ sunt, ut huic quoque studio pro tua humanitate per te consultum uelis: ex istóque præclaro tuorum grege, de quo paulò antè dixi, certos eligas ingenio acres, quibus id muneris omnium iucundissimi atque fructuosissimi committas, ut totam rem mathematicam diligenter amplexi, penitúsque perscrutati, possint cæteros exemplo doctrináque ad sui æmulationem permouere.

Vale. Lutetia Calend. Iulij. 1551.

Errata sic corrigito. Fol.8.uers.9.propositis.fo.15.in fig ε ζ.eod. fol.uers.18.Quare ε met.fo.20.in fig.α ζ.fo.24.b.uers.22.amplius. uers.26.quam.fol.27.b.uers.18.secundã fo.31.uers.ante penul.dele superficiales.fo.34.b.uers.antepen.quàm.fo.43.in fig.lin.α subijce γ.fo.49.ĩ fig.ubi est γ, pone δ.ubi est δ, γ.fo.54.in fig.θ δ υ ζ γ.fo. 74.uer.14.binomiū:alibi.fo.80.uers.19.linea δ β.fo.88.uers.21.eo quod.fo 89.in fig.ι θ λ.fol.95.uers.10.uerbis κj.fol.102.b.uers.13. ideo sic.fol.104.Octogesimū ubiq;.fol.110.b.uers.21.quàm.fo.114 in fig. sub π scribe υ.fol.116.uers.13.per 1.6.fol.127.b.uers.2.quadratum.fol.329.uers.25.linea κ θ.fo.132.uers.14.ad β δ.fol.134. uers.12.lineæ.fo.135, b.uers.24.lineæ, κ λ.fol.136.uers.13.dictarū.

1

EVCLIDIS ELEMENTORVM LIBER DECIMVS.

Petro Montaureo interprete.

COMMENSVRABILES magnitudines dicuntur illæ, quas eadem mensura metitur.

PROPOSITVM *nobis illud est hunc decimū elemẽtorum librum (cuius intelligentiam plerique difficillimam suspicantur, neq; uerò poßibilem absque auxilio eius partis arithmeticæ, quam multorum scriptis illustratã Algebram uocant) sine omnino ullis numeris irrationalibus dictis ostendere, nõ solùm non difficillimū, sed etiam facillimum esse, si quis attentum animum & instructum scientia librorum superiorum* Euclidis *afferat: neque porrò cuiusquam externæ scientiæ, nedum algebræ demonstrationibus indigere: sed ex suis ipsius* Euclidis *tãtum demonstrationibus, & familiarißimo ipsi ordine dependere. Vt autem clarius intelligatur hæc definitio, prius explanãdum puto, si quid in ea subobscurum contineri uideatur. sic enim præcipiunt dialectici. Cum itaque dicitur aliqua mensura magnitudinẽ aliam metiri: illud intelligitur primùm, ut ea mensura sit minor illa quam metitur, aut ei saltem æqualis. maior enim nullo modo metiri minorem potest. Deinde ut ea mensura semel sumpta si æqualis erit, aut si minor fuerit pluribus uicibus repetita: eam magnitudinem quam metitur, præcise referat. id quod ex numeris*

B

Vigeſimumprimum Theorema.

Si rationale ſecundum lineam rationalem applicetur, habebit alterum latus lineam rationalem & commenſurabilem longitudine lineæ, cui rationale parallelogrammum applicatur.

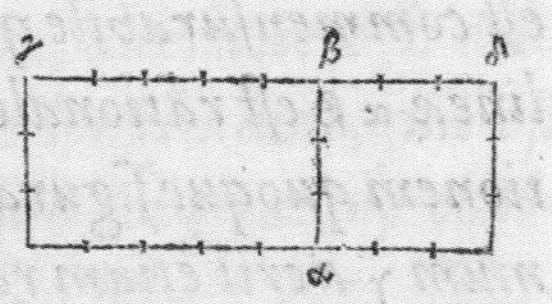

Hoc theorema eſt ueluti ἀντίστροφον *præcedentis.* Rationale enim *parallelogrammum* α γ *applicetur ſecundum lineam* α β *rationalē uno aliquo modo ex antedictis, ſiue ſit illa primo rationalis, ſiue alia ipſi primo rationali commenſurabilis, idq́; longitudine & potentia, uel potentia tātum. his enim tribus modis dicitur linea rationalis.* Dico lineam β γ *eſſe rationalem & longitudine commenſurabilem ipſi lineæ* α β. *Deſcribatur enim quadratum lineæ* α β *quod ſit* α δ. Rationale *eſt igitur quadratum* α δ, *ſed & parallelogrammum* α γ *eſt rationale per poſitionem. Ergo per definitionem rationaliū quæ in ſe conuertitur, ſiue per* 12 *huius, commenſurabile eſt quadratum* α δ *parallelogrammo* α γ. *Eſt autem ſicut quadratum* α δ *ad parallelogrammū* α γ, *ita linea* δ β *ad lineam* β γ, *per primam ſexti. Itaq; per decimam huius, linea* δ β *erit commenſurabilis lineæ* β γ. *ſed linea* β δ, *eſt æqualis lineæ* β α, *commenſurabilis eſt ergo linea* α β, *lineæ* β γ. *Rationalis autem eſt linea* α β, Rationalis *ergo erit & linea* β γ, *& commenſurabilis longitudine lineæ* α β. *Ergo ſi rationale ſecundum lineā rationalem &c.*

Lemma.

Linea

Linea potens ſuperficiem irrationalem, eſt irrationalis. Poſit enim linea α ſuperficiem irrationalem, hoc eſt quadratum quod ab α deſcribitur, æquale eſto areæ irrationali. dico lineam α eſſe irrationalem. Nam ſi linea α eſſet rationalis, rationale quoque eſſet quadratum ab illa deſcriptum: (ſic enim eſt poſitũ inter definitiones) ſed ex poſitione eſt irrationale, irrationalis eſt ergo linea α. quod demonſtrandum erat.

Lemma.

Hîc inſeritur quoddam ſcholium, quod lemmatis inſcriptionem habet, ſed illud nihil aliud eſt quàm demõſtratio quædam ſequentis theorematis.

Vigeſimumſecundum Theorema.

Superficies rectangula contenta duabus lineis rectis rationalibus potẽtia tantum cõmenſurabilibus, irrationalis eſt. Linea autem quæ illam ſuperficiem poteſt, irrationalis & ipſa eſt: uocetur uerò medialis.

Superficies enim rectãgula α γ comprehendatur à duabus lineis rationalibus potentia tantum commẽſurabilibus, quæ ſint α β, β γ. Dico ſuperficiem illam eſſe irrationalem, & lineam quæ illam poteſt, irrationalem etiam eſſe: uocetur autem medialis. Deſcribatur enim à linea α β quadratum α δ. rationale eſt itaq; quadratum α δ. Et quoniam incommẽſurabilis eſt longitudine linea α β

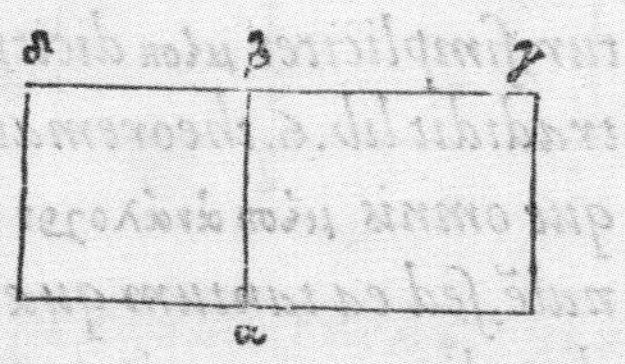

N

1558 **Jean de Tournes** Gabriele Simeoni, *Illustratione de gli epitaffi et medaglie antiche*. Lyon: Jean de Tournes, 1558.

174 pp. 21.5 cm. Illustrator: Bernard Salomon.

Gabriele Simeoni was an Italian humanist who fled to the south of France for religious reasons. In Lyon he published several books with Jean de Tournes, among them this illustrated discourse on antique gravestones and medals. The book – of which a French edition had been published shortly before – was dedicated to Alfonso II d'Este, Duke of Ferrara.

Jean de Tournes (1504–64), a student of Sébastien Gryphe, was a Protestant printer-publisher whose descendants fled to Geneva. De Tournes was one of the most prominent publishers of his time, with an international, mostly humanist list of publications. Many of his books are illustrated with refined woodcuts. A number of the illustrations of the *Illustratione* are attributed to the influential Bernard Salomon (*c.* 1508–*c.* 1561), also of Lyon.

Illustratione de gli epitaffi et medaglie antiche is a typical Renaissance book, both in content and in design. At the same time, this work is characteristic of books made in Lyon after the mid-sixteenth century. There was great interest in the original Roman texts found on tombs and monuments. In this book, the lettering used on these monuments is imitated typographically with letter-spaced small capitals, surrounded by woodcut frames or fleurons. The book is 'modern' in that it hardly contains any decoration except for the illustrations. Only the first page of the dedication was provided with a typically French decorative initial and an ornament.

Books like the *Illustratione* are highly valued by book historians and classic book typographers alike. In his graphic surveys, for example, Stanley Morison paid tribute to De Tournes's work. PD

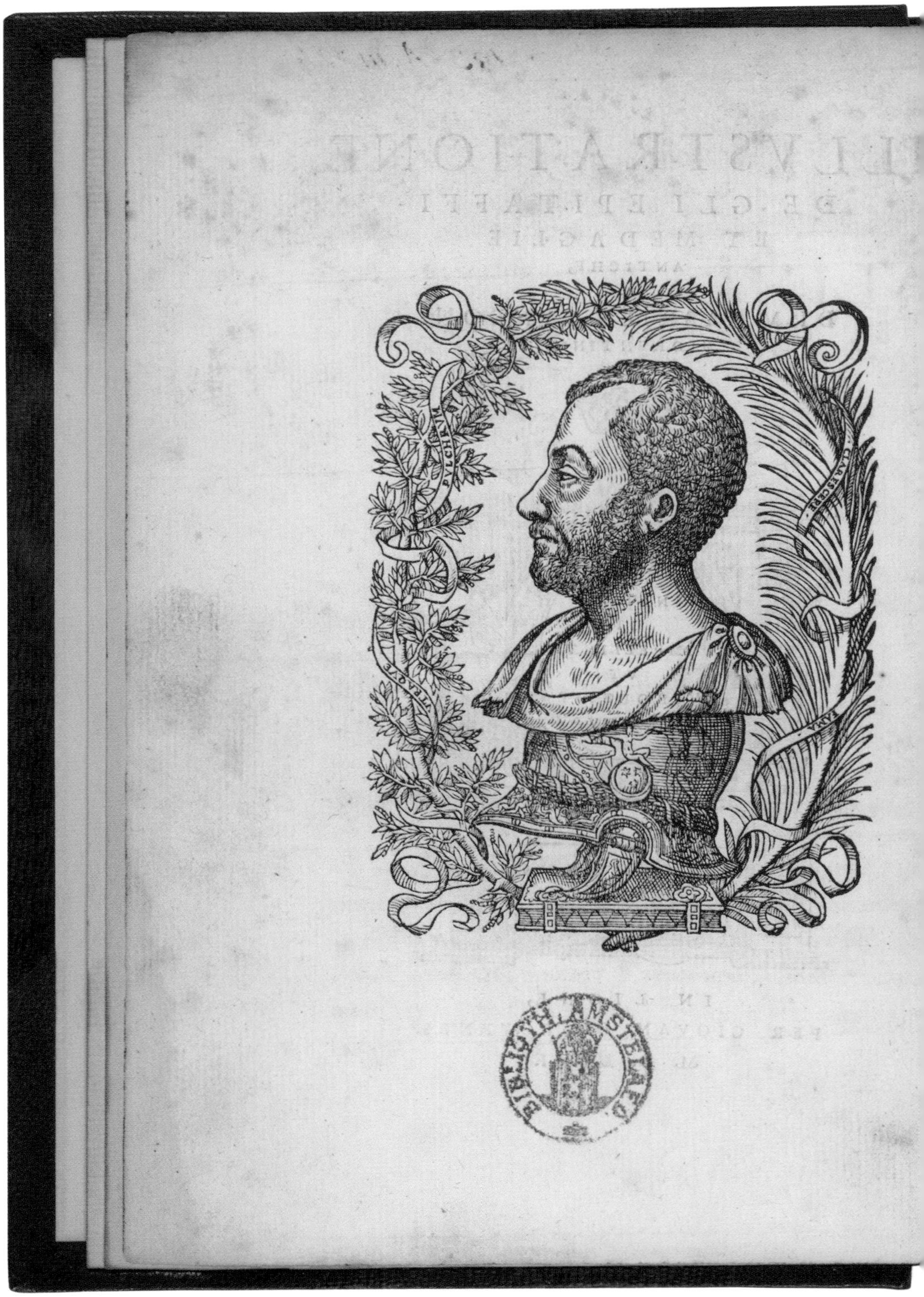

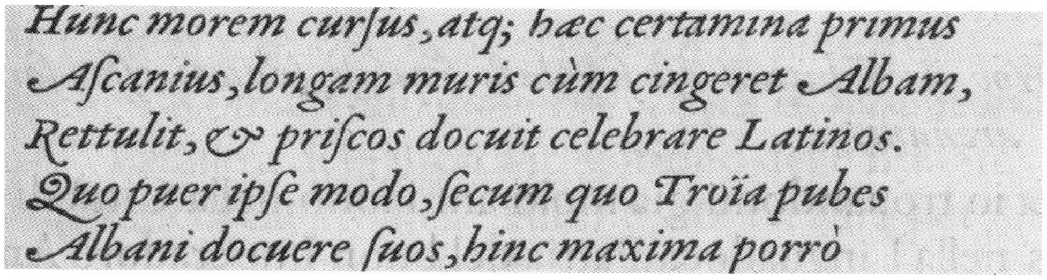
Hunc morem curſus, atq; hæc certamina primus
Aſcanius, longam muris cùm cingeret Albam,
Rettulit, & priſcos docuit celebrare Latinos.
Quo puer ipſe modo, ſecum quo Troïa pubes
Albani docuere ſuos, hinc maxima porrò

Robert Granjon (1512/13–90), one of the best, most prolific and most versatile punchcutters of all time, cut about thirty italics in different styles. He was not quite the first to blend the Aldine and chancery italics, but his version remained the standard into the eighteenth century.

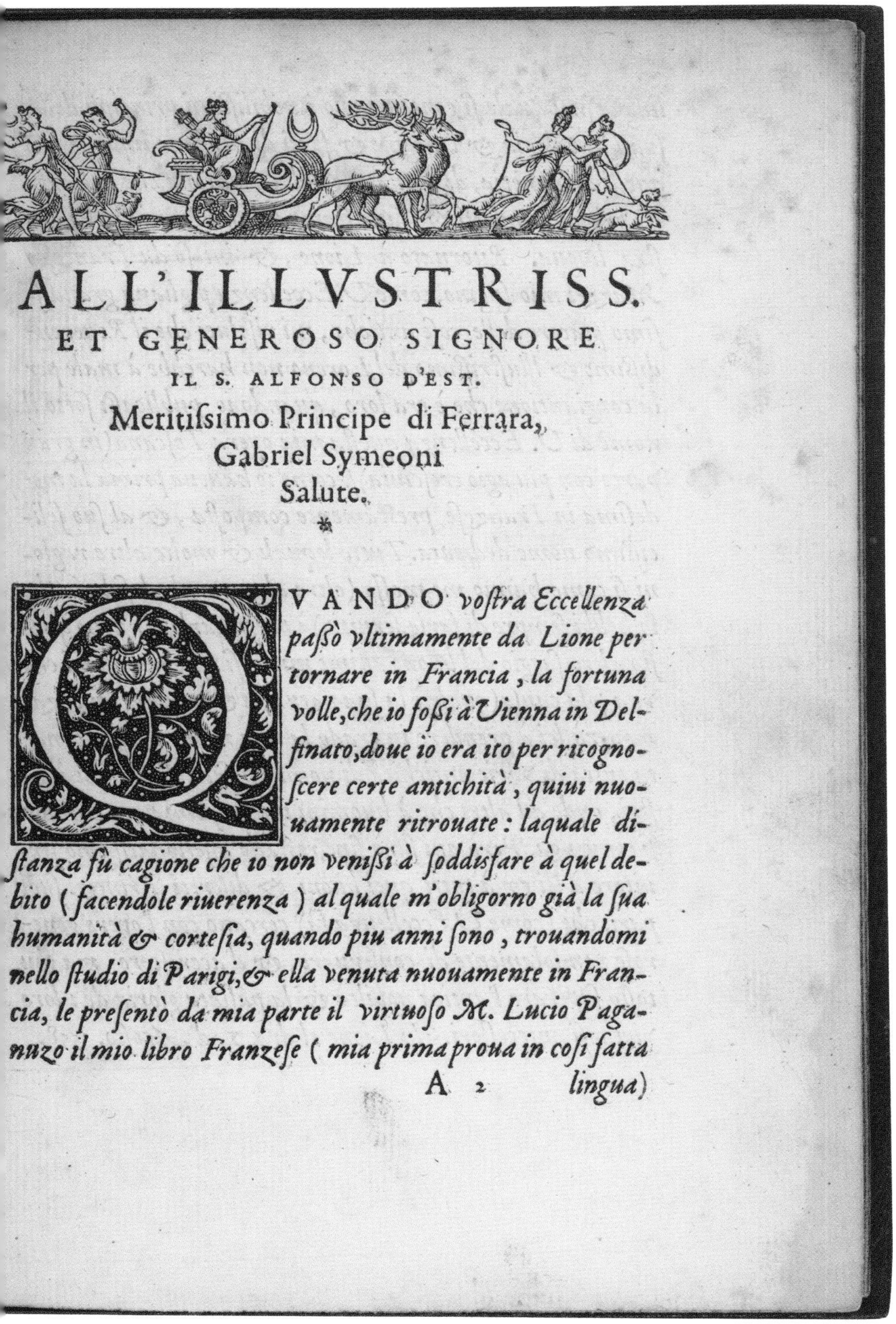
ALL'ILLVSTRISS.
ET GENEROSO SIGNORE
IL S. ALFONSO D'EST.
Meritiſsimo Principe di Ferrara,
Gabriel Symeoni
Salute.

QVANDO voſtra Eccellenza paſsò vltimamente da Lione per tornare in Francia, la fortuna volle, che io foſsi à Vienna in Delfinato, doue io era ito per ricognoſcere certe antichità, quiui nuouamente ritrouate: laquale diſtanza fù cagione che io non veniſsi à ſoddiſfare à quel debito (facendole riuerenza) al quale m'obligorno già la ſua humanità & corteſia, quando piu anni ſono, trouandomi nello ſtudio di Parigi, & ella venuta nuouamente in Francia, le preſentò da mia parte il virtuoſo M. Lucio Paganuzo il mio libro Franzeſe (mia prima proua in coſi fatta
A 2 lingua)

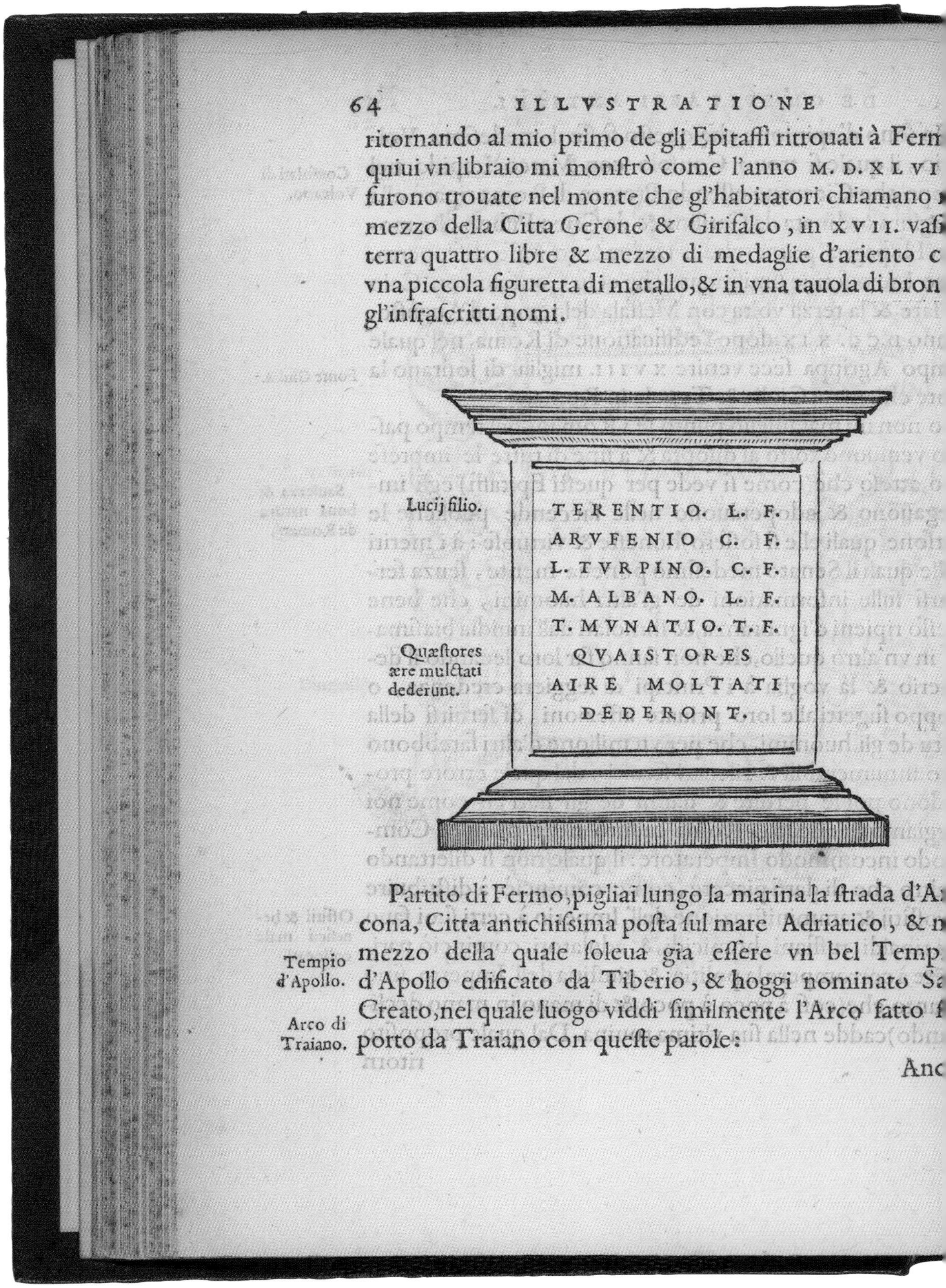
64 ILLVSTRATIONE

ritornando al mio primo de gli Epitaffi ritrouati à Fern
quiui vn libraio mi monstrò come l'anno M. D. X L V I
furono trouate nel monte che gl'habitatori chiamano
mezzo della Citta Gerone & Girifalco, in X V I I. vas
terra quattro libre & mezzo di medaglie d'ariento c
vna piccola figuretta di metallo, & in vna tauola di bron
gl'infrascritti nomi.

Lucij filio.
TERENTIO. L. F.
ARVFENIO C. F.
L. TVRPINO. C. F.
M. ALBANO. L. F.
T. MVNATIO. T. F.
Quæstores ære mulctati dederunt.
QVAISTORES
AIRE MOLTATI
DEDERONT.

Partito di Fermo, pigliai lungo la marina la strada d'A
cona, Citta antichissima posta sul mare Adriatico, & n
Tempio d'Apollo. mezzo della quale soleua gia essere vn bel Temp
d'Apollo edificato da Tiberio, & hoggi nominato Sa
Arco di Traiano. Creato, nel quale luogo viddi similmente l'Arco fatto f
porto da Traiano con queste parole:

Anc

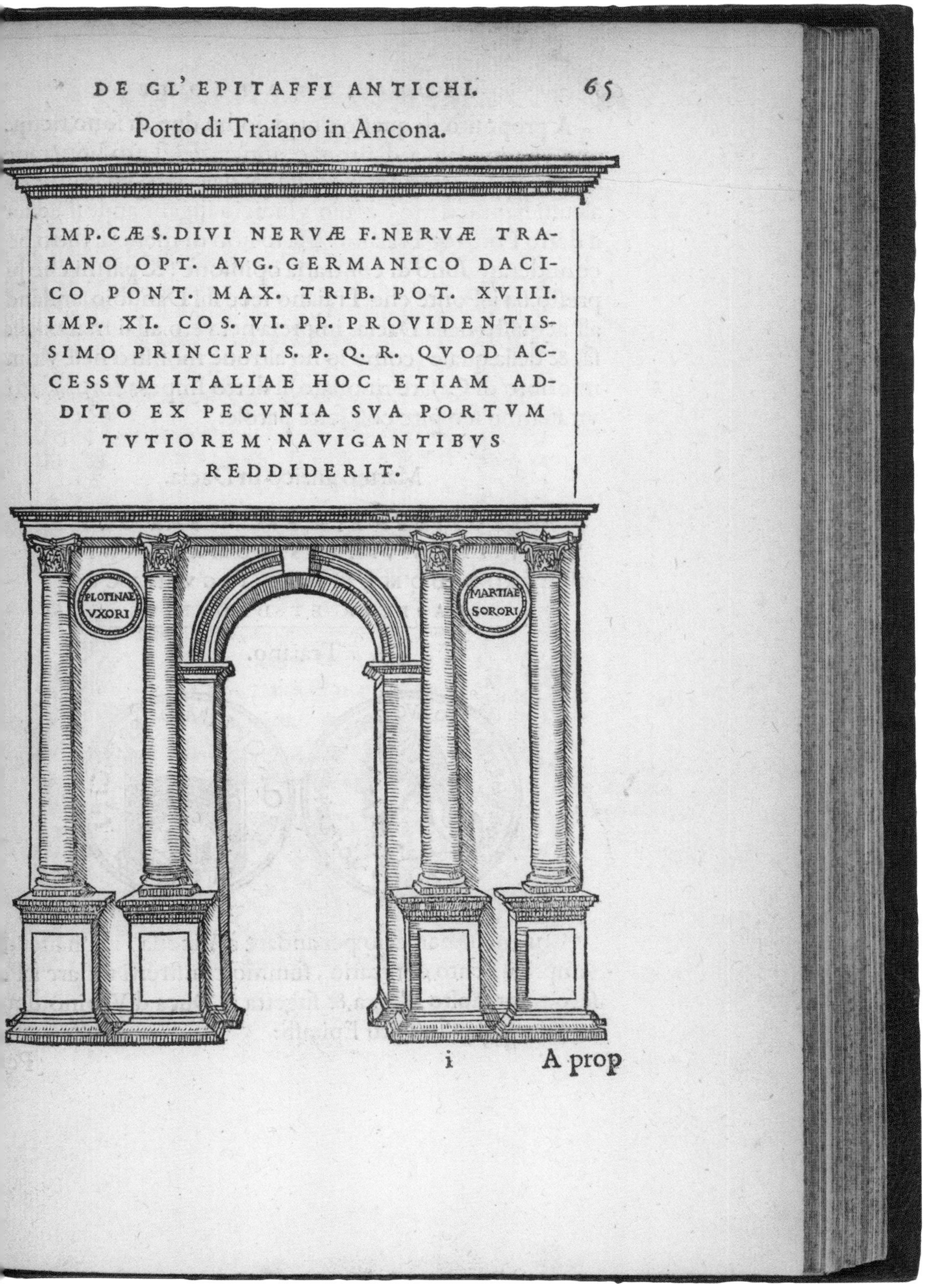

DE GL'EPITAFFI ANTICHI. 65

Porto di Traiano in Ancona.

IMP. CÆS. DIVI NERVÆ F. NERVÆ TRAIANO OPT. AVG. GERMANICO DACICO PONT. MAX. TRIB. POT. XVIII. IMP. XI. COS. VI. PP. PROVIDENTISSIMO PRINCIPI S. P. Q. R. QVOD ACCESSVM ITALIAE HOC ETIAM ADDITO EX PECVNIA SVA PORTVM TVTIOREM NAVIGANTIBVS REDDIDERIT.

i A prop

1558 **Robert Granjon** Palaephatus, *Le premier livre des narrations fabuleuses: avec ses discours de la vérité et histoires d'icelles*; translated by Guillaume Guéroult. Lyon: Robert Granjon, 1558. ii, 59, 60 pp. 19 cm.

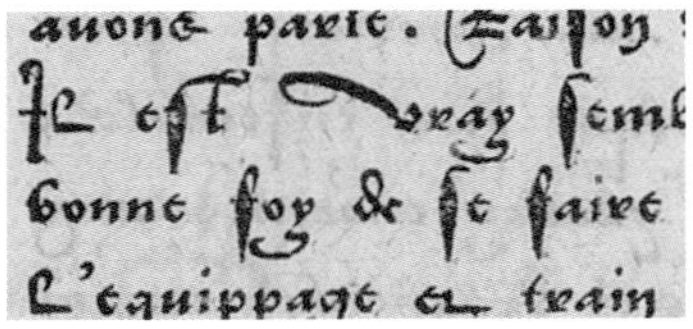

The first civilité type (1557) was cut by Robert Granjon in imitation of the French gothic handwriting of his time. Used for a variety of books, it was considered especially appropriate for children's books, because it matched the handwriting they learned at school.

Robert Granjon (1512/13–1590), son of a Paris printer and bookseller, was apprenticed to a goldsmith. From 1542 to his death he cut more than eighty roman, italic, Greek, Hebrew, Arabic, Syriac, Cyrillic and civilité printing types, plus fleurons: a remarkable output in quantity, quality and variety. He and Claude Garamont cut the best, most widely used and most influential types of their day. While Garamont's staid, traditional types remained Renaissance in their approach, Granjon's were spectacular and innovative, sometimes described as mannerist with even a hint of the baroque. He especially mastered the elaborate forms of italics, Greeks, Arabics, arabesque fleurons and civilités.

Granjon remained primarily a punchcutter for his entire career, working in Paris, Lyon, Antwerp, Rome and probably Geneva and Frankfurt. He supplied punches and matrices to many printers. His own printing and publishing (1549–62/63) served in part as a vehicle for his new types. He introduced what we now call civilité type in 1557, with King Henri II granting him a ten-year privilege for this *'lettre françoise d'art de main'* later that year. Nevertheless, others cut civilité types in Paris (Danfrie, 1558) and Antwerp (Tavernier, 1559). While Granjon launched his civilité with a patriotic appeal for a national hand and used it for literary works, it proved more successful as a body type for children's books, songbooks and religious and other works for less sophisticated readers, including the fable book shown here. As an auxiliary type it remained popular in the Low Countries for two centuries. JAL

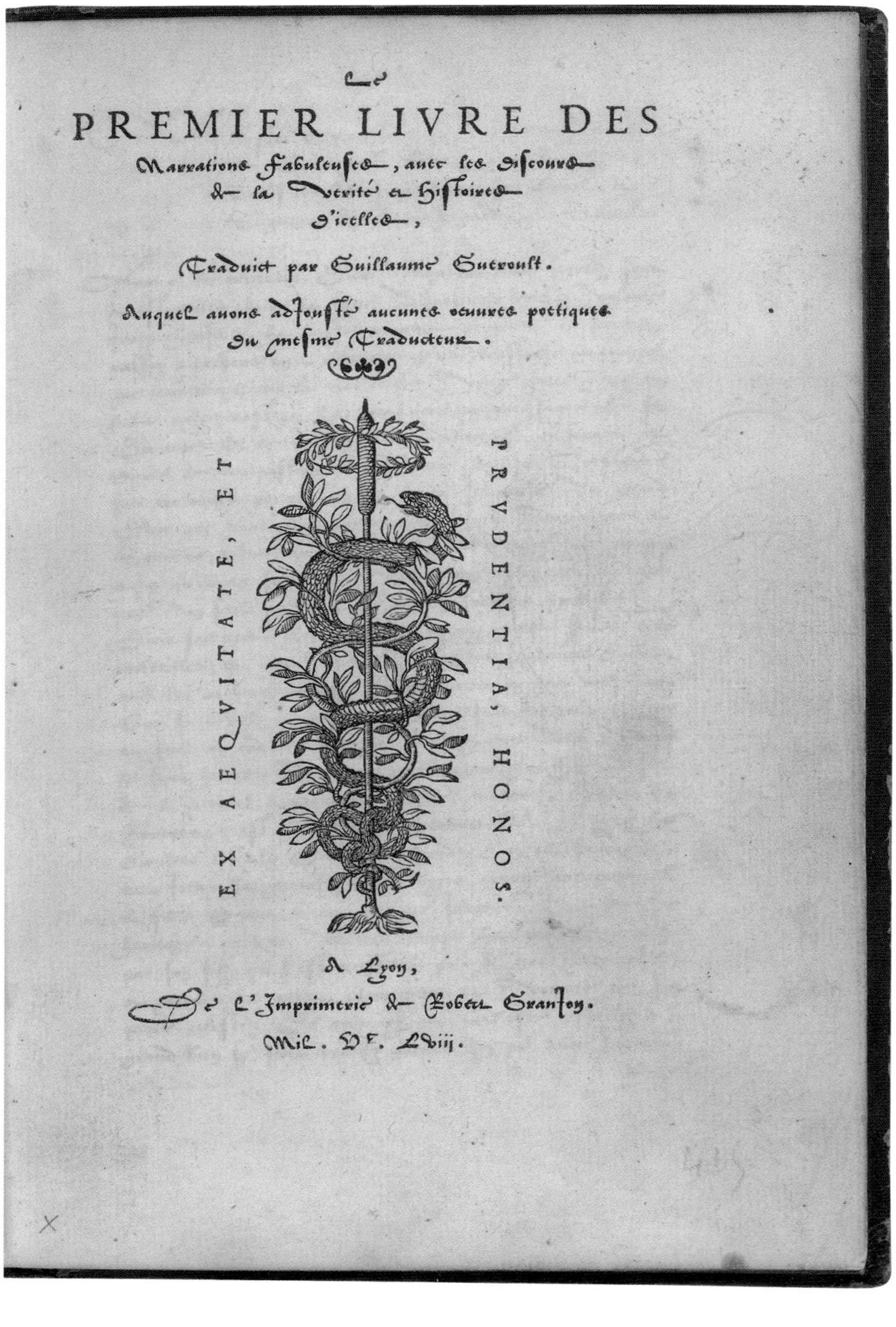

Le

PREMIER LIVRE DES

Narrations fabuleuses, avec ses discours & la Verité et Histoires d'icelles,

Traduict par Guillaume Gueroult.

Auquel avons adjousté aucunes oeuvres poetiques du mesme Traducteur.

EX AEQVITATE, ET PRVDENTIA, HONOS.

A Lyon,

De l'Imprimerie de Robert Granjon.

Mil. D. L. viij.

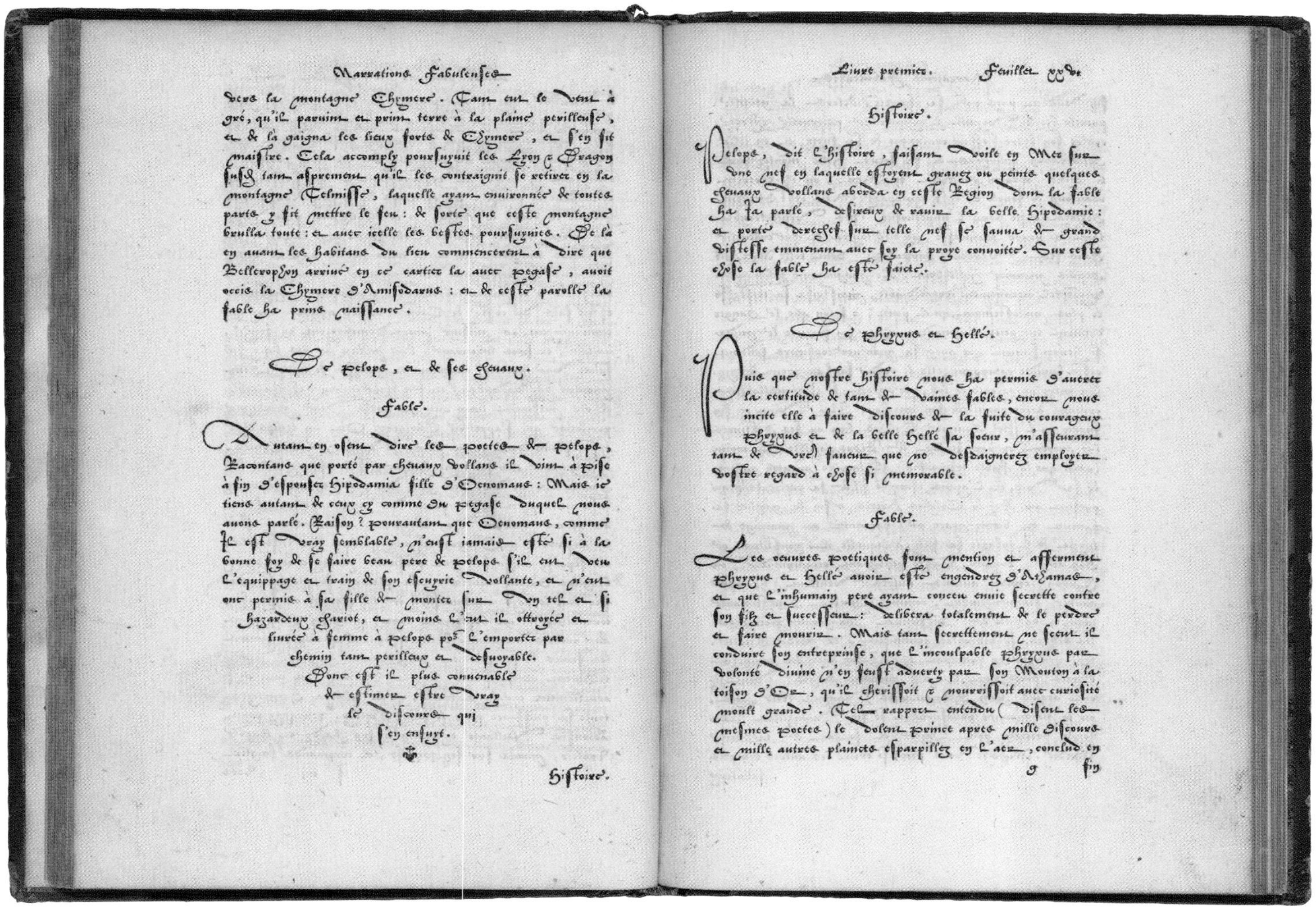

Narrations Fabuleuses

vers la montagne Chymere. Tant eut le vent à gré, qu'il paruint et print terre à la plaine perilleuse, et de la gaigna les lieux forts de Chymere, et s'en fit maistre. Cela accomply poursuyuit les Lyon et Dragon suss tant asprement qu'il les contraignit se retirer en la montagne Telmisse, laquelle ayant enuironnée de toutes parts y fit mettre le feu: de sorte que ceste montagne brulla toute: et auec icelle les bestes poursuyuies. De là en auant les habitans du lieu commencerent à dire que Bellerophon arriué en ce cartier la auec pegase, auoit occis la Chymere d'Amisodarus: et de ceste parolle la fable ha prins naissance.

De pelops, et de ses cheuaux.

Fable.

Autant en osent dire les poetes de pelops, Racontans que porté par cheuaux vollans il vint à pise à fin d'espouser Hipodamia fille d'Oenomaus: Mais ie tiens autant de ceux cy comme du pegase duquel nous auons parlé. Raison? pource autant que Oenomaus, comme Il est vray semblable, n'eust iamais esté si à la bonne foy de se faire beau pere de pelops s'il eut veu l'equippage et train de son escuyrie vollante, et n'eut ont permis à sa fille de monter sur vn tel et si hazardeux chariot, et moins l'eut il ottroyée et liurée à femme à pelops pour l'emporter par chemin tant perilleux et desuoyable. Donc est il plus conuenable de estimer estre vray le discours qui s'en ensuyt.

Histoire.

Liure premier. Feuillet xxv.

Histoire.

Pelops, dit l'histoire, faisant voile en Mer sur vne nef en laquelle estoyent grauez ou peints quelques cheuaux vollans aborda en ceste Region dont la fable ha fait parle, desireux de rauir la belle Hipodamie: et porté derechef sur telle nef se sauua de grand vistesse emmenant auec soy la proye conuoitée. Sur ceste chose la fable ha esté faicte.

De phryxus et Hellé.

Puis que nostre histoire nous ha permis d'auerer la certitude de tant de vaines fables, encor nous incite elle à faire discours de la fuite du courageux phryxus et de la belle Hellé sa soeur, m'asseurant tant de vostre faueur que ne desdaignerez employer vostre regard à chose si memorable.

Fable.

Les oeuures poetiques font mention et affermant phryxus et Hellé auoir esté engendrez d'Athamas, et que l'inhumain pere ayant conceu enuie secrette contre son filz et successeur: delibera totalement de le perdre et faire mourir. Mais tant secrettement ne sceut il conduire son entreprinse, que l'incoulpable phryxus par volonté diuine n'en feust aduerty par son Mouton à la toison d'Or, qu'il cherissoit et nourrissoit auec curiosité moult grande. Tel rapport entendu (disent les mesmes poetes) se dolent prince apres mille discours et mille autres plainctes esparpillez en l'aer, conclud en

g fin

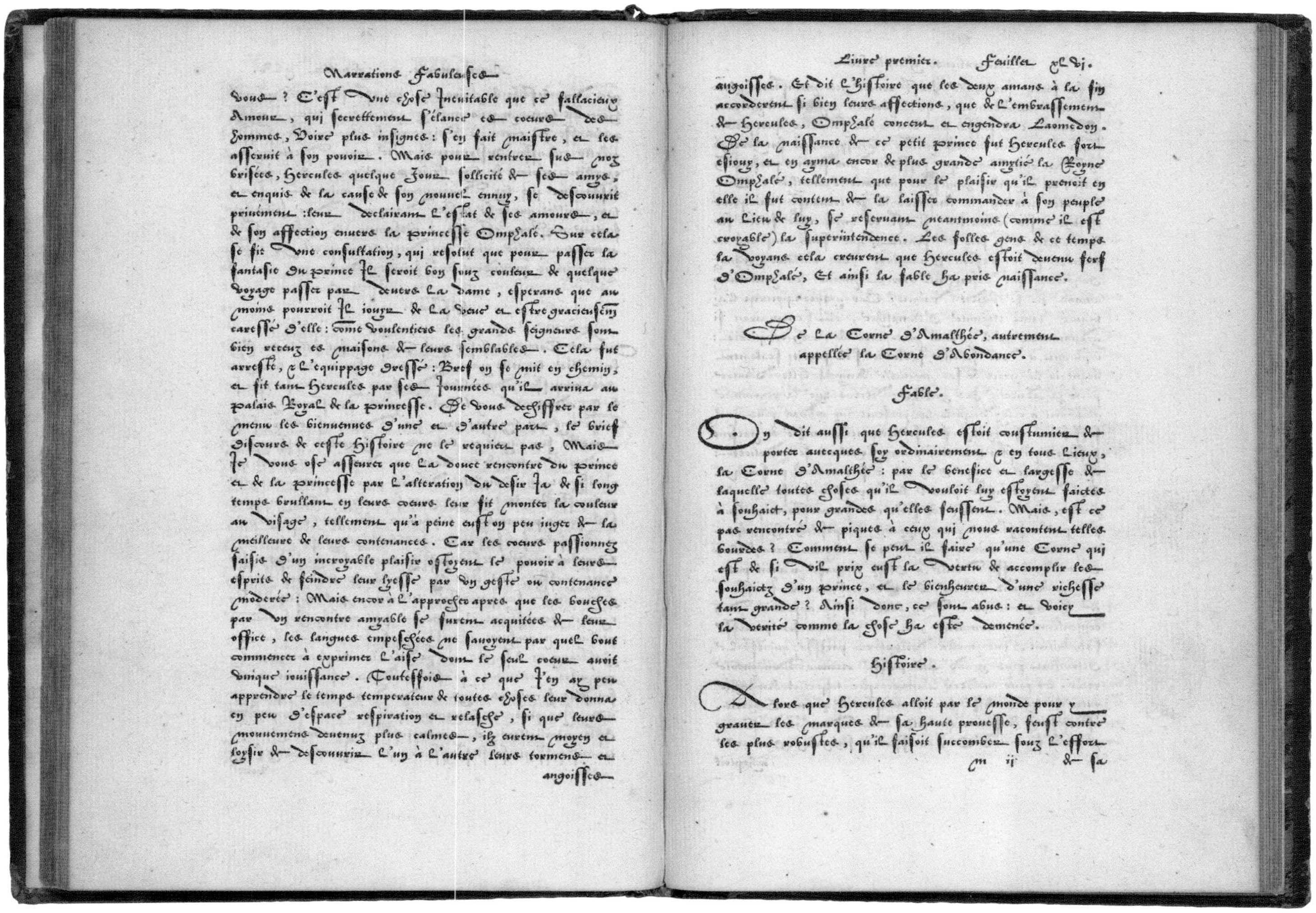

Narrations Fabuleuses

vous? C'est vne chose Inuitable que ce fallacieux Amour, qui secrettement s'elance es coeurs des hommes, voire plus insignes: s'en fait maistre, et les asseruit à son pouuoir. Mais pour rentrer sur noz brisées, Hercules quelque iour sollicité de ses amys, et enquis de la cause de son nouuel ennuy, se descouurit priuement à eux declairant l'estat de ses amours, et de son affection enuers la princesse Omphalé. Sur cela se fit vne consultation, qui resolut que pour passer la fantasie du prince Il seroit bon soubz couleur de quelque voyage passer par deuers la dame, esperant que au moins pourroit Il iouyr de la veue et estre gracieusement caressé d'elle: come vousentiers les grands seigneurs sont bien receuz es maisons de leurs semblables. Cela fut arresté, et l'equippage dressé: Bref on se mit en chemin, et fit tant Hercules par ses iournées qu'il arriua au palais Royal de la princesse. De vous deschiffrer par le menu les bienuenues d'une et d'autre part, le brief discours de ceste histoire ne le requiert pas, Mais Je vous ose asseurer que la douce rencontre du prince et de la princesse par l'alteration du desir sa de si long temps brullant en leurs coeurs leur fit monter la couleur au visage, tellement qu'à peine eust on peu iuger de la meilleure de leurs contenances. Car les coeurs passionnez saisis d'un incroyable plaisir estoyent se pouoir à leurs esprits de feindre leur lyesse par vn geste ou contenance moderée: Mais encor à l'approcher apres que les bouches par vn rencontre amyable se furent acquitées de leur office, les langues empeschées ne sauoyent par quel bout commencer à exprimer l'aise dont le seul coeur auoit vnique iouissance. Toutesfois à ce que i'en ay peu apprendre le temps temperateur de toutes choses leur donna en peu d'espace respiration et relasche, si que leurs mouuemens deuenuz plus calmes, ilz eurent moyen et loysir de descouurir l'un à l'autre leurs tormens et

angoisses

Liure premier. Feuillet xlvi.

angoisses. Et dit l'histoire que les deux amans à la fin accorderent si bien leurs affections, que de l'embrassement de Hercules, Omphalé conceut et engendra Laomedon. De la naissance de ce petit prince fut Hercules fort ioyeux, et en ayma encor de plus grande amytié la Royne Omphalé, tellement que pour le plaisir qu'il prenoit en elle il fut content de la laisser commander à son peuple au Lieu de luy, se reseruant neantmoins (comme il est croyable) la superintendence. Les folles gens de ce temps la voyans cela creurent que Hercules estoit deuenu serf d'Omphalé, Et ainsi la fable ha pris naissance.

De la Corne d'Amalthée, autrement appellée la Corne d'Abondance.

Fable.

On dit aussi que Hercules estoit coustumier de porter auecques soy ordinairement et en tous Lieux, la Corne d'Amalthée: par le benefice et largesse de laquelle toutes choses qu'il vouloit luy estoyent faictes à souhaict, pour grandes qu'elles feussent. Mais, est ce pas rencontre de piques à ceux qui nous racontent telles bourdes? Comment se peut il faire qu'une Corne qui est de si vil prix eust la vertu de accomplir les souhaictz d'un prince, et le bienheureur d'une richesse tant grande? Ainsi donc, ce sont abus: et voicy la verité comme la chose ha esté demenée.

Histoire.

Alors que Hercules alloit par le monde pour y grauer les marques de sa haulte prouesse, feust contre les plus robustes, qu'il faisoit succomber soubz l'effort

m ii de sa

1565 **Christoffel Plantin** Hadrianus Junius, *Emblemata*. Antwerp: Christoffel Plantin, 1565. 149 pp. 17 cm.

Illustrators: Geoffroy Ballain, Pieter Huys. Woodblock cutters: Gerard Jansen van Kampen, Arnold Nicolai.

Emblem books appeared for the first time in the 1630s. An emblem is a pictorial riddle – in woodcut or copper engraving – that can be read in several ways. It illustrates a proverb (sometimes from Erasmus's *Adagia*) and is accompanied by an ingenious poem and explanation in prose. Emblem books were still popular in Europe in the eighteenth century. Hadrianus Junius was one of the Dutch literary masters of the genre.

Christoffel Plantin (1520?–89), the printer and publisher of *Emblemata*, hailed from France and had settled in Antwerp in his late twenties. The title page of this emblem book gives a clear indication that its design is characteristically French. The woodcuts are refined and the layout is elegant. Above each emblem is the number in spaced small capitals; immediately below the number is the proverb in lower case, the illustration, and the epigram in italic. Scholarly commentaries appear in a separate section at the end of the book; they are set in italic.

Each page of the book is framed with an identical border, built up from separate cast ornaments. This strengthens the typographical unity of the book. Surrounding the text and illustrations with a border was a French tradition. This was mainly done in small, illustrated editions such as the early sixteenth-century books of hours, which were copied from handwritten examples dating from the fifteenth century. PD

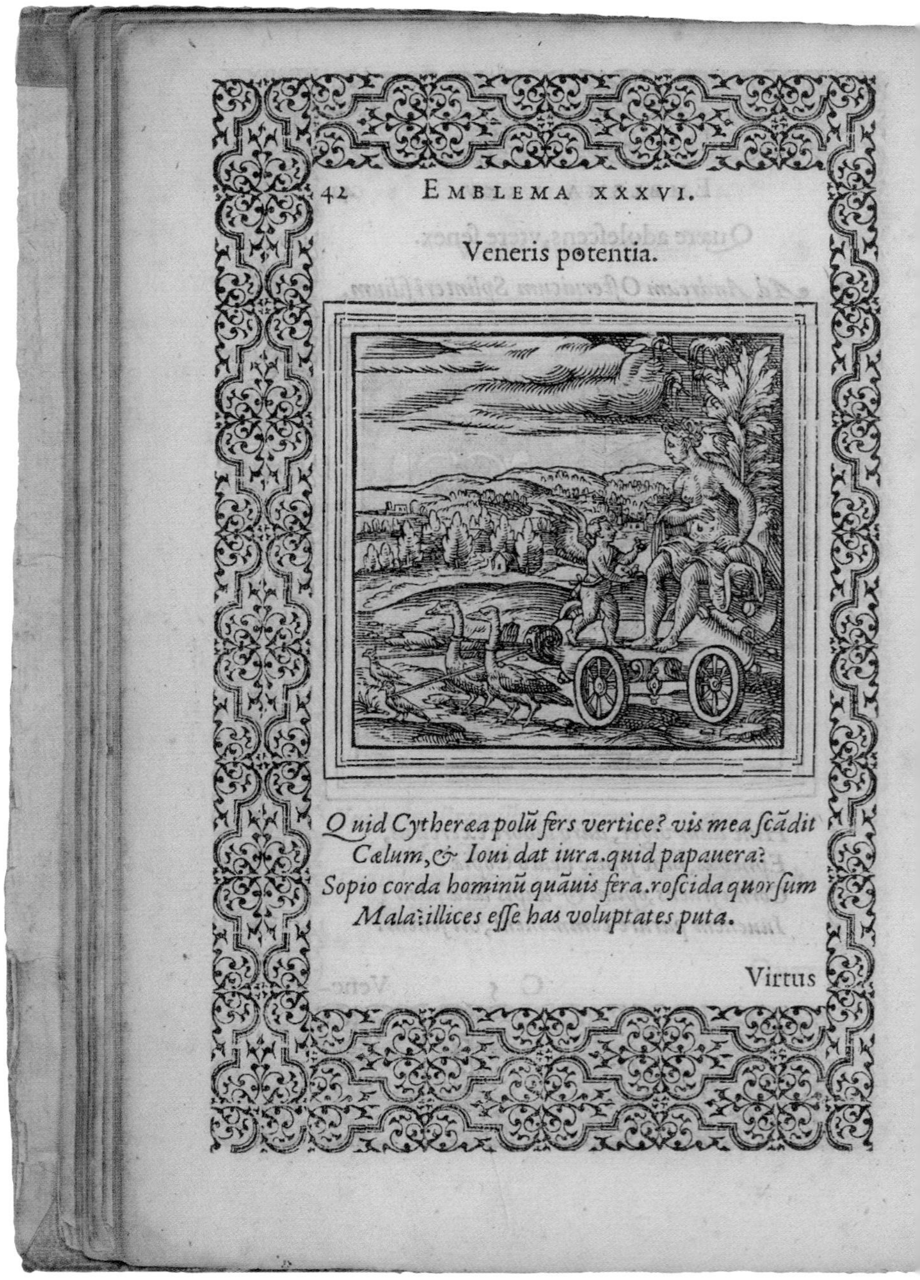

Jean de Tournes in Lyon used Bernard Salomon's arabesque woodblocks and by 1559 arabesques built up from fleurons, probably by Salomon's son-in-law Robert Granjon (1512/13–90), who cut types for De Tournes. Granjon moved to Antwerp in 1563 and likely cut these fleurons, which were later used alongside others he sold to Plantin in 1566.

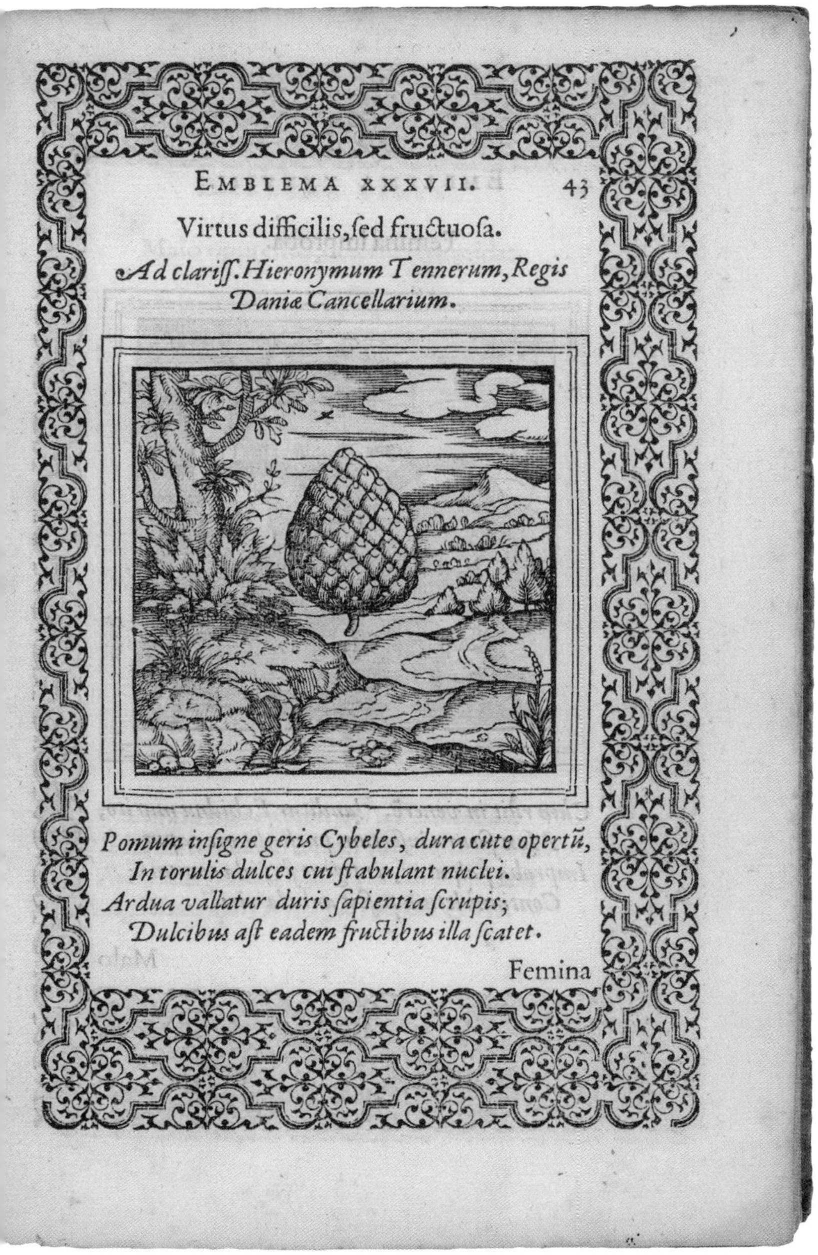

EMBLEMA XXXVII. 43

Virtus difficilis, ſed fructuoſa.

Ad clariſſ. Hieronymum Tennerum, Regis Daniæ Cancellarium.

Pomum inſigne geris Cybeles, dura cute opertū,
In torulis dulces cui ſtabulant nuclei.
Ardua vallatur duris ſapientia ſcrupis;
Dulcibus aſt eadem fructibus illa ſcatet.

Femina

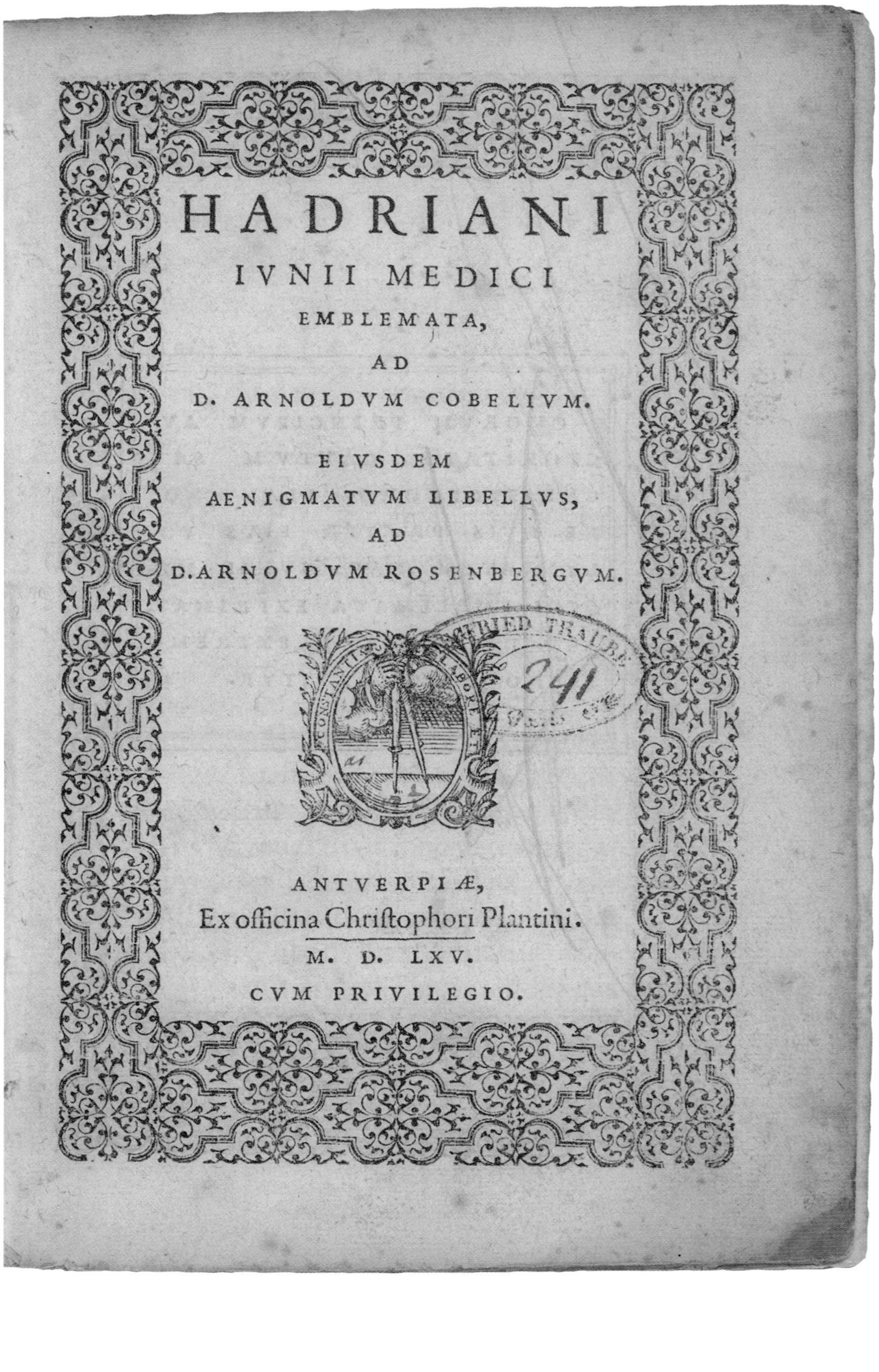

HADRIANI
IVNII MEDICI
EMBLEMATA,
AD
D. ARNOLDVM COBELIVM.
EIVSDEM
AENIGMATVM LIBELLVS,
AD
D. ARNOLDVM ROSENBERGVM.

ANTVERPIÆ,
Ex officina Christophori Plantini.
M. D. LXV.
CVM PRIVILEGIO.

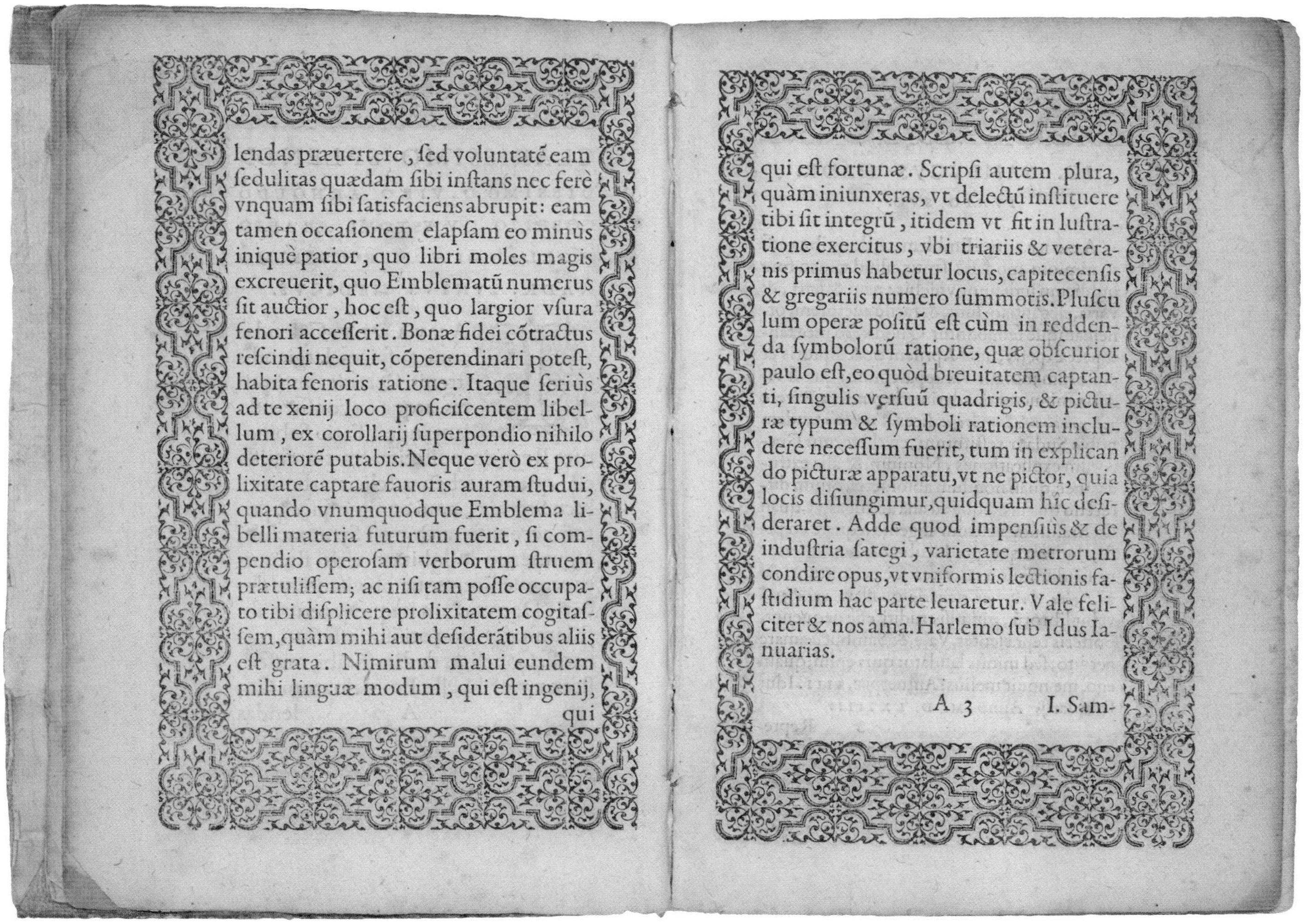

lendas præuertere, ſed voluntatẽ eam ſedulitas quædam ſibi inſtans nec ferè vnquam ſibi ſatisfaciens abrupit: eam tamen occaſionem elapſam eo minùs iniquè patior, quo libri moles magis excreuerit, quo Emblematũ numerus ſit auctior, hoc eſt, quo largior vſura fenori acceſſerit. Bonæ fidei cõtractus reſcindi nequit, cõperendinari poteſt, habita fenoris ratione. Itaque ſeriùs ad te xenij loco proficiſcentem libellum, ex corollarij ſuperpondio nihilo deteriorẽ putabis. Neque verò ex prolixitate captare fauoris auram ſtudui, quando vnumquodque Emblema libelli materia futurum fuerit, ſi compendio operoſam verborum ſtruem prætuliſſem; ac niſi tam poſſe occupato tibi diſplicere prolixitatem cogitaſſem, quàm mihi aut deſiderátibus aliis eſt grata. Nimirum malui eundem mihi linguæ modum, qui eſt ingenij, qui

qui eſt fortunæ. Scripſi autem plura, quàm iniunxeras, vt delectũ inſtituere tibi ſit integrũ, itidem vt fit in luſtratione exercitus, vbi triariis & veteranis primus habetur locus, capitecenſis & gregariis numero ſummotis. Pluſculum operæ poſitũ eſt cùm in reddenda ſymbolorũ ratione, quæ obſcurior paulo eſt, eo quòd breuitatem captanti, ſingulis verſuũ quadrigis, & picturæ typum & ſymboli rationem includere neceſſum fuerit, tum in explicando picturæ apparatu, vt ne pictor, quia locis diſiungimur, quidquam hic deſideraret. Adde quod impenſiùs & de induſtria ſategi, varietate metrorum condire opus, vt vniformis lectionis faſtidium hac parte leuaretur. Vale feliciter & nos ama. Harlemo ſub Idus Ianuarias.

A 3 I. Sam-

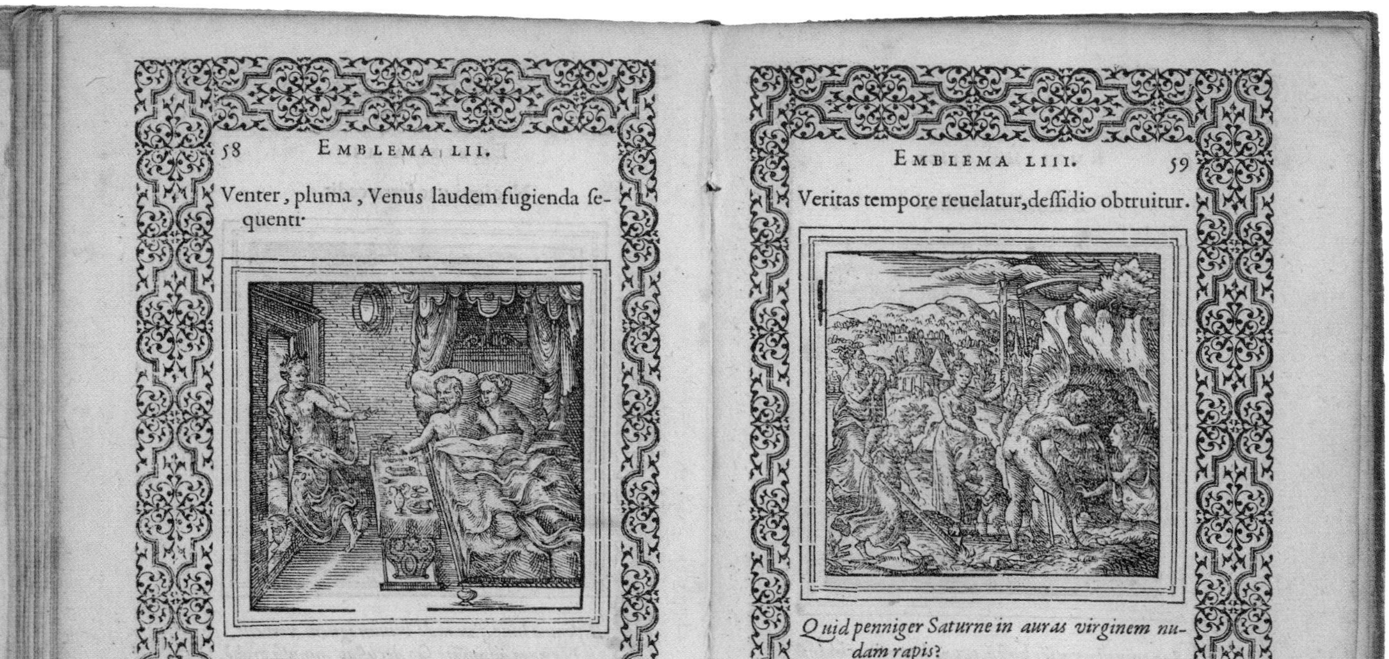

58 EMBLEMA LII.

Venter, pluma, Venus laudem fugienda ſequenti.

Quò fugitiua ruis, quem'ue auerſata relinquis
Gloria clara virum?
Deſero ſuffultum pluma, Veneris'q. miniſtrum,
Mancipium'que gulæ.

Veri-

EMBLEMA LIII. 59

Veritas tempore reuelatur, deſſidio obruitur.

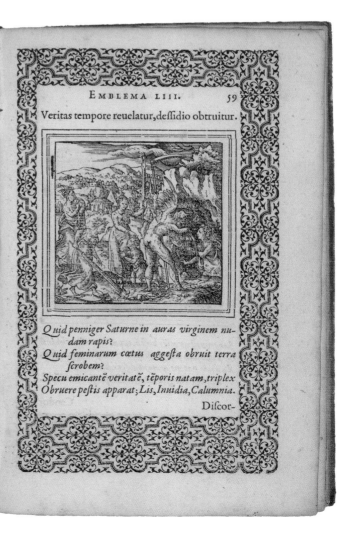

Quid penniger Saturne in auras virginem nudam rapis?
Quid feminarum cœtus aggeſta obruit terra ſcrobem?
Specu emicantẽ veritatẽ, tẽporis natam, triplex
Obruere peſtis apparat; Lis, Inuidia, Calumnia.

Diſcor-

1569 **Plantin Polyglot** *Biblia sacra Hebraice, Chaldaice, Græce, & Latine…* ; ed. Benito Arias Montanus. Antwerp: Christoffel Plantin, 1569–73. 8 volumes. 44 cm. Engravers: Peter van der Heyden, Pieter Huys, Joannes Wiericx, Philip Galle and others.

Plantin's polyglot Bible in Latin, Greek, Hebrew, Syriac and Aramaic is his most ambitious publication and a source for centuries of biblical scholarship. The French-born Christoffel Plantin (1520?–89) accompanied his father to Paris, where he remained to study. Apprenticed in Caen, he came to Antwerp in 1548/49 as a journeyman bookbinder, began selling books, and set up his own printing and publishing office in 1555. With seven presses and at least thirty-five employees in the 1560s, it was one of the world's largest printing houses, profiting from Antwerp's flourishing international trade. Plantin had to dissolve his partnership with Calvinist financiers in 1567, but managed a delicate balancing act, printing for both the Spanish Catholic authorities and his many anti-Spanish Protestant patrons.

The Renaissance and Reformation inspired textual criticism by Catholic and Protestant scholars searching for 'the' correct text of the Bible. By 1565 Plantin was planning a new edition of the Complutensian Polyglot (1514–17; see page 74) to facilitate comparison of the texts, and won sponsorship from King Philip II of Spain. Philip's chaplain Benito Arias Montanus carefully edited and annotated the texts, expanded the Aramaic text, and added a Syriac New Testament and additional Latin translations. Scholarly aids and engraved maps, plans and other illustrations helped the reader interpret the texts and understand their historical context.

Plantin commissioned the two Syriac types from Robert Granjon for this work. He printed 1,213 copies, on vellum and four different sizes and qualities of paper, selling paper copies for between 70 and 200 florins. JAL

Plantin's largest Hebrew type, cut in 1559 by Guillaume Le Bé I (1524/25–1598), following broad-pen calligraphy. He sold the matrices and mould to Plantin in 1562. As an apprentice, Le Bé may have helped Jean Arnoul to cut Robert Estienne's Hebrew types, but his own version surpassed Estienne's and even Bomberg's in Venice.

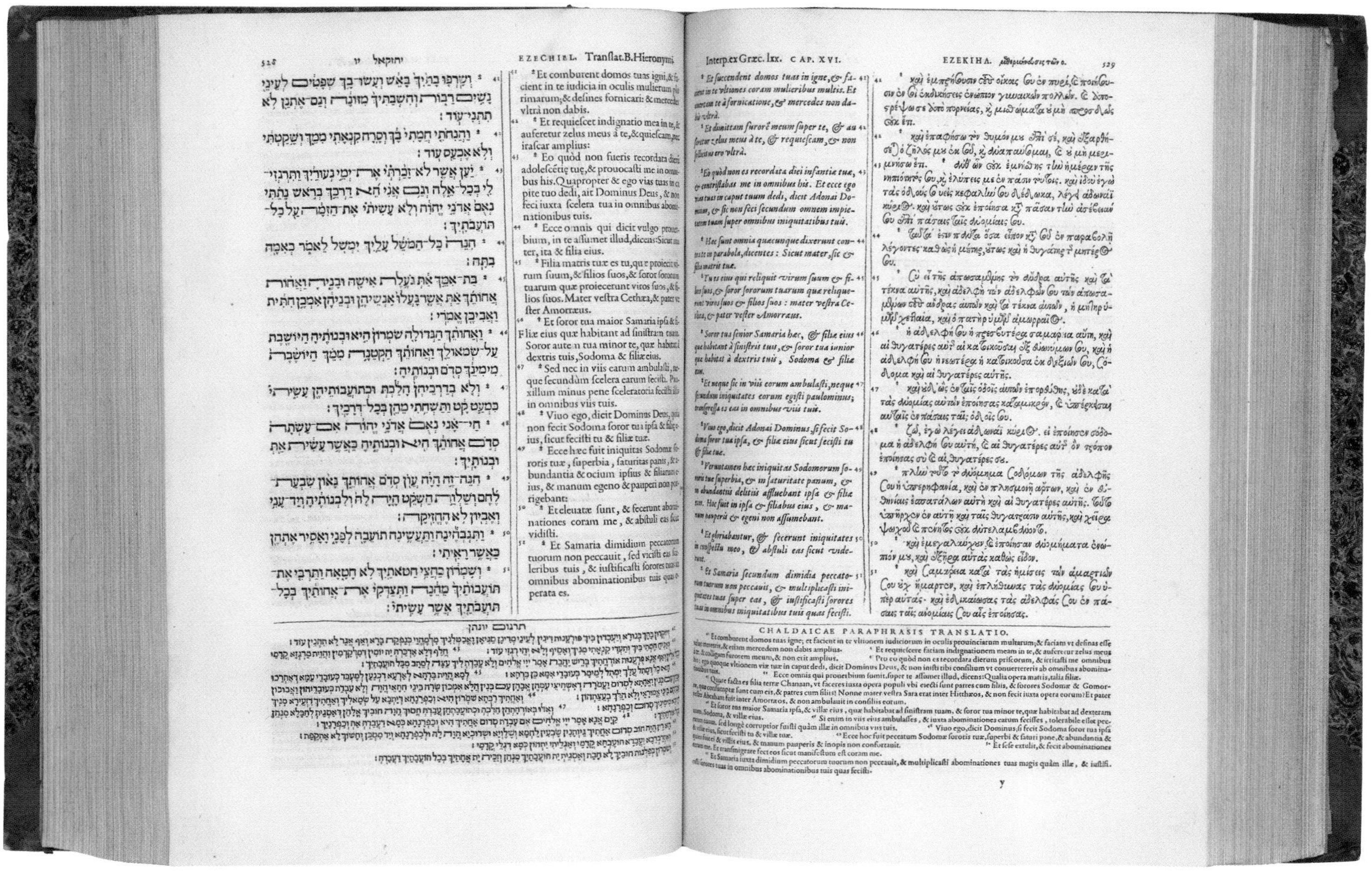

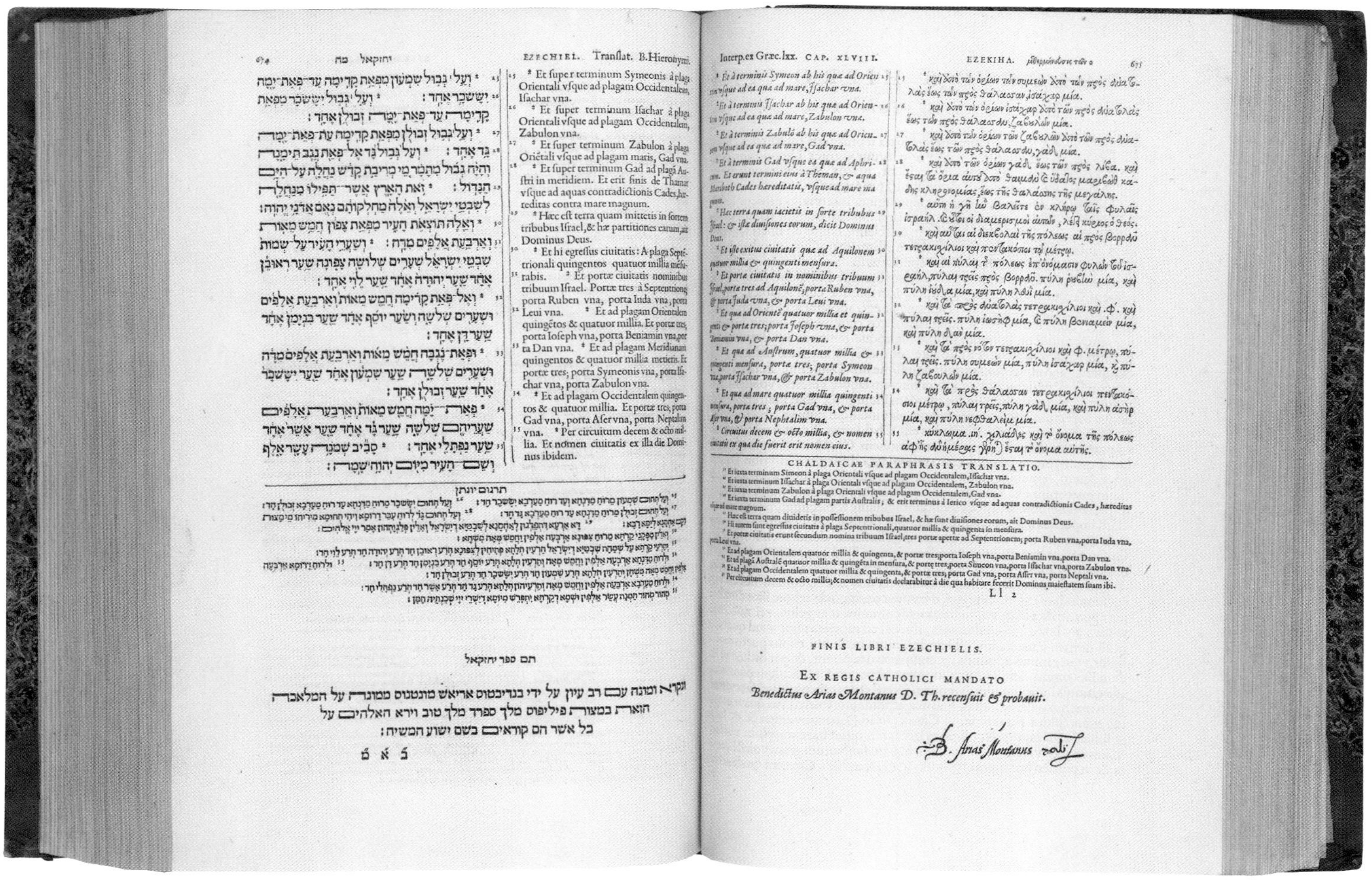

Plantin Polyglot

Henri Estienne II (1531–98) – using the Latinized name of Henricus Stephanus – was one of the great scholars of his day. He mainly published annotated texts from antiquity. His monumental lexicon of classical Greek was still being reprinted in the nineteenth century and remains an important reference work to this day.

The Estienne family, originally from Paris, relocated to Geneva for religious reasons. There, Henri published a number of – often voluminous – Greek text editions and also this *Thesaurus*, which almost caused him to go bankrupt. An epigram at the beginning of the first volume describes how the book turned him into a pauper and an old man, prematurely grey and wrinkled.

Remarkably, Estienne used hardly any of the aspects of his native French typographical tradition. The study in general and the ornaments in particular have all the characteristics of contemporary books printed in Geneva. The pages are not numbered, but the columns are, a customary feature in this genre. Every six centimetres, a letter of the alphabet is placed between the columns. This simplifies research and especially the looking-up of references. Column 2A, for instance, refers to the first paragraph of the right-hand column on the first page of the main text. PD

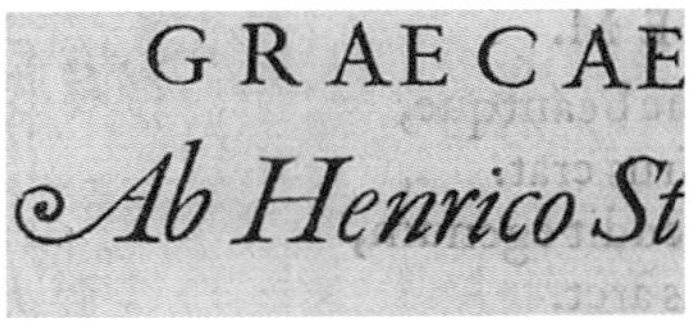

While large 'Canon' (about 42 point) romans quickly became a staple of display typography after their introduction in 1530, printers rarely demanded such a large italic. This 1564 example by Robert Granjon (1512/13–90), the century's greatest master of the italic, had no serious competitors until Jean Jannon cut one in c. 1620.

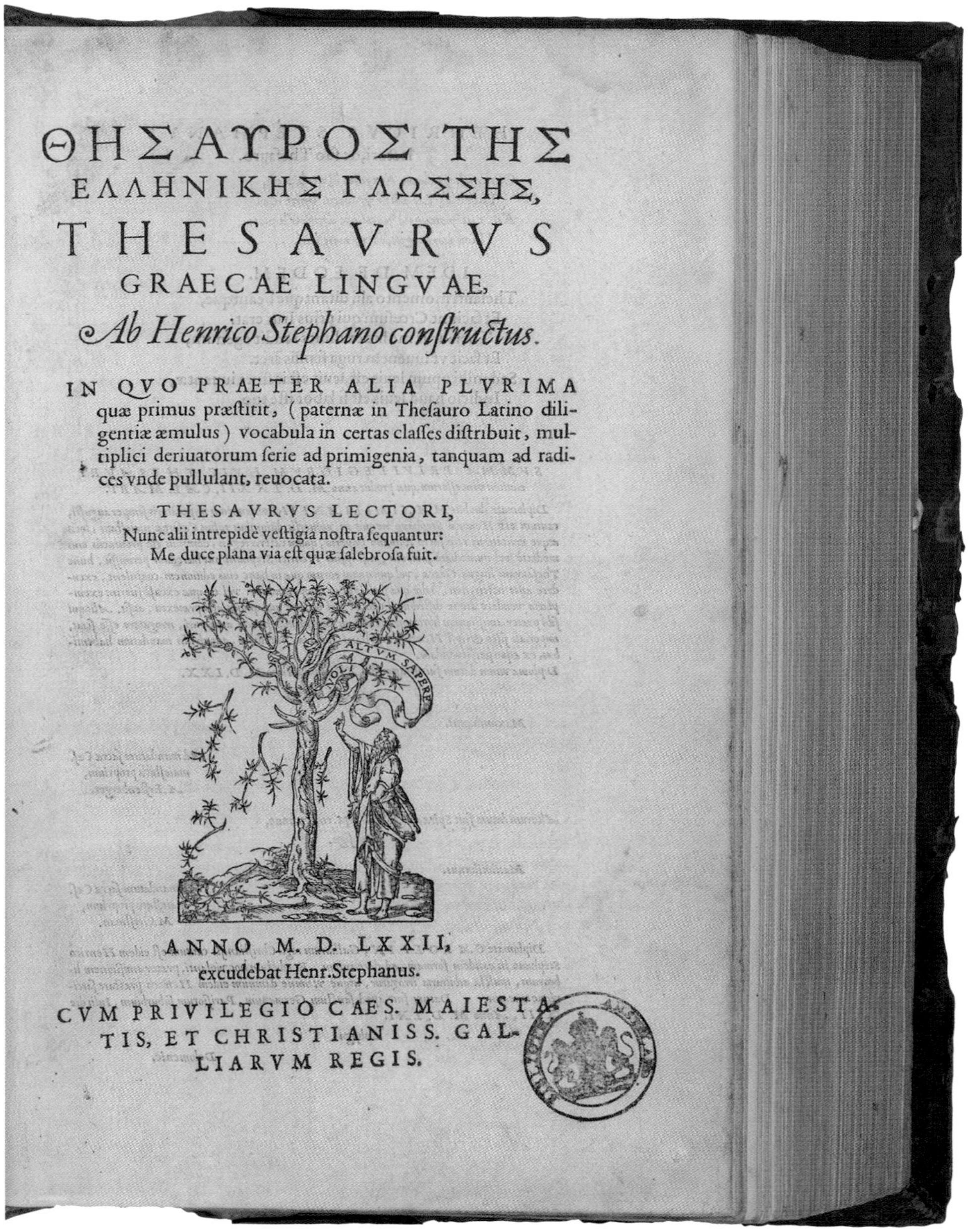

ΘΗΣΑΥΡΟΣ ΤΗΣ
ΕΛΛΗΝΙΚΗΣ ΓΛΩΣΣΗΣ,
THESAVRVS
GRAECAE LINGVAE,
Ab Henrico Stephano constructus.

IN QVO PRAETER ALIA PLVRIMA quæ primus præstitit, (paternæ in Thesauro Latino diligentiæ æmulus) vocabula in certas classes distribuit, multiplici deriuatorum serie ad primigenia, tanquam ad radices vnde pullulant, reuocata.

THESAVRVS LECTORI,
Nunc alii intrepidè vestigia nostra sequantur:
Me duce plana via est quæ salebrosa fuit.

ANNO M. D. LXXII,
excudebat Henr. Stephanus.

CVM PRIVILEGIO CAES. MAIESTATIS, ET CHRISTIANISS. GALLIARVM REGIS.

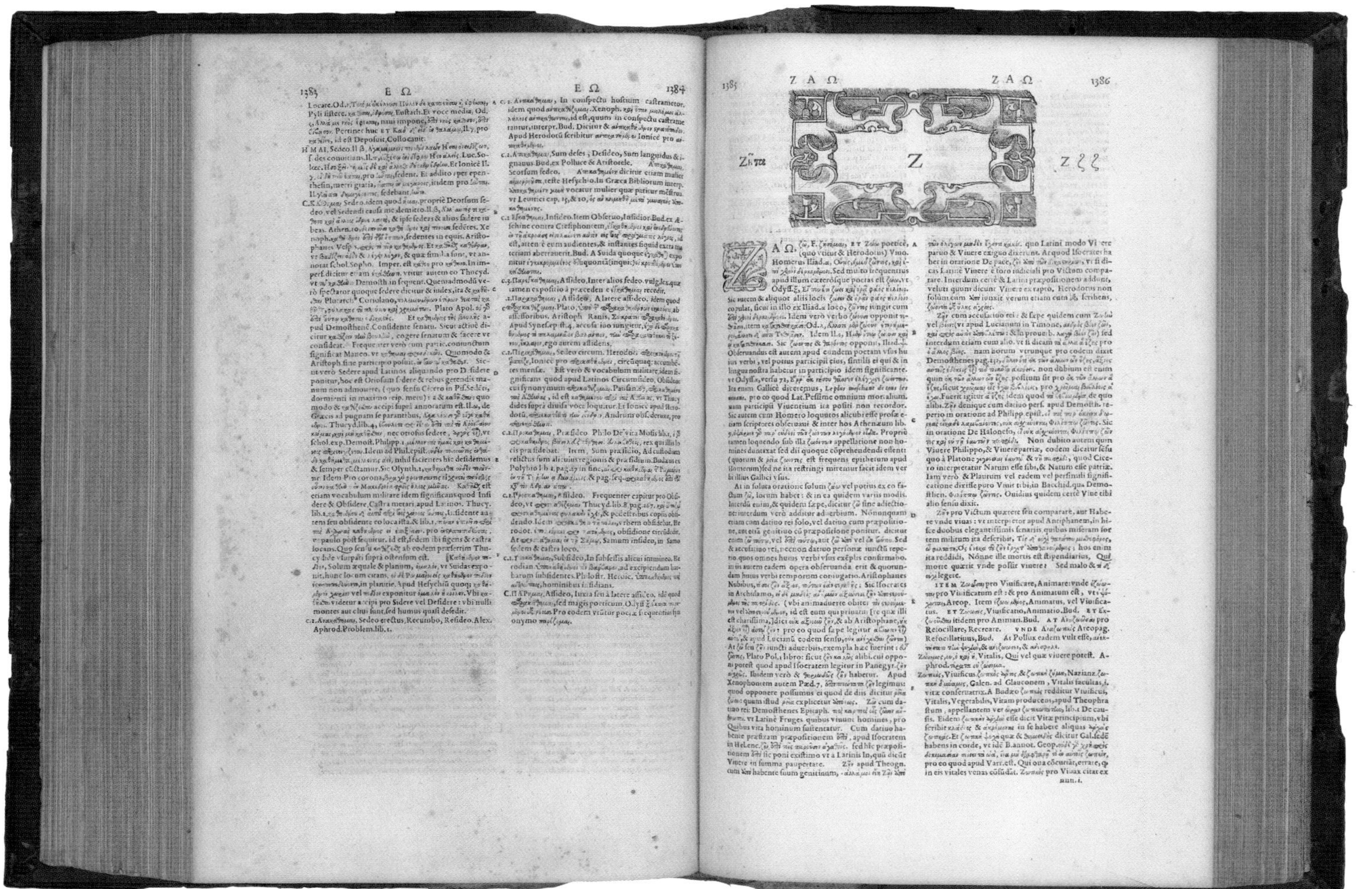

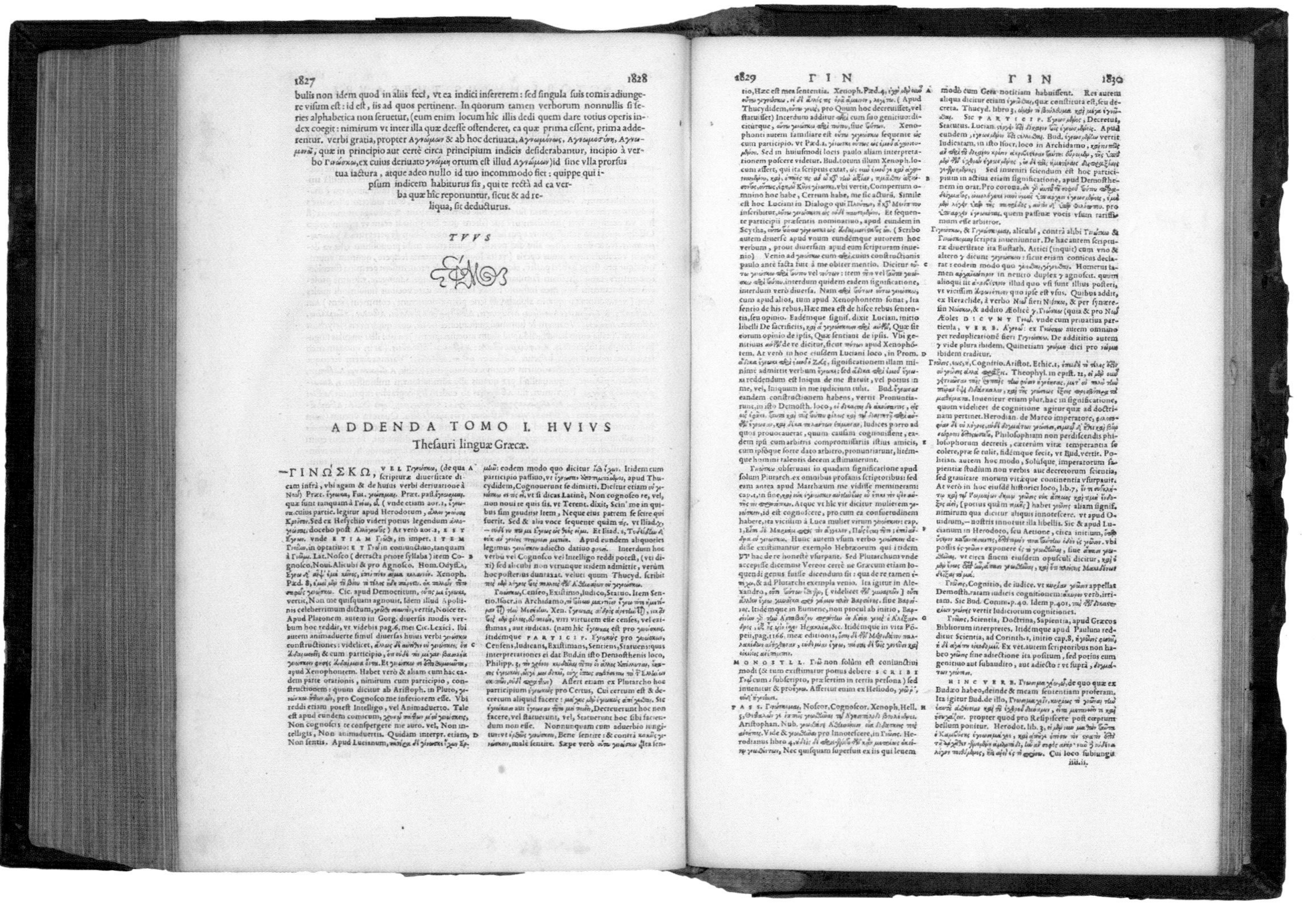

Henri Estienne II

1577 **Giovan Francesco Cresci** Giovan Francesco Cresci, *Il perfetto scrittore*... Venice: Giovanni Antonio degli Antoni, *c.* 1577/80 (?). 48 leaves. 15.5 × 22 cm. 1st ed. Rome, 1571. Woodblock cutter: Giovanni Francesco Aureri. Printer: 'i Rampazetti' = the heirs of Francesco Rampazetto (?)

Giovan Francesco Cresci (*c.* 1530?–*c.* 1607/17), whose father managed affairs for powerful cardinals, studied calligraphy in Milan before moving to Rome in around 1552. By 1556 he worked as a scribe at the Vatican Library and by 1560 as a copyist for the Sistine Chapel. His earliest-known surviving manuscript (1558) shows him pioneering a new style of writing, cutting his pen with a narrower and more flexible nib. Cresci's first printed writing manual and copybook (1560) challenged the traditional scribes and writing masters such as Giovanni Battista Palatino, claiming that his new chancery hand can be written faster than their old-fashioned one and has already been adopted by most of the Roman secretaries.

Il perfetto scrittore was Cresci's second writing manual, first published in Rome in 1571. The copy shown here is an abbreviated Venetian edition, somewhat carelessly printed from the original woodblocks. Besides the chancery type, it includes more formal italics, roman and gothic hands and decorated letters.

Pointed-pen letterforms have clear affinities with copperplate engraving, used by most of Cresci's followers, but he still preferred woodcut blocks for his own manuals.

Cresci's style triumphed, evolving into the pointed-pen script and lettering that dominated until Edward Johnston and others revived broad-nibbed pen calligraphy in around 1900. Typefounders and letterpress printers proved to be more conservative: the influence of the pointed pen infiltrated printing types only gradually over two centuries. Notable turning points were Philippe Grandjean's Romain du Roi (1699; see page 180) and the typefaces of the eccentric English writing master John Baskerville (1754; see page 208). JAL

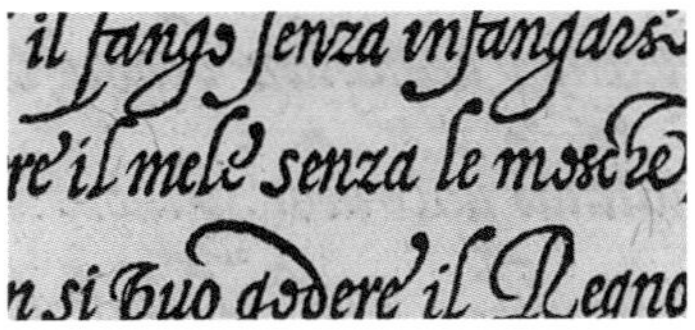

Cresci's chancery hand as cut on wood, probably by Giovanni Francesco Aureri da Crema (*fl.* 1560–78) in Rome. Ball or teardrop terminals replace the flat terminals of the traditional broad-nibbed pen and the swelling strokes show the beginnings of the transition to the flexible pointed pen.

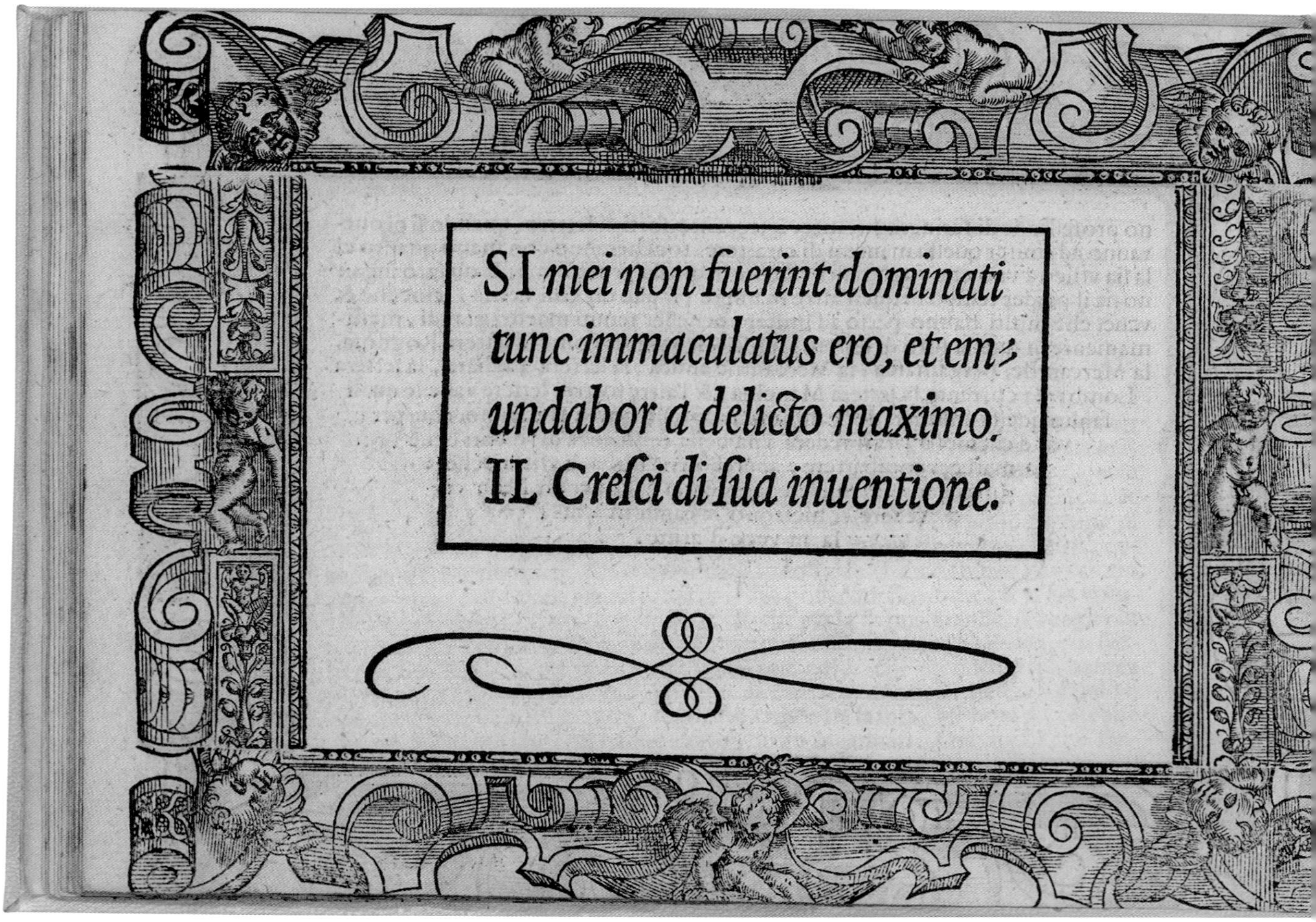

IL PERFETTO SCRITTORE
Di M. Gio. Francesco Cresci Cittadino Milanese.
Doue si veggono i veri Caratteri, & le natural
forme di tutte quelle sorti di lettere, che
à vero scrittor si appartengono.
Con alcun'altre da lui nuouamente ritrouate.
Et i modi, che deue tenere il mastro
per ben insegnare.

AABBCCDDEEFFG
HHIIKKLLMMNN
OOOPPQQRRSSTT.
VVXXXYYZZ. CRESCIVS.

DELLA LETTERA CANCELLARESCA
alquanto corrente.

QVESTA sorte di lettera alquanto corrente studiato che s'haurà li Alfabeti della lettera formatella co suoi essempi quel tempo, che ad ogniuno sarà conueniente potrà per voler venire alla prattica dello scriuere, studiare questa maniera alquanto corrente per cominciar a dar alla lettera maggior dependenza & a pigliar alcuni tratti (come in essa si vede) che conuengono alla lettera corsiua, & in questa maniera studiando, la mano verrà a poco a poco ad acquistare dispositione & grado di uenir alla prattica dello scriuer' veloce & sicuro.

SICOME Non si puo solcare il mare senza pericolo,
caminare per il fango senza infangarsi. ricorre il grano
senza paglia, hauere il mele senza le mosche, la rosa senza
la spina; cosi non si puo godere il Regno di Dio sēza tribol.ni
Il Cresci di mano propria.

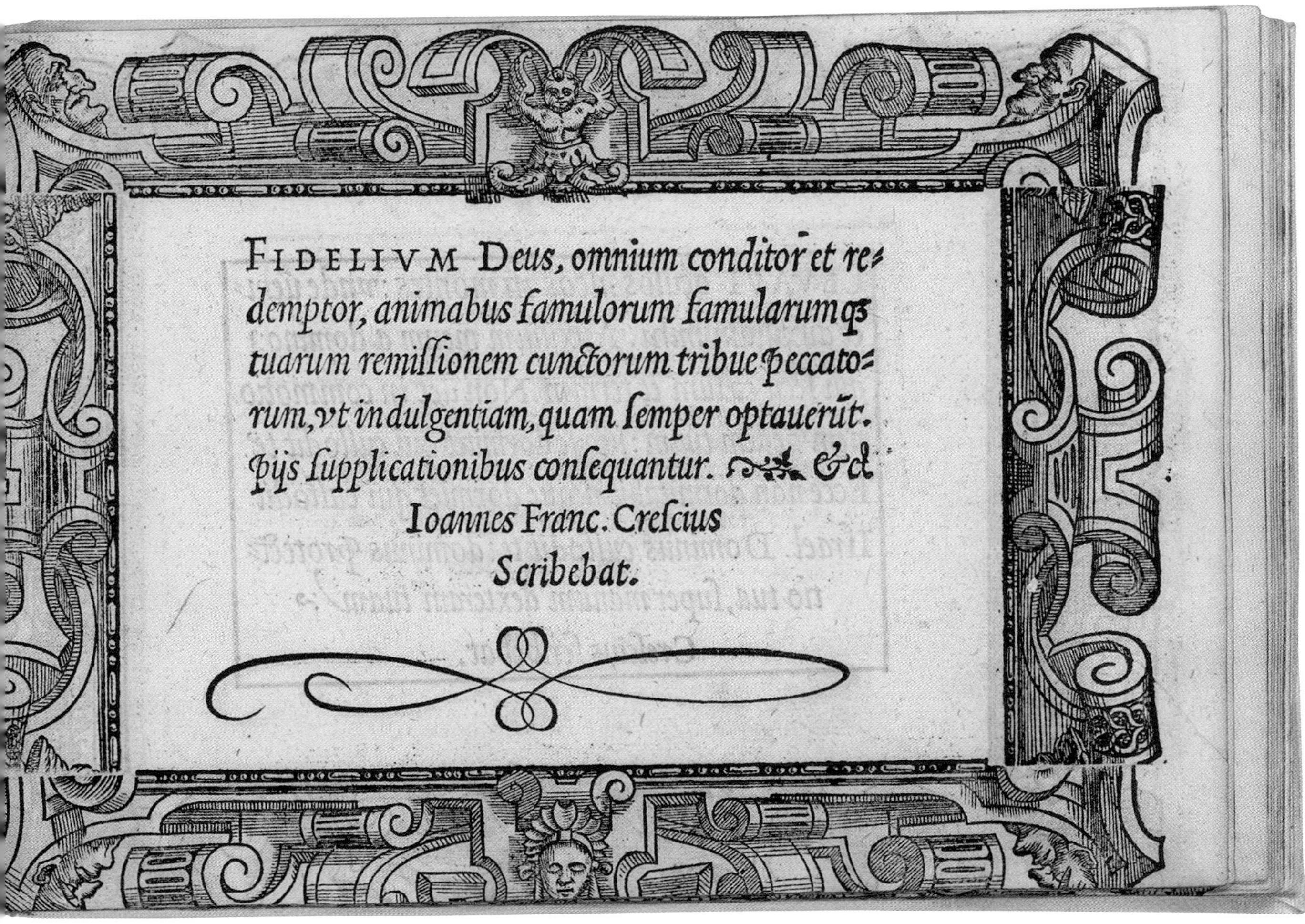

FIDELIVM Deus, omnium conditor et redemptor, animabus famulorum famularumq; tuarum remissionem cunctorum tribue peccatorum, vt indulgentiam, quam semper optauerūt. pijs supplicationibus consequantur. &c.
Ioannes Franc. Crescius
Scribebat.

Aabcdefg
hilmnop
qrstuxyz

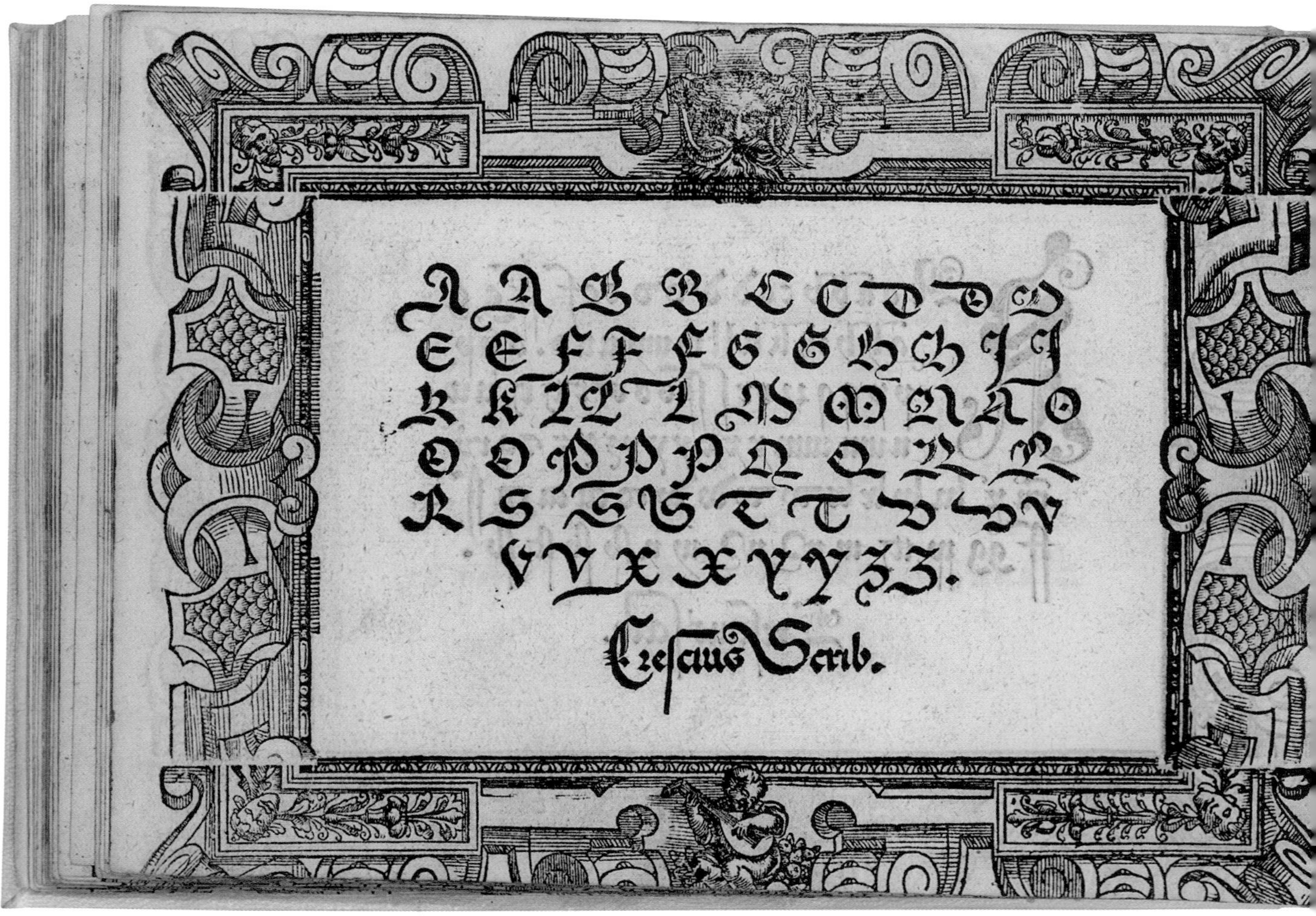

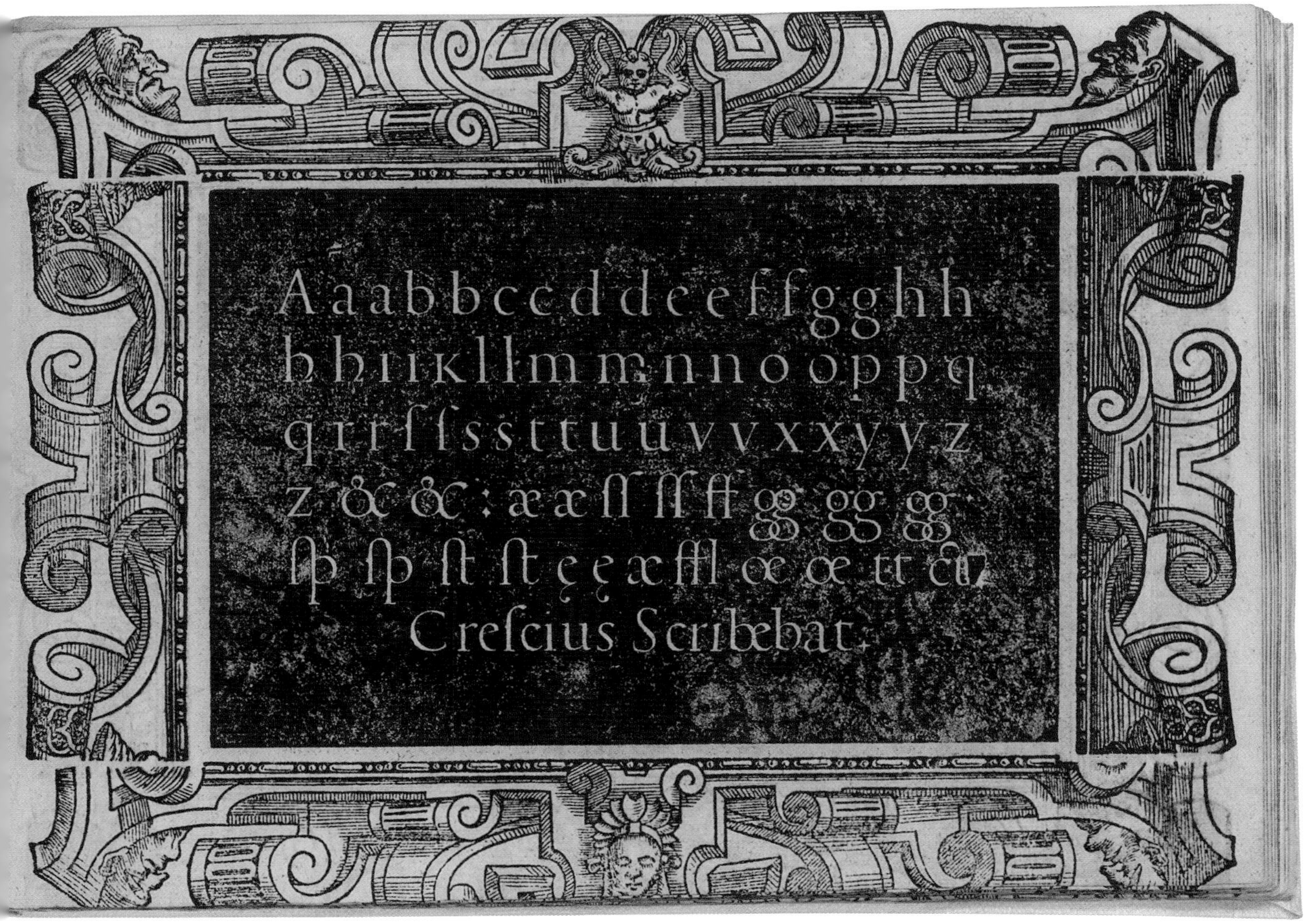
Crescius Scribebat.

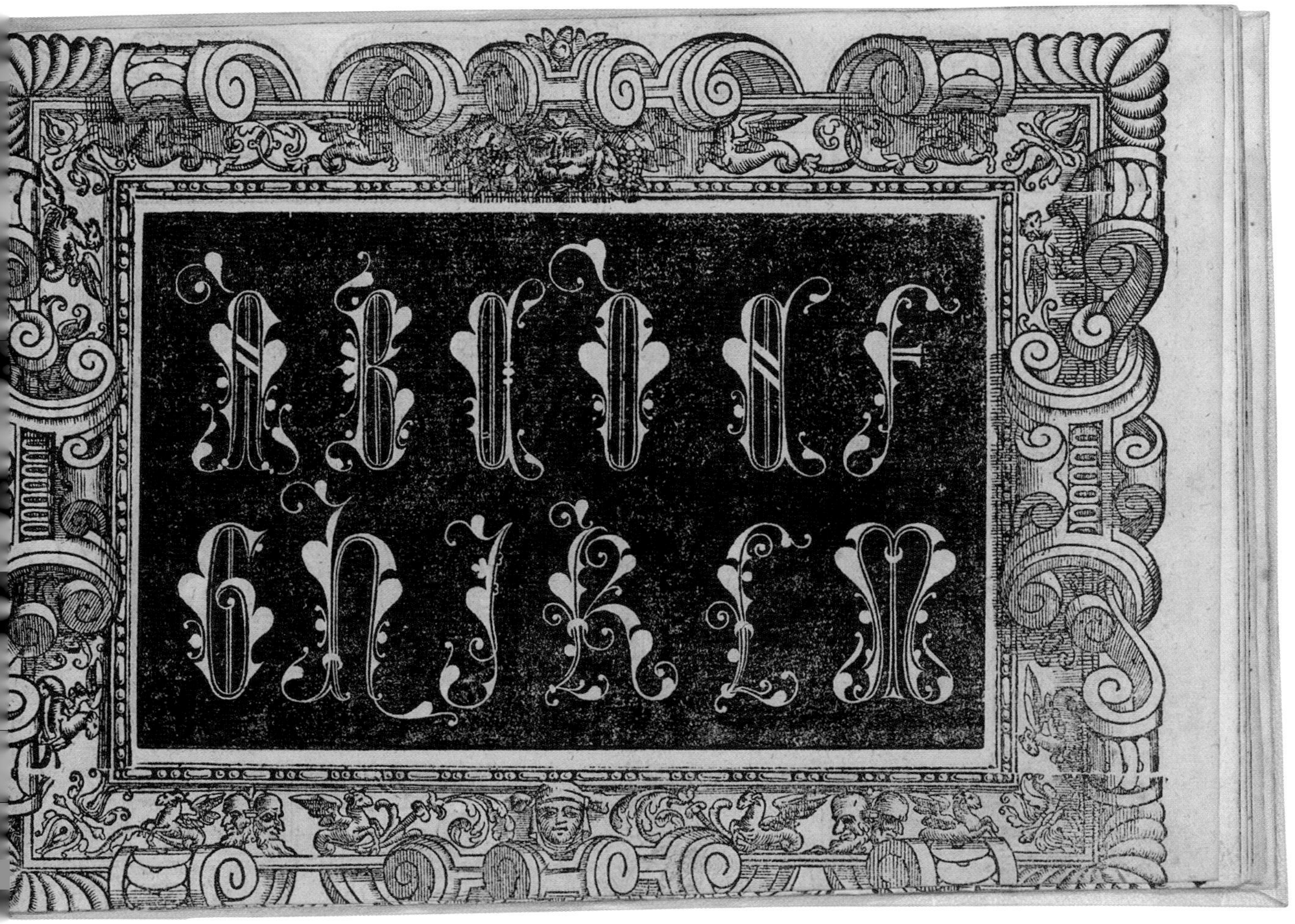

The Dutch Golden Age

Detail of *Académie de l'espée*, printed by the Elzeviers (see p. 158)

GEORGIU
ELECTOR
N. 7
N. 16
N. 15
N. 9
N. 3
N. 4
N. 1

The Dutch Golden Age **In the river port of Antwerp, cultural and commercial heart of the Low Countries in around 1565, Christoffel Plantin played a leading international role among printers. Protestant movements attracted increasing numbers of the book trade's scholars, artisans and merchants, but Spain's Catholic King Philip II repressed them brutally. The resulting revolt and Eighty Years' War established the Dutch Republic in the northern Low Countries but restored Spanish rule in the south. Talent, capital and influence flowed directly or indirectly north to Holland, becoming a deluge when Antwerp fell to Spain in 1585. The Dutch controlled the waterways, decimating Antwerp's shipping, and Holland's book trade gradually filled the void left by the rapidly declining south and particularly flourishing during the Twelve Years' Truce (1609–21).**

With foresight, Plantin had opened a Leiden office in 1583, continued by his son-in-law, Franciscus Raphelengius. Holland's excellent markets, ready capital and unmatched infrastructure drew many others – even Catholics – into its book trade. Printers in the Spanish Low Countries could barely persuade their last typefounder to stay. A relatively tolerant attitude to different religious (and other) beliefs, an important tenet of the revolt, aided both printing and international trade, attracting Jews from Iberia and Eastern Europe, Armenians from the Middle East and Venice, and French Huguenots.

Radical authors, often banned elsewhere, could publish freely in Holland: Böhme, Comenius, Descartes, Cocceius, Spinoza, Balthasar Bekker, Bayle, English Puritans and Polish Socinians. Amsterdam soon took the lead. Willem Jansz Blaeu printed his 1617

Copernicus in the knowledge that its 1616 prohibition stifled foreign competition. Protestant notions that laymen (and even women) should study scripture led to demands for greater education and smaller, cheaper Bibles. Holland's trade and commerce also helped it to attain Europe's highest literacy rate, enlarging the market for political and religious pamphlets, almanacs, newspapers, songbooks, emblem books and popular literature.

In the university town of Leiden, the Elzeviers published scholarly books, student theses and cheap classics. In Amsterdam, whose merchants drove the shipping trade, Blaeu branched out from copperplate globes and maps to publish atlases, copperplate illustrations, astronomy and practical science. Voyagers' discoveries quickly spread via cartographic, topographic and natural history publications. Paulus van Ravesteyn printed the first authorized Dutch Bible. Dutch printers smuggled Bibles to England in tens of thousands. Broer Jansz and Joris Veselar printed the first newspapers. Others specialized in almanacs, government publications, German books, and more. Amsterdam housed the Low Countries' first Jewish (1626) and Armenian (1660) presses. Scholarly presses printed Arabic, Syriac and Samaritan.

Nicolaes Briot, Christoffel van Dijck and others made Amsterdam an international centre of punchcutting and typefounding. Roman types, already the norm for Latin and romance languages, spread to Dutch scholarly works, but Textura held its place in sermons and Bibles. Holland lost its innovative role after 1688, although it retained some of its international market share for a few decades. JAL

1595 **Willem Barentsz** Willem Barentsz, *Nieuwe beschryvinghe ende caertboeck vande Midtlandtsche Zee*.

Amsterdam: Cornelis Claesz, 1595. 43.5 cm. Engravers: Jodocus Hondius; Pieter van den Keere (maps).

This nautical atlas by Willem Barentsz (*c.* 1560–97) was published in 1595. Although the navigator and explorer Barentsz is now best known for the winter months he forcibly spent on Novaya Zemlya in the Barents Sea, he was better acquainted with the Mediterranean. Ever since 1590, there had been a sharp increase in the amount of Dutch naval traffic to ports along the Mediterranean coast via the Strait of Gibraltar. Barentsz's atlas covers the western seacoasts along which the Dutch conducted trade.

The *Caertboeck* ('map book') – the term 'atlas' had not yet been invented – was a natural continuation of the first printed sea atlas, Waghenaer's *Spieghel der zeevaerdt* (1584). Waghenaer's atlas covers the Western European seacoasts from Norway to the Strait of Gibraltar, the area then covered by the Dutch merchant navy.

Barentsz's work should be seen in the context of the explosive dynamism of the circles surrounding Cornelis Claesz and the geographer and theologian Petrus Plancius towards the end of the sixteenth century. The printer and publisher Claesz (*c.* 1551–1609) mainly concentrated on geographic and nautical editions, and until his death he was involved in virtually all atlases, travel journals, and cosmographies that were printed in Amsterdam. With the publication of *Licht der zee-vaert* ('The Light of Navigation') in 1608, Willem Jansz Blaeu announced himself as Claesz's successor in this field. It would not be until 1618 that Barentsz's book became obsolete. In that year, Blaeu included the entire Mediterranean coastline in the third volume of his *Licht der zee-vaert*. JW

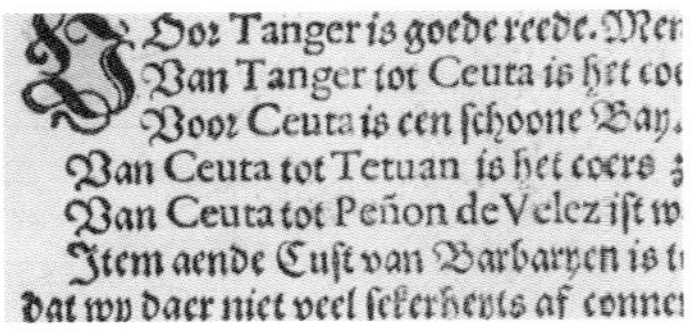
Voor Tanger is goede reede. Mer
Van Tanger tot Ceuta is het co
Voor Ceuta is een schoone Bay.
Van Ceuta tot Tetuan is het coers
Van Ceuta tot Peñon de Velez ist w
Item aende Cust van Barbaryen is t
dat wy daer niet veel sekerheyts af conne

This is a Nuremberg Fraktur (1522/25) cut by Hieronymus Andreae (*c.* 1485?–1556) or a close copy, after lettering by the writing master Johann Neudörffer. Fraktur type was usually used for German texts. Plantin had matrices for this face by 1580 and Willem Silvius had a fount, sold in 1582; both perhaps originated from the Sabon/Berner foundry in Frankfurt.

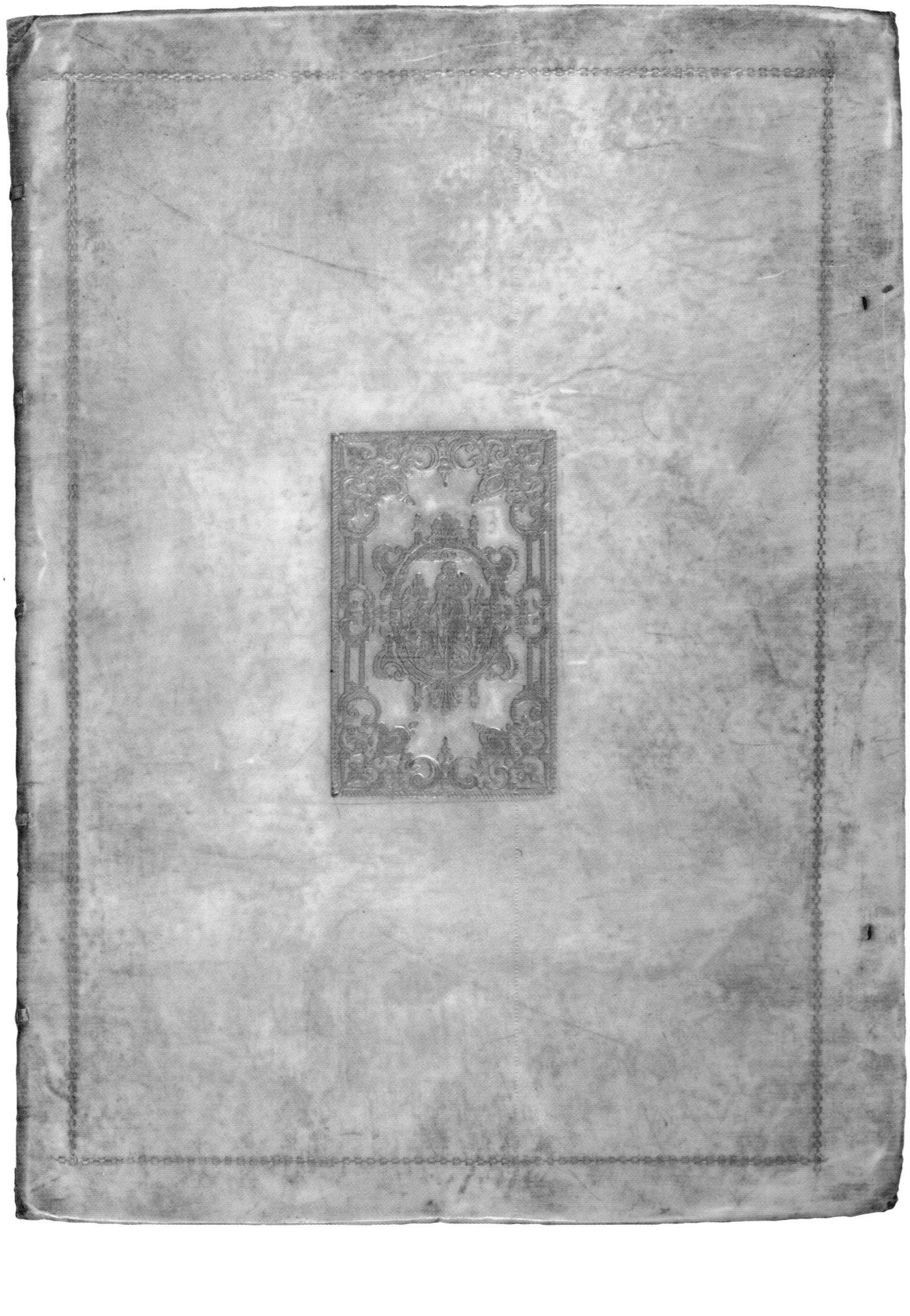

Nieuwe beschryvinghe ende
CAERTBOECK
Vande Midlandtsche Zee
door
Willem Barentzoen.
GENVA.
TOT AMSTELREDAM,
Ghedruct by Cornelis Claesz. op't Water in't Schrijf-boeck/by d'oude Brugghe.
Met Privilegie. M. D. XCV.

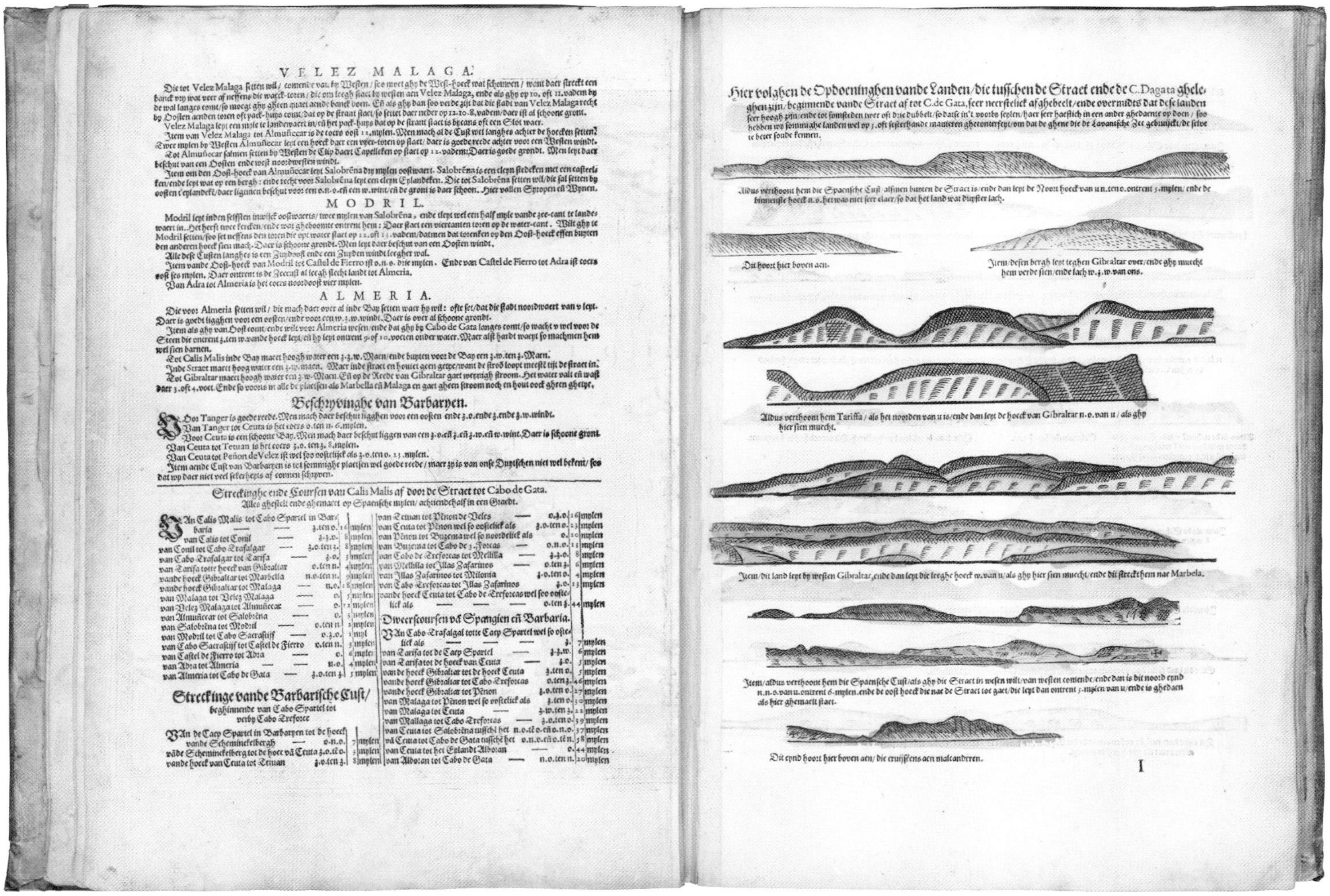
VELEZ MALAGA.
MODRIL.
ALMERIA.
Beschryvinghe van Barbaryen.
I

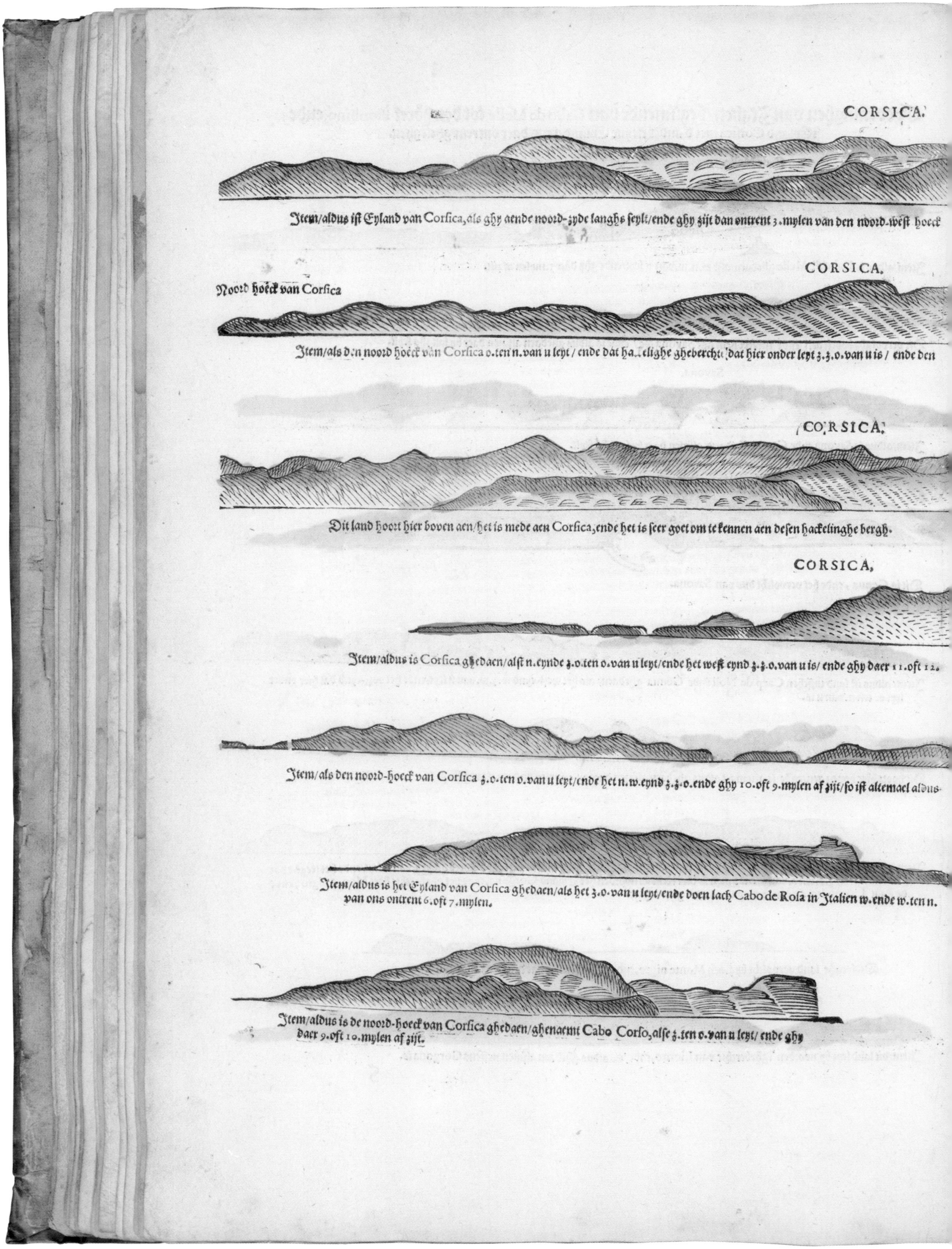
CORSICA.
Item/aldus ist Eyland van Corsica, als ghy aende noord-zyde langhs seylt/ende ghy zijt dan ontrent 3. mylen van den noord-west hoeck
CORSICA.
Noord hoeck van Corsica
Item/als den noord hoeck van Corsica o. ten n. van u leyt / ende dat hackelighe gheberchte dat hier onder leyt z. z. o. van u is / ende den
CORSICA.
Dit land hoort hier boven aen/het is mede aen Corsica, ende het is seer goet om te kennen aen desen hackelinghe bergh.
CORSICA.
Item/aldus is Corsica ghedaen/alst n. eynde z. o. ten o. van u leyt/ende het west eynd z. z. o. van u is/ ende ghy daer 11. oft 12.
Item/als den noord-hoeck van Corsica z. o. ten o. van u leyt/ende het n. w. eynd z. z. o. ende ghy 10. oft 9. mylen af zijt/so ist altemael aldus
Item/aldus is het Eyland van Corsica ghedaen/als het z. o. van u leyt/ende doen lach Cabo de Rosa in Italien w. ende w. ten n. van ons ontrent 6. oft 7. mylen.
Item/aldus is de noord-hoeck van Corsica ghedaen/ghenaemt Cabo Corso, alse z. ten o. van u leyt/ ende ghy daer 9. oft 10. mylen af zijt.

nde leyt dan z.ten o.van u/ ende den noorderschẽ hoeck die lach o.ten z.van ons.

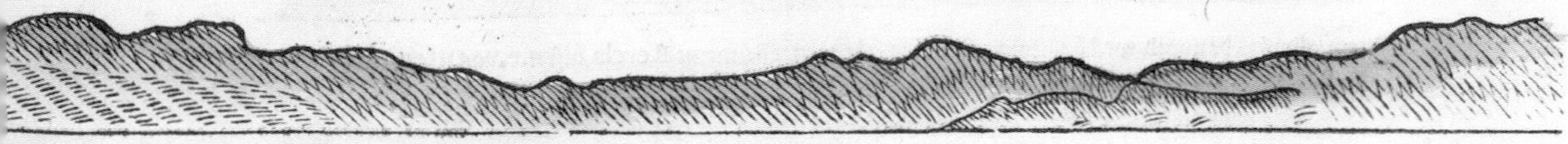

w.hoeck z.ten w.van u is/ so'ist land altemael aldus ghedaen als hier ghemaelt staet.

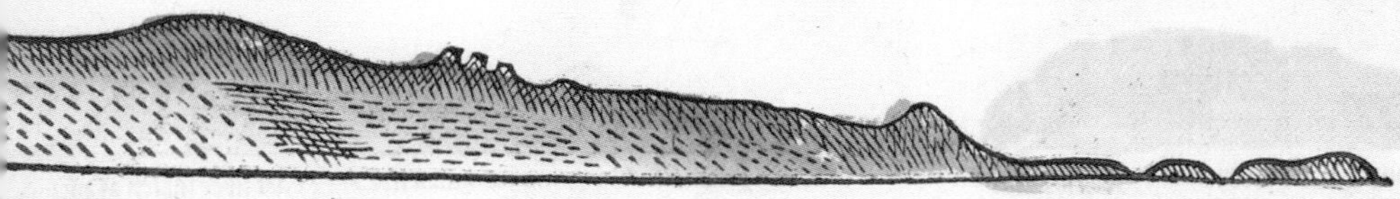

ylen af zijt.

Corsica.

daen. Dit land hier onder/ dat is den noord-hoeck die hooft hier achter aen.

Dit is den Noord-west hoeck van Corsica, ende het hooft boven aen.

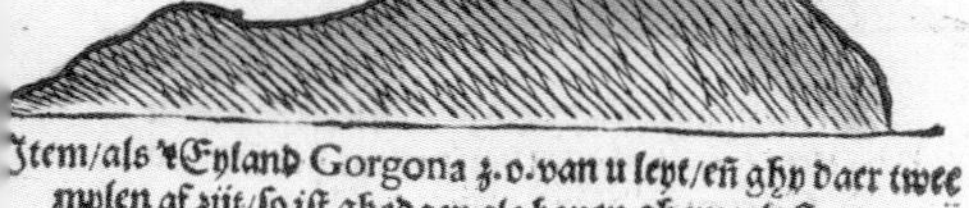

Item/als 't Eyland Gorgona z.o.van u leyt/ eñ ghy daer twee mylen af zijt/ so ist ghedaen als boven ghemaelt staet.

Item/als 't Eyland Gorgona, z.z.o.van u leyt 2. mylen/ so ist aldus ghedaen.

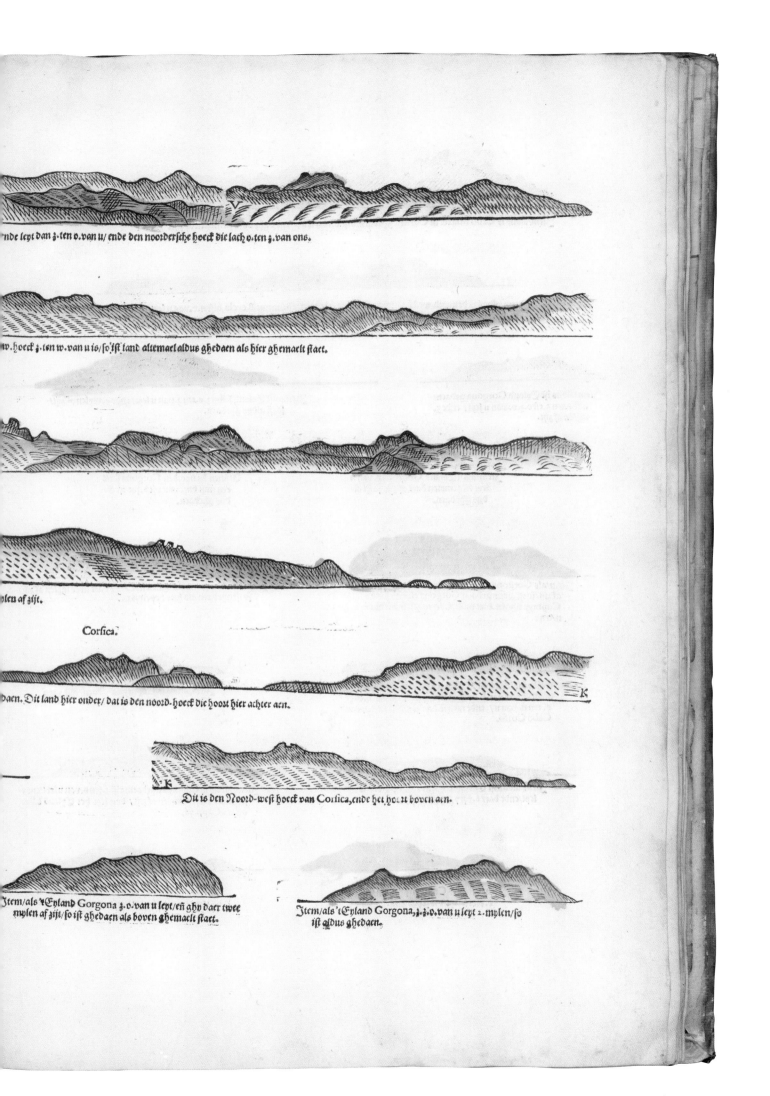

1605 **Jan van den Velde** Jan van den Velde, *Spieghel der schrijfkonste, inden welcken ghesien worden veelderhande gheschriften met hare fondementen ende onderrichtinghe*. Amsterdam (?): Cornelis Claesz (?), c. 1605/06 (?). 73 leaves. 23 × 35 cm. 1st ed. Rotterdam, 1605. Engravers: Simon Wijnhoutsz de Vries (Frisius) and others.

Spieghel der schrijfkonste ('Mirror of the Art of Writing') was the magnum opus of the greatest and most influential Dutch writing master, first published in 1605. Jan van den Velde (1568–1623) credited his father, an Antwerp nail-smith, for setting him to learn penmanship, probably under the great writing master Felix van Sambix. When Antwerp fell to Spain in 1585 he and van Sambix fled to Holland. Though only seventeen, he immediately established a reputation equalled only by van Sambix and one or two others.

As Holland filled the void left by Antwerp's decline, its flourishing international trade demanded scribes who could rapidly execute numerous practical and decorative hands for various documents in many languages (the Dutch East India Company was incorporated in 1602). The move towards the pointed pen signalled by Cresci's 1560 copybook spread to the Low Countries in Clément Perret's manual, printed by Plantin in 1569. By van den Velde's time, pointed-pen running scripts, formal italics and roman letterforms had joined the numerous formal and informal gothic hands in the mandatory repertoire. These new letterforms exerted some influence on seventeenth-century Dutch printing type, but did not come to full flower in the conservative letterpress medium until the late eighteenth century.

Van Waesberghe published the first edition of van den Velde's copybook and illustrated instruction manual but it was Cornelis Claesz who sold it at the Frankfurt bookfair in spring 1605, acquired the plates, and probably published the edition illustrated here (omitting the letterpress text) before his complete editions in several languages. Willem Jansz Blaeu acquired the plates in 1610 and continued to produce editions into the 1620s. JAL

Copperplate engraving perfectly suited the pointed pen's swelling strokes. Van den Velde's surviving manuscript models for this copybook showcase the astonishing skill of the engraver, Simon Frisius (1580–1629), an excellent writing master in his own right. He followed a mirror image of the pen-written original, offset onto the copperplate.

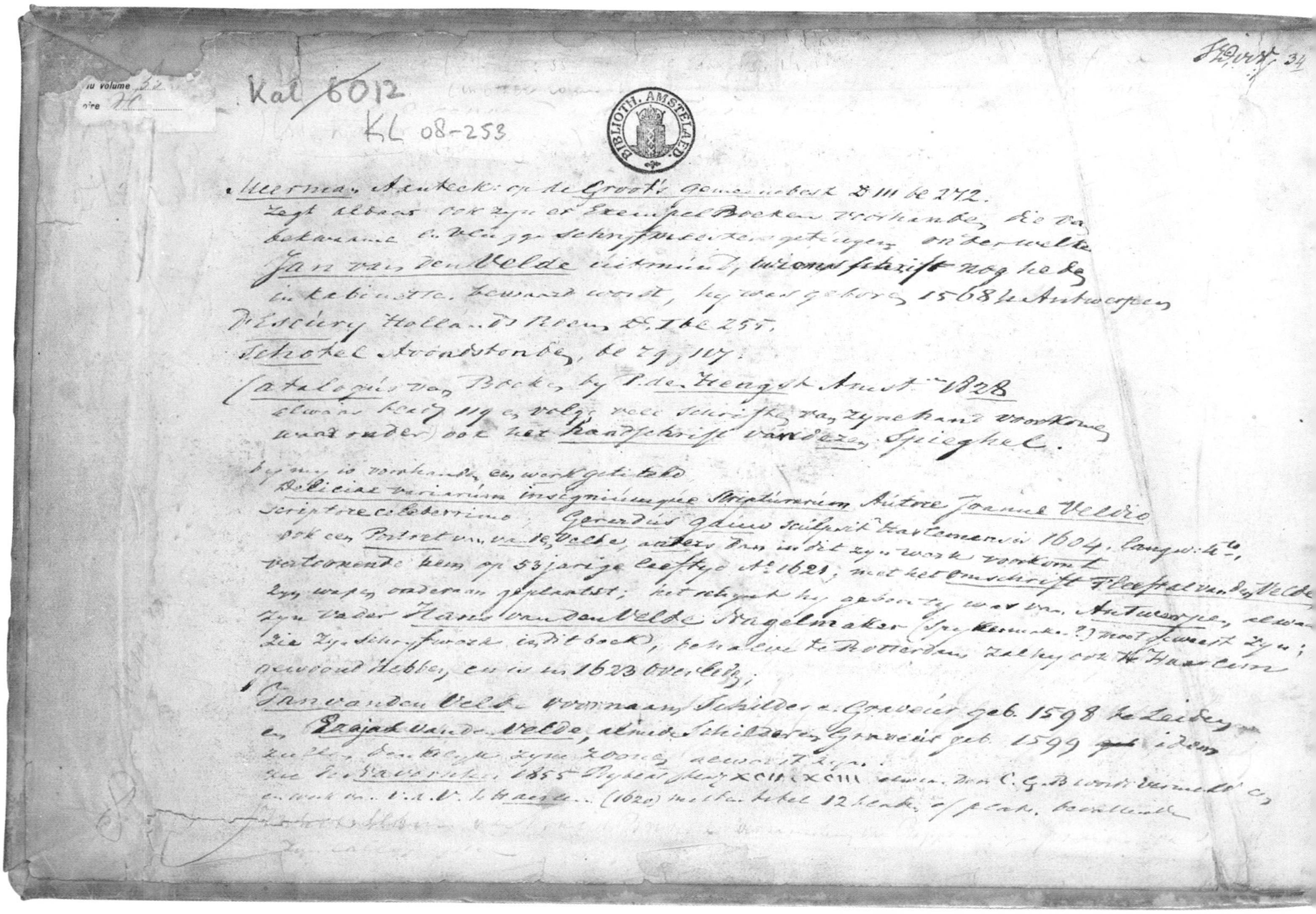

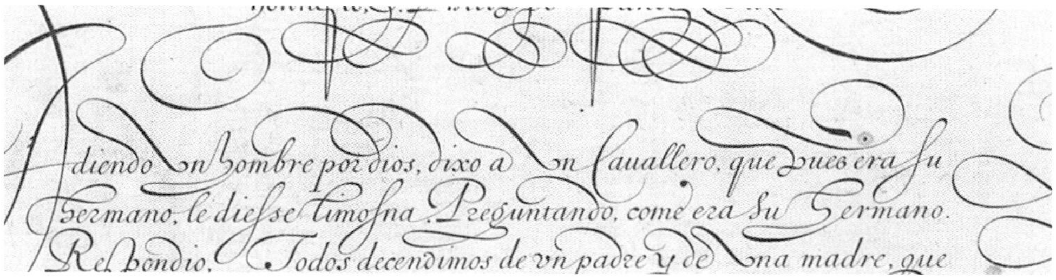
Adiendo vn hombre por dios, dixo a vn Cauallero, que dues era su
Hermano, le diesse limosna. Preguntando, come era su Hermano.
Respondio. Todos decendimos de vn padre y de vna madre, que

SPIEGHEL
Der Schrijfkonste,
Inden welcken ghesien worden veelderhande Gheschriften met hare Fondementen ende onderrichtinghe Wtghegeven
DOOR
Jan vanden Velde Fransoysche-School-Mr. binnen de vermaerde Coopstadt Rotterdam. Anno 1605.

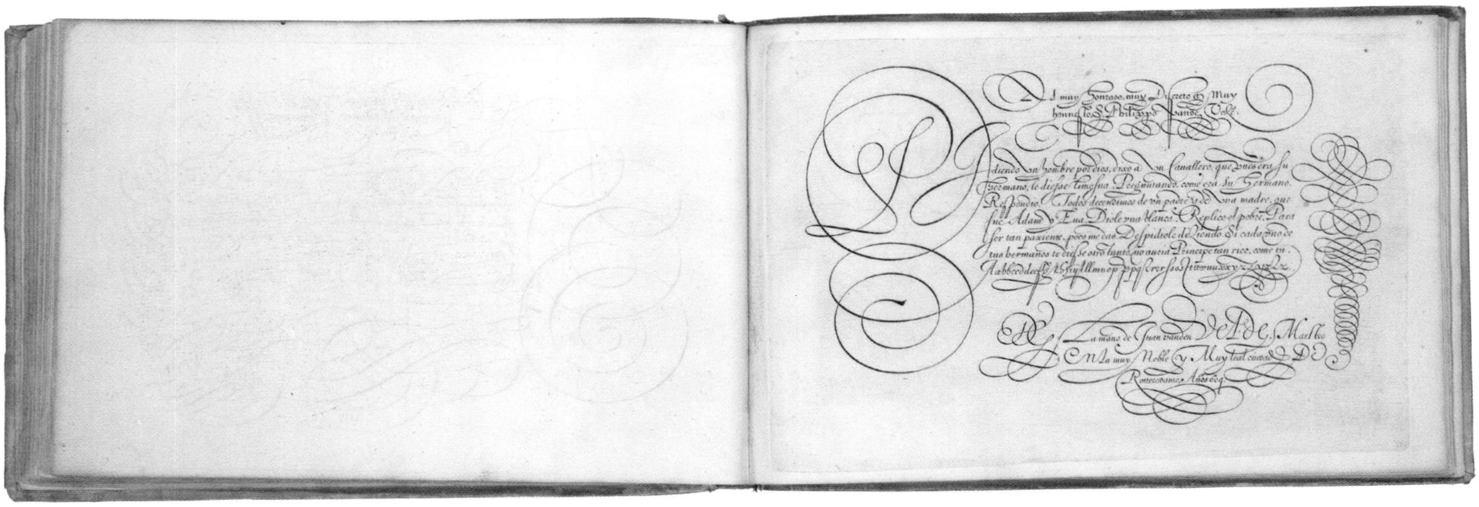

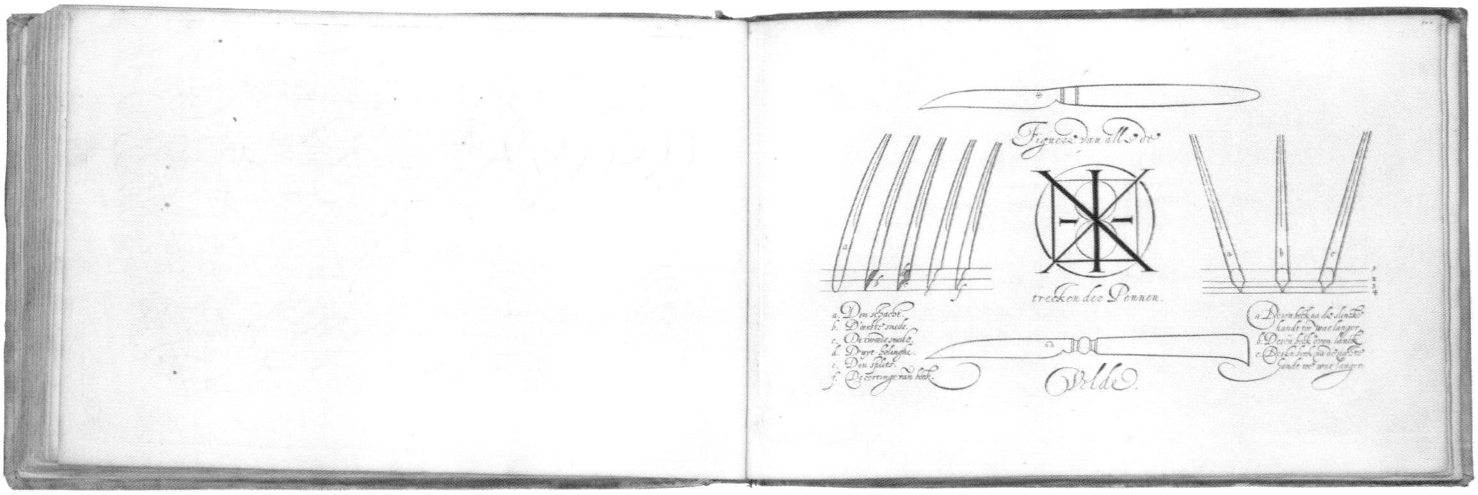

Jan van den Velde

1615 **Vincenzo Scamozzi** Vincenzo Scamozzi, *L'idea della architettura universale*. Venice: Vincenzo Scamozzi, 1615.

2 volumes. 34 cm. Illustrator: Vincenzo Scamozzi. Printer: Giorgio Valentino, Venice.

The architect Vincenzo Scamozzi (1548–1616) of Vicenza was a follower of Andrea Palladio. He began working on his treatise *L'idea della architettura universale* ('The Idea of Universal Architecture') in 1519, including an overview of his designs. Scamozzi had the book printed at his own expense, partly with the aim of promoting his design practice. The illustrations, both woodcuts and engravings, are an important part of the treatise. The woodcuts and the type were printed together; the engravings had to be printed separately on an intaglio press.

The design of the treatise is less interesting. It underlines that early seventeenth-century Venetian printers could not match the skills of predecessors such as Aldus Manutius. The printing is uneven, and the ornaments and decorative initials are a mixture of old sixteenth-century and new baroque materials. The design has some peculiarities. The text is set in roman, the headings in italic, while in most Italian books it was the other way around. The running heads are printed from an older and slightly worn type. Furthermore, the first words of the paragraphs are set in spaced small capitals, which accentuate the paragraph divisions rather heavily.

A new Golden Age of Italian typography would begin in the eighteenth century, with the arrival of Giambattista Bodoni. PD

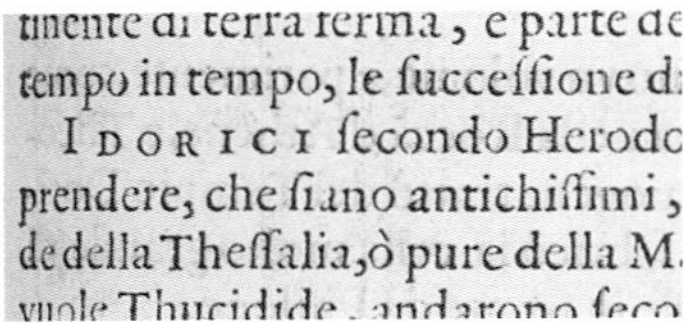
tempo in tempo, le successione d
I D O R I C I secondo Herodo
prendere, che siano antichissimi,
de della Thessalia, ò pure della M.

A Saint Augustin (14 point) roman by the French Calvinist printer-punchcutter Pierre Haultin (*c.* 1510/20–87) in Geneva. It was used in Venice (1559), followed by Geneva (1560), Antwerp (1562), Frankfurt (1563), London and Paris (1566), remaining popular in Italy. Haultin made the x-height larger than Garamont's, a trend Granjon took further.

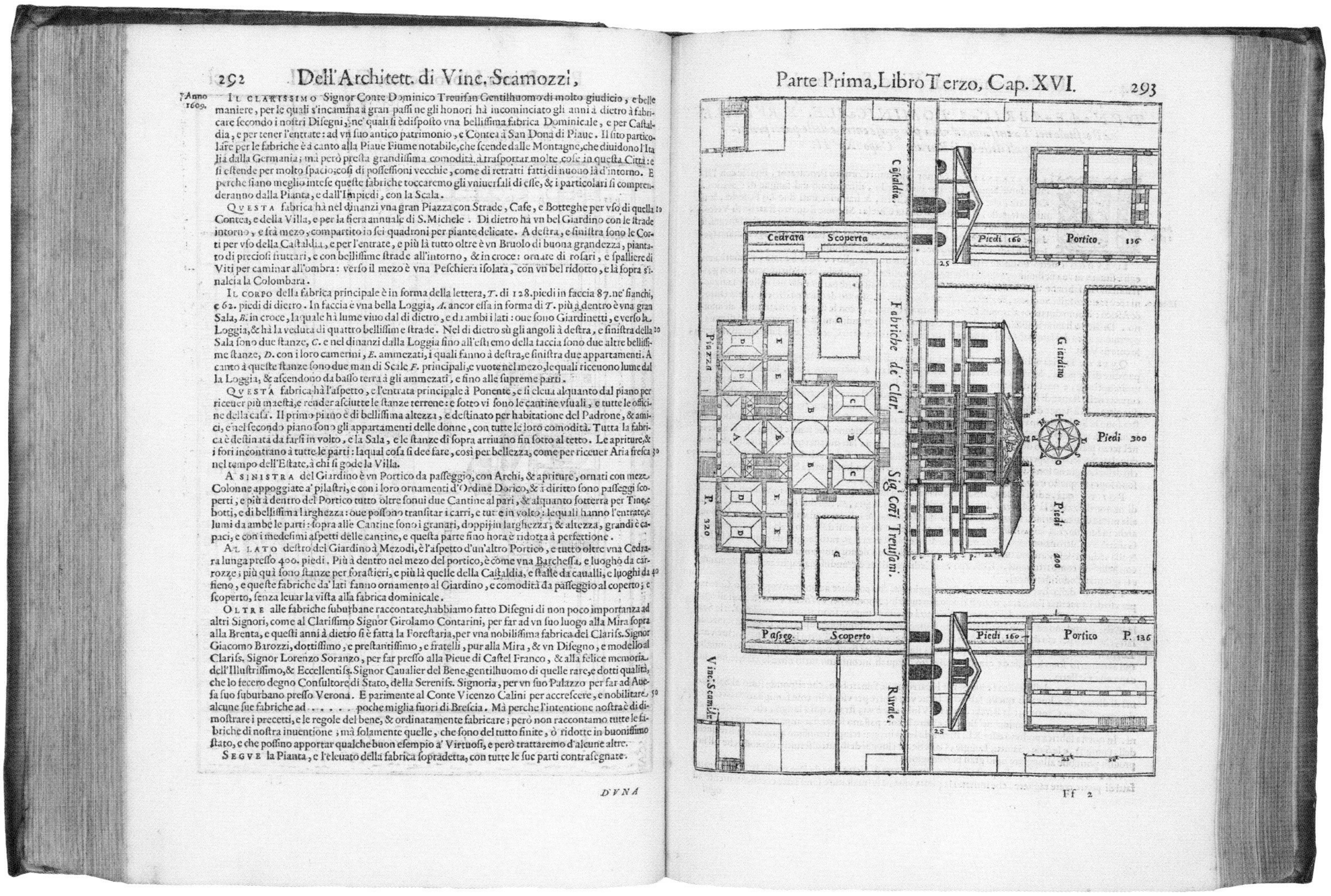

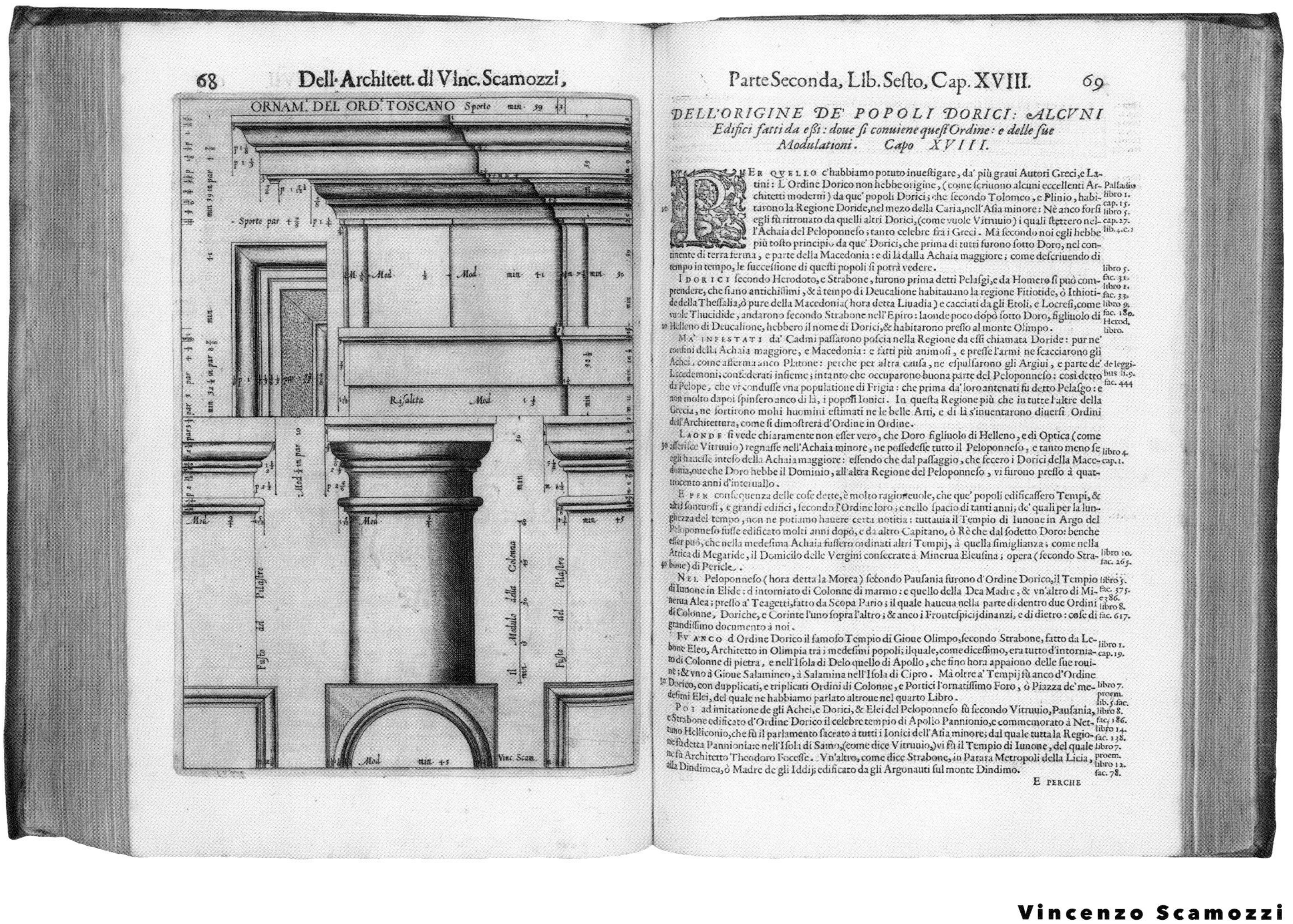

Vincenzo Scamozzi

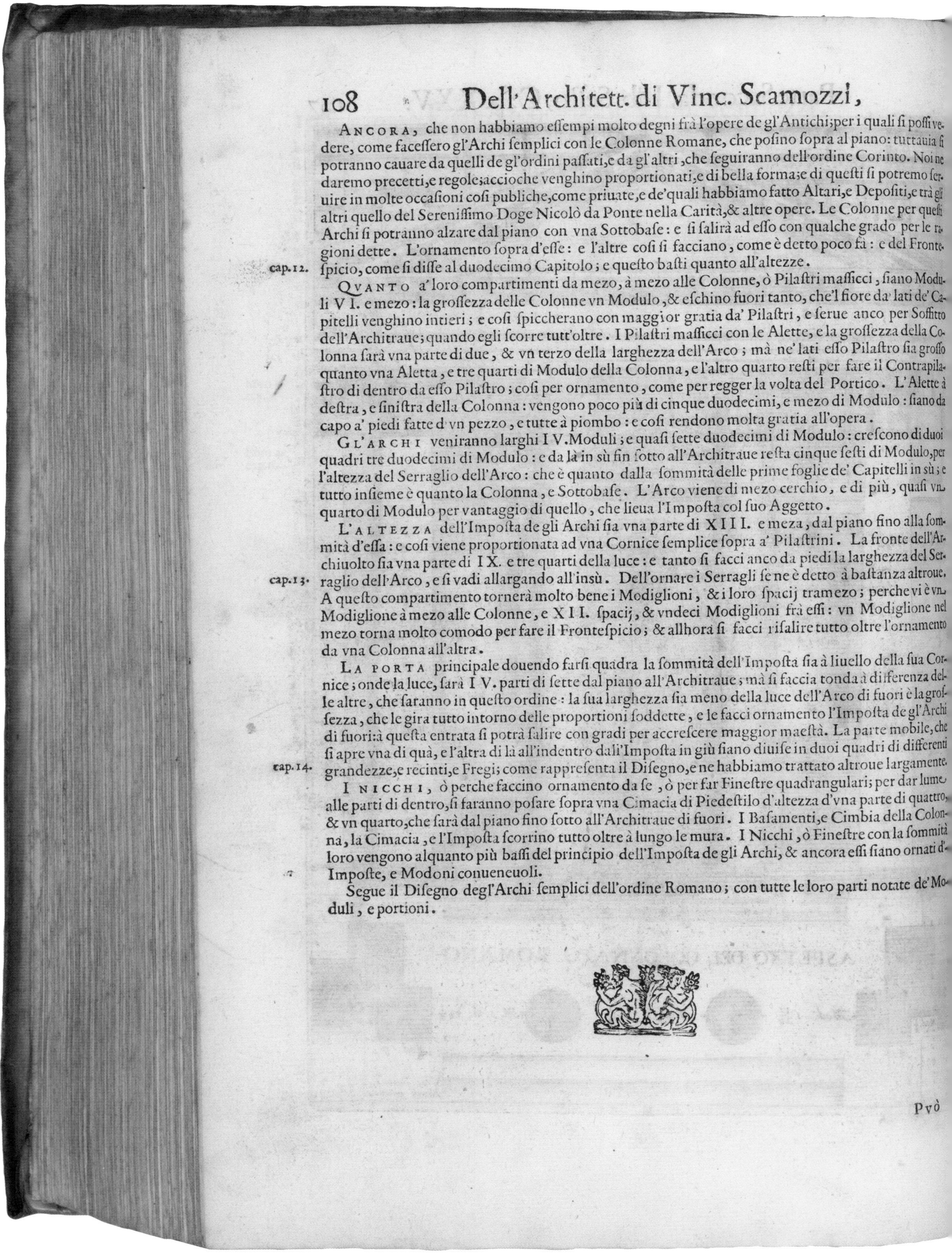

108 Dell'Architett. di Vinc. Scamozzi,

Ancora, che non habbiamo eſſempi molto degni frà l'opere de gl'Antichi;per i quali ſi poſſi vedere, come faceſſero gl'Archi ſemplici con le Colonne Romane, che poſino ſopra al piano: tuttauia ſi potranno cauare da quelli de gl'ordini paſſati,e da gl'altri ,che ſeguiranno dell'ordine Corinto. Noi ne daremo precetti,e regole;accioche venghino proportionati,e di bella forma;e di queſti ſi potremo ſeruire in molte occaſioni coſi publiche,come priuate,e de'quali habbiamo fatto Altari,e Depoſiti,e trà gli altri quello del Sereniſſimo Doge Nicolò da Ponte nella Carità,& altre opere. Le Colonne per queſti Archi ſi potranno alzare dal piano con vna Sottobaſe: e ſi ſalirà ad eſſo con qualche grado per le ragioni dette. L'ornamento ſopra d'eſſe: e l'altre coſi ſi facciano, come è detto poco fà: e del Fronte-

cap.12. ſpicio, come ſi diſſe al duodecimo Capitolo; e queſto baſti quanto all'altezze.

Qvanto a' loro compartimenti da mezo, à mezo alle Colonne, ò Pilaſtri maſſicci, ſiano Moduli V I. e mezo: la groſſezza delle Colonne vn Modulo, & eſchino fuori tanto, che'l fiore da' lati de' Capitelli venghino intieri; e coſi ſpiccherano con maggior gratia da' Pilaſtri, e ſerue anco per Soffitto dell'Architraue; quando egli ſcorre tutt'oltre. I Pilaſtri maſſicci con le Alette, e la groſſezza della Colonna ſarà vna parte di due, & vn terzo della larghezza dell'Arco; mà ne' lati eſſo Pilaſtro ſia groſſo quanto vna Aletta, e tre quarti di Modulo della Colonna, e l'altro quarto reſti per fare il Contrapilaſtro di dentro da eſſo Pilaſtro; coſi per ornamento, come per regger la volta del Portico. L'Alette à deſtra, e ſiniſtra della Colonna: vengono poco più di cinque duodecimi, e mezo di Modulo: ſiano da capo a' piedi fatte d'vn pezzo, e tutte à piombo: e coſi rendono molta gratia all'opera.

Gl'archi veniranno larghi I V. Moduli; e quaſi ſette duodecimi di Modulo: creſcono di duoi quadri tre duodecimi di Modulo: e da là in sù fin ſotto all'Architraue reſta cinque ſeſti di Modulo, per l'altezza del Serraglio dell'Arco: che è quanto dalla ſommità delle prime foglie de' Capitelli in sù; e tutto inſieme è quanto la Colonna, e Sottobaſe. L'Arco viene di mezo cerchio, e di più, quaſi vn quarto di Modulo per vantaggio di quello, che lieua l'Impoſta col ſuo Aggetto.

L'altezza dell'Impoſta de gli Archi ſia vna parte di X I I I. e meza, dal piano fino alla ſommità d'eſſa: e coſi viene proportionata ad vna Cornice ſemplice ſopra a' Pilaſtrini. La fronte dell'Archiuolto ſia vna parte di I X. e tre quarti della luce: e tanto ſi facci anco da piedi la larghezza del Ser-

cap.13. raglio dell'Arco, e ſi vadi allargando all'insù. Dell'ornare i Serragli ſe ne è detto à baſtanza altroue. A queſto compartimento tornerà molto bene i Modiglioni, & i loro ſpacij tramezo; perche vi è vn Modiglione à mezo alle Colonne, e X I I. ſpacij, & vndeci Modiglioni frà eſſi: vn Modiglione nel mezo torna molto comodo per fare il Fronteſpicio; & allhora ſi facci riſalire tutto oltre l'ornamento da vna Colonna all'altra.

La porta principale douendo farſi quadra la ſommità dell'Impoſta ſia à liuello della ſua Cornice; onde la luce, ſarà I V. parti di ſette dal piano all'Architraue; mà ſi faccia tonda à differenza delle altre, che ſaranno in queſto ordine: la ſua larghezza ſia meno della luce dell'Arco di fuori è la groſſezza, che le gira tutto intorno delle proportioni ſoddette, e le facci ornamento l'Impoſta de gl'Archi di fuori: à queſta entrata ſi potrà ſalire con gradi per accreſcere maggior maeſtà. La parte mobile, che ſi apre vna di quà, e l'altra di là all'indentro dall'Impoſta in giù ſiano diuiſe in duoi quadri di differenti

cap.14. grandezze, e recinti, e Fregi; come rappreſenta il Diſegno, e ne habbiamo trattato altroue largamente.

I nicchi, ò perche faccino ornamento da ſe, ò per far Fineſtre quadrangulari; per dar lume alle parti di dentro, ſi faranno poſare ſopra vna Cimacia di Piedeſtilo d'altezza d'vna parte di quattro, & vn quarto, che ſarà dal piano fino ſotto all'Architraue di fuori. I Baſamenti, e Cimbia della Colonna, la Cimacia, e l'Impoſta ſcorrino tutto oltre à lungo le mura. I Nicchi, ò Fineſtre con la ſommità loro vengono alquanto più baſſi del principio dell'Impoſta de gli Archi, & ancora eſſi ſiano ornati d'Impoſte, e Modoni conueneuoli.

Segue il Diſegno degl'Archi ſemplici dell'ordine Romano; con tutte le loro parti notate de' Moduli, e portioni.

Può

Parte Seconda, Libro Sesto, Cap. XXV· 109
Vinc. Scamozzi
ASPETTO DEGL' ARCHI ROMANI
L

1627 **Paulus Aertsz van Ravesteyn** Matthijs van Velden et al., *Amsterdamsche Pegasus*. Amsterdam: Cornelis Willemsz Blaeu-Laken, 1627. 177 pp. 17 cm. Illustrator: Jan van de Velde. Printer: Paulus Aertsz van Ravesteyn, Amsterdam.

In 1627, when the *Amsterdamsche Pegasus* was published, the Golden Age of Dutch printing had only just begun. The names of Blaeu and Elzevier were still relatively obscure, although the printer and publisher Paulus Aertsz van Ravesteyn (*c.* 1586–1655) was already active in Amsterdam. His printed matter counts among the best of its time. Van Ravesteyn was an outstanding and versatile local printer who worked for the municipal theatre and the city government. He also published collections of verse by local poets. His work is exemplary: he used good type and excellent decorative material. Van Ravesteyn most likely owned an intaglio press, enabling him to produce work with etchings or engravings in his own printing firm.

This type of songbook originated from the Netherlands in the beginning of the seventeenth century and quickly became popular. It often had fairly large margins, various typefaces (civilité type in particular), musical scores, and illustrations. The beautiful etchings in the *Amsterdamsche Pegasus* are by Jan van de Velde (*c.* 1593–1641), son of the equally famous calligrapher of the same name (see page 146). Most of these typographically well-designed songbooks were meant for upper-class adolescents, who would sing from them at parties and festivities. The *Amsterdamsche Pegasus* is one of the most splendid examples of its genre. As its price was two florins – equalling two days' pay for the average workman – it was within reach of only a select group of customers. PD

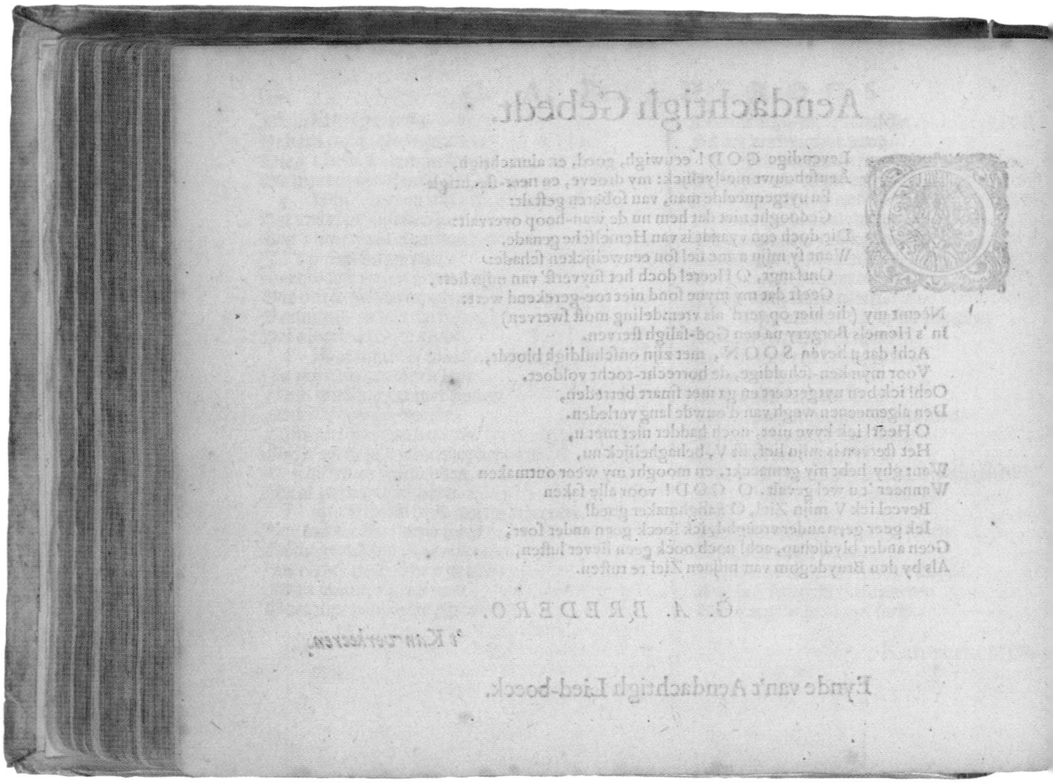

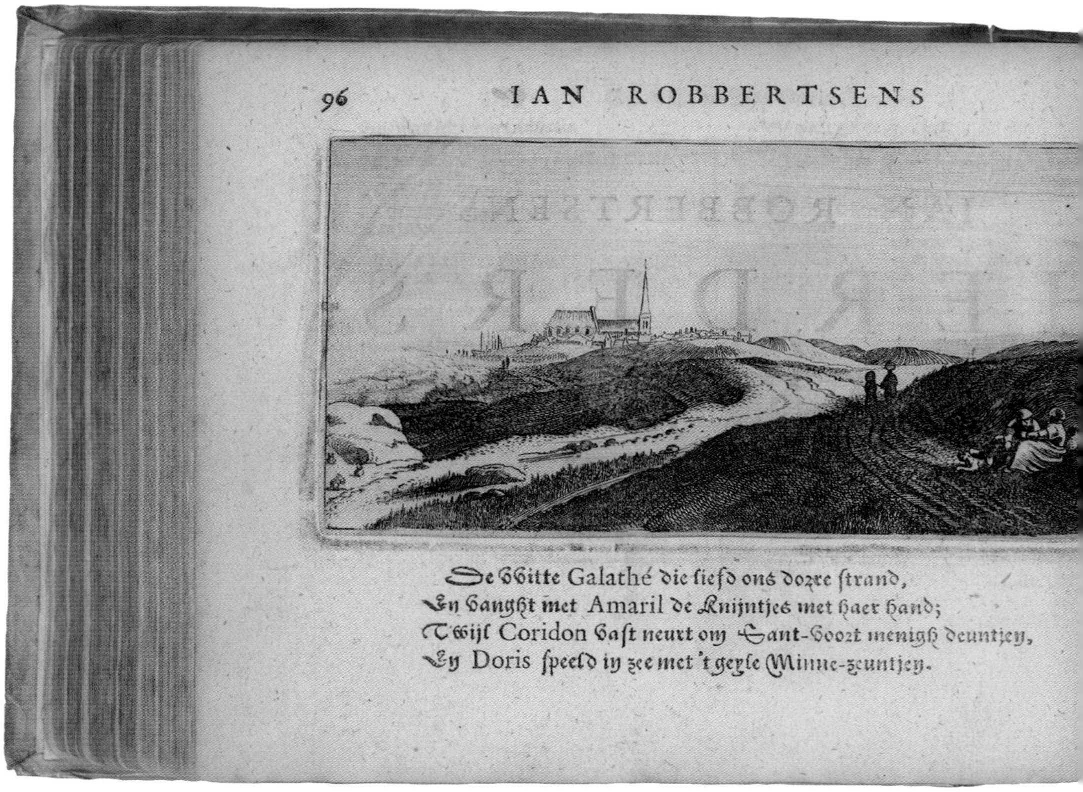

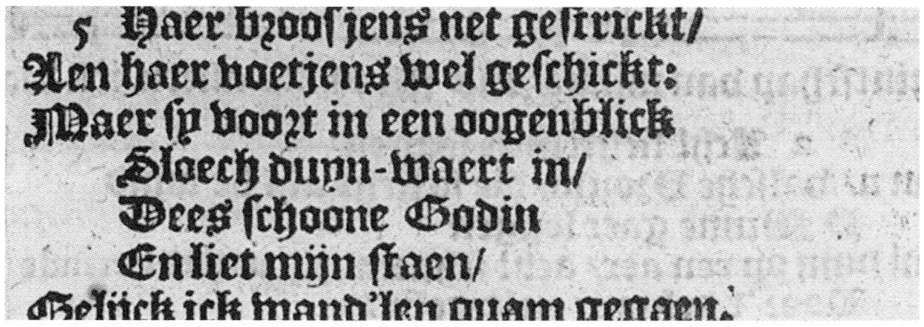
5 Haer broosjens net gestrickt/
Aen haer voetjens wel geschickt:
Maer sy voort in een oogenblick
Sloech duyn-waert in/
Dees schoone Godin
En liet mijn staen/
Gelijck ick wand'len quam gegaen.

A Mediaen (12 point) Textura probably cut by Nicolaes Briot (*c.* 1580/84–1626) in Gouda and later Amsterdam, used from at least 1616. Briot followed the sixteenth-century Texturas of Hendrik van den Keere, but added baroque elements, such as the ball terminals on A, B, J, H, M, N and S.

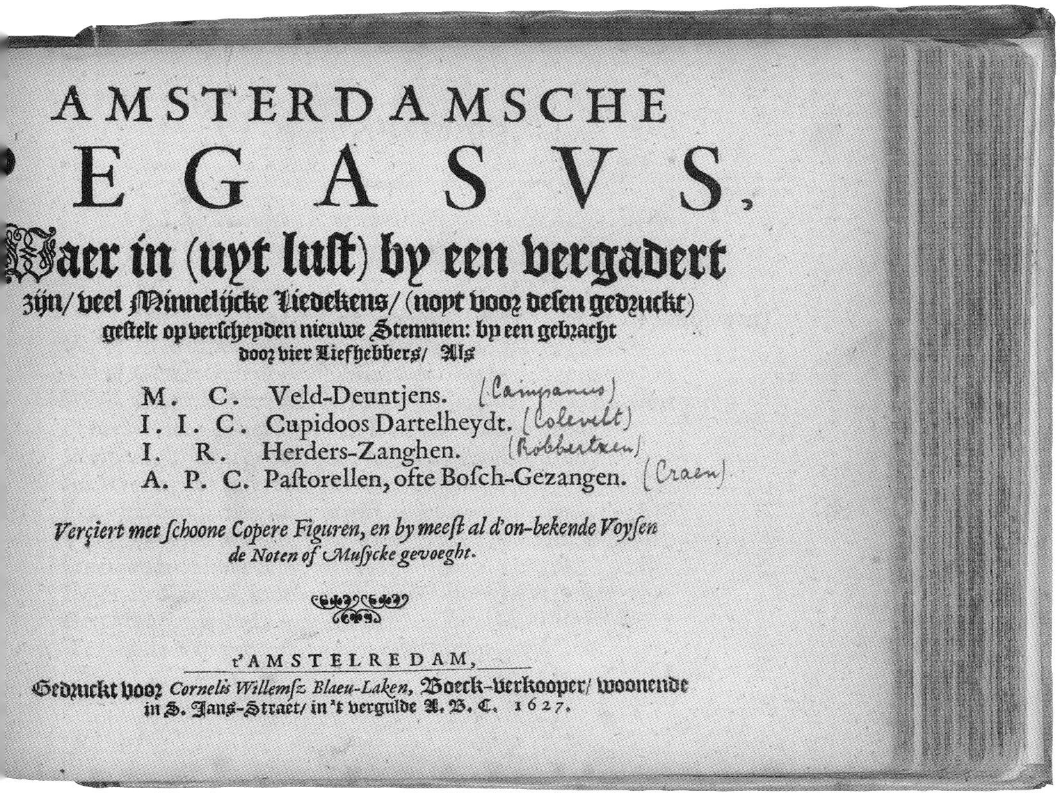
AMSTERDAMSCHE
[P]EGASVS,
[W]aer in (uyt lust) by een vergadert
zijn/ veel Minnelijcke Liedekens/ (noyt voor desen gedruckt)
gestelt op verscheyden nieuwe Stemmen: by een gebracht
door vier Liefhebbers/ Als
M. C. Veld-Deuntjens. (Campanus)
I. I. C. Cupidoos Dartelheydt. (Colevelt)
I. R. Herders-Zanghen. (Robbertzen)
A. P. C. Pastorellen, ofte Bosch-Gezangen. (Craen)
Verçiert met schoone Copere Figuren, en by meest al d'on-bekende Voysen de Noten of Musycke gevoeght.
t'AMSTELREDAM,
Gedruckt voor *Cornelis Willemsz Blaeu-Laken*, Boeck-verkooper/ woonende in S. Jans-Straet/ in 't vergulde A. B. C. 1627.

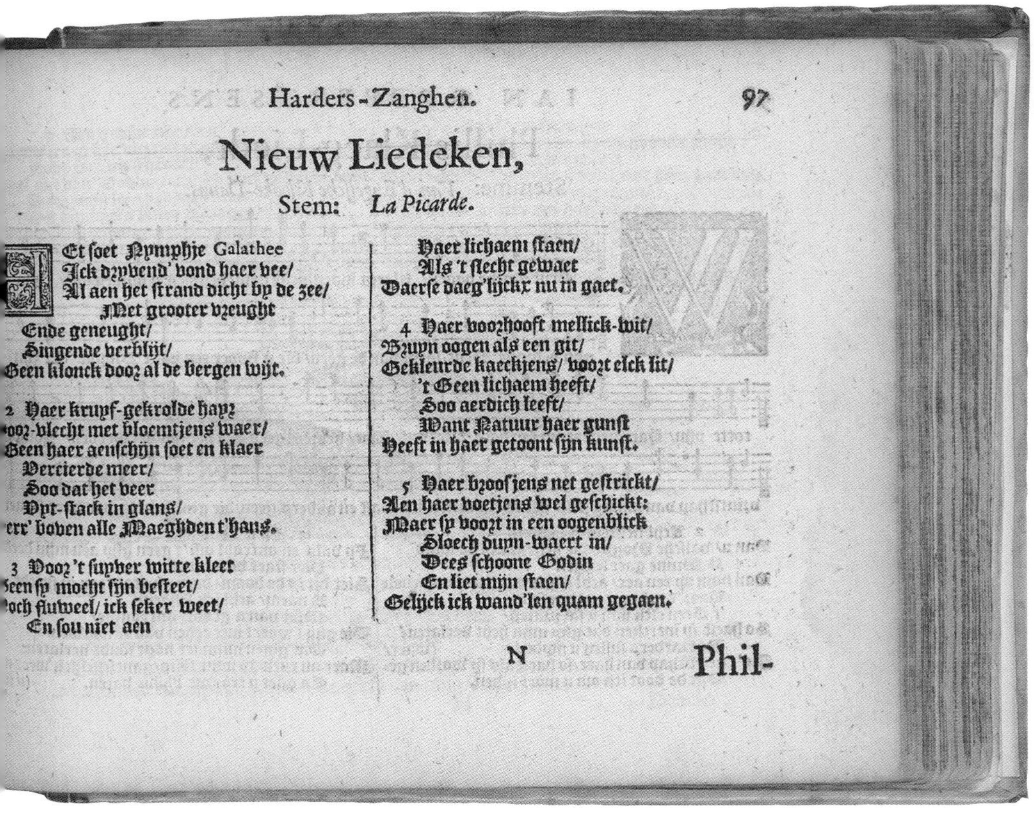
Harders-Zanghen. 97
Nieuw Liedeken,
Stem: *La Picarde.*
Het soet Nymphje Galathee
Ick dryvend' vond haer vee/
Al aen het strand dicht by de zee/
Met grooter vreught
Ende geneught/
Singende verblijt/
Geen klonck door al de bergen wijt.
2 Haer kruyf-gekrolde hayr
...ooz-vlecht met bloemtjens waer/
Geen haer aenschijn soet en klaer
Verçierde meer/
Soo dat het veer
Opt-stack in glans/
...err' boven alle Maeghden t'haus.
3 Door 't suyver witte kleet
...een sy mocht sijn besteet/
...och fluweel/ ick seker weet/
En sou niet aen
Haer lichaem staen/
Als 't slecht gewaet
Daerse daeg'lijckx nu in gaet.
4 Haer voorhooft mellick-wit/
Bruyn oogen als een git/
Geklende kaeckjens/ voor elck lit/
't Geen lichaem heeft/
Soo aerdich leeft/
Want Natuur haer gunst
Heeft in haer getoont sijn kunst.
5 Haer broosjens net gestrickt/
Aen haer voetjens wel geschickt:
Maer sy voort in een oogenblick
Sloech duyn-waert in/
Dees schoone Godin
En liet mijn staen/
Gelijck ick wand'len quam gegaen.
N Phil-

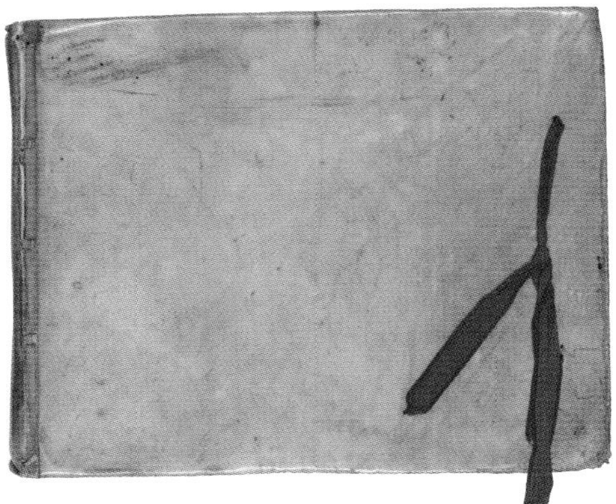

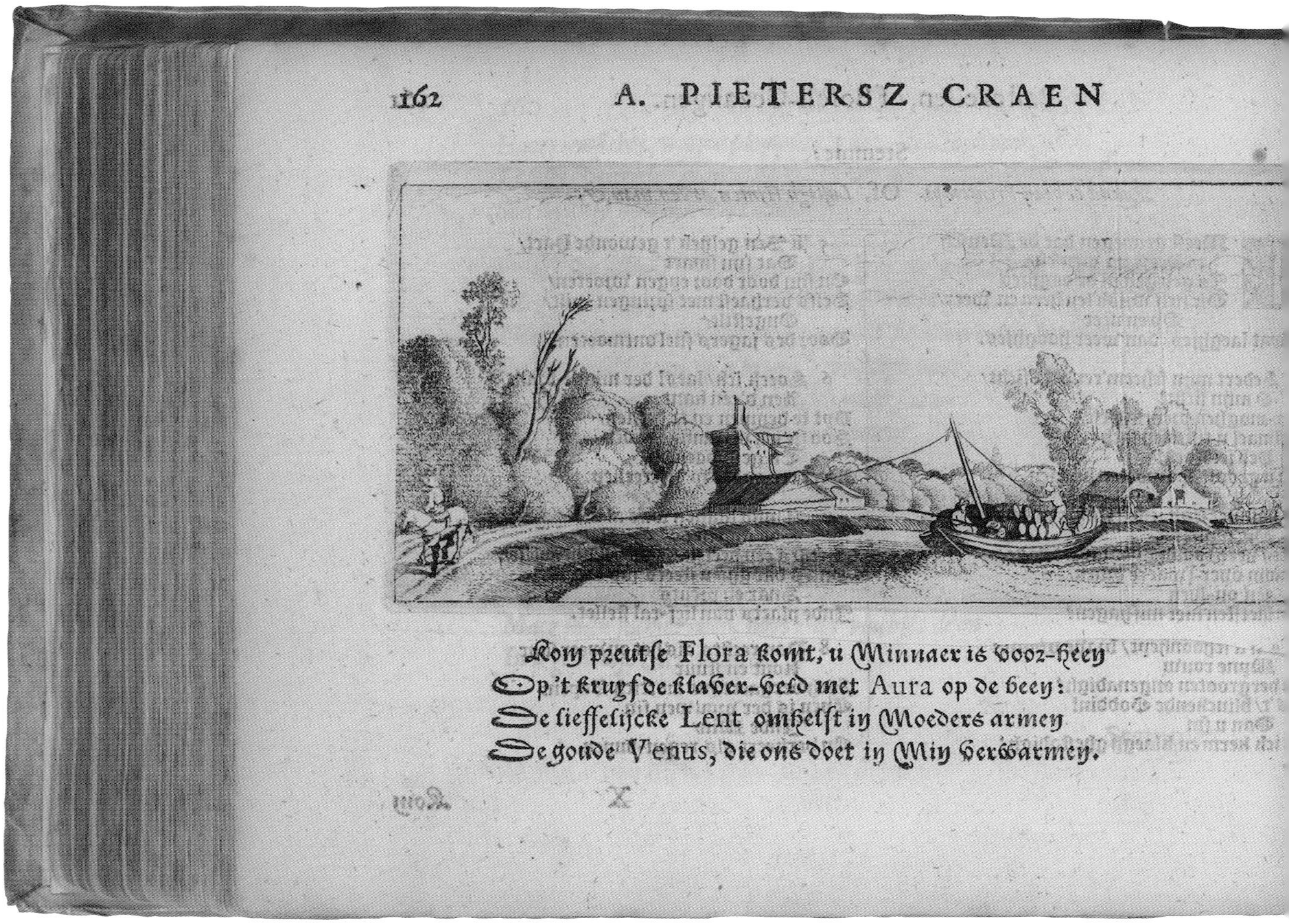
162 A. PIETERSZ CRAEN

Kom preutse Flora komt, u Minnaer is voor-heen
Op 't kruyf de klaver-veld met Aura op de heen:
De lieffelijcke Lent omhelst in Moeders armen
De goude Venus, die ons doet in Min verwarmen.

X

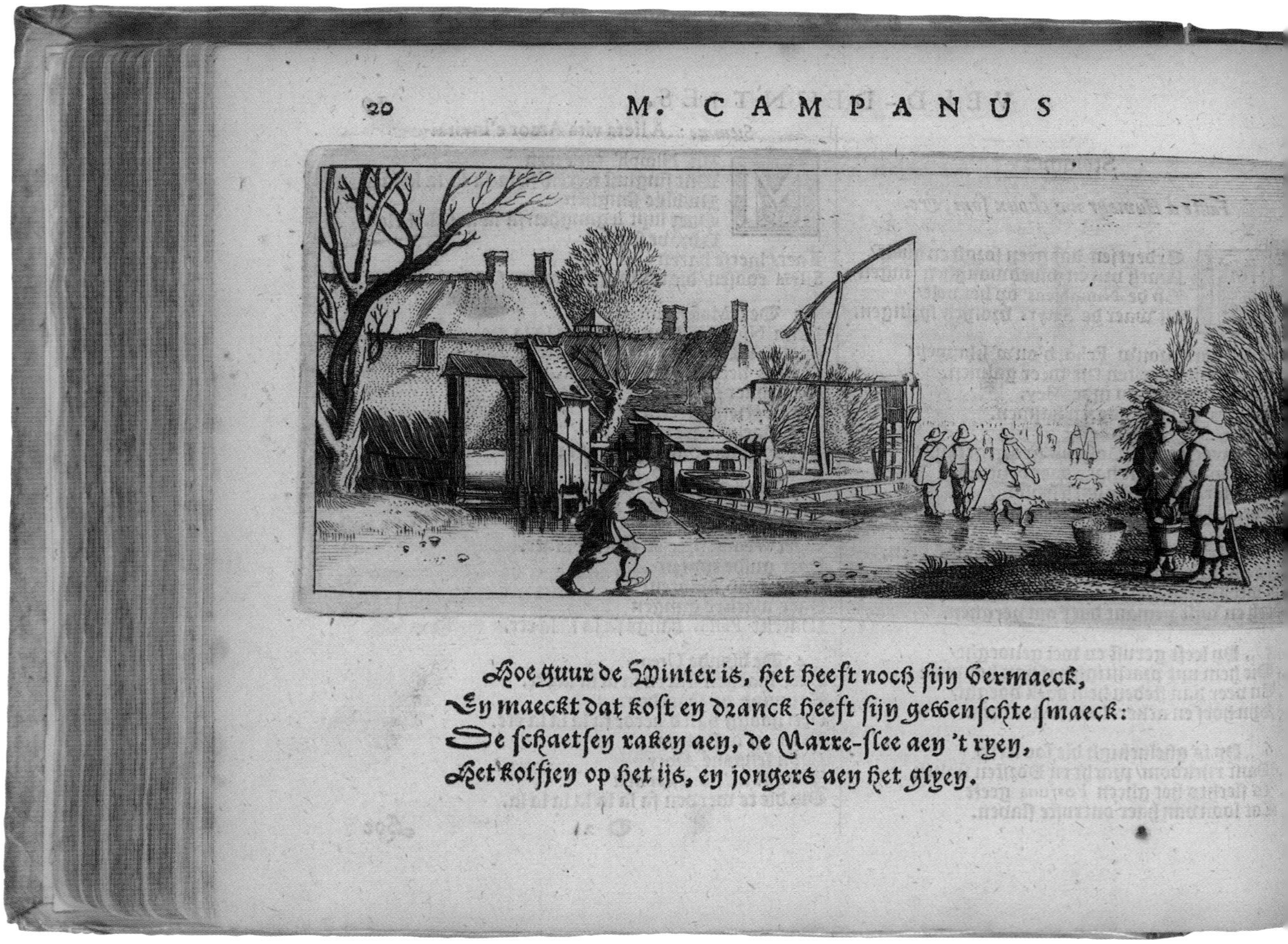
20 M. CAMPANUS

Hoe guur de Winter is, het heeft noch sijn vermaeck,
En maeckt dat kost en dranck heeft sijn gewenschte smaeck:
De schaetsen raken aen, de Narre-slee aen 't ryen,
Het kolfjen op het ijs, en jongers aen het glyen.

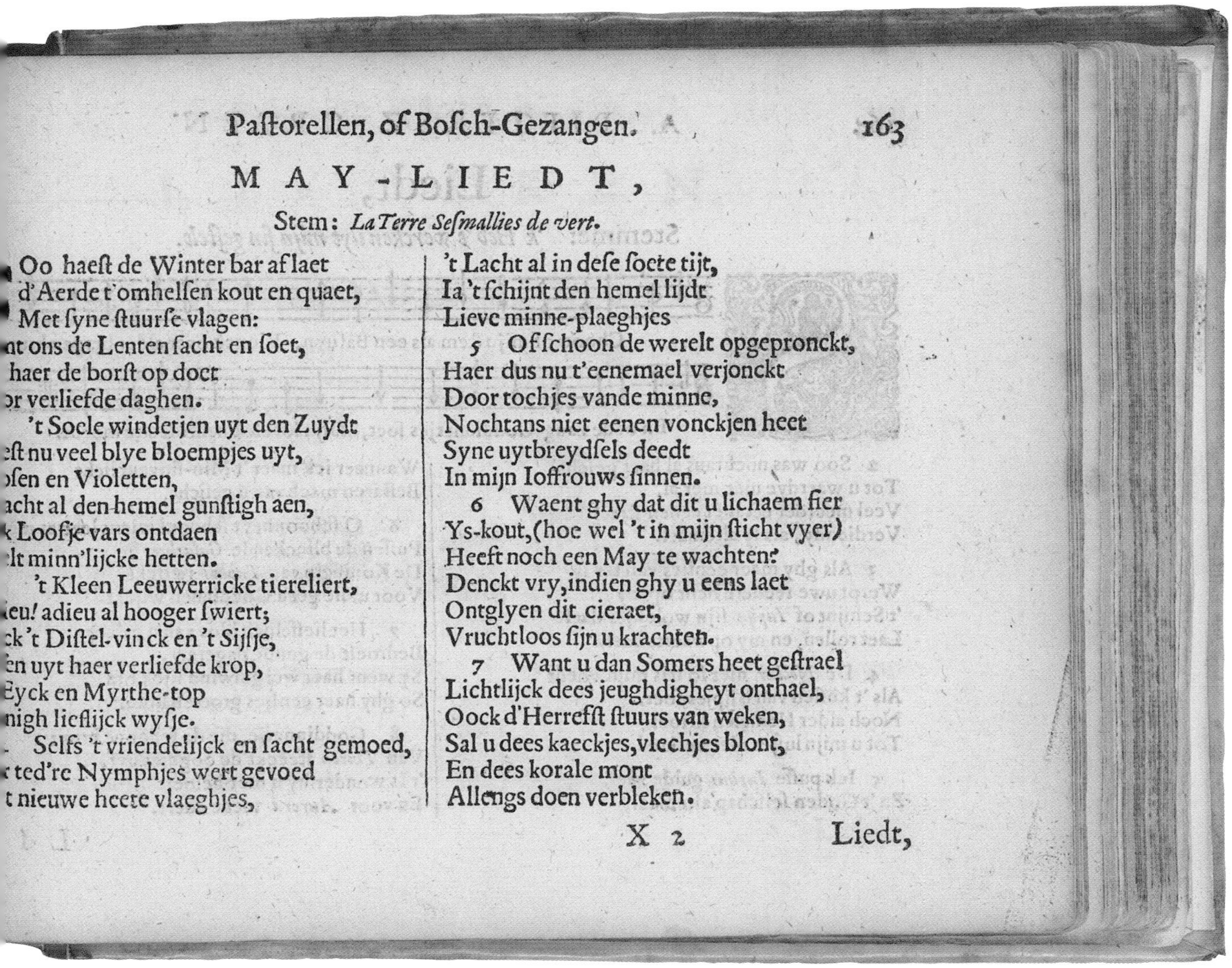
Pastorellen, of Bosch-Gezangen. 163

MAY-LIEDT,

Stem: *La Terre Sesmallies de vert.*

Oo haest de Winter bar af laet
d'Aerde t'omhelsen kout en quaet,
Met syne stuurse vlagen:
nt ons de Lenten sacht en soet,
haer de borst op doet
or verliefde daghen.
't Soele windetjen uyt den Zuydt
est nu veel blye bloempjes uyt,
osen en Violetten,
acht al den hemel gunstigh aen,
Loofje vars ontdaen
lt minn'lijcke hetten.
't Kleen Leeuwerricke tiereliert,
eu! adieu al hooger swiert;
ck 't Distel-vinck en 't Sijsje,
en uyt haer verliefde krop,
Eyck en Myrthe-top
nigh lieflijck wysje.
Selfs 't vriendelijck en sacht gemoed,
ted're Nymphjes wert gevoed
t nieuwe heete vlaeghjes,
't Lacht al in dese soete tijt,
Ia 't schijnt den hemel lijdt
Lieve minne-plaeghjes
5 Of schoon de werelt opgepronckt,
Haer dus nu t'eenemael verjonckt
Door tochjes vande minne,
Nochtans niet eenen vonckjen heet
Syne uytbreydsels deedt
In mijn Ioffrouws sinnen.
6 Waent ghy dat dit u lichaem fier
Ys-kout, (hoe wel 't in mijn sticht vyer)
Heeft noch een May te wachten?
Denckt vry, indien ghy u eens laet
Ontglyen dit cieraet,
Vruchtloos sijn u krachten.
7 Want u dan Somers heet gestrael
Lichtlijck dees jeughdigheyt onthael,
Oock d'Herrefst stuurs van weken,
Sal u dees kaeckjes, vlechjes blont,
En dees korale mont
Allengs doen verbleken.

X 2 Liedt,

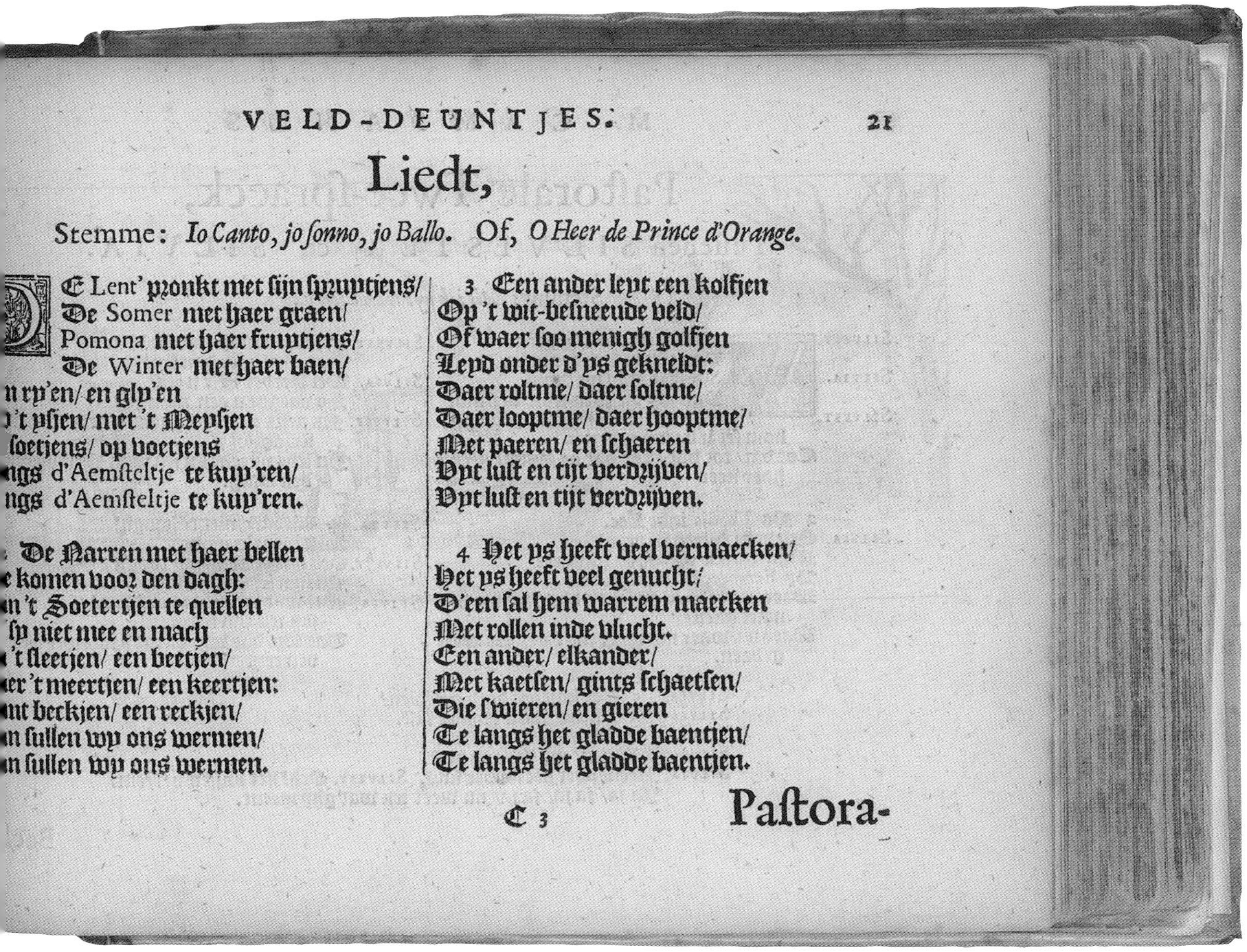
VELD-DEUNTJES. 21

Liedt,

Stemme: *Io Canto, jo sonno, jo Ballo.* Of, *O Heer de Prince d'Orange.*

DE Lent' pronkt met sijn spruytjens/
De Somer met haer graen/
Pomona met haer fruytjens/
De Winter met haer baen/
n ry'en/ en gly'en
'tysjen/ met 't Meysjen
soetjens/ op voetjens
ngs d'Aemsteltje te kuy'ren/
ngs d'Aemsteltje te kuy'ren.
De Narren met haer bellen
e komen voor den dagh:
n 't Soetertjen te quellen
sy niet mee en mach
't sleetjen/ een beetjen/
er 't meertjen/ een keertjen:
nt beckjen/ een reckjen/
n sullen wy ons wermen/
n sullen wy ons wermen.
3 Een ander leyt een kolfjen
Op 't wit-besneeude veld/
Of waer soo menigh golfjen
Leyd onder d'ys gekneldt:
Daer roltme/ daer soltme/
Daer looptme/ daer hooptme/
Met paeren/ en schaeren
Uyt lust en tijt verdrijven/
Uyt lust en tijt verdrijven.
4 Het ys heeft veel vermaecken/
Het ys heeft veel genucht/
D'een sal hem warrem maecken
Met rollen inde vlucht.
Een ander/ elkander/
Met kaetsen/ gints schaetsen/
Die swieren/ en gieren
Te langs het gladde baentjen/
Te langs het gladde baentjen.

C 3 Pastora-

1628 **The Elzeviers** Gerard Thibault, *Académie de l'espée, ou se demonstrent par reigles mathematiques sur le fondement d'un cercle mysterieux la theorie et pratique des vrais et jusqu'a present incognus secrets du maniement des armes a pied et a cheval*. Amsterdam (?): heirs of Gerard Thibault, 1628 (= 1629). Paginated in many short series. 56 cm. Illustrator: Gerard Thibault (?). Engravers: Pieter Serwouter, Jacob van der Borcht, Pieter de Jode and others. Printers: Bonaventura & Abraham Elzevier, Leiden.

Académie de l'espée ('Academy of the Sword') was the greatest fencing manual ever published and the most ambitious book production of its day, intended primarily for noblemen. Gerard Thibault (*c.* 1573/74–1627), from Antwerp, learned a new fencing style in Spain, improved it and introduced it to the Dutch Republic. Mixing analytical tactics with mysticism, he defeated the best swordsmen at Prince Maurits's court. He apparently drew the illustrations for this manual and commissioned the engraving and printing, supported by Dutch and foreign noblemen whose coats-of-arms he included in the book. The book features 63 enormous plates by sixteen engravers (most plates are 50 × 70 cm). King Louis XIII of France, the States-General of the Netherlands and the Emperor Ferdinand II granted the book privileges.

Isaack Elzevier added a printing office to his family's publishing house in 1617 and sold it in 1625 to his uncle and brother, Bonaventura and Abraham Elzevier, famous for their scholarly books for the university and miniature classics for students. They had many woodcut initials made and some types cast specially for *Académie de l'espée*. Thibault intended to publish it in 1626 but died leaving the first part, shown here, probably in press (the second part, on the theme of horseback swordfighting, never appeared). His heirs published it – dated 1628 on the title page – by autumn 1629, when the Frankfurt bookseller Lucas Jennis sold it at the Frankfurt bookfair. The Elzeviers printed each letterpress leaf on a whole sheet of royal paper, the largest common size, and probably had the double-royal paper for the plates specially made. They added three leaves, not in all copies, in around August 1630. JAL

This is the first known use of a narrow Ascendonica (24 point) italic, resembling a wider 1632 Augustijn (14 point). Both accompanied romans by Nicolaes Briot (*c.* 1580/84–1626), who may have cut them. Influenced by pointed-pen calligraphy, they had little influence on later types. The Romain du Roi typeface introduced pointed-pen influences independently in 1699.

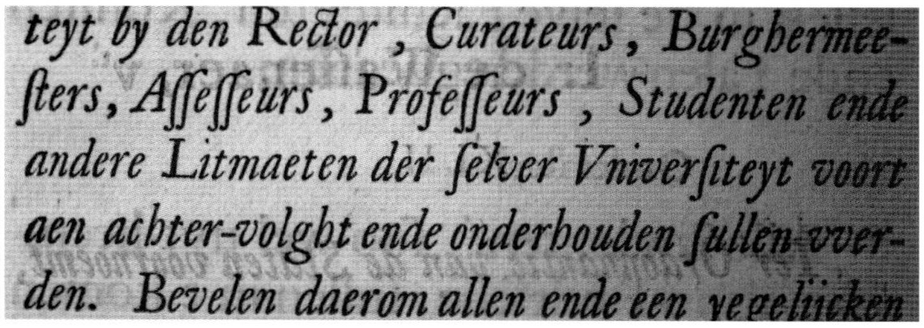
teyt by den Rector, Curateurs, Burghermeesters, Assesseurs, Professeurs, Studenten ende andere Litmaeten der selver Vniversiteyt voort aen achter-volght ende onderhouden sullen-vverden. Bevelen daerom allen ende een vegelijcken

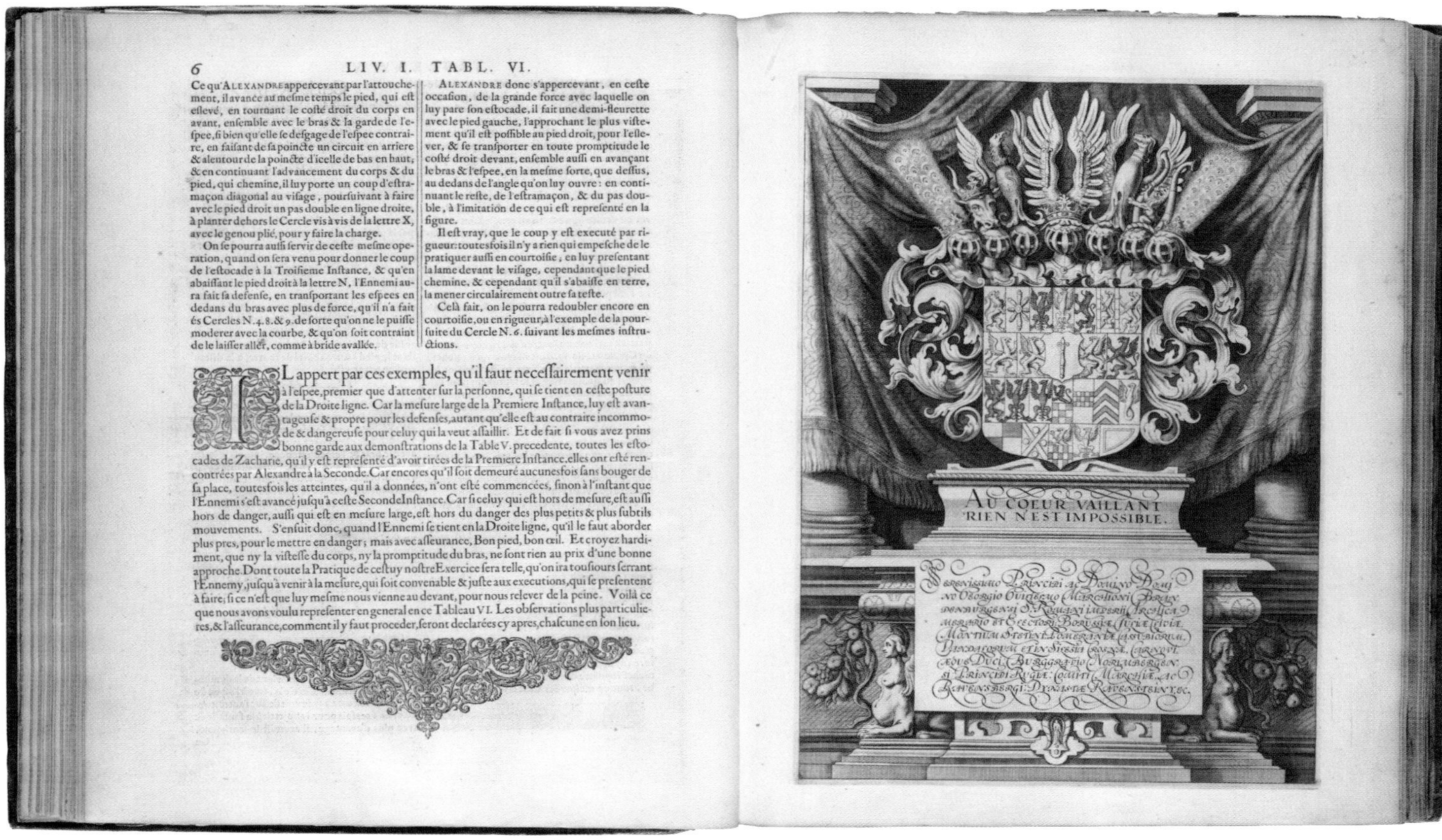
6 LIV. I. TABL. VI.

Ce qu'ALEXANDRE appercevant par l'attouchement, il avance au mesme temps le pied, qui est eslevé, en tournant le costé droit du corps en avant, ensemble avec le bras & la garde de l'espee, si bien qu'elle se desgage de l'espee contraire, en faisant de sa poincte un circuit en arriere & alentour de la poincte d'icelle de bas en haut; & en continuant l'advancement du corps & du pied, qui chemine, il luy porte un coup d'estramaçon diagonal au visage, poursuivant à faire avec le pied droit un pas double en ligne droite, à planter dehors le Cercle vis à vis de la lettre X, avec le genou plié, pour y faire la charge.

On se pourra aussi servir de ceste mesme operation, quand on sera venu pour donner le coup de l'estocade à la Troisieme Instance, & qu'en abaissant le pied droit à la lettre N, l'Ennemi aura fait sa defense, en transportant les espees en dedans du bras avec plus de force, qu'il n'a fait és Cercles N. 4. 8. & 9. de sorte qu'on ne le puisse moderer avec la courbe, & qu'on soit contraint de le laisser aller, comme à bride avallée.

ALEXANDRE donc s'appercevant, en ceste occasion, de la grande force avec laquelle on luy pare son estocade, il fait une demi-fleurette avec le pied gauche, l'approchant le plus vistement qu'il est possible au pied droit, pour l'eslever, & se transporter en toute promptitude le costé droit devant, ensemble aussi en avançant le bras & l'espee, en la mesme sorte, que dessus, au dedans de l'angle qu'on luy ouvre: en continuant le reste, de l'estramaçon, & du pas double, à l'imitation de ce qui est representé en la figure.

Il est vray, que le coup y est executé par rigueur: toutesfois il n'y a rien qui empesche de le pratiquer aussi en courtoisie; en luy presentant la lame devant le visage, cependant que le pied chemine, & cependant qu'il s'abaisse en terre, la mener circulairement outre sa teste.

Celà fait, on le pourra redoubler encore en courtoisie, ou en rigueur, à l'exemple de la poursuite du Cercle N. 6. suivant les mesmes instructions.

IL appert par ces exemples, qu'il faut necessairement venir à l'espee, premier que d'attenter sur la personne, qui se tient en ceste posture de la Droite ligne. Car la mesure large de la Premiere Instance, luy est avantageuse & propre pour les defenses, autant qu'elle est au contraire incommode & dangereuse pour celuy qui la veut assaillir. Et de fait si vous avez prins bonne garde aux demonstrations de la Table V. precedente, toutes les estocades de Zacharie, qu'il y est representé d'avoir tirées de la Premiere Instance, elles ont esté rencontrées par Alexandre à la Seconde. Car encores qu'il soit demeuré aucunesfois sans bouger de sa place, toutesfois les atteintes, qu'il a données, n'ont esté commencées, sinon à l'instant que l'Ennemi s'est avancé jusqu'à ceste Seconde Instance. Car si celuy qui est hors de mesure, est aussi hors de danger, aussi qui est en mesure large, est hors du danger des plus petits & plus subtils mouvements. S'ensuit donc, quand l'Ennemi se tient en la Droite ligne, qu'il le faut aborder plus pres, pour le mettre en danger; mais avec asseurance, Bon pied, bon œil. Et croyez hardiment, que ny la vistesse du corps, ny la promptitude du bras, ne sont rien au prix d'une bonne approche. Dont toute la Pratique de cestuy nostre Exercice sera telle, qu'on ira tousiours serrant l'Ennemy, jusqu'à venir à la mesure, qui soit convenable & juste aux executions, qui se presentent à faire; si ce n'est que luy mesme nous vienne au devant, pour nous relever de la peine. Voilà ce que nous avons voulu representer en general en ce Tableau VI. Les observations plus particulieres, & l'asseurance, comment il y faut proceder, seront declarées cy apres, chascune en son lieu.

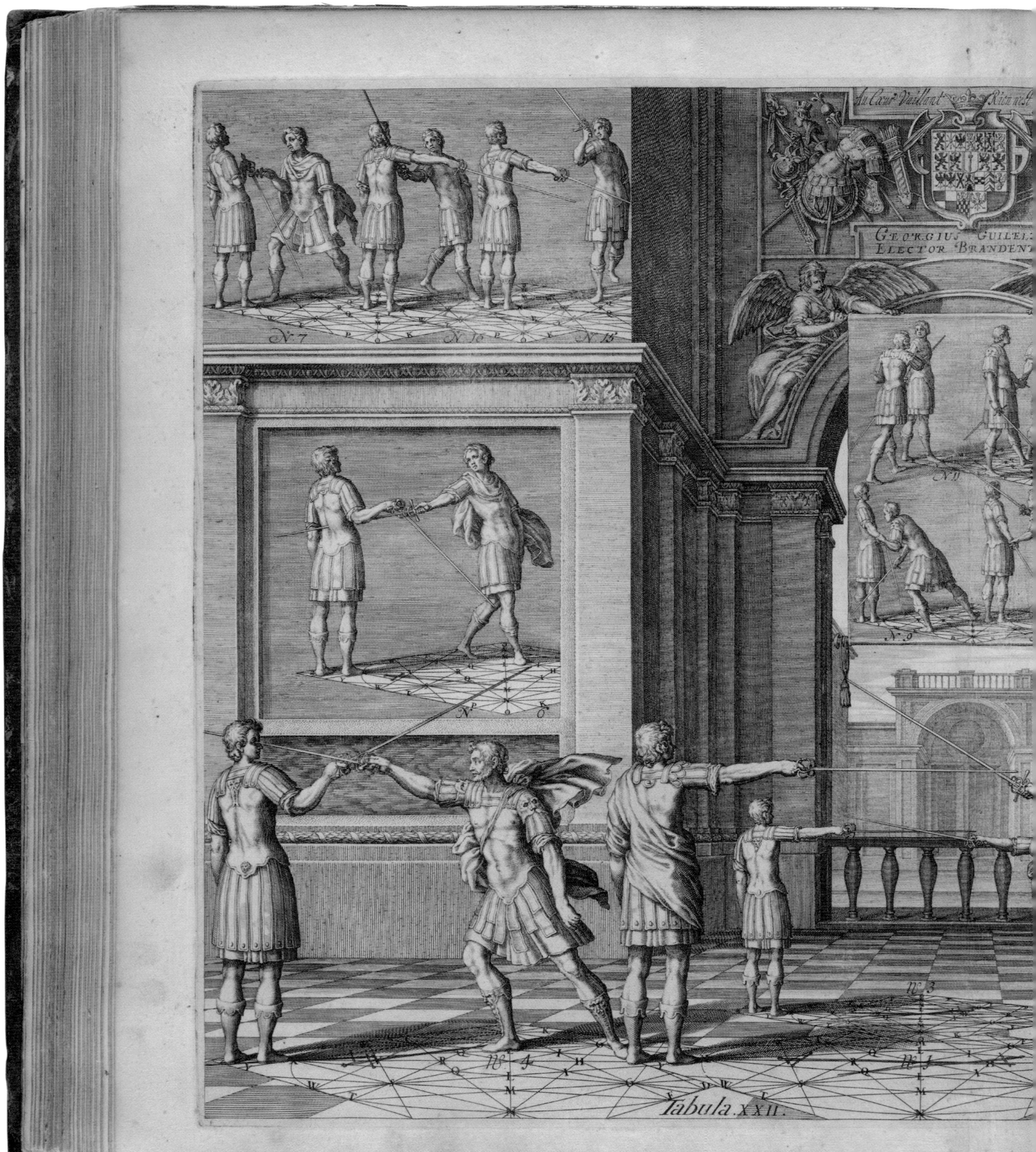
Au Cœur Vaillant Rien n'est
GEORGIUS GUILEL:
ELECTOR BRANDENT
Tabula.XXII.

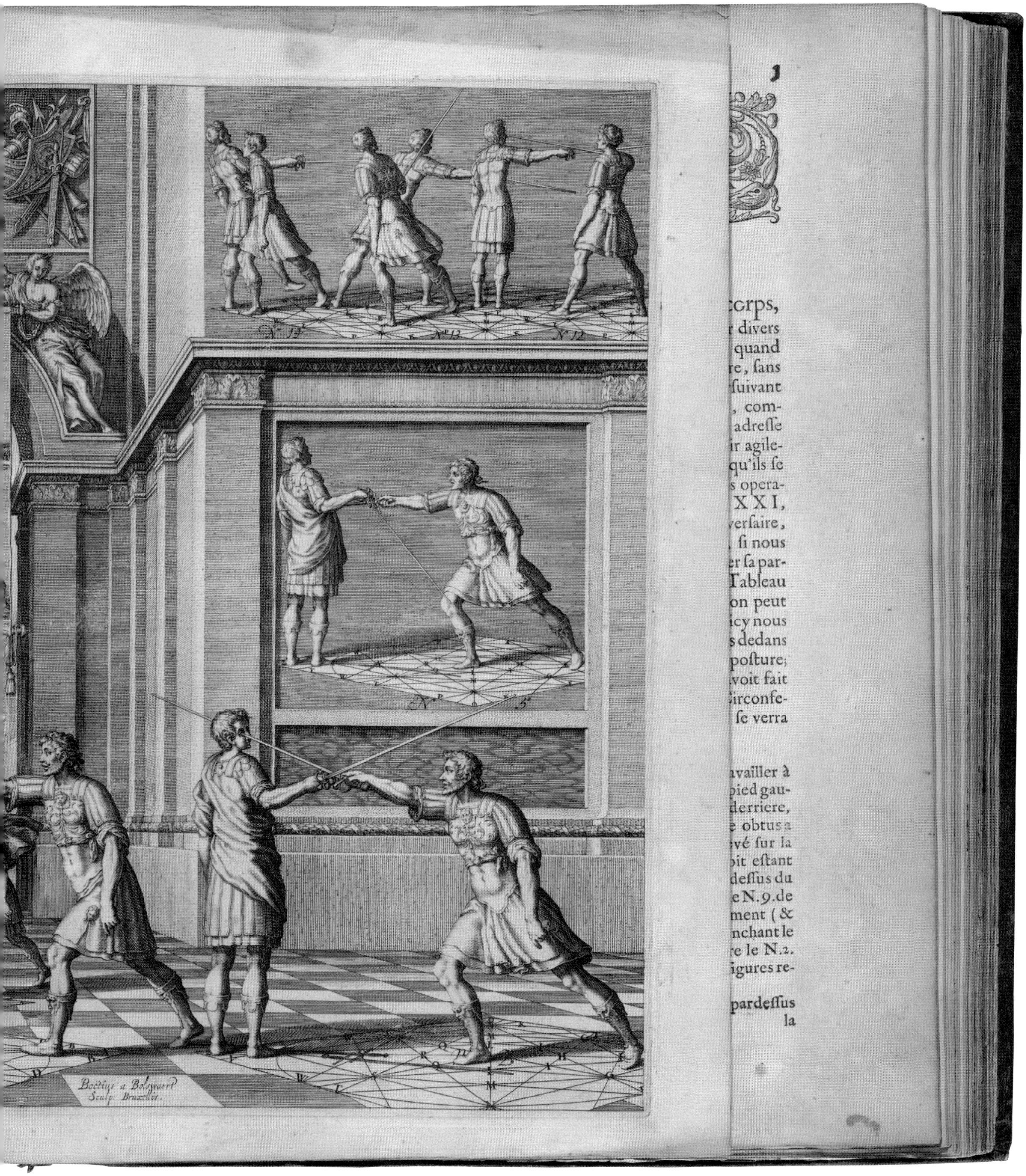
Boëtius a Bolswaert
Sculp: Bruxellis.

1664 **Joan Blaeu** *Grooten atlas, oft werelt-beschrijving, in welcke 't aertryck, de zee, en hemel, wordt vertoond en beschreven*. **Amsterdam: Joan Blaeu, 1664. 9 volumes. 58.5 cm. Illustrator: Hessel Gerritsz ('The walrus and its young').**

Joan Blaeu (1598–1673) reached the apex of his fame as a publisher, printer, and cartographer in 1662, when his *Atlas maior* came on the market: it was the biggest and most expensive atlas internationally available at that time. No other printer was capable of such a monumental performance.

The *Atlas maior* has its roots in the work of Abraham Ortelius and Gerardus Mercator. These cartographers from the Southern Netherlands had paved the way for Blaeu with their atlases in 1570 and 1595, respectively. Blaeu senior, Willem Jansz, picked up the thread in 1630, and this resulted in the relatively plain *Atlantis appendix*. Over the next three decades, the Blaeu atlas evolved into a twelve-volume geographic encyclopedia.

Depending on the edition, an *Atlas maior* contains an abundant variety of around six hundred maps, showing areas around the world. Most of the maps are of the same double folio size: they fold neatly into the atlas binding. Among variant copies of the same edition, there are considerable differences: the maps may be uncoloured or coloured by hand, the colouring can be simple or lavish, and some copies are even 'illuminated' with gold. The maps in the Blaeu atlases are printed from copperplates, and usually the back of the maps includes an explanation in letterpress.

The illustrations shown here come from a nine-volume *Atlas maior* in Dutch, complemented by two city maps of the Northern and Southern Netherlands, which first appeared in 1649. JW

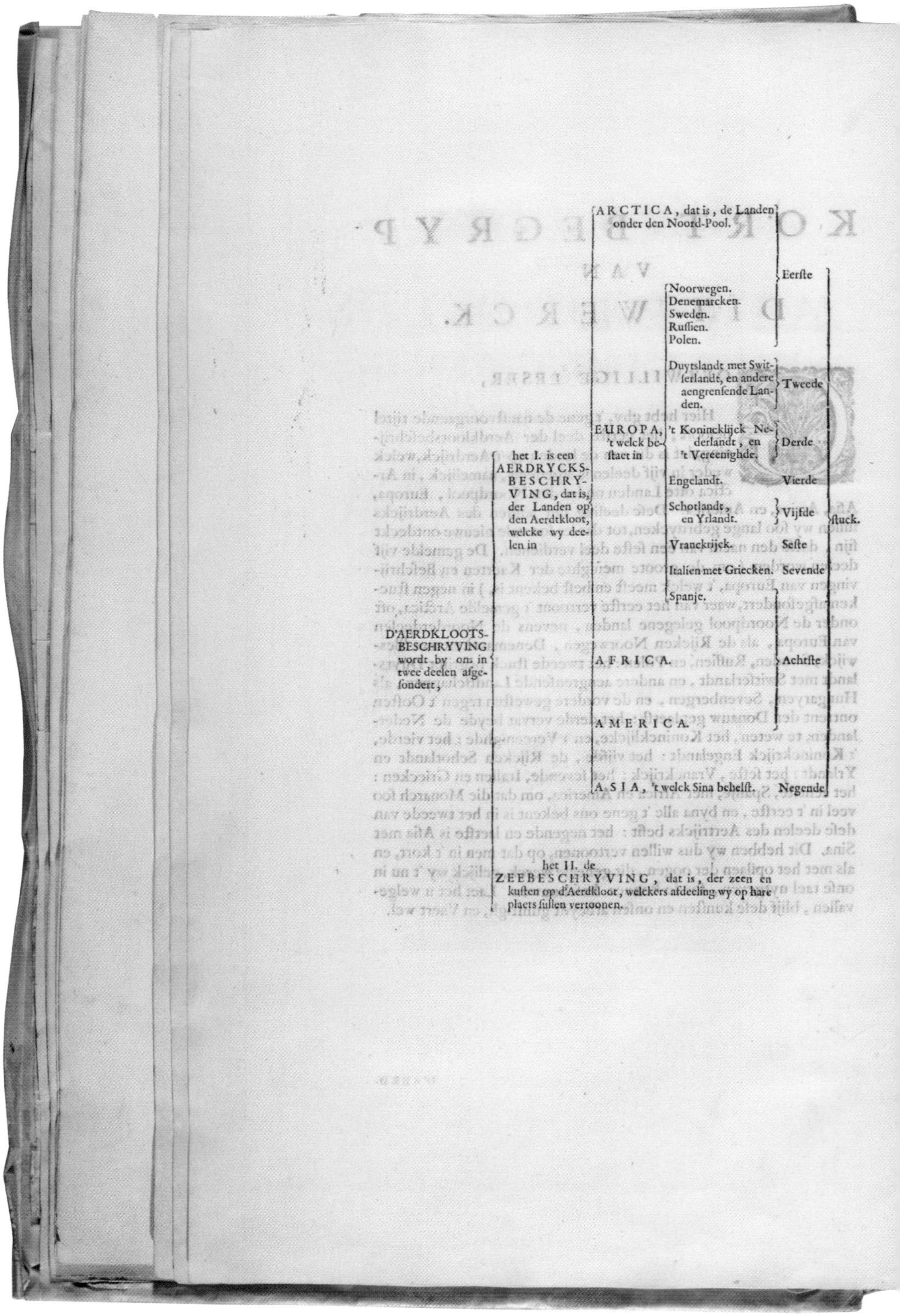

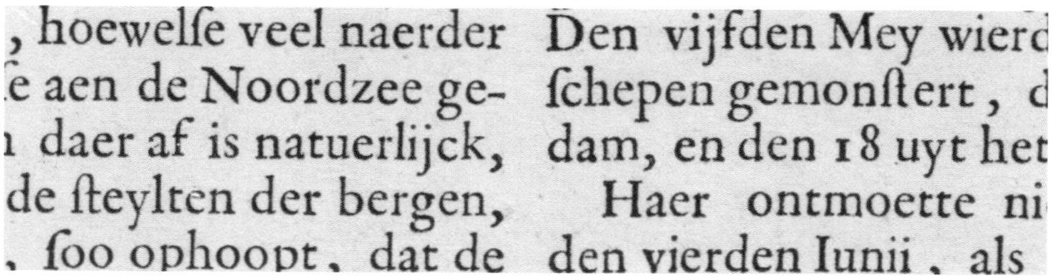
, hoewelſe veel naerder
ſe aen de Noordzee ge-
ı daer af is natuerlijck,
de ſteylten der bergen,
, ſoo ophoopt, dat de

Den vijfden Mey wierd
ſchepen gemonſtert, d
dam, en den 18 uyt het
Haer ontmoette ni
den vierden Iunii, als

This text (17 point) roman by Nicolaes Briot (*c.* 1580/84–1626) was in use by 1622. William Caslon in London modelled his 1728 Great Primer roman on it. Briot and his widow supplied most of the matrices for the in-house typefoundry that Blaeu was setting up in his printing office when Briot died prematurely.

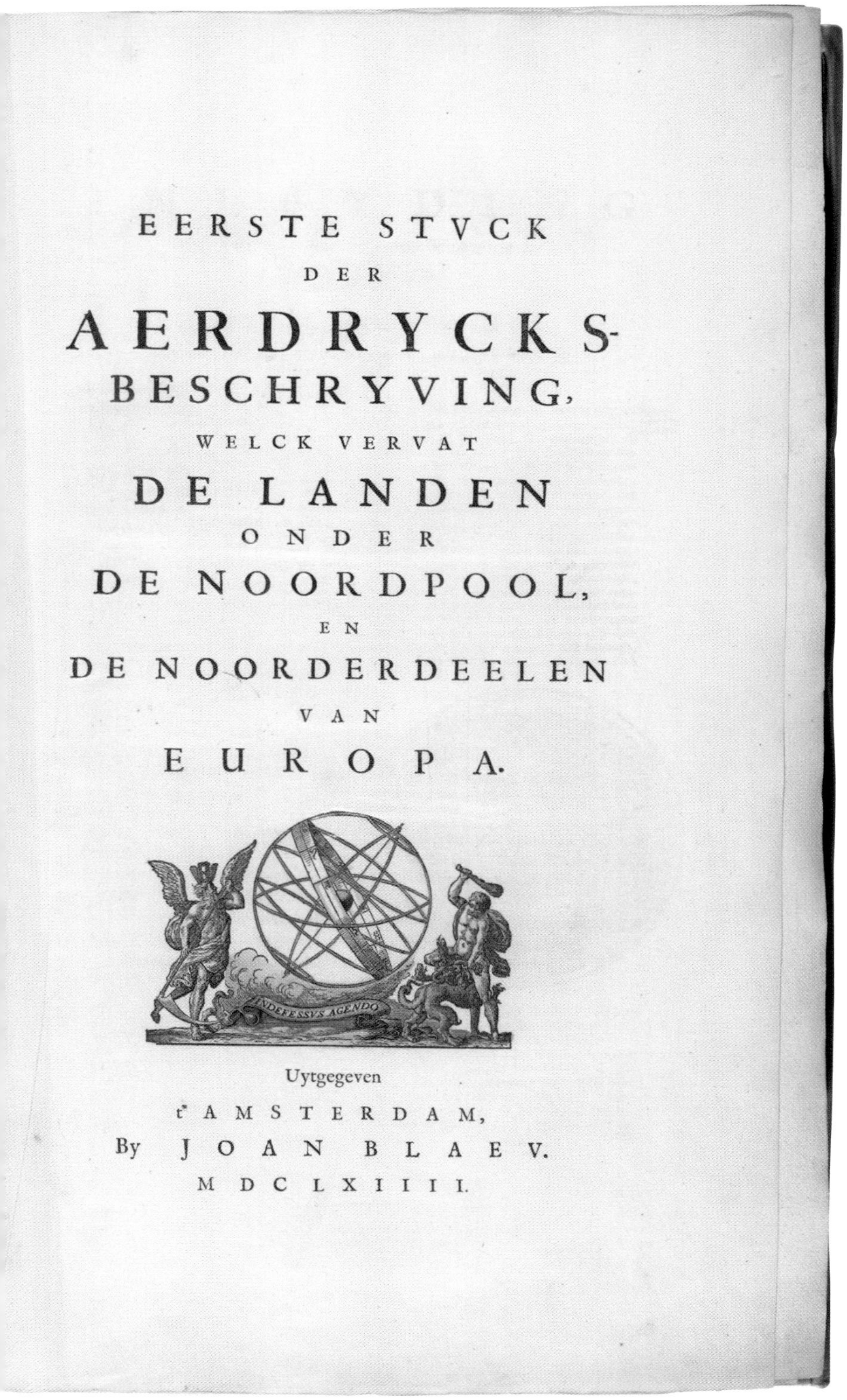
EERSTE STVCK
DER
AERDRYCKS-
BESCHRYVING,
WELCK VERVAT
DE LANDEN
ONDER
DE NOORDPOOL,
EN
DE NOORDERDEELEN
VAN
EUROPA.

Uytgegeven
t'AMSTERDAM,
By JOAN BLAEV.
MDCLXIIII.

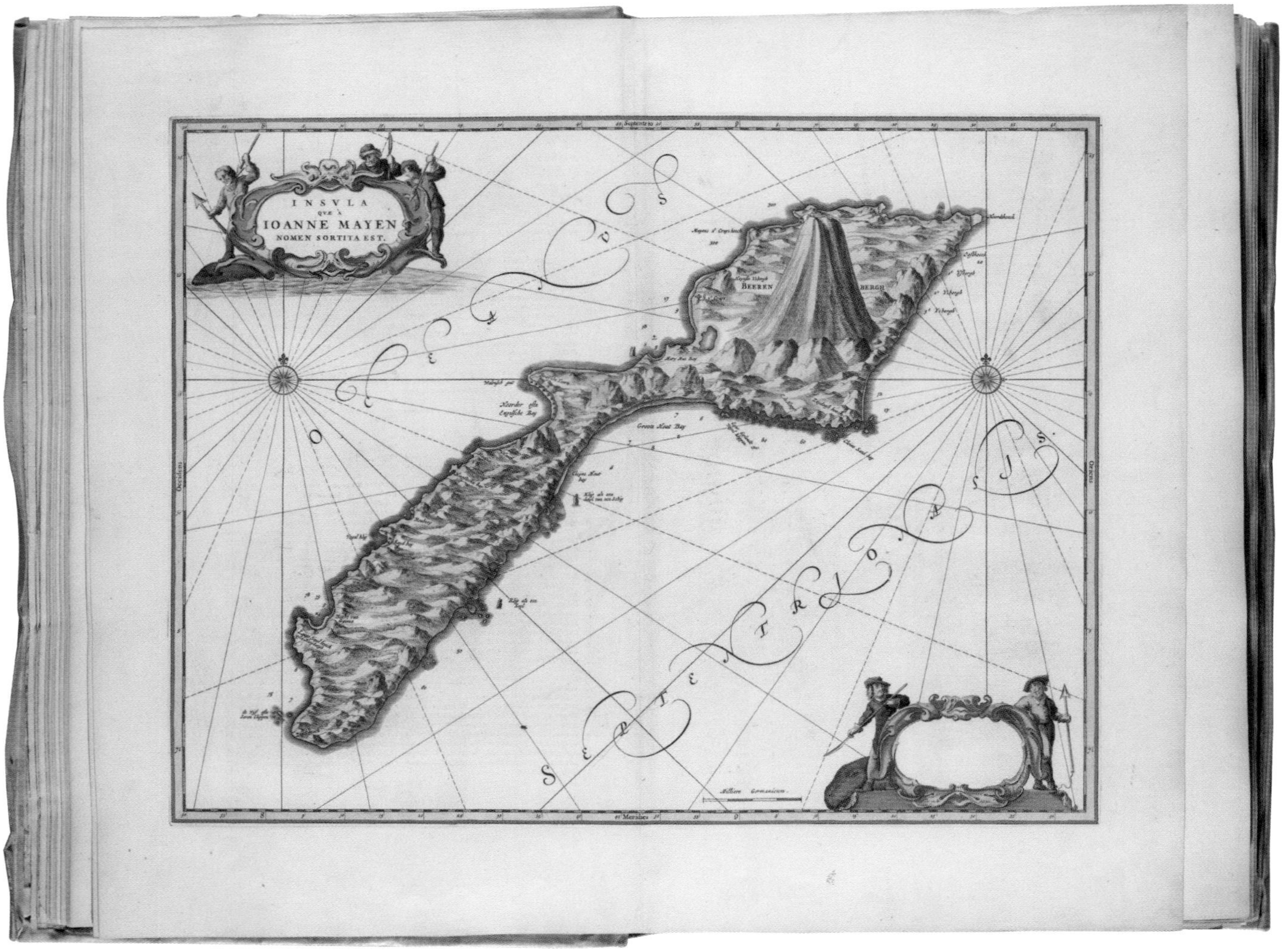
INSULA
QUÆ À
IOANNE MAYEN
NOMEN SORTITA EST.
BEEREN BERGH

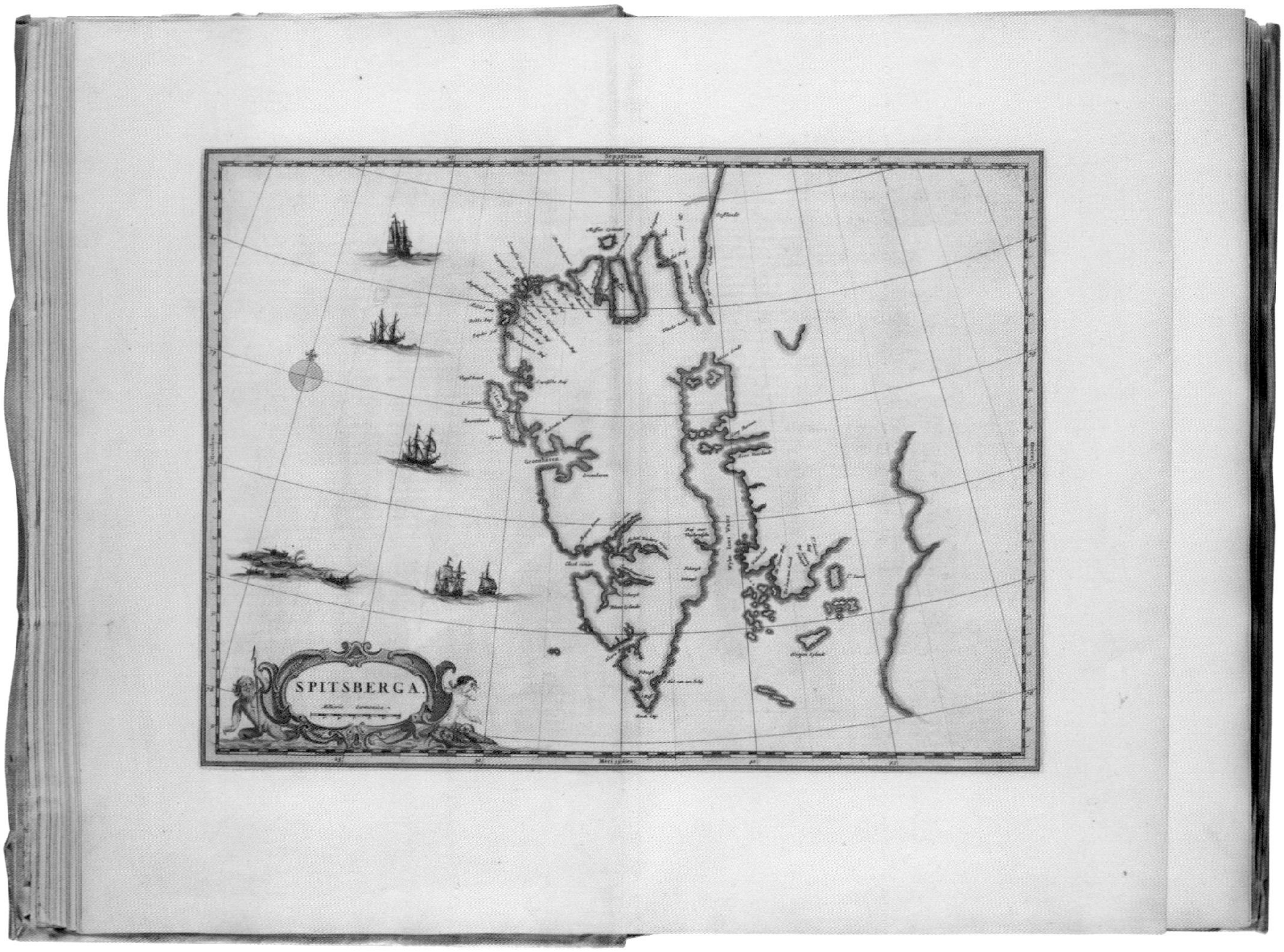
SPITSBERGA

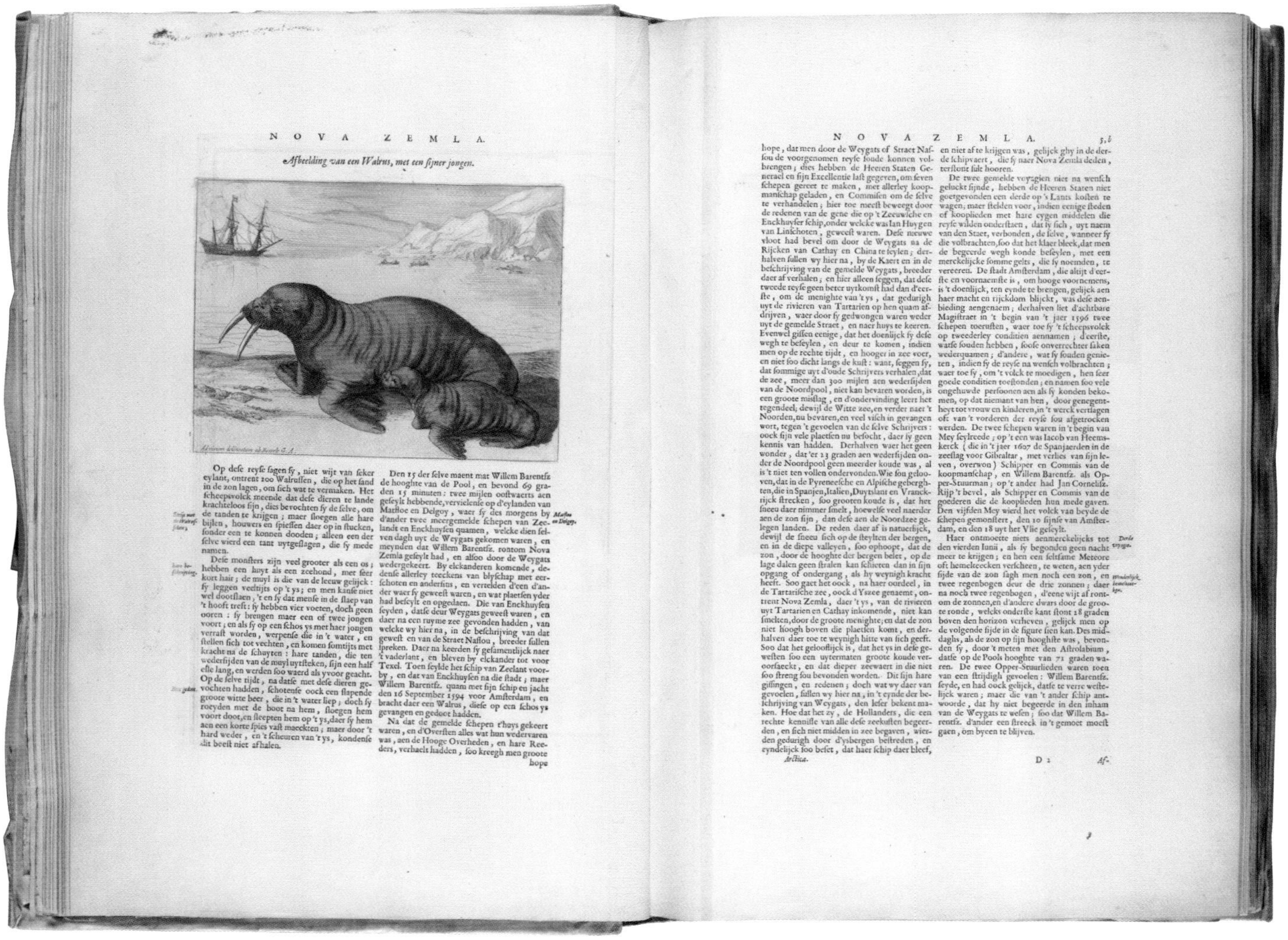
NOVA ZEMLA.
Afbeelding van een Walrus, met een sijner jongen.
NOVA ZEMLA.

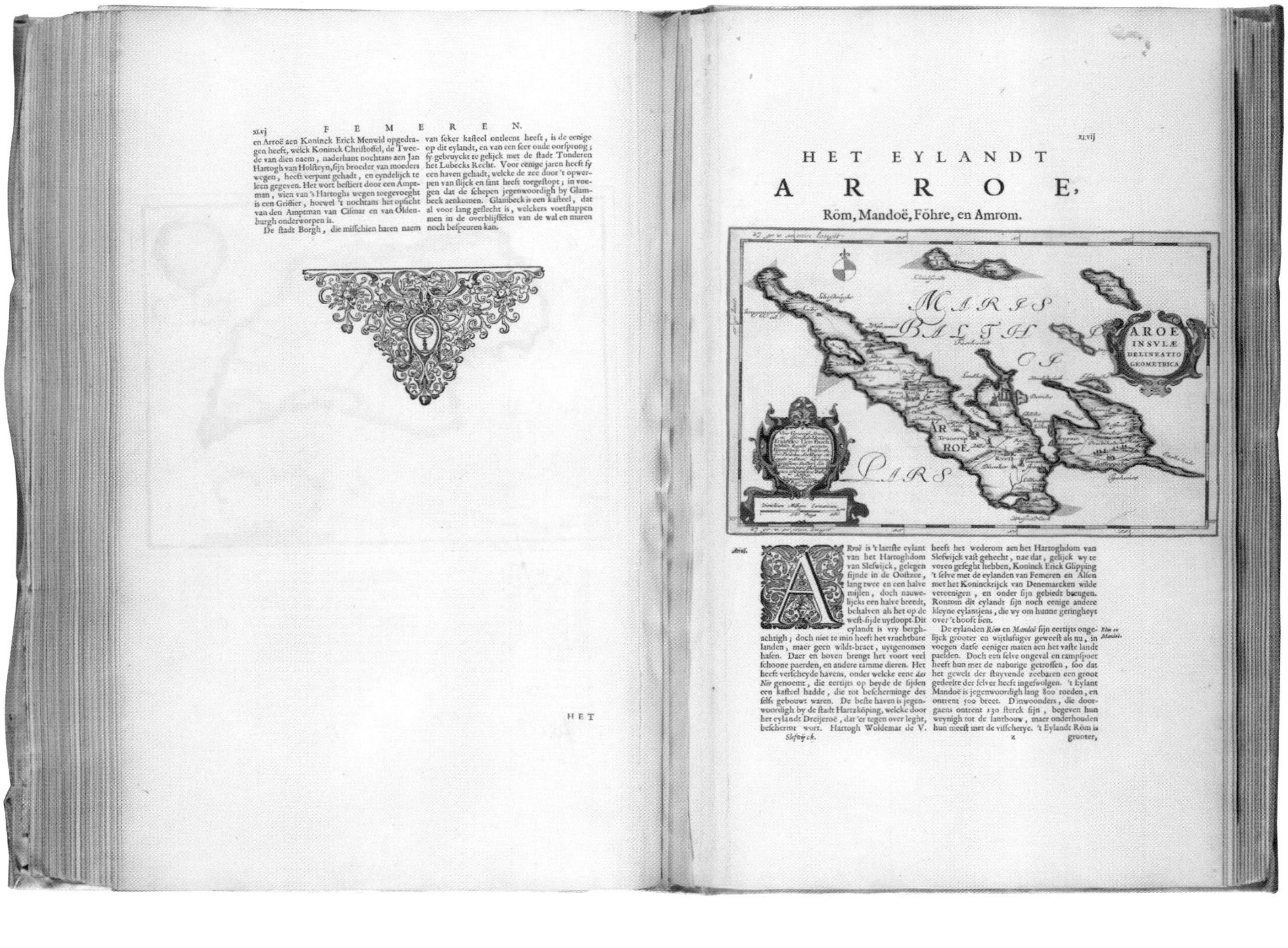
FEMEREN.
HET EYLANDT
ARROE,
Röm, Mandoë, Föhre, en Amrom.
AROE INSULÆ DELINEATIO GEOMETRICA
MARIS BALTHICI
HET

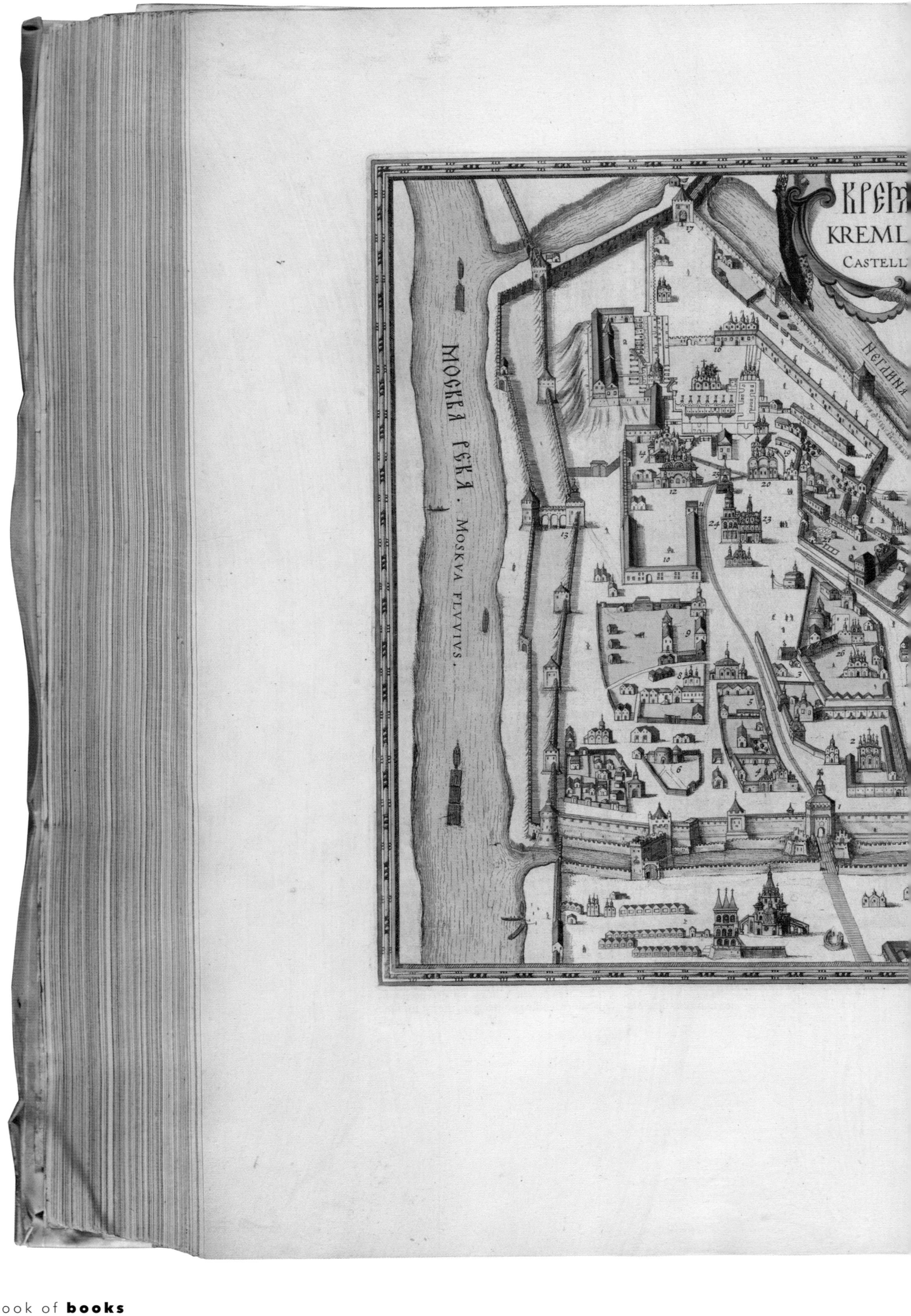
МОСКВА РЕКА.
MOSKVA FLVVIUS.

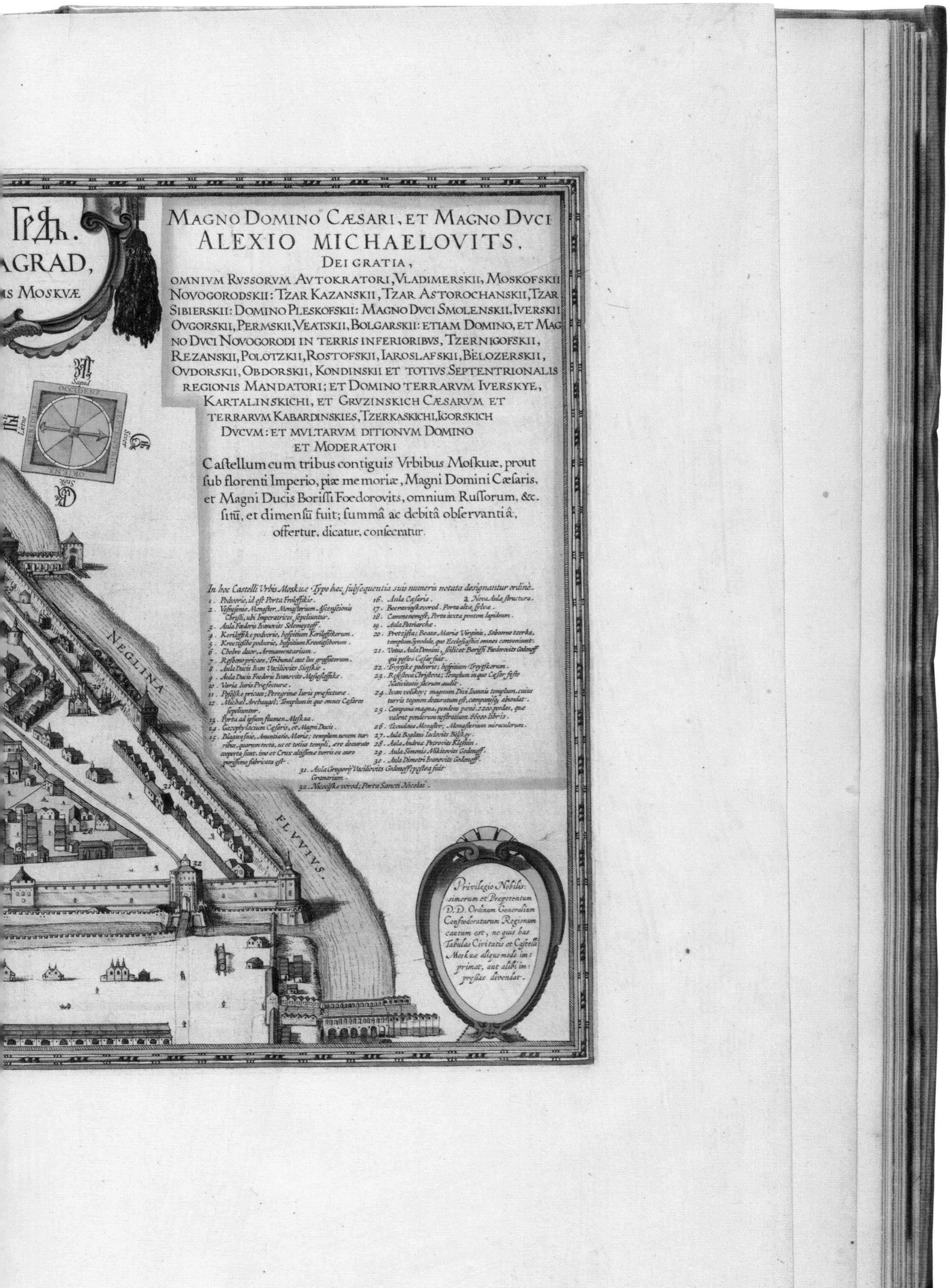
ГрДь.
AGRAD,
S MOSKVÆ
MAGNO DOMINO CÆSARI, ET MAGNO DVCI
ALEXIO MICHAELOVITS,
DEI GRATIA,
OMNIVM RVSSORVM AVTOKRATORI, VLADIMERSKII, MOSKOFSKII
NOVOGORODSKII: TZAR KAZANSKII, TZAR ASTOROCHANSKII, TZAR
SIBIERSKII: DOMINO PLESKOFSKII: MAGNO DVCI SMOLENSKII, IVERSKII
OVGORSKII, PERMSKII, VEATSKII, BOLGARSKII: ETIAM DOMINO, ET MAG
NO DVCI NOVOGORODI IN TERRIS INFERIORIBVS, TZERNIGOFSKII,
REZANSKII, POLOTZKII, ROSTOFSKII, IAROSLAFSKII, BELOZERSKII,
OVDORSKII, OBDORSKII, KONDINSKII ET TOTIVS SEPTENTRIONALIS
REGIONIS MANDATORI; ET DOMINO TERRARVM IVERSKYE,
KARTALINSKICHI, ET GRVZINSKICH CÆSARVM ET
TERRARVM KABARDINSKIES, TZERKASKICHI, IGORSKICH
DVCVM: ET MVLTARVM DITIONVM DOMINO
ET MODERATORI
Castellum cum tribus contiguis Vrbibus Moskuæ, prout
sub florenti Imperio, piæ memoriæ, Magni Domini Cæsaris,
et Magni Ducis Borissi Foedorovits, omnium Russorum, &c.
situ, et dimensu fuit; summâ ac debitâ observantiâ,
offertur, dicatur, consecratur.
In hoc Castelli Vrbis Moskuæ Typo hæc subsequentia suis numeris notata designantur ordine.
NEGLINA
FLVVIVS.
Privilegio Nobilis-
simorum et Præpotentum
D.D. Ordinum Generalium
Confoederatarum Regionum
cautum est, ne quis has
Tabulas Civitatis et Castelli
Moskuæ aliquo modo im-
primat, aut alibi im-
pressas divendat.

1683 **Joseph Moxon** Joseph Moxon, *Mechanick Exercises: or, the Doctrine of Handy-works. Applied to the Art of Printing.*

London: Joseph Moxon, 1683–84. 394 pp. 20 cm.

This first printer's manual was published in London in 1683–84: a guidebook covering every aspect of casting and composing type and printing books. It was the second volume of *Mechanick Exercises*, a planned series of descriptions of various trades, published in instalments. The author was Joseph Moxon (1627–91), publisher, printer, punchcutter, typefounder and globe-maker. Because of the highly detailed and correct descriptions of objects such as the type case, the printing press, the paper press, the type mould, and the way they should be used, this work is mainly a book for craftsmen. However, when the learned Moxon (who was a member of the Royal Society) points out the rational principles of typography, he is also addressing English intellectuals. Moxon had spent part of his life in Holland working for Dutch printers, and in various sections of the book he discusses Dutch tools and customs. It is remarkable that a manual of this kind would be published in a country that, at that time, played a very minor role in book printing. The typographic design of *Mechanick Exercises* is simple but clear.

All English printer's manuals published subsequently, until around 1840, go back to Moxon's work, but the book had little impact in the rest of Europe. However, *Mechanick Exercises* would eventually become the quintessential handbook for historians of printing and typesetting. FAJ

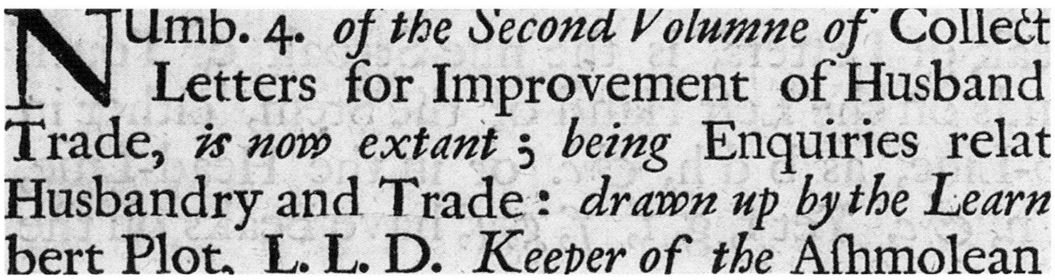

Numb. 4. *of the Second Volumne of* Collect
Letters for Improvement of Husband
Trade, *is now extant*; *being* Enquiries relat
Husbandry and Trade: *drawn up by the Learn*
bert Plot. L. L. D. *Keeper of the* Aſhmolean

Arthur Nicholls (*c.* 1585?–*c.* 1640/53) cut this Great Primer (17 point) roman (1638) and italic (1639) in London. After 1646, even Dutch printers used roman type. Caslon's types, superior in execution, drove these stylistically more modern faces (and better Dutch types) out of use in England by around 1730.

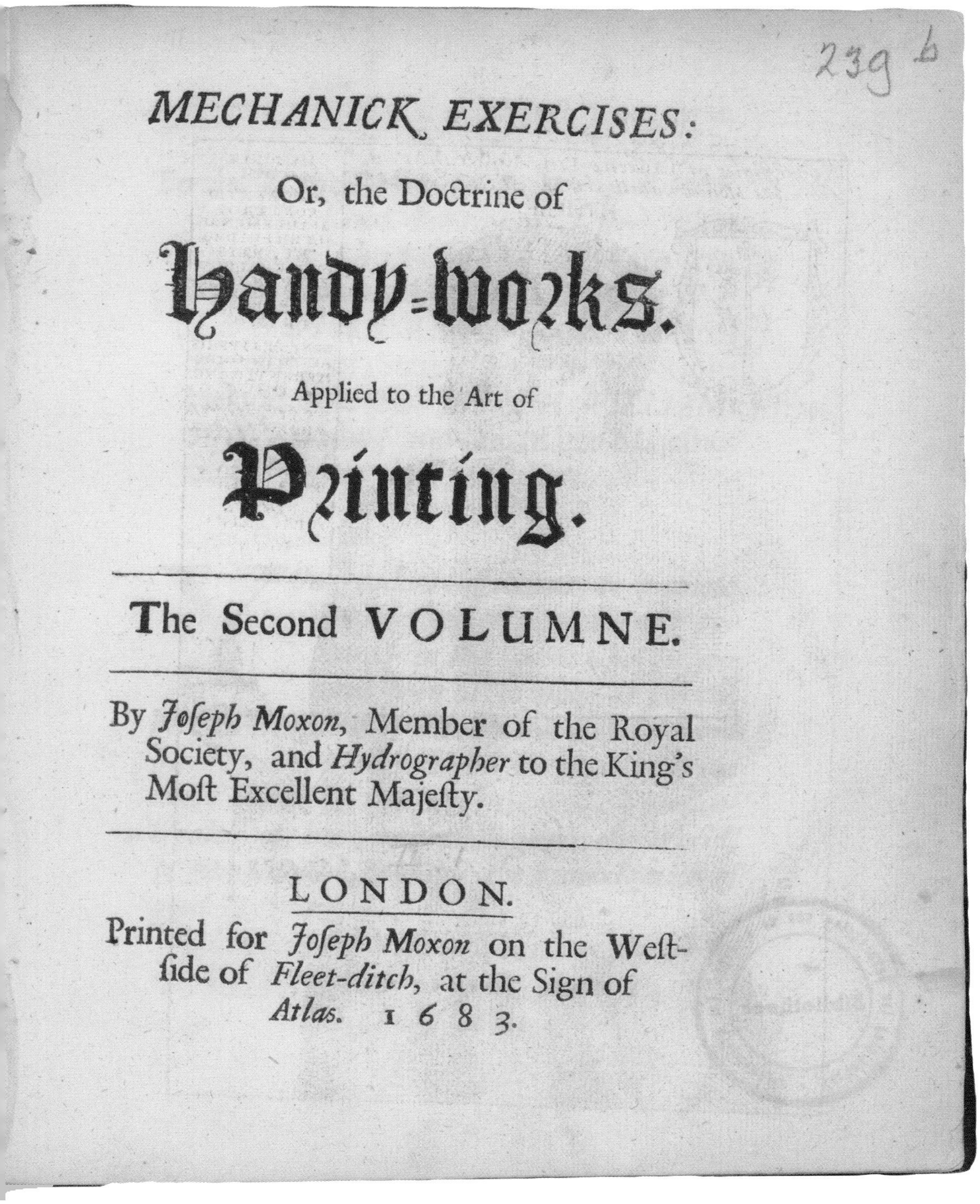

MECHANICK EXERCISES:

Or, the Doctrine of

Handy-works.

Applied to the Art of

Printing.

The Second VOLUMNE.

By *Joſeph Moxon*, Member of the Royal Society, and *Hydrographer* to the King's Moſt Excellent Majeſty.

LONDON.

Printed for *Joſeph Moxon* on the Weſt-ſide of *Fleet-ditch*, at the Sign of *Atlas*. 1683.

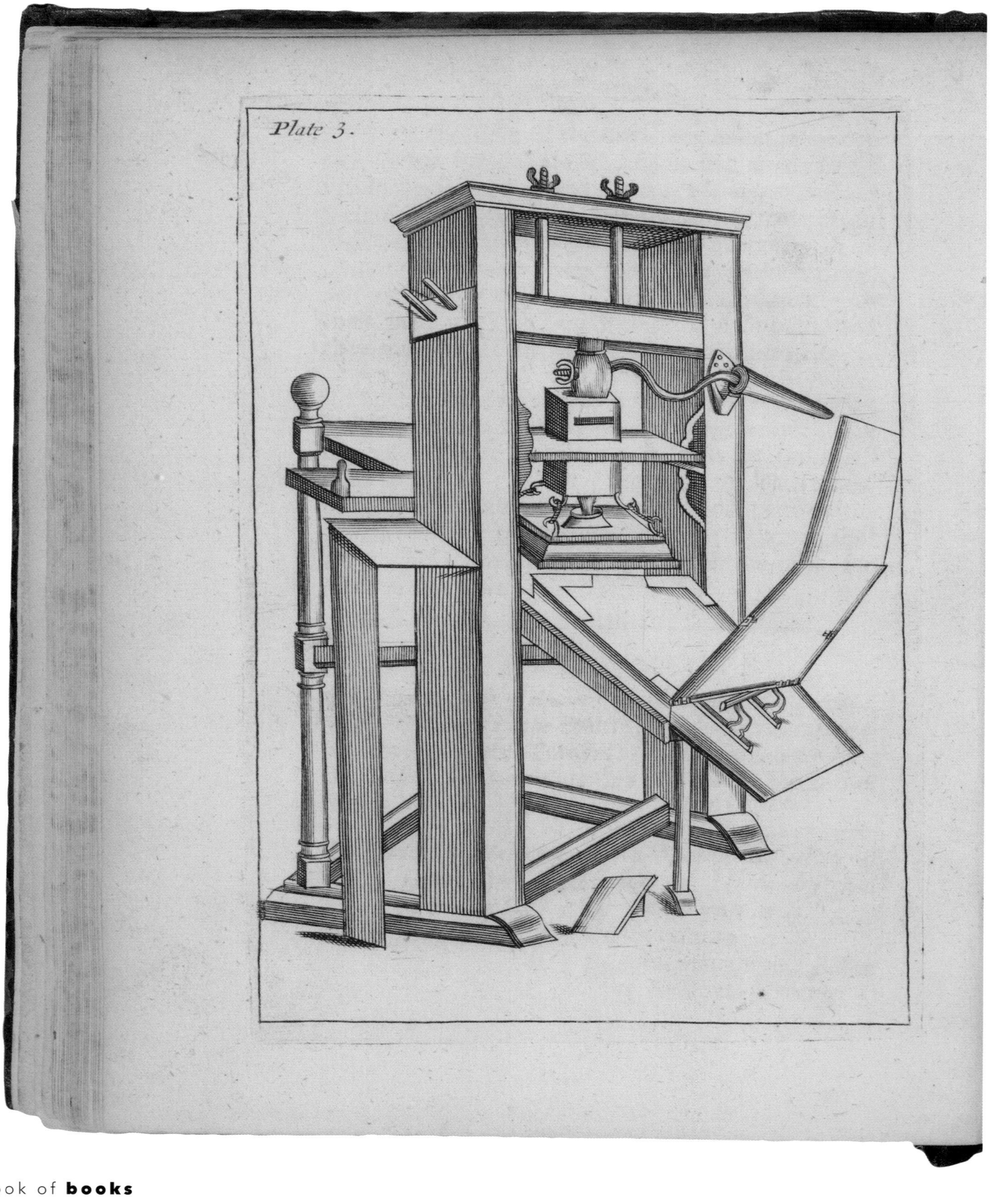
Plate 3.

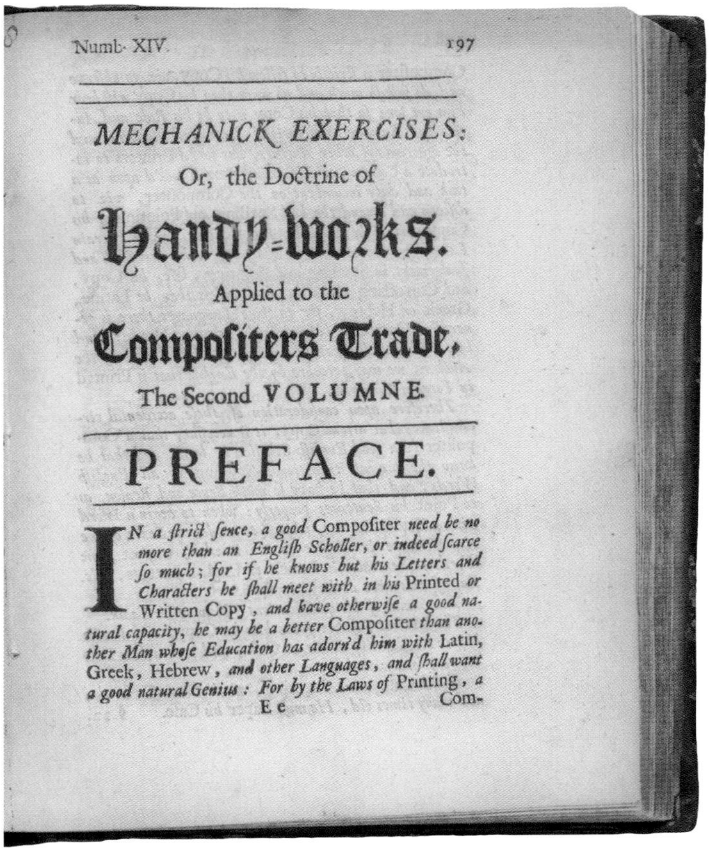

Numb. XIV. 197

MECHANICK EXERCISES:
Or, the Doctrine of
Handy-works.
Applied to the
Compositers Trade.
The Second VOLUMNE.

PREFACE.

IN a *strict sence, a good* Compositer *need be no more than an English Scholler, or indeed scarce so much; for if he knows but his Letters and Characters he shall meet with in his* Printed *or* Written Copy, *and have otherwise a good natural capacity, he may be a better* Compositer *than another Man whose Education has adorn'd him with* Latin, Greek, Hebrew, *and other Languages, and shall want a good natural* Genius: *For by the Laws of* Printing, *a*
Ee Com-

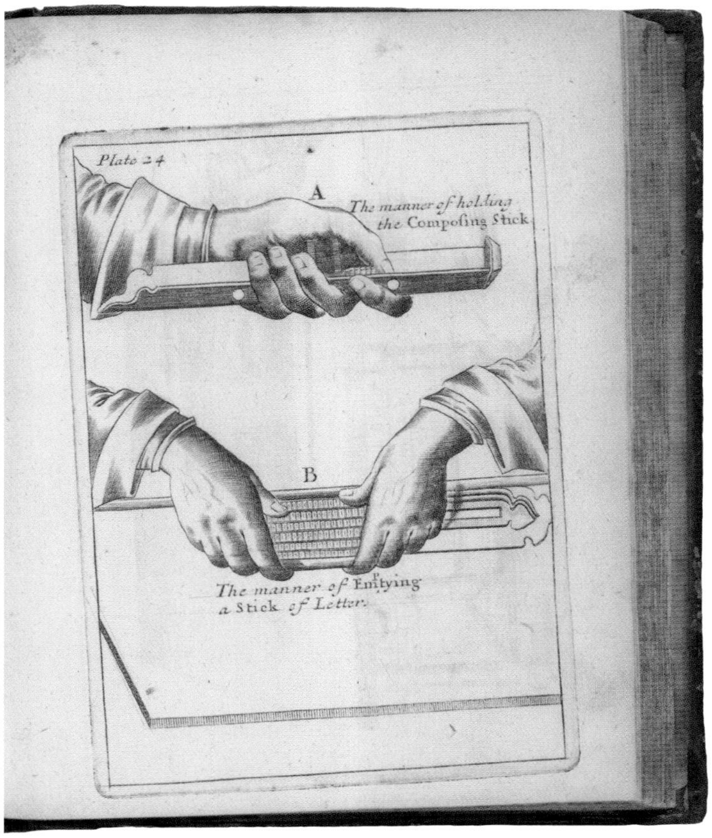

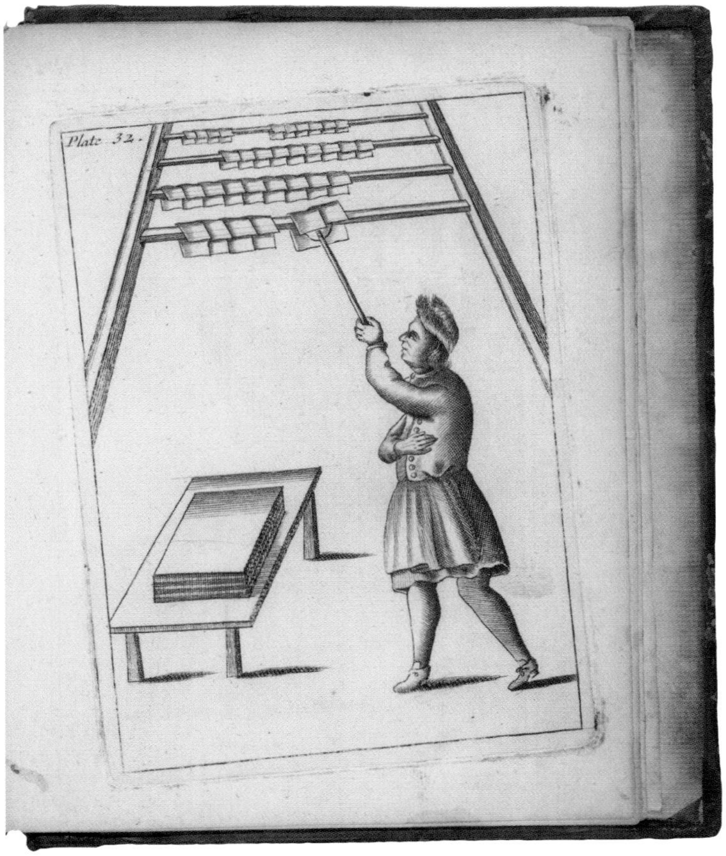

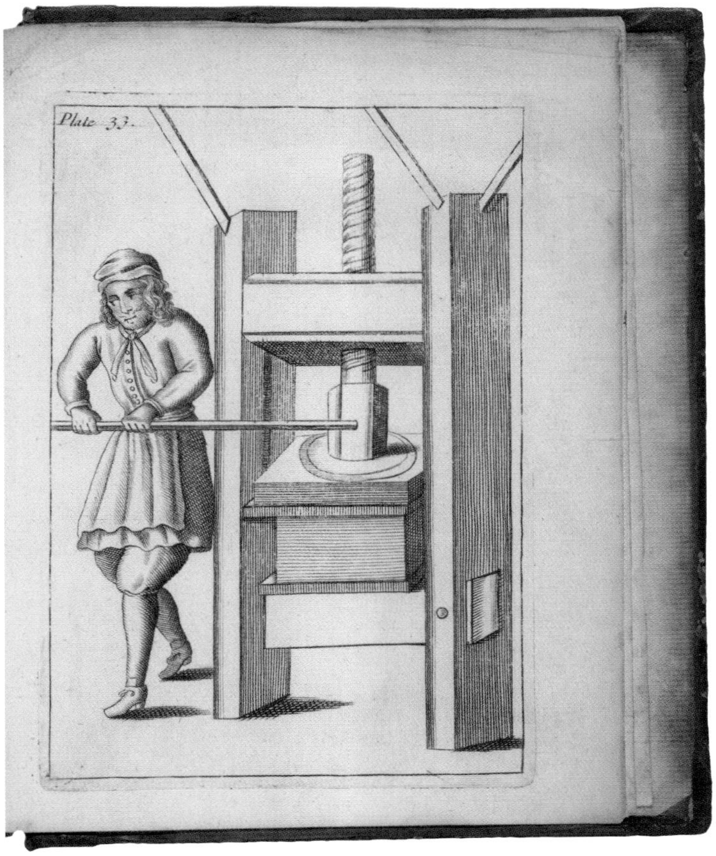

The eighteenth century

Detail of *The Natural History of Carolina, Florida, and the Bahama Islands*, printed and illustrated by Mark Catesby (see p. 192)

The eighteenth century **Trends begun in the seventeenth century continued into the eighteenth with the somewhat heavy 'old face' types of the Englishman William Caslon and of the German-born Joan Michael Fleischman, who worked in the Netherlands. Other currents can be seen in the crowded layout of pages and in the large books with copperplate illustrations by the Imprimerie Royale in Paris and others. Around the middle of the century, the rococo style, with its extravagant ornamentation, held sway in typography, for example in the fleurons of the Paris punchcutter and typefounder Pierre-Simon Fournier.**

After about 1775, a rejuvenating rediscovery of classical antiquity followed the excavations at Pompeii and Herculaneum, and influenced a turn towards a purer, more geometrically constructed typography. Printers such as the Didots in Paris and Giambattista Bodoni in Parma turned away from Fournier's style in the 1780s. They preferred the designs of the English printer John Baskerville, who can be regarded as their forerunner. Pierre Didot and Bodoni also praised the remarkable typography of Joaquín Ibarra, a printer working in Madrid. This neoclassical style uses printing types with a strong contrast in thickness between horizontal and vertical elements, and serifs that form right angles with the strokes. As early as 1700, a scholarly committee – appointed by King Louis XIV of France – had, in consultation with the punchcutter Philippe Grandjean, designed a roman and italic constructed according to a strictly rational pattern.

In the layout of books from the last decades of the eighteenth century, we find an extravagant use of white space: in the margins, in the interlinear spacing, in the

spaces between the words and in the spacing around punctuation marks. Title pages were typographical tours de force, made up of centred lines of capitals surrounded by plenty of space: ornament was reduced to an occasional printed rule. Paris printers in particular – following Enlightenment concepts – saw the simple grandeur of their typography as the supreme perfection. Classic texts by authors such as Virgil and Racine were published in monumental form, mostly accompanied by engravings in the neoclassical style of Jacques-Louis David and his students. These extremely expensive books were intended for the nobility and bourgeoisie, who were already returning by 1796, immediately after the French Revolution.

Traditional books, mostly of a religious nature, continued older traditions. FAJ

1700 **Cornelis de Bruijn** Cornelis de Bruijn, *Voyage au Levant*... Delft: Cornelis de Bruijn, 1700. 408 pp. 41.5 cm.

Illustrator: Cornelis de Bruijn. Printer: Hendrik Krooneveld, Delft.

Cornelis de Bruijn (*c.* 1652–1726/7) was an ardent traveller rather than an explorer: he undertook grand tours away from the usual routes. Among other locations, he travelled to the Mediterranean, Russia, and Persia, where he made copious notes of what he witnessed. He made sketches from life, and later used the results to compile a book. The production of lavishly illustrated editions such as the *Voyage au Levant* was costly. Unable to find a publisher, De Bruijn decided to make use of a sales method that was still relatively unusual in the Netherlands: he sold the book by subscription, with the buyers paying in advance.

Voyage au Levant is the French translation of De Bruijn's original Dutch account of his journey around the Mediterranean. The folio volume is characteristic of contemporary monumental editions published in the Netherlands, which were inspired by the work of French immigrants. The influx of Huguenots, who had left their country by order of Louis XIV after the revocation of the Edict of Nantes, had given the quality of publishing in the Netherlands a new impetus.

This copy of the *Voyage au Levant* is special: it is a milestone in colour printing. Another Dutch printer, Johannes Teyler, had already experimented with printing engravings in colour. Instead of covering the copperplate with black ink, it was painted by hand: blue for the sky, brown for the pyramids, and so on. The plate would then be wiped and printed. Blocks of colour were painted in by hand afterwards. PD

These capitals were used in Amsterdam from 1661, probably printed from sandcastings mounted on woodblocks. They appear in the typefounders' specimens of Bartholomeus Voskens (Hamburg, c. 1665) and Christoffel van Dijck (Amsterdam, c. 1668/69) and resemble the architectural lettering that Van Dijck designed and Michiel Comans painted for Amsterdam's city hall (painter paid 1658).

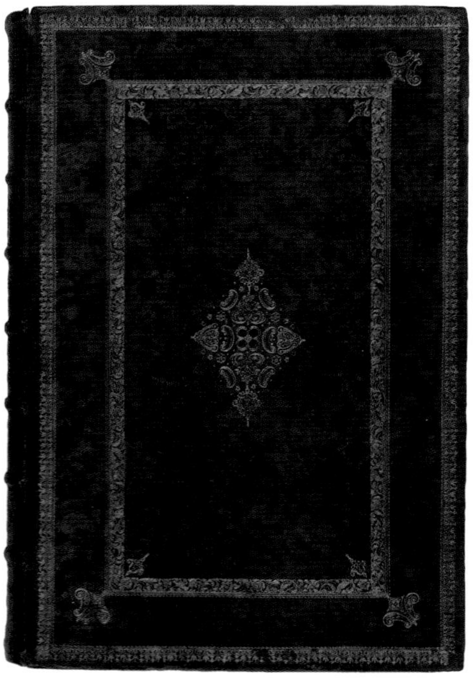

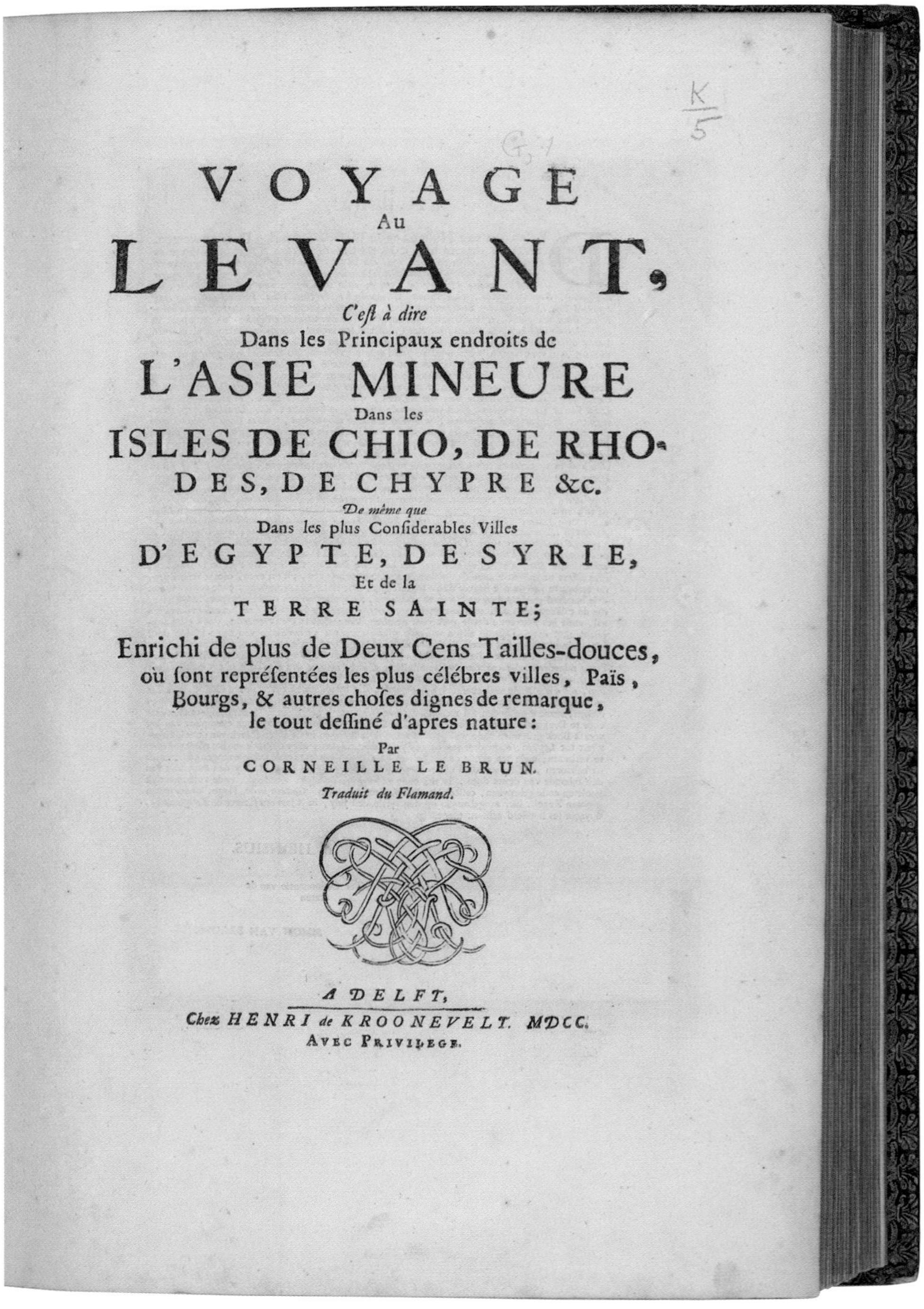

VOYAGE
Au
LEVANT,
C'est à dire
Dans les Principaux endroits de
L'ASIE MINEURE
Dans les
ISLES DE CHIO, DE RHODES, DE CHYPRE &c.
De même que
Dans les plus Considerables Villes
D'EGYPTE, DE SYRIE,
Et de la
TERRE SAINTE;
Enrichi de plus de Deux Cens Tailles-douces, où sont représentées les plus célébres villes, Païs, Bourgs, & autres choses dignes de remarque, le tout dessiné d'apres nature:
Par
CORNEILLE LE BRUN.
Traduit du Flamand.

A DELFT,
Chez *HENRI de KROONEVELT. MDCC.*
AVEC PRIVILEGE.

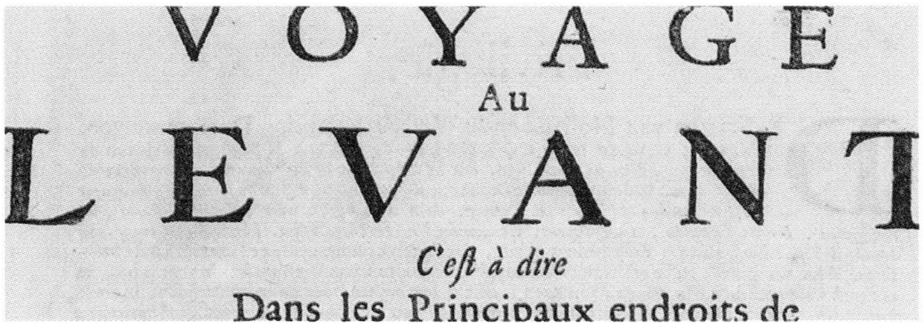

VOYAGE

Au

LEVANT

C'eſt à dire

Dans les Principaux endroits de

170 VOYAGE au LEVANT

etoffe de ſoye brodée fort proprement, à quoi elles s'entendent en perfection. Elles ne ſont pas non plus trop dedaigneuſes ni même trop retenuës à l'egard des hommes: car & dans la ville & à la campagne on les voit aux jours de rejouiſſance, danſer en branle de tous côtez, & même une etranger s'y peut joindre librement, & prendre par la main celle qu'il trouve la plus à ſon gré ſans que perſonne en prenne de la jalouſie. Elles font auſſi tant de civilité aux étranges qu'on a ſujet d'en être ſurpris. Mais pour avoir le plaiſir de les frequenter, & de jouir des douceurs de leur converſation, il faut ſçavoir parler leur langue, parce qu'il y en a tres peu entre elles qui ſachent l'Italien. Pour les hommes ils s'en ſervent paſſablement pour la plus part. La maniere dont ceux ci s'habillent eſt à peu pres telle qu'elle étoit autrefois chez nous, avant que la gravité de nos Hollandois ſe fût laiſſé corrompre en ſuivant les modes inconſtantes des François. Ils portent des Chapeaux pointus à grands bords & un juſtaucorps aſſez court avec quatre grandes baſques. Les manches ſont ouvertes ſur le bras, & gar-

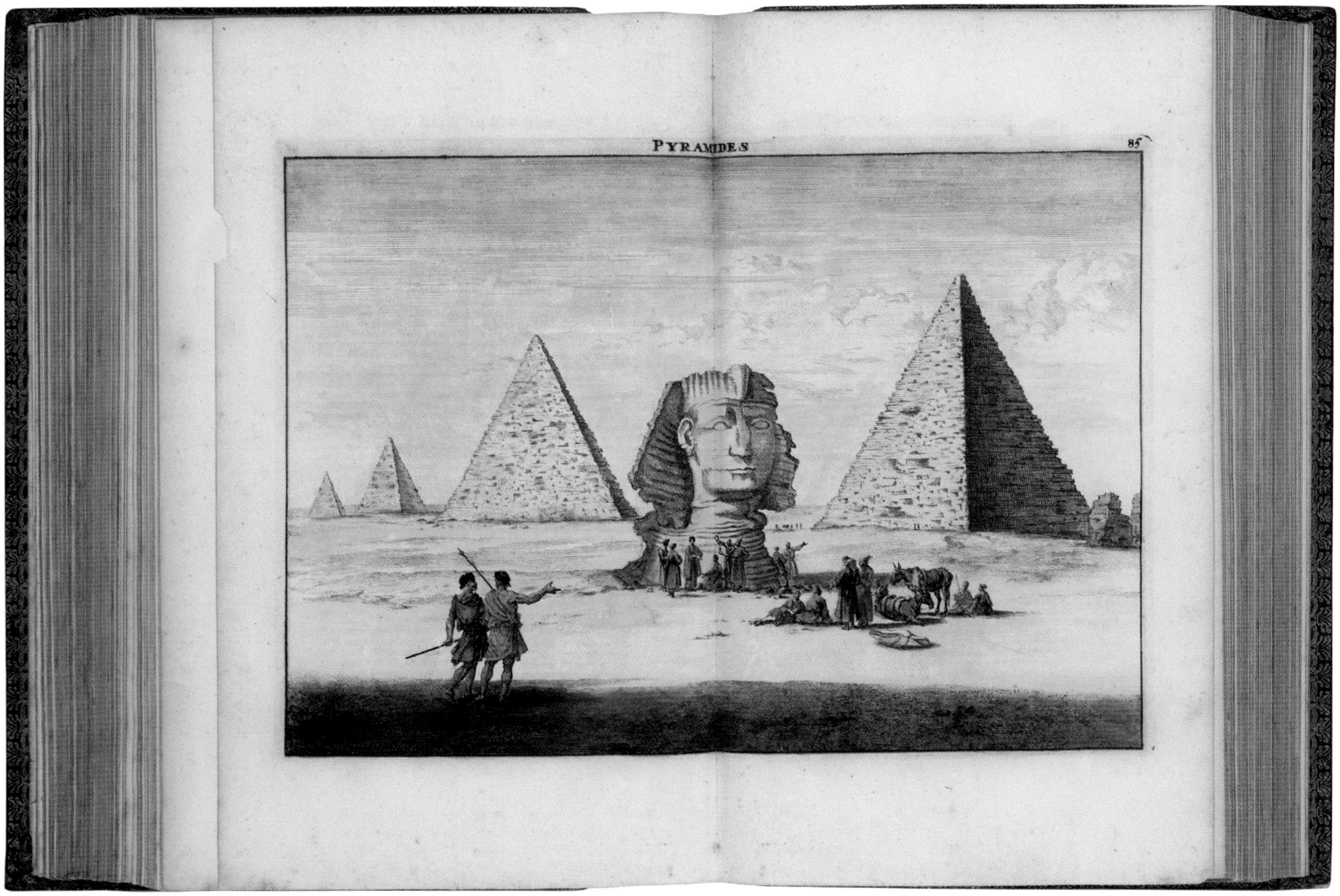
PYRAMIDES
85

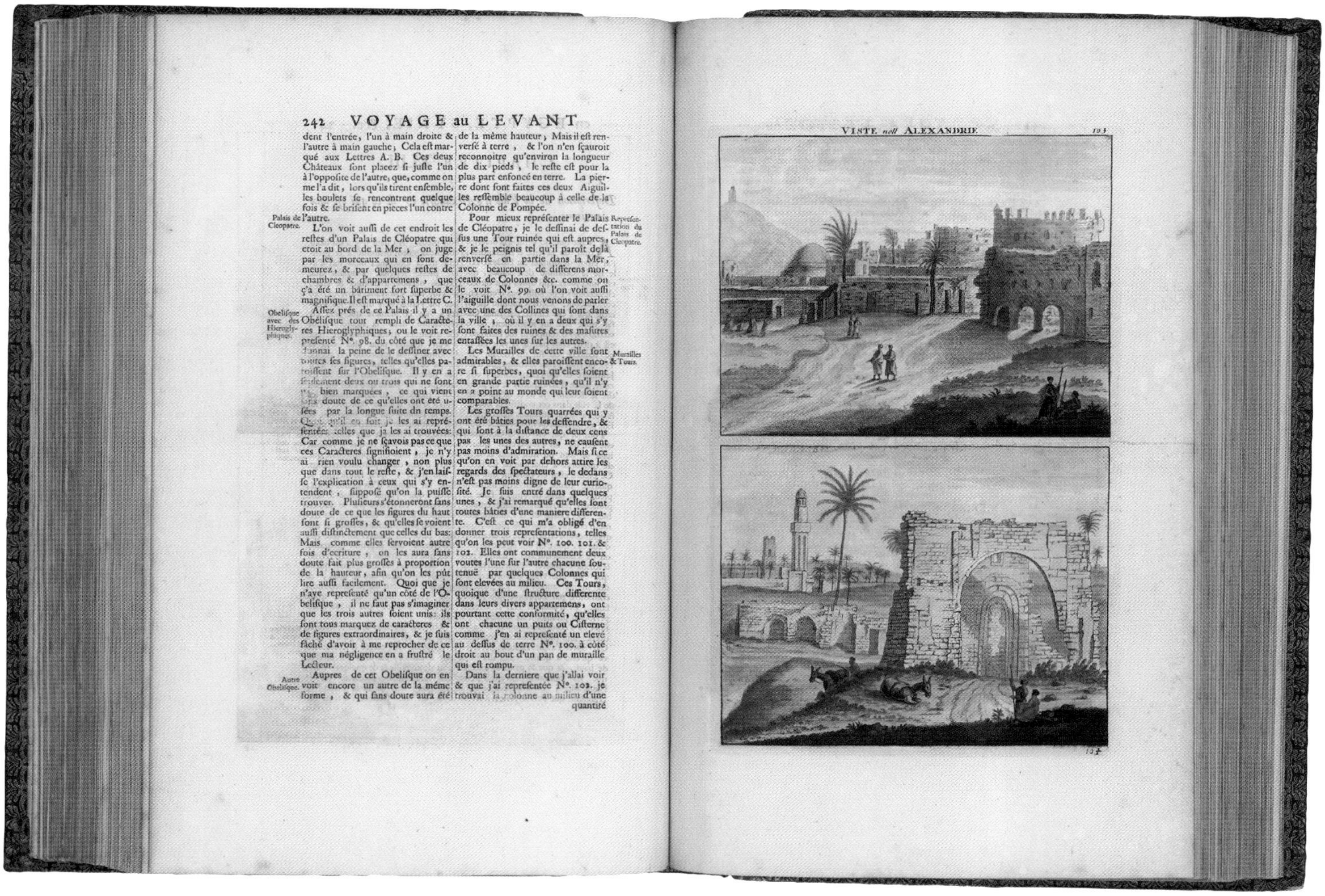
242 VOYAGE au LEVANT
VISTE nell ALEXANDRIE

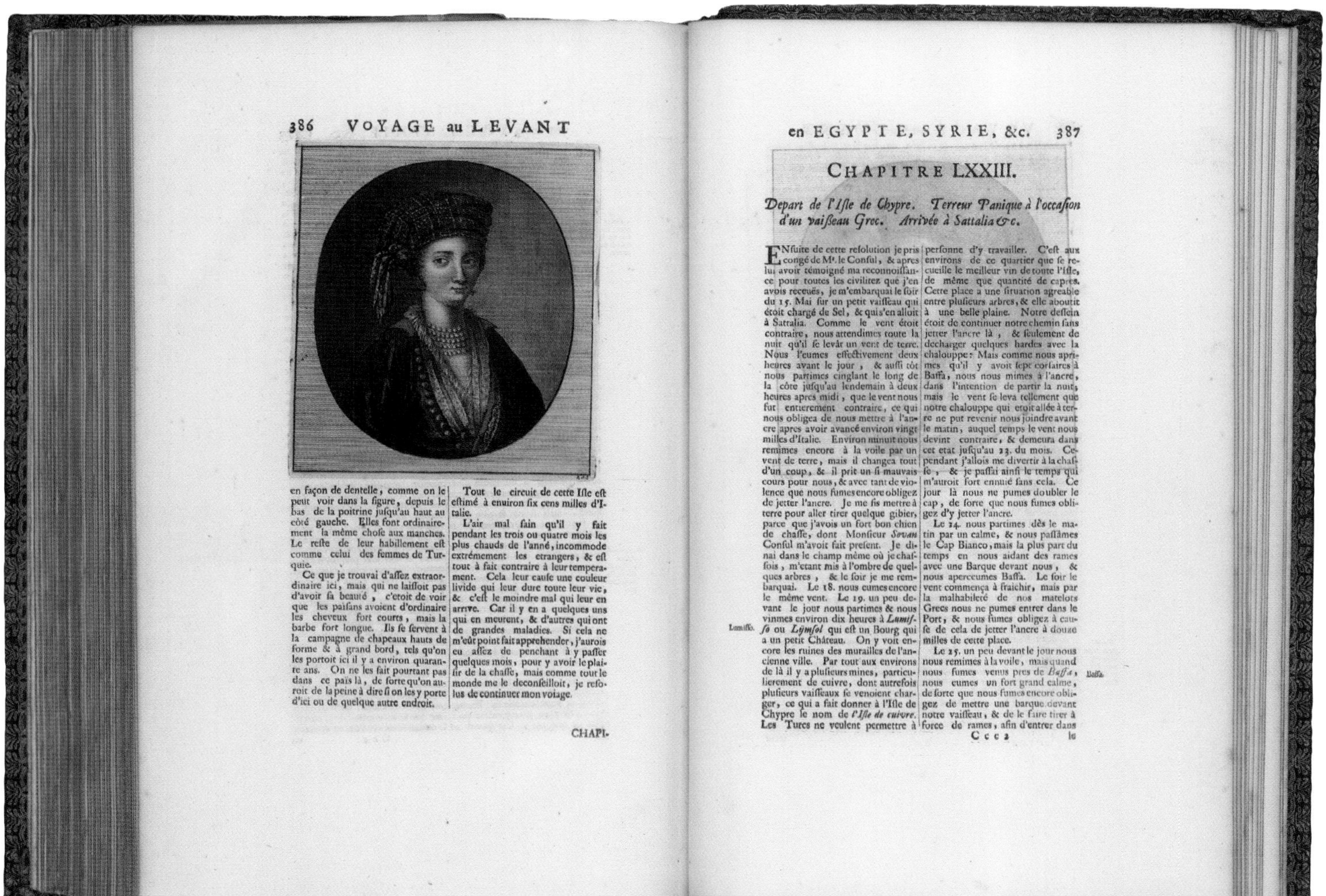
386 VOYAGE au LEVANT
en EGYPTE, SYRIE, &c. 387
CHAPITRE LXXIII.
Depart de l'Isle de Chypre. Terreur Panique à l'occasion d'un vaisseau Grec. Arrivée à Sattalia &c.
CHAPI-

Cornelis de Bruijn

1705 **Charles Plumier & Imprimerie Royale** Charles Plumier, *Traité des fougères de l'Amérique*. Paris: Imprimerie Royale, 1705. xxxvi, 146 pp. 44 cm. Illustrator: Charles Plumier.

French draughtsman and botanist Charles Plumier (1646–1704) was sent to the Caribbean in 1689 on the orders of King Louis XIV to describe the flora. The outcome of his trip was successful and Plumier was appointed royal botanist. This book on American plants, with descriptions of fifty ferns, was published after his second trip to the Antilles. His third trip took him to the Caribbean again and to Brazil. He named some of the species that he discovered after famous botanists. In his systematic naming system, Linnaeus would later adopt these species names, one of which was *Plumiera*, named after Plumier by a friend.

Plumier put the finishing touches to his *Traité des fougères de l'Amérique* ('Treatise on the Ferns of America') just before he died at the beginning of his fourth trip. With its 172 stylized engravings of American ferns, often covering the entire page and depicting the plant in detail, this edition was the first large monograph on this plant variety.

The printing was done by the Imprimerie Royale, which had been founded in 1640 on the initiative of Cardinal Richelieu. During the eighteenth century, this enterprise, managed by the Anisson family, grew into the largest European press, with seventeen presses by around 1725 and over fifty presses after the French Revolution. During the eighteenth century, the Imprimerie Royale set a standard for quality and workmanship in French typography. AP

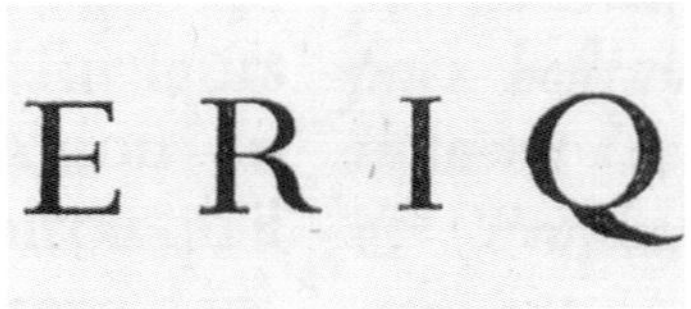

This Romain du Roi was cut by Philippe Grandjean (1666–1714); its first size appeared in a 1699 specimen and a 1702 book. It was the first roman type to be planned by a committee, separating the design from the execution, almost in a modern sense. The other types are older, one dating from 1517.

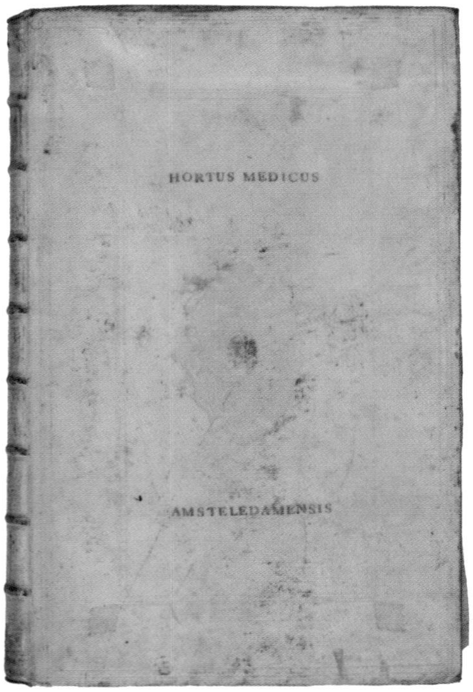

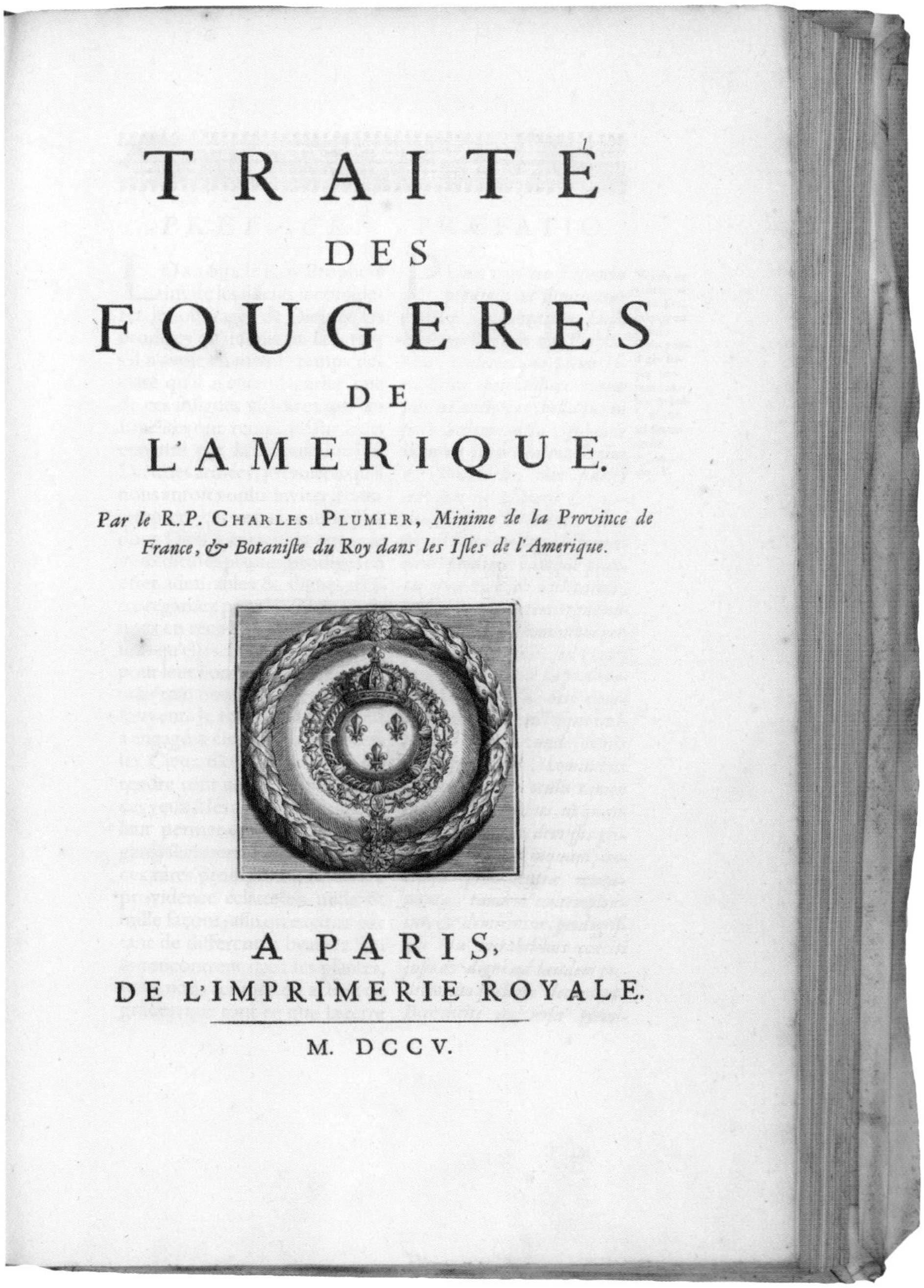
TRAITÉ
DES
FOUGERES
DE
L'AMERIQUE.
Par le R.P. CHARLES PLUMIER, *Minime de la Province de France, & Botaniste du Roy dans les Isles de l'Amerique.*
A PARIS,
DE L'IMPRIMERIE ROYALE.
M. DCCV.

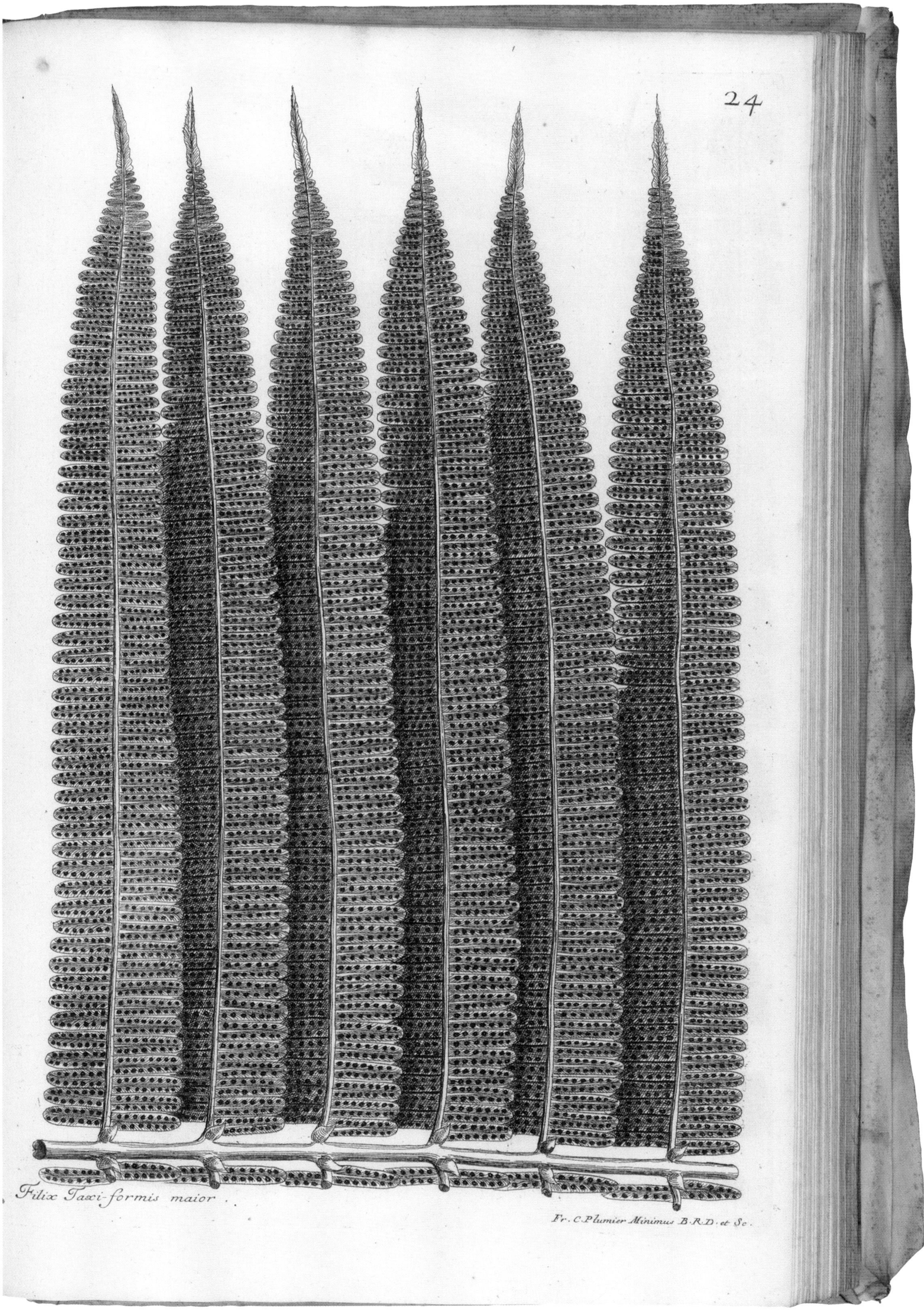
24
Filix Taxi-formis maior.
Fr. C. Plumier Minimus B.R.D. et Sc.

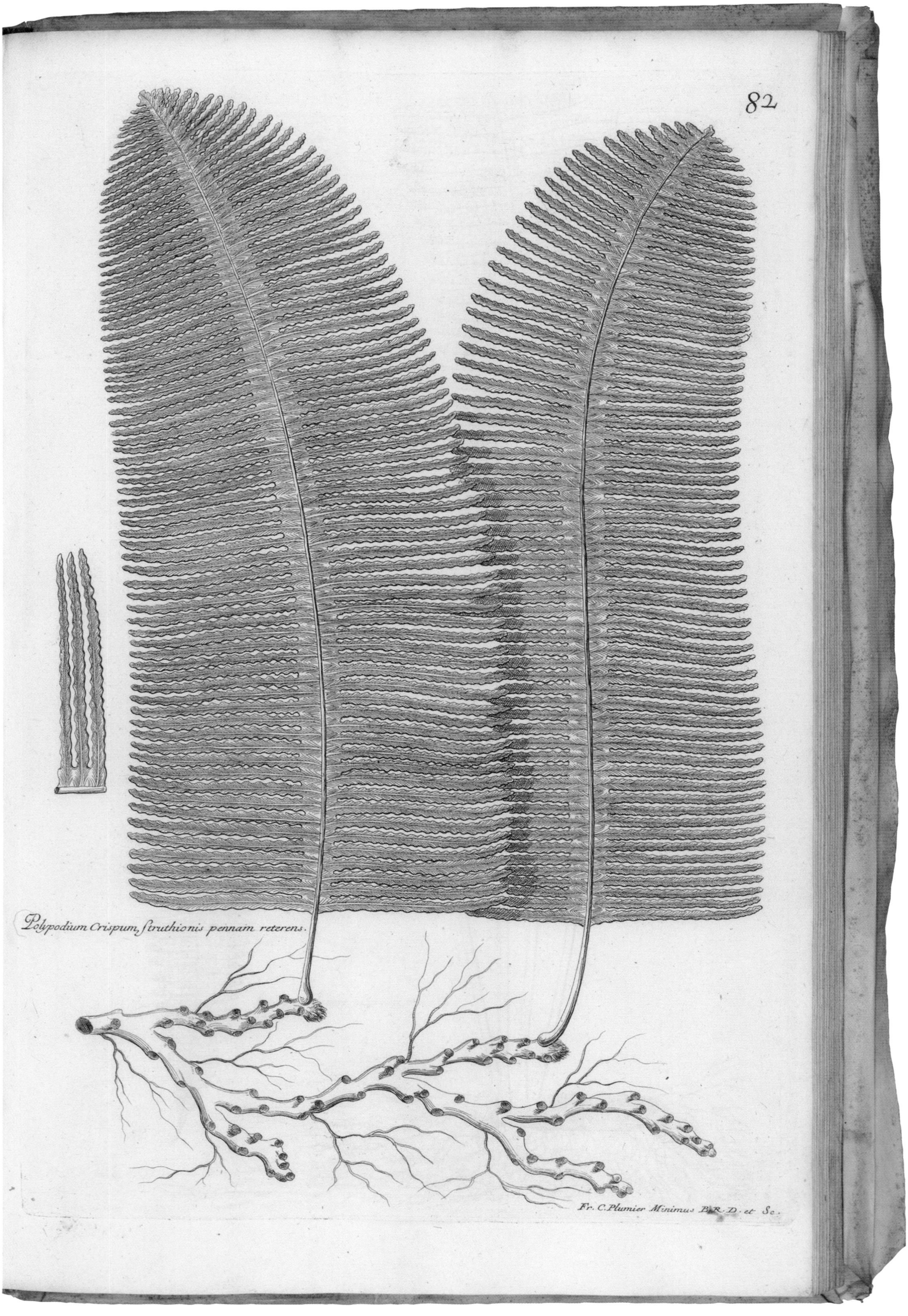
82
Polypodium Crispum, ſtruthionis pennam reterens.
Fr. C. Plumier Minimus P.R. D. et Sc.

112

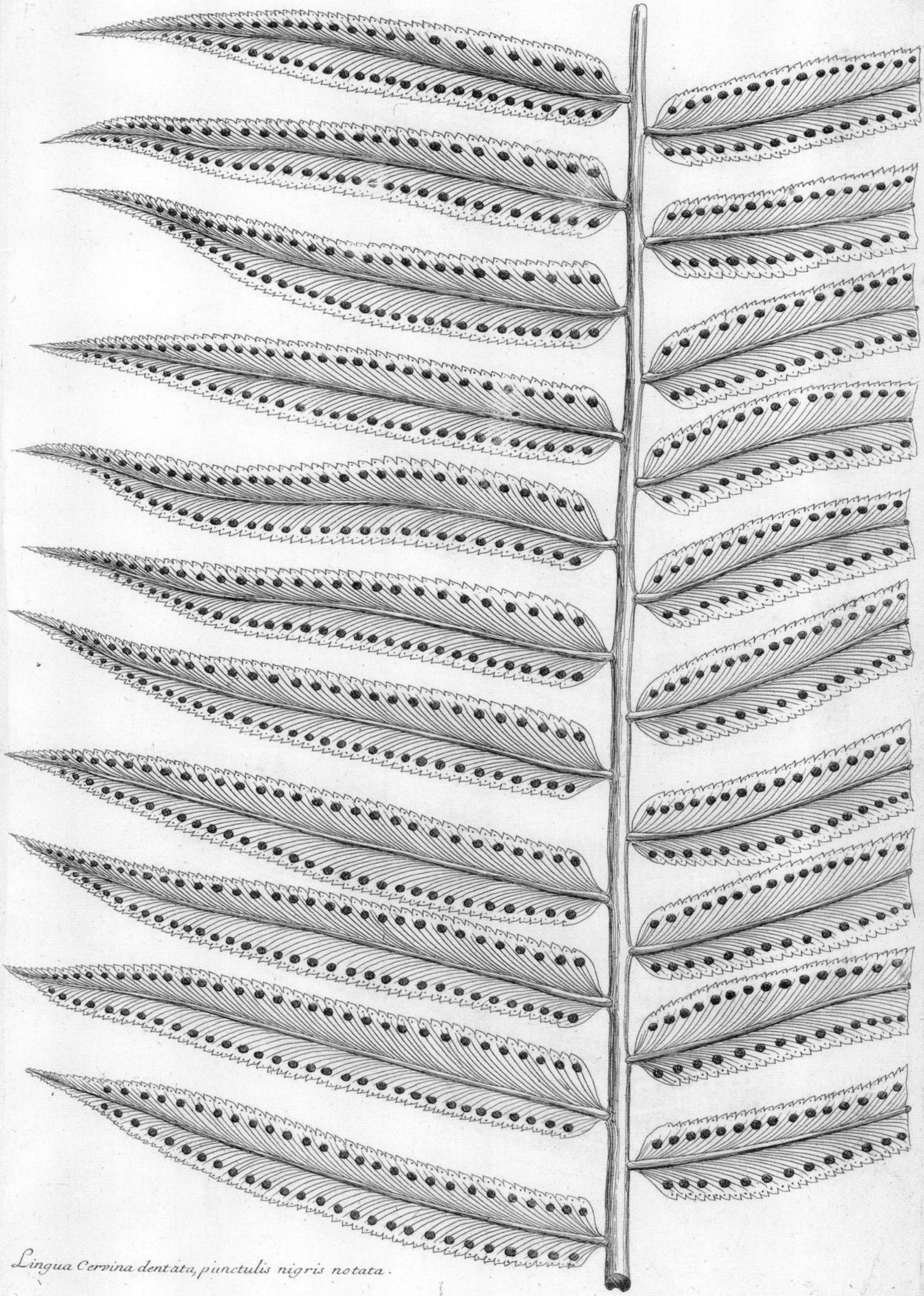

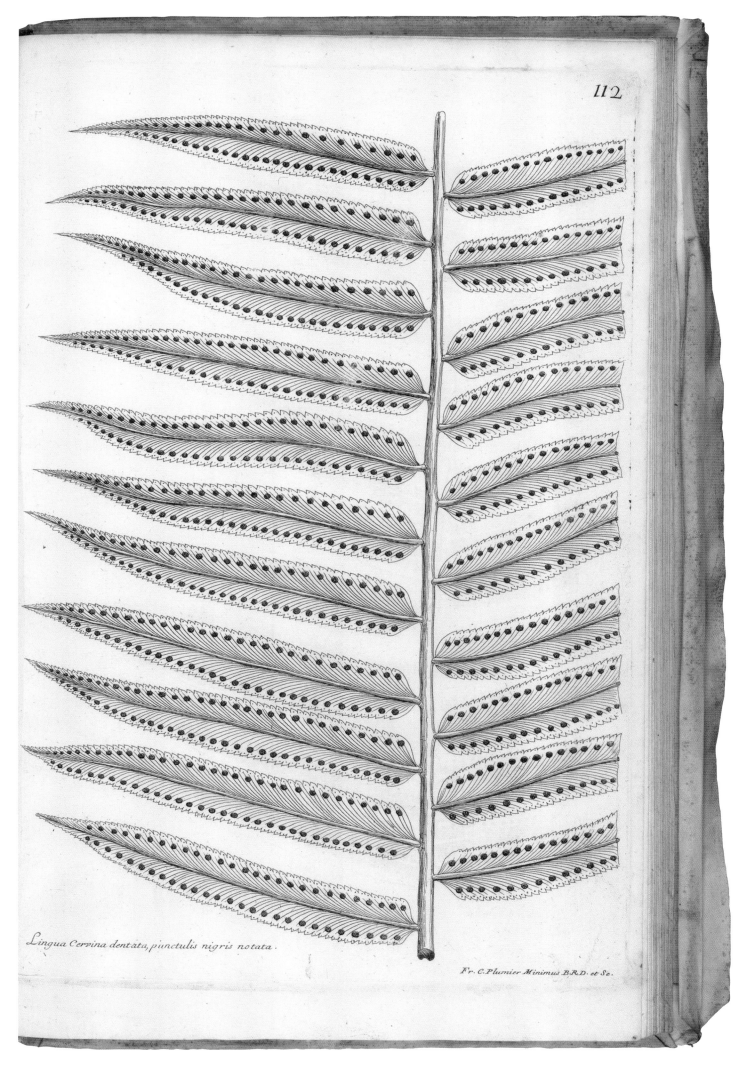

Lingua Cervina dentata, punctulis nigris notata.

Fr. C. Plumier Minimus B.R.D. et Sc.

1719 **Maria Sibylla Merian** Maria Sibylla Merian, *Over de voortteeling en wonderbaerlyke veranderingen der Surinaemsche insecten*. Amsterdam: Johannes Oosterwyk, 1719. 72 pp. 55 cm. Illustrator: Maria Sibylla Merian.

Maria Sibylla Merian (1647–1717) came from a prominent German family of artists and publishers. She grew up in Frankfurt am Main and practised painting and engraving from a young age. She embellished her paintings of flowers, which were often done on parchment, with beetles and butterflies – in this she followed her stepfather, the still-life and flower painter Jacob Marrel. From a young age, Merian was also interested in breeding silkworms; she would research caterpillars and butterflies passionately for the rest of her life.

When Merian joined the Labadist sect in 1686, she heard about the tropical environment in Surinam, where this religious community had a colony. In 1699, she travelled to Surinam with her youngest daughter, but for health reasons she had to return to Amsterdam, where she had a residence. Back in Amsterdam, she published the illustrated results of her research in 1705; the large illustrations were coloured by hand by Merian and her daughter. This edition, which is enlarged with extra illustrations, was published posthumously.

Merian often used counterprints for her hand-coloured illustrations. She would run a blank sheet through the press together with a freshly printed engraving that was still wet. This would give her a lighter mirror image, without plate marks. The colouring of the prints was a costly affair, however. The price for an uncoloured copy was 24 guilders, a coloured copy would cost 45 guilders and a lavishly coloured copy, for which rare pigments had been used, would cost no less than 75 guilders. AP

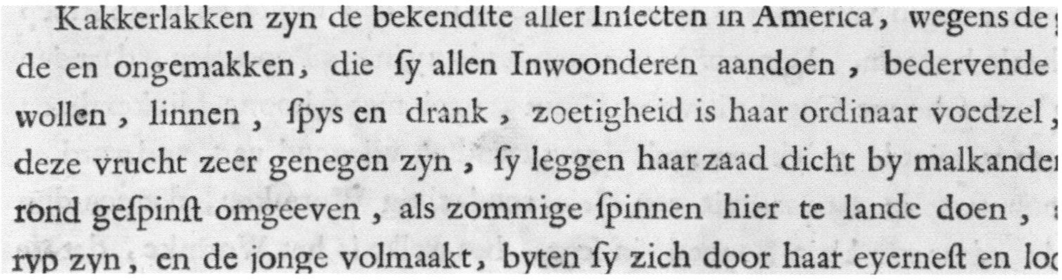

Kakkerlakken zyn de bekendste aller Insecten in America, wegens de
de en ongemakken, die sy allen Inwoonderen aandoen, bedervende
wollen, linnen, spys en drank, zoetigheid is haar ordinaar voedzel,
deze vrucht zeer genegen zyn, sy leggen haar zaad dicht by malkander
rond gespinst omgeeven, als zommige spinnen hier te lande doen,
ryp zyn, en de jonge volmaakt, byten sy zich door haar eyernest en lo

The type styles established by Claude Garamont and especially Robert Granjon (1512/13–90) in sixteenth-century France proved remarkably long-lived, even as newer styles joined them. This is Granjon's Gros Parangon (20 point) roman (1570), cast by the Voskens foundry in Amsterdam and still being produced by their successors in 1781.

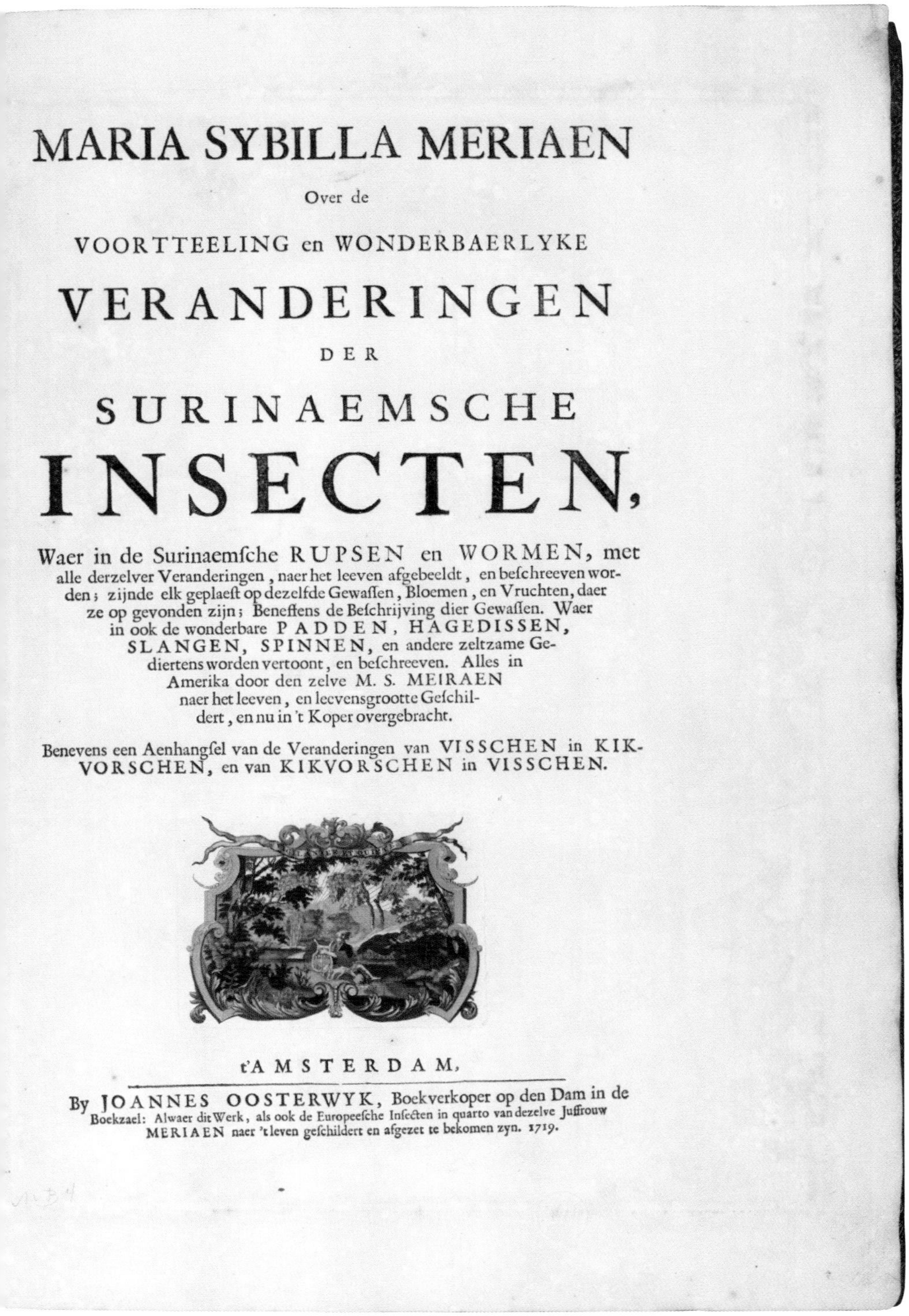

MARIA SYBILLA MERIAEN
Over de
VOORTTEELING en WONDERBAERLYKE
VERANDERINGEN
DER
SURINAEMSCHE
INSECTEN,
Waer in de Surinaemsche RUPSEN en WORMEN, met alle derzelver Veranderingen, naer het leeven afgebeeldt, en beschreeven worden; zijnde elk geplaest op dezelfde Gewassen, Bloemen, en Vruchten, daer ze op gevonden zijn; Beneffens de Beschrijving dier Gewassen. Waer in ook de wonderbare PADDEN, HAGEDISSEN, SLANGEN, SPINNEN, en andere zeltzame Gediertens worden vertoont, en beschreeven. Alles in Amerika door den zelve M. S. MEIRAEN naer het leeven, en leevensgrootte Geschildert, en nu in 't Koper overgebracht.
Benevens een Aenhangsel van de Veranderingen van VISSCHEN in KIKVORSCHEN, en van KIKVORSCHEN in VISSCHEN.
t'AMSTERDAM,
By JOANNES OOSTERWYK, Boekverkoper op den Dam in de Boekzael: Alwaer dit Werk, als ook de Europeesche Insecten in quarto van dezelve Juffrouw MERIAEN naer 't leven geschildert en afgezet te bekomen zyn. 1719.

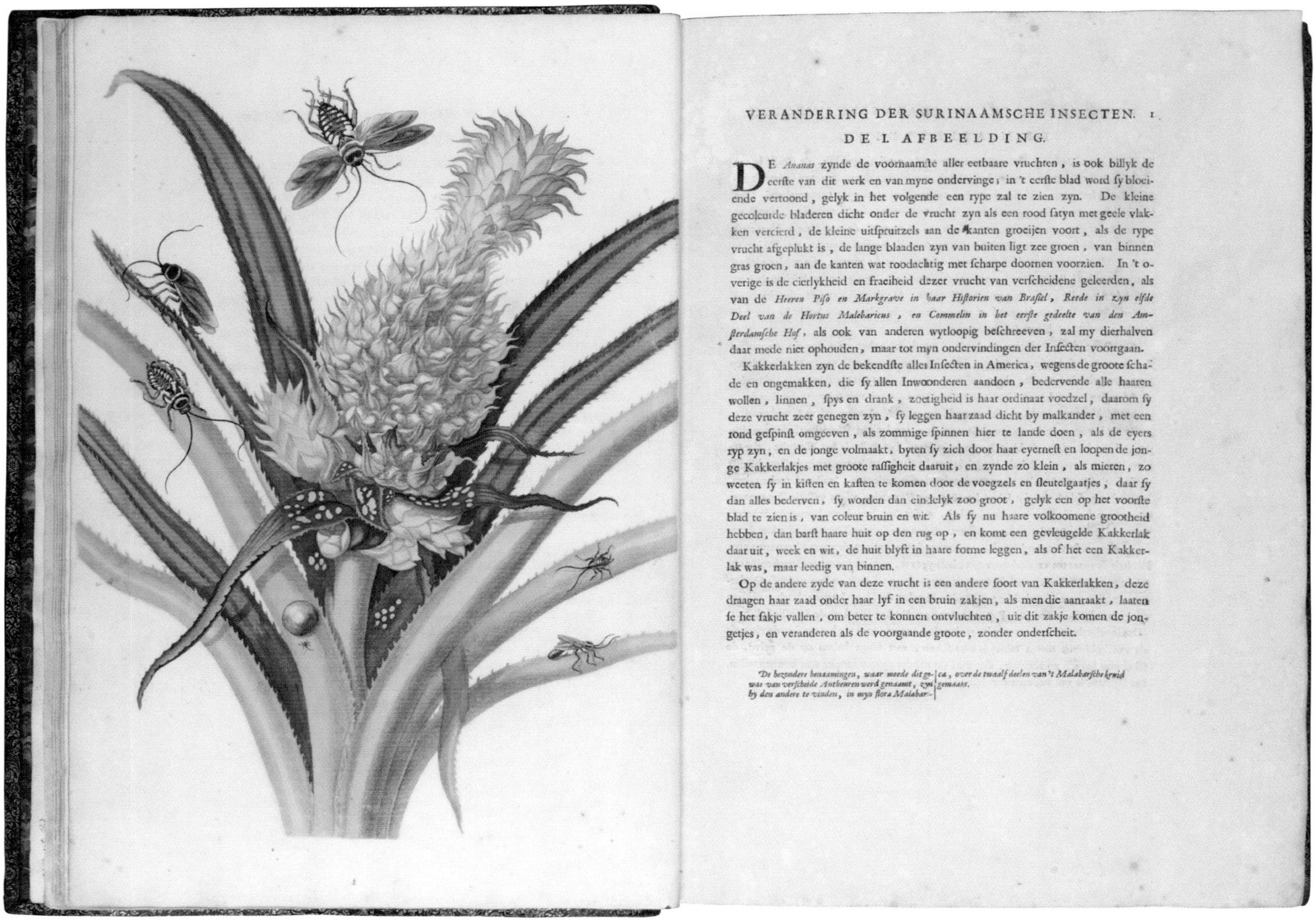

VERANDERING DER SURINAAMSCHE INSECTEN. 1

DE I. AFBEELDING.

DE *Ananas* zynde de voornaamſte aller eetbaare vruchten, is ook billyk de eerſte van dit werk en van myne ondervinge; in 't eerſte blad word ſy bloeiende vertoond, gelyk in het volgende een rype zal te zien zyn. De kleine gecoleurde bladeren dicht onder de vrucht zyn als een rood ſatyn met geele vlakken vercierd, de kleine uitſpruitzels aan de *kanten groeijen voort, als de rype vrucht afgeplukt is, de lange blaaden zyn van buiten ligt zee groen, van binnen gras groen, aan de kanten wat roodachtig met ſcharpe doornen voorzien. In 't overige is de cierlykheid en fraiheid dezer vrucht van verſcheidene geleerden, als van de *Heeren Piſo en Markgrave in haar Hiſtorien van Braſiel, Reede in zyn elfde Deel van de Hortus Malebaricus, en Commelin in het eerſte gedeelte van den Amſterdamſche Hof*, als ook van anderen wytloopig beſchreeven, zal my dierhalven daar mede niet ophouden, maar tot myn ondervindingen der Inſecten voortgaan.

Kakkerlakken zyn de bekendſte aller Inſecten in America, wegens de groote ſchade en ongemakken, die ſy allen Inwoonderen aandoen, bedervende alle haaren wollen, linnen, ſpys en drank, zoetigheid is haar ordinaar voedzel, daarom ſy deze vrucht zeer genegen zyn, ſy leggen haar zaad dicht by malkander, met een rond geſpinſt omgeeven, als zommige ſpinnen hier te lande doen, als de eyers ryp zyn, en de jonge volmaakt, byten ſy zich door haar eyerneſt en loopen de jonge Kakkerlakjes met groote raſſigheit daaruit, en zynde zo klein, als mieren, zo weeten ſy in kiſten en kaſten te komen door de voegzels en ſleutelgaatjes, daar ſy dan alles bederven, ſy worden dan eindelyk zoo groot, gelyk een op het voorſte blad te zien is, van coleur bruin en wit. Als ſy nu haare volkoomene grootheid hebben, dan barſt haare huit op den rug op, en komt een gevleugelde Kakkerlak daar uit, week en wit, de huit blyft in haare forme leggen, als of het een Kakkerlak was, maar leedig van binnen.

Op de andere zyde van deze vrucht is een andere ſoort van Kakkerlakken, deze draagen haar zaad onder haar lyf in een bruin zakjen, als men die aanraakt, laaten ſe het ſakje vallen, om beter te konnen ontvluchten, uit dit zakje komen de jongetjes, en veranderen als de voorgaande groote, zonder onderſcheit.

De bezondere benaamingen, waar meede dit gewas van verſcheide Autheuren werd genaamt, zyn by den andere te vinden, in myn flora Malabarica, over de twaalf deelen van 't Malabarſche kruid gemaakt.

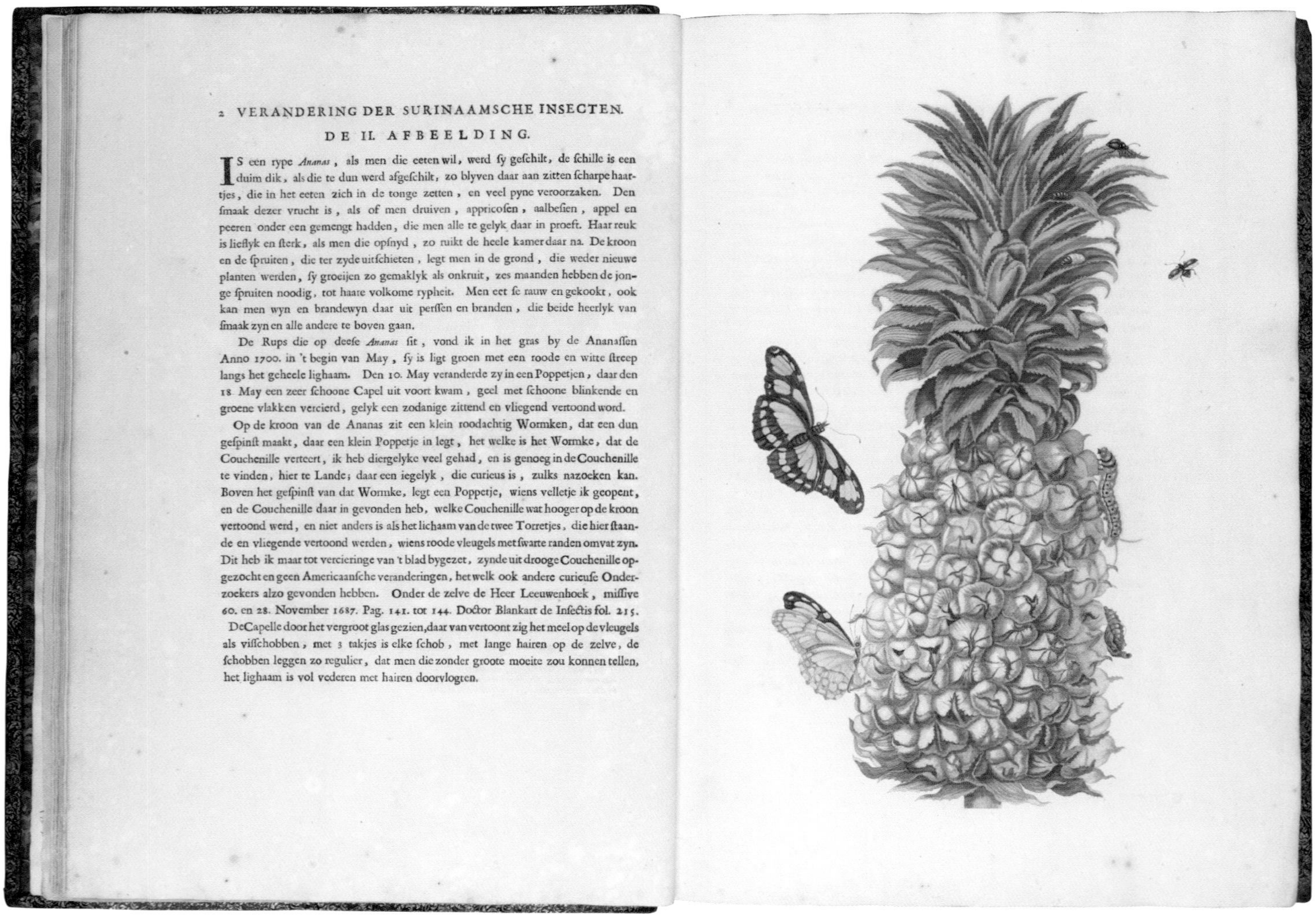

2 VERANDERING DER SURINAAMSCHE INSECTEN.

DE II. AFBEELDING.

IS een rype *Ananas*, als men die eeten wil, werd ſy geſchilt, de ſchille is een duim dik, als die te dun werd afgeſchilt, zo blyven daar aan zitten ſcharpe haartjes, die in het eeten zich in de tonge zetten, en veel pyne veroorzaken. Den ſmaak dezer vrucht is, als of men druiven, appricoſen, aalbeſien, appel en peeren onder een gemengt hadden, die men alle te gelyk daar in proeft. Haar reuk is lieflyk en ſterk, als men die opſnyd, zo ruikt de heele kamer daar na. De kroon en de ſpruiten, die ter zyde uitſchieten, legt men in de grond, die weder nieuwe planten werden, ſy groeijen zo gemaklyk als onkruit, zes maanden hebben de jonge ſpruiten noodig, tot haare volkome rypheit. Men eet ſe rauw en gekookt, ook kan men wyn en brandewyn daar uit perſſen en branden, die beide heerlyk van ſmaak zyn en alle andere te boven gaan.

De Rups die op deeſe *Ananas* ſit, vond ik in het gras by de Ananaſſen Anno 1700. in 't begin van May, ſy is ligt groen met een roode en witte ſtreep langs het geheele lighaam. Den 10. May veranderde zy in een Poppetjen, daar den 18. May een zeer ſchoone Capel uit voort kwam, geel met ſchoone blinkende en groene vlakken vercierd, gelyk een zodanige zittend en vliegend vertoond word.

Op de kroon van de Ananas zit een klein roodachtig Wormken, dat een dun geſpinſt maakt, daar een klein Poppetje in legt, het welke is het Wormke, dat de Couchenille verteert, ik heb diergelyke veel gehad, en is genoeg in de Couchenille te vinden, hier te Lande; daar een iegelyk, die curieus is, zulks nazoeken kan. Boven het geſpinſt van dat Wormke, legt een Poppetje, wiens velletje ik geopent, en de Couchenille daar in gevonden heb, welke Couchenille wat hooger op de kroon vertoond werd, en niet anders is als het lichaam van de twee Torretjes, die hier ſtaande en vliegende vertoond werden, wiens roode vleugels met ſwarte randen omvat zyn. Dit heb ik maar tot vercieringe van 't blad bygezet, zynde uit drooge Couchenille opgezocht en geen Americaanſche veranderingen, het welk ook andere curieuſe Onderzoekers alzo gevonden hebben. Onder de zelve de Heer Leeuwenhoek, miſſive 60. en 28. November 1687. Pag. 141. tot 144. Doctor Blankart de Inſectis fol. 215.

De Capelle door het vergroot glas gezien, daar van vertoont zig het meel op de vleugels als viſſchobben, met 3 takjes is elke ſchob, met lange hairen op de zelve, de ſchobben leggen zo regulier, dat men die zonder groote moeite zou konnen tellen, het lighaam is vol vederen met hairen doorvlogten.

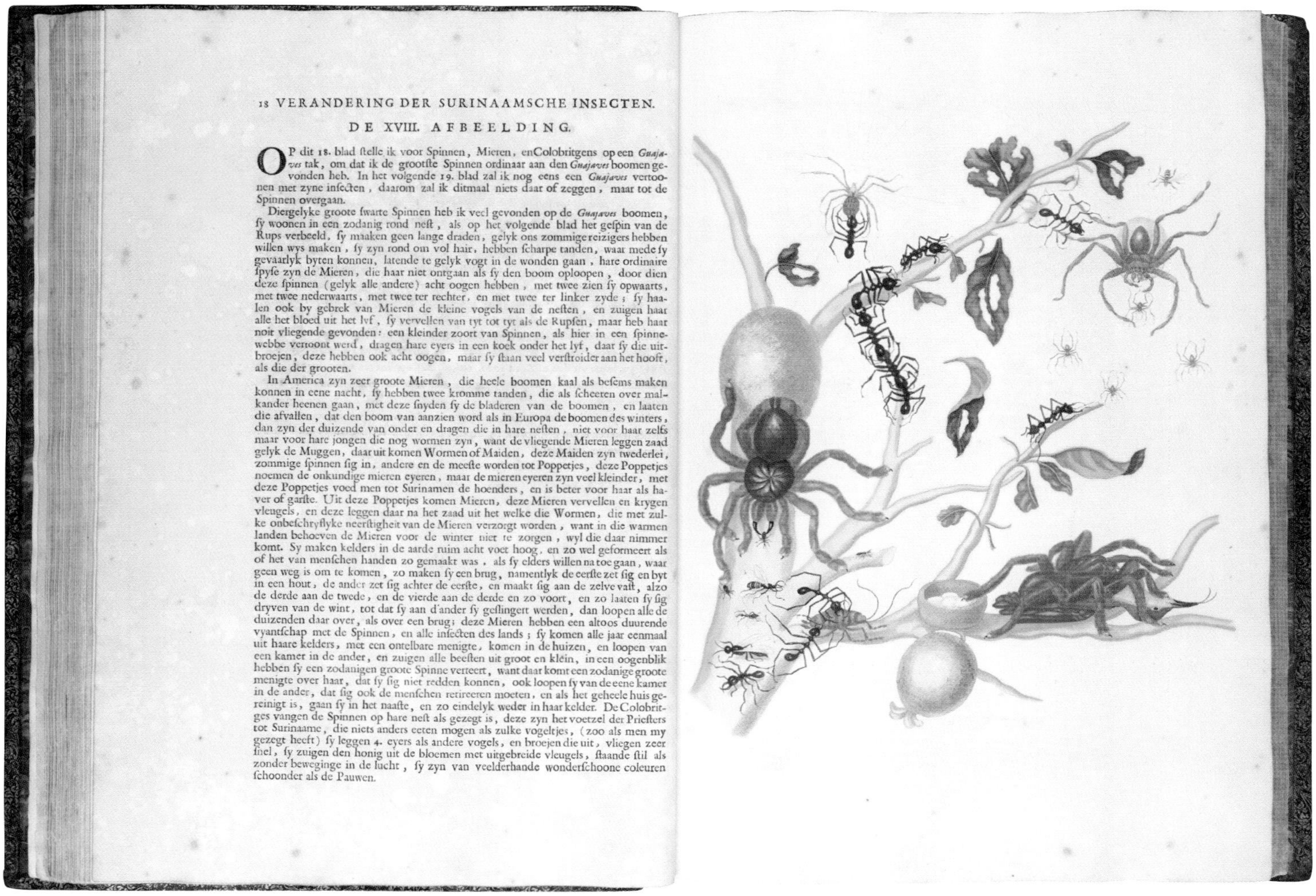

18 VERANDERING DER SURINAAMSCHE INSECTEN.

DE XVIII. AFBEELDING.

OP dit 18. blad ſtelle ik voor Spinnen, Mieren, enColobritgens op een *Guajaves* tak, om dat ik de grootſte Spinnen ordinaar aan den *Guajaves* boomen gevonden heb. In het volgende 19. blad zal ik nog eens een *Guajaves* vertoonen met zyne inſecten, daarom zal ik ditmaal niets daar of zeggen, maar tot de Spinnen overgaan.

Diergelyke groote ſwarte Spinnen heb ik veel gevonden op de *Guajaves* boomen, ſy woonen in een zodanig rond neſt, als op het volgende blad het geſpin van de Rups verbeeld, ſy maaken geen lange draden, gelyk ons zommige reizigers hebben willen wys maken, ſy zyn rond om vol hair, hebben ſcharpe tanden, waar mede ſy gevaarlyk byten konnen, latende te gelyk vogt in de wonden gaan, hare ordinaire ſpyſe zyn de Mieren, die haar niet ontgaan als ſy den boom oploopen, door dien deze ſpinnen (gelyk alle andere) acht oogen hebben, met twee zien ſy opwaarts, met twee nederwaarts, met twee ter rechter, en met twee ter linker zyde; ſy haalen ook by gebrek van Mieren de kleine vogels van de neſten, en zuigen haar alle het bloed uit het lyf, ſy vervellen van tyt tot tyt als de Rupſen, maar heb haar noit vliegende gevonden: een kleinder zoort van Spinnen, als hier in een ſpinnewebbe vertoont werd, dragen hare eyers in een koek onder het lyf, daar ſy die uitbroejen, deze hebben ook acht oogen, maar ſy ſtaan veel verſtroider aan het hooft, als die der grooten.

In America zyn zeer groote Mieren, die heele boomen kaal als beſems maken konnen in eene nacht, ſy hebben twee kromme tanden, die als ſcheeren over malkander heenen gaan, met deze ſnyden ſy de bladeren van de boomen, en laaten die afvallen, dat den boom van aanzien word als in Europa de boomen des winters, dan zyn der duizende van onder en dragen die in hare neſten, niet voor haar zelfs maar voor hare jongen die nog wormen zyn, want de vliegende Mieren leggen zaad gelyk de Muggen, daar uit komen Wormen of Maiden, deze Maiden zyn twederlei, zommige ſpinnen ſig in, andere en de meeſte worden tot Poppetjes, deze Poppetjes noemen de onkundige mieren eyeren, maar de mieren eyeren zyn veel kleinder, met deze Poppetjes voed men tot Surinamen de hoenders, en is beter voor haar als haver of garſte. Uit deze Poppetjes komen Mieren, deze Mieren vervellen en krygen vleugels, en deze leggen daar na het zaad uit het welke die Wormen, die met zulke onbeſchryflyke neerſtigheit van de Mieren verzorgt worden, want in die warmen landen behoeven de Mieren voor de winter niet te zorgen, wyl die daar nimmer komt. Sy maken kelders in de aarde ruim acht voet hoog, en zo wel geformeert als of het van menſchen handen zo gemaakt was, als ſy elders willen na toe gaan, waar geen weg is om te komen, zo maken ſy een brug, namentlyk de eerſte zet ſig en byt in een hout, de ander zet ſig achter de eerſte, en maakt ſig aan de zelve vaſt, alzo de derde aan de twede, en de vierde aan de derde en zo voort, en zo laaten ſy ſig dryven van de wint, tot dat ſy aan d'ander ſy geſlingert werden, dan loopen alle de duizenden daar over, als over een brug; deze Mieren hebben een altoos duurende vyantſchap met de Spinnen, en alle inſecten des lands; ſy komen alle jaar eenmaal uit haare kelders, met een ontelbare menigte, komen in de huizen, en loopen van een kamer in de ander, en zuigen alle beeſten uit groot en klein, in een oogenblik hebben ſy een zodanigen groote Spinne verteert, want daar komt een zodanige groote menigte over haar, dat ſy ſig niet redden konnen, ook loopen ſy van de eene kamer in de ander, dat ſig ook de menſchen retireeren moeten, en als het geheele huis gereinigt is, gaan ſy in het naaſte, en zo eindelyk weder in haar kelder. De Colobritges vangen de Spinnen op hare neſt als gezegt is, deze zyn het voetzel der Prieſters tot Surinaame, die niets anders eeten mogen als zulke vogeltjes, (zoo als men my gezegt heeft) ſy leggen 4. eyers als andere vogels, en broejen die uit, vliegen zeer ſnel, ſy zuigen den honig uit de bloemen met uitgebreide vleugels, ſtaande ſtil als zonder beweginge in de lucht, ſy zyn van veelderhande wonderſchoone coleuren ſchoonder als de Pauwen.

60 VERANDERING DER SURINAAMSCHE INSECTEN.

DE LX. AFBEELDING.

IN January 1701. begaf ik my in het boſch tot Surinaame om te zien of iets ontdekken konde, ik vond deze Bloem aan een Boom, die cierlyk rood was, van naam en eigenſchap aan de Inwoonders des zelven Lands onbekend.

Hier vond ik een ſchoone groote roode Rups, die op elken lid drie blaauwe corallen, en op ieder coral een ſwarten pluim had, ik dachte hem met de bladen van dezen Boom te ſpyſen, maar hy heeft ſig ten eerſten ingeſponnen, en is tot zulk een raare Poppetjen geworden, zo dat ik niet zeeker weet of ik ſijne rechte ſpyſe heb gevonden of niet; Den 14. January quam een zulke ſchoone Cappelle daar uit, ſijn achterſte vleugels zyn van binnen ſchoon blaauw, de voorſte bruin met een witten ſtreep daar door heen, met wat blaauw, gelyk hier vliegend vertoond word, de buitenſte vleugels hebben drie ronde boogen met ſwart, geel en bruin, en zeer ſchoon gevlamt, gelyk hier zittend vertoond word, in Holland word hy de *Groote Atlas* genaamt.

Wilde Weſpe of *Maribonſe* van de Inwoonders genaamt werden op Surinaame overal gevonden, zelfs in de huizen en in het veld, zyn bruinachtig van coleur, ſe ſteeken de menſchen en beeſten die haar naderen, en haar in haar doen verſtooren, ſy maaken huiskens als in Europa van allerlei aardige fabryk, waardig om te beſchouwen, men ziet daar in merkteekenen van voorſigtigheid, hoe ſy tegens regen en wind gebouwt zyn, om haar zaad in zekerheid te leggen, uit dit zaad komt eerſt een witten Worm, gelyk een onder de Rups legt, deze veranderd allenskens in zulke ſoort van wilde Beijen, die een plage des zelven Lands zyn.

1723 **Martin-Dominique Fertel** Martin-Dominique Fertel, *La science pratique de l'imprimerie*. Saint-Omer: Martin-Dominique Fertel, 1723. 292 pp. 24.5 cm.

The manual *La science pratique de l'imprimerie* ('Practical Knowledge of Printing') was written, published, and printed by Martin-Dominique Fertel (1684–1752). Fertel was a local printer in the north of France; he had travelled through Italy and Flanders. It is the second printer's manual to appear in print and the first in French. Fertel was unaware of the book by his predecessor Joseph Moxon (1683–84; see page 168). Unlike Moxon, Fertel gives many instructions for novice craftsmen, especially compositors. It is one of the very few printers' manuals to provide instructions on typographic design, and even gives numerous examples of designs for title pages, poetry, two-column pages and marginalia.

In the typography of his own book, Fertel fully conforms to the layout traditions of the time. The title page is overfull and printed in red and black; the main text is divided into small units.

In 1793, Antoine-François Momoro borrowed parts of this text for his printer's manual, and Dutch translations of these parts are found in their turn in the Dutch manual by David Wardenaar. An English adaptation by Samuel Palmer survives only as a manuscript. FAJ

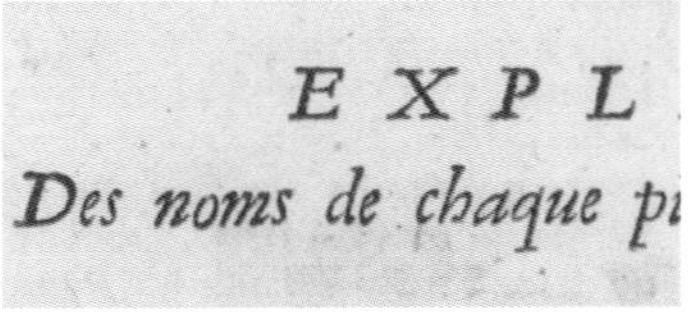

Fertel used various sixteenth- and seventeenth-century types. Jean Jannon (1580–1658) cut this Gros Romain (17 point) italic, shown in his 1621 specimen of types and cut after 1615. Types that he sold to the Imprimerie Royale in Paris were wrongly attributed to Claude Garamont and later served as models for 'Garamond' revivals.

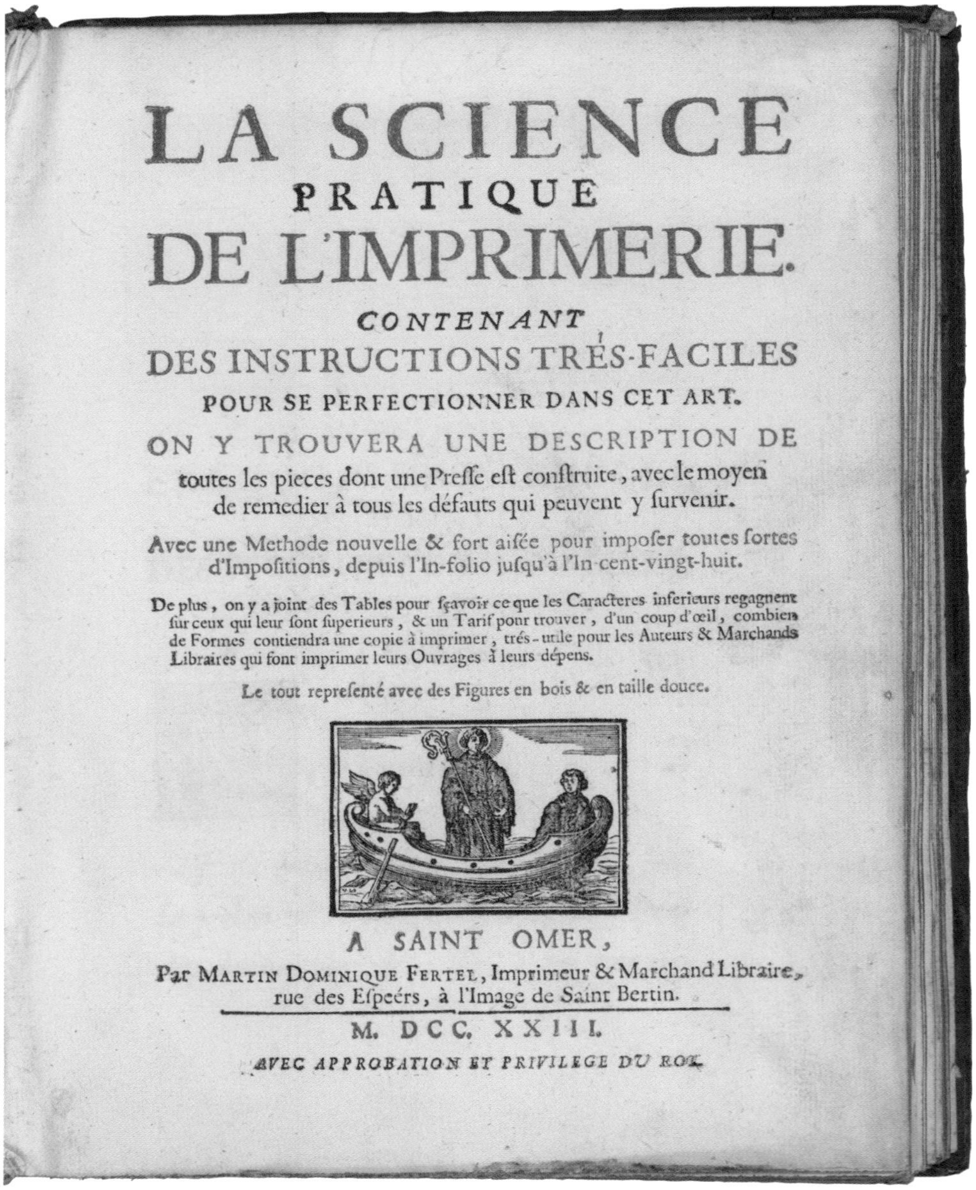

LA SCIENCE
PRATIQUE
DE L'IMPRIMERIE.
CONTENANT
DES INSTRUCTIONS TRÉS-FACILES
POUR SE PERFECTIONNER DANS CET ART.
ON Y TROUVERA UNE DESCRIPTION DE
toutes les pieces dont une Presse est construite, avec le moyen
de remedier à tous les défauts qui peuvent y survenir.
Avec une Methode nouvelle & fort aisée pour imposer toutes sortes
d'Impositions, depuis l'In-folio jusqu'à l'In-cent-vingt-huit.
De plus, on y a joint des Tables pour sçavoir ce que les Caractéres inferieurs regagnent
sur ceux qui leur sont superieurs, & un Tarif pour trouver, d'un coup d'œil, combien
de Formes contiendra une copie à imprimer, trés-utile pour les Auteurs & Marchands
Libraires qui font imprimer leurs Ouvrages à leurs dépens.
Le tout representé avec des Figures en bois & en taille douce.

A SAINT OMER,
Par MARTIN DOMINIQUE FERTEL, Imprimeur & Marchand Libraire,
rue des Espeérs, à l'Image de Saint Bertin.
M. DCC. XXIII.
AVEC APPROBATION ET PRIVILEGE DU ROY.

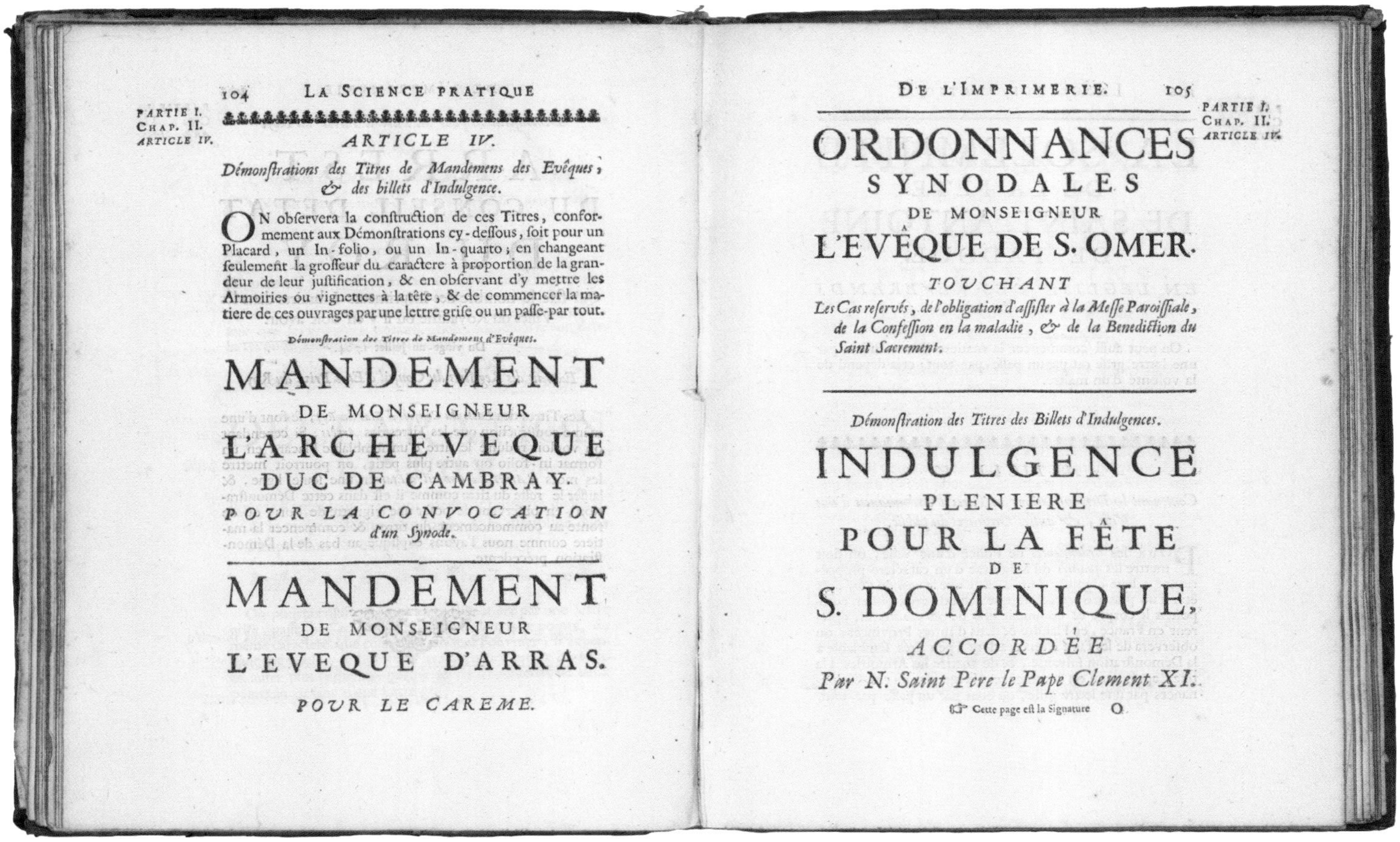

104 LA SCIENCE PRATIQUE

PARTIE I.
CHAP. II.
ARTICLE IV.

ARTICLE IV.

Démonstrations des Titres de Mandemens des Evêques, & des billets d'Indulgence.

ON observera la construction de ces Titres, conformement aux Démonstrations cy-dessous, soit pour un Placard, un In-folio, ou un In-quarto; en changeant seulement la grosseur du caractere à proportion de la grandeur de leur justification, & en observant d'y mettre les Armoiries ou vignettes à la tête, & de commencer la matiere de ces ouvrages par une lettre grise ou un passe-par tout.

Démonstration des Titres de Mandemens d'Evêques.

MANDEMENT
DE MONSEIGNEUR
L'ARCHEVEQUE
DUC DE CAMBRAY.
POUR LA CONVOCATION d'un Synode.

MANDEMENT
DE MONSEIGNEUR
L'EVEQUE D'ARRAS.
POUR LE CAREME.

DE L'IMPRIMERIE. 105

PARTIE I.
CHAP. II.
ARTICLE IV.

ORDONNANCES
SYNODALES
DE MONSEIGNEUR
L'EVÊQUE DE S. OMER.
TOUCHANT
Les Cas reservés, de l'obligation d'assister à la Messe Paroissiale, de la Confession en la maladie, & de la Benediction du Saint Sacrement.

Démonstration des Titres des Billets d'Indulgences.

INDULGENCE
PLENIERE
POUR LA FÊTE
DE
S. DOMINIQUE,
ACCORDÉE
Par N. Saint Pere le Pape Clement XI.

☞ Cette page est la Signature O.

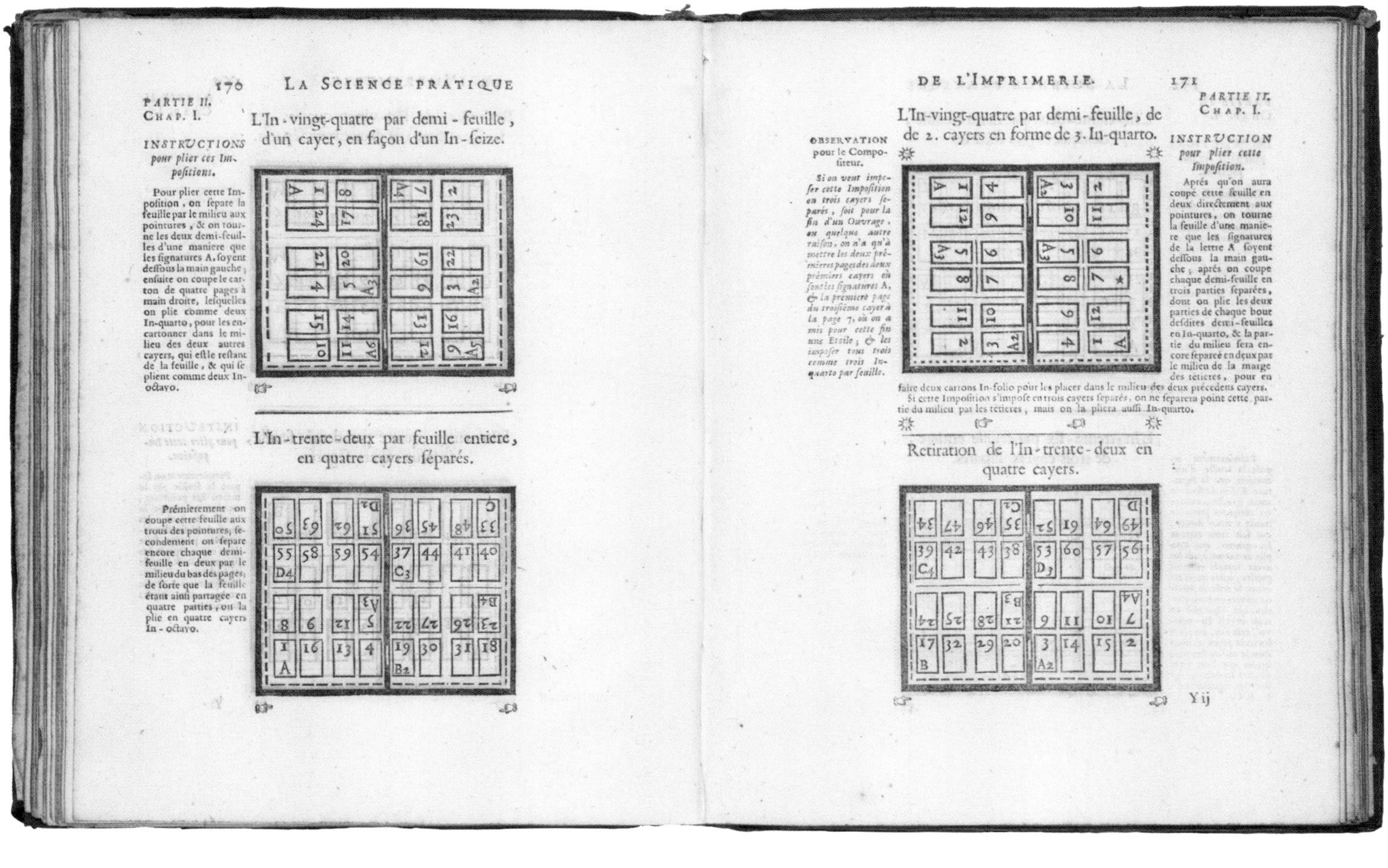

170 LA SCIENCE PRATIQUE

PARTIE II.
CHAP. I.

L'In-vingt-quatre par demi-feuille, d'un cayer, en façon d'un In-seize.

INSTRUCTIONS pour plier ces Impositions.

Pour plier cette Imposition, on separe la feuille par le milieu aux pointures, & on tourne les deux demi-feuilles d'une maniere que les signatures A, soyent dessous la main gauche; ensuite on coupe le carton de quatre pages à main droite, lesquelles on plie comme deux In-quarto, pour les encartonner dans le milieu des deux autres cayers, qui est le restant de la feuille, & qui se plient comme deux In-octavo.

L'In-trente-deux par feuille entiere, en quatre cayers separés.

Prémierement on coupe cette feuille aux trous des pointures; secondement on separe encore chaque demi-feuille en deux par le milieu du bas des pages; de sorte que la feuille étant ainsi partagée en quatre parties, on la plie en quatre cayers In-octavo.

DE L'IMPRIMERIE. 171

PARTIE II.
CHAP. I.

L'In-vingt-quatre par demi-feuille, de de 2. cayers en forme de 3. In-quarto.

OBSERVATION pour le Compositeur.

Si on veut imposer cette Imposition en trois cayers separés, soit pour la fin d'un Ouvrage, ou quelque autre raison, on n'a qu'à mettre les deux prémieres pages des deux prémiers cayers où sont les signatures A, & la premiere page du troisiéme cayer à la page 7, où on a mis pour cette fin une Etoile; & les imposer tous trois comme trois In-quarto par feuille.

INSTRUCTION pour plier cette Imposition.

Aprés qu'on aura coupé cette feuille en deux directement aux pointures, on tourne la feuille d'une maniere que les signatures de la lettre A soyent dessous la main gauche; aprés on coupe chaque demi-feuille en trois parties separées, dont on plie les deux parties de chaque bout desdites demi-feuilles en In-quarto, & la partie du milieu sera encore separeé en deux par le milieu de la marge des tetieres, pour en faire deux cartons In-folio pour les placer dans le milieu des deux précedens cayers.

Si cette Imposition s'impose en trois cayers separés, on ne separera point cette partie du milieu par les tetieres, mais on la plicra aussi In-quarto.

Retiration de l'In-trente-deux en quatre cayers.

Yij

Martin-Dominique Fertel

Pag·230

page 230

EXPLICATION

Des noms de chaque piece dont la Preſſe eſt conſtruite

A *Le train du derriere de la Preſſe.* C'eſt l'aſſemblage qui ſoûtient tout le corps de la Preſſe, & ſur lequel on poſe l'encrier,

B *Les Jumelles.* Ce ſont les deux plus longues pieces qui ſont à plomb, & qui ſoûtiennent la Vis & l'Ecrou de la Preſſe.

C *Le Chapeau de la Preſſe.* C'eſt la piece de bois qui eſt aſſemblée au deſſus des deux Jumelles pour les tenir ſtables.

D *Le Sommier d'en haut.* C'eſt la piece de bois où eſt enchaſſé l'écrou de la Vis de la Preſſe ; cette piece a un double tenon aux deux bouts, qui entrent auſſi dans les doubles mortaiſes qui ſont a chaque côté des deux Jumelles.

E *Le Sommier d'en bas.* C'eſt la piece de bois ſur lequel tout le train de la Preſſe roule ; cette piece a auſſi un double tenon aux deux bouts, de même que la précedente.

F *La Vis de la Preſſe.* C'eſt une piece de fer ronde, & cannelée en ligne ſpirale, & qui entre dans un écrou qui l'eſt de même, en ſorte que s'engageant l'une dans l'autre, ils font un trés-grand effort pour preſſer. La Vis à 4. filets eſt beaucoup meilleure que celle qui n'en a que 3.

G *L'arbre de la Vis.* C'eſt la piece de fer ronde, au bout de laquelle eſt la Vis, qui entre dans l'écroue ; cette piece a trois noms ; ſçavoir depuis ſon commencement juſqu'à l'endroit où ſont les troux pour faire entrer le Bareau, elle s'appelle *Vis* ; le milieu *l'Arbre*, & ſon extremité le *Pivot*.

H *La Boete.* C'eſt un morceau de bois prés d'un pied de long & de quatre pouces en carré, lequel eſt percé d'outre en outre de ſa longueur, en diminuant de largeur ſelon la groſſeur & la forme de l'arbre de la vis, afin que le *Pivot* dudit Arbre deſcende en droite ligne dans la Grenouille.

I *La Clef de la Vis.* C'eſt un morceau de fer plat, plus large par le commencement que par le bout, lequel ſe met au trou de l'Arbre qui eſt au bas de la *Boete* ; c'eſt ce qui ſoûtient la Platine qui eſt attachée aux quatre coins de la *Boete.* Autrefois on mettoit la *Clef* au milieu de la *Boete*, mais cet uſage eſt aboli depuis peu de têms.

K *La Tablette.* Ce ſont deux petites planches qui ſe joignent enſemble ; elles ſont attachées à chaque côté des Jumelles par deux mortaiſes en queue d'aronde. Cette *Tablette* ſert principalement à maintenir la *Boete* dans ſon niveau, afin que la Platine de la Preſſe ſoit toûjours dans ſon équilibre, ſans balancer d'un côté ou d'autre.

L *Le Pivot.* C'eſt l'extremité de l'Arbre de la Vis.

M *La Grenouille.* C'eſt un morceau d'acier creux enchaſſé dans le milieu du ſommet de la Platine, dans lequel le *Pivot* tourne.

N *La Platine.* C'eſt une piece de cuivre ou de bois bien unie, laquelle foule ſur la forme par le moyen de la Vis qui preſſe deſſus, elle eſt attachée au quatre coins avec des ficelles, & dans d'autres endroits avec des vis.

O *Le Bareau.* C'eſt la barre de fer, au bout de laquelle il y a un manche de bois, qui ſert à faire tourner la Vis pour preſſer ſur la Forme.

P *Berceau.* Ce ſont deux longues pieces de bois qui ſont attachées tout le long de la Preſſe, & poſées ſur le Sommier d'en bas, leſquelles ſont faites en façon d'une coulice, pour faire gliſſer le Coffre ſans balancer d'un côté ou d'autre.

Q *Les petites Poutres ou Bandes de fer.* Ce ſont deux pieces de bois qui tiennent enſemble avec le Berceau par un aſſemblage, ſur leſquelles il y a une bande de fer tout le long, afin de faire rouler tout le train de la Preſſe, comme le *Coffre*, le *Marbre*, ſur lequel on poſe les *Formes*, le *Tympan* & la *Friſquette.*

R *Le Rouleau.* C'eſt un rond morceau de bois, où ſont attachées les Cordes, pour faire rouler tout le train de la Preſſe.

S *Les Cordes du Rouleau.*

T *La Manivelle.* C'eſt un manche de bois qui eſt au bout de la broche du Rouleau, elle ſert à faire rouler le train de la Preſſe.

V *Le Coffre.* C'eſt un aſſemblage de 4. pieces de bois de 4. doigts de hauteur & de trois doigts d'épaiſſeur, dans lequel eſt enchaſſé le Marbre.

X *La Table.* C'eſt une planche de chêne, qui eſt attachée deſſous le Coffre.

Y *Cantonnieres.* Ce ſont des morceaux de bois ou de fer qui ſont attachés aux quatre coins au deſſus du Coffre, afin de tenir la Forme dans ſa même ſituation, par le moyen des coins de

1729 **Mark Catesby** Mark Catesby, *The Natural History of Carolina, Florida, and the Bahama Islands; Containing the Figures of Birds, Beasts, Fishes, Serpents, Insects, and Plants; Particularly the Forest-Trees, Shrubs, and Other Plants*. London: Mark Catesby, 1729–47. 2 volumes. 52.5 cm. Illustrator: Mark Catesby.

The English naturalist Mark Catesby (1683–1749) left for Virginia in 1712 and visited Jamaica and Bermuda as well. When he returned after a seven-year voyage, he brought home so many new plants that the members of the Royal Society in London financed his second voyage to America. During this second trip (1722–26), which took him to the Carolinas, Florida and Georgia, among other places, Catesby managed to collect an enormous quantity of plant and animal specimens.

Back in England, he wanted to make a book from this unique material, but his sponsors were not willing to finance its costly production. Catesby then decided to learn to etch, so that he could create the illustrations himself. The first instalment of *The Natural History of Carolina, Florida, and the Bahama Islands* was published in 1729; volume one was completed four years after that. Catesby coloured all of the hundred plates by hand. In the introduction, Catesby apologizes for his mediocre abilities as an artist, but he proudly mentions that his illustrations are superior because instead of using cross-hatching – which was customary in Amsterdam and Leipzig – the hatching follows the 'humour of the feathers'. It took Catesby another fourteen years to finish the 120 illustrations in volume two and the appendix.

Catesby produced the first bird book to be published in colour. It contains over a hundred plates of birds, in most cases the more colourful males. The other plates, numbering more than 170, feature plants, fish, amphibians, reptiles, insects, sponges and mammals. AP

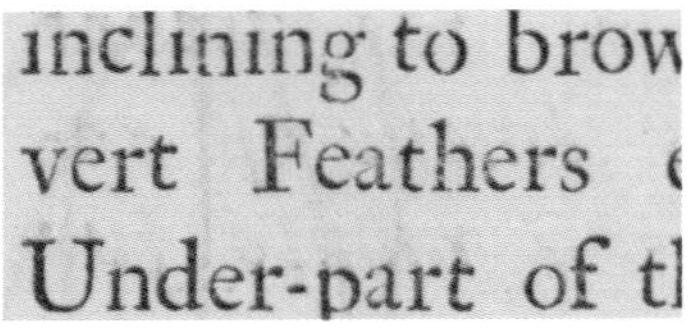

This Double Pica (22 point) roman was cut by the Frankfurt-born Dutchman, Peter de Walpergen (1646–1703) in Oxford for John Fell and his University Press, which used it in 1682. London printers were using it by 1708. It is stylistically more modern than types by Nicholas Kis (*c.* 1688) or William Caslon (*c.* 1730).

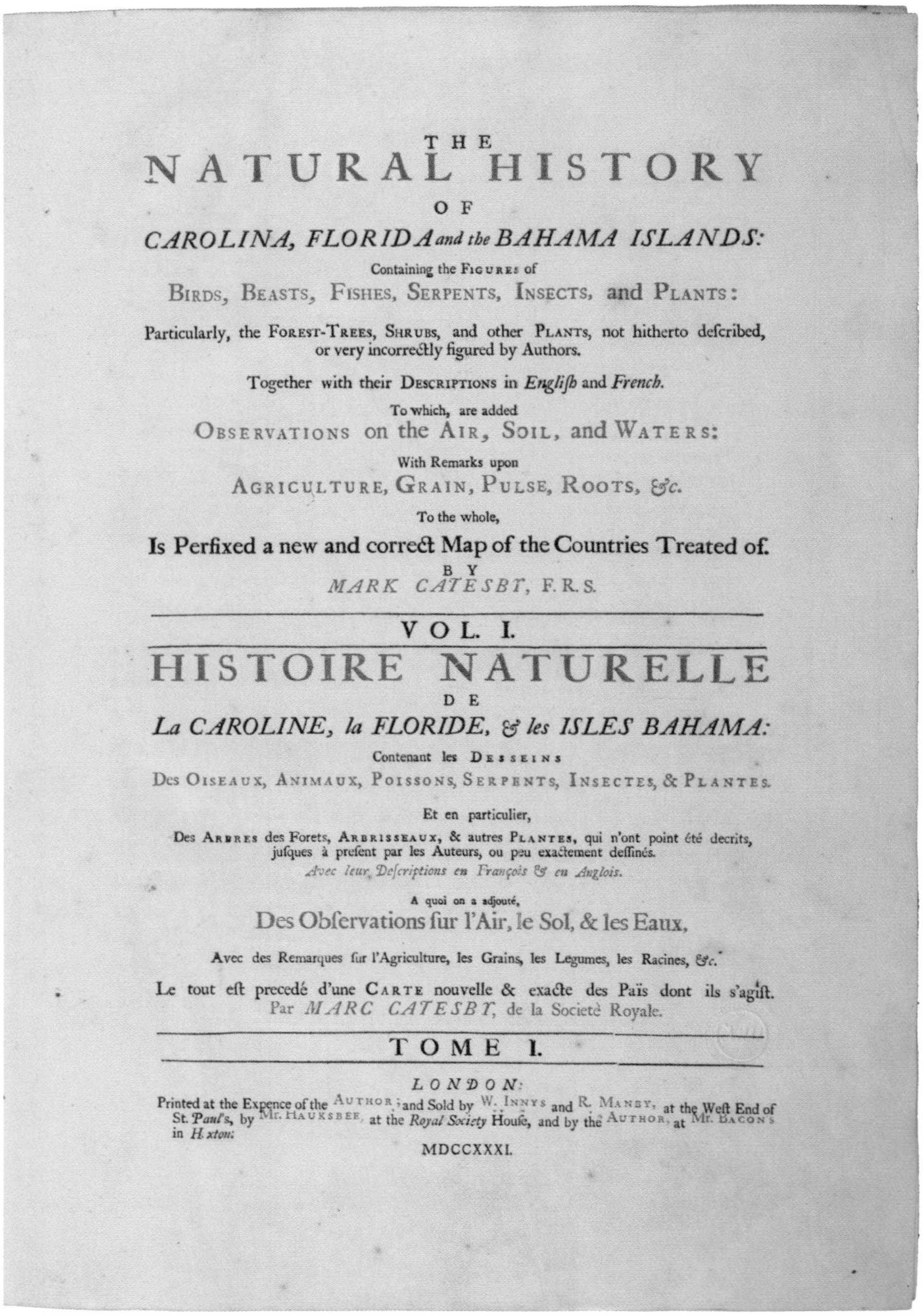

THE
NATURAL HISTORY
OF
CAROLINA, FLORIDA and the BAHAMA ISLANDS:
Containing the FIGURES of
BIRDS, BEASTS, FISHES, SERPENTS, INSECTS, and PLANTS:
Particularly, the FOREST-TREES, SHRUBS, and other PLANTS, not hitherto described, or very incorrectly figured by Authors.
Together with their DESCRIPTIONS in *English* and *French*.
To which, are added
OBSERVATIONS on the AIR, SOIL, and WATERS:
With Remarks upon
AGRICULTURE, GRAIN, PULSE, ROOTS, &c.
To the whole,
Is Perfixed a new and correct Map of the Countries Treated of.
BY
MARK CATESBY, F.R.S.

VOL. I.

HISTOIRE NATURELLE
DE
La CAROLINE, la FLORIDE, & les ISLES BAHAMA:
Contenant les DESSEINS
Des OISEAUX, ANIMAUX, POISSONS, SERPENTS, INSECTES, & PLANTES.
Et en particulier,
Des ARBRES des Forets, ARBRISSEAUX, & autres PLANTES, qui n'ont point été decrits, jusques à present par les Auteurs, ou peu exactement dessinés.
Avec leur Descriptions en François & en Anglois.
A quoi on a adjouté,
Des Observations sur l'Air, le Sol, & les Eaux,
Avec des Remarques sur l'Agriculture, les Grains, les Legumes, les Racines, &c.
Le tout est precedé d'une CARTE nouvelle & exacte des Païs dont ils s'agist.
Par *MARC CATESBY*, de la Societé Royale.

TOME I.

LONDON:
Printed at the Expence of the AUTHOR; and Sold by W. INNYS and R. MANBY, at the West End of St. *Paul's*, by MR. HAUKSBEE, at the *Royal Society* House, and by the AUTHOR, at MR. BACON'S in *Hoxton*.
MDCCXXXI.

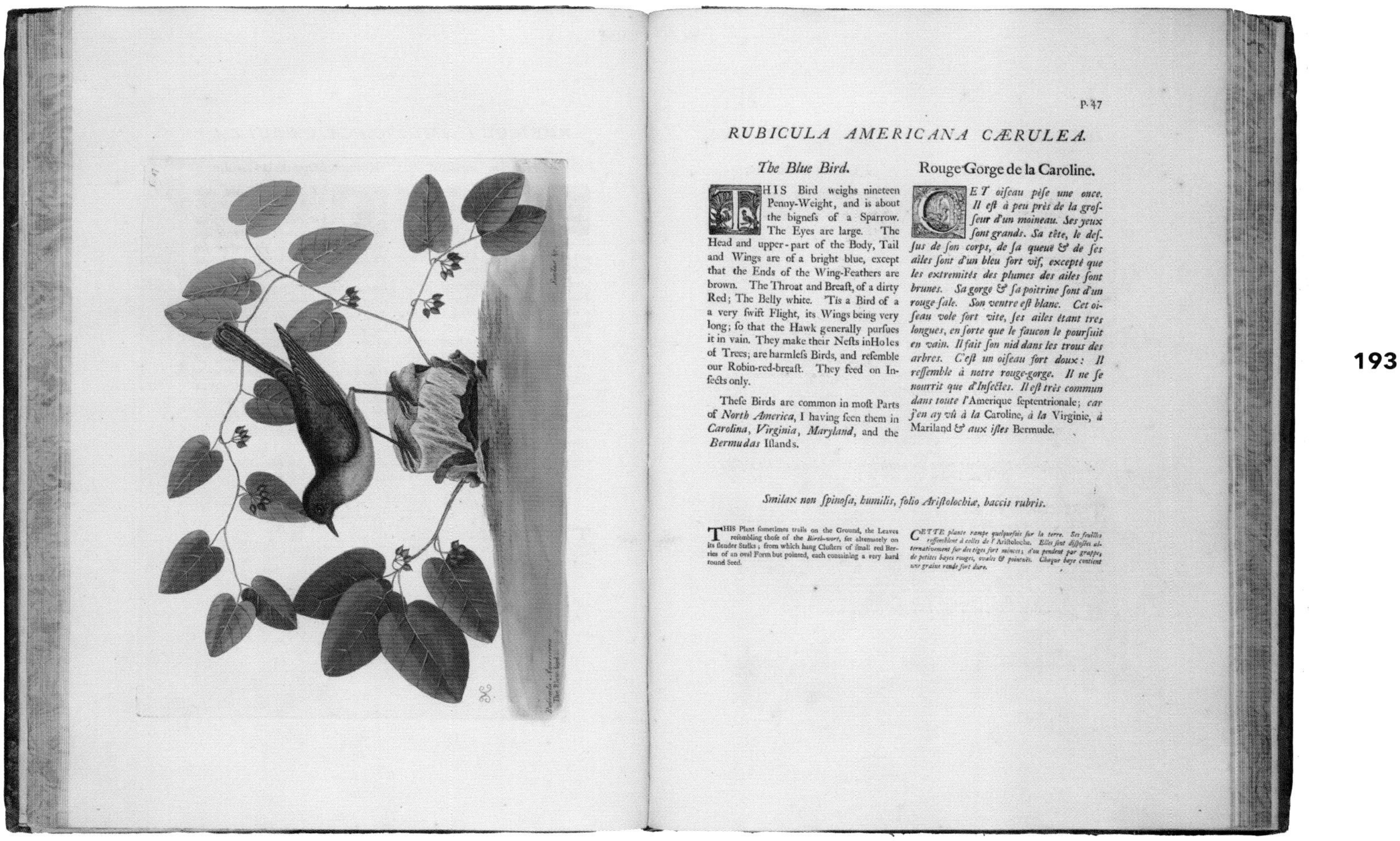
P. 47

RUBICULA AMERICANA CÆRULEA.

The Blue Bird.

THIS Bird weighs nineteen Penny-Weight, and is about the bigneſs of a Sparrow. The Eyes are large. The Head and upper-part of the Body, Tail and Wings are of a bright blue, except that the Ends of the Wing-Feathers are brown. The Throat and Breaſt, of a dirty Red; The Belly white. 'Tis a Bird of a very ſwift Flight, its Wings being very long; ſo that the Hawk generally purſues it in vain. They make their Neſts in Holes of Trees; are harmleſs Birds, and reſemble our Robin-red-breaſt. They feed on Inſects only.

Theſe Birds are common in moſt Parts of *North America*, I having ſeen them in *Carolina*, *Virginia*, *Maryland*, and the *Bermudas* Iſlands.

Rouge-Gorge de la Caroline.

CET oiſeau pèſe une once. Il eſt à peu près de la groſſeur d'un moineau. Ses yeux ſont grands. Sa tête, le deſſus de ſon corps, de ſa queuë & de ſes ailes ſont d'un bleu fort vif, excepté que les extremités des plumes des ailes ſont brunes. Sa gorge & ſa poitrine ſont d'un rouge ſale. Son ventre eſt blanc. Cet oiſeau vole fort vite, ſes ailes étant tres longues, en ſorte que le faucon le pourſuit en vain. Il fait ſon nid dans les trous des arbres. C'eſt un oiſeau fort doux: Il reſſemble à notre rouge-gorge. Il ne ſe nourrit que d'Inſectes. Il eſt très commun dans toute l'Amerique ſeptentrionale; *car j'en ay vû à la* Caroline, *à la* Virginie, *à* Mariland *& aux iſles* Bermude.

Smilax non ſpinoſa, humilis, folio Ariſtolochiæ, baccis rubris.

THIS Plant ſometimes trails on the Ground, the Leaves reſembling thoſe of the *Birth-wort*, ſet alternately on its ſlender Stalks; from which hang Cluſters of ſmall red Berries of an oval Form but pointed, each containing a very hard round Seed.

*CETTE plante rampe quelquefois ſur la terre. Ses feuilles reſſemblent à celles de l'*Ariſtoloche. *Elles ſont diſpoſées alternativement ſur des tiges fort minces; d'où pendent par grappes de petites bayes rouges, ovales & pointuës. Chaque baye contient une graine ronde fort dure.*

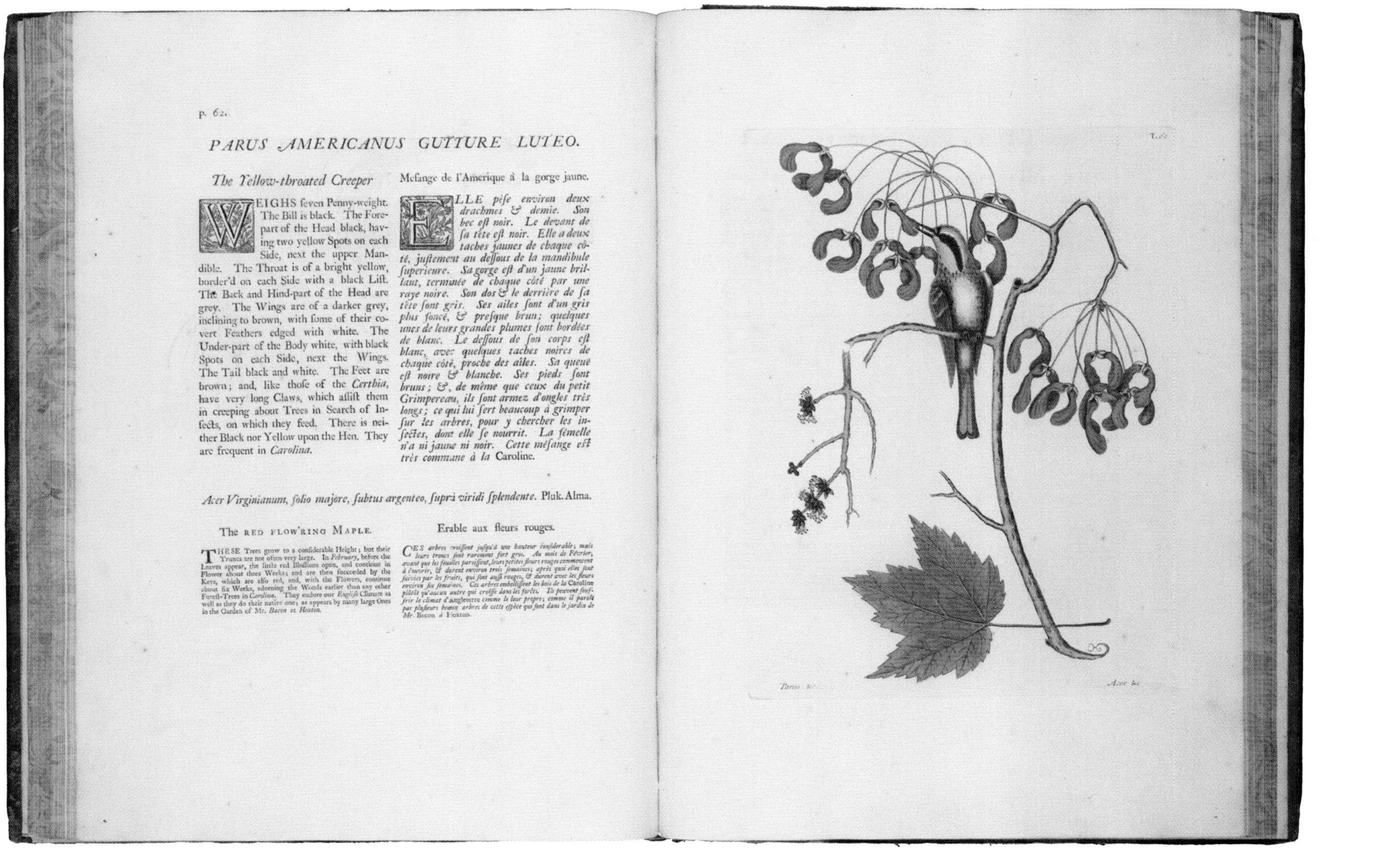
p. 62.

PARUS AMERICANUS GUTTURE LUTEO.

The Yellow-throated Creeper

WEIGHS ſeven Penny-weight. The Bill is black. The Fore-part of the Head black, having two yellow Spots on each Side, next the upper Mandible. The Throat is of a bright yellow, border'd on each Side with a black Liſt. The Back and Hind-part of the Head are grey. The Wings are of a darker grey, inclining to brown, with ſome of their covert Feathers edged with white. The Under-part of the Body white, with black Spots on each Side, next the Wings. The Tail black and white. The Feet are brown; and, like thoſe of the *Certhia*, have very long Claws, which aſſiſt them in creeping about Trees in Search of Inſects, on which they feed. There is neither Black nor Yellow upon the Hen. They are frequent in *Carolina*.

Meſange de l'Amerique à la gorge jaune.

ELLE pèſe environ deux drachmes & demie. Son bec eſt noir. Le devant de ſa tête eſt noir. Elle a deux taches jaunes de chaque côté, juſtement au deſſous de la mandibule ſuperieure. Sa gorge eſt d'un jaune brillant, terminée de chaque côté par une raye noire. Son dos & le derrière de ſa tête ſont gris. Ses ailes ſont d'un gris plus foncé, & preſque brun; quelques unes de leurs grandes plumes ſont bordées de blanc. Le deſſous de ſon corps eſt blanc, avec quelques taches noires de chaque côté, proche des ailes. Sa queuë eſt noire & blanche. Ses pieds ſont bruns; &, de même que ceux du petit Grimpereau, ils ſont armez d'ongles très longs; ce qui lui ſert beaucoup à grimper ſur les arbres, pour y chercher les inſectes, dont elle ſe nourrit. La femelle n'a ni jaune ni noir. Cette méſange eſt très commune à la Caroline.

Acer Virginianum, folio majore, ſubtus argenteo, suprà viridi ſplendente. Pluk. Alma.

The RED FLOW'RING MAPLE.

THESE Trees grow to a conſiderable Height; but their Trunks are not often very large. In *February*, before the Leaves appear, the little red Bloſſoms open, and continue in Flower about three Weeks; and are then ſucceeded by the Keys, which are alſo red, and, with the Flowers, continue about ſix Weeks, adorning the Woods earlier than any other Foreſt-Trees in *Carolina*. They endure our *Engliſh* Climate as well as they do their native one; as appears by many large Ones in the Garden of Mr. *Bacon* at *Hoxton*.

Erable aux fleurs rouges.

CES arbres croiſſent juſqu'à une hauteur conſiderable; mais leurs troncs ſont rarement fort gros. Au mois de Février, avant que les feuilles paroiſſent, leurs petites fleurs rouges commencent à s'ouvrir, & durent environ trois ſemaines; après quoi elles ſont ſuivies par les fruits, qui ſont auſſi rouges, & durent avec les fleurs environ ſix ſemaines. Ces arbres embelliſſent les bois de la Caroline *plûtôt qu'aucun autre qui croiſſe dans les forêts. Ils peuvent ſouffrir le climat d'Angleterre comme le leur propre; comme il paroît par pluſieurs beaux arbres de cette eſpèce qui ſont dans le jardin de* Mr. Bacon *à* Hoxton.

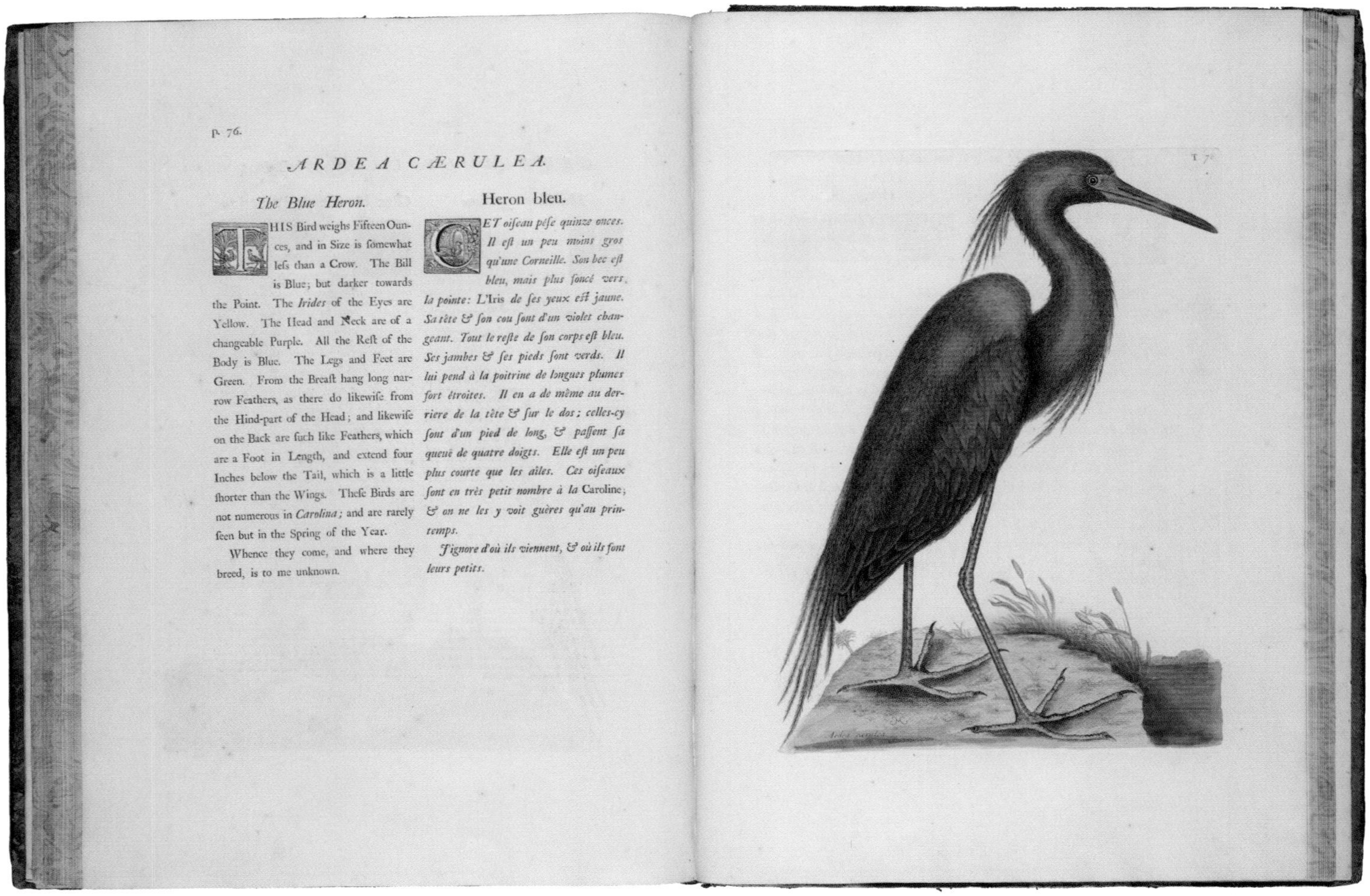

p. 76.

ARDEA CÆRULEA.

The Blue Heron.

THIS Bird weighs Fifteen Ounces, and in Size is ſomewhat leſs than a Crow. The Bill is Blue; but darker towards the Point. The *Irides* of the Eyes are Yellow. The Head and Neck are of a changeable Purple. All the Reſt of the Body is Blue. The Legs and Feet are Green. From the Breaſt hang long narrow Feathers, as there do likewiſe from the Hind-part of the Head; and likewiſe on the Back are ſuch like Feathers, which are a Foot in Length, and extend four Inches below the Tail, which is a little ſhorter than the Wings. Theſe Birds are not numerous in *Carolina*; and are rarely ſeen but in the Spring of the Year.

Whence they come, and where they breed, is to me unknown.

Heron bleu.

CET oiſeau péſe quinze onces. Il eſt un peu moins gros qu'une Corneille. Son bec eſt bleu, mais plus foncé vers la pointe: L'Iris de ſes yeux eſt jaune. Sa tête & ſon cou ſont d'un violet changeant. Tout le reſte de ſon corps eſt bleu. Ses jambes & ſes pieds ſont verds. Il lui pend à la poitrine de longues plumes fort étroites. Il en a de même au derriere de la tête & ſur le dos; celles-cy ſont d'un pied de long, & paſſent ſa queuë de quatre doigts. Elle eſt un peu plus courte que les aîles. Ces oiſeaux ſont en très petit nombre à la Caroline*; & on ne les y voit guères qu'au printemps.*

J'ignore d'où ils viennent, & où ils ſont leurs petits.

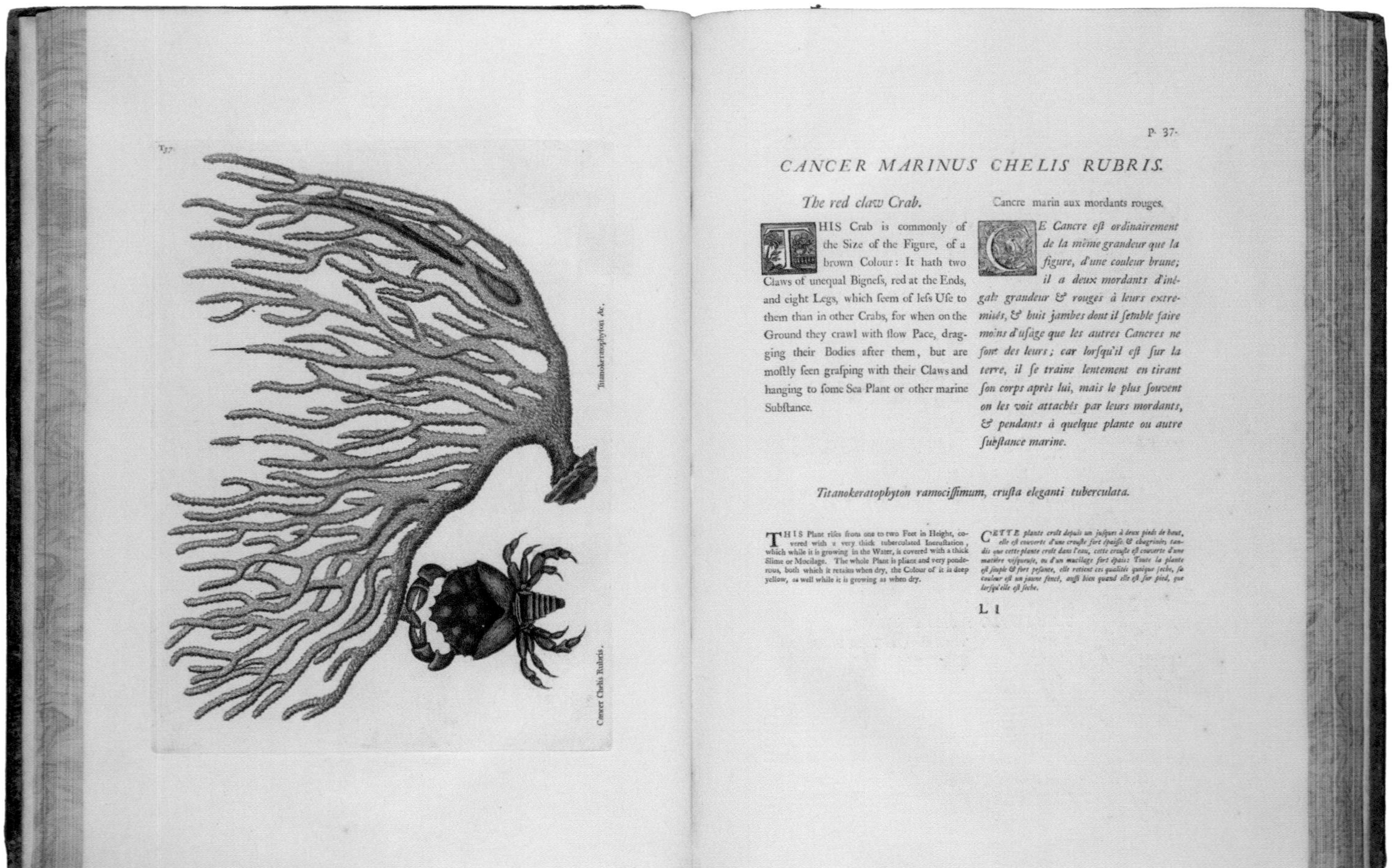

Cancer Chelis Rubris.

Titanokeratophyton &c.

p. 37.

CANCER MARINUS CHELIS RUBRIS.

The red claw Crab.

THIS Crab is commonly of the Size of the Figure, of a brown Colour: It hath two Claws of unequal Bigneſs, red at the Ends, and eight Legs, which ſeem of leſs Uſe to them than in other Crabs, for when on the Ground they crawl with ſlow Pace, dragging their Bodies after them, but are moſtly ſeen graſping with their Claws and hanging to ſome Sea Plant or other marine Subſtance.

Cancre marin aux mordants rouges.

CE Cancre eſt ordinairement de la même grandeur que la figure, d'une couleur brune; il a deux mordants d'inégale grandeur & rouges à leurs extremités, & huit jambes dont il ſemble faire moins d'uſage que les autres Cancres ne font des leurs; car lorſqu'il eſt ſur la terre, il ſe traine lentement en tirant ſon corps après lui, mais le plus ſouvent on les voit attachés par leurs mordants, & pendants à quelque plante ou autre ſubſtance marine.

Titanokeratophyton ramociſſimum, cruſta eleganti tuberculata.

THIS Plant riſes from one to two Feet in Height, covered with a very thick tuberculated Incruſtation, which while it is growing in the Water, is covered with a thick Slime or Mucilage. The whole Plant is pliant and very ponderous, both which it retains when dry, the Colour of it is deep yellow, as well while it is growing as when dry.

CETTE plante croît depuis un juſques à deux pieds de haut, elle eſt couverte d'une crouſte fort épaiſſe & chagrinée; tandis que cette plante croît dans l'eau, cette crouſte eſt couverte d'une matière viſqueuſe, ou d'un mucilage fort épais: Toute la plante eſt ſouple & fort peſante, elle retient ces qualités quoique ſeche, ſa couleur eſt un jaune foncé, auſſi bien quand elle eſt ſur pied, que lorſqu'elle eſt ſeche.

L l

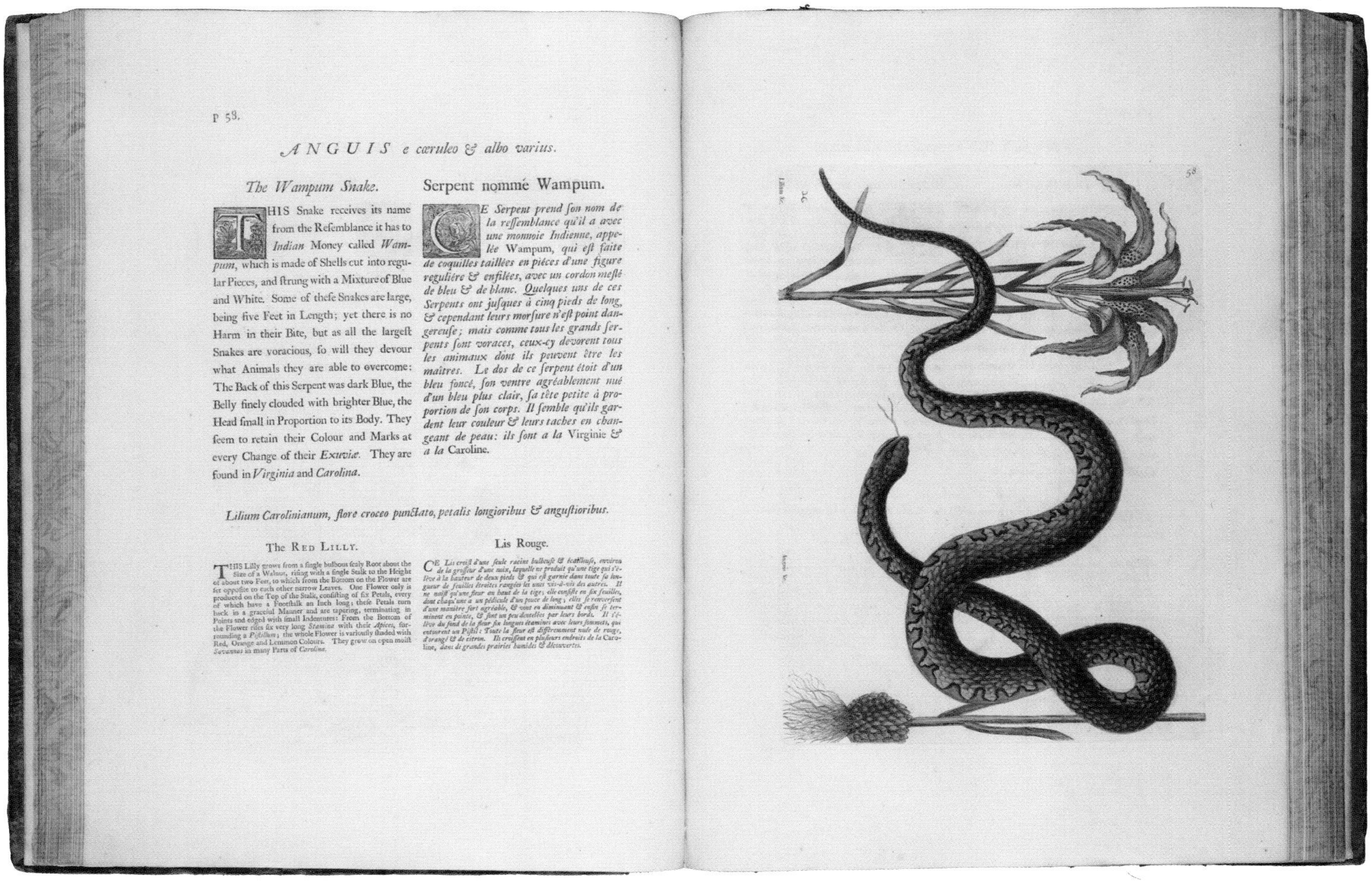
p 58.
ANGUIS e cæruleo & albo varius.
The Wampum Snake.
THIS Snake receives its name from the Refemblance it has to Indian Money called Wampum, which is made of Shells cut into regular Pieces, and ftrung with a Mixture of Blue and White. Some of thefe Snakes are large, being five Feet in Length; yet there is no Harm in their Bite, but as all the largeft Snakes are voracious, fo will they devour what Animals they are able to overcome: The Back of this Serpent was dark Blue, the Belly finely clouded with brighter Blue, the Head fmall in Proportion to its Body. They feem to retain their Colour and Marks at every Change of their Exuviæ. They are found in Virginia and Carolina.
Serpent nommé Wampum.
CE Serpent prend fon nom de la reffemblance qu'il a avec une monnoie Indienne, appelée Wampum, qui eft faite de coquilles taillées en piéces d'une figure reguliére & enfilées, avec un cordon meflé de bleu & de blanc. Quelques uns de ces Serpents ont jufques à cinq pieds de long, & cependant leurs morfure n'eft point dangereufe; mais comme tous les grands ferpents font voraces, ceux-cy devorent tous les animaux dont ils peuvent être les maîtres. Le dos de ce ferpent étoit d'un bleu foncé, fon ventre agréablement nué d'un bleu plus clair, fa tête petite à proportion de fon corps. Il femble qu'ils gardent leur couleur & leurs taches en changeant de peau: ils font a la Virginie & a la Caroline.
Lilium Carolinianum, flore croceo punctato, petalis longioribus & anguftioribus.
The RED LILLY.
Lis Rouge.

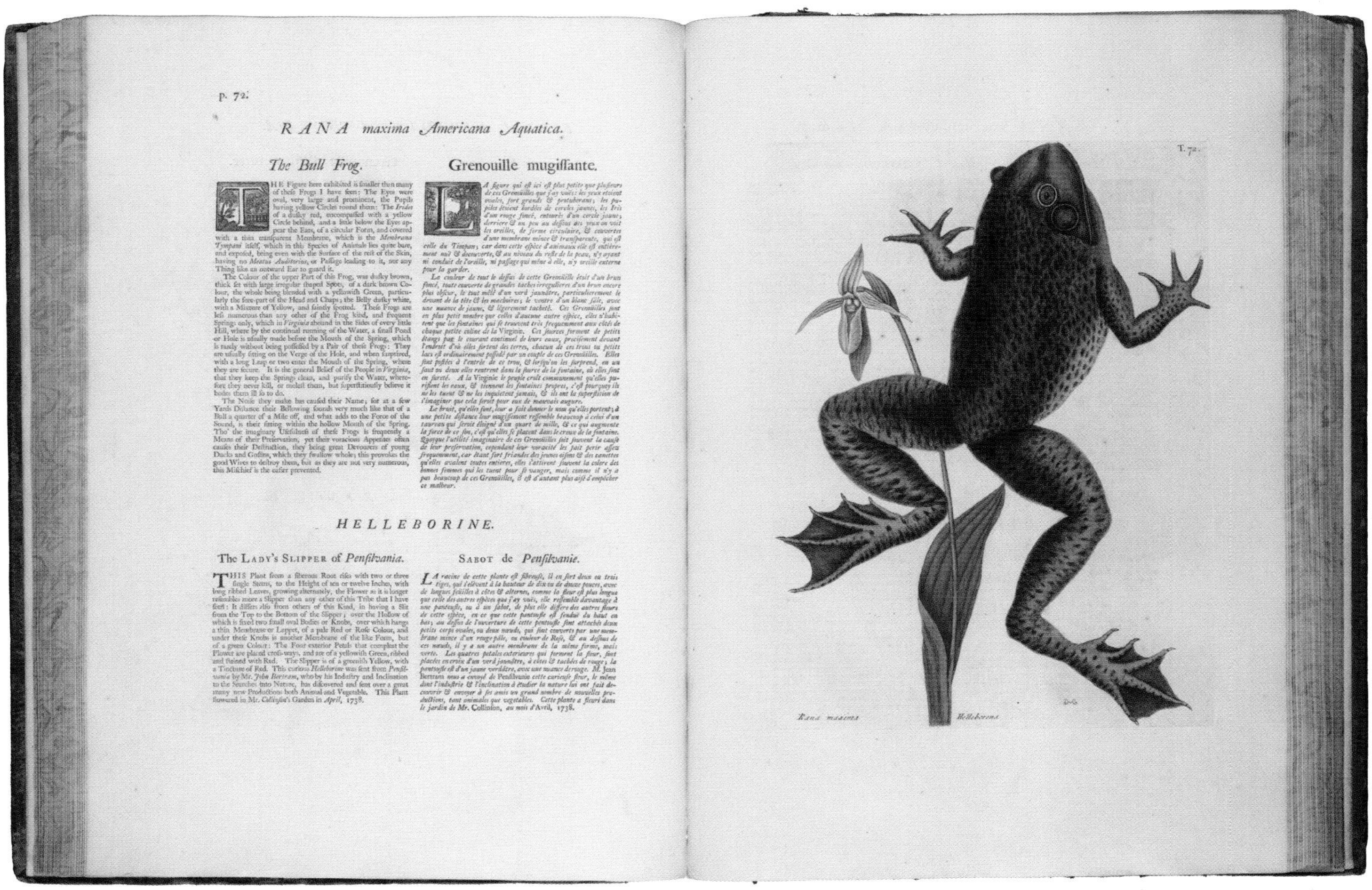
p. 72.
RANA maxima Americana Aquatica.
The Bull Frog.
Grenouille mugiffante.
HELLEBORINE.
The LADY'S SLIPPER of Penfilvania.
SABOT de Penfilvanie.

MAGNOLIA altiſſima, flore ingenti candido.

The Laurel Tree of Carolina.

THESE Trees are commonly two Foot and an half, and ſometimes three Feet in Diameter, riſing with a ſtrait Trunc, to the Height of eighty Feet and upwards, with a regular ſhaped Head. The Leaves are ſhaped like thoſe of the *Lauro-ceraſus*, but much larger, of a ſhining bright Green, except their under Sides, which are of a Ruſſet red Colour, with a hoary roughneſs, like Buff. This Particularity in the Leaves doth not appear before the Tree is large, the young ones having their Leaves green on both Sides. In *May* the Bloſſoms open, which are large, white and very fragrant, ſomewhat reſembling in Form a ſingle Peony: The Petals are uſually ten, and ſometimes eleven and twelve in Number; they are thick and ſucculent, in the midſt of which is placed the *Ovarium*, cloſely ſurrounded with *Apices*, which before the Petals fall off, ſwells to the Size of a Pigeon's Egg, and when fully grown, is formed into an oval Cone, in Size of a Gooſe's Egg. It is green at firſt, but when ripe of a reddiſh Purple. On the Superficies are many little Protuberances, in each of which lies a ſingle Seed, ſomewhat leſs than a Kidney Bean, covered with a red Film: In *Auguſt*, at which Time the Fruit is ripe, every one of theſe little Swellings openeth, and diſchargeth its Seeds, which do not fall immediately to the Ground, but hang pendant by ſmall white Threads, about two Inches long.

This ſtately Tree perfumes the Woods, and diſplays its Beauties from *May* till *November*, producing firſt its fragrant and ample Bloſſoms, ſucceeded by its glittering Fruit. It retains the Leaves all the Year, which being of two Colours have a pretty Effect, when waved by the Wind, diſplaying firſt one Side, and then the other.

What much adds to the Value of this Tree is, that it is ſo far naturalized and become a Denizon to our Country and Climate, as to adorn firſt the Garden of that worthy and curious Baronet, Sir *John Colliton*, of *Exmouth* in *Devonſhire*, where for theſe three Years paſt, it has produced Plenty of Bloſſoms, ſince that and in the Year 1737, one of them bloſſom'd at *Parſons Green*, in the Garden of the Right Honourable Sir *Charles Wager*; one of which Bloſſoms expanded, meaſured eleven Inches over.

Their Native Place is *Florida* and South *Carolina*, to the North of which I have never ſeen any, nor heard that they grow.

Laurier de la Caroline.

CES arbres ont ordinairement deux pieds & demi, & quelquefois trois pieds de diametre, il s'élevent à la hauteur de dix-huit pieds & au deſſus, leur tronc eſt droit & leurs branches forment un bouquet regulier. Leurs feüilles ont la même figure que celles du Laurier-ceriſe; mais elles ſont beaucoup plus grandes, d'un verd clair & vif, excepté que le deſſous en eſt d'un rouge roux, & vélu, comme un eſpece de Buſle; cette ſingularité des feuilles ne paroit que lorſque l'arbre eſt grand, car les feuilles des petits ſont vertes des deux côtés. Les fleurs s'ouvrent en May, *elles ſont grandes, blanches, & de fort bonne odeur; elles reſemblent en quelque ſorte à celles de Pivoine ſimple, elles ſont ordinairement compoſées de dix pétales, quelquefois d'onze, & même de douze; leſquelles petales ſont épaiſſes & ſucculentes; l'ovaire eſt placé au milieu, & entouré de ſommets; avant que les petales tombent, il devient gros comme un œuf de pigeon, & quand il a fini de croître, il prend la forme d'un cône ovale, de la groſſeur d'un œuf d'oye; il eſt verd d'abord, il devient enſuite rouge, avec un melange de verd; ſa ſuperficie eſt ſemée de petites éminences, dans chacune deſquelles une ſemence eſt renfermée, un peu moins groſſe qu'un Phaſeole, couverte d'une membrane rouge: Au mois* d'Aouſt, *tems auquel le fruit eſt mûr, chacune de ces petites éminences s'ouvrent & laiſſent échaper ſa ſemence; elle ne tombe pas pour cela immediatement à terre, mais elle pend par un petit filet blanc, d'environ deux pouces de long.*

Cet arbre magnifique parfume les bois & étale ſes beautés depuis May *juſques en* Novembre, *produiſant d'abord ſes grandes & odoriferantes fleurs, auxquelles ſuccedent ſes fruits brillans. Il garde ſes feuilles toute l'année, & comme elles ſont de deux couleurs, elles produiſent un effet fort agréable lorſqu'elles ſont agitées par le vent, qui expoſe à la vuë tantôt un de leur côtés, & tantôt l'autre.*

Ce qui augmente encore beaucoup le merite de cet arbre, c'eſt qu'il eſt ſi bien naturaliſé dans notre Pays, & qu'il eſt ſi bien accommodé à notre climat, qu'il ſert d'ornemens depuis trois ans, aux jardin de l'illuſtre & curieux Mr. Jean Colliton, *Chevalier Baronet, demeurant à* Exmouth, *dans la Province de* Devon; *là où il étale ſes belles fleurs en abondance depuis ce tems, & dans l'année* 1737, *il en a fleuri un autre à* Parſons Green, *dans le jardin de Mr. l'Admiral* Charles Wager; *une de ces fleurs entierement ouverte avoit onze pouces de diametre.*

Ces arbres ſont originaires de la Floride, *& du Sud de la* Caroline. *Je n'en ai jamais vû dans le Nord de ce Pays, ni n'ai oui dire, qu'il y en euſt.*

R r

1733 **George Bickham** George Bickham, *The Universal Penman; or, The art of writing made useful to the gentleman and scholar, as well as the man of business*. London: Robert Sayer, c. 1760. 212 leaves. 40 cm. Engraved and first published 1733–41.

The most comprehensive copybook of English writing masters was first published as the British Empire rose to power. After 1688, England displaced the Dutch Republic as the leading sea power. Flourishing trade and manufacturing meant more business and financial records and correspondence, and growing literacy spawned more writing. Moreover, *nouveau riche* industrialists and their families often wanted their handwriting to reflect their status.

The Londoner George Bickham the elder (1683/84–1758), apprenticed to the writing master and engraver John Sturt, was the most skilled engraver of writing books of his day, but not the best writing master. He enlisted more than twenty masters to contribute samples for his 'universal' copybook, including every leading figure: Joseph Champion, Willington Clark, Samuel Vaux, Gabriel Brooks, John Bland. The 212 leaves appeared in 52 parts from 1733 to 1741 and were reprinted several times. While roundhand dominates, older gothic hands (still used for legal documents) appear alongside a variety of styles for occasional use (including engraved counterparts to various typographic styles) and for writing foreign languages.

Printing types generally evolve more slowly than handlettering. Shortly before Bickham's first part appeared, moreover, the London punchcutter and typefounder William Caslon had introduced his excellent but conservative types, driving cruder but stylistically more modern types out of use and almost ignoring nearly two centuries of evolution in writing and engraving. In 1754, the writing master John Baskerville brought type more in line with contemporary handwritten forms. However, the new styles did not win a definitive victory in Britain until the 1790s. JAL

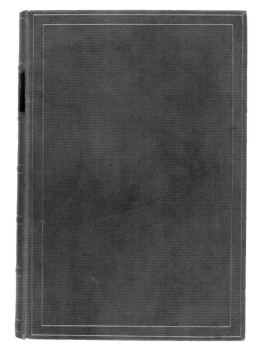

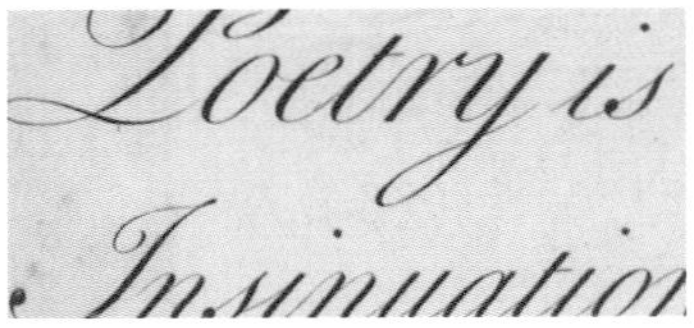

George Shelley, Charles Snell and others adopted and simplified the pointed-pen script of Van den Velde in the Netherlands, Materot in France and others, to evolve the English roundhand in the late seventeenth and early eighteenth centuries. It returned to mainland Europe later in the century, sometimes under the name *lettres anglaises*.

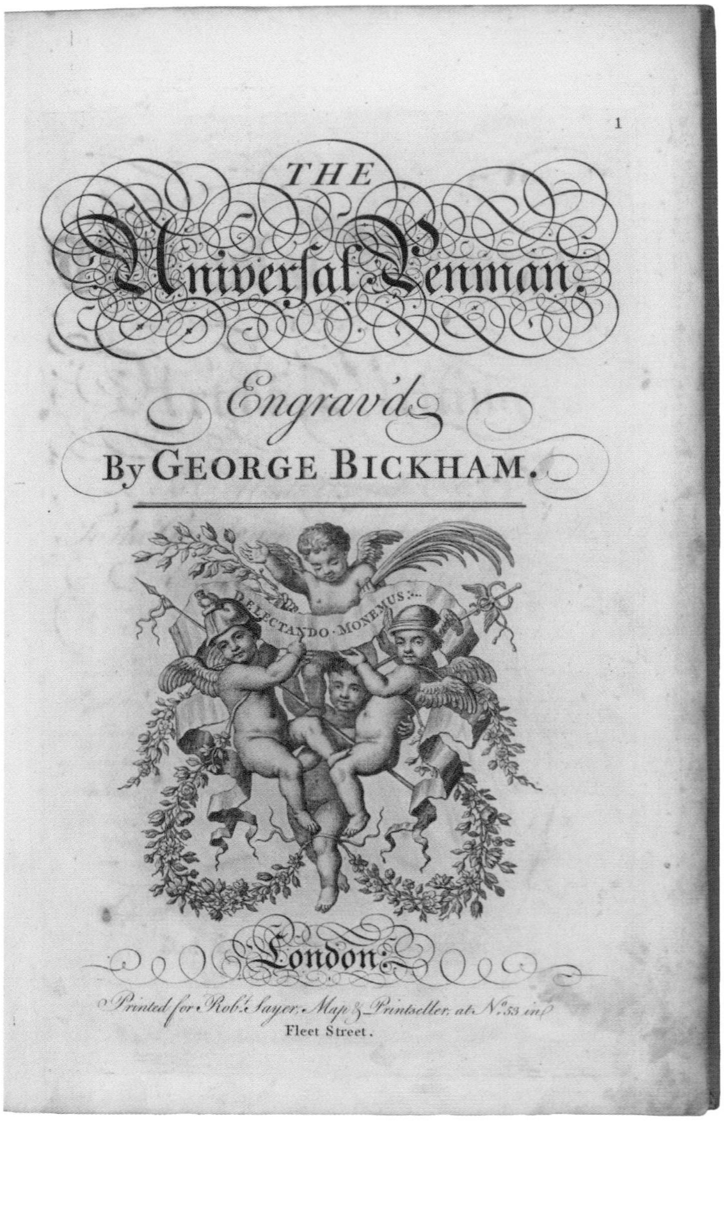

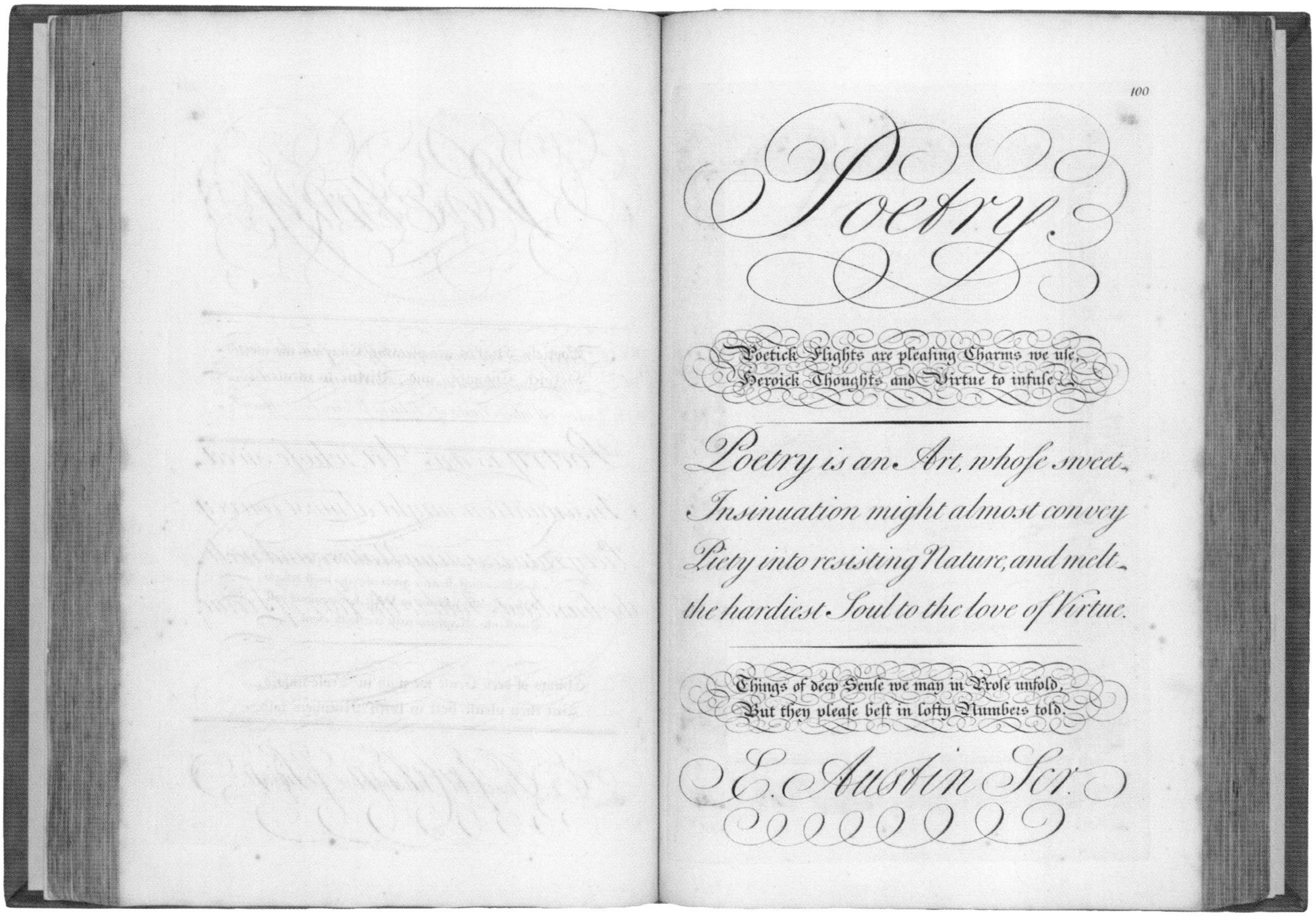
100
Poetry.
Poetick Flights are pleasing Charms we use,
Heroick Thoughts and Virtue to infuse.
Poetry is an Art, whose sweet
Insinuation might almost convey
Piety into resisting Nature, and melt
the hardiest Soul to the love of Virtue.
Things of deep Sense we may in Prose unfold,
But they please best in lofty Numbers told.
E. Austin Scr.

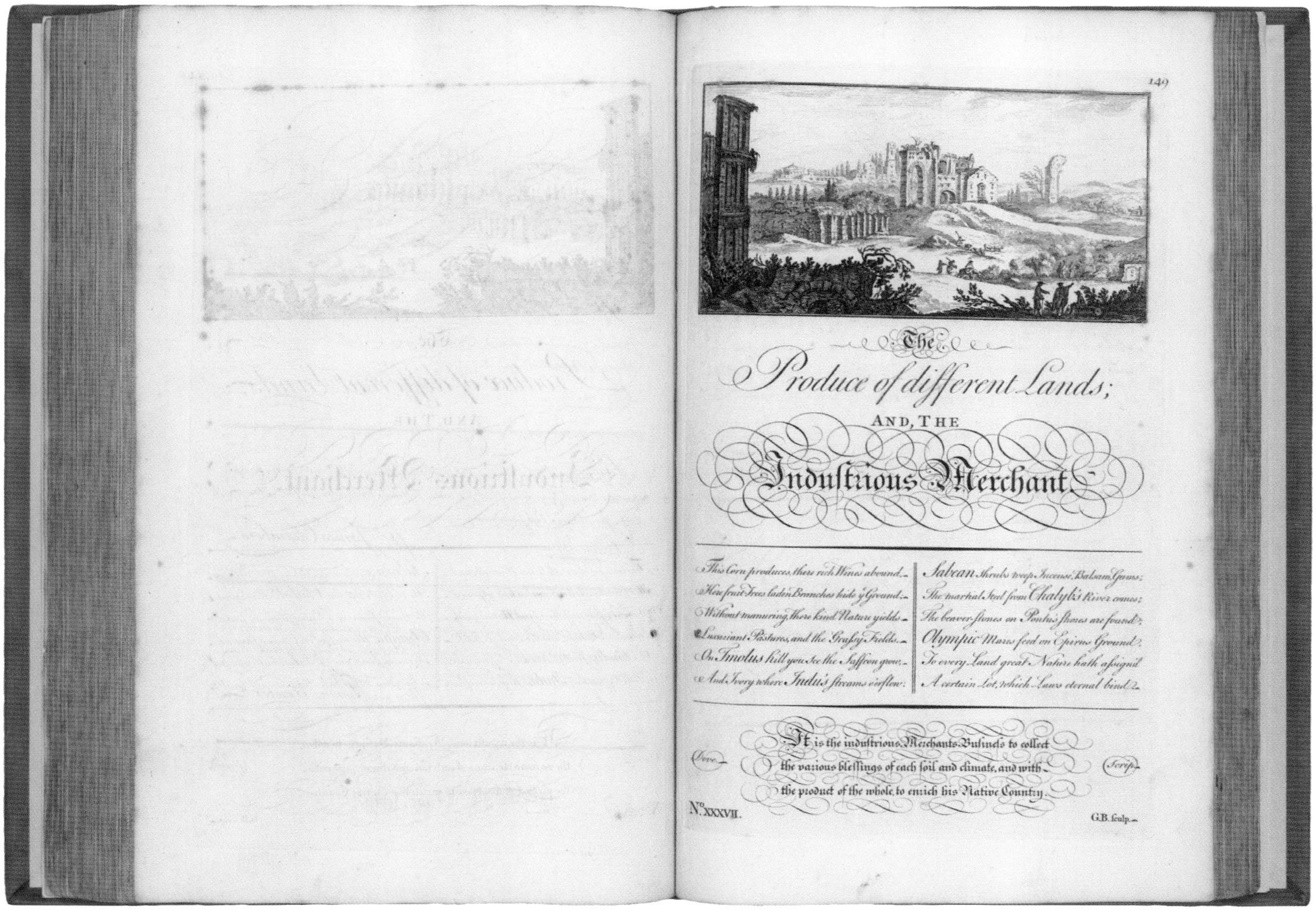
149
The
Produce of different Lands;
AND, THE
Industrious Merchant.
This Corn produces, there rich Wines abound,
Here fruit Trees laden Branches hide y^e Ground:
Without manuring, there kind Nature yields
Luxuriant Pastures, and the Grassy Fields.
On Tmolus hill you see the Saffron grow,
And Ivory where Indu's streams o'erflow:
Sabean Shrubs weep Incense, Balsam, Gums;
The martial Steel from Chalyb's River comes;
The beaver stones on Pontu's shores are found;
Olympic Mares feed on Epirus Ground;
To every Land great Nature hath assign'd
A certain Lot, which Laws eternal bind.
It is the industrious Merchants Business to collect
the various blessings of each soil and climate, and with
the product of the whole, to enrich his Native Country.
N°. XXXVII.
G.B. sculp.

1750 **Giovanni Battista Piranesi** Giovanni Battista Piranesi, *Invenzioni capric di carceri all'acqua forte*.

Rome: Giovanni Bouchard, *c.* 1750. 14 sheets. 52.5 cm. Sheets *c.* 51 x 72 cm. Illustrator: Giovanni Battista Piranesi.

The Italian Giovanni Battista Piranesi (1720–78) was an etcher, engraver, architect and archaeologist. He produced many views of Rome. These *vedute* were sold both separately, as single sheets, and as a series, which buyers could bind according to their own taste. The *Vedute di Roma* is therefore not a book in the traditional sense. Piranesi mainly used etching for his plates. *Invenzioni capric di carceri* occupies a special place in Piranesi's oeuvre. The first edition, published around 1750, consists of fourteen plates. The second edition has two additional etchings, and the plates were numbered.

The plates in *Invenzioni capric di carceri* ('Inventions of Fanciful Prisons') depict imaginary subterranean prisons fitted with machines, the function of which is unclear. The etchings may have been inspired by the excavations in Herculaneum, or by the 'caves' of Nero's Domus Aurea. These mysterious dungeons, executed in a bold and free style of etching, seem to suggest feverish nightmares. At least this was how they were interpreted by Thomas De Quincey, who compared Piranesi's images with his own opium-induced visions. The Surrealists were also influenced by these plates, which have now eclipsed all of Piranesi's other creations, among which are over a thousand etchings. PD

'Poor Piranesi. His dark, brooding fantasies of classical ruins have haunted the architectural imagination for centuries. Yet aside from a minor church renovation in Rome, he never fulfilled his ambitions as an architect and is still known mainly as an engraver. And in recent decades his art has been unjustly associated with postmodernism's tired obsession with classical motifs.' Nicolai Ouroussoff in *The New York Times*, September 28, 2007.

1751 **Encyclopedia of Diderot & d'Alembert** *Encyclopédie, ou dictionnaire raisonné des sciences, des arts et des métiers*; ed. Denis Diderot & Jean Le Rond d'Alembert. Paris: André Le Breton et al., 1751–72. 28 volumes. 40.5 cm (volume of plates). With later supplements. Illustrator: Louis-Jacques Goussier (depicted work). Engraver: Robert Bénard (depicted work).

The *Encyclopédie* of Denis Diderot (1713–84) and Jean Le Rond d'Alembert (1717–83), in 28 volumes, was the single most ambitious publication that had ever been printed in France. Its aim was to give a detailed overview of all available human knowledge. The *Encyclopédie* contained over 70,000 articles written by a team of specialists. Diderot was one of the editors and also one of the encyclopedia's most productive authors. Eleven volumes were devoted to detailed illustrations. The initiator and main publisher was André Le Breton (who also wrote the article on printing ink).

The *Encyclopédie* was originally conceived as a translation of a considerably less extensive English work, but the two editors initially appointed proved to be incompetent. Diderot and d'Alembert then took over. The gigantic work was financed by subscription. The number of subscribers rose, despite problems with the censor. The final print run amounted to 4,250 copies, which at the time was an impressive figure.

The beautifully executed plates offer an insight into eighteenth-century craftsmanship and knowledge of the world. The production of books is also discussed, with detailed illustrations and descriptions of the manufacture of paper and the application of graphic techniques, among other topics. This encyclopedia was a positive catalyst in the spread of the Enlightenment. PD

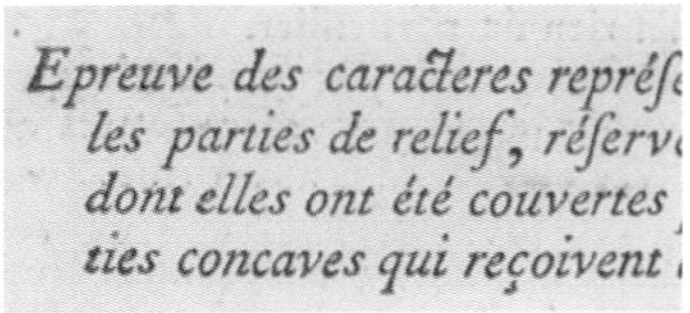
Epreuve des caracteres repré[…]
les parties de relief, réserv[…]
dont elles ont été couvertes […]
ties concaves qui reçoivent […]

This is Pierre-Simon Fournier's Saint Augustin (14 point) italic (c. 1740). Fournier (1712–68) began cutting innovative italics in this style in 1736, perhaps anticipated by Louis Luce in 1732. Influenced by pointed-pen calligraphy and the engraved designs for the Romain du Roi, Fournier's examples set a standard for all that followed.

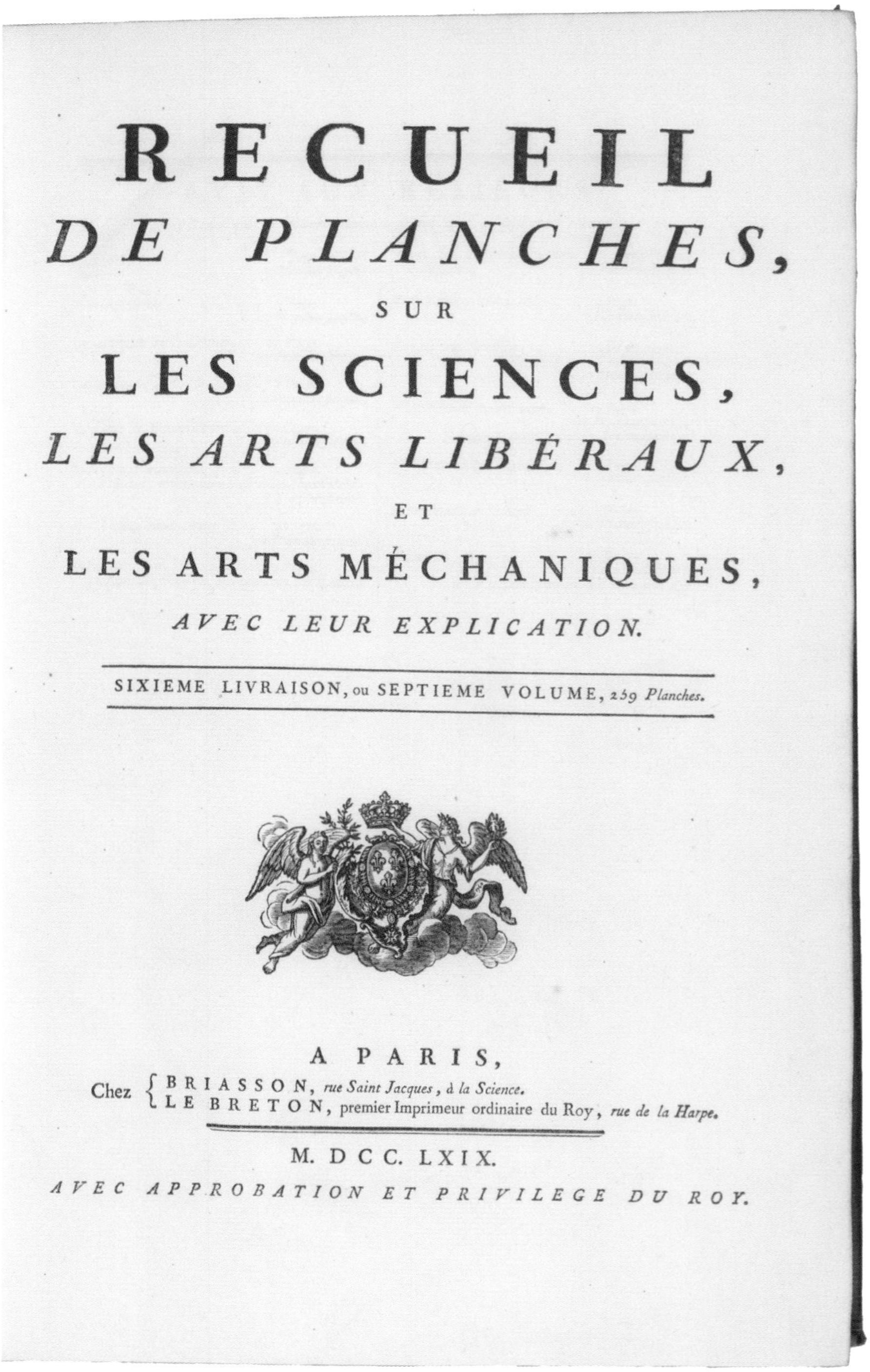
RECUEIL
DE PLANCHES,
SUR
LES SCIENCES,
LES ARTS LIBÉRAUX,
ET
LES ARTS MÉCHANIQUES,
AVEC LEUR EXPLICATION.

SIXIEME LIVRAISON, ou SEPTIEME VOLUME, 259 Planches.

A PARIS,
Chez { BRIASSON, rue Saint Jacques, à la Science.
LE BRETON, premier Imprimeur ordinaire du Roy, rue de la Harpe.

M. DCC. LXIX.
AVEC APPROBATION ET PRIVILEGE DU ROY.

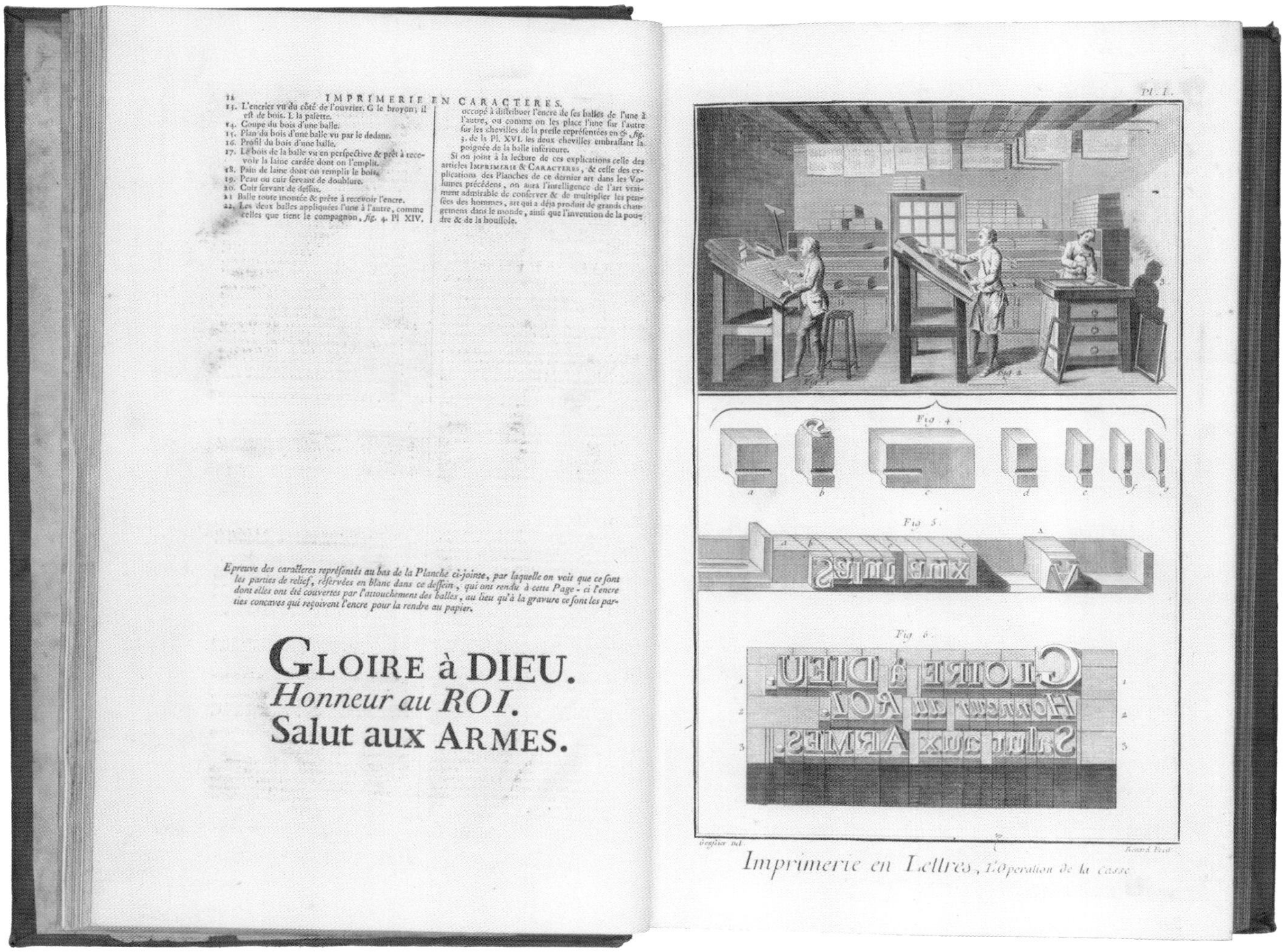
12 IMPRIMERIE EN CARACTERES.
13. L'encrier vu du côté de l'ouvrier. G le broyon; il est de bois. L la palette.
14. Coupe du bois d'une balle.
15. Plan du bois d'une balle vu par le dedans.
16. Profil du bois d'une balle.
17. Le bois de la balle vu en perspective & prêt à recevoir la laine cardée dont on l'emplit.
18. Pain de laine dont on remplit le bois.
19. Peau ou cuir servant de doublure.
20. Cuir servant de dessus.
21 Balle toute montée & prête à recevoir l'encre.
22. Les deux balles appliquées l'une à l'autre, comme celles que tient le compagnon, fig. 4. Pl XIV.
occupé à distribuer l'encre de ses balles de l'une à l'autre, ou comme on les place l'une sur l'autre sur les chevilles de la presse représentées en & , fig. 5. de la Pl. XVI. les deux chevilles embrassant la poignée de la balle inférieure.
Si on joint à la lecture de ces explications celle des articles IMPRIMERIE & CARACTERES, & celle des explications des Planches de ce dernier art dans les Volumes précédens, on aura l'intelligence de l'art vraiment admirable de conserver & de multiplier les pensées des hommes, art qui a déja produit de grands changemens dans le monde, ainsi que l'invention de la poudre & de la boussole.
Epreuve des caracteres représentés au bas de la Planche ci-jointe, par laquelle on voit que ce sont les parties de relief, réservées en blanc dans ce dessein, qui ont rendu à cette Page-ci l'encre dont elles ont été couvertes par l'attouchement des balles, au lieu qu'à la gravure ce sont les parties concaves qui reçoivent l'encre pour la rendre au papier.
GLOIRE à DIEU.
Honneur au ROI.
Salut aux ARMES.
Pl. I.
Fig. 4.
Fig. 5.
Fig. 6.
Imprimerie en Lettres, L'Opération de la Casse

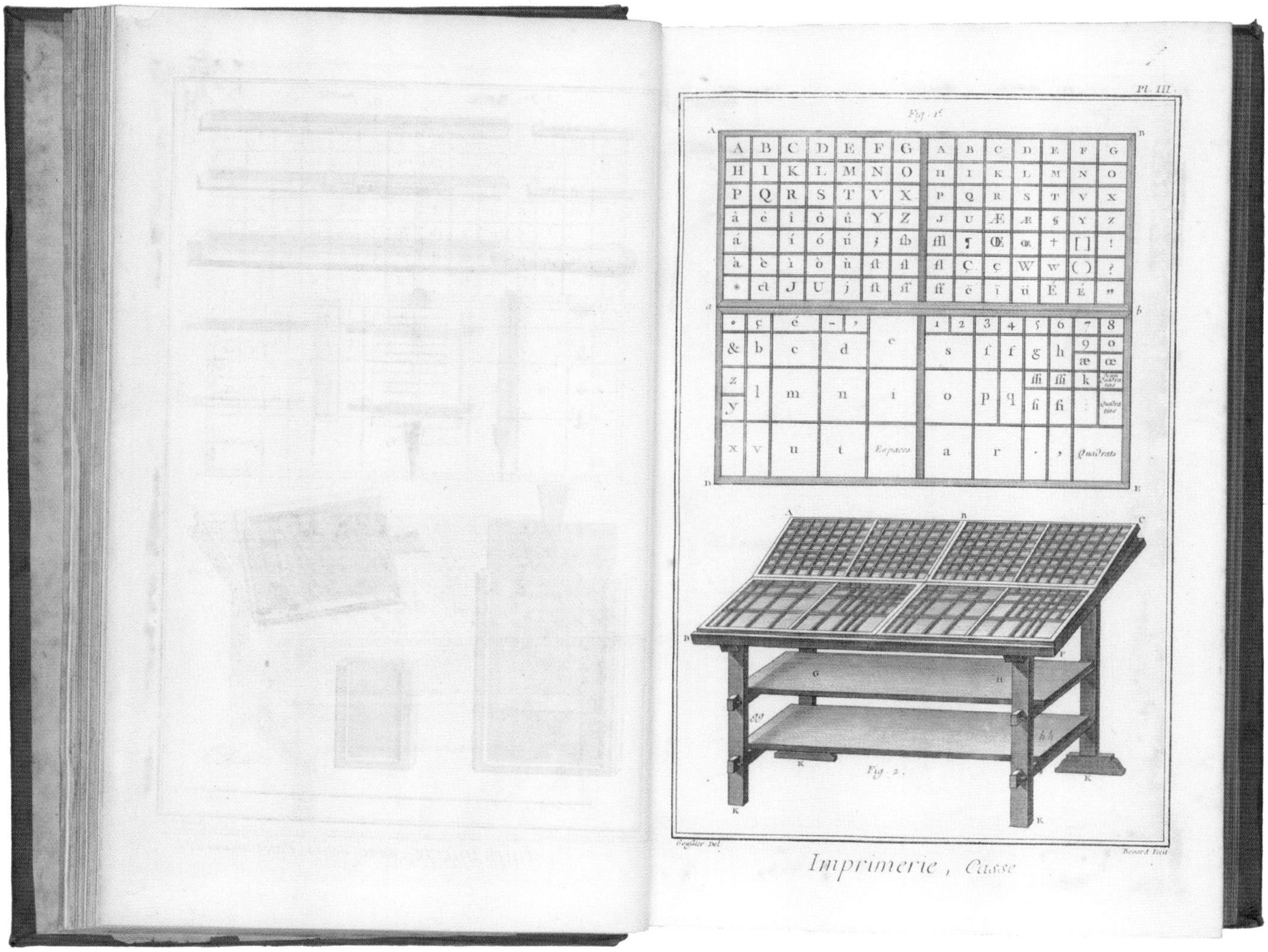
Pl. III.
Fig. 1re
Fig. 2.
Imprimerie, Casse

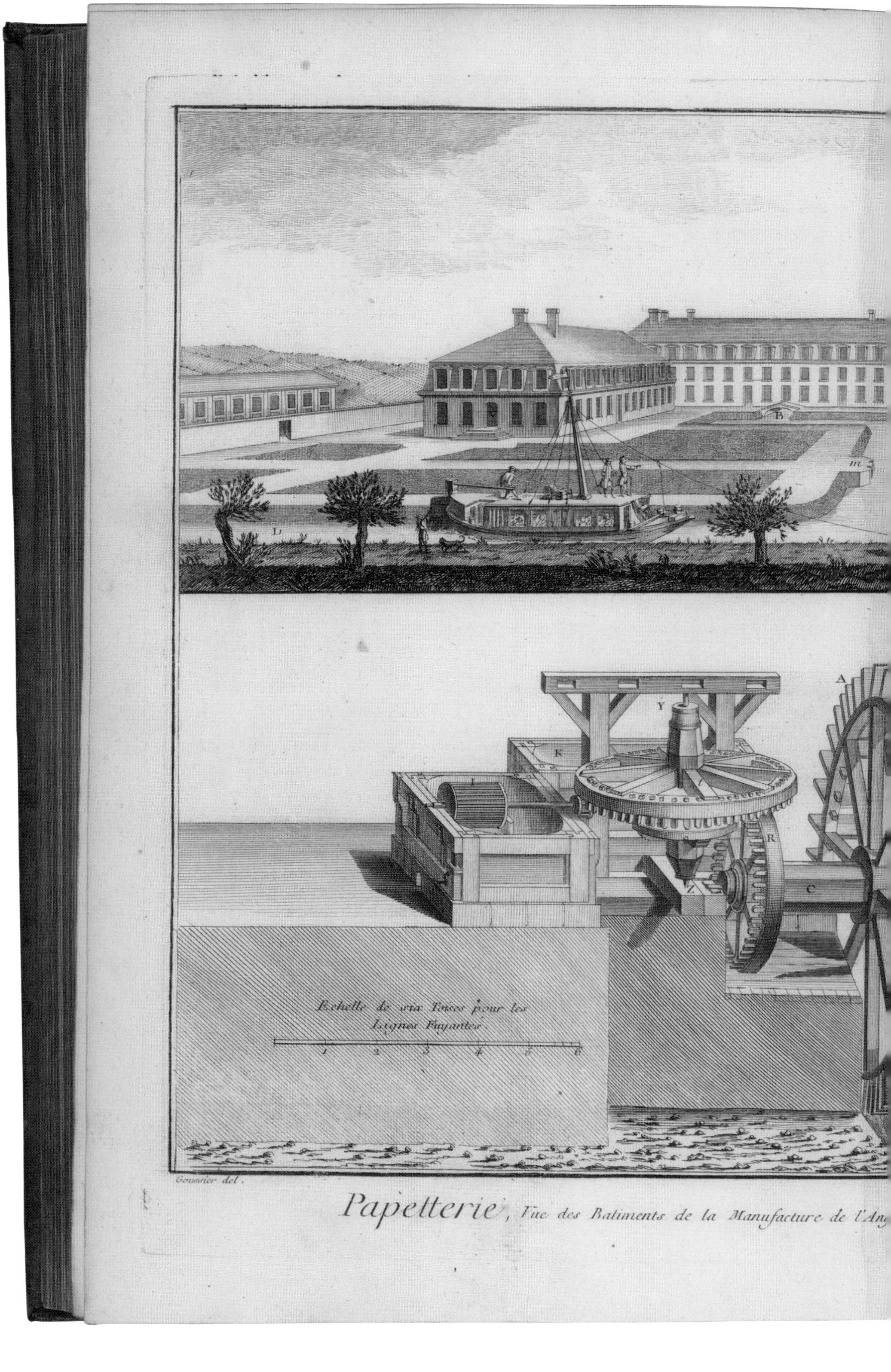
Echelle de six Toises pour les
Lignes Fuyantes.
Goussier del.
Papetterie, Vue des Batiments de la Manufacture de l'Ang

Pl. I.

Benard Fecit

près Montargis. Vue du Rouage d'un des Moulins de cette Manufacture.

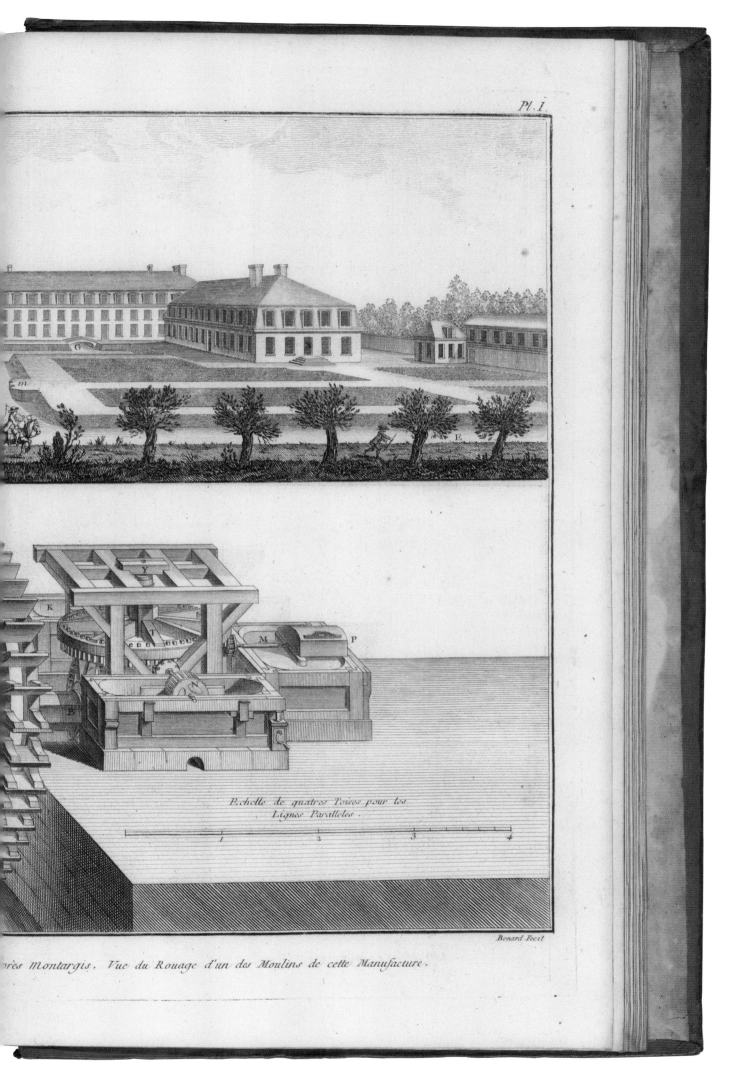

1757 **John Baskerville** Virgil, *Bucolica, Georgica, et Aeneis*. Birmingham: John Baskerville, 1757. x, 432 pp. 29 cm.

The Englishman John Baskerville (1707–75) is famous for the printing types named after him. They were often copied and are now even available in digital form. Baskerville lived most of his life in Birmingham, where he worked first as a writing master and a cutter of letters in stone. A splendid slate that he apparently cut as his shop sign survives with its text in roman, italic and gothic lettering: 'Grave Stones cut in any of the Hands by John Baskervill writing-master'. He later made a fortune as a manufacturer of japanned wares.

In around 1750, Baskerville began working intensely in book production, paying special attention to printing types. In a foreword, he wrote: 'Having been an early admirer of the beauty of Letters, I became insensibly desirous of contributing to the perfection of them.' He followed the style of contemporary calligraphy, influenced by the pointed pen and engraved lettering. His types had a greater contrast and more vertical axis than Caslon's. To retain their refined forms in print, he successfully attempted to improve all aspects of production, from ink and paper to the press and the actual printing.

His first book, shown here, was published in May 1757 in royal quarto format. The list of subscribers included Oxford and Cambridge scholars, along with leading citizens of Birmingham and other cities. Many consider this undecorated Virgil, with its simple elegance, his greatest work. To Baskerville's disappointment, his expensive but editorially sloppy books were never a financial success, but they and his types were extremely influential internationally. ML

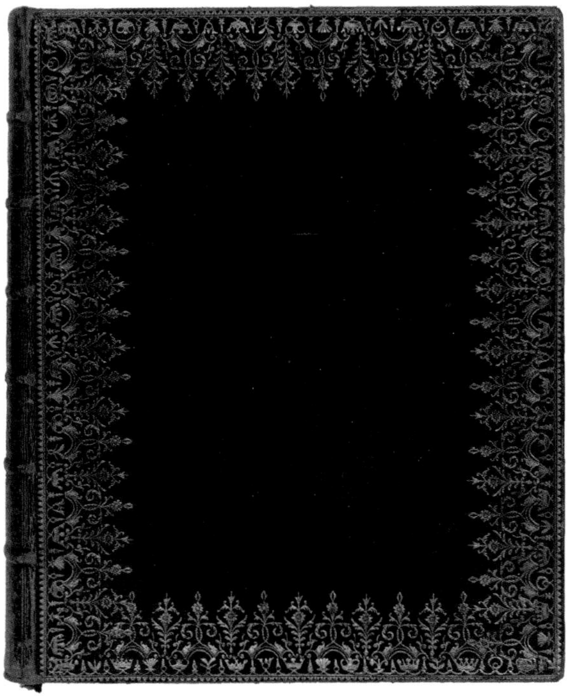

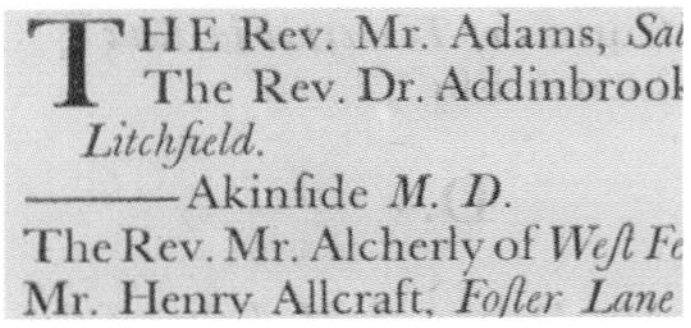

THE Rev. Mr. Adams, *Sa*
The Rev. Dr. Addinbrook
Litchfield.
——— Akinfide *M. D.*
The Rev. Mr. Alcherly of *Weſt F*
Mr. Henry Allcraft, *Foſter Lane*

Baskerville's letters were cut by John Handy (1720?-92/93), who later worked for Baskerville's widow as well. Handy has been described as a 'very honest man which performed all the manual operations both in respect of filing the punches, making the letter moulds and every other improvement which Mr Baskerville made in printing.'

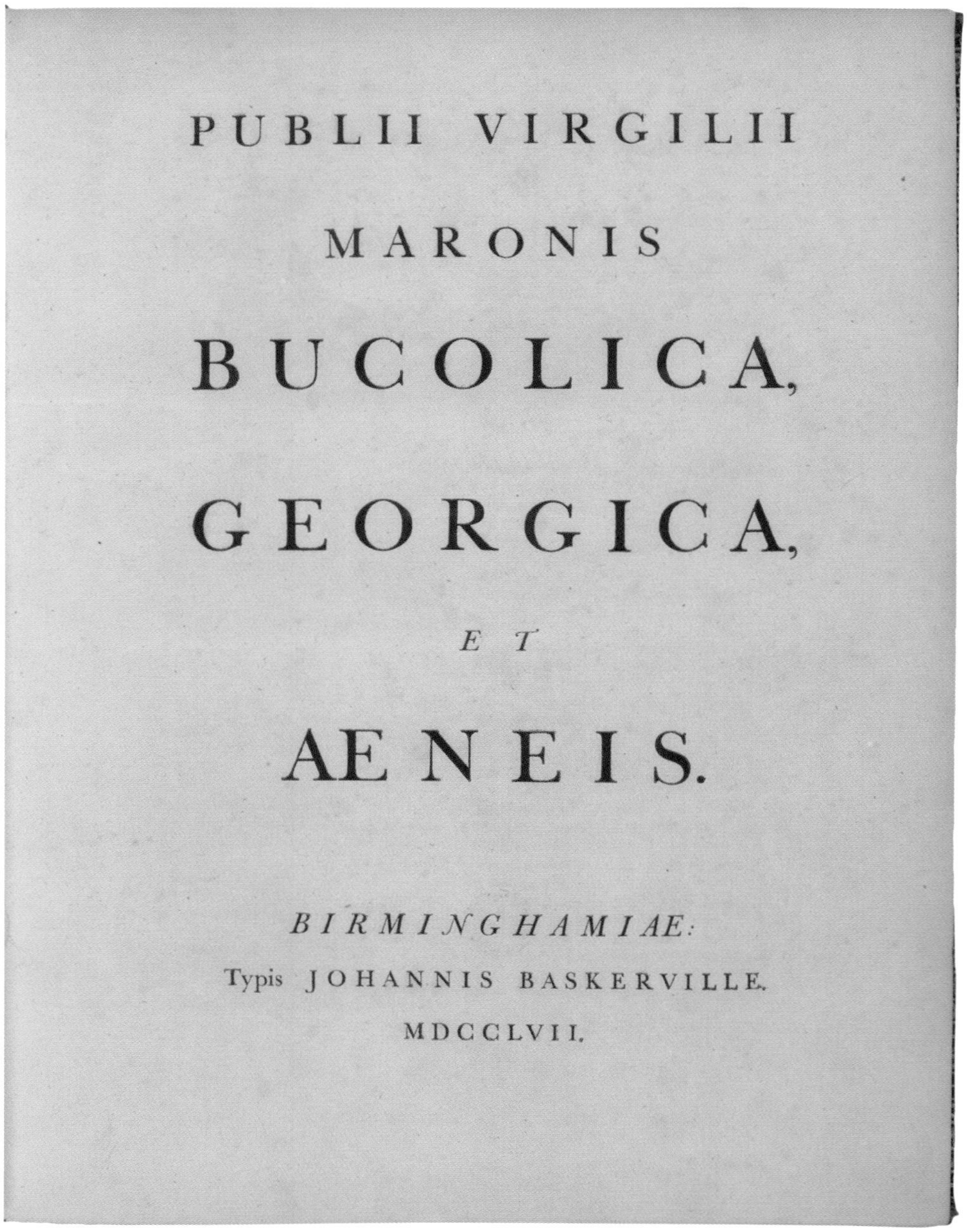

PUBLII VIRGILII
MARONIS
BUCOLICA,
GEORGICA,
ET
AENEIS.

BIRMINGHAMIAE:
Typis JOHANNIS BASKERVILLE.
MDCCLVII.

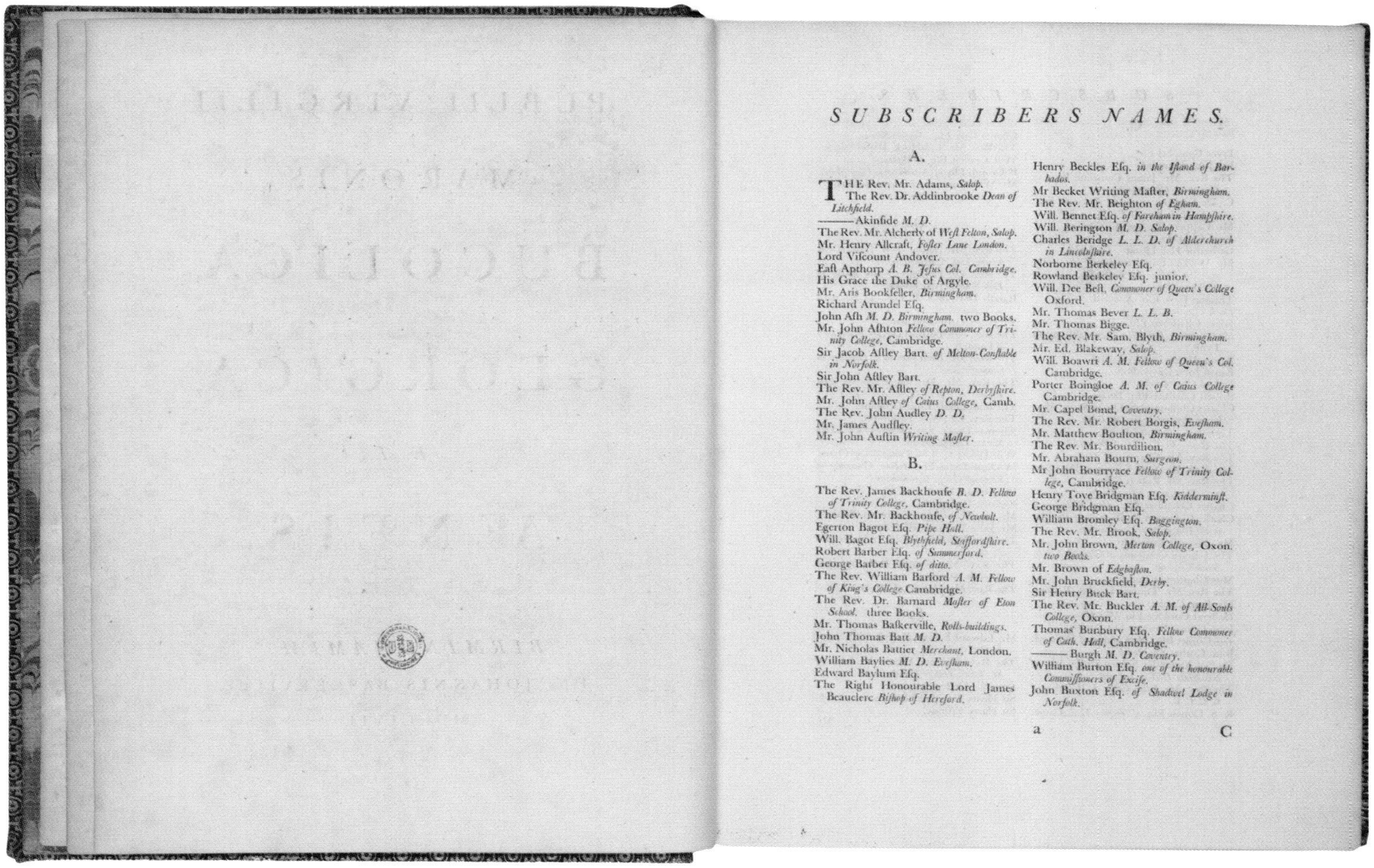

SUBSCRIBERS NAMES.

A.

THE Rev. Mr. Adams, *Salop.*
The Rev. Dr. Addinbrooke *Dean of Litchfield.*
———Akinſide *M. D.*
The Rev. Mr. Alcherly of *Weſt Felton, Salop.*
Mr. Henry Allcraft, *Foſter Lane London.*
Lord Viſcount Andover.
Eaſt Apthorp *A. B. Jeſus Col. Cambridge.*
His Grace the Duke of Argyle.
Mr. Aris Bookſeller, *Birmingham.*
Richard Arundel Eſq.
John Aſh *M. D. Birmingham.* two Books.
Mr. John Aſhton *Fellow Commoner of Trinity College,* Cambridge.
Sir Jacob Aſtley Bart. *of Melton-Conſtable in Norfolk.*
Sir John Aſtley Bart.
The Rev. Mr. Aſtley *of Repton, Derbyſhire.*
Mr. John Aſtley *of Caius College,* Camb.
The Rev. John Audley *D. D.*
Mr. James Audſley.
Mr. John Auſtin *Writing Maſter.*

B.

The Rev. James Backhouſe *B. D. Fellow of Trinity College,* Cambridge.
The Rev. Mr. Backhouſe, *of Newbolt.*
Egerton Bagot Eſq. *Pipe Hall.*
Will. Bagot Eſq. *Blythfield, Staffordſhire.*
Robert Barber Eſq. *of Summerford.*
George Barber Eſq. *of ditto.*
The Rev. William Barford *A. M. Fellow of King's College* Cambridge.
The Rev. Dr. Barnard *Maſter of Eton School.* three Books.
Mr. Thomas Baſkerville, *Rolls-buildings.*
John Thomas Batt *M. D.*
Mr. Nicholas Battier *Merchant,* London.
William Baylies *M. D. Eveſham.*
Edward Baylum Eſq.
The Right Honourable Lord James Beauclerc *Biſhop of Hereford.*
Henry Beckles Eſq. *in the Iſland of Barbados.*
Mr Becket Writing Maſter, *Birmingham.*
The Rev. Mr. Beighton *of Egham.*
Will. Bennet Eſq. *of Fareham in Hampſhire.*
Will. Berington *M. D. Salop.*
Charles Beridge *L. L. D. of Alderchurch in Lincolnſhire.*
Norborne Berkeley Eſq.
Rowland Berkeley Eſq. junior.
Will. Dee Beſt, *Commoner of Queen's College* Oxford.
Mr. Thomas Bever *L. L. B.*
Mr. Thomas Bigge.
The Rev. Mr. Sam. Blyth, *Birmingham.*
Mr. Ed. Blakeway, *Salop.*
Will. Boawri *A. M. Fellow of Queen's Col.* Cambridge.
Porter Boingloe *A. M. of Caius College* Cambridge.
Mr. Capel Bond, *Coventry.*
The Rev. Mr. Robert Borgis, *Eveſham.*
Mr. Matthew Boulton, *Birmingham.*
The Rev. Mr. Bourdilion.
Mr. Abraham Bourn, *Surgeon.*
Mr John Bourryace *Fellow of Trinity College,* Cambridge.
Henry Toye Bridgman Eſq. *Kidderminſt.*
George Bridgman Eſq.
William Bromley Eſq. *Baggington.*
The Rev. Mr. Brook, *Salop.*
Mr. John Brown, *Merton College,* Oxon. *two Books.*
Mr. Brown of *Edgbaſton.*
Mr. John Bruckfield, *Derby.*
Sir Henry Buck Bart.
The Rev. Mr. Buckler *A. M. of All-Souls College,* Oxon.
Thomas Bunbury Eſq. *Fellow Commoner of Cath. Hall,* Cambridge.
——— Burgh *M. D. Coventry.*
William Burton Eſq. *one of the honourable Commiſſioners of Exciſe.*
John Buxton Eſq. *of Shadwel Lodge in Norfolk.*

a C

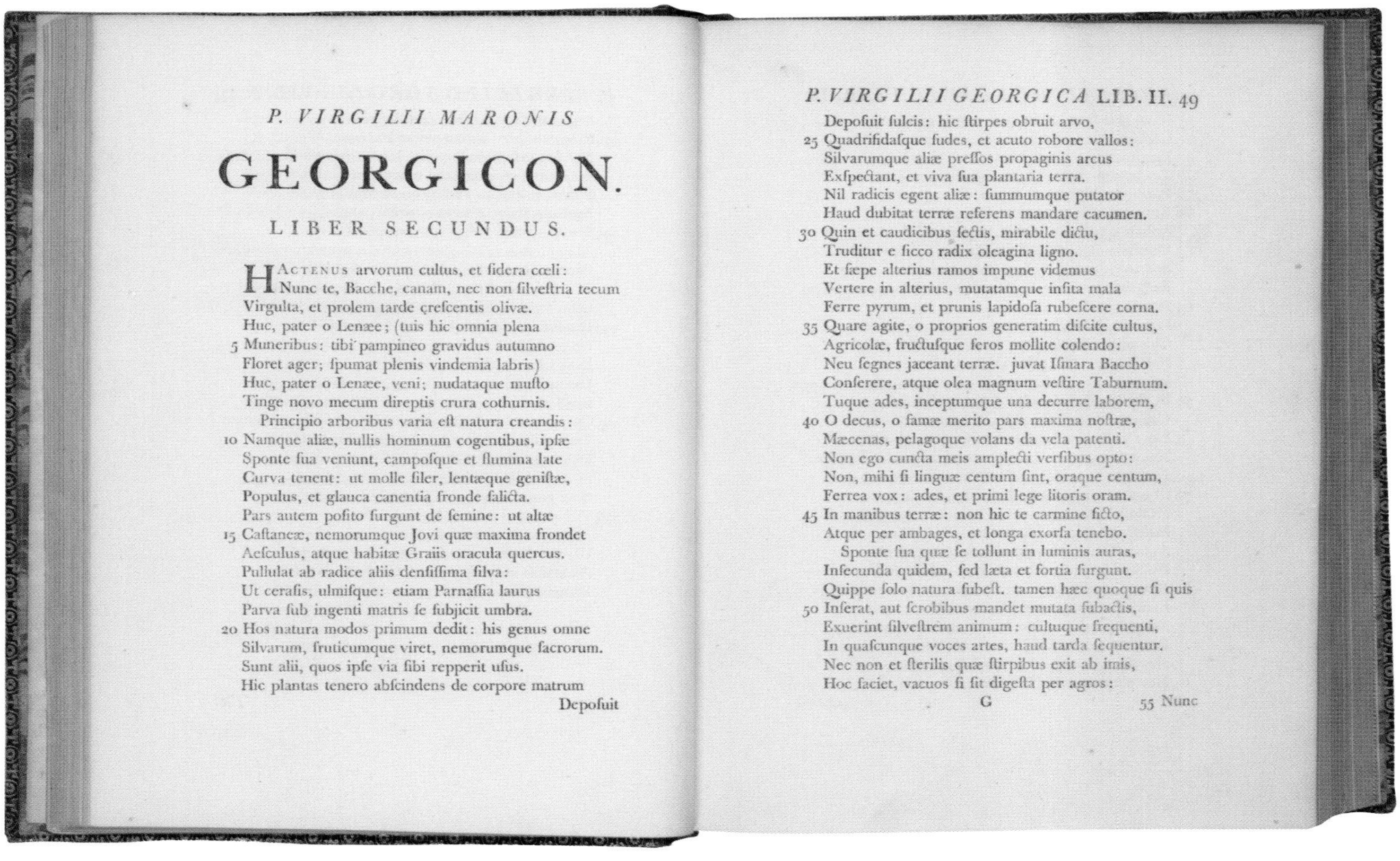

P. VIRGILII MARONIS

GEORGICON.

LIBER SECUNDUS.

HACTENUS arvorum cultus, et ſidera cœli:
Nunc te, Bacche, canam, nec non ſilveſtria tecum
Virgulta, et prolem tarde creſcentis olivæ.
Huc, pater o Lenæe; (tuis hic omnia plena
Muneribus: tibi pampineo gravidus autumno
Floret ager; ſpumat plenis vindemia labris)
Huc, pater o Lenæe, veni; nudataque muſto
Tinge novo mecum direptis crura cothurnis.
Principio arboribus varia eſt natura creandis:
Namque aliæ, nullis hominum cogentibus, ipſæ
Sponte ſua veniunt, campoſque et flumina late
Curva tenent: ut molle ſiler, lentæque geniſtæ,
Populus, et glauca canentia fronde ſalicta.
Pars autem poſito ſurgunt de ſemine: ut altæ
Caſtaneæ, nemorumque Jovi quæ maxima frondet
Aeſculus, atque habitæ Graiis oracula quercus.
Pullulat ab radice aliis denſiſſima ſilva:
Ut ceraſis, ulmiſque: etiam Parnaſſia laurus
Parva ſub ingenti matris ſe ſubjicit umbra.
Hos natura modos primum dedit: his genus omne
Silvarum, fruticumque viret, nemorumque ſacrorum.
Sunt alii, quos ipſe via ſibi repperit uſus.
Hic plantas tenero abſcindens de corpore matrum
Depoſuit

P. VIRGILII GEORGICA LIB. II. 49

Depoſuit ſulcis: hic ſtirpes obruit arvo,
Quadrifidaſque ſudes, et acuto robore vallos:
Silvarumque aliæ preſſos propaginis arcus
Exſpectant, et viva ſua plantaria terra.
Nil radicis egent aliæ: ſummumque putator
Haud dubitat terræ referens mandare cacumen.
Quin et caudicibus ſectis, mirabile dictu,
Truditur e ſicco radix oleagina ligno.
Et ſæpe alterius ramos impune videmus
Vertere in alterius, mutatamque inſita mala
Ferre pyrum, et prunis lapidoſa rubeſcere corna.
Quare agite, o proprios generatim diſcite cultus,
Agricolæ, fructuſque feros mollite colendo:
Neu ſegnes jaceant terræ. juvat Iſmara Baccho
Conſerere, atque olea magnum veſtire Taburnum.
Tuque ades, inceptumque una decurre laborem,
O decus, o famæ merito pars maxima noſtræ,
Mæcenas, pelagoque volans da vela patenti.
Non ego cuncta meis amplecti verſibus opto:
Non, mihi ſi linguæ centum ſint, oraque centum,
Ferrea vox: ades, et primi lege litoris oram.
In manibus terræ: non hic te carmine ficto,
Atque per ambages, et longa exorſa tenebo.
Sponte ſua quæ ſe tollunt in luminis auras,
Infecunda quidem, ſed læta et fortia ſurgunt.
Quippe ſolo natura ſubeſt. tamen hæc quoque ſi quis
Inſerat, aut ſcrobibus mandet mutata ſubactis,
Exuerint ſilveſtrem animum: cultuque frequenti,
In quaſcunque voces artes, haud tarda ſequentur.
Nec non et ſterilis quæ ſtirpibus exit ab imis,
Hoc faciet, vacuos ſi ſit digeſta per agros:
G Nunc

1764 **Pierre-Simon Fournier** Pierre-Simon Fournier, *Manuel typographique, utile aux gens de lettres, & à ceux qui exercent les différentes parties de l'art de l'imprimerie*. Paris: Barbou, 1764–'1766' (= 1768). 2 vols. 18 cm. Illustrators: Pierre-Simon Fournier (?) (16 plates); Hubert François Gravelot and Jacques de Sève (frontispieces). Engraver: Etienne Fessard (frontispieces).

Pierre-Simon Fournier le Jeune (1712–68) learned typefounding in Paris at the former Le Bé foundry, associated with his family since 1698. He first produced wood-engraved vignettes, then large letters for casting, perhaps in sand from wooden patterns.

The Enlightenment encouraged the scientific study of trade practices that had long been passed down by apprenticeship, reflected in the Académie des Sciences's unpublished study of type and printing. It included not only the engraved plates that served as models for the Romain du Roi (1699–*c.* 1730), but also a table of measured body sizes. Fournier published a similar table in 1737, only one year after he began cutting type. He kept his body sizes closer to the traditional ones by setting his point equal to $^1/_{72}$nd of his own inch, somewhat smaller than that based on the *pied du roi*. Fournier distributed specimens by his own foundry in 1739, including a few traditional types cut by the Le Bé family. Those he cut himself combined traditional styles, influences from the Romain du Roi and some innovations of his own, especially in the italic.

Fournier's account of typefounding in Diderot's *Encyclopédie* (1751) may have inspired the more ambitious account illustrated here: the first detailed book devoted to typefounding and punchcutting. Fournier appears not to have known Joseph Moxon's 1683 *Mechanick Exercises* (see page 168), which included chapters on the same subjects. In 1764, Fournier issued an extensive specimen for his foundry, reissuing its specimens in this manual. JAL

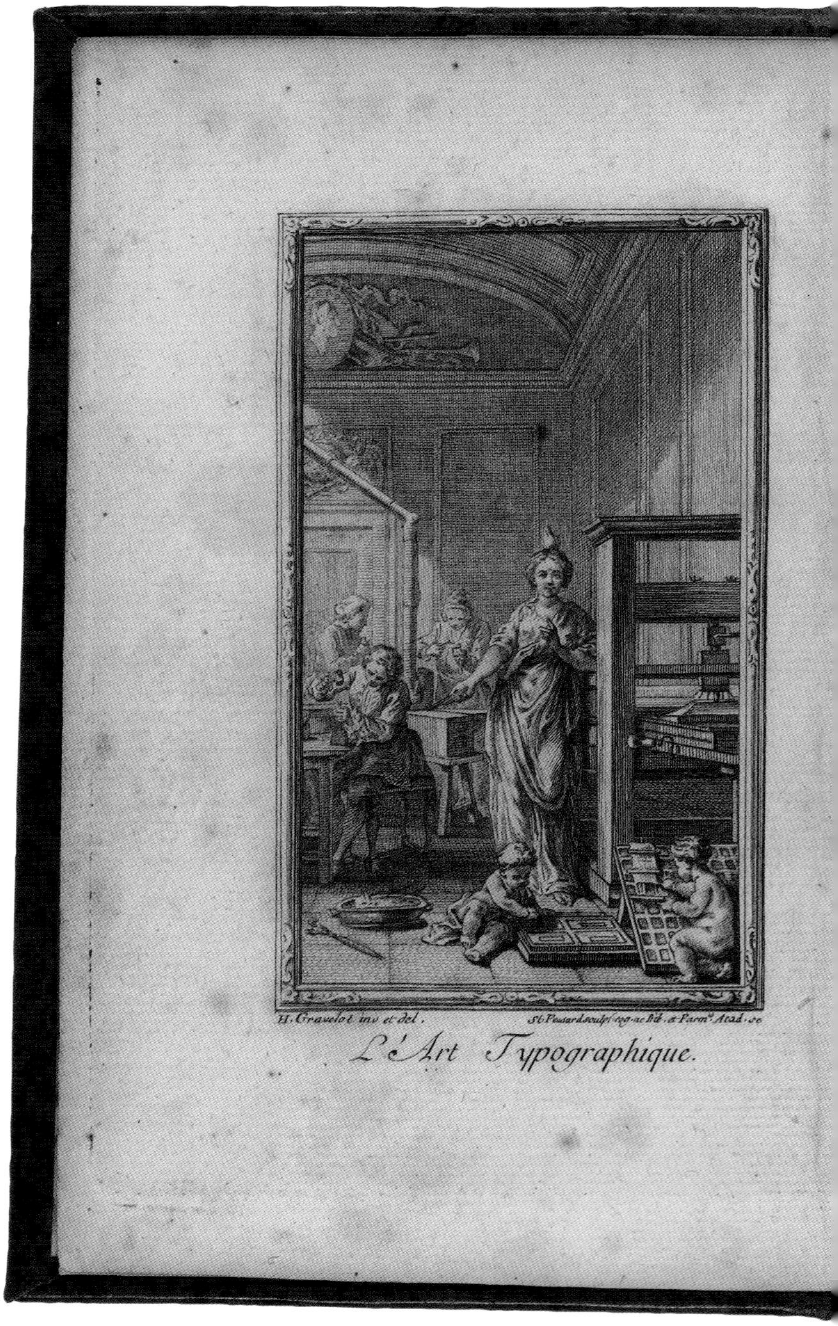

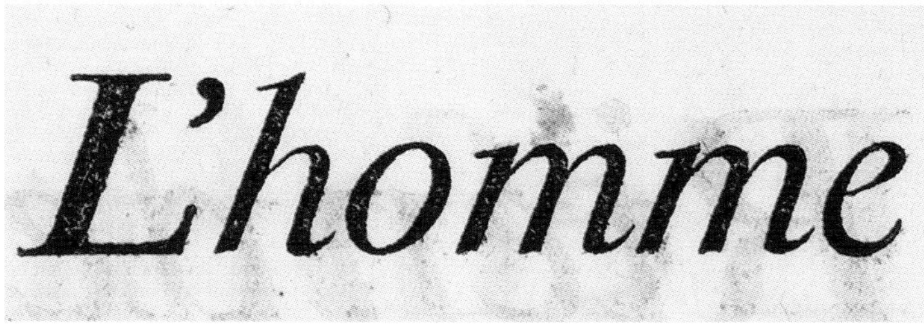

This is Fournier's first italic (cut 1736, used 1737). The roman-like serifs that replaced the traditional arched leading strokes in the i, j, m, n, p, q, r and u established what would remain a standard French characteristic for more than a century. Louis Luce may have anticipated this in his lost 1732 specimen.

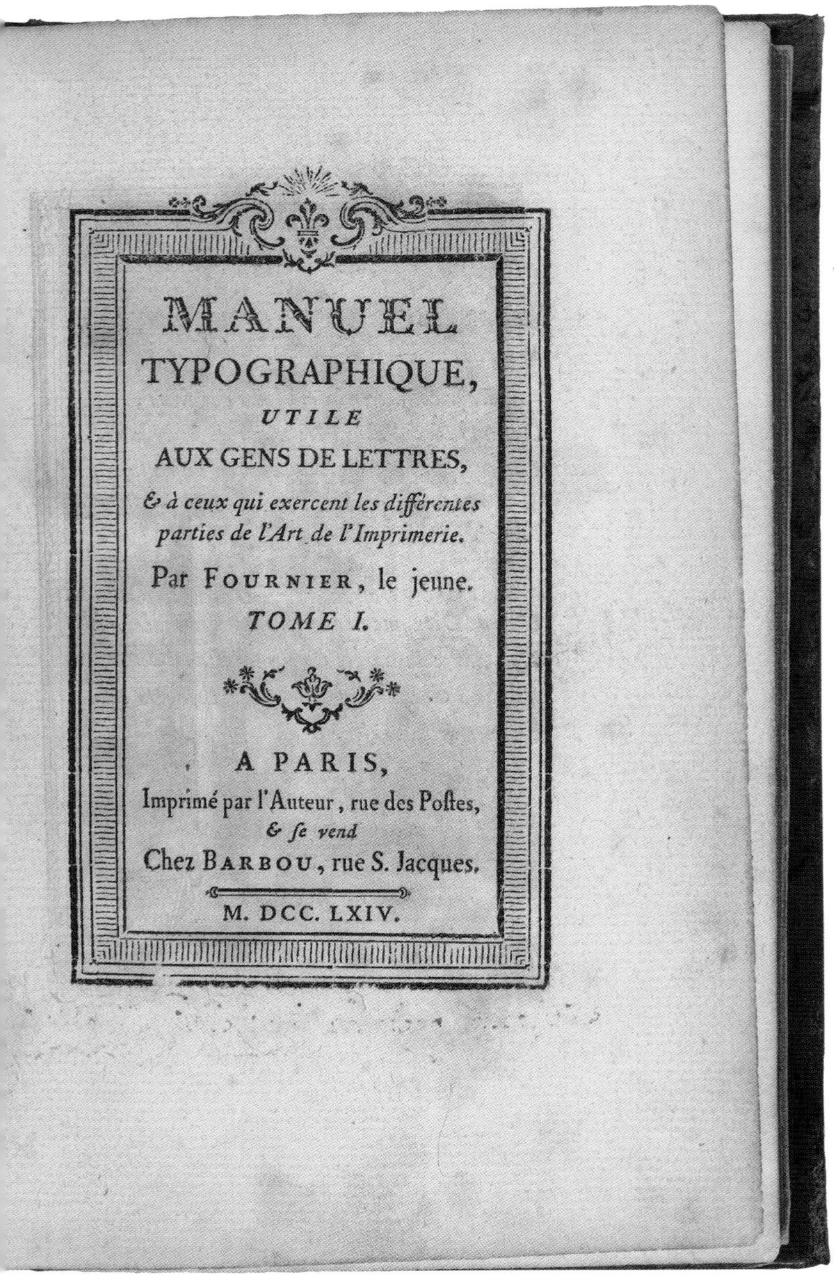
MANUEL
TYPOGRAPHIQUE,
UTILE
AUX GENS DE LETTRES,
& à ceux qui exercent les différentes parties de l'Art de l'Imprimerie.
Par FOURNIER, le jeune.
TOME I.
A PARIS,
Imprimé par l'Auteur, rue des Poftes,
& fe vend
Chez BARBOU, rue S. Jacques.
M. DCC. LXIV.

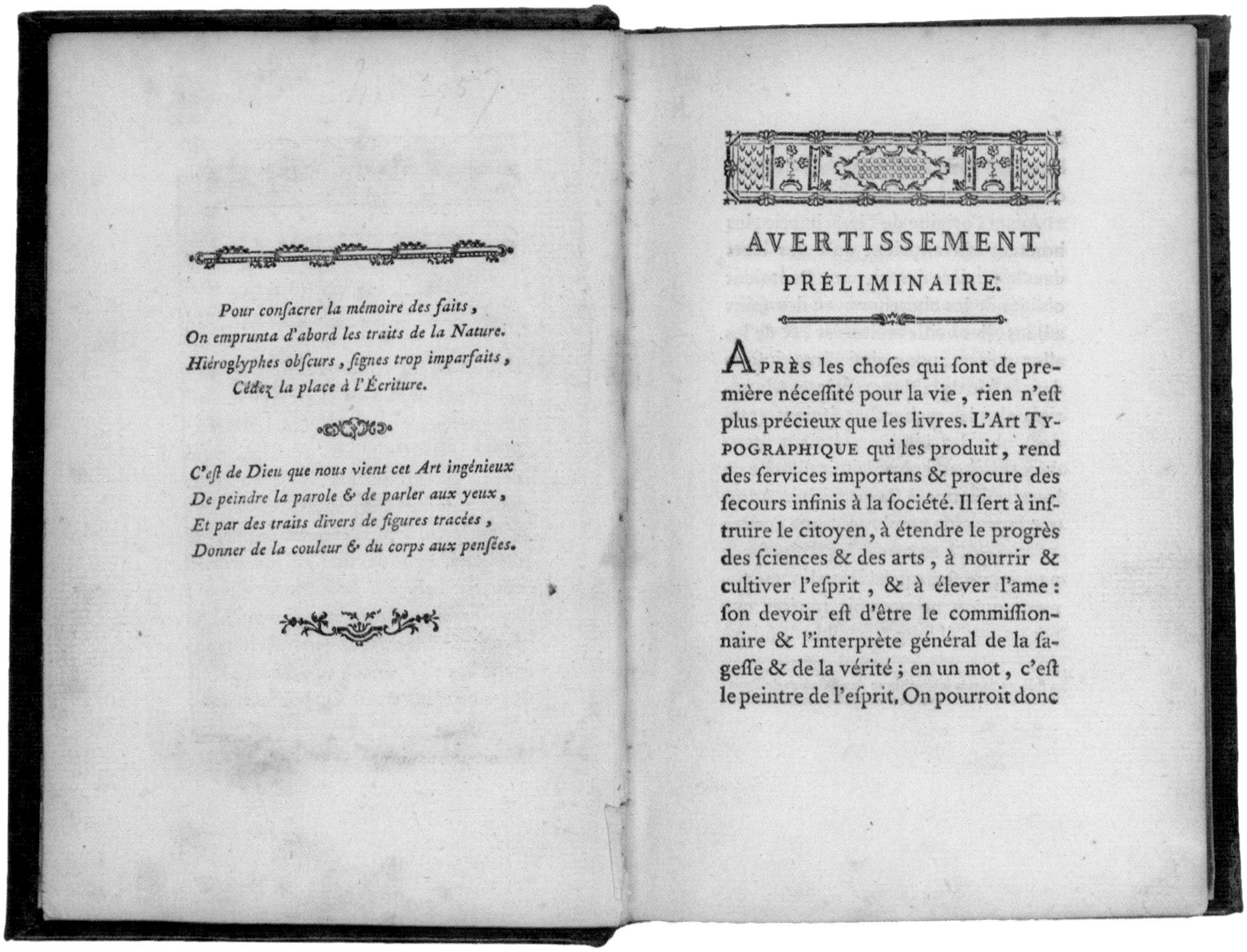
Pour consacrer la mémoire des faits,
On emprunta d'abord les traits de la Nature.
Hiéroglyphes obscurs, signes trop imparfaits,
Cédez la place à l'Écriture.
C'est de Dieu que nous vient cet Art ingénieux
De peindre la parole & de parler aux yeux,
Et par des traits divers de figures tracées,
Donner de la couleur & du corps aux pensées.
AVERTISSEMENT
PRÉLIMINAIRE.
APRÈS les choses qui sont de première nécessité pour la vie, rien n'est plus précieux que les livres. L'Art TYPOGRAPHIQUE qui les produit, rend des services importans & procure des secours infinis à la société. Il sert à instruire le citoyen, à étendre le progrès des sciences & des arts, à nourrir & cultiver l'esprit, & à élever l'ame: son devoir est d'être le commissionnaire & l'interprète général de la sagesse & de la vérité; en un mot, c'est le peintre de l'esprit. On pourroit donc

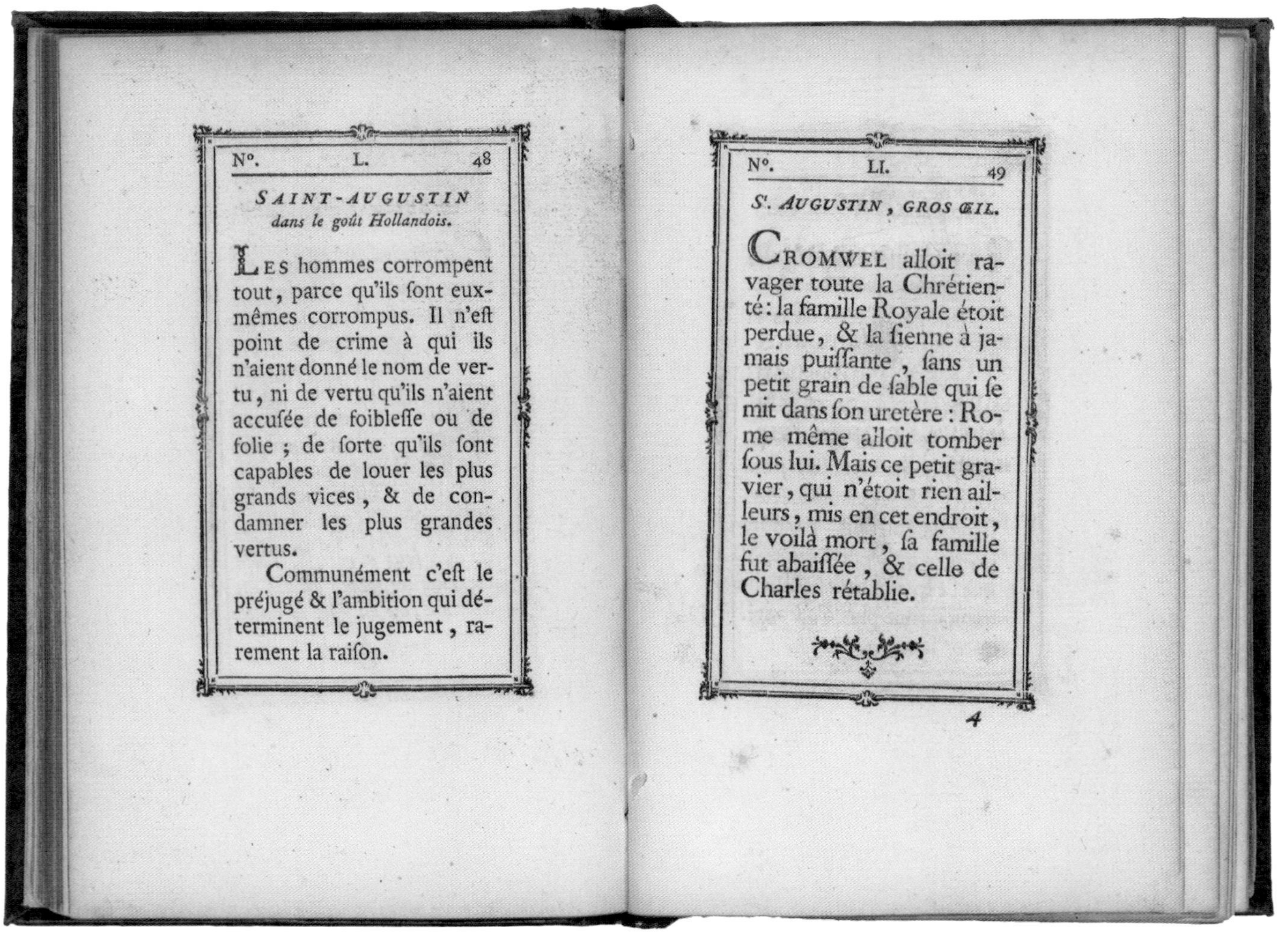
N°. L. 48
SAINT-AUGUSTIN
dans le goût Hollandois.
LES hommes corrompent tout, parce qu'ils sont eux-mêmes corrompus. Il n'est point de crime à qui ils n'aient donné le nom de vertu, ni de vertu qu'ils n'aient accusée de foiblesse ou de folie; de sorte qu'ils sont capables de louer les plus grands vices, & de condamner les plus grandes vertus.
Communément c'est le préjugé & l'ambition qui déterminent le jugement, rarement la raison.
N°. LI. 49
S'. AUGUSTIN, GROS ŒIL.
CROMWEL alloit ravager toute la Chrétienté: la famille Royale étoit perdue, & la sienne à jamais puissante, sans un petit grain de sable qui se mit dans son uretère: Rome même alloit tomber sous lui. Mais ce petit gravier, qui n'étoit rien ailleurs, mis en cet endroit, le voilà mort, sa famille fut abaissée, & celle de Charles rétablie.
4

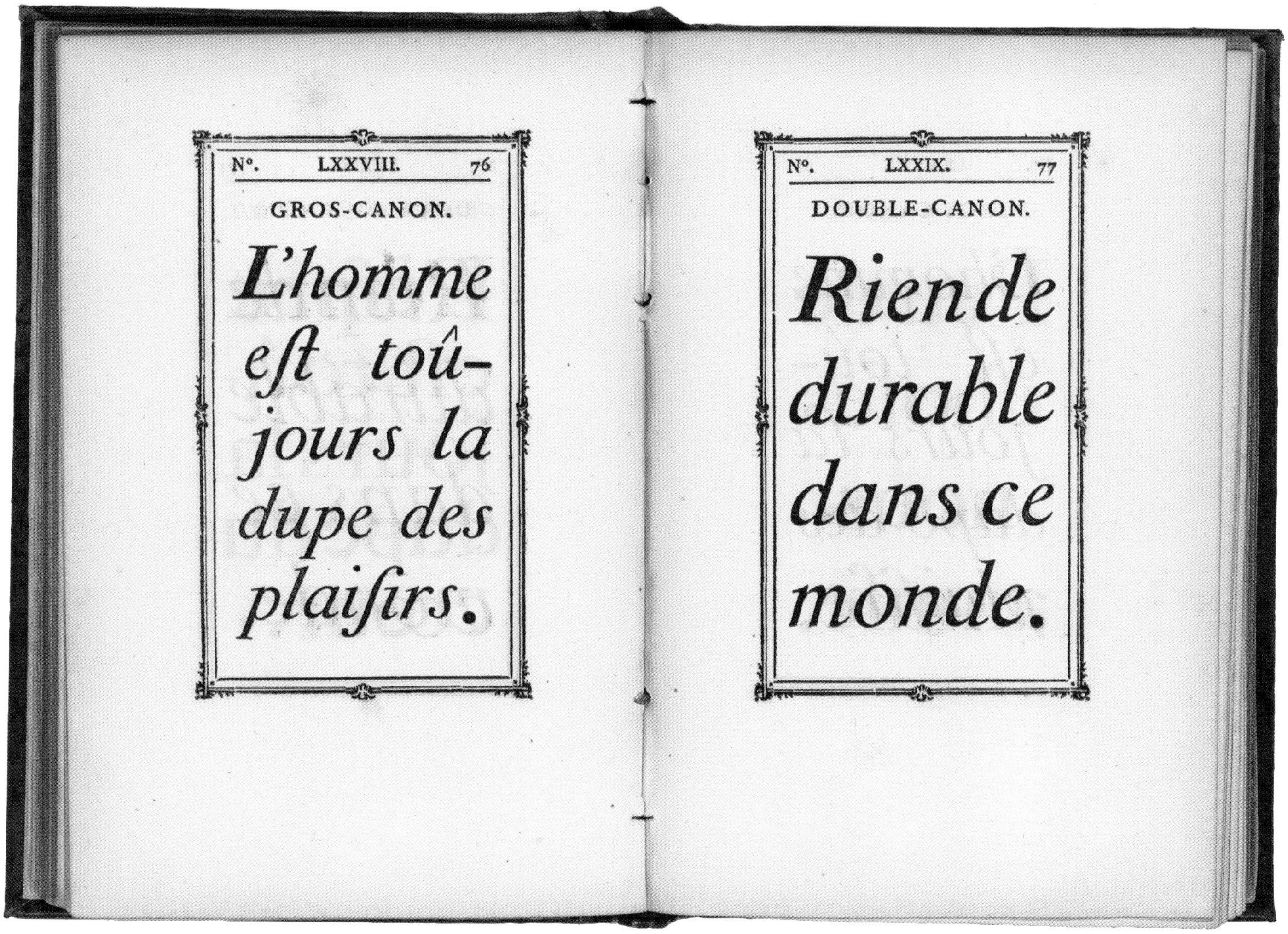
N°. LXXVIII. 76
GROS-CANON.
L'homme eſt toû-jours la dupe des plaiſirs.
N°. LXXIX. 77
DOUBLE-CANON.
Rien de durable dans ce monde.

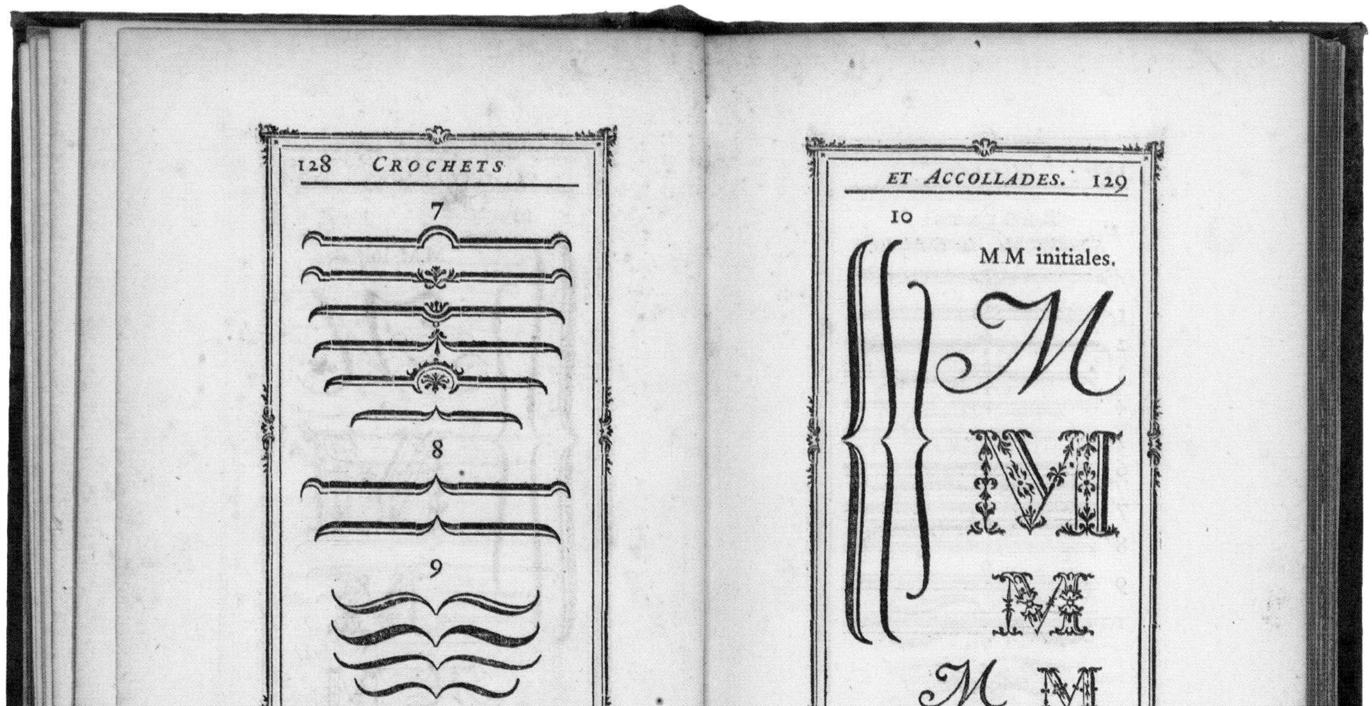
128 CROCHETS
7
8
9
ET ACCOLLADES. 129
10
MM initiales.
9

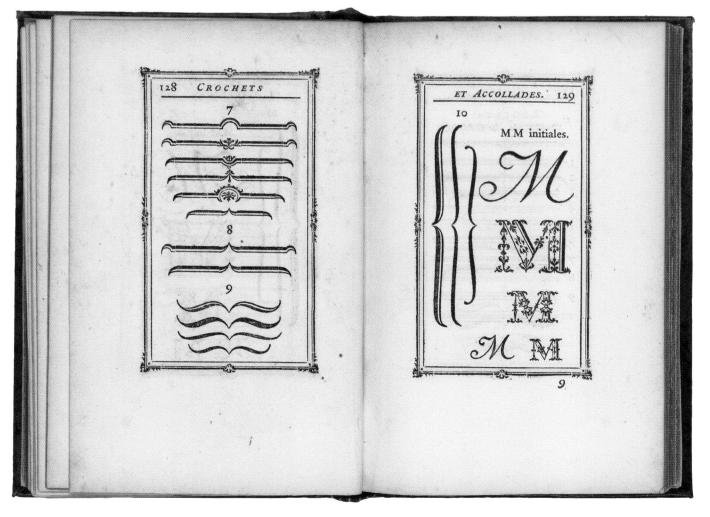

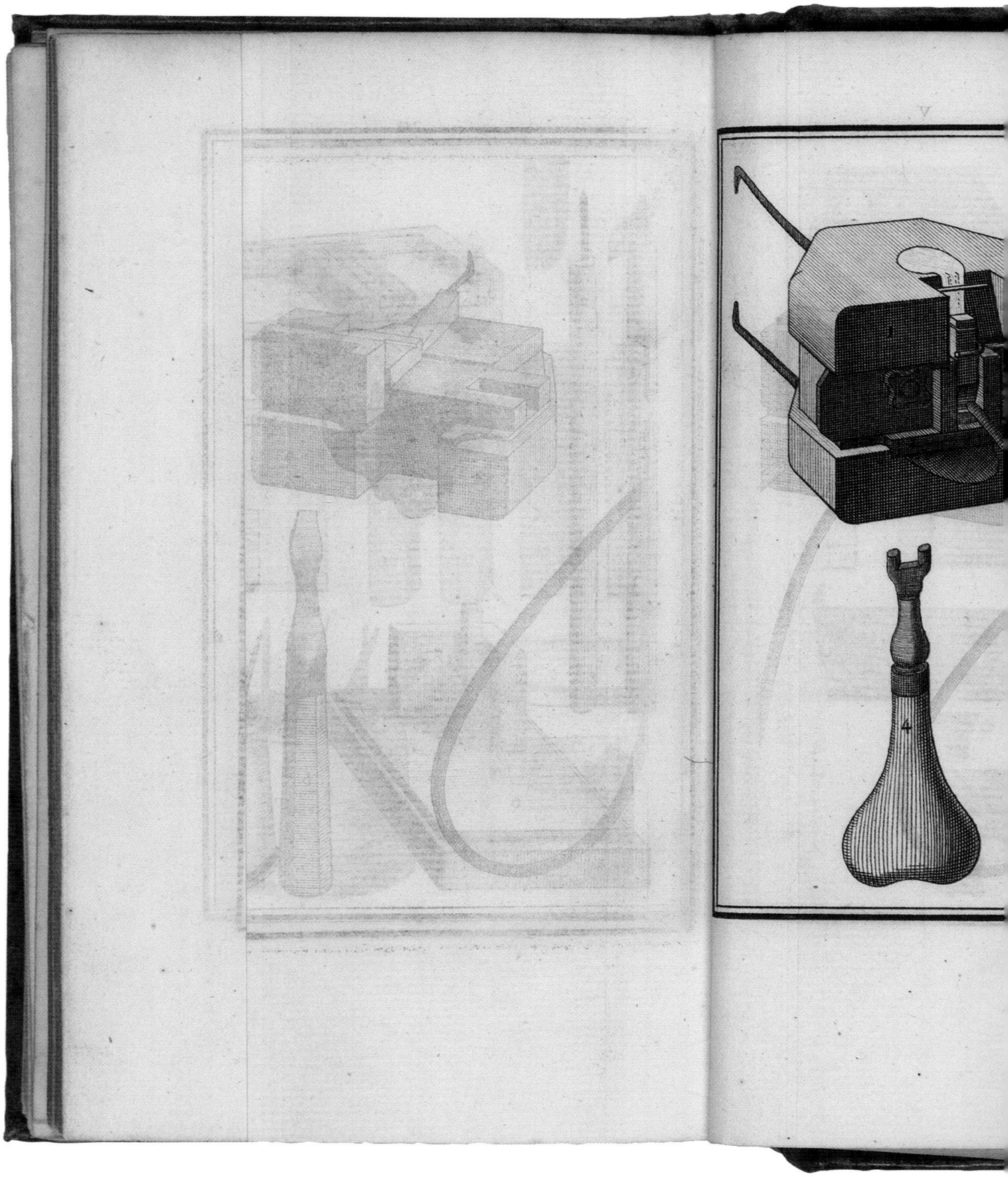
4

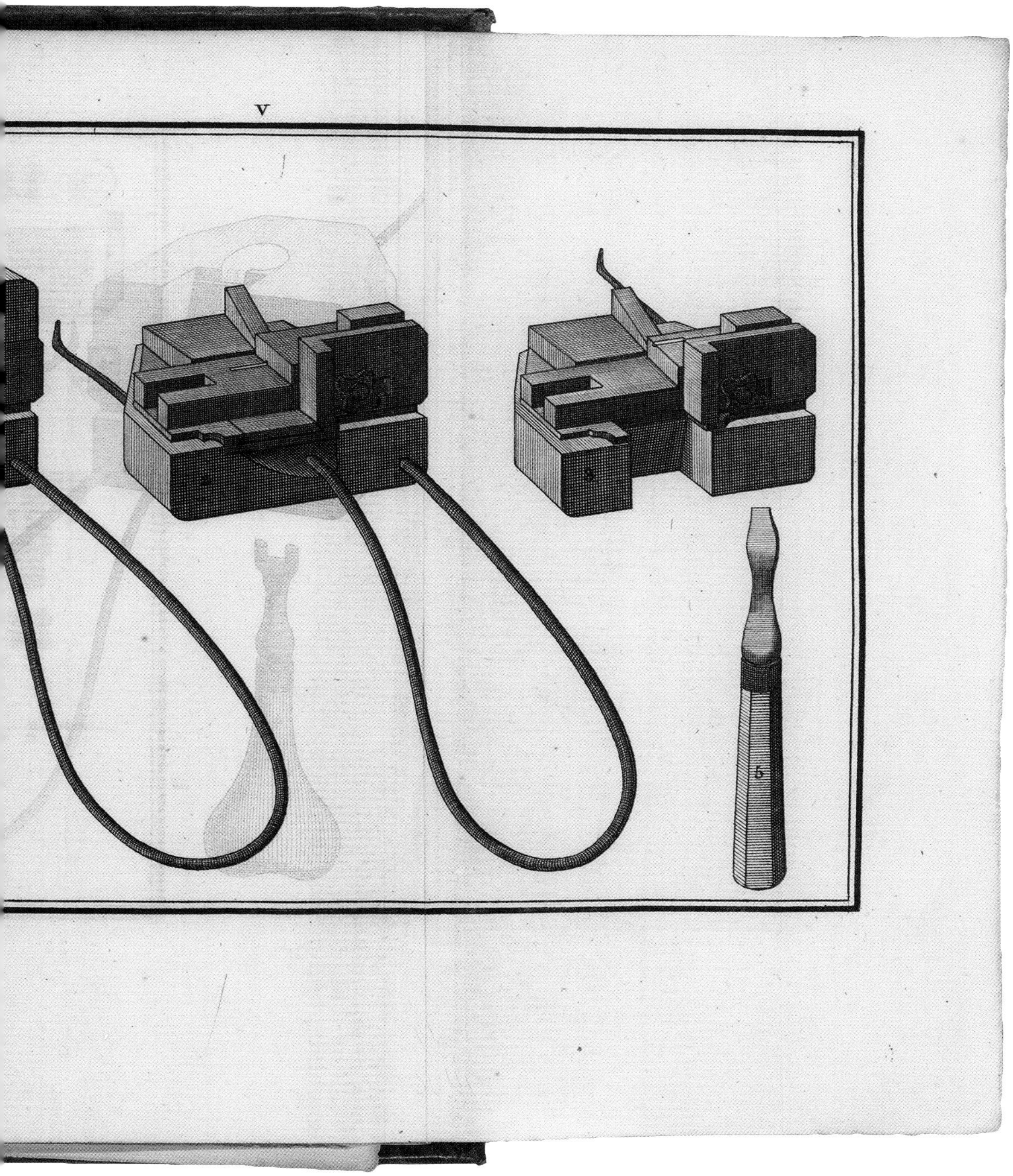
V

1766 **Johannes Enschedé** **Leopold Mozart, *Grondig onderwijs in het behandelen der viool*. Haarlem: Johannes Enschedé, 1766. 20, 259 pp. 26 cm. Engraver: Cornelis van Noorde, after anonymous illustrations in the first edition.**

This is the first Dutch edition of Leopold Mozart's famous and influential violin instruction book, *A Treatise on the Fundamental Principles of Violin Playing*, and surpasses the original 1756 German edition typographically. It was published following the 1765/66 Dutch concert tour by Leopold's precocious son Wolfgang Amadeus, born in the year that the German edition first appeared.

Early music types required one impression for the notes and another for the staves, increasing costs and requiring care to ensure that the two impressions registered properly. Single-impression music type appeared in about 1527, each piece of type including one note on a vertical slice of the staff. Ill-suited to intricate music, this system lost ground to engraved copperplates and punched pewter plates, which could render the most elaborate polyphonic music, but whose higher costs and limited press runs begged a better solution.

From 1753 to 1766, at least seven typefounders issued letterpress music types that divided the staff with notes not only vertically but also horizontally, allowing printers to build up polyphonic or other complicated music from a grid of cast elements. Jacques François Rosart made the first (1753), but Breitkopf (1756) and Fournier (1756, whose system initially required two impressions) received more acclaim. The German-born Joan Michael Fleischman (1707–68) worked more than two years on his type for Enschedé, completing the 226 punches and 240 matrices in 1760. His extraordinary technical skill ensured that the separately cast elements joined almost seamlessly. The difficulty and expense of setting the type limited its use, but it proved so difficult to copy that Enschedé used its elements to create borders for security printing in 1794. JAL

The best music type of its kind, cut by Joan Michael Fleischman for Johannes Enschedé, was first used in 1761. The staves and notes are built up from a grid of cast elements, each on a Parel (5½ point) body. Only the final chapters feature examples of polyphonic music.

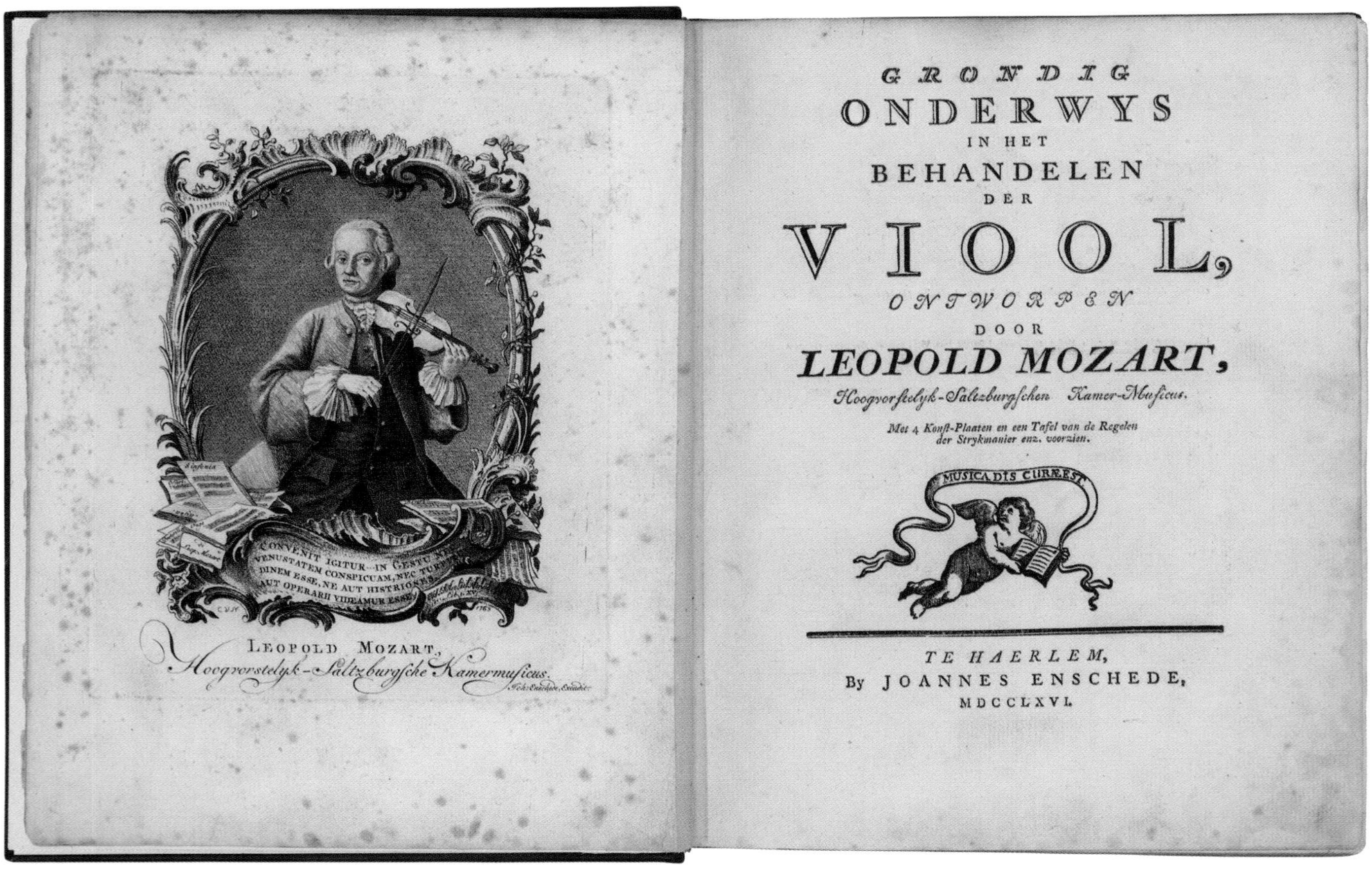

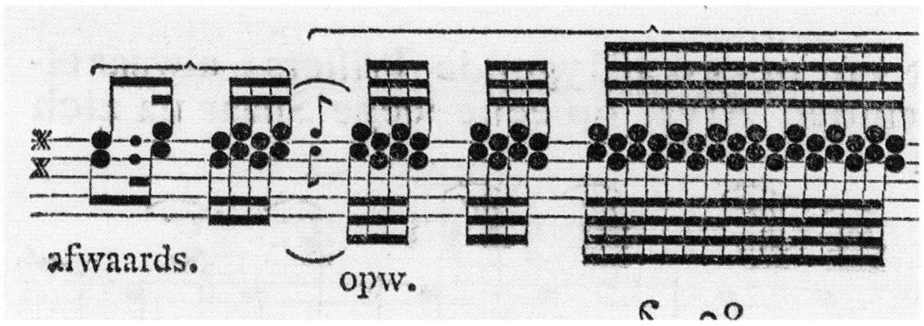

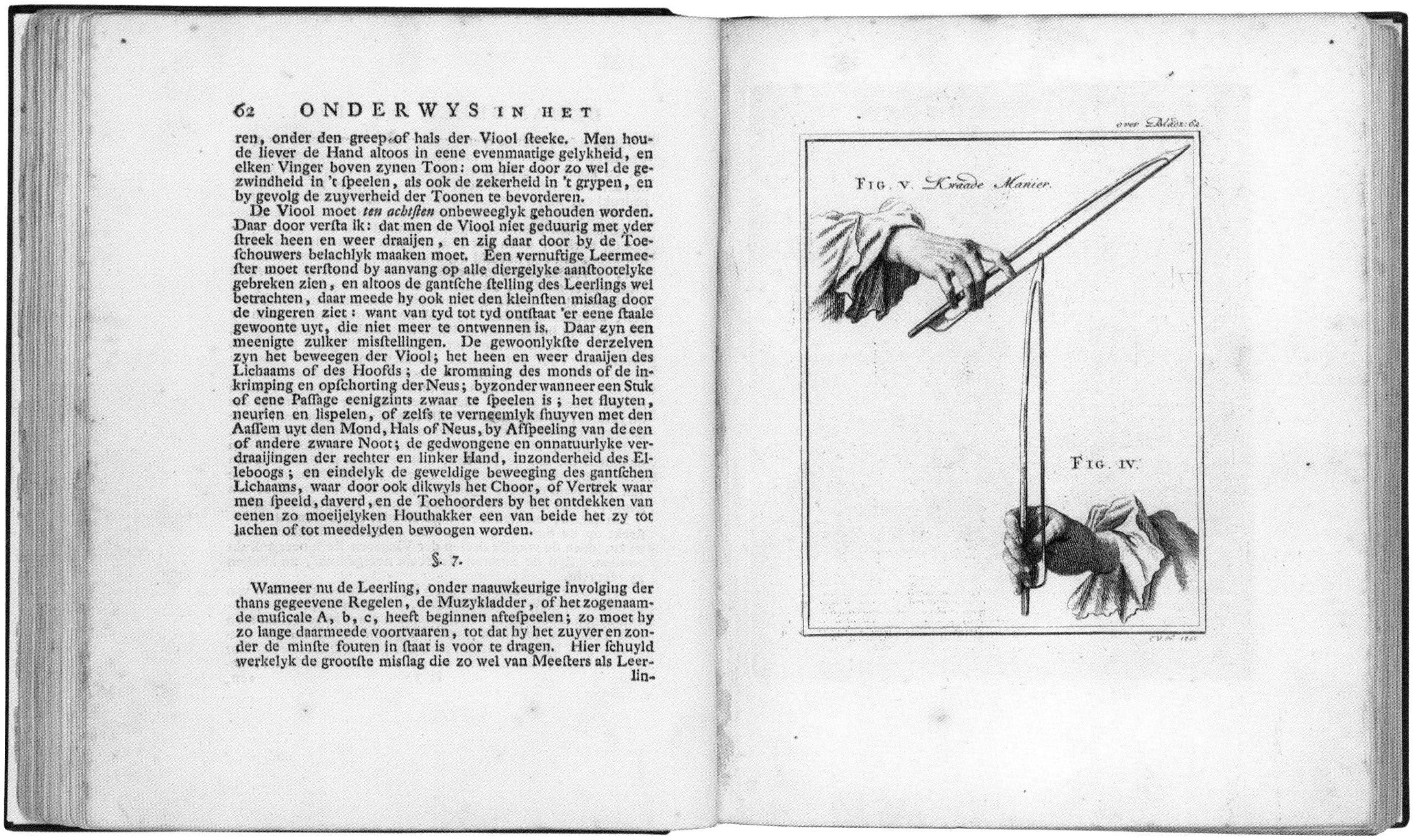
62 ONDERWYS IN HET

ren, onder den greep of hals der Viool ſteeke. Men houde liever de Hand altoos in eene evenmaatige gelykheid, en elken Vinger boven zynen Toon: om hier door zo wel de gezwindheid in 't ſpeelen, als ook de zekerheid in 't grypen, en by gevolg de zuyverheid der Toonen te bevorderen.

De Viool moet *ten achtſten* onbeweeglyk gehouden worden. Daar door verſta ik: dat men de Viool niet geduurig met yder ſtreek heen en weer draaijen, en zig daar door by de Toeſchouwers belachlyk maaken moet. Een vernuftige Leermeeſter moet terſtond by aanvang op alle diergelyke aanſtootelyke gebreken zien, en altoos de gantſche ſtelling des Leerlings wel betrachten, daar meede hy ook niet den kleinſten miſſlag door de vingeren ziet: want van tyd tot tyd ontſtaat 'er eene ſtaale gewoonte uyt, die niet meer te ontwennen is. Daar zyn een meenigte zulker misſtellingen. De gewoonlykſte derzelven zyn het beweegen der Viool; het heen en weer draaijen des Lichaams of des Hoofds; de kromming des monds of de inkrimping en opſchorting der Neus; byzonder wanneer een Stuk of eene Paſſage eenigzints zwaar te ſpeelen is; het fluyten, neurien en lispelen, of zelfs te verneemlyk ſnuyven met den Aaſſem uyt den Mond, Hals of Neus, by Afſpeeling van de een of andere zwaare Noot; de gedwongene en onnatuurlyke verdraaijingen der rechter en linker Hand, inzonderheid des Elleboogs; en eindelyk de geweldige beweeging des gantſchen Lichaams, waar door ook dikwyls het Choor, of Vertrek waar men ſpeeld, daverd, en de Toehoorders by het ontdekken van eenen zo moeijelyken Houthakker een van beide het zy tot lachen of tot meedelyden bewoogen worden.

§. 7.

Wanneer nu de Leerling, onder naauwkeurige involging der thans gegeevene Regelen, de Muzykladder, of het zogenaamde muſicale A, b, c, heeft beginnen afteſpeelen; zo moet hy zo lange daarmeede voortvaaren, tot dat hy het zuyver en zonder de minſte fouten in ſtaat is voor te dragen. Hier ſchuyld werkelyk de grootſte miſſlag die zo wel van Meeſters als Leerlin-

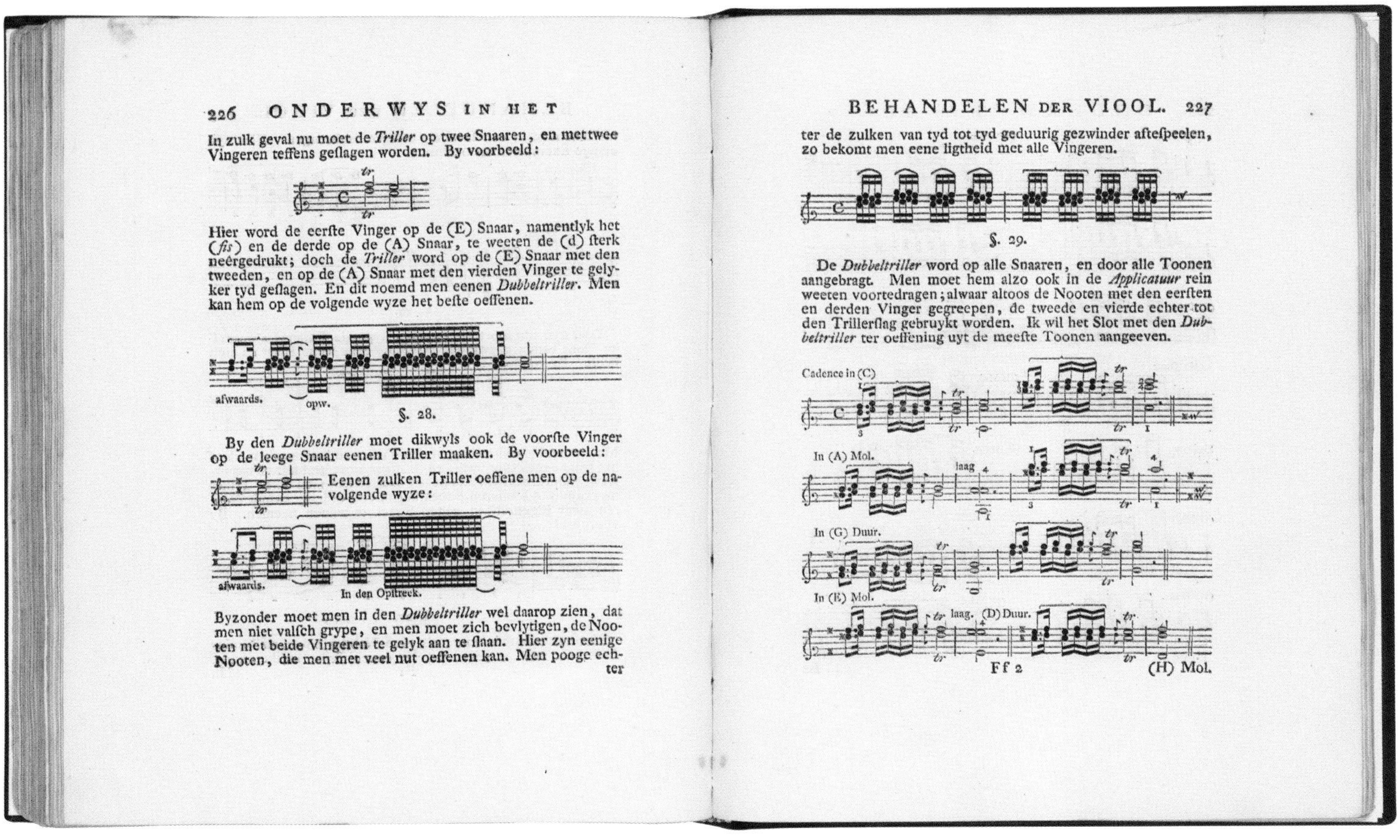
226 ONDERWYS IN HET

In zulk geval nu moet de *Triller* op twee Snaaren, en met twee Vingeren teſſens geſlagen worden. By voorbeeld:

Hier word de eerſte Vinger op de (E) Snaar, namentlyk het (*fis*) en de derde op de (A) Snaar, te weeten de (d) ſterk neêrgedrukt; doch de *Triller* word op de (E) Snaar met den tweeden, en op de (A) Snaar met den vierden Vinger te gelyker tyd geſlagen. En dit noemd men eenen *Dubbeltriller*. Men kan hem op de volgende wyze het beſte oeffenen.

afwaards. opw.

§. 28.

By den *Dubbeltriller* moet dikwyls ook de voorſte Vinger op de leege Snaar eenen Triller maaken. By voorbeeld:

Eenen zulken Triller oeffene men op de navolgende wyze:

afwaards. In den Opſtreek.

Byzonder moet men in den *Dubbeltriller* wel daarop zien, dat men niet valſch grype, en men moet zich bevlytigen, de Nooten met beide Vingeren te gelyk aan te ſlaan. Hier zyn eenige Nooten, die men met veel nut oeffenen kan. Men pooge ech-ter

BEHANDELEN DER VIOOL. 227

ter de zulken van tyd tot tyd geduurig gezwinder afteſpeelen, zo bekomt men eene ligtheid met alle Vingeren.

§. 29.

De *Dubbeltriller* word op alle Snaaren, en door alle Toonen aangebragt. Men moet hem alzo ook in de *Applicatuur* rein weeten voortedragen; alwaar altoos de Nooten met den eerſten en derden Vinger gegreepen, de tweede en vierde echter tot den Trillerſlag gebruykt worden. Ik wil het Slot met den *Dubbeltriller* ter oeffening uyt de meeſte Toonen aangeeven.

Cadence in (C)

In (A) Mol. laag

In (G) Duur.

In (E) Mol. laag. (D) Duur.

Ff 2 (H) Mol.

1771 **Louis-René Luce** Louis-René Luce, *Essai d'une nouvelle typographie, ornée de vignettes, fleurons, trophées, filets, cadres & cartels inventés, dessinés & exécutés par L. Luce, graveur du roi, pour son Imprimerie Royale*. Paris: J. Barbou, 1771 (= 1772). 97 leaves. 26 cm.

Phillipe Grandjean cut the first thirteen sizes of the French Imprimerie Royale's Romain du Roi and its italic, the first appearing in a 1699 specimen. Jean Alexandre assisted Grandjean from 1712, then succeeded him. Louis-René Luce (*c.* 1695?–1774) assisted Alexandre from 1726, married his daughter and succeeded him as *graveur du roi* in 1738. Luce cut the final sizes of the Romain du Roi (the largest and smallest) between 1737 and *c.* 1745. The styles of the Romain du Roi changed over the years, especially the italics, so all of these punchcutters made important contributions. Luce's Perle (about 5 point) roman and italic were neither the smallest nor the best miniature types – perhaps three romans and one italic as small or smaller preceded them in France and Holland – but they nevertheless demonstrated remarkable skill.

Although Luce describes the types in the specimen shown here as being cut for the Imprimerie Royale, he also worked on his own account, issuing specimens between 1732 (unfortunately lost) and 1771 before the Imprimerie Royale acquired his materials in 1773. The fleurons and probably the italics in his 1732 specimen influenced those of Pierre-Simon Fournier. JAL

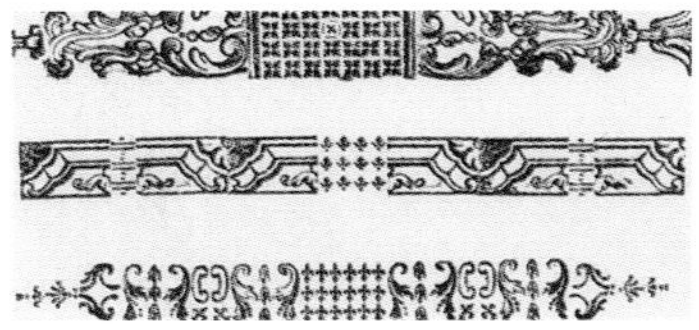

Rococo decorations assembled from Luce's small cast elements (fleurons or printers' flowers). Pierre-Simon Fournier, the greatest master of rococo fleurons, acknowledged Luce as the first to introduce them, but Luce's 1732 specimen is not known to survive. The arabesque fleurons popular since the 1560s had fallen out of fashion.

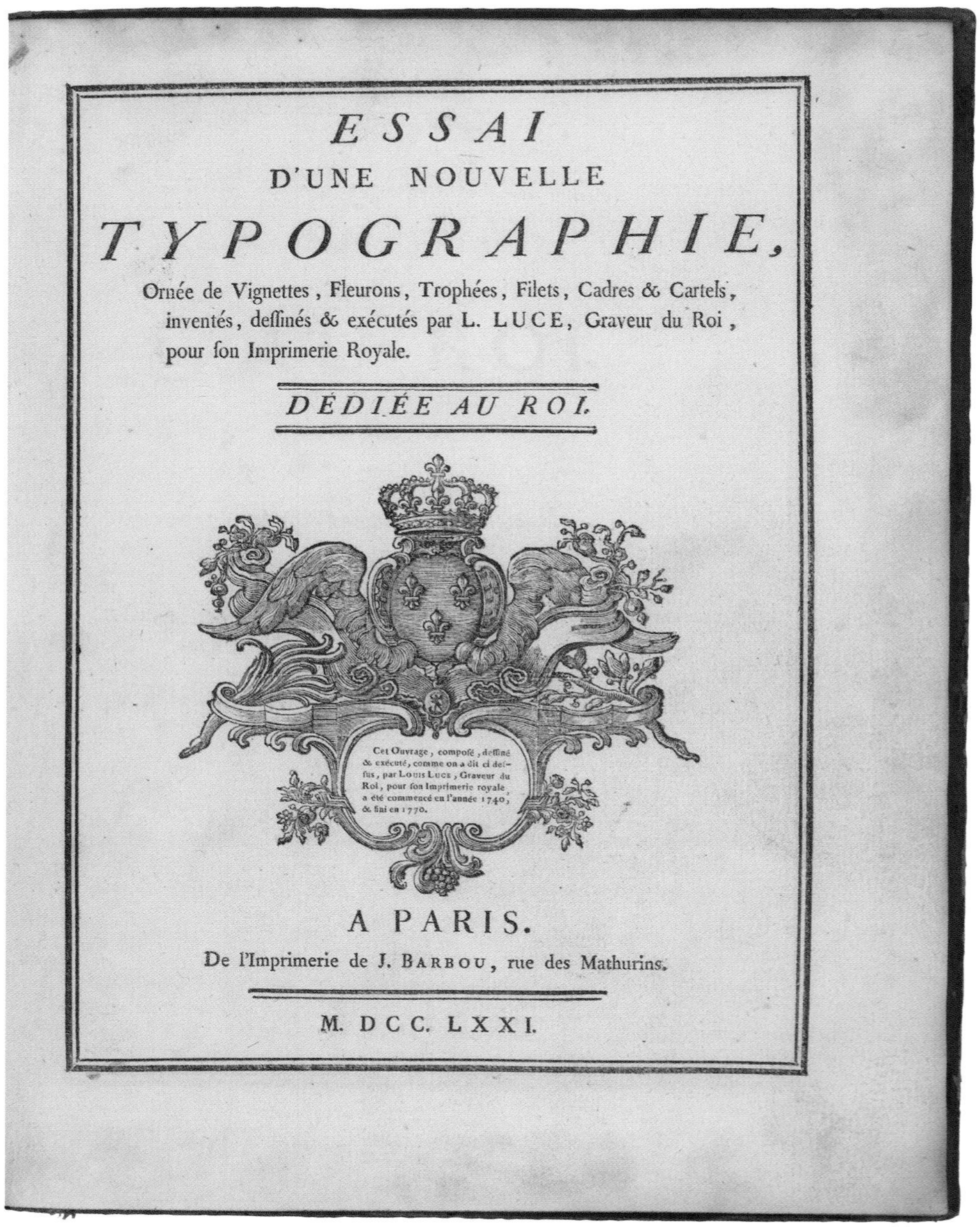

ESSAI
D'UNE NOUVELLE
TYPOGRAPHIE,
Ornée de Vignettes, Fleurons, Trophées, Filets, Cadres & Cartels, inventés, deſſinés & exécutés par L. LUCE, Graveur du Roi, pour ſon Imprimerie Royale.

DÉDIÉE AU ROI.

Cet Ouvrage, composé, deſſiné & exécuté, comme on a dit ci-deſſus, par LOUIS LUCE, Graveur du Roi, pour ſon Imprimerie royale a été commencé en l'année 1740, & fini en 1770.

A PARIS.
De l'Imprimerie de J. BARBOU, rue des Mathurins.

M. DCC. LXXI.

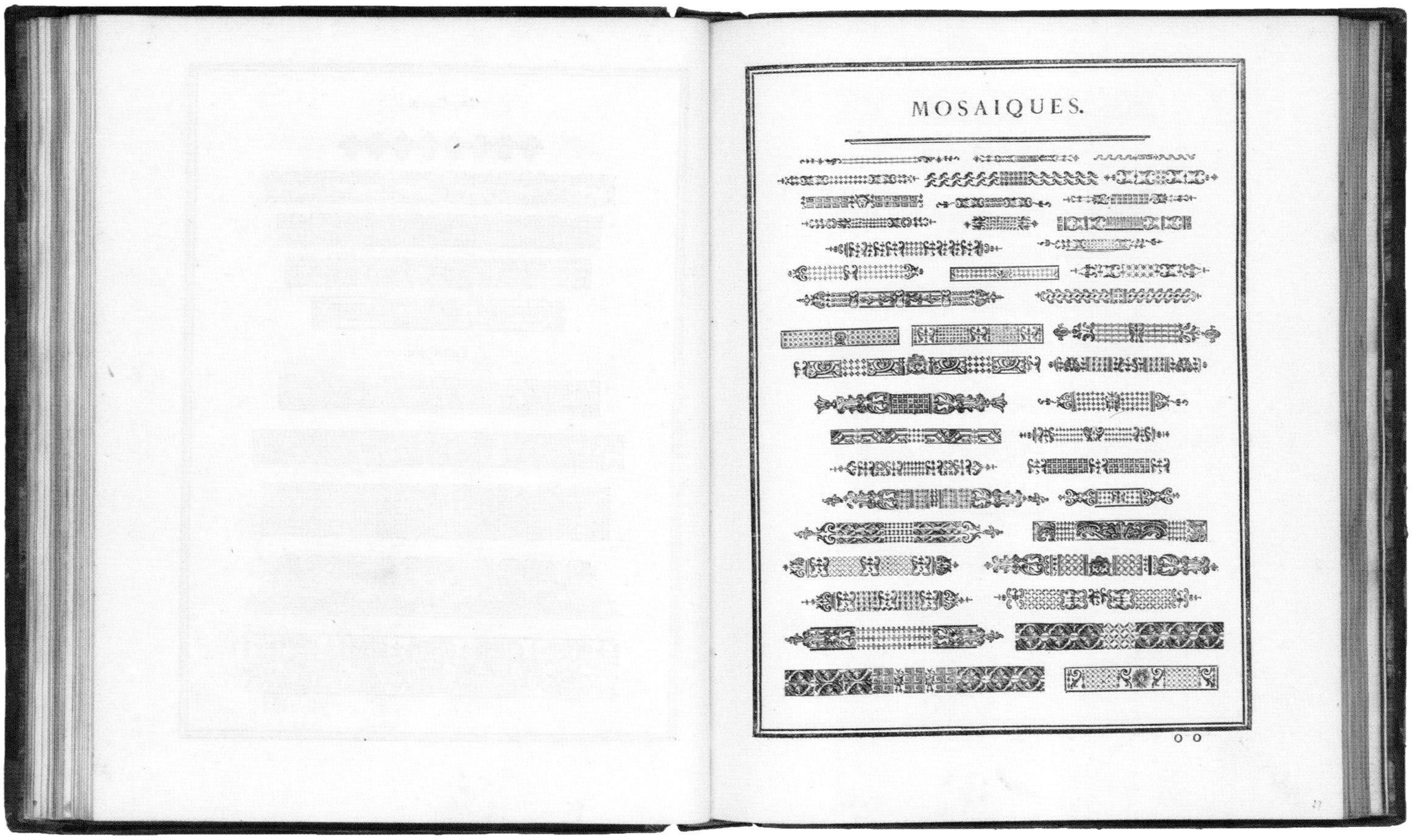
MOSAIQUES.

O O

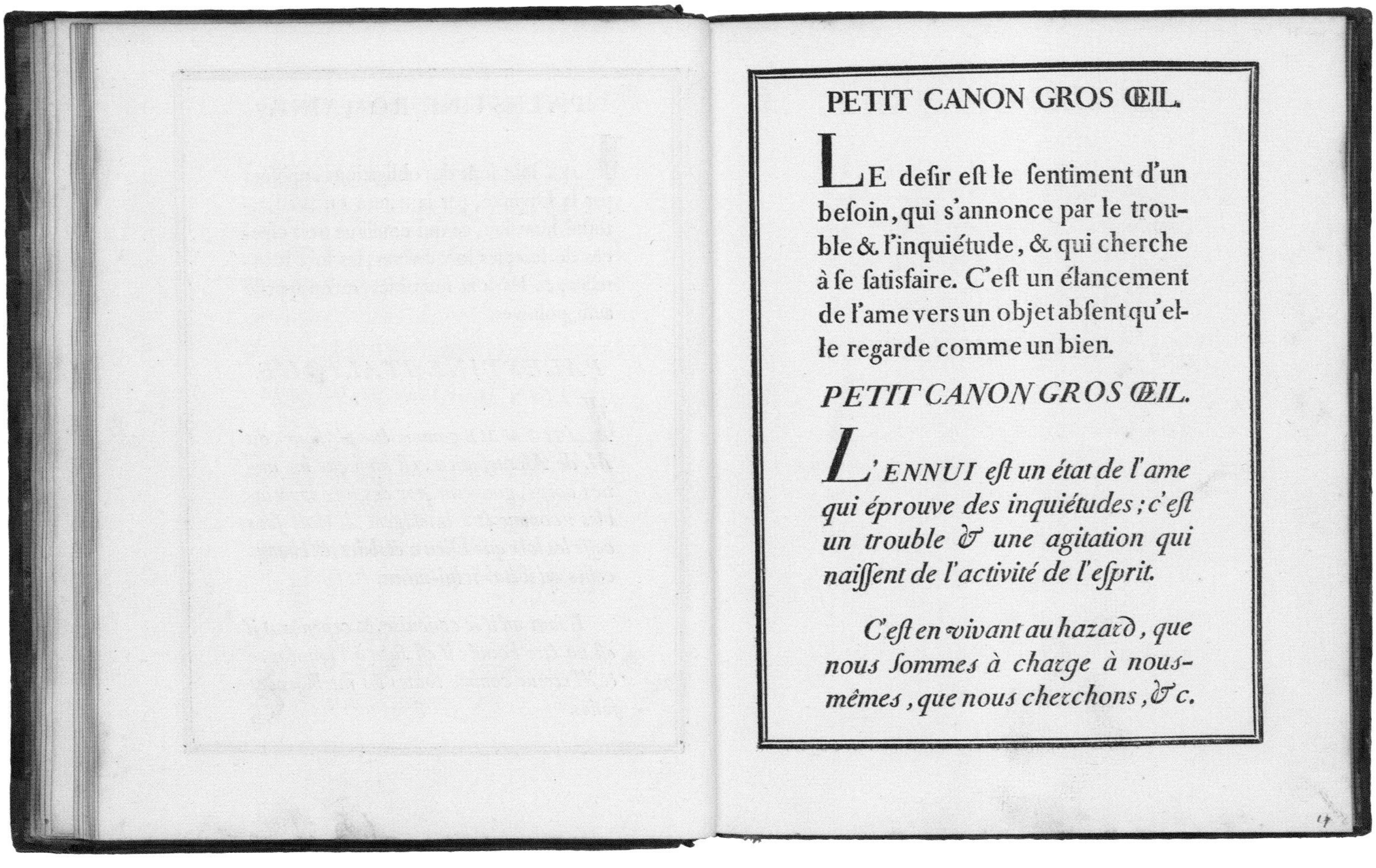
PETIT CANON GROS ŒIL.

LE deſir eſt le ſentiment d'un beſoin, qui s'annonce par le trouble & l'inquiétude, & qui cherche à ſe ſatisfaire. C'eſt un élancement de l'ame vers un objet abſent qu'elle regarde comme un bien.

PETIT CANON GROS ŒIL.

L'ENNUI eſt un état de l'ame qui éprouve des inquiétudes ; c'eſt un trouble & une agitation qui naiſſent de l'activité de l'eſprit.

C'eſt en vivant au hazard, que nous ſommes à charge à nous-mêmes, que nous cherchons, &c.

1772 **Joaquín Ibarra** **Gaius Sallustius Crispus, *La conjuración de Catilina y La guerra de Jugurta*. Madrid: Joaquín Ibarra, 1772. 395 pp. 37 cm. Illustrators: Isidro Carnicero, Mariano Salvador Maélla. Engravers: Fernando Selma, José Joaquín Fabregat, Francisco Muntaner and others (illustrations). Draftsman & engraver: Juan de la Cruz Cano y Olmedilla (map).**

This deluxe Spanish edition of Sallust's history of Catiline's rebellion against the Roman Republic and of the Republic's war in North Africa established Joaquín Ibarra (1725–85) of Zaragoza as Spain's greatest printer. Apprenticed to his brother, printer to the University of Cervera, Ibarra left in 1742, perhaps working in his uncle's Madrid printing office until he established his own in 1753. King Carlos III appointed him Printer to the Court in 1766. Two years later Carlos's nephew Ferdinand, Duke of Parma, enlisted Giambattista Bodoni to manage his new Stamperia Reale in Parma, beginning with type acquired from Pierre-Simon Fournier in Paris. The two presses certainly influenced each other, though Baskerville in England and François-Ambroise Didot in Paris influenced both.

Ibarra originally used many sixteenth-century types from France and the Low Countries, but he had begun to replace them even before his royal appointment. In 1764 he introduced decorated titling capitals by Fournier and from 1765 to 1771 new romans and italics by Eudald Pradell in Madrid, resembling some by Jacques François Rosart in Brussels. This edition of Sallust adds an italic and some titling capitals by Antonio Espinosa with acknowledged Fournier influences, but which also strongly reflect pointed-pen calligraphy and engraved lettering. The Sallust's prominent engraved illustrations may have suggested the cutting of a type to suit them, and the printing office enlisted the help of a calligrapher to advise the punchcutter.

Besides the large format, new type and numerous illustrations, the excellent paper and very black ink add to this book's grandeur. JAL

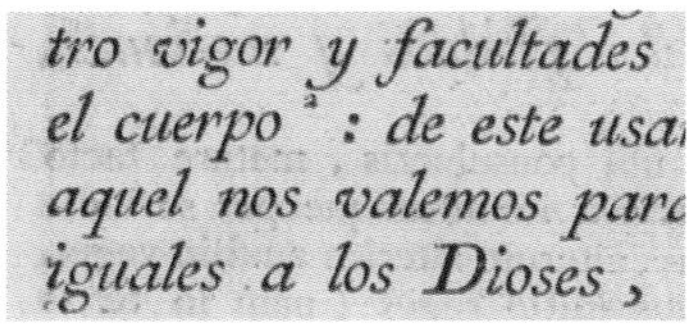
tro vigor y facultades
el cuerpo [2] *: de este usa*
aquel nos valemos para
iguales a los Dioses ,

Antonio Espinosa de los Monteros (1731–1812) studied drawing and engraving at the Royal Academy of San Fernando in Madrid, worked at the Spanish royal mint, then set up a typefoundry by 1764. He cut this italic, possible commissioned for the book shown here, with advice from the calligrapher José de Anduaga y Garimberti (1751–1822).

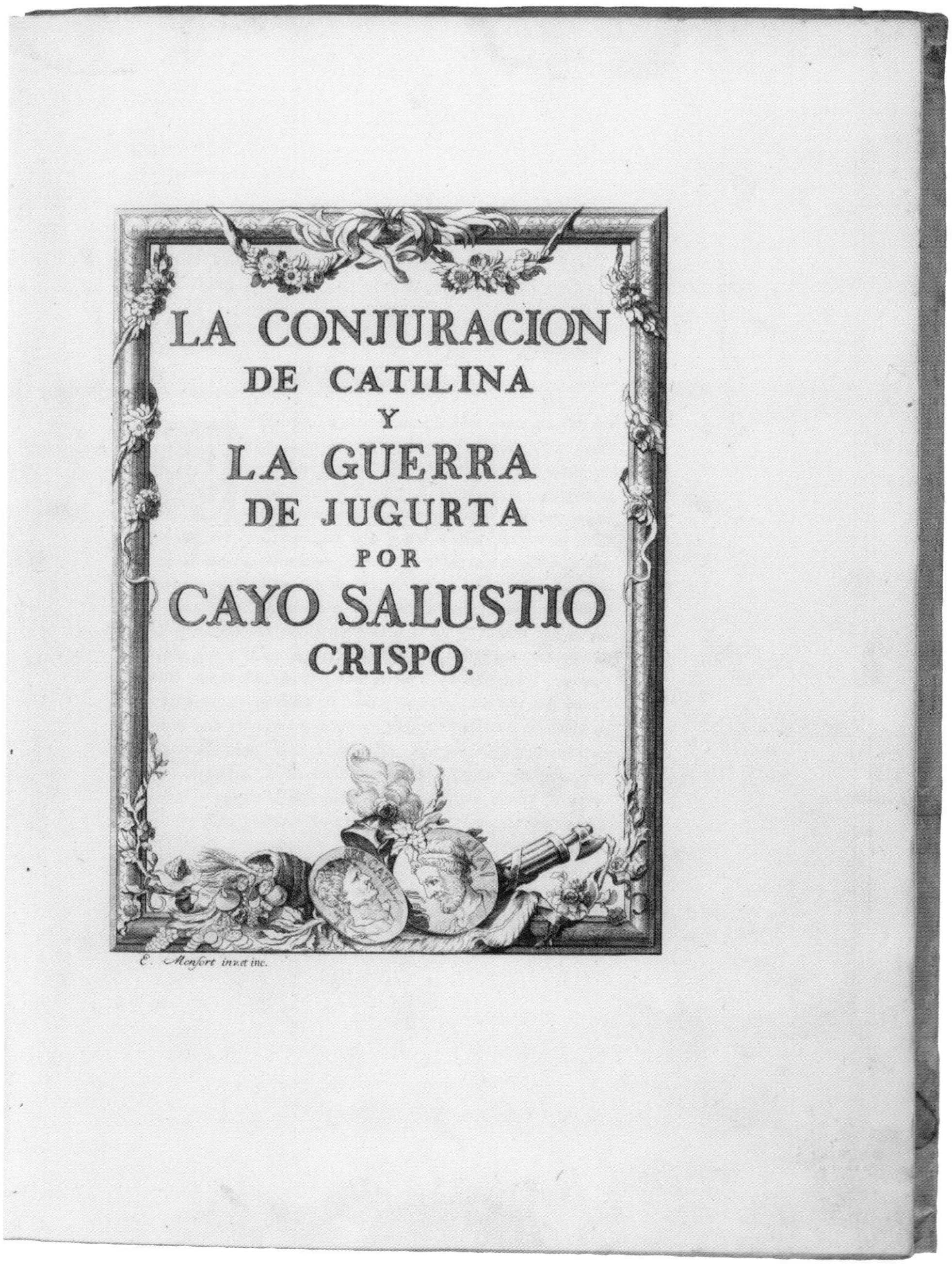
LA CONJURACION
DE CATILINA
Y
LA GUERRA
DE JUGURTA
POR
CAYO SALUSTIO
CRISPO.

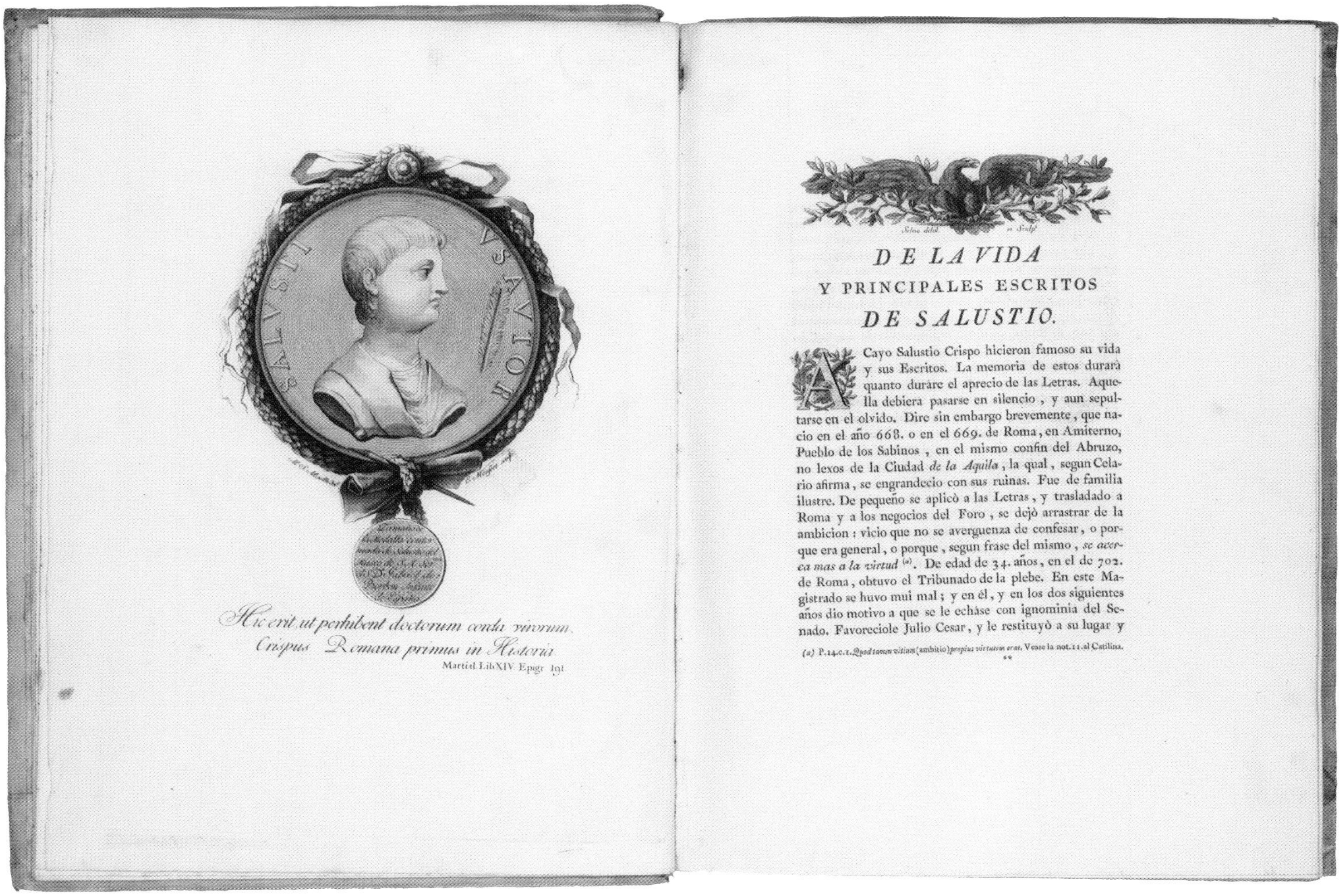

Hic erit, ut perhibent doctorum corda virorum,
Crispus Romana primus in Historia.
Martial. Lib. XIV Epigr. 191

DE LA VIDA
Y PRINCIPALES ESCRITOS
DE SALUSTIO.

A Cayo Salustio Crispo hicieron famoso su vida y sus Escritos. La memoria de estos durarà quanto duràre el aprecio de las Letras. Aquella debiera pasarse en silencio, y aun sepultarse en el olvido. Dire sin embargo brevemente, que nacio en el año 668. o en el 669. de Roma, en Amiterno, Pueblo de los Sabinos, en el mismo confin del Abruzo, no lexos de la Ciudad *de la Aquila*, la qual, segun Celario afirma, se engrandecio con sus ruinas. Fue de familia ilustre. De pequeño se aplicò a las Letras, y trasladado a Roma y a los negocios del Foro, se dejò arrastrar de la ambicion: vicio que no se averguenza de confesar, o porque era general, o porque, segun frase del mismo, *se acerca mas a la virtud* (a). De edad de 34. años, en el de 702. de Roma, obtuvo el Tribunado de la plebe. En este Magistrado se huvo mui mal; y en él, y en los dos siguientes años dio motivo a que se le echàse con ignominia del Senado. Favoreciole Julio Cesar, y le restituyò a su lugar y

(a) P.14.c.1. *Quod tamen vitium* (ambitio) *propius virtutem erat.* Vease la not. 11. al Catilina.

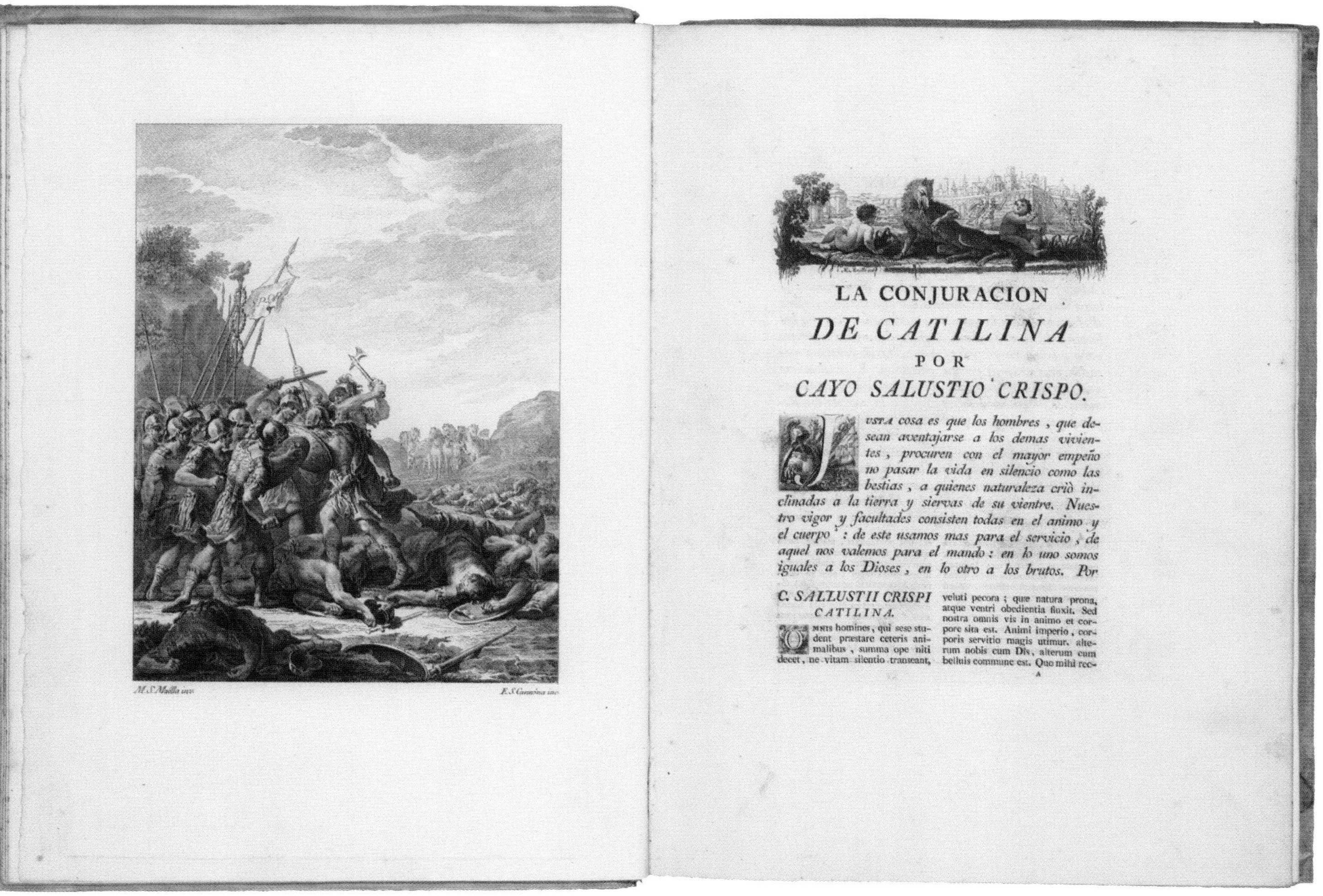

LA CONJURACION
DE CATILINA
POR
CAYO SALUSTIO CRISPO.

Justa cosa es que los hombres, que desean aventajarse a los demas vivientes, procuren con el mayor empeño no pasar la vida en silencio como las bestias, a quienes naturaleza criò inclinadas a la tierra y siervas de su vientre. Nuestro vigor y facultades consisten todas en el animo y el cuerpo : de este usamos mas para el servicio, de aquel nos valemos para el mando: en lo uno somos iguales a los Dioses, en lo otro a los brutos. Por

C. SALLUSTII CRISPI
CATILINA.

Omnis homines, qui sese student præstare ceteris animalibus, summa ope niti decet, ne vitam silentio transeant, veluti pecora; quæ natura prona, atque ventri obedientia finxit. Sed nostra omnis vis in animo et corpore sita est. Animi imperio, corporis servitio magis utimur. alterum nobis cum Dis, alterum cum belluis commune est. Quo mihi rec-

1784 **François-Ambroise Didot** Torquato Tasso, *La Gerusalemme liberata*. Paris: François-Ambroise Didot l'Aîné, 1784–86. 2 volumes. 30.5 cm. Illustrator: Charles-Nicolas Cochin. Engravers: Jean-Baptiste Tilliard and others.

This edition of Tasso's *La Gerusalemme liberata* was part of a series of deluxe editions of classical texts, published and printed in Paris from 1783 onwards by members of the Didot family: François-Ambroise l'Aîné, his brother Pierre-François le Jeune, and his sons Pierre and Firmin. They each owned a press, a typefoundry, and a publishing house. The series is the typographic expression of a new movement in the arts: neoclassicism. The layout is clear and monumental, with dominant white spaces around the text; the type is more rationally designed and smooth woven paper is used.

François-Ambroise Didot (1730–1804) was the first to use this new design style. He had his new types cut by Pierre-Louis Vafflard (*c.* 1750?–*c.* 1824). The type in this Tasso edition represents the first accomplished form of the 'modern face'; the large capitals on the title page were cut by Firmin Didot, who had studied under Vafflard. Although Pierre-François Didot was the regular printer for 'Monsieur' (the king's younger brother, see the title page), this book was printed by his brother François-Ambroise, who was already famous by then. Collectors' editions of this kind often had impressive engravings; in this edition, the engravings are after drawings by Charles-Nicolas Cochin (1715–90).

In 1785–86, François-Ambroise Didot also published a reprint of this highlight of Italian literature, with the same typographic design. FAJ

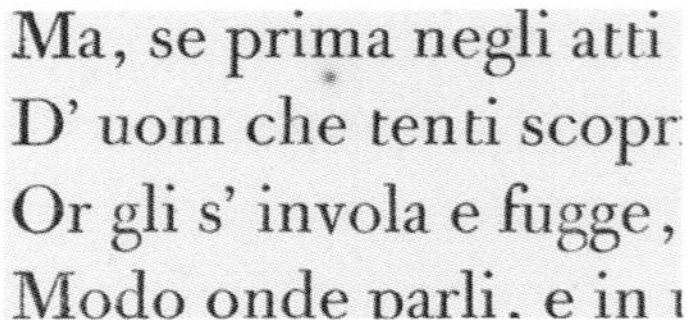

Ma, se prima negli atti
D' uom che tenti scopr
Or gli s' invola e fugge,
Modo onde parli, e in

This Gros Romain (17 point) roman by Pierre-Louis Vafflard heralded the new Didot and Bodoni style. Surpassing the innovations of the Romain du Roi, Fournier and Baskerville, it combined the pointed pen's quick transitions from thick to thin with long unbracketed horizontal serifs and a vertical axis.

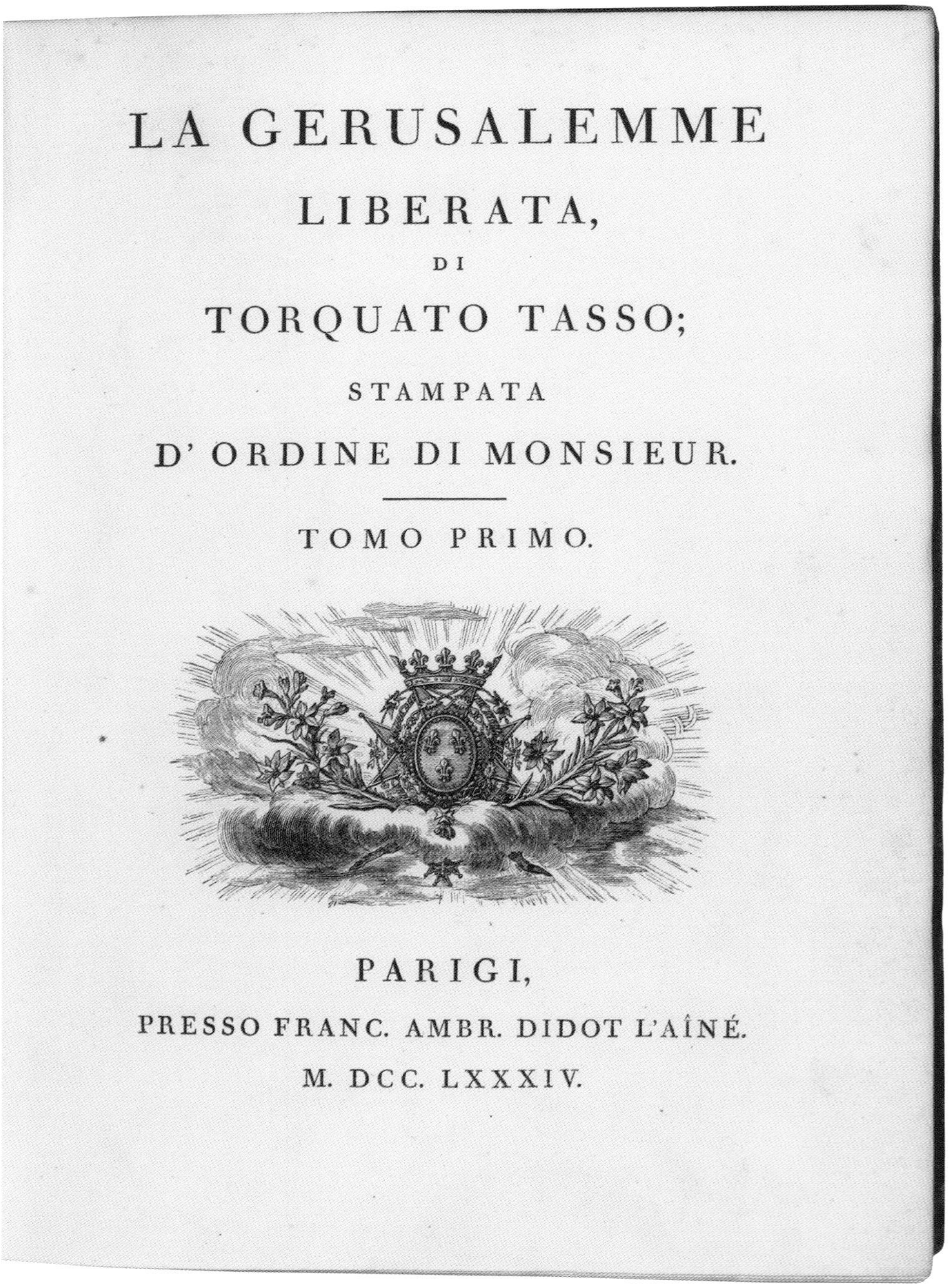

LA GERUSALEMME
LIBERATA,
DI
TORQUATO TASSO;
STAMPATA
D' ORDINE DI MONSIEUR.

TOMO PRIMO.

PARIGI,
PRESSO FRANC. AMBR. DIDOT L'AÎNÉ.
M. DCC. LXXXIV.

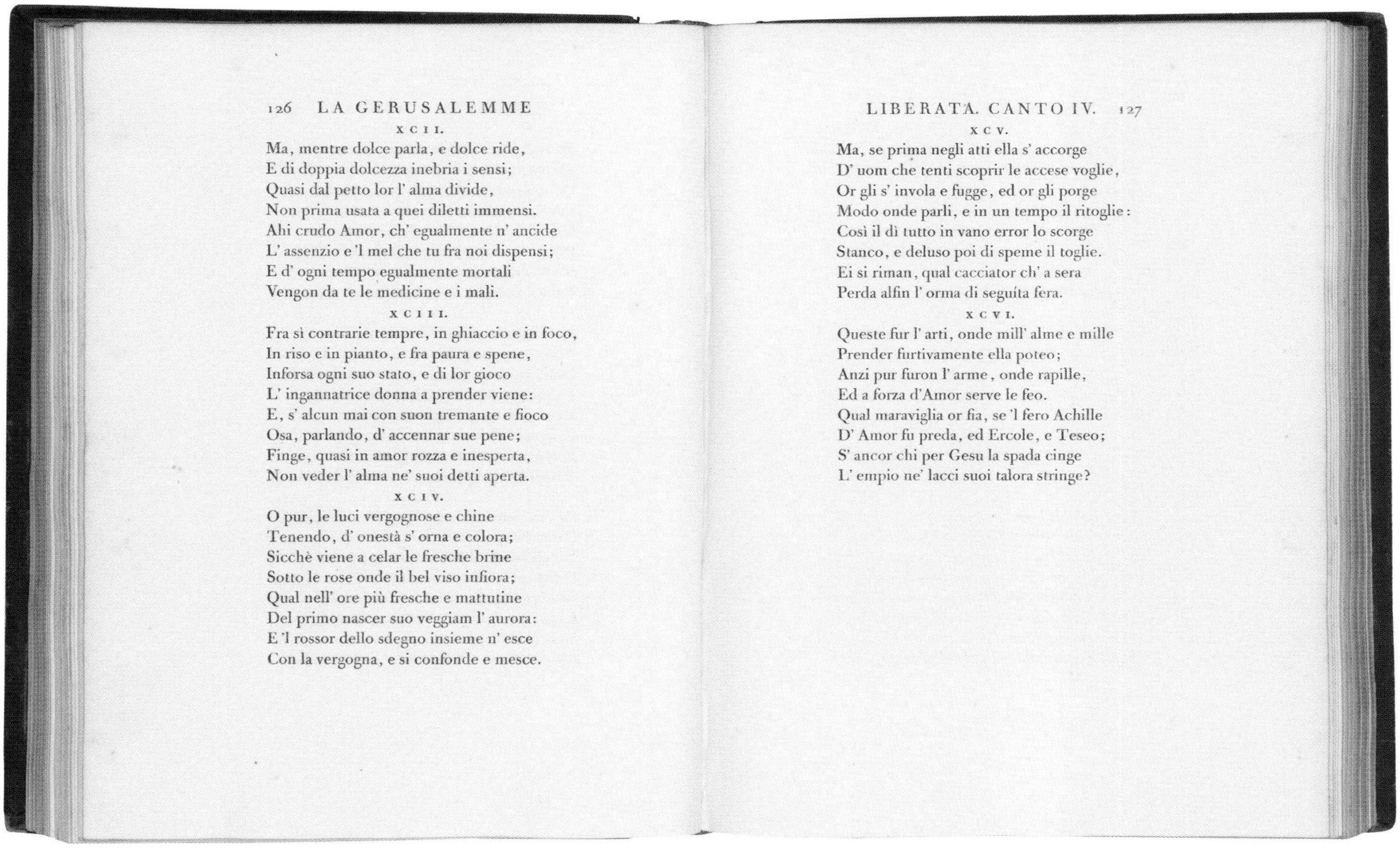

126 LA GERUSALEMME

XCII.

Ma, mentre dolce parla, e dolce ride,
E di doppia dolcezza inebria i sensi;
Quasi dal petto lor l' alma divide,
Non prima usata a quei diletti immensi.
Ahi crudo Amor, ch' egualmente n' ancide
L' assenzio e 'l mel che tu fra noi dispensi;
E d' ogni tempo egualmente mortali
Vengon da te le medicine e i mali.

XCIII.

Fra sì contrarie tempre, in ghiaccio e in foco,
In riso e in pianto, e fra paura e spene,
Inforsa ogni suo stato, e di lor gioco
L' ingannatrice donna a prender viene:
E, s' alcun mai con suon tremante e fioco
Osa, parlando, d' accennar sue pene;
Finge, quasi in amor rozza e inesperta,
Non veder l' alma ne' suoi detti aperta.

XCIV.

O pur, le luci vergognose e chine
Tenendo, d' onestà s' orna e colora;
Sicchè viene a celar le fresche brine
Sotto le rose onde il bel viso infiora;
Qual nell' ore più fresche e mattutine
Del primo nascer suo veggiam l' aurora:
E 'l rossor dello sdegno insieme n' esce
Con la vergogna, e si confonde e mesce.

LIBERATA. CANTO IV. 127

XCV.

Ma, se prima negli atti ella s' accorge
D' uom che tenti scoprir le accese voglie,
Or gli s' invola e fugge, ed or gli porge
Modo onde parli, e in un tempo il ritoglie:
Così il dì tutto in vano error lo scorge
Stanco, e deluso poi di speme il toglie.
Ei si riman, qual cacciator ch' a sera
Perda alfin l' orma di seguita fera.

XCVI.

Queste fur l' arti, onde mill' alme e mille
Prender furtivamente ella poteo;
Anzi pur furon l' arme, onde rapille,
Ed a forza d'Amor serve le feo.
Qual maraviglia or fia, se 'l fero Achille
D' Amor fu preda, ed Ercole, e Teseo;
S' ancor chi per Gesu la spada cinge
L' empio ne' lacci suoi talora stringe?

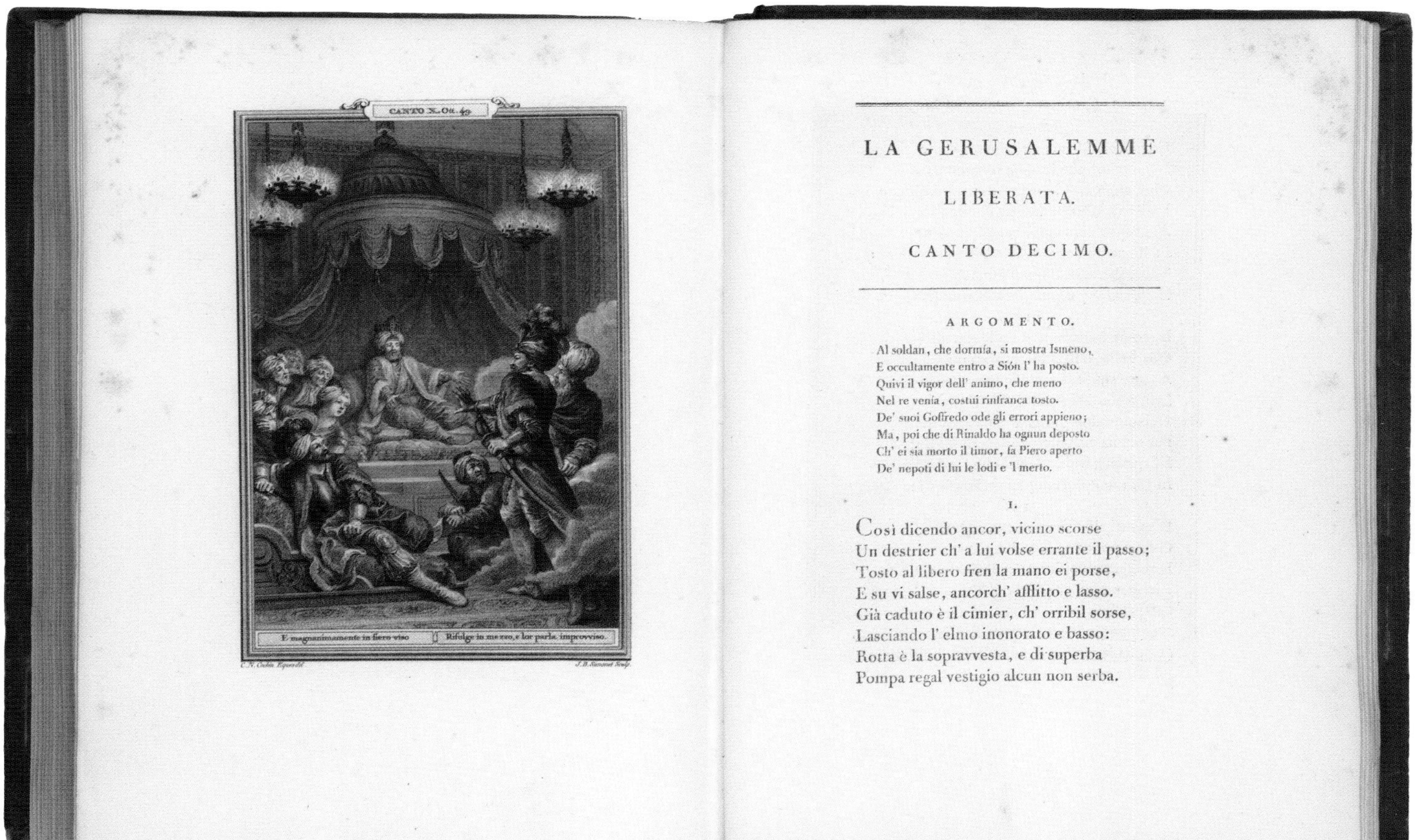

CANTO X. Ot. 40

E magnanimamente in fiero viso | Rifulge in mezzo, e lor parla improviso.

LA GERUSALEMME

LIBERATA.

CANTO DECIMO.

ARGOMENTO.

Al soldan, che dormía, si mostra Ismeno,
E occultamente entro a Sión l' ha posto.
Quivi il vigor dell' animo, che meno
Nel re venía, costui rinfranca tosto.
De' suoi Goffredo ode gli errori appieno;
Ma, poi che di Rinaldo ha ognun deposto
Ch' ei sia morto il timor, fa Piero aperto
De' nepoti di lui le lodi e 'l merto.

I.

Così dicendo ancor, vicino scorse
Un destrier ch' a lui volse errante il passo;
Tosto al libero fren la mano ei porse,
E su vi salse, ancorch' afflitto e lasso.
Già caduto è il cimier, ch' orribil sorse,
Lasciando l' elmo inonorato e basso:
Rotta è la sopravvesta, e di superba
Pompa regal vestigio alcun non serba.

1793 **Giambattista Bodoni** Virgil, *Opera*. Parma: Giambattista Bodoni, 1793. 2 volumes. 47.5 cm.

The Italian Giambattista Bodoni (1740–1813) was the major competitor to the Didot family in the market of collector's editions for rich bibliophiles. He worked at the court of the Count of Parma; 'in aedibus Palatinis' ('in the palace complex'), as it often says on his title pages. Bodoni produced deluxe editions of classical works, such as this Virgil from 1793. This monumental edition of the works of the Roman poet, who was considered the greatest writer of all time, was not meant to be read (the volume is rather bulky and heavy) but rather to prove that the owner belonged to the cultural elite. In consequence, the scholarly aspects of an ostentatious edition like this Virgil were considered less important. Bodoni's edition has many textual errors, for which Pierre Didot criticized him five years later, in the preface to his own edition of Virgil.

The typographic design of Bodoni's Virgil is one of the highlights of neoclassicism: the layout is geometric and the letters seem to swim in a sea of white. The printing is perfect in all technical aspects: a sharp print on white paper, which has been pressed after printing.

Bodoni is most famous for his hundreds of Latin and non-Latin alphabets, for which he indefatigably cut thousands of punches. Twice, he collected them in a type specimen book, the *Manuale tipografico* from 1788 and from 1818. But Bodoni did not sell his typefaces: these books only served their maker's vanity. FAJ

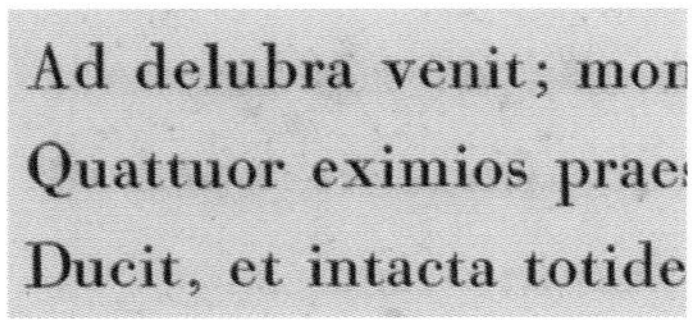
Ad delubra venit; mon
Quattuor eximios prae
Ducit, et intacta totide

Bodoni admired Baskerville's 1757 Virgil, but used and then copied Fournier's types for his earliest books in c. 1770. After c. 1785, he vied with the Didot family to produce the most spectacular and refined types ever seen. Didot and Bodoni's influence overthrew the traditional roman and italic internationally by 1800.

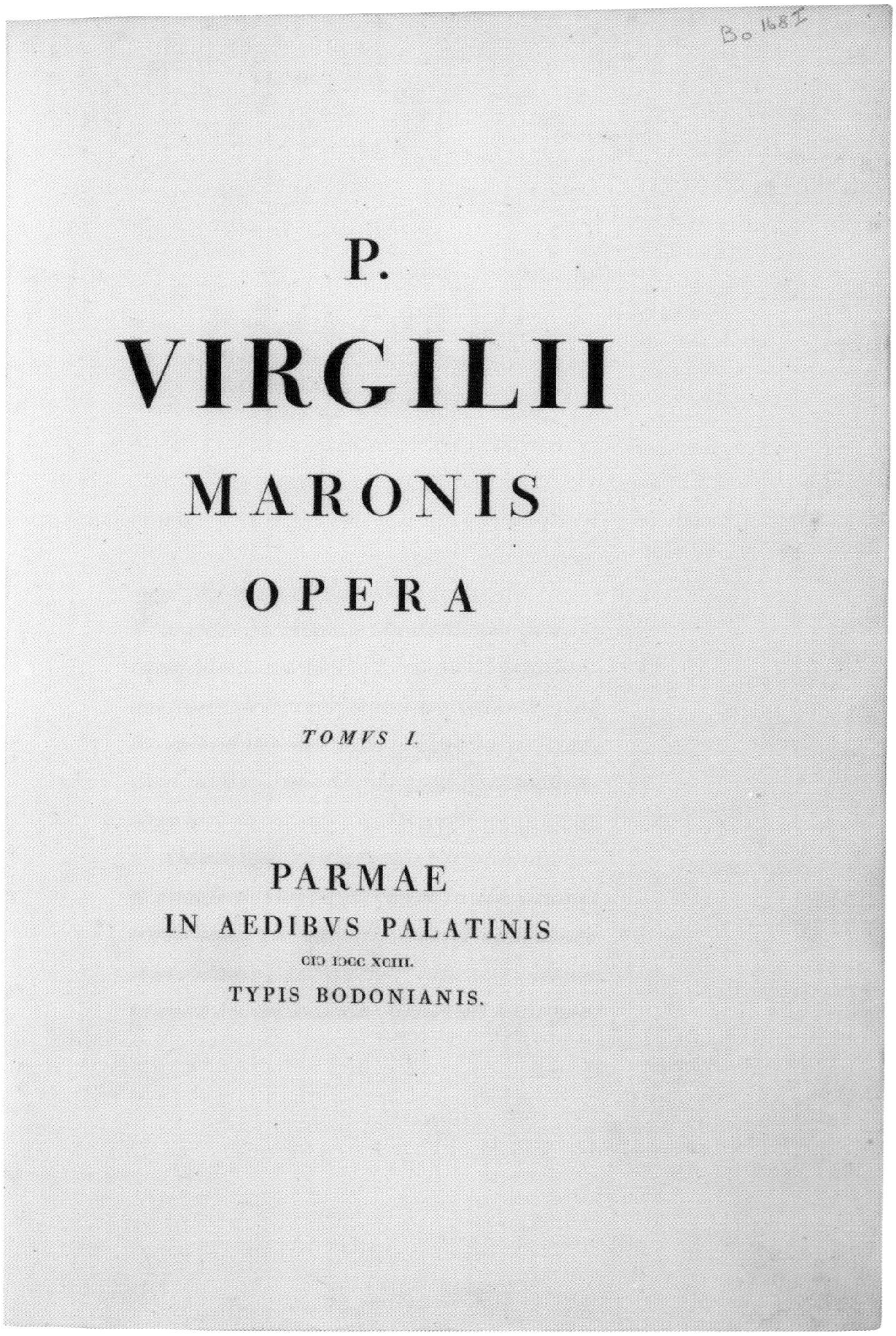
P.
VIRGILII
MARONIS
OPERA

TOMVS I.

PARMAE
IN AEDIBVS PALATINIS
CIↃ IↃCC XCIII.
TYPIS BODONIANIS.

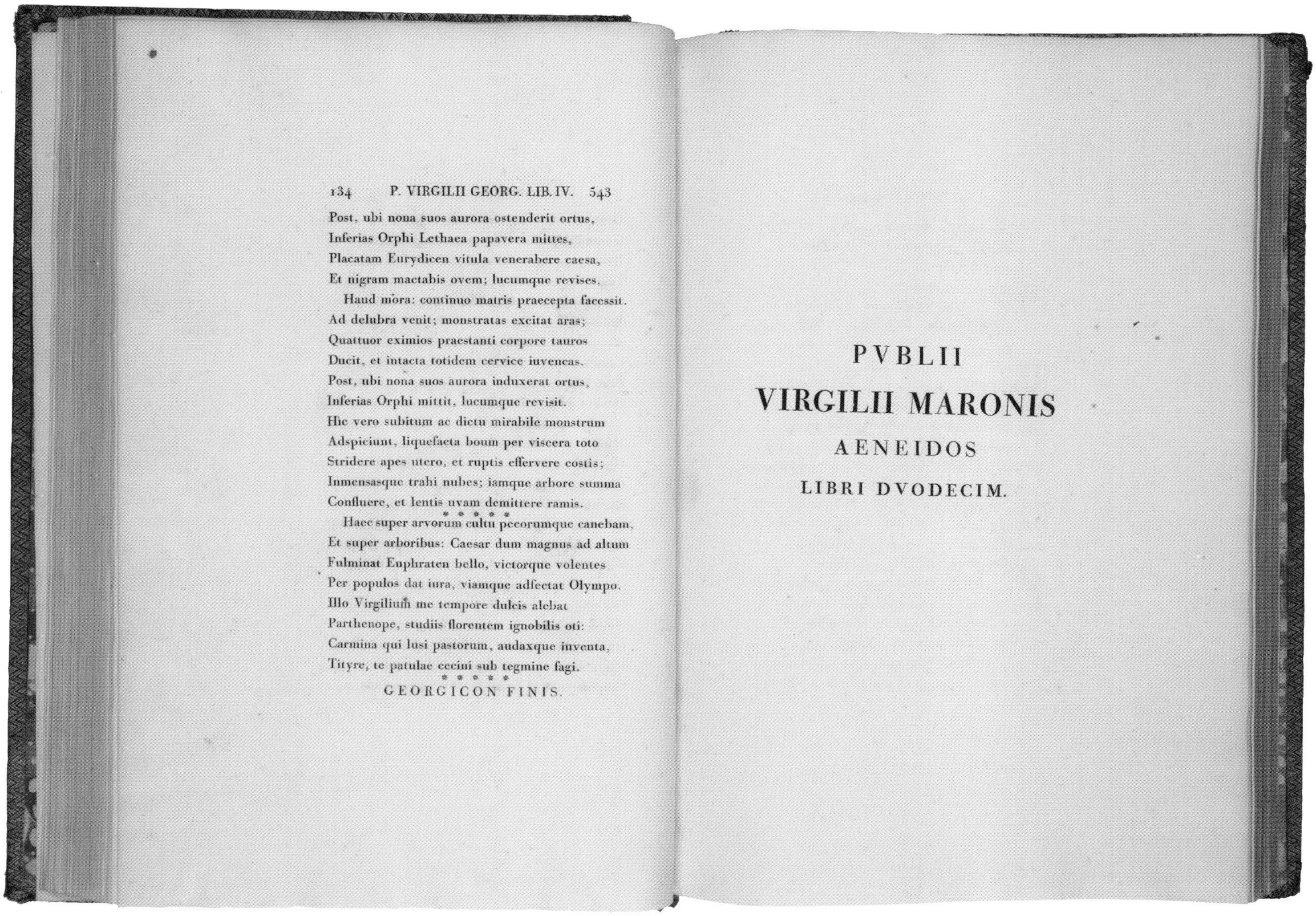

134 P. VIRGILII GEORG. LIB. IV. 543

Post, ubi nona suos aurora ostenderit ortus,
Inferias Orphi Lethaea papavera mittes,
Placatam Eurydicen vitula venerabere caesa,
Et nigram mactabis ovem; lucumque revises.
Haud mora: continuo matris praecepta facessit.
Ad delubra venit; monstratas excitat aras;
Quattuor eximios praestanti corpore tauros
Ducit, et intacta totidem cervice iuvencas.
Post, ubi nona suos aurora induxerat ortus,
Inferias Orphi mittit, lucumque revisit.
Hic vero subitum ac dictu mirabile monstrum
Adspiciunt, liquefacta boum per viscera toto
Stridere apes utero, et ruptis effervere costis;
Inmensasque trahi nubes; iamque arbore summa
Confluere, et lentis uvam demittere ramis.

* * * * *

Haec super arvorum cultu pecorumque canebam,
Et super arboribus: Caesar dum magnus ad altum
Fulminat Euphraten bello, victorque volentes
Per populos dat iura, viamque adfectat Olympo.
Illo Virgilium me tempore dulcis alebat
Parthenope, studiis florentem ignobilis oti:
Carmina qui lusi pastorum, audaxque iuventa,
Tityre, te patulae cecini sub tegmine fagi.

* * * * *

GEORGICON FINIS.

PVBLII
VIRGILII MARONIS
AENEIDOS
LIBRI DVODECIM.

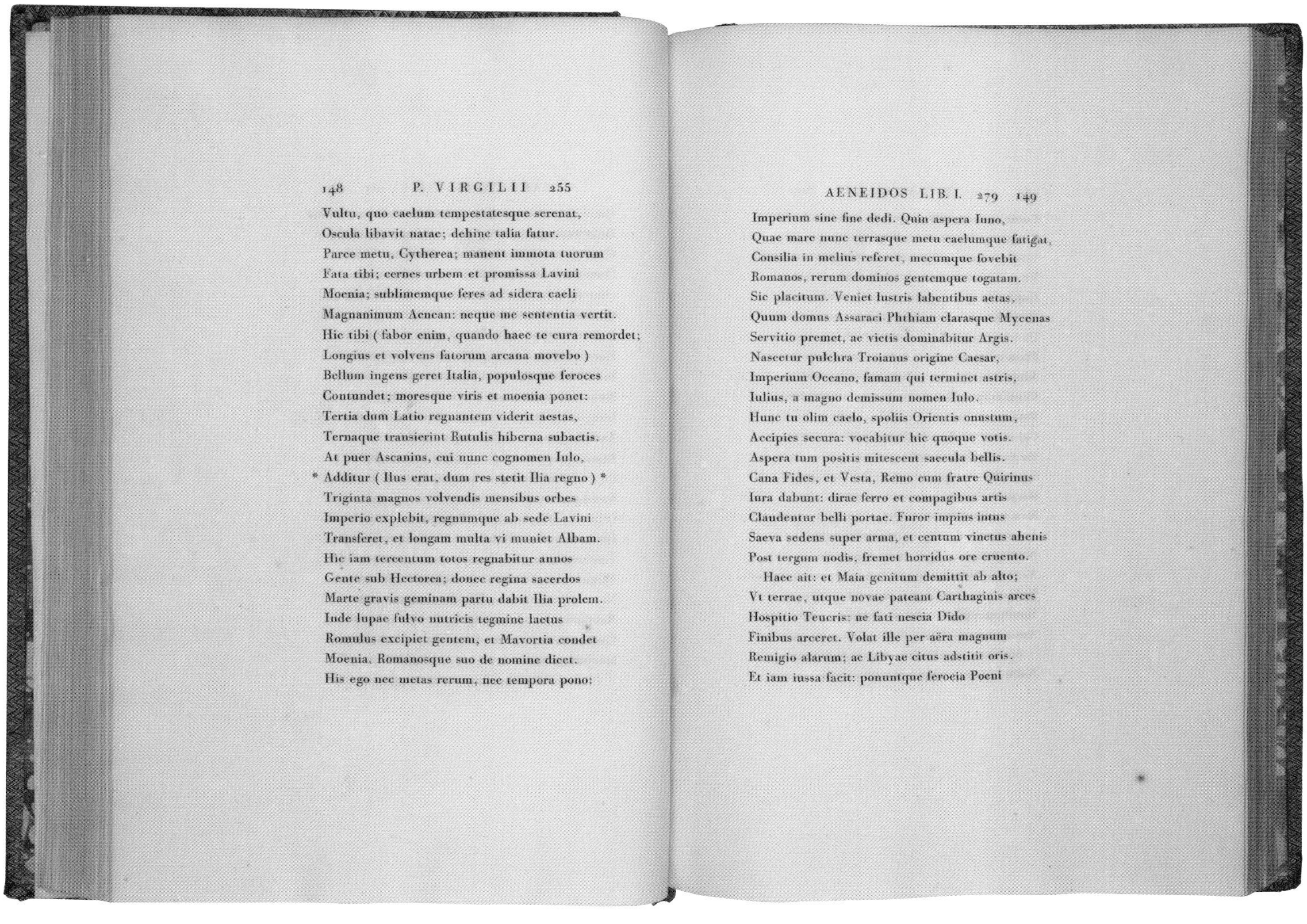

148 P. VIRGILII 255

Vultu, quo caelum tempestatesque serenat,
Oscula libavit natae; dehinc talia fatur.
Parce metu, Cytherea; manent immota tuorum
Fata tibi; cernes urbem et promissa Lavini
Moenia; sublimemque feres ad sidera caeli
Magnanimum Aenean: neque me sententia vertit.
Hic tibi (fabor enim, quando haec te cura remordet;
Longius et volvens fatorum arcana movebo)
Bellum ingens geret Italia, populosque feroces
Contundet; moresque viris et moenia ponet:
Tertia dum Latio regnantem viderit aestas,
Ternaque transierint Rutulis hiberna subactis.
At puer Ascanius, cui nunc cognomen Iulo,
* Additur (Ilus erat, dum res stetit Ilia regno) *
Triginta magnos volvendis mensibus orbes
Imperio explebit, regnumque ab sede Lavini
Transferet, et longam multa vi muniet Albam.
Hic iam tercentum totos regnabitur annos
Gente sub Hectorea; donec regina sacerdos
Marte gravis geminam partu dabit Ilia prolem.
Inde lupae fulvo nutricis tegmine laetus
Romulus excipiet gentem, et Mavortia condet
Moenia, Romanosque suo de nomine dicet.
His ego nec metas rerum, nec tempora pono:

AENEIDOS LIB. I. 279 149

Imperium sine fine dedi. Quin aspera Iuno,
Quae mare nunc terrasque metu caelumque fatigat,
Consilia in melius referet, mecumque fovebit
Romanos, rerum dominos gentemque togatam.
Sic placitum. Veniet lustris labentibus aetas,
Quum domus Assaraci Phthiam clarasque Mycenas
Servitio premet, ac victis dominabitur Argis.
Nascetur pulchra Troianus origine Caesar,
Imperium Oceano, famam qui terminet astris,
Iulius, a magno demissum nomen Iulo.
Hunc tu olim caelo, spoliis Orientis onustum,
Accipies secura: vocabitur hic quoque votis.
Aspera tum positis mitescent saecula bellis.
Cana Fides, et Vesta, Remo cum fratre Quirinus
Iura dabunt: dirae ferro et compagibus artis
Claudentur belli portae. Furor impius intus
Saeva sedens super arma, et centum vinctus ahenis
Post tergum nodis, fremet horridus ore cruento.
Haec ait: et Maia genitum demittit ab alto;
Vt terrae, utque novae pateant Carthaginis arces
Hospitio Teucris: ne fati nescia Dido
Finibus arceret. Volat ille per aëra magnum
Remigio alarum; ac Libyae citus adstitit oris.
Et iam iussa facit: ponuntque ferocia Poeni

1797 **Thomas Bewick** *History of British Birds: Containing the History and Description of Water Birds.* Newcastle-upon-Tyne: T. Bewick; London: Longman and Rees, 1804. xx, 400 pp. 21.5 cm. Volume 2. Volume 1, from 1797, is *Containing the History and Description of Land Birds.* Illustrator & engraver: Thomas Bewick. Printer: Edward Walker, Newcastle.

In the eighteenth century, book illustrations were often etchings or copperplate engravings. These were printed from metal plates, while the text was printed from cast metal type. The illustrations (intaglio) and the text (letterpress) had to be printed on two different presses. Therefore, wood engravings became popular towards the end of the eighteenth century: the metal type and the block of wood could be printed simultaneously. Wood engraving as an illustration technique went on to dominate the market for books and magazines for a century.

The Englishman Thomas Bewick (1753–1828), 'the father of modern wood engraving', played an important role in this development. At fourteen, Bewick had been apprenticed to the engraver Ralph Beilby in Newcastle in the north of England. Beilby taught him copperplate engraving and the decoration and lettering of silver and other metal objects. In 1777, Bewick became Beilby's business partner. Bewick became interested in wood engraving, a technique for which he managed to find both technical and artistic improvements. In a wood engraving, the design is cut away with a graver or burin; the lines cut away will not print. Fine detailing is possible when a burin is used to work on the end grain of hardwoods.

Bewick rose to national fame with the *General History of Quadrupeds* (1790) and especially with the two-volume *History of British Birds* (1797, 1804). Both editions were reprinted during Bewick's lifetime. The public admired the true-to-life illustrations in *History of British Birds* and the often witty vignettes. These editions were the result of many years of work that Bewick did at night, after his regular work hours and for his own pleasure. ML

Two-line Brevier (16 point) open titling capitals, as shown in Vincent Figgins's 1801 specimen. Continental typefounders introduced open roman capitals (usually shaded to suggest a roman inscription lit from the top right) in the 1750s and 60s, but they became popular in Britain after the Fry foundry introduced them in 1788.

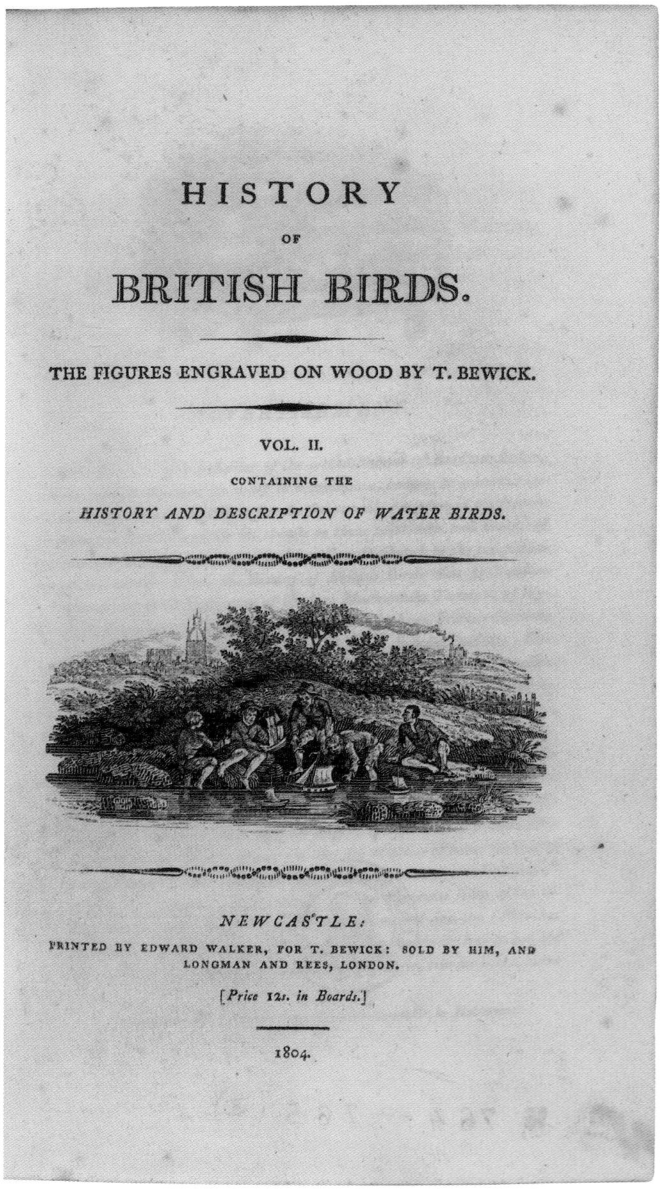
HISTORY

OF

BRITISH BIRDS.

THE FIGURES ENGRAVED ON WOOD BY T. BEWICK.

VOL. II.

CONTAINING THE

HISTORY AND DESCRIPTION OF WATER BIRDS.

NEWCASTLE:

PRINTED BY EDWARD WALKER, FOR T. BEWICK: SOLD BY HIM, AND LONGMAN AND REES, LONDON.

[*Price 12s. in Boards.*]

1804.

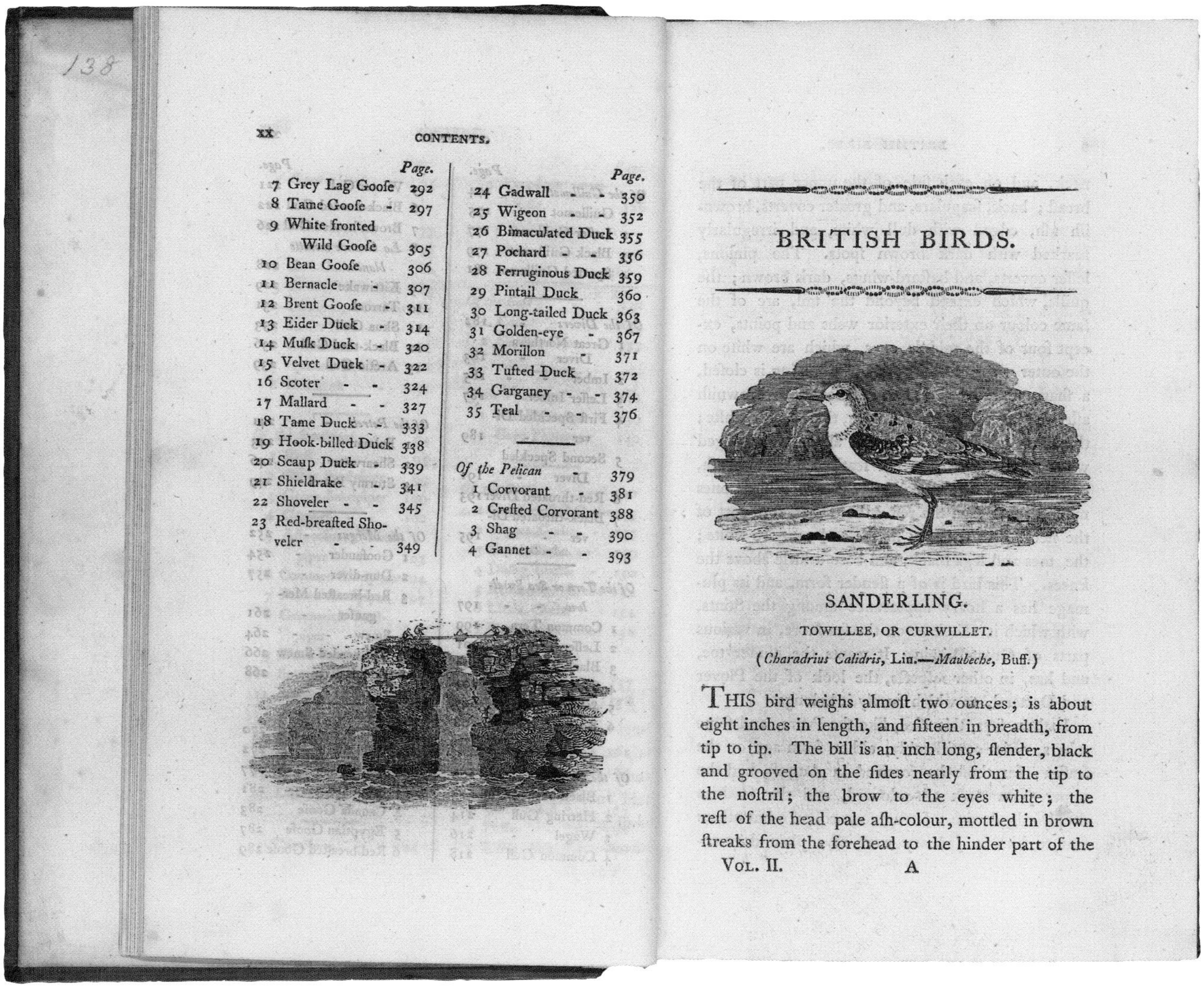

BRITISH BIRDS.

SANDERLING.

TOWILLEE, OR CURWILLET.

(*Charadrius Calidris*, Lin.—*Maubeche*, Buff.)

THIS bird weighs almoſt two ounces; is about eight inches in length, and fifteen in breadth, from tip to tip. The bill is an inch long, ſlender, black and grooved on the ſides nearly from the tip to the noſtril; the brow to the eyes white; the reſt of the head pale aſh-colour, mottled in brown ſtreaks from the forehead to the hinder part of the

VOL. II. A

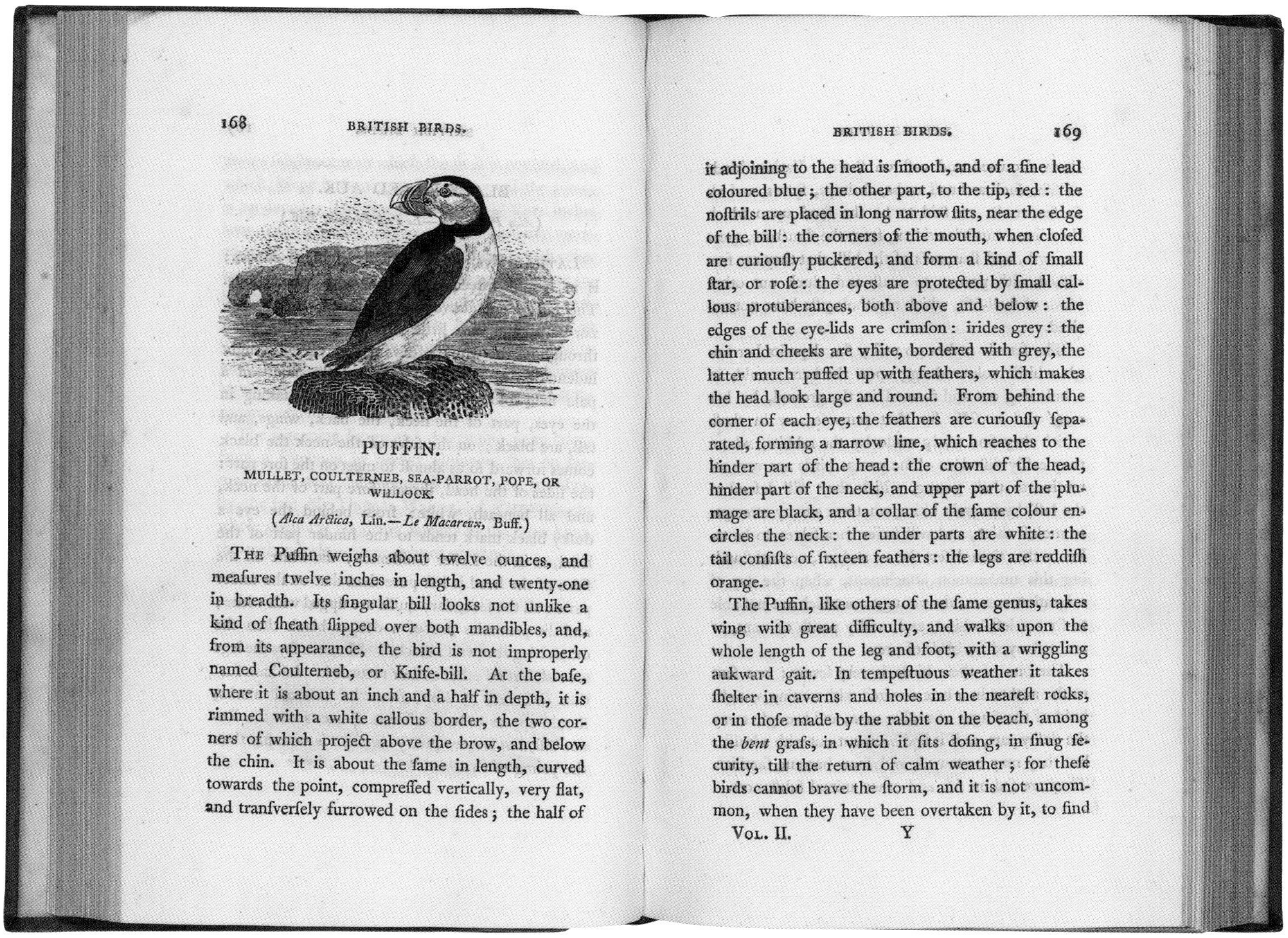

PUFFIN.

MULLET, COULTERNEB, SEA-PARROT, POPE, OR WILLOCK.

(*Alca Arctica*, Lin.—*Le Macareux*, Buff.)

THE Puffin weighs about twelve ounces, and meaſures twelve inches in length, and twenty-one in breadth. Its ſingular bill looks not unlike a kind of ſheath ſlipped over both mandibles, and, from its appearance, the bird is not improperly named Coulterneb, or Knife-bill. At the baſe, where it is about an inch and a half in depth, it is rimmed with a white callous border, the two corners of which project above the brow, and below the chin. It is about the ſame in length, curved towards the point, compreſſed vertically, very flat, and tranſverſely furrowed on the ſides; the half of

it adjoining to the head is ſmooth, and of a fine lead coloured blue; the other part, to the tip, red: the noſtrils are placed in long narrow ſlits, near the edge of the bill: the corners of the mouth, when cloſed are curiouſly puckered, and form a kind of ſmall ſtar, or roſe: the eyes are protected by ſmall callous protuberances, both above and below: the edges of the eye-lids are crimſon: irides grey: the chin and cheeks are white, bordered with grey, the latter much puffed up with feathers, which makes the head look large and round. From behind the corner of each eye, the feathers are curiouſly ſeparated, forming a narrow line, which reaches to the hinder part of the head: the crown of the head, hinder part of the neck, and upper part of the plumage are black, and a collar of the ſame colour encircles the neck: the under parts are white: the tail conſiſts of ſixteen feathers: the legs are reddiſh orange.

The Puffin, like others of the ſame genus, takes wing with great difficulty, and walks upon the whole length of the leg and foot, with a wriggling aukward gait. In tempeſtuous weather it takes ſhelter in caverns and holes in the neareſt rocks, or in thoſe made by the rabbit on the beach, among the *bent* graſs, in which it ſits doſing, in ſnug ſecurity, till the return of calm weather; for theſe birds cannot brave the ſtorm, and it is not uncommon, when they have been overtaken by it, to find

VOL. II. Y

227

1802 **Redouté & Didot le Jeune** Pierre-Joseph Redouté, *Les Liliacées*. Paris: P.-J. Redouté, 1802–16. 8 volumes. 52.5 cm. Illustrator: Pierre-Joseph Redouté. Printer: Didot jeune, Paris.

Pierre-Joseph Redouté (1759–1840) was born in Saint-Hubert, a small town in what is now Belgium. After his father had taught him the principles of the painter's trade, he continued his education in Liège. As a travelling portrait painter he came to the Netherlands, where the floral still lifes of Jan van Huysum made a deep impression on him. In 1782, he settled in Paris and learned the art of engraving. An encounter with Charles Louis L'Héritier de Brutelle proved very influential. This civil servant, botanist and bibliophile educated Redouté in the art of scientific botanical illustrations and hired him.

At the invitation of L'Héritier, Redouté visited England in 1787, where he first saw stipple engravings. Stipple engravings, which are built up from small cavities in the copperplate, allow for inking with different colours without adjacent colours blending during a print run. The stipple also gives the image a lightness and faithfulness that line engravings cannot match. During this period, Redouté became the most important botanical artist of his time.

Employed by Empress Joséphine, Napoleon's wife, Redouté worked in the gardens at Malmaison, just outside of Paris. *Les Liliacées* ('Lilies') was published in this period, and printed by the firm of Didot le Jeune, of the famous printing family. This is Redouté's biggest and most ambitious work. He even managed to refine his technique of stipple engraving; after printing, the illustrations were coloured by hand. *Les Liliacées* is only matched by Redouté's later books on roses. AP

These 64D (68 point) roman titling capitals were cut by Firmin Didot (1764–1836). Pierre Didot introduced several sizes on the title page of his magnificent folio Virgil in 1798. The refined letterforms with fine hairlines and unbracketed serifs displayed a technical brilliance never seen before: the archetypal Didot style.

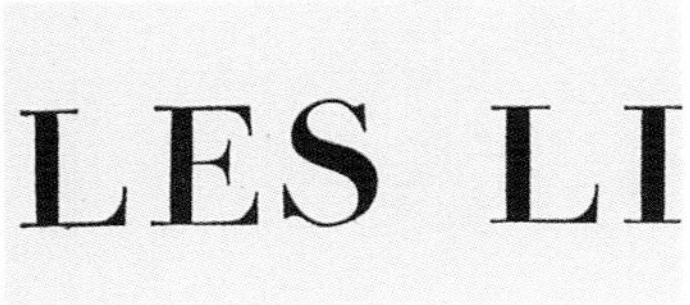

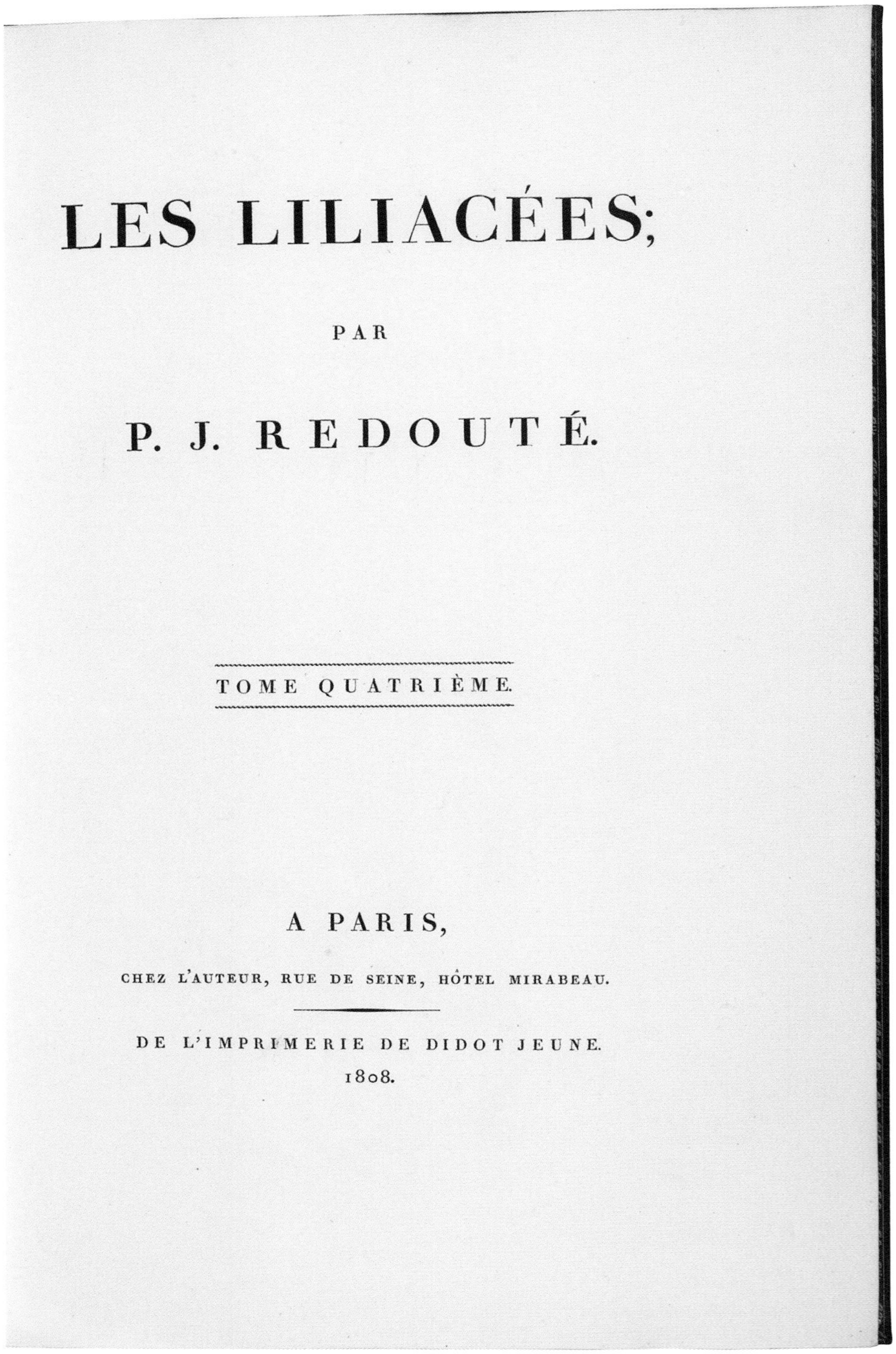
LES LILIACÉES;

PAR

P. J. REDOUTÉ.

TOME QUATRIÈME.

A PARIS,

CHEZ L'AUTEUR, RUE DE SEINE, HÔTEL MIRABEAU.

DE L'IMPRIMERIE DE DIDOT JEUNE.

1808.

CRINUM GIGANTEUM.
CRINUM GÉANT.
Crinum Giganteum
Crinum Géant

TULIPA OCULUS-SOLIS.
TULIPE ŒIL-DE-SOLEIL.
DESCRIPTION.
Tulipa oculus-Solis
Tulipe œil de Soleil

1809 **Imprimerie Impériale** *Description de l'Égypte: ou, recueil des observations et des recherches qui ont été faites en Égypte pendant l'expédition de l'armée française*; published on the orders of His Majesty the Emperor Napoleon. Paris: Imprimerie Impériale, 1809–28. 20 volumes. 42 cm (text volume), 109 cm (volumes of plates). Illustrator: André Dutertre (work shown here). Engravers: (Jean-Jérôme?) Beaugean, Berthault, André Dutertre (work shown here).

In the summer of 1798, a French army of almost 50,000 troops under the command of Napoleon left for Egypt, followed in its wake by a group of scientists, artists, mathematicians, orientalists and cartographers. The main purpose of the campaign was to block the British trade route with India, which mainly followed an overland route via Egypt. Although the campaign was a military debacle for the French, it was a scientific success. The artefacts retrieved at the excavation sites had been processed and recorded.

In a short space of time, the artists managed to record enormous amounts of visual information on the land, its history and its natural history. They made drawings of pyramids, palaces and depictions on graves. Among the group of artists who travelled along with the army was André Dutertre (1753–1842), who made the drawings for the two prints that are depicted here. During the voyage to Egypt, Dutertre, who was the son of a Parisian intaglio printer, drew many portraits of officers and other expedition members. He also became known for his reproductions of work by old masters.

Back in France, a committee was established in 1802 to prepare a momentous publication. The first volume of the series, by order of Napoleon (who had become emperor by then), was published in 1809 by the Imprimerie Impériale. The buyers were virtually forced to have a cabinet made to size for the series, which included three atlas volumes on double elephant folio (109 × 73 cm) – at the time the largest printed books ever – plus nine text volumes (42 × 28 cm) and eight more volumes of plates (73 × 56 cm). In Europe, the campaign resulted in an 'Egyptomania' craze as well as a continuing scientific interest in Egyptian culture. AP

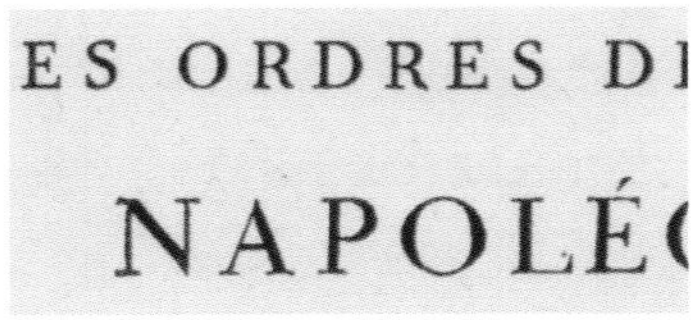
ES ORDRES DI
NAPOLÉ(

Napoleon's Egyptian campaign (1798–1801) awakened a new interest in the ancient world among both scholars and the public, an led to stylistic revivals. Quite appropriately, the Imprimerie Impériale revived Philippe Grandjean's neoclassical Romain du Roi (1699–1711) for this magnificent presentation including the results of the campaign's archaeological research.

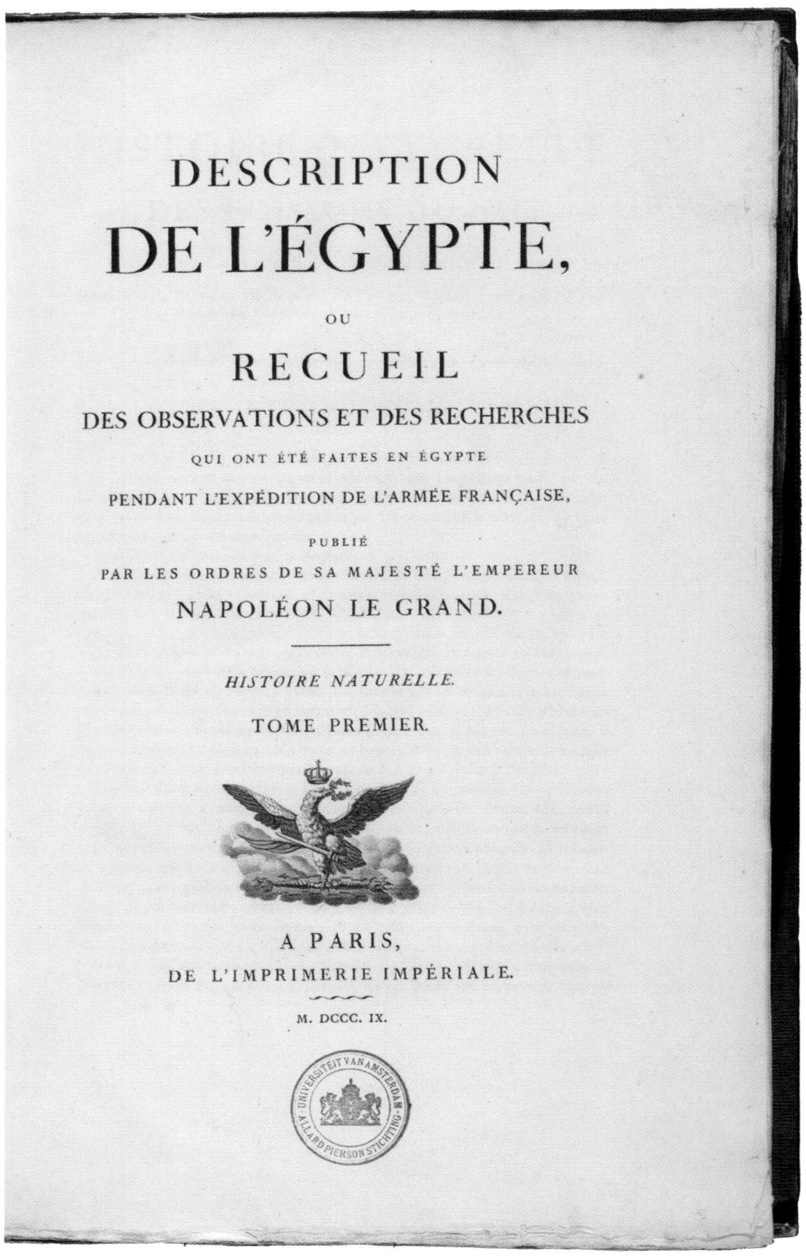
DESCRIPTION
DE L'ÉGYPTE,
OU
RECUEIL
DES OBSERVATIONS ET DES RECHERCHES
QUI ONT ÉTÉ FAITES EN ÉGYPTE
PENDANT L'EXPÉDITION DE L'ARMÉE FRANÇAISE,
PUBLIÉ
PAR LES ORDRES DE SA MAJESTÉ L'EMPEREUR
NAPOLÉON LE GRAND.
HISTOIRE NATURELLE.
TOME PREMIER.
A PARIS,
DE L'IMPRIMERIE IMPÉRIALE.
M. DCCC. IX.

A. Vol. I. EDFOU (APOLLINOPOLIS MAGNA.) Pl. 49

VUE DU GRAND TEMPLE.

E.M. Vol. I. LE KAIRE. Pl. 41.

VUE DE LA PLACE EZBEKYEH; CÔTÉ DU SUD.

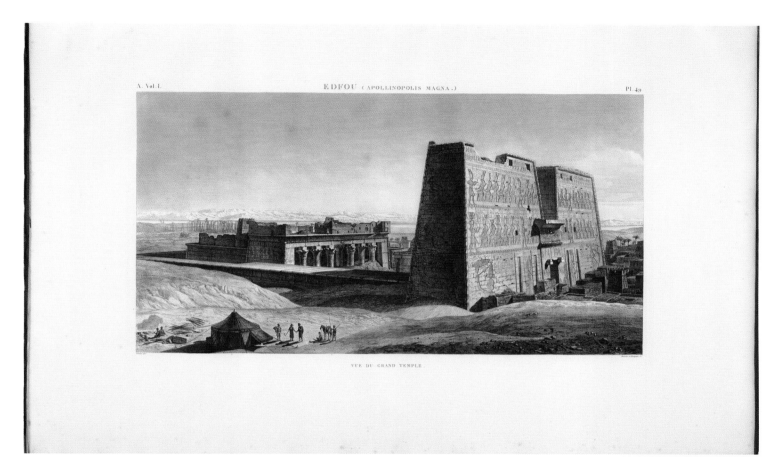

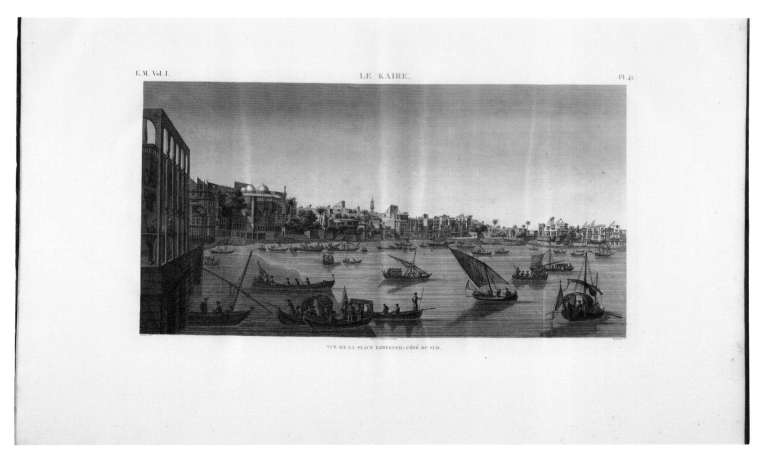

Nineteenth-century graphic techniques

Detail of *Spécimen des écritures modernes*, designed by Jean Midolle **(see p. 244)**

ALPHABET LAPIDAIRE MONSTRE.

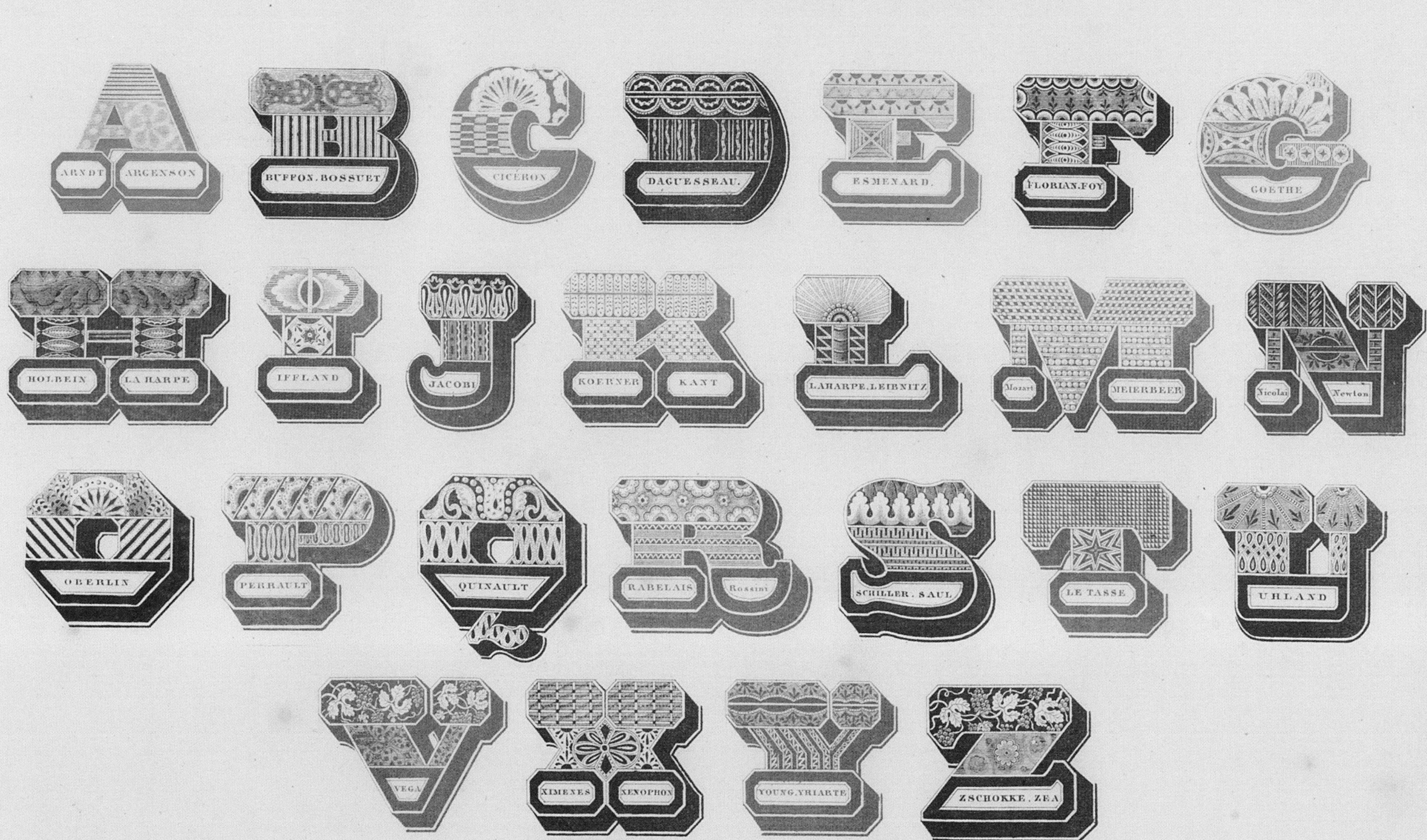

C. Fasoli

Midolle Ecrivⁿ Compositᵉ

Lith. de E. Simon à Strasbg.

Nineteenth-century graphic techniques **The early nineteenth century added an entirely new printing process to the range of options for the production of graphic images: lithography. This technique, invented by the German Alois Senefelder in the late eighteenth century, evolved to become one of the most versatile of printing processes. In lithography, the artist or illustrator could draw with chalk or a special ink directly on the stone that served as the printing surface. Compared to wood engraving, this system gave the artist or draughtsman unprecedented freedom. Lithography, moreover, proved extremely well-suited to colour printing, even though it was initially cost-effective only for large print runs.**

One disadvantage was that the application of lithography to book illustration required a separate pass through the press: the illustrations could not be printed together with letterpress text set in metal type. The lithographic stones had to be printed with a different kind of press and often even in a different printing house! After printing, the lithographs were therefore inserted as plates in the printed and folded sheets that carried the letterpress text of the book. Lithography became the method of choice for producing colour posters and commercial printed items such as labels, letterheads and menus.

In the late eighteenth century, Thomas Bewick in England had developed the technique of wood engraving. This relief printing process, where the image was engraved in the hard end grain of the woodblock, gave finer control over the image than the traditional woodcut (which was cut on the plank) and made longer press runs possible. The introduction of electrotyping soon after 1839 removed the last hurdle for the mass production of illustrated works. It allowed printers to duplicate printing blocks or plates and the copper duplicates also resisted wear better than woodblocks. This invention signals the beginning of the illustrated popular periodical.

But the most important discovery of the nineteenth century was surely photography, in 1839. Suddenly reality could be captured without the intervention

of a painter or draughtsman. Not until about 1860, however, was it possible to reproduce photographic images in print on a large scale. Several processes emerged in succession, including photolithography (1855), collotype (1868), process engraving (actually a kind of etching, *c.* 1870) and photogravure (1879). The initial difficulties with the reproduction of grey tones in book illustration met a practical solution with the invention of the halftone block (1882).

In the course of the twentieth century, photolithography was further developed with the offset technique, which saw expanding use for the production of books from the 1950s onwards. JDZ

1818 **Alois Senefelder** **Alois Senefelder, *Vollständiges Lehrbuch der Steindruckerey*. Munich: Karl Thienemann; Vienna: Karl Gerold, 1818. xiv, 370 pp. 27 cm. With 'Musterblätter', 32.5 cm.**

The German Alois Senefelder (1771–1834), the inventor of lithography, wrote this manual when lithography was already being used by a large number of printers. Rumours that the technique had been developed in Paris or London may have lead him to publish a book about his printmaking technique, staking his claim once and for all.

The *Vollständiges Lehrbuch der Steindruckerey* ('Complete Manual of Lithography') constitutes a milestone in the history of printing. In the first part of the book, Senefelder describes his invention and the possibilities it offers, while the second part contains practical instructions. The supplement contains twenty specimens, or *Musterblätter*, which illustrate the various methods.

Senefelder's book was also published in French and English, in 1819, followed by a number of manuals by great contemporary lithographers: Godefroy Engelmann, in France (1822), and Charles Joseph Hullmandel, in England (1824). These new manuals proved quite influential as regards the spread of the new printmaking technique, especially because they focused on the artist who drew on the stone, rather than on the practical side of a lithographic printing office. JDZ

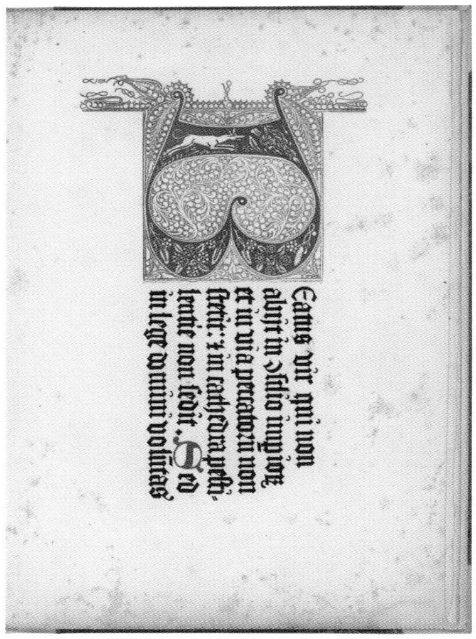

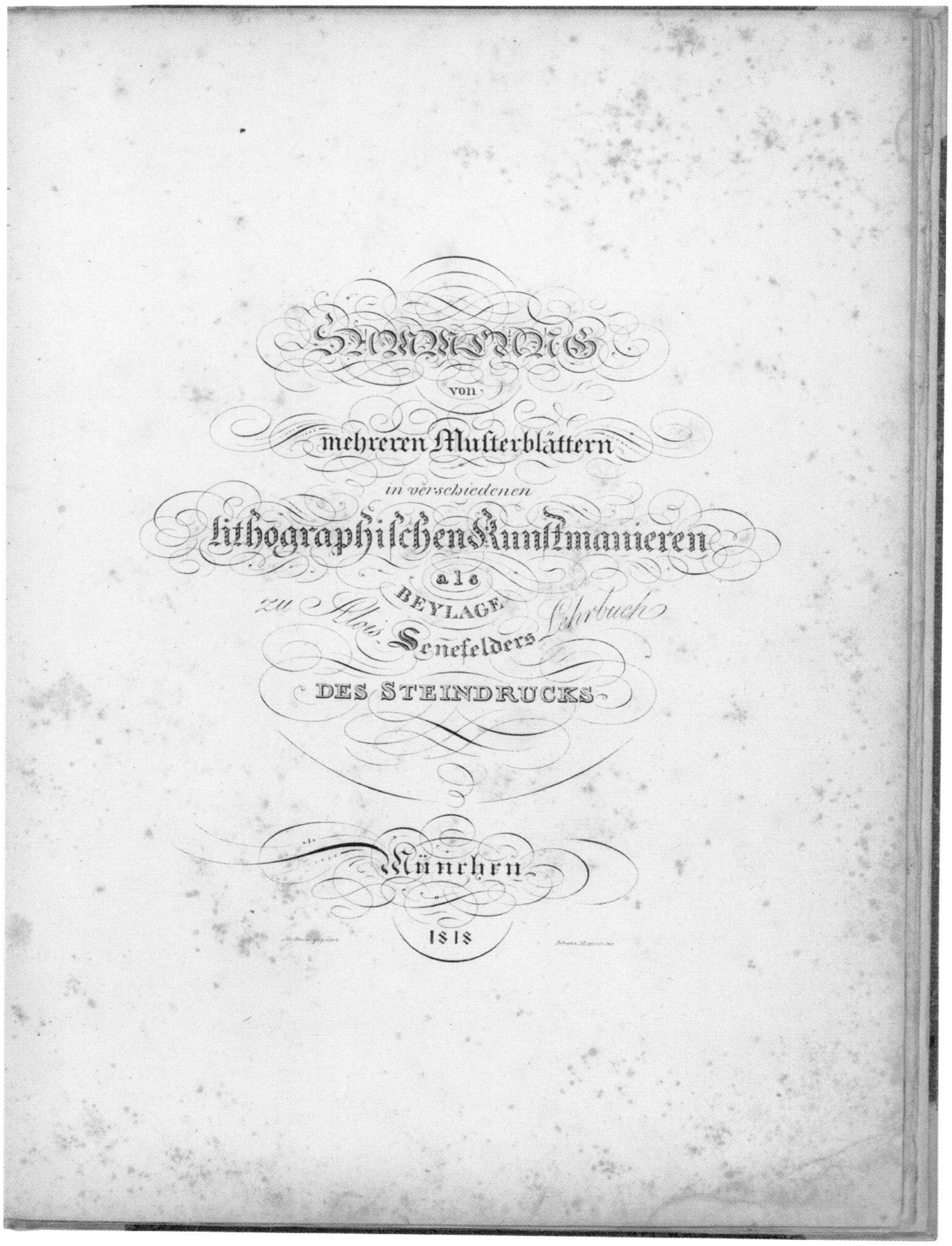

Lithography is a printing technique based on the mutual repulsion of water and fat. The lithographer or artist makes a drawing on a thick limestone plate using a fat or oil-based medium, such as ink or crayons. Then the stone is wetted, and when printing ink is rolled onto the stone, only the greasy parts take the ink. Offset printing developed from lithography and came to dominate the world of books after the Second World War.

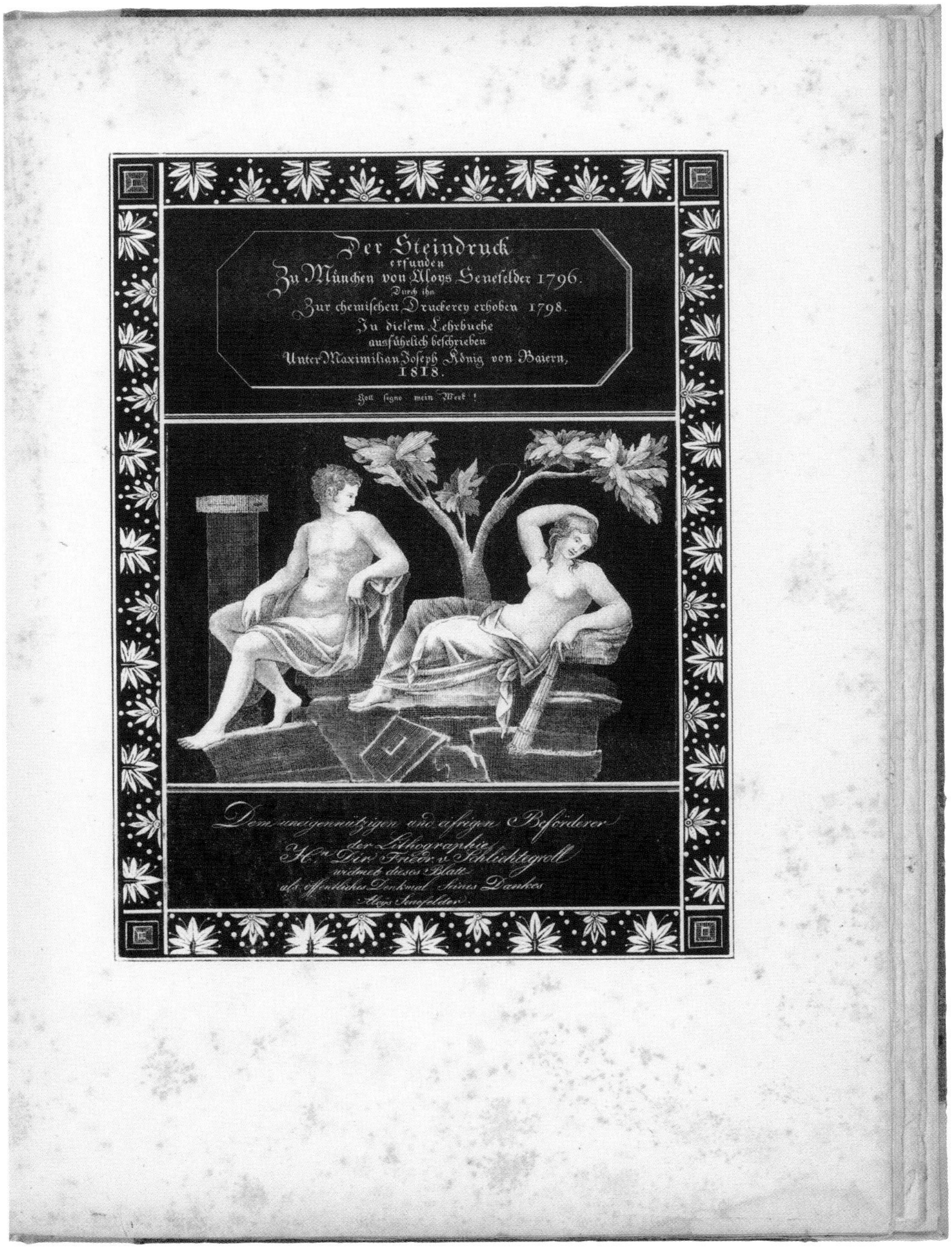

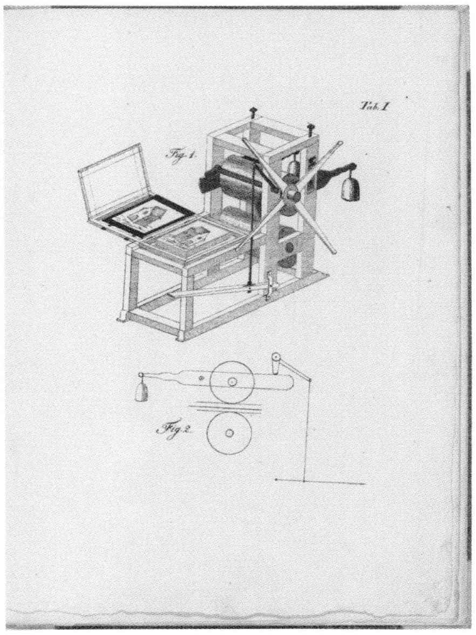

1822 **William Savage** **William Savage, *Practical Hints on Decorative Printing, with Illustrations Engraved on Wood, and Printed in Colours at the Type Press*. London: Longman, Hurst, Rees, Orme and Brown et al., 1822. vi, 118 pp. 38 cm.**

Printer: William Savage, London.

The professional literature on printers' manuals generally speaks highly of *Practical Hints on Decorative Printing*. At the beginning of the nineteenth century, the printing of colour illustrations was still in its infancy. One of the problems was the inferior quality of printing ink. The letterpress printer and engraver William Savage (1770–1843) had applied himself to colour printing for decorative purposes (not for book illustrations). In his text, he phrases this as follows: '[that] the imitation of coloured drawings be attempted with success, as to give facsimiles of the productions of different masters, at a small expense, to serve as studies, or for the decoration of rooms, where, if framed and glazed, the eye should not be able to distinguish them from drawings.'

Despite its many pleas for and directions on beautiful printing and striving for superior craftsmanship, Savage's book is not exactly a prime example. The inking is uneven and the text contains quite a few typesetter's errors. The principal flaw of contemporary ink manufacture that Savage mentions, oil and pigment separation after printing, is quite prominent in the plates of his

book. This could be a result of the book's age, but in a sense, *Practical Hints on Decorative Printing* is, in its current state, at odds with the intentions of the author.

Colour printing went on to expand immensely with the arrival of the cylinder press, which made it much easier to register the colours exactly. JDZ

This is Caslon & Catherwood's Canon (42 point) roman (*c.* 1812) with the stem width of about 38% of the cap height, from a series produced *c.* 1808–14. British foundries produced these 'fat face' types for the advertising boom that accompanied the industrial revolution. From a two-leaf type specimen in part 1 (1818).

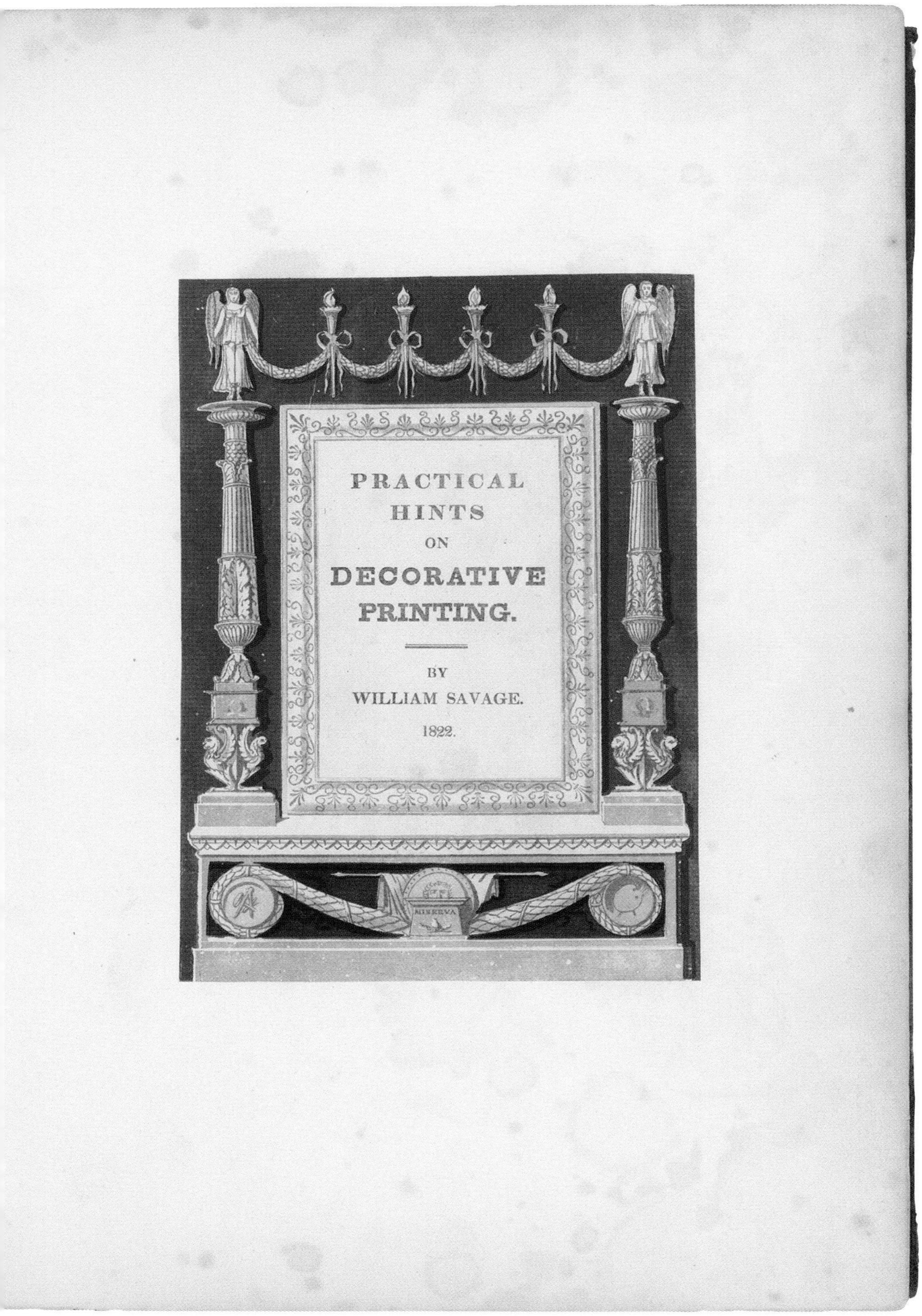

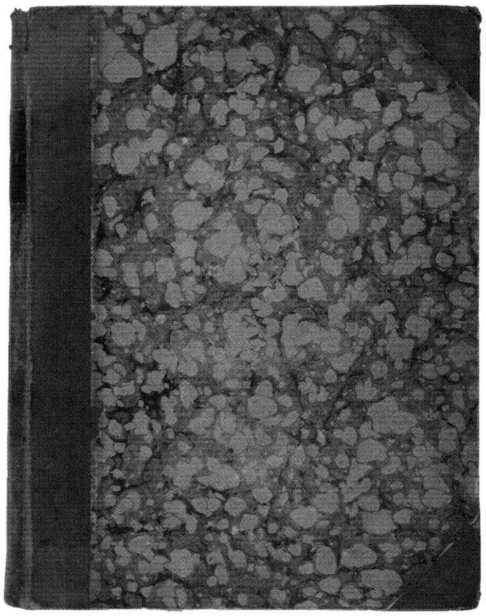

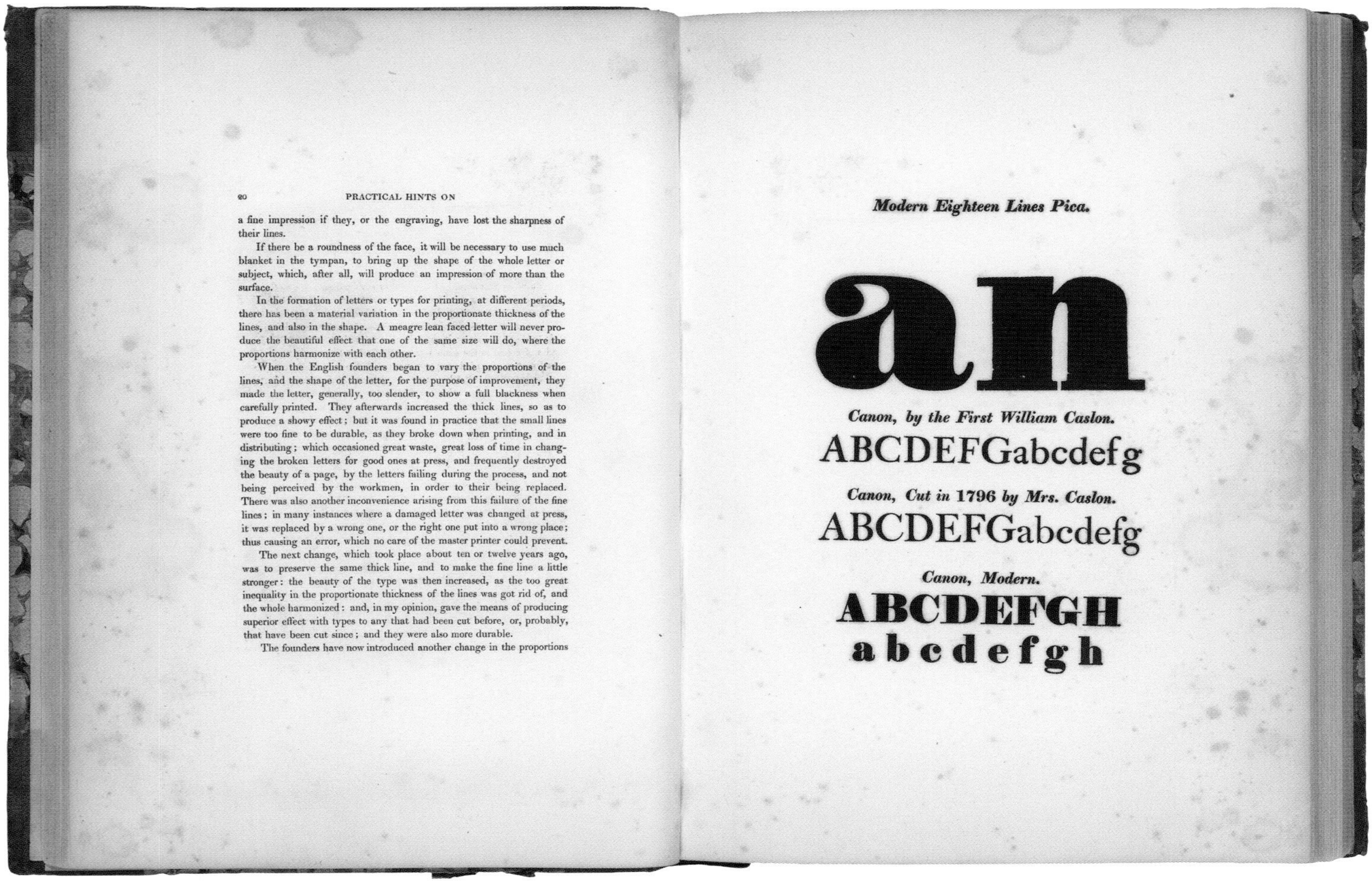

20 PRACTICAL HINTS ON

a fine impression if they, or the engraving, have lost the sharpness of their lines.

If there be a roundness of the face, it will be necessary to use much blanket in the tympan, to bring up the shape of the whole letter or subject, which, after all, will produce an impression of more than the surface.

In the formation of letters or types for printing, at different periods, there has been a material variation in the proportionate thickness of the lines, and also in the shape. A meagre lean faced letter will never produce the beautiful effect that one of the same size will do, where the proportions harmonize with each other.

When the English founders began to vary the proportions of the lines, and the shape of the letter, for the purpose of improvement, they made the letter, generally, too slender, to show a full blackness when carefully printed. They afterwards increased the thick lines, so as to produce a showy effect; but it was found in practice that the small lines were too fine to be durable, as they broke down when printing, and in distributing; which occasioned great waste, great loss of time in changing the broken letters for good ones at press, and frequently destroyed the beauty of a page, by the letters failing during the process, and not being perceived by the workmen, in order to their being replaced. There was also another inconvenience arising from this failure of the fine lines; in many instances where a damaged letter was changed at press, it was replaced by a wrong one, or the right one put into a wrong place; thus causing an error, which no care of the master printer could prevent.

The next change, which took place about ten or twelve years ago, was to preserve the same thick line, and to make the fine line a little stronger: the beauty of the type was then increased, as the too great inequality in the proportionate thickness of the lines was got rid of, and the whole harmonized: and, in my opinion, gave the means of producing superior effect with types to any that had been cut before, or, probably, that have been cut since; and they were also more durable.

The founders have now introduced another change in the proportions

Modern Eighteen Lines Pica.

an

Canon, by the First William Caslon.

ABCDEFGabcdefg

Canon, Cut in 1796 by Mrs. Caslon.

ABCDEFGabcdefg

Canon, Modern.

ABCDEFGH
abcdefgh

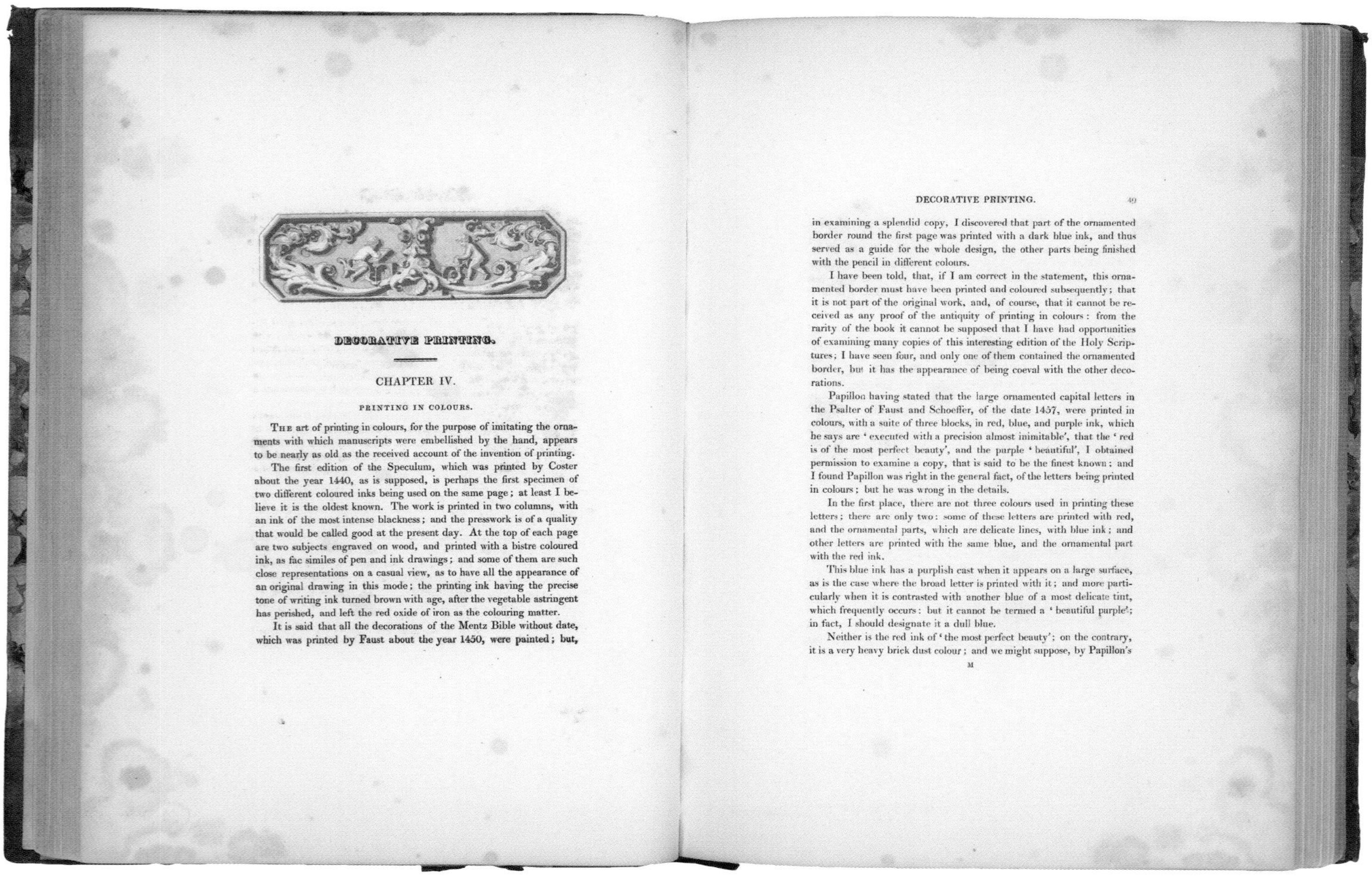

DECORATIVE PRINTING.

CHAPTER IV.

PRINTING IN COLOURS.

THE art of printing in colours, for the purpose of imitating the ornaments with which manuscripts were embellished by the hand, appears to be nearly as old as the received account of the invention of printing.

The first edition of the Speculum, which was printed by Coster about the year 1440, as is supposed, is perhaps the first specimen of two different coloured inks being used on the same page; at least I believe it is the oldest known. The work is printed in two columns, with an ink of the most intense blackness; and the presswork is of a quality that would be called good at the present day. At the top of each page are two subjects engraved on wood, and printed with a bistre coloured ink, as fac similes of pen and ink drawings; and some of them are such close representations on a casual view, as to have all the appearance of an original drawing in this mode; the printing ink having the precise tone of writing ink turned brown with age, after the vegetable astringent has perished, and left the red oxide of iron as the colouring matter.

It is said that all the decorations of the Mentz Bible without date, which was printed by Faust about the year 1450, were painted; but,

DECORATIVE PRINTING. 49

in examining a splendid copy, I discovered that part of the ornamented border round the first page was printed with a dark blue ink, and thus served as a guide for the whole design, the other parts being finished with the pencil in different colours.

I have been told, that, if I am correct in the statement, this ornamented border must have been printed and coloured subsequently; that it is not part of the original work, and, of course, that it cannot be received as any proof of the antiquity of printing in colours: from the rarity of the book it cannot be supposed that I have had opportunities of examining many copies of this interesting edition of the Holy Scriptures; I have seen four, and only one of them contained the ornamented border, but it has the appearance of being coeval with the other decorations.

Papillon having stated that the large ornamented capital letters in the Psalter of Faust and Schoeffer, of the date 1457, were printed in colours, with a suite of three blocks, in red, blue, and purple ink, which he says are 'executed with a precision almost inimitable', that the 'red is of the most perfect beauty', and the purple 'beautiful', I obtained permission to examine a copy, that is said to be the finest known; and I found Papillon was right in the general fact, of the letters being printed in colours; but he was wrong in the details.

In the first place, there are not three colours used in printing these letters; there are only two: some of these letters are printed with red, and the ornamental parts, which are delicate lines, with blue ink; and other letters are printed with the same blue, and the ornamental part with the red ink.

This blue ink has a purplish cast when it appears on a large surface, as is the case where the broad letter is printed with it; and more particularly when it is contrasted with another blue of a most delicate tint, which frequently occurs: but it cannot be termed a 'beautiful purple'; in fact, I should designate it a dull blue.

Neither is the red ink of 'the most perfect beauty'; on the contrary, it is a very heavy brick dust colour; and we might suppose, by Papillon's

M

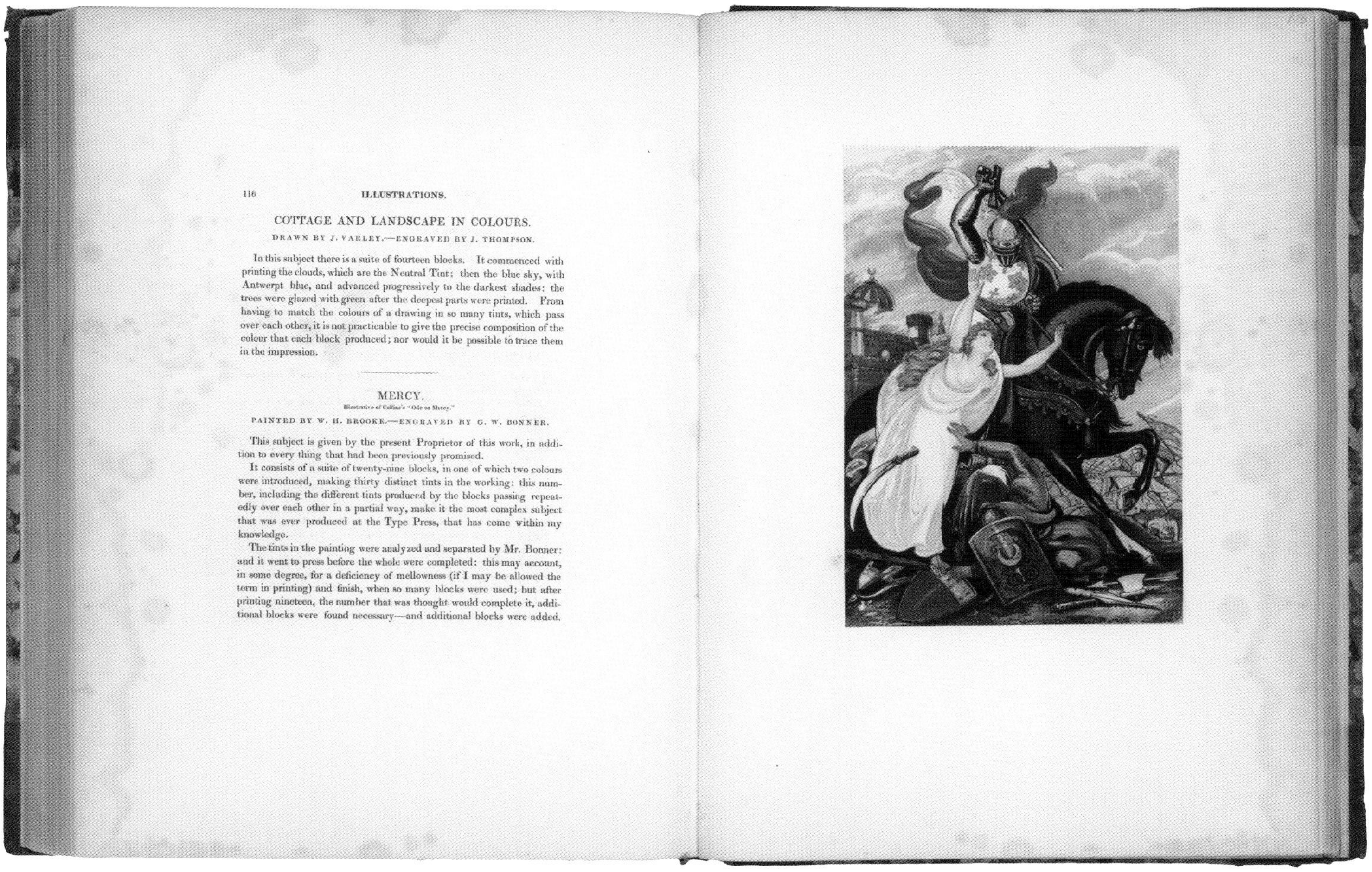

116 ILLUSTRATIONS.

COTTAGE AND LANDSCAPE IN COLOURS.

DRAWN BY J. VARLEY.—ENGRAVED BY J. THOMPSON.

In this subject there is a suite of fourteen blocks. It commenced with printing the clouds, which are the Neutral Tint; then the blue sky, with Antwerpt blue, and advanced progressively to the darkest shades: the trees were glazed with green after the deepest parts were printed. From having to match the colours of a drawing in so many tints, which pass over each other, it is not practicable to give the precise composition of the colour that each block produced; nor would it be possible to trace them in the impression.

MERCY.

Illustrative of Collins's "Ode on Mercy."

PAINTED BY W. H. BROOKE.—ENGRAVED BY G. W. BONNER.

This subject is given by the present Proprietor of this work, in addition to every thing that had been previously promised.

It consists of a suite of twenty-nine blocks, in one of which two colours were introduced, making thirty distinct tints in the working: this number, including the different tints produced by the blocks passing repeatedly over each other in a partial way, make it the most complex subject that was ever produced at the Type Press, that has come within my knowledge.

The tints in the painting were analyzed and separated by Mr. Bonner: and it went to press before the whole were completed: this may account, in some degree, for a deficiency of mellowness (if I may be allowed the term in printing) and finish, when so many blocks were used; but after printing nineteen, the number that was thought would complete it, additional blocks were found necessary—and additional blocks were added.

114 ILLUSTRATIONS.

2. Fennel plant, Antwerpt blue and chrome yellow; the umbel of the plant a little more yellow. The eyes in the wings of the Butterfly, vermilion.

3. Dark yellow in the wings, Indian yellow.

4. Light yellow in the wings, and in the flowers of the plant, chrome yellow.

5. Brown in the Butterfly, burnt Sienna, rose pink, Indian red, and black ink.

6. Deep shaded brown in the Butterfly, the same colours, with the addition of a little black ink.

7. Darkest colour in the under wings, the same colours, with a little more black ink.

For the Specimen from which the drawing was made, I beg leave to return my thanks to Mr. Hatchett, of the Bank of England, on account of the kind and friendly manner he entrusted me with a rare and scarce insect from his Cabinet.

ROSE HILL PARROT.

From New South Wales.

DRAWN FROM LIFE BY J. P. NEALE.—ENGRAVED BY BRANSTON.

This beautiful, and in England, scarce bird, took its name from a hill, called Rose Hill, in New South Wales, on account of the numbers of them resorting to it. Mr. Dalziel, of Princes Street, Rotherhithe, politely gave permission for a drawing to be made, which Mr. Neale undertook to execute.

There are seven blocks.

This was a subject that I thought peculiarly applicable to the process, and which would prove one of the happiest efforts in the book; and I was particularly anxious that it should be so; for the owner of the bird is a

William Savage

1828 **Vincent Figgins** *Specimen of Printing Types*. London: Vincent Figgins, 1828. 137 leaves plus 3 specimen leaves and a price list loosely inserted. 24 cm.

Vincent Figgins (1767–1844) was apprenticed in 1782 to the London typefounder and punchcutter Joseph Jackson, and managed the foundry from 1789, but cut no punches himself. He established good relations with Jackson's customers, but could not afford to purchase the foundry when Jackson died in 1792. When William Caslon III purchased Jackson's stock in February 1792, Figgins set up independently, apparently in his father's house in London.

In June 1792 the Oxford University Press asked Figgins to complete Jackson's modernization of its Greek matrices. With difficulty he located Jackson's anonymous freelance punchcutter, who went on to cut type for Figgins for thirty years. Cutting several new types took more than a year, but starting from scratch had advantages: Richard Austin and William Martin, introducing Didot and Bodoni's influences to Britain, rapidly made older types obsolete.

Gaining patronage from leading printers (John Nichols from April 1793 and Thomas Bensley II soon after), Figgins's typefoundry quickly flourished, offering up-to-date romans and italics, many non-Latin types, and a range of decorated types. William Caslon IV introduced the first sans serif in around 1812/14 – following architectural lettering derived from classical Roman inscriptions – but Figgins's 'Antique' (slab serif) variant (*c*. 1818, rarely found in earlier lettering) at first met with greater commercial success. Slab serif types spread through British and European typefoundries before Figgins introduced the second sans serif in 1828. Influenced by contemporary romans, his sans serif abandoned inscriptional forms, setting the style for British (and from 1836 continental) foundries into the twentieth century. Figgins's foundry flourished under his sons and grandson until 1907. JAL

This second sans serif (Figgins, 1828) established the style that dominated before Edward Johnston's sans (1916) and returned with Univers and Helvetica (1957). The first sans serif (Caslon, *c*. 1812/14) followed lettering in architectural drawings (*c*. 1779) and London's 'Egyptian' shop signs (1805, named after Napoleon's Egyptian campaign), but nothing similar appeared until 1916.

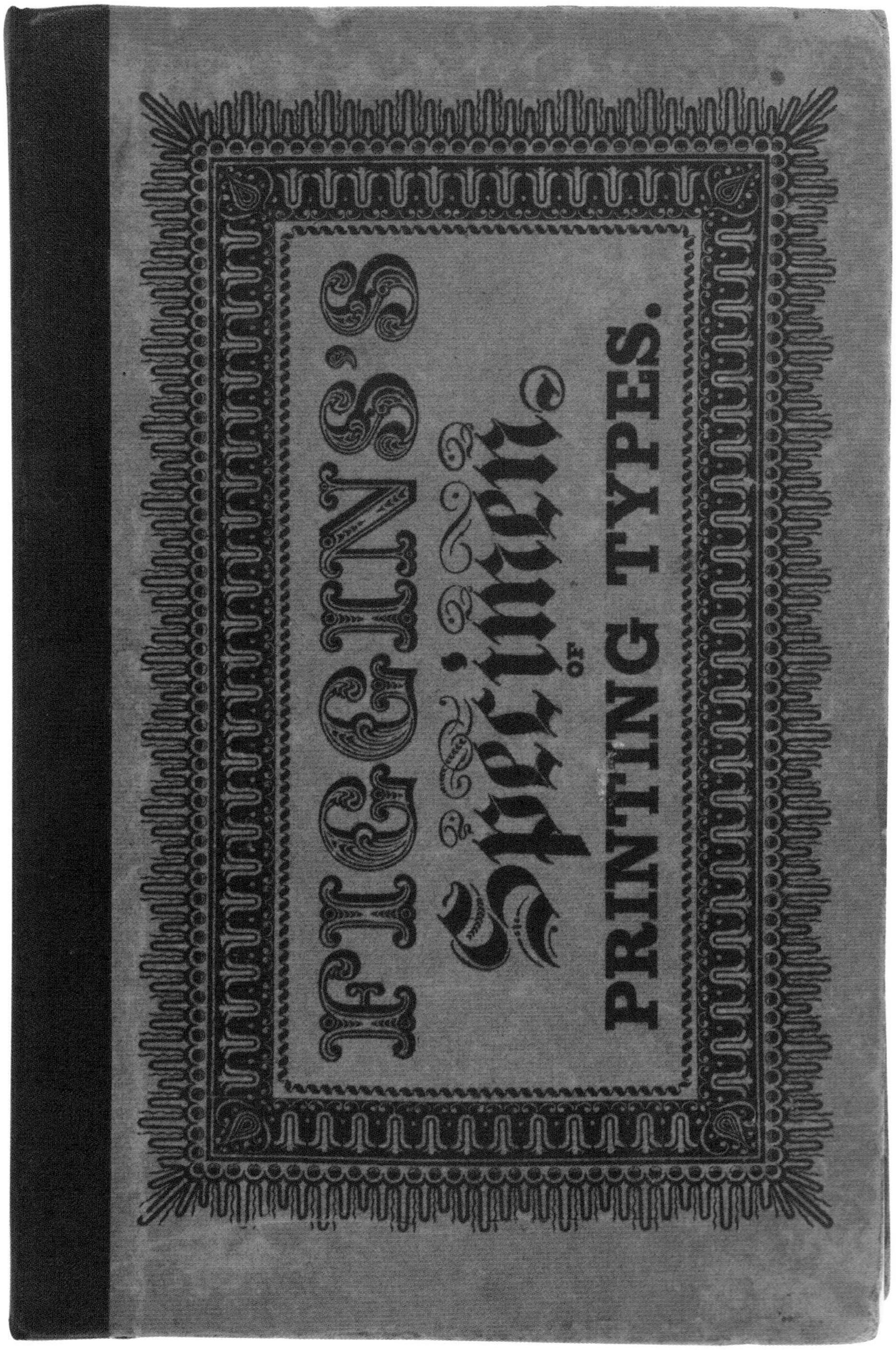

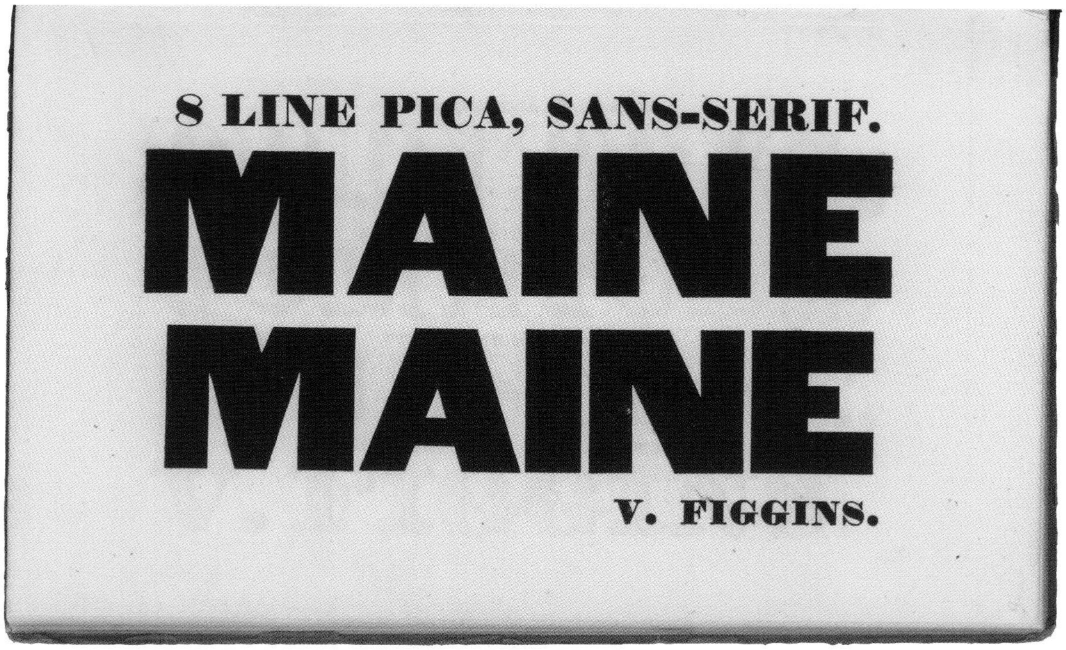
8 LINE PICA, SANS-SERIF.

MAINE

MAINE

V. FIGGINS.

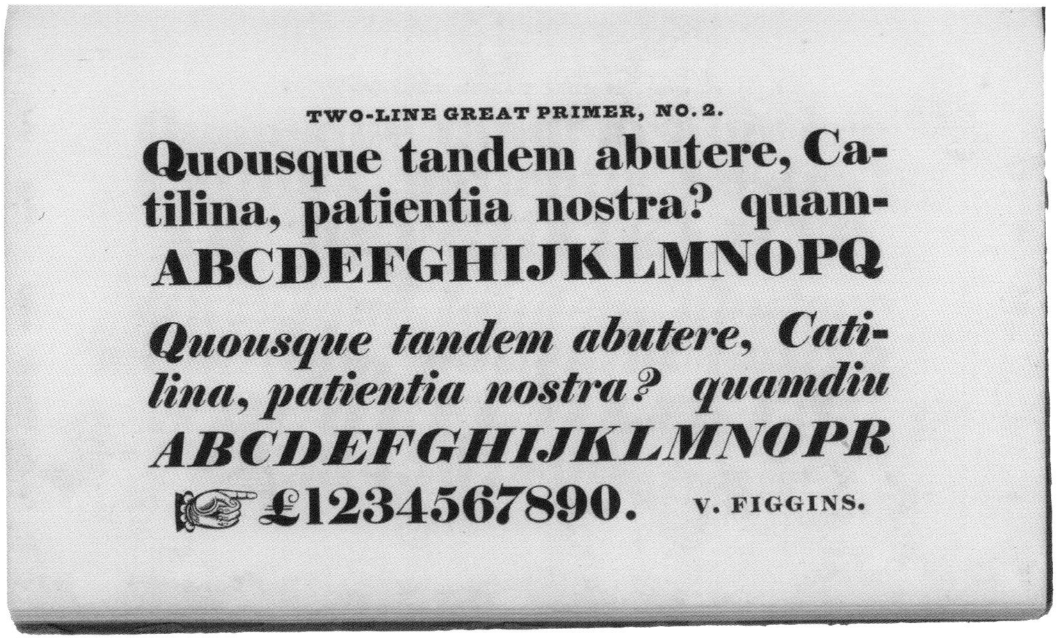
TWO-LINE GREAT PRIMER, NO. 2.

Quousque tandem abutere, Catilina, patientia nostra? quam-
ABCDEFGHIJKLMNOPQ

*Quousque tandem abutere, Cati-
lina, patientia nostra? quamdiu
ABCDEFGHIJKLMNOPR*

☞ £1234567890. V. FIGGINS.

SIXTEEN-LINE PICA, ANTIQUE.

MIN

V. FIGGINS. 1825.

1834 **Jean Midolle** Jean Midolle, *Spécimen des écritures modernes comprenant les romaines fleuronnées, gothiques nouvelles, fractures, françaises, anglaise, italienne et allemande*. Strasbourg: Fc. Emile Simon fils, 1834–35. 40 leaves. 28 × 40 cm. Lettering artist: Jean Midolle. Chromolithographers: Auguste Ehrhardt, C. Fasoli, E. Lemaître. Printer: Frédéric Emile Simon fils, Strasbourg.

A spectacular demonstration of pioneering chromolithographic techniques applied to decorative letters. Jean Midolle (*fl.* 1830–46), a lettering artist and palaeographer also active in Geneva and St Gallen, had these examples of calligraphy and alphabets printed and published as both black and white lithographs and as the chromolithographs shown here.

The lithographers used four different techniques to achieve wide-ranging effects. Some stones were inked *à la poupée*, like earlier copperplates: different colours were dabbed onto different parts of the stone with a swab, so that they could be printed together. Sometimes different parts of a stone were inked and transferred to different stones that could then be used to print each colour separately. Sometimes bands of ink in different colours were partially blended on the inking slab without completely mixing them. That rainbow of colour could then be rolled onto the stone, either for a background tint or for a complex image. Finally, gold or other metallic dust was sprinkled on some of the freshly-printed leaves, sticking to the wet ink. Some leaves combined more than one technique. Simon's labour-intensive methods never saw widespread use, four-colour chromolithographs (patented 1837) proving more practical.

The convenience and economy of typefounders' reusable decorative letters restricted the lithographer's freedom of form and layout to certain genres. The decorative alphabets of Midolle's *Ecritures modernes* therefore won less of a following than his accompanying *Ecritures anciens* and *Galerie: Compositions*, which included non-Latin lettering, pages from medieval manuscripts and other forms of composition less amenable to the typefounder's art. JAL

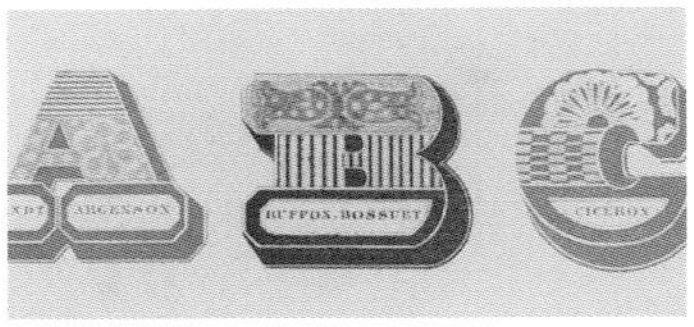

The letters from the original stone were transferred to two new stones, with no adjacent letters on the same stone. The new stones were then rainbow-inked, one from blue at the head to pink at the foot, the other from orange at the head to green at the foot.

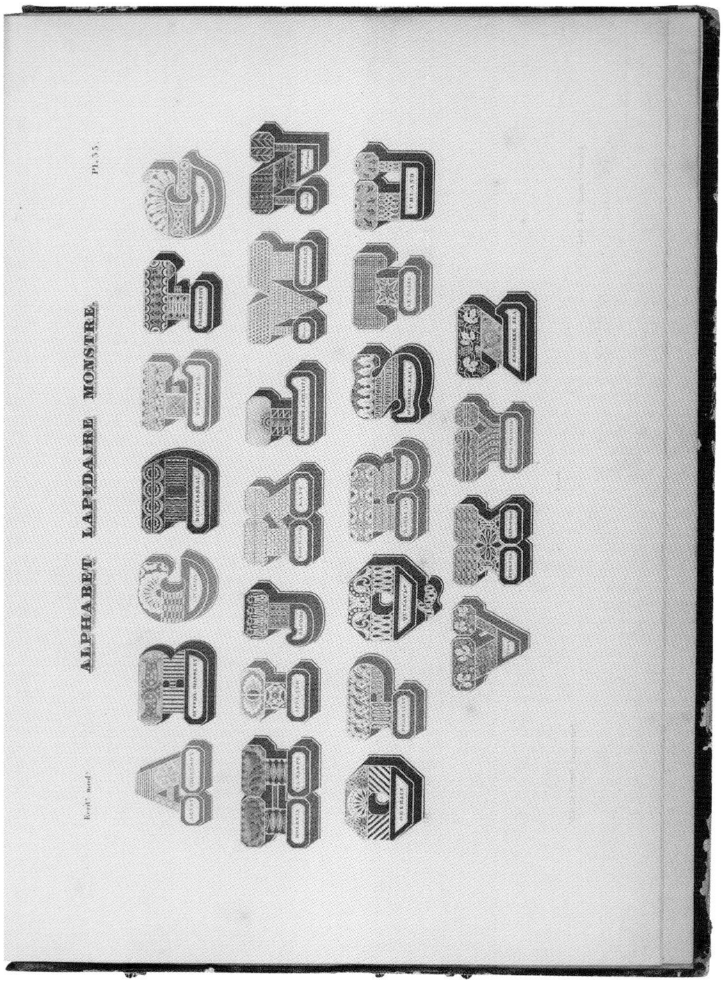
ALPHABET LAPIDAIRE MONSTRE

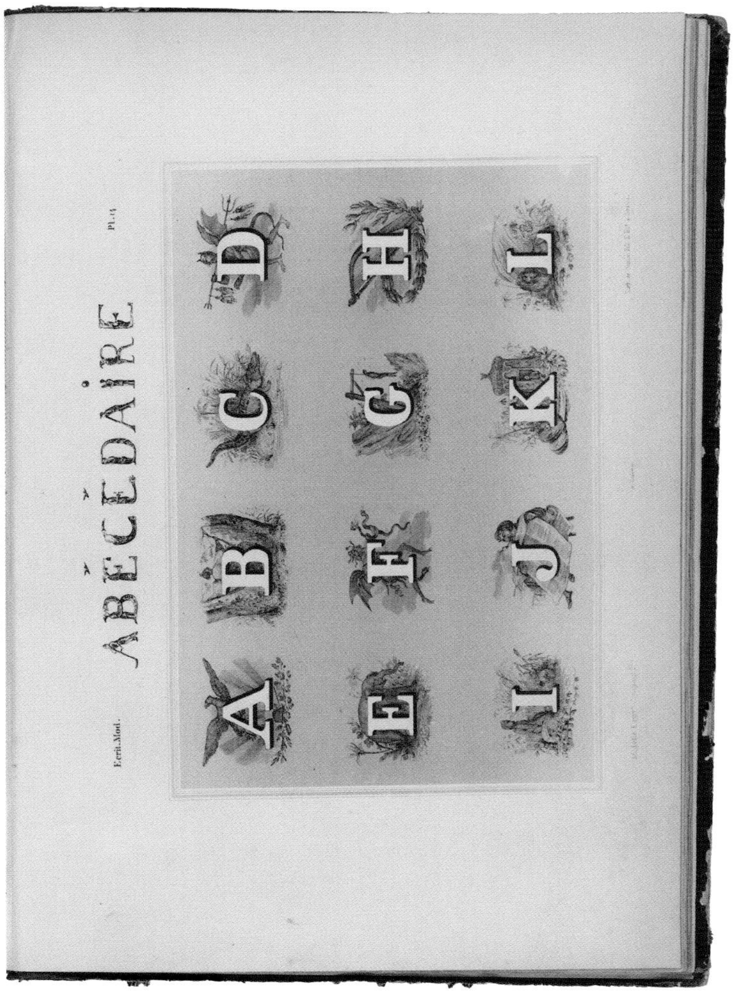
ABÉCÉDAIRE

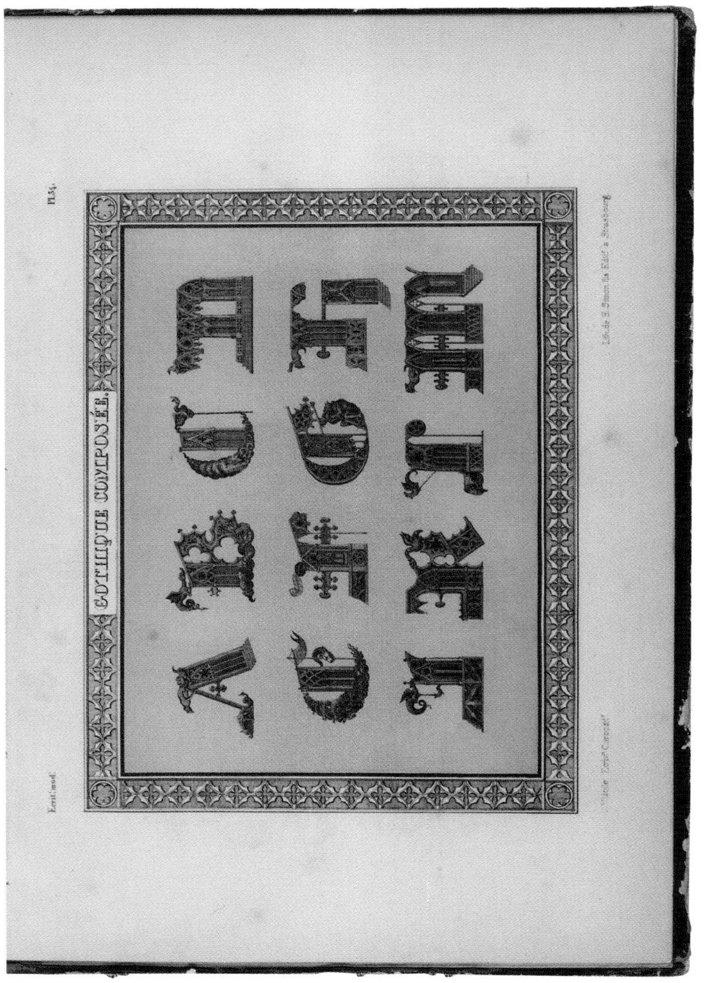
GOTHIQUE COMPOSÉE

1840 **John Gould** **John Gould, *The Birds of Australia*. London: John Gould, 1840–48, 1869. 7 volumes. 56.5 cm. Illustrator: John Gould. Lithographer: Elizabeth Gould and others. Printers: C. Hullmandel, London / (after *c.* 1843) Hullmandel & Walton, London (lithography); Richard & John E. Taylor, London (letterpress).**

John Gould (1804–81), who worked at the Zoological Society museum in London, was a specialist in ornithology and bird painting. In May 1838, Gould travelled by boat to Australia, with his wife and child, to record Australian birds for a standard book that had been planned. In 1840, the family returned to England with specimens of eight hundred bird species, nests and eggs of over seventy species, and with records on habitat and behaviour. Gould also took a great number of parakeet pairs home, a species he had come to enjoy in Australia, both as a pet and as a meat.

The Birds of Australia began to appear in December 1840, in tri-monthly instalments. In contrast to his predecessors, Gould used lithography instead of engravings or etchings. He drew rough sketches for all the plates, which were finished in detail by his wife Elizabeth (and by others, after her death in 1841) and then transferred to the lithographic stone. The plates were hand-coloured at Gould's home in London.

With his first book, released in the early 1830s, Gould had been forced to finance the publication himself. He did well out of it: his business instinct and his demands for high-quality illustrations and text ensured that his projects were profitable. *The Birds of Australia*, which contains six hundred colour illustrations, is generally seen as the most important of Gould's eighteen larger publications. AP

The Fry and Steele typefoundry's French Canon (51 point) no. 2 (1807/08) is an excellent display face. Opened in 1764, Fry's foundry first cut types following Baskerville's style, then closely copied Caslon after 1780. In around 1804, fifteen years after Didot and Bodoni's influence reached Britain, Fry and Steele began their 'modern face' series.

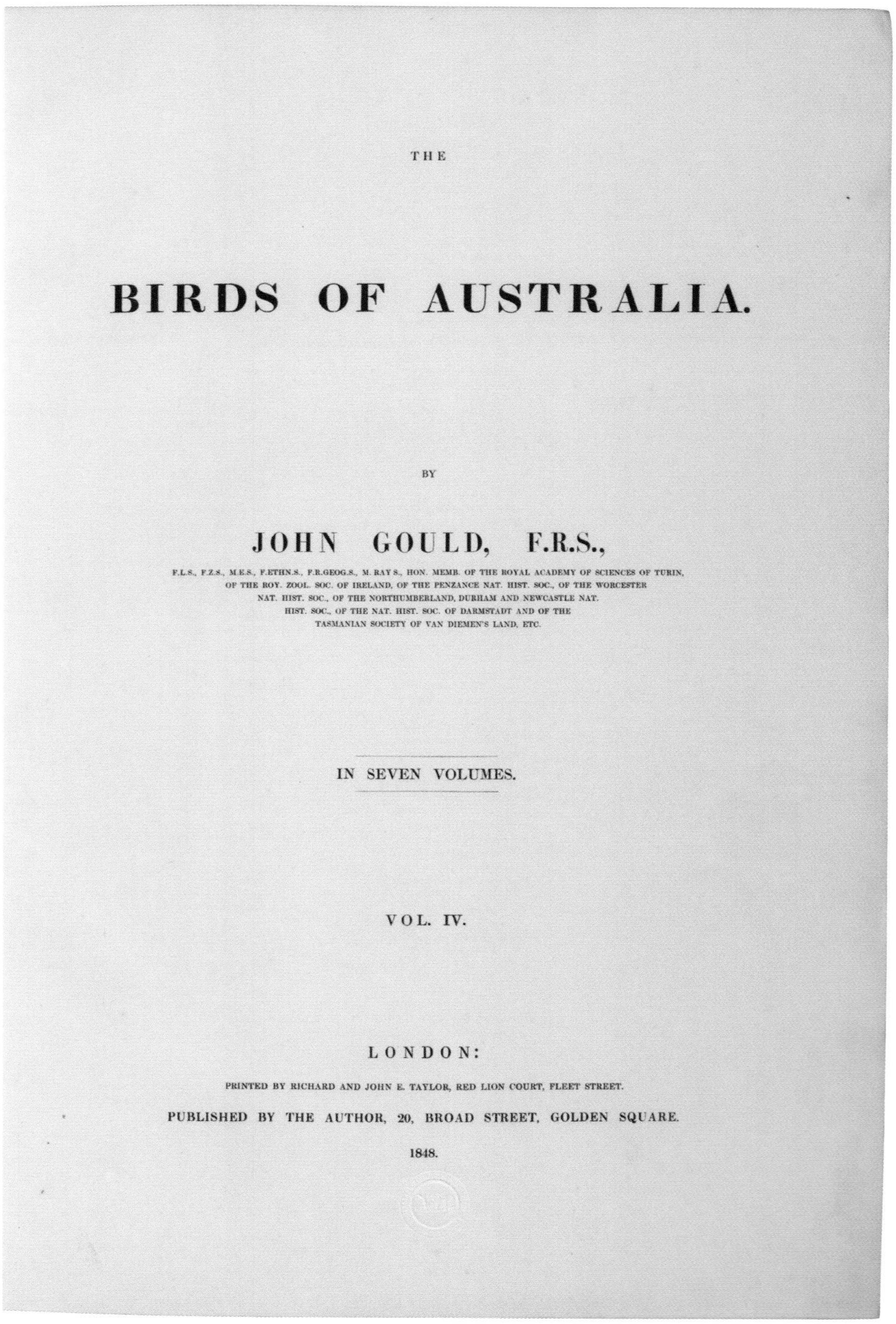

THE

BIRDS OF AUSTRALIA.

BY

JOHN GOULD, F.R.S.,

F.L.S., F.Z.S., M.E.S., F.ETHN.S., F.R.GEOG.S., M. RAY S., HON. MEMB. OF THE ROYAL ACADEMY OF SCIENCES OF TURIN, OF THE ROY. ZOOL. SOC. OF IRELAND, OF THE PENZANCE NAT. HIST. SOC., OF THE WORCESTER NAT. HIST. SOC., OF THE NORTHUMBERLAND, DURHAM AND NEWCASTLE NAT. HIST. SOC., OF THE NAT. HIST. SOC. OF DARMSTADT AND OF THE TASMANIAN SOCIETY OF VAN DIEMEN'S LAND, ETC.

IN SEVEN VOLUMES.

VOL. IV.

LONDON:

PRINTED BY RICHARD AND JOHN E. TAYLOR, RED LION COURT, FLEET STREET.

PUBLISHED BY THE AUTHOR, 20, BROAD STREET, GOLDEN SQUARE.

1848.

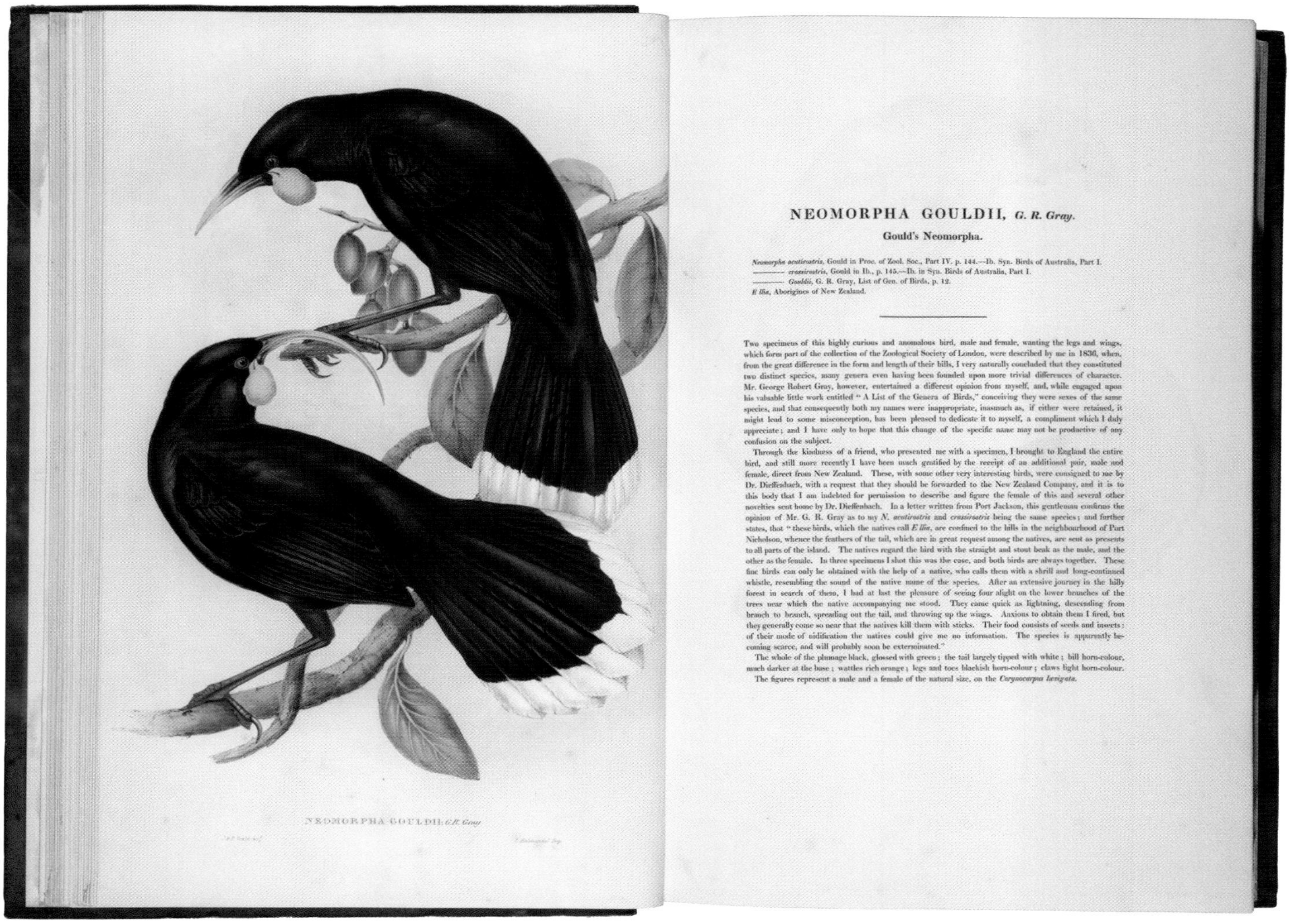

NEOMORPHA GOULDII, *G. R. Gray.*

Gould's Neomorpha.

Neomorpha acutirostris, Gould in Proc. of Zool. Soc., Part IV. p. 144.—Ib. Syn. Birds of Australia, Part I.
——— *crassirostris*, Gould in Ib., p. 145.—Ib. in Syn. Birds of Australia, Part I.
——— *Gouldii*, G. R. Gray, List of Gen. of Birds, p. 12.
E llia, Aborigines of New Zealand.

Two specimens of this highly curious and anomalous bird, male and female, wanting the legs and wings, which form part of the collection of the Zoological Society of London, were described by me in 1836, when, from the great difference in the form and length of their bills, I very naturally concluded that they constituted two distinct species, many genera even having been founded upon more trivial differences of character. Mr. George Robert Gray, however, entertained a different opinion from myself, and, while engaged upon his valuable little work entitled "A List of the Genera of Birds," conceiving they were sexes of the same species, and that consequently both my names were inappropriate, inasmuch as, if either were retained, it might lead to some misconception, has been pleased to dedicate it to myself, a compliment which I duly appreciate; and I have only to hope that this change of the specific name may not be productive of any confusion on the subject.

Through the kindness of a friend, who presented me with a specimen, I brought to England the entire bird, and still more recently I have been much gratified by the receipt of an additional pair, male and female, direct from New Zealand. These, with some other very interesting birds, were consigned to me by Dr. Dieffenbach, with a request that they should be forwarded to the New Zealand Company, and it is to this body that I am indebted for permission to describe and figure the female of this and several other novelties sent home by Dr. Dieffenbach. In a letter written from Port Jackson, this gentleman confirms the opinion of Mr. G. R. Gray as to my *N. acutirostris* and *crassirostris* being the same species; and further states, that "these birds, which the natives call *E llia*, are confined to the hills in the neighbourhood of Port Nicholson, whence the feathers of the tail, which are in great request among the natives, are sent as presents to all parts of the island. The natives regard the bird with the straight and stout beak as the male, and the other as the female. In three specimens I shot this was the case, and both birds are always together. These fine birds can only be obtained with the help of a native, who calls them with a shrill and long-continued whistle, resembling the sound of the native name of the species. After an extensive journey in the hilly forest in search of them, I had at last the pleasure of seeing four alight on the lower branches of the trees near which the native accompanying me stood. They came quick as lightning, descending from branch to branch, spreading out the tail, and throwing up the wings. Anxious to obtain them I fired, but they generally come so near that the natives kill them with sticks. Their food consists of seeds and insects: of their mode of nidification the natives could give me no information. The species is apparently becoming scarce, and will probably soon be exterminated."

The whole of the plumage black, glossed with green; the tail largely tipped with white; bill horn-colour, much darker at the base; wattles rich orange; legs and toes blackish horn-colour; claws light horn-colour.

The figures represent a male and a female of the natural size, on the *Corynocarpus lævigata.*

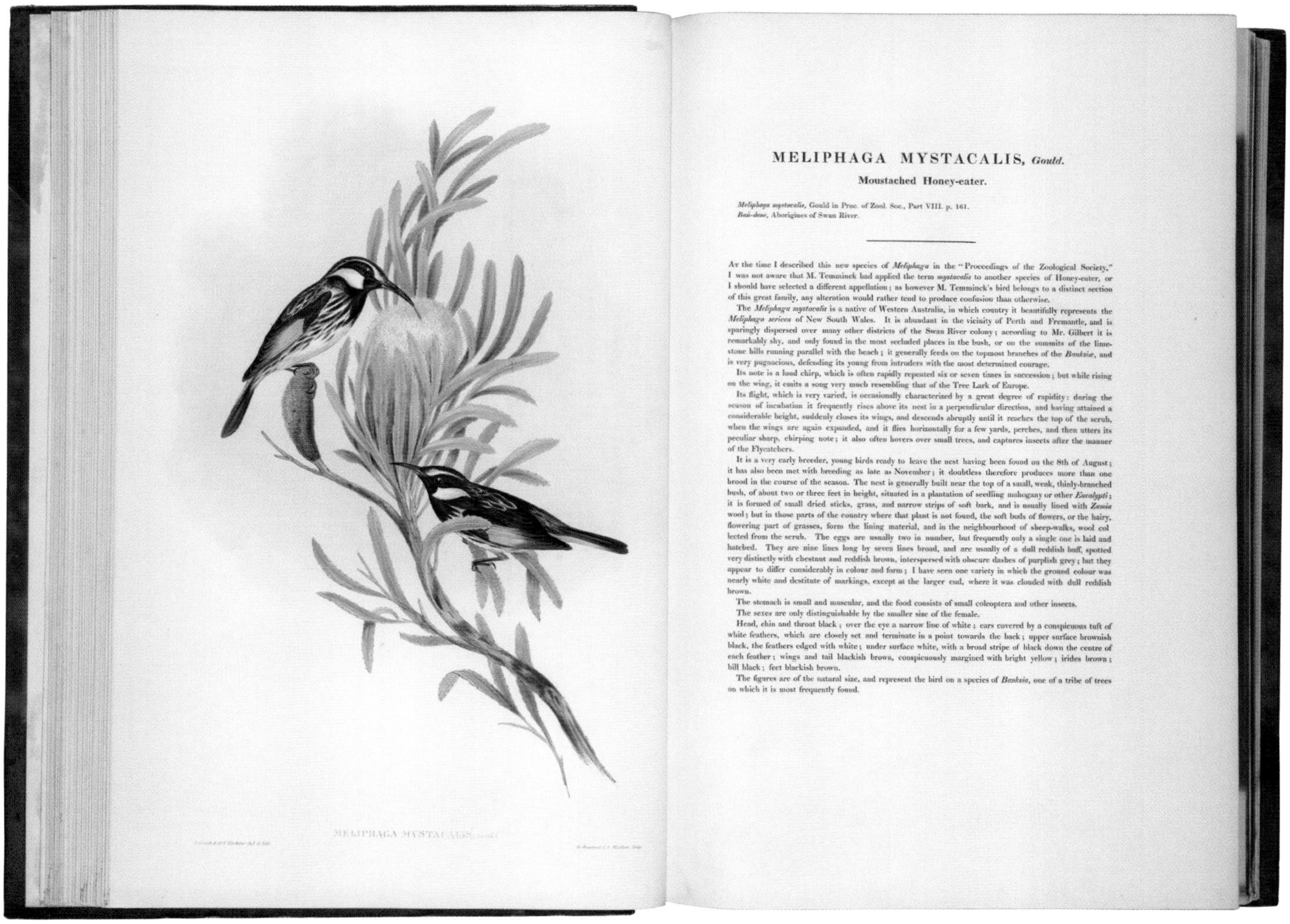

MELIPHAGA MYSTACALIS, *Gould.*

Moustached Honey-eater.

Meliphaga mystacalis, Gould in Proc. of Zool. Soc., Part VIII. p. 161.
Bui-dene, Aborigines of Swan River.

At the time I described this new species of *Meliphaga* in the "Proceedings of the Zoological Society," I was not aware that M. Temminck had applied the term *mystacalis* to another species of Honey-eater, or I should have selected a different appellation; as however M. Temminck's bird belongs to a distinct section of this great family, any alteration would rather tend to produce confusion than otherwise.

The *Meliphaga mystacalis* is a native of Western Australia, in which country it beautifully represents the *Meliphaga sericea* of New South Wales. It is abundant in the vicinity of Perth and Fremantle, and is sparingly dispersed over many other districts of the Swan River colony; according to Mr. Gilbert it is remarkably shy, and only found in the most secluded places in the bush, or on the summits of the limestone hills running parallel with the beach; it generally feeds on the topmost branches of the *Banksiæ*, and is very pugnacious, defending its young from intruders with the most determined courage.

Its note is a loud chirp, which is often rapidly repeated six or seven times in succession; but while rising on the wing, it emits a song very much resembling that of the Tree Lark of Europe.

Its flight, which is very varied, is occasionally characterized by a great degree of rapidity: during the season of incubation it frequently rises above its nest in a perpendicular direction, and having attained a considerable height, suddenly closes its wings, and descends abruptly until it reaches the top of the scrub, when the wings are again expanded, and it flies horizontally for a few yards, perches, and then utters its peculiar sharp, chirping note; it also often hovers over small trees, and captures insects after the manner of the Flycatchers.

It is a very early breeder, young birds ready to leave the nest having been found on the 8th of August; it has also been met with breeding as late as November; it doubtless therefore produces more than one brood in the course of the season. The nest is generally built near the top of a small, weak, thinly-branched bush, of about two or three feet in height, situated in a plantation of seedling mahogany or other *Eucalypti*; it is formed of small dried sticks, grass, and narrow strips of soft bark, and is usually lined with *Zamia* wool; but in those parts of the country where that plant is not found, the soft buds of flowers, or the hairy, flowering part of grasses, form the lining material, and in the neighbourhood of sheep-walks, wool collected from the scrub. The eggs are usually two in number, but frequently only a single one is laid and hatched. They are nine lines long by seven lines broad, and are usually of a dull reddish buff, spotted very distinctly with chestnut and reddish brown, interspersed with obscure dashes of purplish grey; but they appear to differ considerably in colour and form; I have seen one variety in which the ground colour was nearly white and destitute of markings, except at the larger end, where it was clouded with dull reddish brown.

The stomach is small and muscular, and the food consists of small coleoptera and other insects.

The sexes are only distinguishable by the smaller size of the female.

Head, chin and throat black; over the eye a narrow line of white; ears covered by a conspicuous tuft of white feathers, which are closely set and terminate in a point towards the back; upper surface brownish black, the feathers edged with white; under surface white, with a broad stripe of black down the centre of each feather; wings and tail blackish brown, conspicuously margined with bright yellow; irides brown; bill black; feet blackish brown.

The figures are of the natural size, and represent the bird on a species of *Banksia*, one of a tribe of trees on which it is most frequently found.

PTILONORHYNC

OLOSERICEUS: Kuhl.
C. Hullmandel Imp.

1842 **Gottlieb Haase Söhne** *Affiche-Zierschriften*. Prague: Gottlieb Haase Söhne, *c.* 1842. Leaves 140–44. 28.5 cm.

In histories of type design, the nineteenth century usually comes off rather badly. For enthusiasts of classic book faces, this era has little to offer: it was the age of large poster types. In competition with lithography, with its total freedom of drawing, these types were sometimes lavishly decorated. Few images are able to evoke the early nineteenth century as directly as these display types do. Moreover, revivals of these types still come in and out of fashion.

Type in large sizes for commercial printing has been around for some time. A beautiful example is a huge blackletter in capital and lower case, which was designed in around 1580 by the punchcutter Hendrik van den Keere of Ghent. The Antwerp printer, Christoffel Plantin, occasionally used this Grosse Flamande for initials in books and probably for posters as well. The type was sand-cast using wooden pattern letters.

The typefoundry of Gottlieb Haase Söhne in Prague had a better method for producing large letters: dabbing. An engraver would cut an alphabet in wooden blocks, which were then struck into solidifying type-metal. The stereotype castings thus obtained were mounted type-high on wood and sold by the piece. Copying was a customary practice at the time. The exuberant floral type (no. 1574) in this specimen, for example, is copied from a design by Louis John Pouchée (1782–1845).

Mass production of wood type became feasible in the second quarter of the nineteenth century. This was mainly due to the invention of the router; shortly after its introduction, it was combined with a pantograph. ML

This typeface is a direct or indirect copy of a design from the London foundry of Louis John Pouchée (1782–1845). His ornamented types from around 1825 rank among the best of their kind. The fine detail, however, would have been too complex to produce using a router.

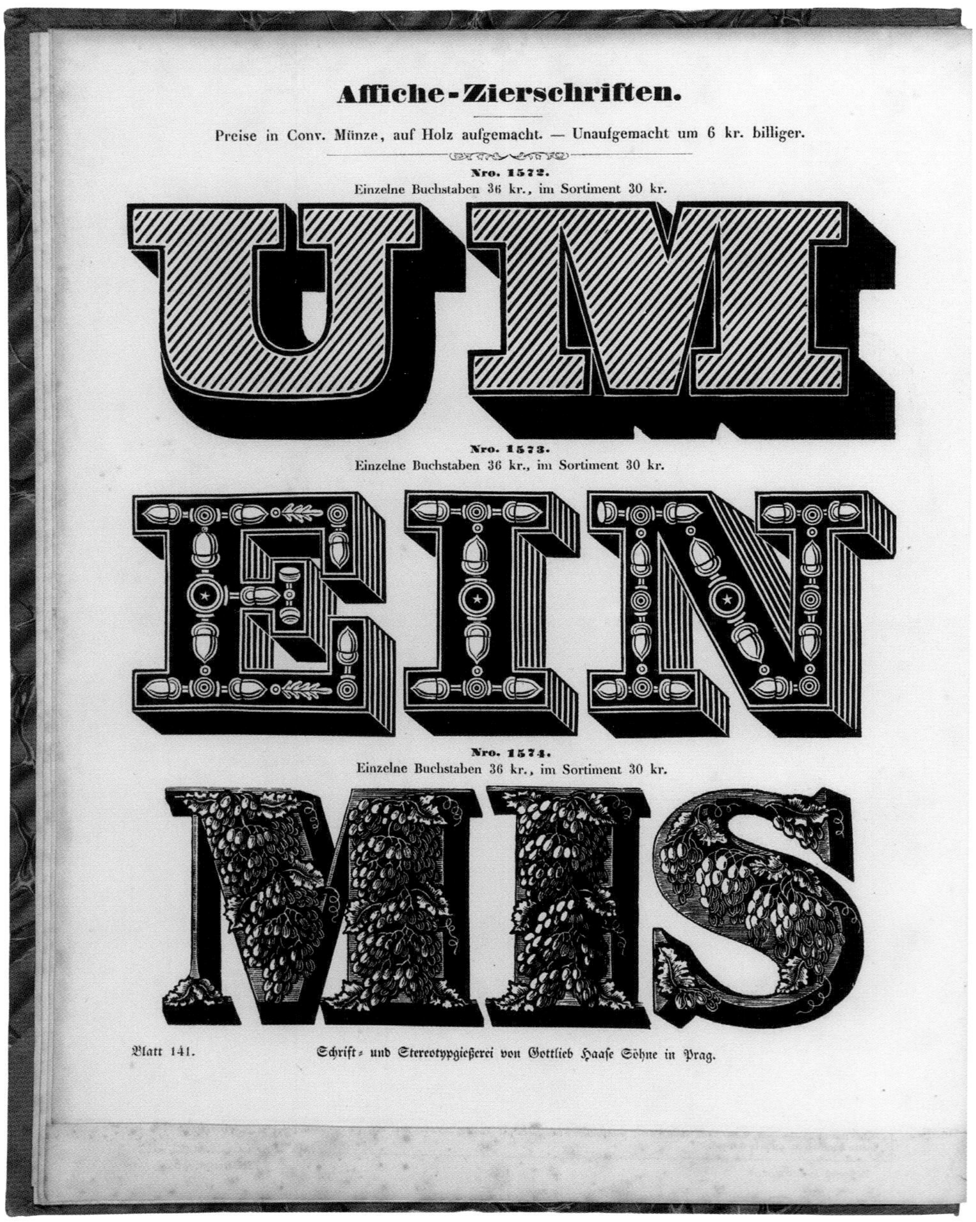

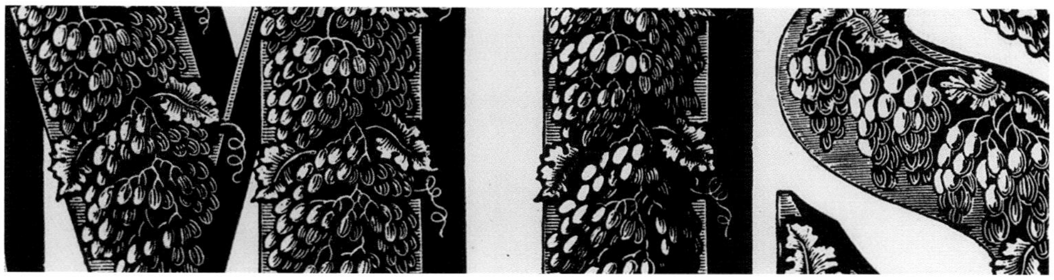

Zierschriften.

Preise in Conv. Münze.

Nr. 1551. — Minimum 12 Pf. à 2 fl.

Ein Leben ohne Geselligkeit ist ein lebendiger Tod.

Nr. 1552. — Minimum 15 Pf. à 1 fl. 40 kr.

In seinen Thaten malt sich stets der Mensch.

Nr. 1553. — Minimum 18 Pf. à 1 fl. 30 kr.

Die Religion ist das Band der Liebe.

Nr. 1554. — Minimum 20 Pf. à 1 fl. 30 kr.

Mineralbad

Nr. 1555. — Minimum 6 Pf. à 1 fl. 15 kr.

DIE STRENGE ZEIT DER PRÜFUNG IST

Nr. 1556. — Minimum 8 Pf. à 1 fl. 15. kr.

DAS LEBEN. ENDE GUT

Nr. 1557. — Minimum 8 Pf. à 1 fl. 15 kr.

FRANKREICH. LONDON.

Nr. 1558. — Minimum 10 Pf. à 1 fl. 15 kr.

NORD-DEUTSCHLAND.

Nr. 1559. — Minimum 10 Pf. à 1 fl. 15 kr.

BERLIN. AMBERG.

Nr. 1560. — Minimum 10 Pf. à 1 fl. 15 kr.

DAS VATERLAND.

Nr. 1561. — Minimum 12 Pf. à 1 fl. 15 kr.

DAENEMARK.

Nr. 1562. — Minimum 10 Pf. à 1 fl. 15 kr.

OESTERREICH. RUSSLAND.

Nr. 1563. — Minimum 10 Pf. à 1 fl. 15 kr.

WÜRZBURG. ARAU.

Nr. 1564. — Minimum 10 Pf. à 1 fl. 15 kr.

PREUSSEN. BERLIN.

Nr. 1565. — Minimum 12 Pf. à 1 fl. 15 kr.

KOPENHAGEN.

Nr. 1566. — Minimum 15 Pf. à 1 fl. 15 kr.

BOEHMEN. PRAG.

Nr. 167. — Pr. Buchstabe 15 kr., im Sortiment 12 kr.

OFEN.

Ecken und Mittelstücke.

Nr. 1571. — 4 St. 1 fl. Nr. 1568. — 4 St. 40 kr. Nr. 1569. — 4 St. 40 kr. Nr. 1570. — 4 St. 1 fl.

Blatt 140. Schrift- und Stereotypgießerei von Gottlieb Haase Söhne in Prag.

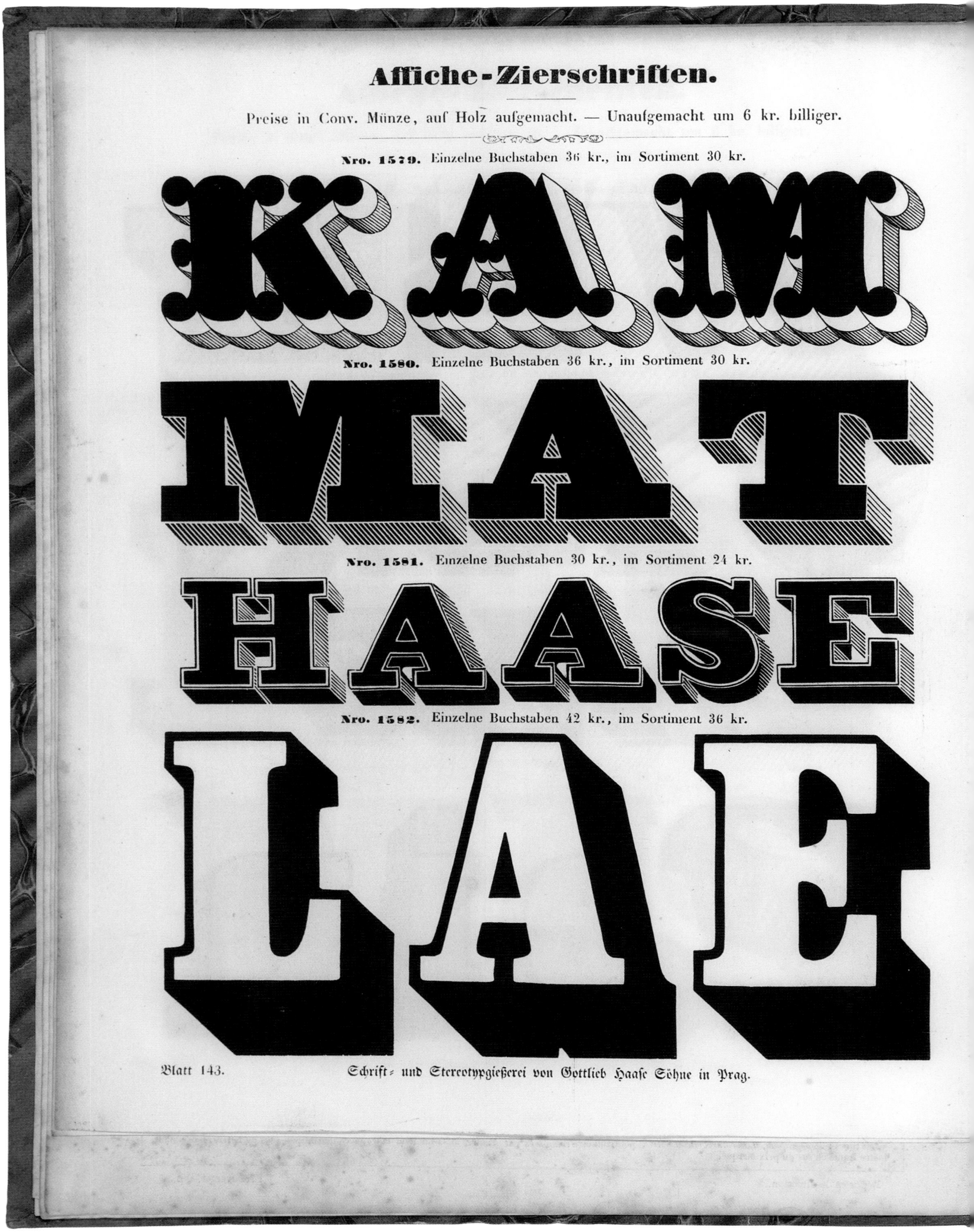

Affiche-Zierschriften.

Preise in Conv. Münze, auf Holz aufgemacht. — Unaufgemacht um 6 kr. billiger.

Nro. 1579. Einzelne Buchstaben 36 kr., im Sortiment 30 kr.

KAM

Nro. 1580. Einzelne Buchstaben 36 kr., im Sortiment 30 kr.

MAT

Nro. 1581. Einzelne Buchstaben 30 kr., im Sortiment 24 kr.

HAASE

Nro. 1582. Einzelne Buchstaben 42 kr., im Sortiment 36 kr.

LAE

Blatt 143.

Schrift- und Stereotypgießerei von Gottlieb Haase Söhne in Prag.

Affiche-Zierschriften.

Preise in Conv. Münze, auf Holz aufgemacht. — Unaufgemacht um 6 kr. billiger.

Nro. 1575. Einzelne Buchstabeu 36 kr., im Sortiment 30 kr.

WEH

Nro. 1576. Einzelne Buchstaben 36 kr., im Sortiment 30 kr.

OFEN

Nro. 1577. Einzelne Buchstaben 48 kr., im Sortiment 36 kr.

DIE

Nro. 1578. Einzelne Buchstaben 36 kr., im Sortiment 30 kr.

Wein

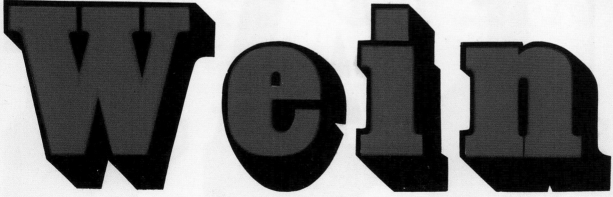

Blatt 142. Schrift- und Stereotypgießerei von Gottlieb Haase Söhne in Prag.

1844 **Chiswick Press** **Hannah Mary Rathbone, *So much of the Diary of Lady Willoughby as relates to her Domestic History, & to the Eventful Period of the Reign of Charles the First*. London: Longman, Brown, Green, & Longmans, 1844. 174 pp. 21.5 cm.**

Printer: Chiswick Press, London.

In 1844, publisher Thomas Longman presented *The Diary of Lady Willoughby*, allegedly written in the first half of the seventeenth century by Elizabeth, Lady Willoughby. To increase the edition's attractiveness, Longman advertised that the interior and binding were in keeping with the era in question. Nevertheless, some readers doubted the authenticity of the diary, and during the following year, it was revealed to be fiction. Hannah Mary Rathbone, who was forty-six years old at the time, turned out to be the author. The book earned its lasting fame for its typography, not least because it reintroduced Caslon, a typeface dating from the beginning of the eighteenth century that had fallen out of fashion.

The Diary of Lady Willoughby was printed by the Chiswick Press. The owner, Charles Whittingham (1795–1876) specialized in producing unusual books in limited editions. Since speed was not of paramount importance for this kind of quality printing, Chiswick Press continued to use hand presses for a relatively long period. One of the main customers was friend and publisher William Pickering, whose interest in historically inspired design went down well with Whittingham. Caslon was recast for Whittingham and Pickering, and both of them started using the type on title pages in 1840. It was purely accidental that the first book that Chiswick Press set entirely in Caslon was not commissioned by Pickering but by another publisher, Longman.

Historically allusive typography was popular in the first decades of the twentieth century under the name 'period typography'. ML

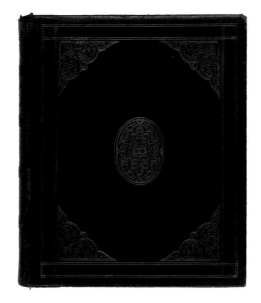

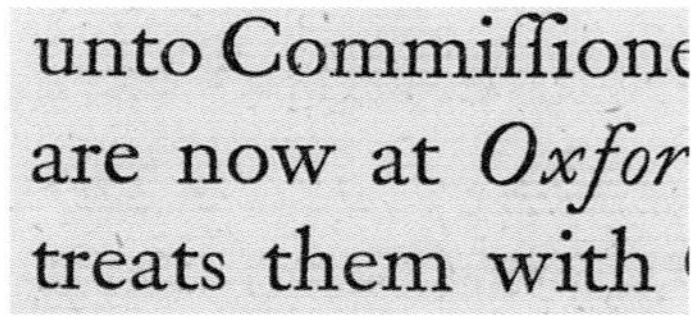

unto Commiffione
are now at *Oxfor*
treats them with

The London punchcutter and typefounder William Caslon (1693–1766) based his romans on seventeenth-century Dutch type. As his types were commercially successful, his work was frequently copied. In the twentieth century, modern versions of Caslon became exceptionally popular with British printers: 'When in doubt, use Caslon.'

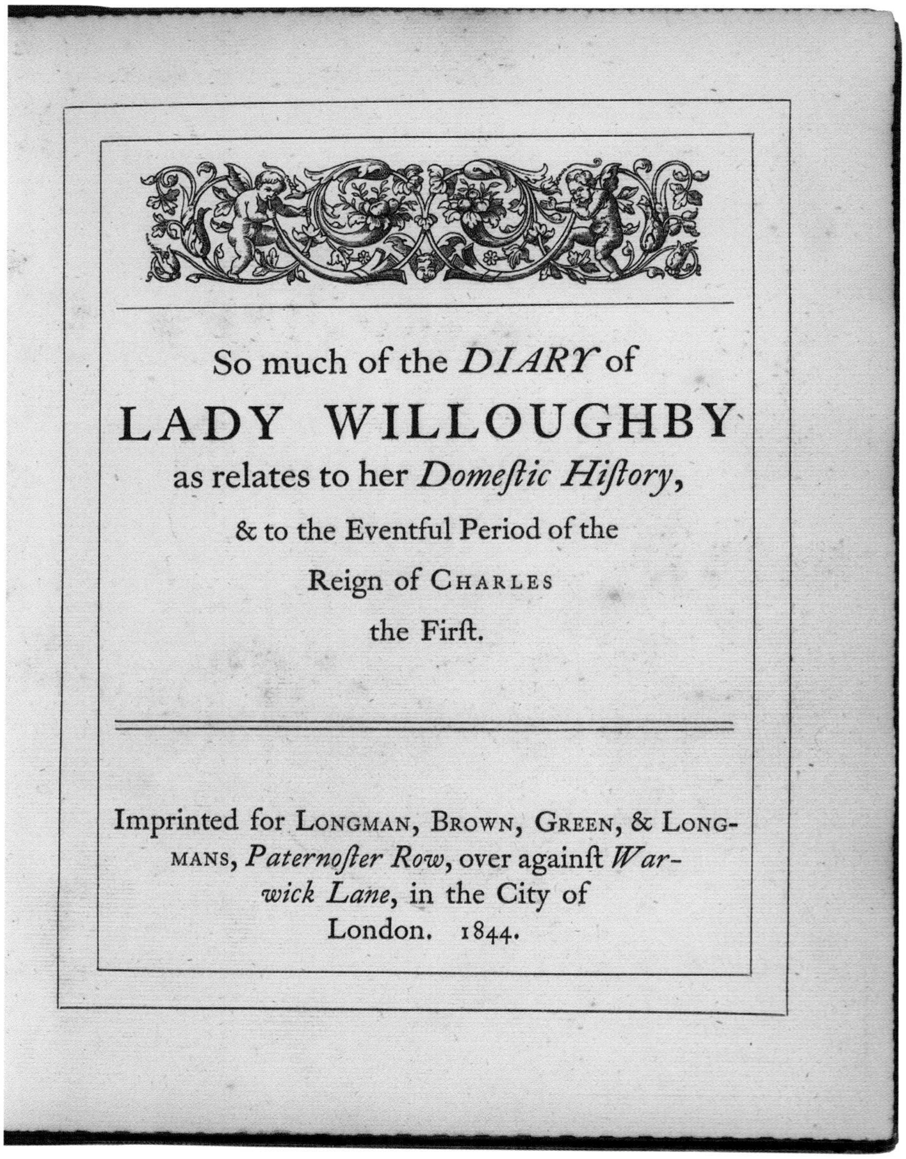

So much of the *DIARY* of
LADY WILLOUGHBY
as relates to her *Domeftic Hiftory*,
& to the Eventful Period of the
Reign of CHARLES
the Firft.

Imprinted for LONGMAN, BROWN, GREEN, & LONG-
MANS, *Paternofter Row*, over againft *War-
wick Lane*, in the City of
London. 1844.

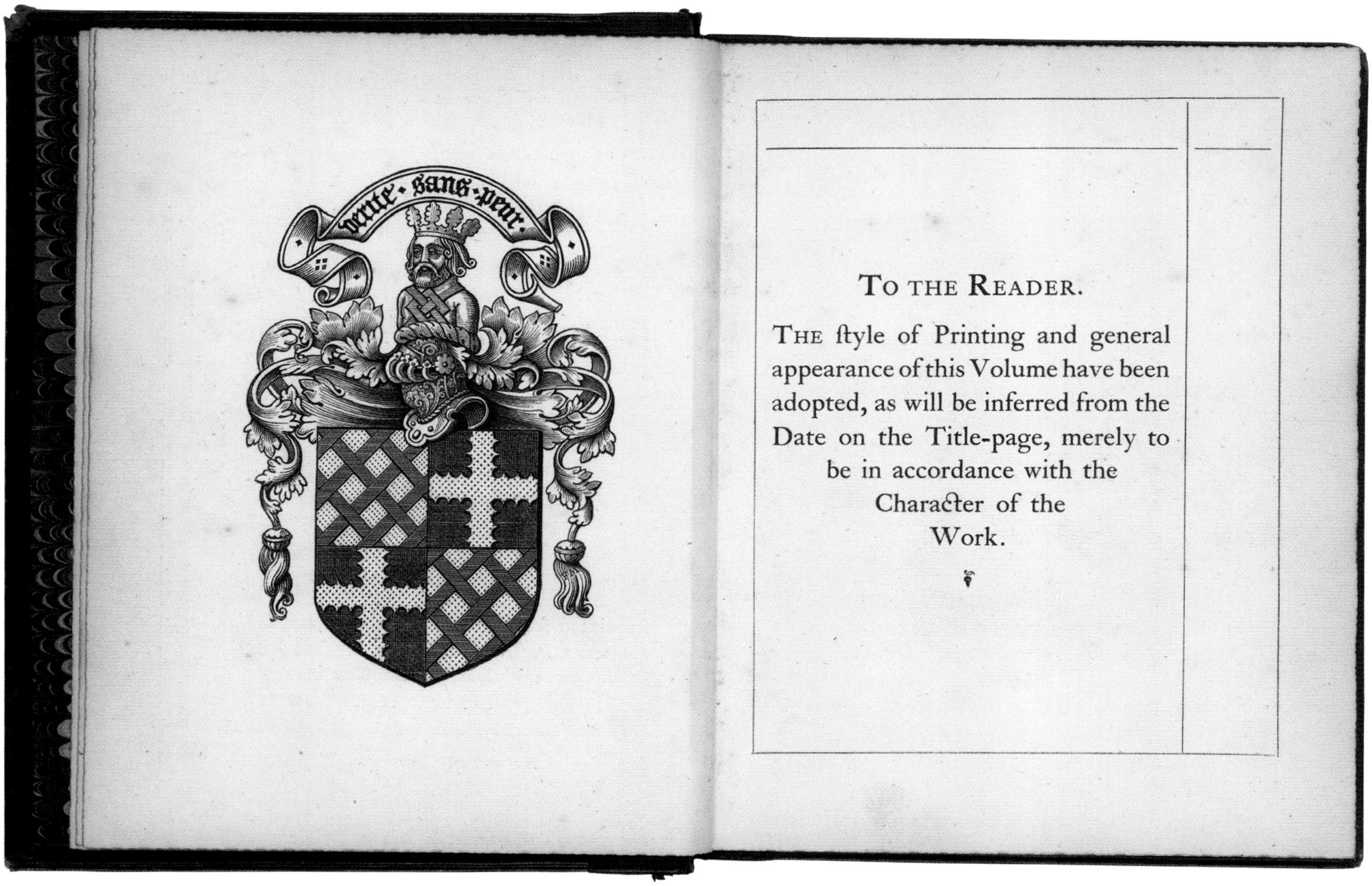
verite · sans · peur
To the Reader.
The ſtyle of Printing and general appearance of this Volume have been adopted, as will be inferred from the Date on the Title-page, merely to be in accordance with the Character of the Work.

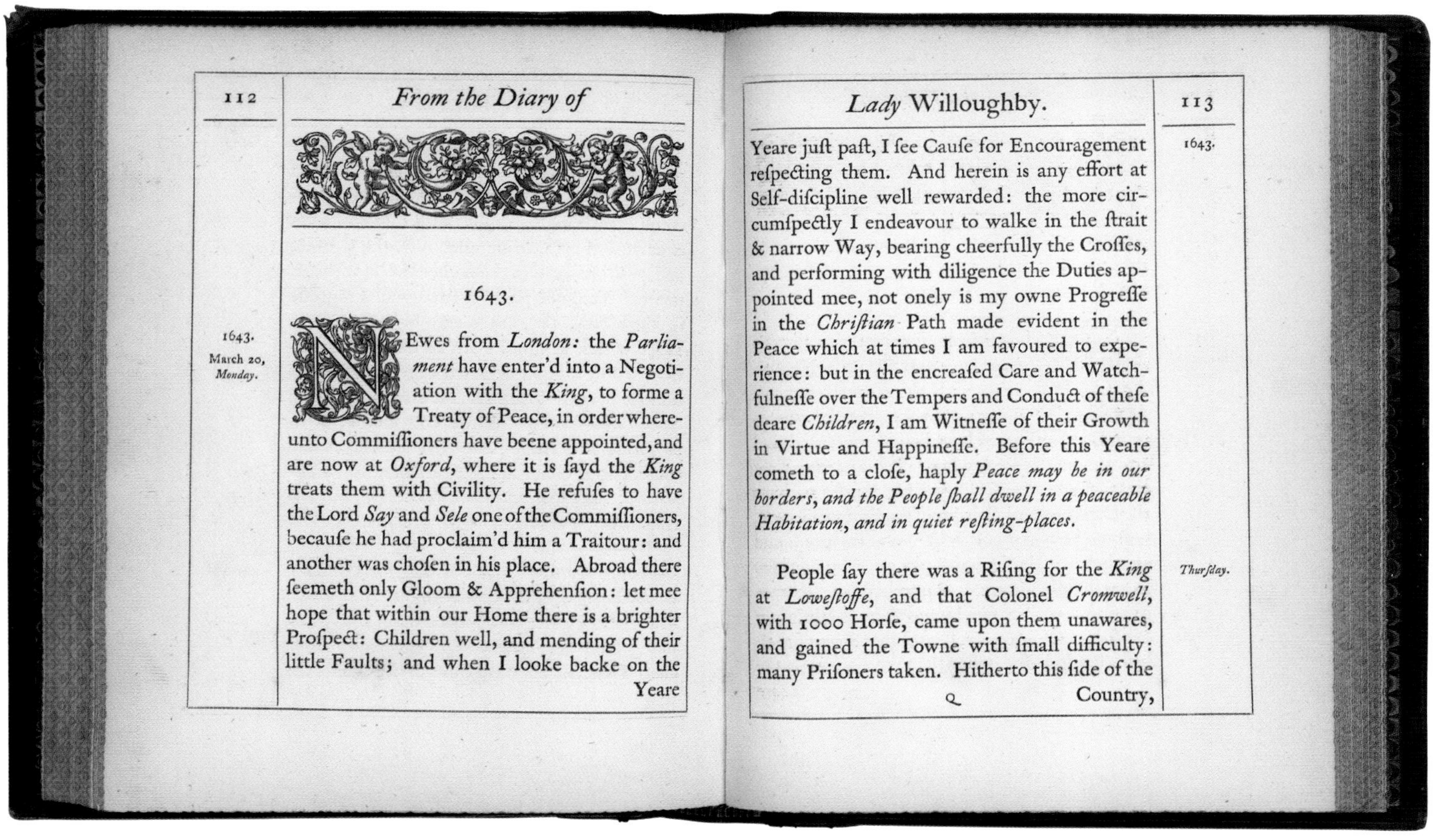
112
From the Diary of
1643.
1643. March 20, Monday.
NEwes from London: the Parliament have enter'd into a Negotiation with the King, to forme a Treaty of Peace, in order whereunto Commiſſioners have beene appointed, and are now at Oxford, where it is ſayd the King treats them with Civility. He refuſes to have the Lord Say and Sele one of the Commiſſioners, becauſe he had proclaim'd him a Traitour: and another was choſen in his place. Abroad there ſeemeth only Gloom & Apprehenſion: let mee hope that within our Home there is a brighter Proſpect: Children well, and mending of their little Faults; and when I looke backe on the Yeare
Lady Willoughby.
113
1643.
Yeare juſt paſt, I ſee Cauſe for Encouragement reſpecting them. And herein is any effort at Self-diſcipline well rewarded: the more circumſpectly I endeavour to walke in the ſtrait & narrow Way, bearing cheerfully the Croſſes, and performing with diligence the Duties appointed mee, not onely is my owne Progreſſe in the Chriſtian Path made evident in the Peace which at times I am favoured to experience: but in the encreaſed Care and Watchfulneſſe over the Tempers and Conduct of theſe deare Children, I am Witneſſe of their Growth in Virtue and Happineſſe. Before this Yeare cometh to a cloſe, haply Peace may be in our borders, and the People ſhall dwell in a peaceable Habitation, and in quiet reſting-places.
Thurſday.
People ſay there was a Riſing for the King at Loweſtoffe, and that Colonel Cromwell, with 1000 Horſe, came upon them unawares, and gained the Towne with ſmall difficulty: many Priſoners taken. Hitherto this ſide of the Country,
Q

1858 **John Sliegh & Birket Foster** *Odes and Sonnets*. London: George Routledge & Co., 1859 (= 1858). 107 pp.

22.5 cm. Illustrators: John Sliegh (decorations), Birket Foster (illustrations). Wood engraver & printer: Brothers Dalziel, London.

During the gift-giving month of December, the display windows of the bookshops were filled to the brim with deluxe editions. These editions had colour illustrations – wood engravings or lithographs – and were handsomely bound. English production of deluxe editions reached a high level, and Routledge specialized in them. The anthology *Odes and Sonnets*, gilt-edged and decorated in neo-gothic style by John Sliegh (*fl.* 1841–79) is one such gift book. About Sliegh himself, little is known, but his two wood-engraved preliminary pages speak volumes. At first sight they look like chromolithographs. He also designed the gold-stamped publisher's binding; his monogram is on the front cover. The nature scenes were drawn by Birket Foster (1825–99), one of the most popular illustrators of poetry at the time in England.

The London firm Brothers Dalziel, founded in 1840, did the engravings of the designs by Sliegh and Foster, and the book was printed by the Camden Press, which was owned by Dalziel. The illustrations were printed in three colours, while the title page includes no less than six: two blues, purple, green, pink and red. Dalziel was one of the leading firms for wood engravings, and their work appeared in many magazines, among them *The Illustrated London News*. The firm often initiated and financed projects, and it may very well have done so in the case of *Odes and Sonnets*. Brothers Dalziel had been collaborating with publisher George Routledge since 1850. An American edition of *Odes and Sonnets* was printed by the Camden Press for the New York publisher D. Appleton & Co. ML

WHEN that the fields put
Thou silent sitt'st nea
Whilst the gay thrush

In the 1840s, typefounders adapted the characteristic British 'modern-face' romans and italics of around 1810, introducing longer serifs, rounded bracketing and some narrower capitals. Reducing the weight of these forms (especially in the italic lowercase) adds a hint of earlier types, such as Richard Austin's for John Bell in 1788.

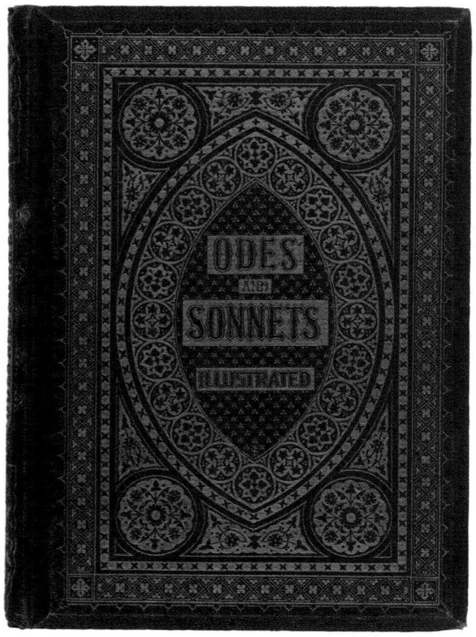

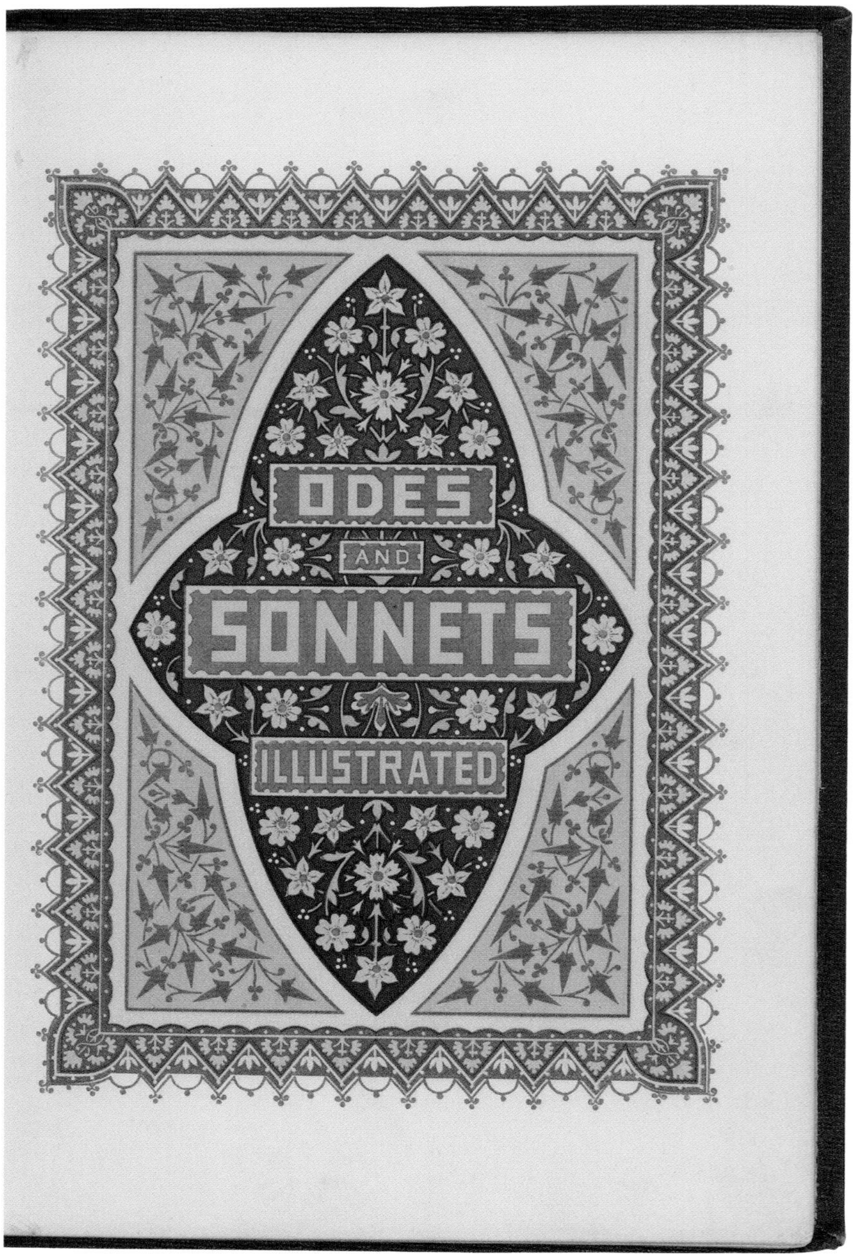

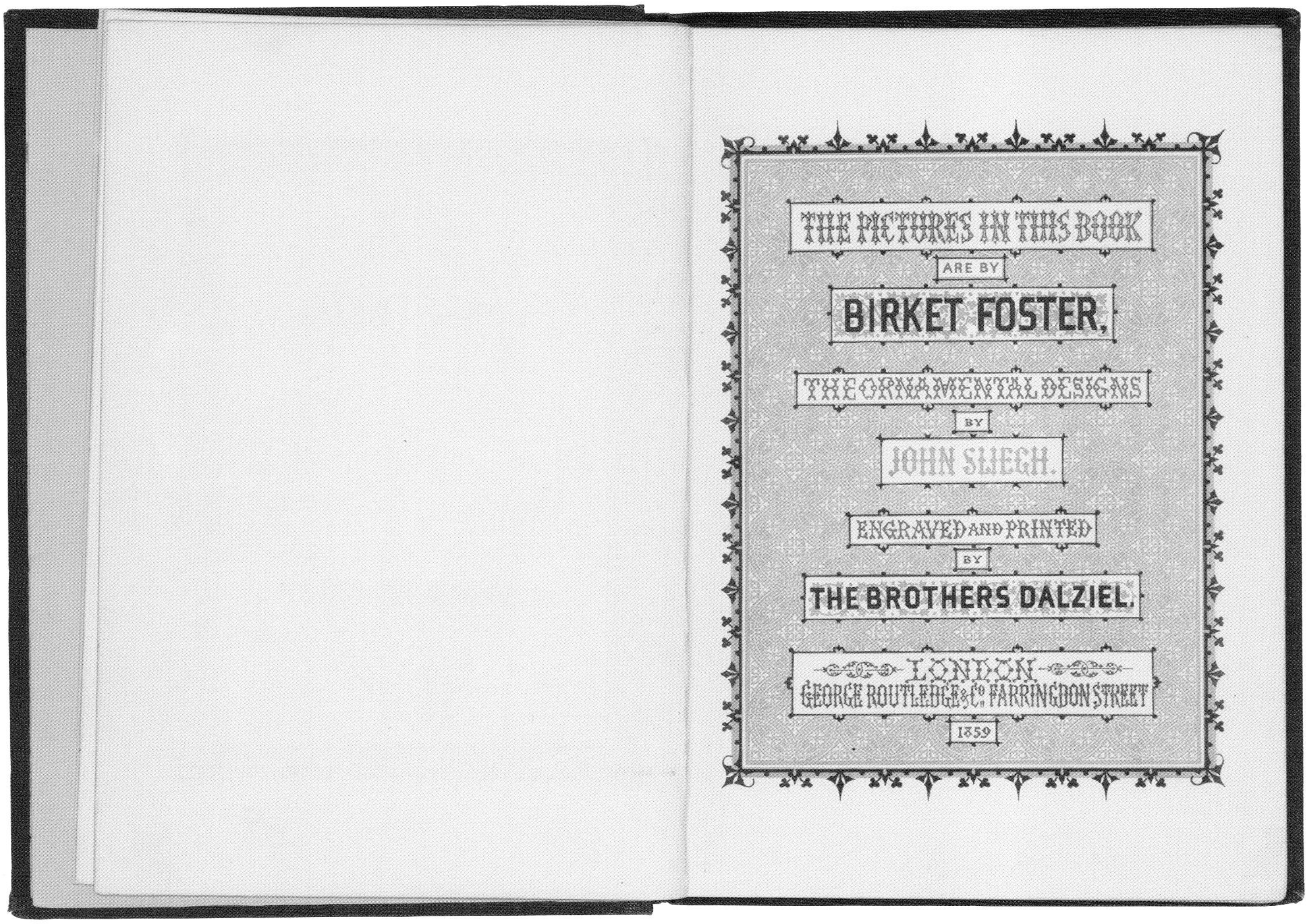

THE PICTURES IN THIS BOOK
ARE BY
BIRKET FOSTER,
THE ORNAMENTAL DESIGNS
BY
JOHN SLIEGH.
ENGRAVED AND PRINTED
BY
THE BROTHERS DALZIEL.
LONDON
GEORGE ROUTLEDGE & Co. FARRINGDON STREET
1859

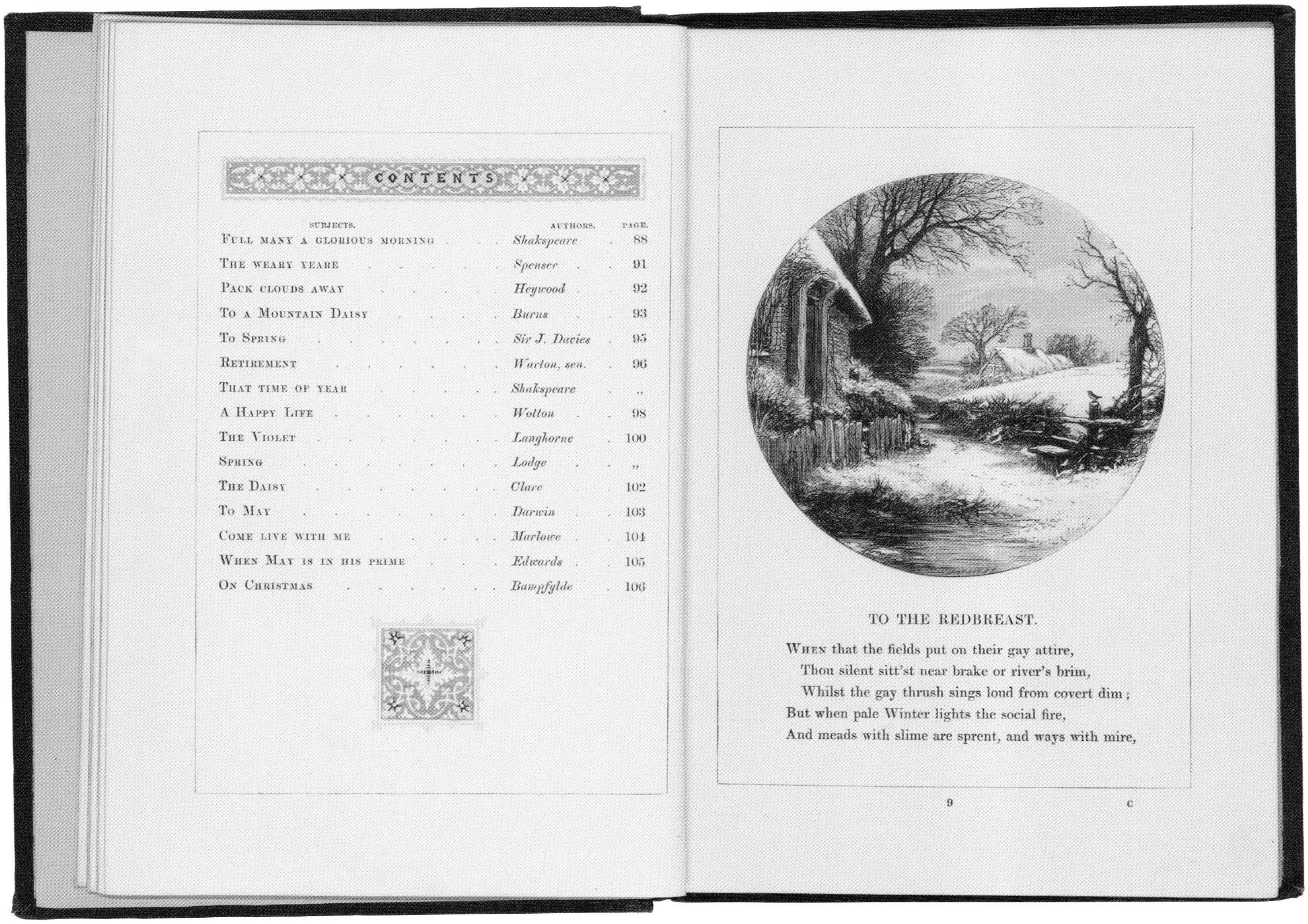

CONTENTS

SUBJECTS.	AUTHORS.	PAGE.
Full many a glorious morning	*Shakspeare*	88
The weary yeare	*Spenser*	91
Pack clouds away	*Heywood*	92
To a Mountain Daisy	*Burns*	93
To Spring	*Sir J. Davies*	95
Retirement	*Warton, sen.*	96
That time of year	*Shakspeare*	,,
A Happy Life	*Wotton*	98
The Violet	*Langhorne*	100
Spring	*Lodge*	,,
The Daisy	*Clare*	102
To May	*Darwin*	103
Come live with me	*Marlowe*	104
When May is in his prime	*Edwards*	105
On Christmas	*Bampfylde*	106

TO THE REDBREAST.

When that the fields put on their gay attire,
Thou silent sitt'st near brake or river's brim,
Whilst the gay thrush sings loud from covert dim;
But when pale Winter lights the social fire,
And meads with slime are sprent, and ways with mire,

9 c

1860 **Victorian gift book** Anne Lydia Bond, *Three Gems in One Setting: The Poet's Song, Tennyson; Field Flowers, Campbell; Pilgrim Fathers, Mrs. Hemans*. London: W. Kent & Co., 1860. 18 leaves. 22 cm. Illustrator: Anne Lydia Bond. Chromolithographer: David Brand, London. Bookbinder: Leighton, Son and Hodge, London.

The Victorians liked to read poetry, and selections from the work of British poets found an eager market every Christmas. The gift book *Three Gems in One Setting*, including work by the poet laureate Alfred Tennyson, appeared in 1860. Already in November the publisher was advertising the collection in the newspaper: 'This book, as its name implies, is a perfect gem. It needs but an inspection to make every lover of the fine arts anxious to possess a copy.' *Three Gems* is indeed a luxurious production.

The publisher certainly did not skimp on the cloth binding: it displays lavish blind and gold blocking, and a chromolithograph is mounted, recessed, on the front board. The edges are gilt. Because the edition was bound in batches, there are variant issues, for example using different colours of cloth. A binder's ticket on the back paste-down shows it was bound by Leighton, Son and Hodge. This London firm was one of the great industrial bookbinders of the time. The designer of the binding is unknown. The publisher also offered the book, at a considerably higher price, bound in goatskin.

The illustrations and decorations on the eighteen leaves, which are printed only on one side, were drawn by Anne Lydia Bond, who also worked for the publishing house Routledge. The lithographer rendered Bond's drawings on stone in various colours and gold. Chromolithography was the pre-eminent colour printing process of the second half of the nineteenth century, though it met formidable competition from the colour wood engraving throughout that period. ML

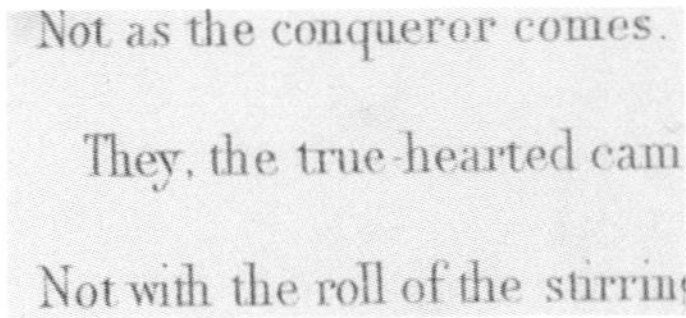

The text was handwritten in the style of nineteenth-century typefaces and printed lithographically. This allowed the text and illustrations to be executed with a single graphic technique.

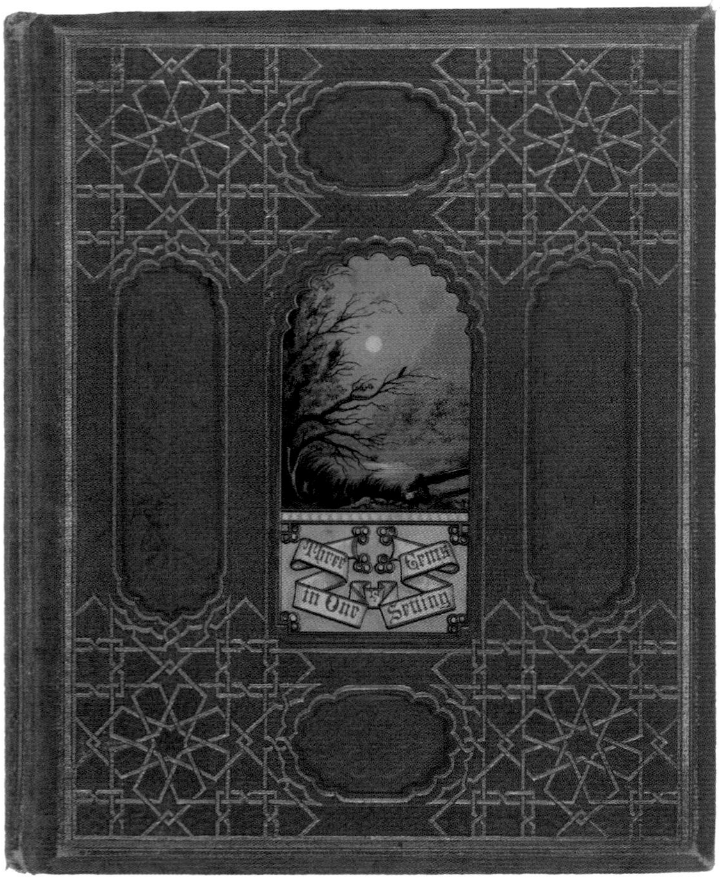

Even now what affections the violet
awakes;
What loved little islands, twice seen
in their lakes,
Can the wild water-lily restore;
What landscapes I read in the
primrose's looks,
And what pictures of pebbled and
minnowy brooks,
In the vetches that tangled their shore.
11

Not as the conqueror comes,
They, the true hearted came;
Not with the roll of the stirring drums,
And the trumpet that sings of fame.
Not as the flying come,
In silence and in fear;
They shook the depths of the desert gloom
With their hymns of lofty cheer.

Victorian gift book

1882 **Julius Klinkhardt** *Proben-Album der Accidenz-, Buch- und Noten-Druckerei von Julius Klinkhardt und Lithogr. Kunstanstalt J.G. Bach (Besitzer Julius Klinkhardt).* **Leipzig: Julius Klinkhardt, 1882. 36 cm. Printer & bookbinder: Julius Klinkhardt, Leipzig.**

The nineteenth century saw the emergence of big firms engaged in all aspects of book publishing. A typical example is the German company of Julius Klinkhardt. Klinkhardt, who started out as a bookseller in 1834, expanded his activities considerably over the decades that followed. In 1882 the firm, in which four hundred people were employed, had a composing room and a printing office, a typefoundry with punchcutting department, a wood-engraving and an electrotyping department, a lithography printing office, and a bookbindery. Klinkhardt was therefore able to tend to the entire book production process. Klinkhardt also had a publishing house, which specialized in schoolbooks and teaching aids.

In 1882, Klinkhardt distributed this gilt-edged *Proben-Album* (specimen book) in order to acquire print jobs from other publishers. It served both as a concise printer's type specimen book and as a sample book of the various types of printed matter that Klinkhardt produced. Printers usually took care of typographic design as well, and Klinkhardt wanted to showcase the abilities of its typesetters. The *Proben-Album* covered all areas, from books and illustrated magazines to music printing. The catalogue closes with specimens from the firm's lithographic printing office.

The title page is set in an architectural style that was in vogue at the time, with a base, columns and a cornice. It has decorations in the Renaissance fashion. During the second half of the nineteenth century, typefoundries issued many ornaments and decorative borders in historical styles. It was not until the 1890s that American examples of 'artistic printing' ended the historicizing epoch of German commercial printing. The firm of Julius Klinkhardt still exists as a publishing house, specializing in books on teaching. ML

The title page shows some recent styles, among them new display types. The publisher's name is set in a so-called Latin: a narrow type with low contrast and triangular serifs, apparently first introduced in Britain in c. 1875, though with French precursors.

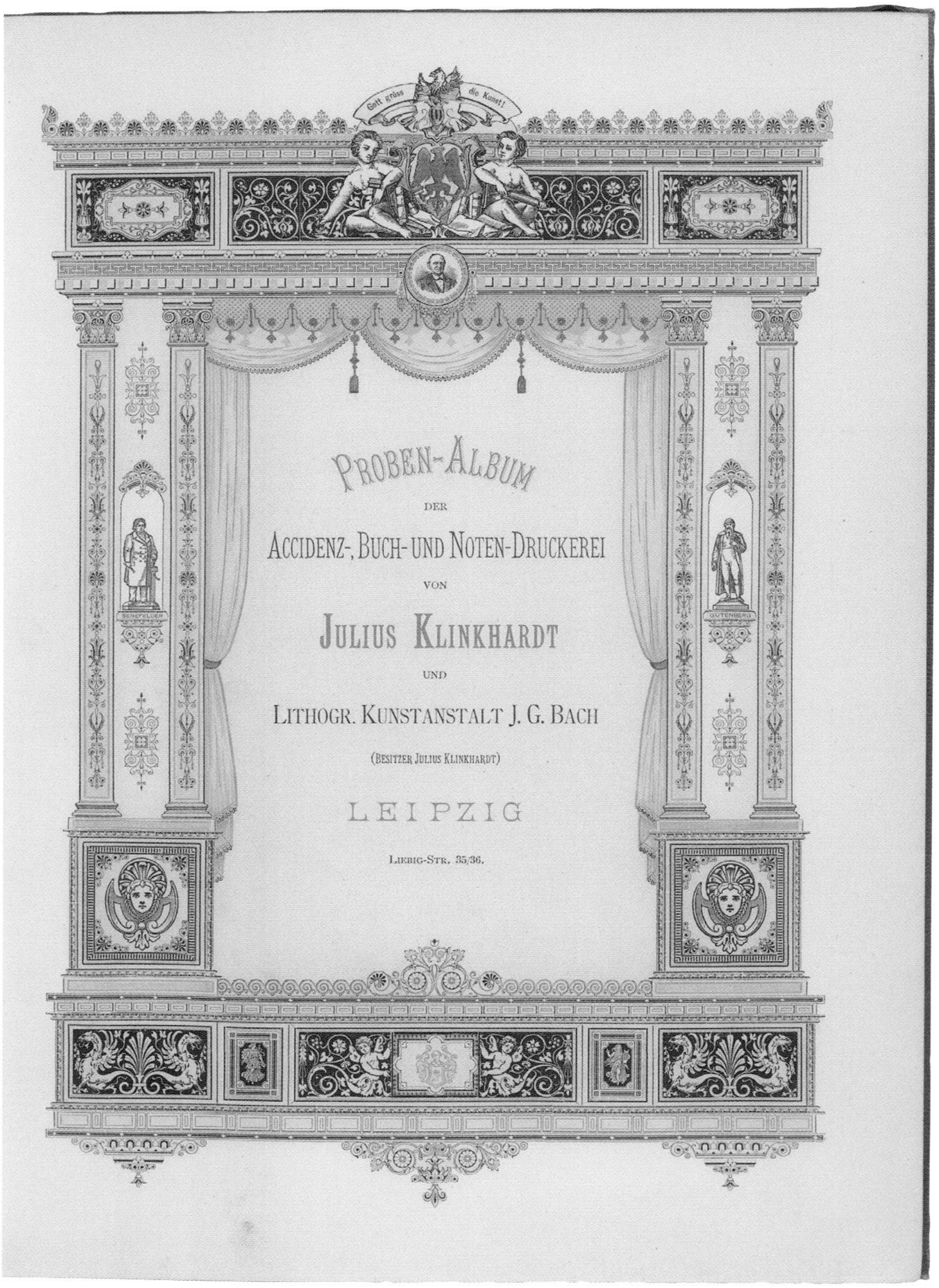

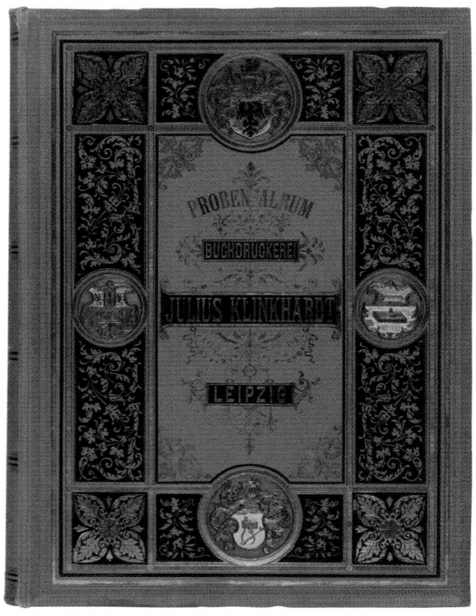

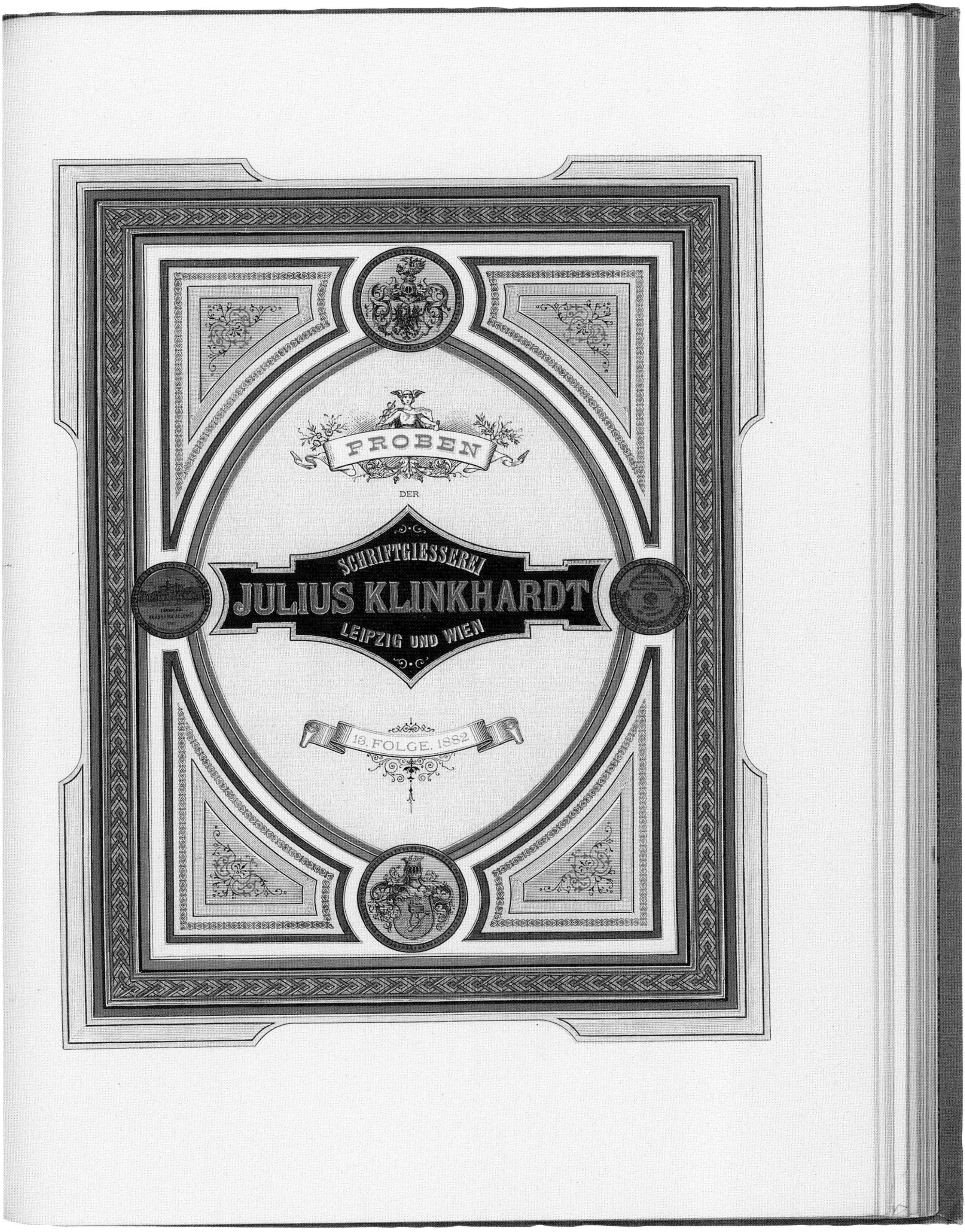
PROBEN
DER
SCHRIFTGIESSEREI
JULIUS KLINKHARDT
LEIPZIG UND WIEN
13. FOLGE. 1882

1887 **Eadweard Muybridge** Eadweard Muybridge, *Animal Locomotion: An Electro-photographic Investigation of Consecutive Phases of Animal Movements: 1872–1885*. Philadelphia: University of Pennsylvania, 1887. 49.5 x 61 cm. Separate prospectus and catalogue of plates. Photographer: Eadweard Muybridge. Printer: Photo-gravure Company, New York.

The pioneering photographer Eadweard Muybridge (1830–1904) took dramatic photographs of Yosemite Valley, which contributed to the mythical image of the American West. He photographed the war with the Native Americans and made panoramas of San Francisco. However, he owes his fame to his studies of the body in motion, which have inspired many artists, including Edgar Degas and Francis Bacon.

Muybridge was born in England. He emigrated to New York in his early twenties, where he opened a bookstore selling imported books and came in contact with the daguerreotype, a photographic process. During a stay in England, he learned the wet collodion process, with which high-quality negatives – and therefore many prints – can be made. Armed with this knowledge, Muybridge started concentrating on photography in around 1866, in San Francisco.

In 1872, Leland Stanford gave him a commission that would determine the course of his life. The wealthy entrepreneur owned a racing stable and asked Muybridge to try and prove that a trotting horse has all four legs off the ground at some point in its stride. They succeeded the same year. Muybridge later continued his experiments, sponsored by Stanford, using a row of cameras to record consecutive movements. Muybridge would project these images mounted in sequence on a rotating disc; this made him a pioneer of film as well. New studies of motion were done between 1884 and 1885, with the support of some financiers and under the auspices of the University of Pennsylvania, resulting in *Animal Locomotion*, published in 1887. Since then, reprints have been published that have been targeted at cartoonists and illustrators, among others. ML

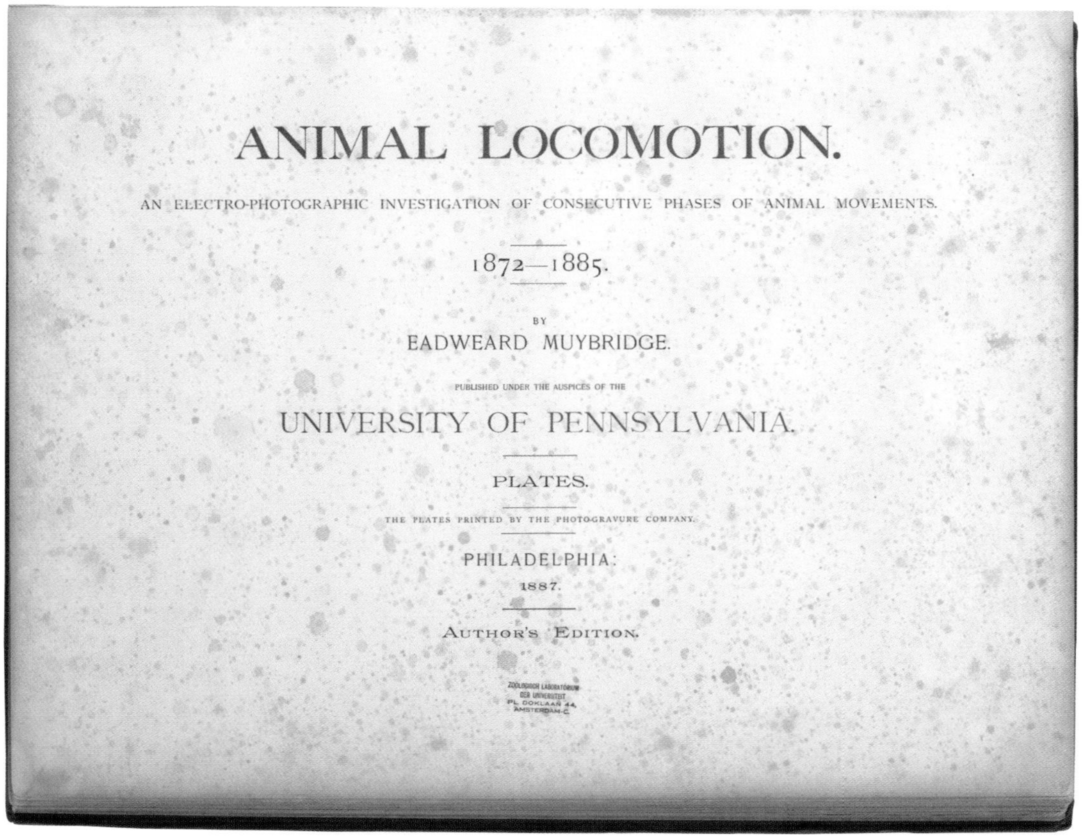
ANIMAL LOCOMOTION.

AN ELECTRO-PHOTOGRAPHIC INVESTIGATION OF CONSECUTIVE PHASES OF ANIMAL MOVEMENTS.

1872—1885.

BY

EADWEARD MUYBRIDGE.

PUBLISHED UNDER THE AUSPICES OF THE

UNIVERSITY OF PENNSYLVANIA.

PLATES.

THE PLATES PRINTED BY THE PHOTOGRAVURE COMPANY.

PHILADELPHIA:

1887.

AUTHOR'S EDITION.

The Photo-gravure Company in New York reproduced the photographs in collotype. This was a planographic technique using photosensitized gelatine. The first collotype dates from 1868. The technique was still used in the twentieth century for high-quality art publications and for reproductions of photographs, paintings, and manuscripts.

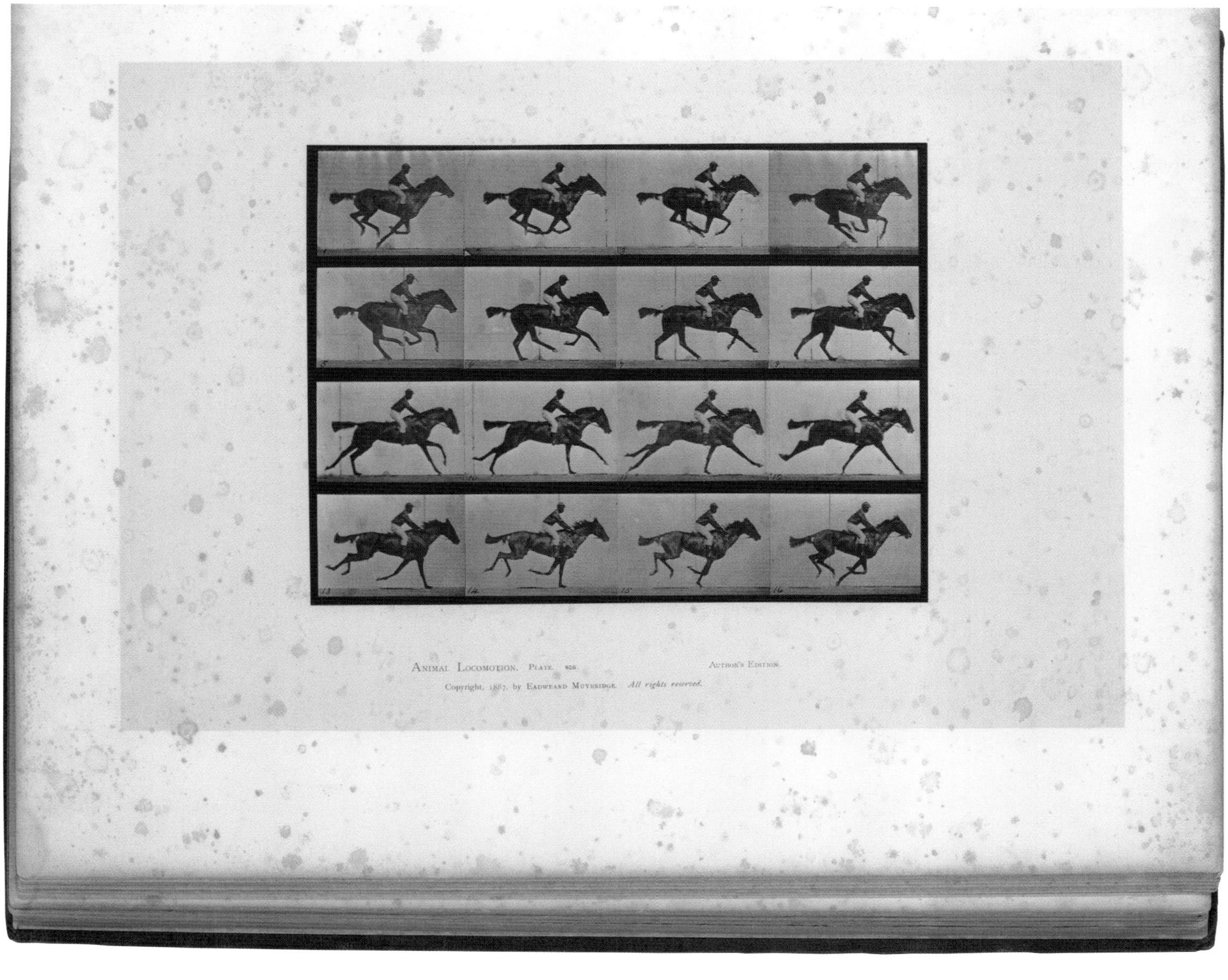

Animal Locomotion. Plate 347
Author's Edition.
Copyright, 1887, by Eadweard Muybridge. All rights reserved.

1890 **James McNeill Whistler** James McNeill Whistler, *The Gentle Art of Making Enemies: as pleasingly exemplified in many instances, wherein the serious ones of this earth, carefully exasperated, have been prettily spurred on to unseemliness and indiscretion, while overcome by an undue sense of right*. London: William Heinemann, 1890. xvi, 292 pp. 21 cm. Designer: James McNeill Whistler. Printer: Ballantyne Press, London and Edinburgh.

The typographic design of *The Gentle Art of Making Enemies* attracted attention from the moment it was published. Despite the plain brown paper covers, it was a rather bizarre book. One critic wrote: 'The book is altogether so curious, so dainty in all externals, so absolutely unlike anything that ever before has proceeded from a printing press, that probably the bibliophile of the future who is without a copy of the first edition on his shelves will be as unhappy as those Flemish amateurs of etchings and tulips in the seventeenth century are represented to have been when their collections lacked a first state of Rembrandt's *Little Juno with the Crown*, or a bulb of the famous Semper Augustus tulip.' (*Academy*, 1890). The asymmetric design of the cover and the title page was definitely striking, as was the placement of the notes, which start in the back or fore-edge margins and sometimes run on into the foot margins.

The front cover and title page have a small butterfly instead of the author's name. Dozens of specially drawn butterflies are placed throughout the book. The American painter and printmaker, James McNeill Whistler (1834–1903), used vignettes like these to sign all his work. Whistler was both the author and the designer of this collection of texts: the front of the book states that it was 'printed under his own immediate care and supervision'. Prior to *The Gentle Art*, Whistler had already done some typographic design. He wanted control over everything connected with his art, from catalogues to exhibition designs. The asymmetry betrays his Japonisme; he was a dandy who used to wear kimonos. Whistler's typography had many followers, including Charles Ricketts.

The Gentle Art of Making Enemies contains miscellaneous texts by Whistler and other items such as reviews and letters to newspapers. His innovative art had been ridiculed for a long time and Whistler the artist did not let anything pass: with this book, Whistler meant to cut his critics down to size. ML

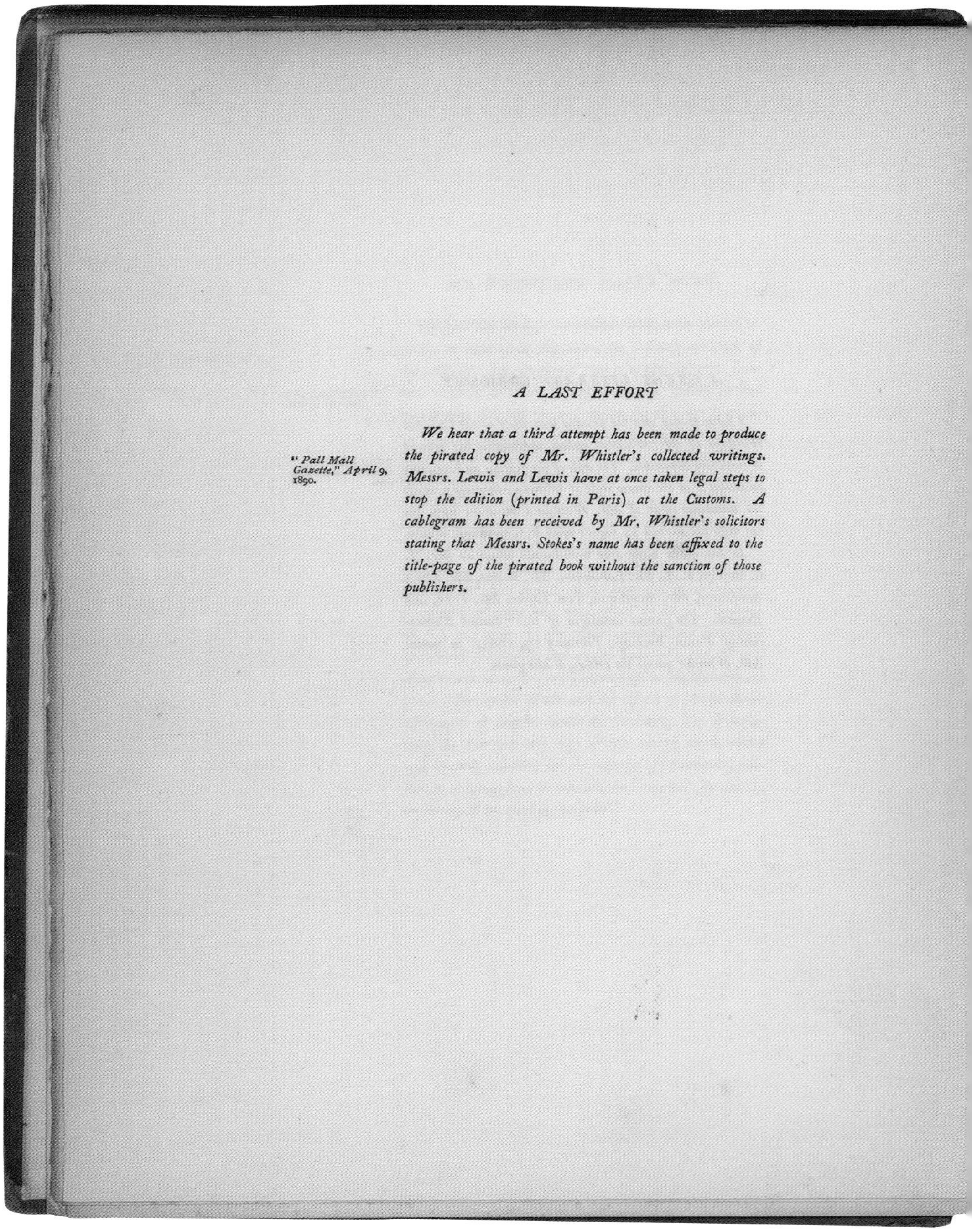

A LAST EFFORT

"Pall Mall Gazette," April 9, 1890.

We hear that a third attempt has been made to produce the pirated copy of Mr. Whistler's collected writings. Messrs. Lewis and Lewis have at once taken legal steps to stop the edition (printed in Paris) at the Customs. A cablegram has been received by Mr. Whistler's solicitors stating that Messrs. Stokes's name has been affixed to the title-page of the pirated book without the sanction of those publishers.

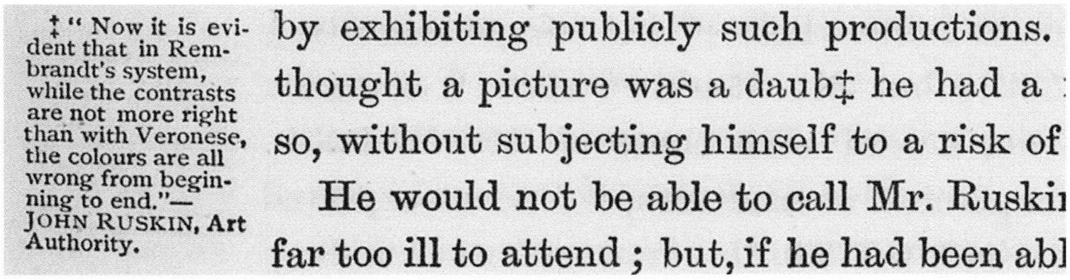

‡ " Now it is evident that in Rembrandt's system, while the contrasts are not more right than with Veronese, the colours are all wrong from beginning to end."— JOHN RUSKIN, Art Authority.

by exhibiting publicly such productions.
thought a picture was a daub‡ he had a
so, without subjecting himself to a risk of
He would not be able to call Mr. Ruski
far too ill to attend ; but, if he had been abl

The main text is set in an English 'modern face' type of the style introduced in the 1840s, but here it is combined with an 'old style' type, a style introduced by Alexander Phemister for the Miller & Richard typefoundry in around 1860, in the wake of the Caslon revival.

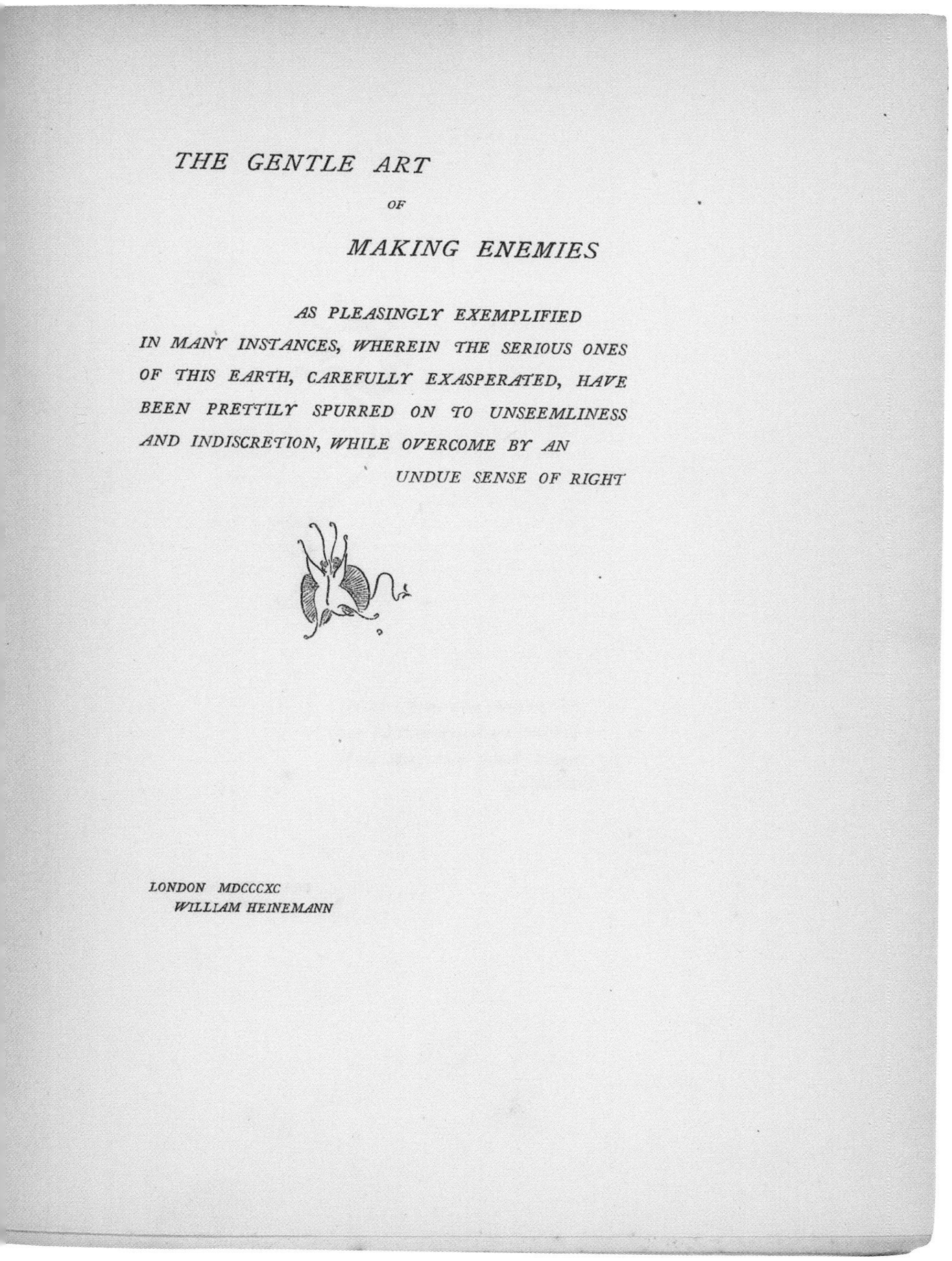

THE GENTLE ART

OF

MAKING ENEMIES

AS PLEASINGLY EXEMPLIFIED
IN MANY INSTANCES, WHEREIN THE SERIOUS ONES
OF THIS EARTH, CAREFULLY EXASPERATED, HAVE
BEEN PRETTILY SPURRED ON TO UNSEEMLINESS
AND INDISCRETION, WHILE OVERCOME BY AN
UNDUE SENSE OF RIGHT

LONDON MDCCCXC
WILLIAM HEINEMANN

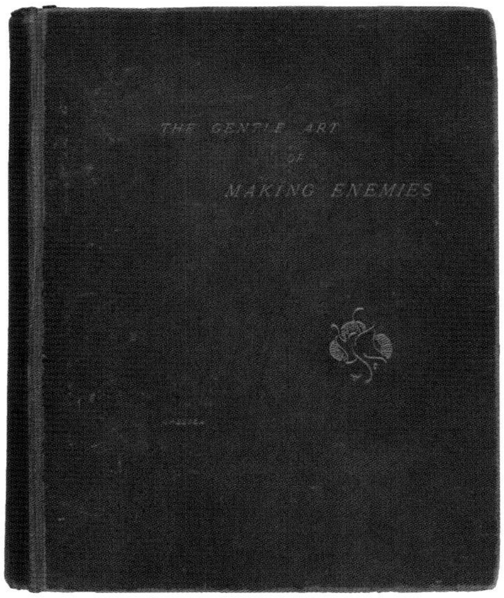

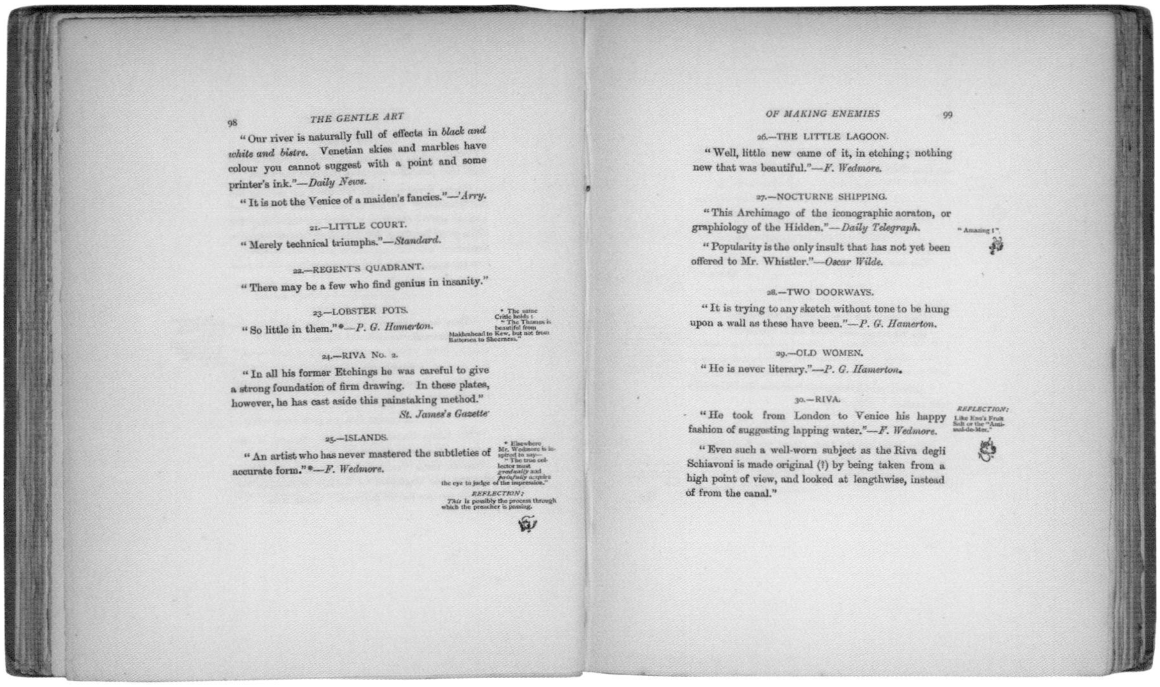

98 THE GENTLE ART

"Our river is naturally full of effects in *black and white and bistre.* Venetian skies and marbles have colour you cannot suggest with a point and some printer's ink."—*Daily News.*

"It is not the Venice of a maiden's fancies."—*'Arry.*

21.—LITTLE COURT.

"Merely technical triumphs."—*Standard.*

22.—REGENT'S QUADRANT.

"There may be a few who find genius in insanity."

23.—LOBSTER POTS.

"So little in them."*—*P. G. Hamerton.*

* The same Critic holds:—"The Thames is beautiful from Maidenhead to Kew, but not from Battersea to Sheerness."

24.—RIVA No. 2.

"In all his former Etchings he was careful to give a strong foundation of firm drawing. In these plates, however, he has cast aside this painstaking method."
St. James's Gazette

25.—ISLANDS.

"An artist who has never mastered the subtleties of accurate form."*—*F. Wedmore.*

* Elsewhere Mr. Wedmore is inspired to say—"The true collector must *gradually* and *painfully* acquire the eye to judge of the impression."

REFLECTION:
This is possibly the process through which the preacher is passing.

OF MAKING ENEMIES 99

26.—THE LITTLE LAGOON.

"Well, little new came of it, in etching; nothing new that was beautiful."—*F. Wedmore.*

27.—NOCTURNE SHIPPING.

"This Archimago of the iconographic aoraton, or graphiology of the Hidden."—*Daily Telegraph.*

"Amazing!"

"Popularity is the only insult that has not yet been offered to Mr. Whistler."—*Oscar Wilde.*

28.—TWO DOORWAYS.

"It is trying to any sketch without tone to be hung upon a wall as these have been."—*P. G. Hamerton.*

29.—OLD WOMEN.

"He is never literary."—*P. G. Hamerton.*

30.—RIVA.

"He took from London to Venice his happy fashion of suggesting lapping water."—*F. Wedmore.*

REFLECTION:
Like Eno's Fruit Salt or the "Animal-de-Mer."

"Even such a well-worn subject as the Riva degli Schiavoni is made original (?) by being taken from a high point of view, and looked at lengthwise, instead of from the canal."

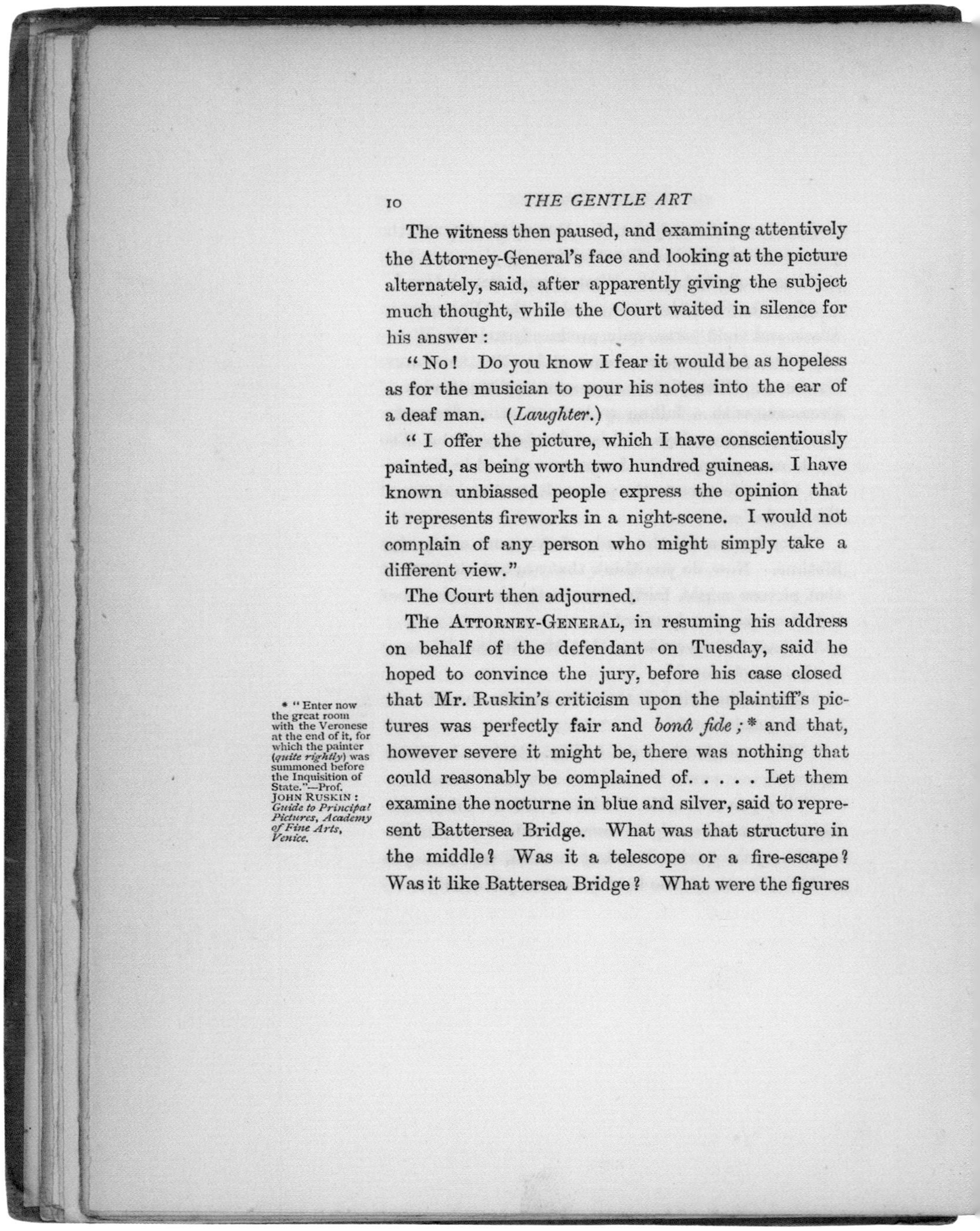

10 THE GENTLE ART

The witness then paused, and examining attentively the Attorney-General's face and looking at the picture alternately, said, after apparently giving the subject much thought, while the Court waited in silence for his answer:

"No! Do you know I fear it would be as hopeless as for the musician to pour his notes into the ear of a deaf man. (*Laughter.*)

"I offer the picture, which I have conscientiously painted, as being worth two hundred guineas. I have known unbiassed people express the opinion that it represents fireworks in a night-scene. I would not complain of any person who might simply take a different view."

The Court then adjourned.

The ATTORNEY-GENERAL, in resuming his address on behalf of the defendant on Tuesday, said he hoped to convince the jury, before his case closed that Mr. Ruskin's criticism upon the plaintiff's pictures was perfectly fair and *bonâ fide;** and that, however severe it might be, there was nothing that could reasonably be complained of. . . . . Let them examine the nocturne in blue and silver, said to represent Battersea Bridge. What was that structure in the middle? Was it a telescope or a fire-escape? Was it like Battersea Bridge? What were the figures

* "Enter now the great room with the Veronese at the end of it, for which the painter (*quite rightly*) was summoned before the Inquisition of State."—Prof. JOHN RUSKIN: *Guide to Principal Pictures, Academy of Fine Arts, Venice.*

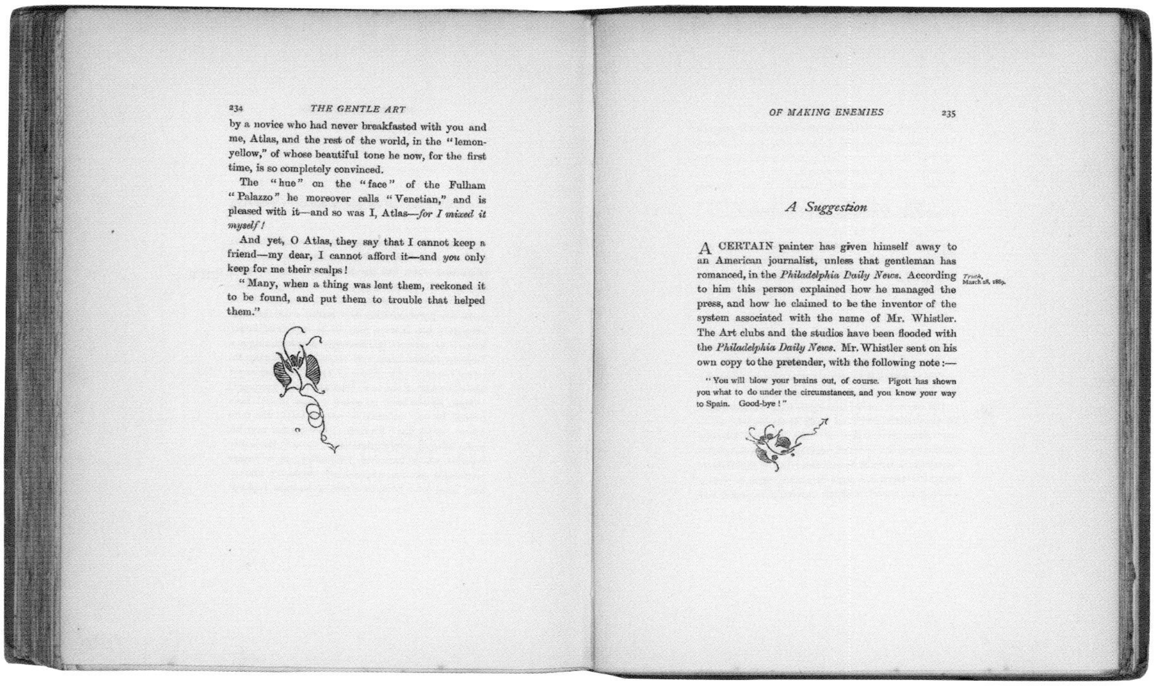

234 THE GENTLE ART

by a novice who had never breakfasted with you and me, Atlas, and the rest of the world, in the "lemon-yellow," of whose beautiful tone he now, for the first time, is so completely convinced.

The "hue" on the "face" of the Fulham "Palazzo" he moreover calls "Venetian," and is pleased with it—and so was I, Atlas—*for I mixed it myself!*

And yet, O Atlas, they say that I cannot keep a friend—my dear, I cannot afford it—and *you* only keep for me their scalps!

"Many, when a thing was lent them, reckoned it to be found, and put them to trouble that helped them."

OF MAKING ENEMIES 235

A Suggestion

A CERTAIN painter has given himself away to an American journalist, unless that gentleman has romanced, in the *Philadelphia Daily News*. According to him this person explained how he managed the press, and how he claimed to be the inventor of the system associated with the name of Mr. Whistler. The Art clubs and the studios have been flooded with the *Philadelphia Daily News*. Mr. Whistler sent on his own copy to the pretender, with the following note:—

Truth, March 28, 1889.

"You will blow your brains out, of course. Pigott has shown you what to do under the circumstances, and you know your way to Spain. Good-bye!"

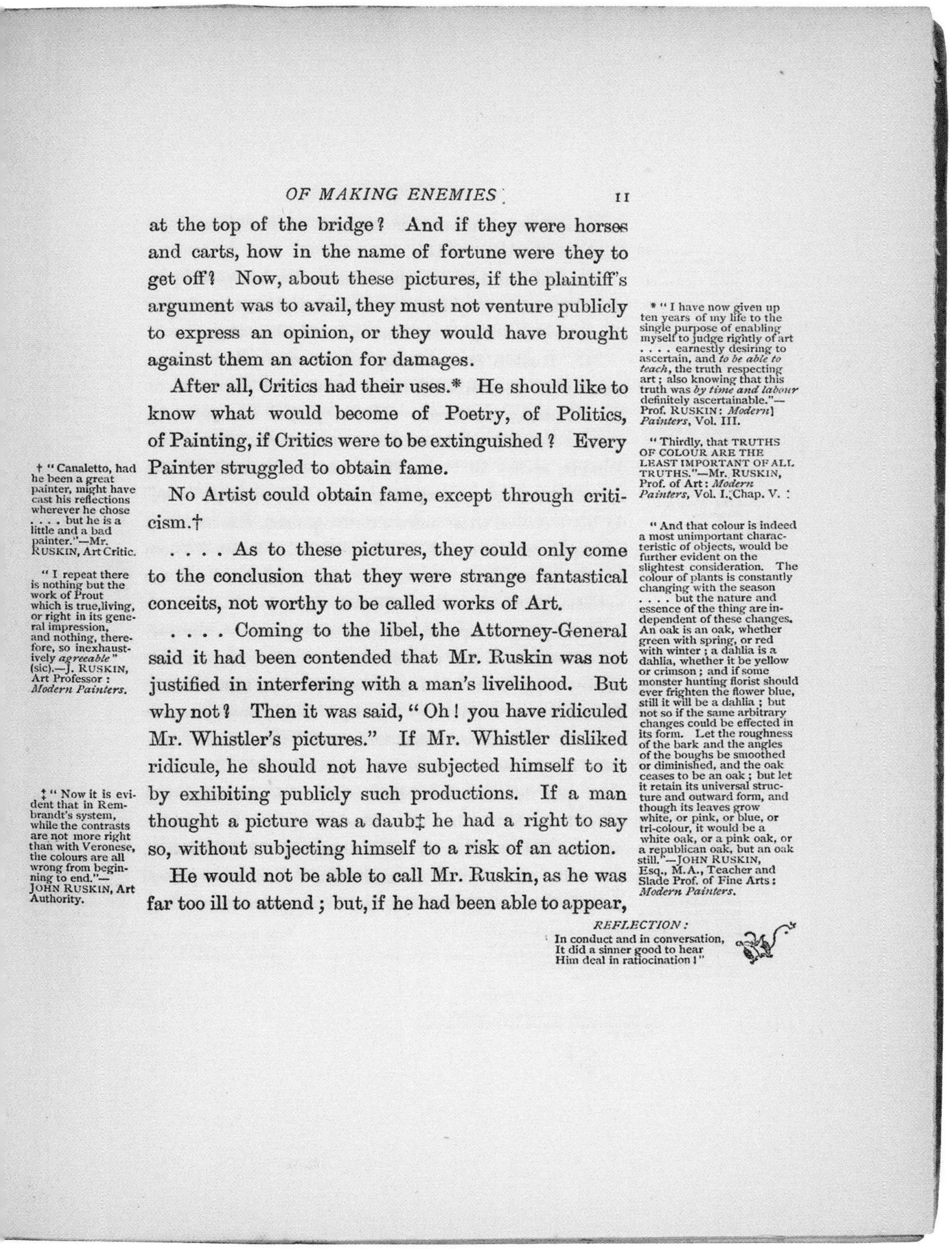

OF MAKING ENEMIES 11

at the top of the bridge? And if they were horses and carts, how in the name of fortune were they to get off? Now, about these pictures, if the plaintiff's argument was to avail, they must not venture publicly to express an opinion, or they would have brought against them an action for damages.

After all, Critics had their uses.* He should like to know what would become of Poetry, of Politics, of Painting, if Critics were to be extinguished? Every Painter struggled to obtain fame.

No Artist could obtain fame, except through criticism.†

. . . . As to these pictures, they could only come to the conclusion that they were strange fantastical conceits, not worthy to be called works of Art.

. . . . Coming to the libel, the Attorney-General said it had been contended that Mr. Ruskin was not justified in interfering with a man's livelihood. But why not? Then it was said, "Oh! you have ridiculed Mr. Whistler's pictures." If Mr. Whistler disliked ridicule, he should not have subjected himself to it by exhibiting publicly such productions. If a man thought a picture was a daub‡ he had a right to say so, without subjecting himself to a risk of an action.

He would not be able to call Mr. Ruskin, as he was far too ill to attend; but, if he had been able to appear,

* "I have now given up ten years of my life to the single purpose of enabling myself to judge rightly of art . . . . earnestly desiring to ascertain, and *to be able to teach*, the truth respecting art; also knowing that this truth was *by time and labour* definitely ascertainable."—Prof. RUSKIN: *Modern Painters*, Vol. III.

"Thirdly, that TRUTHS OF COLOUR ARE THE LEAST IMPORTANT OF ALL TRUTHS."—Mr. RUSKIN, Prof. of Art: *Modern Painters*, Vol. I. Chap. V.

"And that colour is indeed a most unimportant characteristic of objects, would be further evident on the slightest consideration. The colour of plants is constantly changing with the season . . . . but the nature and essence of the thing are independent of these changes. An oak is an oak, whether green with spring, or red with winter; a dahlia is a dahlia, whether it be yellow or crimson; and if some monster hunting florist should ever frighten the flower blue, still it will be a dahlia; but not so if the same arbitrary changes could be effected in its form. Let the roughness of the bark and the angles of the boughs be smoothed or diminished, and the oak ceases to be an oak; but let it retain its universal structure and outward form, and though its leaves grow white, or pink, or blue, or tri-colour, it would be a white oak, or a pink oak, or a republican oak, but an oak still."—JOHN RUSKIN, Esq., M.A., Teacher and Slade Prof. of Fine Arts: *Modern Painters*.

† "Canaletto, had he been a great painter, might have cast his reflections wherever he chose . . . . but he is a little and a bad painter."—Mr. RUSKIN, Art Critic.

"I repeat there is nothing but the work of Prout which is true, living, or right in its general impression, and nothing, therefore, so inexhaustively *agreeable*" (sic).—J. RUSKIN, Art Professor: *Modern Painters*.

‡ "Now it is evident that in Rembrandt's system, while the contrasts are not more right than with Veronese, the colours are all wrong from beginning to end."—JOHN RUSKIN, Art Authority.

REFLECTION:
"In conduct and in conversation,
It did a sinner good to hear
Him deal in ratiocination!"

1894 **Gerrit Dijsselhof** Walter Crane, *Kunst en samenleving*; ed. Jan Veth. Amsterdam: Scheltema en Holkema, 1894. ix, 171 pp. 23 cm. Translation of *The Claims of Decorative Art*, 1892. Designer: Gerrit Dijsselhof (binding & decorations). Printer: Joh. Enschedé en Zonen, Haarlem.

Art Nouveau was a movement in the applied arts and architecture that flowered in the 1890s. It broke with both tradition and academic historicism. Japanese prints were an important inspiration for its advertising posters. Often costly, Art Nouveau products – glass, ceramics, and furniture – were in high demand with the bourgeoisie. The German version of this style is known as 'Jugendstil', while the wayward Dutch variant is now called 'Nieuwe Kunst' (New Art).

One of the leaders of the international movement was Walter Crane, a popular illustrator of children's books. Crane's *The Claims of Decorative Art* (1892) would, in an adaptation by the artist and art critic Jan Veth, become the handbook of Nieuwe Kunst. Crane argued that the arts could not flourish in industrial society because machines deliver soulless products. Likewise, Veth had written that industrialization had virtually destroyed the art of the book, in terms of its decoration and the truth of the materials.

Although the design of this Dutch translation was inspired by the original, it faithfully reflects the ideas of Veth and the artist Gerrit Dijsselhof (1866–1924). For instance, woodblocks cut by Dijsselhof himself were used for the decorations on the half leather binding. For the chapters' head- and tailpieces, woodcuts by Dijsselhof, inspired by folk art, were also used. The interior was printed on heavy handmade paper. The construction of the binding was made evident in the decoration: the binding cords are depicted on the spine. They grow into lobsters on the front and back covers and seem to hold the book block together. The proud cockerel on the title page announces a new age. ML

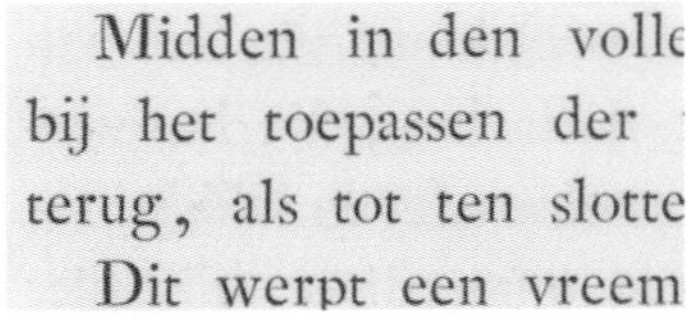
Midden in den volle
bij het toepassen der
terug, als tot ten slotte
Dit werpt een vreem

This type, from 1743, was made by the German punchcutter Joan Michael Fleischman (1707–68), who worked in the Netherlands for most of his life. The printer, Enschedé, had many of Fleischman's punches and matrices in his foundry. Fleischman's typefaces were frequently used in collector's editions at the beginning of the twentieth century.

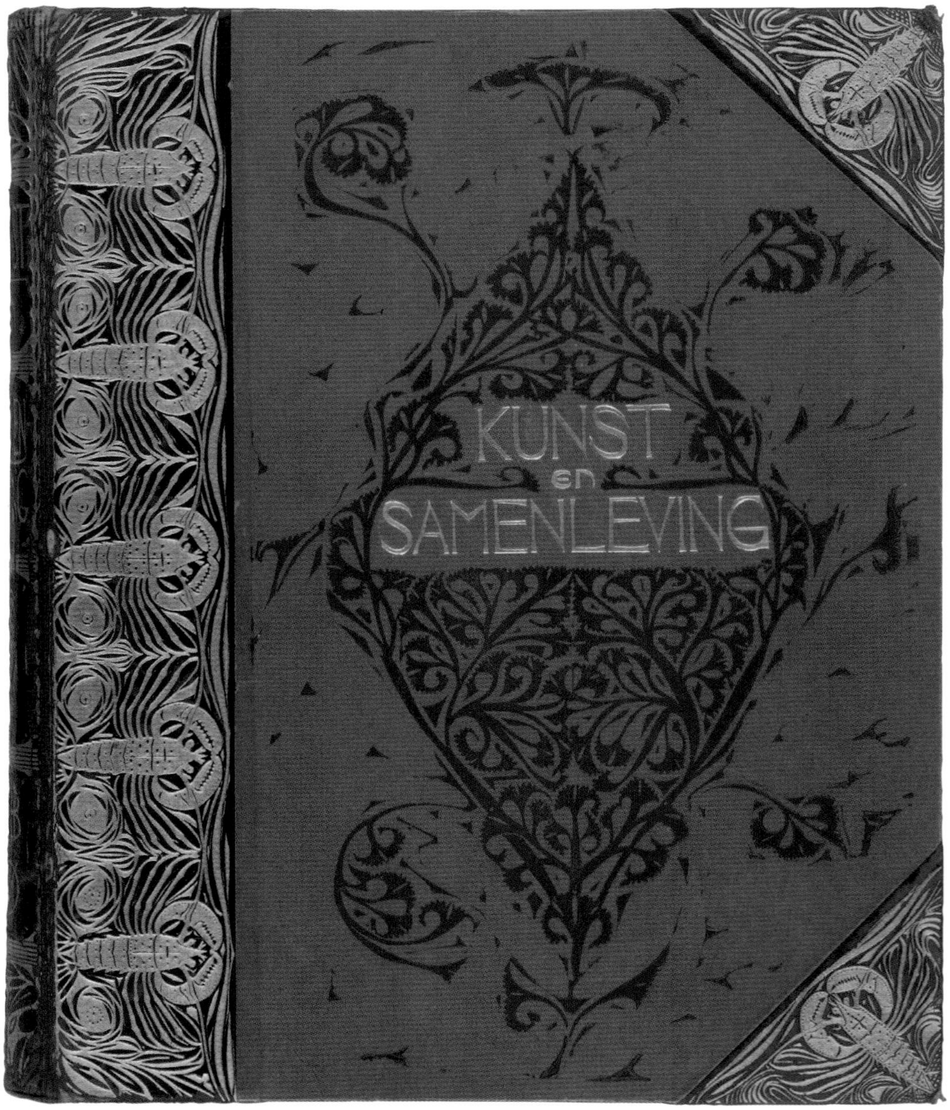

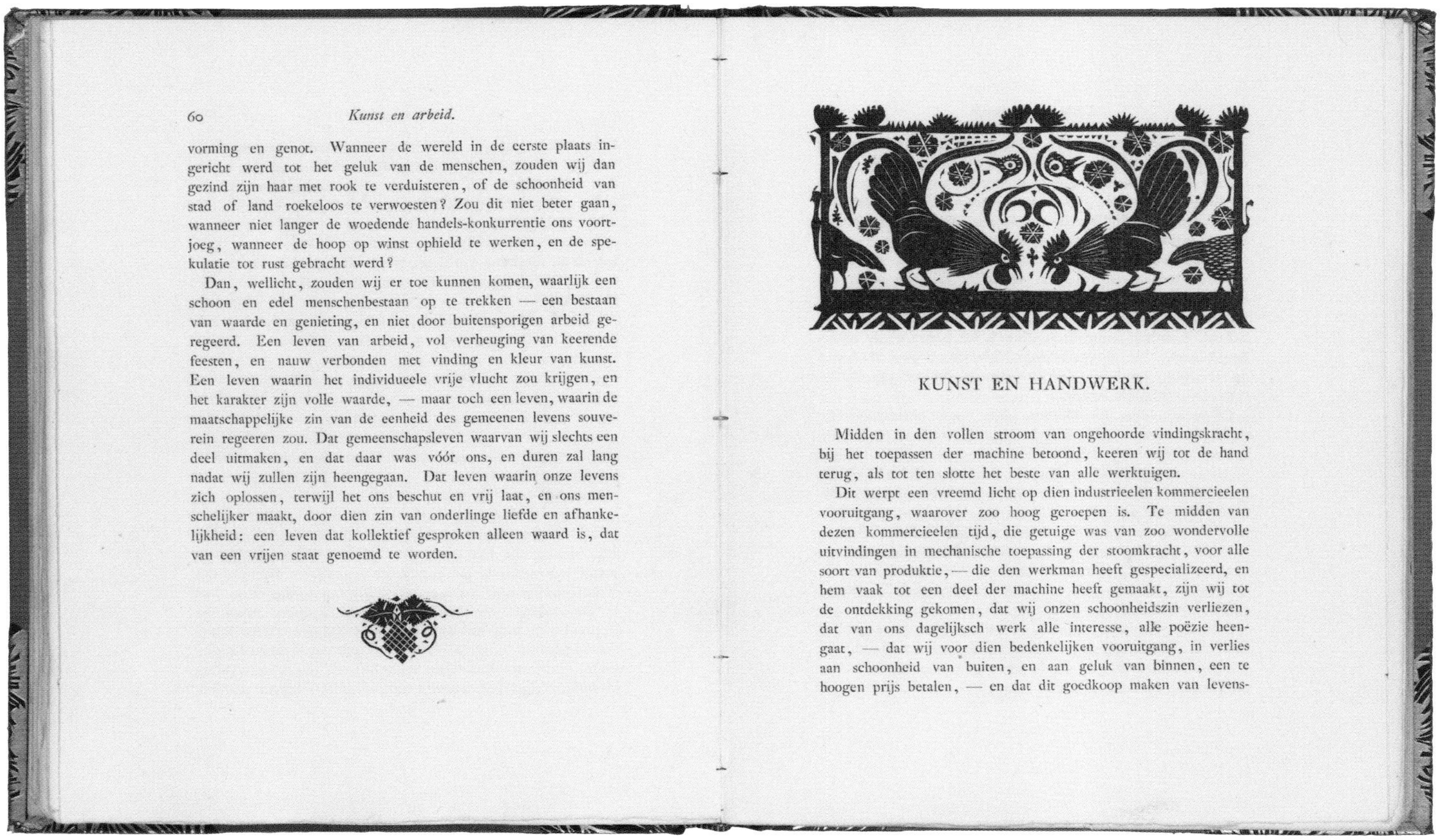

60 *Kunst en arbeid.*

vorming en genot. Wanneer de wereld in de eerste plaats ingericht werd tot het geluk van de menschen, zouden wij dan gezind zijn haar met rook te verduisteren, of de schoonheid van stad of land roekeloos te verwoesten? Zou dit niet beter gaan, wanneer niet langer de woedende handels-konkurrentie ons voortjoeg, wanneer de hoop op winst ophield te werken, en de spekulatie tot rust gebracht werd?

Dan, wellicht, zouden wij er toe kunnen komen, waarlijk een schoon en edel menschenbestaan op te trekken — een bestaan van waarde en genieting, en niet door buitensporigen arbeid geregeerd. Een leven van arbeid, vol verheuging van keerende feesten, en nauw verbonden met vinding en kleur van kunst. Een leven waarin het individueele vrije vlucht zou krijgen, en het karakter zijn volle waarde, — maar toch een leven, waarin de maatschappelijke zin van de eenheid des gemeenen levens souverein regeeren zou. Dat gemeenschapsleven waarvan wij slechts een deel uitmaken, en dat daar was vóór ons, en duren zal lang nadat wij zullen zijn heengegaan. Dat leven waarin onze levens zich oplossen, terwijl het ons beschut en vrij laat, en ons menschelijker maakt, door dien zin van onderlinge liefde en afhankelijkheid: een leven dat kollektief gesproken alleen waard is, dat van een vrijen staat genoemd te worden.

KUNST EN HANDWERK.

Midden in den vollen stroom van ongehoorde vindingskracht, bij het toepassen der machine betoond, keeren wij tot de hand terug, als tot ten slotte het beste van alle werktuigen.

Dit werpt een vreemd licht op dien industrieelen kommercieelen vooruitgang, waarover zoo hoog geroepen is. Te midden van dezen kommercieelen tijd, die getuige was van zoo wondervolle uitvindingen in mechanische toepassing der stoomkracht, voor alle soort van produktie, — die den werkman heeft gespecializeerd, en hem vaak tot een deel der machine heeft gemaakt, zijn wij tot de ontdekking gekomen, dat wij onzen schoonheidszin verliezen, dat van ons dagelijksch werk alle interesse, alle poëzie heengaat, — dat wij voor dien bedenkelijken vooruitgang, in verlies aan schoonheid van buiten, en aan geluk van binnen, een te hoogen prijs betalen, — en dat dit goedkoop maken van levens-

KUNST EN SAMENLEVING. NAAR WALTER CRANE'S CLAIMS OF DECORATIVE ART, IN HET NEDERLANDSCH BEWERKT DOOR JAN VETH, EN VERCIERD MET TALRIJKE VIGNETTEN, IN HOUT GESNEDEN DOOR G. W. DIJSSELHOF.

UITGEGEVEN TE AMSTERDAM DOOR SCHELTEMA EN HOLKEMA'S BOEKHANDEL — MDCCCXCIV

Private presses and traditional book typography

Detail of *Moralités légendaires*, designed by Lucien and Esther Pissarro **(see p. 282)**

Private presses and traditional book typography **Nineteenth-century art and architecture reflected a broad interest in the past. Styles from several historical periods were revived, leading to what we know as neo-Gothic, neo-Renaissance, and so on. In the typographical world, historical typefaces were rediscovered, especially for the better class of books. In around 1840, English typophiles began to bring some original materials of the eighteenth-century typefounder William Caslon back into use, and they liked to use them in historically allusive typographic designs.**

The most frequently used printing types of the nineteenth century nevertheless remained the so-called Didones – rather mechanical designs that followed the course set by Didot and Bodoni. In the middle of the nineteenth century, a fringe market developed for new book faces with a more historical character, known as 'old-style types' in Britain and 'Elzévirs' in France. Their market share remained limited.

The Englishman William Morris (1834–96), a representative of the Arts and Crafts Movement, disliked the compressed and engineered Didones. This socialist, who did good business with his exclusive designs for wallpaper and textiles, had been obsessed with the Middle Ages since his youth and took a critical stand against industrial production. In 1891 he founded his own printing office, the Kelmscott Press. His 'ideal book' was printed on a hand press with his own types, based on fifteenth-century models, using deep black ink on handmade paper. A double-page spread formed a graphic whole and the woodcut illustrations and decorations perfectly suited the text block set in Morris's heavy types. The Kelmscott Press was internationally admired and imitated. Two of Morris's friends established the

influential Doves Press, whose publications were less heavily decorated and more typographically refined.

William Morris's ideas and the private press movement gave a younger generation impetus towards a practically orientated typography that accepted the role of the machine. Designers such as the American Bruce Rogers (1870–1957), the Dutchman Jan van Krimpen (1892–1958) and the Englishman Stanley Morison (1889–1967) turned their attention to literary, religious and scholarly publications. They were interested in books in which text played the leading role, taking little or no interest in photobooks. In *First Principles of Typography* (1930), Morison codified the design philosophy of traditional book typography. Following typographic conventions and serving the reader were essential for this anti-modernist. His soulmate and friend Beatrice Warde coined the catchphrase: 'Printing should be invisible.' As typographic adviser to the Monotype Corporation, the typesetting machine manufacturers, Morison played an important role in bringing many historical (and other) typefaces onto the market, and in the development of the widely used Times New Roman (1932). ML

1895 **William Morris** Dante Gabriel Rossetti, *Hand and Soul*. Hammersmith: Kelmscott Press; Chicago: Way and Williams, 1895. 56 pp. 15 cm. Designer & illustrator: William Morris. Printer: Kelmscott Press, Hammersmith (London).

'I began printing books,' wrote William Morris in 1896, 'with the hope of producing some which would have a definite claim to beauty, while at the same time they should be easy to read and should not dazzle the eye, or trouble the intellect of the reader by eccentricity of form in the letters.' By founding a private press, the Englishman Morris (1834–96) gave his interest in books a new impetus. Before that, in the 1870s, he had calligraphed and illuminated books by hand. Also, he abhorred the cheap paper, thin typefaces and abominable layouts of contemporary books.

When Morris, in his fifties, started the Kelmscott Press (1891–98), he was already a successful man. He was well known as a writer, as an Arts and Crafts artist, and as a socialist. His firm, Morris & Co., produced stained glass, furniture, wallpaper and fabrics, and boasted more than a hundred employees. For his private press, Morris designed heavy types, using photographic enlargements of historic types. The production of his books was done according to traditional methods: a hand press was used to print on handmade paper or parchment. Woodcuts were used for the decorations. The expensive Kelmscott editions were in great demand with book collectors and librarians.

Hand and Soul is an early text by the painter and poet Dante Gabriel Rossetti, who was an old friend of Morris. The ornamental borders had already been used for another book. *Hand and Soul* is the only Kelmscott publication that also appeared in an American edition. Kelmscott Press had many admirers and followers outside of Great Britain, mostly in the United States. ML

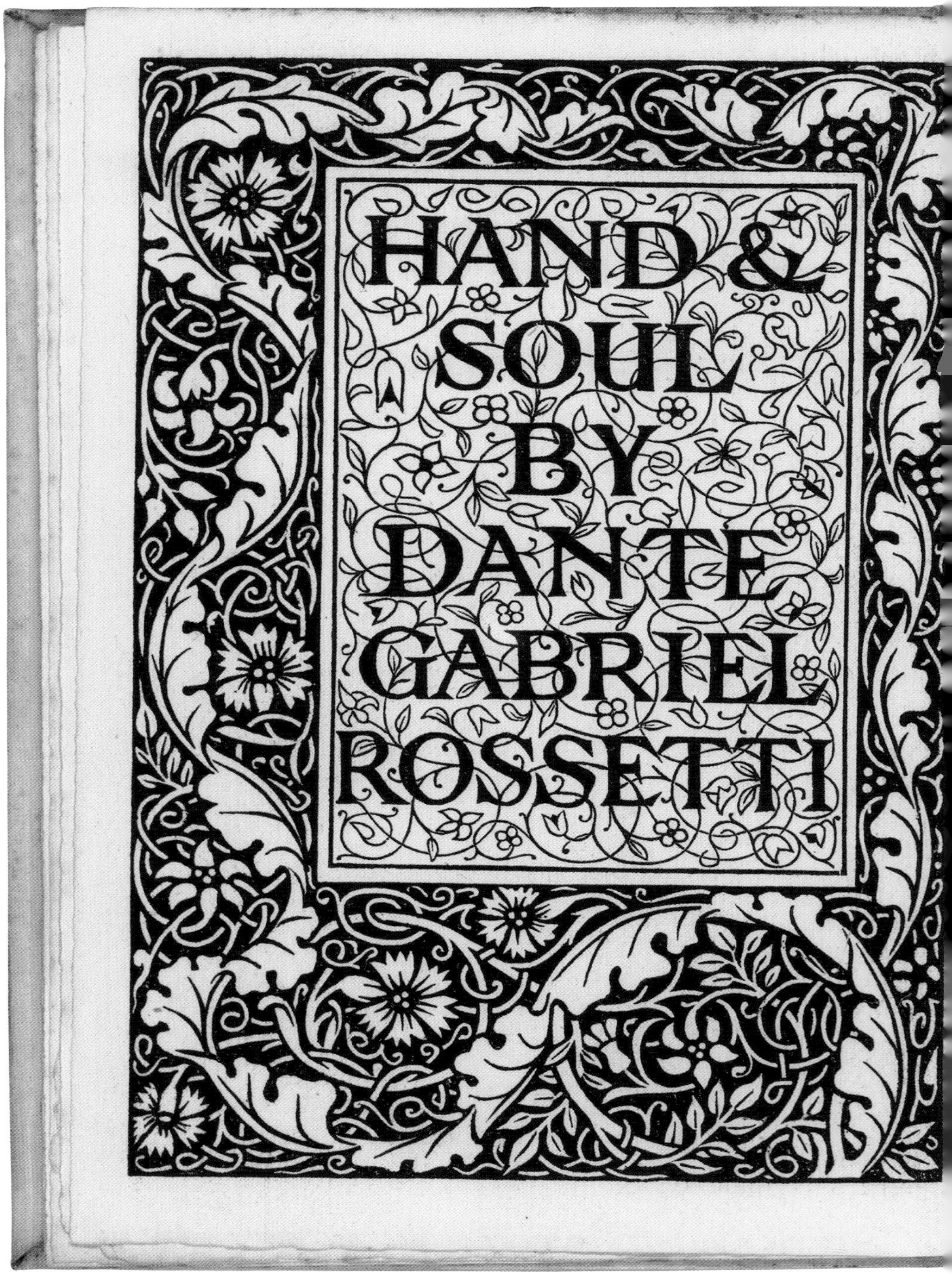

Towards the end of 1889, William Morris started designing the Golden Type (1891), which he initially called 'Jenson-Morris.' Nicolas Jenson's roman from 1470 served as an example; Emery Walker, a friend who lived near Morris in Hammersmith, had furnished photographic enlargements of historic types. Edward Prince (1846–1923) cut the punches.

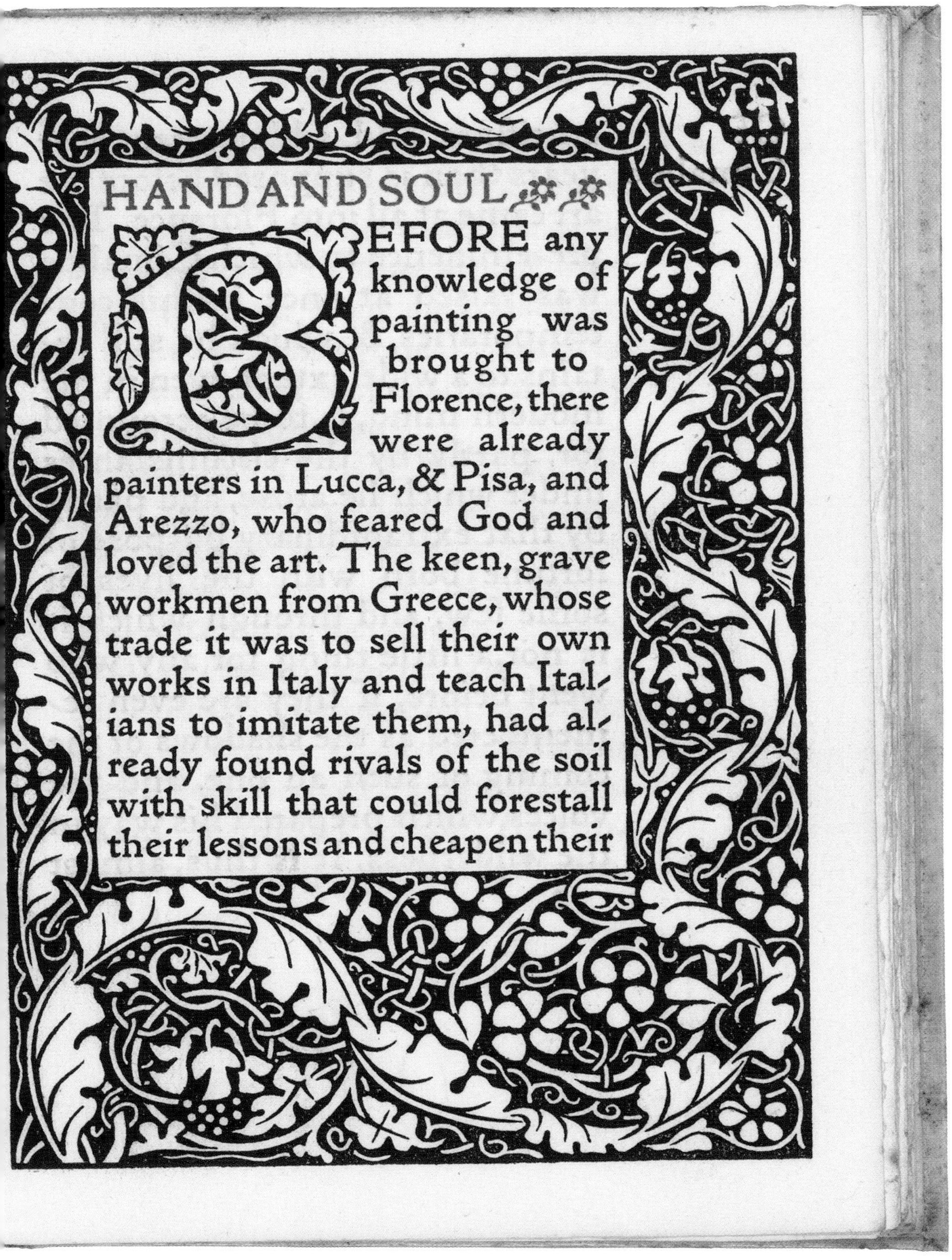

HAND AND SOUL

BEFORE any knowledge of painting was brought to Florence, there were already painters in Lucca, & Pisa, and Arezzo, who feared God and loved the art. The keen, grave workmen from Greece, whose trade it was to sell their own works in Italy and teach Italians to imitate them, had already found rivals of the soil with skill that could forestall their lessons and cheapen their

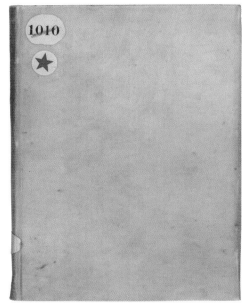

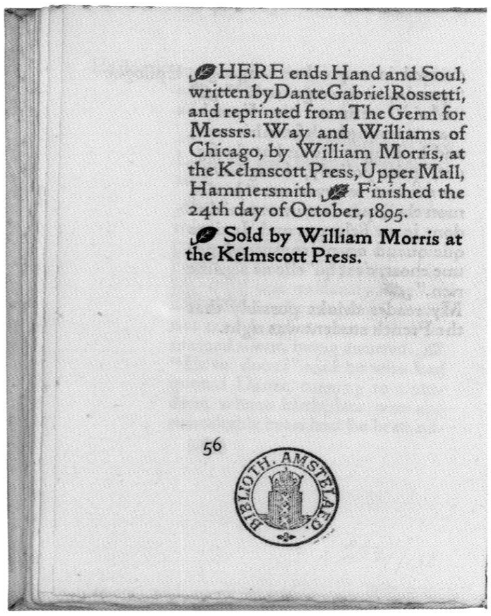

HERE ends Hand and Soul, written by Dante Gabriel Rossetti, and reprinted from The Germ for Messrs. Way and Williams of Chicago, by William Morris, at the Kelmscott Press, Upper Mall, Hammersmith. Finished the 24th day of October, 1895.

Sold by William Morris at the Kelmscott Press.

56

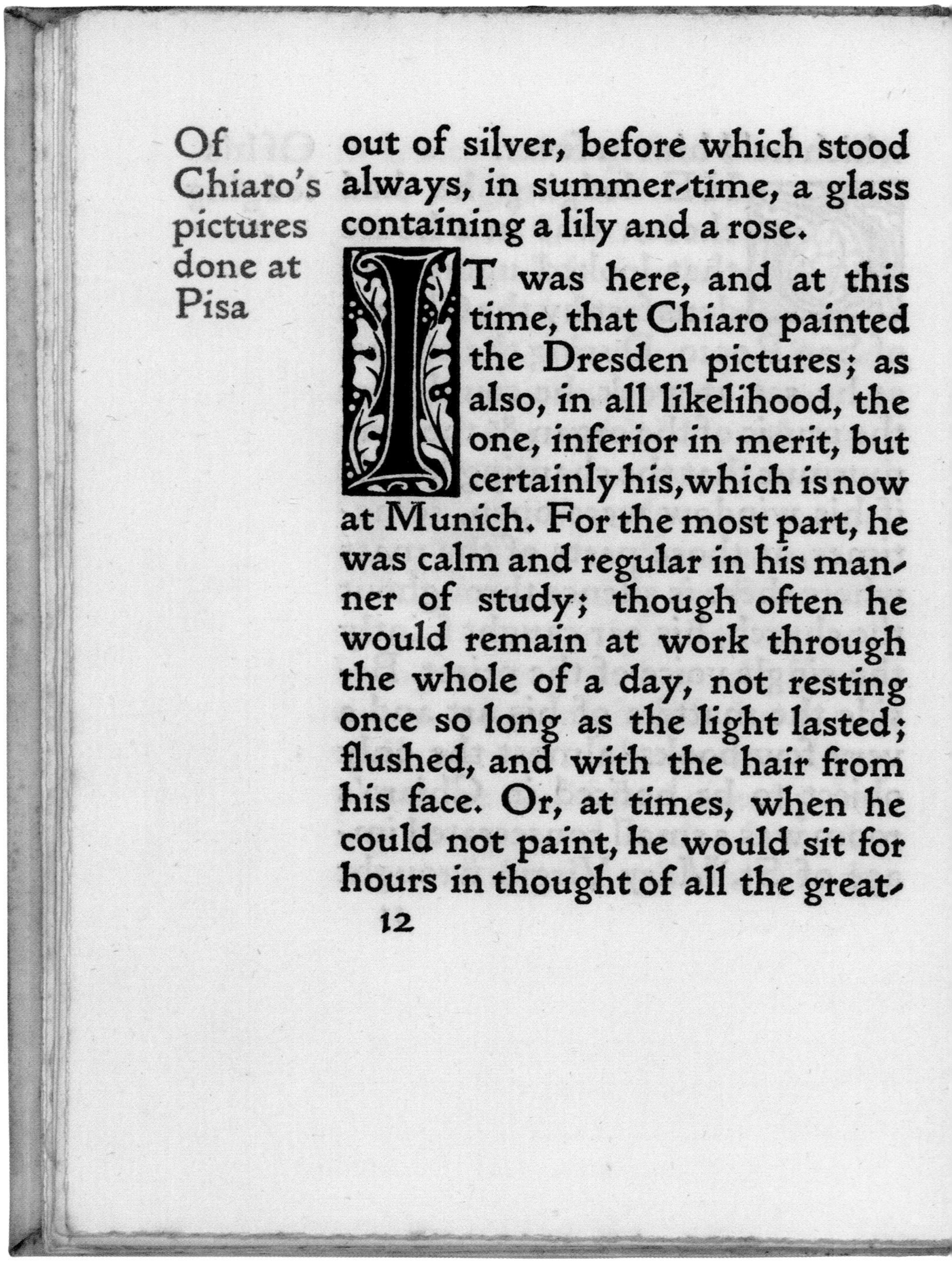

Of Chiaro's pictures done at Pisa

out of silver, before which stood always, in summer-time, a glass containing a lily and a rose.

IT was here, and at this time, that Chiaro painted the Dresden pictures; as also, in all likelihood, the one, inferior in merit, but certainly his, which is now at Munich. For the most part, he was calm and regular in his manner of study; though often he would remain at work through the whole of a day, not resting once so long as the light lasted; flushed, and with the hair from his face. Or, at times, when he could not paint, he would sit for hours in thought of all the great-

12

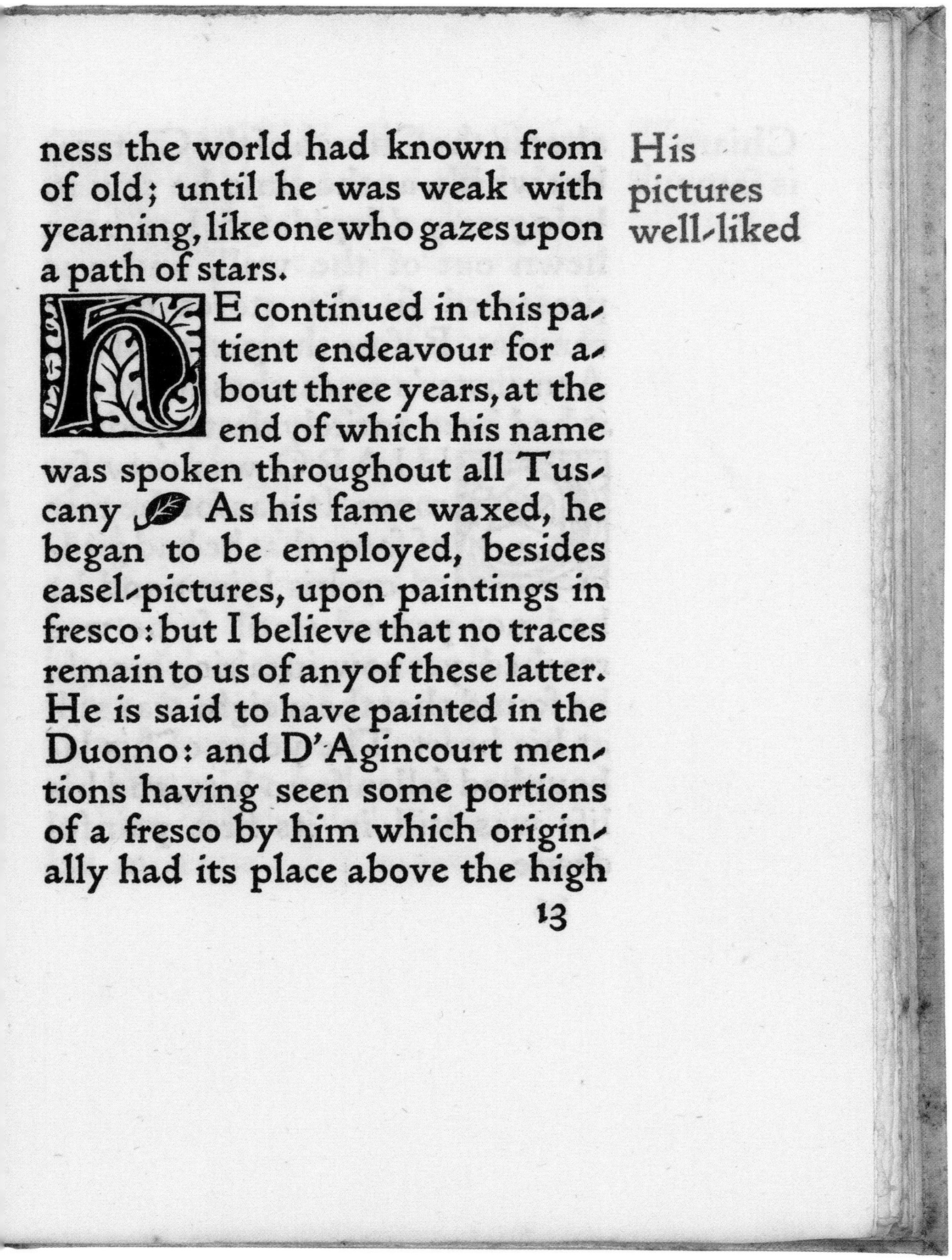

ness the world had known from of old; until he was weak with yearning, like one who gazes upon a path of stars.

His pictures well-liked

HE continued in this patient endeavour for about three years, at the end of which his name was spoken throughout all Tuscany ¶ As his fame waxed, he began to be employed, besides easel-pictures, upon paintings in fresco: but I believe that no traces remain to us of any of these latter. He is said to have painted in the Duomo: and D'Agincourt mentions having seen some portions of a fresco by him which originally had its place above the high

13

'This type [Jenson's] I studied with much care, getting it photographed to a big scale, and drawing it over many times before I began designing my own letter; so that though I think I mastered the essence of it, I did not copy it servilely; in fact, my Roman type, especially in the lower-case, tends rather more to the Gothic than does Jenson's.' William Morris in *A note … on his aims in founding the Kelmscott Press*, 1898.

1895 **Théo van Rysselberghe** Émile Verhaeren, *Almanach: cahier de vers*. Brussels: Dietrich & Co.; Paris: en vente à l'Estampe originale, 1895. 44 pp. 22 cm. Illustrator: Théo van Rysselberghe. Printer: Mme Vve Monnom, Brussels.

The wealthy city of Brussels was a centre of Art Nouveau during the last decade of the nineteenth century. This poetry collection from 1895 was produced by two of the leading figures in the movement: the poet Émile Verhaeren and the artist Théo van Rysselberghe (1862–1926). The booklet, set entirely in italic, is printed on luxury paper but the finishing is simple saddle-stitching. A second colour is also used: purple (as shown here), orange, blue or green. The decorations of the *Almanach* show the influence of English private presses. There is some restraint in the handdrawn lettering. In his lettering for posters, however, Van Rysselberghe could be more experimental, displaying the influences of Japanese calligraphy and Toulouse-Lautrec.

Van Rysselberghe had started to focus more heavily on the decorative arts. In 1895 he worked for the Paris gallery L'Art Nouveau, run by Siegfried Bing. He produced graphic work for magazines, catalogues and books, and also designed posters. He worked with Georges Lemmen and Henry van de Velde on decorations for the Flemish avant-garde magazine *Van nu en straks*; the first issue appeared in 1893.

In the fields of the visual and applied arts, van Rysselberghe felt a connection with Verhaeren. Together they had admired Seurat's painting *A Sunday on La Grande Jatte* in Paris in 1886, and it had not taken long for van Rysselberghe to begin working with Seurat's neo-Impressionist pointillist technique himself. Verhaeren supported modern movements as an art critic, and promoted the group Les XX (1883–93) as well as its successor, Libre Esthétique. Van Rysselberghe belonged to both groups. ML

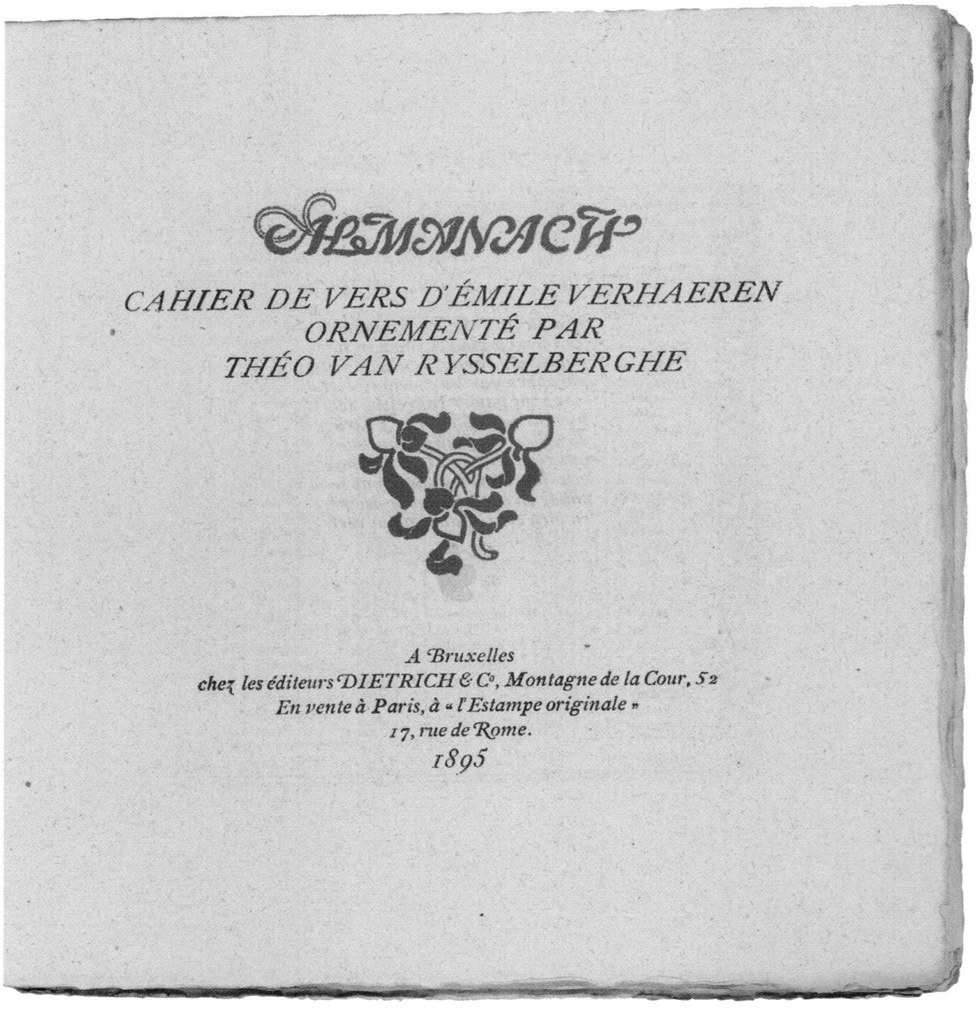

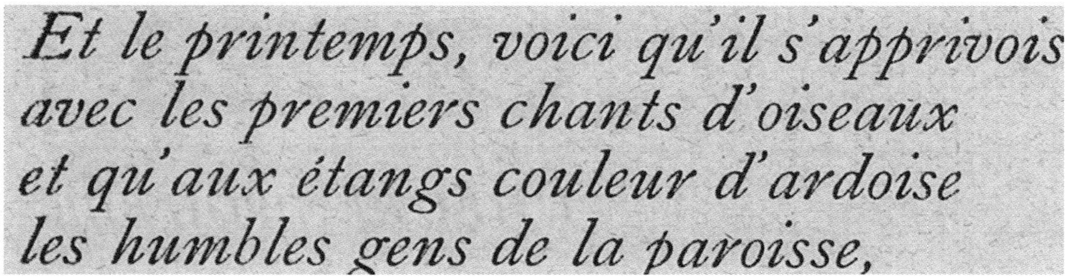
Et le printemps, voici qu'il s'apprivois
avec les premiers chants d'oiseaux
et qu'aux étangs couleur d'ardoise
les humbles gens de la paroisse,

Caslon's 1730 Great Primer italic, the first to fully display his mature style, is shown here in a newly revised form. The Caslon foundry announced in 1878 that they were adapting the original Caslon faces for machine casting and made further revisions to this size in 1893. They opened a Paris branch by 1883.

C'est Mars!
L'ombre du soir incline aux longs miroirs
des lacs pensifs ses bras qui glissent
et s'enfoncent sous les eaux lisses.

C'est Mars!
Et le printemps, voici qu'il s'apprivoise
avec les premiers chants d'oiseaux
et qu'aux étangs couleur d'ardoise
les humbles gens de la paroisse,
pour abriter les toits et border les closeaux,
coupent de pauvres blancs roseaux.

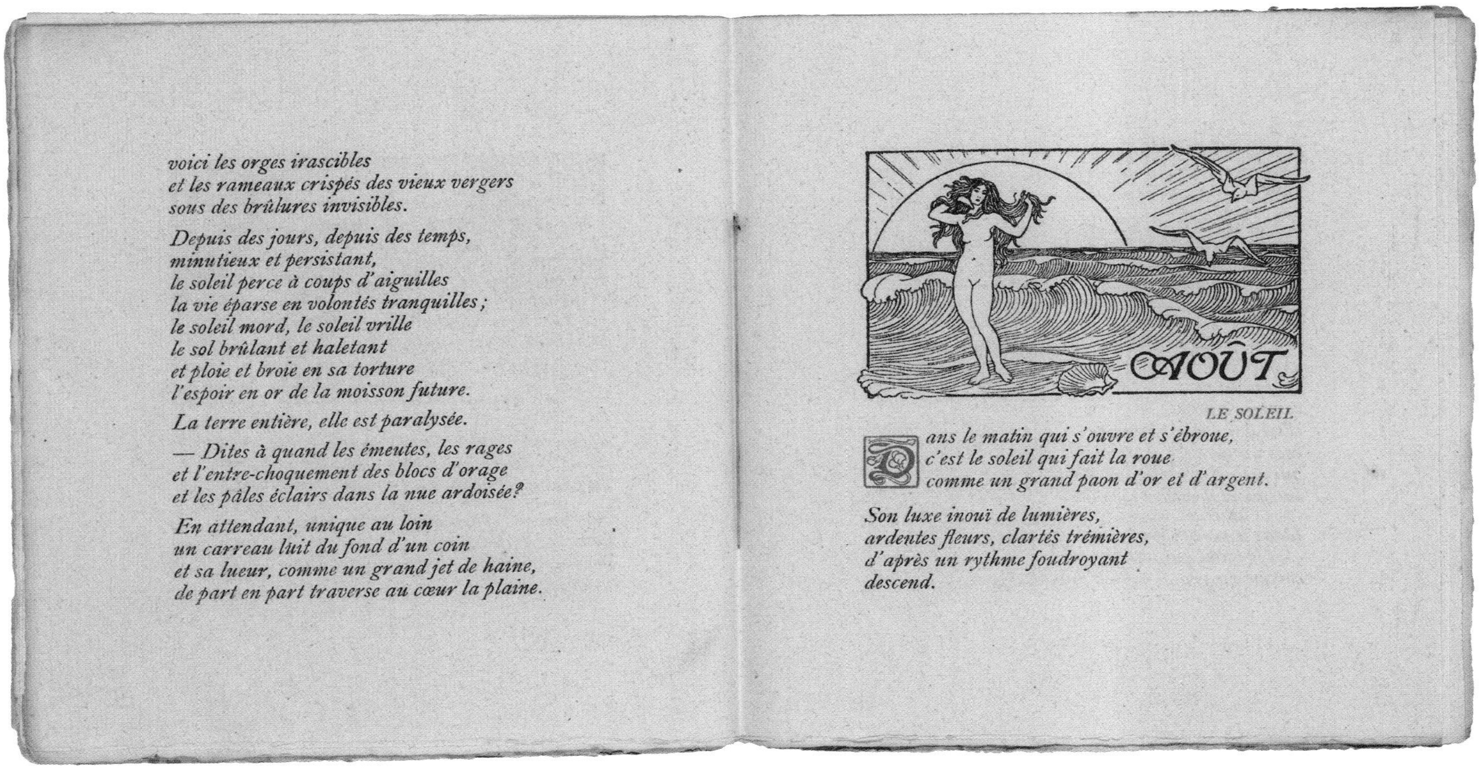
voici les orges irascibles
et les rameaux crispés des vieux vergers
sous des brûlures invisibles.

Depuis des jours, depuis des temps,
minutieux et persistant,
le soleil perce à coups d'aiguilles
la vie éparse en volontés tranquilles;
le soleil mord, le soleil vrille
le sol brûlant et haletant
et ploie et broie en sa torture
l'espoir en or de la moisson future.

La terre entière, elle est paralysée.

— Dites à quand les émeutes, les rages
et l'entre-choquement des blocs d'orage
et les pâles éclairs dans la nue ardoisée?

En attendant, unique au loin
un carreau luit du fond d'un coin
et sa lueur, comme un grand jet de haine,
de part en part traverse au cœur la plaine.

LE SOLEIL

Dans le matin qui s'ouvre et s'ébroue,
c'est le soleil qui fait la roue
comme un grand paon d'or et d'argent.

Son luxe inouï de lumières,
ardentes fleurs, clartés trémières,
d'après un rythme foudroyant
descend.

1897 **Lucien & Esther Pissarro** Jules Laforgue, *Moralités légendaires*. London: Hacon & Ricketts; Paris: Société du Mercure de France, 1897–98. 2 volumes. 22 cm. Illustrator: Lucien Pissarro. Engraver: Esther Pissarro. Printer: Eragny Press, London.

Towards the end of the nineteenth century and at the beginning of the twentieth, a number of private presses emerged – primarily in Great Britain, the United States and Germany – which modelled themselves after the Kelmscott Press. The married couple Lucien (1863–1944) and Esther (1870–1951) Pissarro were early followers. Lucien was the eldest son of the French painter Camille Pissarro, and father and son had both worked in the pointillist style in Eragny in Normandy.

To break away from his famous father's artistic influences, Lucien Pissarro turned to illustrating books and became a skilled wood engraver; his wood engravings are often in several colours. Towards the end of 1890, he settled in England, where he became friends with the painter and art connoisseur Charles Ricketts. Ricketts worked for publishers as a book designer in the Art Nouveau style. In 1893, he and his partner started designing limited editions (later under the name Vale Press). When, a year later, the Pissarro couple launched the Eragny Press, they decided to join forces with Ricketts.

Starting with the second volume of Laforgue's *Moralités légendaires* ('Moral Tales'), the printing was done in the Pissarros' printing shop. This stayed close to the tenets of the Arts and Crafts movement, although they received occasional help from a professional printer. *Moralités* was set in Vale type, which was put at their disposal by Ricketts. The initials, borders and illustrations printed in one colour were – as was often the case – cut into wood by Esther Pissarro. Lucien Pissarro focused on painting once more when the press closed in 1914. ML

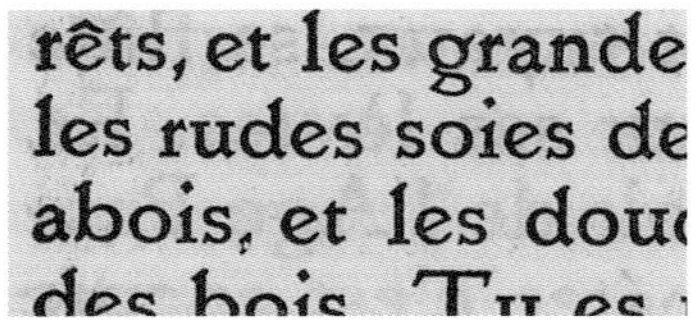

The rather heavy Vale Type (1895) was designed by Charles Ricketts (1866–1931) and took inspiration from Nicolas Jenson's 1470 roman. The type was cut by Edward Prince (1846–1923), who frequently made punches for private presses. The type was cast by Sir Charles Reed and Sons, London.

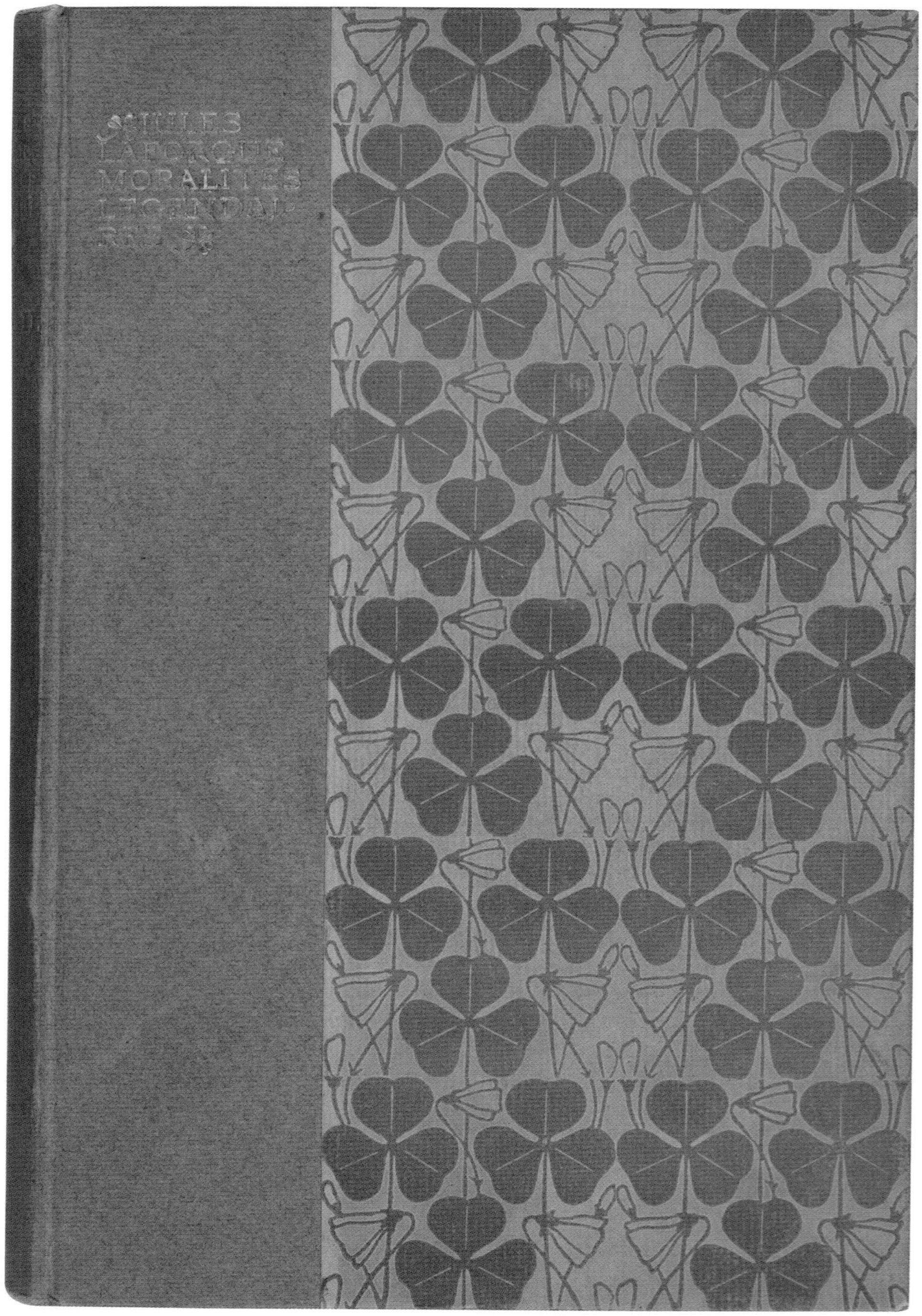

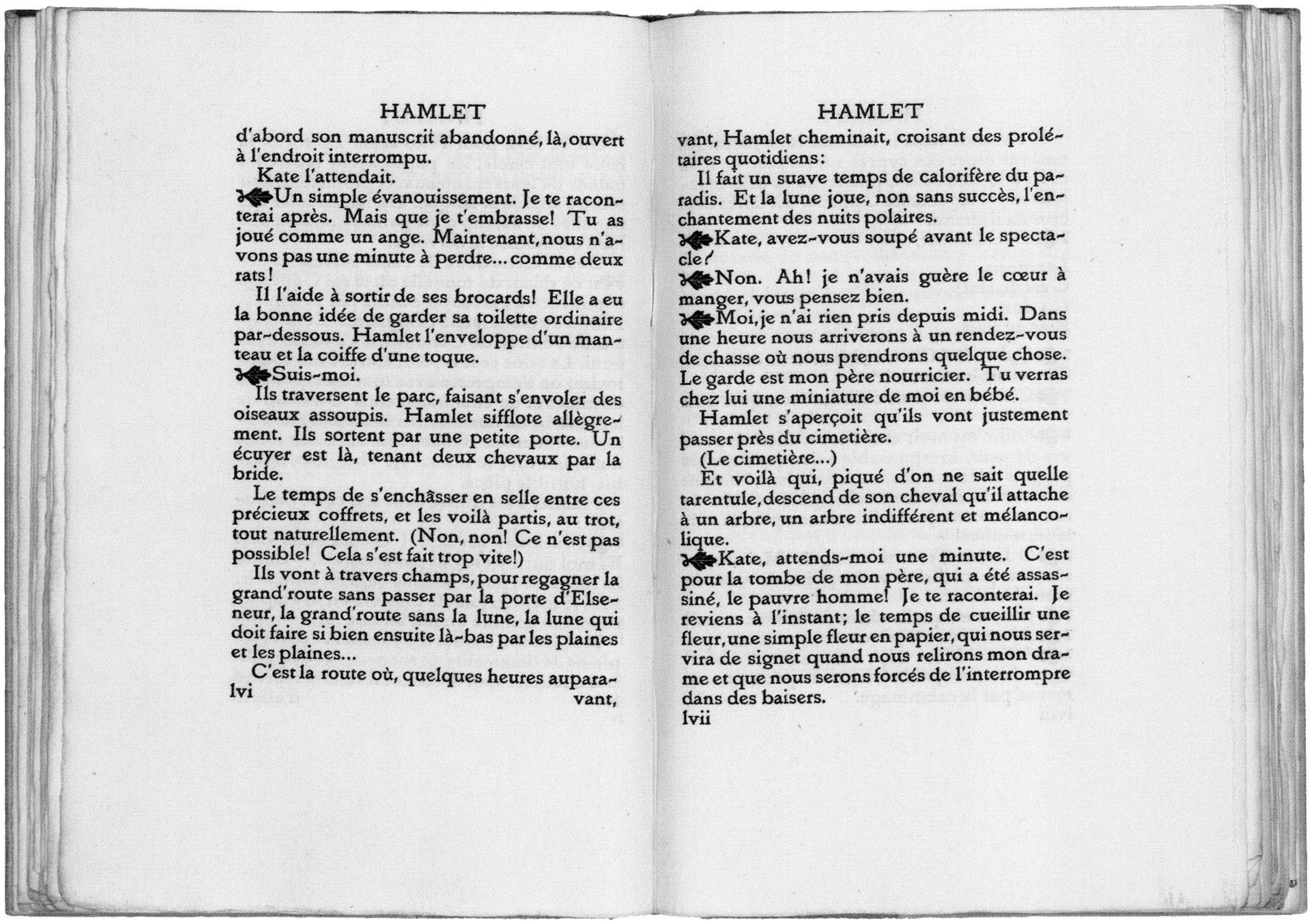

HAMLET

d'abord son manuscrit abandonné, là, ouvert à l'endroit interrompu.

Kate l'attendait.

Un simple évanouissement. Je te raconterai après. Mais que je t'embrasse! Tu as joué comme un ange. Maintenant, nous n'avons pas une minute à perdre... comme deux rats!

Il l'aide à sortir de ses brocards! Elle a eu la bonne idée de garder sa toilette ordinaire par-dessous. Hamlet l'enveloppe d'un manteau et la coiffe d'une toque.

Suis-moi.

Ils traversent le parc, faisant s'envoler des oiseaux assoupis. Hamlet sifflote allègrement. Ils sortent par une petite porte. Un écuyer est là, tenant deux chevaux par la bride.

Le temps de s'enchâsser en selle entre ces précieux coffrets, et les voilà partis, au trot, tout naturellement. (Non, non! Ce n'est pas possible! Cela s'est fait trop vite!)

Ils vont à travers champs, pour regagner la grand'route sans passer par la porte d'Elseneur, la grand'route sans la lune, la lune qui doit faire si bien ensuite là-bas par les plaines et les plaines...

C'est la route où, quelques heures auparavant,

lvi

HAMLET

vant, Hamlet cheminait, croisant des prolétaires quotidiens:

Il fait un suave temps de calorifère du paradis. Et la lune joue, non sans succès, l'enchantement des nuits polaires.

Kate, avez-vous soupé avant le spectacle?

Non. Ah! je n'avais guère le cœur à manger, vous pensez bien.

Moi, je n'ai rien pris depuis midi. Dans une heure nous arriverons à un rendez-vous de chasse où nous prendrons quelque chose. Le garde est mon père nourricier. Tu verras chez lui une miniature de moi en bébé.

Hamlet s'aperçoit qu'ils vont justement passer près du cimetière.

(Le cimetière...)

Et voilà qui, piqué d'on ne sait quelle tarentule, descend de son cheval qu'il attache à un arbre, un arbre indifférent et mélancolique.

Kate, attends-moi une minute. C'est pour la tombe de mon père, qui a été assassiné, le pauvre homme! Je te raconterai. Je reviens à l'instant; le temps de cueillir une fleur, une simple fleur en papier, qui nous servira de signet quand nous relirons mon drame et que nous serons forcés de l'interrompre dans des baisers.

lvii

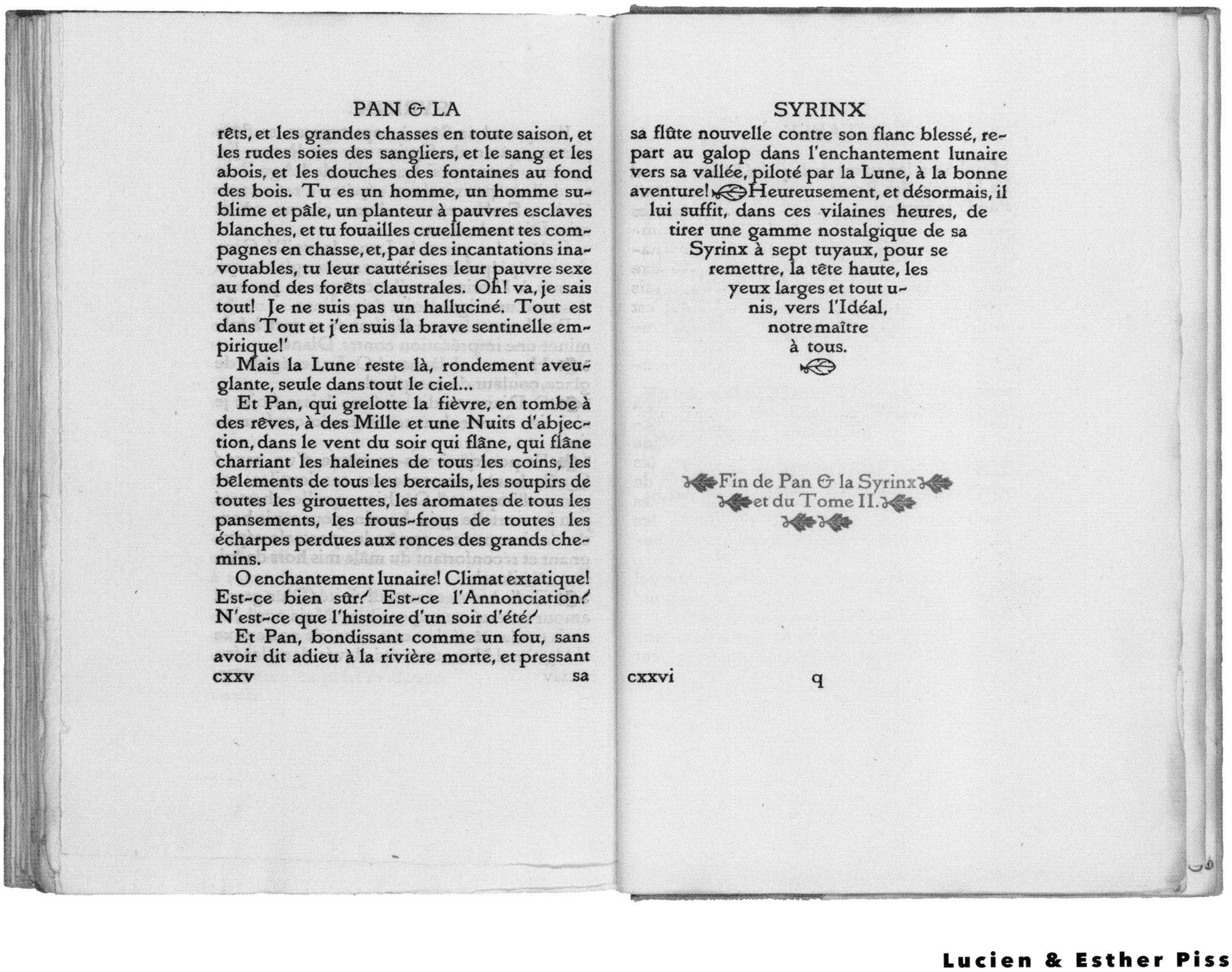

PAN & LA

rêts, et les grandes chasses en toute saison, et les rudes soies des sangliers, et le sang et les abois, et les douches des fontaines au fond des bois. Tu es un homme, un homme sublime et pâle, un planteur à pauvres esclaves blanches, et tu fouailles cruellement tes compagnes en chasse, et, par des incantations inavouables, tu leur cautérises leur pauvre sexe au fond des forêts claustrales. Oh! va, je sais tout! Je ne suis pas un halluciné. Tout est dans Tout et j'en suis la brave sentinelle empirique!'

Mais la Lune reste là, rondement aveuglante, seule dans tout le ciel...

Et Pan, qui grelotte la fièvre, en tombe à des rêves, à des Mille et une Nuits d'abjection, dans le vent du soir qui flâne, qui flâne charriant les haleines de tous les coins, les bêlements de tous les bercails, les soupirs de toutes les girouettes, les aromates de tous les pansements, les frous-frous de toutes les écharpes perdues aux ronces des grands chemins.

O enchantement lunaire! Climat extatique! Est-ce bien sûr? Est-ce l'Annonciation? N'est-ce que l'histoire d'un soir d'été?

Et Pan, bondissant comme un fou, sans avoir dit adieu à la rivière morte, et pressant

cxxv sa

SYRINX

sa flûte nouvelle contre son flanc blessé, repart au galop dans l'enchantement lunaire vers sa vallée, piloté par la Lune, à la bonne aventure! Heureusement, et désormais, il lui suffit, dans ces vilaines heures, de tirer une gamme nostalgique de sa Syrinx à sept tuyaux, pour se remettre, la tête haute, les yeux larges et tout unis, vers l'Idéal, notre maître à tous.

Fin de Pan & la Syrinx et du Tome II.

cxxvi q

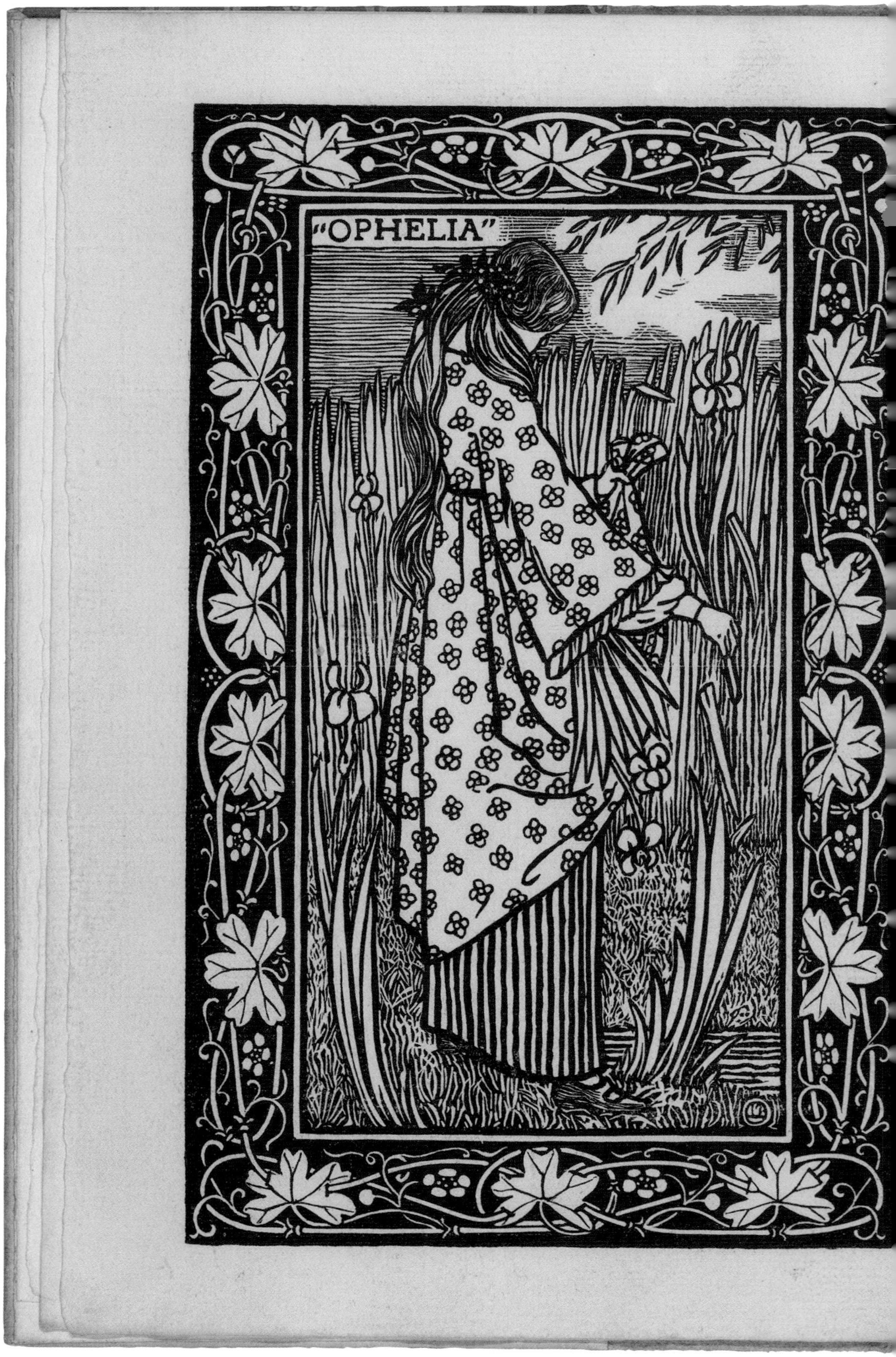
"OPHELIA"

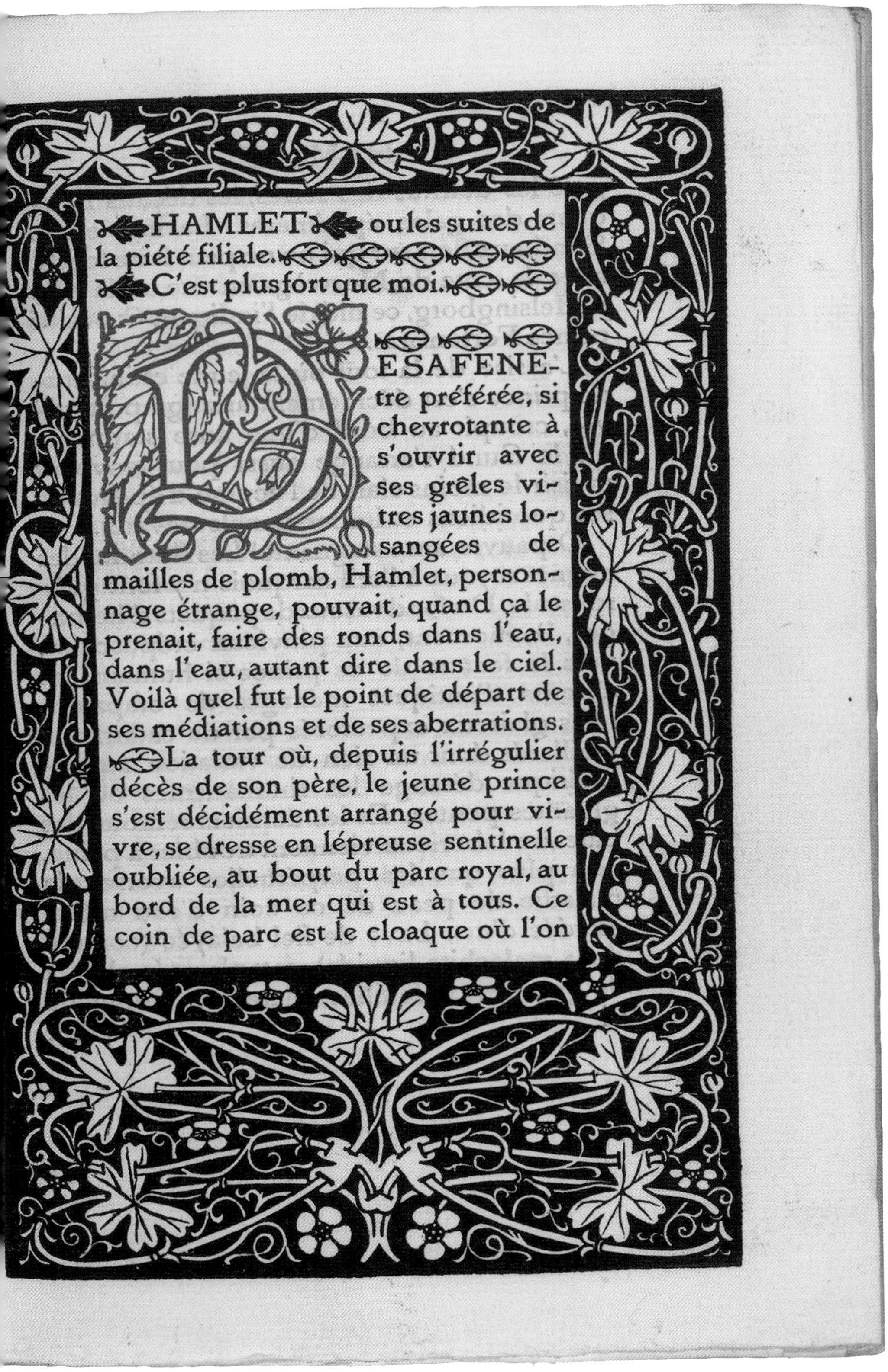

HAMLET ou les suites de la piété filiale.

C'est plus fort que moi.

DE SA FENETRE préférée, si chevrotante à s'ouvrir avec ses grêles vitres jaunes losangées de mailles de plomb, Hamlet, personnage étrange, pouvait, quand ça le prenait, faire des ronds dans l'eau, dans l'eau, autant dire dans le ciel. Voilà quel fut le point de départ de ses médiations et de ses aberrations.

La tour où, depuis l'irrégulier décès de son père, le jeune prince s'est décidément arrangé pour vivre, se dresse en lépreuse sentinelle oubliée, au bout du parc royal, au bord de la mer qui est à tous. Ce coin de parc est le cloaque où l'on

1904 **Theodore Low De Vinne** Theodore Low De Vinne, *Modern Methods of Book Composition: A Treatise on Type-setting by Hand and by Machine and on the Proper Arrangement and Imposition of Pages*. New York: The Century Co., 1904. xi, 477 pp. 19.5 cm. Volume from *The Practice of Typography*. Designer: Theodore Low De Vinne. Printer: The De Vinne Press, New York.

The monumental De Vinne Press Building in lower Manhattan, with its impressive arches, is now a designated New York City landmark. The eight-storey redbrick structure (1886) in Lafayette Street was designed by the firm of Babb, Cook and Willard and was commissioned by entrepreneur Theodore Low De Vinne (1828–1914), a self-made printer.

De Vinne – who had started out as a teenager working for a printer with only one hand press – welcomed the technological developments that characterized the second half of the nineteenth century. Due to mechanization, typesetting and printing could be done on an industrial scale. The De Vinne Press with its modern presses was able to produce magazines for a mass market, such as *The Century Illustrated Monthly Magazine*, of which no less than 250,000 copies had to be printed at times. Linn Boyd Benton cooperated with De Vinne in designing the Century typeface especially for this magazine.

De Vinne also owed his renown to his many publications, in particular to his four-volume printing manual *The Practice of Typography* (1900–4). The volume on *Modern Methods of Book Composition* was obviously addressed primarily to apprentice typesetters. Besides practical issues, the book also discusses issues of typographic design, such as title pages and tables. In his preface, De Vinne wrote that he was mainly concerned with 'the plain book made to be used and read more than to be decorated and admired as an exhibit of typographical skill.' ML

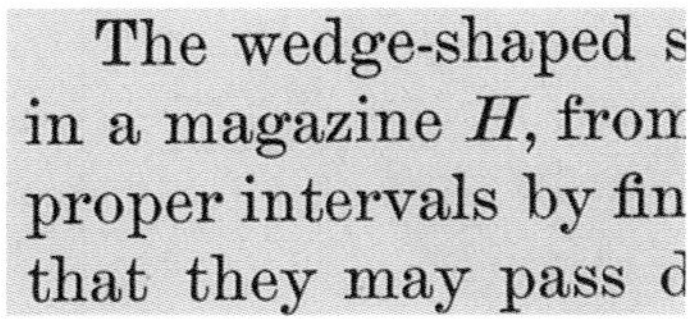

The wedge-shaped s
in a magazine *H*, from
proper intervals by fin
that they may pass d

Linn Boyd Benton (1844–1932) devised Century, a slightly heavier and more readable text face, with Theodore Low De Vinne. The typeface was meant for use in *The Century Magazine*. Century (1895) was issued by the American Type Founders and soon became available for hot-metal composing machines. It was highly successful and was developed, over the course of the years, into a huge family.

'… but when he [the printer] has a free hand and is asked to do the composition of a new book in workmanlike manner, he will make no mistake in adhering to methods of simplicity that have prevailed for centuries. It will be safer to accept the leadership of Bodoni and Didot, of Pickering and Whittingham, than that of many recent reformers of typography.' (p. 110)

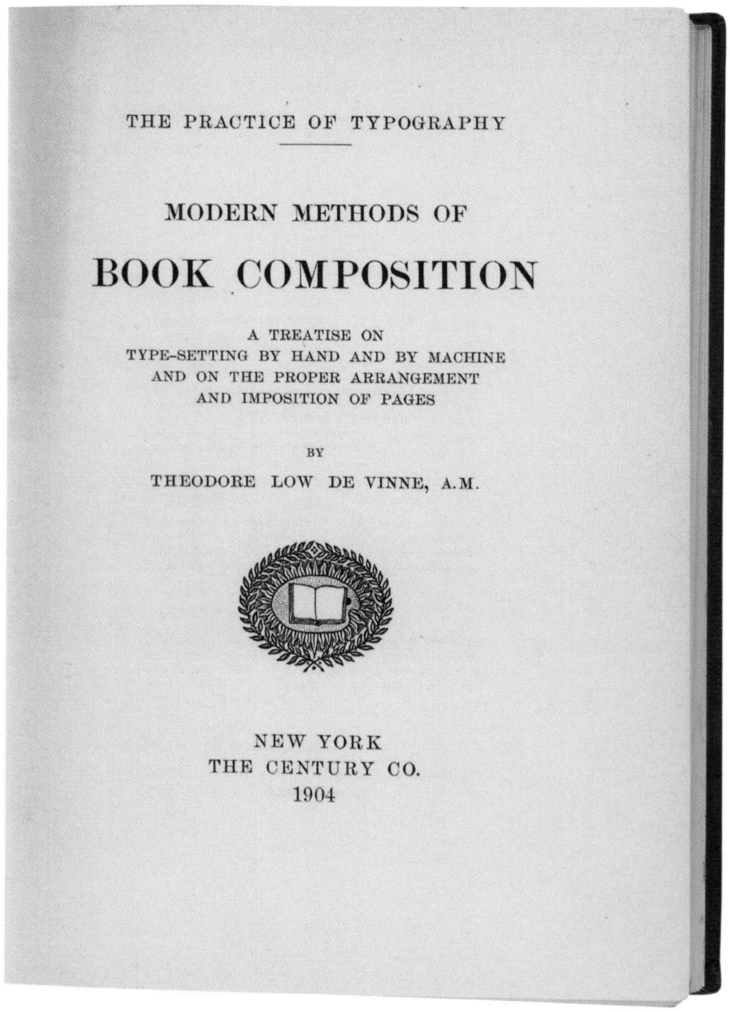

THE PRACTICE OF TYPOGRAPHY

MODERN METHODS OF

BOOK COMPOSITION

A TREATISE ON
TYPE-SETTING BY HAND AND BY MACHINE
AND ON THE PROPER ARRANGEMENT
AND IMPOSITION OF PAGES

BY

THEODORE LOW DE VINNE, A.M.

NEW YORK
THE CENTURY CO.
1904

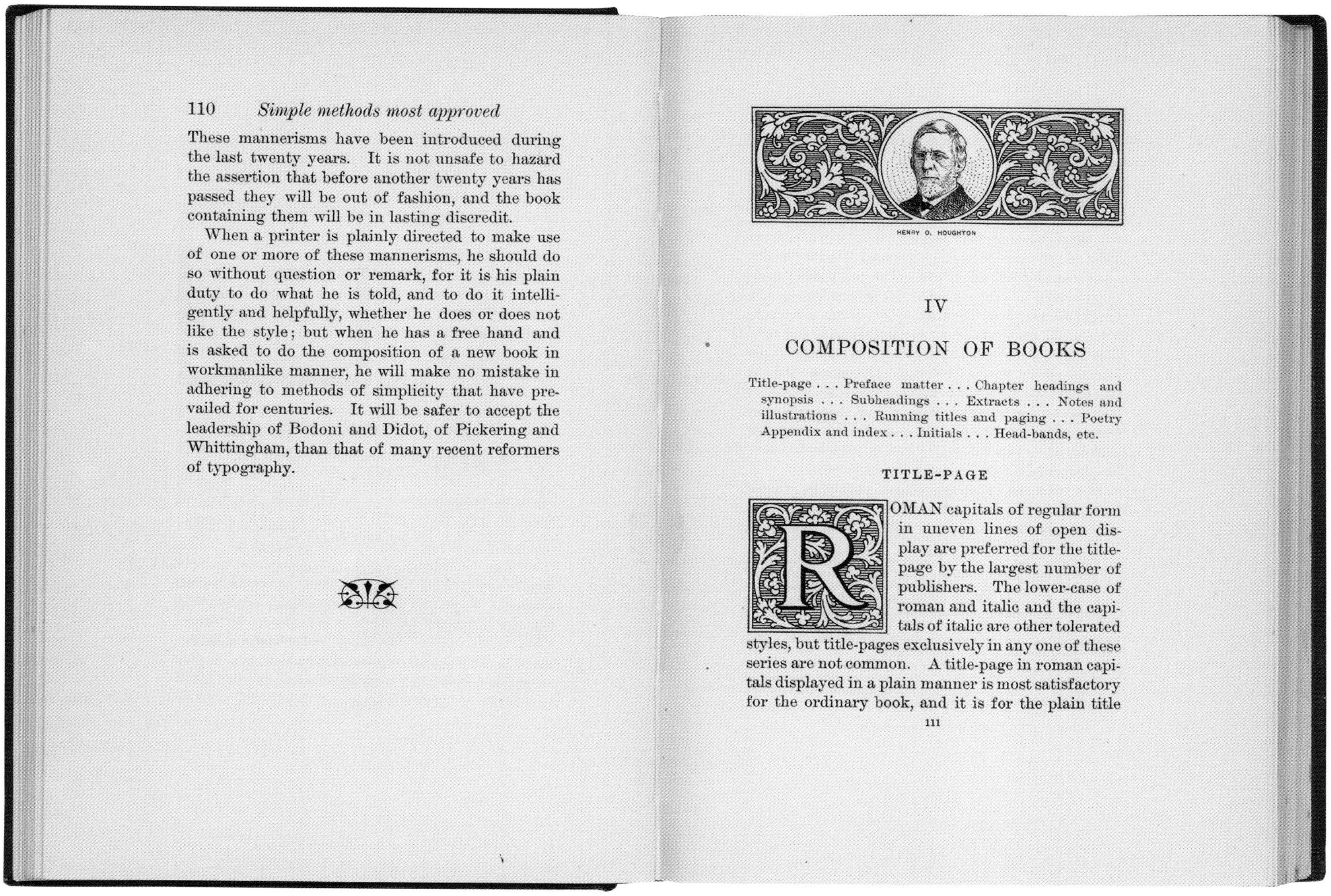

110 *Simple methods most approved*

These mannerisms have been introduced during the last twenty years. It is not unsafe to hazard the assertion that before another twenty years has passed they will be out of fashion, and the book containing them will be in lasting discredit.

When a printer is plainly directed to make use of one or more of these mannerisms, he should do so without question or remark, for it is his plain duty to do what he is told, and to do it intelligently and helpfully, whether he does or does not like the style; but when he has a free hand and is asked to do the composition of a new book in workmanlike manner, he will make no mistake in adhering to methods of simplicity that have prevailed for centuries. It will be safer to accept the leadership of Bodoni and Didot, of Pickering and Whittingham, than that of many recent reformers of typography.

HENRY O. HOUGHTON

IV

COMPOSITION OF BOOKS

Title-page . . . Preface matter . . . Chapter headings and synopsis . . . Subheadings . . . Extracts . . . Notes and illustrations . . . Running titles and paging . . . Poetry Appendix and index . . . Initials . . . Head-bands, etc.

TITLE-PAGE

ROMAN capitals of regular form in uneven lines of open display are preferred for the title-page by the largest number of publishers. The lower-case of roman and italic and the capitals of italic are other tolerated styles, but title-pages exclusively in any one of these series are not common. A title-page in roman capitals displayed in a plain manner is most satisfactory for the ordinary book, and it is for the plain title

111

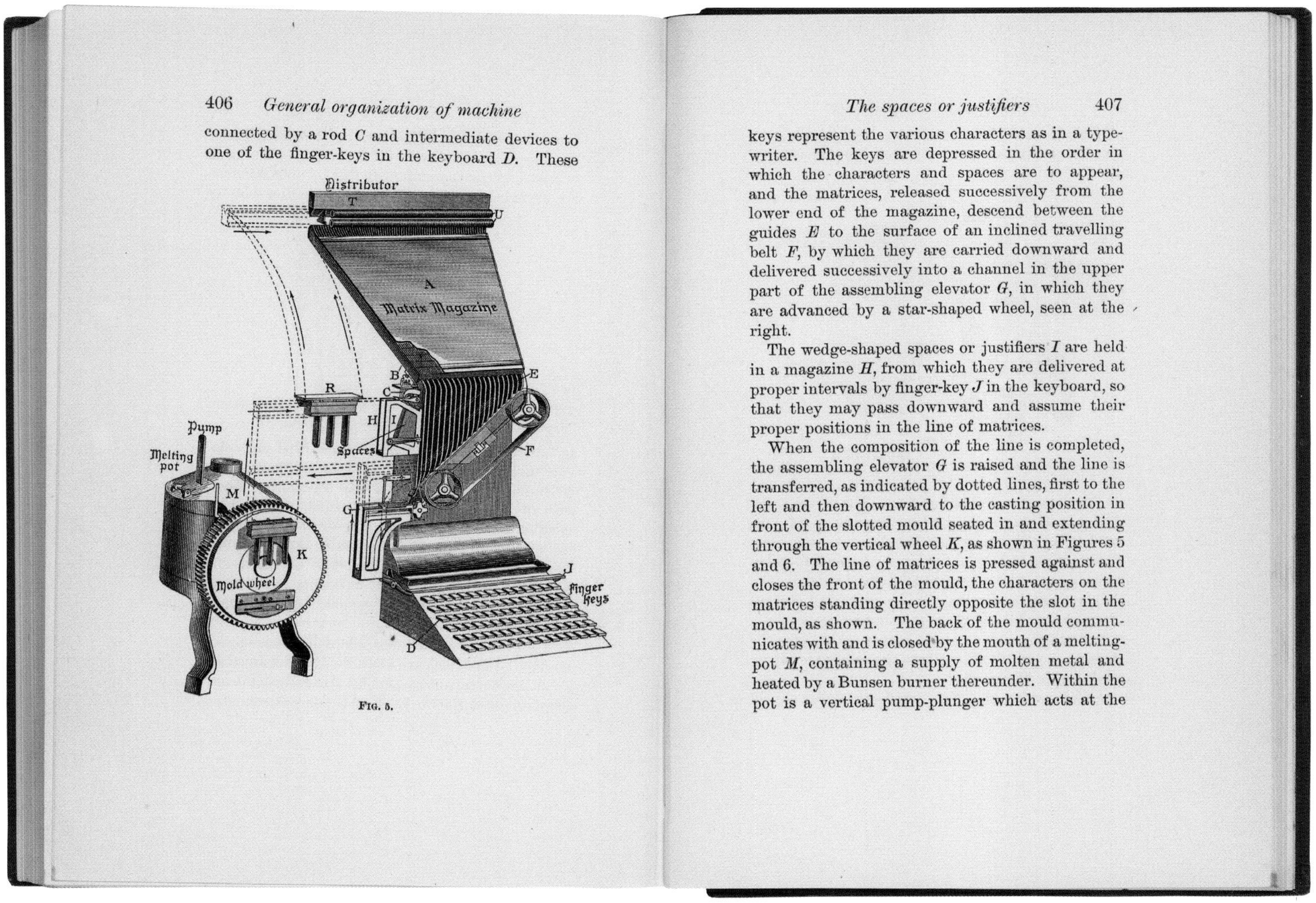

406 *General organization of machine*

connected by a rod *C* and intermediate devices to one of the finger-keys in the keyboard *D*. These

Fig. 5.

The spaces or justifiers 407

keys represent the various characters as in a typewriter. The keys are depressed in the order in which the characters and spaces are to appear, and the matrices, released successively from the lower end of the magazine, descend between the guides *E* to the surface of an inclined travelling belt *F*, by which they are carried downward and delivered successively into a channel in the upper part of the assembling elevator *G*, in which they are advanced by a star-shaped wheel, seen at the right.

The wedge-shaped spaces or justifiers *I* are held in a magazine *H*, from which they are delivered at proper intervals by finger-key *J* in the keyboard, so that they may pass downward and assume their proper positions in the line of matrices.

When the composition of the line is completed, the assembling elevator *G* is raised and the line is transferred, as indicated by dotted lines, first to the left and then downward to the casting position in front of the slotted mould seated in and extending through the vertical wheel *K*, as shown in Figures 5 and 6. The line of matrices is pressed against and closes the front of the mould, the characters on the matrices standing directly opposite the slot in the mould, as shown. The back of the mould communicates with and is closed by the mouth of a melting-pot *M*, containing a supply of molten metal and heated by a Bunsen burner thereunder. Within the pot is a vertical pump-plunger which acts at the

1905 **Count Harry Kessler & Emery Walker** *Schopenhauer's sämmtliche Werke*, vols. 1 & 2 (= *Welt als Wille & Vorstellung*); ed. Eduard Grisebach. Leipzig: Insel Verlag, 1905. 1,462 pp. 17 cm. From the series *Grossherzog Wilhelm Ernst Ausgabe*. Designers: Count Harry Kessler (concept), Emery Walker. Lettering artist: Eric Gill. Book designer: Douglas Cockerell. Printer: Poeschel & Trepte, Leipzig.

The wealthy dandy Count Harry Kessler (1868–1937) was a man of consequence in the German art world. In 1903, he founded the avant-garde forum, the Deutscher Künstlerbund (which still exists), in protest against the reactionary cultural politics. Kessler was a great bibliophile, and it was around this time that he acted as project leader for the *Grossherzog Wilhelm Ernst Ausgabe* ('Grand Duke Wilhelm Ernst Edition'). He himself came up with the concept for the series, consisting of classics from German literature and philosophy.

As an idealist, Kessler wanted to stimulate a new cultural climate with this ambitious series, which was named after its Weimar patron. The volumes were therefore not in the decorative Art Nouveau style but had a clear and restrained design instead, to enhance readability. The compact paperbacks, printed on thin India paper, were meant to be within reach of a broad audience. Although the series was published under scholarly supervision, the editors elected not to include any commentary or scholarly apparatus, as these would only impede the reader's own critical reflections.

While book production took place in Germany, Kessler looked to London for the design. Emery Walker (1851–1933) – who was, according to Kessler, the greatest typographical genius since the Renaissance – took care of typography, Edward Johnston (1872–1944) and Eric Gill (1882–1940) designed the lettering, and Douglas Cockerell (1870–1945) designed the flexible, tomato-red binding. Walker was co-founder of the Doves Press, whose editions were typeset with the greatest care. Not only was the design of the *Grossherzog Wilhelm Ernst Ausgabe* deemed un-German, the choice of type was too: not a blackletter type, but a Latin type with better readability. The cosmopolitan Kessler abhorred the idea of using blackletter for purely nationalistic reasons. ML

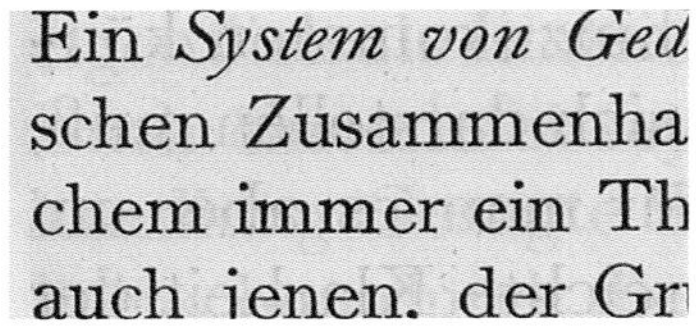

Monotype Old Style (1901) was an adaptation of a type designed around 1860 for Miller & Richard by Alexander Phemister (1829–94). Printer Carl Ernst Poeschel reputedly acquired the Monotype hot-metal composing machine especially for the *Grossherzog Wilhelm Ernst Ausgabe*. For Kessler's series concept, this Old Style was the most suitable typeface available for Monotype.

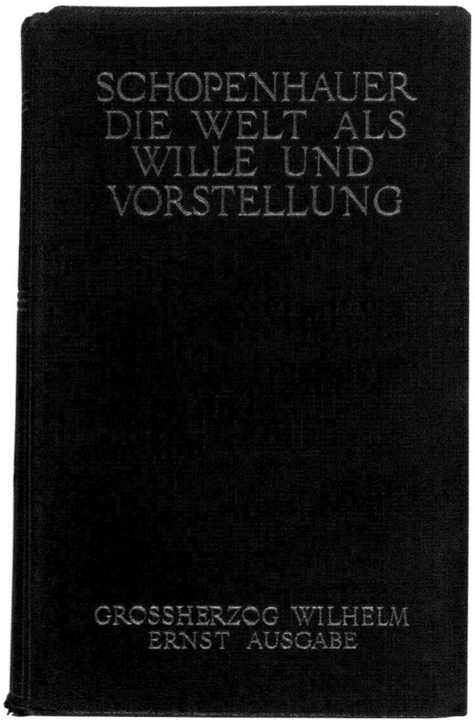

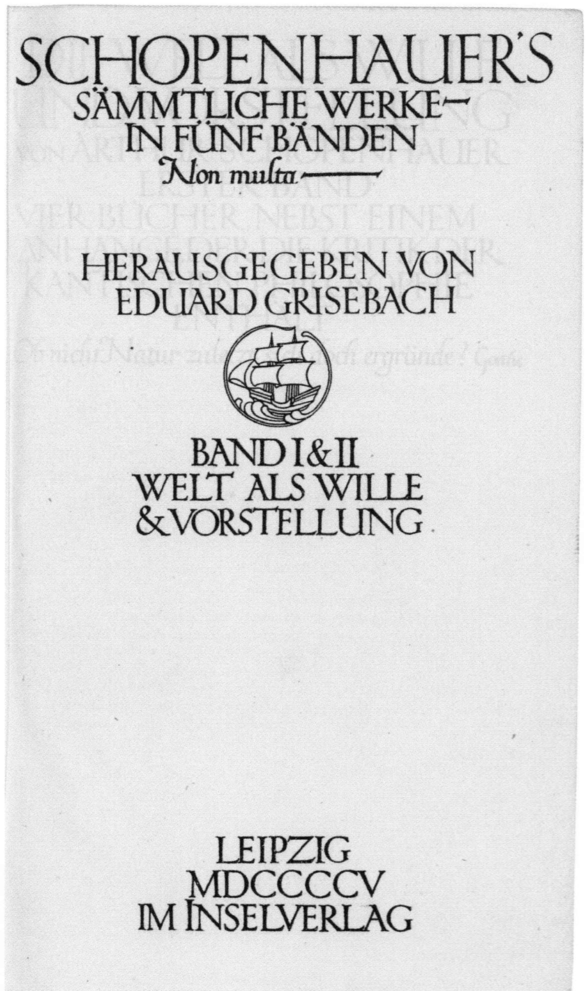

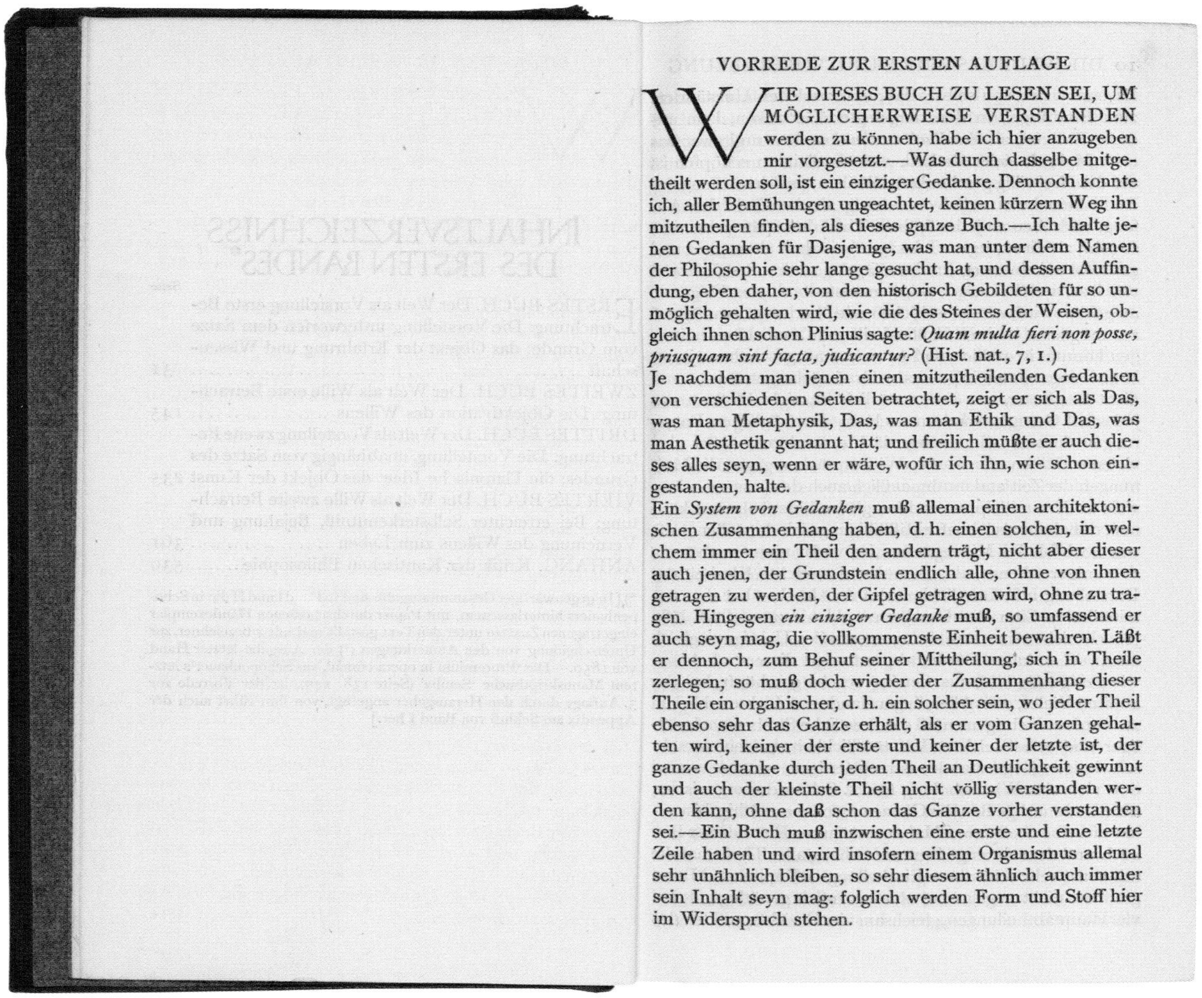

VORREDE ZUR ERSTEN AUFLAGE

WIE DIESES BUCH ZU LESEN SEI, UM MÖGLICHERWEISE VERSTANDEN werden zu können, habe ich hier anzugeben mir vorgesetzt.—Was durch dasselbe mitgetheilt werden soll, ist ein einziger Gedanke. Dennoch konnte ich, aller Bemühungen ungeachtet, keinen kürzern Weg ihn mitzutheilen finden, als dieses ganze Buch.—Ich halte jenen Gedanken für Dasjenige, was man unter dem Namen der Philosophie sehr lange gesucht hat, und dessen Auffindung, eben daher, von den historisch Gebildeten für so unmöglich gehalten wird, wie die des Steines der Weisen, obgleich ihnen schon Plinius sagte: *Quam multa fieri non posse, priusquam sint facta, judicantur?* (Hist. nat., 7, 1.)
Je nachdem man jenen einen mitzutheilenden Gedanken von verschiedenen Seiten betrachtet, zeigt er sich als Das, was man Metaphysik, Das, was man Ethik und Das, was man Aesthetik genannt hat; und freilich müßte er auch dieses alles seyn, wenn er wäre, wofür ich ihn, wie schon eingestanden, halte.
Ein *System von Gedanken* muß allemal einen architektonischen Zusammenhang haben, d. h. einen solchen, in welchem immer ein Theil den andern trägt, nicht aber dieser auch jenen, der Grundstein endlich alle, ohne von ihnen getragen zu werden, der Gipfel getragen wird, ohne zu tragen. Hingegen *ein einziger Gedanke* muß, so umfassend er auch seyn mag, die vollkommenste Einheit bewahren. Läßt er dennoch, zum Behuf seiner Mittheilung, sich in Theile zerlegen; so muß doch wieder der Zusammenhang dieser Theile ein organischer, d. h. ein solcher sein, wo jeder Theil ebenso sehr das Ganze erhält, als er vom Ganzen gehalten wird, keiner der erste und keiner der letzte ist, der ganze Gedanke durch jeden Theil an Deutlichkeit gewinnt und auch der kleinste Theil nicht völlig verstanden werden kann, ohne daß schon das Ganze vorher verstanden sei.—Ein Buch muß inzwischen eine erste und eine letzte Zeile haben und wird insofern einem Organismus allemal sehr unähnlich bleiben, so sehr diesem ähnlich auch immer sein Inhalt seyn mag: folglich werden Form und Stoff hier im Widerspruch stehen.

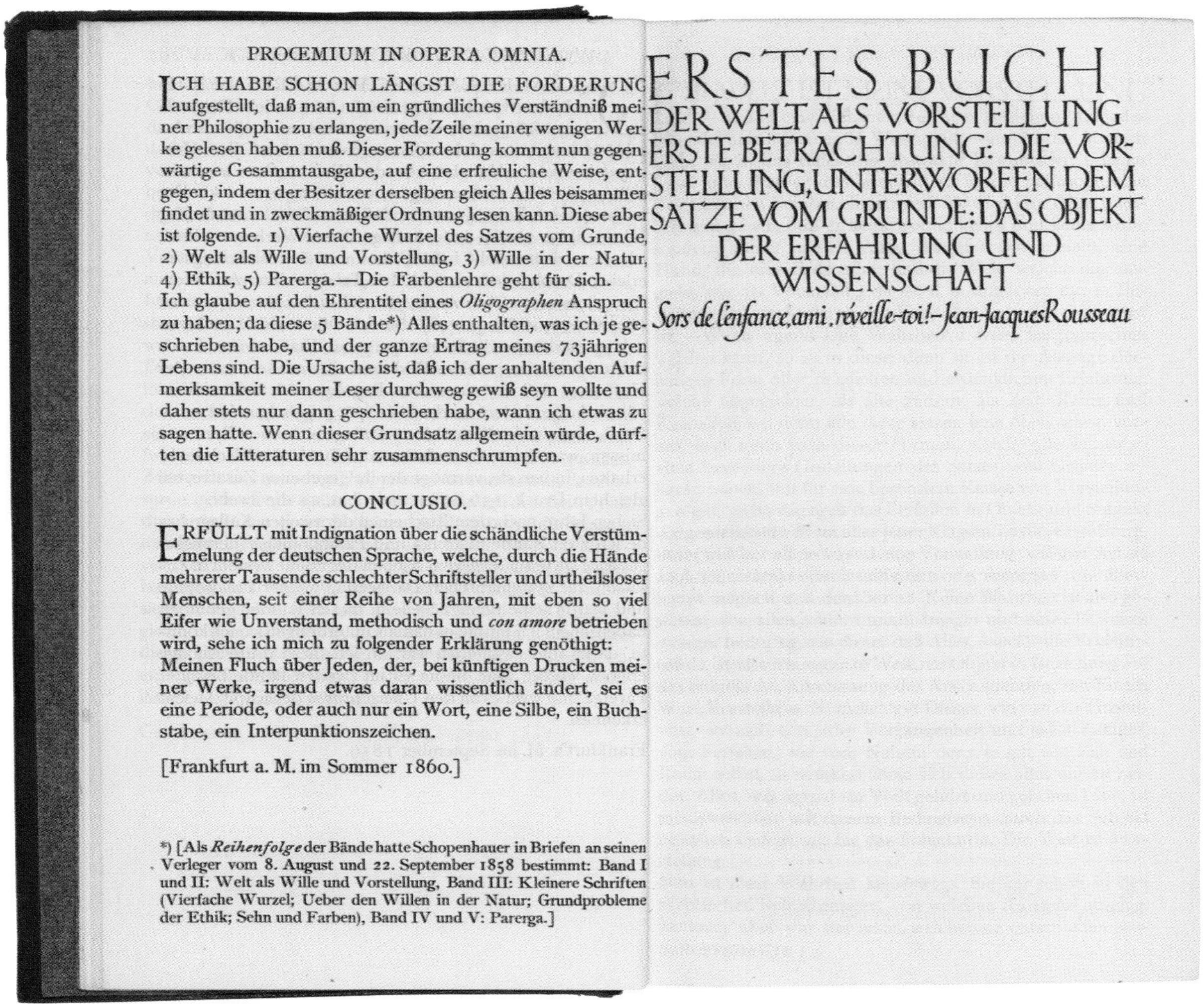

PROŒMIUM IN OPERA OMNIA.

ICH HABE SCHON LÄNGST DIE FORDERUNG aufgestellt, daß man, um ein gründliches Verständniß meiner Philosophie zu erlangen, jede Zeile meiner wenigen Werke gelesen haben muß. Dieser Forderung kommt nun gegenwärtige Gesammtausgabe, auf eine erfreuliche Weise, entgegen, indem der Besitzer derselben gleich Alles beisammen findet und in zweckmäßiger Ordnung lesen kann. Diese aber ist folgende. 1) Vierfache Wurzel des Satzes vom Grunde, 2) Welt als Wille und Vorstellung, 3) Wille in der Natur, 4) Ethik, 5) Parerga.—Die Farbenlehre geht für sich.
Ich glaube auf den Ehrentitel eines *Oligographen* Anspruch zu haben; da diese 5 Bände*) Alles enthalten, was ich je geschrieben habe, und der ganze Ertrag meines 73jährigen Lebens sind. Die Ursache ist, daß ich der anhaltenden Aufmerksamkeit meiner Leser durchweg gewiß seyn wollte und daher stets nur dann geschrieben habe, wann ich etwas zu sagen hatte. Wenn dieser Grundsatz allgemein würde, dürften die Litteraturen sehr zusammenschrumpfen.

CONCLUSIO.

ERFÜLLT mit Indignation über die schändliche Verstümmelung der deutschen Sprache, welche, durch die Hände mehrerer Tausende schlechter Schriftsteller und urtheilsloser Menschen, seit einer Reihe von Jahren, mit eben so viel Eifer wie Unverstand, methodisch und *con amore* betrieben wird, sehe ich mich zu folgender Erklärung genöthigt:
Meinen Fluch über Jeden, der, bei künftigen Drucken meiner Werke, irgend etwas daran wissentlich ändert, sei es eine Periode, oder auch nur ein Wort, eine Silbe, ein Buchstabe, ein Interpunktionszeichen.

[Frankfurt a. M. im Sommer 1860.]

*) [Als *Reihenfolge* der Bände hatte Schopenhauer in Briefen an seinen Verleger vom 8. August und 22. September 1858 bestimmt: Band I und II: Welt als Wille und Vorstellung, Band III: Kleinere Schriften (Vierfache Wurzel; Ueber den Willen in der Natur; Grundprobleme der Ethik; Sehn und Farben), Band IV und V: Parerga.]

ERSTES BUCH
DER WELT ALS VORSTELLUNG
ERSTE BETRACHTUNG: DIE VORSTELLUNG, UNTERWORFEN DEM SATZE VOM GRUNDE: DAS OBJEKT DER ERFAHRUNG UND WISSENSCHAFT

Sors de l'enfance, ami, réveille-toi!—Jean-Jacques Rousseau

1905 **Rudolf von Larisch** Rudolf von Larisch, *Unterricht in ornamentaler Schrift*. Vienna: K.K. Hof- und Staatsdruckerei, 1905. 85 pp. 24 cm.

This is the first edition of the German-speaking world's foremost guide to lettering and calligraphy, with eleven editions up to the author's death. Only Edward Johnston's *Writing & Illuminating & Lettering*, published in 1906 (German edition 1910), had a comparable influence on twentieth-century lettering.

Rudolf von Larisch (1856–1934), son of a noble Austrian officer, may have discovered medieval art and heraldry working for a Knight of Malta. He studied at the Arts and Crafts School in Vienna and worked in the imperial peerage archives, admiring lettering as art and decoration in heraldic and other documents. Attracted to progressive social and artistic movements, he worked with Jugendstil artists from the Wiener Secession (established 1897), taught at the Vienna Arts and Crafts School (1902) and elsewhere, and joined the Wiener Werkstätte (1903).

Johnston studied traditional craft techniques in early manuscripts, offering numerous model alphabets based on historical styles for students to follow, nearly all written with a broad-nibbed pen held at a (theoretically) constant angle. Larisch viewed lettering as a form of self-expression, and featured no alphabets but instead gave examples of drawn and written lettering using various tools and materials, sometimes with a variable pen angle. His first publication on lettering (1899) discussed legibility and spacing, while the manual for students shown here calls blackletter type 'illegible', includes examples of sans serif lettering (with more in the second edition, 1909) and emphasizes lettering's flat areas. This attracted the emerging modernists. Peter Behrens wrote: 'No better plan could be set out to attain noble simplicity, good proportions and proper arrangement of lettering.' JAL

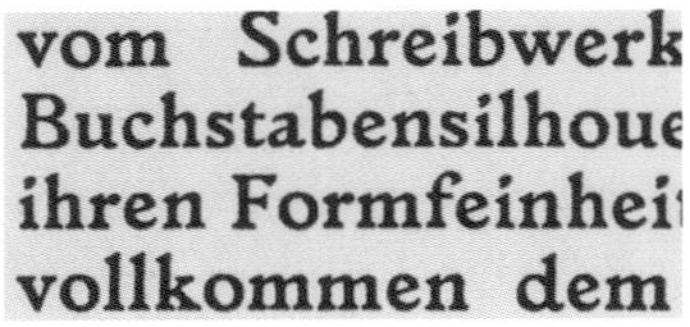
vom Schreibwerk
Buchstabensilhoue
ihren Formfeinhei
vollkommen dem

Rudolf von Larisch's proprietary Plinius Antiqua for the Austrian state printing office, introduced in their festschrift *Die k.k. Hof- und Staatsdruckerei 1804–1904*, was perhaps the first revival of Jenson's 1470 roman outside of private presses. German speakers, accustomed to blackletter type, accepted it without an italic, setting words in capitals for emphasis.

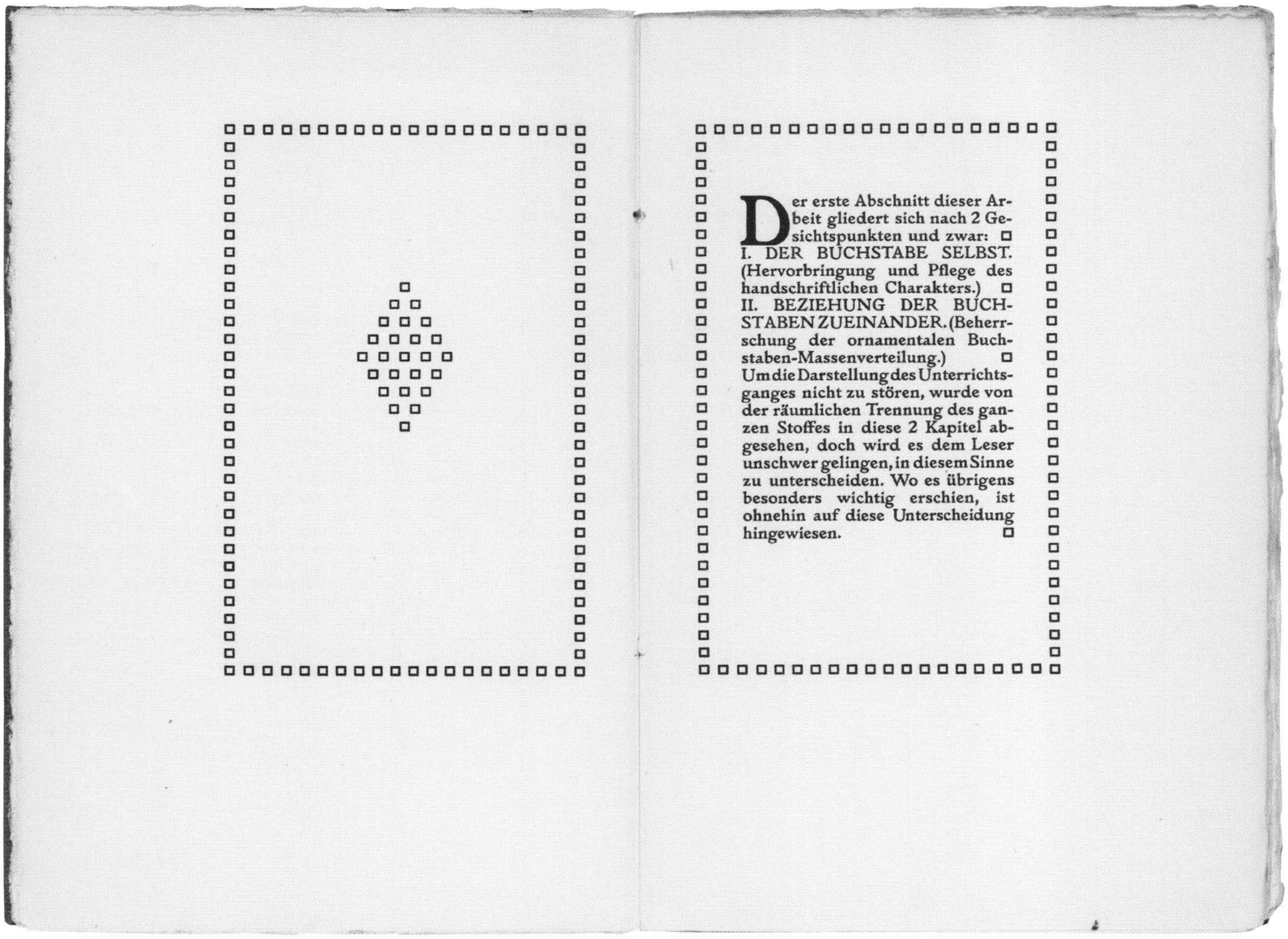
Der erste Abschnitt dieser Arbeit gliedert sich nach 2 Gesichtspunkten und zwar: □
I. DER BUCHSTABE SELBST. (Hervorbringung und Pflege des handschriftlichen Charakters.) □
II. BEZIEHUNG DER BUCHSTABEN ZUEINANDER. (Beherrschung der ornamentalen Buchstaben-Massenverteilung.) □
Um die Darstellung des Unterrichtsganges nicht zu stören, wurde von der räumlichen Trennung des ganzen Stoffes in diese 2 Kapitel abgesehen, doch wird es dem Leser unschwer gelingen, in diesem Sinne zu unterscheiden. Wo es übrigens besonders wichtig erschien, ist ohnehin auf diese Unterscheidung hingewiesen. □

291

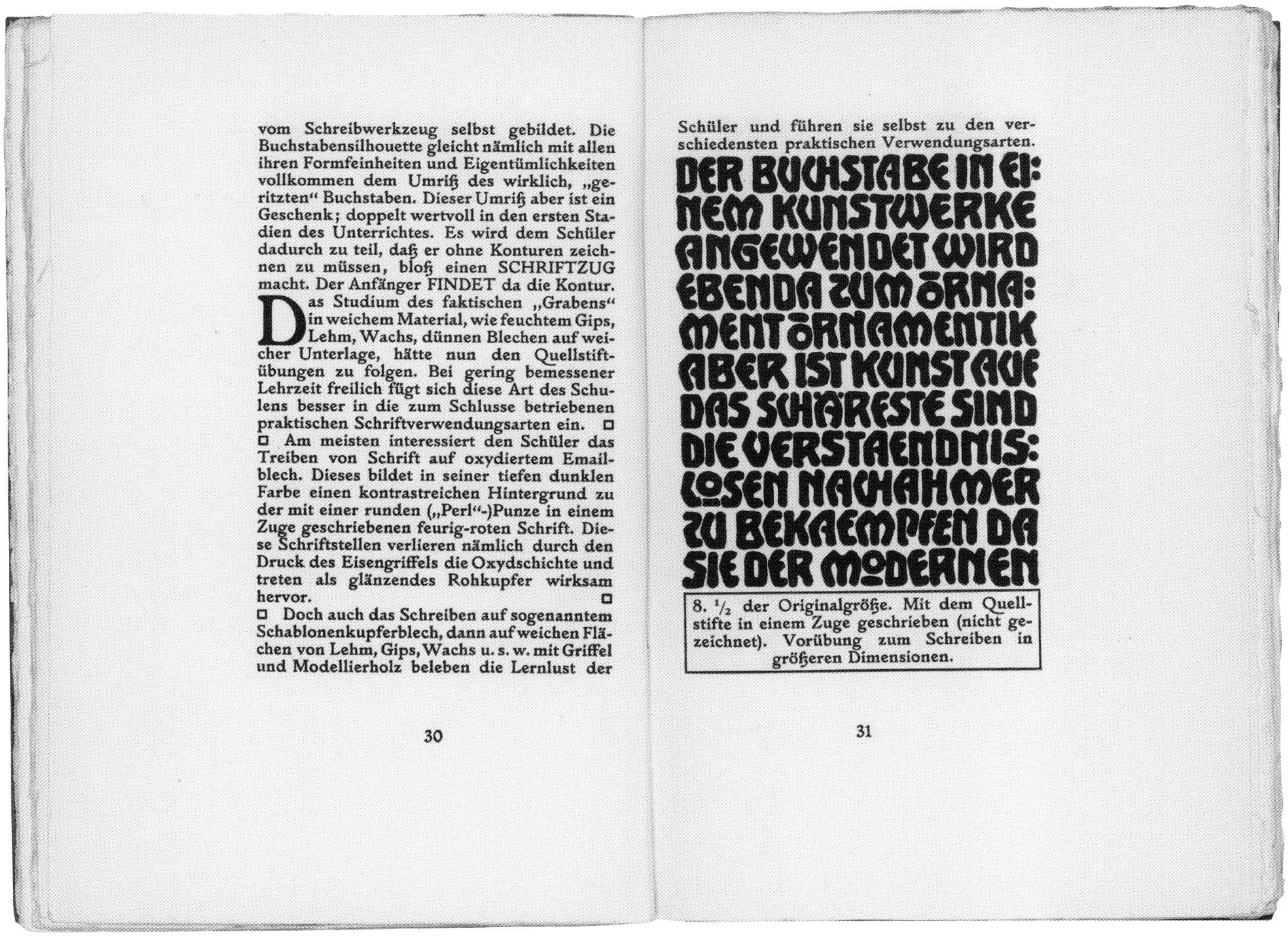
vom Schreibwerkzeug selbst gebildet. Die Buchstabensilhouette gleicht nämlich mit allen ihren Formfeinheiten und Eigentümlichkeiten vollkommen dem Umriß des wirklich, „geritzten" Buchstaben. Dieser Umriß aber ist ein Geschenk; doppelt wertvoll in den ersten Stadien des Unterrichtes. Es wird dem Schüler dadurch zu teil, daß er ohne Konturen zeichnen zu müssen, bloß einen SCHRIFTZUG macht. Der Anfänger FINDET da die Kontur.

Das Studium des faktischen „Grabens" in weichem Material, wie feuchtem Gips, Lehm, Wachs, dünnen Blechen auf weicher Unterlage, hätte nun den Quellstiftübungen zu folgen. Bei gering bemessener Lehrzeit freilich fügt sich diese Art des Schulens besser in die zum Schlusse betriebenen praktischen Schriftverwendungsarten ein. □

□ Am meisten interessiert den Schüler das Treiben von Schrift auf oxydiertem Emailblech. Dieses bildet in seiner tiefen dunklen Farbe einen kontrastreichen Hintergrund zu der mit einer runden („Perl"-)Punze in einem Zuge geschriebenen feurig-roten Schrift. Diese Schriftstellen verlieren nämlich durch den Druck des Eisengriffels die Oxydschichte und treten als glänzendes Rohkupfer wirksam hervor. □

□ Doch auch das Schreiben auf sogenanntem Schablonenkupferblech, dann auf weichen Flächen von Lehm, Gips, Wachs u. s. w. mit Griffel und Modellierholz beleben die Lernlust der

30

Schüler und führen sie selbst zu den verschiedensten praktischen Verwendungsarten.

DER BUCHSTABE IN EI: NEM KUNSTWERKE ANGEWENDET WIRD EBENDA ZUM ORNA: MENT ORNAMENTIK ABER IST KUNST AUF DAS SCHÄRFSTE SIND DIE VERSTAENDNIS: LOSEN NACHAHMER ZU BEKAEMPFEN DA SIE DER MODERNEN

8. $^1/_2$ der Originalgröße. Mit dem Quellstifte in einem Zuge geschrieben (nicht gezeichnet). Vorübung zum Schreiben in größeren Dimensionen.

31

1906 Doves Press Johann Wolfgang von Goethe, *Faust: eine Tragoedie*. Hammersmith: The Doves Press, 1906–10. 2 volumes. 23.5 cm. Designers: T. J. Cobden-Sanderson, Emery Walker. Lettering artist: Edward Johnston. Typesetters: J. H. Mason, W. Jenkins (Doves Press). Printers: H. Gage-Cole, Albert Lewis (Doves Press).

Between 1900 and 1916, the English Doves Press, owned by bookbinder Thomas Cobden-Sanderson (1840–1922) and graphic entrepreneur Emery Walker (1851–1933), published around forty books that were produced on a hand press. Both men had been friends of William Morris, the founder of the very first private press, the Kelmscott Press. Their books were both a continuation of the example of the Kelmscott Press and a criticism of some aspects of its typographical design. In book design, the Doves Press aspired to pure, unadorned beauty.

The typography of this two-volume edition of *Faust* is based on examples from around 1500. The type was designed by Walker (and Cobden-Sanderson) and modelled after Jenson's. Every publication by the Doves Press was set in this typeface. In imitation of books printed around 1500, only one typeface was used, in one size, and an italic was absent, although the printing world in 1900 knew typefaces that were made in many sizes and variants. The initials, often printed in red, were based on drawn lettering and served to articulate the text. They were designed by the famous calligrapher Edward Johnston (1872–1944), whose student Eric Gill did the woodcuts. Shoulder notes are printed in red. Word spacing is tight and there is no leading. The Doves Press used handmade paper; the vellum binding is simple.

This is one of the fifteen copies that were printed on vellum; the beauty of printing is obvious. FAJ

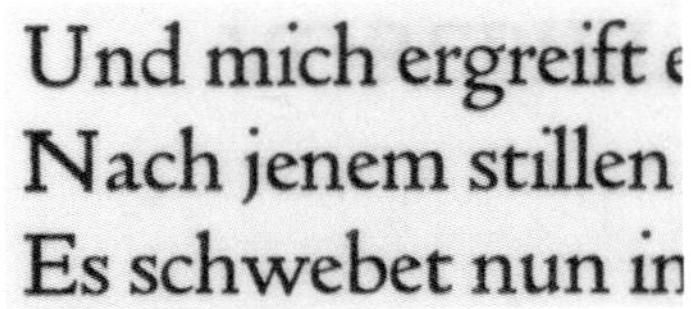
Und mich ergreift e
Nach jenem stillen
Es schwebet nun in

In 1891 William Morris initiated a fashion for private and later commercial Jenson revivals. Emery Walker, who inspired Morris, largely designed the Doves Type (1900) for his and Cobden-Sanderson's own press. His typographic experience, skill and taste yielded a finer and subtler result, cut (like Morris's) by Edward Prince.

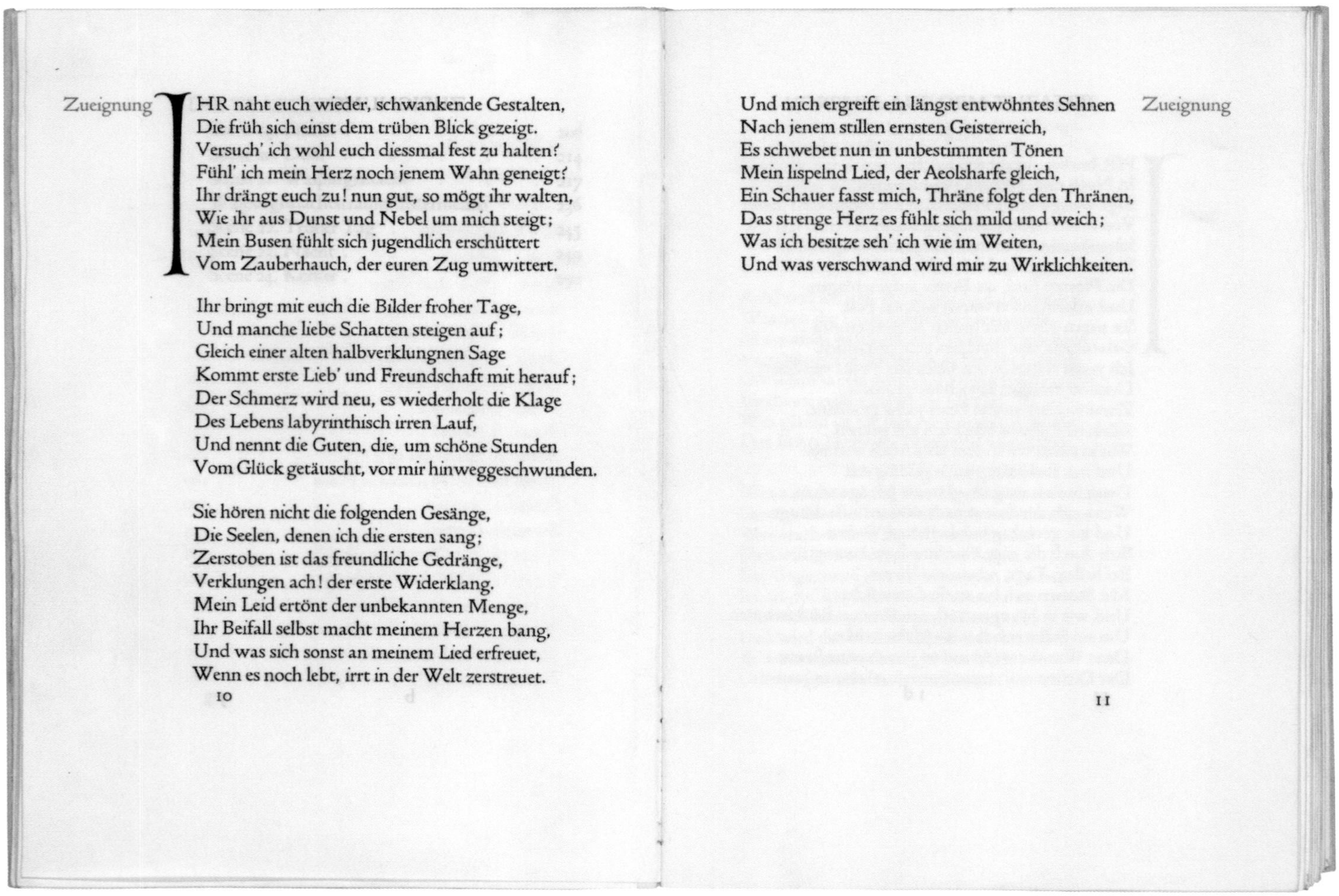
Zueignung

IHR naht euch wieder, schwankende Gestalten,
Die früh sich einst dem trüben Blick gezeigt.
Versuch' ich wohl euch diessmal fest zu halten?
Fühl' ich mein Herz noch jenem Wahn geneigt?
Ihr drängt euch zu! nun gut, so mögt ihr walten,
Wie ihr aus Dunst und Nebel um mich steigt;
Mein Busen fühlt sich jugendlich erschüttert
Vom Zauberhauch, der euren Zug umwittert.

Ihr bringt mit euch die Bilder froher Tage,
Und manche liebe Schatten steigen auf;
Gleich einer alten halbverklungnen Sage
Kommt erste Lieb' und Freundschaft mit herauf;
Der Schmerz wird neu, es wiederholt die Klage
Des Lebens labyrinthisch irren Lauf,
Und nennt die Guten, die, um schöne Stunden
Vom Glück getäuscht, vor mir hinweggeschwunden.

Sie hören nicht die folgenden Gesänge,
Die Seelen, denen ich die ersten sang;
Zerstoben ist das freundliche Gedränge,
Verklungen ach! der erste Widerklang.
Mein Leid ertönt der unbekannten Menge,
Ihr Beifall selbst macht meinem Herzen bang,
Und was sich sonst an meinem Lied erfreuet,
Wenn es noch lebt, irrt in der Welt zerstreuet.

10

Und mich ergreift ein längst entwöhntes Sehnen
Nach jenem stillen ernsten Geisterreich,
Es schwebet nun in unbestimmten Tönen
Mein lispelnd Lied, der Aeolsharfe gleich,
Ein Schauer fasst mich, Thräne folgt den Thränen,
Das strenge Herz es fühlt sich mild und weich;
Was ich besitze seh' ich wie im Weiten,
Und was verschwand wird mir zu Wirklichkeiten.

Zueignung

11

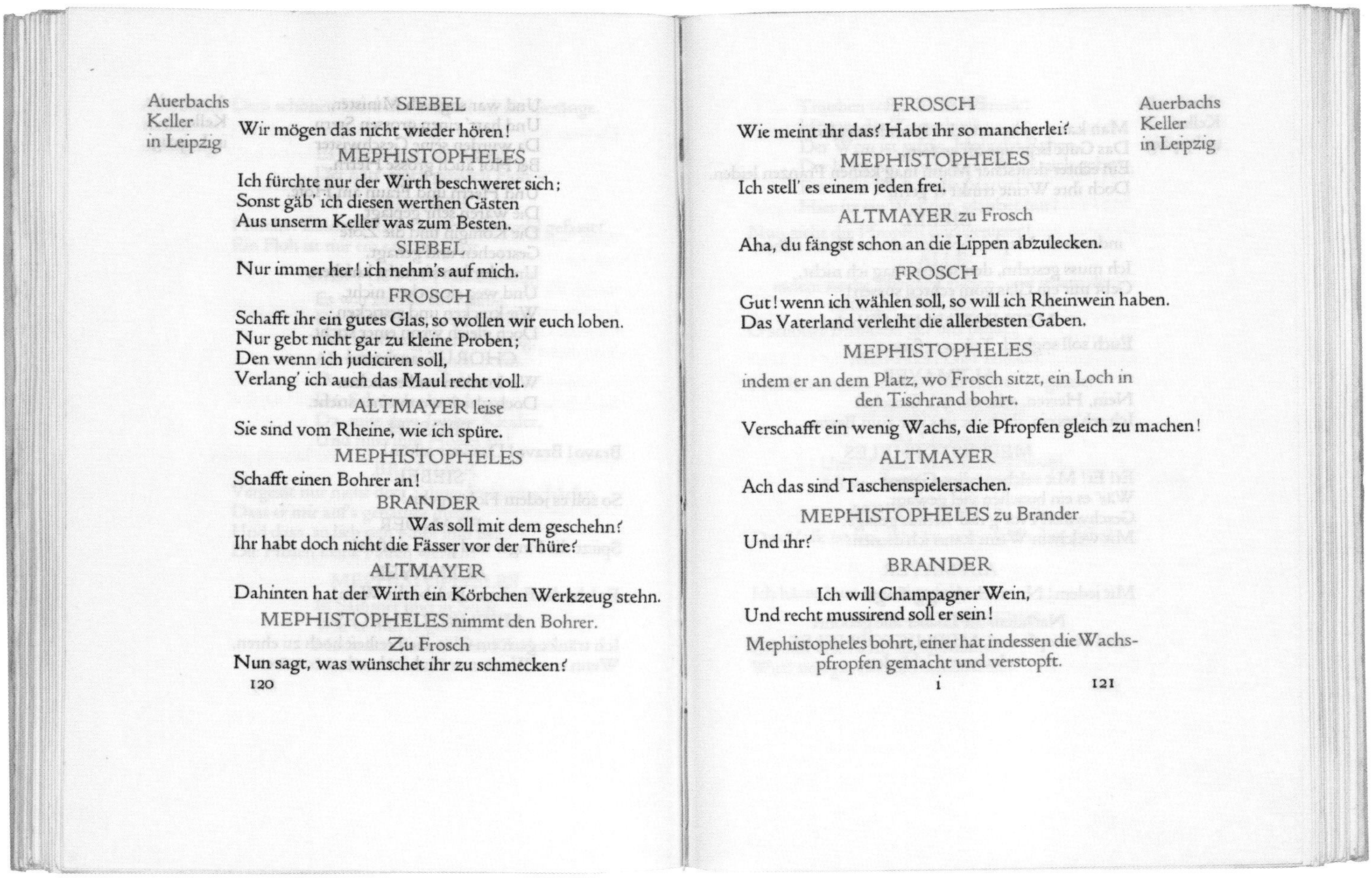

Auerbachs Keller in Leipzig

SIEBEL

Wir mögen das nicht wieder hören!

MEPHISTOPHELES

Ich fürchte nur der Wirth beschweret sich;
Sonst gäb' ich diesen werthen Gästen
Aus unserm Keller zum Besten.

SIEBEL

Nur immer her! ich nehm's auf mich.

FROSCH

Schafft ihr ein gutes Glas, so wollen wir euch loben.
Nur gebt nicht gar zu kleine Proben;
Den wenn ich judiciren soll,
Verlang' ich auch das Maul recht voll.

ALTMAYER leise

Sie sind vom Rheine, wie ich spüre.

MEPHISTOPHELES

Schafft einen Bohrer an!

BRANDER

Was soll mit dem geschehn?
Ihr habt doch nicht die Fässer vor der Thüre?

ALTMAYER

Dahinten hat der Wirth ein Körbchen Werkzeug stehn.

MEPHISTOPHELES nimmt den Bohrer.

Zu Frosch

Nun sagt, was wünschet ihr zu schmecken?

120

FROSCH

Wie meint ihr das? Habt ihr so mancherlei?

MEPHISTOPHELES

Ich stell' es einem jeden frei.

ALTMAYER zu Frosch

Aha, du fängst schon an die Lippen abzulecken.

FROSCH

Gut! wenn ich wählen soll, so will ich Rheinwein haben.
Das Vaterland verleiht die allerbesten Gaben.

MEPHISTOPHELES

indem er an dem Platz, wo Frosch sitzt, ein Loch in den Tischrand bohrt.

Verschafft ein wenig Wachs, die Pfropfen gleich zu machen!

ALTMAYER

Ach das sind Taschenspielersachen.

MEPHISTOPHELES zu Brander

Und ihr?

BRANDER

Ich will Champagner Wein,
Und recht mussirend soll er sein!

Mephistopheles bohrt, einer hat indessen die Wachspfropfen gemacht und verstopft.

i 121

Auerbachs Keller in Leipzig

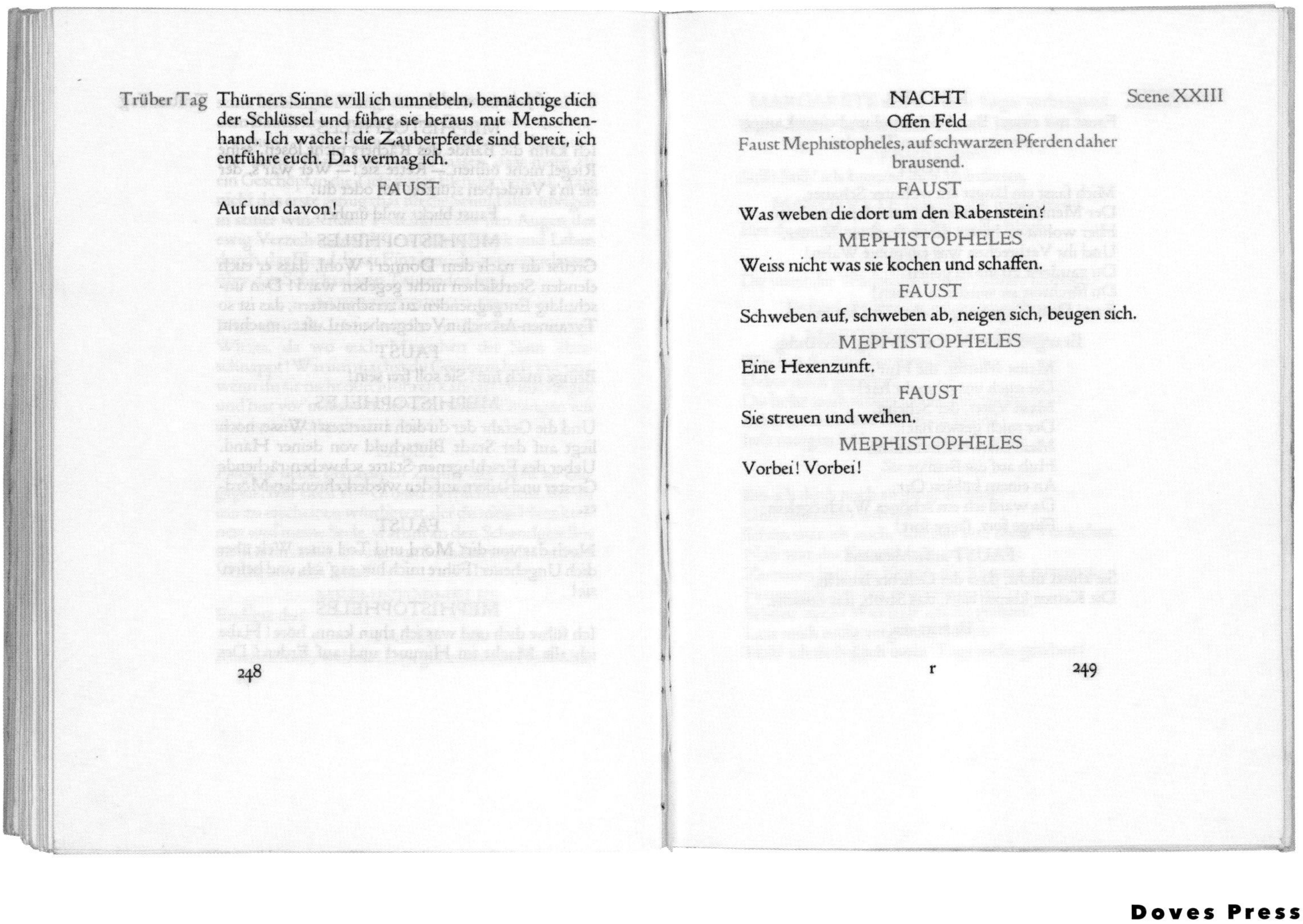

Trüber Tag

Thürners Sinne will ich umnebeln, bemächtige dich der Schlüssel und führe sie heraus mit Menschenhand. Ich wache! die Zauberpferde sind bereit, ich entführe euch. Das vermag ich.

FAUST

Auf und davon!

248

Scene XXIII

NACHT

Offen Feld

Faust Mephistopheles, auf schwarzen Pferden daher brausend.

FAUST

Was weben die dort um den Rabenstein?

MEPHISTOPHELES

Weiss nicht was sie kochen und schaffen.

FAUST

Schweben auf, schweben ab, neigen sich, beugen sich.

MEPHISTOPHELES

Eine Hexenzunft.

FAUST

Sie streuen und weihen.

MEPHISTOPHELES

Vorbei! Vorbei!

r 249

1908 **Henry van de Velde** **Friedrich Nietzsche, *Also sprach Zarathustra: ein Buch für Alle und Keinen*. Leipzig: Insel-Verlag, 1908. 160 pp. 37 cm. Designers: Henry van de Velde (binding, decoration & typography), Georges Lemmen (typeface). Printer: W. Drugulin, Leipzig.**

Ever since Art Nouveau had reached its peak, Count Harry Kessler had a monumental edition of Nietzsche's *Zarathustra* in mind, for which he commissioned, in 1898, the renowned Belgian Art Nouveau artists Henry van de Velde (1863–1957) and Georges Lemmen (1865–1916). By the time that the edition, which is overlaid with gold ornaments, was finally ready, a decade had passed, Art Nouveau was on the wane, and the architect and cultural critic Adolf Loos, one of the pioneers of modernism, had already categorized the use of ornaments as a 'crime'.

The multitalented van de Velde, who started out as a painter, had mainly worked on design and architecture since the 1890s and was highly successful in those fields. His most acclaimed graphic works from that period are posters and packaging designs for the Tropon food company. In 1902, van de Velde relocated to Weimar, Germany, where he was appointed advisor to the Grand Duke; Kessler was appointed museum director in Weimar. Hardly any work was done on the *Zarathustra* edition between 1901 and 1906.

The project was restarted in 1907. They experimented with a two-column layout and with various ornament forms and printing colours. Although the original idea was to have the decoration engraved in wood – in the Arts and Crafts tradition – ordinary zinc etchings were used. On Kessler's instructions, the golden section was taken into account in the design. The much revered *Zarathustra* is van de Velde's most important book design. This edition had a print run of 530 copies, and despite its high price, it sold well. ML

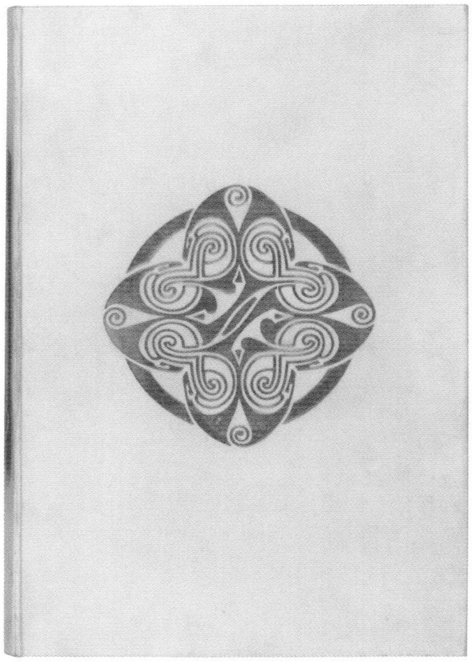

The Lemmen Schrift typeface was designed especially for this edition of *Zarathustra* by the Belgian Art Nouveau artist Georges Lemmen (1865–1916), in cooperation with Count Harry Kessler (1868–1937). The type was cut in Leipzig, possibly by the typefoundry of W. Drugulin. The first proof was ready in 1901.

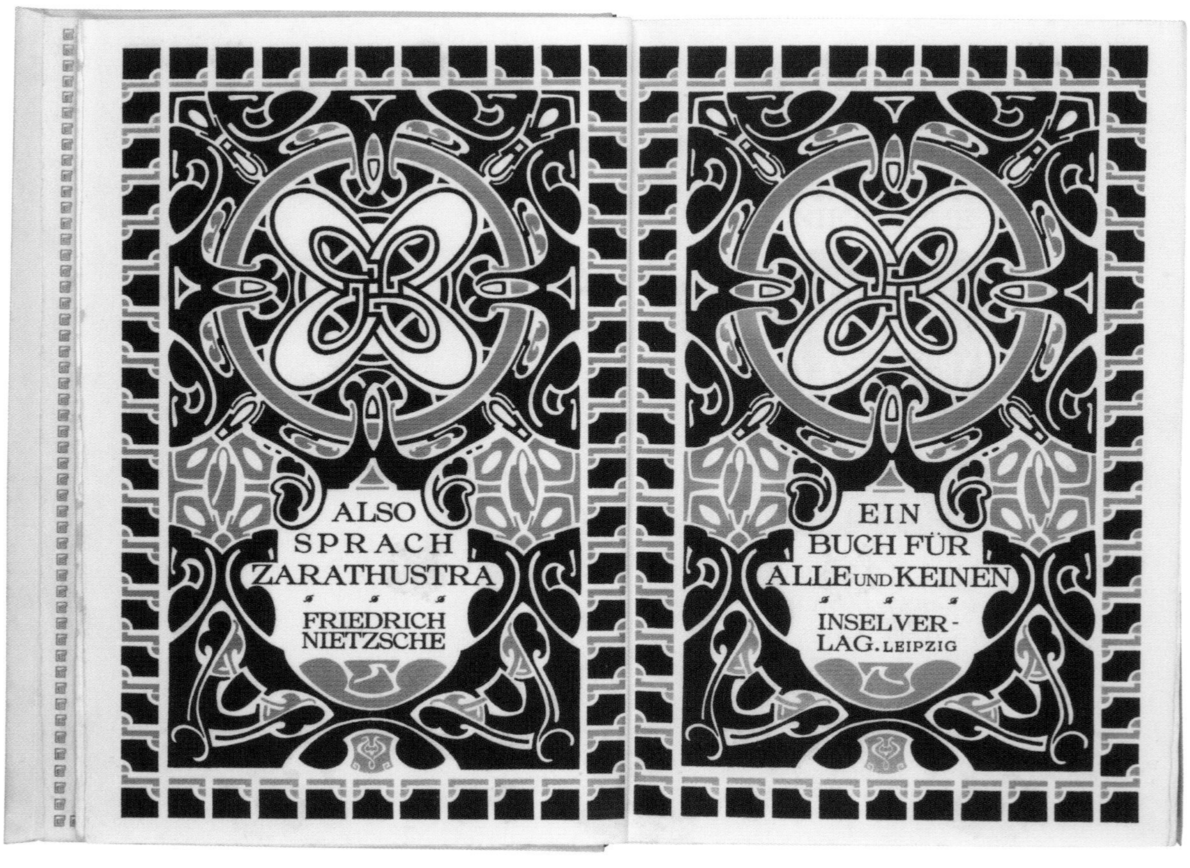

Eines Morgens, nicht lange nach seiner Rückkehr zur Höhle, sprang Zarathustra von seinem Lager auf wie ein Toller, schrie mit furchtbarer Stimme und gebärdete sich, als ob noch Einer auf dem Lager läge, der nicht davon aufstehn wolle; und also tönte Zarathustra's Stimme, daß seine Thiere erschreckt hinzukamen, und daß aus allen Höhlen und Schlupfwinkeln, die Zarathustra's Höhle benachbart waren, alles Gethier davon huschte, – fliegend, flatternd, kriechend, springend, wie ihm nur die Art von Fuß und Flü-

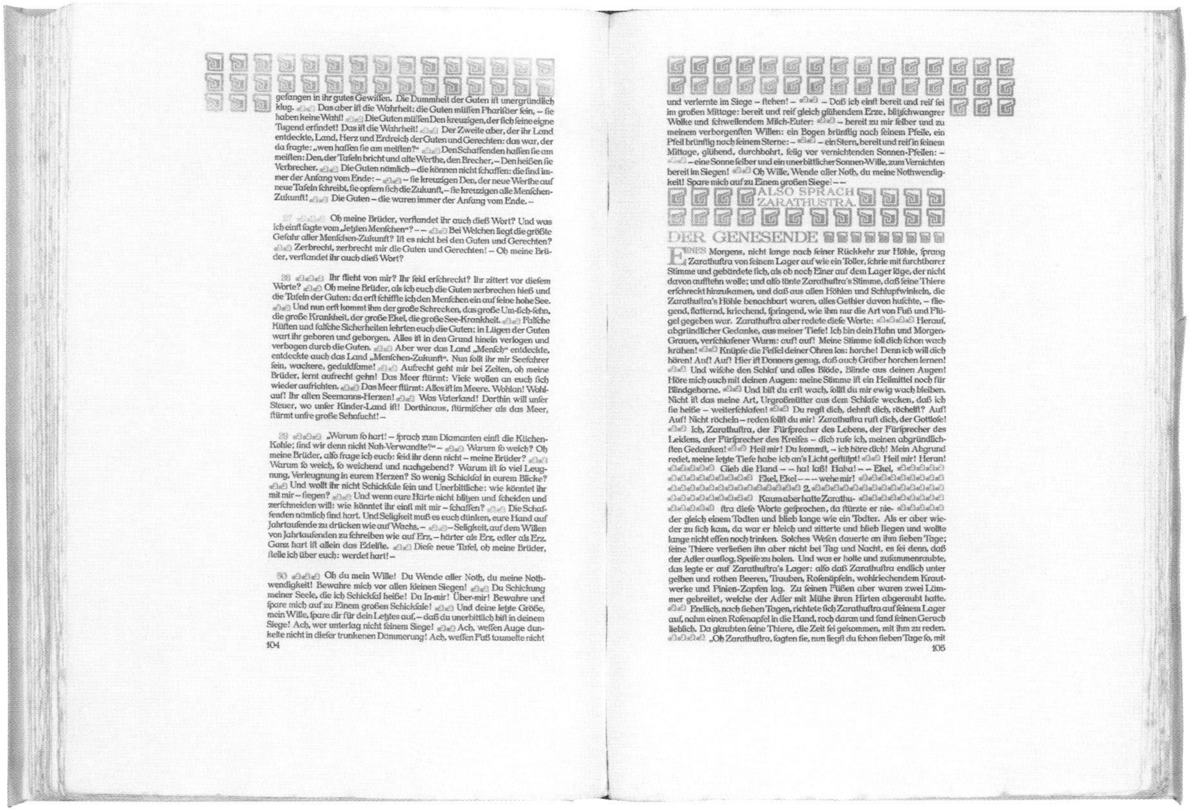

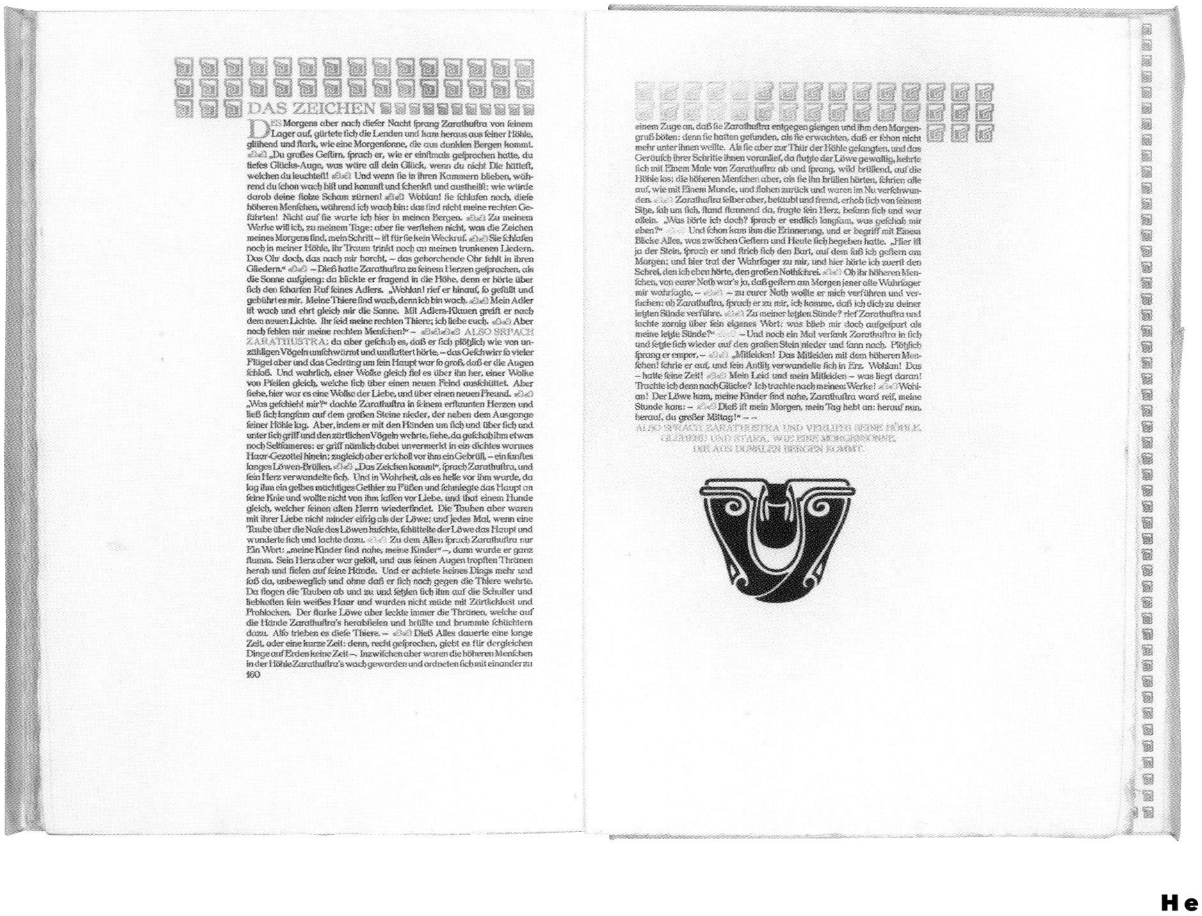

1909 **Peter Behrens** *Bogenlampenliste No. 4*. Berlin: Allgemeine Elektricitäts-Gesellschaft, 1909. 16 pp. 27 cm.

Designer: Peter Behrens.

Originally a painter, Peter Behrens (1868–1940) switched to design toward the end of the 1890s. In 1907, he was one of the co-founders of the Deutscher Werkbund. The goal of this association was the improvement of industrial products by integrating arts, crafts, and industry; also with the aim of increasing national exports. Under the motto 'Vom Sofakissen zum Städtebau' ('from sofa cushions to cities'), all fields of design and architecture were covered.

Earlier in 1907, Behrens was hired as artistic consultant by AEG (Allgemeine Elektricitäts-Gesellschaft). Due to his work for the German electrical company, he is now considered to be the first designer to create a corporate identity. He had the opportunity to put his mark on virtually everything: on the logo and printed matter, on products such as lamps, dental drills, and kettles, and on factories and cottages for factory workers. His turbine factory in the Berlin Moabit district, which dates from the same year as this brochure, is an icon of modern architecture. Among his assistants at the time were Walter Gropius and Ludwig Mies van der Rohe, who both became famous architects in their own right.

Behrens was particularly interested in type, and some of his earliest designs are typefaces. His Behrens Antiqua, which was used frequently in AEG printed matter, was issued in 1908 by typefoundry Gebr. Klingspor in Offenbach am Main. For large sizes, such as the lettering used for the cover of the lighting brochure shown here, the letterforms were drawn separately. A special AEG capitals alphabet presumably served as an example. Behrens accepted commissions from AEG until his death in 1940. ML

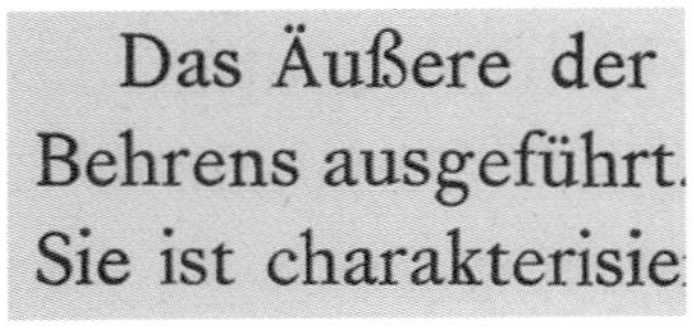

This is not Behrens Antiqua, the type that was used frequently in AEG printed matter. This is a roman based ultimately on the Fonderie Générale's Elzévir introduced by Théophile Beaudoire (reputedly in 1858), in the wake of the Caslon revival in Britain and Louis Perrin's Augustaux. This version eliminates some of Elzévir's Didone characteristics.

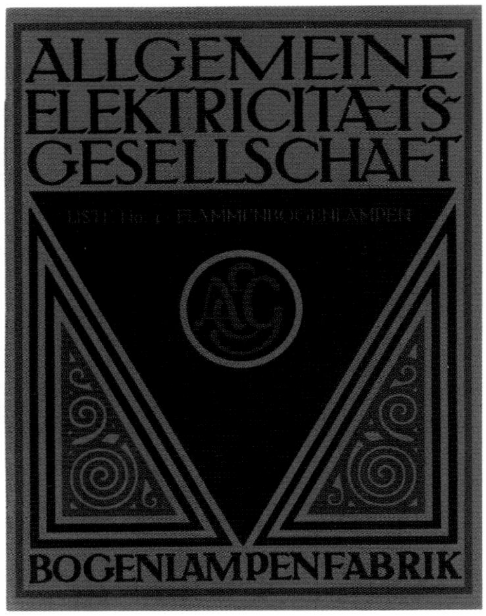

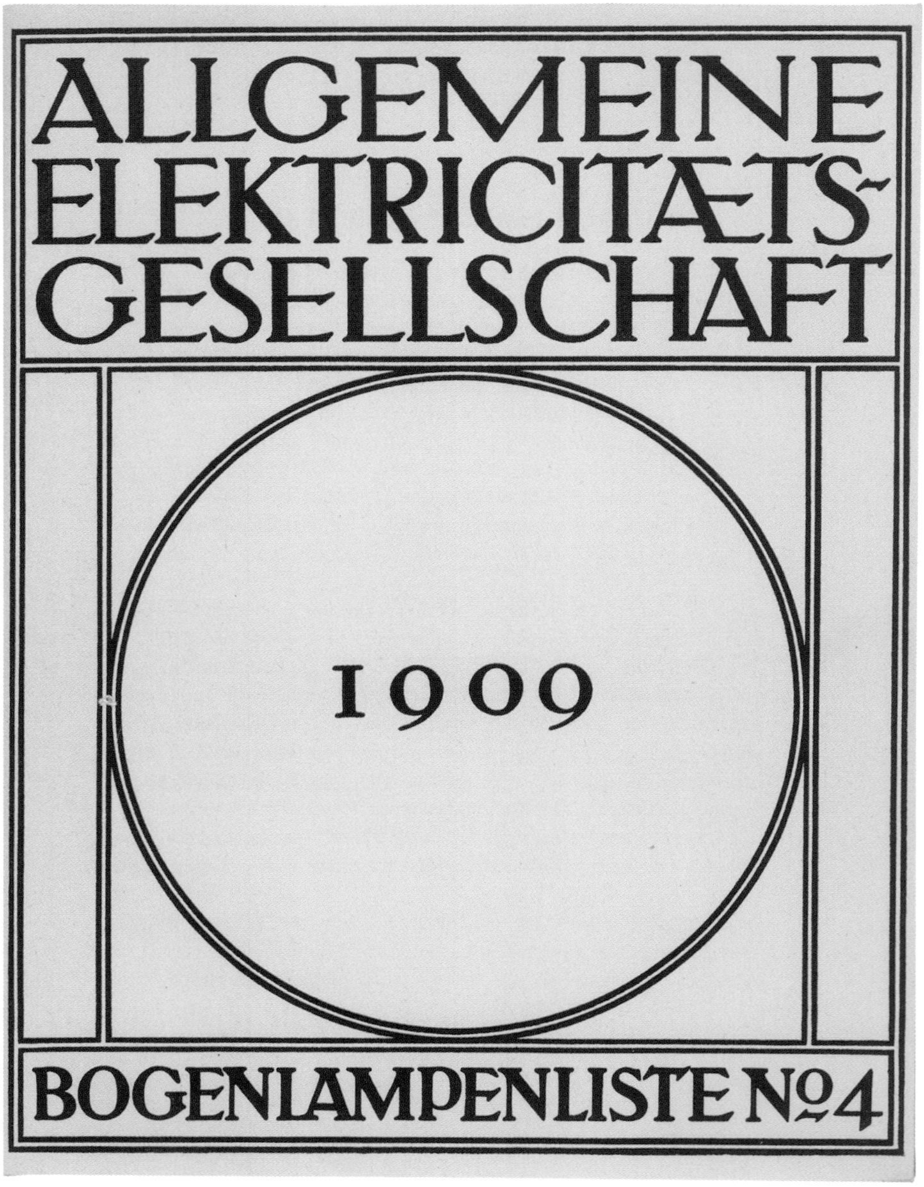

Fortschritte der Berliner Straßenbeleuchtung", Journal für Gasbeleuchtung 1908, Nr. 45. Sonderabdrücke stehen Interessenten zur Verfügung).

Die Höchst-Brenndauer der Duplex-Flammenbogenlampe kommt derjenigen der Intensivlampe gleich; die Triplex-Flammenbogenlampe wird bis zu 22stündiger Brenndauer geliefert, bei keineswegs großen Abmessungen.

Das Äußere der Lampen ist nach Entwürfen von Professor Peter Behrens ausgeführt. Nebenstehendes Bild zeigt die komplette Lampe. Sie ist charakterisiert durch möglichst glatte Oberflächen, durch die sanft nach außen geschweifte Form, welche sich nach unten fast unmerklich verbreitert; die nach außen geschwungene Linie nimmt der Reflektor-Ansatz nochmals auf. Die Lampe präsentiert sich im schlichten Dunkelgrün, mit Zierringen aus Tombak, welche die Farbenwirkung wesentlich erhöhen, zumal im Vergleich mit dem bisher fast allein herrschenden, nüchternen Schwarz.

Der neuen Lampenform ist die Glocke angepaßt, ein Zylinder, gerade weit genug, um das Gestänge der Lampe zu umfassen. Je kleiner eine Glocke, desto größer der Glanz der Lichtquelle, und damit ihr Lichteffekt. Deshalb war die Intensiv-Flammenbogenlampe mit ihrer kleinen stark leuchtenden Glocke bisher unerreicht, wo es auf starke Effekte ankam, wie z. B. für Front- und Schaufensterbeleuchtungen. Mit der neuen Glockenform übertrifft die Triplexflammenlampe noch diese Wirkung. Der enge Glaszylinder wird vom Licht fast gleichmäßig erfüllt, und die brennende Lampe erscheint wie eine Feuersäule, die das Auge von weitem anzieht und fesselt.

Nur bei den Lampen längster Bauart hat man es zweckmäßiger gefunden, runde Glocken anzuwenden. Um auch diese möglichst klein zu halten, ist der Kunstgriff angewendet, daß die Glocke das Gestänge nicht ganz umfaßt, und durch einen verlängerten Aschenteller abgeschlossen wird.

4

A·E·G-FLAMMENBOGENLAMPE

TRIPLEX-FLAMMENBOGENLAMPEN

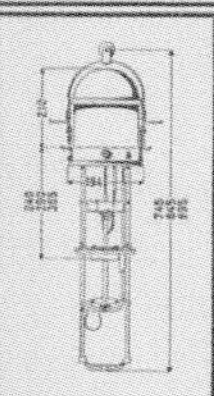

Für Gleichstrom, mit ca. 30 Volt Lampenspannung

P. L. Nr. der Lampe	Stromstärke Amp.	Brenndauer im Freien ca. Stunden	Länge jeder Kohle mm	Gewicht netto ca. kg	Preis per Stück ohne Laterne mit Kappe und Bügel: Grünlackiert ℳ	Tombak ℳ
67320	6, 8, 10, 12, 15	11½–12½	200	9	54.—	62.—
67322		15½–16½	250	9,1	55.—	63.—
67324		21½–22½	325	9,25	56.—	64.—

Zugehörige Laternen P. L. Nr. 68320/22/24, siehe Seite 12

Kohlenstärken

Stromstärke . . . . Amp.	6	8	10	12	15
Lampenspannung . . . . . ca. Volt	28	30	31	32	33
T. B. Kohlen Nr. 1530 weiß oder gelb: oben — ϕ	12	13	15	16	18
unten + ϕ	13	14	16	17	20

Schaltung

Die Triplex-Flammenbogenlampen brennen unter möglichster Ausnutzung der Netzspannung an 110—120 Volt in Dreischaltung, an 220 Volt in Fünf- oder Sechsschaltung. Zubehör s. Seite 13.

Bei Serienschaltung von mehr als drei Lampen an Netzspannungen von 130 Volt aufwärts, soll jede Lampe einen automatischen Ersatzwiderstand P. L. Nr. 2870 erhalten, der die Nebenschlußwicklung der ersteren vor Verbrennen bei unvorhergesehenem Verlöschen schützt und die übrigen Lampen der Serie brennend erhält.

Automatische Ersatzwiderstände

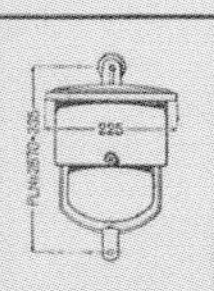

P. L. Nr. des Ersatzwiderstandes	Stromstärke Amp.	Lampenspannung Volt	Gewicht netto ca. kg	Preis ℳ
2870	6, 8, 10, 12, 15	28, 30, 31, 32, 33	4,5	28.—

Zur Aufhängung über der Lampe eingerichtet; doch kann der Apparat auch an beliebiger Stelle montiert und die Anschlüsse parallel zu der Lampe abgezweigt werden.

8

DUPLEX-FLAMMENBOGENLAMPEN

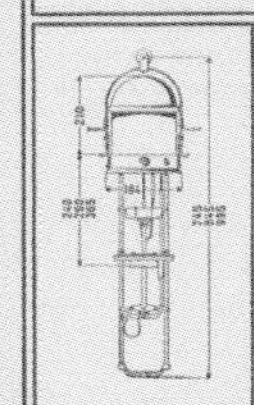

Für Gleichstrom, mit ca. 40 Volt Lampenspannung

P. L. Nr. der Lampe	Stromstärke Amp.	Brenndauer im Freien ca. Stunden	Länge jeder Kohle mm	Gewicht netto ca. kg	Preis per Stück ohne Laterne mit Kappe und Bügel: Grünlackiert ℳ	Tombak ℳ
67320	6, 8,10, 12,15	8½–10½	200	9	54.—	62.—
67322		11½–13½	250	9,1	55.—	63.—
67324		16–18	325	9,25	56.—	64.—

Zugehörige Laternen P. L. Nr. 68320/22/24, siehe Seite 12

Kohlenstärken

Stromstärke . . . . Amp.	6	8	10	12	15
Lampenspannung . . . . . ca. Volt	40	40	40	41	42
T. B. Kohlen Nr. 1440 weiß oder gelb: oben — ϕ	12	13	15	16	18
unten + ϕ	13	14	16	17	20

Schaltung

Die Duplex-Flammenbogenlampen brennen unter möglichster Ausnutzung der Netzspannung an 110—120 Volt in Zweischaltung, an 220 Volt in Vierschaltung. Zubehör s. Seite 14.

Bei Serienschaltung von mehr als 2 Lampen an Netzspannungen von 130 Volt aufwärts, soll jede Lampe einen autom. Ersatzwiderstand P. L. Nr. 2899—2900 erhalten, der die Nebenschlußwicklung der ersteren vor Verbrennen bei unvorhergesehenem Verlöschen schützt und die übrigen Lampen der Serie brennend erhält.

Automatische Ersatzwiderstände

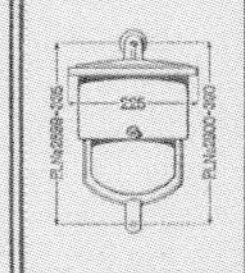

P. L. Nr. des Ersatzwiderstandes	Stromstärke Amp.	Lampenspannung Volt	Gewicht netto ca. kg	Preis ℳ
2899	6, 8, 10	40	4,5	28.—
2900	12, 15	41, 42	5	34.—

Zur Aufhängung über der Lampe eingerichtet; doch kann der Apparat auch an beliebiger Stelle montiert und die Anschlüsse parallel zur Lampe abgezweigt werden

9

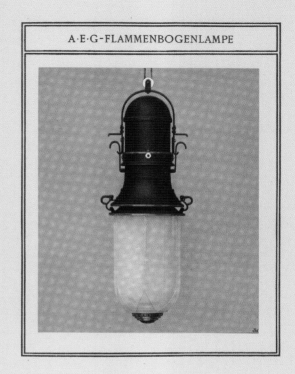

1912 **American Type Founders Company** *American Specimen Book of Type Styles: Complete Catalogue of Printing Machinery and Printing Supplies*. Jersey City, NJ: American Type Founders Company, 1912. 1,301 pp. 28.5 cm.

In 1886, a brand new kind of machine made its appearance in the composing room of the *New York Tribune* newspaper: a Linotype. With this machine, there was no need to gather the individual letters from the little boxes in the type cases; the text could simply be typed in and the Linotype (line-of-type) would cast complete lines of type. The success of this hot-metal typesetting machine was immense. For the typefoundries it meant the end of the vast market for text types for newspapers and magazines. They now focused more on the production of fashionable display types, along with accompanying initials and ornaments.

In the second half of the nineteenth century, the United States boasted over two dozen traditional typefoundries. Besides type, these companies traded in all equipment used in printing offices, such as presses and cutting machines. Among the foundries there was cut-throat competition, and the speedy acceptance of the Linotype caused a serious decline in sales. Most foundries, therefore, decided to merge into the American Type Founders Company (ATF), founded in 1892. The *American Specimen Book of Type Styles* was the most extensive catalogue ever published by the ATF. Production of the book, which runs to over 1,300 pages, must have taken many man-hours.

The work of Morris F. Benton (1872–1948) is well represented in the catalogue. He was head of typeface development at ATF. Benton was a prolific type designer and some of his typefaces, including Franklin Gothic (1902), are still popular today. ML

'Study this book page by page. It is not a mere price list, but a veritable encyclopedia of typographic styles. Here are the type faces which have established the typographic fashions, and also beautiful examples of how these type faces can be used to please the printer's customers.' (p. 16)

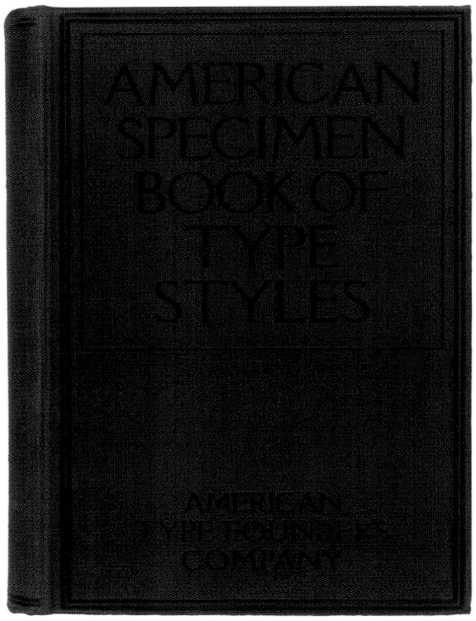

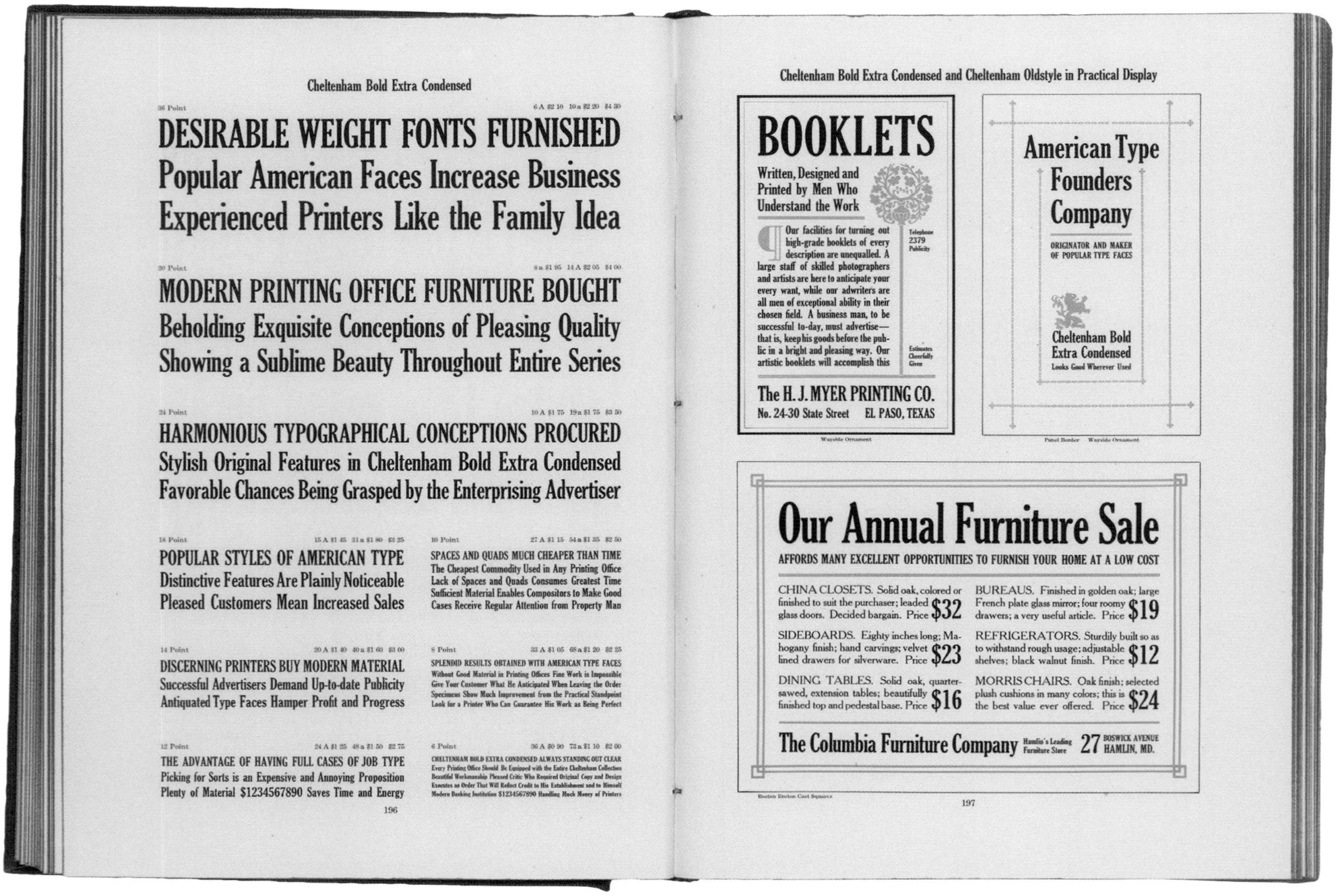
Cheltenham Bold Extra Condensed

DESIRABLE WEIGHT FONTS FURNISHED
Popular American Faces Increase Business
Experienced Printers Like the Family Idea

MODERN PRINTING OFFICE FURNITURE BOUGHT
Beholding Exquisite Conceptions of Pleasing Quality
Showing a Sublime Beauty Throughout Entire Series

HARMONIOUS TYPOGRAPHICAL CONCEPTIONS PROCURED
Stylish Original Features in Cheltenham Bold Extra Condensed
Favorable Chances Being Grasped by the Enterprising Advertiser

POPULAR STYLES OF AMERICAN TYPE
Distinctive Features Are Plainly Noticeable
Pleased Customers Mean Increased Sales

SPACES AND QUADS MUCH CHEAPER THAN TIME
The Cheapest Commodity Used in Any Printing Office
Lack of Spaces and Quads Consumes Greatest Time
Sufficient Material Enables Compositors to Make Good
Cases Receive Regular Attention from Property Man

DISCERNING PRINTERS BUY MODERN MATERIAL
Successful Advertisers Demand Up-to-date Publicity
Antiquated Type Faces Hamper Profit and Progress

THE ADVANTAGE OF HAVING FULL CASES OF JOB TYPE
Picking for Sorts is an Expensive and Annoying Proposition
Plenty of Material $1234567890 Saves Time and Energy

196

Cheltenham Bold Extra Condensed and Cheltenham Oldstyle in Practical Display

BOOKLETS
Written, Designed and Printed by Men Who Understand the Work

The H. J. MYER PRINTING CO.
No. 24-30 State Street EL PASO, TEXAS

American Type Founders Company
ORIGINATOR AND MAKER OF POPULAR TYPE FACES
Cheltenham Bold Extra Condensed
Looks Good Wherever Used

Our Annual Furniture Sale
AFFORDS MANY EXCELLENT OPPORTUNITIES TO FURNISH YOUR HOME AT A LOW COST

CHINA CLOSETS. Solid oak, colored or finished to suit the purchaser; leaded glass doors. Decided bargain. Price $32
BUREAUS. Finished in golden oak; large French plate glass mirror; four roomy drawers; a very useful article. Price $19
SIDEBOARDS. Eighty inches long; Mahogany finish; hand carvings; velvet lined drawers for silverware. Price $23
REFRIGERATORS. Sturdily built so as to withstand rough usage; adjustable shelves; black walnut finish. Price $12
DINING TABLES. Solid oak, quarter-sawed, extension tables; beautifully finished top and pedestal base. Price $16
MORRIS CHAIRS. Oak finish; selected plush cushions in many colors; this is the best value ever offered. Price $24

The Columbia Furniture Company 27 BOSWICK AVENUE HAMLIN, MD.

197

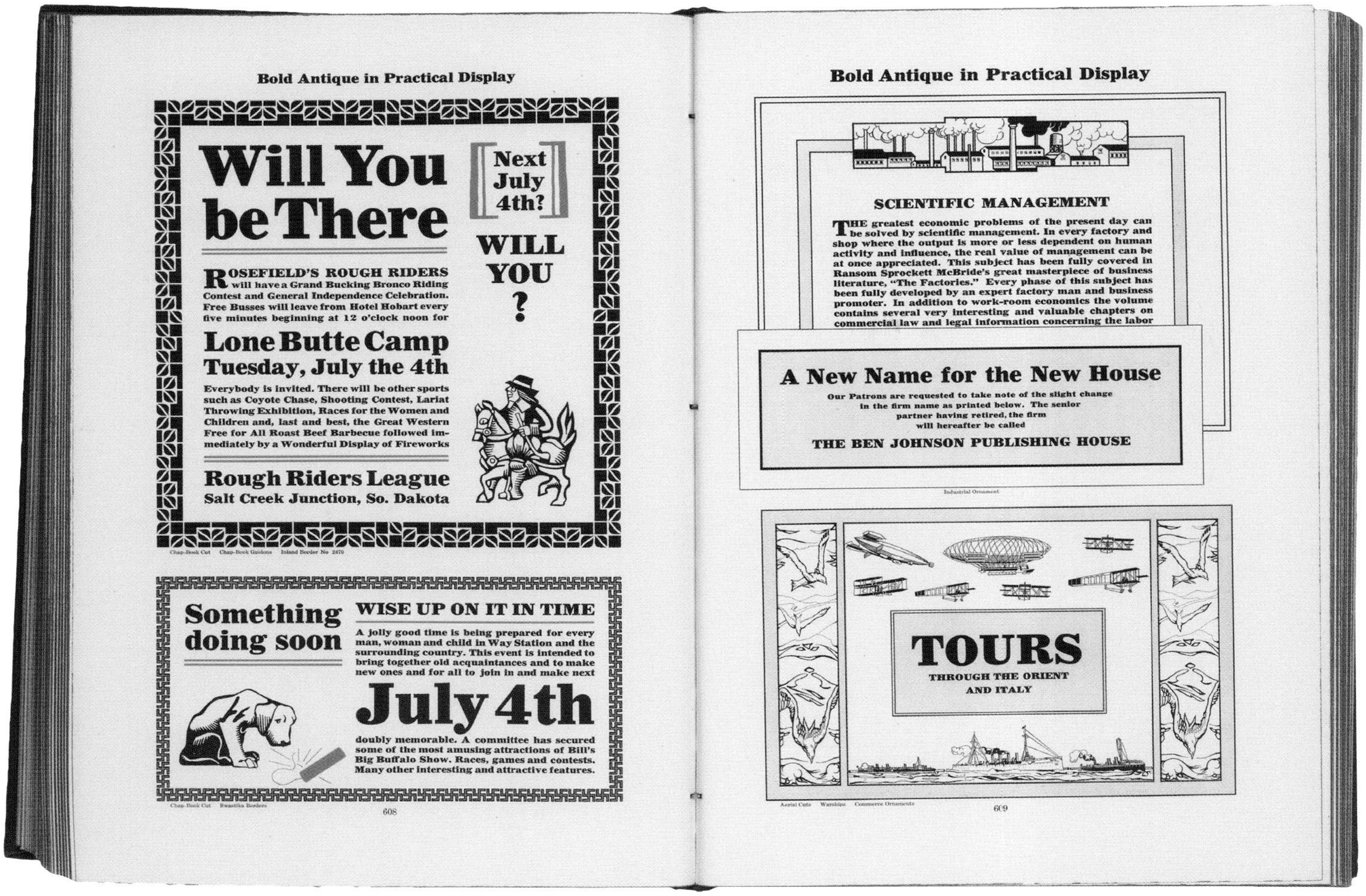
Bold Antique in Practical Display

Will You be There

Next July 4th? WILL YOU ?

ROSEFIELD'S ROUGH RIDERS will have a Grand Bucking Bronco Riding Contest and General Independence Celebration. Free Busses will leave from Hotel Hobart every five minutes beginning at 12 o'clock noon for

Lone Butte Camp

Tuesday, July the 4th

Everybody is invited. There will be other sports such as Coyote Chase, Shooting Contest, Lariat Throwing Exhibition, Races for the Women and Children and, last and best, the Great Western Free for All Roast Beef Barbecue followed immediately by a Wonderful Display of Fireworks

Rough Riders League

Salt Creek Junction, So. Dakota

Something doing soon

WISE UP ON IT IN TIME

A jolly good time is being prepared for every man, woman and child in Way Station and the surrounding country. This event is intended to bring together old acquaintances and to make new ones and for all to join in and make next

July 4th

doubly memorable. A committee has secured some of the most amusing attractions of Bill's Big Buffalo Show. Races, games and contests. Many other interesting and attractive features.

608

Bold Antique in Practical Display

SCIENTIFIC MANAGEMENT

THE greatest economic problems of the present day can be solved by scientific management. In every factory and shop where the output is more or less dependent on human activity and influence, the real value of management can be at once appreciated. This subject has been fully covered in Ransom Sprockett McBride's great masterpiece of business literature, "The Factories." Every phase of this subject has been fully developed by an expert factory man and business promoter. In addition to work-room economics the volume contains several very interesting and valuable chapters on commercial law and legal information concerning the labor

A New Name for the New House

Our Patrons are requested to take note of the slight change in the firm name as printed below. The senior partner having retired, the firm will hereafter be called

THE BEN JOHNSON PUBLISHING HOUSE

TOURS

THROUGH THE ORIENT AND ITALY

609

299

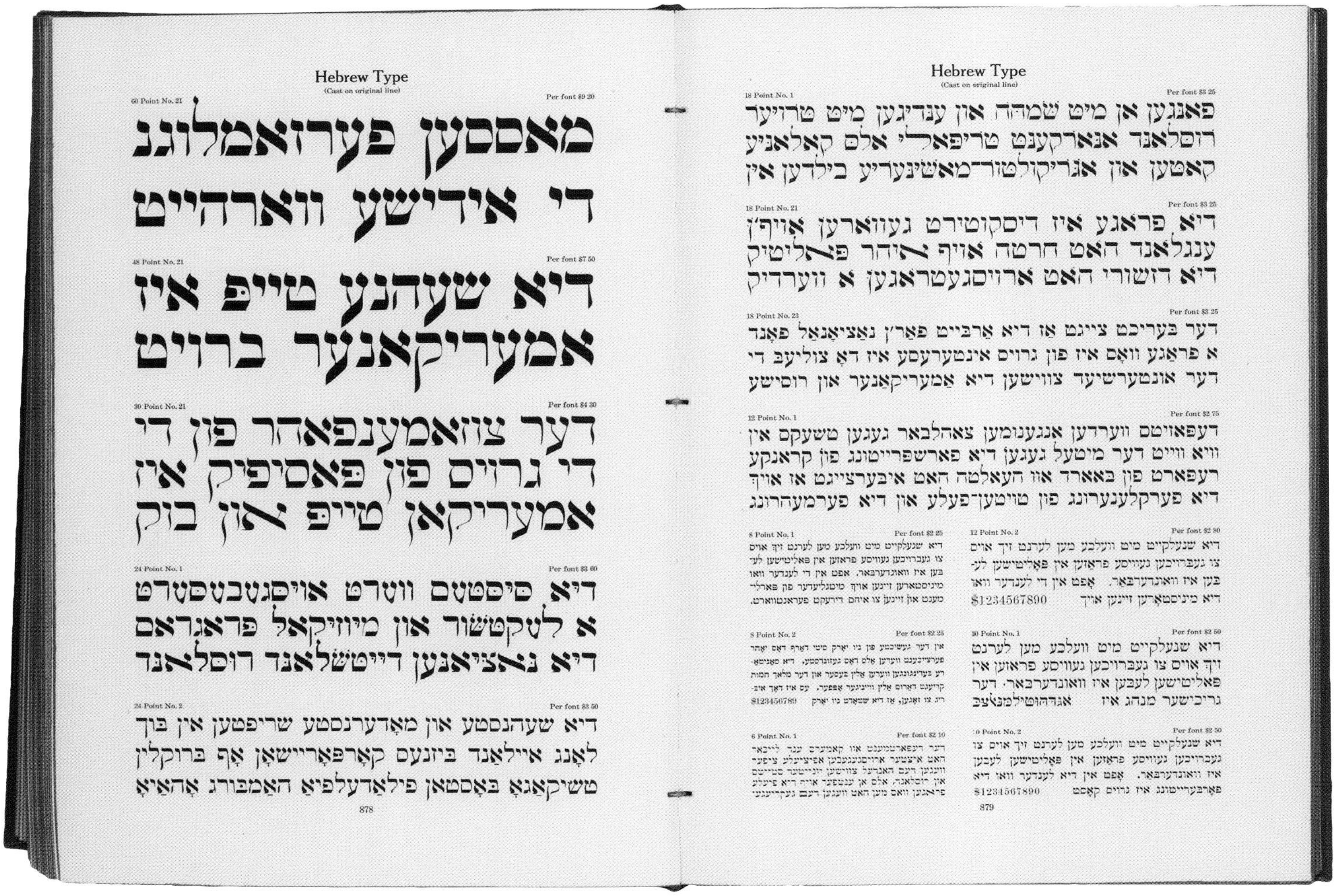
Hebrew Type
(Cast on original line)

מאססען פערזאמלונג
די אידישע ווארהייט

דיא שעהנע טייפ איז
אמעריקאנער ברויט

דער צוזאמענפאהר פון די
די גרויס פון פאסיפיק איז
אמעריקאן טייפ און בוק

דיא סיסטעם ווערט אויסגעבעססערט
א לעקטשור און מיוזיקאל פראגראם
דיא נאציאנען דייטשלאנד רוסלאנד

דיא שעהנסטע און מאָדערנסטע שריפטען אין בוך
לאַנג איילאַנד ביזנעס קארפארײשאן אף ברוקלין
טשיקאגא באָסטאן פילאַדעלפיא האמבורג אהאיא

878

Hebrew Type
(Cast on original line)

879

Avant-garde and New Typography

Detail of *Dlja golosa*,
designed by El Lissitzky
(see p. 314)

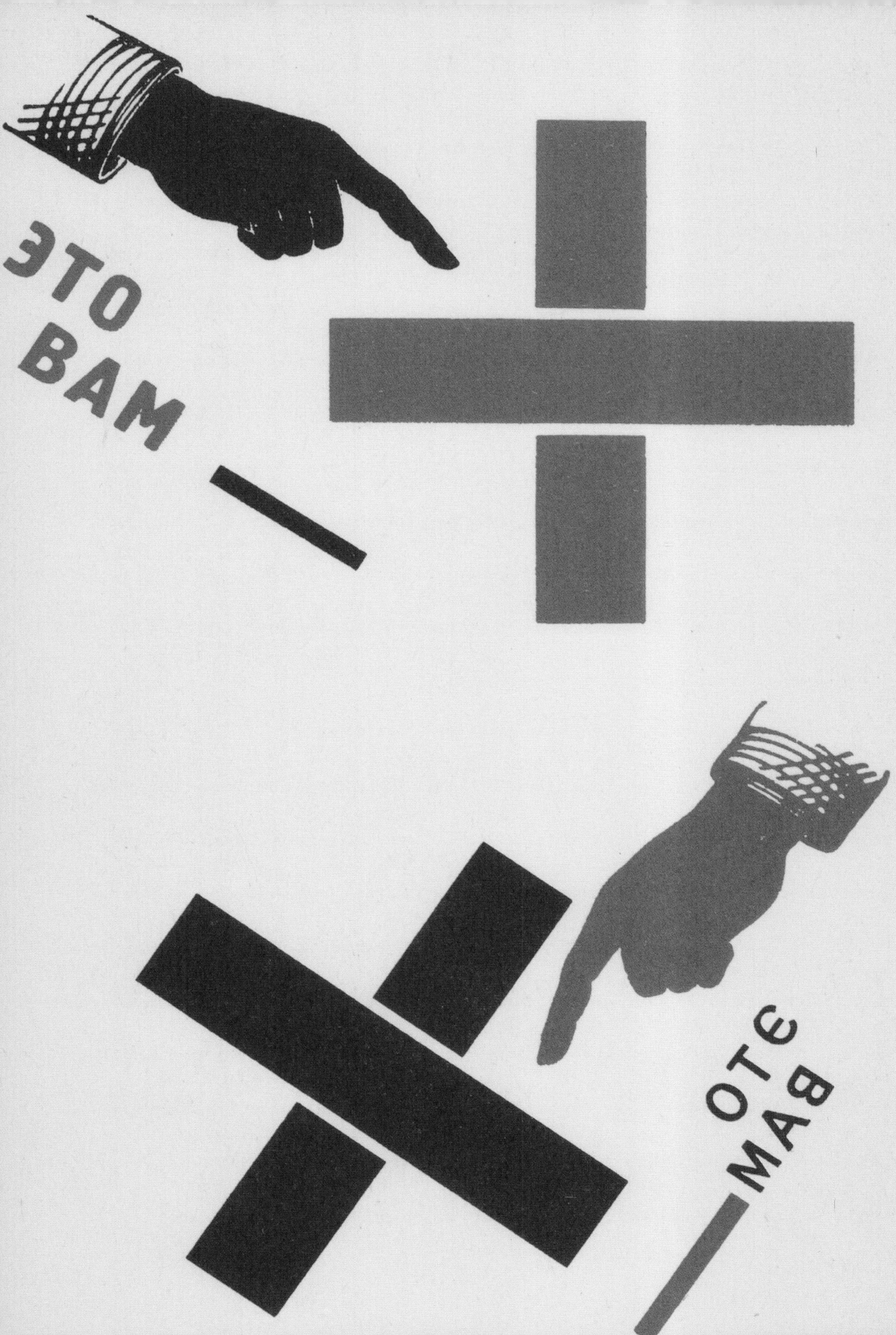
ЭТО ВАМ
ЭТО ВАМ

Avant-garde and New Typography **While William Morris's followers refined book typography in the first decades of the twentieth century, a relatively small group of European artists devoted themselves to visual experiments in a wide variety of printed matter. This often politically motivated avant-garde – Futurists, Dadaists, Constructivists and others – emphatically rejected traditional aesthetic views.**

Italian Futurists including Filippo Tommaso Marinetti and Francesco Cangiullo broke with linguistic and typographic rules for their 'words at liberty'. The German Dadaist John Heartfield, appalled by the First World War, rejected all conventions and made innovative photomontages, including some for book covers. Among the Constructivists were the Dutchman Theo van Doesburg, the Czech Karel Teige and the influential Russian visionary El Lissitzky. In the books he designed, Lissitzky searched for new way of reading: 'optics not phonetics'.

In 1925 Jan Tschichold, a young German with a solid training in the graphic arts, brought together statements and designs by the international avant-garde in *elementare typographie*. This small publication included work by Lissitzky, Kurt Schwitters and a teacher at the Bauhaus, Herbert Bayer. More influential still was Tschichold's *The New Typography* (1928), a manual in A5 format. The title, taken from a phrase that was already being used, clearly presented graphic design as a counterpart to modern movements such as the New Architecture and the New Photography. The model for Tschichold was 'the engineer', the creator of the 'automobile, airplane, telephone, radio, department store, neon lights, New York!' The New Typography stood for the functional, the machine-made, the standardized and the use of

photography (typofoto). Its stylistic characteristics included asymmetry, the machine aesthetic and sans serif letterforms. The didactic Tschichold, moreover, was never reticent in proclaiming do's and don'ts. He himself practised the New Typography not only in books but also in posters and other ephemeral forms of printing. The typeface of this movement was without a doubt Futura, issued by the Bauer typefoundry in 1927. Paul Renner designed this 'geometric' sans serif. At that time he was already an old hand in the field and had converted to modernism in the 1920s.

After Hitler came to power in 1933, several designers left Germany either for political reasons or because they were Jewish. Heartfield and Schwitters finally ended up in England. Otto Neurath and Marie Reidemeister left the anti-democratic Austria in 1934 and went via the Netherlands to England. Bayer emigrated quite late to the United States, receiving as his first commission the landmark Bauhaus exhibition at MoMA in New York (1938). By 1933, Tschichold had already left for Switzerland. There, designers of the older and younger guard formalized modernism to establish what became known as Swiss typography or the International Typographic Style: the avant-garde became the corporate mainstream. ML

1919 **Francesco Cangiullo** Francesco Cangiullo, *Caffeconcerto: alfabeto a sorpresa*. Milan: Edizioni futuriste di 'Poesia', 1919. 48 pp. 25 cm. Designer: Francesco Cangiullo. Printer: Luigi Pierro & figlio, Naples.

In 1909, the Italian poet Filippo Tommaso Marinetti published his first Futurist manifesto. It spoke of a new poetry and a new way of life. Futurism aimed to shock the public, to break with all traditions, and to get rid of museums and libraries. It glorified war, technology and speed: 'a roaring car, sounding like gunfire as it drives along, is more beautiful than the Victory of Samothrace.' Soon, artists also began to join the movement, and although the Futurists were nationalists, they also fostered international innovation.

The French poet Mallarmé was a predecessor of the movement, but the linguistic and typographic expressions of Futurism were more radical. Marinetti talked about '*parole in libertà*' (words at liberty). The expressive formal possibilities of typography were fully exploited: letters and words in varying sizes, weights, and styles were arranged in curved or diagonal lines or were scattered freely on the page. Sometimes collages were made on paper, with typographic fragments and line drawings, after which a page-sized relief line block would be made from a photo negative of the work.

PROPRIETÀ LETTERARIA
Stab. d'Arti Grafiche Luigi Pierro & Figlio - Via Roma, 402 - Napoli

The Neapolitan Futurist Francesco Cangiullo (1888–1977) used the concept of *parole in libertà* for theatre, poetry and paintings. *Caffeconcerto*, his most acclaimed work in print, appeared in 1919; it is reputed to have been designed four years earlier. The booklet is printed on paper of various colours. Figures have been formed using numerals, letters and other materials from the printer's type case, supplemented by drawings. From the pages emerges the story of a night of variety theatre, including acrobats and dancers. Although Cangiullo left Futurism in the 1920s, he did keep in touch with Marinetti. ML

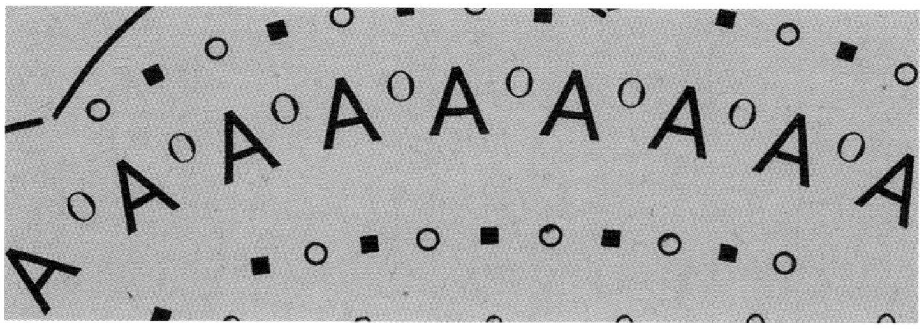

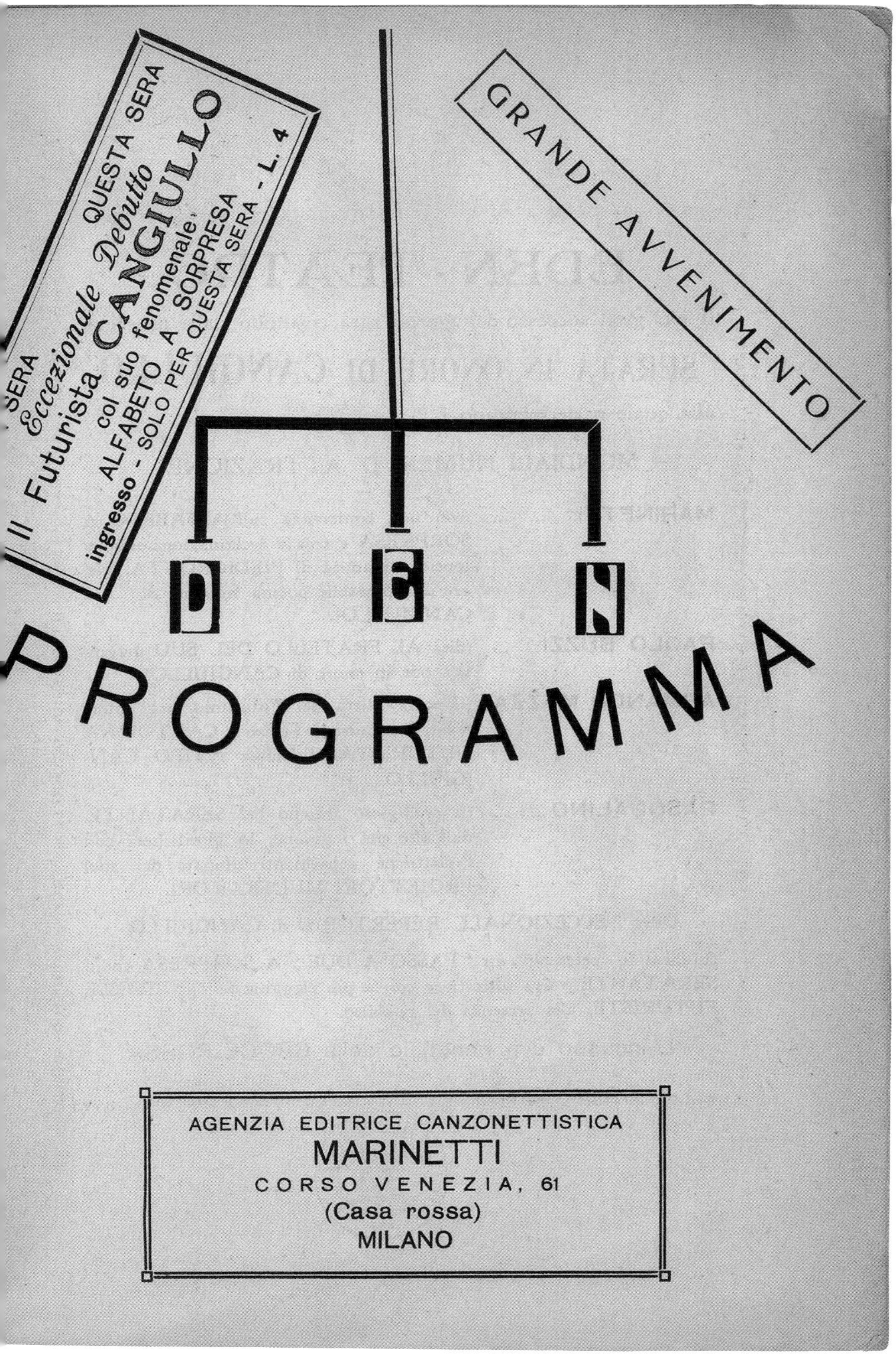
SERA
Il Futurista Eccezionale Debutto
QUESTA SERA
CANGIULLO
col suo fenomenale
ALFABETO A SORPRESA
ingresso - SOLO PER QUESTA SERA - L. 4
GRANDE AVVENIMENTO
D E N
PROGRAMMA
AGENZIA EDITRICE CANZONETTISTICA
MARINETTI
CORSO VENEZIA, 61
(Casa rossa)
MILANO

CANGIULLO
FUTURISTA
CAFFECONCERTO
ALFABETO A SORPRESA
Cangiullo
EDIZIONI FUTURISTE
DI
"POESIA"
CORSO VENEZIA, 61
MILANO

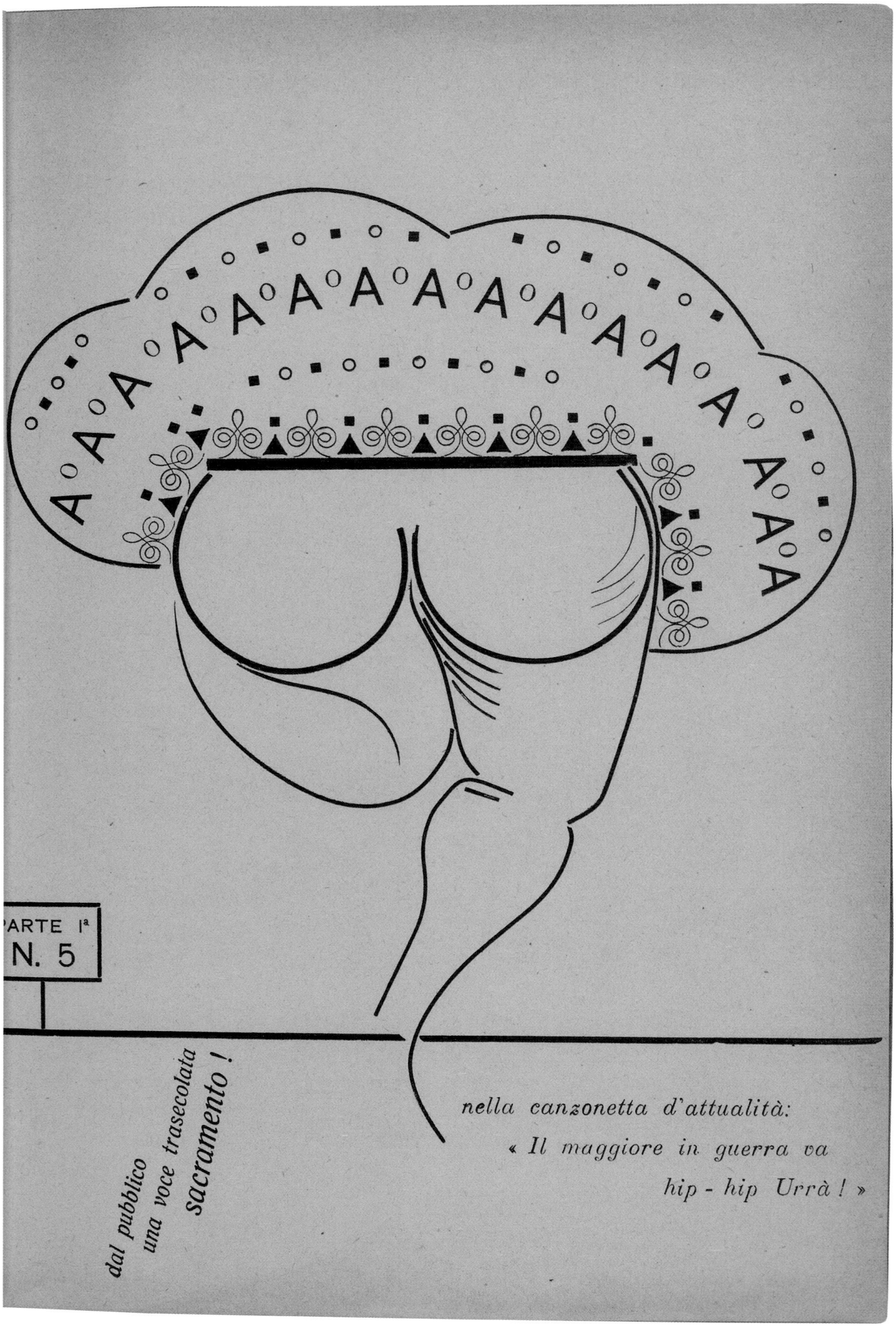
A A A A A A A A A A A A A A A A A
PARTE Iª
N. 5
dal pubblico
una voce trasecolata
sacramento !
nella canzonetta d'attualità:
« Il maggiore in guerra va
hip - hip Urrà ! »

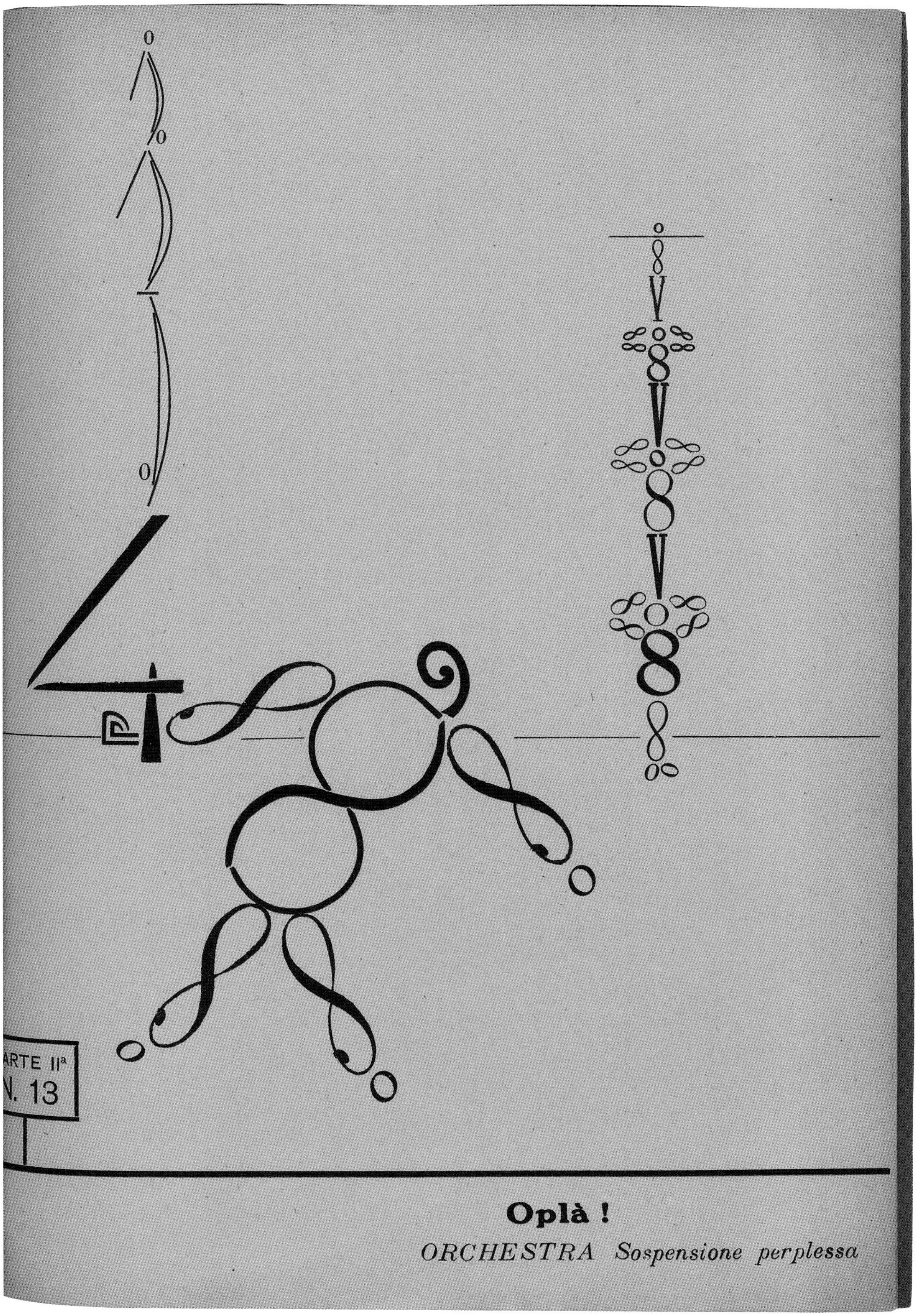
ARTE IIª
N. 13
Oplà !
ORCHESTRA Sospensione perplessa

1919 **Fernand Léger** Blaise Cendrars, *La fin du monde filmée par l'ange N.-D: roman*. Paris: Éditions de la Sirène, 1919.

60 pp. 32 cm. Designer & illustrator: Fernand Léger. Printers: Frazier-Soye, Paris (letterpress); Richard, Paris (pochoir).

Blaise Cendrars and Fernand Léger, the writer and illustrator of this book respectively, were close friends. Before the First World War (1914–18), in which they both fought, they often met in Paris. Cendrars thought film was the quintessential medium of the modern age. His satirical *La fin du monde filmée par l'ange N.-D.* ('The end of the world filmed by the angel Notre-Dame') from 1919 reads like a film script rather than a story: it has numbered fragments and is told in the simple present tense. God, personified as an American businessman, observes that the war has been profitable for him. He decides to destroy the earth and commissions an angel to film the apocalypse. But at the end, the film plays in reverse and God is back in his office.

Like Cendrars, the painter Léger (1881–1955) was highly interested in advertising and lettering in public spaces. For him, the modern, fragmented city was symbolized by the billboard, which is often seen only for a moment from a car or a train. In his illustrations for *La fin du monde* he predominantly used stencilling and other kinds of urban lettering. Léger had produced an oil painting called *The Typographer* in 1918; now it was he himself who was designing a layout.

The translucent colours are pochoir-printed. This stencil technique was popular in France for deluxe editions and magazines. During the period between the wars, Paris and its suburbs were home to some thirty firms that specialized in this technique. ML

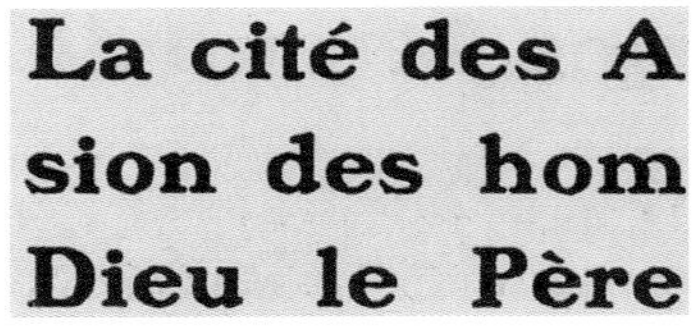

Morland was issued in 1900 by the London typefoundry H.W. Caslon & Co. This bold roman with italic has irregular outlines, which stand out at the bigger sizes. The design of this display type is based on Blanchard, by the Inland Type Foundry of Saint Louis, Missouri.

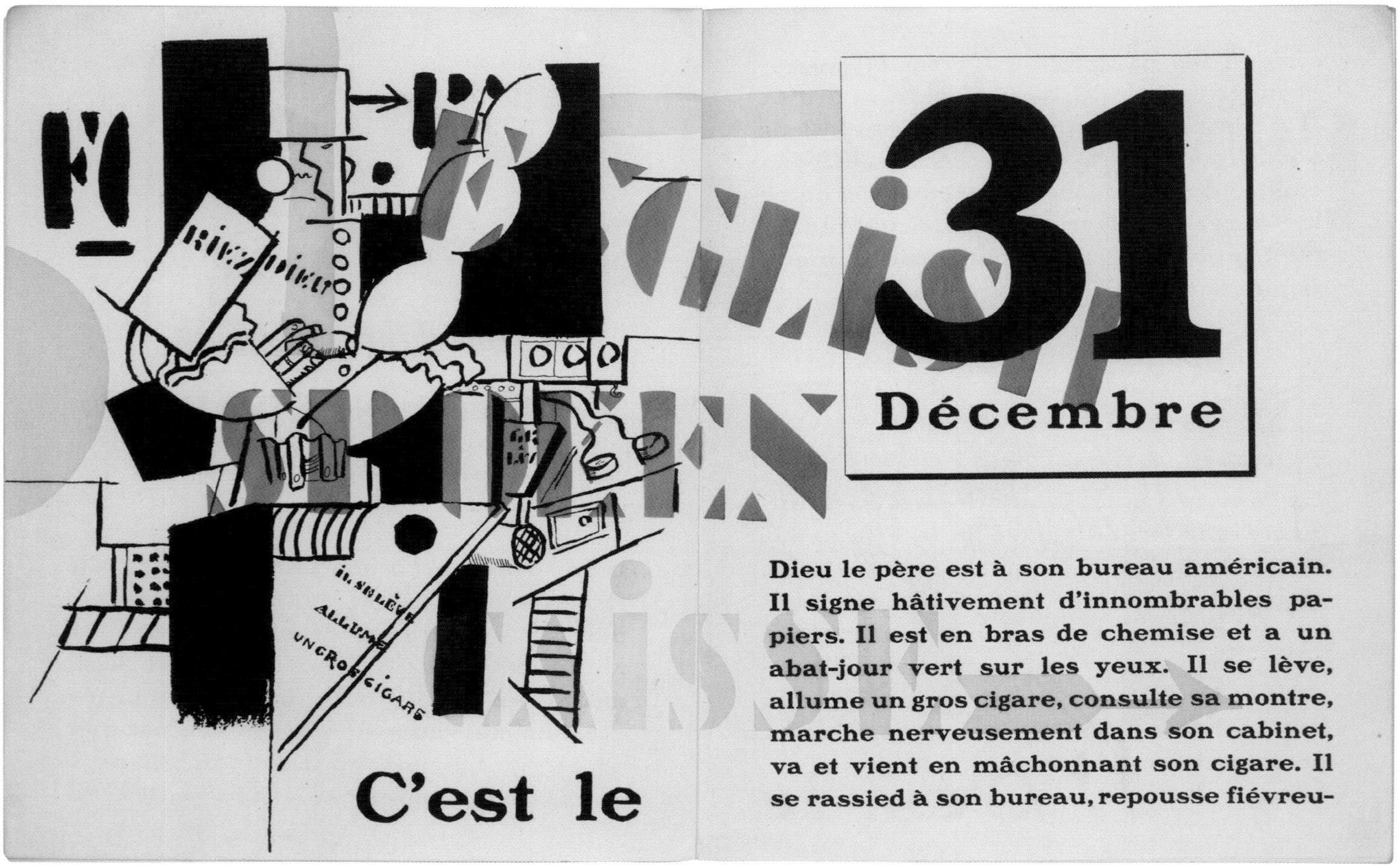

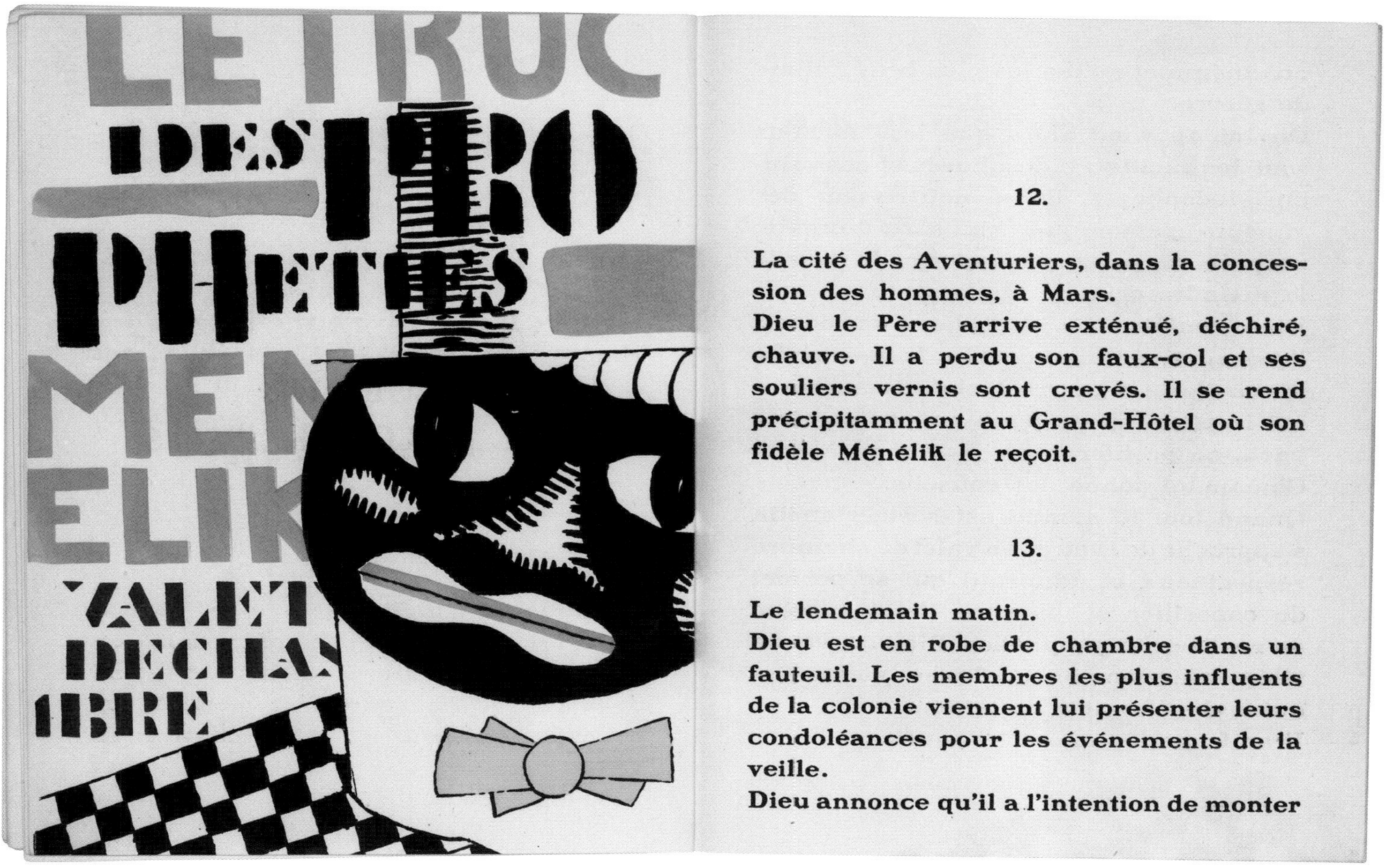

12.

La cité des Aventuriers, dans la concession des hommes, à Mars.
Dieu le Père arrive exténué, déchiré, chauve. Il a perdu son faux-col et ses souliers vernis sont crevés. Il se rend précipitamment au Grand-Hôtel où son fidèle Ménélik le reçoit.

13.

Le lendemain matin.
Dieu est en robe de chambre dans un fauteuil. Les membres les plus influents de la colonie viennent lui présenter leurs condoléances pour les événements de la veille.
Dieu annonce qu'il a l'intention de monter

1923 **Bruce Rogers** Ernest Dowson, *The Pierrot of the Minute*. New York: The Grolier Club, 1923. 49 pp. 18.5 cm.

Designer: Bruce Rogers. Printer: William Edwin Rudge, Mount Vernon, New York. In slipcase.

In Indianapolis, when he was in his early twenties, Bruce Rogers (1870–1957) saw an edition by William Morris's Kelmscott Press. He was won over immediately: illustration – which had seemed to be his calling – was forgotten, and from then on he decided to focus on book design.

In 1896, Rogers started to work for the Riverside Press in Cambridge, Massachusetts. At this large printing company, which was affiliated with the publishing house Houghton, Mifflin and Company, he learned all there was to know about the technical aspects of book production. He even managed to persuade management to start a series of special Riverside Press editions: books with small print runs and unusual designs, which varied with each edition. After he left the Riverside Press in 1911, he worked as an independent designer in the United States and in the UK.

Rogers, once dubbed 'America's typographic playboy' by his colleague Carl Purington Rollins, loved to use 'period typography' for literary works, designing in the characteristic style of the period in which the work was written. He often made use of plain and decorated rules, as well as ornaments. His most beautiful work in this field may well be Dowson's small *The Pierrot of the Minute*, a stage play set in the Parc du Petit Trianon in Versailles. Rogers lavishly decorated the edition with Fournier ornaments. The book, which appeared as part of a small series for the bibliophile Grolier Club, was typeset and printed by William Edwin Rudge. Rogers was friendly with this idealistic, high-quality printer, and it was with Rudge during the 1920s that Rogers did some of his best work. ML

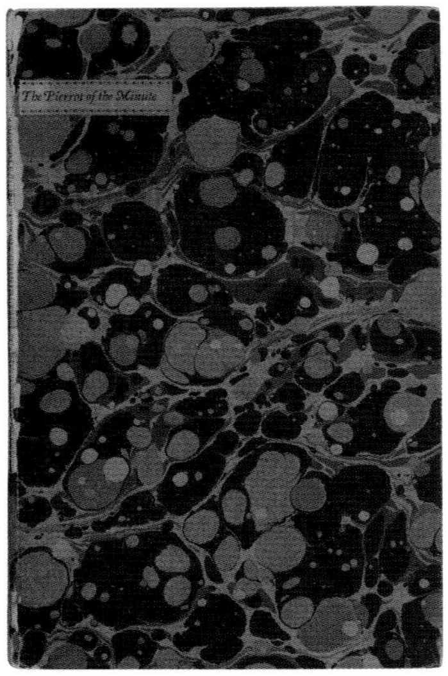

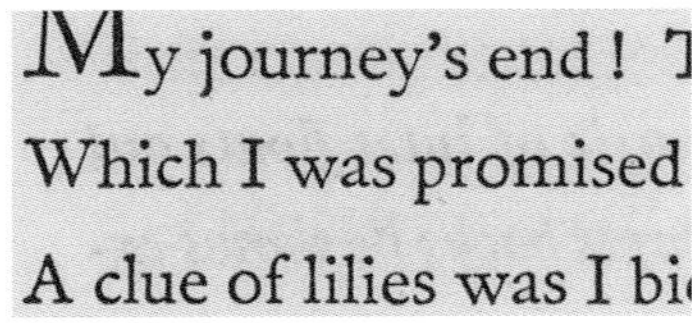

Deberny's Ancien Romain and its italic form (1899?), perhaps mixing influences from William Caslon in *c.* 1730 (the Caslon foundry had opened a Paris branch by 1883) and earlier French types. It and the rococo ornaments, copied from those in Fournier's 1766 *Manuel Typographique*, were imported from France.

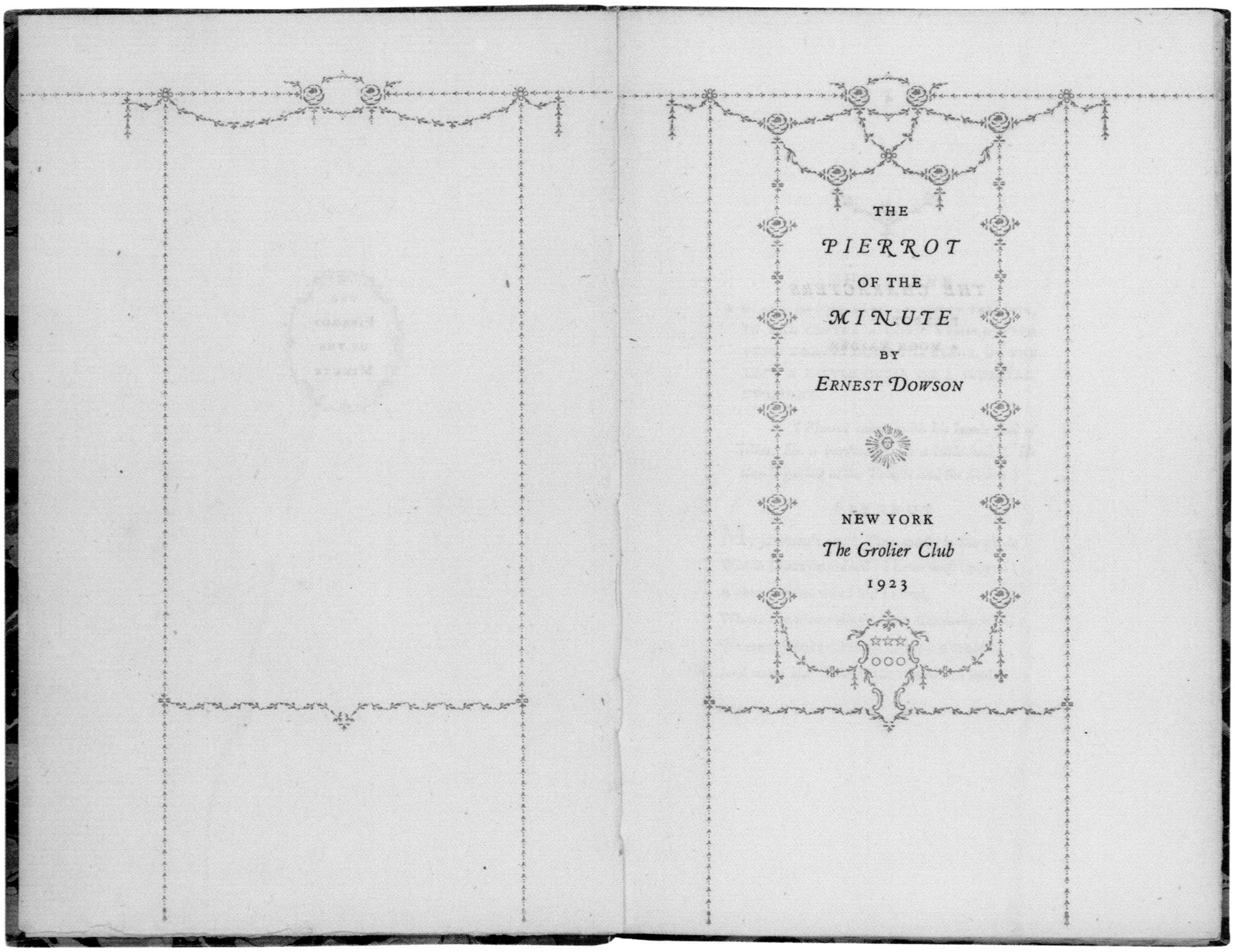

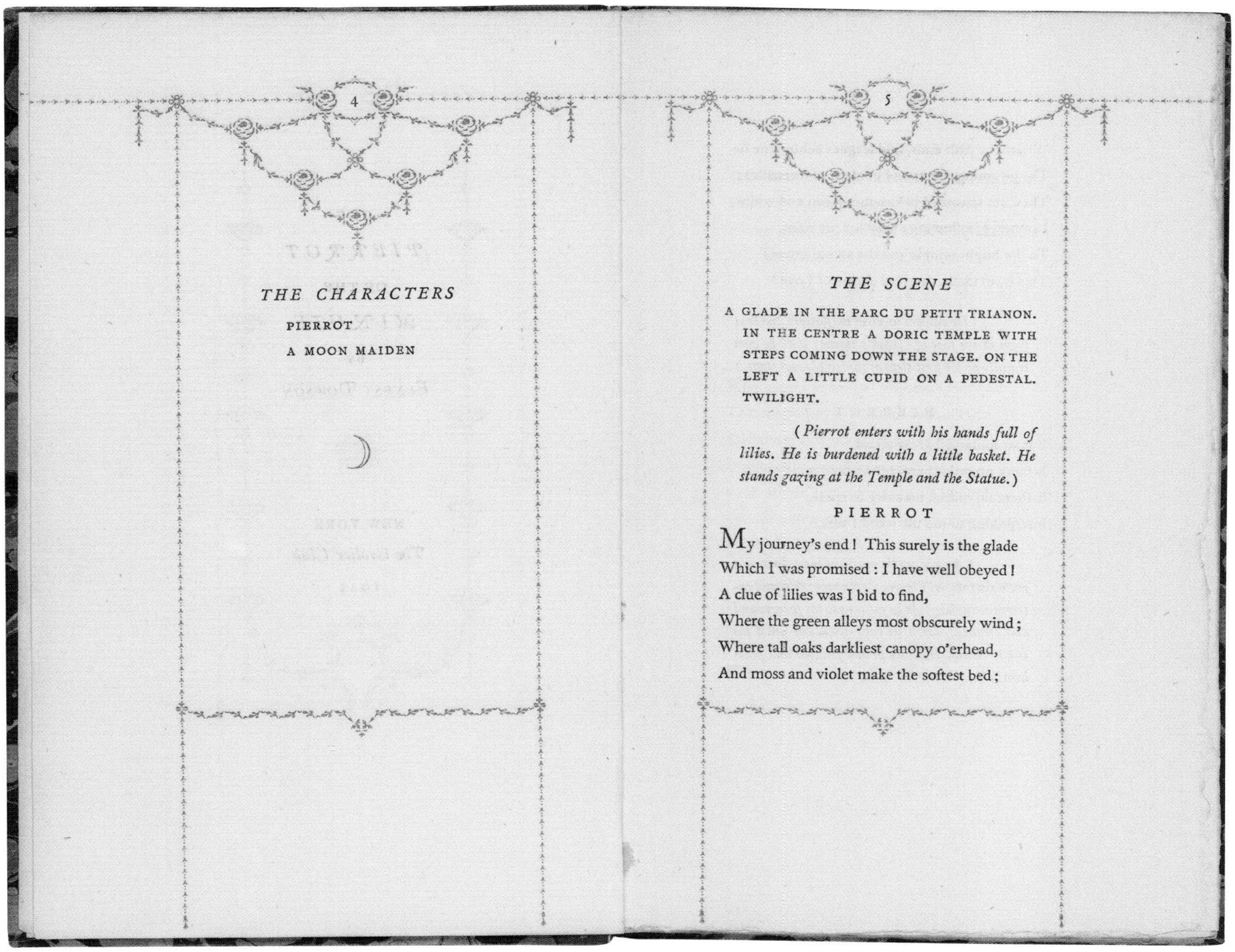

4

THE CHARACTERS

PIERROT

A MOON MAIDEN

5

THE SCENE

A GLADE IN THE PARC DU PETIT TRIANON. IN THE CENTRE A DORIC TEMPLE WITH STEPS COMING DOWN THE STAGE. ON THE LEFT A LITTLE CUPID ON A PEDESTAL. TWILIGHT.

(Pierrot enters with his hands full of lilies. He is burdened with a little basket. He stands gazing at the Temple and the Statue.)

PIERROT

My journey's end! This surely is the glade
Which I was promised: I have well obeyed!
A clue of lilies was I bid to find,
Where the green alleys most obscurely wind;
Where tall oaks darkliest canopy o'erhead,
And moss and violet make the softest bed;

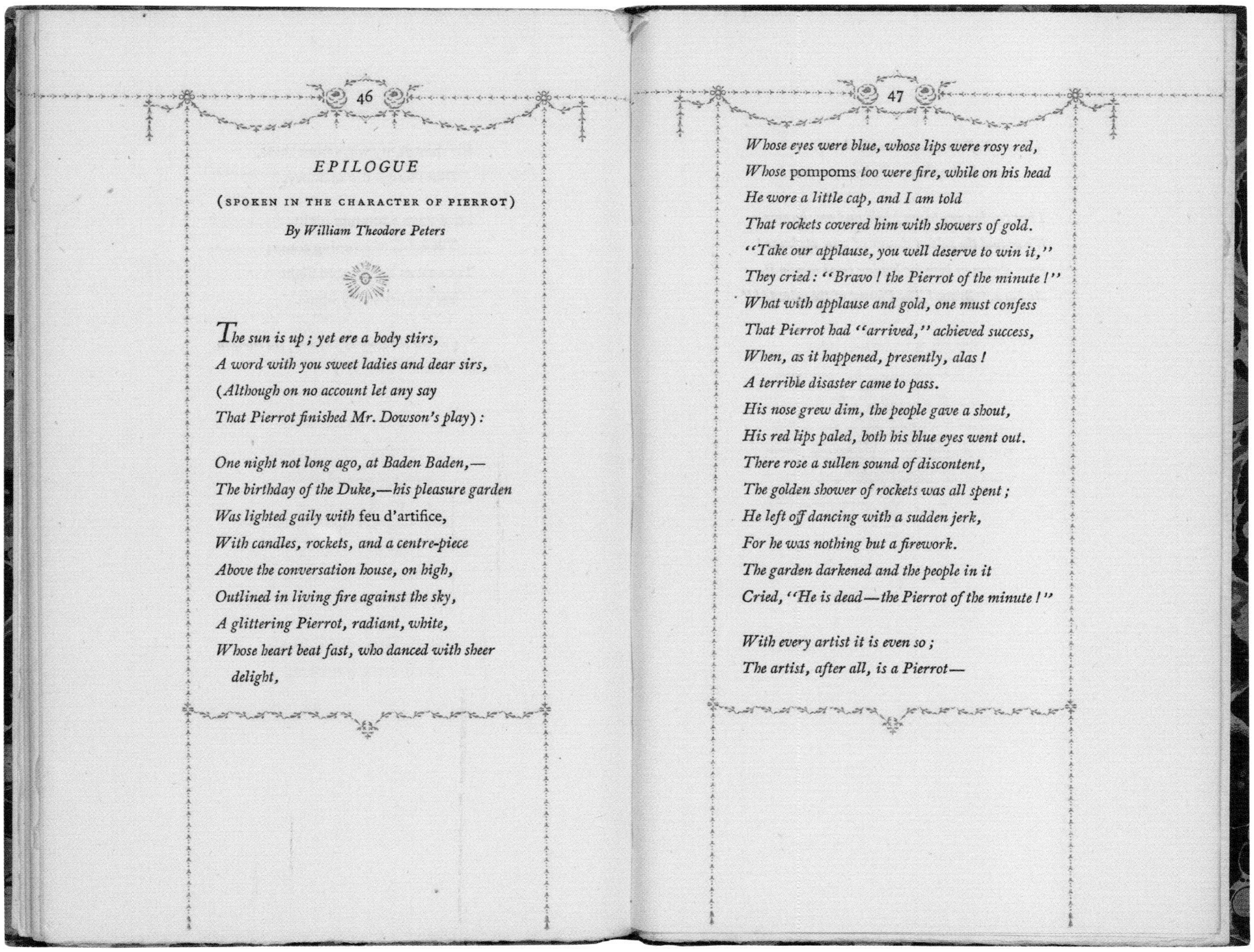

46

EPILOGUE

(SPOKEN IN THE CHARACTER OF PIERROT)

By William Theodore Peters

The sun is up; yet ere a body stirs,
A word with you sweet ladies and dear sirs,
(Although on no account let any say
That Pierrot finished Mr. Dowson's play):

One night not long ago, at Baden Baden,—
The birthday of the Duke,—his pleasure garden
Was lighted gaily with feu d'artifice,
With candles, rockets, and a centre-piece
Above the conversation house, on high,
Outlined in living fire against the sky,
A glittering Pierrot, radiant, white,
Whose heart beat fast, who danced with sheer
delight,

47

Whose eyes were blue, whose lips were rosy red,
Whose pompoms *too were fire, while on his head*
He wore a little cap, and I am told
That rockets covered him with showers of gold.
"Take our applause, you well deserve to win it,"
They cried: "Bravo! the Pierrot of the minute!"
What with applause and gold, one must confess
That Pierrot had "arrived," achieved success,
When, as it happened, presently, alas!
A terrible disaster came to pass.
His nose grew dim, the people gave a shout,
His red lips paled, both his blue eyes went out.
There rose a sullen sound of discontent,
The golden shower of rockets was all spent;
He left off dancing with a sudden jerk,
For he was nothing but a firework.
The garden darkened and the people in it
Cried, "He is dead—the Pierrot of the minute!"

With every artist it is even so;
The artist, after all, is a Pierrot—

1923 **El Lissitzky** Vladimir Mayakovsky, *Dlja golosa*. Berlin: RSFSR Gosudarstvennoe izdatel'stvo, 1923. 61 pp. 19 cm.

Designer ('book constructor'): El Lissitzky. Typesetter & printer: Lutze & Vogt, Berlin.

Vladimir Mayakovsky and El Lissitzky (1890–1941) were leading figures of the Russian avant-garde in the beginning of the last century. After the Bolshevik revolution of 1917, the poet Mayakovsky had placed his work in the service of social reform. For the architect, artist, designer and photographer Lissitzky revolutionary art became a theme in 1919, after he personally met the painter Kazimir Malevich and became acquainted with his geometric Suprematism. Lissitzky started to apply ideas of Suprematism to political printed matter such as the famous propaganda poster *Beat the Whites with the Red Wedge* (1919–20). He further developed Malevich's ideas in a three-dimensional direction.

During the early 1920s, Lissitzky, who was fluent in German, began travelling through Western Europe to make contacts and work with kindred spirits, including Theo van Doesburg, Kurt Schwitters, Jan Tschichold and Piet Zwart. Lissitzky and the artist Jean Arp produced the book *Die Kunstismen / Les ismes de l'art / The isms of art* (1925), which contains a survey of contemporary avant-garde movements.

Lissitzky's best-known graphic work, *Dlja golosa* ('For the Voice'), was created in 1923 in Berlin, which was at the time a vibrant city of art and hosted a large community of Russian expatriates. This anthology of Mayakovsky's revolutionary poetry was published by the Berlin affiliate of the Soviet publishing house Gosizdat. A small printer executed the layout sketch, and even the complex illustrations were built up entirely from material from the type case. A striking feature is the thumb index with abbreviated titles, which replaces the usual index. More importantly, Mayakovsky's poems gain directness from Lissitzky's visual representations. ML

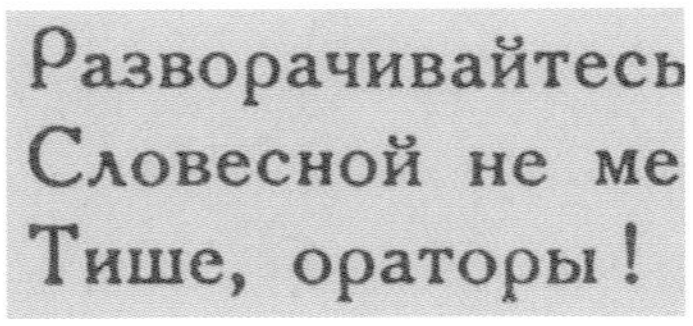

From 1904 to 1915 Morris F. Benton at American Type Founders created the first major typeface family: 22 variants of the architect Bertram Goodhue's 1890s Cheltenham. The Berthold typefoundry in Berlin copied several variants as Sorbonne in 1907, eliminating a few of the original's eccentricities and adding the Cyrillic shown here.

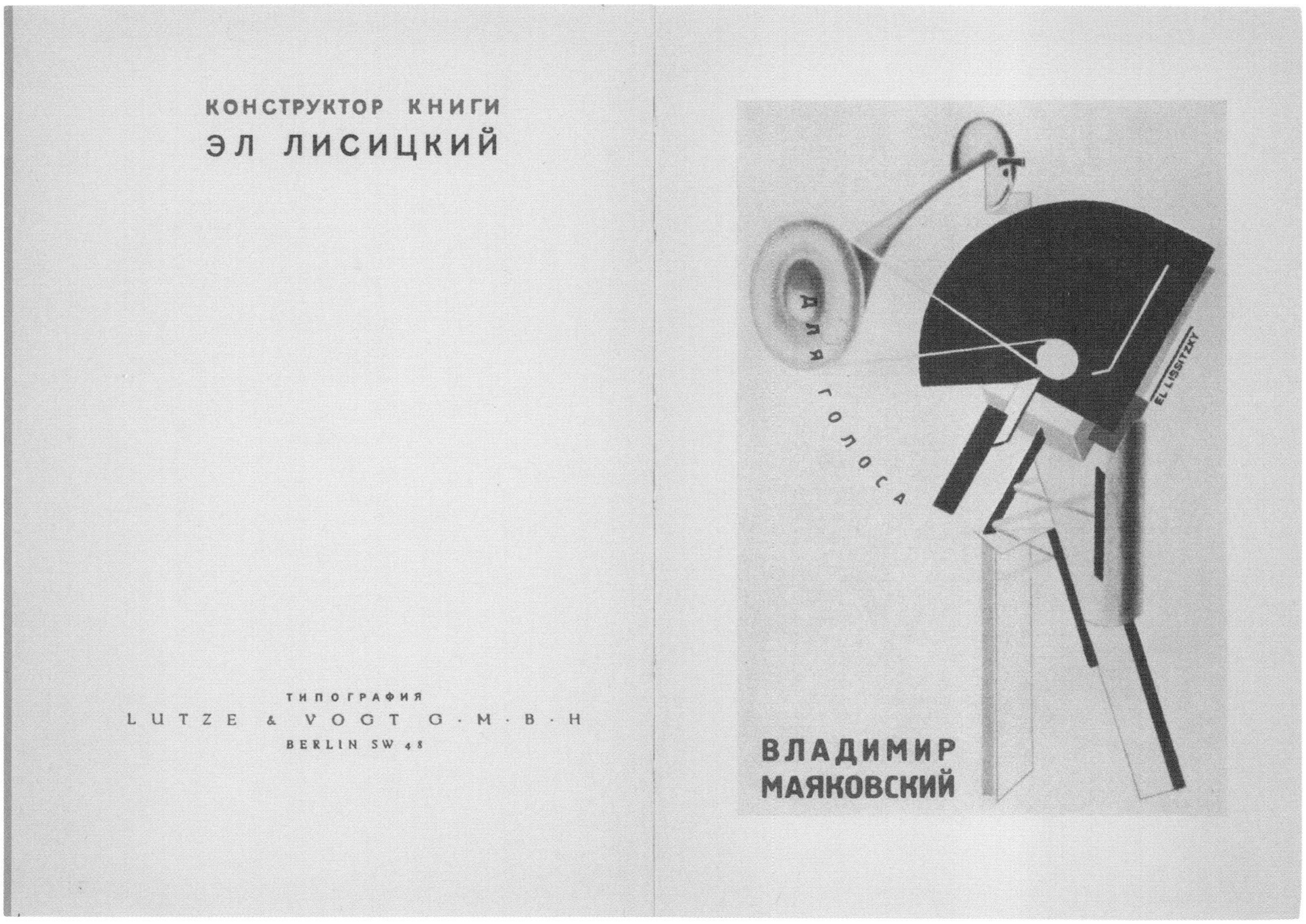
КОНСТРУКТОР КНИГИ
ЭЛ ЛИСИЦКИЙ
ТИПОГРАФИЯ
LUTZE & VOGT G·M·B·H
BERLIN SW 48
ДЛЯ ГОЛОСА
EL LISSITZKY
ВЛАДИМИР
МАЯКОВСКИЙ

315

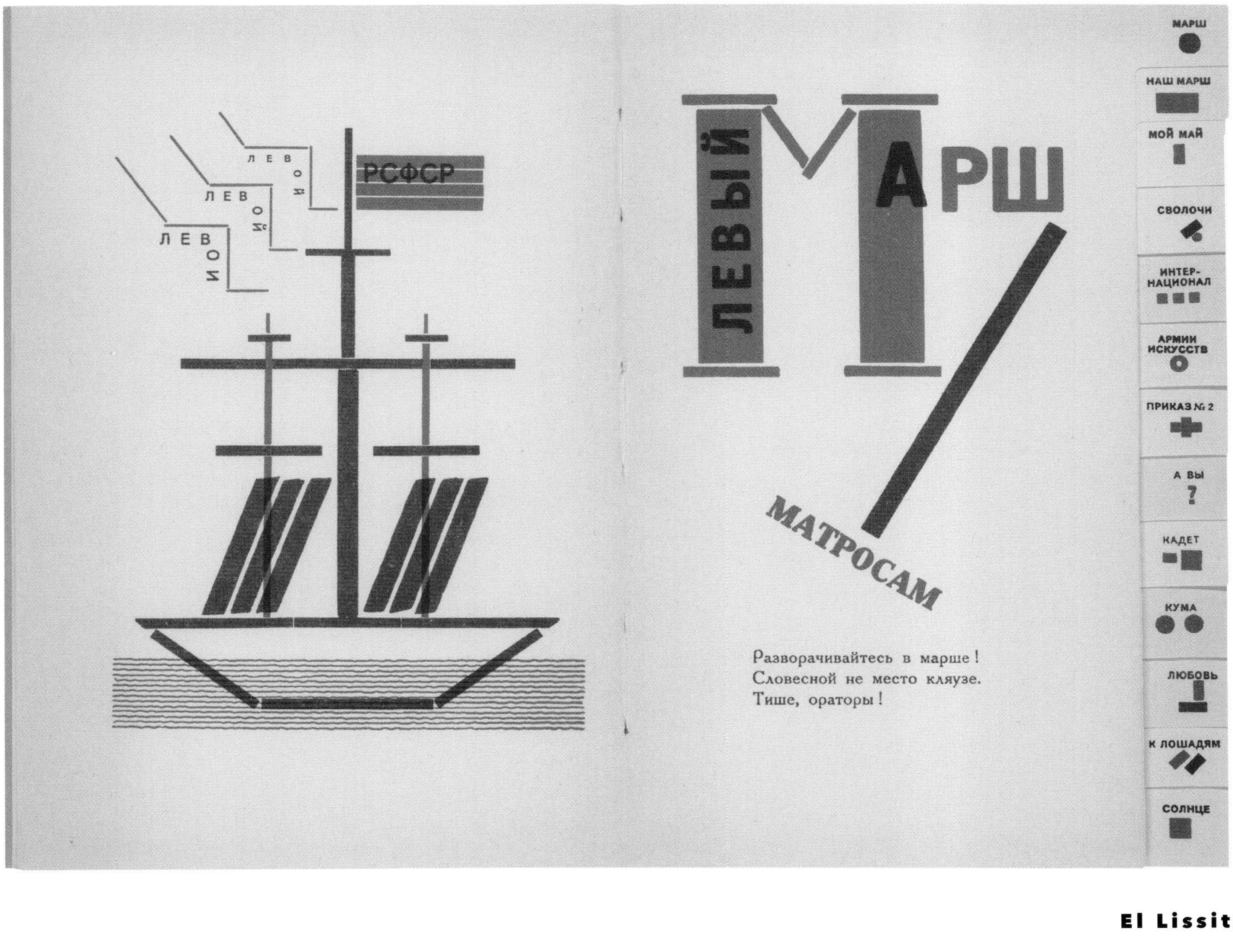
ЛЕВ
ОЙ
РСФСР
ЛЕВЫЙ
МАРШ
МАТРОСАМ
Разворачивайтесь в марше!
Словесной не место кляузе.
Тише, ораторы!
МАРШ
НАШ МАРШ
МОЙ МАЙ
СВОЛОЧИ
ИНТЕР-
НАЦИОНАЛ
АРМИИ
ИСКУССТВ
ПРИКАЗ № 2
А ВЫ
?
КАДЕТ
КУМА
ЛЮБОВЬ
К ЛОШАДЯМ
СОЛНЦЕ

ЭТО
ВАМ
ЭТО
ВАМ
ПРИКАЗ
№ 2
ПО АРМИЯМ ИСКУССТВ
ПРИКАЗ № 2
А ВЫ
?
КАДЕТ
КУМА
ЛЮБОВЬ
К ЛОШАДЯМ
СОЛНЦЕ

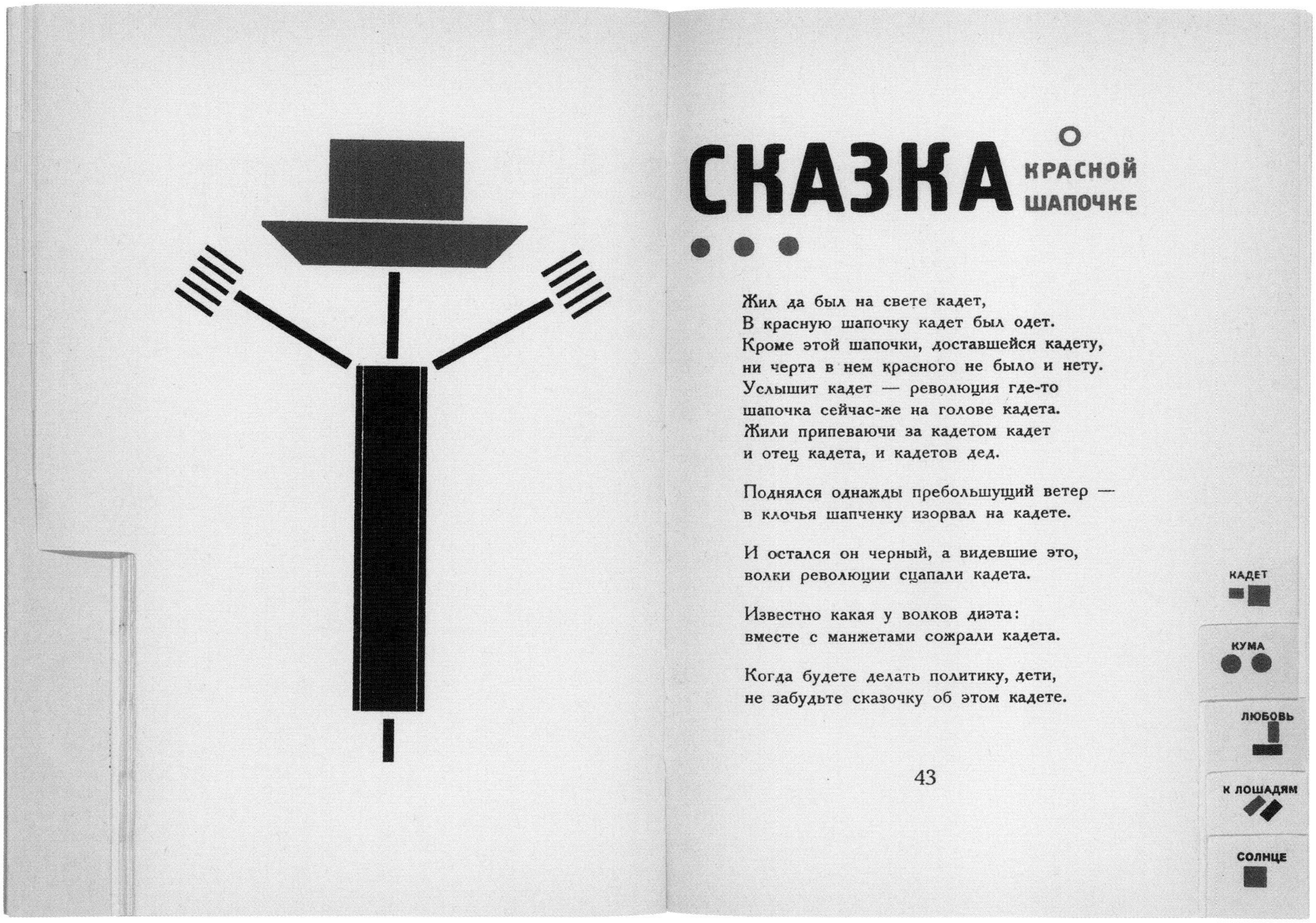
СКАЗКА о красной шапочке

Жил да был на свете кадет,
В красную шапочку кадет был одет.
Кроме этой шапочки, доставшейся кадету,
ни черта в нем красного не было и нету.
Услышит кадет — революция где-то
шапочка сейчас-же на голове кадета.
Жили припеваючи за кадетом кадет
и отец кадета, и кадетов дед.

Поднялся однажды пребольшущий ветер —
в клочья шапченку изорвал на кадете.

И остался он черный, а видевшие это,
волки революции сцапали кадета.

Известно какая у волков диэта:
вместе с манжетами сожрали кадета.

Когда будете делать политику, дети,
не забудьте сказочку об этом кадете.

43

КАДЕТ
КУМА
ЛЮБОВЬ
К ЛОШАДЯМ
СОЛНЦЕ

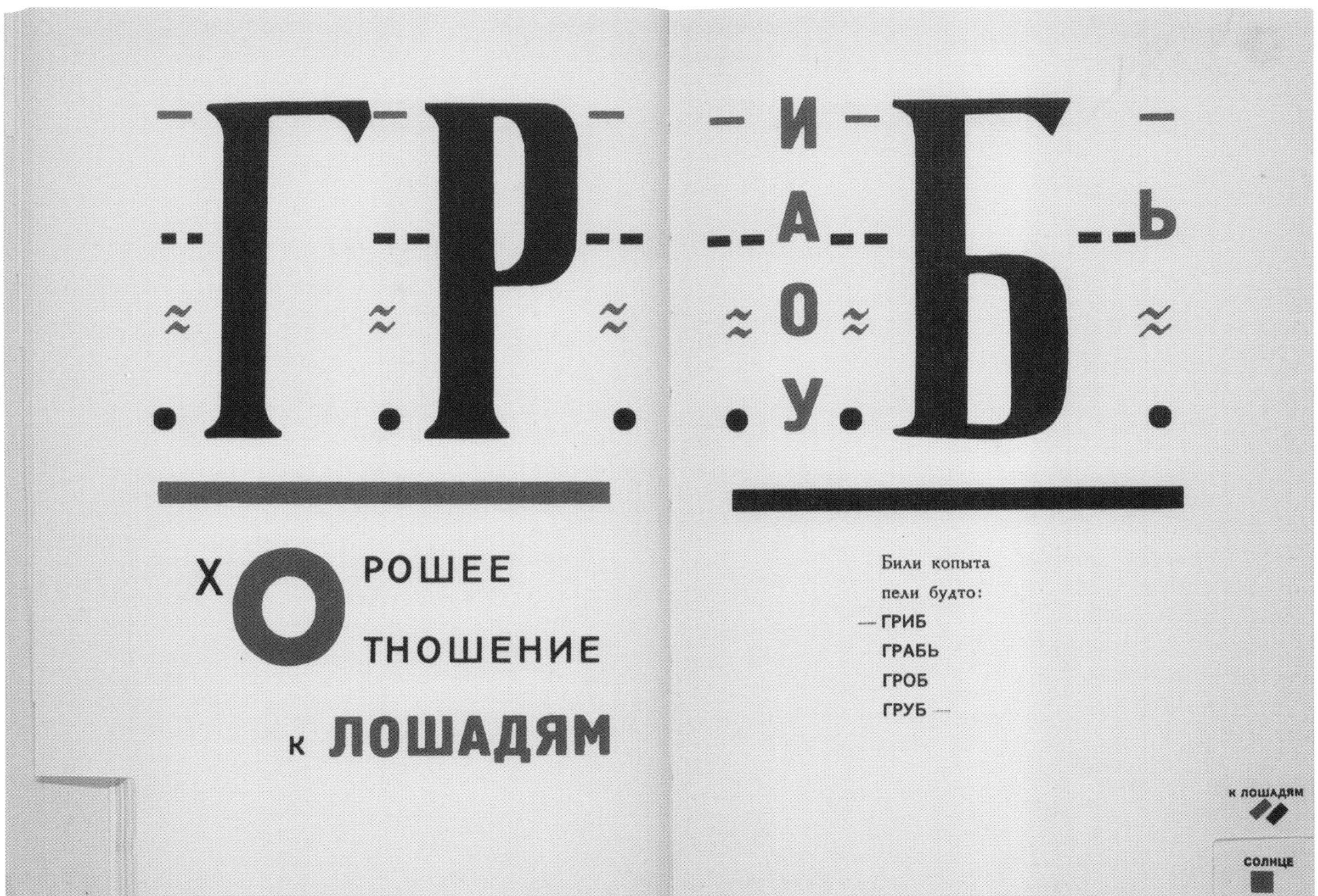
Г. Р. И А О У. Б Ь

Хорошее отношение к лошадям

Били копыта
пели будто:
— ГРИБ
ГРАБЬ
ГРОБ
ГРУБ —

К ЛОШАДЯМ
СОЛНЦЕ

1923 **Rudolf Koch** *Das Evangelium des Markus*. Offenbach am Main: Wilhelm Gerstung, 1923. 75 pp. 30 cm.

Rudolfinischer Druck, no. 19.

Rudolf Koch (1876–1934), born in Nuremberg, abandoned plans for a classical education when his father, a sculptor and museum inspector, died in 1886. Apprenticed as a metal chaser, he left to study drawing, intending to teach art. In 1898 he began designing and drawing in the Jugendstil spirit for a lithographic company and then a bookbinding firm, working freelance from 1902. Art journals led him to try lettering with a broad-nibbed pen and to apply to the Rudhard typefoundry (renamed Klingspor after 1906) in Offenbach, pioneers of 'artistic' type for the commercial market. He designed type there from 1906 to his death and from 1908 taught lettering at Offenbach's Arts and Crafts School.

A devoted teacher with a love of medieval craft traditions, he developed a strong personal bond with his students and employers. In the spirit of Rudolf von Larisch, he found inspiration for personal expression in historical tradition. Already spiritually inclined, he turned devoutly Lutheran during his traumatic military service in the First World War. In 1921 he and several students founded the Offenbacher Werkgemeinschaft for collaborative handwork (drawing, lettering, woodblock cutting, type design and punchcutting, book design and production, and textiles), often with a rich liturgical flavour and always bearing the strong personal stamp of the makers. Several of his students became leading designers internationally.

With the publisher Rudolf Gerstung, Koch began a series of small books in 1911. This edition of the Gospel according to St Mark, with hand-lettered coloured initials and headings in the tradition of early printing, was the nineteenth in the series. JAL

Rudolf Koch designed the Klingspor typefoundry's Maximilian Gotisch (first size used in 1914) for a 1917 Bible (never produced) intended to commemorate the Lutheran Reformation. Gustav Eichenauer (1891–1982) probably cut the type, with small sizes in steel and large in type metal for electrotyping. The design is tailored to each size.

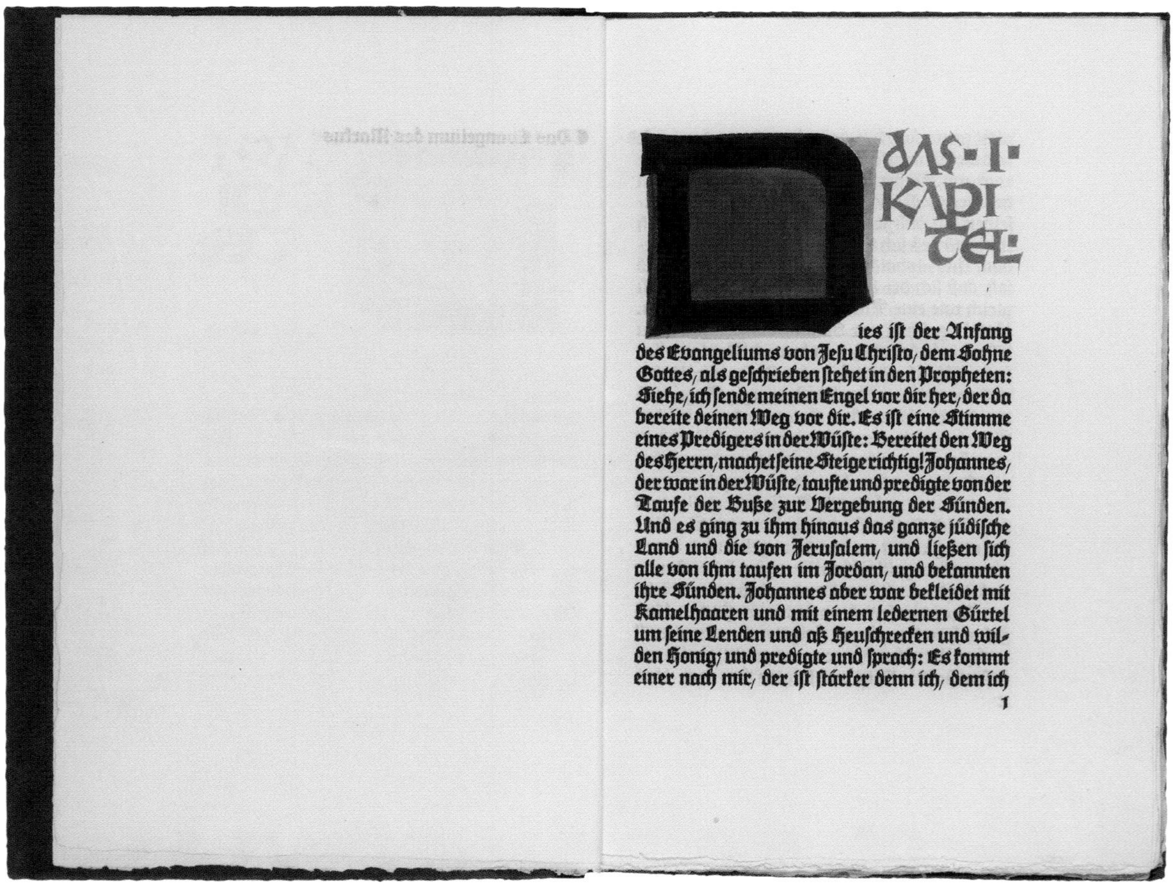

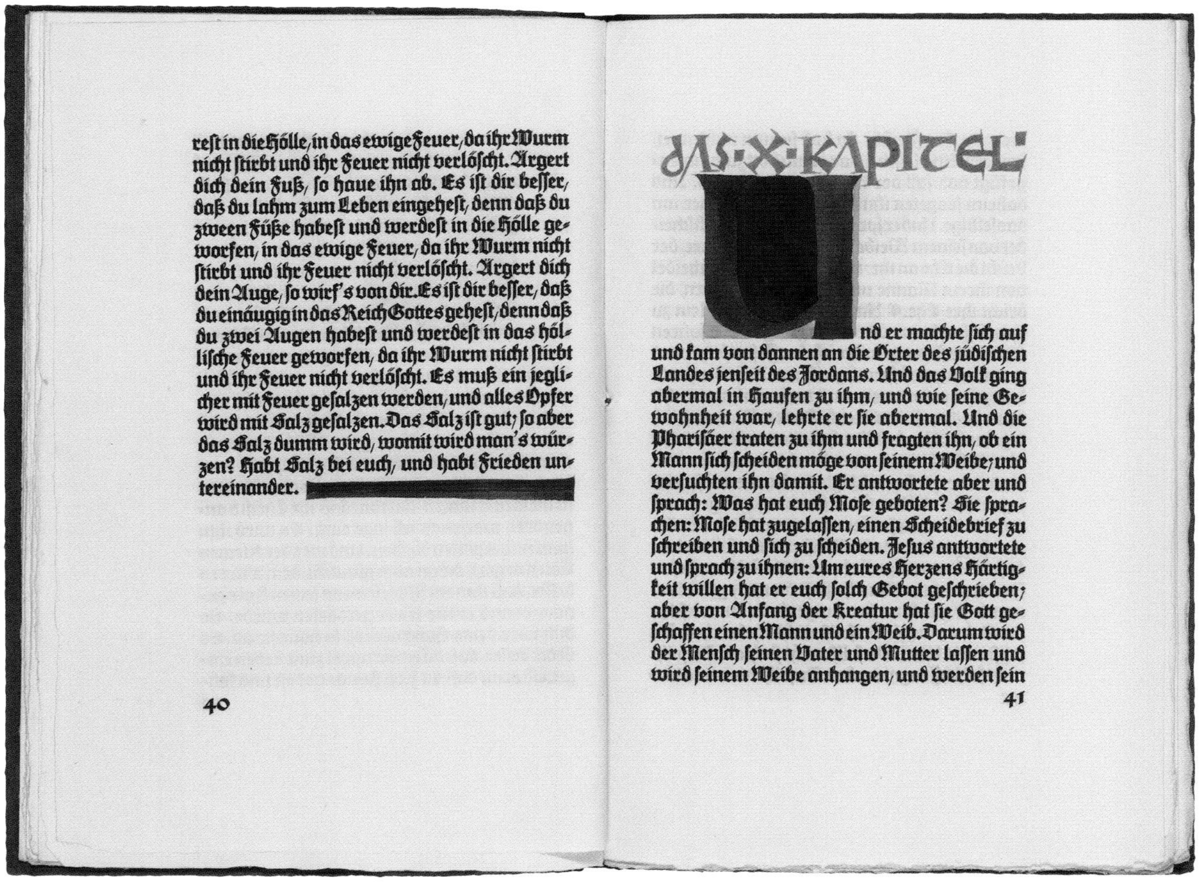

rest in die Hölle, in das ewige Feuer, da ihr Wurm nicht stirbt und ihr Feuer nicht verlöscht. Ärgert dich dein Fuß, so haue ihn ab. Es ist dir besser, daß du lahm zum Leben eingehest, denn daß du zween Füße habest und werdest in die Hölle geworfen, in das ewige Feuer, da ihr Wurm nicht stirbt und ihr Feuer nicht verlöscht. Ärgert dich dein Auge, so wirf's von dir. Es ist dir besser, daß du einäugig in das Reich Gottes gehest, denn daß du zwei Augen habest und werdest in das höllische Feuer geworfen, da ihr Wurm nicht stirbt und ihr Feuer nicht verlöscht. Es muß ein jeglicher mit Feuer gesalzen werden, und alles Opfer wird mit Salz gesalzen. Das Salz ist gut; so aber das Salz dumm wird, womit wird man's würzen? Habt Salz bei euch, und habt Frieden untereinander.

40

DAS·X·KAPITEL

Und er machte sich auf und kam von dannen an die Örter des jüdischen Landes jenseit des Jordans. Und das Volk ging abermal in Haufen zu ihm, und wie seine Gewohnheit war, lehrte er sie abermal. Und die Pharisäer traten zu ihm und fragten ihn, ob ein Mann sich scheiden möge von seinem Weibe; und versuchten ihn damit. Er antwortete aber und sprach: Was hat euch Mose geboten? Sie sprachen: Mose hat zugelassen, einen Scheidebrief zu schreiben und sich zu scheiden. Jesus antwortete und sprach zu ihnen: Um eures Herzens Härtigkeit willen hat er euch solch Gebot geschrieben; aber von Anfang der Kreatur hat sie Gott geschaffen einen Mann und ein Weib. Darum wird der Mensch seinen Vater und Mutter lassen und wird seinem Weibe anhangen, und werden sein

41

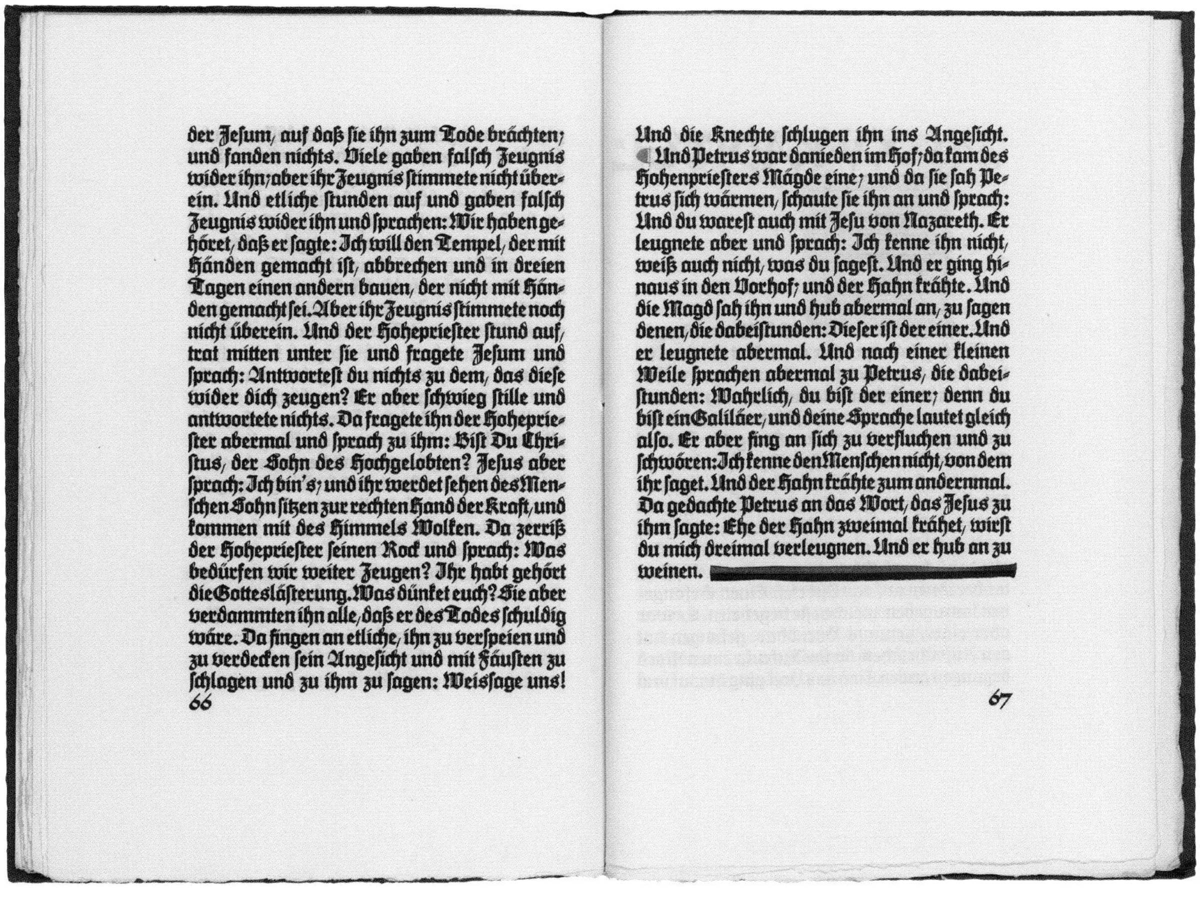

der Jesum, auf daß sie ihn zum Tode brächten; und fanden nichts. Viele gaben falsch Zeugnis wider ihn; aber ihr Zeugnis stimmete nicht überein. Und etliche stunden auf und gaben falsch Zeugnis wider ihn und sprachen: Wir haben gehöret, daß er sagte: Ich will den Tempel, der mit Händen gemacht ist, abbrechen und in dreien Tagen einen andern bauen, der nicht mit Händen gemacht sei. Aber ihr Zeugnis stimmete noch nicht überein. Und der Hohepriester stund auf, trat mitten unter sie und fragete Jesum und sprach: Antwortest du nichts zu dem, das diese wider dich zeugen? Er aber schwieg stille und antwortete nichts. Da fragete ihn der Hohepriester abermal und sprach zu ihm: Bist Du Christus, der Sohn des Hochgelobten? Jesus aber sprach: Ich bin's; und ihr werdet sehen des Menschen Sohn sitzen zur rechten Hand der Kraft, und kommen mit des Himmels Wolken. Da zerriß der Hohepriester seinen Rock und sprach: Was bedürfen wir weiter Zeugen? Ihr habt gehört die Gotteslästerung. Was dünket euch? Sie aber verdammten ihn alle, daß er des Todes schuldig wäre. Da fingen an etliche, ihn zu verspeien und zu verdecken sein Angesicht und mit Fäusten zu schlagen und zu ihm zu sagen: Weissage uns!

66

Und die Knechte schlugen ihn ins Angesicht. ¶ Und Petrus war danieden im Hof; da kam des Hohenpriesters Mägde eine; und da sie sah Petrus sich wärmen, schaute sie ihn an und sprach: Und du warest auch mit Jesu von Nazareth. Er leugnete aber und sprach: Ich kenne ihn nicht, weiß auch nicht, was du sagest. Und er ging hinaus in den Vorhof; und der Hahn krähte. Und die Magd sah ihn und hub abermal an, zu sagen denen, die dabeistunden: Dieser ist der einer. Und er leugnete abermal. Und nach einer kleinen Weile sprachen abermal zu Petrus, die dabeistunden: Wahrlich, du bist der einer; denn du bist ein Galiläer, und deine Sprache lautet gleich also. Er aber fing an sich zu verfluchen und zu schwören: Ich kenne den Menschen nicht, von dem ihr saget. Und der Hahn krähte zum andernmal. Da gedachte Petrus an das Wort, das Jesus zu ihm sagte: Ehe der Hahn zweimal krähet, wirst du mich dreimal verleugnen. Und er hub an zu weinen.

67

1924 **Francis Thibaudeau** Francis Thibaudeau, *Manuel français de typographie moderne: faisant suite à 'La lettre d'imprimerie'*. Paris: Bureau de l'édition, 1924. xvi, 583 pp. 22.5 cm. Designer: Francis Thibaudeau. Photo-engraver: Gillot, Paris. Typesetter: Deberny & Peignot, Paris. Printer: G. de Malherbe & Cie, Paris. Bookbinder: Engel, Paris.

The typographer and specialist author Francis Thibaudeau (1860–1925) left the countryside for Paris in the 1890s. For five years, he was an apprentice of Claude Motteroz, one of the largest and best-known printers in Paris of that time. Motteroz also published on the graphic arts and had designed a typeface based on a legibility study. In 1900, Thibaudeau began working for the Parisian typefoundry Peignot, where he was in charge of the composing room. He worked at the firm until his death.

In addition to his work at the typefoundry, which would eventually operate under the name Deberny & Peignot, Thibaudeau wrote two books in the period 1915–24. These were hefty volumes: *La lettre d'imprimerie* from 1921, which contained Thibaudeau's system for classifying typefaces, and the *Manuel français de typographie moderne* from 1924. The former was dedicated to George Auriol, 'innovateur français de l'écriture typographiée', the latter to (among others) Eugène Grasset. These artists were leading figures in French Art Nouveau, and Deberny & Peignot sold typefaces designed by them.

The *Manuel* is a typesetter's manual which pays ample attention to design. It covers the practical aspects of typesetting, the history and form of typefaces, and various design styles for things such as book covers and other kinds of small printed matter. Towards the end of the book, Thibaudeau discusses and illustrates the method he developed for making detailed typographical sketches. The *Manuel* still breathes the spirit of Art Nouveau, with a title page that uses 'typographie des groupes', line-filling ornaments at the end of paragraphs, and Auriol as the text face. ML

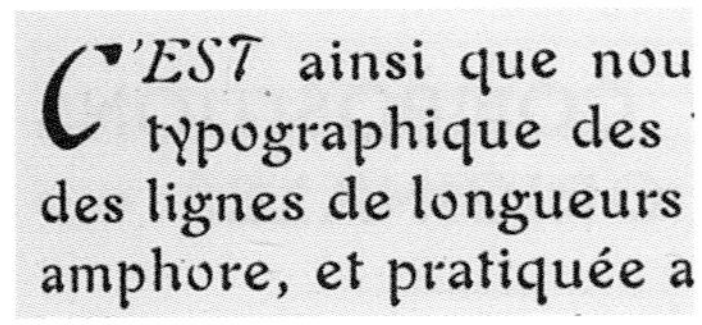
C'EST ainsi que nou
typographique des
des lignes de longueurs
amphore, et pratiquée a

The illustrator, graphic designer, and writer, George Auriol (1863–1938), designed several typefaces for G. Peignot & Fils in Paris. This Auriol, dating from 1902 and named after its designer, clearly has Japanese influences. Eugène Parmentier cut the punches, as he had earlier, for the Art Nouveau typeface Grasset.

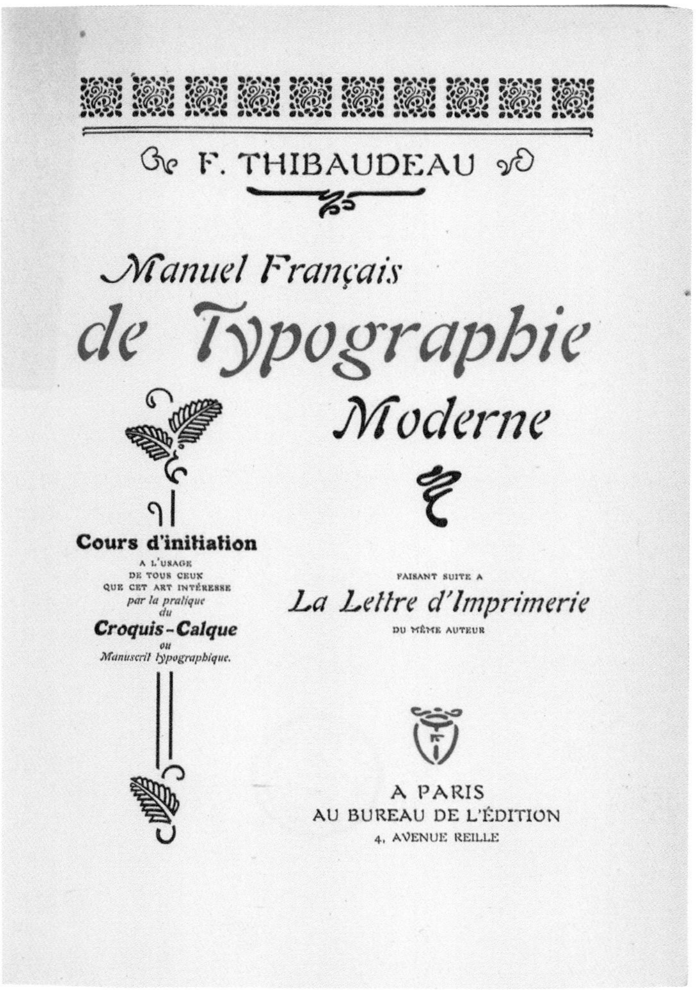

F. THIBAUDEAU

Manuel Français
de Typographie
Moderne

Cours d'initiation
A L'USAGE
DE TOUS CEUX
QUE CET ART INTÉRESSE
par la pratique
du
Croquis-Calque
ou
Manuscrit typographique.

FAISANT SUITE A
La Lettre d'Imprimerie
DU MÊME AUTEUR

A PARIS
AU BUREAU DE L'ÉDITION
4, AVENUE REILLE

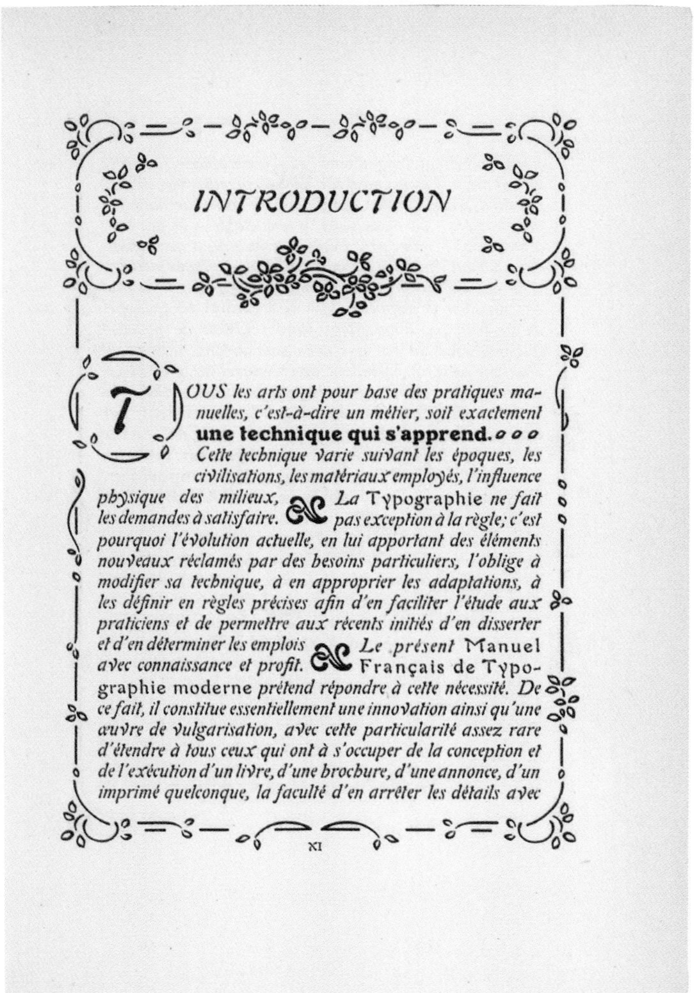

INTRODUCTION

TOUS les arts ont pour base des pratiques manuelles, c'est-à-dire un métier, soit exactement **une technique qui s'apprend.** *Cette technique varie suivant les époques, les civilisations, les matériaux employés, l'influence physique des milieux, les demandes à satisfaire. La* Typographie *ne fait pas exception à la règle; c'est pourquoi l'évolution actuelle, en lui apportant des éléments nouveaux réclamés par des besoins particuliers, l'oblige à modifier sa technique, à en approprier les adaptations, à les définir en règles précises afin d'en faciliter l'étude aux praticiens et de permettre aux récents initiés d'en disserter et d'en déterminer les emplois avec connaissance et profit. Le présent* Manuel Français de Typographie moderne *prétend répondre à cette nécessité. De ce fait, il constitue essentiellement une innovation ainsi qu'une œuvre de vulgarisation, avec cette particularité assez rare d'étendre à tous ceux qui ont à s'occuper de la conception et de l'exécution d'un livre, d'une brochure, d'une annonce, d'un imprimé quelconque, la faculté d'en arrêter les détails avec*

XI

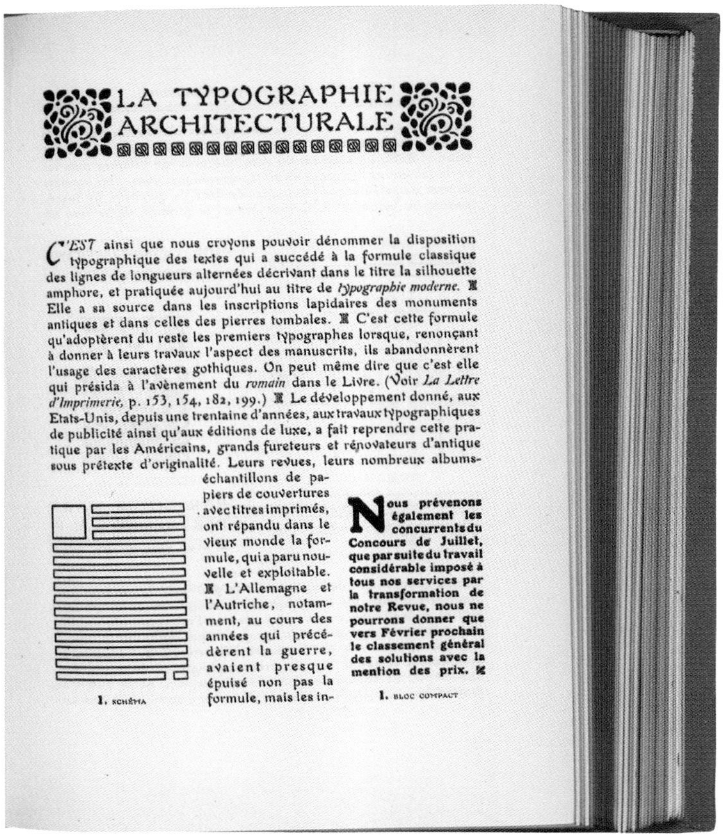

LA TYPOGRAPHIE ARCHITECTURALE

C'EST ainsi que nous croyons pouvoir dénommer la disposition typographique des textes qui a succédé à la formule classique des lignes de longueurs alternées décrivant dans le titre la silhouette amphore, et pratiquée aujourd'hui au titre de *typographie moderne.* Elle a sa source dans les inscriptions lapidaires des monuments antiques et dans celles des pierres tombales. C'est cette formule qu'adoptèrent du reste les premiers typographes lorsque, renonçant à donner à leurs travaux l'aspect des manuscrits, ils abandonnèrent l'usage des caractères gothiques. On peut même dire que c'est elle qui présida à l'avènement du *romain* dans le Livre. (Voir *La Lettre d'Imprimerie,* p. 153, 154, 182, 199.) Le développement donné, aux Etats-Unis, depuis une trentaine d'années, aux travaux typographiques de publicité ainsi qu'aux éditions de luxe, a fait reprendre cette pratique par les Américains, grands fureteurs et rénovateurs d'antique sous prétexte d'originalité. Leurs revues, leurs nombreux albums-échantillons de papiers de couvertures avec titres imprimés, ont répandu dans le vieux monde la formule, qui a paru nouvelle et exploitable. L'Allemagne et l'Autriche, notamment, au cours des années qui précédèrent la guerre, avaient presque épuisé non pas la formule, mais les in-

1. SCHÉMA

Nous prévenons également les concurrents du Concours de Juillet, que par suite du travail considérable imposé à tous nos services par la transformation de notre Revue, nous ne pourrons donner que vers Février prochain le classement général des solutions avec la mention des prix.

1. BLOC COMPACT

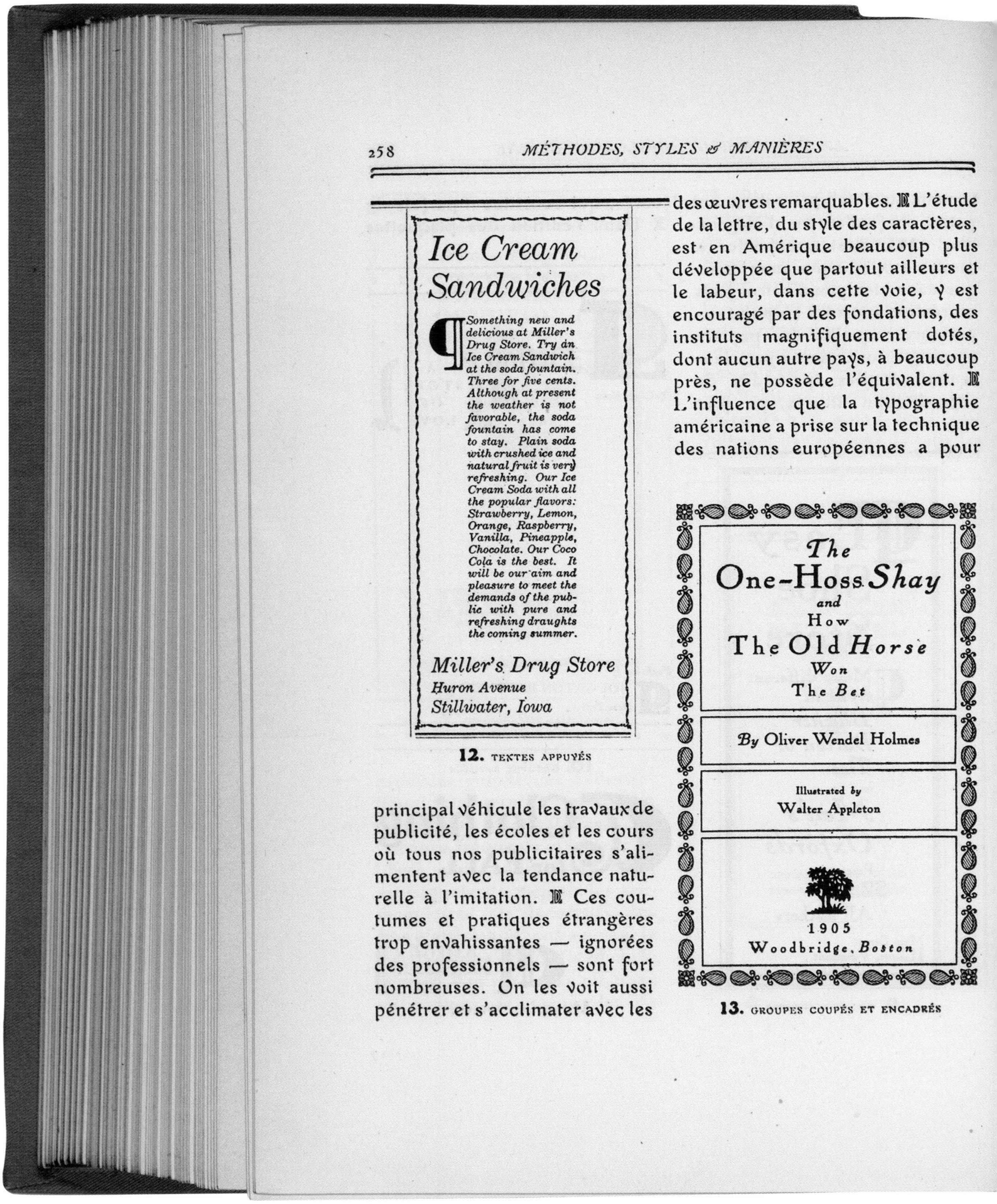

258 MÉTHODES, STYLES & MANIÈRES

Ice Cream Sandwiches

¶ Something new and delicious at Miller's Drug Store. Try an Ice Cream Sandwich at the soda fountain. Three for five cents. Although at present the weather is not favorable, the soda fountain has come to stay. Plain soda with crushed ice and natural fruit is very refreshing. Our Ice Cream Soda with all the popular flavors: Strawberry, Lemon, Orange, Raspberry, Vanilla, Pineapple, Chocolate. Our Coco Cola is the best. It will be our aim and pleasure to meet the demands of the public with pure and refreshing draughts the coming summer.

Miller's Drug Store
Huron Avenue
Stillwater, Iowa

12. TEXTES APPUYÉS

des œuvres remarquables. ❧ L'étude de la lettre, du style des caractères, est en Amérique beaucoup plus développée que partout ailleurs et le labeur, dans cette voie, y est encouragé par des fondations, des instituts magnifiquement dotés, dont aucun autre pays, à beaucoup près, ne possède l'équivalent. ❧ L'influence que la typographie américaine a prise sur la technique des nations européennes a pour principal véhicule les travaux de publicité, les écoles et les cours où tous nos publicitaires s'alimentent avec la tendance naturelle à l'imitation. ❧ Ces coutumes et pratiques étrangères trop envahissantes — ignorées des professionnels — sont fort nombreuses. On les voit aussi pénétrer et s'acclimater avec les

The
One-Hoss *Shay*
and
How
The Old *Horse*
Won
The *Bet*

By Oliver Wendel Holmes

Illustrated *by*
Walter Appleton

1905
Woodbridge, *Boston*

13. GROUPES COUPÉS ET ENCADRÉS

instructions sur les objets d'importation comme les machines à écrire, les machines à composer et autres appareils graphiques d'invention américaine. ¶ Certaines d'entre elles sont souvent anti-professionnelles, notamment la *mode* innovée ces dernières années dans la papeterie commerciale et industrielle, qui prouve peut-être plus que toute autre l'intervention dans son lancement de non-techniciens

14. GROUPES COUPÉS ET ENCADRÉS

15. FONDS DE VIGNETTES

de l'imprimerie, nous voulons parler de l'encadrement des têtes-de-lettres et factures à la façon des tableaux, à l'aide de filets ou de bordures variées imprimées à l'extrême limite des marges. ¶ Quand on connaît les difficultés d'exécution que comporte cette fantaisie, les tours de mains que suppose sa réussite, on peut affirmer que ce n'est pas un professionnel

1925 **Theo van Doesburg & Käte Steinitz** Kurt Schwitters, *Die Scheuche: Märchen*. Hanover: Apossverlag, 1925.

12 pp. 21 x 25 cm. Designers: Theo van Doesburg, Käte Steinitz. Typesetter: Paul Vogt (Peuvag). Printer: Peuvag, Hanover.

The two artists Theo van Doesburg (1883–1931) and Kurt Schwitters (1887–1948) were close friends. They had performed together during a Dada tour of Holland, at the beginning of the 1920s. During these gatherings, van Doesburg would read his manifesto, *Wat is Dada*? (What is Dada?), and he would be frequently interrupted by a barking, croaking, and hissing Schwitters, sitting at the back of the auditorium. Both of them worked as graphic designers, although van Doesburg only did so occasionally, while it was a major source of income for Schwitters. From 1924 onwards, he owned an advertising agency in Hanover, Merz Werbezentrale. Ink manufacturer Pelican was an important client.

Schwitters published illustrated fairy tales with his neighbour and friend Käte Steinitz (1889–1975). When van Doesburg visited his friend in 1925 and saw their work, he reacted enthusiastically. Perhaps the three of them could collaborate on a similar but more radical book that was completely typographical? An example of this was *Dlja golosa*, designed by El Lissitzky (see page 314), which had been published two years before. Like *Dlja golosa*, *Die Scheuche* ('The Scarecrow') was built up almost exclusively from material from the type case. The text was written by Schwitters. The character of the 'Bauer' (farmer) is depicted with a bold, sans serif B, with rules for the limbs and perpendicular b's for feet, thus creating unity between text and image. Although the cover mentions all three of them as typographers, the typography should mainly be attributed to van Doesburg.

In the age of metal type, printing was entirely based on rectangles. Oblique positioning of elements, which frequently occurs in *Die Scheuche*, was complicated. For that reason, the back cover credits the compositor by name. ML

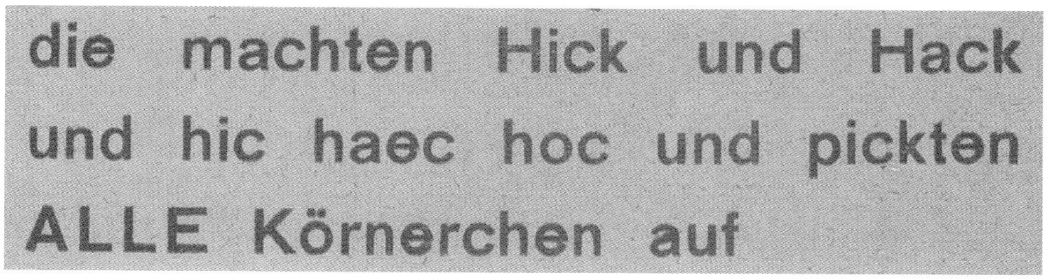
die machten Hick und Hack
und hic haec hoc und pickten
ALLE Körnerchen auf

An unidentified sans serif of the style introduced by many typefoundries in the 1900–10 period. It does not exactly match Berthold's Akzidenz-Grotesk, Stempel's Reform-Grotesk, Bauer's Venus – all German designs – or Antieke by the Dutch Typefoundry Amsterdam.

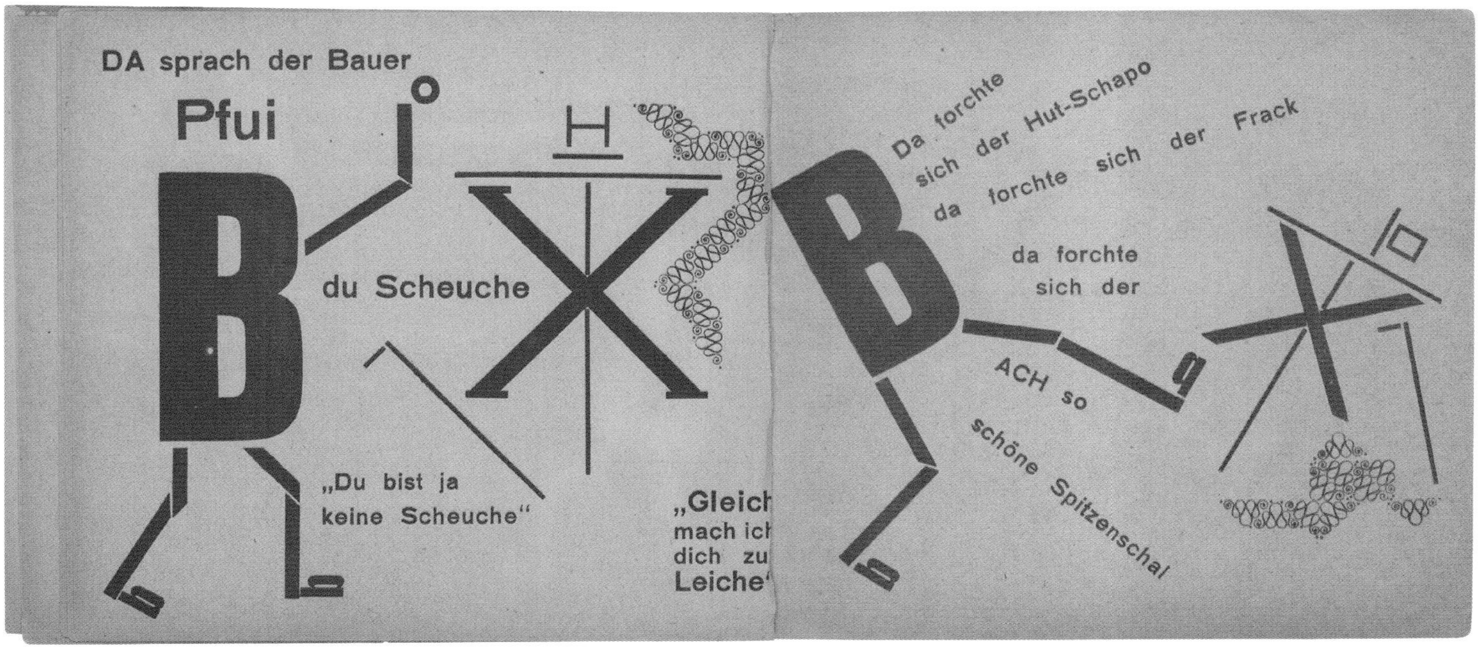

1926 **Karel Teige** **Vítězslav Nezval, *Abeceda*. Prague: J. Otto, 1926. 57 pp. 30 cm. Designer: Karel Teige. Choreographer: Milča Mayerová. Photographer: Karel Paspa.**

Abeceda (Alphabet) is a collective artwork, created by Devětsil. This Czech avant-garde group, active between 1920 and 1931, consisted of architects, painters, writers, photographers, and performing artists. Karel Teige (1900–51) was one of the founders and the group's main theoretician and spokesman. Since the twenties he had been working as a book designer and he was well acquainted with recent developments in Russian Constructivism and at the Bauhaus.

Abeceda was an expression of the Devětsil group's so called 'Poetism', to which Teige had devoted an essay in 1924. Poetism's aim was a playful, entertaining and optimistic kind of art, intended for the streets rather than for museums. Poetism used experimental forms such as visual poetry, which were more appropriate to this new art than the usual paintings and poems. In *Abeceda*, Teige orchestrated a combination of poetry and image (photomontage). He had worked with the poet Nezval before.

The third participant in the *Abeceda* project was choreographer-dancer Milča Mayerová (1901–77), whose name is credited on the cover. Her dance compositions for Nezval's poems consisted of three to four poses for each quatrain, ranging from playful to provocative. Mayerová was probably the one who suggested publication, since the book was beyond the usual scope of its publishing house, Otto, which was owned by her family. The studio photographs show Mayerová, who gives the impression of a confident and modern woman, posing in glossy gym shorts and singlet with a matching cap. With these montages of poetry and photography, Karel Teige created a cheerful typo-photo book. ML

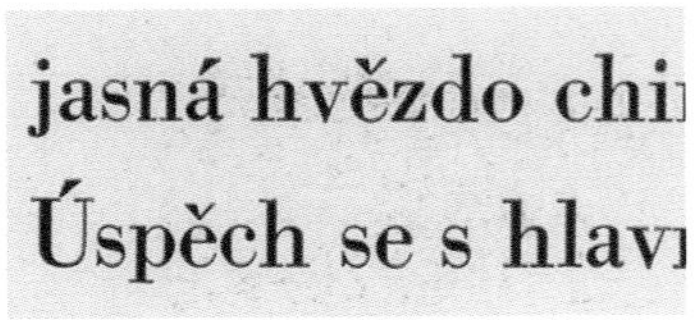

This version of Bodoni is an adaptation of the types cut by Giambattista Bodoni (1740–1813). Many Bodoni revivals were issued in the twentieth century; Morris F. Benton's, dating from 1909 for American Type Founders, was frequently copied. Bodoni remained popular with modernists, including Massimo Vignelli.

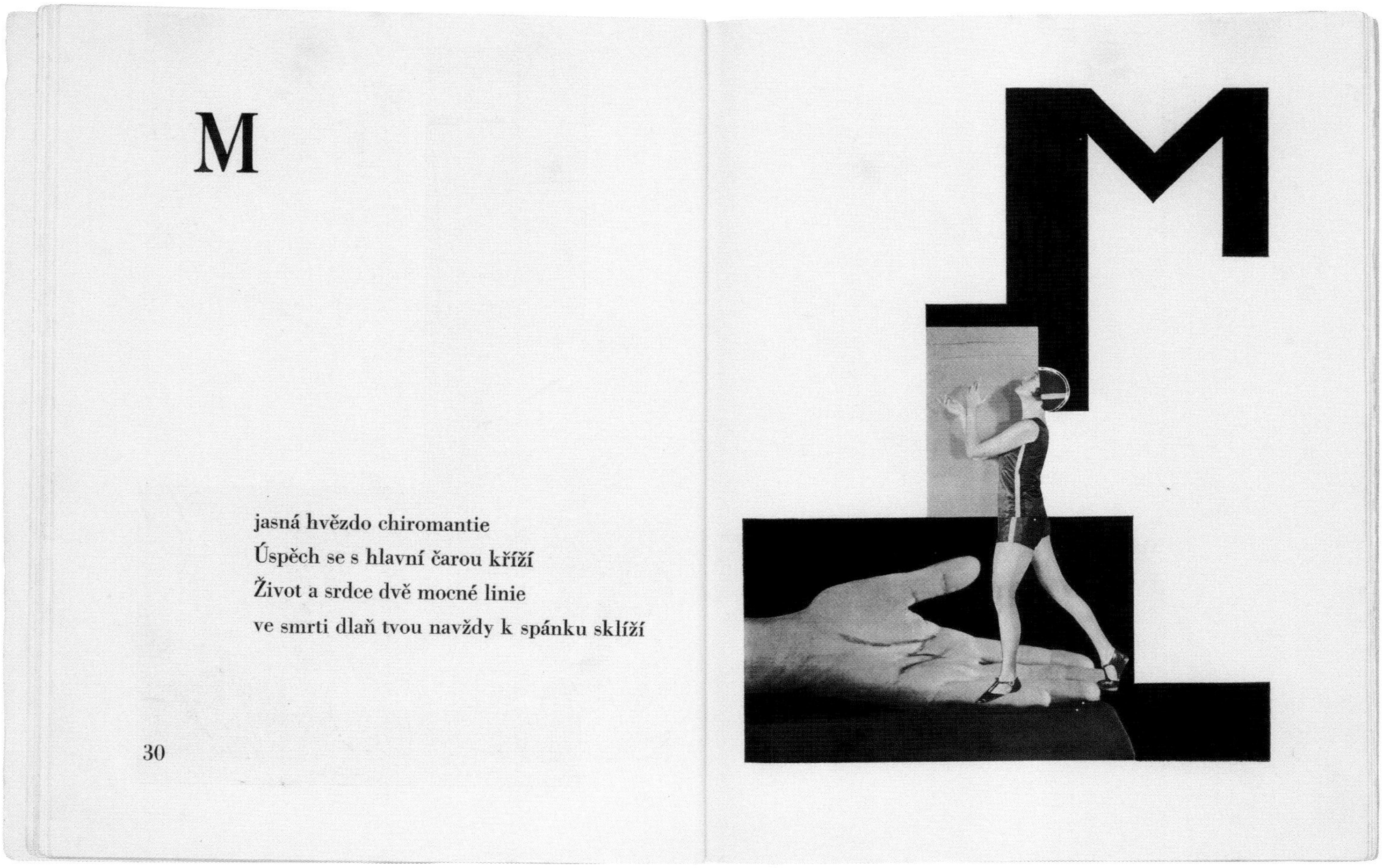

M

jasná hvězdo chiromantie
Úspěch se s hlavní čarou kříží
Život a srdce dvě mocné linie
ve smrti dlaň tvou navždy k spánku sklíží

30

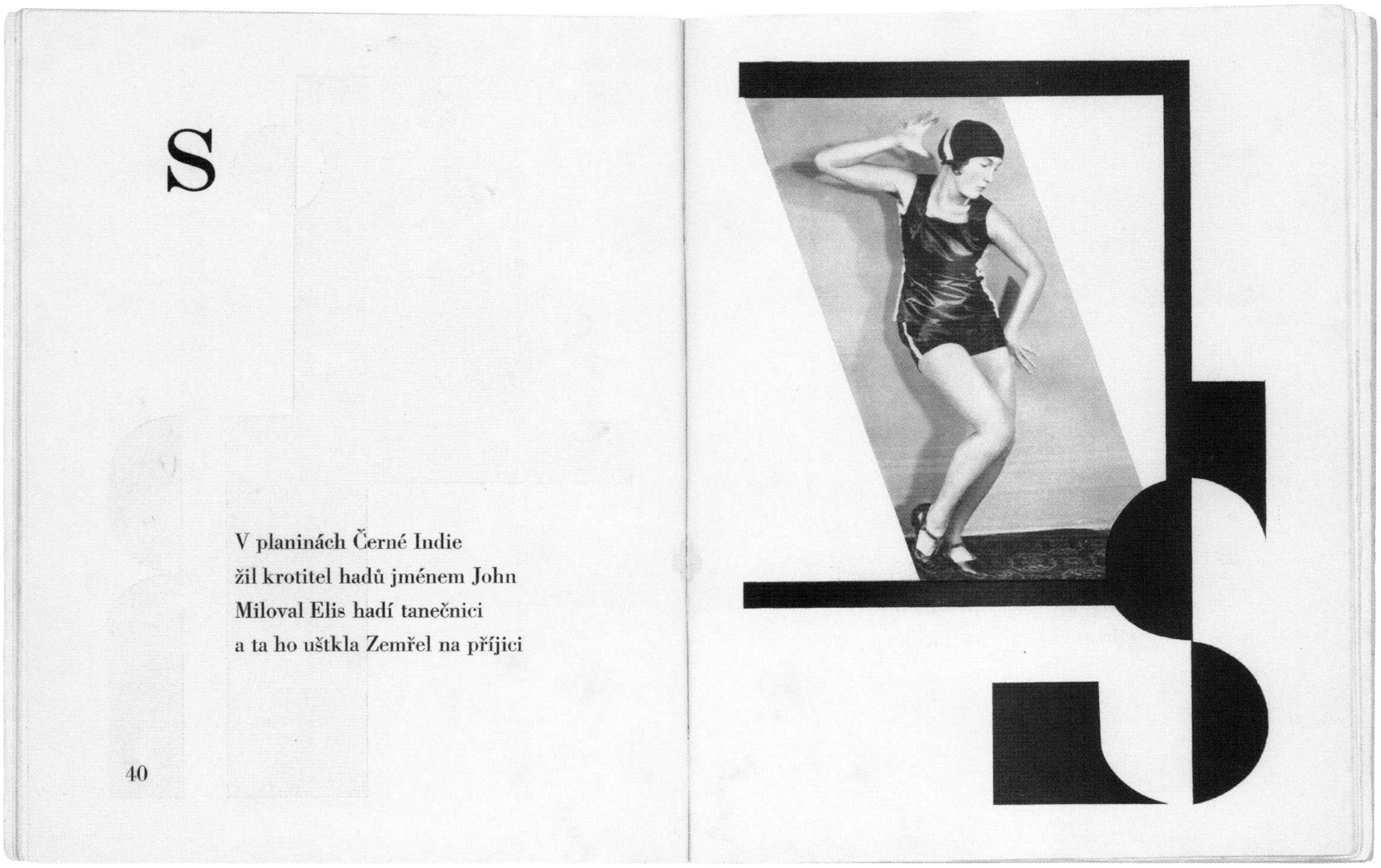

S

V planinách Černé Indie
žil krotitel hadů jménem John
Miloval Elis hadí tanečnici
a ta ho uštkla Zemřel na příjici

40

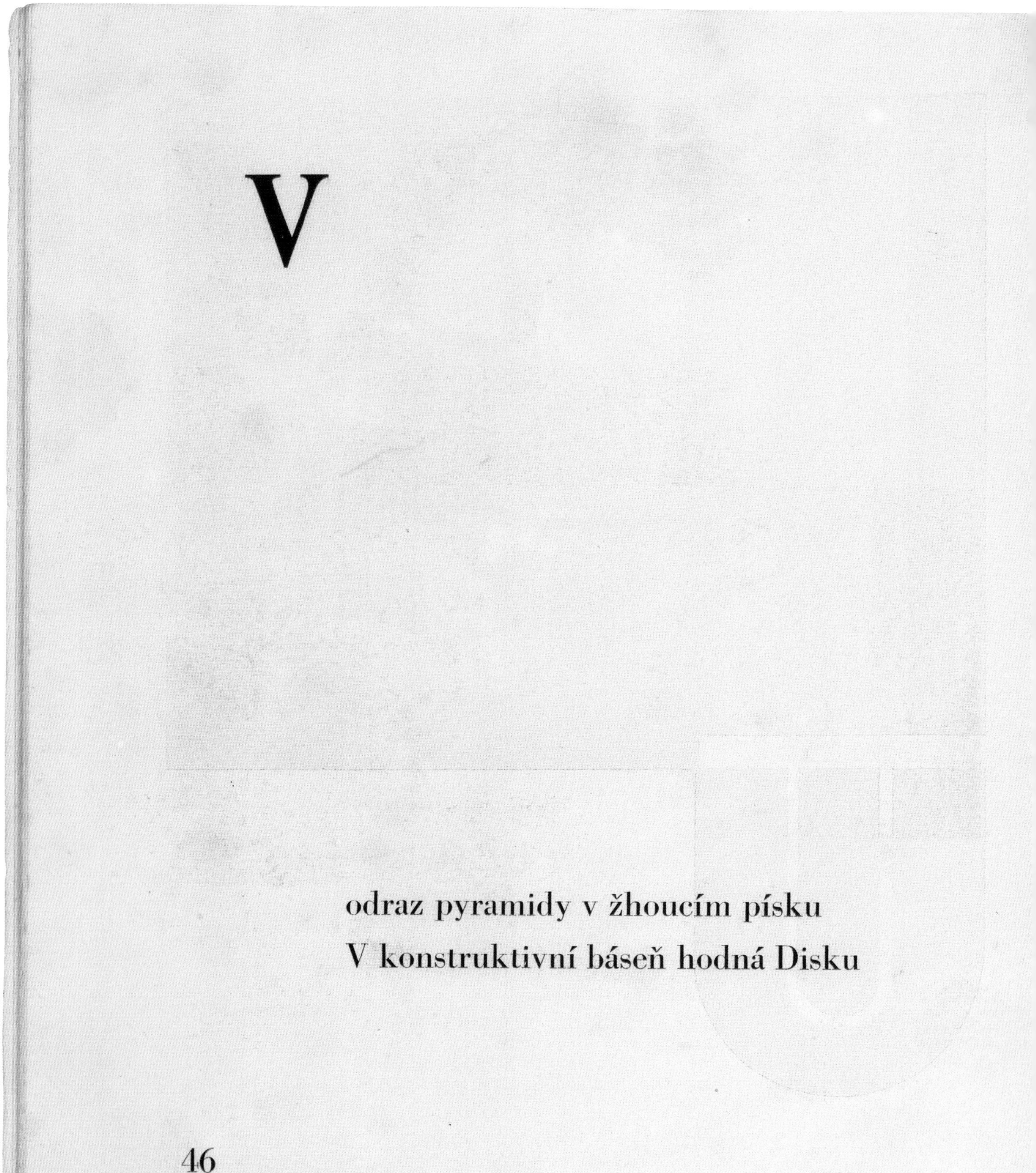

V

odraz pyramidy v žhoucím písku
V konstruktivní báseň hodná Disku

46

1927 **H. N. Werkman** Johan Dijkstra, *De Ploeg Groningen Holland 1927*. Groningen: De Ploeg, 1927. 26 pp. 37 cm.

Designer & printer: H. N. Werkman, Groningen.

Hendrik Werkman (1882–1945) was a part-time artist who owned a commercial printing firm in the provincial town of Groningen. He had no talent for business and his firm barely escaped bankruptcy in 1926–27. He was a painter, and had been a founder member of De Ploeg (The Plough), a group of artists influenced by German Expressionism. Werkman was also impressed by the abstract work of De Stijl; he visited a De Stijl exhibition in Groningen in 1922.

In 1923, Werkman began to use his firm's hand press to make artist's prints, graphic compositions in various techniques (later including stencilling), utilizing materials from the composing room as well as other objects. In this period he started publishing *The Next Call* (1923–26), which had an international distribution although its print run was small. In this magazine, which mainly contains texts written by Werkman, wood type and numerals are used autonomously. Werkman's print work at this time was orientated towards the Constructivist avant-garde. Werkman also printed and designed posters, invitations and catalogues for De Ploeg. *De Ploeg Groningen Holland 1927*, shown here, contains black-and-white reproductions of work by the members and a manifesto in German by painter Johan Dijkstra, typographically interpreted by Werkman.

Werkman's famous *Chassidische legenden* ('Hassidic Legends') was produced during the German occupation of the Netherlands. Werkman was arrested by the Nazis in 1945, when the war was almost over, and was executed by firing squad some weeks later; the occupying forces may have suspected him of producing illegal printed matter. Willem Sandberg, designer and museum director, made significant efforts to establish Werkman's reputation. ML

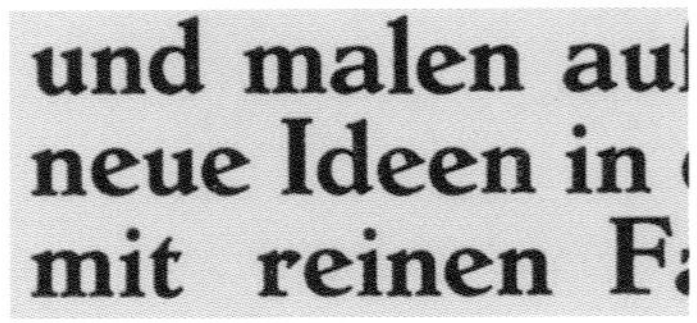

Hollandse Mediæval (1912, Intertype Medieval) by S.H. de Roos (1877–1962) was the most popular typeface in the Netherlands during the first half of the twentieth century. A Jenson revival with German influences, it was used for books and commercial printing, and was issued by Typefoundry Amsterdam.

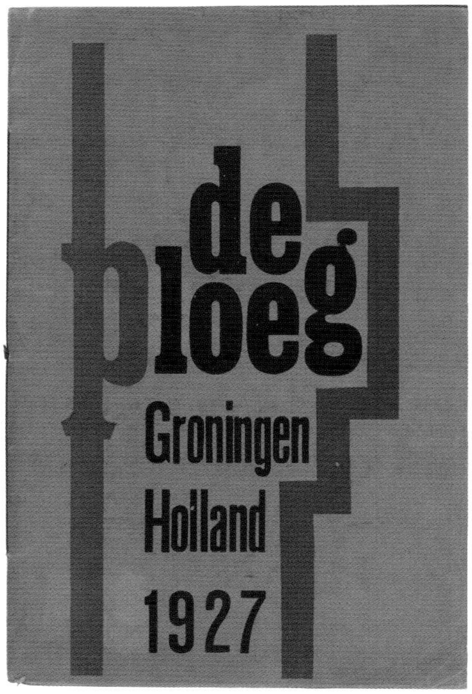

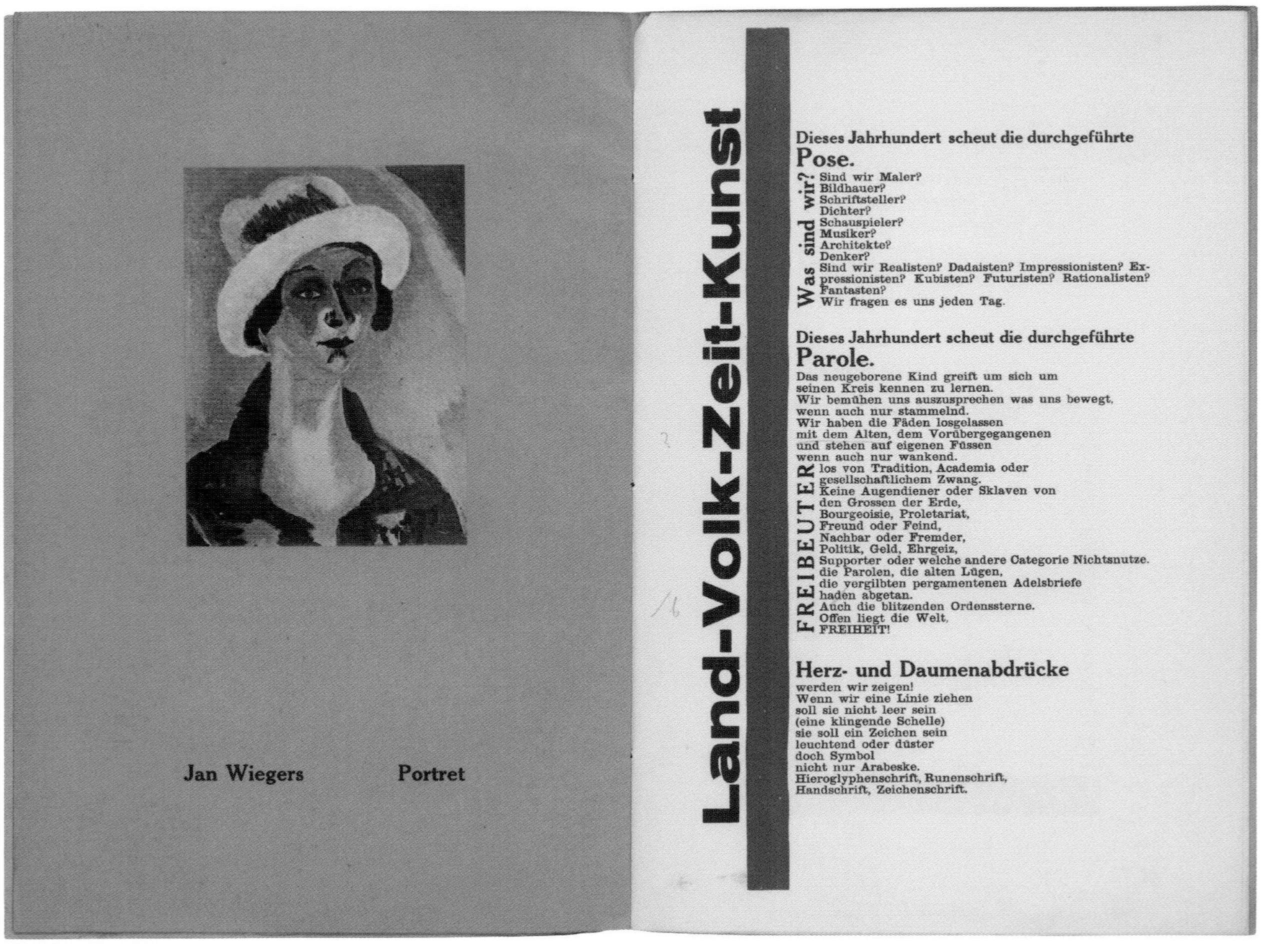

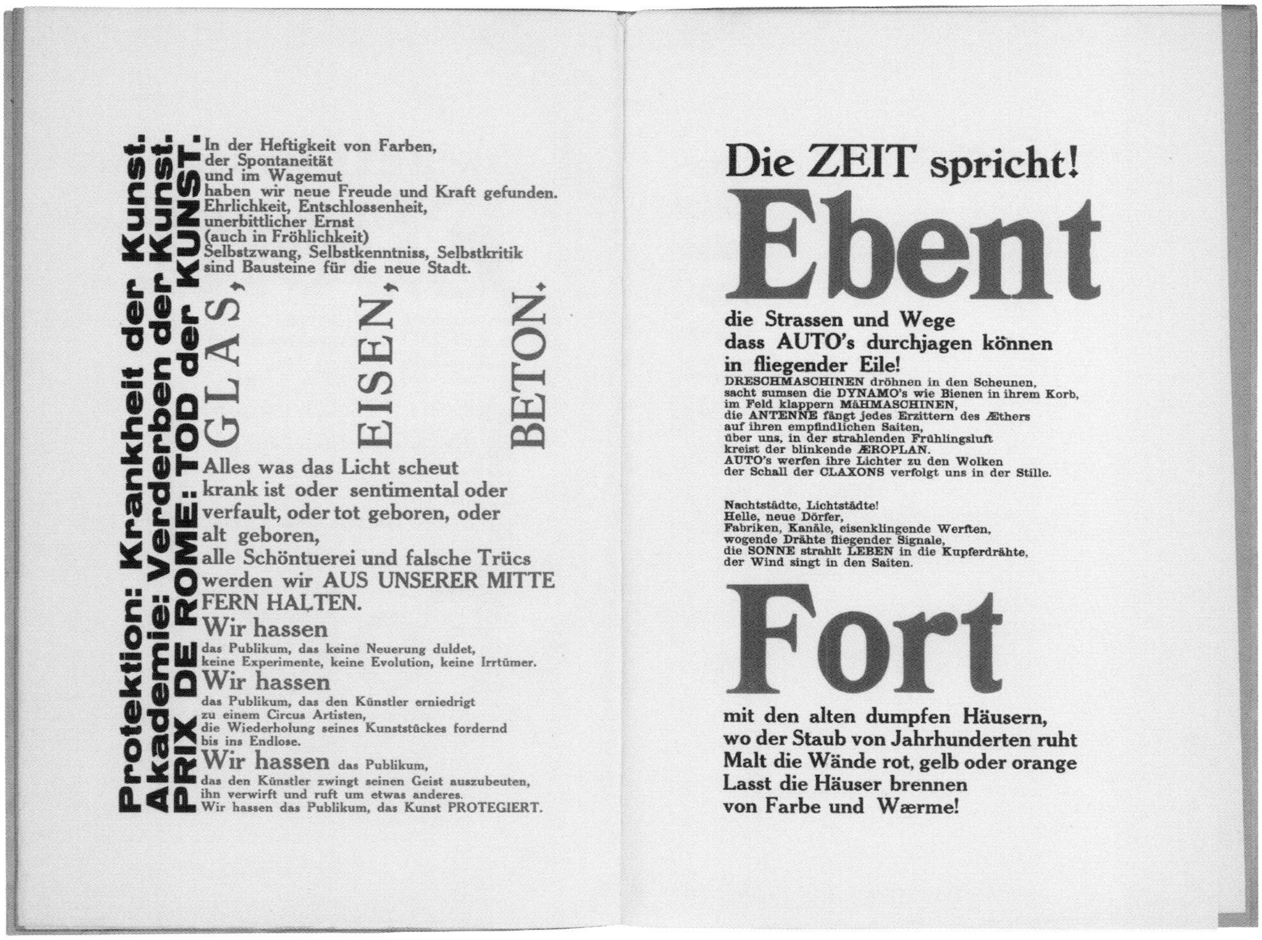

Protektion: Krankheit der Kunst.
Akademie: Verderben der Kunst.
PRIX DE ROME: TOD der KUNST.

In der Heftigkeit von Farben,
der Spontaneität
und im Wagemut
haben wir neue Freude und Kraft gefunden.
Ehrlichkeit, Entschlossenheit,
unerbittlicher Ernst
(auch in Fröhlichkeit)
Selbstzwang, Selbstkenntniss, Selbstkritik
sind Bausteine für die neue Stadt.

GLAS, EISEN, BETON.

Alles was das Licht scheut
krank ist oder sentimental oder
verfault, oder tot geboren, oder
alt geboren,
alle Schöntuerei und falsche Trücs
werden wir AUS UNSERER MITTE
FERN HALTEN.
Wir hassen
das Publikum, das keine Neuerung duldet,
keine Experimente, keine Evolution, keine Irrtümer.
Wir hassen
das Publikum, das den Künstler erniedrigt
zu einem Circus Artisten,
die Wiederholung seines Kunststückes fordernd
bis ins Endlose.
Wir hassen das Publikum,
das den Künstler zwingt seinen Geist auszubeuten,
ihn verwirft und ruft um etwas anderes.
Wir hassen das Publikum, das Kunst PROTEGIERT.

Die ZEIT spricht!
Ebent
die Strassen und Wege
dass AUTO's durchjagen können
in fliegender Eile!
DRESCHMASCHINEN dröhnen in den Scheunen,
sacht sumsen die DYNAMO's wie Bienen in ihrem Korb,
im Feld klappern MÄHMASCHINEN,
die ANTENNE fängt jedes Erzittern des Æthers
auf ihren empfindlichen Saiten,
über uns, in der strahlenden Frühlingsluft
kreist der blinkende ÆROPLAN.
AUTO's werfen ihre Lichter zu den Wolken
der Schall der CLAXONS verfolgt uns in der Stille.

Nachtstädte, Lichtstädte!
Helle, neue Dörfer,
Fabriken, Kanäle, eisenklingende Werften,
wogende Drähte fliegender Signale,
die SONNE strahlt LEBEN in die Kupferdrähte,
der Wind singt in den Saiten.

Fort
mit den alten dumpfen Häusern,
wo der Staub von Jahrhunderten ruht
Malt die Wände rot, gelb oder orange
Lasst die Häuser brennen
von Farbe und Wærme!

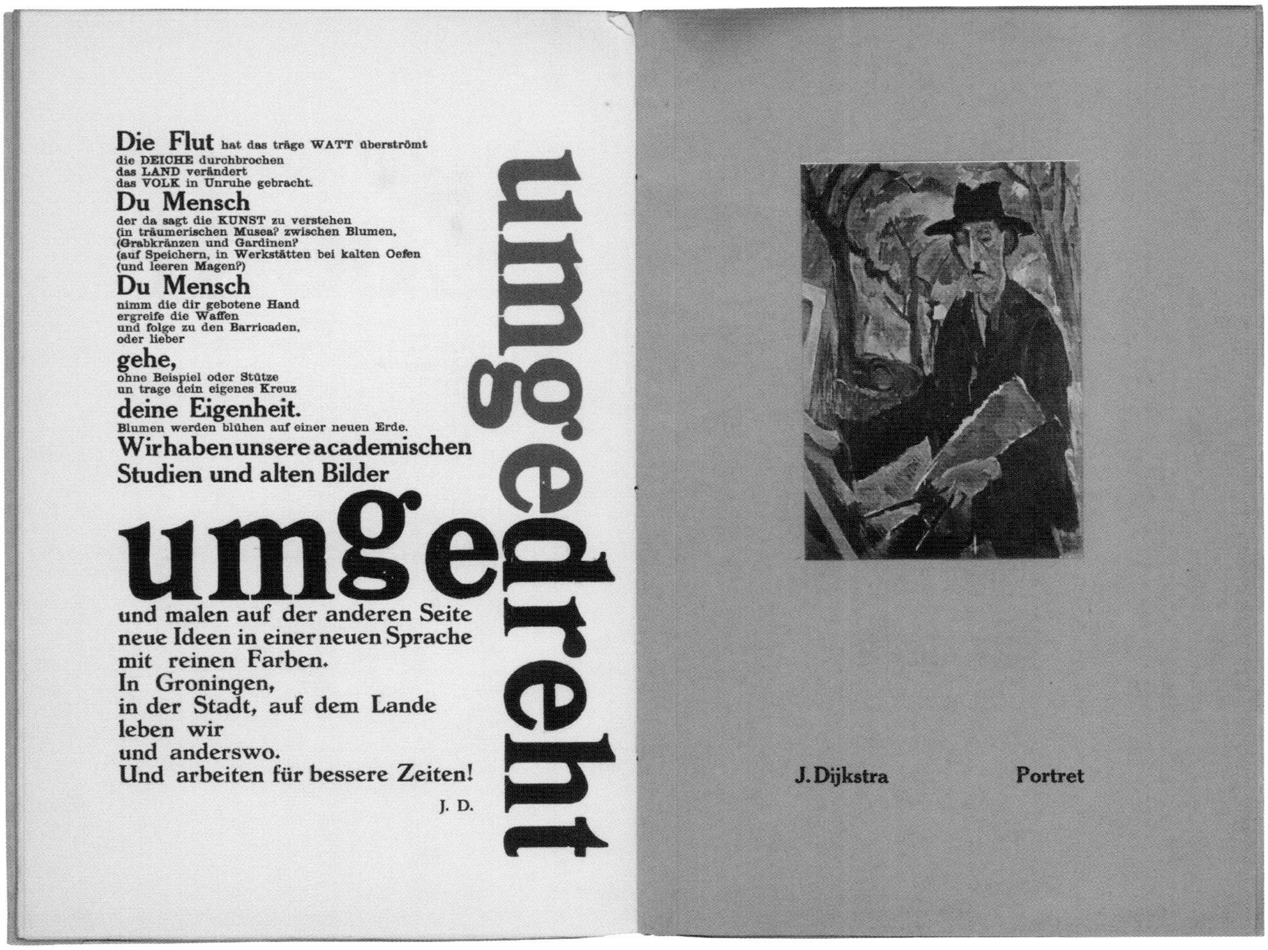

Die Flut hat das träge WATT überströmt
die DEICHE durchbrochen
das LAND verändert
das VOLK in Unruhe gebracht.
Du Mensch
der da sagt die KUNST zu verstehen
(in träumerischen Musea? zwischen Blumen,
(Grabkränzen und Gardinen?
(auf Speichern, in Werkstätten bei kalten Oefen
(und leeren Magen?)
Du Mensch
nimm die dir gebotene Hand
ergreife die Waffen
und folge zu den Barricaden,
oder lieber
gehe,
ohne Beispiel oder Stütze
un trage dein eigenes Kreuz
deine Eigenheit.
Blumen werden blühen auf einer neuen Erde.
Wirhabenunsereacademischen
Studien und alten Bilder
umge
umgedreht
und malen auf der anderen Seite
neue Ideen in einer neuen Sprache
mit reinen Farben.
In Groningen,
in der Stadt, auf dem Lande
leben wir
und anderswo.
Und arbeiten für bessere Zeiten!
J. D.

J. Dijkstra Portret

1928 **W. A. Dwiggins** W. A. Dwiggins, *Layout in Advertising*. New York, London: Harper and Brothers, 1928. 200 pp. 23.5 cm. Designer & illustrator: W. A. Dwiggins.

W. A. Dwiggins (1880–1956) – also known as Dwig or WAD – was trained as an illustrator in Chicago, where one of his teachers was type designer Frederic Goudy. As his private press did not bring in much money, Dwiggins started working as an advertising illustrator and specialized in hand-drawn lettering. At the beginning of the twenties, after being diagnosed as a diabetic, he decided to devote more time to things that he considered worthwhile, and designing, decorating and illustrating books became his main activity. His work for publisher Alfred A. Knopf became well-known; particularly his stencilled Art Deco decorations and distinctive lettering style.

Dwiggins, who had a versatile pen, has many publications to his name. (The term 'graphic designer' reputedly found general acceptance after he used it in 1922.) He believed that advertising should not just seduce, but inform as well. In this 1928 manual, *Layout in Advertising*, he hoped to offer a method of design rather than ready-made solutions. Contrary to what the title suggests, the book offers a broad introduction to the field of graphic design. It is illustrated with specially produced drawings by Dwiggins. A revised edition appeared in 1948, and *Layout in Advertising* remained the dominant manual in the field throughout the fifties.

As a result of Dwiggins's remark in *Layout in Advertising* that there was a need for a good sans serif type, composing-machine manufacturer Mergenthaler Linotype asked him to design one for them. In January 1930, Metro was published. It was followed by, among others, the typefaces Electra (1935) and Caledonia (1939). Dwiggins was most influential as a type designer and a lettering artist. ML

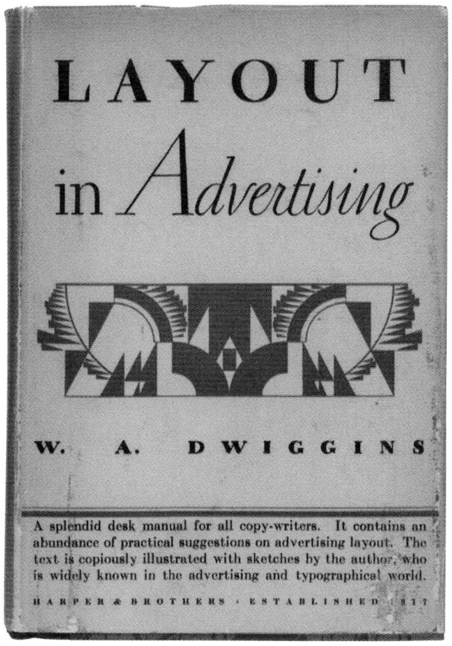

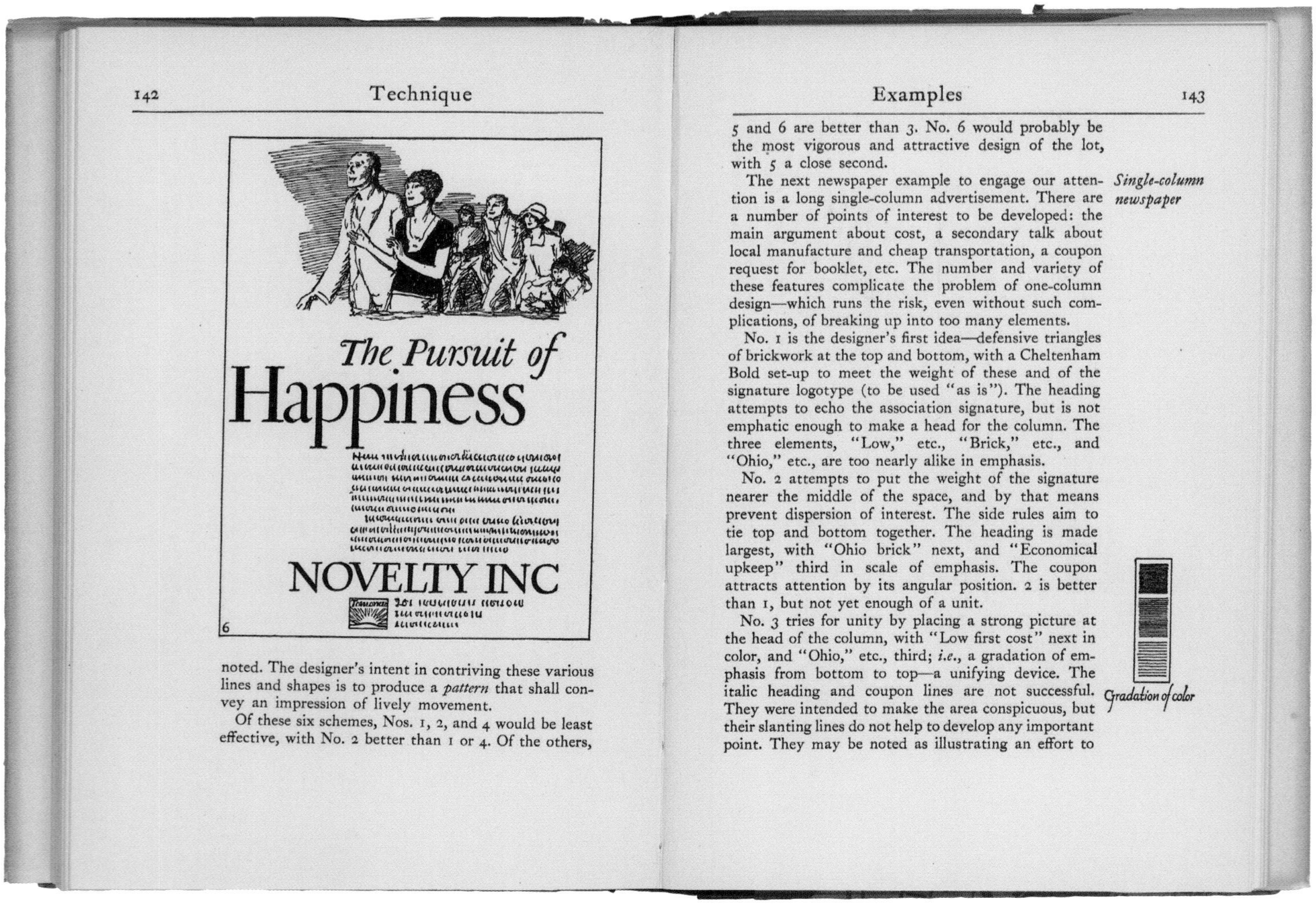
142 Technique

noted. The designer's intent in contriving these various lines and shapes is to produce a *pattern* that shall convey an impression of lively movement.

Of these six schemes, Nos. 1, 2, and 4 would be least effective, with No. 2 better than 1 or 4. Of the others,

Examples 143

5 and 6 are better than 3. No. 6 would probably be the most vigorous and attractive design of the lot, with 5 a close second.

The next newspaper example to engage our attention is a long single-column advertisement. There are a number of points of interest to be developed: the main argument about cost, a secondary talk about local manufacture and cheap transportation, a coupon request for booklet, etc. The number and variety of these features complicate the problem of one-column design—which runs the risk, even without such complications, of breaking up into too many elements. *Single-column newspaper*

No. 1 is the designer's first idea—defensive triangles of brickwork at the top and bottom, with a Cheltenham Bold set-up to meet the weight of these and of the signature logotype (to be used "as is"). The heading attempts to echo the association signature, but is not emphatic enough to make a head for the column. The three elements, "Low," etc., "Brick," etc., and "Ohio," etc., are too nearly alike in emphasis.

No. 2 attempts to put the weight of the signature nearer the middle of the space, and by that means prevent dispersion of interest. The side rules aim to tie top and bottom together. The heading is made largest, with "Ohio brick" next, and "Economical upkeep" third in scale of emphasis. The coupon attracts attention by its angular position. 2 is better than 1, but not yet enough of a unit.

No. 3 tries for unity by placing a strong picture at the head of the column, with "Low first cost" next in color, and "Ohio," etc., third; *i.e.*, a gradation of emphasis from bottom to top—a unifying device. The italic heading and coupon lines are not successful. They were intended to make the area conspicuous, but their slanting lines do not help to develop any important point. They may be noted as illustrating an effort to *Gradation of color*

The next newspaper example to engage our attention is a long single-column advertisement. There are a number of points of interest to be developed: the main argument about cost, a secondary talk about local manufacture and cheap transportation, a coupon request for booklet, etc. The number and variety of

Linotype Caslon Old Face (with short descenders) is used alongside the mostly marginal headings in Frederic Goudy's American Monotype Garamont; both typefaces were apparently issued in 1923. Caslon Old Face is Linotype's closest copy of William Caslon's types cut in c. 1730. The Garamont follows Jean Jannon's types (1615–21).

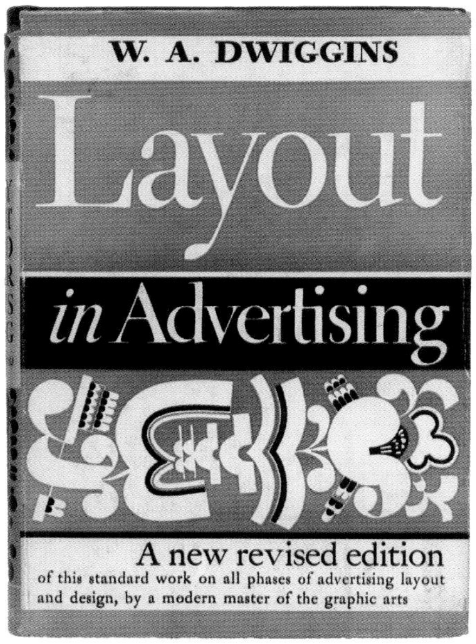

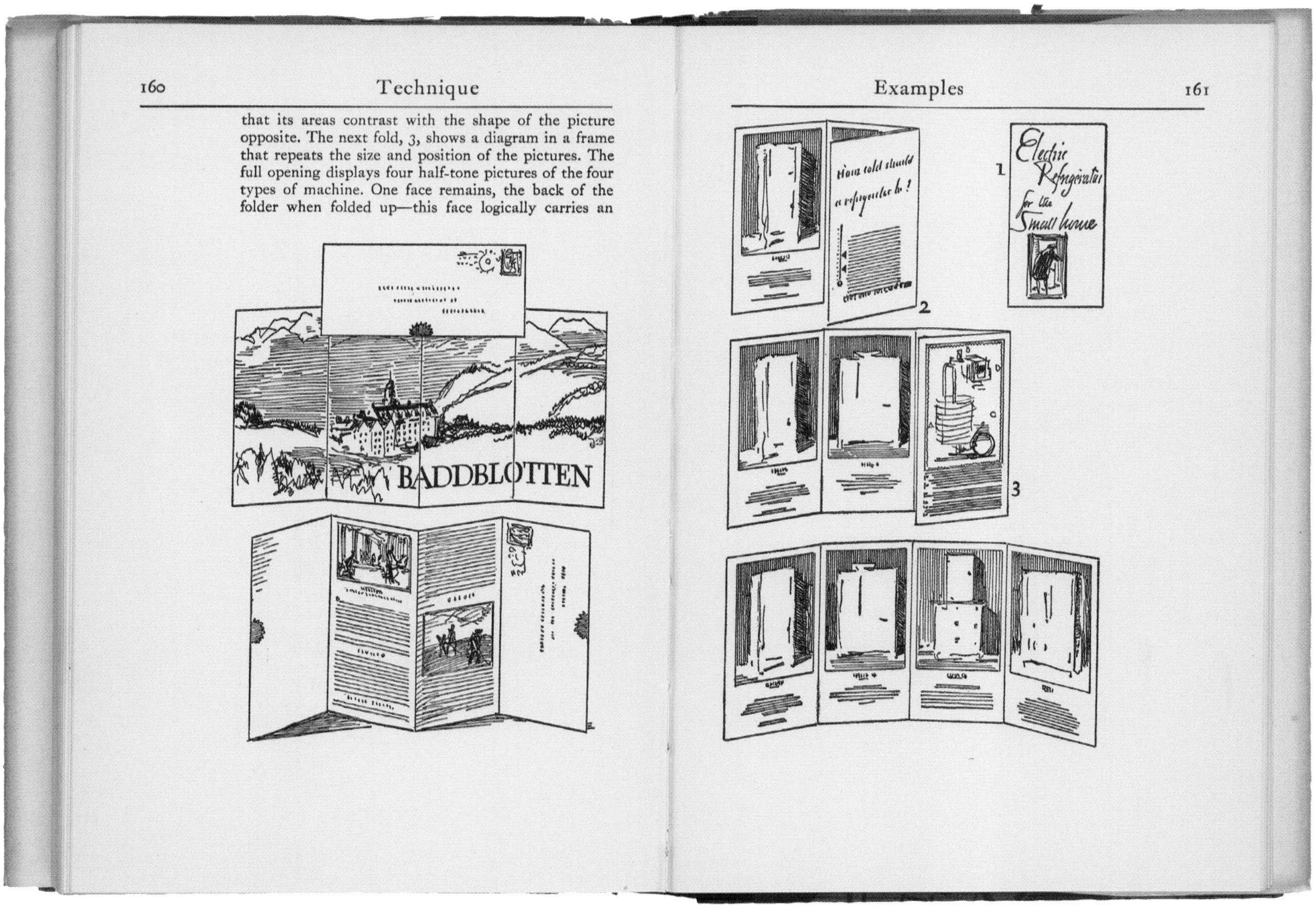
160 Technique

that its areas contrast with the shape of the picture opposite. The next fold, 3, shows a diagram in a frame that repeats the size and position of the pictures. The full opening displays four half-tone pictures of the four types of machine. One face remains, the back of the folder when folded up—this face logically carries an

Examples 161

1929 **Wiener Werkstätte** Mathilde Flögl, *Die Wiener Werkstätte 1903–1928: modernes Kunstgewerbe und sein Weg.*

Vienna: Krystall-Verlag, 1929. 71 pp. 23 cm. Designer: Mathilde Flögl. Binding designers: Vally Wieselthier, Gudrun Baudisch.

Printer: J. Gerstmayer, Vienna. Bookbinder: Karl Scheibe, Vienna. In box.

This deluxe edition – almost square – was published on the occasion of the 25th anniversary of the Wiener Werkstätte (Vienna Workshops) in 1928. This group of painters, sculptors, architects and craftsmen designed and produced a great many products, ranging from cutlery and jewelry to complete interiors, which were viewed as a *Gesamtkunstwerk* or 'total work of art'. The group's principles came from the work of William Morris – who is explicitly cited in this jubilee edition – and the Arts and Crafts movement; stylistic influences included Japanese art and the geometric designs of Charles Rennie Mackintosh. Despite its international prestige, the Wiener Werkstätte had to close its doors in 1932.

The cover is papier-mâché; the front design is by Vally Wieselthier (1895–1945), who had worked with papier-mâché before; the back design is by Gudrun Baudisch (1907–82). Both designers are now primarily known for their ceramics. On the cover are stylized female figures, animals and objects, all in relief. The decorated endpapers may be a design by Josef Hoffmann, co-founder of the Werkstätte. Editor Mathilde Flögl (1893–1958) designed the interior. She had joined the Werkstätte in 1916 and was one of its most versatile members, known also for her posters and advertising designs.

The typography of the book interior is distinctive. The lines of main text are extremely long, with type running to within a hair's breadth of the edge of the page; the margins are minimal. The captions, which are often extensive, are in capitals and set in blocks, sometimes crosswise. Occasionally, two different captions overlap. An exciting sequence of spreads was achieved using typography, photography, and black, red, golden, and silver areas. ML

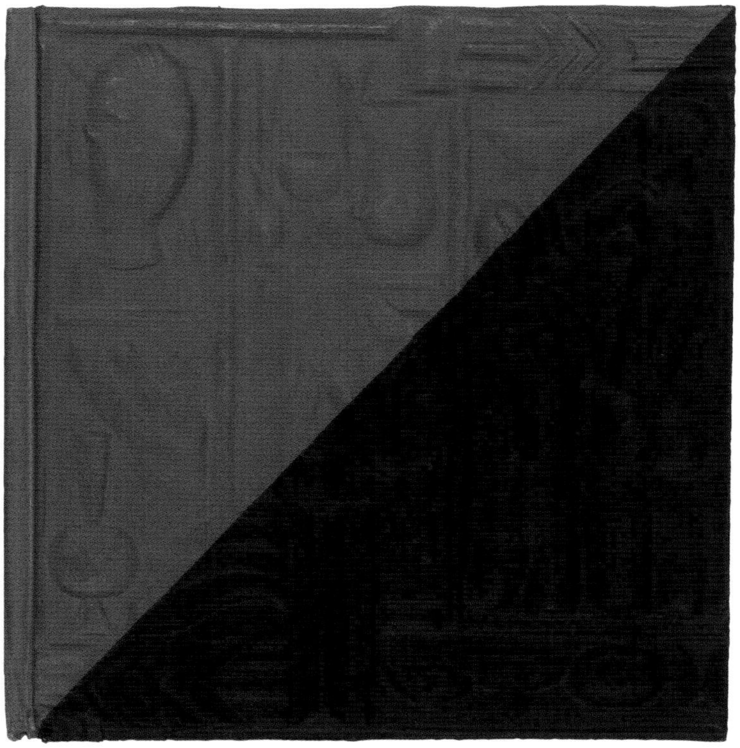

JOSEF HOFFMANN: AUFGANG EINER VILLA IN WIEN-DÖBLING. 1902—1903. J. HOFFMANN: ENTRANCE TO A VILLA, VIENNA-DÖBLING. 1902—1903. J. HOFFMANN: PERRON ET ESCALIER D'UNE VILLA, VIENNE-DÖBLING. 1902—1903.

J. HOFFMANN: DACHGARTEN DES 1905 BIS 1911 ERBAUTEN STOCLET-PALAIS IN BRÜSSEL. DIE WÄNDE SIND MIT PLATTEN AUS WEISSEM NORWEGISCHEM MARMOR BELEGT. DIE KANTEN MIT GEPRÄGTEM UND VERGOLDETEM METALL EINGEFASST. BAU, EINRICHTUNG UND DIE GEBRAUCHSGEGENSTÄNDE STAMMEN AUS DER WIENER WERKSTÄTTE. HERR STOCLET FREUT SICH DIESES HAUSES WIE AM ERSTEN TAG. »FÜR MICH IST ES DAS SCHÖNSTE HAUS DER WELT.« JOSEF HOFFMANN: ROOF GARDEN OF THE STOCKLET PALAIS, BRUSSELS, BUILT IN 1905 TO 1911. THE WALLS ARE FACED WITH SLABS OF WHITE NORWEGIAN MARBLE. THE EDGES ARE FRAMED WITH CHASED BURNISHED METAL. THE ENTIRE BUILDING, FURNISHINGS AND ALL OTHER EQUIMENTS WERE MADE BY THE WIENER WERKSTÄTTE. OF THIS HOUSE MR. STOCKLET SAYS, "I THINK, IT THE MOST BEAUTIFUL HOME IN THE WORLD. I FIND MORE AND MORE HAPPINESS IN IT". JOSEF HOFFMANN: JARDIN SUR LA TERRASSE DU PALAIS STOCLET A BRUXELLES, CONSTRUIT DE 1905 A 1911. LES MURS SONT COUVERTS DE PLAQUES DE MARBRE BLANC DE NORVEGE, BORDES DE METAL DORE ET FRAPPE. LA CONSTRUCTION, L'AMEUBLEMENT ET LES ACCESSOIRES PROVIENNENT DES ATELIERS DE LA WIENER WERKSTÄTTE. M. STOCLET A TOUJOURS ENCORE LA JOIE DU PREMIER JOUR DE SA MAISON ET LA TROUVE LA PLUS BELLE AU MONDE.

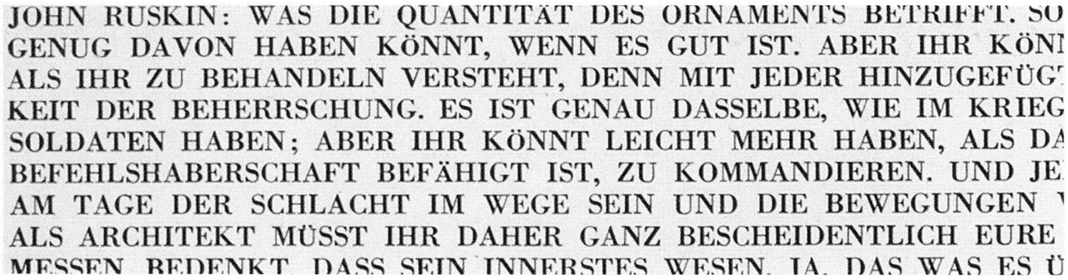
JOHN RUSKIN: WAS DIE QUANTITÄT DES ORNAMENTS BETRIFFT. SO
GENUG DAVON HABEN KÖNNT, WENN ES GUT IST. ABER IHR KÖN
ALS IHR ZU BEHANDELN VERSTEHT, DENN MIT JEDER HINZUGEFÜG
KEIT DER BEHERRSCHUNG. ES IST GENAU DASSELBE, WIE IM KRIEG
SOLDATEN HABEN; ABER IHR KÖNNT LEICHT MEHR HABEN, ALS DA
BEFEHLSHABERSCHAFT BEFÄHIGT IST, ZU KOMMANDIEREN. UND JE
AM TAGE DER SCHLACHT IM WEGE SEIN UND DIE BEWEGUNGEN
ALS ARCHITEKT MÜSST IHR DAHER GANZ BESCHEIDENTLICH EURE
MESSEN BEDENKT, DASS SEIN INNERSTES WESEN, JA, DAS WAS ES Ü

The type is probably Haas Bodoni (*c.* 1924), also issued for Linotype use at around the time this book appeared. It largely followed Morris F. Benton's 1909 version for American Type Founders, which was based on Bodoni's later types, cut between *c.* 1806 and his death in 1813.

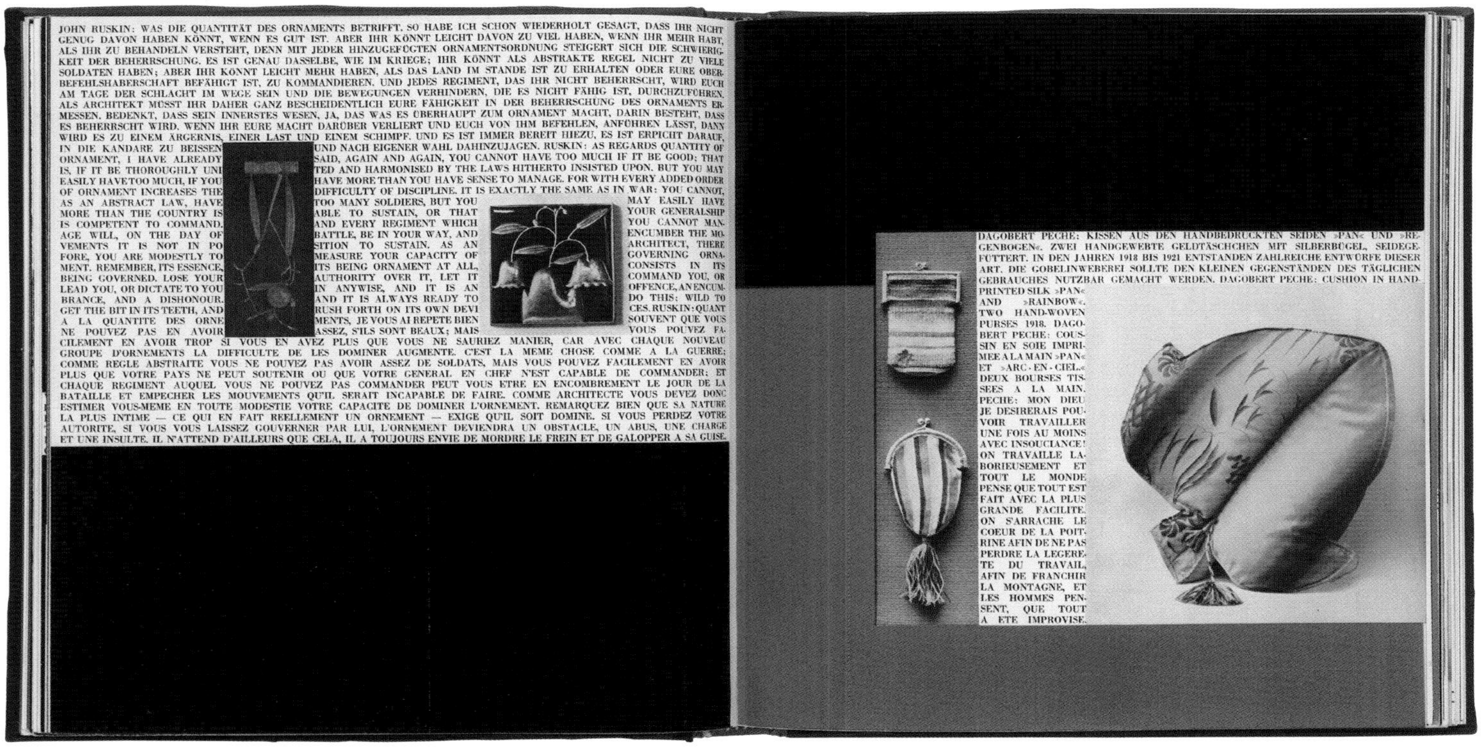

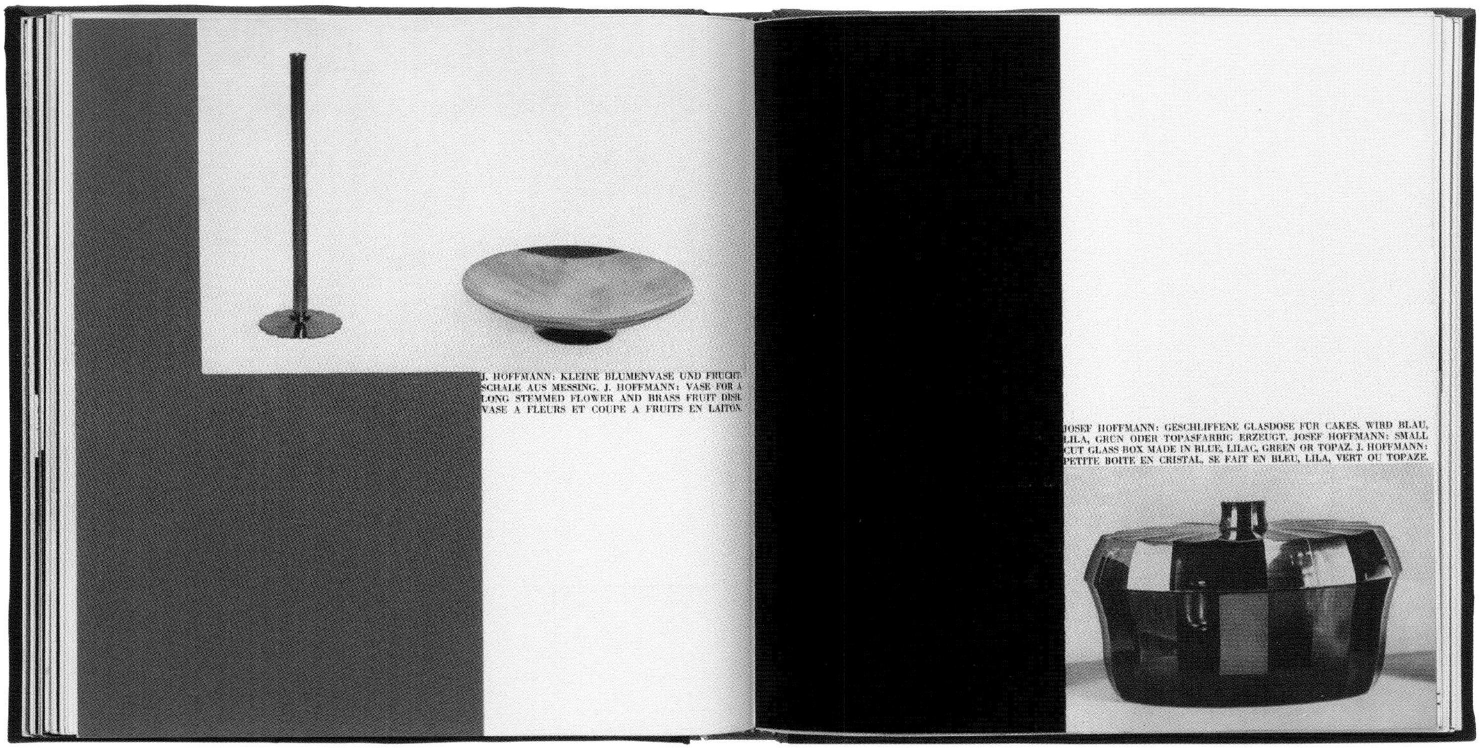

1929 **Count Harry Kessler & Edward Gordon Craig** William Shakespeare, *Die tragische Geschichte von Hamlet Prinzen von Dänemark*; translated by Gerhart Hauptmann. Leipzig: Insel-Verlag; Berlin: S. Fischer, 1928 (= 1929). 204 pp. 35.5 cm. This copy is an incomplete proof. English edition 1930. Designer: Count Harry Kessler. Illustrator & engraver: Edward Gordon Craig. Lettering artist: Eric Gill. Printer: Cranach Presse, Weimar.

Count Harry Kessler (1868–1937) already owned a small printing press by the time he was twelve, and he went on to have a lifelong fascination with making books. In 1913, he started a private press in Weimar, the Cranach Presse, after having supervised the production of such monumental editions as the *Grossherzog Wilhelm Ernst Ausgabe* (1904; see page 288) and Henry van de Velde's *Zarathustra* (1908; see page 294). To equip the press, J. H. Mason came over from England, on the recommendation of Emery Walker. Mason had worked for the Doves Press before. When the First World War broke out in 1914, Kessler – who first served in the army as an officer and then became a diplomat – had no time for his private press for several years.

Virgil's *Eclogues* (1926) and the *Hamlet* shown here are among the most acclaimed editions by the Cranach Presse. The illustrations are by Edward Gordon Craig (1872–1966), who also engraved the blocks. As a theatre director, Craig wanted to create a modern, more abstract, 'total' theatre. His 1912 Moscow production of *Hamlet* was famous and many elements of the illustrations are derived from this production. Apart from the original text, the Cranach edition also contains the sources of Shakespeare's *Hamlet*, in a smaller type size. Fitting Craig's illustrations into this mosaic was not easy, and at the last moment, some of the illustrations had to be adapted or replaced by new engravings.

An Englishman who once was an apprentice at the Kelmscott Press helped out with the printing of this *Hamlet*. In order to obtain perfect prints of the illustrations, a lot of time was spent in make-ready. ML

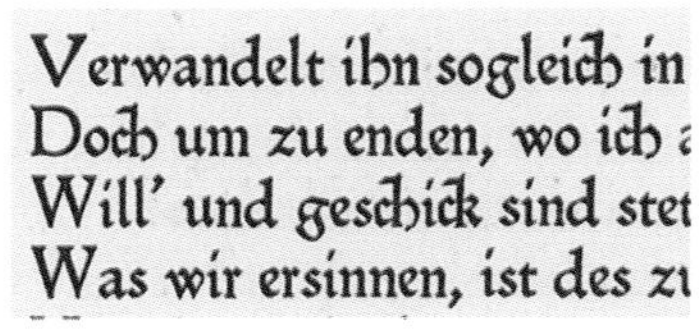

The Hamlet-Fraktur type, in three sizes, was designed by calligrapher Edward Johnston (1872–1944). An image from a fifteenth-century book by Fust & Schoeffer, which Kessler had supplied, served as a model. Edward Prince started cutting punches in 1913, a job that would only be finished in 1927, by George Friend.

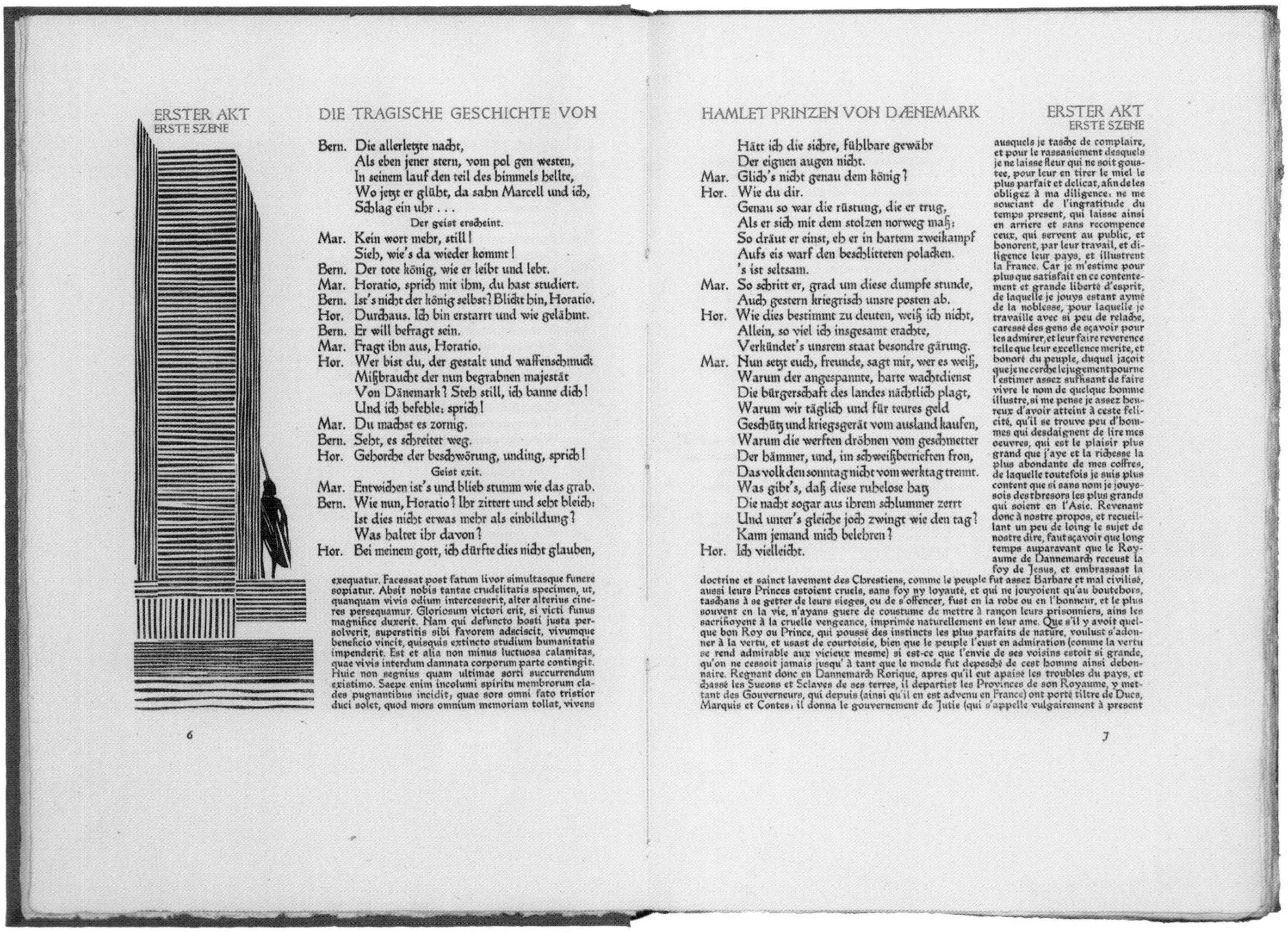

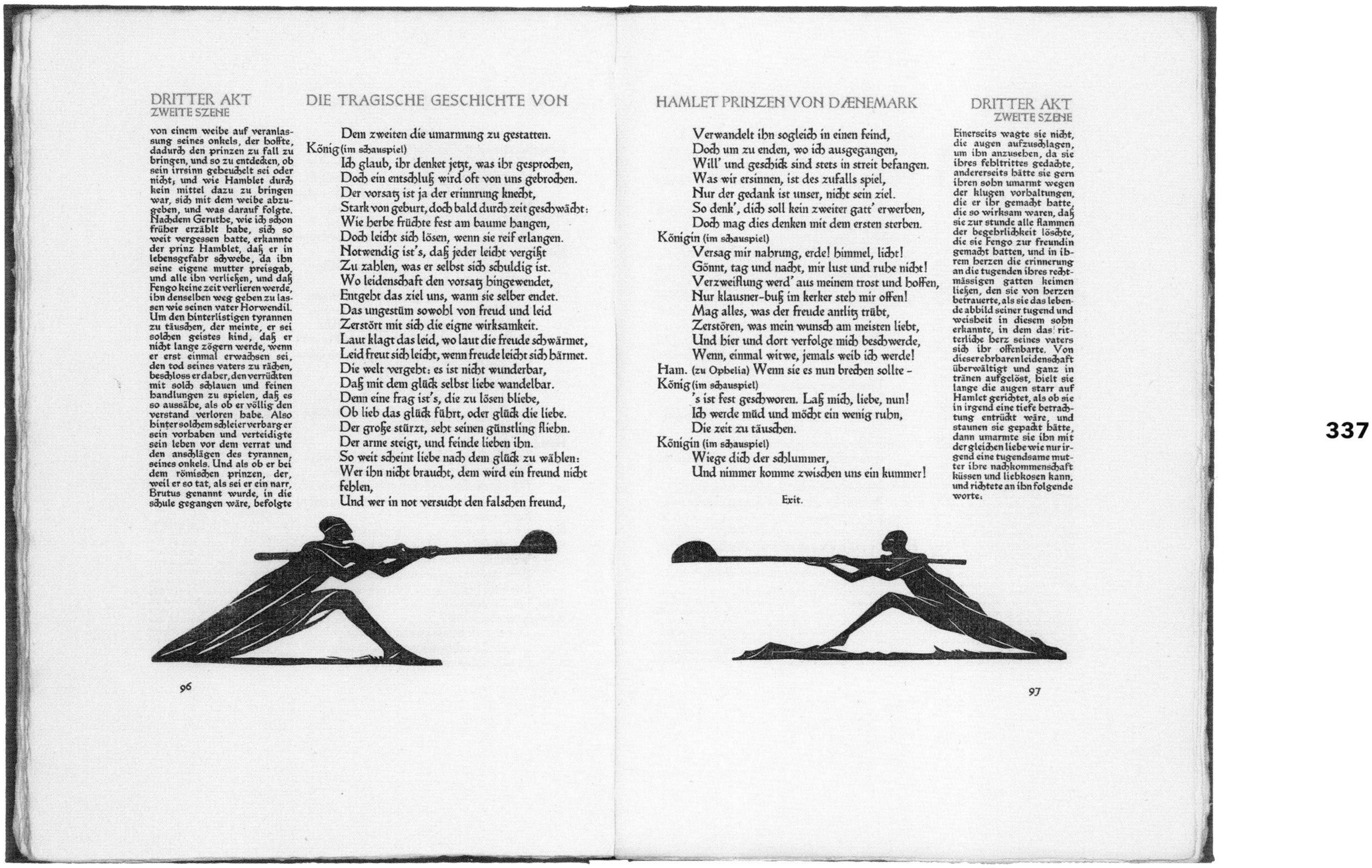

DRITTER AKT
ZWEITE SZENE

von einem weibe auf veranlassung seines onkels, der hoffte, dadurch den prinzen zu fall zu bringen, und so zu entdecken, ob sein irrsinn geheuchelt sei oder nicht; und wie Hamblet durch kein mittel dazu zu bringen war, sich mit dem weibe abzugeben, und was darauf folgte. Nachdem Geruthe, wie ich schon früher erzählt habe, sich so weit vergessen hatte, erkannte der prinz Hamblet, daß er in lebensgefahr schwebe, da ihn seine eigene mutter preisgab, und alle ihn verließen, und daß Fengo keine zeit verlieren werde, ihn denselben weg gehen zu lassen wie seinen vater Horwendil. Um den hinterlistigen tyrannen zu täuschen, der meinte, er sei solchen geistes kind, daß er nicht lange zögern werde, wenn er erst einmal erwachsen sei, den tod seines vaters zu rächen, beschloss er daher, den verrückten mit solch schlauen und feinen handlungen zu spielen, daß es so aussähe, als ob er völlig den verstand verloren habe. Also hinter solchem schleier verbarg er sein vorhaben und verteidigte sein leben vor dem verrat und den anschlägen des tyrannen, seines onkels. Und als ob er bei dem römischen prinzen, der, weil er so tat, als sei er ein narr, Brutus genannt wurde, in die schule gegangen wäre, befolgte

DIE TRAGISCHE GESCHICHTE VON

Dem zweiten die umarmung zu gestatten.
König (im schauspiel)
Ich glaub, ihr denket jetzt, was ihr gesprochen,
Doch ein entschluß wird oft von uns gebrochen.
Der vorsatz ist ja der erinnrung knecht,
Stark von geburt, doch bald durch zeit geschwächt:
Wie herbe früchte fest am baume hangen,
Doch leicht sich lösen, wenn sie reif erlangen.
Notwendig ist's, daß jeder leicht vergißt
Zu zahlen, was er selbst sich schuldig ist.
Wo leidenschaft den vorsatz hingewendet,
Entgeht das ziel uns, wann sie selber endet.
Das ungestüm sowohl von freud und leid
Zerstört mit sich die eigne wirksamkeit.
Laut klagt das leid, wo laut die freude schwärmet,
Leid freut sich leicht, wenn freude leicht sich härmet.
Die welt vergeht: es ist nicht wunderbar,
Daß mit dem glück selbst liebe wandelbar.
Denn eine frag ist's, die zu lösen bliebe,
Ob lieb das glück führt, oder glück die liebe.
Der große stürzt, seht seinen günstling fliehn.
Der arme steigt, und feinde lieben ihn.
So weit scheint liebe nach dem glück zu wählen:
Wer ihn nicht braucht, dem wird ein freund nicht fehlen,
Und wer in not versucht den falschen freund,

96

HAMLET PRINZEN VON DÆNEMARK

Verwandelt ihn sogleich in einen feind,
Doch um zu enden, wo ich ausgegangen,
Will' und geschick sind stets in streit befangen.
Was wir ersinnen, ist des zufalls spiel,
Nur der gedank ist unser, nicht sein ziel.
So denk', dich soll kein zweiter gatt' erwerben,
Doch mag dies denken mit dem ersten sterben.
Königin (im schauspiel)
Versag mir nahrung, erde! himmel, licht!
Gönnt, tag und nacht, mir lust und ruhe nicht!
Verzweiflung werd' aus meinem trost und hoffen,
Nur klausner-buß im kerker steh mir offen!
Mag alles, was der freude antlitz trübt,
Zerstören, was mein wunsch am meisten liebt,
Und hier und dort verfolge mich beschwerde,
Wenn, einmal witwe, jemals weib ich werde!
Ham. (zu Ophelia) Wenn sie es nun brechen sollte –
König (im schauspiel)
's ist fest geschworen. Laß mich, liebe, nun!
Ich werde müd und möcht ein wenig ruhn,
Die zeit zu täuschen.
Königin (im schauspiel)
Wiege dich der schlummer,
Und nimmer komme zwischen uns ein kummer!

Exit.

DRITTER AKT
ZWEITE SZENE

Einerseits wagte sie nicht, die augen aufzuschlagen, um ihn anzusehen, da sie ihres fehltrittes gedachte, andererseits hätte sie gern ihren sohn umarmt wegen der klugen vorhaltungen, die er ihr gemacht hatte, die so wirksam waren, daß sie zur stunde alle flammen der begehrlichkeit löschte, die sie Fengo zur freundin gemacht hatten, und in ihrem herzen die erinnerung an die tugenden ihres rechtmässigen gatten keimen ließen, den sie von herzen betrauerte, als sie das lebende abbild seiner tugend und weisheit in diesem sohn erkannte, in dem das ritterliche herz seines vaters sich ihr offenbarte. Von dieser ehrbaren leidenschaft überwältigt und ganz in tränen aufgelöst, hielt sie lange die augen starr auf Hamlet gerichtet, als ob sie in irgend eine tiefe betrachtung entrückt wäre, und staunen sie gepackt hätte, dann umarmte sie ihn mit der gleichen liebe wie nur irgend eine tugendsame mutter ihre nachkommenschaft küssen und liebkosen kann, und richtete an ihn folgende worte:

97

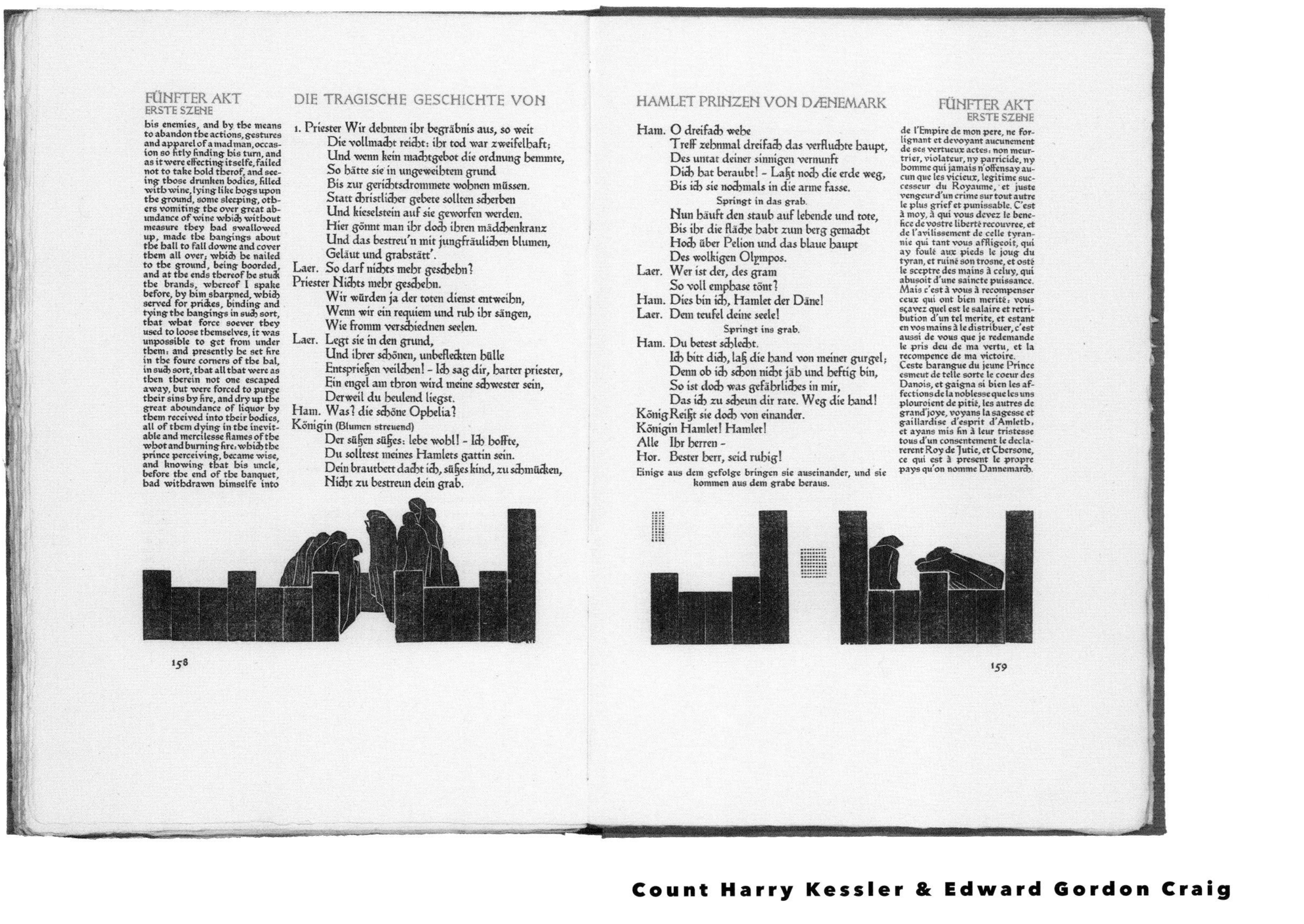

FÜNFTER AKT
ERSTE SZENE

his enemies, and by the means to abandon the actions, gestures and apparel of a madman, occasion so fitly finding his turn, and as it were effecting itselfe, failed not to take hold therof, and seeing those drunken bodies, filled with wine, lying like hogs upon the ground, some sleeping, others vomiting the over great abundance of wine which without measure they had swallowed up, made the hangings about the hall to fall downe and cover them all over; which he nailed to the ground, being boorded, and at the ends thereof he stuck the brands, whereof I spake before, by him sharpned, which served for prickes, binding and tying the hangings in such sort, that what force soever they used to loose themselves, it was unpossible to get from under them: and presently he set fire in the foure corners of the hal, in such sort, that all that were as then therein not one escaped away, but were forced to purge their sins by fire, and dry up the great aboundance of liquor by them received into their bodies, all of them dying in the inevitable and mercilesse flames of the whot and burning fire: which the prince perceiving, became wise, and knowing that his uncle, before the end of the banquet, had withdrawn himselfe into

DIE TRAGISCHE GESCHICHTE VON

1. Priester Wir dehnten ihr begräbnis aus, so weit
Die vollmacht reicht: ihr tod war zweifelhaft;
Und wenn kein machtgebot die ordnung hemmte,
So hätte sie in ungeweihtem grund
Bis zur gerichtsdrommete wohnen müssen.
Statt christlicher gebete sollten scherben
Und kieselstein auf sie geworfen werden.
Hier gönnt man ihr doch ihren mädchenkranz
Und das bestreu'n mit jungfräulichen blumen,
Geläut und grabstätt'.
Laer. So darf nichts mehr geschehn?
Priester Nichts mehr geschehn.
Wir würden ja der toten dienst entweihn,
Wenn wir ein requiem und ruh ihr sängen,
Wie fromm verschiednen seelen.
Laer. Legt sie in den grund,
Und ihrer schönen, unbefleckten hülle
Entsprießen veilchen! – Ich sag dir, harter priester,
Ein engel am thron wird meine schwester sein,
Derweil du heulend liegst.
Ham. Was? die schöne Ophelia?
Königin (Blumen streuend)
Der süßen süßes: lebe wohl! – Ich hoffte,
Du solltest meines Hamlets gattin sein.
Dein brautbett dacht ich, süßes kind, zu schmücken,
Nicht zu bestreun dein grab.

158

HAMLET PRINZEN VON DÆNEMARK

Ham. O dreifach wehe
Treff zehnmal dreifach das verfluchte haupt,
Des untat deiner sinnigen vernunft
Dich hat beraubt! – Laßt noch die erde weg,
Bis ich sie nochmals in die arme fasse.
Springt in das grab.
Nun häuft den staub auf lebende und tote,
Bis ihr die fläche habt zum berg gemacht
Hoch über Pelion und das blaue haupt
Des wolkigen Olympos.
Laer. Wer ist der, des gram
So voll emphase tönt?
Ham. Dies bin ich, Hamlet der Däne!
Laer. Dem teufel deine seele!
Springt ins grab.
Ham. Du betest schlecht.
Ich bitt dich, laß die hand von meiner gurgel;
Denn ob ich schon nicht jäh und heftig bin,
So ist doch was gefährliches in mir,
Das ich zu scheun dir rate. Weg die hand!
König Reißt sie doch von einander.
Königin Hamlet! Hamlet!
Alle Ihr herren –
Hor. Bester herr, seid ruhig!
Einige aus dem gefolge bringen sie auseinander, und sie kommen aus dem grabe heraus.

FÜNFTER AKT
ERSTE SZENE

de l'Empire de mon pere, ne forlignant et devoyant aucunement de ses vertueux actes: non meurtrier, violateur, ny parricide, ny homme qui jamais n'offensay aucun que les vicieux, legitime successeur du Royaume, et juste vengeur d'un crime sur tout autre le plus grief et punissable. C'est à moy, à qui vous devez le benefice de vostre liberté recouvree, et de l'avilissement de celle tyrannie qui tant vous affligeoit, qui ay foulé aux pieds le joug du tyran, et ruiné son trosne, et osté le sceptre des mains à celuy, qui abusoit d'une saincte puissance. Mais c'est à vous à recompenser ceux qui ont bien merité: vous sçavez quel est le salaire et retribution d'un tel merite, et estant en vos mains à le distribuer, c'est aussi de vous que je redemande le pris deu de ma vertu, et la recompence de ma victoire.
Ceste harangue du jeune Prince esmeut de telle sorte le coeur des Danois, et gaigna si bien les affections de la noblesse que les uns plouroient de pitié, les autres de grand'joye, voyans la sagesse et gaillardise d'esprit d'Amleth, et ayans mis fin à leur tristesse tous d'un consentement le declarerent Roy de Jutie, et Chersone, ce qui est à present le propre pays qu'on nomme Dannemarch.

159

1929 **A. M. Cassandre** *Bifur: caractère de publicité*. Paris: Deberny & Peignot, 1929. 28 pp. 26.5 cm.

Designer: A. M. Cassandre. Printer: Deberny & Peignot, Paris.

'After all, our epoch can boast only one A. M. Cassandre', his colleague Paul Rand once declared. Cassandre, the pseudonym of Frenchman Adolphe Jean-Marie Mouron (1901–68), was one of the most successful graphic designers of the period between the wars. His advertising posters are considered the epitome of Art Deco. Cassandre did work for department stores in Paris, for liquor distilleries, and for shipping and railroad companies. His work is characterized by geometry, abstraction, airbrush technique and by the central role of lettering.

The lettering for the posters – only capitals, without exception – was designed by Cassandre himself. The letters are usually bold, constructed sans serifs that clearly display their drawing-board origins. The Parisian typefounder Charles Peignot was captivated by Cassandre's work and the two men met in around 1925. Cassandre went on to design a number of typefaces for Deberny & Peignot, of which Bifur (1929) was the first. An early version of this typeface seems to have been used four years earlier in a poster for the aperitif Pivolo.

Bifur is a series of sans serif capitals from which about half of each letter is missing. The N, for instance, consists only of a diagonal line. The forms become more readable when a hatched shading is added. It is a typeface for advertising, meant for texts consisting of only a few words, such as posters. As this small but striking type specimen shows, Deberny & Peignot paid a great deal of attention to publicity material. At the time, even the firm's vans were painted with a design by Cassandre: 'le graphisme dans la rue'. ML

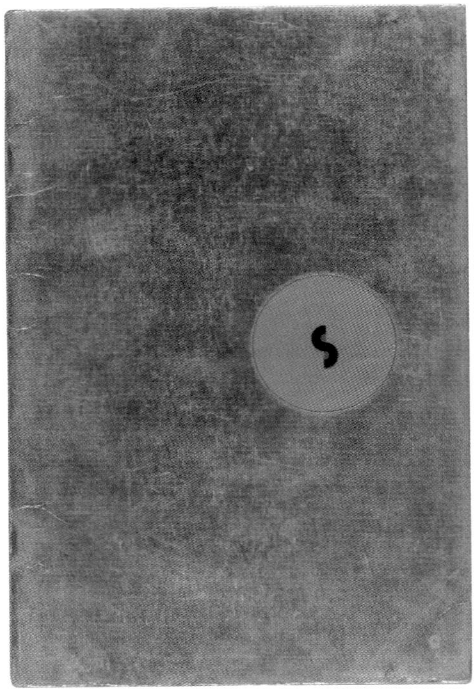

This is the hand-set metal Bifur, but Cassandre's typeface now exists in digital variants. Richard Kegler (b. 1965), the American founder of the digital typefoundry P22, added a lower case to his version.

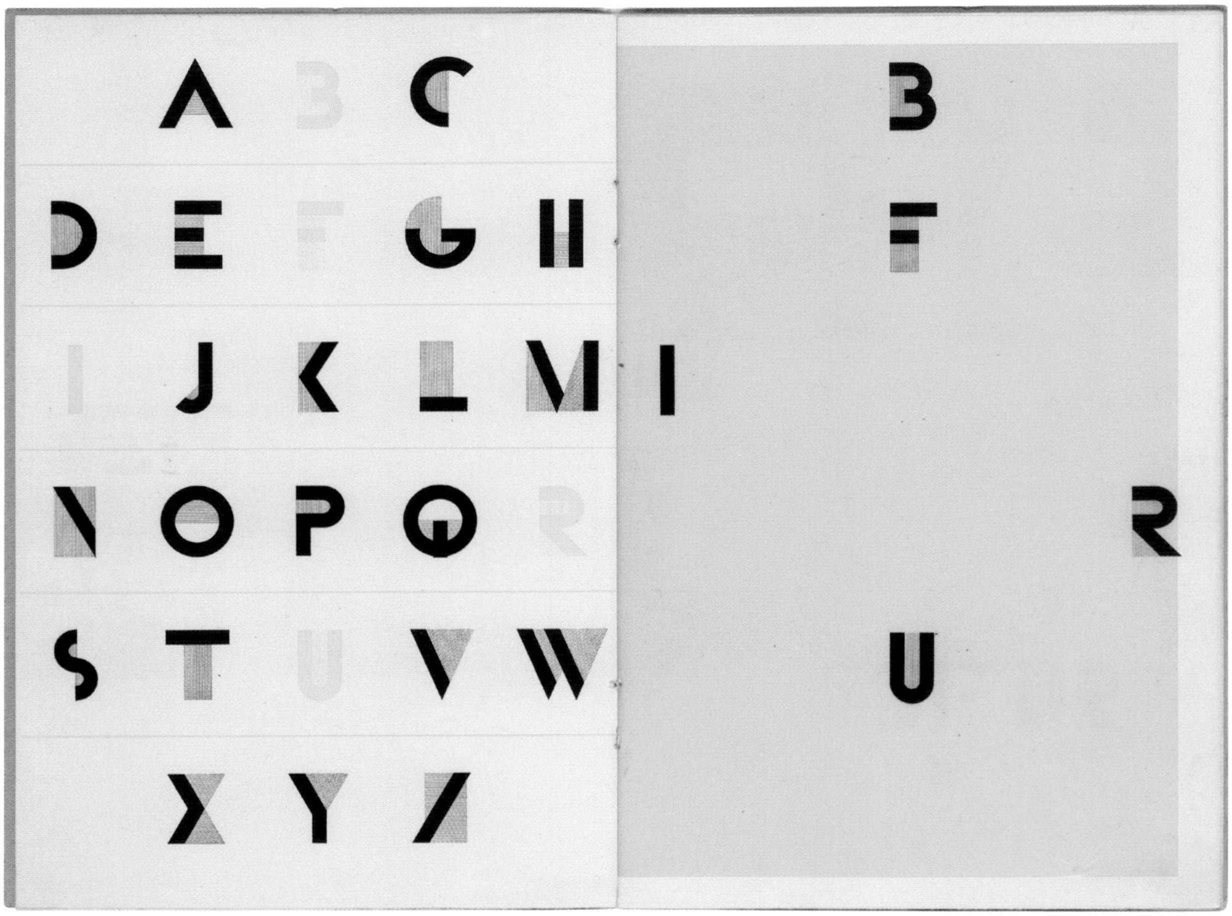

MAIS
DANGER
NE LE RENDS PAS ILLISIBLE

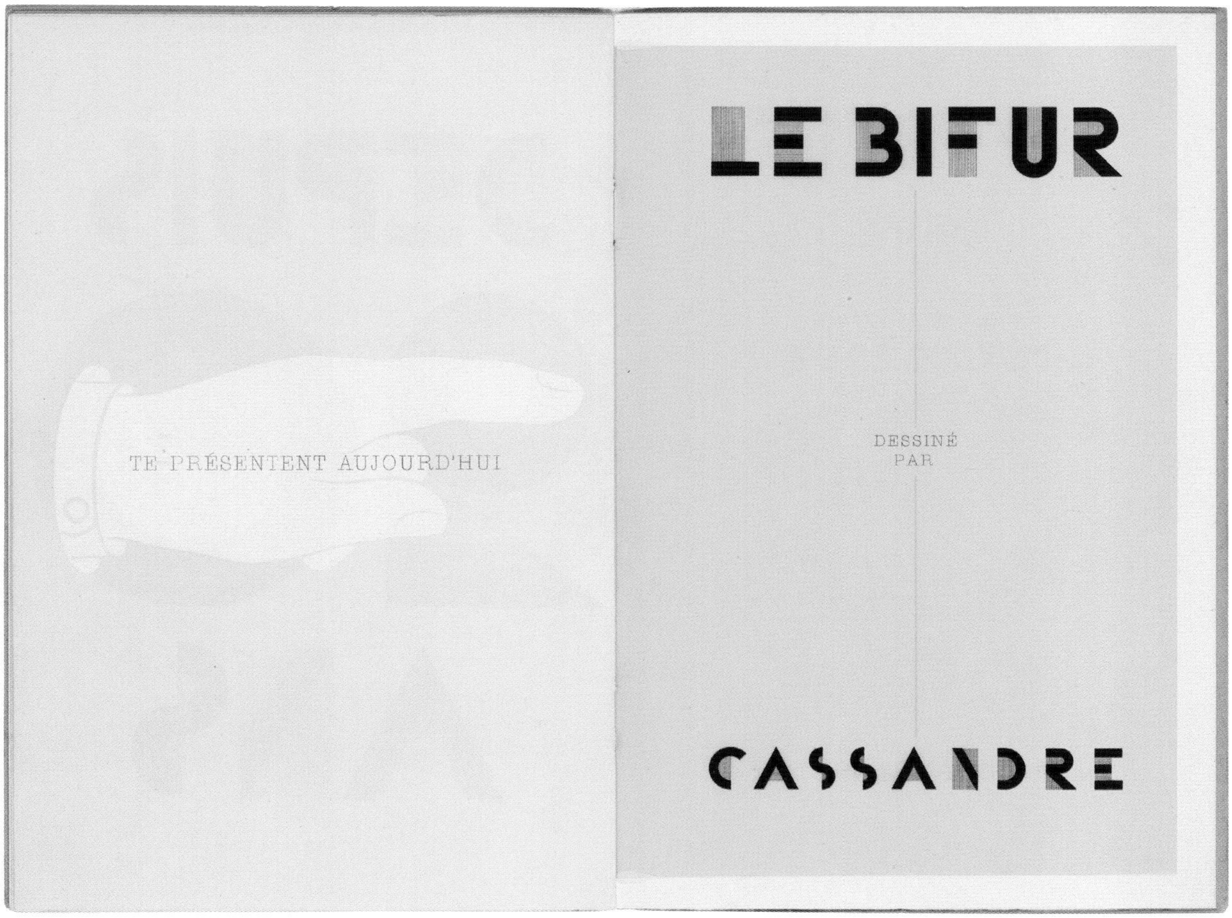
TE PRÉSENTENT AUJOURD'HUI
LE BIFUR
DESSINÉ
PAR
CASSANDRE

1929 **John Heartfield** Kurt Tucholsky, *Deutschland, Deutschland über alles: ein Bilderbuch*. Berlin: Neuer Deutscher Verlag, 1929. 231 pp. 24 cm. Designer & illustrator: John Heartfield. Printer: Pass & Garleb, Berlin.

Deutschland, Deutschland über alles is a provocative book. In its pages, the writer and journalist Kurt Tucholsky speaks out against militarism, social injustice and class conflict in the Weimar Republic (1918/19–1933). Using many literary forms – from poem to parable – Tucholsky tried to shake his countrymen awake and to warn them of the dangers of National Socialism.

John Heartfield's masterly design manages to make Tucholsky's message clear before the book is even opened. His satirical photomontages fill both the front and the back cover – a remarkable feature at this date. The front shows a montage of a bust of a man wearing a top hat on top of an army helmet, half bourgeois, half military, his eyes blindfolded with a German flag. The colours used make the conflicting flags immediately clear. The old imperial flag (preferred by the National Socialists) was black, white and red, while the republican flag was black, red and gold. The title is presented like a speech bubble and is set in archetypal German blackletter type. Inside the book, Heartfield also provides a running commentary in the form of photographs.

John Heartfield (1891–1968), born Helmut Herzfeld, had come to know the artist George Grosz in 1915. They became friends and were both active in Berlin's Dada scene. In this period Heartfield and his brother Wieland established the Malik-Verlag, a left-wing publishing house. He made his name with photomontages for books and for the Communist paper *Arbeiter-Illustrierte-Zeitung*, issued in large press runs. After Hitler took power in 1933, Heartfield fled via Prague to England. He returned in 1950 and settled in East Germany. ML

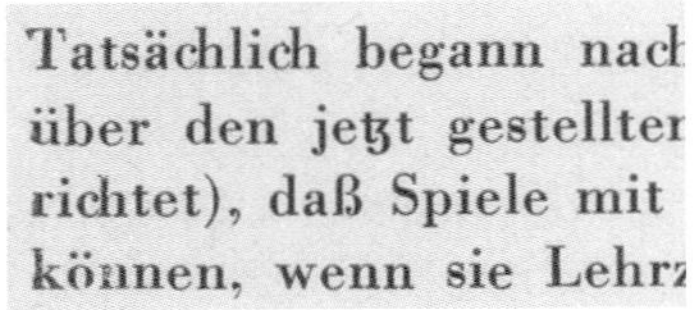
Tatsächlich begann nach
über den jetzt gestellten
richtet), daß Spiele mit
können, wenn sie Lehrz

This Linotype Bodoni (*c.* 1928) is based on that of the Haas typefoundry in Basel, Switzerland, which was in turn a revised version of American Type Founders' Bodoni (1909) by Morris F. Benton (1872–1948).

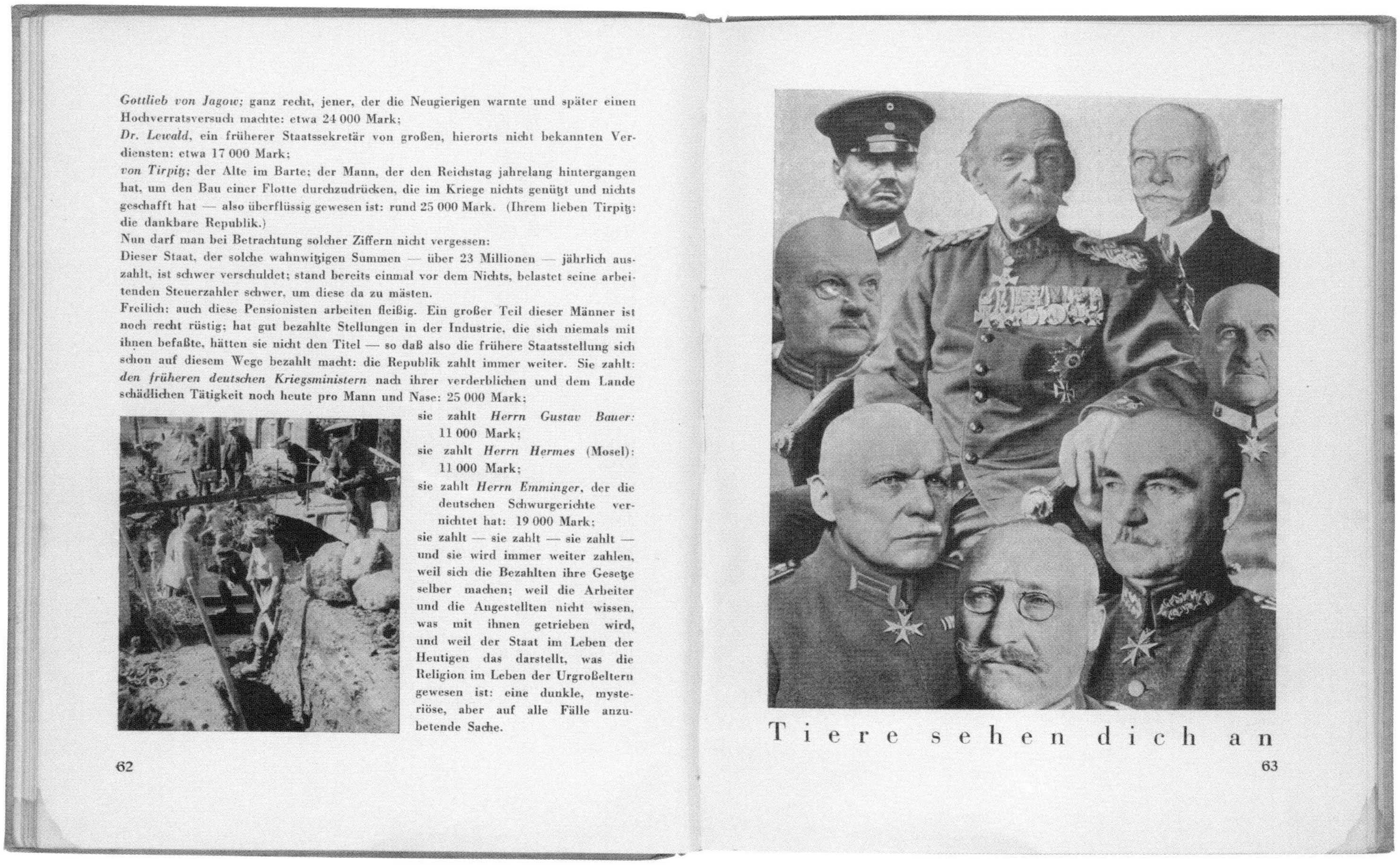

Gottlieb von Jagow; ganz recht, jener, der die Neugierigen warnte und später einen Hochverratsversuch machte: etwa 24 000 Mark;
Dr. Lewald, ein früherer Staatssekretär von großen, hierorts nicht bekannten Verdiensten: etwa 17 000 Mark;
von Tirpitz; der Alte im Barte; der Mann, der den Reichstag jahrelang hintergangen hat, um den Bau einer Flotte durchzudrücken, die im Kriege nichts genützt und nichts geschafft hat — also überflüssig gewesen ist: rund 25 000 Mark. (Ihrem lieben Tirpitz: die dankbare Republik.)
Nun darf man bei Betrachtung solcher Ziffern nicht vergessen:
Dieser Staat, der solche wahnwitzigen Summen — über 23 Millionen — jährlich auszahlt, ist schwer verschuldet; stand bereits einmal vor dem Nichts, belastet seine arbeitenden Steuerzahler schwer, um diese da zu mästen.
Freilich: auch diese Pensionisten arbeiten fleißig. Ein großer Teil dieser Männer ist noch recht rüstig; hat gut bezahlte Stellungen in der Industrie, die sich niemals mit ihnen befaßte, hätten sie nicht den Titel — so daß also die frühere Staatsstellung sich schon auf diesem Wege bezahlt macht: die Republik zahlt immer weiter. Sie zahlt: *den früheren deutschen Kriegsministern* nach ihrer verderblichen und dem Lande schädlichen Tätigkeit noch heute pro Mann und Nase: 25 000 Mark;
sie zahlt *Herrn Gustav Bauer:* 11 000 Mark;
sie zahlt *Herrn Hermes* (Mosel): 11 000 Mark;
sie zahlt *Herrn Emminger,* der die deutschen Schwurgerichte vernichtet hat: 19 000 Mark;
sie zahlt — sie zahlt — sie zahlt — und sie wird immer weiter zahlen, weil sich die Bezahlten ihre Gesetze selber machen; weil die Arbeiter und die Angestellten nicht wissen, was mit ihnen getrieben wird, und weil der Staat im Leben der Heutigen das darstellt, was die Religion im Leben der Urgroßeltern gewesen ist: eine dunkle, mysteriöse, aber auf alle Fälle anzubetende Sache.

62

T i e r e   s e h e n   d i c h   a n

63

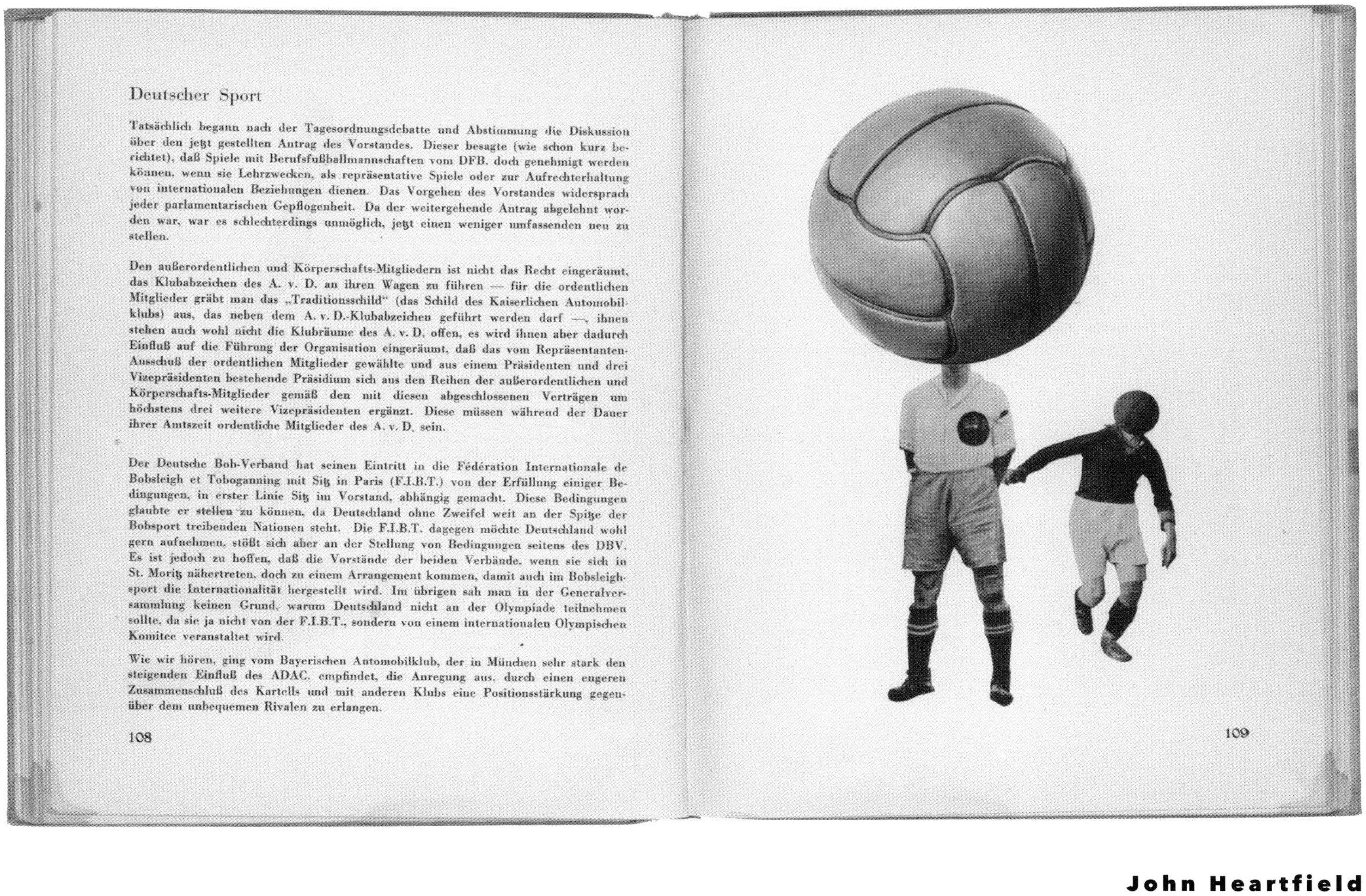

Deutscher Sport

Tatsächlich begann nach der Tagesordnungsdebatte und Abstimmung die Diskussion über den jetzt gestellten Antrag des Vorstandes. Dieser besagte (wie schon kurz berichtet), daß Spiele mit Berufsfußballmannschaften vom DFB. doch genehmigt werden können, wenn sie Lehrzwecken, als repräsentative Spiele oder zur Aufrechterhaltung von internationalen Beziehungen dienen. Das Vorgehen des Vorstandes widersprach jeder parlamentarischen Gepflogenheit. Da der weitergehende Antrag abgelehnt worden war, war es schlechterdings unmöglich, jetzt einen weniger umfassenden neu zu stellen.

Den außerordentlichen und Körperschafts-Mitgliedern ist nicht das Recht eingeräumt, das Klubabzeichen des A. v. D. an ihren Wagen zu führen — für die ordentlichen Mitglieder gräbt man das „Traditionsschild" (das Schild des Kaiserlichen Automobilklubs) aus, das neben dem A. v. D.-Klubabzeichen geführt werden darf —, ihnen stehen auch wohl nicht die Klubräume des A. v. D. offen, es wird ihnen aber dadurch Einfluß auf die Führung der Organisation eingeräumt, daß das vom Repräsentanten-Ausschuß der ordentlichen Mitglieder gewählte und aus einem Präsidenten und drei Vizepräsidenten bestehende Präsidium sich aus den Reihen der außerordentlichen und Körperschafts-Mitglieder gemäß den mit diesen abgeschlossenen Verträgen um höchstens drei weitere Vizepräsidenten ergänzt. Diese müssen während der Dauer ihrer Amtszeit ordentliche Mitglieder des A. v. D. sein.

Der Deutsche Bob-Verband hat seinen Eintritt in die Fédération Internationale de Bobsleigh et Toboganning mit Sitz in Paris (F.I.B.T.) von der Erfüllung einiger Bedingungen, in erster Linie Sitz im Vorstand, abhängig gemacht. Diese Bedingungen glaubte er stellen zu können, da Deutschland ohne Zweifel weit an der Spitze der Bobsport treibenden Nationen steht. Die F.I.B.T. dagegen möchte Deutschland wohl gern aufnehmen, stößt sich aber an der Stellung von Bedingungen seitens des DBV. Es ist jedoch zu hoffen, daß die Vorstände der beiden Verbände, wenn sie sich in St. Moritz nähertreten, doch zu einem Arrangement kommen, damit auch im Bobsleighsport die Internationalität hergestellt wird. Im übrigen sah man in der Generalversammlung keinen Grund, warum Deutschland nicht an der Olympiade teilnehmen sollte, da sie ja nicht von der F.I.B.T., sondern von einem internationalen Olympischen Komitee veranstaltet wird.

Wie wir hören, ging vom Bayerischen Automobilklub, der in München sehr stark den steigenden Einfluß des ADAC. empfindet, die Anregung aus, durch einen engeren Zusammenschluß des Kartells und mit anderen Klubs eine Positionsstärkung gegenüber dem unbequemen Rivalen zu erlangen.

108

109

aus —? August Friedrich Wilhelm Schulze (1821—1889). Ein bebarteter, alter, bescheidener Mann, mit Brille und schütterm weißen Haar; Arbeit und Alter haben ihn leicht geduckt, aus seinen Augen blickt alles Mögliche, verglommene Herrschsucht, Traurigkeit, ein langes Leben — ein Mensch, mit dem man sprechen kann. In pace.
Hans Erich Schulze (1854—1915). Blanke Augen und der mächtige Schädel eines tatkräftigen Mannes; in diesen Augen ist vielerlei: ererbte Familienzüge, List, sicherlich Güte. Für den ist der deutsche Humanismus nicht umsonst gewesen — er hat eine Beziehung zu dem Besten gehabt, was Deutschland zu geben hatte. Aber schon nicht mehr so wie der Alte, sein Vater. In pace.
Dr. iur. Ernst Emil Schulze (geb. 1885). Donnerwetter!
Ein glatt rasierter Schweineschädel: zwei kleine Knopfaugen; ein erbarmungsloser Kragen; ein Zahnbürstenschnurrbart . . . und um die Wein-Unterlippe jener Zug von Kälte und Korrektheit, der die Hülle aller neudeutschen Herzlosigkeit ist. In pace? In bello. „Und der Hermundure flüstert beklommen: Gott, ist die Gegend runtergekommen . . ."
Die gute alte Zeit hats nie gegeben. Die schlechte neue? Allemal. So, wie der alte Jahrgang der deutschen Strafrichter immer noch angeht, weil es doch oft noch einen winzigen Weg zum Herzen dieser Männer gibt und vor allem, weil sie eines haben, jedoch die Brutalität der neuen Jahrgänge unerträglich ist: so ist auch der Typus der deutschen Kaufleute des neunzehnten Jahrhunderts, das vielfach aus Neusilber gewesen ist, eitel Gold gegen das Nickel dieser Tage. Wie das blitzt? Wie hart das funkelt! Und wie gelb das einmal werden wird . . .!
Gesichter, die in die Hose gehören. Aber wir zeigen sie der Welt — mit einem herausfordernden Ausruf aus dem Götz, und wundern uns, daß alle, alle dagegen sind.

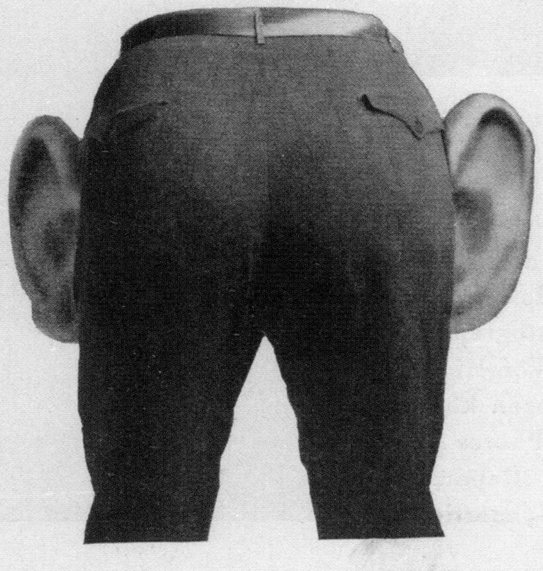

176

Die Pose der Kraft

Eine leicht verweichlichte Generation junger Leute, die nicht bis zehn boxen kann, stellt auf den Bühnen der großen Städte Kraft dar. Es gibt eine ganze Literatur solcher Stücke, in denen der Wilde Westen, die Maschinen und neuerdings auch das Proletariat dazu herhalten müssen, Vorwand für eine Schaustellung zu sein, die verlogen ist bis in ihre weichen Knochen. Welch trutzig gereckte Arme! hintenüber geworfene Köpfe! So ist die neue Zeit gar nicht. So sieht sie nicht einmal aus. So wird sie nur dargestellt.

Am schauerlichsten aber ist es, wenn die Schwächlinge in weibischer Anbetung der Kraft sich am Nationalismus hochranken und brünstig die erigierten Fahnen umarmen; das geht von den schreibenden Marineleutnants bis zu den jüngeren Autoren, ihren Namen sollt Ihr nie erfahren, einer beginnt mit dem Anfangsbuchstaben Bronnen. Hei, da gehts zu!

Dieser, der da oben boxt, tut es sicherlich ethisch — ich höre die gezackten, gerafften, geballten und gesteilten Verse, die keine sind, aber sicherlich mit der Internationale schließen. Kost ja nischt.

Dann gibts welche, die boxen mehr aus sauberer Freude am Blut. Es wird ein bißchen viel geschlagen in der neueren deutschen Literatur — der Riesenerfolg so eines Schmarrens wie des Lönsschen „Wehrwolfs" ist auf latenten Sadismus zurückzuführen. Es hat einmal in der verblichenen Zeitschrift „Der Drache" die Geschichte eines gestanden, dem zeigte ein Stahlhelmer ein koloriertes Photo von der Erschießung Schlageters. „Wissen Sie", sagte der Held, „wenn ich sowas Racheaktjes, dann . . ." er meinte, dann würde ihm sehr wohl zumute — aber ich mag das nicht hierher setzen, es ist nicht schön. Deckt aber den tiefen Zusammenhang zwischen Wollust und Blutlust auf das eindeutigste auf. Was dem einen seine Ludmilla, ist dem andern sein Einmarsch in München.

1929 **Jan Tschichold** Franz Roh & Jan Tschichold, *Foto-Auge: 76 Fotos der Zeit; Oeil et photo: 76 photographies de notre temps; Photo-eye: 76 Photos of the Period*. Stuttgart: Dr. Fritz Wedekind & Co., 1929. 18 pp. 30 cm. Designer: Jan Tschichold. Photographer (cover): El Lissitzky. Printer: Heinrich Fink, Stuttgart. With the folds at the fore-edge.

When Jan Tschichold (1902–74) designed *Foto-Auge*, he had already made his reputation, even though he was still in his twenties. To some extent, this was due to his publications, in particular to his manual *Die neue Typographie*, which had appeared the year before. After visiting a Bauhaus exhibition in Weimar, in 1923, Tschichold became increasingly influenced by modernism.

In 1928, he was a selection committee member for 'Film und Foto' (Fifo). This travelling international exhibition, which opened in Stuttgart in 1929, focused on several fields of photography, including advertising. Tschichold's friends El Lissitzky and Piet Zwart took care of selections for the Russian and Dutch sections respectively. The groundbreaking exhibition was accompanied by a modest catalogue. The photobook *Foto-Auge*, which Tschichold helped to compile, was a spin-off from this exhibition. It contains work by László Moholy-Nagy, Zwart, Tschichold, and others. Lissitzky's self-portrait featured on the front cover, *The Constructor* (1924), has become iconic.

Tschichold advocated the use of DIN standard paper sizes for reasons of efficiency. *Die neue Typographie* appeared in A5 size, *Foto-Auge* in A4. *Foto-Auge* is an example of New Typography in other aspects as well: the layout is asymmetric, lower-case type is used exclusively, and the book, although refined, is not a luxury edition. A Japanese binding – with folds at the fore-edge – was used to give the book some bulk (it has only 94 pages). To this end, the leaves were stapled through the back margins. ML

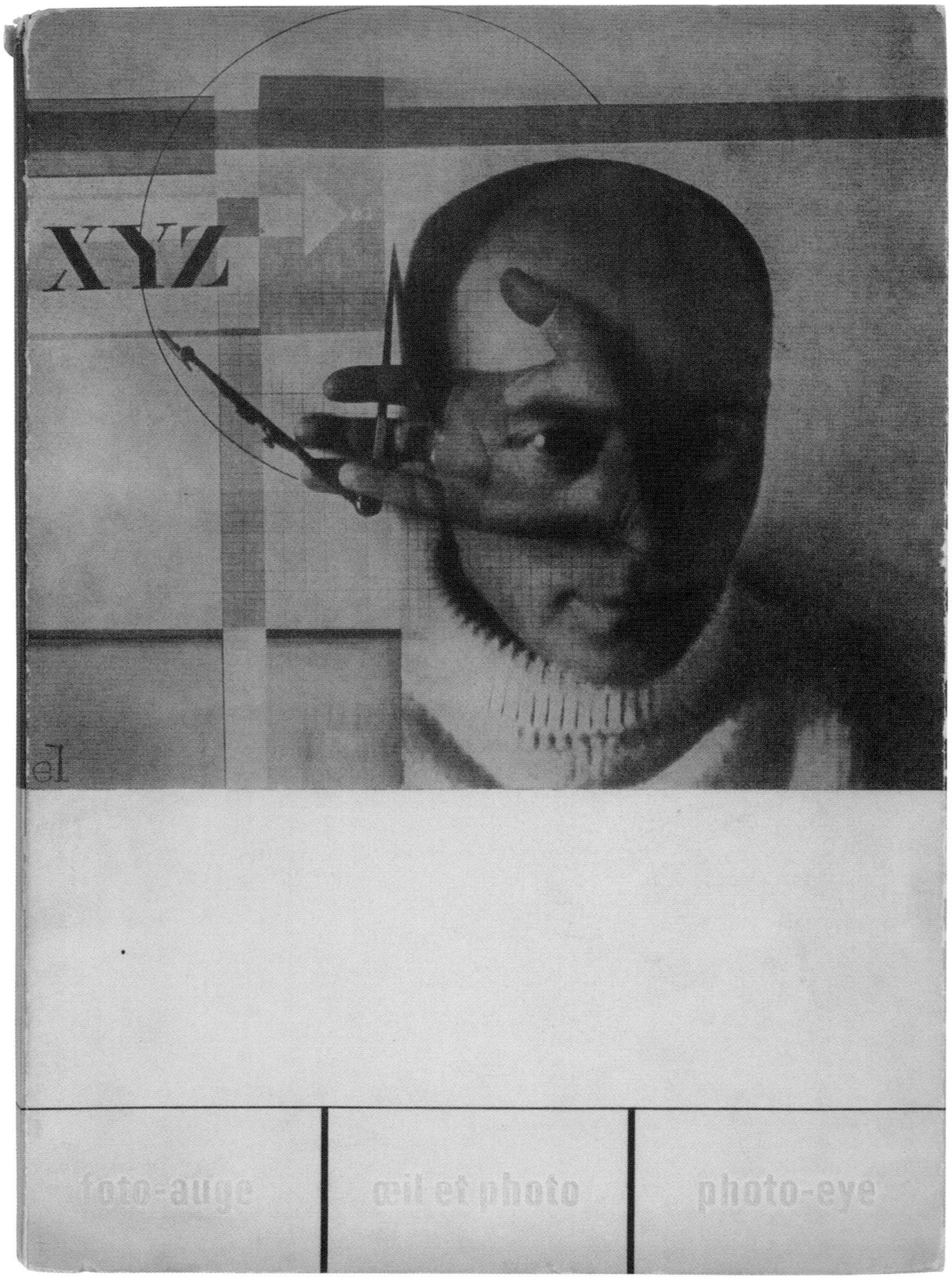

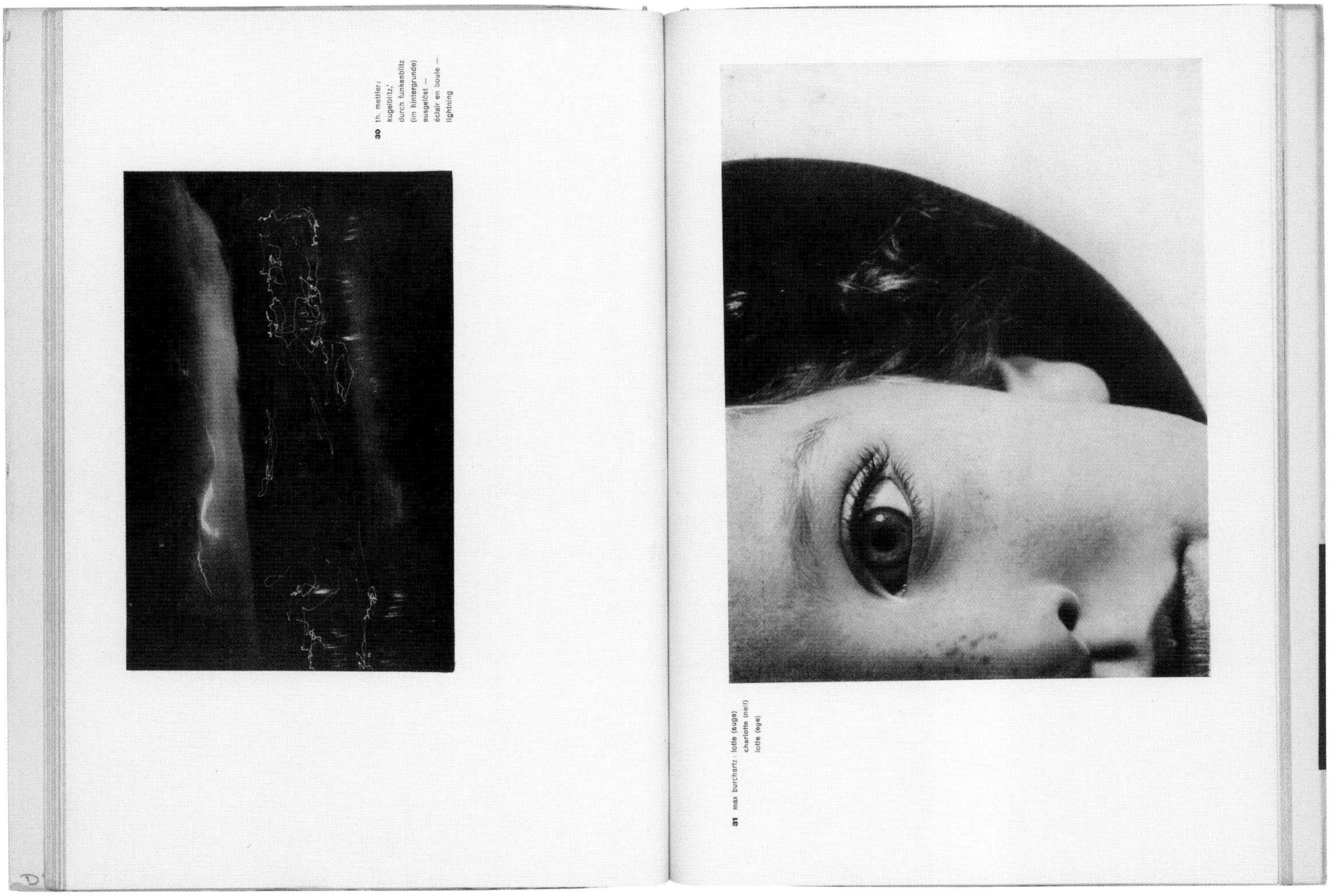
30 th. mettler:
kugelblitz,'
durch funkenblitz
(im hintergrunde)
ausgelöst —
éclair en boule —
lightning
31 max burchartz: lotte (auge)
charlotte (oeil)
lotte (eye)

34 ereit weston: wellblechdächer — toits de tôle ondulée — roofs of corrugated iron
35 herbert bayer: beine — jambes — legs

1931 **Eric Gill** Eric Gill, *An Essay on Typography*. London: Sheed & Ward, 1931. 120 pp. 21 cm. Designer: Eric Gill. Printer: René Hague & Eric Gill, Pigotts.

Like Tschichold's *Die neue Typographie* (1928) and Morison's *First Principles of Typography* (1936, in book form), Eric Gill's *An Essay on Typography* is a designer's manual. Since the days of William Morris, typographic design had been seen as an independent discipline. Here, however, typography is placed within the context of cultural criticism, focusing on the positions of artists and craftsmen in an industrial society. The dust cover of this first edition from 1931 says: 'Printing & Piety: An essay on life and works in the England of 1931, & particularly typography.'

In this book by Eric Gill (1882–1940), artist and graphic designer, everything is different. Gill's statements are firm and sometimes sarcastic. The title page simultaneously serves as a table of contents. The text is set in Joanna, designed by the author, who was also involved in the printing of the book. Paragraphs start at the beginning of the lines and are preceded by a pilcrow, which is sometimes used in the middle of a line as well. A conspicuous feature is the conscious and consistent use of unjustified line endings, giving the text a ragged right edge. In the book, Gill defends this unjustified typesetting by pointing out its regularity and serenity, as the variations in word spacing that we always see when text is justified do not occur. FAJ

Edward Johnston's Railway Type (designed 1916, but not made available commercially) abandoned nineteenth-century forms in favour of those of Renaissance Florence. The success of German sans serifs that combined Johnston's influence with 'constructive' principles led Monotype to invite Johnston's pupil Eric Gill to design Gill Sans, shown here and first used in 1928.

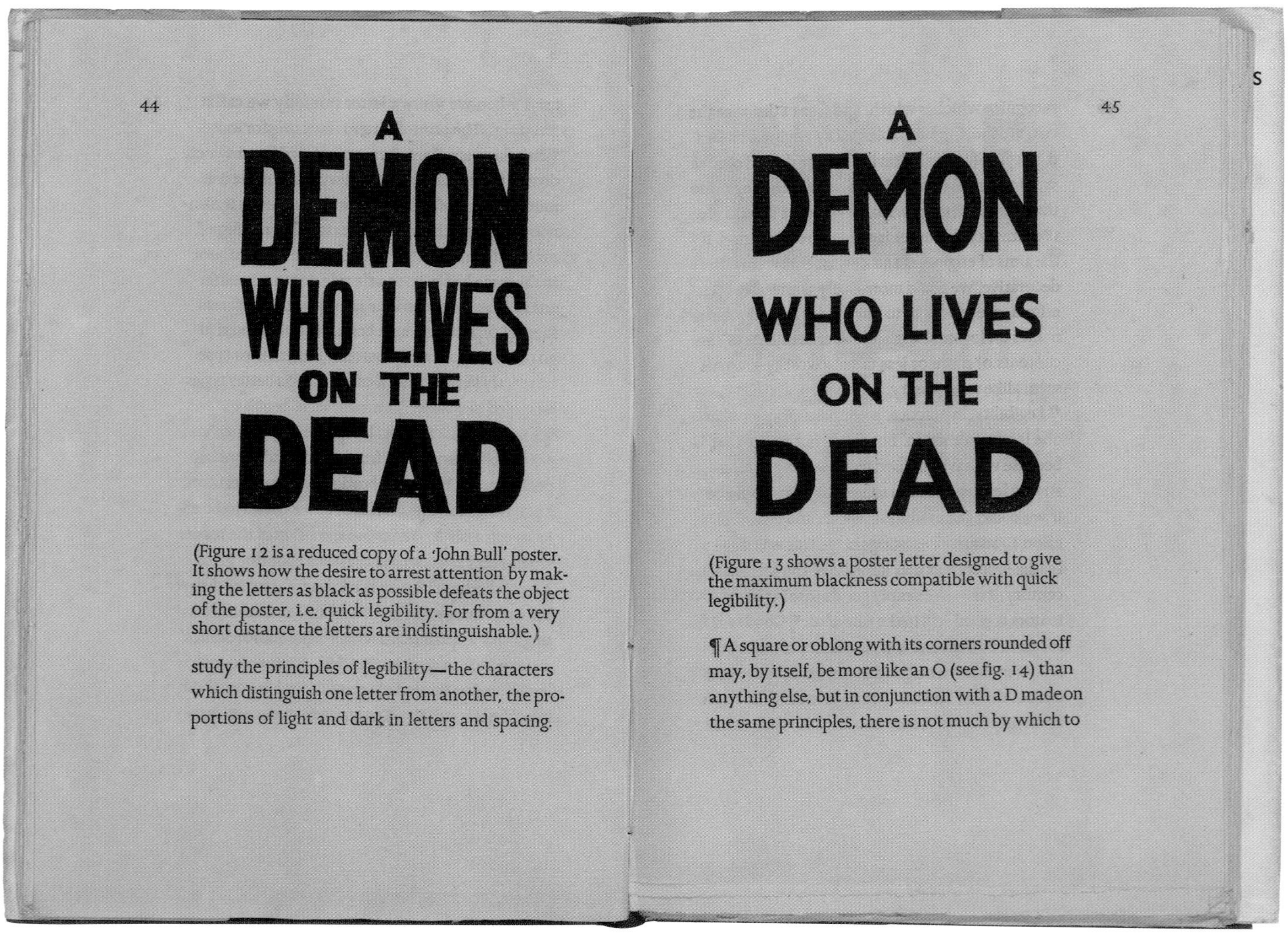

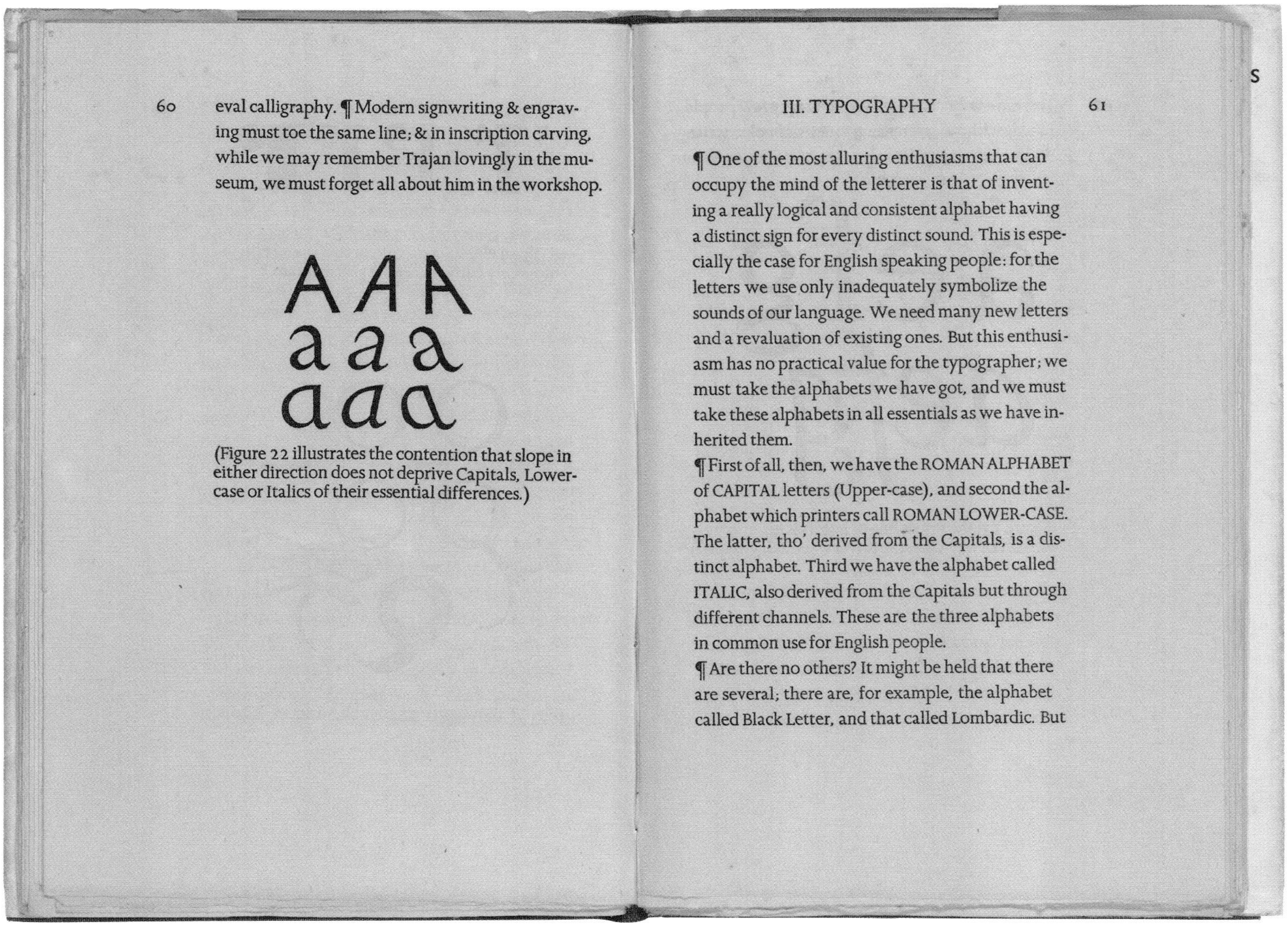
60 eval calligraphy. ¶ Modern signwriting & engraving must toe the same line; & in inscription carving, while we may remember Trajan lovingly in the museum, we must forget all about him in the workshop.

(Figure 22 illustrates the contention that slope in either direction does not deprive Capitals, Lower-case or Italics of their essential differences.)

III. TYPOGRAPHY 61

¶ One of the most alluring enthusiasms that can occupy the mind of the letterer is that of inventing a really logical and consistent alphabet having a distinct sign for every distinct sound. This is especially the case for English speaking people: for the letters we use only inadequately symbolize the sounds of our language. We need many new letters and a revaluation of existing ones. But this enthusiasm has no practical value for the typographer; we must take the alphabets we have got, and we must take these alphabets in all essentials as we have inherited them.

¶ First of all, then, we have the ROMAN ALPHABET of CAPITAL letters (Upper-case), and second the alphabet which printers call ROMAN LOWER-CASE. The latter, tho' derived from the Capitals, is a distinct alphabet. Third we have the alphabet called ITALIC, also derived from the Capitals but through different channels. These are the three alphabets in common use for English people.

¶ Are there no others? It might be held that there are several; there are, for example, the alphabet called Black Letter, and that called Lombardic. But

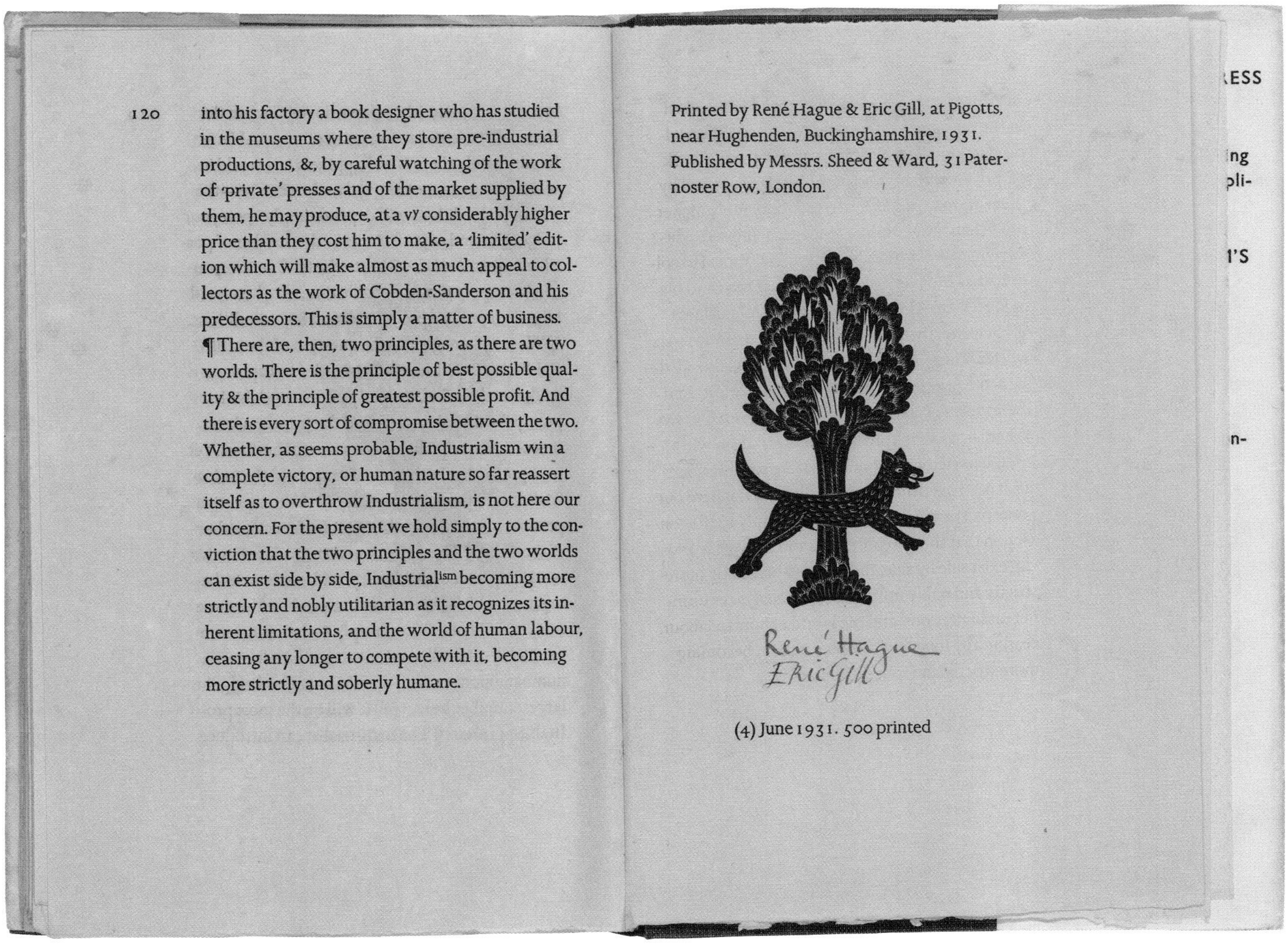
120 into his factory a book designer who has studied in the museums where they store pre-industrial productions, &, by careful watching of the work of 'private' presses and of the market supplied by them, he may produce, at a vy considerably higher price than they cost him to make, a 'limited' edition which will make almost as much appeal to collectors as the work of Cobden-Sanderson and his predecessors. This is simply a matter of business. ¶ There are, then, two principles, as there are two worlds. There is the principle of best possible quality & the principle of greatest possible profit. And there is every sort of compromise between the two. Whether, as seems probable, Industrialism win a complete victory, or human nature so far reassert itself as to overthrow Industrialism, is not here our concern. For the present we hold simply to the conviction that the two principles and the two worlds can exist side by side, Industrialism becoming more strictly and nobly utilitarian as it recognizes its inherent limitations, and the world of human labour, ceasing any longer to compete with it, becoming more strictly and soberly humane.

Printed by René Hague & Eric Gill, at Pigotts, near Hughenden, Buckinghamshire, 1931. Published by Messrs. Sheed & Ward, 31 Paternoster Row, London.

René Hague
Eric Gill

(4) June 1931. 500 printed

1931 **Piet Zwart** *Reclame*. Rotterdam: Nijgh en Van Ditmar (advertising consultants), 1931. 32 pp. 18 x 25 cm.

Designer: Piet Zwart. Photographers: Nijgh en Van Ditmar, Piet Zwart. Printer: Nijgh en Van Ditmar, Rotterdam.

Piet Zwart (1885–1977) is the most famous Dutch designer of the twentieth century. In the twenties and thirties he was part of the international graphic avant-garde, and with Kurt Schwitters and Jan Tschichold he belonged to the Ring neue Werbegestalter (Circle of New Advertising Designers). Zwart also worked as photographer and industrial designer. His Bruynzeel kitchen design (1938) – based on standard dimensions – became a household item in the Netherlands both in the literal and the figurative sense, and it was reissued as a design classic in the new millennium.

A 2008 monograph on Piet Zwart by Yvonne Brentjens questions his role as an innovator and points out that his early work was heavily influenced by that of El Lissitzky. Zwart's advertisements for the Nederlandsche Kabelfabriek (NKF), for instance, contain visual quotes from El Lissitzky's *Dlja golosa* (1923; see page 314), a copy of which the Russian had given to Zwart as a gift. In the ensuing discussion, Zwart's son and several design historians spoke in his defence.

When Piet Zwart took up typographic design in 1921, he was in his late thirties. Among his regular advertising clients were the NKF, Bruynzeel, and PTT (the Dutch national postal and telecom services). The brochure illustrated here – with folds at the fore-edge – is targeted at potential new clients for advertising campaigns. It was published in 1931, the year Zwart designed his much discussed photomontage stamps for the PTT. The photomontages in *Reclame* contain slogans such as 'In the rattling of the typesetting machine resounds the speed of these times.' For the avant-garde of that era, the use of mechanization was a matter of principle. ML

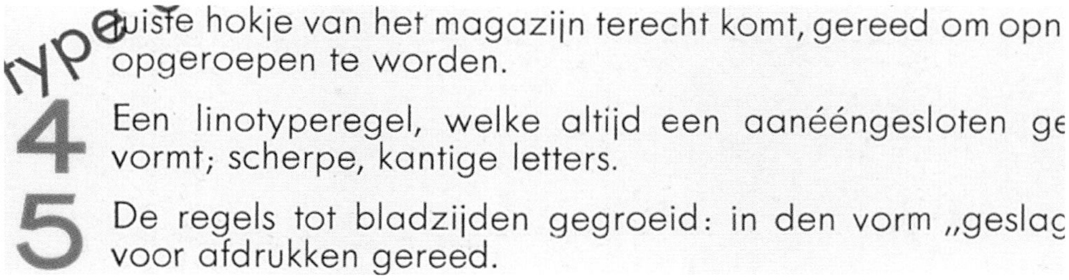

type
uiste hokje van het magazijn terecht komt, gereed om opn
opgeroepen te worden.
4 Een linotyperegel, welke altijd een aanééngesloten ge
vormt; scherpe, kantige letters.
5 De regels tot bladzijden gegroeid: in den vorm „geslag
voor afdrukken gereed.

According to Piet Zwart, the only modern and therefore usable type was a neutral sans serif that harmonized with photographs. He was not particularly fond of Futura (Bauersche Giesserei, 1927), designed by Paul Renner (1878–1956), but the main text shown here is nonetheless set in this geometric sans serif.

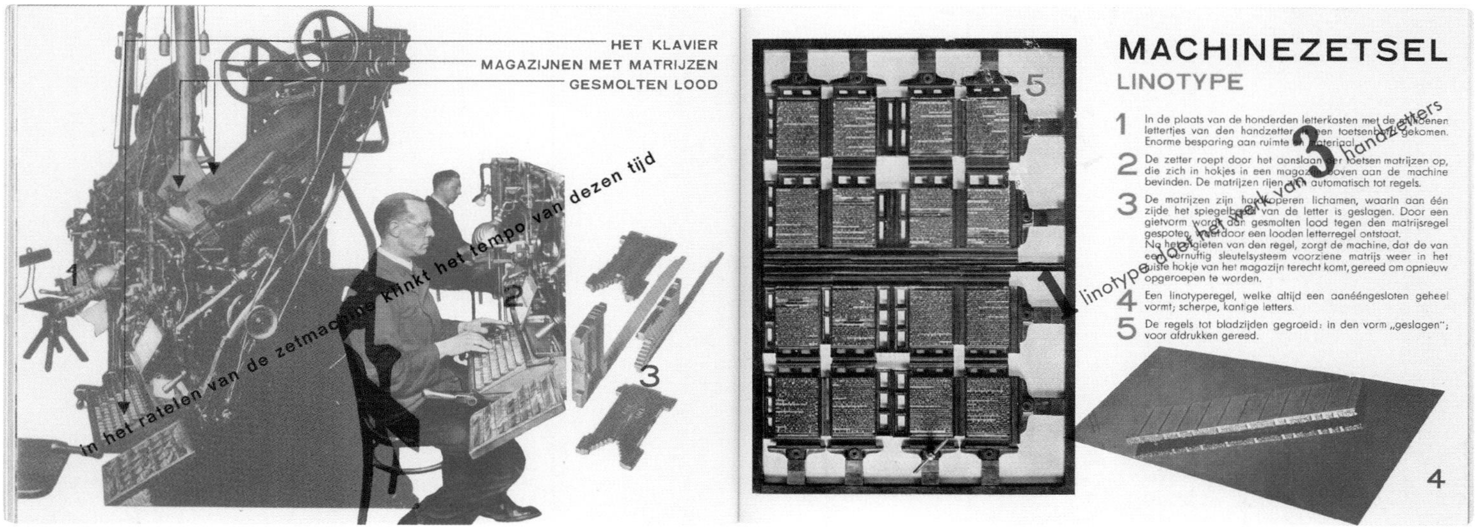

1937 **Jan van Krimpen** **Aristophanes, *The Frogs*; translated by William James Hickie. New York: The Limited Editions Club, 1937. 62 pp. 30 cm. Designer: Jan van Krimpen. Illustrator: John Austen. Printer: Joh. Enschedé en Zonen, Haarlem. In case.**

The Limited Editions Club (LEC), publisher of *The Frogs*, was an American club for book collectors. The illustrated, machine made, 'fine press' editions, printed on quality paper, were issued once a month in print runs of 1,500 copies. For the most part, the books were world literature classics – or, according to the club's newsletter: 'the books *every* man should want to own in a beautiful format.' Three years before it published *The Frogs*, the LEC – perhaps inspired by French *livres d'artiste* publishers – had published another play by Aristophanes for its members: *Lysistrata*, with illustrations by Picasso, including six original etchings.

The LEC worked with prominent printers and designers from the United States and abroad. The publisher had of course spotted the Haarlem company Joh. Enschedé en Zonen, founded in the eighteenth century. Their in-house designer Jan van Krimpen (1892–1958) had an international reputation as a type and book designer. Serious textbooks for the cultural elite were van Krimpen's speciality. He fully endorsed the ideas of his friend Stanley Morison, who advocated restrained and classical book typography. Van Krimpen's work was unadorned; it has been characterized as 'Calvinist' for its austerity.

Since this Aristophanes comedy was represented in *The Work of Jan van Krimpen* (1952), it may be supposed that the book's designer was satisfied with his work. The simple but powerful wood engravings were made by the Englishman John Austen (1886–1948). His work matches the colour of the type pages, which are set with little or no leading. ML

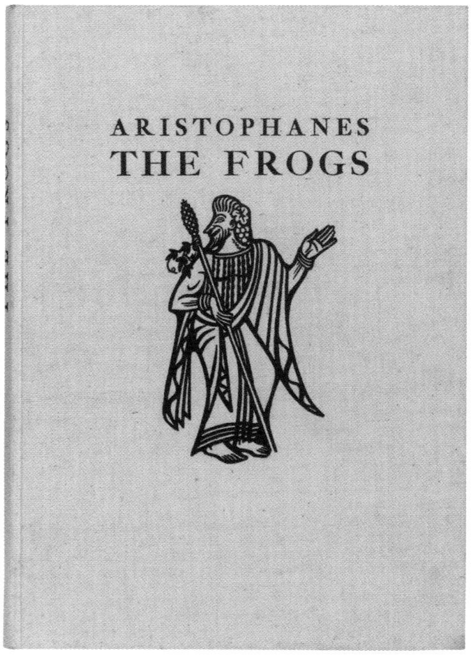

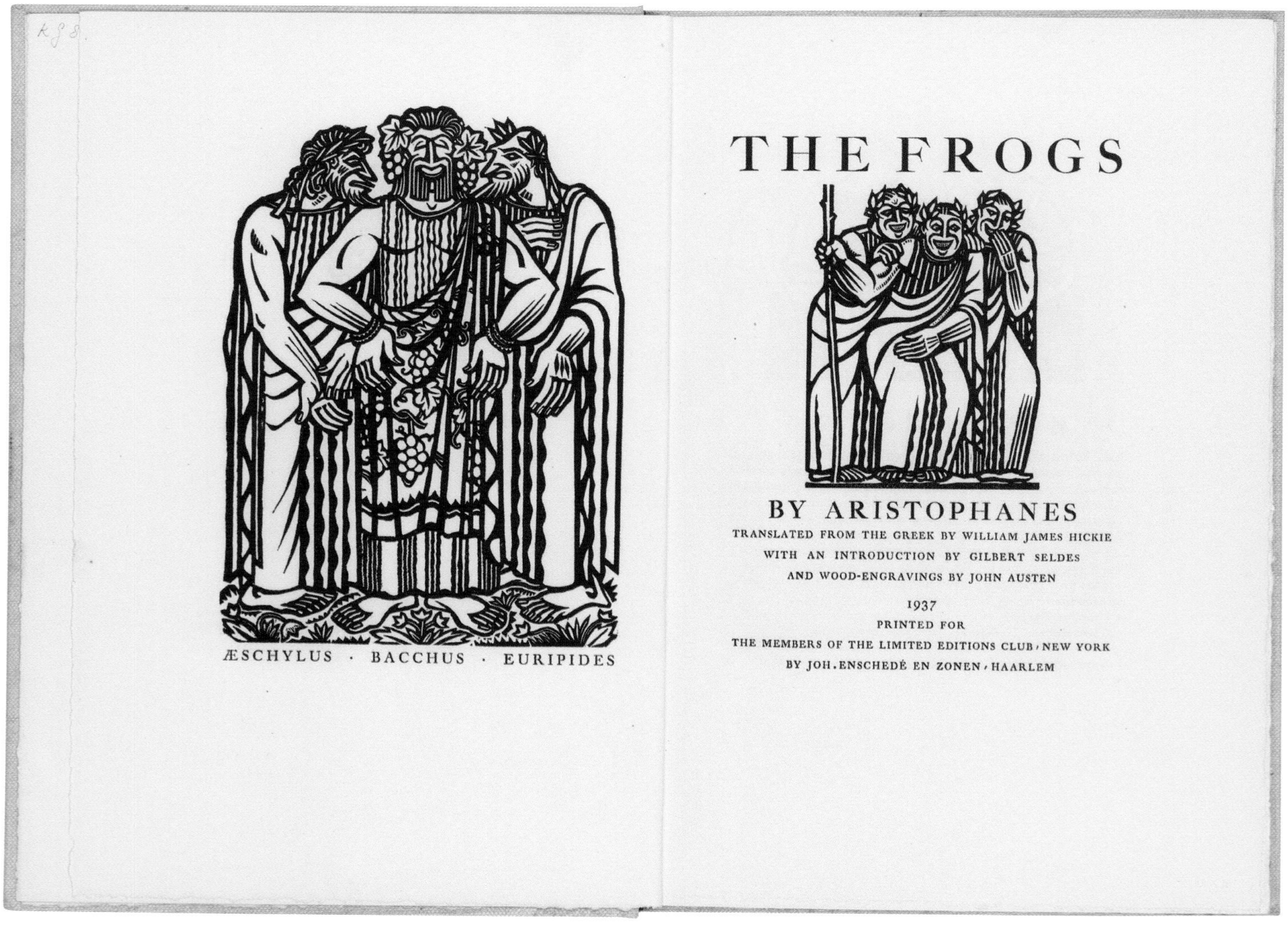

is fitting that the sacred chorus should jointly recommend and teach what is useful for the state. In the first place therefore we move that you put the citizens on a level, and remove their fears. And if any one has erred, having been deceived somewhat by the artifices of Phrynichus, I assert that it ought to be allowed those who made a false step at that time to do away with their former transgressions by pleading their cause. In the next place

This book was set in eighteenth-century typefaces for which the foundry of Enschedé still possessed the original matrices. The large capitals were cut by the Belgian-born Jacques François Rosart (1714–77) and the text face by the German Joan Michael Fleischman (1707–68). Both punchcutters had worked in the Netherlands for an extended period.

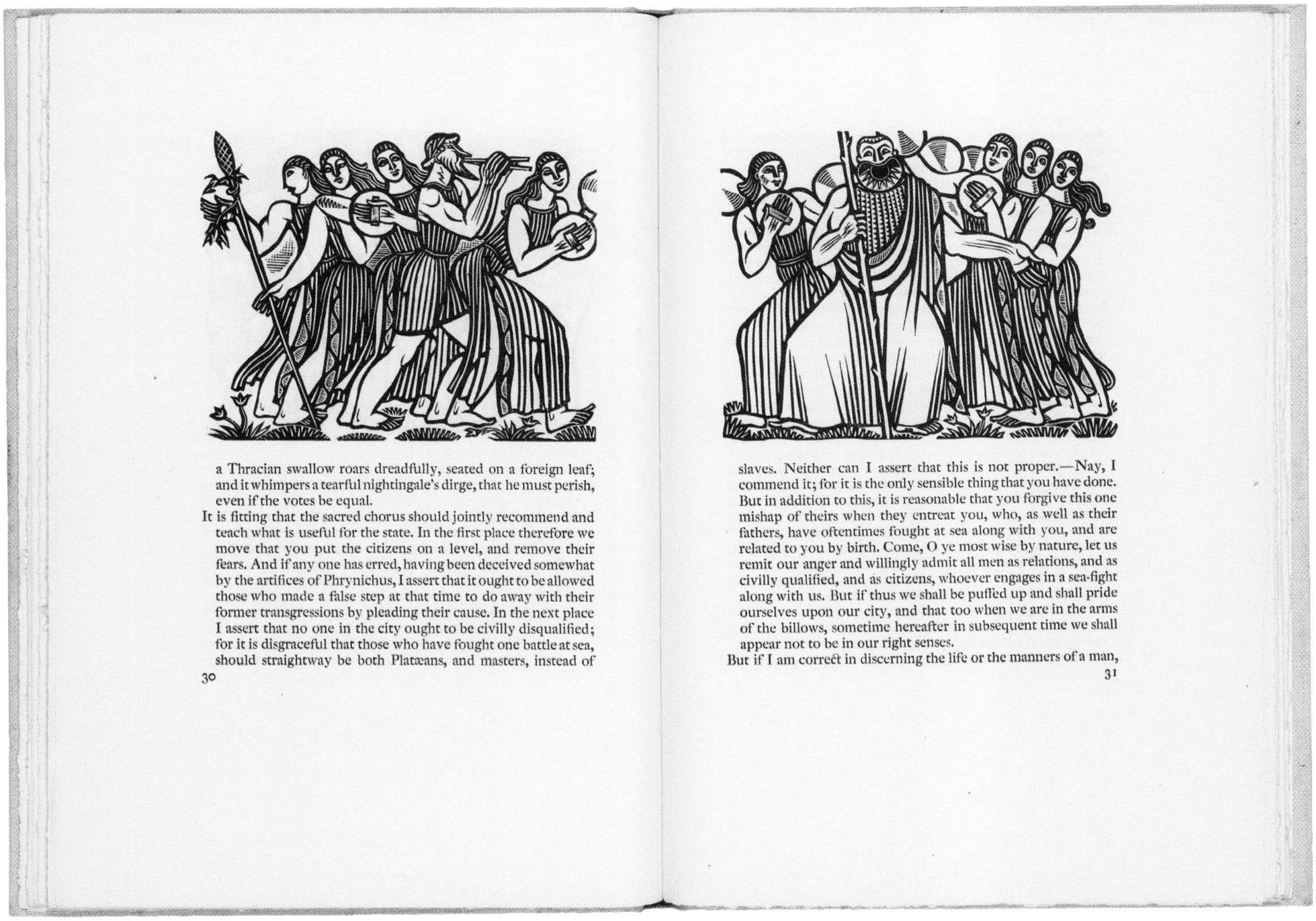

a Thracian swallow roars dreadfully, seated on a foreign leaf; and it whimpers a tearful nightingale's dirge, that he must perish, even if the votes be equal.

It is fitting that the sacred chorus should jointly recommend and teach what is useful for the state. In the first place therefore we move that you put the citizens on a level, and remove their fears. And if any one has erred, having been deceived somewhat by the artifices of Phrynichus, I assert that it ought to be allowed those who made a false step at that time to do away with their former transgressions by pleading their cause. In the next place I assert that no one in the city ought to be civilly disqualified; for it is disgraceful that those who have fought one battle at sea, should straightway be both Platæans, and masters, instead of

30

slaves. Neither can I assert that this is not proper.—Nay, I commend it; for it is the only sensible thing that you have done. But in addition to this, it is reasonable that you forgive this one mishap of theirs when they entreat you, who, as well as their fathers, have oftentimes fought at sea along with you, and are related to you by birth. Come, O ye most wise by nature, let us remit our anger and willingly admit all men as relations, and as civilly qualified, and as citizens, whoever engages in a sea-fight along with us. But if thus we shall be puffed up and shall pride ourselves upon our city, and that too when we are in the arms of the billows, sometime hereafter in subsequent time we shall appear not to be in our right senses.

But if I am correct in discerning the life or the manners of a man,

31

1948 **Pierre Faucheux** Henri Pichette, *Les épiphanies*. Paris: K éditeur, 1948. 137 pp. 24.5 cm. Designer: Pierre Faucheux. Printer: André Tournon et Cie, Paris.

Pierre Faucheux (1924–99) and Robert Massin set the tone in French book design after the Second World War. Book design flourished in those years, particularly due to a number of book clubs, whose members had pledged to buy. People were hungry for books, and club memberships grew rapidly. Faucheux had studied book design and typography for three years at the École Estienne in Paris. He was appointed art director of the Club Français du Livre in 1946, and later worked for another book club. In contrast to the restrained typographical exercises of the Swiss, French book clubs indulged in the use of eye-catching materials and expressive designs. Industrially produced books became an item for collectors.

Faucheux produced this striking book design for the experimental play *Les épiphanies* by his contemporary Henri Pichette. The play was performed for the first time towards the end of 1947 in a small Paris theatre, albeit with a director and a cast of some renown. Despite its long monologues and the absence of a real plot, the play managed to impress and enchant the audience. One year later, the text was published by K éditeur. Faucheux created a typographical interpretation of the play and indicated each of the characters by an odd letter or vignette from the type case. The experimental design clearly shows that Dada and Surrealism were sources of inspiration for him in that period.

At the beginning of the sixties, he opened a design office, Atelier Pierre Faucheux, enabling him to accept larger commissions. An example was the *Livre de Poche* (*LDP*) series for Hachette, which showcases a sampling of his varied and often daring typography. ML

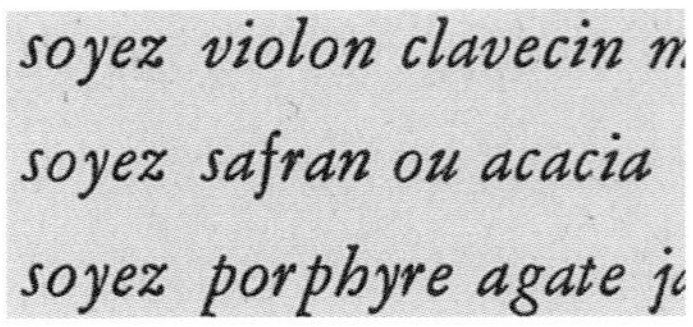

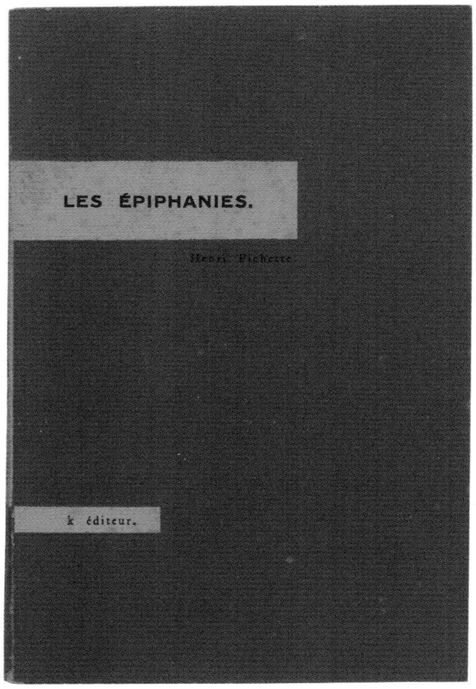

Intertype Garamond (1926) is adapted from the American Type Founders' Garamond (*c.* 1918), designed by Morris F. Benton and Thomas M. Cleland. The roman and the italic are adapted from the early seventeenth-century work of French punchcutter Jean Jannon (1580–1658).

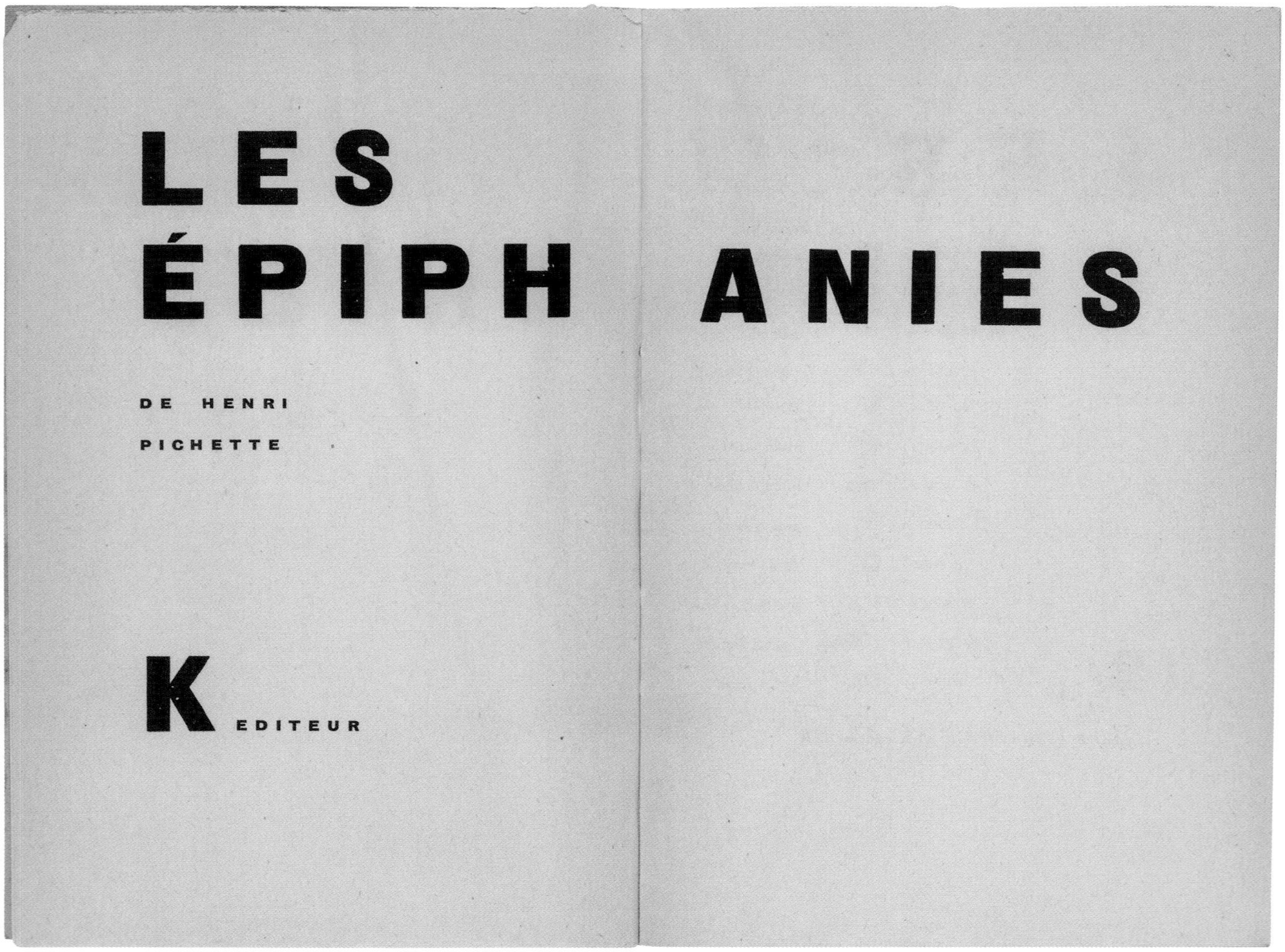

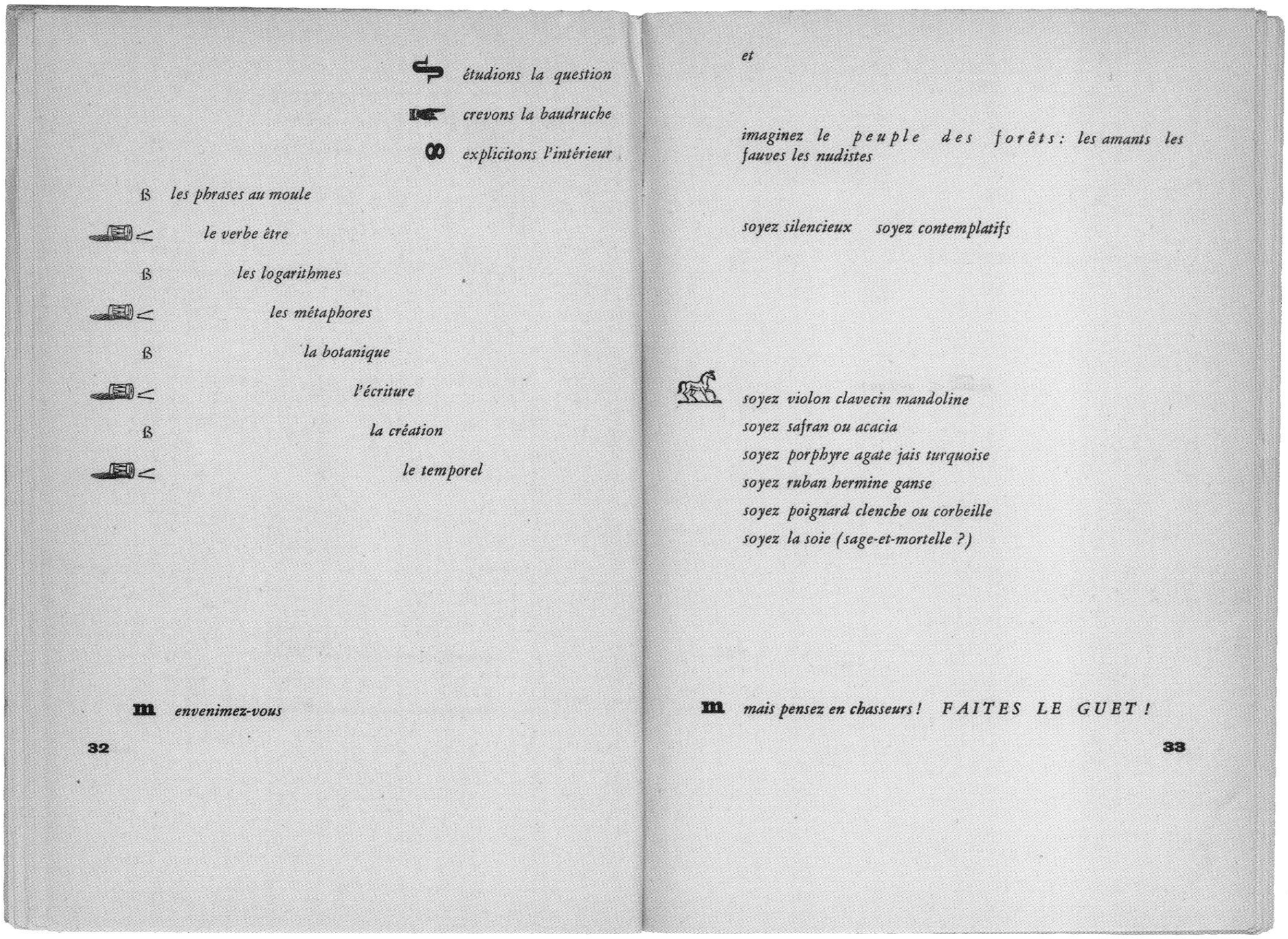
étudions la question

crevons la baudruche

explicitons l'intérieur

ß *les phrases au moule*

le verbe être

ß *les logarithmes*

les métaphores

ß *la botanique*

l'écriture

ß *la création*

le temporel

m *envenimez-vous*

32

et

imaginez le p e u p l e d e s f o r ê t s : les amants les fauves les nudistes

soyez silencieux soyez contemplatifs

soyez violon clavecin mandoline
soyez safran ou acacia
soyez porphyre agate jais turquoise
soyez ruban hermine ganse
soyez poignard clenche ou corbeille
soyez la soie (sage-et-mortelle ?)

m *mais pensez en chasseurs ! F A I T E S L E G U E T !*

33

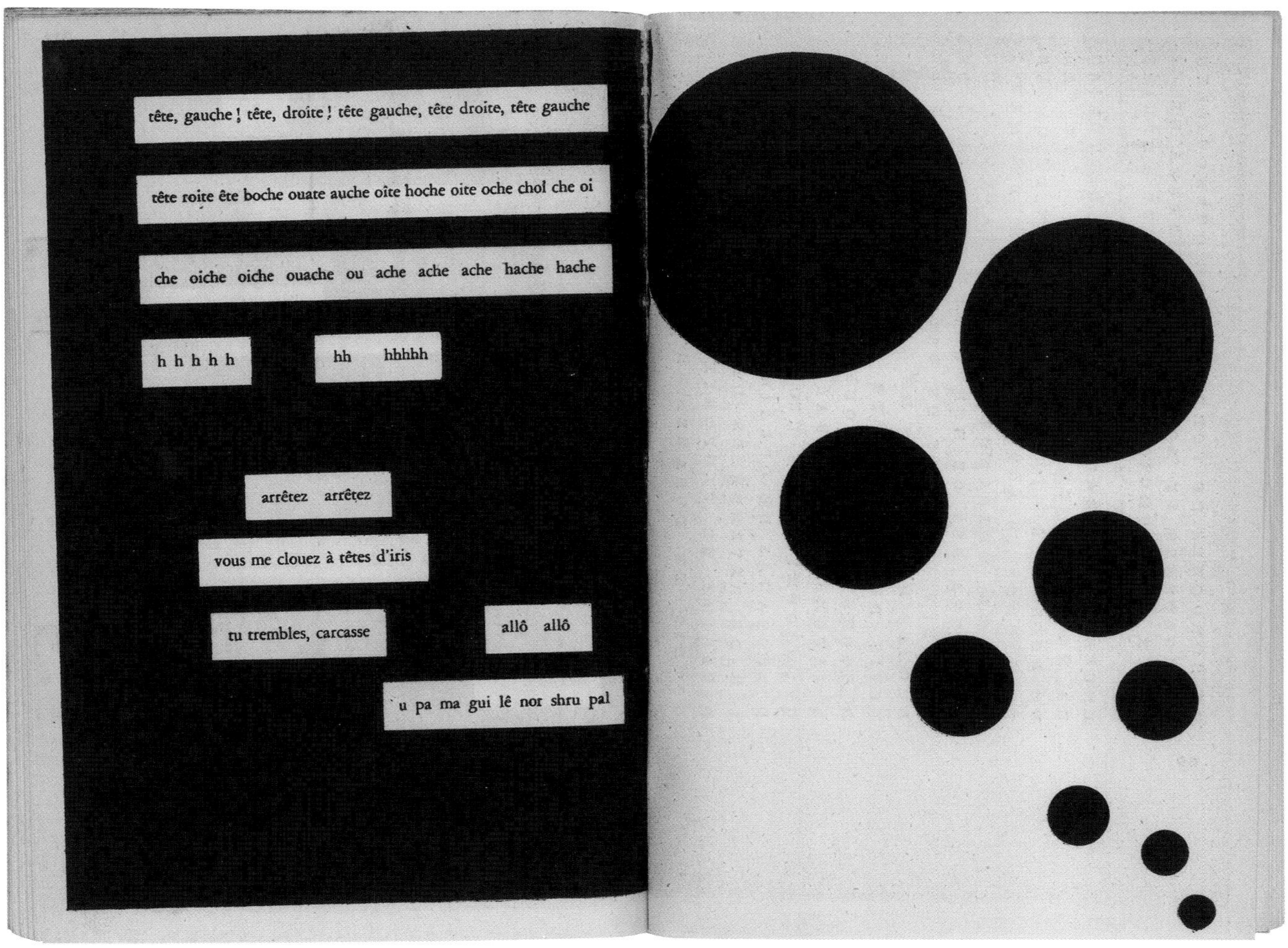
tête, gauche ! tête, droite ! tête gauche, tête droite, tête gauche

tête roite ête boche ouate auche oîte hoche oite oche chol che oi

che oiche oiche ouache ou ache ache ache hache hache

h h h h h

hh hhhhh

arrêtez arrêtez

vous me clouez à têtes d'iris

tu trembles, carcasse

allô allô

u pa ma gui lê nor shru pal

353

Modernism and Swiss typography

Detail of *World Geo-graphic Atlas*, designed by Herbert Bayer (see p. 362)

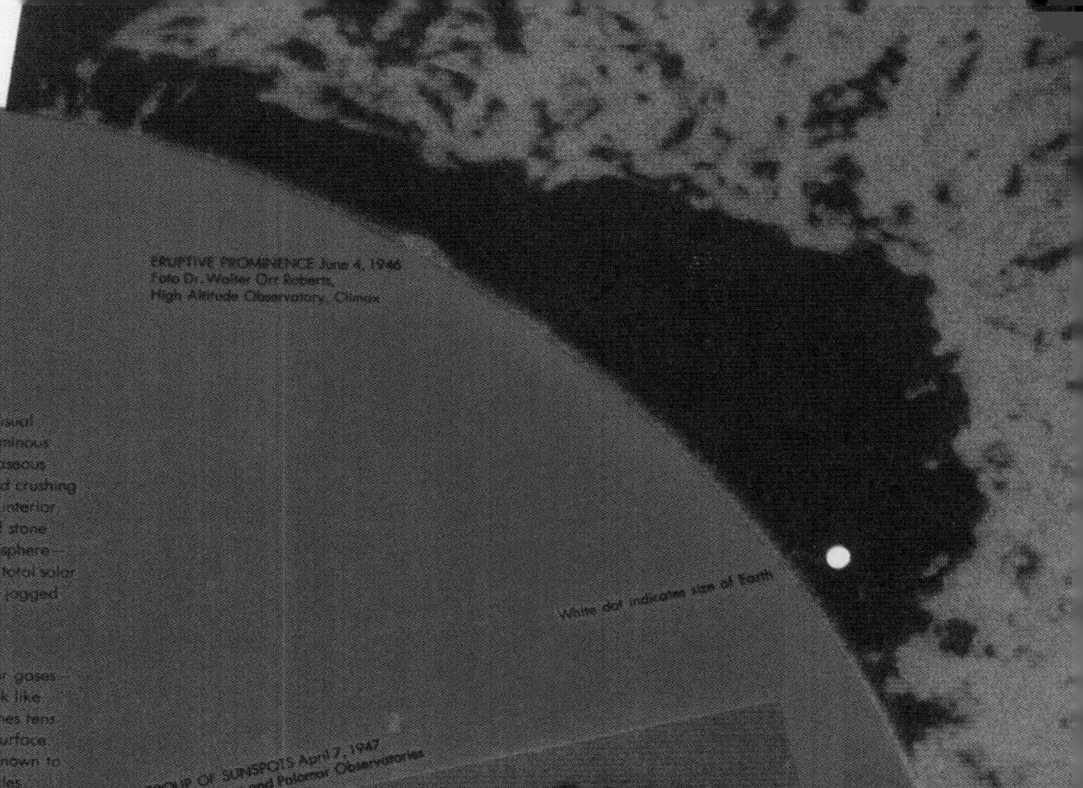

ERUPTIVE PROMINENCE June 4, 1946
Foto Dr. Walter Orr Roberts,
High Altitude Observatory, Climax

SUN DATA. The Sun is a star of generous but not unusual proportions. Like other stars, and unlike most non-luminous astronomical bodies, it is gaseous throughout. But gaseous interior, by virtue of its massive size, temperature and crushing gravitational forces, is wholly opaque. Boundary of interior, known as Photosphere, is as sharp as though made of stone. Surmounting opaque sphere is mysterious solar atmosphere—visible to the naked eye only during brief moments of total solar eclipses—made up of tenuous and extensive Corona, jagged flame-like Prominences and narrow color fringe of Chromosphere.

PROMINENCES—giant clouds of hydrogen and other gases—are irregularly scattered over Sun's surface. They look like great tongues of brilliant red flame reaching sometimes tens or even hundreds of thousands of miles above Sun's surface. They travel as though directed by magnetic forces known to exist in Sun. Their speeds reach many hundreds of miles per second.

SUNSPOTS. Coldest places in the Sun are sunspots, relatively small areas whose temperature may, for unknown reasons, drop to a mere 7,000° F. Sunspots occur periodically, rising and falling in number, in cycles of about a decade. They are symptoms of solar disturbances. When most numerous, electrical and magnetic conditions of earth's upper atmosphere respond with disturbances which affect, among other things, radio communications.

GROUP OF SUNSPOTS April 7, 1947
Foto Mt. Wilson and Palomar Observatories

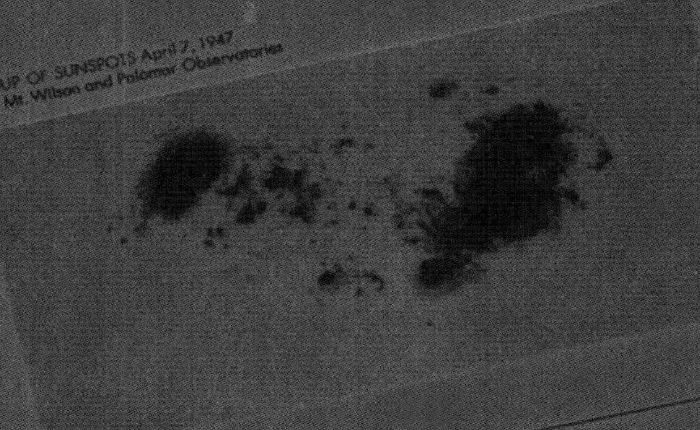

RADIUS OF SUN 432,000 MILES

CHROMOSPHERE. Directly above luminous Photosphere surface from which Sun radiates main supply of energy, lies brilliant Chromosphere, a narrow layer of radiant gas completely enveloping Sun. It glows for a few seconds at start and end of total eclipse as a brilliant red fringe at moon's dark edge.

CORONA, seen brilliantly during eclipse, concealed by sunlight at other times, hides numerous scientific riddles in its pale white glow. It contains atoms of high temperature and low pressure utterly unattainable on earth. It consists in part of electrons speeding thousands of miles per second. Wholly consistent explanation of Corona's behavior eludes even most advanced efforts of astrophysics. Corona changes from day to day in synchronism with solar causes yet unknown. (Effects range from interference with radar reception to faintly flickering auroras over polar regions of earth.)

ENERGY SOURCE. Exact process by which Sun's vast store of energy is released still eludes astrophysicists. Fuel, however, is hydrogen, most abundant element of Sun. Deep beneath the surface exist enormous temperatures (as high as 30,000,000° F.). Pressures reach many millions of tons per square inch. There in the vast atomic retort hydrogen atoms fuse together to form helium—a process which releases energy that lights solar system. According to best estimates, hydrogen of Sun is sufficient to provide sunlight at present rate for the next 10 billion years.

From most ancient times man has recognized vastness of energy store received from the Sun, but only recently have scientists begun to understand complicated processes by which Sun operates. The earth captures prodigious amounts of heat from Sun. 5×10^{20} kilocalories of radiant heat reach earth every year. One person eats approximately 3,000 kilocalories per day in form of food, and utilizes, in the United States, about 150,000 kilocalories per day for light, house heat, locomotion, factory operations, and all other energy-consuming processes of life. Thus store of energy received from Sun exceeds, by thousands, total needs of mankind. All other circumstances of life depend upon unstinting, infallible flow of energy from Sun to earth.

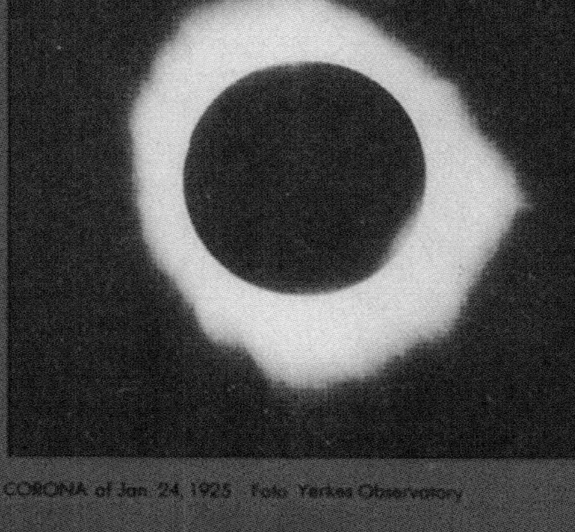

CORONA of Jan. 24, 1925 Foto Yerkes Observatory

SMALL ERUPTIVE PROMINENCE →

CORONA

Modernism and Swiss typography **After the Second World War, an international modernist style grew out of the European avant-garde. Its breeding ground was politically neutral Switzerland, where designers had been able to function almost undisturbed during the war years. The cities of Zurich and Basel also offered thorough courses in graphic design. Herbert Matter, Richard Paul Lohse and Max Bill were the leading modernists of the old guard, although Matter had settled in the United States in 1936. Bill, a former Bauhaus student, gave the movement its initial theoretical impetus. In 1946 he attacked Jan Tschichold, who had switched to a critical view of the New Typography and was promoting classical, symmetrical typography in books for continuous reading.**

The fifties saw the establishment of the graphic designer as a recognized professional. In Switzerland, publications about contemporary typography began to appear, often with trilingual text in German, French and English. The internationally influential journal *New Graphic Design* (1958–65), published in Zurich, included Lohse on its editorial staff. In addition, the young Basel designer Karl Gerstner appeared as co-author of *The New Graphic Art* (1959), which included recent work but also provided an historical context. The movement's first manual was Josef Müller-Brockmann's *The Graphic Artist and His Design Problems* (1961). It featured asymmetrical layouts using grids, sans serif typefaces and photography. In its new Swiss form, modernism was depoliticized and made 'neutral'.

The movement turned back to the older sans serif faces, Akzidenz-Grotesk – sold in English-speaking countries under the name Standard – and Monotype Grotesque

no. 215. These typefaces soon met with stiff competition from new sans serifs such as Helvetica (the Latin word for Swiss) and Univers, which came on the market in 1957.

Among the best-known practitioners of Swiss typography, also called the International Typographic Style, were the Dutchman Wim Crouwel and the Italian-American Massimo Vignelli. Crouwel, nicknamed Mr Gridnik, represented (in his own words) 'an analytical approach that makes an objective contribution to the communication process' (1972). There were also, of course, modernists who kept more distance from the Swiss style, including Paul Rand in the US, Willem Sandberg in the Netherlands, Giovanni Pintori in Italy and Robert Massin in France. Their work is more individual and less minimalist, still leaving room for illustrative elements.

Just as the architectural International Style left its mark on skyscrapers and apartment buildings, its graphic counterpart attained ubiquity through advertising and the house styles of multinational corporations and governments or government-affiliated organizations. In the world of books, it was used on the covers of Penguin paperbacks and more generally in catalogues and books about art and architecture.

Designers and the general public showed a growing resistance to this style in the seventies, often finding it cold, but it never completely disappeared. ML

1948 **Richard Paul Lohse** Richard Wright, *Wir Neger in Amerika*. Zurich: Büchergilde Gutenberg, 1948. 157 pp. 24 cm.

German translation of *12 Million Black Voices* (1941). Designer: Richard Paul Lohse. Photographers: Dorothea Lange and others.

Typesetter: Berichthaus, Zurich. Printer: Héliographia, Lausanne.

In 1924, the Büchergilde Gutenberg was founded in Germany, with the aim of making interesting books affordable to people living on a budget. The book club's typography was progressive, owing to designers that included the young Jan Tschichold. Richard Paul Lohse designed over a hundred books (both fiction and non-fiction) for the club's Swiss affiliate, which became independent after the 1933 book burning in Nazi Germany.

Among Lohse's best work for the Büchergilde Gutenberg is this 1948 translation of Richard Wright's *12 Million Black Voices*. The cover design shows that the square and the grid were crucial for this designer. Apart from the text, which is notable for its social criticism, the book contains photographs of African-Americans during the Great Depression. To obtain the best possible reproduction quality, gravure printing was used. The refined asymmetrical sans serif layout strives for an ideal ratio of text and image on each spread, resulting in a variable number of text lines per page.

Richard Paul Lohse (1902–88) was educated at the Arts and Crafts School in Zurich. He worked for publishers and cultural institutions as well as for firms in industries such as construction. At the same time, he was a well-respected painter, exploring a geometric abstraction approach since 1940. His 'constructive' typography is closely linked to his systematic, objective paintings, which consist of horizontal and vertical elements.

In Zurich, Lohse edited the magazine *Neue Grafik* (1958–65) with Josef Müller-Brockmann, Hans Neuburg and Carlo Vivarelli. For its international readership, the trilingual magazine in German, English and French was an excellent means of getting acquainted with modern Swiss typography. ML

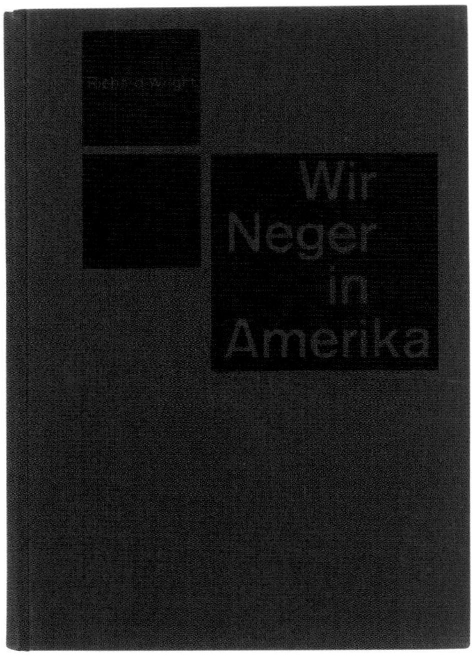

This text was first set in metal type, a sturdy sans serif from around 1900/10, and printed on paper. It was then screened and gravure printed with the images. Of course, the result of gravure printing is that the type contours lack sharpness in comparison to letterpress printing.

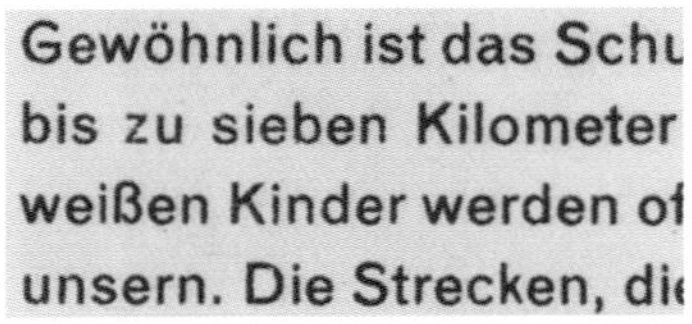
Gewöhnlich ist das Schu
bis zu sieben Kilometer
weißen Kinder werden of
unsern. Die Strecken, di

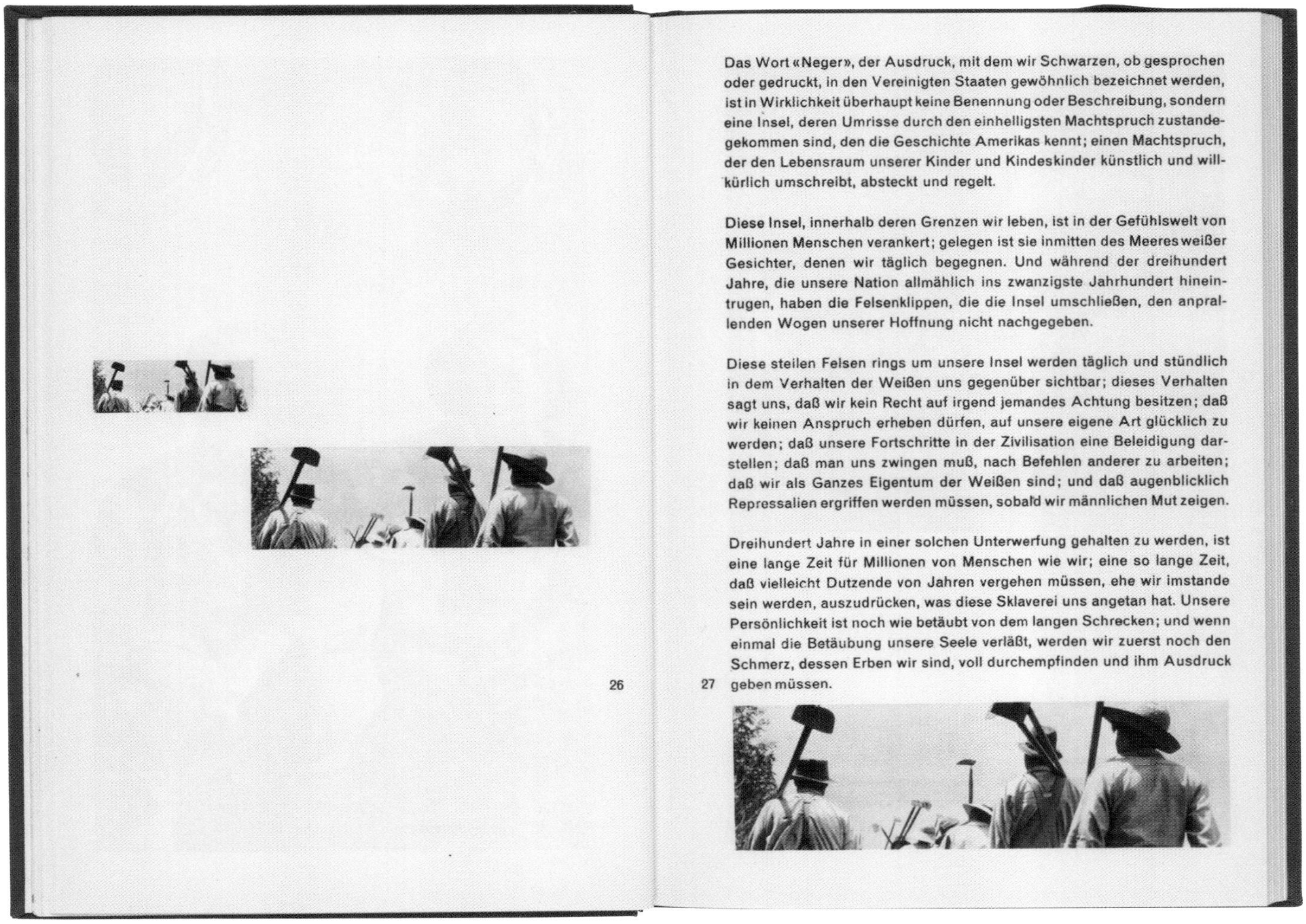

26

27

Das Wort «Neger», der Ausdruck, mit dem wir Schwarzen, ob gesprochen oder gedruckt, in den Vereinigten Staaten gewöhnlich bezeichnet werden, ist in Wirklichkeit überhaupt keine Benennung oder Beschreibung, sondern eine Insel, deren Umrisse durch den einhelligsten Machtspruch zustandegekommen sind, den die Geschichte Amerikas kennt; einen Machtspruch, der den Lebensraum unserer Kinder und Kindeskinder künstlich und willkürlich umschreibt, absteckt und regelt.

Diese Insel, innerhalb deren Grenzen wir leben, ist in der Gefühlswelt von Millionen Menschen verankert; gelegen ist sie inmitten des Meeres weißer Gesichter, denen wir täglich begegnen. Und während der dreihundert Jahre, die unsere Nation allmählich ins zwanzigste Jahrhundert hineintrugen, haben die Felsenklippen, die die Insel umschließen, den anprallenden Wogen unserer Hoffnung nicht nachgegeben.

Diese steilen Felsen rings um unsere Insel werden täglich und stündlich in dem Verhalten der Weißen uns gegenüber sichtbar; dieses Verhalten sagt uns, daß wir kein Recht auf irgend jemandes Achtung besitzen; daß wir keinen Anspruch erheben dürfen, auf unsere eigene Art glücklich zu werden; daß unsere Fortschritte in der Zivilisation eine Beleidigung darstellen; daß man uns zwingen muß, nach Befehlen anderer zu arbeiten; daß wir als Ganzes Eigentum der Weißen sind; und daß augenblicklich Repressalien ergriffen werden müssen, sobald wir männlichen Mut zeigen.

Dreihundert Jahre in einer solchen Unterwerfung gehalten zu werden, ist eine lange Zeit für Millionen von Menschen wie wir; eine so lange Zeit, daß vielleicht Dutzende von Jahren vergehen müssen, ehe wir imstande sein werden, auszudrücken, was diese Sklaverei uns angetan hat. Unsere Persönlichkeit ist noch wie betäubt von dem langen Schrecken; und wenn einmal die Betäubung unsere Seele verläßt, werden wir zuerst noch den Schmerz, dessen Erben wir sind, voll durchempfinden und ihm Ausdruck geben müssen.

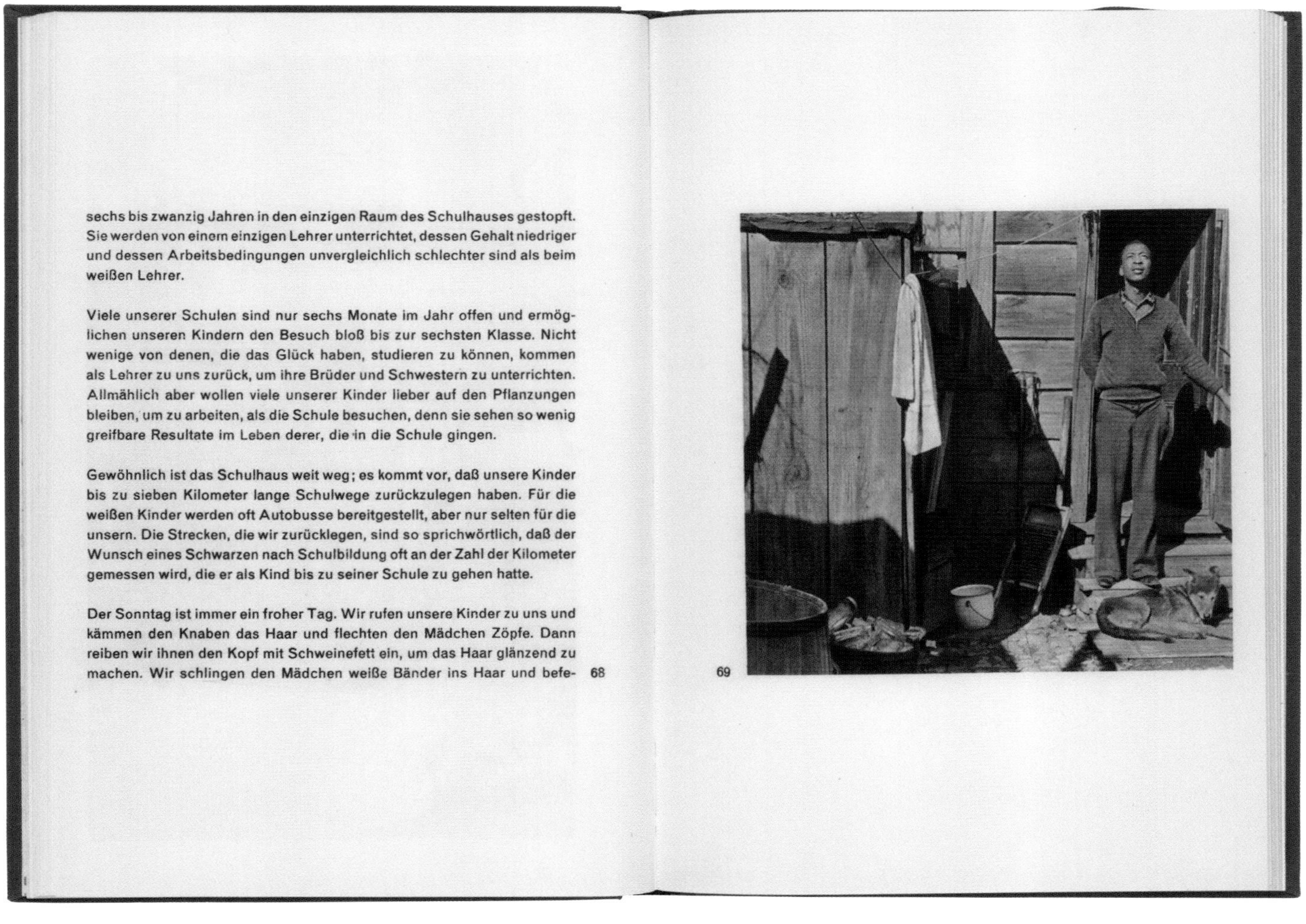

sechs bis zwanzig Jahren in den einzigen Raum des Schulhauses gestopft. Sie werden von einem einzigen Lehrer unterrichtet, dessen Gehalt niedriger und dessen Arbeitsbedingungen unvergleichlich schlechter sind als beim weißen Lehrer.

Viele unserer Schulen sind nur sechs Monate im Jahr offen und ermöglichen unseren Kindern den Besuch bloß bis zur sechsten Klasse. Nicht wenige von denen, die das Glück haben, studieren zu können, kommen als Lehrer zu uns zurück, um ihre Brüder und Schwestern zu unterrichten. Allmählich aber wollen viele unserer Kinder lieber auf den Pflanzungen bleiben, um zu arbeiten, als die Schule besuchen, denn sie sehen so wenig greifbare Resultate im Leben derer, die in die Schule gingen.

Gewöhnlich ist das Schulhaus weit weg; es kommt vor, daß unsere Kinder bis zu sieben Kilometer lange Schulwege zurückzulegen haben. Für die weißen Kinder werden oft Autobusse bereitgestellt, aber nur selten für die unsern. Die Strecken, die wir zurücklegen, sind so sprichwörtlich, daß der Wunsch eines Schwarzen nach Schulbildung oft an der Zahl der Kilometer gemessen wird, die er als Kind bis zu seiner Schule zu gehen hatte.

Der Sonntag ist immer ein froher Tag. Wir rufen unsere Kinder zu uns und kämmen den Knaben das Haar und flechten den Mädchen Zöpfe. Dann reiben wir ihnen den Kopf mit Schweinefett ein, um das Haar glänzend zu machen. Wir schlingen den Mädchen weiße Bänder ins Haar und befe-

68

69

1949 **Jan Tschichold** Kate O'Brien, *Without My Cloak*. Harmondsworth: Penguin Books/William Heinemann, 1949.

509 pp. 18 cm. Penguin Books no. 716. Designer: Jan Tschichold. Printer: Wyman and Sons, London, Fakenham, Reading.

Because of his publications and the high quality of his work, Jan Tschichold (1902–74) was a leading international designer. His *Die neue Typographie* (1928) and *Typographische Gestaltung* (1935) were the typographic manuals of modernism.

While many representatives of New Typography started working as designers in advertising without any professional training, Tschichold had studied classic book typography at Leipzig Academy and had learned typesetting as a volunteer. He was also an exceptionally gifted calligrapher and lettering artist from a young age. Furthermore, aside from his education and practical experience, he was well read in the history of graphic design, all of which made him eminently qualified to translate new ideas onto the shop floor.

When the Nazis rose to power in Germany in 1933, Tschichold – who was denounced as a cultural bolshevist – went into exile in Basel with his wife and child. The books he made in Switzerland clearly show a return to traditional and symmetrical typography. In a lecture he gave in 1945, Tschichold was very clear about this: New Typography, which he now associated with fascism, was suitable for advertising, but unsuitable for literature. A fierce argument then broke loose in the trade journals.

In 1947, Tschichold relocated to London, to improve typography and production of the various Penguin Books series. During the two and a half years he worked for Penguin – as their best-paid employee – he took on every aspect of design, from interiors and covers to the Penguin logo. He was directly involved in the design of over five hundred books. After he left, the publishing house continued to work with his cover formats and detailed composition rules. ML

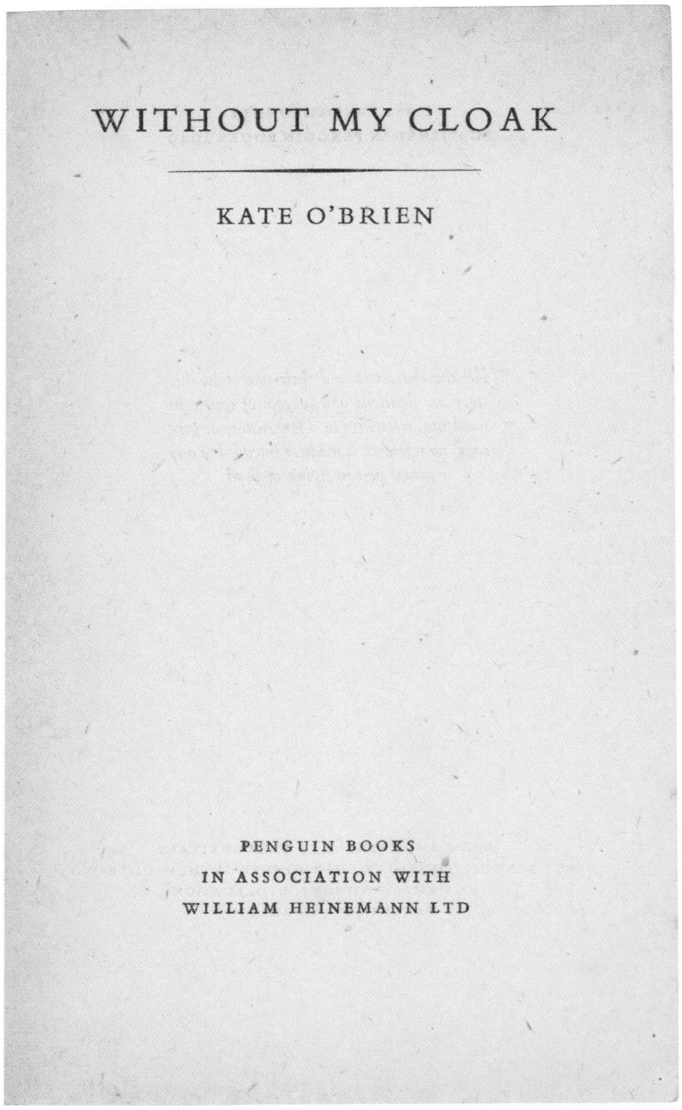

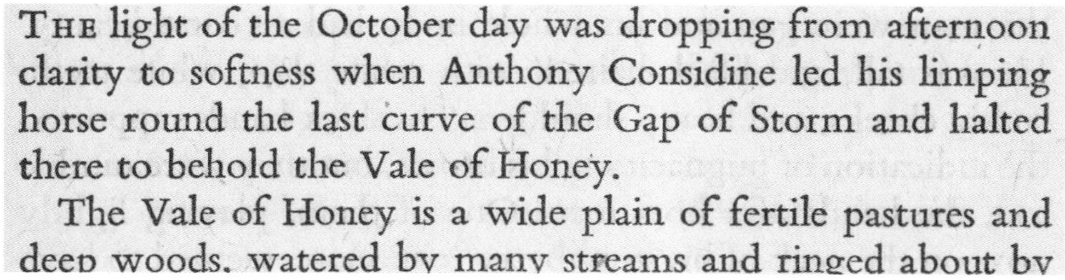

THE light of the October day was dropping from afternoon clarity to softness when Anthony Considine led his limping horse round the last curve of the Gap of Storm and halted there to behold the Vale of Honey.

The Vale of Honey is a wide plain of fertile pastures and deep woods, watered by many streams and ringed about by

Monotype Bembo (1929) – a perennial favourite of classic book typographers – is based on a roman by Francesco Griffo (*fl.* 1475?–1518) and an italic by Giovanni Tagliente (*fl.* 1491–1531). The name refers to Pietro Bembo, the author of the work in which the original roman was first used in 1495/96.

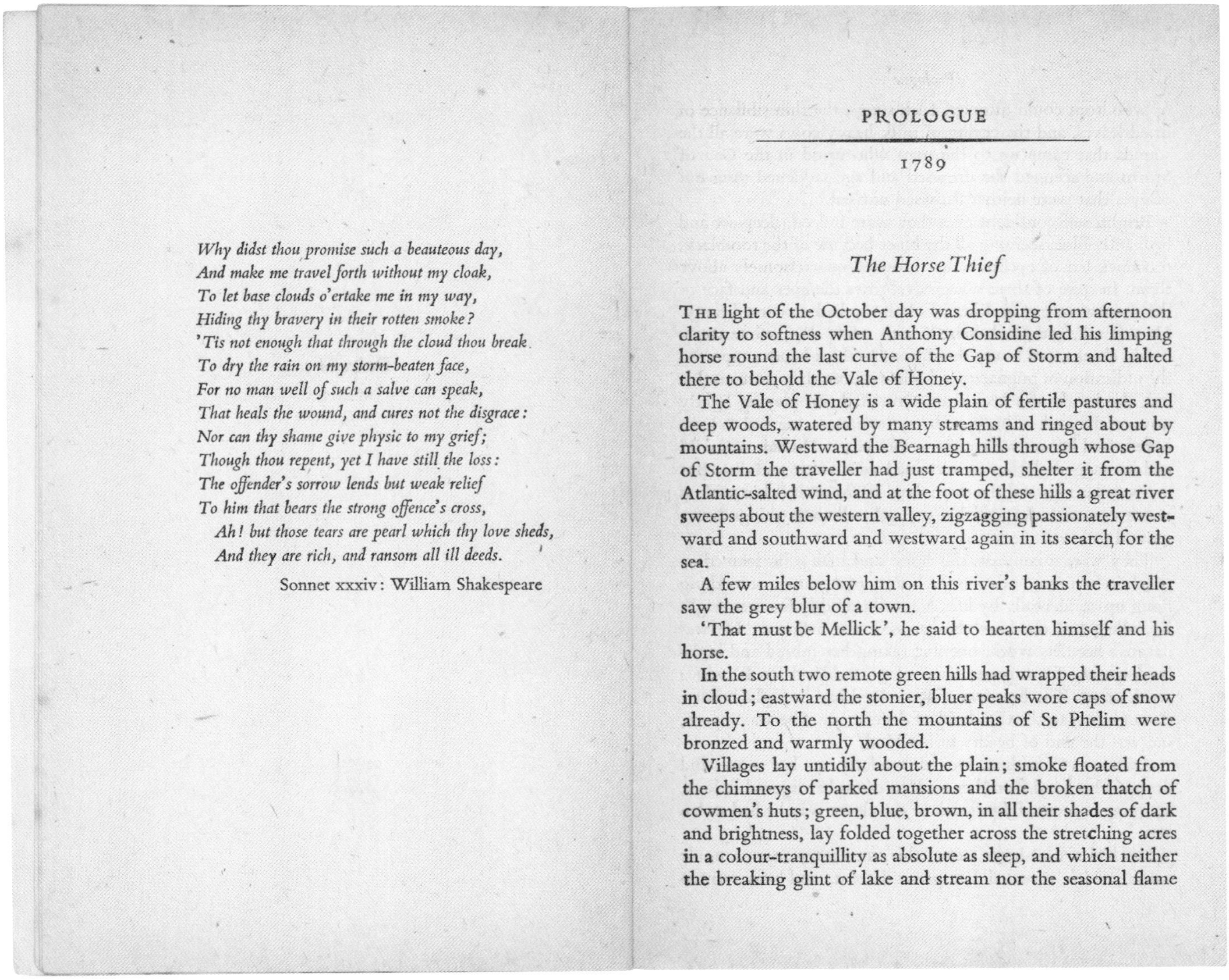

Why didst thou promise such a beauteous day,
And make me travel forth without my cloak,
To let base clouds o'ertake me in my way,
Hiding thy bravery in their rotten smoke?
'Tis not enough that through the cloud thou break
To dry the rain on my storm-beaten face,
For no man well of such a salve can speak,
That heals the wound, and cures not the disgrace:
Nor can thy shame give physic to my grief;
Though thou repent, yet I have still the loss:
The offender's sorrow lends but weak relief
To him that bears the strong offence's cross,
Ah! but those tears are pearl which thy love sheds,
And they are rich, and ransom all ill deeds.

Sonnet xxxiv: William Shakespeare

PROLOGUE

1789

The Horse Thief

THE light of the October day was dropping from afternoon clarity to softness when Anthony Considine led his limping horse round the last curve of the Gap of Storm and halted there to behold the Vale of Honey.

The Vale of Honey is a wide plain of fertile pastures and deep woods, watered by many streams and ringed about by mountains. Westward the Bearnagh hills through whose Gap of Storm the traveller had just tramped, shelter it from the Atlantic-salted wind, and at the foot of these hills a great river sweeps about the western valley, zigzagging passionately westward and southward and westward again in its search for the sea.

A few miles below him on this river's banks the traveller saw the grey blur of a town.

'That must be Mellick', he said to hearten himself and his horse.

In the south two remote green hills had wrapped their heads in cloud; eastward the stonier, bluer peaks wore caps of snow already. To the north the mountains of St Phelim were bronzed and warmly wooded.

Villages lay untidily about the plain; smoke floated from the chimneys of parked mansions and the broken thatch of cowmen's huts; green, blue, brown, in all their shades of dark and brightness, lay folded together across the stretching acres in a colour-tranquillity as absolute as sleep, and which neither the breaking glint of lake and stream nor the seasonal flame

1953 **Herbert Bayer** *World Geo-graphic Atlas: A Composite of Man's Environment*; ed. Herbert Bayer. Chicago: Container Corporation of America, 1953. 368 pp. 41 cm. Designer: Herbert Bayer. Printers: Instituto Geografico de Agostini, Novara; Rand McNally and Company, Chicago. Bookbinder: Rand McNally and Company, Chicago. In case.

In 1953, customers of the Container Corporation of America were the exclusive recipients of the monumental *World Geo-graphic Atlas*, edited and designed by Herbert Bayer. The *Geographical Review* was very clear in its opinion: 'the handsomest and best atlas ever published in America.' Bayer (1900–85) was a former Bauhaus teacher of graphic design and had been working as a designer, visual artist, and architect in the United States since 1938.

Container Corporation of America (CCA), producer of corrugated boxes, was Bayer's main client. The general director of the CCA, Walter Paepcke, wanted his company to have a human face, and he wanted it to be equated with good design. The famous CCA advertising campaign *Great Ideas of Western Man* fully satisfied these objectives: in the ads, designers and artists interpreted quotes from thinkers, poets, and the like, while the company name was modestly placed at the bottom. As Bayer explained to *Time* in 1953: 'It isn't necessary to tell people how boxes are made. Advertising is just to remind them that there is an industry making boxes.'

Bayer and a few other designers worked on the *World Geo-graphic Atlas* for five years; much of the research was done by Bayer himself. The maps were primarily selected from available material, such as the renowned *Goode's School Atlas*. More important were the new cartographic techniques used in the atlas, such as R. Buckminster Fuller's Dymaxion map (or Fuller map), which represents the globe on a flat plane without major distortions. The atlas also makes use of infographics, following Otto Neurath's Isotype method. Finally, Bayer shows himself to be a forerunner of the environmental movement of the 1960s: the atlas focuses heavily on global environmental problems. ML

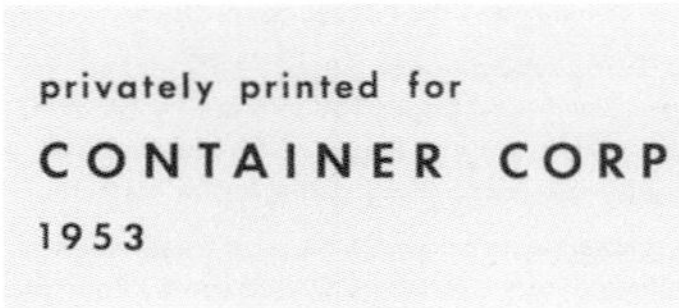

Futura, designed Paul Renner (1878–1956), was first issued in 1927 by the Bauersche Giesserei in Frankfurt am Main. Herbert Bayer was working at the time on his experimental universal alphabet, a geometrically inspired sans serif that consisted, on principle, of only lower-case letters.

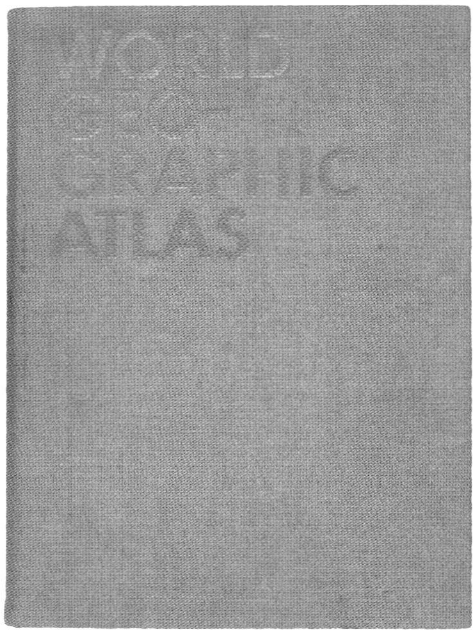

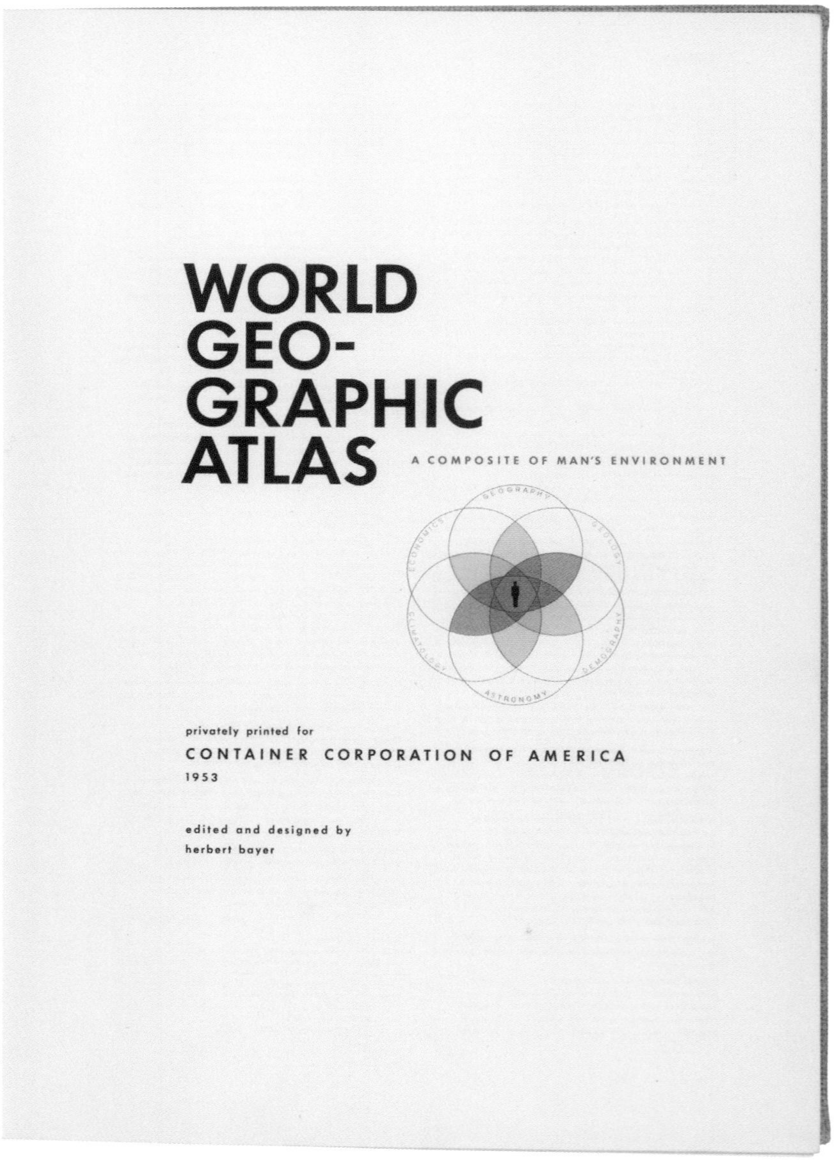

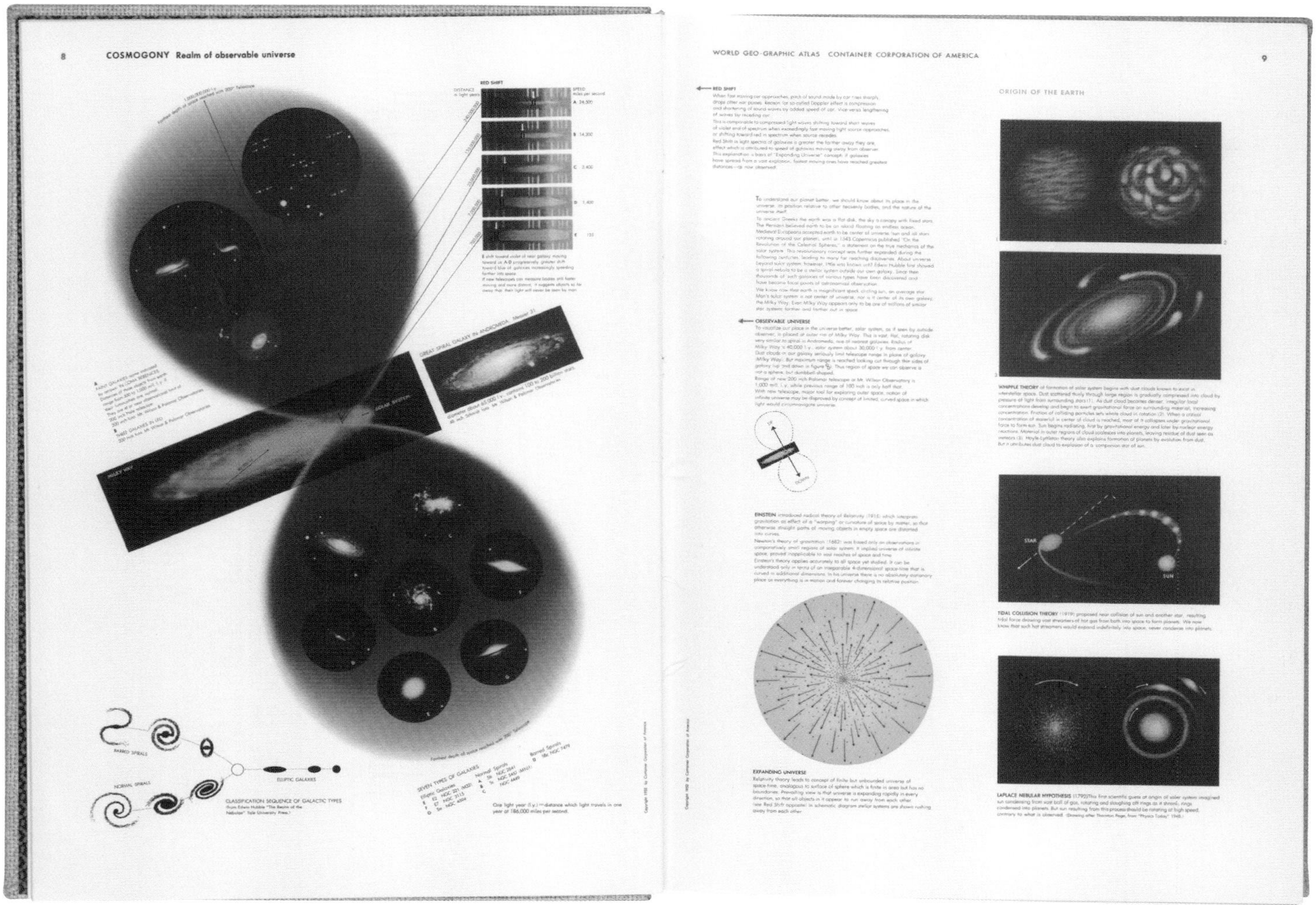
8
COSMOGONY Realm of observable universe
WORLD GEO-GRAPHIC ATLAS CONTAINER CORPORATION OF AMERICA
9
ORIGIN OF THE EARTH

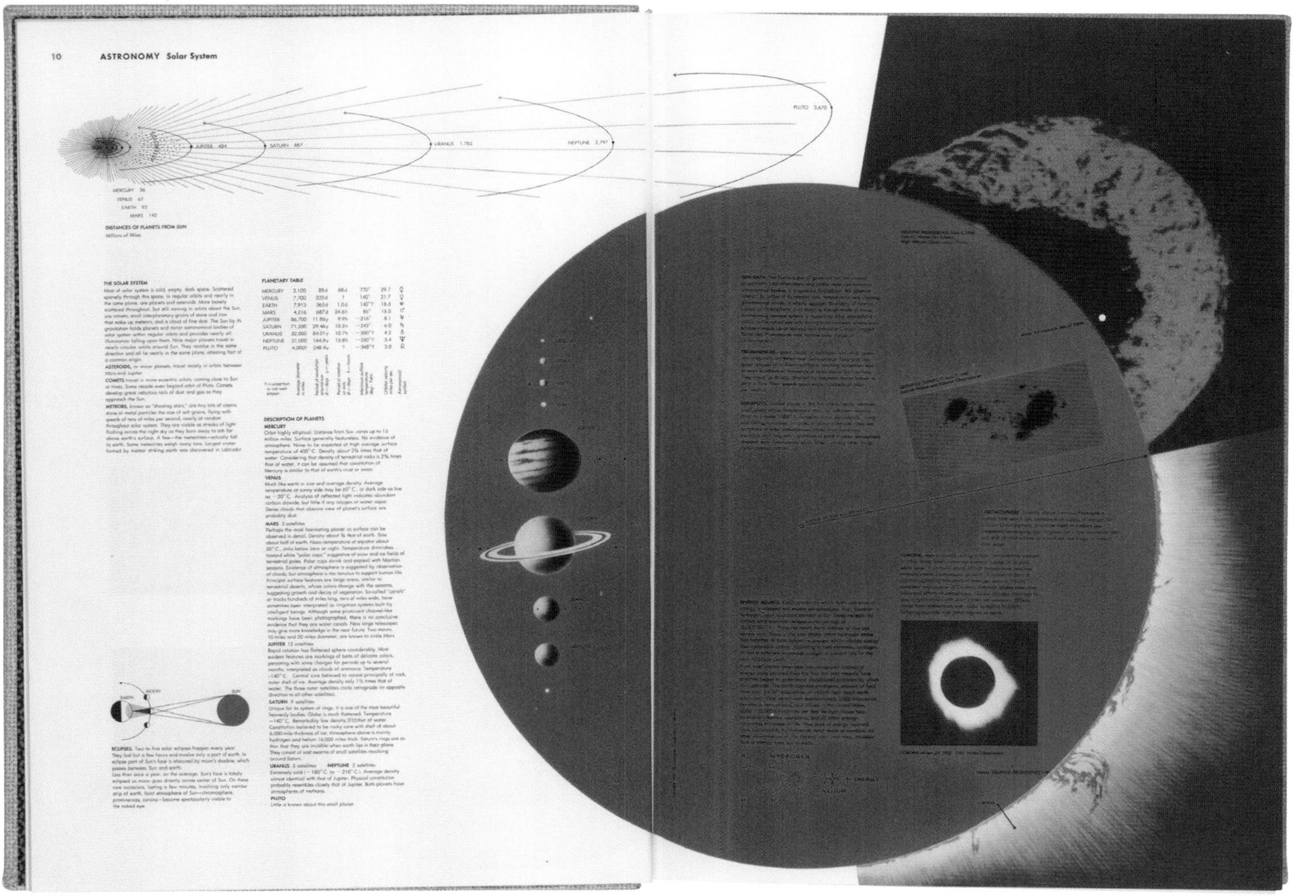
10
ASTRONOMY Solar System

364

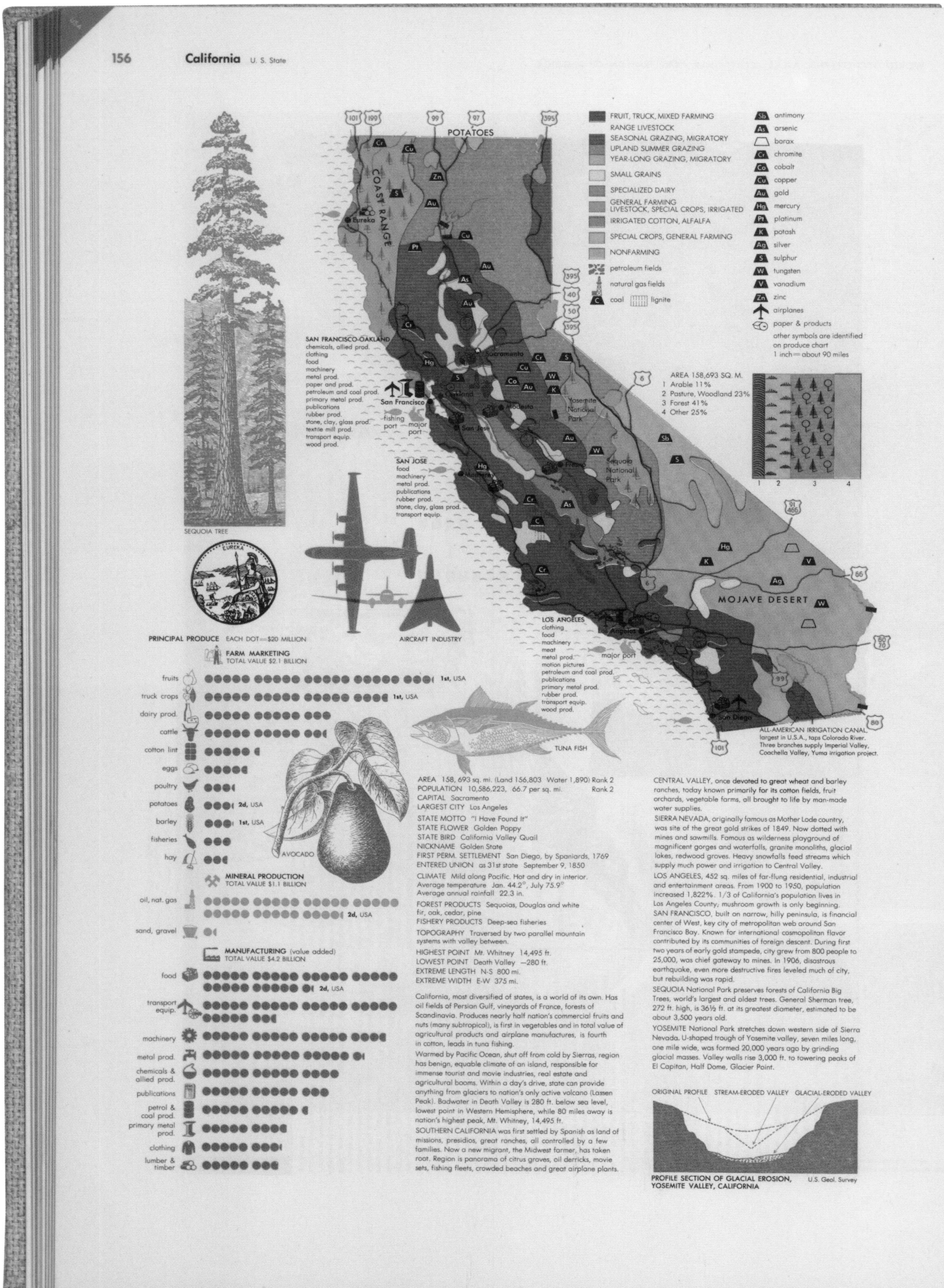

FRUIT, TRUCK, MIXED FARMING
RANGE LIVESTOCK
SEASONAL GRAZING, MIGRATORY
UPLAND SUMMER GRAZING
YEAR-LONG GRAZING, MIGRATORY
SMALL GRAINS
SPECIALIZED DAIRY
GENERAL FARMING
LIVESTOCK, SPECIAL CROPS, IRRIGATED
IRRIGATED COTTON, ALFALFA
SPECIAL CROPS, GENERAL FARMING
NONFARMING
petroleum fields
natural gas fields
coal lignite

Sb antimony
As arsenic
borax
Cr chromite
Co cobalt
Cu copper
Au gold
Hg mercury
Pt platinum
K potash
Ag silver
S sulphur
W tungsten
V vanadium
Zn zinc
airplanes
paper & products
other symbols are identified on produce chart
1 inch = about 90 miles

AREA 158,693 SQ. M.
1 Arable 11%
2 Pasture, Woodland 23%
3 Forest 41%
4 Other 25%

SAN FRANCISCO-OAKLAND
chemicals, allied prod.
clothing
food
machinery
metal prod.
paper and prod.
primary metal prod.
publications
rubber prod.
stone, clay, glass prod.
textile mill prod.
transport equip.
wood prod.

SAN JOSE
food
machinery
metal prod.
publications
rubber prod.
stone, clay, glass prod.
transport equip.

LOS ANGELES
clothing
food
machinery
meat
metal prod.
motion pictures
petroleum and coal prod.
publications
primary metal prod.
rubber prod.
transport equip.
wood prod.

ALL-AMERICAN IRRIGATION CANAL, largest in U.S.A., taps Colorado River. Three branches supply Imperial Valley, Coachella Valley, Yuma irrigation project.

SEQUOIA TREE

AIRCRAFT INDUSTRY

TUNA FISH

AVOCADO

PRINCIPAL PRODUCE EACH DOT = $20 MILLION

FARM MARKETING
TOTAL VALUE $2.1 BILLION
fruits — 1st, USA
truck crops — 1st, USA
dairy prod.
cattle
cotton lint
eggs
poultry
potatoes — 2d, USA
barley — 1st, USA
fisheries
hay

MINERAL PRODUCTION
TOTAL VALUE $1.1 BILLION
oil, nat. gas — 2d, USA
sand, gravel

MANUFACTURING (value added)
TOTAL VALUE $4.2 BILLION
food — 2d, USA
transport equip.
machinery
metal prod.
chemicals & allied prod.
publications
petrol & coal prod.
primary metal prod.
clothing
lumber & timber

AREA 158, 693 sq. mi. (Land 156,803 Water 1,890) Rank 2
POPULATION 10,586,223, 66.7 per sq. mi. Rank 2
CAPITAL Sacramento
LARGEST CITY Los Angeles

STATE MOTTO "I Have Found It"
STATE FLOWER Golden Poppy
STATE BIRD California Valley Quail
NICKNAME Golden State
FIRST PERM. SETTLEMENT San Diego, by Spaniards, 1769
ENTERED UNION as 31st state September 9, 1850

CLIMATE Mild along Pacific. Hot and dry in interior.
Average temperature Jan. 44.2°, July 75.9°
Average annual rainfall 22.3 in.

FOREST PRODUCTS Sequoias, Douglas and white fir, oak, cedar, pine
FISHERY PRODUCTS Deep-sea fisheries

TOPOGRAPHY Traversed by two parallel mountain systems with valley between.

HIGHEST POINT Mt. Whitney 14,495 ft.
LOWEST POINT Death Valley —280 ft.
EXTREME LENGTH N-S 800 mi.
EXTREME WIDTH E-W 375 mi.

California, most diversified of states, is a world of its own. Has oil fields of Persian Gulf, vineyards of France, forests of Scandinavia. Produces nearly half nation's commercial fruits and nuts (many subtropical), is first in vegetables and in total value of agricultural products and airplane manufactures, is fourth in cotton, leads in tuna fishing.

Warmed by Pacific Ocean, shut off from cold by Sierras, region has benign, equable climate of an island, responsible for immense tourist and movie industries, real estate and agricultural booms. Within a day's drive, state can provide anything from glaciers to nation's only active volcano (Lassen Peak). Badwater in Death Valley is 280 ft. below sea level, lowest point in Western Hemisphere, while 80 miles away is nation's highest peak, Mt. Whitney, 14,495 ft.

SOUTHERN CALIFORNIA was first settled by Spanish as land of missions, presidios, great ranches, all controlled by a few families. Now a new migrant, the Midwest farmer, has taken root. Region is panorama of citrus groves, oil derricks, movie sets, fishing fleets, crowded beaches and great airplane plants.

CENTRAL VALLEY, once devoted to great wheat and barley ranches, today known primarily for its cotton fields, fruit orchards, vegetable farms, all brought to life by man-made water supplies.

SIERRA NEVADA, originally famous as Mother Lode country, was site of the great gold strikes of 1849. Now dotted with mines and sawmills. Famous as wilderness playground of magnificent gorges and waterfalls, granite monoliths, glacial lakes, redwood groves. Heavy snowfalls feed streams which supply much power and irrigation to Central Valley.

LOS ANGELES, 452 sq. miles of far-flung residential, industrial and entertainment areas. From 1900 to 1950, population increased 1,822%. 1/3 of California's population lives in Los Angeles County, mushroom growth is only beginning.

SAN FRANCISCO, built on narrow, hilly peninsula, is financial center of West, key city of metropolitan web around San Francisco Bay. Known for international cosmopolitan flavor contributed by its communities of foreign descent. During first two years of early gold stampede, city grew from 800 people to 25,000, was chief gateway to mines. In 1906, disastrous earthquake, even more destructive fires leveled much of city, but rebuilding was rapid.

SEQUOIA National Park preserves forests of California Big Trees, world's largest and oldest trees. General Sherman tree, 272 ft. high, is 36½ ft. at its greatest diameter, estimated to be about 3,500 years old.

YOSEMITE National Park stretches down western side of Sierra Nevada. U-shaped trough of Yosemite valley, seven miles long, one mile wide, was formed 20,000 years ago by grinding glacial masses. Valley walls rise 3,000 ft. to towering peaks of El Capitan, Half Dome, Glacier Point.

ORIGINAL PROFILE STREAM-ERODED VALLEY GLACIAL-ERODED VALLEY

PROFILE SECTION OF GLACIAL EROSION, YOSEMITE VALLEY, CALIFORNIA
U.S. Geol. Survey

WORLD GEO-GRAPHIC ATLAS CONTAINER CORPORATION OF AMERICA
CALIFORNIA
157
San Francisco
Oakland
Sacramento
Stockton
San Jose
Los Angeles
Long Beach
San Diego
Pacific Ocean
Santa Barbara Channel
Lambert Conformal Conic Projection
SCALE 1:3,733,000 1 Inch = 59 Statute Miles
Statute Miles
Kilometers
Longitude West of Greenwich

1954 **Willem Sandberg** *9 jaar Stedelijk Museum Amsterdam, 1945–54*. **Amsterdam: Stedelijk Museum, 1954. 46 pp. 26 cm. Designer: Willem Sandberg. Printer: Stadsdrukkerij Amsterdam.**

During the thirties, Willem Sandberg (1897–1984) had worked as a designer for the Dutch postal and telecom services PTT and for the Amsterdam printer C.A. Spin & Zoon. His early work is a free interpretation of the New Typography. In his role as director of the Stedelijk Museum in Amsterdam, Sandberg attracted a great deal of attention. He made sure the gloomy entrance hall was painted white, curated a controversial exhibition featuring the avant-garde art group COBRA in 1949, and also designed almost all of the museum's printed matter. While the press criticized his groundbreaking policies vehemently, the public came flocking in.

Sandberg was not just a museum director and designer. During the German occupation, for instance, he forged identity papers. Straight after the liberation of the Netherlands in 1945, he was appointed chairman of the new designers' union, the GKf. As a graphic designer, he acquired international fame for both his museum catalogues and posters as well as for his *experimenta typografica*, a series of booklets with short texts that he had begun to design during the war.

Sandberg wanted his printed matter to have a friendly and lively character: 'It had rather not be all neat and shiny.' His trademarks were the use of ordinary brown paper and of letters and shapes torn out of paper. Both elements are present in this catalogue, *9 jaar Stedelijk Museum Amsterdam*. Diagrams of staff and visitor numbers are evidence of his familiarity with infographics: in Vienna, during the twenties, he had studied Otto Neurath's work. The exclusive use of sans serif lower case in a municipal publication of this period is remarkable. ML

This sans serif was issued by Typefoundry Amsterdam under the name Antieke Vet Cursief (grotesque bold italic). It was probably copied, either with or without consent, from a face produced by J. John Söhne's typefoundry in Hamburg in the early 1890s.

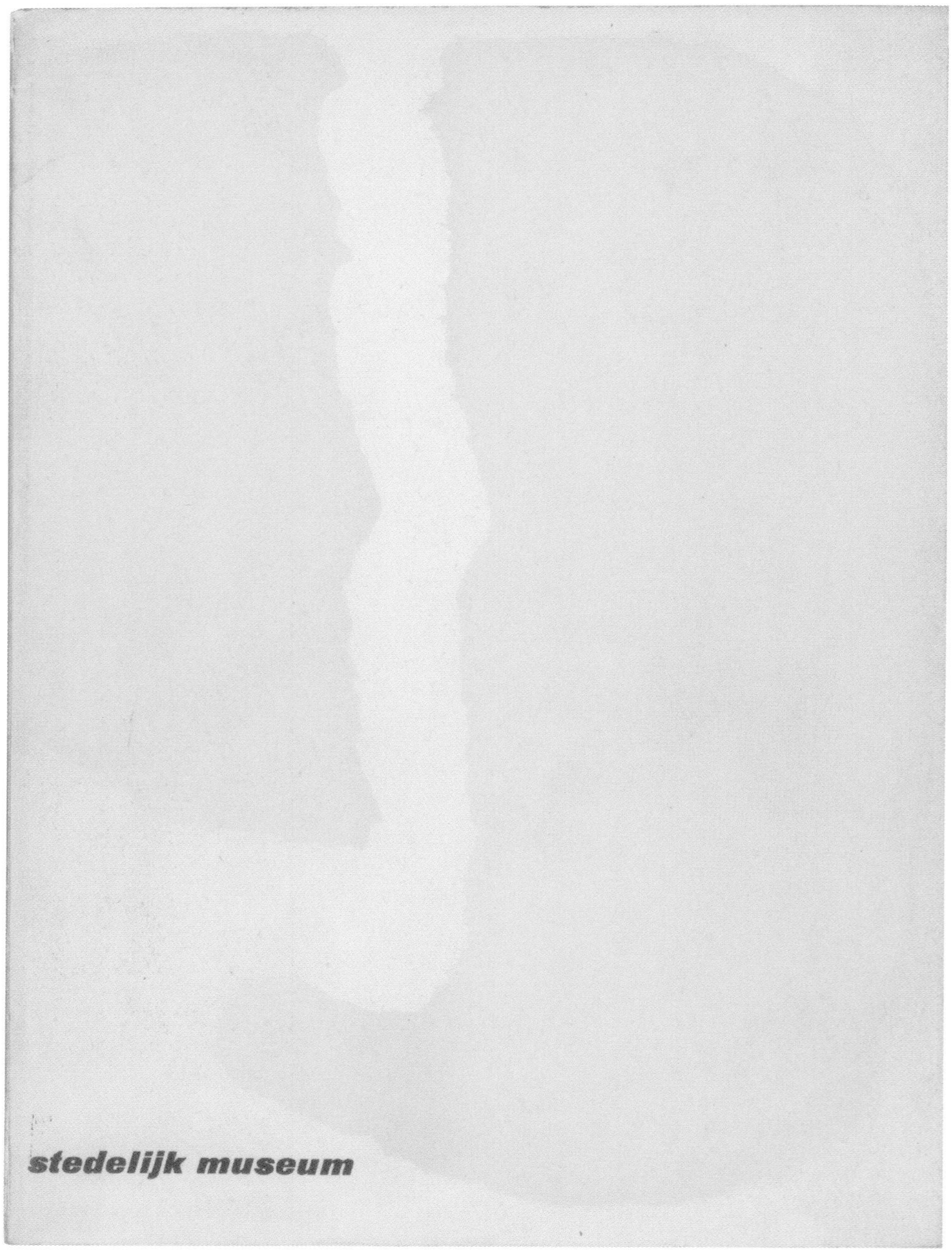

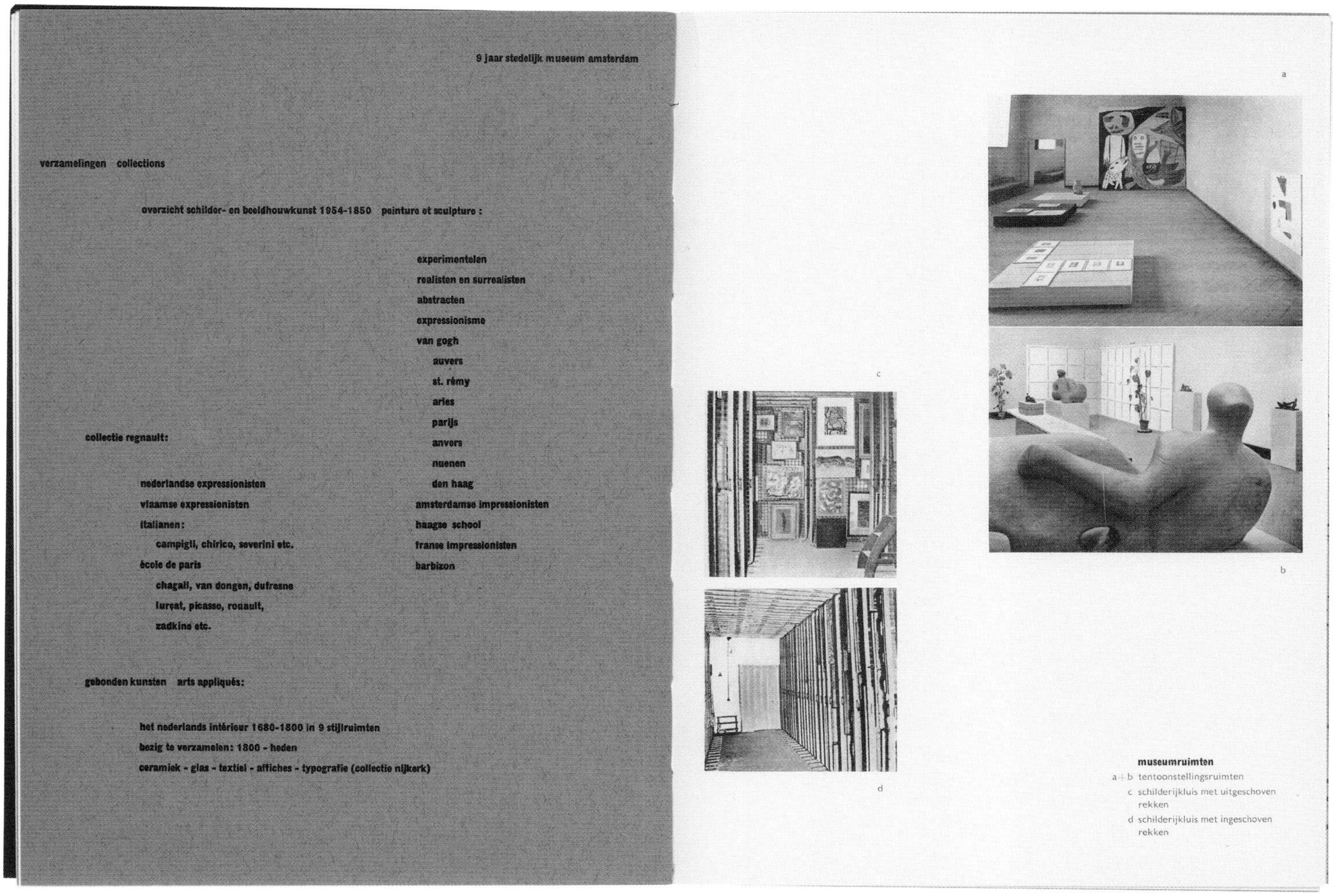

9 jaar stedelijk museum amsterdam

verzamelingen collections

overzicht schilder- en beeldhouwkunst 1954-1850 peinture et sculpture :

experimentelen
realisten en surrealisten
abstracten
expressionisme
van gogh
auvers
st. rémy
arles
parijs
anvers
nuenen
den haag
amsterdamse impressionisten
haagse school
franse impressionisten
barbizon

collectie regnault:

nederlandse expressionisten
vlaamse expressionisten
italianen:
campigli, chirico, severini etc.
école de paris
chagall, van dongen, dufresne
lurçat, picasso, rouault,
zadkine etc.

gebonden kunsten arts appliqués:

het nederlands intérieur 1680-1800 in 9 stijlruimten
bezig te verzamelen: 1800 - heden
ceramiek - glas - textiel - affiches - typografie (collectie nijkerk)

a
c
b
d

museumruimten
a+b tentoonstellingsruimten
c schilderijkluis met uitgeschoven rekken
d schilderijkluis met ingeschoven rekken

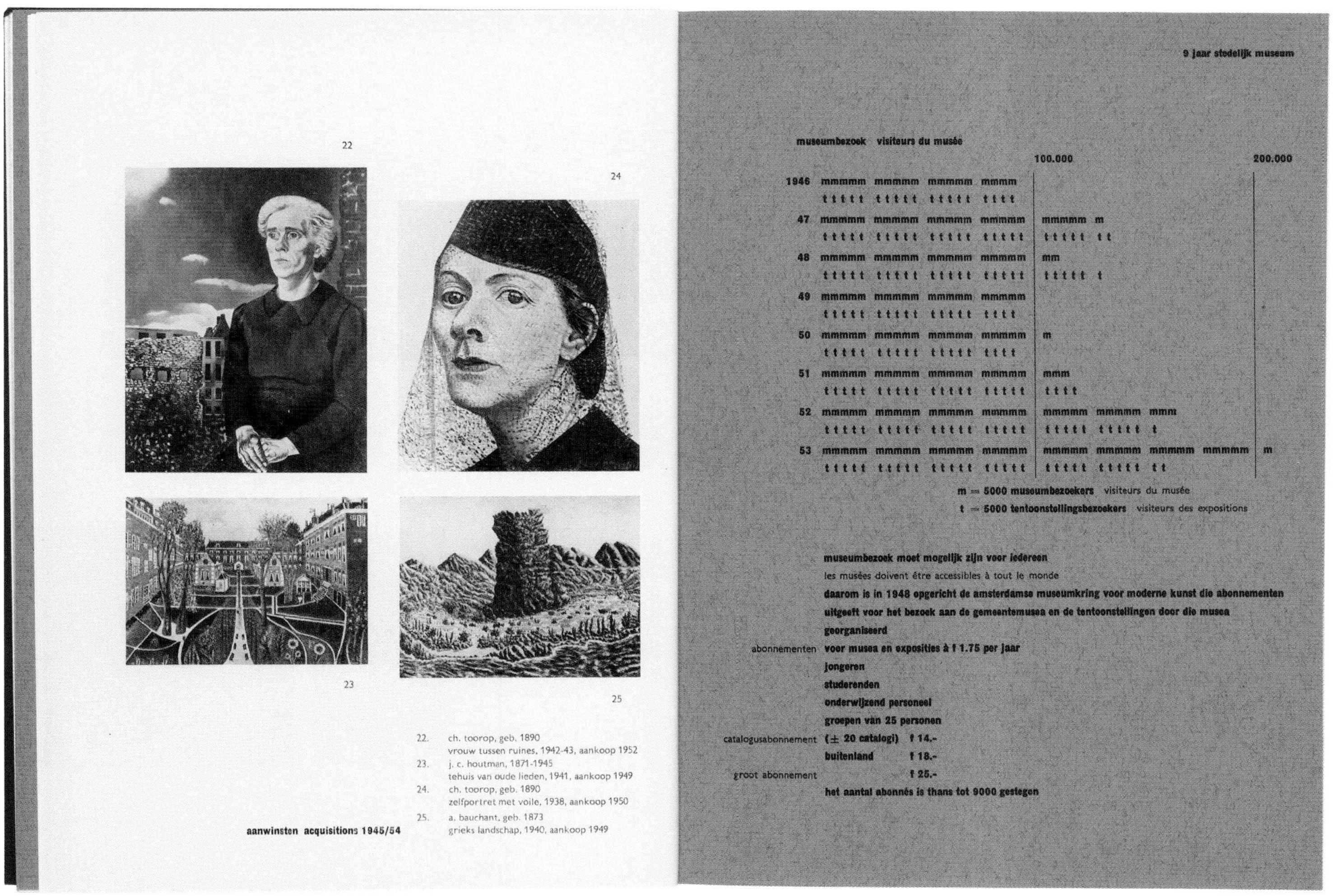

22
24
23
25

22. ch. toorop, geb. 1890
vrouw tussen ruines, 1942-43, aankoop 1952
23. j. c. houtman, 1871-1945
tehuis van oude lieden, 1941, aankoop 1949
24. ch. toorop, geb. 1890
zelfportret met voile, 1938, aankoop 1950
25. a. bauchant, geb. 1873
grieks landschap, 1940, aankoop 1949

aanwinsten acquisitions 1945/54

9 jaar stedelijk museum

museumbezoek visiteurs du musée

100.000 200.000

1946 mmmmm mmmmm mmmmm mmmm
ttttt ttttt ttttt tttt
47 mmmmm mmmmm mmmmm mmmmm | mmmmm m
ttttt ttttt ttttt ttttt | ttttt tt
48 mmmmm mmmmm mmmmm mmmmm | mm
ttttt ttttt ttttt ttttt | ttttt t
49 mmmmm mmmmm mmmmm mmmmm
ttttt ttttt ttttt tttt
50 mmmmm mmmmm mmmmm mmmmm | m
ttttt ttttt ttttt tttt
51 mmmmm mmmmm mmmmm mmmmm | mmm
ttttt ttttt ttttt ttttt | tttt
52 mmmmm mmmmm mmmmm mmmmm | mmmmm mmmmm mmm
ttttt ttttt ttttt ttttt | ttttt ttttt t
53 mmmmm mmmmm mmmmm mmmmm | mmmmm mmmmm mmmmm mmmmm | m
ttttt ttttt ttttt ttttt | ttttt ttttt tt

m = 5000 museumbezoekers visiteurs du musée
t = 5000 tentoonstellingsbezoekers visiteurs des expositions

museumbezoek moet mogelijk zijn voor iedereen
les musées doivent être accessibles à tout le monde
daarom is in 1948 opgericht de amsterdamse museumkring voor moderne kunst die abonnementen uitgeeft voor het bezoek aan de gemeentemusea en de tentoonstellingen door die musea georganiseerd

abonnementen voor musea en exposities à f 1.75 per jaar
jongeren
studerenden
onderwijzend personeel
groepen van 25 personen
catalogusabonnement (± 20 catalogi) f 14.-
buitenland f 18.-
groot abonnement f 25.-
het aantal abonnés is thans tot 9000 gestegen

1945-54
jaar

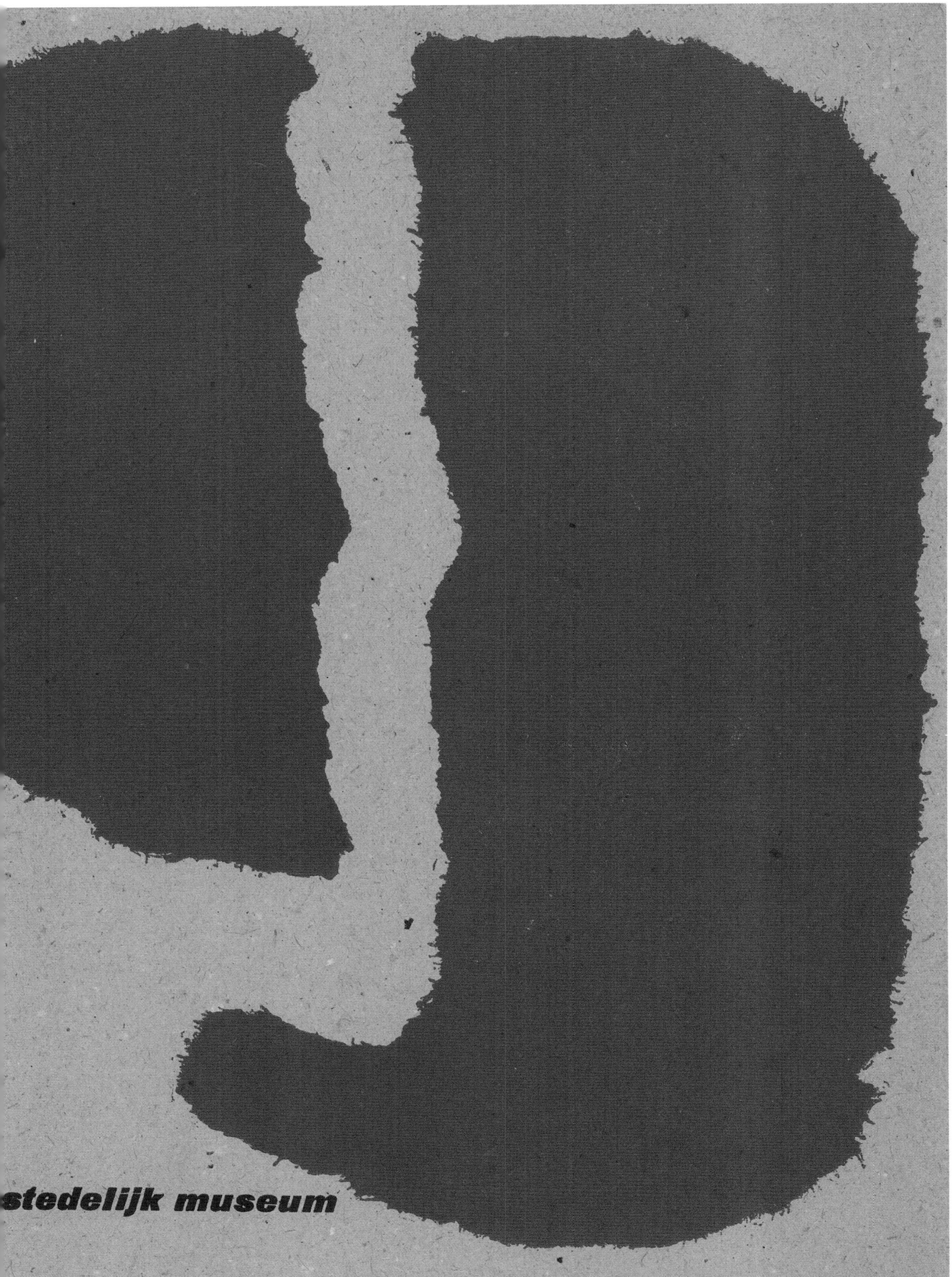

Willem Sandberg

1956 **Marie Neurath** (Isotype) Marie Neurath, *Außen – innen: Was ist drinnen?* Vienna: Schönbrunn Verlag, 1956. 32 pp. 21 cm. *Wunder der Welt*. Translation of *If You Could See Inside*, 1948. Designer: Marie Neurath (Isotype Institute). Printer: Graphikon, Vienna.

Marie Neurath (1898–1986) was born Marie Reidemeister in Braunschweig, northern Germany. While still a student in 1924, she met the sociologist and philosopher Otto Neurath during a field trip to Vienna. Immediately impressed by his work, she decided to start working for him. In his Gesellschafts- und Wirtschaftsmuseum, the 'Vienna Method of Pictorial Statistics' – later renamed Isotype (International System of Typographic Picture Education) – was used to produce infographics for publications and exhibitions.

In the Isotype system, data and ideas were clearly represented by graphic symbols to make information objectively accessible to a broad audience. In the words of Otto Neurath: 'Words divide, images unite.' Isotype was a team effort. Marie had the role of designer ('transformer'), mediating between the subject specialists and the draughtsmen who executed her sketches. Gerd Arntz was the group's main artist.

The political situation, which was fraught with tension, led Otto and Maria to emigrate from their beloved Vienna to the Netherlands in 1934. After the German invasion in 1940, they fled to England, where they married. After the death of her husband in 1945, Marie was in sole charge of the Isotype Institute, which continued in London until the early seventies. Its educational picture books were an international success; the series *They Lived Like This*, for instance, includes twenty volumes. This German translation, *Außen – innen* was produced by the left-wing Austrian publisher Schönbrunn Verlag in a series for children aged from six to sixteen; it was designed according to the 'Neurath Method'. ML

The spread below is entitled *A Strange Way to Look at a House*: 'We have all been inside a house, but how different it looks when it is cut through with our magic knife! Here you can see how long the chimneys really are, how the water gets to the tap and where it runs when you pull the bath-plug.'

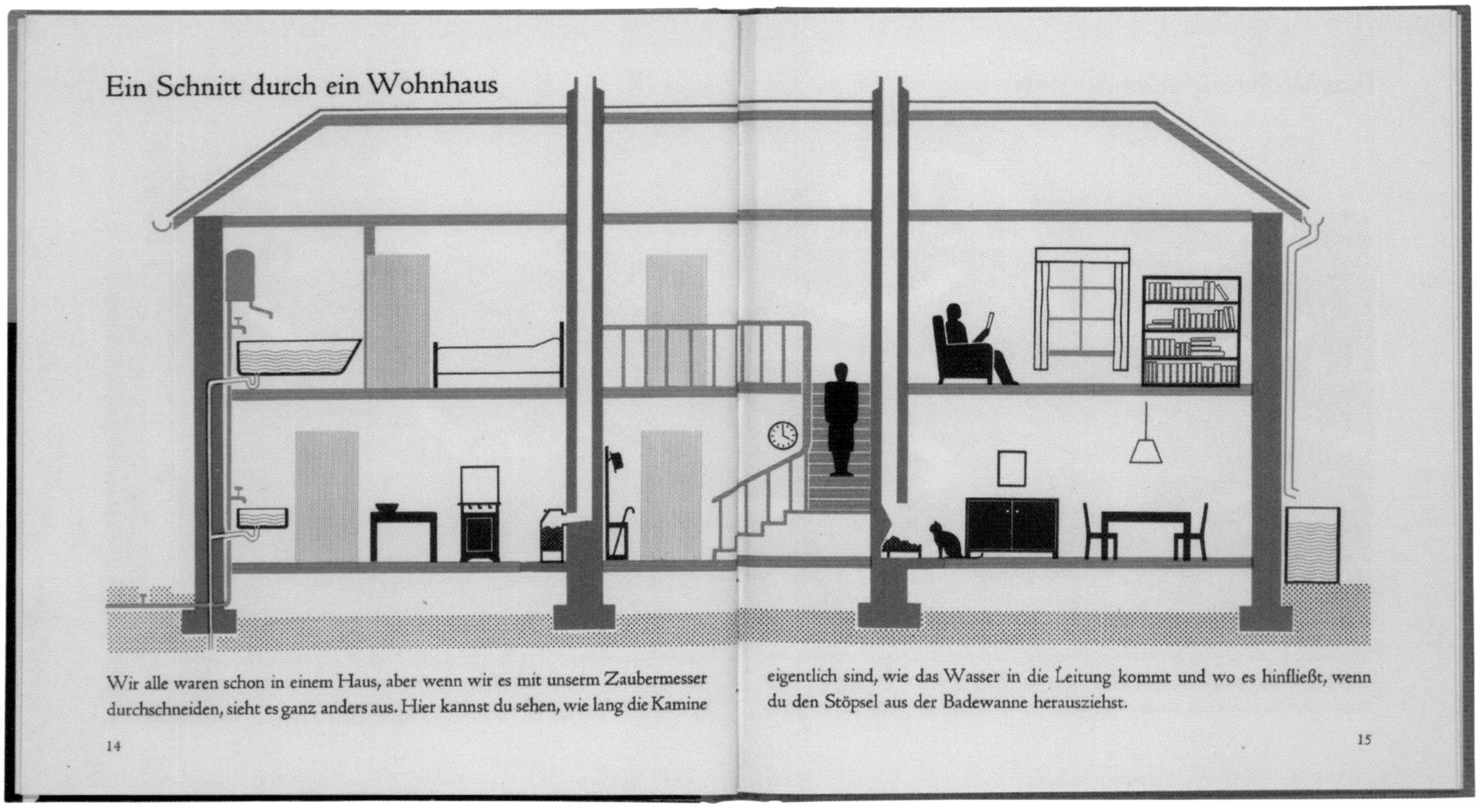

Ein Schnitt durch ein Wohnhaus
Wir alle waren schon in einem Haus, aber wenn wir es mit unserm Zaubermesser durchschneiden, sieht es ganz anders aus. Hier kannst du sehen, wie lang die Kamine
14
eigentlich sind, wie das Wasser in die Leitung kommt und wo es hinfließt, wenn du den Stöpsel aus der Badewanne herausziehst.
15

Wenn man im tiefen Meer auf Entdeckungen geht, verwendet man eine große Stahlkugel mit dicken Glasfenstern, die Taucherkugel genannt wird. Sie wird von einem Schiff aus an einem starken Stahl-

Eusebius by Ernst F. Detterer (1888–1947) was issued solely as a roman in 1924 by the Ludlow Typograph Co. in Chicago. Robert Hunter Middleton (1898–1985) expanded the type with an italic and two weights. It is one of the many revivals based on Nicolas Jenson's 1470 roman.

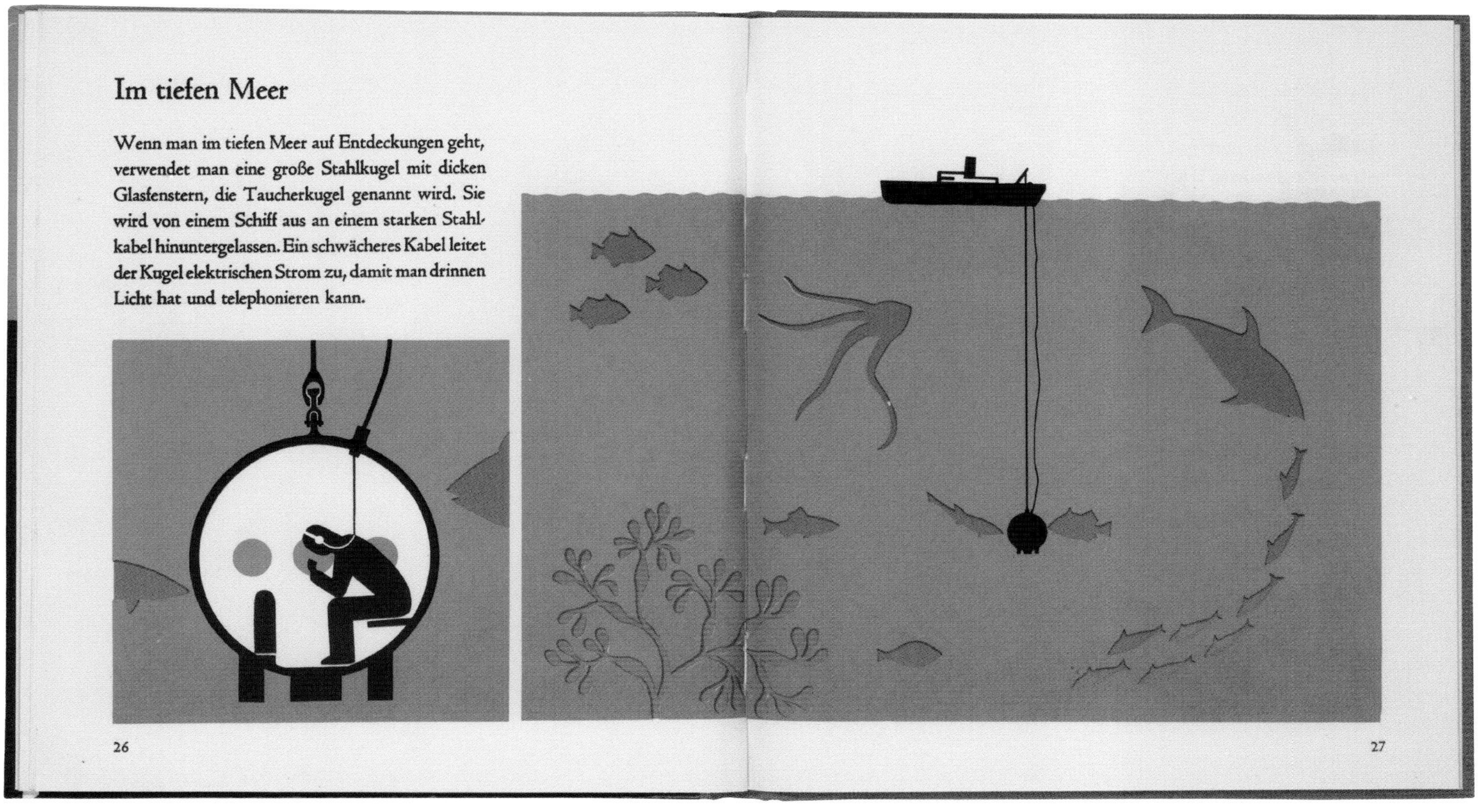

Im tiefen Meer

Wenn man im tiefen Meer auf Entdeckungen geht, verwendet man eine große Stahlkugel mit dicken Glasfenstern, die Taucherkugel genannt wird. Sie wird von einem Schiff aus an einem starken Stahlkabel hinuntergelassen. Ein schwächeres Kabel leitet der Kugel elektrischen Strom zu, damit man drinnen Licht hat und telephonieren kann.

26

27

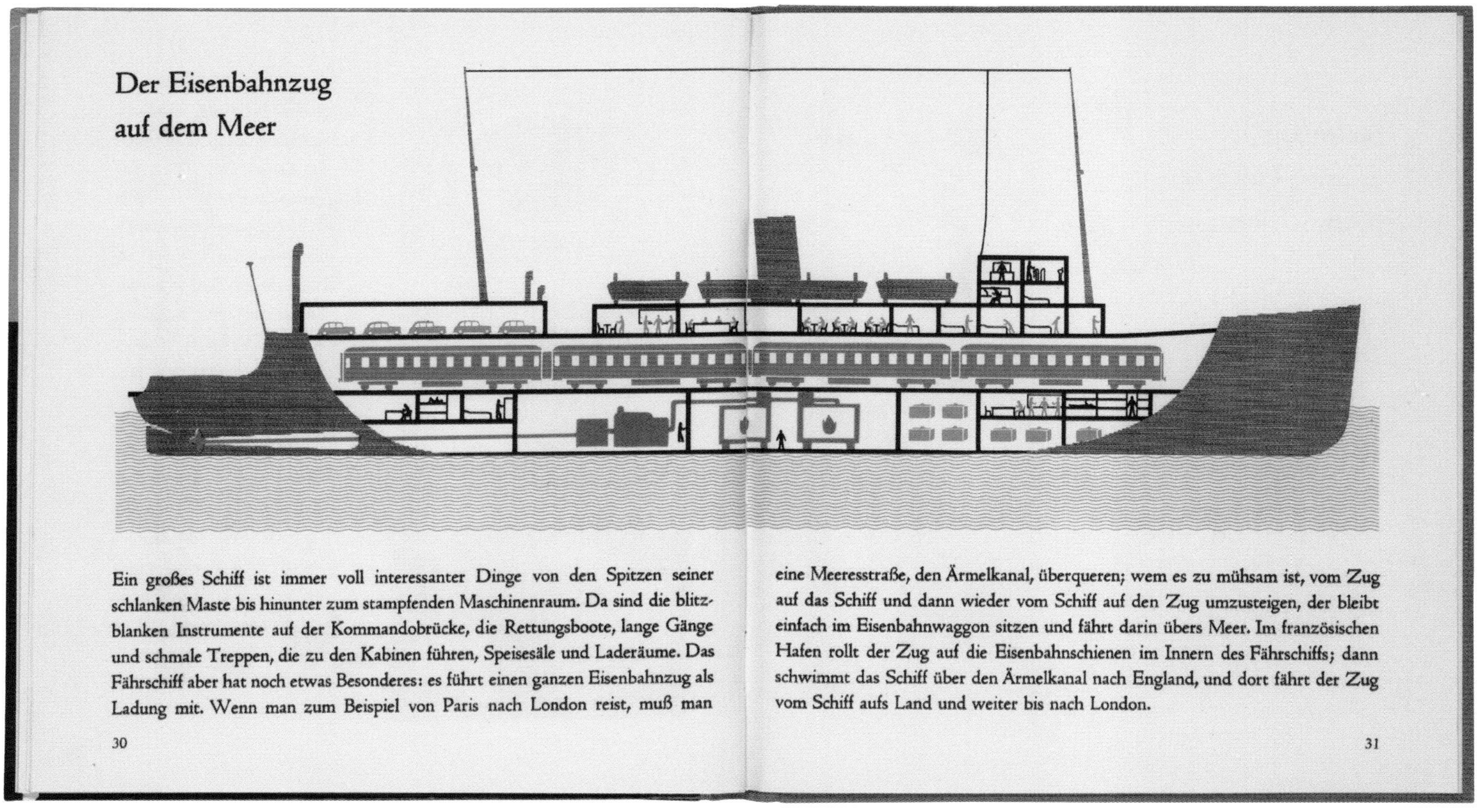

Der Eisenbahnzug auf dem Meer

Ein großes Schiff ist immer voll interessanter Dinge von den Spitzen seiner schlanken Maste bis hinunter zum stampfenden Maschinenraum. Da sind die blitzblanken Instrumente auf der Kommandobrücke, die Rettungsboote, lange Gänge und schmale Treppen, die zu den Kabinen führen, Speisesäle und Laderäume. Das Fährschiff aber hat noch etwas Besonderes: es führt einen ganzen Eisenbahnzug als Ladung mit. Wenn man zum Beispiel von Paris nach London reist, muß man eine Meeresstraße, den Ärmelkanal, überqueren; wem es zu mühsam ist, vom Zug auf das Schiff und dann wieder vom Schiff auf den Zug umzusteigen, der bleibt einfach im Eisenbahnwaggon sitzen und fährt darin übers Meer. Im französischen Hafen rollt der Zug auf die Eisenbahnschienen im Innern des Fährschiffs; dann schwimmt das Schiff über den Ärmelkanal nach England, und dort fährt der Zug vom Schiff aufs Land und weiter bis nach London.

30

31

1956 **Robert Massin** Blaise Cendrars, *L'Or: la merveilleuse histoire du général Johann August Suter*. Paris: Club du Meilleur Livre, 1956. 176 pp. 20 cm. Designer: Robert Massin. Printer: Tournon, Paris. Bookbinder: Babouot, Paris.

Massin, who rarely used his first name Robert, was born in 1925 as the son of an engraver, sculptor and stonemason. In 1948 he was working as an editor for the Club Français du Livre where he began to design printed matter, though not as the result of a studied decision. At the book club he met designer Pierre Faucheux: 'it was watching Faucheux "sell" his layouts, explaining and justifying them with the same fire, that I started to want to make some myself.' There would always be a spirit of creative rivalry between the two men. When a colleague founded the Club du Meilleur Livre in 1952, Massin joined him. Before long he was working at the new book club as an art director.

In Massin's book designs for the Club du Meilleur Livre, there is only one constant: the height. Everything else is variable: the elements that bibliophiles love – cover materials and endpapers – as well as the typography. The prelims of some of the novels have a highly cinematic feel and consist of multiple pages, in some cases up to twenty. In *L'Or*, a biographical novel about a nineteenth-century American pioneer, the decorative use of numerals is striking. A real eye-catcher is the cloth cover printed in rainbow colours. Massin emulates the typographical style of nineteenth-century posters. He would always remain partial to the display typography of that era.

In 1958, Massin also began working for the big Paris publisher Gallimard; the printers had taken care of its graphic design until that point. For over two decades, he would leave his mark on their house style and on several series of books. Massin is perhaps best known for his expressive interpretation of Ionesco's play *La cantatrice chauve* (*The Bald Prima Donna*), published by Gallimard in 1964. ML

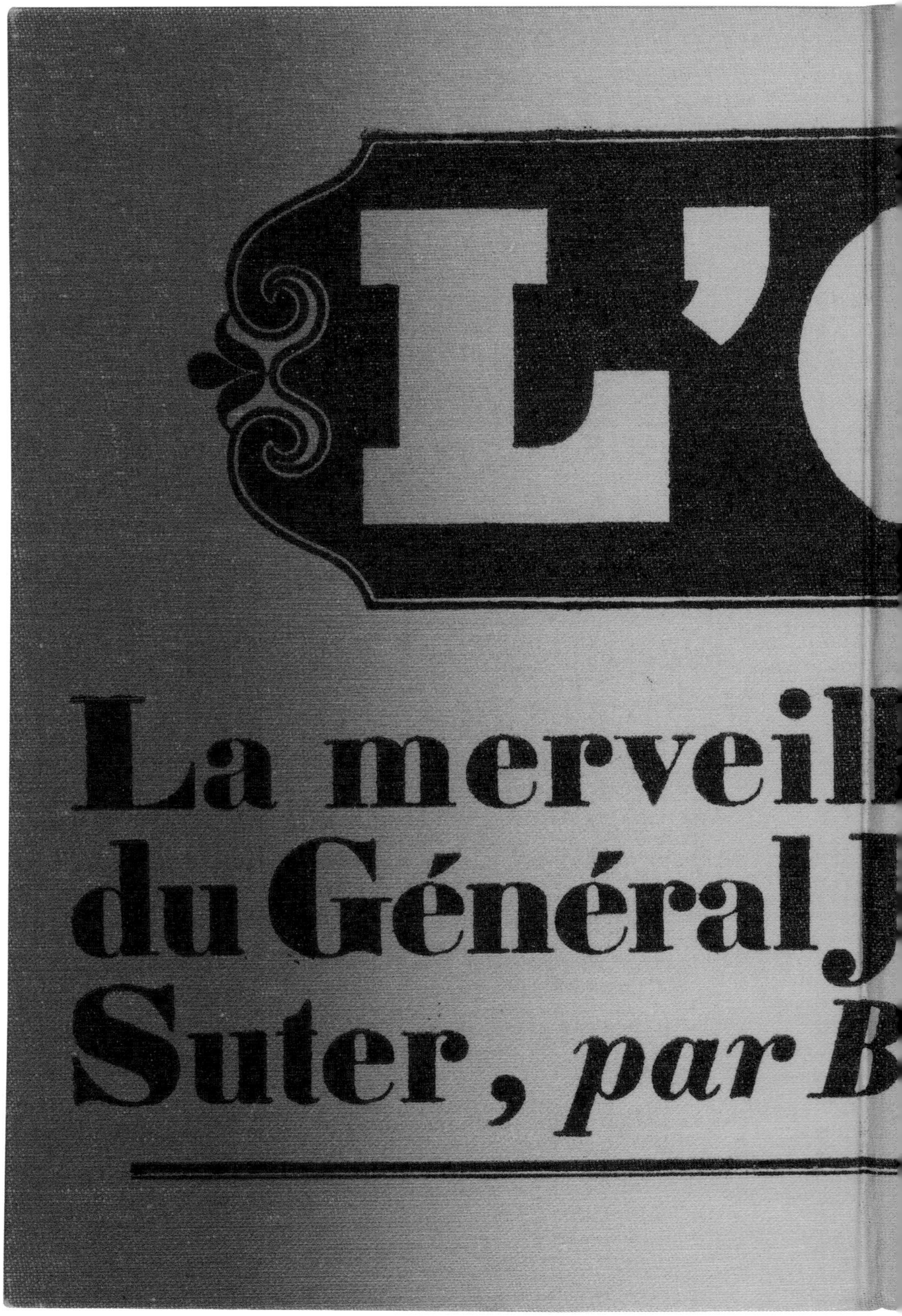

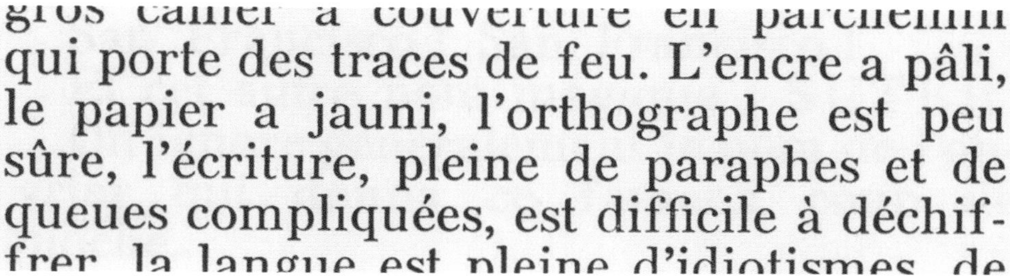
gros cahier à couverture en parchemin
qui porte des traces de feu. L'encre a pâli, le papier a jauni, l'orthographe est peu sûre, l'écriture, pleine de paraphes et de queues compliquées, est difficile à déchiffrer, la langue est pleine d'idiotismes, de

The text type Didot (alluding to the Didot typefoundries in Paris, active 1781–1837) is probably Deberny & Cie's series 16 (the roman g differs), which was listed as a 'création nouvelle' in their 1908 specimen, one year before American Type Founders' Bodoni.

Blaise Cendrars

L'OR

La merveilleuse histoire du Général Johann August Suter

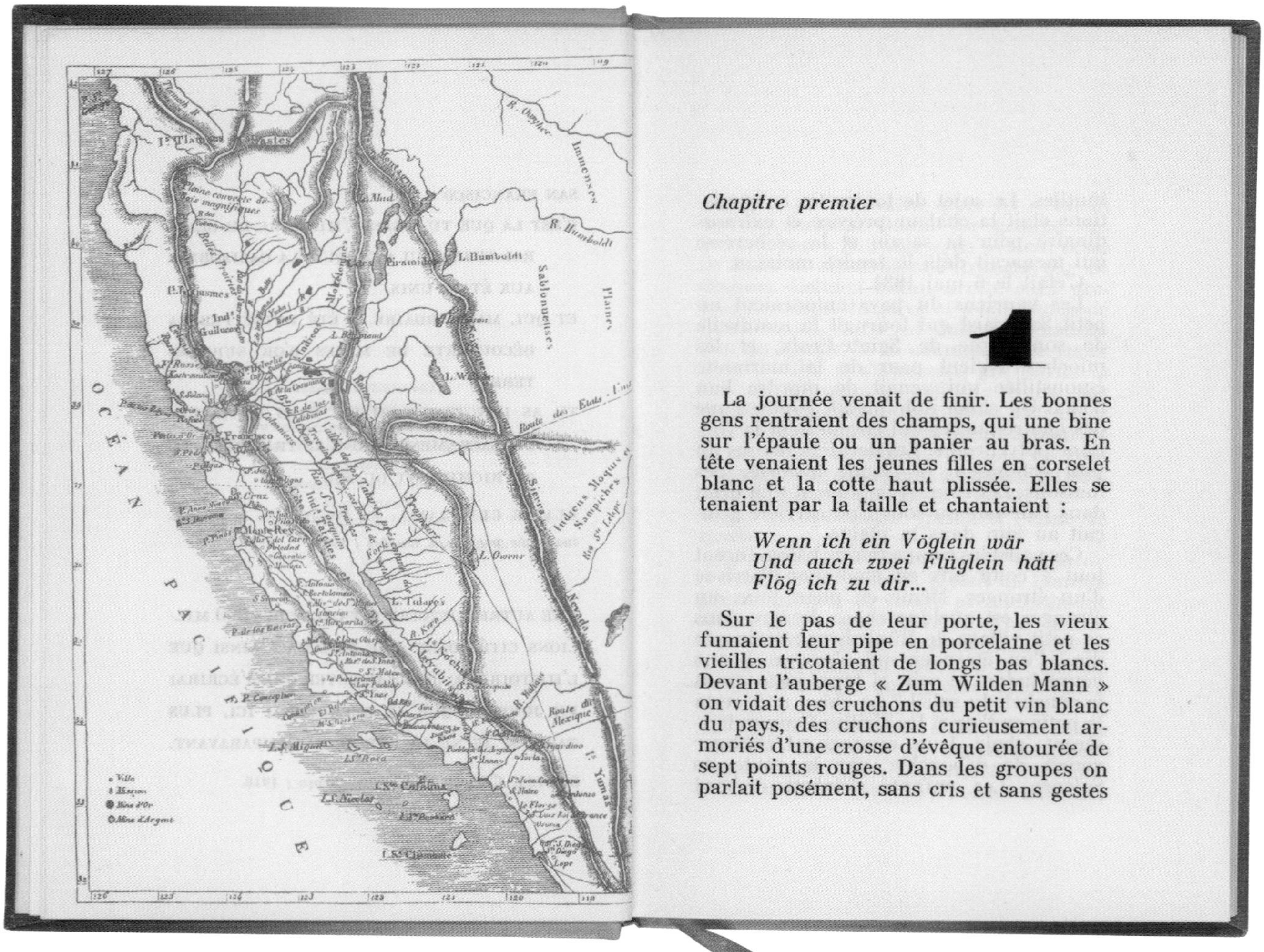

Chapitre premier

1

La journée venait de finir. Les bonnes gens rentraient des champs, qui une bine sur l'épaule ou un panier au bras. En tête venaient les jeunes filles en corselet blanc et la cotte haut plissée. Elles se tenaient par la taille et chantaient :

Wenn ich ein Vöglein wär
Und auch zwei Flüglein hätt
Flög ich zu dir...

Sur le pas de leur porte, les vieux fumaient leur pipe en porcelaine et les vieilles tricotaient de longs bas blancs. Devant l'auberge « Zum Wilden Mann » on vidait des cruchons du petit vin blanc du pays, des cruchons curieusement armoriés d'une crosse d'évêque entourée de sept points rouges. Dans les groupes on parlait posément, sans cris et sans gestes

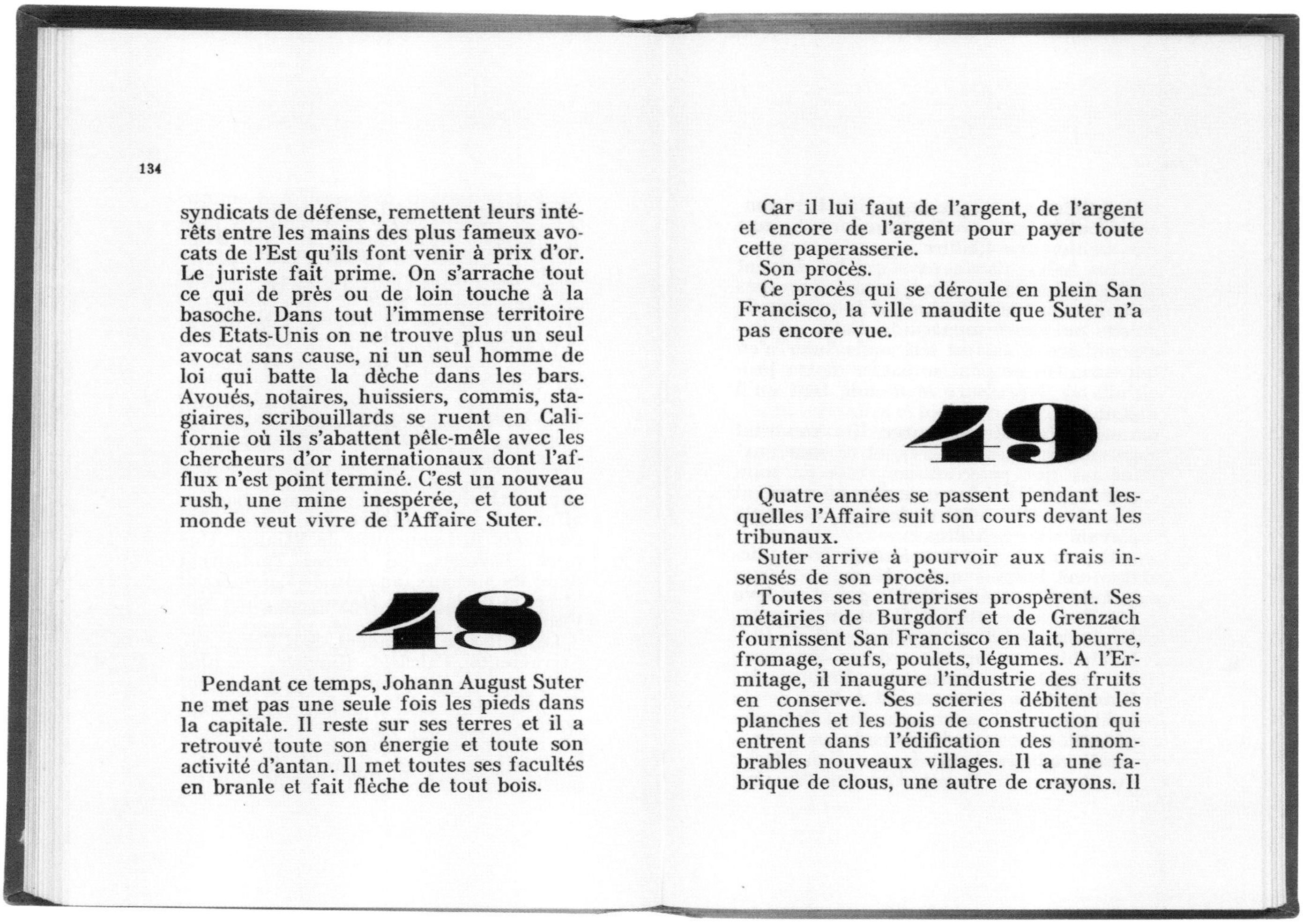

134

syndicats de défense, remettent leurs intérêts entre les mains des plus fameux avocats de l'Est qu'ils font venir à prix d'or. Le juriste fait prime. On s'arrache tout ce qui de près ou de loin touche à la basoche. Dans tout l'immense territoire des Etats-Unis on ne trouve plus un seul avocat sans cause, ni un seul homme de loi qui batte la dèche dans les bars. Avoués, notaires, huissiers, commis, stagiaires, scribouillards se ruent en Californie où ils s'abattent pêle-mêle avec les chercheurs d'or internationaux dont l'afflux n'est point terminé. C'est un nouveau rush, une mine inespérée, et tout ce monde veut vivre de l'Affaire Suter.

48

Pendant ce temps, Johann August Suter ne met pas une seule fois les pieds dans la capitale. Il reste sur ses terres et il a retrouvé toute son énergie et toute son activité d'antan. Il met toutes ses facultés en branle et fait flèche de tout bois.

Car il lui faut de l'argent, de l'argent et encore de l'argent pour payer toute cette paperasserie.

Son procès.

Ce procès qui se déroule en plein San Francisco, la ville maudite que Suter n'a pas encore vue.

49

Quatre années se passent pendant lesquelles l'Affaire suit son cours devant les tribunaux.

Suter arrive à pourvoir aux frais insensés de son procès.

Toutes ses entreprises prospèrent. Ses métairies de Burgdorf et de Grenzach fournissent San Francisco en lait, beurre, fromage, œufs, poulets, légumes. A l'Ermitage, il inaugure l'industrie des fruits en conserve. Ses scieries débitent les planches et les bois de construction qui entrent dans l'édification des innombrables nouveaux villages. Il a une fabrique de clous, une autre de crayons. Il

375

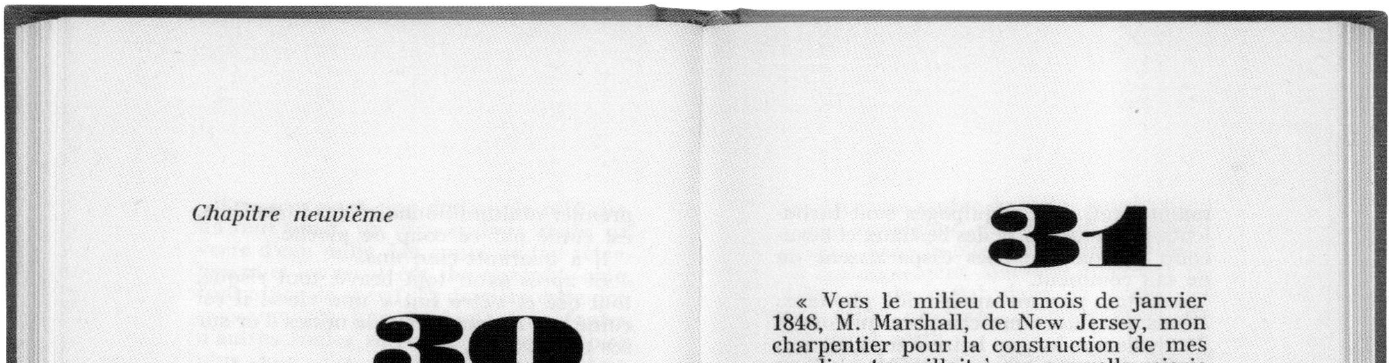

Chapitre neuvième

30

Mais laissons la parole à Johann August Suter.

Je copie le chapitre suivant dans un gros cahier à couverture en parchemin qui porte des traces de feu. L'encre a pâli, le papier a jauni, l'orthographe est peu sûre, l'écriture, pleine de paraphes et de queues compliquées, est difficile à déchiffrer, la langue est pleine d'idiotismes, de termes de dialecte bâlois, d'amerenglish. Si la main, d'une gaucherie attendrissante, a souvent hésité, le récit suit son cours, simplement, bêtement. L'homme qui l'a tracé n'a pas une plainte. Il se borne à raconter les événements, à énumérer les faits tels qu'ils se sont passés. Il reste toujours en deçà de la réalité.

Je traduis humblement :

31

« Vers le milieu du mois de janvier 1848, M. Marshall, de New Jersey, mon charpentier pour la construction de mes moulins, travaillait à ma nouvelle scierie de Coloma, en haut, dans la montagne, à dix-huit heures du fort. Quand la charpente fut dressée, j'envoyai M. Wimmer et famille, plus quelques ouvriers, là-haut ; M. Bennet, d'Oregon, les accompagnait pour s'occuper des attelages et de l'installation mécanique. Mme Wimmer faisait la cuisine pour tout le monde. J'avais encore besoin d'une scierie, car il me manquait des planches pour mon grand moulin à vapeur qui était également en construction, à Brighton, et dont la chaudière et la machinerie venaient d'arriver après dix-huit mois de voyage. Dieu soit béni, jamais je n'aurais cru voir réussir cette entreprise et tous les bœufs vont bien, merci. J'avais également besoin de planches pour la construction d'autres bâtiments et surtout pour établir la clôture du village de Yerba Buena, au fond de la baie, car il y a beaucoup de navires

1956 **Lester Beall** S. S. Field, *DF: A Place in the Country*. Brookfield Center, CT: Lester Beall Design Group, 1956. 18 pp. 29 cm. Designer: Lester Beall.

In 1927, Lester Beall started his career as a freelance advertising designer in Chicago. Beall (1903–69), who had studied art history, had very little practical experience. However, through reading books and magazines, he became well acquainted with avant-garde visual art and graphic design in Europe. Among other things, he studied Werner Gräff's photobook *Es kommt der neue Fotograf!* (1929). In his advertising designs, he used the techniques gleaned from his reading, such as photomontage, in a unique way.

By the mid-1930s, Beall had made a name for himself and relocated to New York, which offered more possibilities for work. He accepted commissions for advertisements, brochures, posters, magazines and packaging. After the Depression, the number of commissions grew dramatically, and Beall, who preferred to work alone, had to hire staff. In 1950, he bought a farm in Connecticut, about sixty miles from New York City. Both his family and his offices moved to Dumbarton Farm (DF). In the years after the move, the agency developed into a trendsetter in corporate identities.

DF: A Place in the Country is a deluxe glossy brochure, printed in colour on a heavy grade paper. Addressing potential clients, Beall expands on the design philosophy of his agency: 'we have a concept of design here that is based upon the idea of the "whole" rather than upon specialization in any of its components.' The company's location was of overall importance: 'we have here an *environment* for work that is good. …This is a "machine" for working in the graphic arts and industrial design.' Nevertheless, he also kept a flock of sheep at Dumbarton Farm – his beloved Cheviots. ML

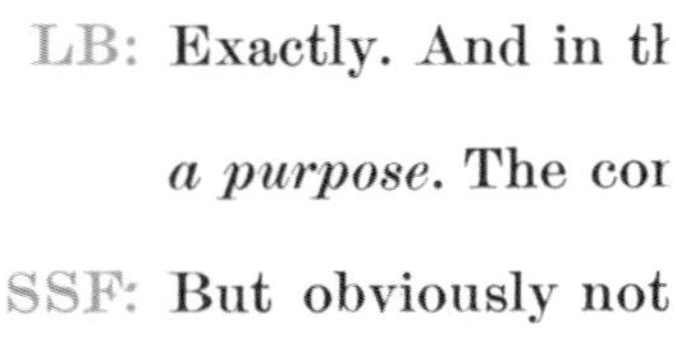

This is a 'modern face' of the kind introduced in the 1840s and common in books for several decades after (an 1869 specimen from the Bruce typefoundry in New York includes many). Like the Stephenson Blake typefoundry's Modern no. 20, this example has rather short descenders.

LB: To the extent that ideas are perceptual, yes. For every *perceptual* idea exists first, last and only as design.

SSF: For instance?

LB: For instance, that chair. It is first of all an idea. It invites you to sit down. Then, in addition, it conveys the idea of comfort and luxury, for it is a good chair... That's where the designer entered the picture. Up to that time it was only so much carpentry.

SSF: What you are saying, then, is that design – any form of design – is essentially the telling of a story.

LB: Exactly. And in the field of applied arts, it is the telling of a story *for a purpose*. The conveying of a calculated message.

SSF: But obviously not all of the messages of design are effective. What are the factors that determine effectiveness?

LB: I believe that the essential character and effectiveness of any design – whether simple or complex, feeble or emphatic – is the inevitable product of two points of view, two attitudes toward life, two philosophies: That of the designer/creator and that of the owner/user.

SSF: Whom do you mean by the owner/user?

LB: The person who commissions the design or buys it or sanctions it. Let's take that chair. Its manufacturer had certain personal and professional standards of taste. He employed a designer who could satisfy or exceed

Library

Secretary's office

1957 **Paul Rand** Ann & Paul Rand, *Sparkle and Spin: A book about words*. New York: Harcourt Brace & World, 1957.

30 pp. 26 cm. Designer & illustrator: Paul Rand.

The most famous American graphic designer of the twentieth century is Paul Rand (1914–96). Born Peretz Rosenbaum, he discovered that his obviously Jewish background would not always get him the commissions he was after in WASP society, so he changed his name in 1935. He is best known for the corporate logos he designed in the fifties and sixties for IBM, United Parcel Service, and the ABC television network. Logos were already an integral component of advertising campaigns he designed in the forties.

Rand was a strong adherent of modernism and a follower of Jan Tschichold. European trade magazines such as the German *Gebrauchsgraphik* had exposed him to this movement. As a student, he dreamed of studying at the Bauhaus in Germany. He and Lester Beall were primarily responsible for introducing the European avant-garde into American graphic design, alongside the work of emigrants such as László Moholy-Nagy, Ladislav Sutnar and Herbert Bayer. Rand used various techniques such as handwritten lettering, collage and photomontage.

In the fifties, Rand developed an illustration style utilizing simplified forms and colour fields that yielded powerful images. His drawings, which were often witty, were used for advertisements and book covers. Rand's style perfectly suited the four children's books he wrote with his wife Ann between 1956 and 1970, picturebooks for their daughter and other young children. *Sparkle and Spin: A book about words* turned out to be an ideal platform for illustrations with typographical elements. ML

This is Futura (Bauersche Giesserei, 1927), designed by German book and type designer Paul Renner (1878–1956), who became a late convert to modernism. The geometric sans serif may seem entirely constructed, but it has many optical refinements. The capitals are partly based on capitals in Roman inscriptions.

Words are "Yes I will"
and "No I won't,"
but they are polite too

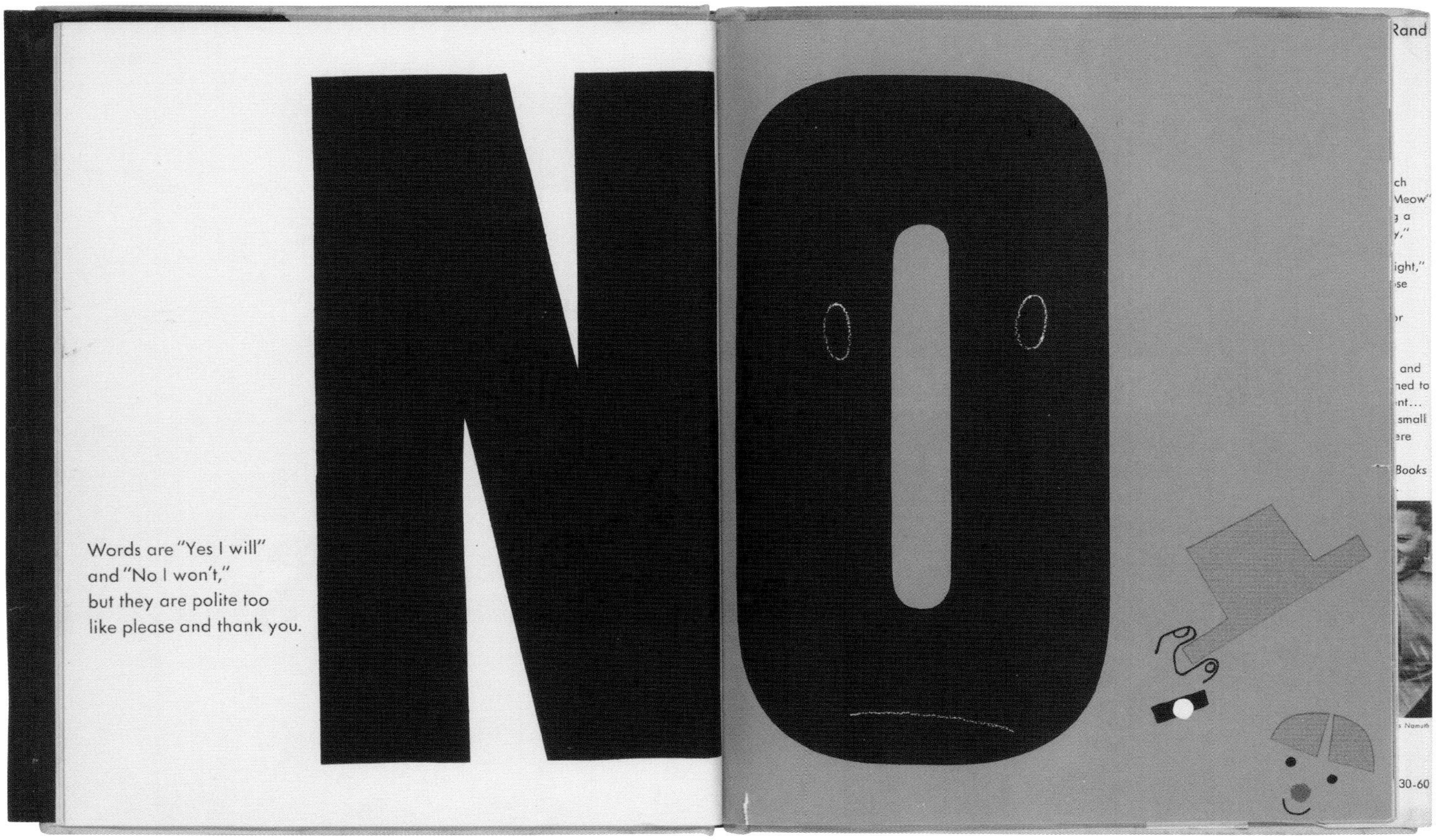

Words are "Yes I will"
and "No I won't,"
but they are polite too
like please and thank you.

b
o
A word is something you shout,
bang! or boo!
when you jump out
from behind a chair,
or something to whisper softly
as the little breeze
that says "hush hush"
as it rustles the leaves.
A word can warn that
someone's sick
or bring somebody running quick!
o

1958 **Karl Gerstner** *Geigy heute: die jüngste Geschichte, der gegenwärtige Aufbau und die heutige Tätigkeit der J.R. Geigy A.G., Basel ...*; ed. Markus Kutter. Basel: Geigy, 1958. 288, xxxii pp. 26 cm. Designer: Karl Gerstner. Photographer (colour): René Groebli. Typesetter & printer: Birkhäuser, Basel. Bookbinder: Max Grollimund, Basel.

The jubilee book *Geigy heute* is a model of Swiss typography. It shows the nearly square format in a binding with a flat spine, the flush left text in a sans serif type, the black and white photos overprinted with transparent areas of colour, and a layout clearly based on a grid. And the innovative diagrams are also notable. The design department of the Basel chemical company Geigy had a name to uphold with their printed matter. Enthusiastic articles about the 'Geigy style' appeared in international design magazines beginning in the early fifties. Within its modernist approach to design the house style provided leeway for a wide variety of designers, both on the permanent staff and working freelance. Talent could always be found nearby: the city's Allgemeine Gewerbeschule (AGS) could boast an international reputation with teachers including Armin Hofmann and Emil Ruder.

Karl Gerstner (b. 1930) grew up in Basel and studied at the AGS. Ruder's classes gave him his first introduction to the Bauhaus – which fascinated him – and with the pre-war New Typography. In 1959, Gerstner and the copywriter Markus Kutter founded an advertising agency and later that year they jointly published *Die neue Graphic*. This was the first design manual to discuss the historical context and principles of Swiss typography, devoting special attention to advertising design.

Like other Swiss modernist designers, including Richard Paul Lohse, Max Bill and Carlo Vivarelli, Gerstner continued to create abstract art in addition to his commissioned design work throughout his life. These Constructivist works with mathematical foundations have been exhibited in museums all over the world. ML

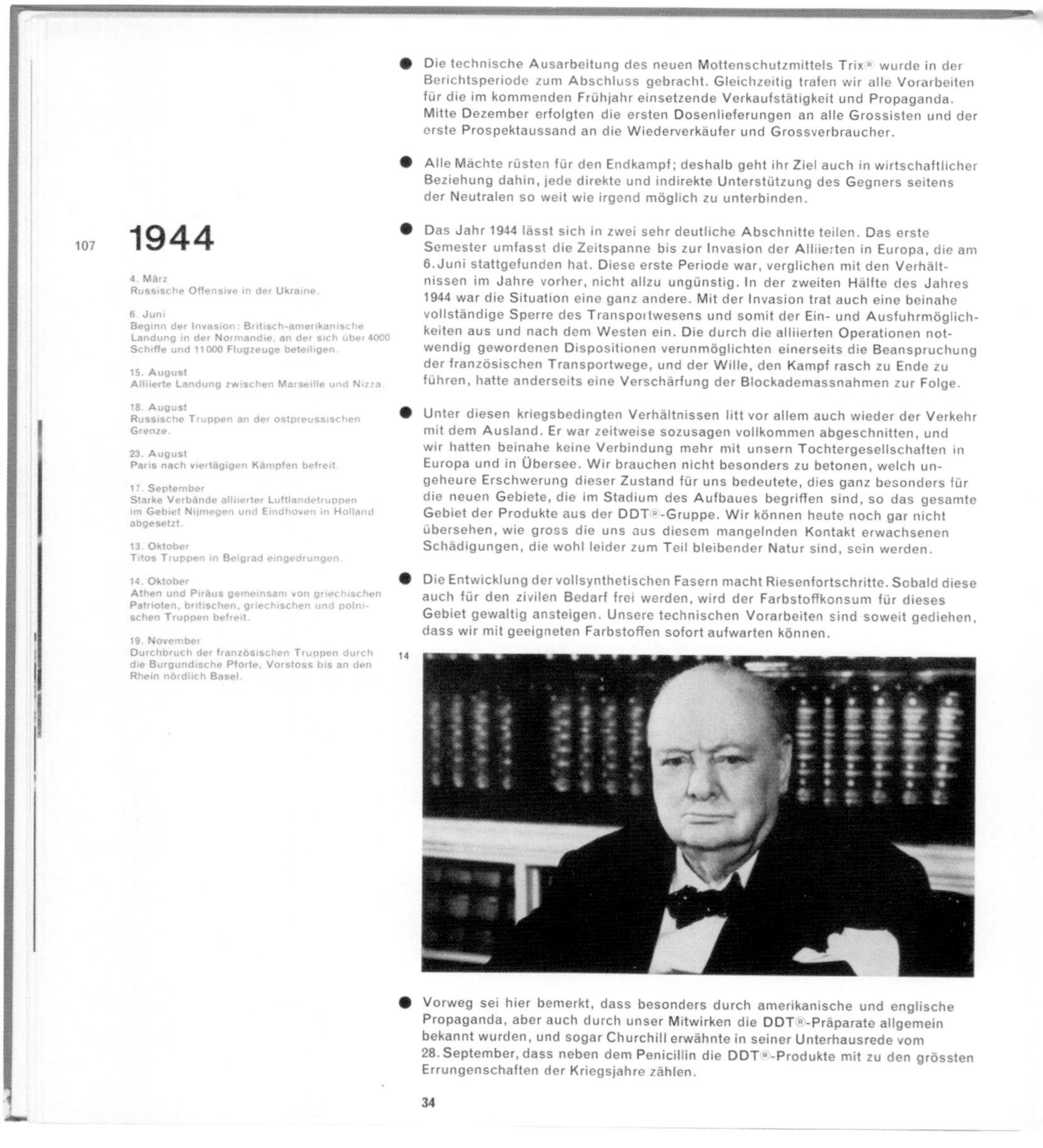

107 **1944**

4. März
Russische Offensive in der Ukraine.

6. Juni
Beginn der Invasion: Britisch-amerikanische Landung in der Normandie, an der sich über 4000 Schiffe und 11000 Flugzeuge beteiligen.

15. August
Alliierte Landung zwischen Marseille und Nizza.

18. August
Russische Truppen an der ostpreussischen Grenze.

23. August
Paris nach viertägigen Kämpfen befreit.

17. September
Starke Verbände alliierter Luftlandetruppen im Gebiet Nijmegen und Eindhoven in Holland abgesetzt.

13. Oktober
Titos Truppen in Belgrad eingedrungen.

14. Oktober
Athen und Piräus gemeinsam von griechischen Patrioten, britischen, griechischen und polnischen Truppen befreit.

19. November
Durchbruch der französischen Truppen durch die Burgundische Pforte, Vorstoss bis an den Rhein nördlich Basel.

- Die technische Ausarbeitung des neuen Mottenschutzmittels Trix® wurde in der Berichtsperiode zum Abschluss gebracht. Gleichzeitig trafen wir alle Vorarbeiten für die im kommenden Frühjahr einsetzende Verkaufstätigkeit und Propaganda. Mitte Dezember erfolgten die ersten Dosenlieferungen an alle Grossisten und der erste Prospektaussand an die Wiederverkäufer und Grossverbraucher.
- Alle Mächte rüsten für den Endkampf; deshalb geht ihr Ziel auch in wirtschaftlicher Beziehung dahin, jede direkte und indirekte Unterstützung des Gegners seitens der Neutralen so weit wie irgend möglich zu unterbinden.
- Das Jahr 1944 lässt sich in zwei sehr deutliche Abschnitte teilen. Das erste Semester umfasst die Zeitspanne bis zur Invasion der Alliierten in Europa, die am 6. Juni stattgefunden hat. Diese erste Periode war, verglichen mit den Verhältnissen im Jahre vorher, nicht allzu ungünstig. In der zweiten Hälfte des Jahres 1944 war die Situation eine ganz andere. Mit der Invasion trat auch eine beinahe vollständige Sperre des Transportwesens und somit der Ein- und Ausfuhrmöglichkeiten aus und nach dem Westen ein. Die durch die alliierten Operationen notwendig gewordenen Dispositionen verunmöglichten einerseits die Beanspruchung der französischen Transportwege, und der Wille, den Kampf rasch zu Ende zu führen, hatte anderseits eine Verschärfung der Blockademassnahmen zur Folge.
- Unter diesen kriegsbedingten Verhältnissen litt vor allem auch wieder der Verkehr mit dem Ausland. Er war zeitweise sozusagen vollkommen abgeschnitten, und wir hatten beinahe keine Verbindung mehr mit unsern Tochtergesellschaften in Europa und in Übersee. Wir brauchen nicht besonders zu betonen, welch ungeheure Erschwerung dieser Zustand für uns bedeutete, dies ganz besonders für die neuen Gebiete, die im Stadium des Aufbaues begriffen sind, so das gesamte Gebiet der Produkte aus der DDT®-Gruppe. Wir können heute noch gar nicht übersehen, wie gross die uns aus diesem mangelnden Kontakt erwachsenen Schädigungen, die wohl leider zum Teil bleibender Natur sind, sein werden.
- Die Entwicklung der vollsynthetischen Fasern macht Riesenfortschritte. Sobald diese auch für den zivilen Bedarf frei werden, wird der Farbstoffkonsum für dieses Gebiet gewaltig ansteigen. Unsere technischen Vorarbeiten sind soweit gediehen, dass wir mit geeigneten Farbstoffen sofort aufwarten können.

14

- Vorweg sei hier bemerkt, dass besonders durch amerikanische und englische Propaganda, aber auch durch unser Mitwirken die DDT®-Präparate allgemein bekannt wurden, und sogar Churchill erwähnte in seiner Unterhausrede vom 28. September, dass neben dem Penicillin die DDT®-Produkte mit zu den grössten Errungenschaften der Kriegsjahre zählen.

34

■ Die klinische Bearbeitung eines Chinaldinderivates wurde abgesc
laufenden Berichtsjahr dieses Therapeutikum als Sterosan® in Form
Salbe in den Handel gebracht. Das Hauptanwendungsgebiet der St
umfasst alle Hauterkrankungen, die durch Staphylo- und Streptoko
sind.

Geigy heute
Die jüngste Geschichte,
der gegenwärtige Aufbau
und die heutige Tätigkeit
der J.R. Geigy A.G., Basel
und der ihr nahestehenden Gesellschaften
Jubiläumsschrift
zum 200jährigen Bestehen
des Geigy-Unternehmens 1958

The text is set in Monotype Grotesque (1926), while the headings are in Akzidenz-Grotesk (Berthold, 1898). Both typefaces are based on nineteenth-century sans serifs and were popular with Swiss modernist typographers.

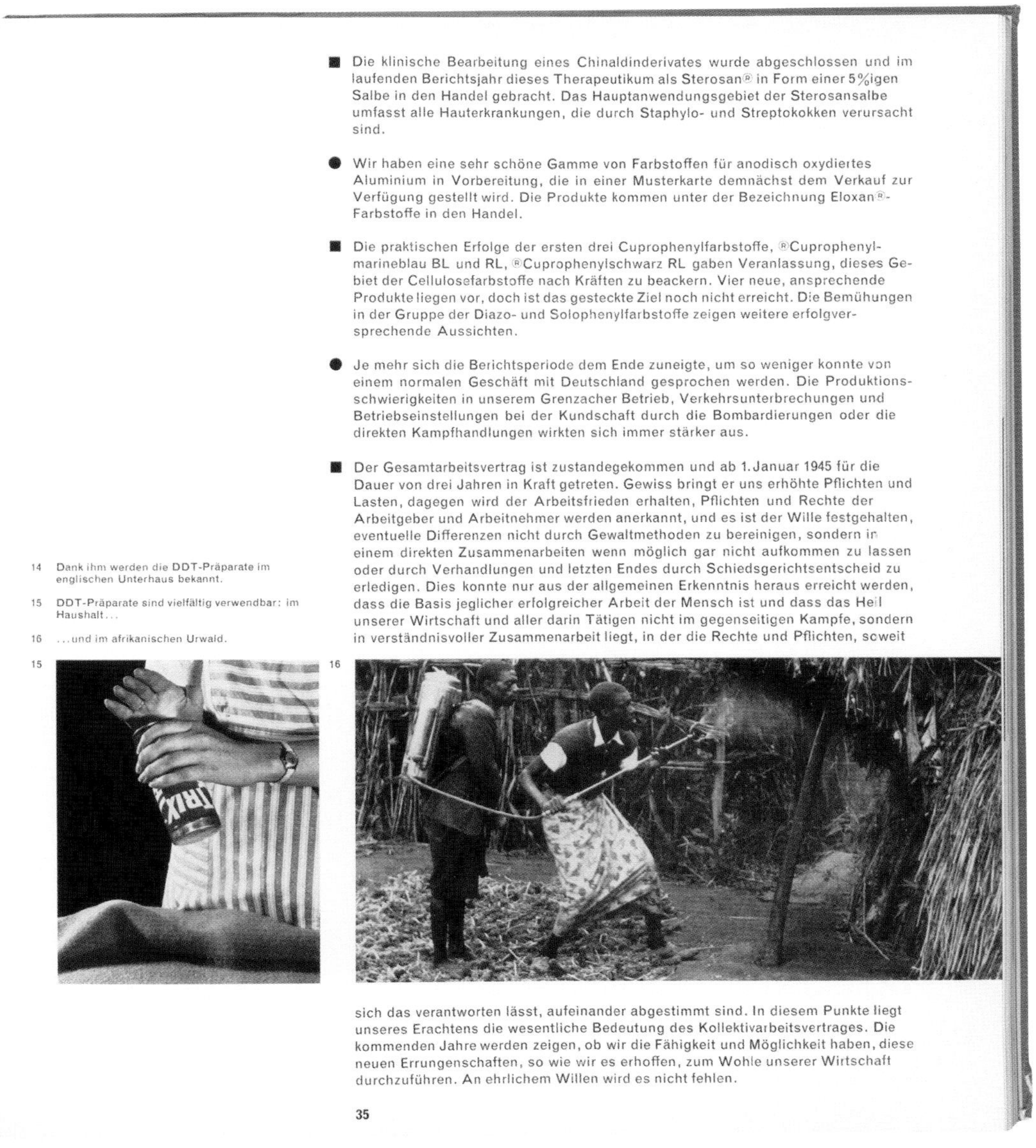

■ Die klinische Bearbeitung eines Chinaldinderivates wurde abgeschlossen und im laufenden Berichtsjahr dieses Therapeutikum als Sterosan® in Form einer 5%igen Salbe in den Handel gebracht. Das Hauptanwendungsgebiet der Sterosansalbe umfasst alle Hauterkrankungen, die durch Staphylo- und Streptokokken verursacht sind.

● Wir haben eine sehr schöne Gamme von Farbstoffen für anodisch oxydiertes Aluminium in Vorbereitung, die in einer Musterkarte demnächst dem Verkauf zur Verfügung gestellt wird. Die Produkte kommen unter der Bezeichnung Eloxan®-Farbstoffe in den Handel.

■ Die praktischen Erfolge der ersten drei Cuprophenylfarbstoffe, ®Cuprophenyl-marineblau BL und RL, ®Cuprophenylschwarz RL gaben Veranlassung, dieses Gebiet der Cellulosefarbstoffe nach Kräften zu beackern. Vier neue, ansprechende Produkte liegen vor, doch ist das gesteckte Ziel noch nicht erreicht. Die Bemühungen in der Gruppe der Diazo- und Solophenylfarbstoffe zeigen weitere erfolgversprechende Aussichten.

● Je mehr sich die Berichtsperiode dem Ende zuneigte, um so weniger konnte von einem normalen Geschäft mit Deutschland gesprochen werden. Die Produktionsschwierigkeiten in unserem Grenzacher Betrieb, Verkehrsunterbrechungen und Betriebseinstellungen bei der Kundschaft durch die Bombardierungen oder die direkten Kampfhandlungen wirkten sich immer stärker aus.

■ Der Gesamtarbeitsvertrag ist zustandegekommen und ab 1. Januar 1945 für die Dauer von drei Jahren in Kraft getreten. Gewiss bringt er uns erhöhte Pflichten und Lasten, dagegen wird der Arbeitsfrieden erhalten, Pflichten und Rechte der Arbeitgeber und Arbeitnehmer werden anerkannt, und es ist der Wille festgehalten, eventuelle Differenzen nicht durch Gewaltmethoden zu bereinigen, sondern in einem direkten Zusammenarbeiten wenn möglich gar nicht aufkommen zu lassen oder durch Verhandlungen und letzten Endes durch Schiedsgerichtsentscheid zu erledigen. Dies konnte nur aus der allgemeinen Erkenntnis heraus erreicht werden, dass die Basis jeglicher erfolgreicher Arbeit der Mensch ist und dass das Heil unserer Wirtschaft und aller darin Tätigen nicht im gegenseitigen Kampfe, sondern in verständnisvoller Zusammenarbeit liegt, in der die Rechte und Pflichten, soweit sich das verantworten lässt, aufeinander abgestimmt sind. In diesem Punkte liegt unseres Erachtens die wesentliche Bedeutung des Kollektivarbeitsvertrages. Die kommenden Jahre werden zeigen, ob wir die Fähigkeit und Möglichkeit haben, diese neuen Errungenschaften, so wie wir es erhoffen, zum Wohle unserer Wirtschaft durchzuführen. An ehrlichem Willen wird es nicht fehlen.

14 Dank ihm werden die DDT-Präparate im englischen Unterhaus bekannt.

15 DDT-Präparate sind vielfältig verwendbar: im Haushalt...

16 ...und im afrikanischen Urwald.

15

16

35

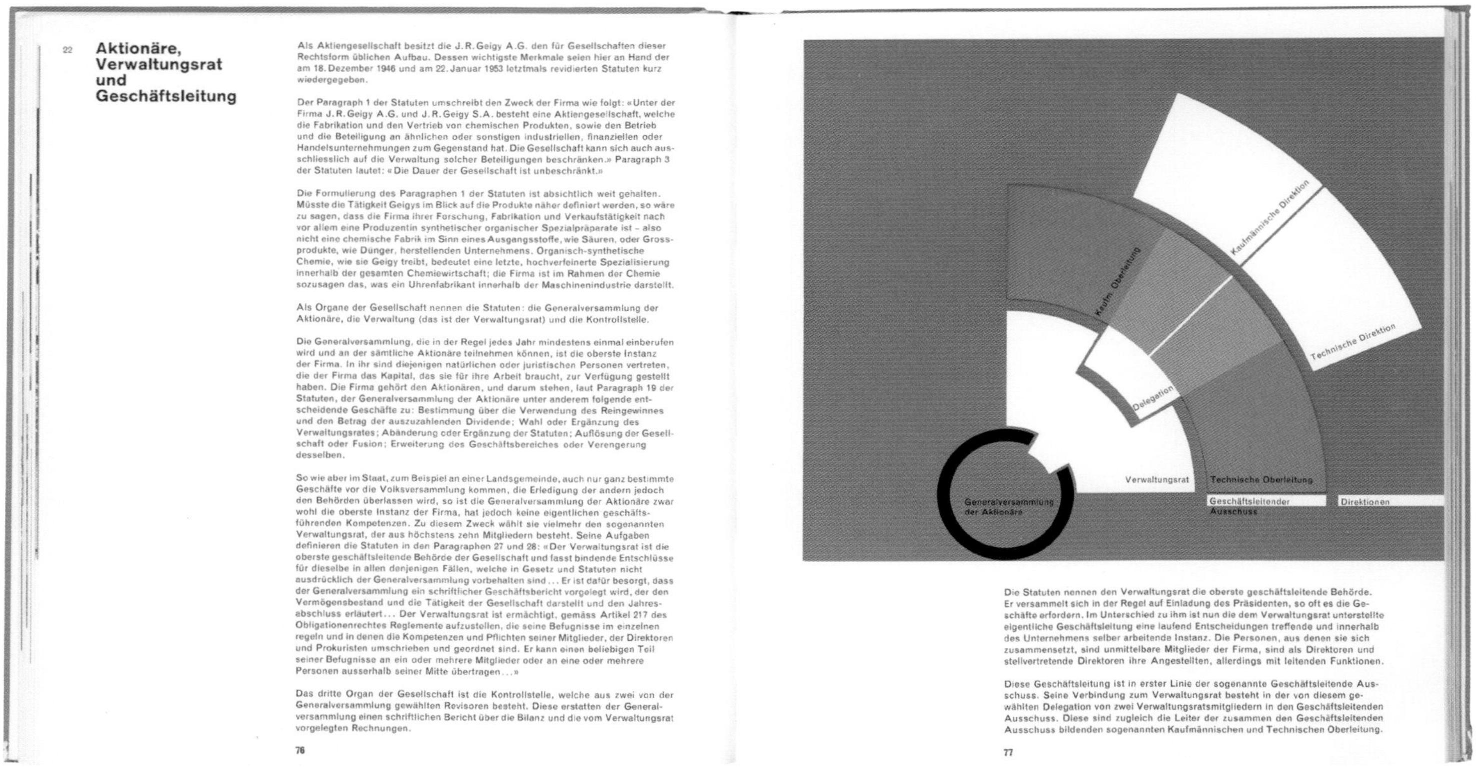

22 **Aktionäre, Verwaltungsrat und Geschäftsleitung**

Als Aktiengesellschaft besitzt die J. R. Geigy A.G. den für Gesellschaften dieser Rechtsform üblichen Aufbau. Dessen wichtigste Merkmale seien hier an Hand der am 18. Dezember 1946 und am 22. Januar 1953 letztmals revidierten Statuten kurz wiedergegeben.

Der Paragraph 1 der Statuten umschreibt den Zweck der Firma wie folgt: «Unter der Firma J. R. Geigy A.G. und J. R. Geigy S.A. besteht eine Aktiengesellschaft, welche die Fabrikation und den Vertrieb von chemischen Produkten, sowie den Betrieb und die Beteiligung an ähnlichen oder sonstigen industriellen, finanziellen oder Handelsunternehmungen zum Gegenstand hat. Die Gesellschaft kann sich auch ausschliesslich auf die Verwaltung solcher Beteiligungen beschränken.» Paragraph 3 der Statuten lautet: «Die Dauer der Gesellschaft ist unbeschränkt.»

Die Formulierung des Paragraphen 1 der Statuten ist absichtlich weit gehalten. Müsste die Tätigkeit Geigys im Blick auf die Produkte näher definiert werden, so wäre zu sagen, dass die Firma ihrer Forschung, Fabrikation und Verkaufstätigkeit nach vor allem eine Produzentin synthetischer organischer Spezialpräparate ist – also nicht eine chemische Fabrik im Sinn eines Ausgangsstoffe, wie Säuren, oder Grossprodukte, wie Dünger, herstellenden Unternehmens. Organisch-synthetische Chemie, wie sie Geigy treibt, bedeutet eine letzte, hochverfeinerte Spezialisierung innerhalb der gesamten Chemiewirtschaft; die Firma ist im Rahmen der Chemie sozusagen das, was ein Uhrenfabrikant innerhalb der Maschinenindustrie darstellt.

Als Organe der Gesellschaft nennen die Statuten: die Generalversammlung der Aktionäre, die Verwaltung (das ist der Verwaltungsrat) und die Kontrollstelle.

Die Generalversammlung, die in der Regel jedes Jahr mindestens einmal einberufen wird und an der sämtliche Aktionäre teilnehmen können, ist die oberste Instanz der Firma. In ihr sind diejenigen natürlichen oder juristischen Personen vertreten, die der Firma das Kapital, das sie für ihre Arbeit braucht, zur Verfügung gestellt haben. Die Firma gehört den Aktionären, und darum stehen, laut Paragraph 19 der Statuten, der Generalversammlung der Aktionäre unter anderem folgende entscheidende Geschäfte zu: Bestimmung über die Verwendung des Reingewinnes und den Betrag der auszuzahlenden Dividende; Wahl oder Ergänzung des Verwaltungsrates; Abänderung oder Ergänzung der Statuten; Auflösung der Gesellschaft oder Fusion; Erweiterung des Geschäftsbereiches oder Verengerung desselben.

So wie aber im Staat, zum Beispiel an einer Landsgemeinde, auch nur ganz bestimmte Geschäfte vor die Volksversammlung kommen, die Erledigung der andern jedoch den Behörden überlassen wird, so ist die Generalversammlung der Aktionäre zwar wohl die oberste Instanz der Firma, hat jedoch keine eigentlichen geschäftsführenden Kompetenzen. Zu diesem Zweck wählt sie vielmehr den sogenannten Verwaltungsrat, der aus höchstens zehn Mitgliedern besteht. Seine Aufgaben definieren die Statuten in den Paragraphen 27 und 28: «Der Verwaltungsrat ist die oberste geschäftsleitende Behörde der Gesellschaft und fasst bindende Entschlüsse für dieselbe in allen denjenigen Fällen, welche in Gesetz und Statuten nicht ausdrücklich der Generalversammlung vorbehalten sind ... Er ist dafür besorgt, dass der Generalversammlung ein schriftlicher Geschäftsbericht vorgelegt wird, der den Vermögensbestand und die Tätigkeit der Gesellschaft darstellt und den Jahresabschluss erläutert ... Der Verwaltungsrat ist ermächtigt, gemäss Artikel 217 des Obligationenrechtes Reglemente aufzustellen, die seine Befugnisse im einzelnen regeln und in denen die Kompetenzen und Pflichten seiner Mitglieder, der Direktoren und Prokuristen umschrieben und geordnet sind. Er kann einen beliebigen Teil seiner Befugnisse an ein oder mehrere Mitglieder oder an eine oder mehrere Personen ausserhalb seiner Mitte übertragen ...»

Das dritte Organ der Gesellschaft ist die Kontrollstelle, welche aus zwei von der Generalversammlung gewählten Revisoren besteht. Diese erstatten der Generalversammlung einen schriftlichen Bericht über die Bilanz und die vom Verwaltungsrat vorgelegten Rechnungen.

76

Die Statuten nennen den Verwaltungsrat die oberste geschäftsleitende Behörde. Er versammelt sich in der Regel auf Einladung des Präsidenten, so oft es die Geschäfte erfordern. Im Unterschied zu ihm ist nun die dem Verwaltungsrat unterstellte eigentliche Geschäftsleitung eine laufend Entscheidungen treffende und innerhalb des Unternehmens selber arbeitende Instanz. Die Personen, aus denen sie sich zusammensetzt, sind unmittelbare Mitglieder der Firma, sind als Direktoren und stellvertretende Direktoren ihre Angestellten, allerdings mit leitenden Funktionen.

Diese Geschäftsleitung ist in erster Linie der sogenannte Geschäftsleitende Ausschuss. Seine Verbindung zum Verwaltungsrat besteht in der von diesem gewählten Delegation von zwei Verwaltungsratsmitgliedern in den Geschäftsleitenden Ausschuss. Diese sind zugleich die Leiter der zusammen den Geschäftsleitenden Ausschuss bildenden sogenannten Kaufmännischen und Technischen Oberleitung.

77

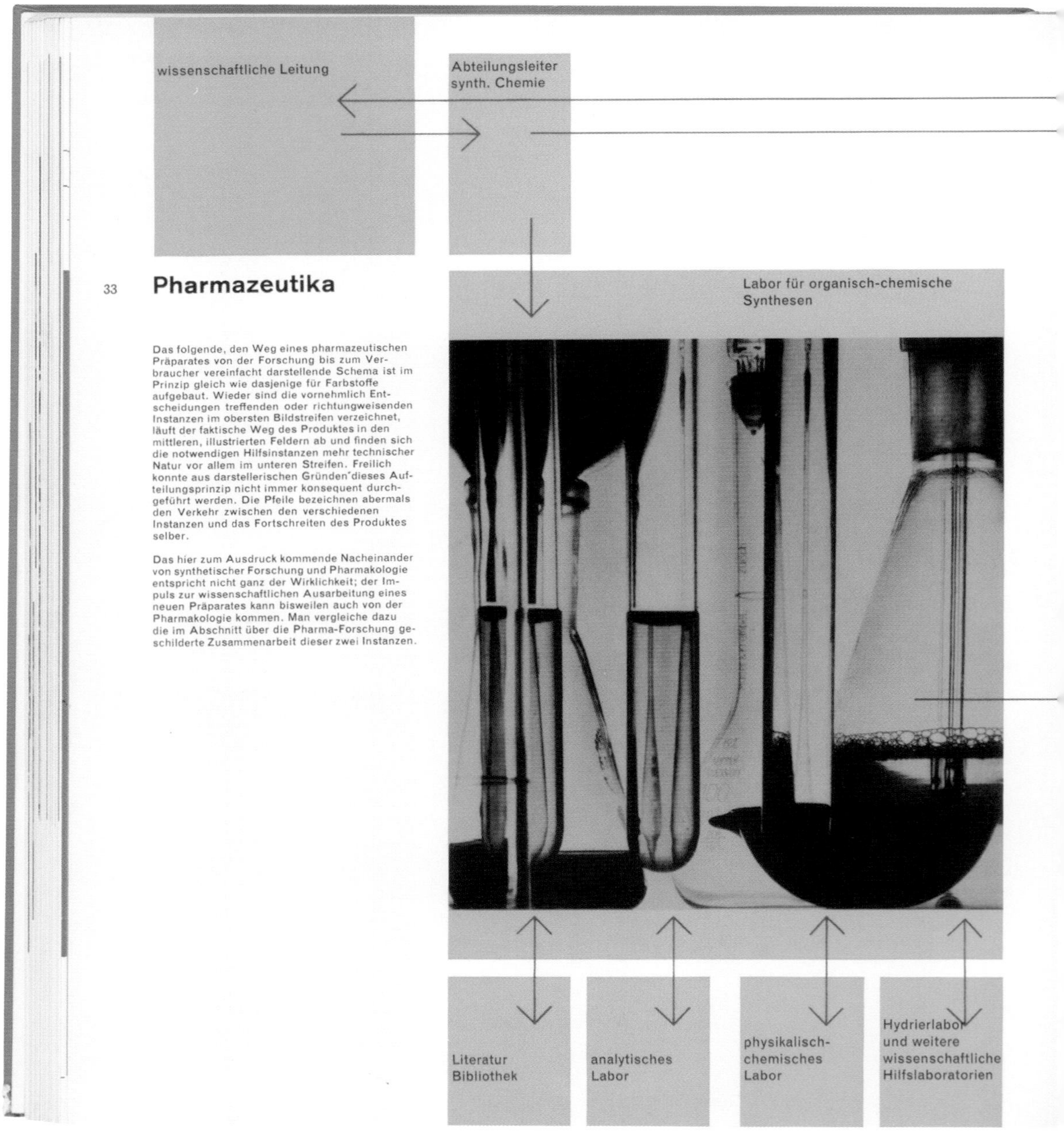

33 **Pharmazeutika**

Das folgende, den Weg eines pharmazeutischen Präparates von der Forschung bis zum Verbraucher vereinfacht darstellende Schema ist im Prinzip gleich wie dasjenige für Farbstoffe aufgebaut. Wieder sind die vornehmlich Entscheidungen treffenden oder richtungweisenden Instanzen im obersten Bildstreifen verzeichnet, läuft der faktische Weg des Produktes in den mittleren, illustrierten Feldern ab und finden sich die notwendigen Hilfsinstanzen mehr technischer Natur vor allem im unteren Streifen. Freilich konnte aus darstellerischen Gründen dieses Aufteilungsprinzip nicht immer konsequent durchgeführt werden. Die Pfeile bezeichnen abermals den Verkehr zwischen den verschiedenen Instanzen und das Fortschreiten des Produktes selber.

Das hier zum Ausdruck kommende Nacheinander von synthetischer Forschung und Pharmakologie entspricht nicht ganz der Wirklichkeit; der Impuls zur wissenschaftlichen Ausarbeitung eines neuen Präparates kann bisweilen auch von der Pharmakologie kommen. Man vergleiche dazu die im Abschnitt über die Pharma-Forschung geschilderte Zusammenarbeit dieser zwei Instanzen.

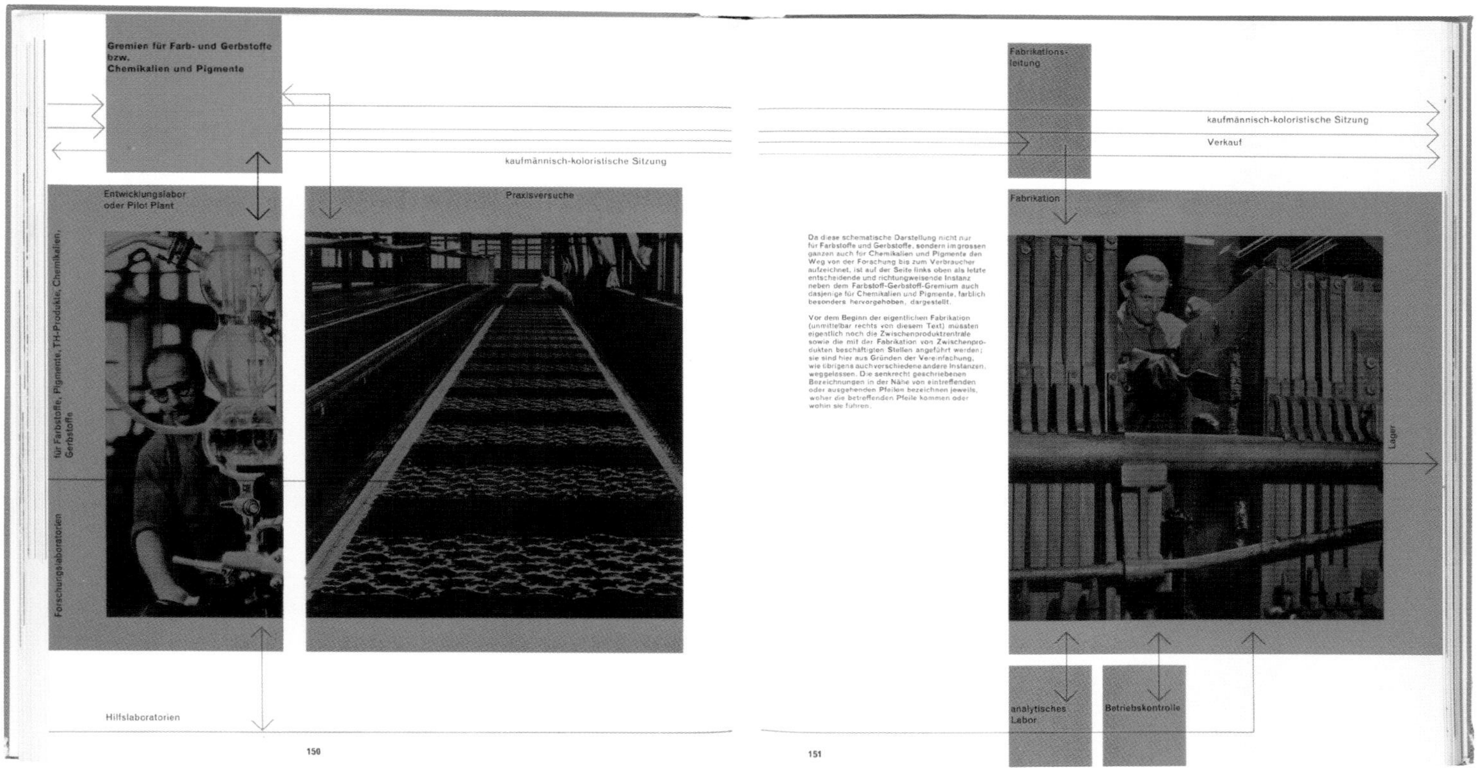

Gremien für Farb- und Gerbstoffe bzw. Chemikalien und Pigmente
kaufmännisch-koloristische Sitzung
Entwicklungslabor oder Pilot Plant
Praxisversuche
Forschungslaboratorien für Farbstoffe, Pigmente, TH-Produkte, Chemikalien, Gerbstoffe
Hilfslaboratorien
150
Da diese schematische Darstellung nicht nur für Farbstoffe und Gerbstoffe, sondern im grossen ganzen auch für Chemikalien und Pigmente den Weg von der Forschung bis zum Verbraucher aufzeichnet, ist auf der Seite links oben als letzte entscheidende und richtungweisende Instanz neben dem Farbstoff-Gerbstoff-Gremium auch dasjenige für Chemikalien und Pigmente, farblich besonders hervorgehoben, dargestellt.
Vor dem Beginn der eigentlichen Fabrikation (unmittelbar rechts von diesem Text) müssten eigentlich noch die Zwischenproduktzentrale sowie die mit der Fabrikation von Zwischenprodukten beschäftigten Stellen angeführt werden; sie sind hier aus Gründen der Vereinfachung, wie übrigens auch verschiedene andere Instanzen, weggelassen. Die senkrecht geschriebenen Bezeichnungen in der Nähe von eintreffenden oder ausgehenden Pfeilen bezeichnen jeweils, woher die betreffenden Pfeile kommen oder wohin sie führen.
Fabrikationsleitung
kaufmännisch-koloristische Sitzung
Verkauf
Fabrikation
Lager
analytisches Labor
Betriebskontrolle
151

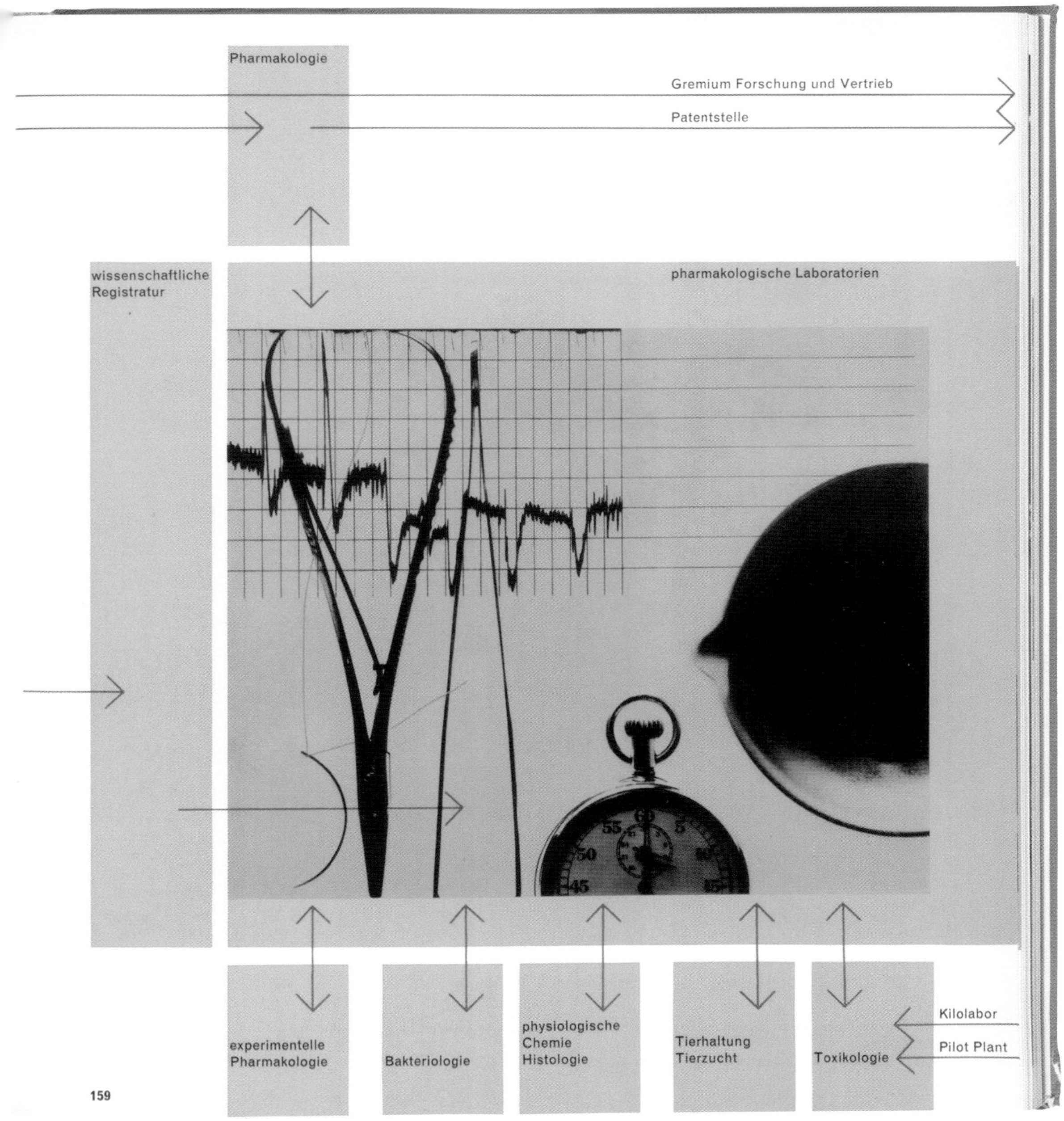

Pharmakologie
Gremium Forschung und Vertrieb
Patentstelle
wissenschaftliche Registratur
pharmakologische Laboratorien
experimentelle Pharmakologie
Bakteriologie
physiologische Chemie Histologie
Tierhaltung Tierzucht
Toxikologie
Kilolabor
Pilot Plant
159

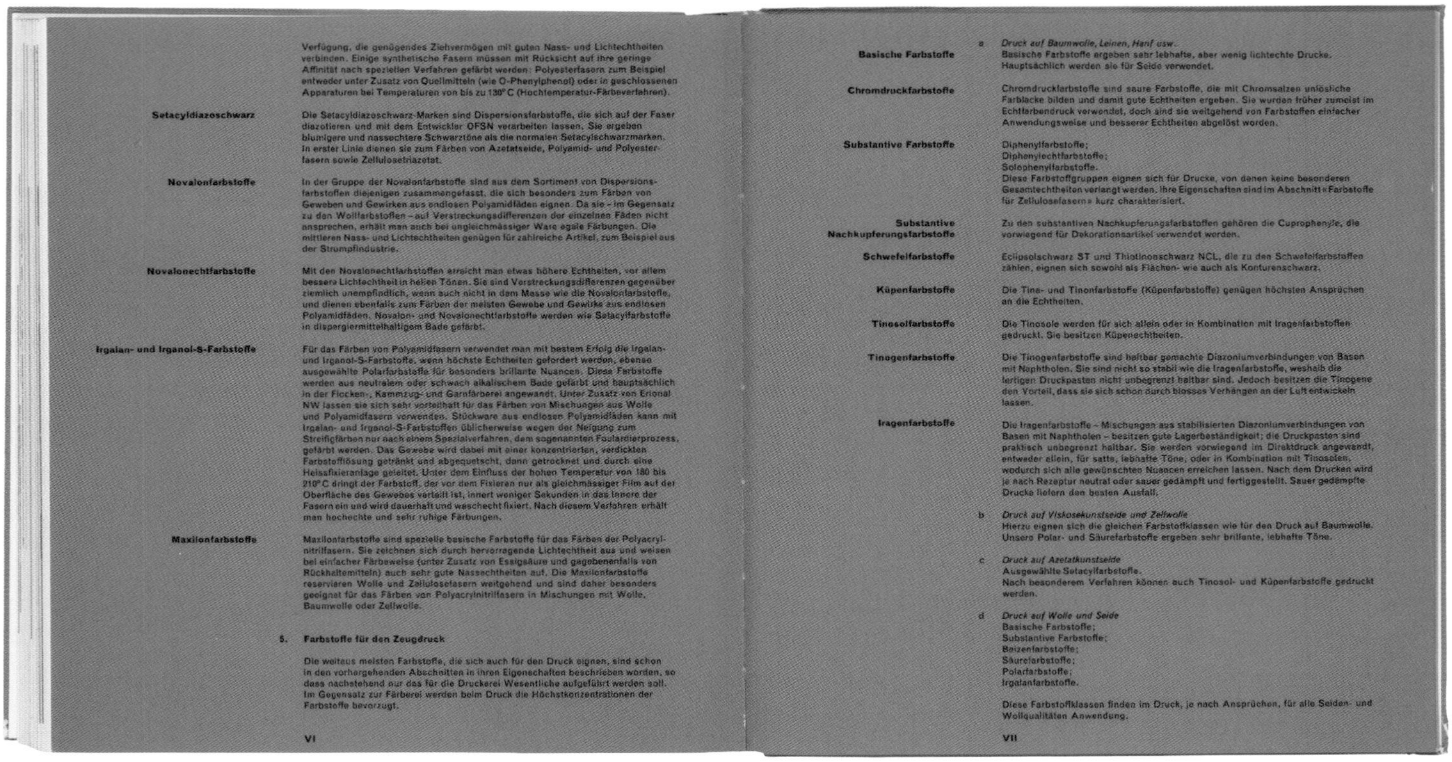

Verfügung, die genügendes Ziehvermögen mit guten Nass- und Lichtechtheiten verbinden. Einige synthetische Fasern müssen mit Rücksicht auf ihre geringe Affinität nach speziellen Verfahren gefärbt werden: Polyesterfasern zum Beispiel entweder unter Zusatz von Quellmitteln (wie O-Phenylphenol) oder in geschlossenen Apparaturen bei Temperaturen von bis zu 130° C (Hochtemperatur-Färbeverfahren).

Setacyldiazoschwarz
Die Setacyldiazoschwarz-Marken sind Dispersionsfarbstoffe, die sich auf der Faser diazotieren und mit dem Entwickler OFSN verarbeiten lassen. Sie ergeben blumigere und nassechtere Schwarztöne als die normalen Setacylschwarzmarken. In erster Linie dienen sie zum Färben von Azetatseide, Polyamid- und Polyesterfasern sowie Zellulosetriazetat.

Novalonfarbstoffe
In der Gruppe der Novalonfarbstoffe sind aus dem Sortiment von Dispersionsfarbstoffen diejenigen zusammengefasst, die sich besonders zum Färben von Geweben und Gewirken aus endlosen Polyamidfäden eignen. Da sie – im Gegensatz zu den Wollfarbstoffen – auf Verstreckungsdifferenzen der einzelnen Fäden nicht ansprechen, erhält man auch bei ungleichmässiger Ware egale Färbungen. Die mittleren Nass- und Lichtechtheiten genügen für zahlreiche Artikel, zum Beispiel aus der Strumpfindustrie.

Novalonechtfarbstoffe
Mit den Novalonechtfarbstoffen erreicht man etwas höhere Echtheiten, vor allem bessere Lichtechtheit in hellen Tönen. Sie sind Verstreckungsdifferenzen gegenüber ziemlich unempfindlich, wenn auch nicht in dem Masse wie die Novalonfarbstoffe, und dienen ebenfalls zum Färben der meisten Gewebe und Gewirke aus endlosen Polyamidfäden. Novalon- und Novalonechtfarbstoffe werden wie Setacylfarbstoffe in dispergiermittelhaltigem Bade gefärbt.

Irgalan- und Irganol-S-Farbstoffe
Für das Färben von Polyamidfasern verwendet man mit bestem Erfolg die Irgalan- und Irganol-S-Farbstoffe, wenn höchste Echtheiten gefordert werden, ebenso ausgewählte Polarfarbstoffe für besonders brillante Nuancen. Diese Farbstoffe werden aus neutralem oder schwach alkalischem Bade gefärbt und hauptsächlich in der Flocken-, Kammzug- und Garnfärberei angewandt. Unter Zusatz von Erional NW lassen sie sich sehr vorteilhaft für das Färben von Mischungen aus Wolle und Polyamidfasern verwenden. Stückware aus endlosen Polyamidfäden kann mit Irgalan- und Irganol-S-Farbstoffen üblicherweise wegen der Neigung zum Streifigfärben nur nach einem Spezialverfahren, dem sogenannten Foulardierprozess, gefärbt werden. Das Gewebe wird dabei mit einer konzentrierten, verdickten Farbstofflösung getränkt und abgequetscht, dann getrocknet und durch eine Heissfixieranlage geleitet. Unter dem Einfluss der hohen Temperatur von 180 bis 210° C dringt der Farbstoff, der vor dem Fixieren nur als gleichmässiger Film auf der Oberfläche des Gewebes verteilt ist, innert weniger Sekunden in das Innere der Fasern ein und wird dauerhaft und waschecht fixiert. Nach diesem Verfahren erhält man hochechte und sehr ruhige Färbungen.

Maxilonfarbstoffe
Maxilonfarbstoffe sind spezielle basische Farbstoffe für das Färben der Polyacrylnitrilfasern. Sie zeichnen sich durch hervorragende Lichtechtheit aus und weisen bei einfacher Färbeweise (unter Zusatz von Essigsäure und gegebenenfalls von Rückhaltemitteln) auch sehr gute Nassechtheiten auf. Die Maxilonfarbstoffe reservieren Wolle und Zellulosefasern weitgehend und sind daher besonders geeignet für das Färben von Polyacrylnitrilfasern in Mischungen mit Wolle, Baumwolle oder Zellwolle.

5. Farbstoffe für den Zeugdruck

Die weitaus meisten Farbstoffe, die sich auch für den Druck eignen, sind schon in den vorhergehenden Abschnitten in ihren Eigenschaften beschrieben worden, so dass nachstehend nur das für die Druckerei Wesentliche aufgeführt werden soll. Im Gegensatz zur Färberei werden beim Druck die Höchstkonzentrationen der Farbstoffe bevorzugt.

VI

a *Druck auf Baumwolle, Leinen, Hanf usw.*

Basische Farbstoffe
Basische Farbstoffe ergeben sehr lebhafte, aber wenig lichtechte Drucke. Hauptsächlich werden sie für Seide verwendet.

Chromdruckfarbstoffe
Chromdruckfarbstoffe sind saure Farbstoffe, die mit Chromsalzen unlösliche Farblacke bilden und damit gute Echtheiten ergeben. Sie wurden früher zumeist im Echtfarbendruck verwendet, doch sind sie weitgehend von Farbstoffen einfacher Anwendungsweise und besserer Echtheiten abgelöst worden.

Substantive Farbstoffe
Diphenylfarbstoffe;
Diphenylechtfarbstoffe;
Solophenylfarbstoffe.
Diese Farbstoffgruppen eignen sich für Drucke, von denen keine besonderen Gesamtechtheiten verlangt werden. Ihre Eigenschaften sind im Abschnitt «Farbstoffe für Zellulosefasern» kurz charakterisiert.

Substantive Nachkupferungsfarbstoffe
Zu den substantiven Nachkupferungsfarbstoffen gehören die Cuprophenyle, die vorwiegend für Dekorationsartikel verwendet werden.

Schwefelfarbstoffe
Eclipsolschwarz ST und Thiotinonschwarz NCL, die zu den Schwefelfarbstoffen zählen, eignen sich sowohl als Flächen- wie auch als Konturenschwarz.

Küpenfarbstoffe
Die Tina- und Tinonfarbstoffe (Küpenfarbstoffe) genügen höchsten Ansprüchen an die Echtheiten.

Tinosolfarbstoffe
Die Tinosole werden für sich allein oder in Kombination mit Iragenfarbstoffen gedruckt. Sie besitzen Küpenechtheiten.

Tinogenfarbstoffe
Die Tinogenfarbstoffe sind haltbar gemachte Diazoniumverbindungen von Basen mit Naphtholen. Sie sind nicht so stabil wie die Iragenfarbstoffe, weshalb die fertigen Druckpasten nicht unbegrenzt haltbar sind. Jedoch besitzen die Tinogene den Vorteil, dass sie sich schon durch blosses Verhängen an der Luft entwickeln lassen.

Iragenfarbstoffe
Die Iragenfarbstoffe – Mischungen aus stabilisierten Diazoniumverbindungen von Basen mit Naphtholen – besitzen gute Lagerbeständigkeit; die Druckpasten sind praktisch unbegrenzt haltbar. Sie werden vorwiegend im Direktdruck angewandt, entweder allein, für satte, lebhafte Töne, oder in Kombination mit Tinosolen, wodurch sich alle gewünschten Nuancen erreichen lassen. Nach dem Drucken wird je nach Rezeptur neutral oder sauer gedämpft und fertiggestellt. Sauer gedämpfte Drucke liefern den besten Ausfall.

b *Druck auf Viskosekunstseide und Zellwolle*
Hierzu eignen sich die gleichen Farbstoffklassen wie für den Druck auf Baumwolle. Unsere Polar- und Säurefarbstoffe ergeben sehr brillante, lebhafte Töne.

c *Druck auf Azetatkunstseide*
Ausgewählte Setacylfarbstoffe.
Nach besonderem Verfahren können auch Tinosol- und Küpenfarbstoffe gedruckt werden.

d *Druck auf Wolle und Seide*
Basische Farbstoffe;
Substantive Farbstoffe;
Beizenfarbstoffe;
Säurefarbstoffe;
Polarfarbstoffe;
Irgalanfarbstoffe.

Diese Farbstoffklassen finden im Druck, je nach Ansprüchen, für alle Seiden- und Wollqualitäten Anwendung.

VII

11, 12, 13 Das Laborgebäude, das Laboratorium, der einzelne Chemiker an seinem Arbeitsplatz – es sind innerste denkende und kontrollierende Zellen des Werkes, in denen sich jeden Tag das Geschick des Unternehmens entscheidet.

224

Anwendung führt zu Schädigungen; das Zahnfleisch wird gelockert, es bilden sich Taschen, in denen sich die Bakterien ansiedeln. Der Sitz der Zähne wird locker, schliesslich kann es sogar zu örtlichen Blutungen kommen.
Im Selgin steht eine Zahnpasta zur Verfügung, die sich prinzipiell von den sonst üblichen Zahnpasten unterscheidet. Sie ist frei von unphysiologischen Komponenten wie Netzmitteln oder Seifen; ihr wirksames Prinzip beruht auf den hygroskopischen und osmotischen Eigenschaften des Meersalzes, enthält sie doch in geeigneter Zusammensetzung eine Aufschwemmung von natürlichen Salzen. Dank der osmotischen Wirkung wird bei der Anwendung von Selgin das Zahnfleisch besser durchblutet und damit besser ernährt. Es festigt sich und beginnt den gegen Karies besonders empfindlichen Zahnhals besser zu umschliessen. Auf Grund seines hohen Salzgehaltes wirkt Selgin blutstillend, fäulnishemmend, desodorierend und hinterlässt ein wohltuendes Gefühl der Mundfrische.
Selgin reinigt wie jede andere Zahnpaste, jedoch ohne schädliche Nebenwirkungen auszulösen. Selgin ist daher die Zahnpaste zur physiologischen Mundpflege, zur einwandfreien Reinigung von Zahnfleisch und Zähnen und zur Stärkung des Zahnfleisches.
Anwendungsform: Paste.

9. Pharma-Farben

Im grösseren Rahmen der Pharma-Vertriebsabteilung, doch als selbständige und von den eigentlichen Pharmazeutika unabhängige Produktengruppe werden die sogenannten Pharma-Farben vertrieben. Zu ihnen gehören die Lebensmittelfarbstoffe die Kosmetikfarbstoffe und die Farbstoffe für Mikroskopie.

a *Lebensmittelfarbstoffe*
Es handelt sich bei ihnen um Farbstoffe, die nicht so sehr zum eigentlichen Färben von Lebensmitteln dienen wie dazu, der natürlichen Färbung von Nahrungs- und Genussmitteln in wohlüberlegter Weise nachzuhelfen. Die Qualität des betreffenden Produktes wird dabei in keiner Weise beeinträchtigt.

b *Kosmetikfarbstoffe*
Die meisten kosmetischen Präparate sind gefärbt oder enthalten zumindest Spuren von Farbstoffen. Neben den verschiedenen Arten von Pudern, Fond-de-Teints, Crèmen werden hauptsächlich für die Herstellung von Lippenstiften Farbstoffe in vielen Schattierungen benötigt. Das Sortiment der fixierenden Lippenstiftfarbstoffe umfasst eine vollständige Gamme, mit der allein oder in Kombination mit Pigmenten und Lackfällungen alle wünschbaren Nuancen erzielt werden können. Auch bei der Herstellung von Seifen, Shampoos, Badezusätzen usw. werden Farbstoffe mitverarbeitet; desgleichen verlangt die Nagellackherstellung nach besonders geeigneten, nicht sedimentierenden Farbstoffen.

Zur Ausarbeitung von Haarfärbemitteln dienen verschiedene entsprechende Zwischenprodukte.

c *Farbstoffe für Mikroskopie*
Unter dieser Gruppe sind die Farbstoffe für Histologie, Bakteriologie, Botanik, desgleichen Farbstoffe für medizinische und analytische Zwecke neben den Indikatoren und einigen Reagenzien zusammengefasst.

Mit wenigen Ausnahmen, zu denen auch die Speziallösungen zur Krebsdiagnose nach Papanicolaou gehören, werden diese Farbstoffe nur in Substanz geliefert.

Unter den Farbstoffen für Mikroskopie befinden sich auch Extraktfarbstoffe natürlichen Ursprungs, welche seit den Anfängen der Farbstoffherstellung bei Geigy stets zu den Standardprodukten gehört haben.

XXVI

Schädlings-bekämpfungsmittel

I. Wirksubstanzen

1. Insektizide

DDT-Wirksubstanz
Die DDT-Produkte sind spezifische Kontaktinsektizide und zeichnen sich aus durch ihre langdauernde Wirksamkeit in Form von Spritz- und Stäubebelägen bei relativ geringer Toxizität für Warmblüter. Sie finden Verwendung im Pflanzenschutz, Vorrats- und Materialschutz, in der Hygiene und in Haushaltpräparaten.

Methoxychlor
In ausseramerikanischen Ländern nur von geringer Bedeutung, stellt Methoxychlor eine spezifisch amerikanische Weiterentwicklung der DDT-Wirksubstanz für gewisse Spezialgebiete dar. Die insektizide Wirkung von Methoxychlor ist eher schwächer als diejenige entsprechender DDT-Produkte; seine hervorstechendste Eigenschaft ist die ausserordentlich geringe Giftigkeit für Warmblüter, speziell auch bei chronischer Exposition. Methoxychlor wird vor allem zur Herstellung von Haushalt- und Veterinärprodukten sowie zur Lösung ganz spezieller Probleme der landwirtschaftlichen Schädlingsbekämpfung verwendet.

Urethane
Das Wirkungsspektrum der DDT-Wirksubstanz weist einige Lücken auf, die es durch Produkte mit spezifischer Wirkung auszufüllen galt. Diese Rolle kommt, was die Blattlausbekämpfung betrifft, den Urethanen (Dimetan, Pyrolan, Isolan) zu, die teils in Kombinationsprodukten, teils als reine spezifische Aphizide im Handel sind.

Diazinon
Diazinon gehört zur Klasse der Thiophosphorsäureester; es ist gekennzeichnet durch hohe insektizide Wirksamkeit bei breitem Wirkungsspektrum, durch eine gewisse Tiefenwirkung und relativ geringe Warmblütertoxizität. Seine wichtigsten Anwendungsgebiete liegen in der Bekämpfung sogenannter resistenter Fliegen, von Haustierektoparasiten und zahlreichen Pflanzenschädlingen, die mit Insektiziden aus der Gruppe der chlorierten Kohlenwasserstoffe nicht oder nur ungenügend bekämpft werden können. Besonders aussichtsreich erscheint Diazinon zur Bekämpfung der Olivenfliege. Als interessant erweisen sich in manchen Fällen Kombinationsprodukte von Diazinon und DDT-Wirksubstanz.

2. Akarizide

Die Bekämpfung von Milben der verschiedensten Arten auf Nutzpflanzen hat in den letzten Jahren immer mehr an Bedeutung gewonnen, so dass es sich als notwendig erwies, gleichzeitig mit den üblichen Spritzbehandlungen gegen schädliche Pilze und Insekten auch diese Parasiten zu bekämpfen.

Chlorbenzilat
Das chemisch der DDT-Wirksubstanz entfernt verwandte Chlorbenzilat weist eine vorzügliche Wirkung gegen alle Entwicklungsstadien der Milben (exklusive Wintereier) auf. Für Warmblüter ist Chlorbenzilat praktisch ungiftig. Chlorbenzilat hat spezifische Anwendungsgebiete im Tee- und Zitrusbau sowie zur Bekämpfung der Bienenmilben gefunden. Seiner breiten Verwendung als Allround-Akarizid steht jedoch seine gelegentliche Phytotoxizität hindernd im Wege.

Phenkapton
Aus diesem Grunde wurde das Phenkapton entwickelt. Dieser Phosphorsäureester besitzt vorzügliche akarizide Eigenschaften (er wirkt auch gegen die Sommereier der Spinnmilben) und erwies sich bis jetzt bei ausgezeichneter Dauerwirkung als ausserordentlich pflanzenverträglich.

XXVII

225

1958 **Max Huber & Giovanni Pintori** Adriano Olivetti et al., *Olivetti 1908–1958*. Ivrea: C. Olivetti & C., 1958. 190 pp. 28.5 cm. German edition. Designer: Max Huber. Cover designer: Giovanni Pintori. Printer: Tiefdruckanstalt Imago, Zurich. Bookbinder: G. Wolfensberger, Zurich.

Italian industry modernized after the Second World War; in design, functionalism reigned. Olivetti and IBM were the international leaders in the field of typewriters and other office equipment. The progressive cultural ideals of Olivetti's management were not just reflected in the architecture of the factories and the workers' housing, but also in product and graphic design. Typewriters such as Marcello Nizzoli's portable Lettera 22 became design icons in the 1950s.

Olivetti had a design department from 1928. Giovanni Pintori (1912–99) had worked there since 1936, and was an art director for many years, designing posters, brochures, and advertisements. The firm also worked with freelancers, such as Imre Reiner and A. M. Cassandre, who designed fonts for typewriters. Max Huber received various typographic commissions from Olivetti, including those for brochures and packaging. In 1958, he designed this anniversary book, which Pintori gave a dust jacket.

Max Huber (1919–92) had been educated at the Arts and Crafts School Zurich. He had worked at the famous Studio Boggeri in Milan, and set up shop as a freelance designer in the forties. Like Max Bill and Richard Paul Lohse, he was a member of the Allianz artists' association, which had a Constructivist orientation. Huber's company photobook *Olivetti 1908–1958* has an asymmetric layout, with a classic serif typeface for the text (normal and bold), and a Clarendon for the headings. The photographs, primarily of interiors and exteriors, vary in size and often bleed off the page. The illustrations are gravure printed, while the text of the various language editions is letterpress printed. ML

Monotype Garamond (1922), despite its name, is not adapted from the types of the sixteenth-century punchcutter Claude Garamont. The attribution to Garamont was a mistake. This 'Garamond' is based on types by Jean Jannon (1580–1658), created between 1615 and 1621.

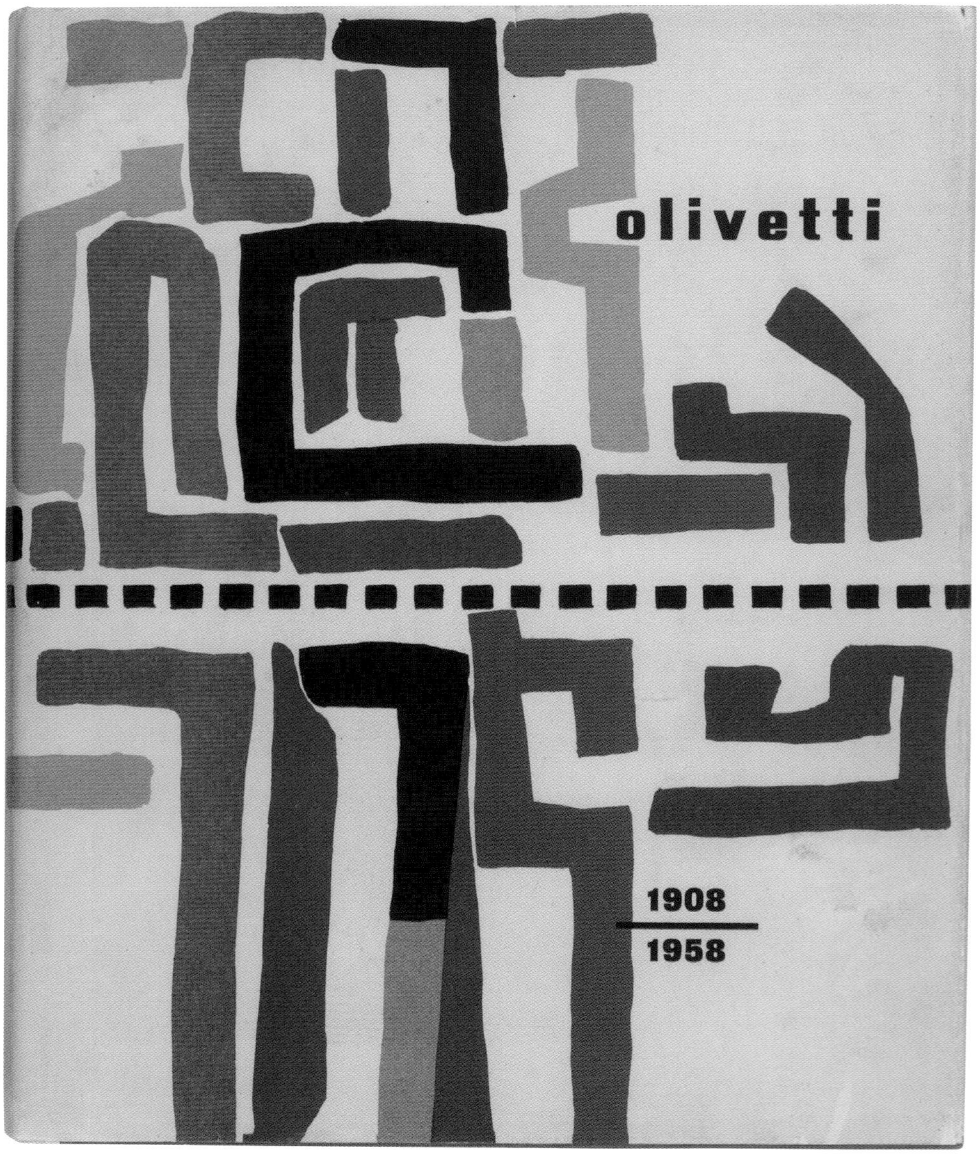

Wenn in den Fachzeitschriften oder in der Umgangssprache vom Olivetti-Stil die Rede ist und damit eine bestimmte Geschmacksrichtung gekennzeichnet wird, so ist dies immer von neuem eine Bestätigung dafür, daß dieser Stil mehr ist als nur Ausdruck einer herrschenden Moderichtung oder einer genialen Improvisation. Dieser Stil ist heute zu einem kulturellen Faktor

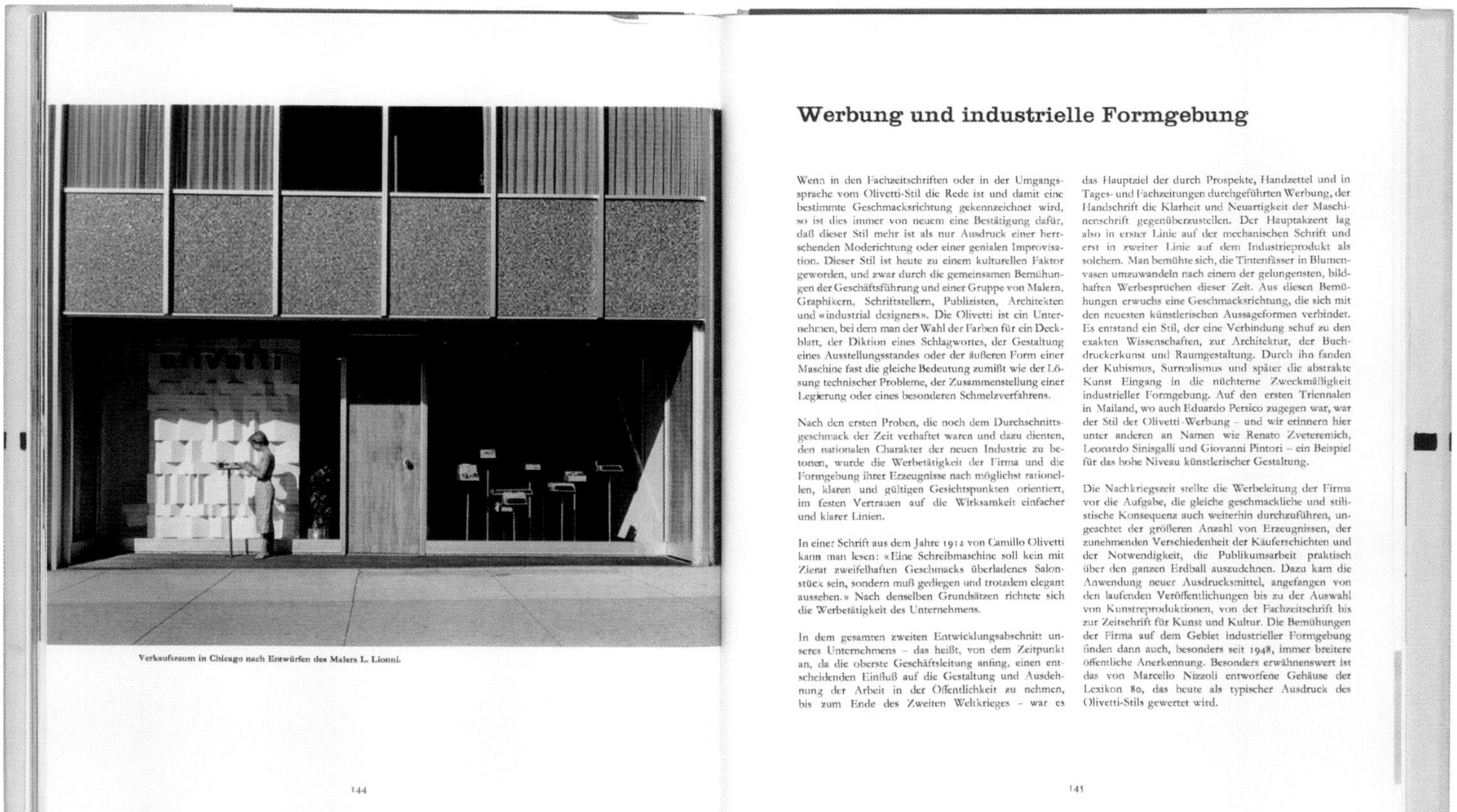

Verkaufsraum in Chicago nach Entwürfen des Malers L. Lionni.

144

Werbung und industrielle Formgebung

Wenn in den Fachzeitschriften oder in der Umgangssprache vom Olivetti-Stil die Rede ist und damit eine bestimmte Geschmacksrichtung gekennzeichnet wird, so ist dies immer von neuem eine Bestätigung dafür, daß dieser Stil mehr ist als nur Ausdruck einer herrschenden Moderichtung oder einer genialen Improvisation. Dieser Stil ist heute zu einem kulturellen Faktor geworden, und zwar durch die gemeinsamen Bemühungen der Geschäftsführung und einer Gruppe von Malern, Graphikern, Schriftstellern, Publizisten, Architekten und «industrial designers». Die Olivetti ist ein Unternehmen, bei dem man der Wahl der Farben für ein Deckblatt, der Diktion eines Schlagwortes, der Gestaltung eines Ausstellungsstandes oder der äußeren Form einer Maschine fast die gleiche Bedeutung zumißt wie der Lösung technischer Probleme, der Zusammenstellung einer Legierung oder eines besonderen Schmelzverfahrens.

Nach den ersten Proben, die noch dem Durchschnittsgeschmack der Zeit verhaftet waren und dazu dienten, den nationalen Charakter der neuen Industrie zu betonen, wurde die Werbetätigkeit der Firma und die Formgebung ihrer Erzeugnisse nach möglichst rationellen, klaren und gültigen Gesichtspunkten orientiert, im festen Vertrauen auf die Wirksamkeit einfacher und klarer Linien.

In einer Schrift aus dem Jahre 1912 von Camillo Olivetti kann man lesen: «Eine Schreibmaschine soll kein mit Zierat zweifelhaften Geschmacks überladenes Salonstück sein, sondern muß gediegen und trotzdem elegant aussehen.» Nach denselben Grundsätzen richtete sich die Werbetätigkeit des Unternehmens.

In dem gesamten zweiten Entwicklungsabschnitt unseres Unternehmens – das heißt, von dem Zeitpunkt an, da die oberste Geschäftsleitung anfing, einen entscheidenden Einfluß auf die Gestaltung und Ausdehnung der Arbeit in der Öffentlichkeit zu nehmen, bis zum Ende des Zweiten Weltkrieges – war es das Hauptziel der durch Prospekte, Handzettel und in Tages- und Fachzeitungen durchgeführten Werbung, der Handschrift die Klarheit und Neuartigkeit der Maschinenschrift gegenüberzustellen. Der Hauptakzent lag also in erster Linie auf der mechanischen Schrift und erst in zweiter Linie auf dem Industrieprodukt als solchem. Man bemühte sich, die Tintenfässer in Blumenvasen umzuwandeln nach einem der gelungensten, bildhaften Werbesprüchen dieser Zeit. Aus diesen Bemühungen erwuchs eine Geschmacksrichtung, die sich mit den neuesten künstlerischen Aussageformen verbindet. Es entstand ein Stil, der eine Verbindung schuf zu den exakten Wissenschaften, zur Architektur, der Buchdruckerkunst und Raumgestaltung. Durch ihn fanden der Kubismus, Surrealismus und später die abstrakte Kunst Eingang in die nüchterne Zweckmäßigkeit industrieller Formgebung. Auf den ersten Triennalen in Mailand, wo auch Eduardo Persico zugegen war, war der Stil der Olivetti-Werbung – und wir erinnern hier unter anderen an Namen wie Renato Zveteremich, Leonardo Sinisgalli und Giovanni Pintori – ein Beispiel für das hohe Niveau künstlerischer Gestaltung.

Die Nachkriegszeit stellte die Werbeleitung der Firma vor die Aufgabe, die gleiche geschmackliche und stilistische Konsequenz auch weiterhin durchzuführen, ungeachtet der größeren Anzahl von Erzeugnissen, der zunehmenden Verschiedenheit der Käuferschichten und der Notwendigkeit, die Publikumsarbeit praktisch über den ganzen Erdball auszudehnen. Dazu kam die Anwendung neuer Ausdrucksmittel, angefangen von den laufenden Veröffentlichungen bis zu der Auswahl von Kunstreproduktionen, von der Fachzeitschrift bis zur Zeitschrift für Kunst und Kultur. Die Bemühungen der Firma auf dem Gebiet industrieller Formgebung finden dann auch, besonders seit 1948, immer breitere öffentliche Anerkennung. Besonders erwähnenswert ist das von Marcello Nizzoli entworfene Gehäuse der Lexikon 80, das heute als typischer Ausdruck des Olivetti-Stils gewertet wird.

145

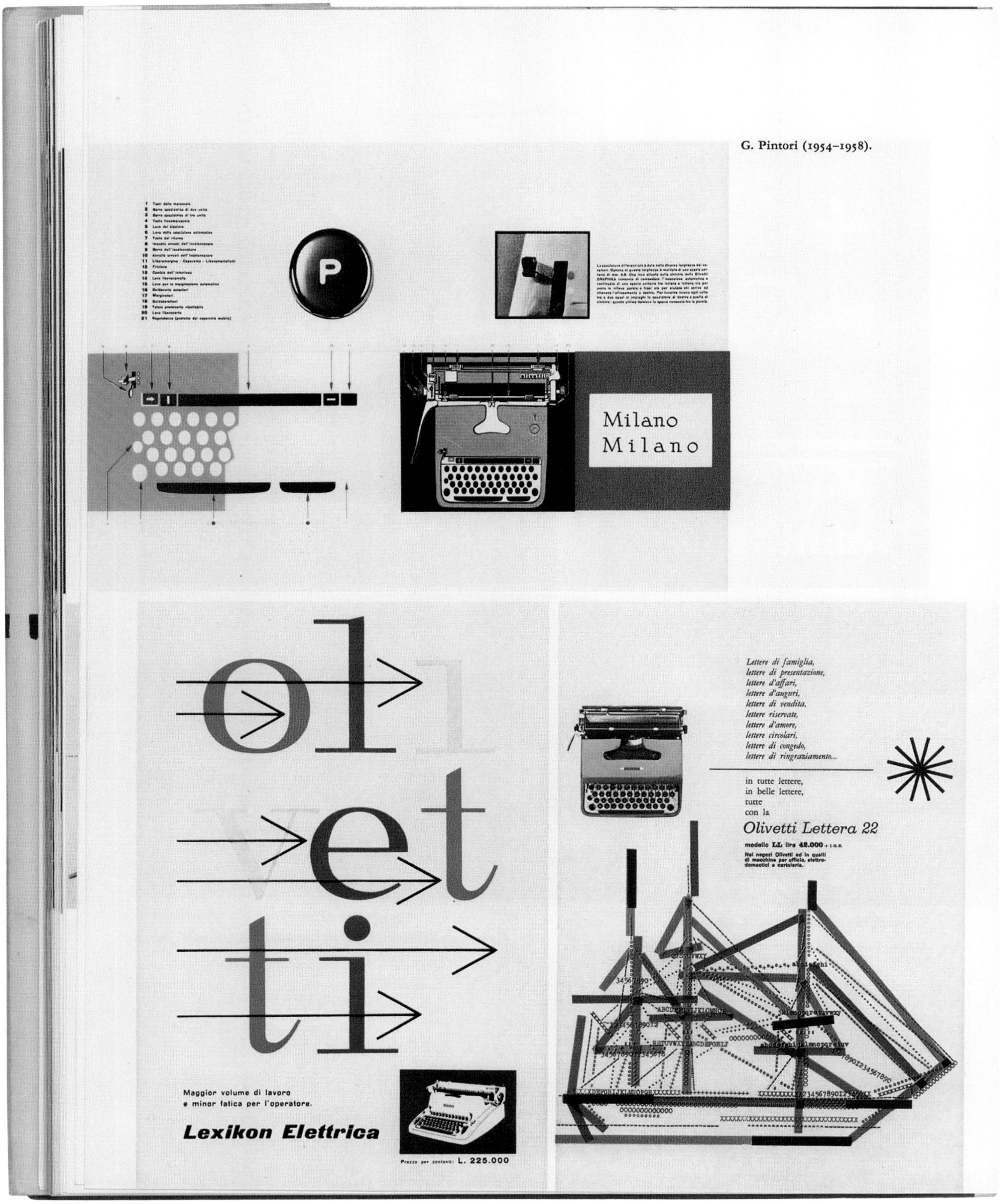
G. Pintori (1954–1958).
Milano
Milano
olivetti
Maggior volume di lavoro
e minor fatica per l'operatore.
Lexikon Elettrica
Prezzo per contanti: L. 225.000
Lettere di famiglia,
lettere di presentazione,
lettere d'affari,
lettere d'auguri,
lettere di vendita,
lettere riservate,
lettere d'amore,
lettere circolari,
lettere di congedo,
lettere di ringraziamento...
in tutte lettere,
in belle lettere,
tutte
con la
Olivetti Lettera 22
modello LL lire 42.000 + I.G.E.
Nei negozi Olivetti ed in quelli
di macchine per ufficio, elettro-
domestici e cartolerie.

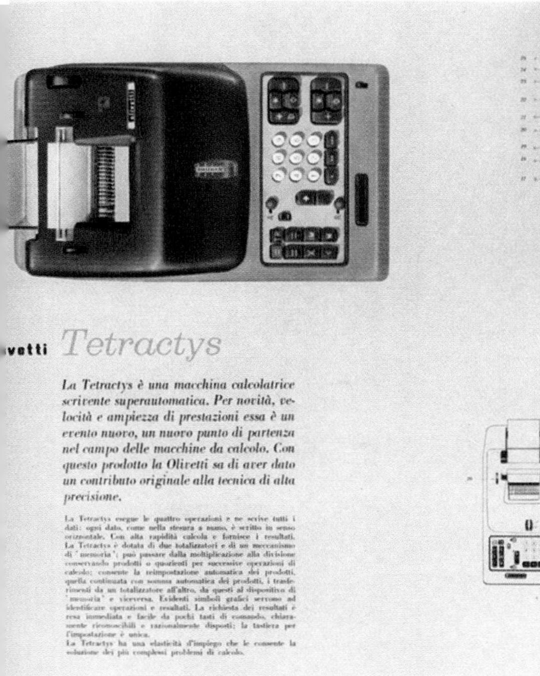

vetti
Tetractys
La Tetractys è una macchina calcolatrice scrivente superautomatica. Per novità, velocità e ampiezza di prestazioni essa è un evento nuovo, un nuovo punto di partenza nel campo delle macchine da calcolo. Con questo prodotto la Olivetti sa di aver dato un contributo originale alla tecnica di alta precisione.

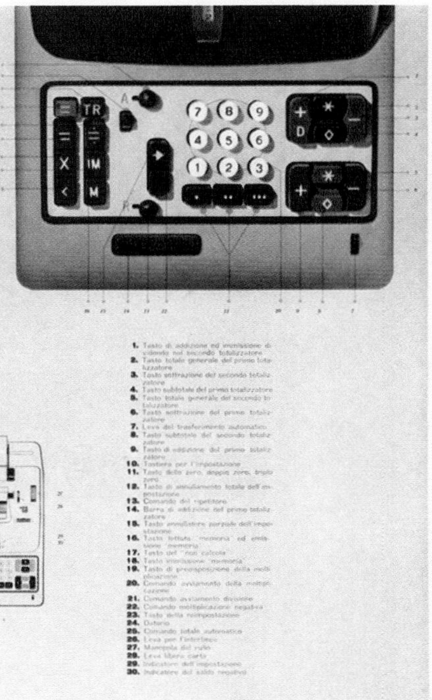

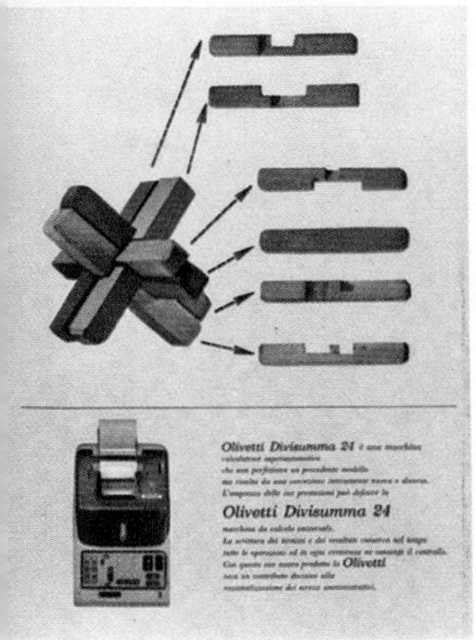

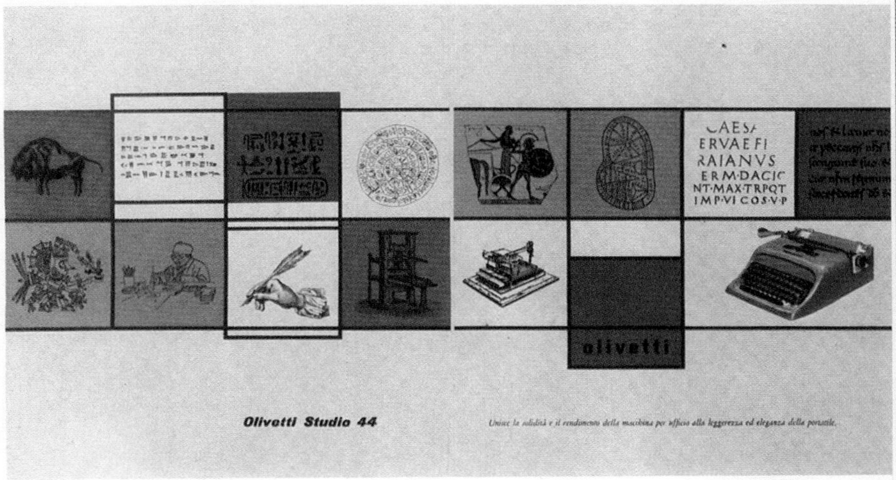

G. Pintori, 1954–1956.

Oben rechts: F. Bassi, 1955.

1963 **Willy Fleckhaus** *edition suhrkamp*. Frankfurt am Main: Suhrkamp Verlag, 1963 on. 18 cm. Designer: Willy Fleckhaus.

edition suhrkamp – always written in lower case – is the best-known book series in postwar Germany. Launched in 1963, and featuring both literary and theoretical texts, it is nicknamed the 'Rainbow series'. The 48 volumes published in one year form a rainbow when they are put in order in a bookcase: from violet, red, orange, yellow, green, and blue to indigo. The standard cover design of the series – exclusively typographic, restricted to one type size and left-aligned – also attracted attention, since most pocket books in the sixties featured a photograph or a drawing on the front. This daringly minimalist concept was created by the self-taught Willy Fleckhaus (1925–83), an admirer of Max Bill. After 1959, he maintained increasing control over the graphic identity of the literary publisher Suhrkamp.

Suhrkamp still publishes the Rainbow series, although with modified typography. The first modification was made in 1980 by Fleckhaus: the cover typography became symmetrical. Fleckhaus's shining, laminated, white dust jacket with colour band for the series *Bibliothek Suhrkamp* pre-dates the *edition suhrkamp* by a few years; the *Bibliothek* series was launched in 1959, and its dust jacket design has not changed since.

Still, it was not his book designs that won Fleckhaus his place in the history of graphic design: he owes his international fame to the cult magazine *Twen* (1959–71). Both the content and look of this lifestyle magazine for young people over twenty – covering subjects such as relationships, fashion, and culture – were revolutionary in the narrow-minded 1960s. The photography, which often had a white or black background, dominated the magazine; the framing was exciting and the sequence of spreads evocative. Because of *Twen*, Willy Fleckhaus became known as Germany's first art director. ML

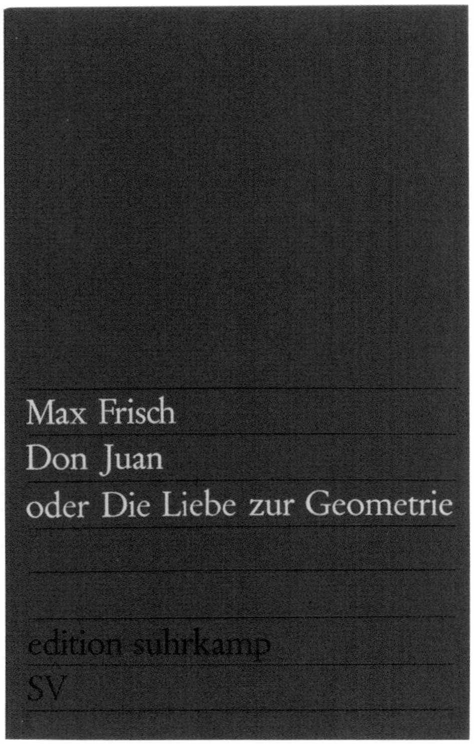

This Garamond is an adaptation of the type cut by the sixteenth-century French punchcutter Claude Garamont. Produced by the German typefoundry D. Stempel in 1924, under supervision of Rudolf Wolf (1895–1942). Subsequently, in 1926, Stempel Garamond was made available for the Linotype composing machine. The italic and the semibold were issued between 1926 and 1933.

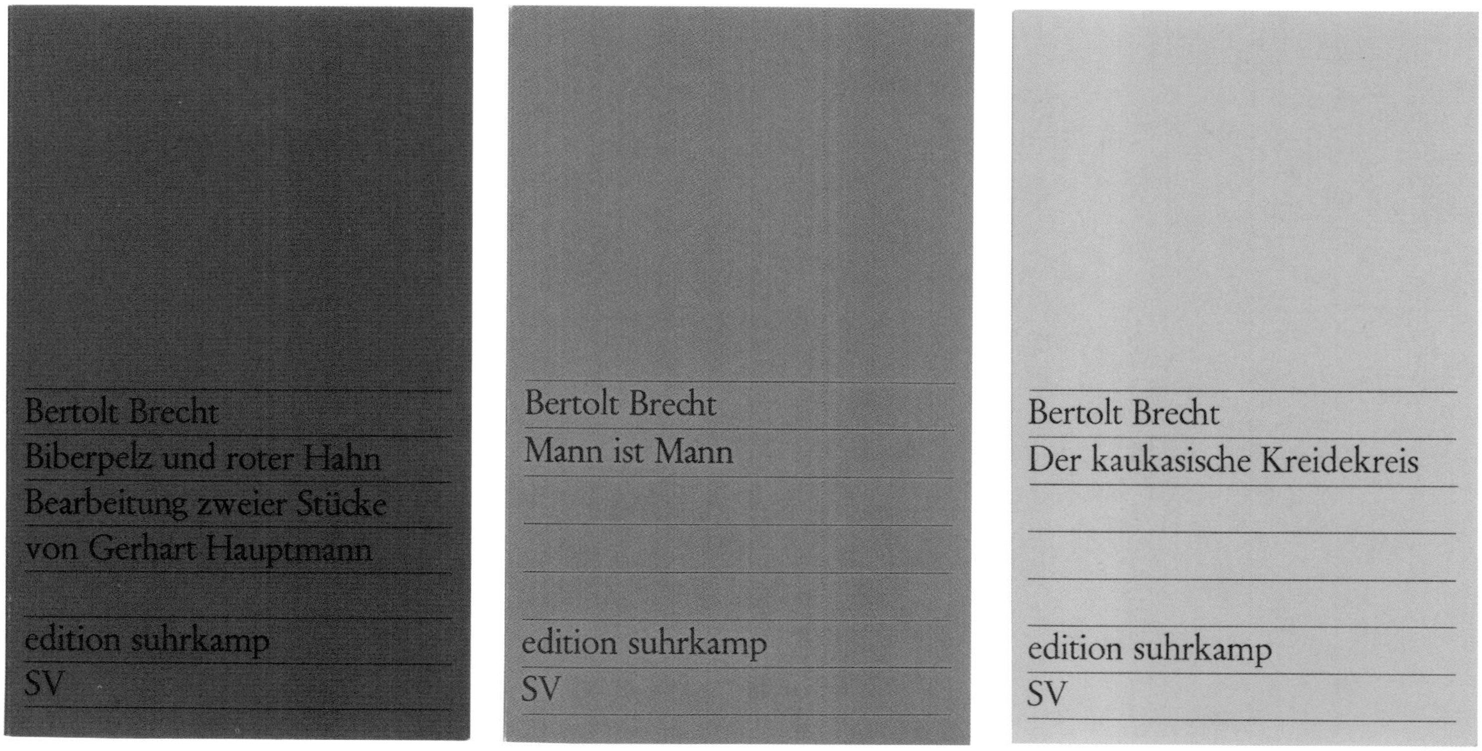
Bertolt Brecht
Biberpelz und roter Hahn
Bearbeitung zweier Stücke
von Gerhart Hauptmann
edition suhrkamp
SV
Bertolt Brecht
Mann ist Mann
edition suhrkamp
SV
Bertolt Brecht
Der kaukasische Kreidekreis
edition suhrkamp
SV

Kevin Vennemann Nahe Jedenew 2450
Bänziger/Duttweiler/Sarasin/Wellmann (Hg.) Fragen Sie Dr. Sex! 2595
Peter Rudolf Das »neue« Amerika 2596
Thomas Kapielski Mischwald 2597
Slavoj Žižek Auf verlorenem Posten 2562
Barbara Nolte/Jan Heidtmann Die da oben 2599
Franco Moretti Kurven, Karten, Stammbäume 2564
Boris Buden Zone des Übergangs 2601
Serhij Zhadan Depeche Mode 2494
Frank Schirrmacher/Thomas Strobl (Hg.) Die Zukunft des Kapitalismus 2603
Hans Magnus Enzensberger Im Irrgarten der Intelligenz 2532
Ann Cotten Fremdwörterbuchsonette 2497
Werner Schiffauer Nach dem Islamismus 2570
Honegger/Neckel/Magnin Strukturierte Verantwortungslosigkeit 2607
Pablo Alabarces Für Messi sterben? 2608
Dietmar Dath Heute keine Konferenz 2501
Peter Sloterdijk Derrida ein Ägypter 2502
n+1-Research (Hg.) Ein Schritt weiter 2539
Colin Crouch Postdemokratie 2540

1964 **Rémy Peignot & Adrian Frutiger** *Univers: 21 variations sur un thème unique*. Paris: Deberny & Peignot, 1964.

21 leaves. 29 cm. Designer: Rémy Peignot.

This type specimen was published by Deberny & Peignot, a typefoundry dating back to the eighteenth century. This Paris firm, directed by Charles Peignot, steered an artistic and progressive course, producing, for example, the typefaces of poster designer A. M. Cassandre. After the Second World War, letterpress (relief printing) started to lose ground to offset lithography (planography). It was in this environment that Peignot embarked on phototypesetting (Lumitype), which served the offset litho market, and he hired Adrian Frutiger for font production in 1952.

The Swiss Frutiger (b. 1928) had to adapt popular metal typefaces such as Garamont, Baskerville and Bodoni, for use in photocomposition. However, Frutiger managed to convince his boss not to use the bestselling Futura as the sans serif type for the program, but instead a new design from his own hand. This type would become Univers (1957). The concept for this type family included 21 numbered variations of width and weight. This competitor of Akzidenz-Grotesk and Helvetica was also made available for use on the Monotype machine in the early sixties.

The Univers specimen was designed by Charles's son Rémy Peignot (1924–86). In 1946, after an internship and attending classes at the Arts and Crafts School in St Gallen, he began working for his father's company as a designer. The specimen promotes the metal Univers for hand setting and consists of loose, letterpress-printed sheets with several variations. The trifold wrapper is eye-catching. The Univers diagram with its blocks of colour was probably also designed by Rémy Peignot. In 1968, several years before Deberny & Peignot closed, he opened his own design agency. ML

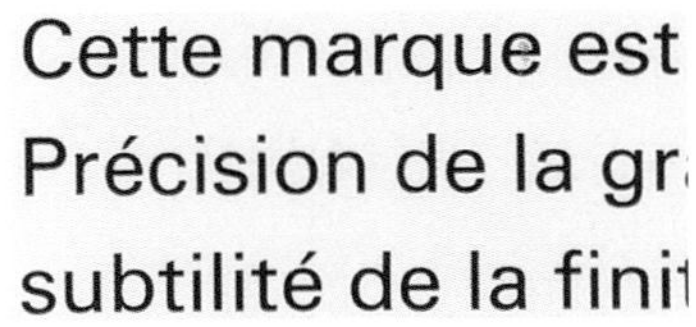
Cette marque est
Précision de la gr
subtilité de la finit

This is the metal Univers for hand setting (foundry type). This highly popular sans serif family designed by Adrian Frutiger has, of course, been expanded and modified over the years; since the 1980s, developments in digital typography have naturally been taken into account.

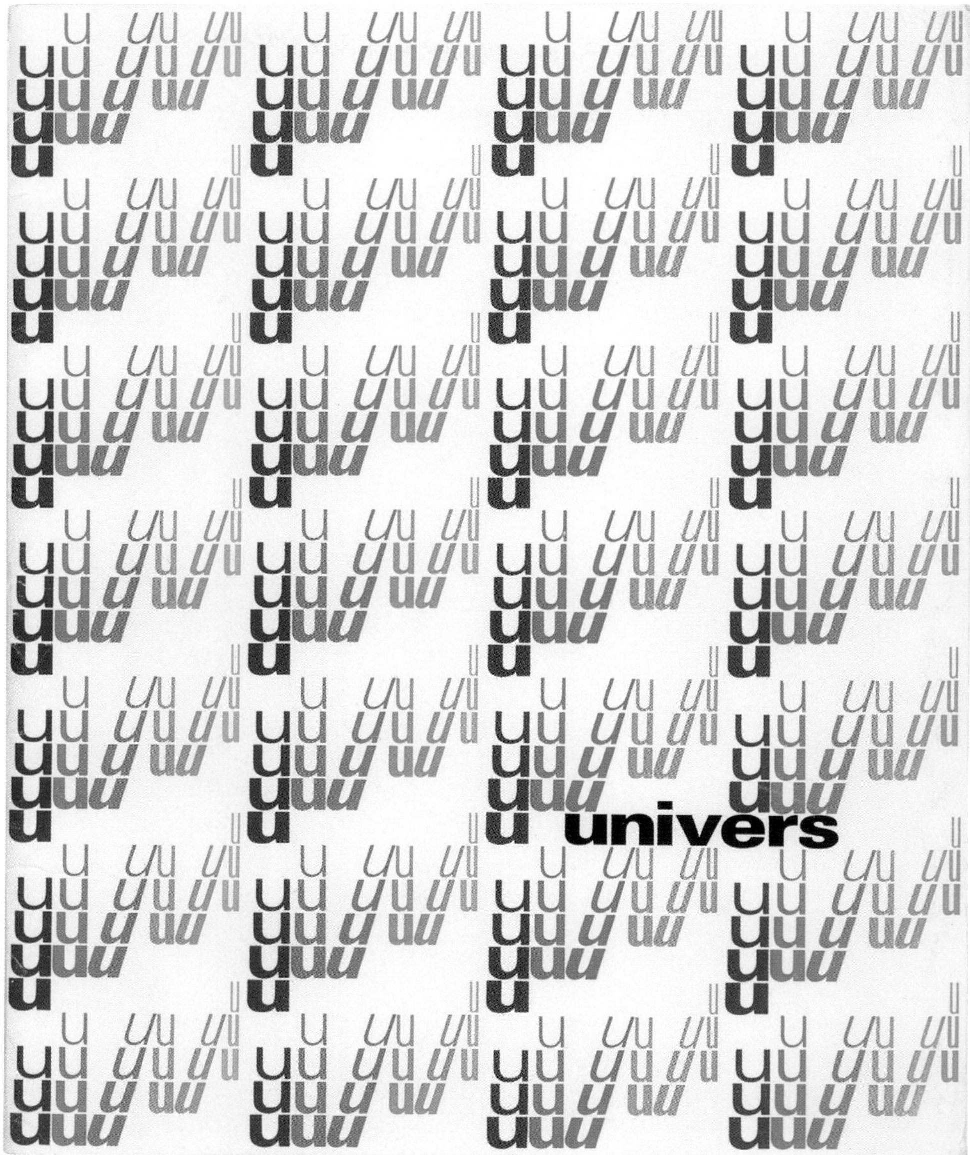
univers

DP

Marque déposée

Cette marque est notre symbole de qualité.
Précision de la gravure mécanique,
subtilité de la finition manuelle,
étroites limites des tolérances, un nouvel alliage
et un parc de machines modernisées
sont les garants de la qualité de nos fontes.

Univers 49
LA TYPOGRAPHIE EST UN ART APPLIQUÉ QUI RÉPOND A DES BESOINS UTILITAIRES ET CHERCHE A TOUCHER PAR LA BEAUTÉ
VOICI EN UN RYTHME CONTINU LE PANORAMA FOISONNANT DES EXPOSITIONS DE LA SAISON PARISIENNE
UNE FORMATION SUCCESSIVE DU PEUPLE DE CE LIEU A FAIT LA COMPOSITION REMARQUABLE
CERTAINE RELATION IMMÉDIATE ENTRE LA MAIN DE L'HOMME ET SON CERVEAU
Nos constructeurs des grandes époques ont conçu les édifices d'un seul jet et non en deux mouvements de l'esprit et en deux séries d'opérations, les unes relatives à la forme et les autres à la matière. La belle qualité de la pierre et l'intelligence de l'architecte
MAGNIFIQUE OUVRAGE POUR LA VULGARISATION ARTISTIQUE
Le bureau d'administration de la société et les membres participants vous prient d'honorer de votre présence la grande matinée artistique à l'occasion de laquelle une exposition de gravures sera organisée
POUR DES EXCURSIONS AVEC ITINÉRAIRES FIXES
chaque membre de notre société a le droit de modifier le parcours à sa convenance sous certaines conditions
EXPOSITION UNIVERSELLE DE LONDRES
la résistance de divers matériaux en aviation démonstration au stand de la fleur artificielle
UNE CONFORTABLE AUTOMOBILE
nous emportera rapidement en toute sécurité vers le gai soleil provençal
GRANDE CONSTRUCTION
modernisation des habitats

Univers 83
LE DÉCOR INTÉRIEUR
Bien que par son style et sa structure ce petit ensemble, qu'il ne faut
DANS LE DERNIER BOURG
Bien que par son style et sa structure ce petit ensemble qu'il ne faut pas surestimer s'apparente à la gravure de
UNE NEIGE MAGNIFIQUE DE BLANCHEUR
Bien que par son style et sa structure ce petit ensemble qu'il ne faut pas surestimer s'apparente aux gravures de la première
DERNIÈRES LIMITES DE L'HORIZON
Bien que par son style et sa structure ce petit ensemble, qu'il ne faut pas surestimer, s'apparente à la gravure
NOTRE ROLE EST D'INFORMER
Bien que par son style et sa structure cet ensemble, qu'il ne faut pas surestimer s'apparente
DANS UN DERNIER ADIEU
Bien que par son style et sa structure cet ensemble qu'il ne faut pas surestimer
UN TEMPS SI LONG
pour construire un tel monument qu'il fallu
POUR ADMIRER
la promenade qui me conduit à son
DIMINUTION
le soleil perd un peu de son
MENUISER
un si grand projet sera
FOURMI
invasion
DEBERNY ET PEIGNOT PARIS

6-4-67
Deberny & Peignot, 18 rue Ferrus, Paris 14

Univers 63
POUR UNE EXÉCUTION
La neige fraîche tranchée par nos pieds, se détacha tout à coup et glissa sur
REFLET BLEUTÉ DU SAPHIR
La neige fraîche, tranchée par nos pieds, se détacha tout à coup et glissa sur l'ancienne neige avec une violence et un
NOUS CONTINUONS CET ÉTRANGE CHEMIN
La neige fraîche, tranchée par nos pieds, se détacha tout à coup et glissa sur l'ancienne neige avec une violence et un bruit d'avalanche
UNE FOULE NOMBREUSE SUR LE QUAI
La neige fraîche, tranchée par nos pieds se détacha tout à coup et glissa sur la neige ancienne avec une violence et un
LEUR DANGEREUSE EXCURSION
La neige fraîche, tranchée par nos pieds, se détacha tout à coup et glissa sur la neige ancienne avec
POUR SON DERNIER ADIEU
La neige fraîche, tranchée par nos pieds se détacha d'un seul coup et glissa sur l'ancienne
MALGRÉ UNE RAISON
incontestable qui sera pour notre corporation
DANS LE JARDIN
près de la maison règne de nouveau
IMPRÉCISION
pour réaliser la marche de son
BRICOLEUR
pour faire la restauration
LISERON
nestorien
DEBERNY ET PEIGNOT PARIS

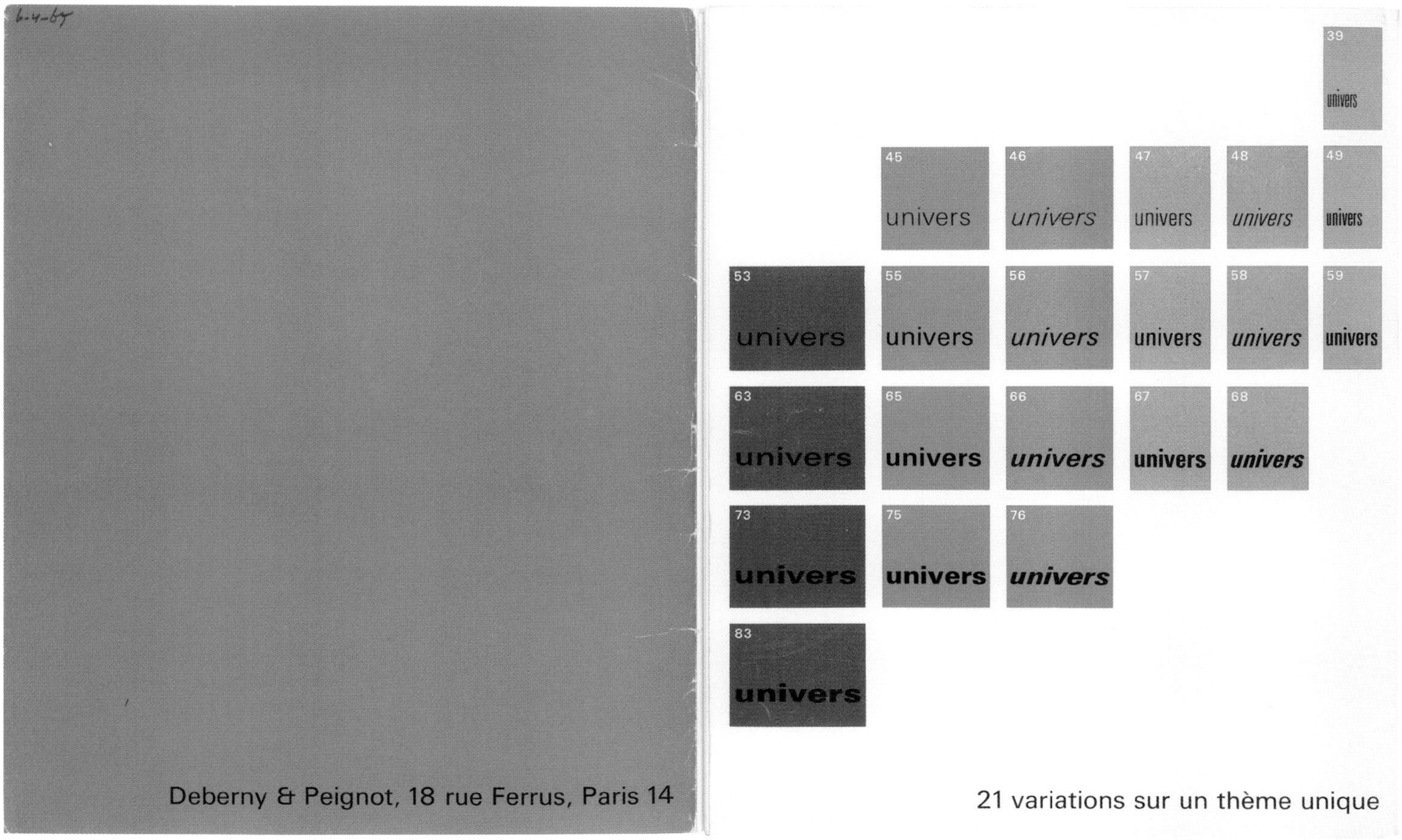

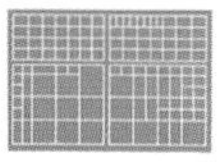
Casse

Univers servira à la composition à la main, à la composition mécanique et à la photocomposition.
Cette nouvelle sera saluée avec joie par les Imprimeurs, les Editeurs et les Artistes.
Cette généreuse et lucide coopération ouvre de nouveau, à l'Art Typographique, les voies de l'avenir.

Maximilien Vox

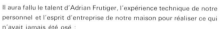

Il aura fallu le talent d'Adrian Frutiger, l'expérience technique de notre personnel et l'esprit d'entreprise de notre maison pour réaliser ce qui n'avait jamais été osé :
3 ans d'études et de recherches, 4 000 dessins, 150 000 heures de gravure à la machine, 50 000 heures de retouches et de finition de poinçons à la main, 35 000 matrices et plus de 150 tonnes de caractères à fondre pour constituer le stock de départ, voilà ce que représente l'Univers. 21 séries, romains et italiques en 4 graisses et 4 chasses différentes. C'est la plus extraordinaire «palette typographique» qui ait jamais été mise à la disposition de l'imprimerie.
L'Univers n'est pas un regroupement d'antiques existantes plus ou moins «rafistolées». Il résulte d'une conception d'ensemble et d'études approfondies des détails. Chacune de ses 21 séries tient sa place dans un ensemble typographique cohérent et harmonieux dont l'origine est l'alphabet romain normal (série 55).
Chaque lettre a été construite pour assurer la lisibilité la plus parfaite aussi bien dans le double gras large série 83 que dans le fin serré série 39. Les blancs intérieurs de chaque lettre (les contrepoinçons) ont été méticuleusement étudiés de façon à réduire, sinon supprimer, au strict minimum les différences de chasse du maigre au gras. Cette répartition rigoureuse des blancs a permis d'ouvrir l'œil des lettres et assure à la ligne une respiration régulière et rythmée. Ainsi la chasse très réduite dans toutes les séries et tous les corps assure à l'Univers une permanence dans la densité des valeurs. La gravure à talus très vertical qui constitue une nouveauté technique fait de l'Univers un caractère qui peut s'user régulièrement sans qu'un engraissement vienne modifier son aspect. L'œil très ouvert ne se bouche pas.
Tous les problèmes de composition peuvent être résolus avec l'Univers : quel que soit le nombre de lettres ou la justification de la ligne il y aura toujours une variante de la famille Univers qui permettra de «tenir dans la justification».
L'Univers est réellement nouveau, c'est une typographie de base, d'un usage universel pour le présent et pour l'avenir.
Nous pensons sincèrement avoir fait œuvre utile en offrant aux Imprimeurs un tel outil et ne pas avoir failli à la mission que nous nous sommes donnée : être au service de la Typographie.

Mono

Film

Les dessins et modèle de ce caractère ont fait l'objet des dépôts internationaux le protégeant des contrefacteurs.
La Lumitype-Photon pour la photocomposition et la Monotype pour la composition mécanique et photographique ont acquis les droits de reproduction de l'Univers.

1966 **Wim Crouwel** Remco Campert, *De letter... n*. Amsterdam: Den Ouden, 1966. 26 pp. 15 x 21 cm. Designer: Wim Crouwel (Total Design). Printer: Den Ouden, Amsterdam. With the folds at the fore-edge.

This publication is a linguistic and graphic game with the letter n. The designer Wim Crouwel (b. 1928) illustrates a short text by the Dutch poet and author Remco Campert. The booklet, printed in letterpress, was a New Year's publication by an Amsterdam printing office. A few years before it appeared, Crouwel and others had founded Total Design (TD), a multidisciplinary bureau. Influenced by the Swiss style of typography, TD worked according to a rational design method. Based in Amsterdam, the bureau received large and complicated commissions, including house styles for governments, businesses and museums. TD became so influential in the Netherlands that the 1970s saw a backlash against its dominant 'functional' style. The criticism, from both the design world and the media, was directed primarily against Crouwel, who was the public face of the bureau.

Even though many regarded his work as rational at the time, Crouwel still found opportunities to experiment, especially in a publication like this, printed in a small edition. In these years Crouwel was also working on a typeface for the new cathode ray tube (CRT) typesetters. This research resulted in his New Alphabet (1967), which broke with all conventions of legibility. Hardly used – technical advances quickly overtook the concept – the alphabet and its printed specimen have since attained a cult status.

De letter... n is partly set in the sans serif Helvetica, sometimes called 'the faceless typeface'. TD preferred to work with sans serif type. Helvetica is based on typefaces from around 1900, but gives a more mechanical, neutral impression. In his preference for 'neutral' design and machine aesthetic, Crouwel shows himself to be a true modernist. ML

raket

Helvetica (1957) was developed by Eduard Hoffmann (1892–1980), director of Haas'sche Schriftgiesserei near Basel, in collaboration with the designer Max Miedinger (1910–80). In fact, it is a completely redrawn version of Akzidenz-Grotesk. From 1961 it was also available from Stempel and Linotype, and was expanded into a family with many variations in weight and width.

n
de letter . . .
geschreven door remco campert
verbeeld door wim crouwel (total design)
gedrukt door drukkerij den ouden

alleen is maar alleen
hoewel je ook met andere letters
samen niets kunt zijn
raket
natuurlijk zijn er woorden die ik niet lust
BOM
als mensen iets te zeggen hebben
ben ik van de partij
zonder pochen
ik sta mijn mannetje
mes
als E voor mij gaat staan
plak ik zin en onzin aan elkaar
OORLOG
e n

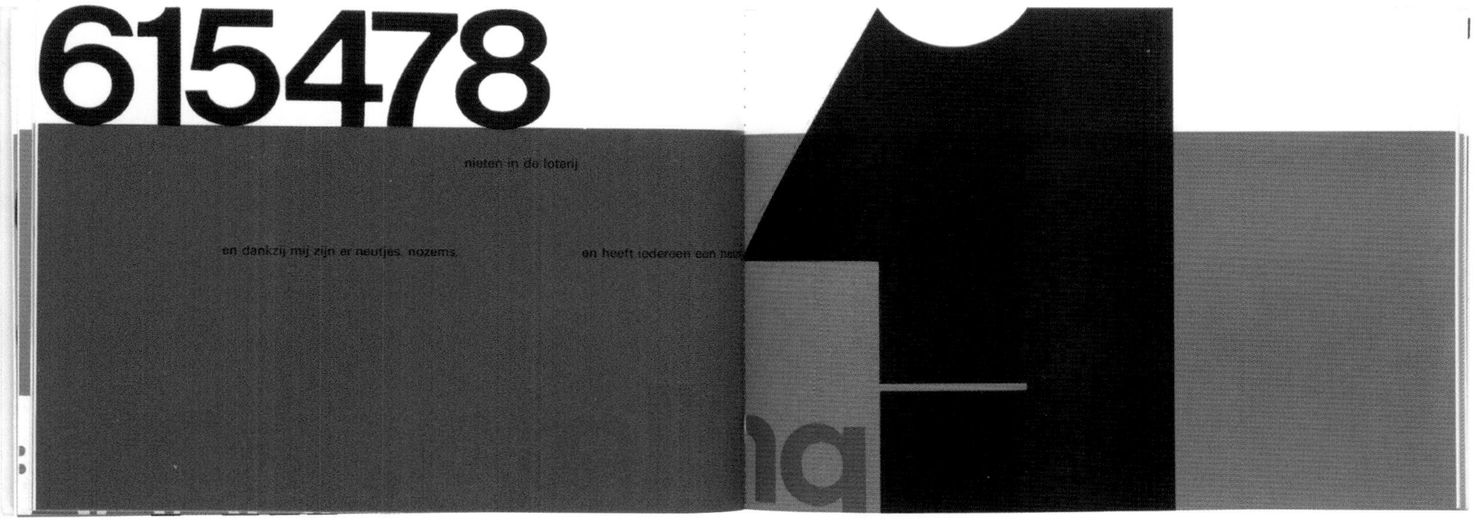
615478
nieten in de loterij
en dankzij mij zijn er neutjes, nozems,

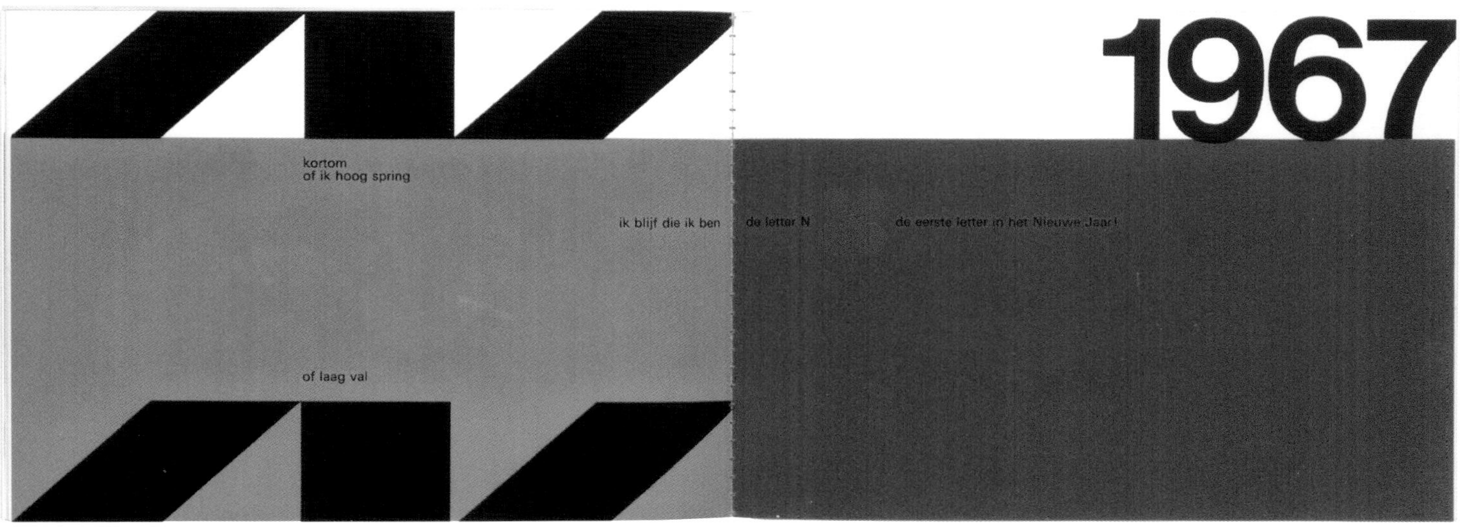
1967
kortom
of ik hoog spring
ik blijf die ik ben
de letter N
de eerste letter in het Nieuwe Jaar!
of laag val

1967 **Quentin Fiore** Marshall McLuhan & Quentin Fiore, *The Medium is the Massage: An Inventory of Effects*; coordinated by Jerome Agel. New York: Bantam Books, 1967. 159 pp. 18 cm. Large hardcover edition later published by Random House. Designer: Quentin Fiore. Printed in the United States.

In Woody Allen's movie *Annie Hall* (1977), the protagonist Alvy Singer gets irritated by a loud conversation while waiting in line for movie tickets. When the man starts to spout nonsense about Marshall McLuhan's theory of the mass media, he's had enough. Alvy pulls the real McLuhan from behind a billboard so McLuhan himself can put the man in his place.

The Canadian professor, McLuhan, who always wanted to reach a wide audience, must have enjoyed doing this cameo. In the sixties he coined the term 'global village' and foresaw that the electronic media would dominate our lives. He stressed the importance of understanding the new media and stated that the influence the medium exerts is in the medium itself rather than in its content or message. His exaggeration 'the medium is the message' became a famous slogan.

The Medium is the Massage was an initiative of the American designer Quentin Fiore (b. 1920). The variation in the title was initially a printer's error on the cover that McLuhan thought felicitous and therefore didn't correct. Fiore was not just the designer but also the editor of the book, which was unusual at the time. He gave the text fragments visual impact with expressive typography and many full-bleed photographic images. A number of short statements, set in a large size, continue over several spreads. Of course, this rather magazine-like book was criticized by traditionalists: it was seen as anti-intellectual and at risk of encouraging illiteracy and even drug abuse. Although McLuhan liked to popularize his message, he was chagrined that *The Medium is the Massage* was his bestselling title. ML

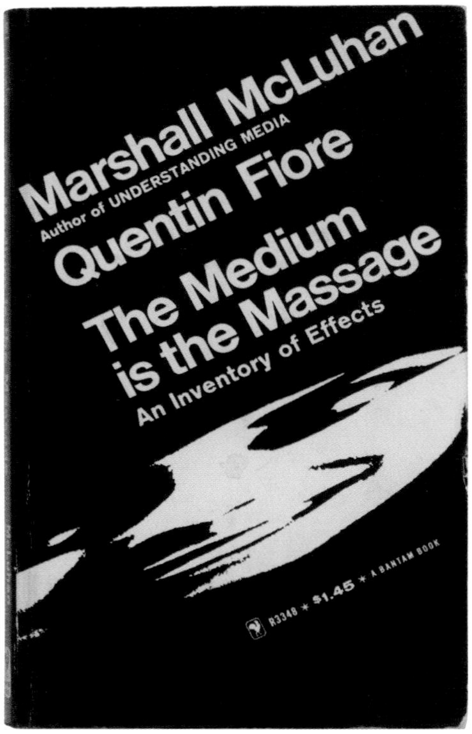

Akzidenz-Grotesk (the large sans serif in the interior) is based on late nineteenth-century types that were all issued under one name by the Berlin foundry Berthold since 1898. Over time, the design of this type family was increasingly unified. It was available in the English-speaking world under the telling name Standard.

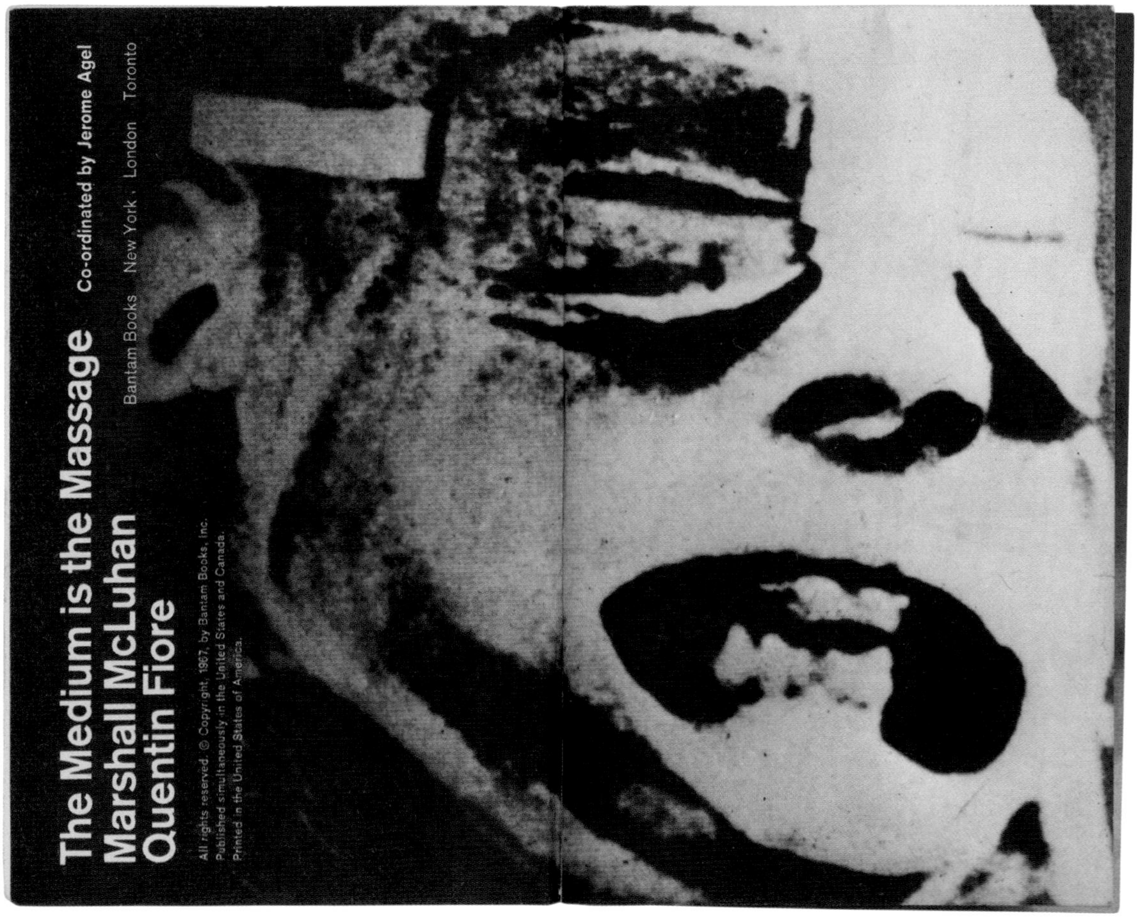

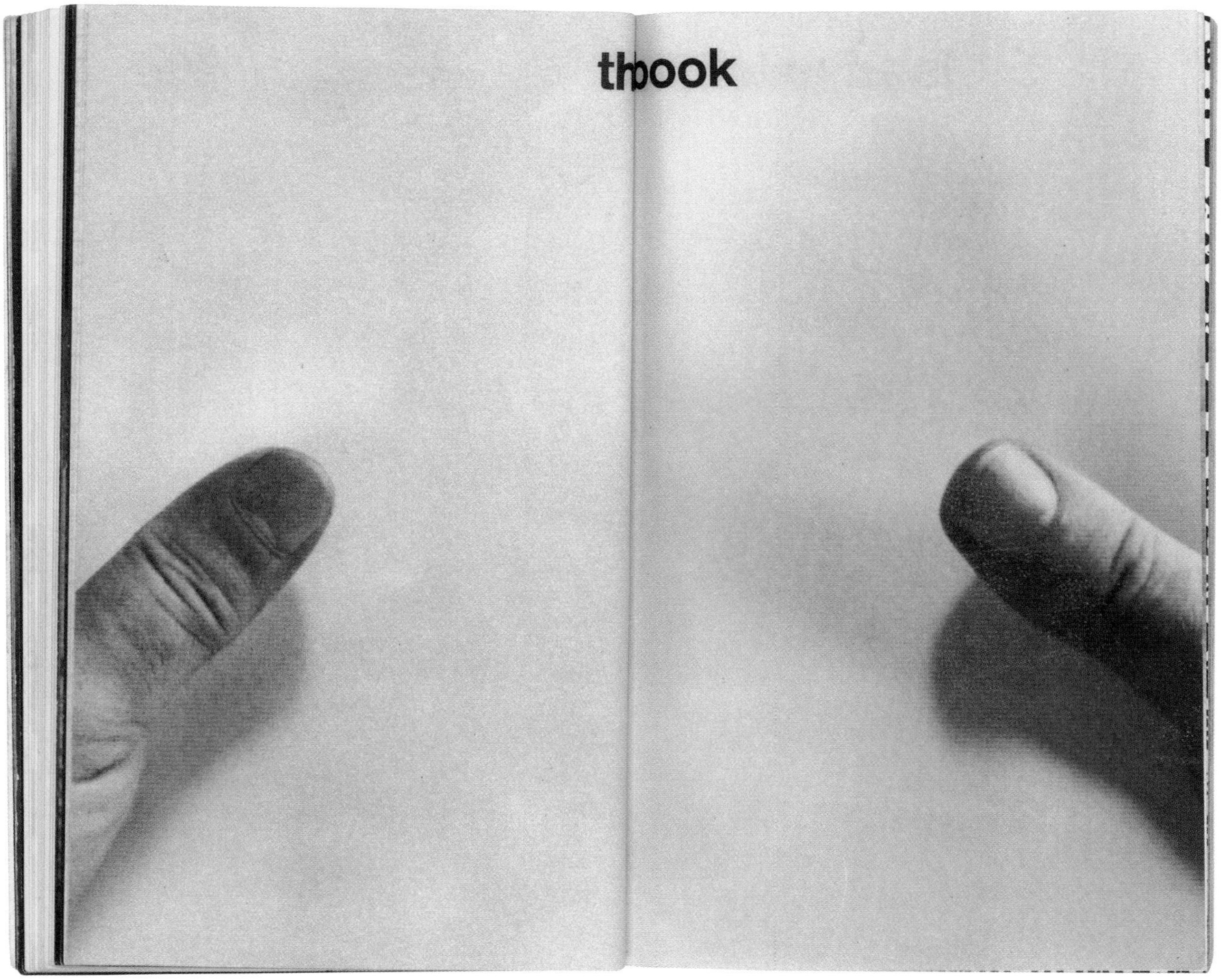
thbook

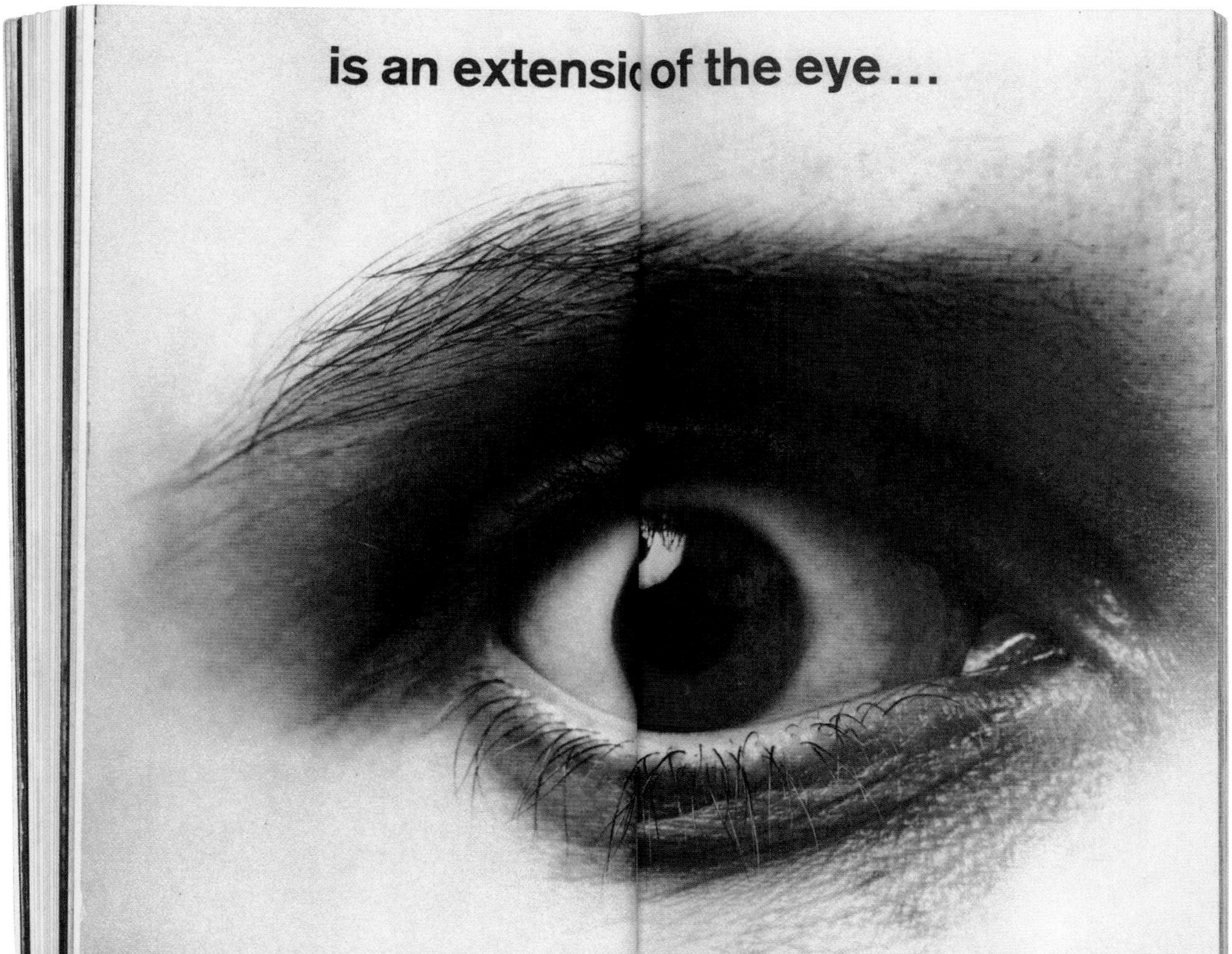
is an extensi of the eye...

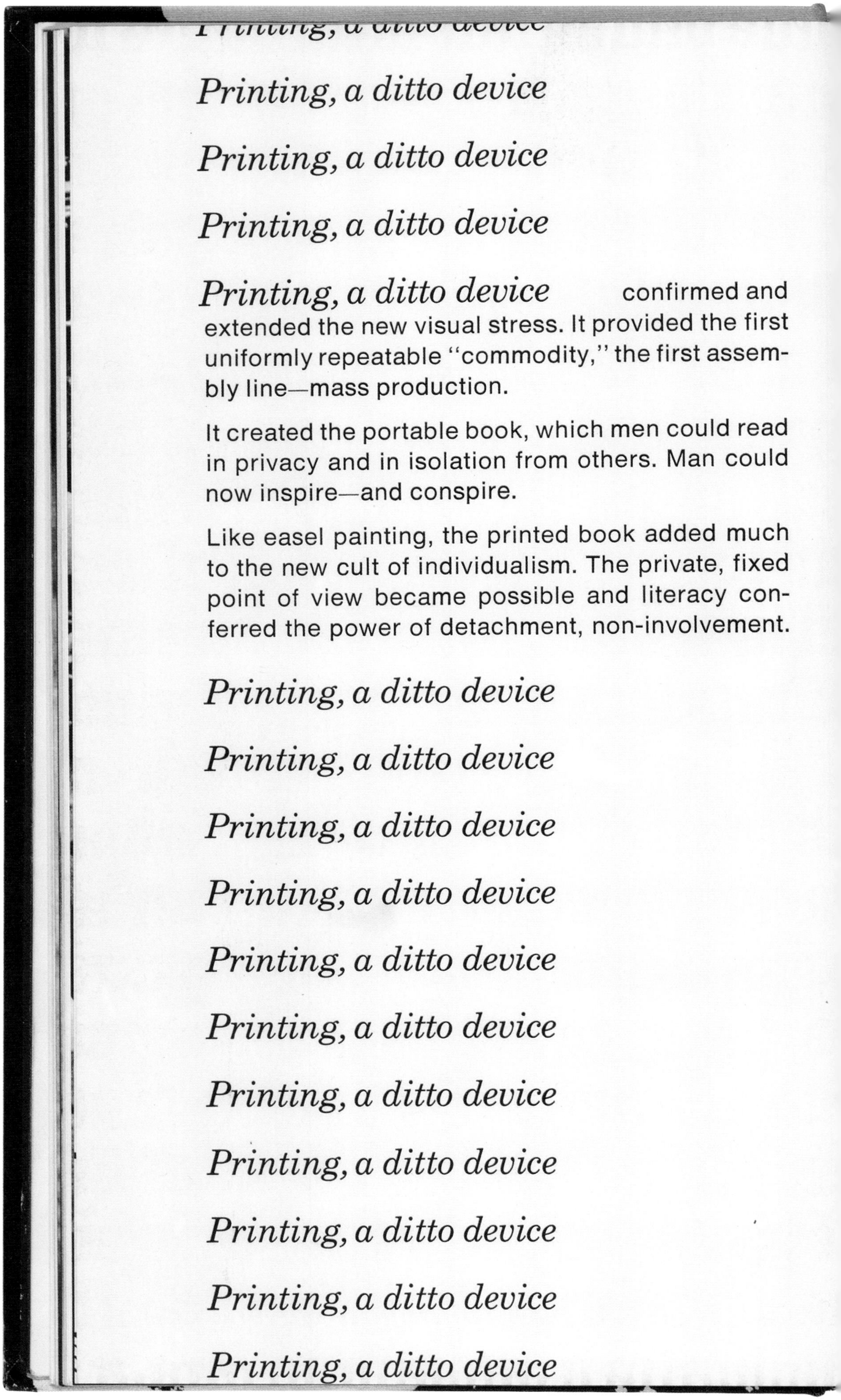

Printing, a ditto device

Printing, a ditto device

Printing, a ditto device

Printing, a ditto device

Printing, a ditto device confirmed and extended the new visual stress. It provided the first uniformly repeatable "commodity," the first assembly line—mass production.

It created the portable book, which men could read in privacy and in isolation from others. Man could now inspire—and conspire.

Like easel painting, the printed book added much to the new cult of individualism. The private, fixed point of view became possible and literacy conferred the power of detachment, non-involvement.

Printing, a ditto device

Printing, a ditto device

Printing, a ditto device

Printing, a ditto device

Printing, a ditto device

Printing, a ditto device

Printing, a ditto device

Printing, a ditto device

Printing, a ditto device

Printing, a ditto device

Printing, a ditto device

Hardcover edition.
Random House, 1967.
28.5 cm.

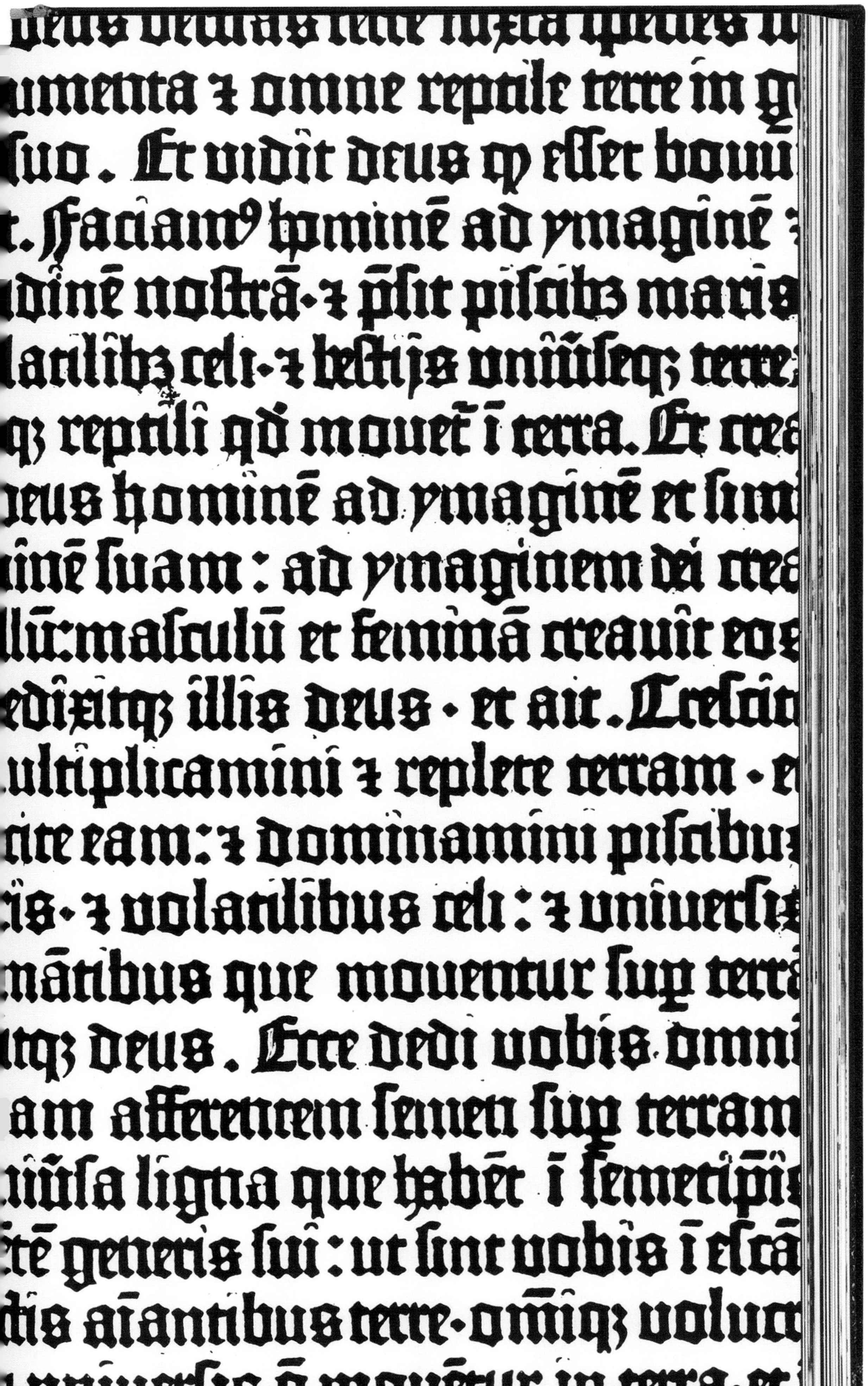
eus bestias terre iuxta species su
umenta & omne reptile terre in g
suo. Et vidit deus q esset bonu
t. Faciamus hominē ad ymaginē &
dinē nostrā. & psit piscibz maris
latilibz celi & bestijs uniūseqz terre
qz reptili qd mouet i terra. Et crea
eus hominē ad ymaginē et simi
inē suam: ad ymaginem dei crea
llū: masculū et feminā creavit eos
edixitqz illis deus. et ait. Crescit
ultiplicamini & replete terram. e
cite eam: & dominamini piscibus
is & volatilibus celi: & universis
mātibus que mouentur sup terra
itqz deus. Ecce dedi vobis omni
am afferentem semen sup terram
uiūsa ligna que habēt i semetipis
tē generis sui: ut sint vobis i esca
ctis aīantibus terre. omniqz volucr
& universis q mouētur in terra. et

1968 **Christian Chruxin** Rainer Langhans & Fritz Teufel, *Klau mich: StPO der Kommune 1*. Frankfurt am Main and Berlin: Edition Voltaire, 1968. 208 pp. 21 cm. *Voltaire Handbuch*, no. 2. Designer: Christian Chruxin.

In the 1960s, Berlin was an enclave of the West within communist East Germany. The student protest movement was strong in this city, and its main themes were the Vietnam War and Germany's Nazi past that had not been dealt with. The protest movement partly obtained its theoretical input from a number of small alternative publishers whose left-wing political publications were often perfectly in tune with the issues discussed in the movement.

The documentary book *Klau mich* ('Steal Me'), about the infamous Kommune 1 criminal case, appeared in 1968 as a volume in the series *Voltaire Handbücher*. The editorial board and design department for the book series was located in Berlin. Members of the Berlin commune K1 had released pamphlets that called on the public to commit arson in department stores during opening hours, in order to denounce the Vietnam War and consumer society. The criminal case did not end in convictions. In *Klau mich*, two of the accused commune members, Rainer Langhans and Fritz Teufel, gave a description of the criminal proceedings and exhibited a playful attitude towards the judicial system.

The anti-aesthetic design by Christian Chruxin (1937–2006) dovetailed with the subject. Chruxin had made his name with his experimental typography, in which words were broken off mid-letter. The image of a large shadowy hand on the cover of *Klau mich* visually expresses the title's invitation to steal. The left-hand pages, with text in a sans serif, document the court proceedings, while the right-hand pages constitute a kind of scrapbook in which various materials pertaining to the trial are reproduced. *Klau mich*, which has a pornographic supplement, appeared just before the Frankfurt Book Fair, in the hope that it would be confiscated. That plan failed: the book sold out on the first day. ML

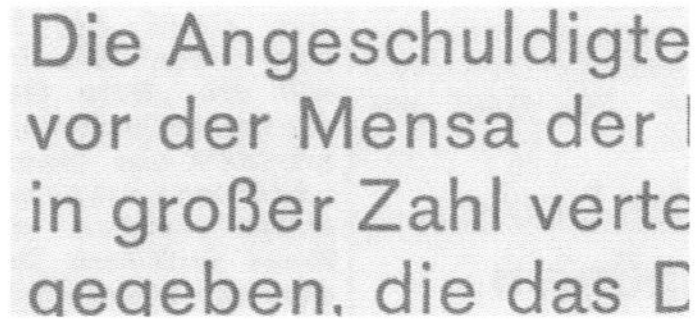

Akzidenz-Grotesk (Berthold) is based on a family of late nineteenth-century sans serifs that had been released under one name since 1898. Eventually, the types were modified to achieve more unity. Additional variants were designed by, among others, Günter Gerhard Lange (1921–2008), who had worked for Berthold in Berlin since 1950.

daß man zwischen ihm und Teufel etwas differenzieren muß. Ich habe bei ihm ausgesprochene Lässigkeit beobachtet. Er hat viel sparsamere Ausdrucksformen. Er hatte z. B. Akten in der Hand, ein Blatt fiel runter, er sah hinterher, na, vielleicht kommste, und dann hat er sich ganz lässig gebückt. Als weiteres Symptom, das diese Tendenz unterstreicht: An einem Verhandlungstag nahm er den Stuhl so, daß ein lautes Geräusch hörbar wurde. Ich bringe einzelne Symptome.

TEUFEL: Aber das ist doch nicht ausreichend für die Lässigkeit!

SPENGLER: Weitere Symptome, Langhans war geladen zur Untersuchung und erschien nicht. Er hat sich auch nicht entschuldigt. Gegen acht Uhr sollte er kommen, gegen zwölf Uhr rief er an, er habe verschlafen. Darauf habe ich gebeten, daß er am nächsten Morgen um 7.45 Uhr kommen solle, darauf hat er gesagt, daß er so früh nicht aufstehen würde. Das ist ein Symptom. Es kamen immer exaltierte und aufgebauschte Symptome heraus. Ich möchte das auch verwerten. Auch das Wort „In Pose stellen“. Ich beobachtete, wie die Fotos für die Zeitung zustande kamen. Das war ein echtes Aufbauen wegen der Publizität. Das beurteile ich psychiatrisch als Effekthascherei. Auch ist mir immer ein spezifisches Lächeln aufgefallen, daß sie immer aufsetzen, sowohl Langhans als auch Sie, auch das ist vom psychiatrischen Standpunkt, daß Sie danach streben, Souveränität zu zeigen, über den Dingen zu stehen, wohingegen L. ein ausgesprochen müdes Lächeln zeigt. Sie unterscheiden sich, der eine neigt mehr zur Steigerung, der andere mehr zur Lässigkeit. – Das sind feste Begriffe, die in der Psychiatrie gelten. Das ist alles an Krankenmaterial erprobt und ich jongliere damit. – Aus den einzelnen Symptomen habe ich das Bild entwickelt und meine Schlüsse gezogen. Auch das Grimassieren läßt auf eine geringe Einsatztiefe der Gefühle schließen.

TEUFEL: Darf ich Sie so verstehen, daß Sie ein Lächeln in einer Gerichtsverhandlung, die Sie zum Weinen finden, schon als Zeichen einer abnormen Persönlichkeit vielleicht mit Recht nehmen?

SPENGLER: L. grimassiert tatsächlich, das ist doch kein

ihr seid in einer Kommune!

Besorgt ihre Sachen, während sie sitzen, es sei denn,

Gegen den Rhf

Warum wird nicht für jeden Tag Ordnungsstrafe 20,- vom Rechtshilfefonds ausgesetzt?

Warum gibt es keinen Haftfonds?

Irgendwann erwischt es uns alle mal. Da muß man denn via Ordnungsstrafen geübt haben. Man kann auch kurzfristige Verkehrsstrafen absitzen.

Der Rechtshilfefonds will ermöglichen, aus Prozessen politische Aktionen zu machen.

Post

Kann er das, wenn er nur für die juristische Durchführung da ist?

Nein!

Dazu gehören die Folgen, die U-Haft unter Umständen und dann auch die Strafhaft.

Technische und politische Hilfe!

Schickt Bücher!

Holt sie ab, wenn sie rauskommen, sorgt für regelmäßigen Anwaltsbesuch.

Wer Milde in Kauf nimmt muß Härte spüren

173

zu einer Zeit, während welcher Menschen in denselben sich aufzuhalten pflegen. Die Aufforderung ist bisher ohne Erfolg geblieben.

Die Angeschuldigten haben am 24. Mai 1967 vor der Mensa der Freien Universität Berlin in großer Zahl verteilte Flugblätter herausgegeben, die das Datum dieses Tages tragen und mit den Zahlen 6 bis 9 sowie mit der Verfasserbezeichnung „Kommune I“ versehen sind. Die Flugblätter nehmen einen Warenhausbrand, der sich am 22. Mai 1967 in Brüssel ereignet hat, zum Anlaß, Brandstiftungen in Berliner Warenhäusern anzuregen, um dadurch wirklichkeitsnahe Vorstellungen von den Kämpfen in Vietnam zu vermitteln. Sie wollen damit das amerikanische Vorgehen in Vietnam anprangern.

Die Flugblätter haben folgenden Text:

Der gesamte Inhalt der Flugblätter läßt erkennen, daß die Verfasser davon ausgehen, der Warenhausbrand in Brüssel sei durch Brandstiftung hervorgerufen worden und daß es angesichts der überzeugenden Wirkung einer solchen „Demonstration“ ihr Bestreben ist, eine nach Größe und Zusammensetzung unbestimmter Gruppe Gleichgesinnter zu gewinnen, die aufgefordert werden, auch in Berliner Warenhäusern – und zwar während der Verkaufszeiten – Brände zu legen.

Verbrechen, gem. §§ 306 Nr. 3, 111 Abs. 2, 47 StGB, § 19 des Berliner Pressegesetzes vom 15. Juni 1965

Geplant

Donnerstag, 6. April 1967 – 15 Pf

Bild Zeitung Berlin

Berlin: Bomben-Anschlag auf US-Vizepräsidenten

● Elf Verschwörer gefaßt

Verfahren eingestellt

„Ihr Enkelkind läßt Sie grüßen“

7

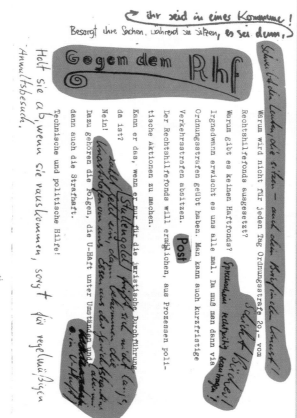

1970 **Wolf Vostell** *Kunst der sechziger Jahre: Sammlung Ludwig im Wallraf-Richartz-Museum, Köln*; eds. Gert von der Osten & Horst Keller. Cologne: Wallraf-Richartz-Museum, 1970. 4th enlarged ed. 36, 169 pp., 4 leaves. 30.5 cm. 1st ed. 1969. Designer ('Visualization'): Wolf Vostell. Graphic production: K. G. Lohse, Frankfurt am Main.

This catalogue showcases work from the collection of the art patrons Irene and Peter Ludwig. This German couple, who made their fortune in the chocolate trade, assembled a very extensive and eclectic collection. In the early sixties the Ludwigs began to take a special interest in contemporary American and international art, which eventually led to *Kunst der sechziger Jahre* ('Art of the Sixties'), a crowd-pulling 1969 exhibition in Cologne that included work by Joseph Beuys, Ellsworth Kelly, Andy Warhol and others.

The designer of the catalogue, Wolf Vostell (1932–98), also appears in it as an artist. Vostell had studied typography and occasionally designed books, but he was primarily an artist. He organized happenings and was a member of Fluxus, an international avant-garde movement. One of Vostell's works shown in Cologne was the 'décollage' *Coca-Cola* (1961). Décollage refers to a process of destructive modification, removing fragments of street posters that have been pasted over others to reveal hidden images and create new associations.

Just as Vostell had sought active participation from the viewer in his art with décollage, he did so graphically in the *Kunst der sechziger Jahre* catalogue. The black-and white-photographic portraits of the artists are printed on acetate sheets and form a link with the catalogue information (when the sheet is turned to the left) and with the tipped-in colour reproductions (when the sheet is turned to the right). This 5-cm-thick book, printed mostly on brown wrapping paper, is held together by two book screws that pass through the soft plastic covers, the plexiglas spine and the book block. The catalogue sold well and was reprinted several times. ML

Folio-Grotesk (1956) was designed by Konrad F. Bauer (1903–70) and Walter Baum (1921–2007). The Bauer typefoundry in Frankfurt am Main continued to expand the family with additional versions until 1969. Bauer and Baum also co-designed the text face Imprimatur (1952) and the Clarendon font Volta (1956).

Kunst der sechziger Jahre
4. verbesserte Auflage
Art of the Sixties
4th revised edition

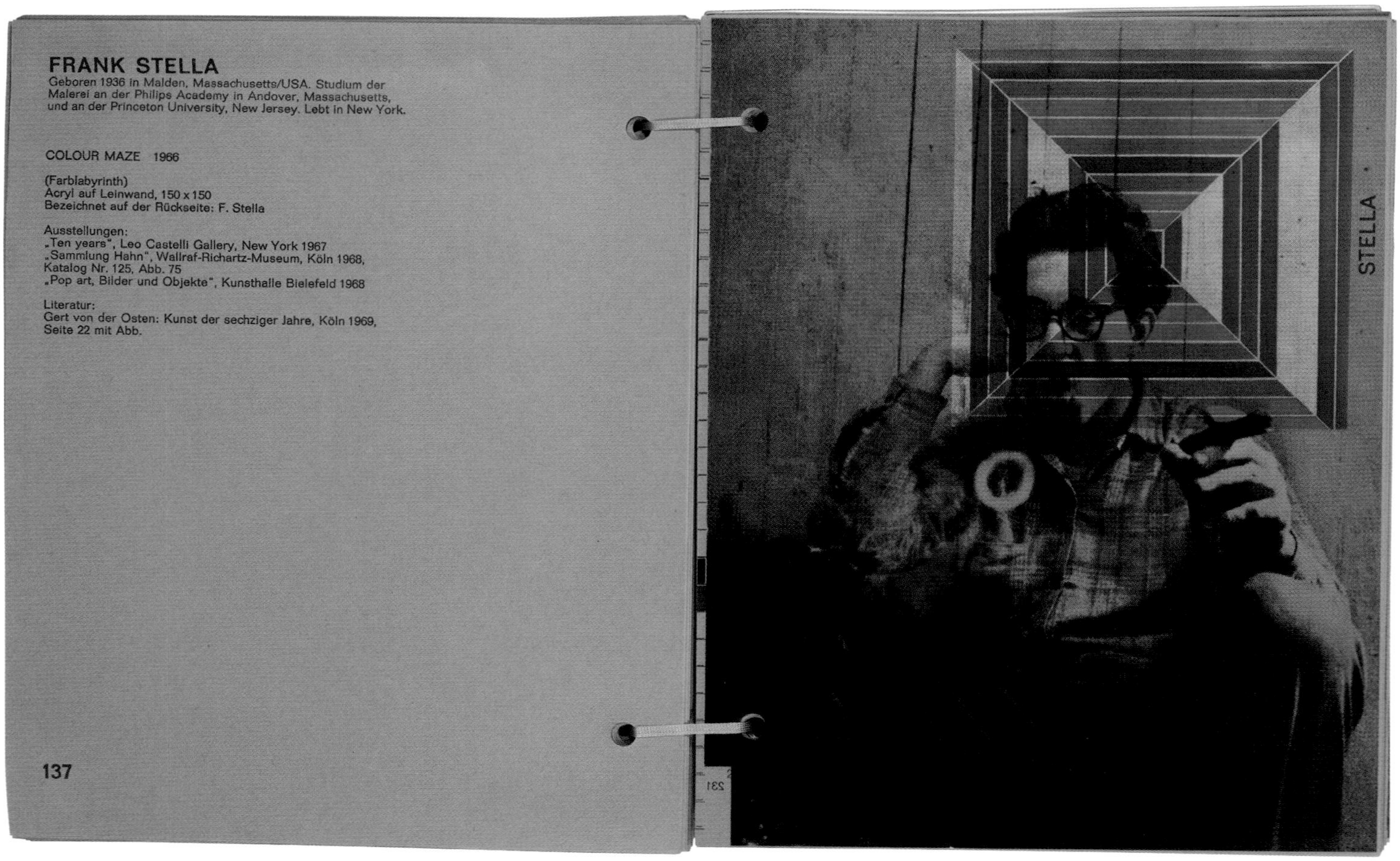

FRANK STELLA
Geboren 1936 in Malden, Massachusetts/USA. Studium der Malerei an der Philips Academy in Andover, Massachusetts, und an der Princeton University, New Jersey. Lebt in New York.
COLOUR MAZE 1966
(Farblabyrinth)
Acryl auf Leinwand, 150 x 150
Bezeichnet auf der Rückseite: F. Stella
Ausstellungen:
„Ten years", Leo Castelli Gallery, New York 1967
„Sammlung Hahn", Wallraf-Richartz-Museum, Köln 1968, Katalog Nr. 125, Abb. 75
„Pop art, Bilder und Objekte", Kunsthalle Bielefeld 1968
Literatur:
Gert von der Osten: Kunst der sechziger Jahre, Köln 1969, Seite 22 mit Abb.
137
STELLA

To make repro-photography of the interior possible, the leaves are held together with ribbons through the screw holes.

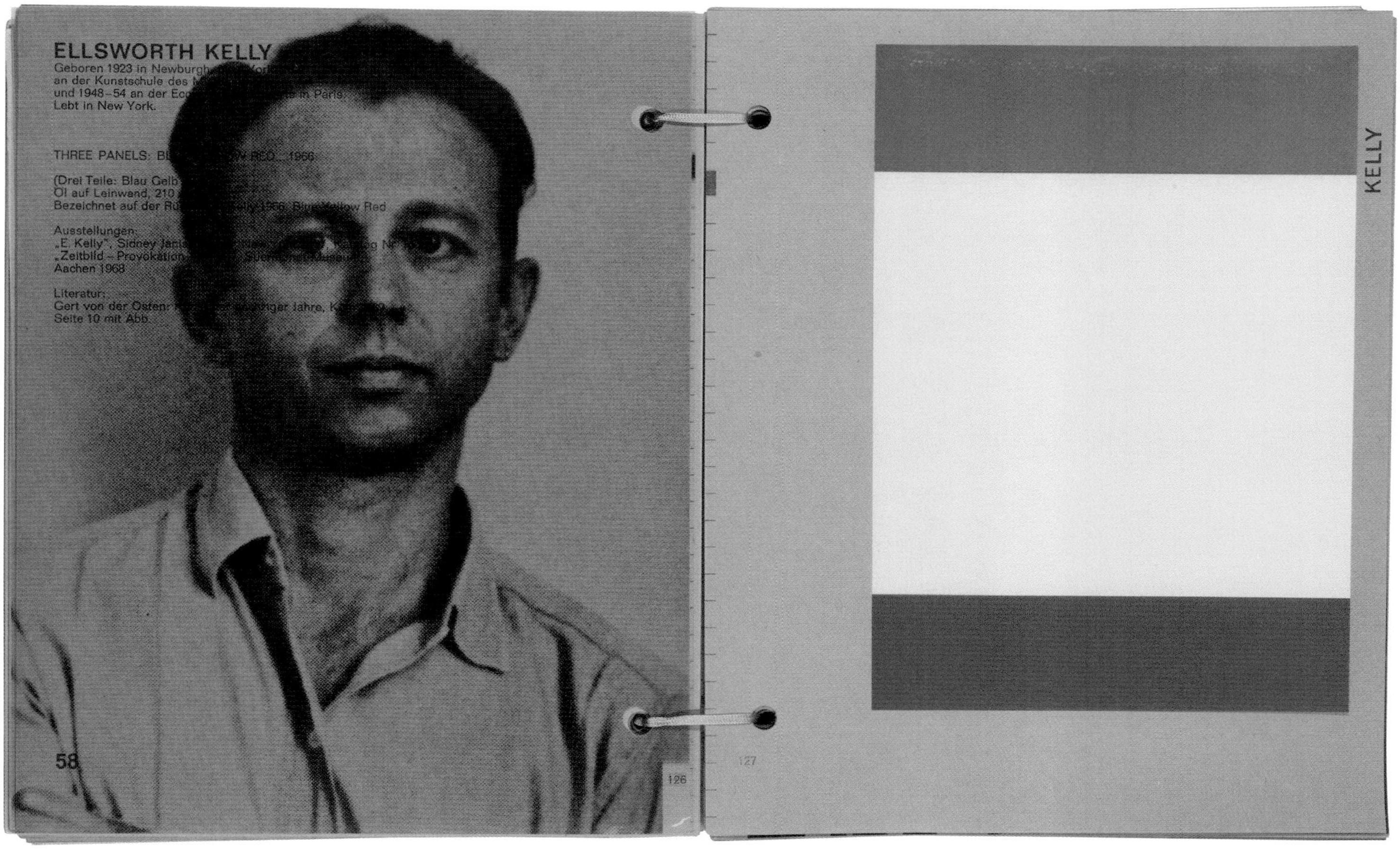

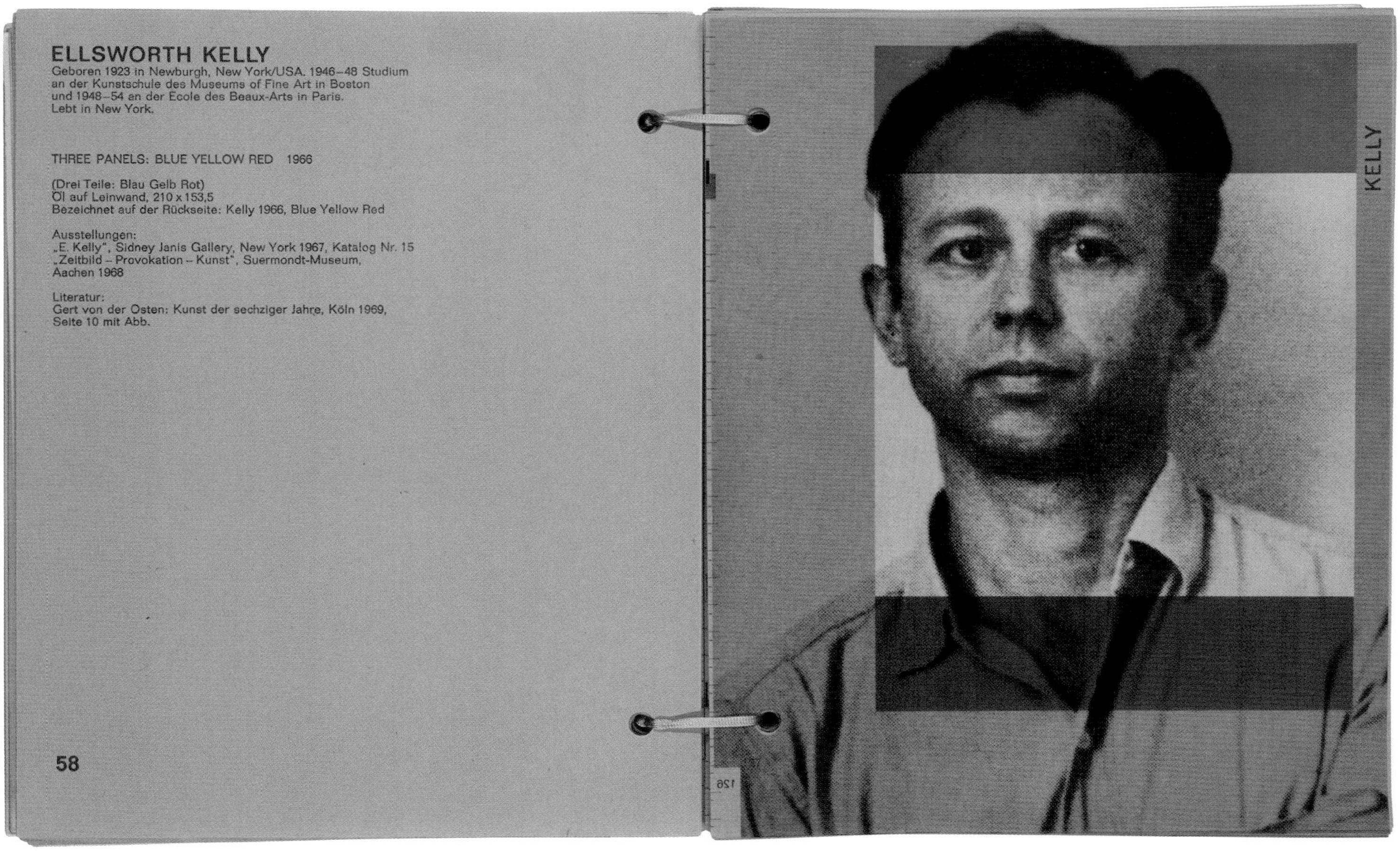

TOM WESSELMANN

Geboren 1931 in Cincinnati, Ohio/USA. Psychologie-Diplom der University of Cincinnati. 1955 Eintritt in die Cooper Union School of Art. Lebt in New York.

BATHTUB 3   1963

(Badewanne Nr. 3)
Öl, Leinwand, Plastik und verschiedene Objekte,
u. a. Badezimmertür, Handtuch und Wäschekasten,

213 x 270 x 45
Bezeichnet unten links: Wesselmann 63,
auf der Rückseite: Bathtub Collage 1963

Ausstellungen:
„Amerikansk Pop Konst“, Moderna Museet, Stockholm 1964
„Tom Wesselmann“, Galerie Ileana Sonnabend, Paris 1966, Abb. im Katalog
„Mostra internazionale d'arte contemporanea“, Campo vitale, Palazzo Grassi, Venedig 1967
„Zeitbild – Provokation – Kunst“, Suermondt-Museum, Aachen 1968

Literatur:
Art International VII 2 1964, Abb. Seite 54 (Besprechung der Ausstellung in Stockholm)
S. R. Swenson: What is Pop Art, in: Art News, 62 10 1964, Seite 40–45, Abb. Seite 40
J. Rublowsky: Pop Art, New York 1965, Seite 115
Art International XI 1 1967, Abb. Seite 70 (Besprechung der Ausstellung Sonnabend)
L. R. Lippard: Pop Art, London 1967, Seite 111, Farbabb. 92, Seite 160
J.-L. Ferrier: Le Nouveau Paysage de Tom Wesselmann, in: Metro 12 1967, Seite 42–45, Abb. 43
Gerhard Bott: Malerei unserer Zeit, Versuch einer Übersicht und Deutung, Vortrag in Bad Wildungen am 24. April 1967, Bad Homburg–Berlin–Zürich 1967, Abb. Seite 25
Sam Hunter: Neorealismo, Assemblage, Pop Art in America (L'arte moderna Nr. 112, Band 13), Milano 1967, Farbabb. Seite 142
Klaus Honnef: Die neue Kunst ist Trumpf, Die Sammlung Ludwig, in: Das Kunstwerk XXII 3–4 1968/69, Seite 39–48, Farbabb. Seite 42
Gert von der Osten: Kunst der sechziger Jahre, Köln 1969, Seite 27 mit Abb.
H. H. Hofstetter: Malerei und Graphik der Gegenwart, Baden-Baden 1969, Farbabb. Seite 277
J. F. Michelet, Pop-Maleri, in: Kunsten Idag 89 1969, Seite 26–37, Abb. Seite 32
Peter Knorr, Die neue Lust in der Kunst, in: Pardon 9, Heft 3, 1970, Seite 47–53, Farbabb. Seite 53

Gezeigt in der Fernsehsendung „Pop Art in USA“ am 8. 8. 1969 um 20.30 Uhr im 3. Programm des WDR

164

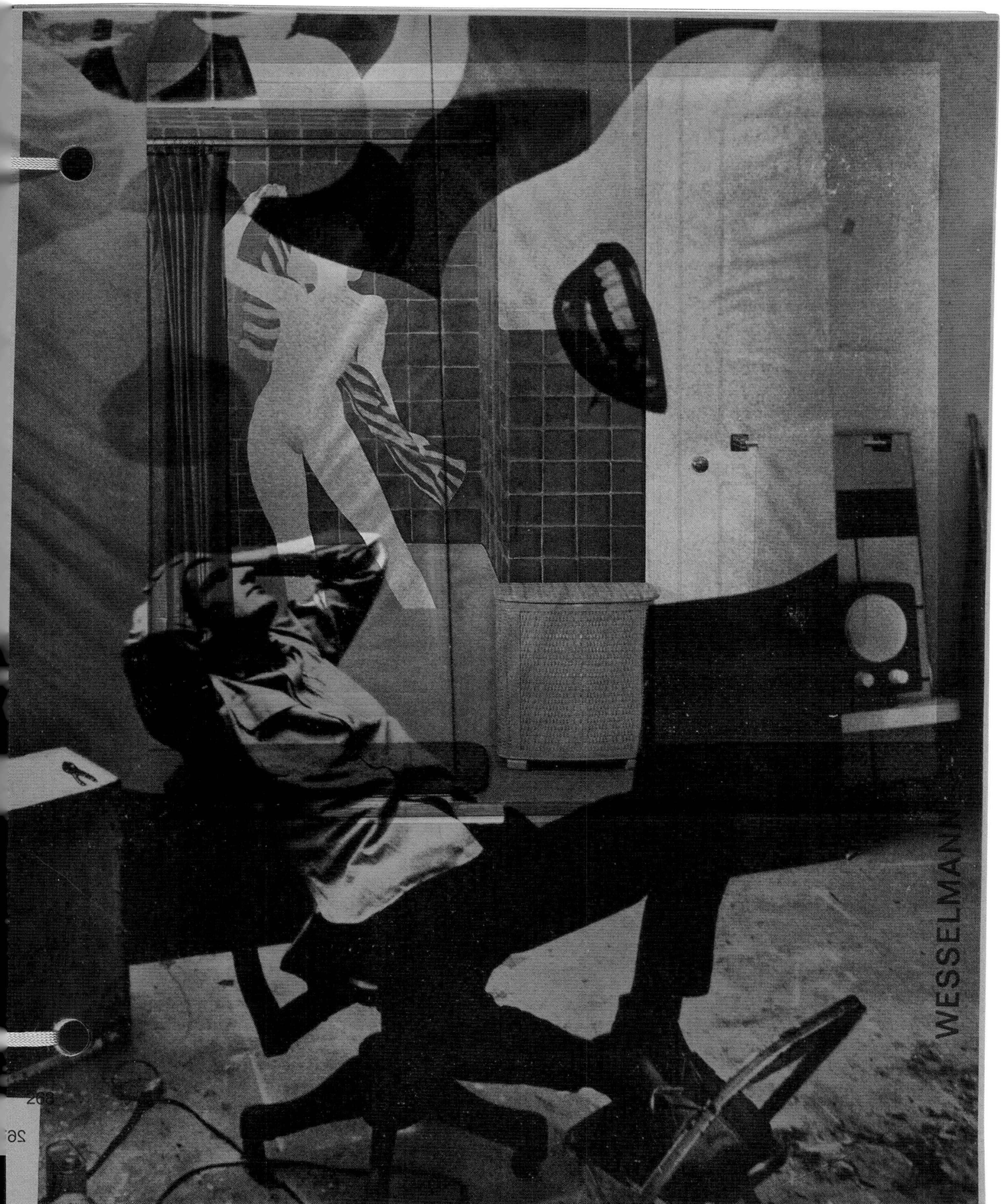
WESSELMAN

1971 **Katy Hepburn** *Monty Python's Big Red Book*; ed. Eric Idle. London: Methuen, 1971. 70 pp. 28.5 cm.

Designer: Katy Hepburn (art editor and layout); Derek Birdsall (art director). Illustrator: Terry Gilliam.

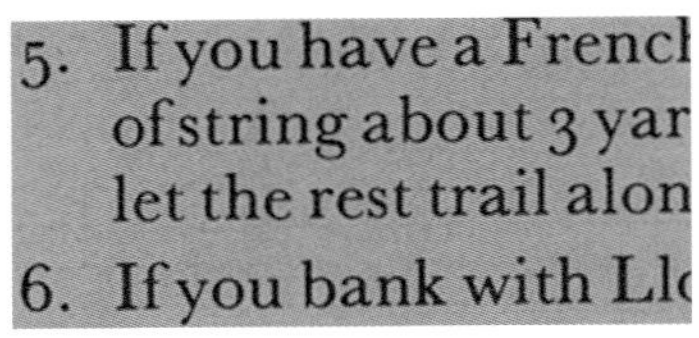

5. If you have a Frencl
of string about 3 yar
let the rest trail alon
6. If you bank with Ll

'**Knickers.** This is just a cheap advertising ploy to draw your attention to *Monty Python's Big Red Book*, get you into a bookshop and relieve you of £1.50.
Single young lady seeks *Monty Python's Big Red Book*. Part time.
For sale. Quantity of pink paper, newsprint, purple ink, Eric Idle, John Cleese, Terry Jones, Michael Palin, Graham Chapman and the illustrated Terry Gilliam. Worth £822, now offered by Methuen at only £1.50 for quick sale.'

Publisher Methuen used these small ads in *The Times* on 4 November 1971 to draw the public's attention to a new title on its list: *Monty Python's Big Red Book* (which has a blue cover). The Pythons were hugely popular for the surreal, absurdist comedy sketches featured on their BBC TV show *Monty Python's Flying Circus*; a book was to be expected. Just as the Python's sketches were often pastiches of television genres such as news and talk shows, the *Big Red Book* was a pastiche of print media. The layout of the *Radio Times* magazine, for instance, was parodied in an article about the 'Upper Class Twit of the Year' race. In *Flying Circus*, the title credits sometimes appeared far ahead of the end of the show; in the book, the colophon pops up after the first few pages.

Looking back, Derek Birdsall credits Katy Hepburn (b. 1947) with the design. She was still a student at the Royal College of Art in London at the time, but she worked as a freelancer on the Monty Python animations. Hepburn, who had feminist sympathies, had some trouble regarding the book's sexism as purely ironic. ML

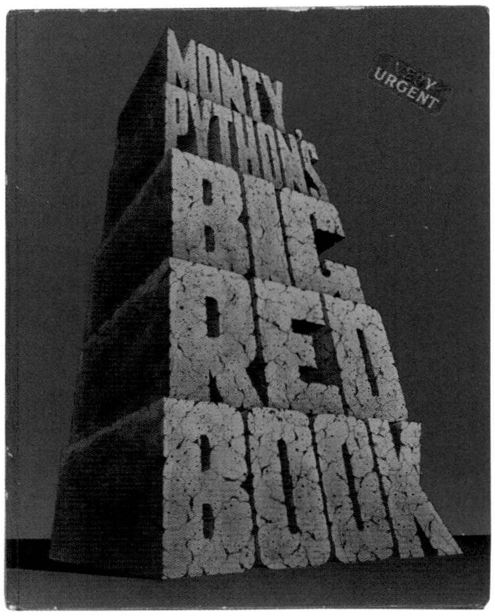

This Baskerville is one of the many twentieth-century adaptations of the work of the English printer and type designer John Baskerville (1707–75). The English Monotype Corporation cut this revival typeface in 1923 and later also made it available for photocomposition. Zuzana Licko designed a free interpretation of Baskerville, named Mrs Eaves, in 1996.

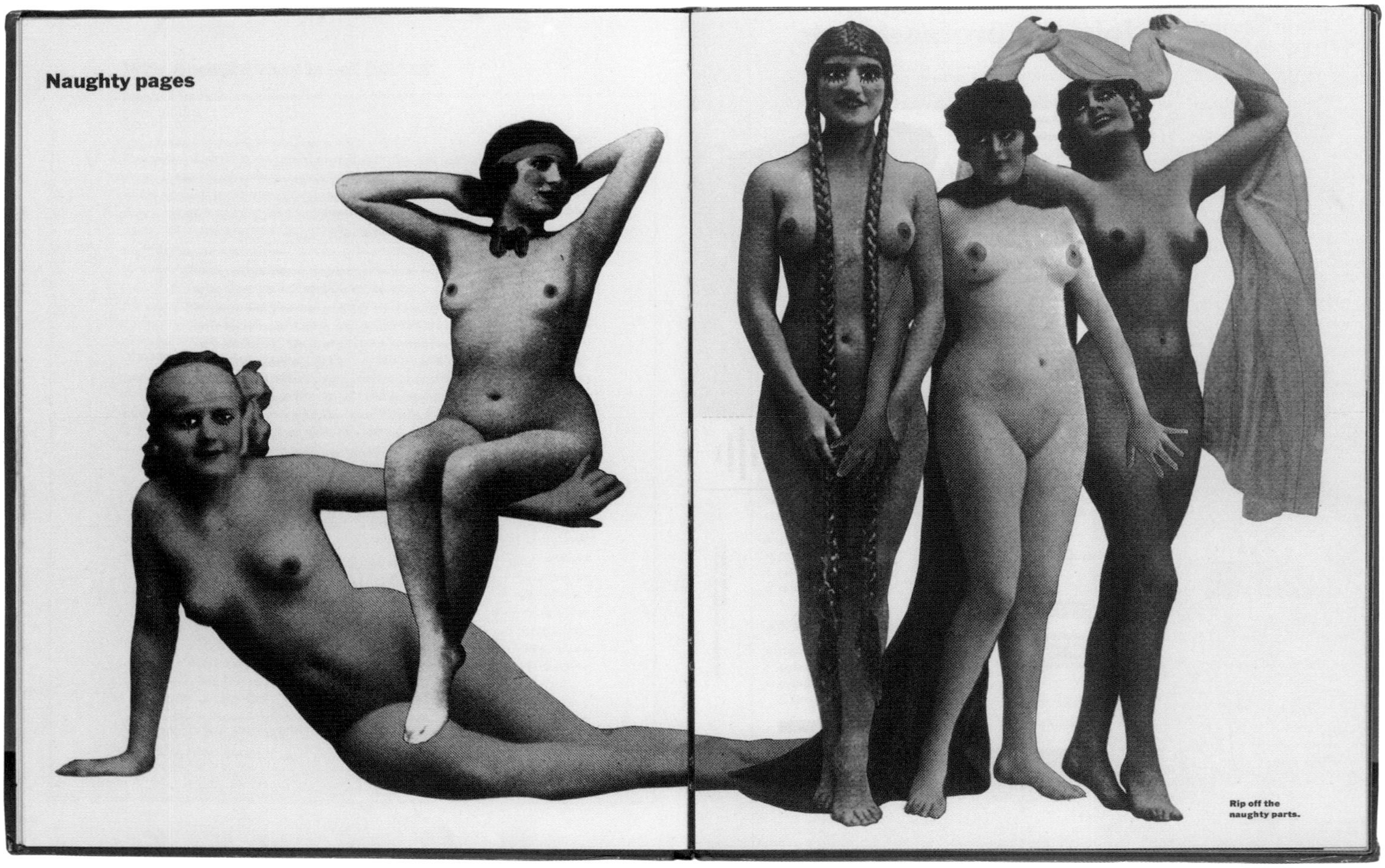

Naughty pages
Rip off the naughty parts.

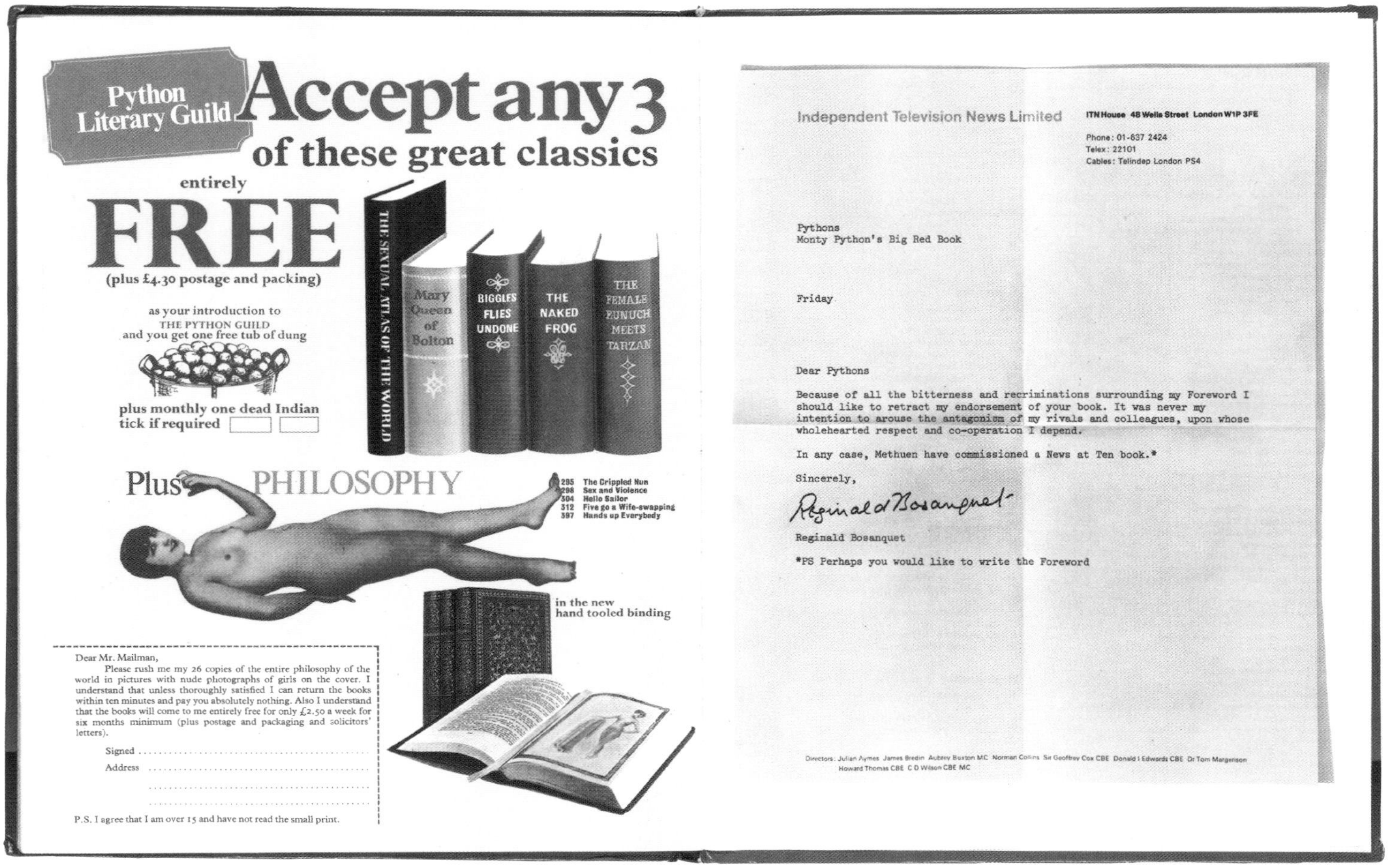

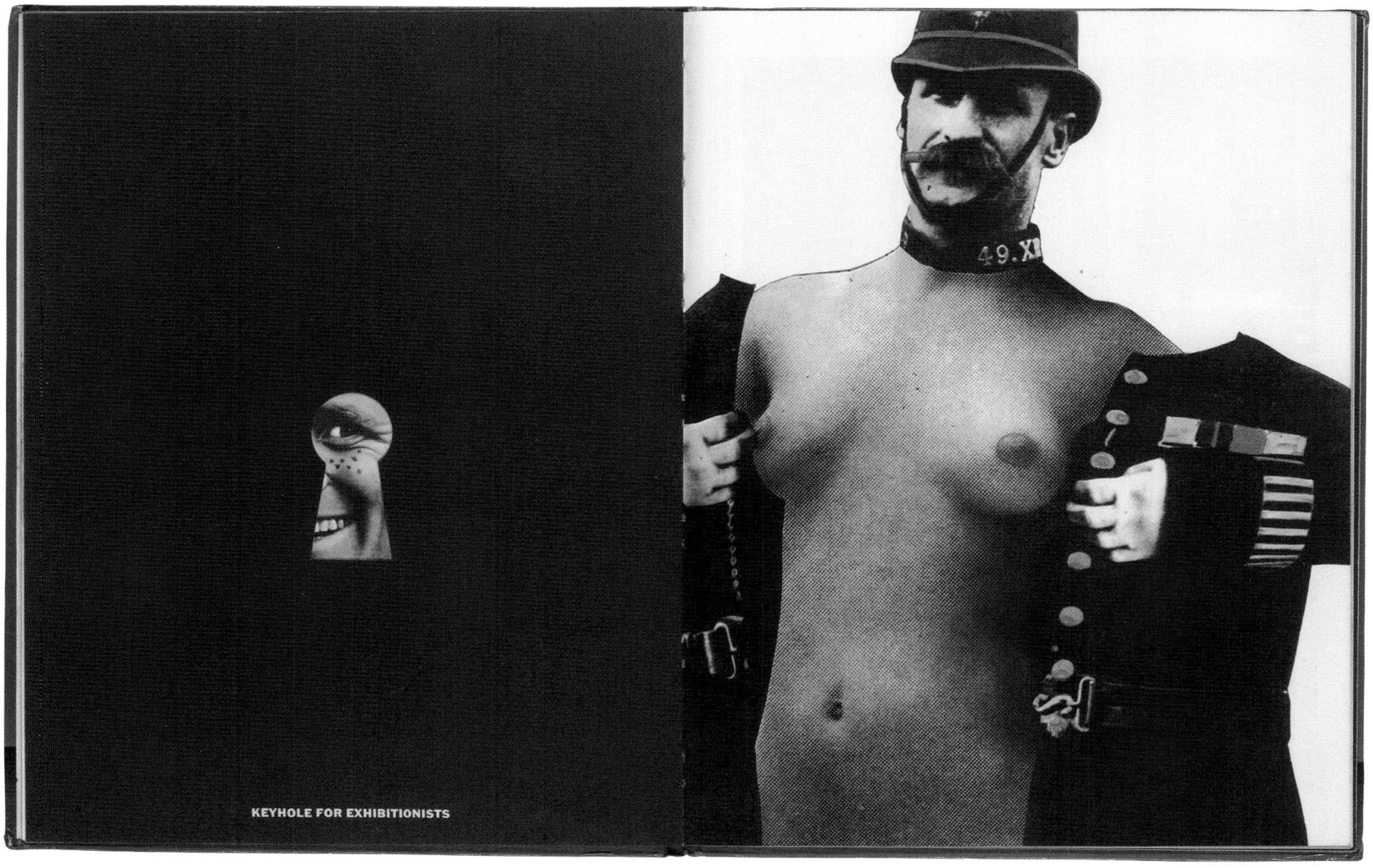

Katy Hepburn

ANSWERS TO THE "ACNE" PATENT QUIZ
by E. D. Silly
1. They're all foreigners.
2. A Bachelor.
3. I did.
4. Smartass.
5. Coventry. (All the rest are in Asia).
6. There's no point in taking this seriously you know.
7. Bad luck – it *was* the obvious one.
8. Ah well – you persisted you poor fool.

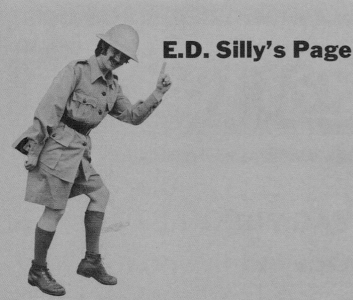

E.D. Silly's Page

SILLY THINGS TO DO by E. D. Silly

1. Take a piece of blue notepaper and stick it on the side of a chicken. Then frighten the chicken.
2. If you live in Birmingham, Nottingham or Leeds go: "Boinggg!"
3. Put a chair in the front garden and put a television on it.
4. Buy a packet of winegums and leave them outside Buckingham Palace.
5. If you have a French *au pair* staying with you, get a piece of string about 3 yards long, tie one end to your finger and let the rest trail along the ground.
6. If you bank with Lloyds, go to see the Manager on Jan. 4th 1972, and talk in a very high voice.

SILLY THINGS TO DO ON A RAINY AFTERNOON

1. Stand out in the rain.

SILLY GAMES by E. D. Silly

1. 4 or more players sit round in a circle. The player nearest the one next to him deals. Whilst the deal is going on the other players have to impersonate either General Franco or any member of the P.L.F. (Palestine Liberation Front).
   Each player has 7 cards, apart from the eldest one who has 9 and the other 3, who have 6. Then the player nearest the one who last went to the lavatory runs out of the room, taking his cards with him and goes to see a film. The next player must either go and see the film as well or, if he has a Jack, Queen or King of any *Black* suit, he must go to the pub. The 2 remaining players can either go to the pub or go to see a film.
   The Winner is the one nearest the mantelpiece.
2. The Francis Of Assisi Game
   The player pretending to be Francis of Assisi deals 6 cards to each player. They all then see who can remain motionless longest. The first player to move then becomes Francis of Assisi.
3. Drabble. A word game for 2 to 4 players. The four players sit from left to right and the first person to write a novel wins.

THE "ACNE" PATENT QUIZ by E. D. Silly

1. What have the following in common? a) Moshe Dayan b) Sammy Davis Jnr. c) The Nawab of Pataudi.
2. Edward Heath is a what?
3. Who wrote "The gushing leaves that through the argent windows blush?"?
4. Can you name seven planets?
5. Which of the following is not in Asia? Lahore, Singapore, Dacca, Bangkok, Coventry.
6. How many fingers am I holding up? a) 1 b) 2 c) 3 d) 46
7. What is "a hen."?
   a) a small sprochett near the tamping wopple of a Keighley trunion?
   b) a regenerative cell in the Aquarian life-support system of the Apollo Space Capsule.
   c) An egg-laying female domestic fowl.
   (Careful with this one – it might not be the obvious E.D.)
8. How do you tell a boy scout?
   a) by b) b) by c) c) in a quiet even voice so as not to frighten him until you've told him.

QUICK CROSSWORD by E. D. Silly

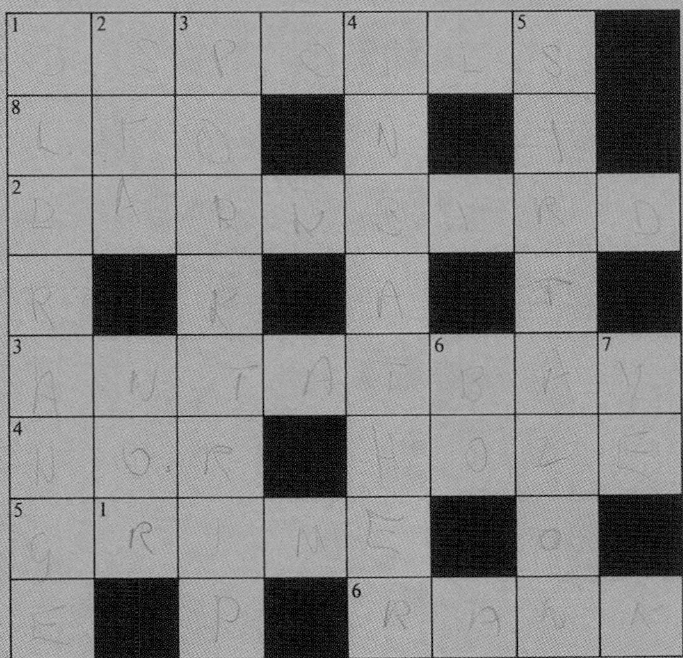

ACROSS
1. O Spoils! (1,6)
2. Dark bird (4,4)
3. Ant at bay (3,2,3)
4. Nor (3)
5. Grime (5)
6. Rank (4)
7. Hole (4)
8. London Philharmonic Orchestra (1,1,1)

DOWN
1. Old range (3,5)
2. Spa (3)
3. Pork trip (4,4)
4. In bather (2,6)
5. Sir talon (3,5)
6. B.O. (1,1)
7. Ye (2)

UP
1. Ron (3)

Katy Hepburn

1977 **Massimo Vignelli** Miklos D. F. Udvardy, *The Audubon Society Field Guide to North American Birds: Western Region*; visual key by Susan Rayfield. New York: Alfred A. Knopf, 1987. 852 pp. 19.5 cm. 1st edition 1977. Designer: Massimo Vignelli. Lithographer: Nievergelt Repro, Zurich. Typesetter: Dix Type, Syracuse, NY. Printed and bound in Japan.

Massimo Vignelli (b. 1931), born in Milan, has never stopped preaching the modernist creed. In *Vignelli: From A to Z*, an autobiographical monograph from 2007, he presents under E of 'Education' nine pictures of work by designers and architects that have had a major influence on his own development. Among them are an architecture book by Max Bill from 1935, a car racing poster by Max Huber from 1948, a book about exhibition design by Richard Paul Lohse from 1953, and a designers' manual by Josef Müller-Brockmann from 1961. All of these designers were key figures in Swiss typography.

At the end of the seventies, when the Audubon Society's bird guides were published, Massimo and his partner Lella Vignelli were running a leading multidisciplinary design studio in New York: Vignelli Associates. The studio, which has survived in a slimmed-down version, not only did graphic design – from books to corporate identities – but also interior, product and furniture design. To Vignelli, graphic design means organizing information, so he likes to use the 'neutral' Helvetica. Towards the end of the sixties he played an important part in popularizing this sans serif in the US.

The guide is pocket-sized, because it is meant for bird identification in the field. It has no jacket but a bellyband, which leaves the waterproof vinyl cover immediately visible to potential buyers. The book (over 850 pages) has a full-colour photo section at the front, and a text section printed on thin India paper to limit the book's final size. ML

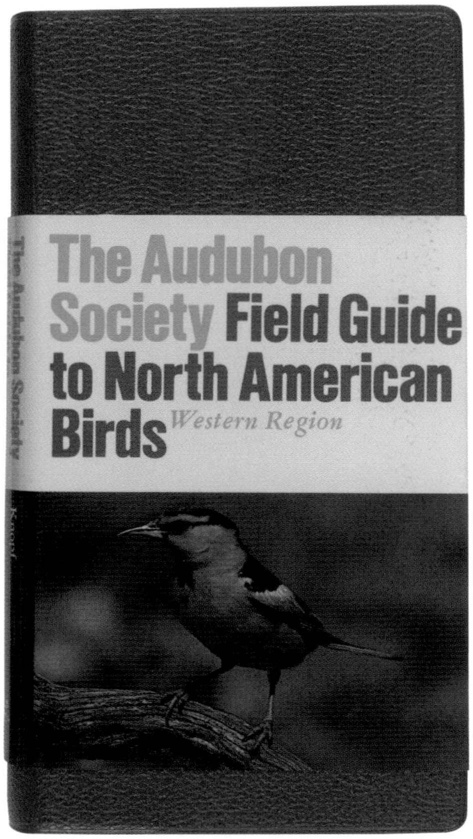

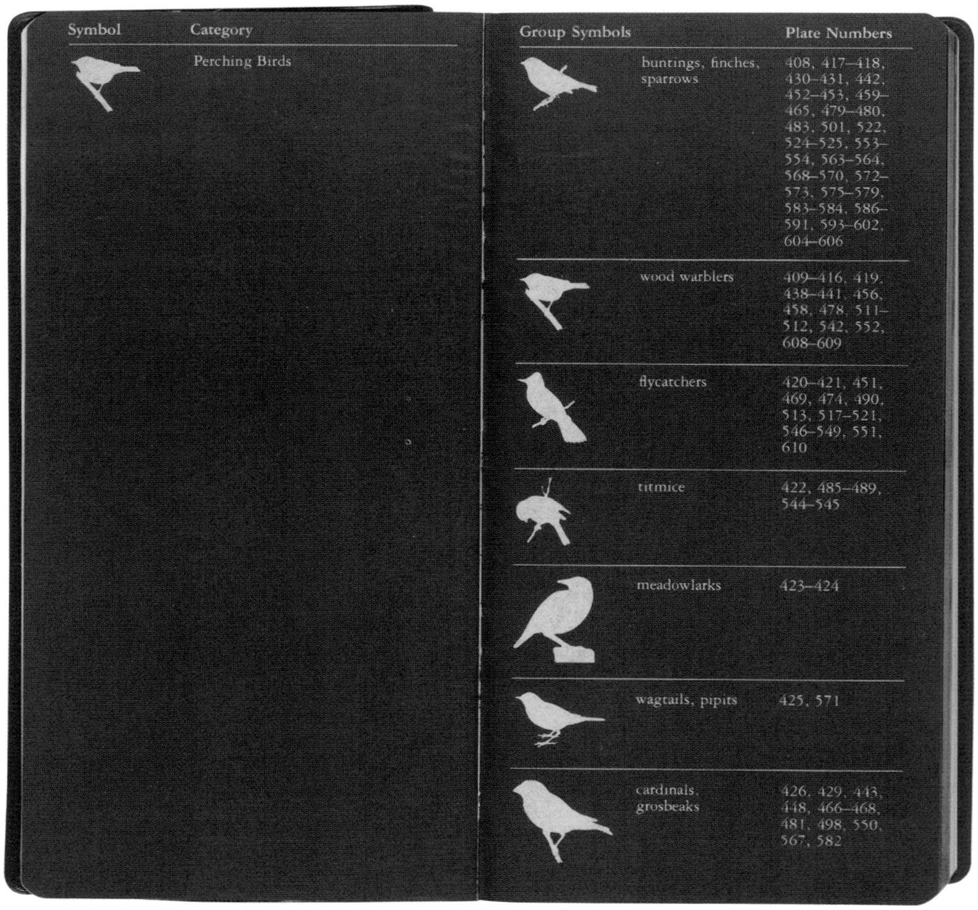

Goldfinches are late nesters, waiting
until plants and weeds have grown,
bloomed, and gone to seed so the sof
fresh seeds can be fed to the young.
Lawrence's nests late in May. It bree

It is well known that Massimo Vignelli feels that six typefaces are all one needs. On his list are: Garamond, Bodoni, Century Expanded, Futura, Times New Roman and Helvetica, which is according to him 'the ultimate typeface'. In the Audubon guide, he combined a Garamond (interior) with a condensed bold Helvetica (cover/ banderole).

Perching Birds
420 Tropical Kingbird, 8–9½″, p. 654
423 Western Meadowlark, 8½–11″, p. 547
421 Western Kingbird, 8–9″, p. 545
424 Eastern Meadowlark, 8½–11″, p. 548
422 Verdin, 4–4½″, p. 514
425 Yellow Wagtail, 6½″, p. 766

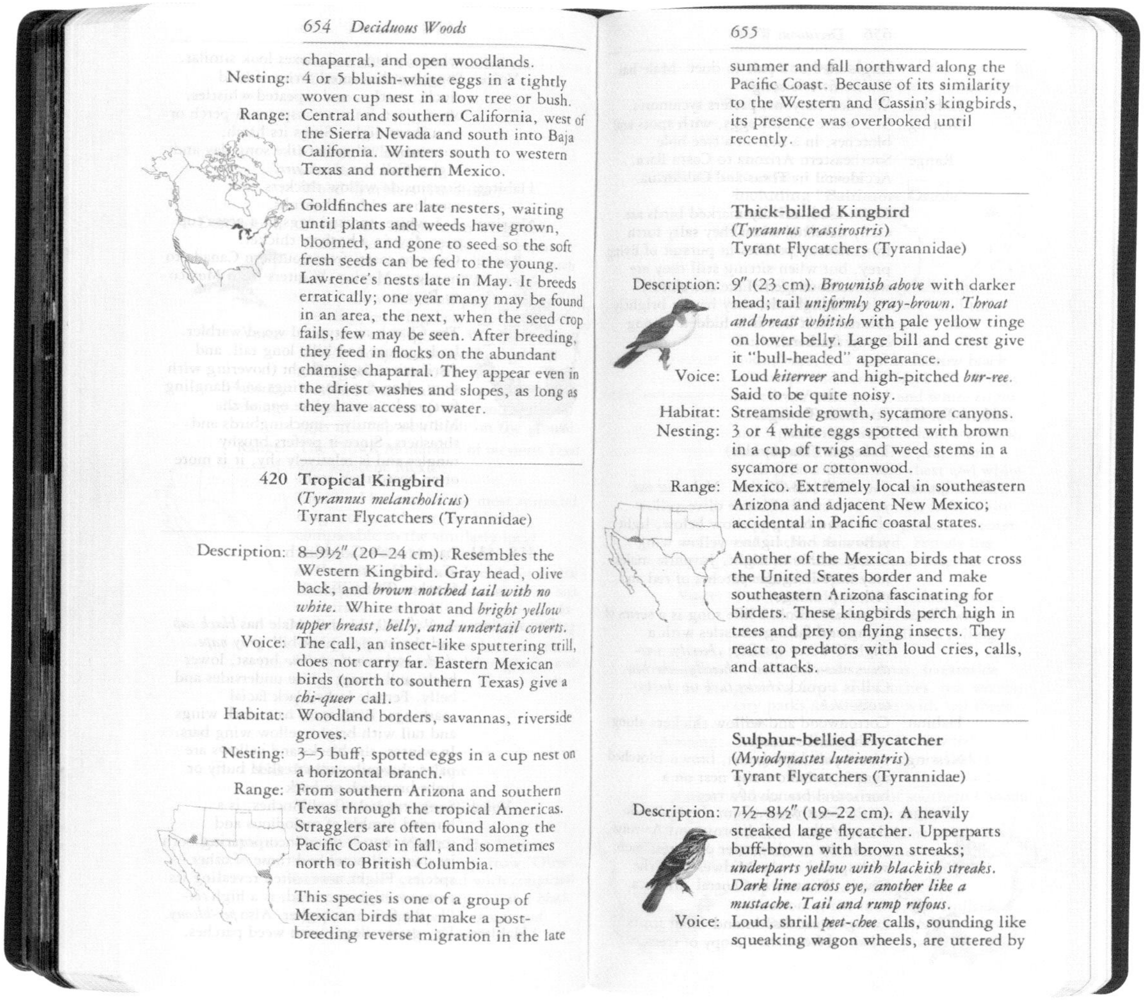

654 *Deciduous Woods*

chaparral, and open woodlands.

Nesting: 4 or 5 bluish-white eggs in a tightly woven cup nest in a low tree or bush.

Range: Central and southern California, west of the Sierra Nevada and south into Baja California. Winters south to western Texas and northern Mexico.

Goldfinches are late nesters, waiting until plants and weeds have grown, bloomed, and gone to seed so the soft fresh seeds can be fed to the young. Lawrence's nests late in May. It breeds erratically; one year many may be found in an area, the next, when the seed crop fails, few may be seen. After breeding, they feed in flocks on the abundant chamise chaparral. They appear even in the driest washes and slopes, as long as they have access to water.

420 Tropical Kingbird
(*Tyrannus melancholicus*)
Tyrant Flycatchers (Tyrannidae)

Description: 8–9½" (20–24 cm). Resembles the Western Kingbird. Gray head, olive back, and *brown notched tail with no white.* White throat and *bright yellow upper breast, belly, and undertail coverts.*

Voice: The call, an insect-like sputtering trill, does not carry far. Eastern Mexican birds (north to southern Texas) give a *chi-queer* call.

Habitat: Woodland borders, savannas, riverside groves.

Nesting: 3–5 buff, spotted eggs in a cup nest on a horizontal branch.

Range: From southern Arizona and southern Texas through the tropical Americas. Stragglers are often found along the Pacific Coast in fall, and sometimes north to British Columbia.

This species is one of a group of Mexican birds that make a post-breeding reverse migration in the late

655

summer and fall northward along the Pacific Coast. Because of its similarity to the Western and Cassin's kingbirds, its presence was overlooked until recently.

Thick-billed Kingbird
(*Tyrannus crassirostris*)
Tyrant Flycatchers (Tyrannidae)

Description: 9" (23 cm). *Brownish above* with darker head; tail *uniformly gray-brown. Throat and breast whitish* with pale yellow tinge on lower belly. Large bill and crest give it "bull-headed" appearance.

Voice: Loud *kiterreer* and high-pitched *bur-ree.* Said to be quite noisy.

Habitat: Streamside growth, sycamore canyons.

Nesting: 3 or 4 white eggs spotted with brown in a cup of twigs and weed stems in a sycamore or cottonwood.

Range: Mexico. Extremely local in southeastern Arizona and adjacent New Mexico; accidental in Pacific coastal states.

Another of the Mexican birds that cross the United States border and make southeastern Arizona fascinating for birders. These kingbirds perch high in trees and prey on flying insects. They react to predators with loud cries, calls, and attacks.

Sulphur-bellied Flycatcher
(*Myiodynastes luteiventris*)
Tyrant Flycatchers (Tyrannidae)

Description: 7½–8½" (19–22 cm). A heavily streaked large flycatcher. Upperparts buff-brown with brown streaks; *underparts yellow with blackish streaks. Dark line across eye, another like a mustache. Tail and rump rufous.*

Voice: Loud, shrill *peet-chee* calls, sounding like squeaking wagon wheels, are uttered by

1981 **Helmut Brade** Wieland Herzfelde & Hans Marquardt, *Pass auf! Hier kommt Grosz: Bilder, Rhythmen und Gesänge, 1915–1918*. Leipzig: Philipp Reclam jun., 1981. 111 pp. 25 cm. Designer: Helmut Brade. Typesetter & bookbinder: Interdruck, Leipzig. Printer: H.F. Jütte, Leipzig.

The designer Helmut Brade (b. 1937) was born and educated in the city of Halle, near Leipzig. He later taught at the art academy there. Besides books, Brade designs posters for cultural events, as well as scenery for theatre and opera. The 1981 anthology *Pass auf! Hier kommt Grosz* was produced in East Germany, at that time still the German Democratic Republic (DDR).

The DDR, under communist control and with a relatively weak economy made worse by the oil crisis of 1979, was no stranger to censorship. The facilities for graphic production there were limited. The often unmotivated personnel had to work with obsolete equipment, and good paper and good bookbinding cloth were scarce. The government even limited the size of the (unprinted) margins of book pages! There was nevertheless a strong typographic tradition, especially in the cities of East Berlin and Leipzig, and books were greatly esteemed.

The collection *Pass auf! Hier kommt Grosz* ('Watch Out! Here Comes Grosz') contains texts and drawings by the anti-bourgeois artist George Grosz (1893–1959). This material dates from the 1910s and 1920s. The afterword notes that the book's design was inspired by a prospectus, designed by John Heartfield and printed in three colours, for the 1917 *Kleine Grosz Mappe*. Although Brade's design alludes to this prospectus's use of colour and images, he does not produce a Dada pastiche. *Pass auf! Hier kommt Grosz* shows Brade's own distinctive use of symmetry and asymmetry, and of Gill Sans (normal and bold) for the main text. In the largely anti-modernist art climate of the DDR, it must have been a daring piece of work. ML

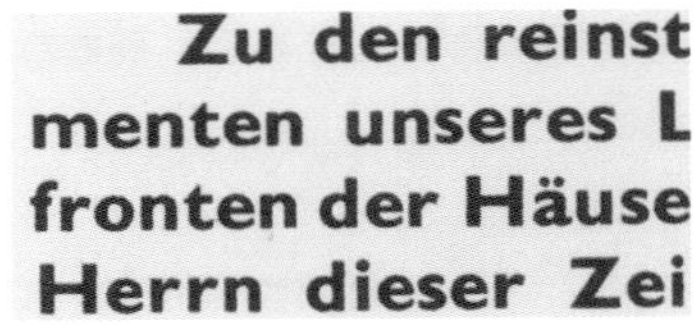
Zu den reinst
menten unseres L
fronten der Häuse
Herrn dieser Zei

The sans serif Gill Sans (1928) is one of the typefaces that the artist, designer and essayist Eric Gill (1882–1940) designed for the English Monotype Corporation. It appears here in a photo-typeset variant, offset-printed.

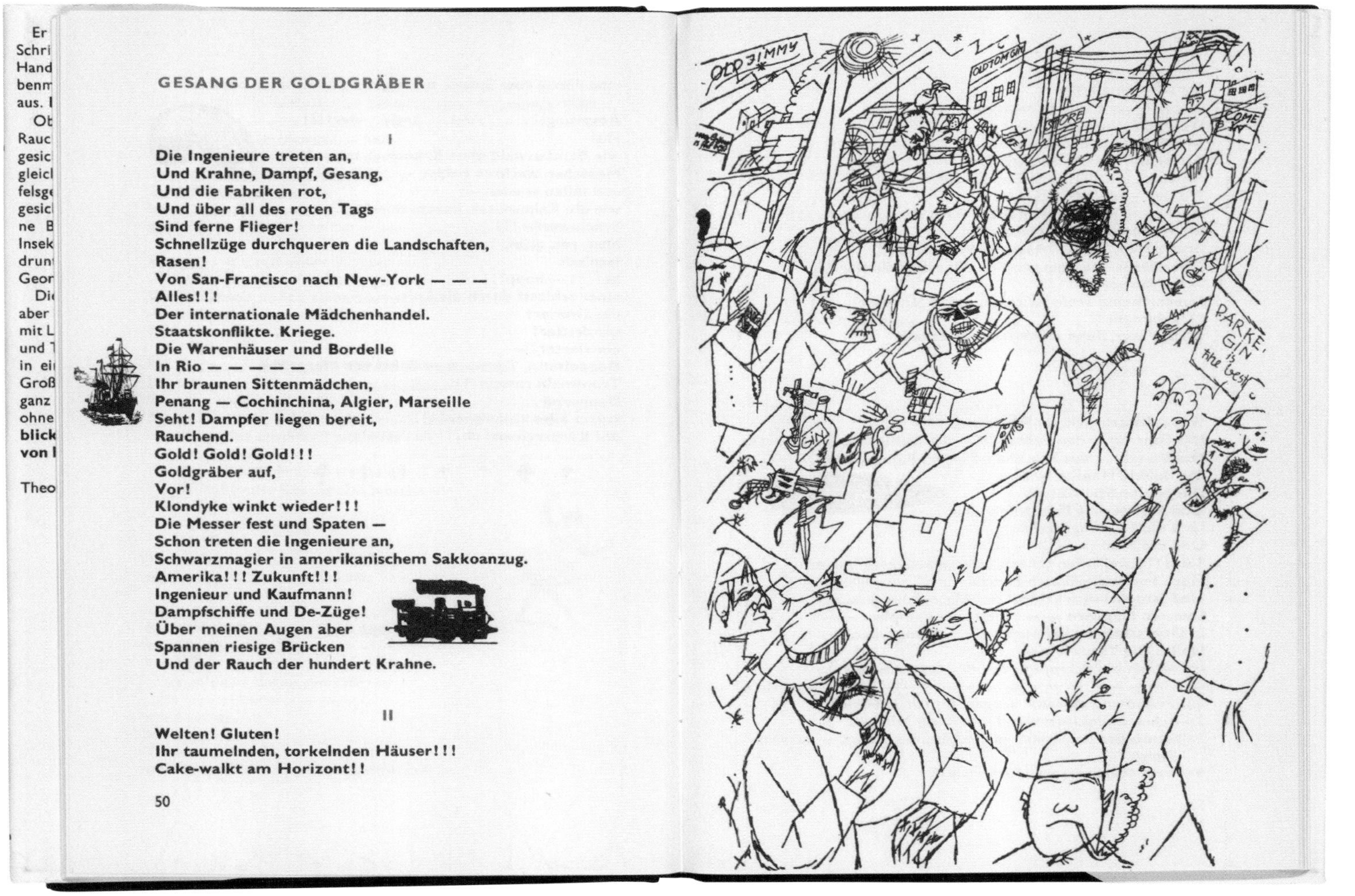
GESANG DER GOLDGRÄBER
I
Die Ingenieure treten an,
Und Krahne, Dampf, Gesang,
Und die Fabriken rot,
Und über all des roten Tags
Sind ferne Flieger!
Schnellzüge durchqueren die Landschaften,
Rasen!
Von San-Francisco nach New-York — — —
Alles!!!
Der internationale Mädchenhandel.
Staatskonflikte. Kriege.
Die Warenhäuser und Bordelle
In Rio — — — — —
Ihr braunen Sittenmädchen,
Penang — Cochinchina, Algier, Marseille
Seht! Dampfer liegen bereit,
Rauchend.
Gold! Gold! Gold!!!
Goldgräber auf,
Vor!
Klondyke winkt wieder!!!
Die Messer fest und Spaten —
Schon treten die Ingenieure an,
Schwarzmagier in amerikanischem Sakkoanzug.
Amerika!!! Zukunft!!!
Ingenieur und Kaufmann!
Dampfschiffe und De-Züge!
Über meinen Augen aber
Spannen riesige Brücken
Und der Rauch der hundert Krahne.
II
Welten! Gluten!
Ihr taumelnden, torkelnden Häuser!!!
Cake-walkt am Horizont!!
50
OLD JIMMY
COME IN
BARKE GIN is the best

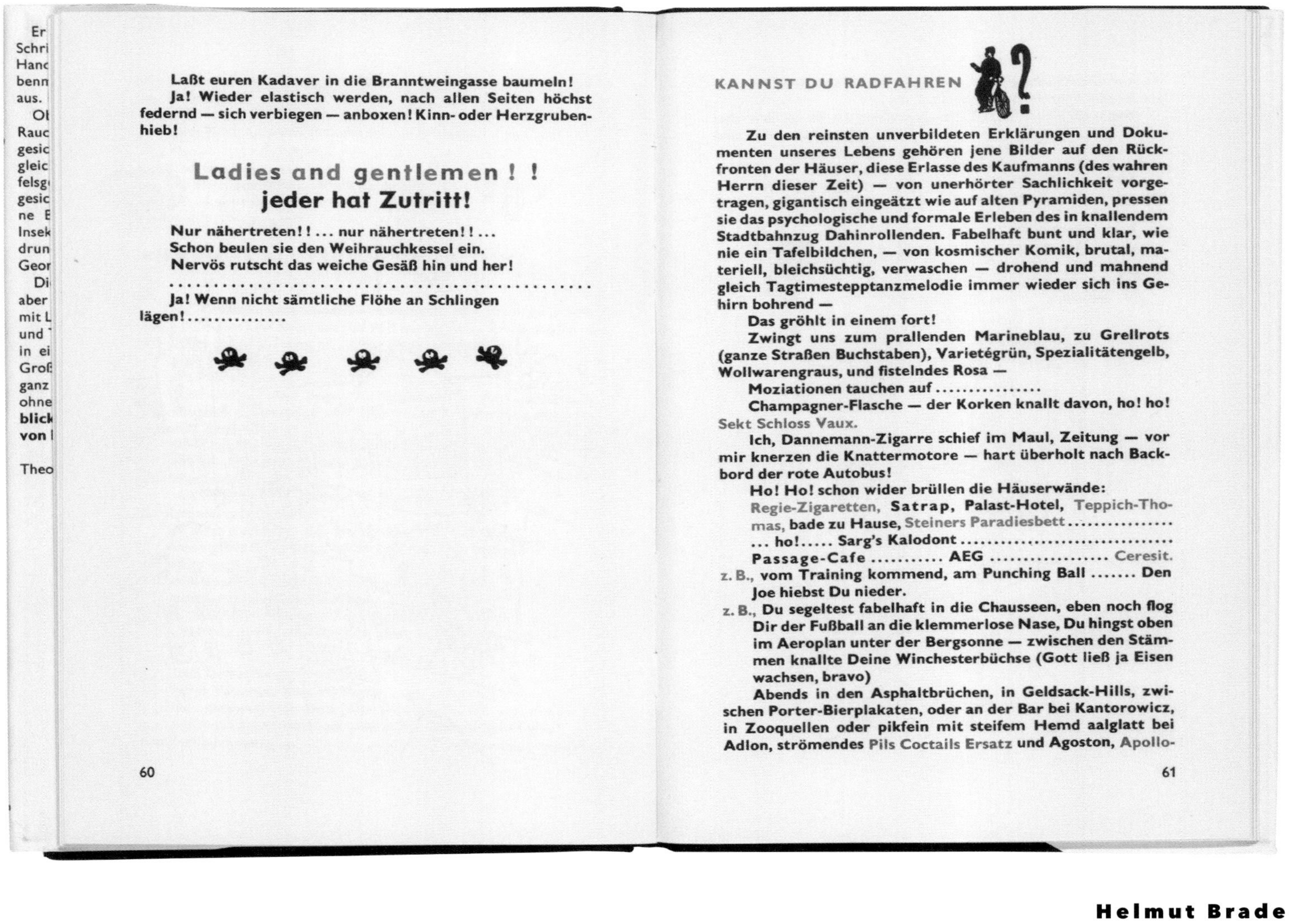
Laßt euren Kadaver in die Branntweingasse baumeln!
Ja! Wieder elastisch werden, nach allen Seiten höchst federnd — sich verbiegen — anboxen! Kinn- oder Herzgrubenhieb!
Ladies and gentlemen!!
jeder hat Zutritt!
Nur nähertreten!!... nur nähertreten!!...
Schon beulen sie den Weihrauchkessel ein.
Nervös rutscht das weiche Gesäß hin und her!
Ja! Wenn nicht sämtliche Flöhe an Schlingen lägen!...............
60
KANNST DU RADFAHREN ?
Zu den reinsten unverbildeten Erklärungen und Dokumenten unseres Lebens gehören jene Bilder auf den Rückfronten der Häuser, diese Erlasse des Kaufmanns (des wahren Herrn dieser Zeit) — von unerhörter Sachlichkeit vorgetragen, gigantisch eingeätzt wie auf alten Pyramiden, pressen sie das psychologische und formale Erleben des in knallendem Stadtbahnzug Dahinrollenden. Fabelhaft bunt und klar, wie nie ein Tafelbildchen, — von kosmischer Komik, brutal, materiell, bleichsüchtig, verwaschen — drohend und mahnend gleich Tagtimestepptanzmelodie immer wieder sich ins Gehirn bohrend —
Das gröhlt in einem fort!
Zwingt uns zum prallenden Marineblau, zu Grellrots (ganze Straßen Buchstaben), Varietégrün, Spezialitätengelb, Wollwarengraus, und fistelndes Rosa —
Moziationen tauchen auf ....
Champagner-Flasche — der Korken knallt davon, ho! ho! Sekt Schloss Vaux.
Ich, Dannemann-Zigarre schief im Maul, Zeitung — vor mir knerzen die Knattermotore — hart überholt nach Backbord der rote Autobus!
Ho! Ho! schon wider brüllen die Häuserwände:
Regie-Zigaretten, Satrap, Palast-Hotel, Teppich-Thomas, bade zu Hause, Steiners Paradiesbett ....
... ho!..... Sarg's Kalodont ....
Passage-Cafe .... AEG .... Ceresit.
z. B., vom Training kommend, am Punching Ball .... Den Joe hiebst Du nieder.
z. B., Du segeltest fabelhaft in die Chausseen, eben noch flog Dir der Fußball an die klemmerlose Nase, Du hingst oben im Aeroplan unter der Bergsonne — zwischen den Stämmen knallte Deine Winchesterbüchse (Gott ließ ja Eisen wachsen, bravo)
Abends in den Asphaltbrüchen, in Geldsack-Hills, zwischen Porter-Bierplakaten, oder an der Bar bei Kantorowicz, in Zooquellen oder pikfein mit steifem Hemd aalglatt bei Adlon, strömendes Pils Coctails Ersatz und Agoston, Apollo-
61

Postmodernism

Detail of ***Those Lips, Those Eyes*, designed by Paula Scher** **(see p. 426)**

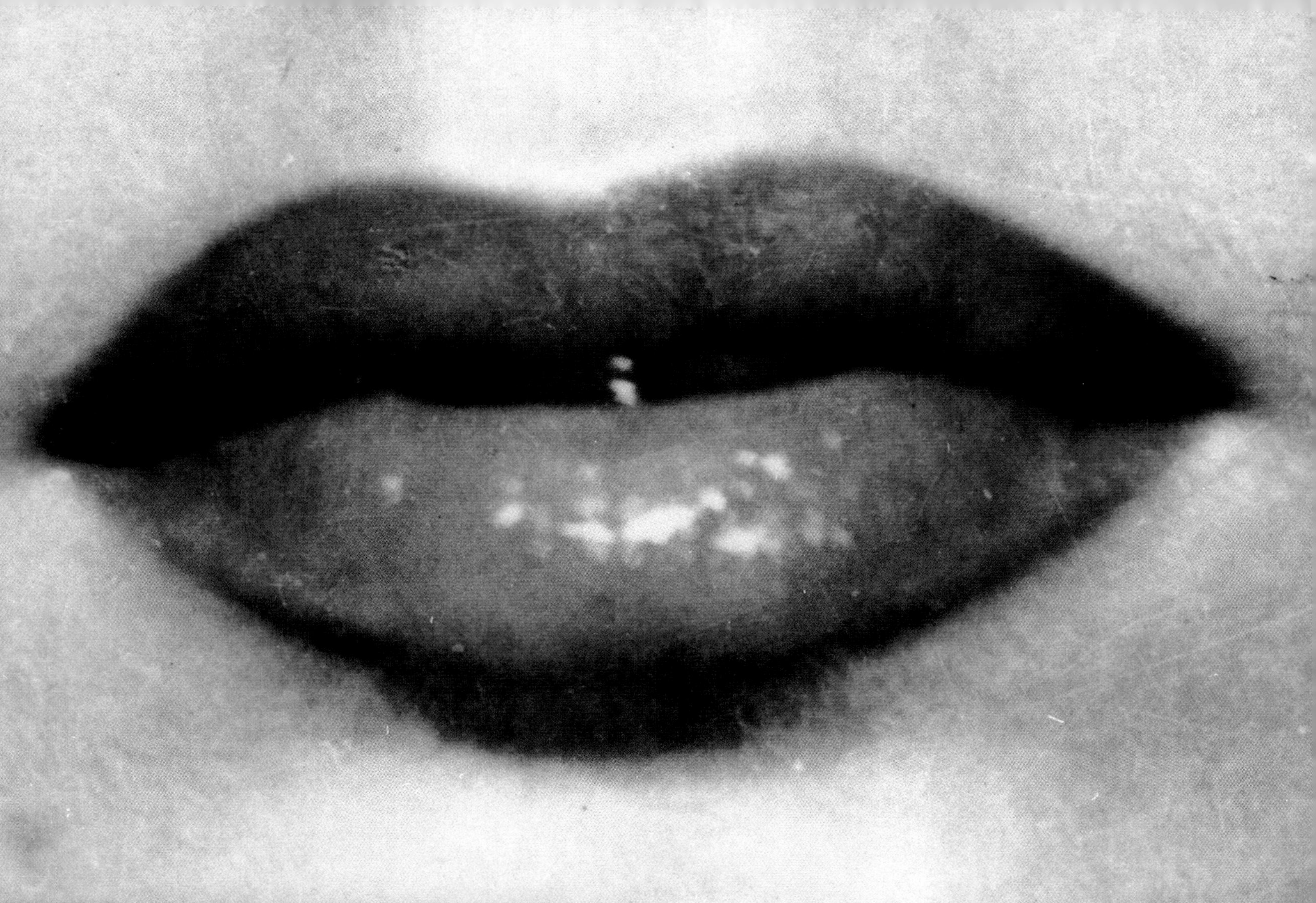

Postmodernism **In the late 1970s, designers and architects reacted strongly against the modernism that was internationally dominant, with its rational approach and highbrow minimalism. This diverse and wide-ranging movement, dubbed postmodernism, flourished into the 1990s. The modernist motto 'Less is more' was satirized as 'Less is a bore' and a new appreciation of pop culture emerged. Some graphic designers were inspired by anonymous, often older commercial printed matter, such as advertisements and machine parts catalogues, as well as street graphics. The clarity that modernists strove to achieve had to make way for layering. Rules were made to be broken.**

Postmodernism found particular expression in album covers, posters and magazines. Frequently reproduced examples include Paula Scher's 1984 Swatch poster and Anton Beeke's 1995 Holland Festival poster. Both are pastiches of the work of famous avant-garde artists: inside jokes for the graphic world. The American magazine *Emigre*, later distributed internationally, began using the new Apple Macintosh for experimental digital typography in 1984. A less ephemeral expression of postmodernism is *Nederlandse postzegels 87+88* (1988). This commission from a government corporation, which eventually funded the very expensive production, gave the book designer Irma Boom the utmost freedom. The rules of legibility are provocatively broken: this aesthetic catalogue verges on autonomous design that subordinates function. Boom – like Bruce Mau and others in the same generation – prefers to be involved in a project at an early stage and to function as an editor.

The introduction of software such as Fontographer in the mid-eighties greatly expanded the creative opportunities for type designers. Max Kisman made fun of the

typographic tradition with his cut-and-paste font Fudoni (1991) for FontShop, a collage made up of Futura and Bodoni. Barry Deck took inspiration from stencil lettering at a laundromat for his 'imperfect' Template Gothic (1990), issued by Emigre Fonts, which proved a commercial success, becoming the postmodernist typeface of the nineties.

Modernism continued to exist along side postmodernism and retained its validity for quite a few designers of books and catalogues who began work in the eighties or later, including the now defunct London studio 8vo – with Wim Crouwel producing major commissions – and the Amsterdam studios Joost Grootens and Experimental Jetset. Grootens, specializing in atlases, deeply believes in 'the absence of the designer'. His 2010 designer's monograph ends on a completely modern note with the credo: 'Whatever role he chooses, the designer above all needs to have clarity about the material he works with and subsequently provide clarity in his translation of data into representation.' ML

1988 **Irma Boom** Paul Hefting, *Nederlandse postzegels 87+88*. The Hague: Staatsbedrijf der PTT/SDU uitgeverij, 1988. 2 volumes. 25 cm. Designer: Irma Boom (SDU Ontwerpgroep). Photolithographer: Van der Poort, Pijnacker. Typesetter: IGS, Rotterdam. Printer: SDU drukkerij, The Hague. Bookbinder: Wöhrmann, Zutphen. With the folds at the fore-edge.

Nederlandse postzegels 87+88 could be viewed as the debut of designer Irma Boom (b. 1960). It is a two-volume publication in a series of books on stamp design, backgrounds and philatelic issue data. The publication was produced by the SDU, where Boom was employed as a designer at the time. In many ways these volumes constituted a break from more usual design styles. The photo typefaces used are all sans serifs: Frutiger, Univers and Gill Sans. The italic forms of these faces are not used: accentuation is done by either using another body size or by underlining. The layout is characterized by a varying type area, text and illustrations bleeding over the edges of the pages and continuing on the next page, paragraphs indicated by setting the first seven letters in a bigger body size, and the absence of hyphens. A Japanese-style binding has been used, and the translucency of the thin offset paper has been taken advantage of by printing mirror images of illustrations on the versos. The subject of Paul Hefting's text is inspiration, so Boom added a wealth of illustrations that could be seen, she believed, as sources of inspiration for the stamp designers. This visual presentation in particular shows that the designer in fact played the role of co-editor or even co-author.

Although the readability of these books was criticized, they turned out to be the first of an impressive sequence of book designs by Irma Boom. FAJ

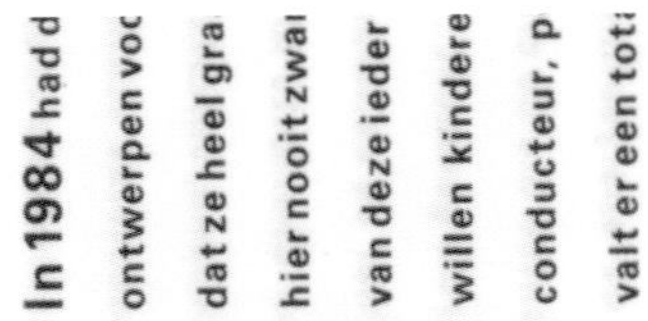

Univers (1957), designed by Adrian Frutiger (b. 1928), is still a very successful typeface internationally. This extensive family was developed as a photosetting and a metal foundry version by Deberny & Peignot in Paris. Soon, Univers was adapted for Monotype composing machines (hot metal and film).

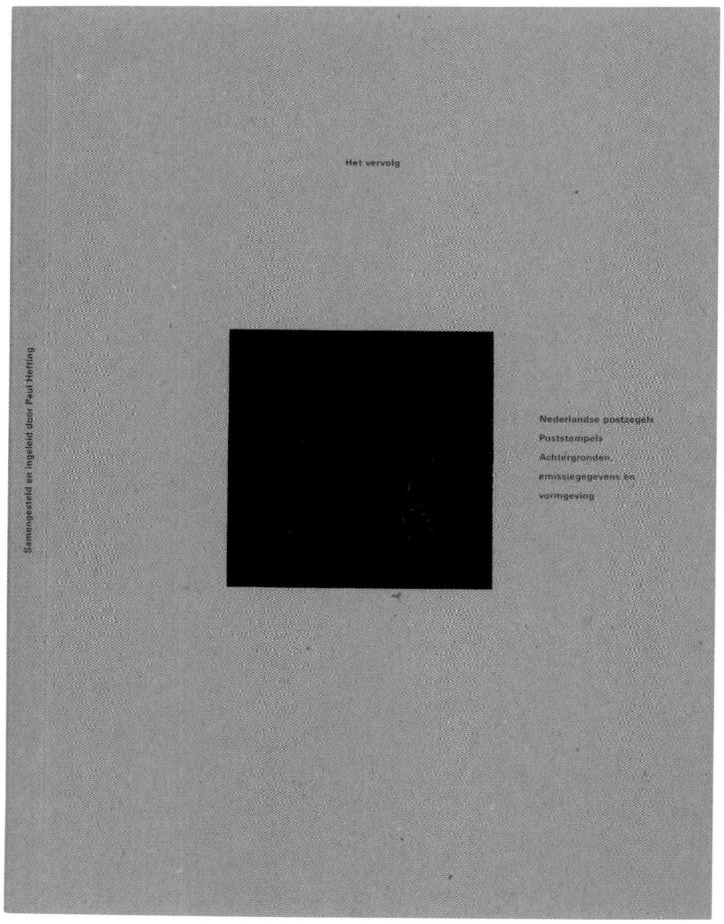

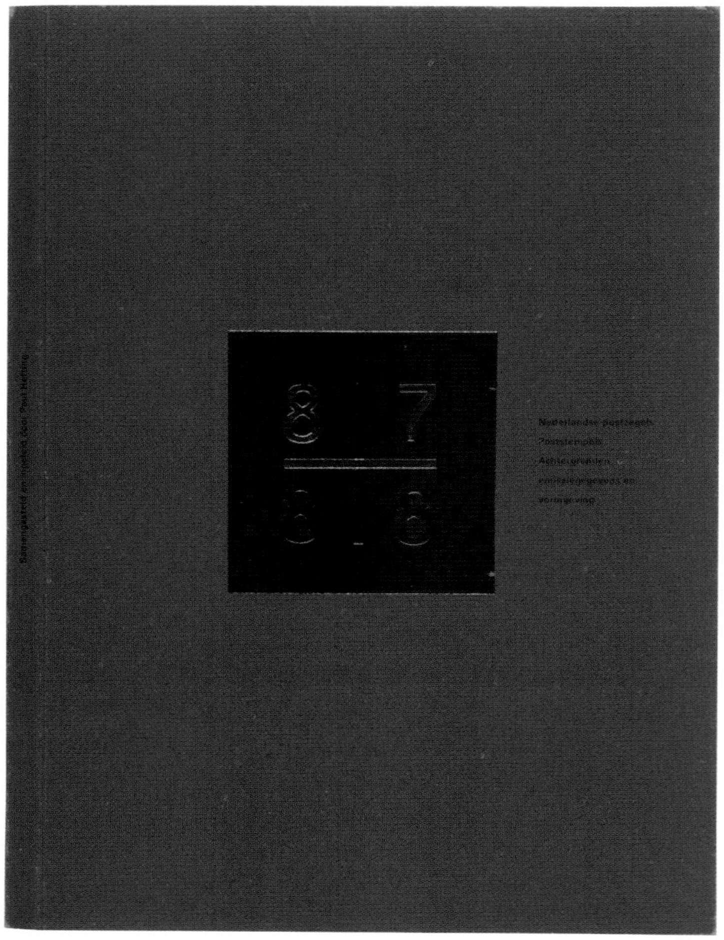

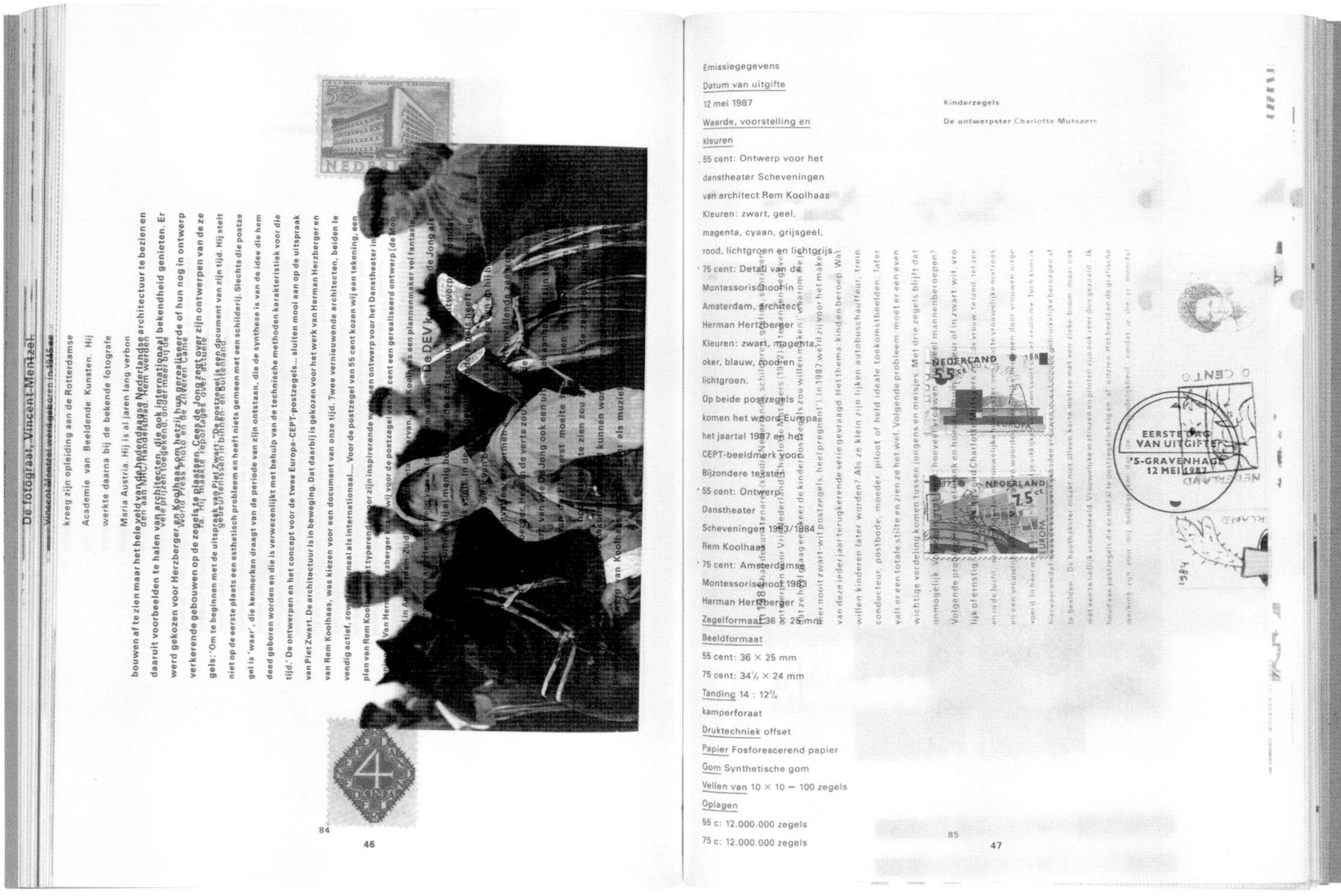
Emissiegegevens
Datum van uitgifte
12 mei 1987
Waarde, voorstelling en kleuren
55 cent: Ontwerp voor het danstheater Scheveningen van architect Rem Koolhaas
Kleuren: zwart, geel, magenta, cyaan, grijsgeel, rood, lichtgroen en lichtgrijs.
75 cent: Detail van de Montessorischool in Amsterdam, architect Herman Hertzberger
Kleuren: zwart, magenta, oker, blauw, rood en lichtgroen.
Op beide postzegels komen het woord Europa, het jaartal 1987 en het CEPT-beeldmerk voor.
Bijzondere teksten
55 cent: Ontwerp Danstheater Scheveningen 1983/1984 Rem Koolhaas
75 cent: Amsterdamse Montessorischool 1983 Herman Hertzberger
Zegelformaat 36 × 25 mm
Beeldformaat
55 cent: 36 × 25 mm
75 cent: 34½ × 24 mm
Tanding 14 : 12¾
kamperforaat
Druktechniek offset
Papier Fosforescerend papier
Gom Synthetische gom
Vellen van 10 × 10 — 100 zegels
Oplagen
55 c: 12.000.000 zegels
75 c: 12.000.000 zegels
Kinderzegels
De ontwerpster Charlotte Mutsaers
De fotograaf, Vincent Mentzel
EERSTE DAG VAN UITGIFTE 'S-GRAVENHAGE 12 MEI 1987
84
46
85
47

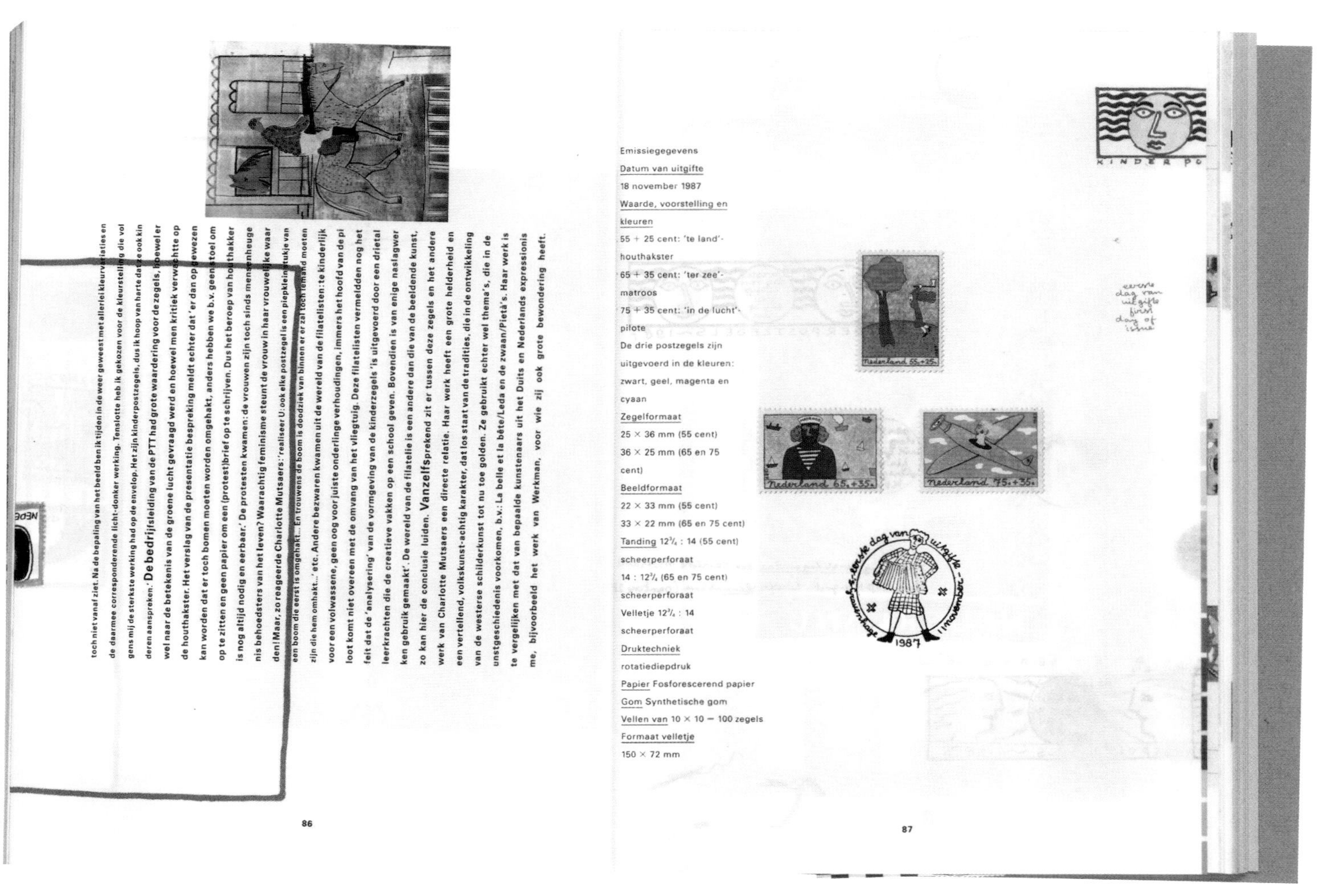
Emissiegegevens
Datum van uitgifte
18 november 1987
Waarde, voorstelling en kleuren
55 + 25 cent: 'te land'- houthakster
65 + 35 cent: 'ter zee'- matroos
75 + 35 cent: 'in de lucht'- pilote
De drie postzegels zijn uitgevoerd in de kleuren: zwart, geel, magenta en cyaan
Zegelformaat
25 × 36 mm (55 cent)
36 × 25 mm (65 en 75 cent)
Beeldformaat
22 × 33 mm (55 cent)
33 × 22 mm (65 en 75 cent)
Tanding 12¾ : 14 (55 cent) scheerperforaat
14 : 12¾ (65 en 75 cent) scheerperforaat
Velletje 12¾ : 14 scheerperforaat
Druktechniek rotatiediepdruk
Papier Fosforescerend papier
Gom Synthetische gom
Vellen van 10 × 10 — 100 zegels
Formaat velletje
150 × 72 mm
86
87

eerste dag van uitgifte first day of issue
STZEGELS 1987
nederland 75c+35c
1987
6 x 17
2 1/2 x 8 1/2
5 x 17
75c 55
NEDERLAND
NEDERLAND
NEDERLAND
NEDERLAND
NEDERLAND 50c
88

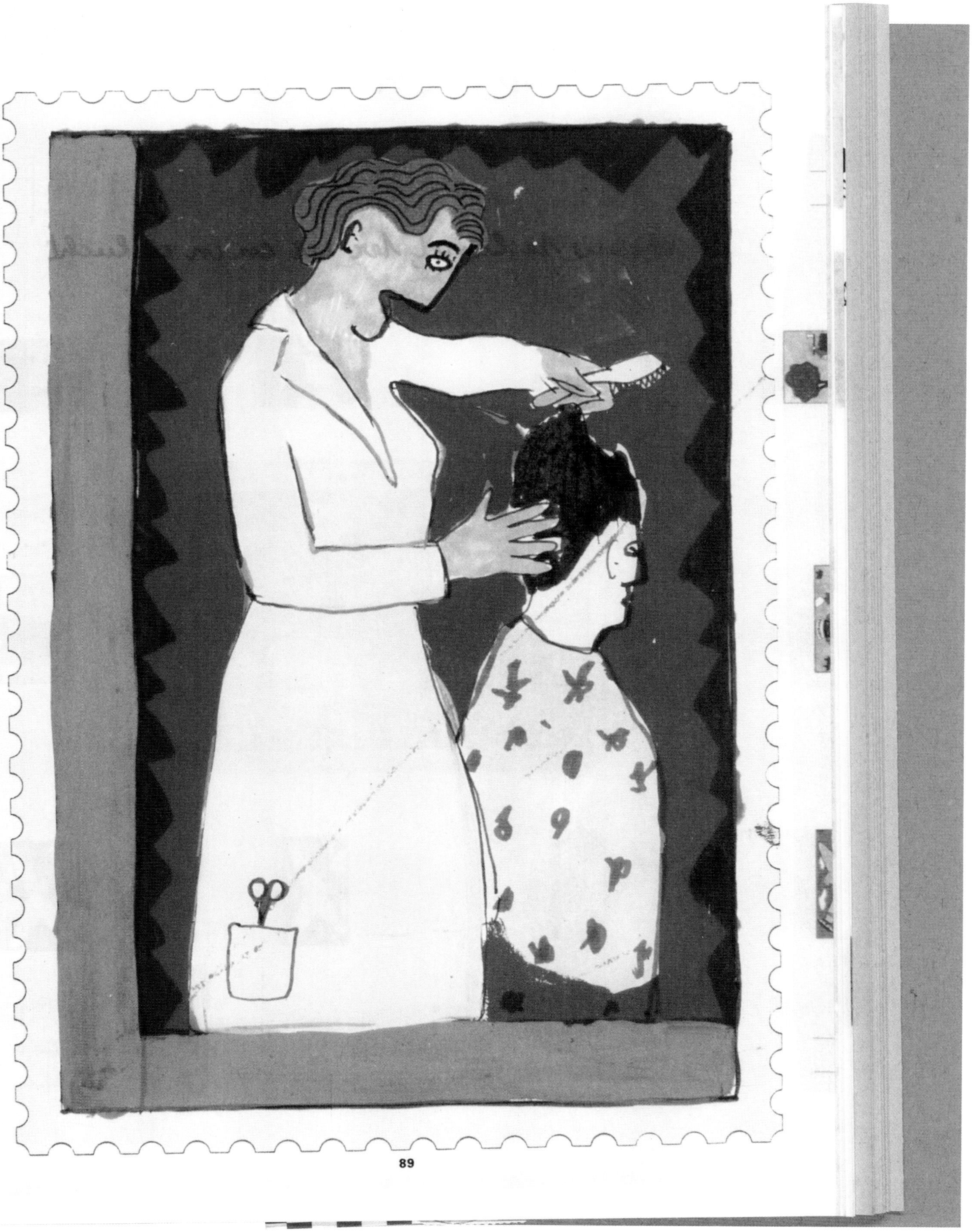

1992 **Paula Scher** Edward Z. Epstein & Lou Valentino, *Those Lips, Those Eyes: A Celebration of Classic Hollywood Sensuality*. New York: Carol Publishing Group, 1992. 96 pp. 31 cm. Designers: Paula Scher, David Matt (Pentagram, NY).

Paula Scher (b. 1948) lives and works in New York, the city she calls her great source of inspiration. In 1991 she became a partner in Pentagram, a multidisciplinary design bureau that carries out a wide variety of commissions: from architecture and product design to visual identity and book design. Their clients have included United Airlines, Bausch + Lomb and Penguin Books. At Pentagram, Scher always works in a small team, so that even as a partner in the firm she remains active in the actual design process.

Her 1984 poster for the Swiss company Swatch made her the talk of the design world. Scher had already experimented with historical design styles earlier, but in her Swatch poster she 'reused' a travel poster by Swiss designer Herbert Matter, a design icon from the thirties. Insiders certainly didn't miss the reference; this sort of appropriation was quite common among postmodernists. But much to Scher's surprise, it set off a debate among colleagues: should it be considered parody or plagiarism? Since then, her Swatch poster has been given a permanent place in histories of graphic design.

Those Lips, Those Eyes must have been one of the first commissions that Scher took on at Pentagram. The book, with no text except for the introduction, is a collection of studio photos of Hollywood stars such as Ava Gardner, Rita Hayworth and Bette Davis. Scher took the title literally, with aesthetic blowups and compositions of eyes and mouths, larger than life. The endpapers may allude to Jan Tschichold's *Der Berufsphotograph* (1938), an exhibition poster that features a portrait of a woman in the form of a film negative. ML

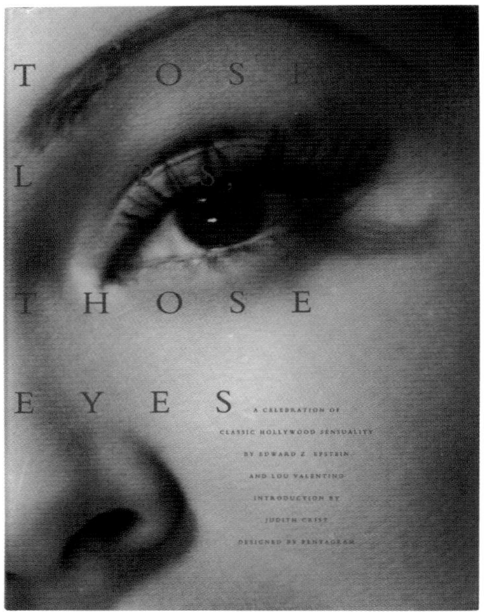

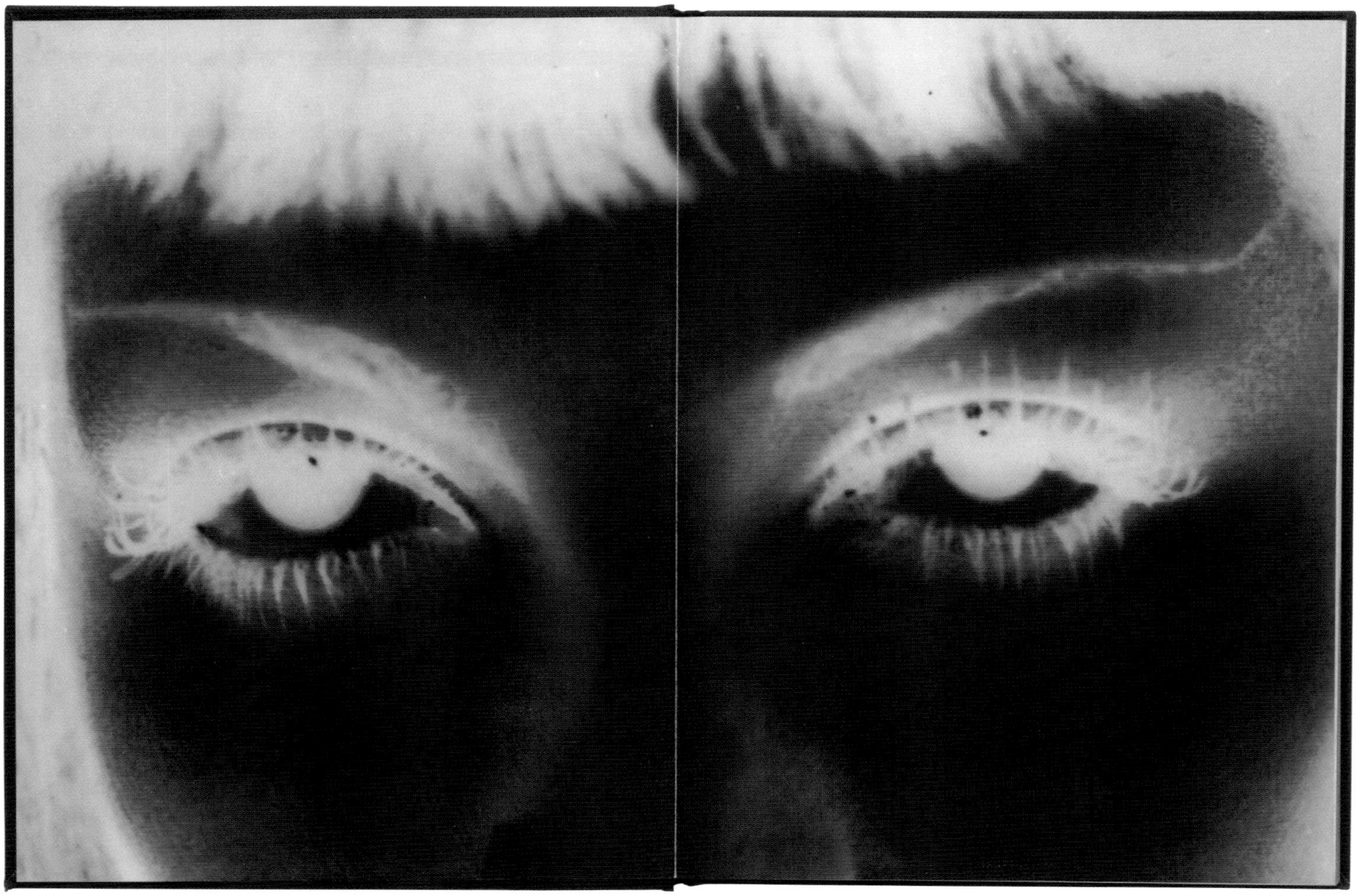

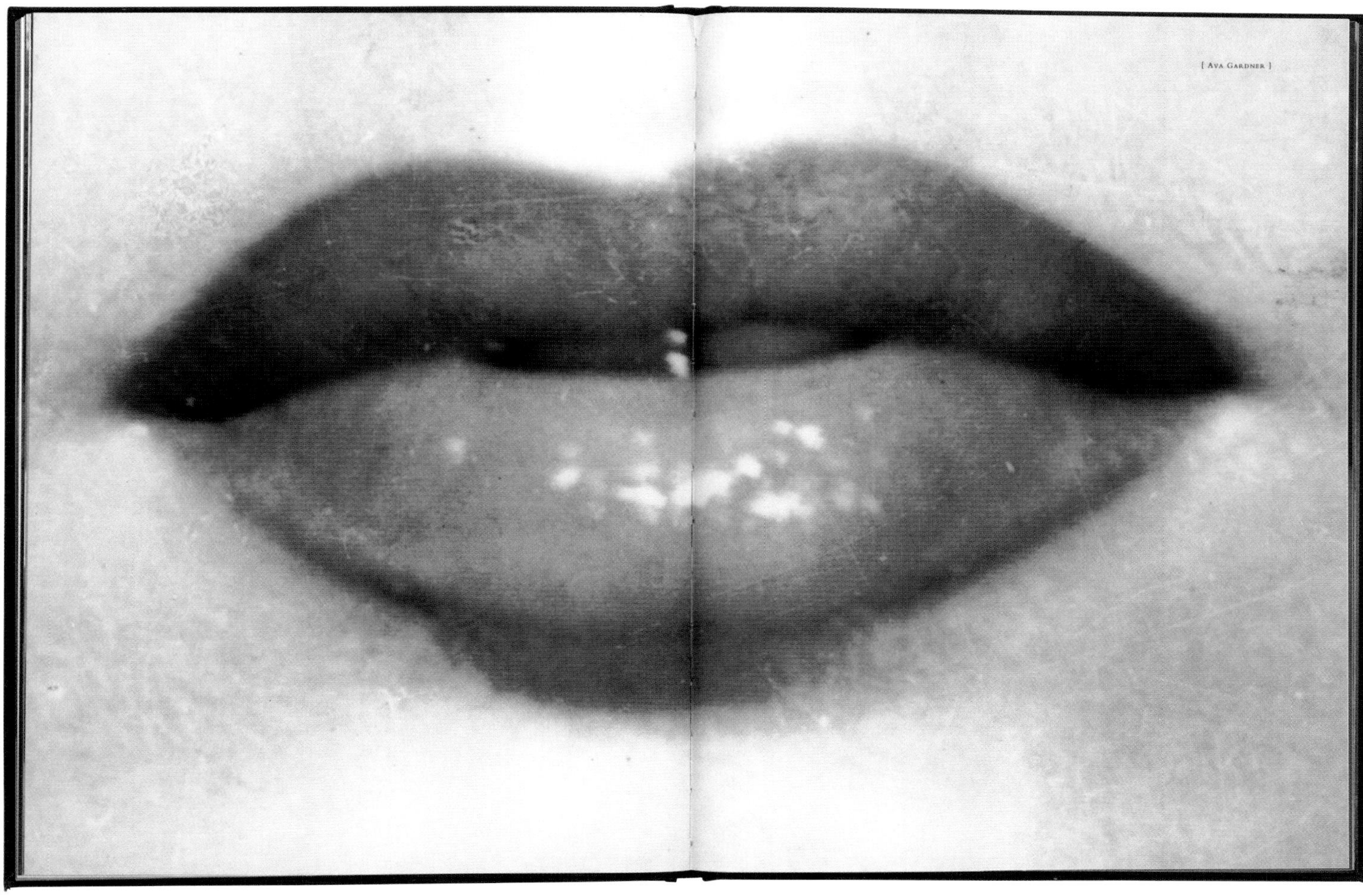

Introduction by Judith Crist

Those lips, those eyes! They do indeed hypnotize us – as do the brow, the nose, the chin, the cheekbones, the tip of the ear, the cleft, the hint of dimple. After all, some three hundred years ago Alexander Pope pointed out, "Tis not a lip or eye we beauty call / But the joint force and full result of all."

But oh, those lips and eyes and the forceful results therefrom! At this writing, from the cluttered bulletin board above my desk, on greeting cards and announcements, a pensive Charles Boyer casts me a heavy-lidded shiny-lipped come-hither; a melancholy lush-mouthed Greta Garbo looks wistfully aside; a near-smiling Cary Grant ducks his head slightly for a flirt-look; Jean Harlow offers a tight-lipped tough-as-nails stare; and Marlene Dietrich presents a pouting kiss-me-you-fool profile above a film preservation group's ominous statistic: "Of the 21,000 films made in America before 1951, only half survive."

But, fortunately, photographs do survive, and they preserve for us the stuff this century's cinematic dreams were made on. The photos that Edward Z. Epstein and Lou Valentino offer us in this book are not stills from motion pictures. They are the carefully composed, meticulously posed, stylishly lit and beautifully dressed – or half-dressed – Hollywood studio portraits intended strictly for the big sell: publicity to promote the stars' sex appeal. Simply put: love for sale in fulfillment of dreams and desires – and millions of moviegoers bought it. (And, for ultimate irony, so did art collectors, for many of these exquisite examples of commercial contrivance – advertising art from the twenties through the early sixties – have become works of art in themselves.)

Hollywood's stars were sold – and bought – as sheiks and Greek gods and he-men and dreamboats, as America's sweethearts, as sweater, sarong, and oomph girls, love goddesses, sex kittens, vamps (as in "vampires"), as The Face, The Body, The Look. The girl or boy next door? We should be so lucky!

They were sold to tantalize and entrap the dreamers by offering, in varying degrees, the grace, the loveliness, the sensuality, the voluptuousness, the bewitchment, the suggestiveness, the radiance, the licentiousness, the dazzlement, the hint of danger, the glimmer of mystery, even the flicker of intelligence, and above all, the enticing eye and the lickerish lips of our fantasy lovers.

But it's far more than the eyes mythologized as the windows of the soul or Tracy Lord's "withering glance of the goddess," more than the "eternity" Shakespeare saw in lovers' "lips and eyes" or e. e. cummings's "profound and fragile lips," more even than the totality summed up by Philip Marlowe's "the kind of look I could feel in my hip pocket." And it's more than a love affair between camera and subject. "The camera might love Hollywood's darlings," Dorothy Parker once noted, "but no camera will ever love any of them as much as they love themselves." And perhaps that's the secret of it all.

"We didn't need dialogue," Norma Desmond said. "We had *faces*." And more. And herewith the proof thereof.

[Claudette Colbert]

[Ava Gardner]

1995 **Bruce Mau** Rem Koolhaas & Bruce Mau, *Small, Medium, Large, Extra-Large: Office for Metropolitan Architecture*; ed. Jennifer Sigler. Rotterdam: 010 Publishers, 1995. xxxi, 1344 pp. 24 cm. Cover and spine title: *S,M,L,XL*. Designers: Bruce Mau, Kevin Sugden (Bruce Mau Design Inc.). Photographer: Hans Werlemann. Printed and bound in Italy.

The appearance of the bulky *S,M,L,XL* (over 1,300 pages) by Rem Koolhaas and Bruce Mau was quite an event. Of course Koolhaas already enjoyed cult status in architectural circles, but even in the long tradition of the architecture book, a book of this size was remarkable. As the title suggests, the projects are not presented in chronological order, but according to size: from small to large. This is a book made for browsing, rather than linear reading.

The attention of the design world was caught by the fact that the name of Bruce Mau (b. 1959) was on the cover, next to that of Koolhaas. The Canadian Mau wanted to do more than just look after the design of edited text and illustrations; instead, he wanted to work on projects in which he was involved from the start and could have serious input. Mau and Koolhaas worked in this way on *S,M,L,XL* for years, and Mau's studio almost went bankrupt over the project.

When *S,M,L,XL* appeared, Irma Boom had just put the finishing touches on an even bulkier book as designer and co-author: a corporate history of the multinational SHV. She had mixed feelings, standing in line in an Amsterdam bookshop to have her copy of *S,M,L,XL* signed when her own magnum opus of over 2,000 pages was about to be printed. *S,M,L,XL* seems to have initiated a trend of design monographs that are as thick as a fist. *Pentagram Book Five* (1999) runs to almost 500 pages, Mau's *Life Style* (2000) is over 600 pages, and Alan Fletcher's *The Art of Looking Sideways* (2001) is over 500 pages. ML

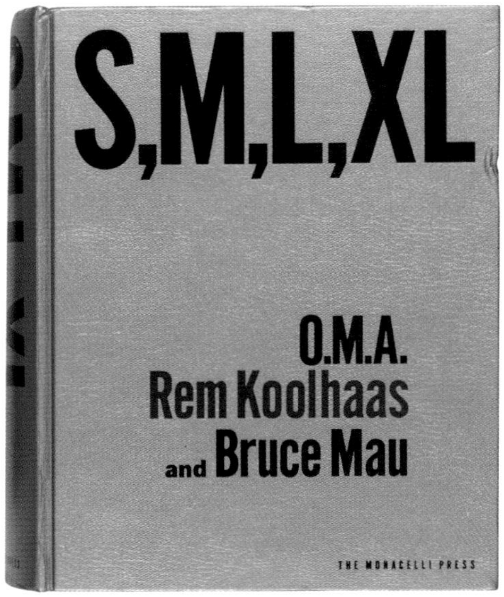

The authorship of Times New Roman (Monotype, 1932) is generally attributed to Stanley Morison (1889-1967), typographical advisor to Monotype, and Victor Lardent (1905-68), a draughtsman at *The Times* specialized in lettering who made the drawings. The typeface was developed for the newspaper, but in the pre-digital age it was often used for books.

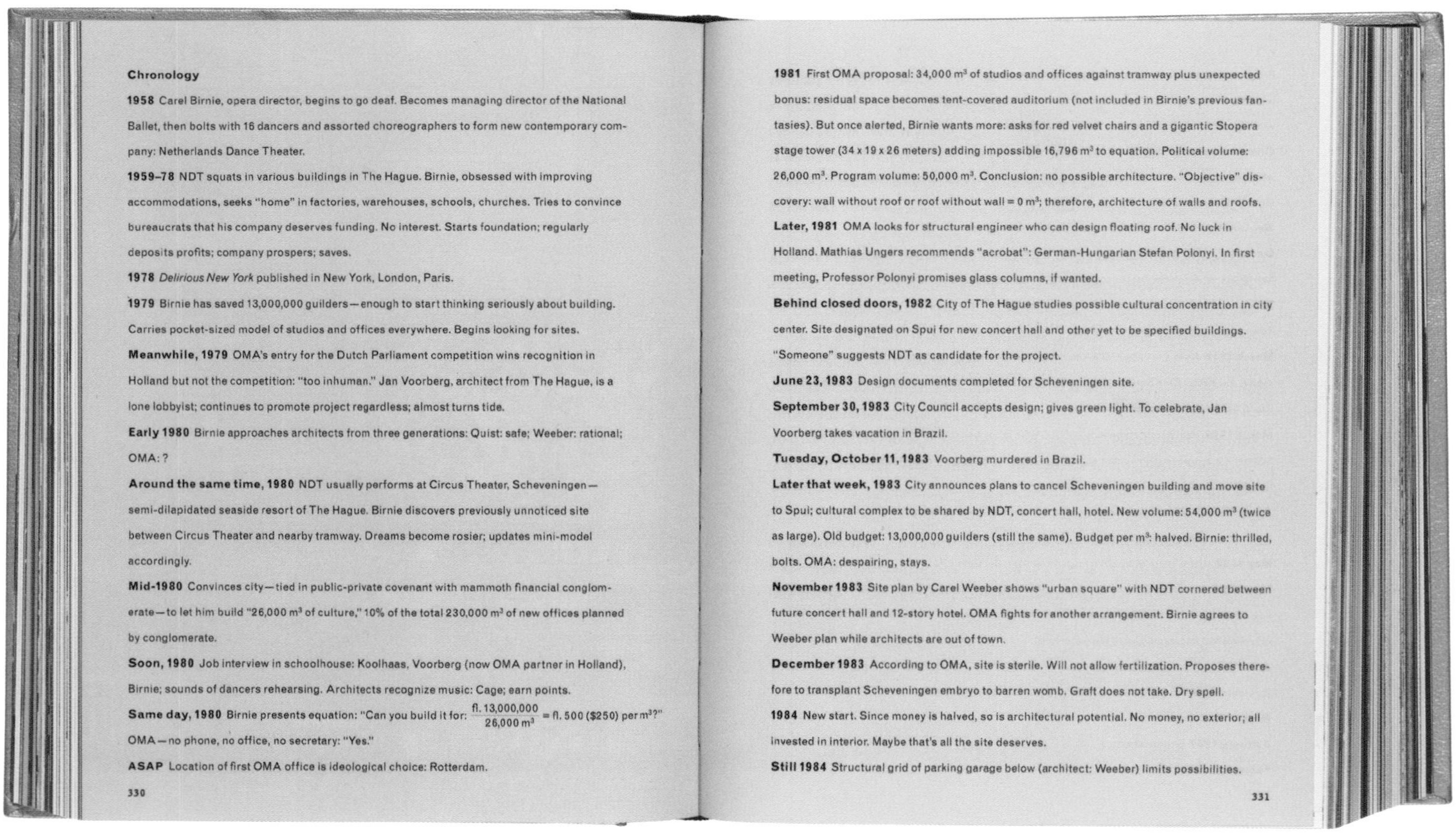

Chronology

1958 Carel Birnie, opera director, begins to go deaf. Becomes managing director of the National Ballet, then bolts with 16 dancers and assorted choreographers to form new contemporary company: Netherlands Dance Theater.

1959–78 NDT squats in various buildings in The Hague. Birnie, obsessed with improving accommodations, seeks "home" in factories, warehouses, schools, churches. Tries to convince bureaucrats that his company deserves funding. No interest. Starts foundation; regularly deposits profits; company prospers; saves.

1978 *Delirious New York* published in New York, London, Paris.

1979 Birnie has saved 13,000,000 guilders—enough to start thinking seriously about building. Carries pocket-sized model of studios and offices everywhere. Begins looking for sites.

Meanwhile, 1979 OMA's entry for the Dutch Parliament competition wins recognition in Holland but not the competition: "too inhuman." Jan Voorberg, architect from The Hague, is a lone lobbyist; continues to promote project regardless; almost turns tide.

Early 1980 Birnie approaches architects from three generations: Quist: safe; Weeber: rational; OMA: ?

Around the same time, 1980 NDT usually performs at Circus Theater, Scheveningen—semi-dilapidated seaside resort of The Hague. Birnie discovers previously unnoticed site between Circus Theater and nearby tramway. Dreams become rosier; updates mini-model accordingly.

Mid-1980 Convinces city—tied in public-private covenant with mammoth financial conglomerate—to let him build "26,000 m^3 of culture," 10% of the total 230,000 m^3 of new offices planned by conglomerate.

Soon, 1980 Job interview in schoolhouse: Koolhaas, Voorberg (now OMA partner in Holland), Birnie; sounds of dancers rehearsing. Architects recognize music: Cage; earn points.

Same day, 1980 Birnie presents equation: "Can you build it for: $\frac{\text{fl. } 13{,}000{,}000}{26{,}000 \text{ m}^3}$ = fl. 500 ($250) per m^3?" OMA—no phone, no office, no secretary: "Yes."

ASAP Location of first OMA office is ideological choice: Rotterdam.

330

1981 First OMA proposal: 34,000 m^3 of studios and offices against tramway plus unexpected bonus: residual space becomes tent-covered auditorium (not included in Birnie's previous fantasies). But once alerted, Birnie wants more: asks for red velvet chairs and a gigantic Stopera stage tower (34 x 19 x 26 meters) adding impossible 16,796 m^3 to equation. Political volume: 26,000 m^3. Program volume: 50,000 m^3. Conclusion: no possible architecture. "Objective" discovery: wall without roof or roof without wall = 0 m^3; therefore, architecture of walls and roofs.

Later, 1981 OMA looks for structural engineer who can design floating roof. No luck in Holland. Mathias Ungers recommends "acrobat": German-Hungarian Stefan Polonyi. In first meeting, Professor Polonyi promises glass columns, if wanted.

Behind closed doors, 1982 City of The Hague studies possible cultural concentration in city center. Site designated on Spui for new concert hall and other yet to be specified buildings. "Someone" suggests NDT as candidate for the project.

June 23, 1983 Design documents completed for Scheveningen site.

September 30, 1983 City Council accepts design; gives green light. To celebrate, Jan Voorberg takes vacation in Brazil.

Tuesday, October 11, 1983 Voorberg murdered in Brazil.

Later that week, 1983 City announces plans to cancel Scheveningen building and move site to Spui; cultural complex to be shared by NDT, concert hall, hotel. New volume: 54,000 m^3 (twice as large). Old budget: 13,000,000 guilders (still the same). Budget per m^3: halved. Birnie: thrilled, bolts. OMA: despairing, stays.

November 1983 Site plan by Carel Weeber shows "urban square" with NDT cornered between future concert hall and 12-story hotel. OMA fights for another arrangement. Birnie agrees to Weeber plan while architects are out of town.

December 1983 According to OMA, site is sterile. Will not allow fertilization. Proposes therefore to transplant Scheveningen embryo to barren womb. Graft does not take. Dry spell.

1984 New start. Since money is halved, so is architectural potential. No money, no exterior; all invested in interior. Maybe that's all the site deserves.

Still 1984 Structural grid of parking garage below (architect: Weeber) limits possibilities.

331

ıatches supply and demand. Orgasm instead of agony: there
ıe possibilities are announced in the cleanest typograph
ıographic. **17. End** **17.1** Imagine a Hollywood movie at
ıere in the Holy Land. Market scene: from left and right e

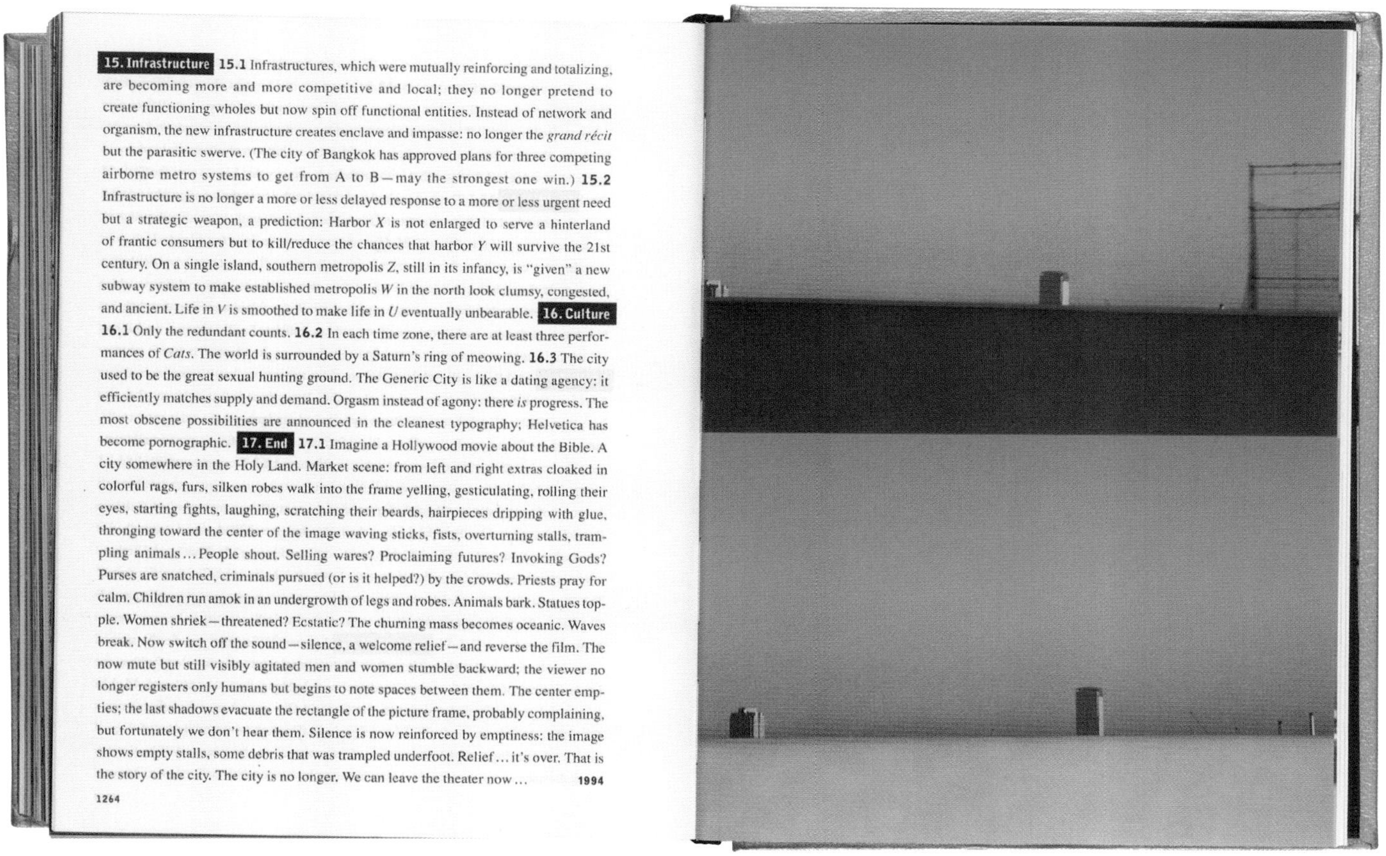

15. Infrastructure **15.1** Infrastructures, which were mutually reinforcing and totalizing, are becoming more and more competitive and local; they no longer pretend to create functioning wholes but now spin off functional entities. Instead of network and organism, the new infrastructure creates enclave and impasse: no longer the *grand récit* but the parasitic swerve. (The city of Bangkok has approved plans for three competing airborne metro systems to get from A to B—may the strongest one win.) **15.2** Infrastructure is no longer a more or less delayed response to a more or less urgent need but a strategic weapon, a prediction: Harbor *X* is not enlarged to serve a hinterland of frantic consumers but to kill/reduce the chances that harbor *Y* will survive the 21st century. On a single island, southern metropolis *Z*, still in its infancy, is "given" a new subway system to make established metropolis *W* in the north look clumsy, congested, and ancient. Life in *V* is smoothed to make life in *U* eventually unbearable. **16. Culture** **16.1** Only the redundant counts. **16.2** In each time zone, there are at least three performances of *Cats*. The world is surrounded by a Saturn's ring of meowing. **16.3** The city used to be the great sexual hunting ground. The Generic City is like a dating agency: it efficiently matches supply and demand. Orgasm instead of agony: there *is* progress. The most obscene possibilities are announced in the cleanest typography; Helvetica has become pornographic. **17. End** **17.1** Imagine a Hollywood movie about the Bible. A city somewhere in the Holy Land. Market scene: from left and right extras cloaked in colorful rags, furs, silken robes walk into the frame yelling, gesticulating, rolling their eyes, starting fights, laughing, scratching their beards, hairpieces dripping with glue, thronging toward the center of the image waving sticks, fists, overturning stalls, trampling animals… People shout. Selling wares? Proclaiming futures? Invoking Gods? Purses are snatched, criminals pursued (or is it helped?) by the crowds. Priests pray for calm. Children run amok in an undergrowth of legs and robes. Animals bark. Statues topple. Women shriek—threatened? Ecstatic? The churning mass becomes oceanic. Waves break. Now switch off the sound—silence, a welcome relief—and reverse the film. The now mute but still visibly agitated men and women stumble backward; the viewer no longer registers only humans but begins to note spaces between them. The center empties; the last shadows evacuate the rectangle of the picture frame, probably complaining, but fortunately we don't hear them. Silence is now reinforced by emptiness: the image shows empty stalls, some debris that was trampled underfoot. Relief… it's over. That is the story of the city. The city is no longer. We can leave the theater now… **1994**

1264

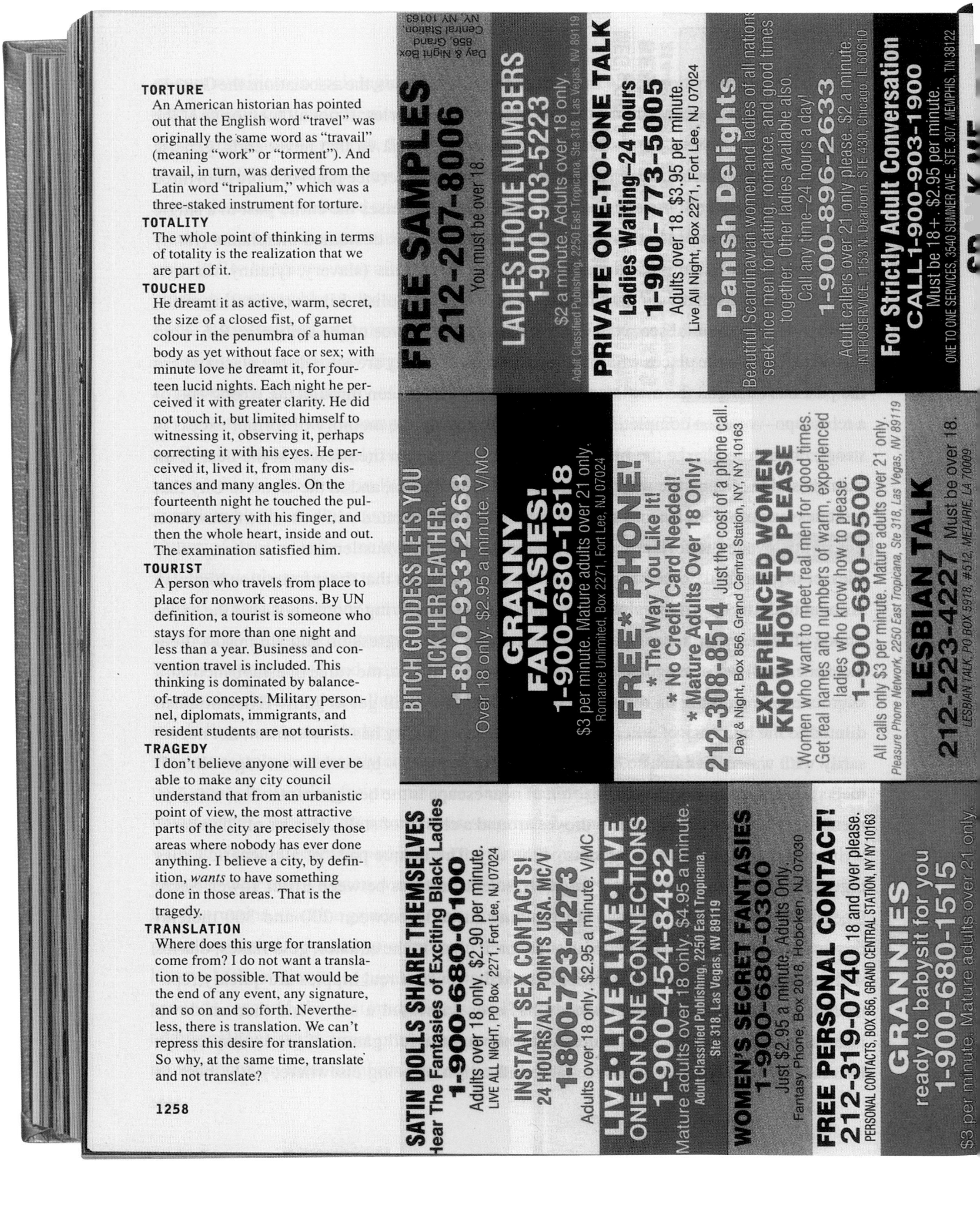

TORTURE
An American historian has pointed out that the English word "travel" was originally the same word as "travail" (meaning "work" or "torment"). And travail, in turn, was derived from the Latin word "tripalium," which was a three-staked instrument for torture.

TOTALITY
The whole point of thinking in terms of totality is the realization that we are part of it.

TOUCHED
He dreamt it as active, warm, secret, the size of a closed fist, of garnet colour in the penumbra of a human body as yet without face or sex; with minute love he dreamt it, for fourteen lucid nights. Each night he perceived it with greater clarity. He did not touch it, but limited himself to witnessing it, observing it, perhaps correcting it with his eyes. He perceived it, lived it, from many distances and many angles. On the fourteenth night he touched the pulmonary artery with his finger, and then the whole heart, inside and out. The examination satisfied him.

TOURIST
A person who travels from place to place for nonwork reasons. By UN definition, a tourist is someone who stays for more than one night and less than a year. Business and convention travel is included. This thinking is dominated by balance-of-trade concepts. Military personnel, diplomats, immigrants, and resident students are not tourists.

TRAGEDY
I don't believe anyone will ever be able to make any city council understand that from an urbanistic point of view, the most attractive parts of the city are precisely those areas where nobody has ever done anything. I believe a city, by definition, *wants* to have something done in those areas. That is the tragedy.

TRANSLATION
Where does this urge for translation come from? I do not want a translation to be possible. That would be the end of any event, any signature, and so on and so forth. Nevertheless, there is translation. We can't repress this desire for translation. So why, at the same time, translate and not translate?

1258

215-474-2885
Strictly adults over 21. No Credit Card needed.
LESBIAN TALK, PO BOX 5918, #512, METAIRIE, LA 70009
BORED HOUSEWIVES
Women who want to cheat on their husbands confess their fantasies
1-900-680-2100
$3 per minute. Mature adults over 21 only.
Fantasy Phone, Box 2018, Hoboken, NJ 07030
FREE FANTASIES
• NO CREDIT CARD NEEDED!
• THE ULTIMATE FREE SAMPLES!
213-346-1075
Adults over 18 only. Just the cost of a phone call.
Vortex Communications, 4540 S. Arville, Las Vegas, Nevada 89103
I Want To Make You Come
1-800-945-4569
$2.95 a minute. Adults 18+ only. MC/V
HOME PHONE NUMBERS
girls who want to connect with you!
1-900-884-5005
Over 18 only please. $2.90 a minute.
MIX 'N MATCH 2520 Welsh Road, STE 500, Philadelphia, PA 19152
Listen to me Scream in Ecstasy
I love to Masturbate while you're Listening
1-800-766-4688
Adults 18+ only. $2.95 a minute. MC/V
FULFILL YOUR FANTASIES
NO CREDIT CARD NEEDED!
215-474-2290 Adults over 18.
MIX 'N MATCH 2520 Welsh Road, STE 500, Philadelphia, PA 19152
Talk Live
THE ULTIMATE PHONE
1-900-740-6423
1-900-288-6399
$3.95 a minute. Adults over 18 only.
Live All Night, Box 2271, Fort Lee, NJ 07024
WOMEN'S FANTASIES!
1-900-680-1414 Adults over 18. $2.90 per minute.
Vortex Communications, 4540 S. Arville, Las Vegas, Nevada 89103
Ebony Angel Fantasies
1-900-903-1414
Over 18 only please. $2.90 per minute.
Vortex Communications, 4540 S. Arville, Las Vegas, Nevada 89103
Lusty Lesbos Lap It Up-1-800-374-9994
$2.95 a minute. 18+ only. V/MC
Meet Real Girls Who Want To Meet You
Listen to personal messages from real girls and then leave your private message! Meet someone special!
1-900-773-3233
Adults over 18. $2.90 per minute.
Live All Night, Box 2271, Fort Lee, NJ 07024
WOMEN'S PRIVATE CONFESSIONS
1-900-903-1717
All calls just $2.95 a minute. Adults only
Fantasy Phone, Box 2018, Hoboken, NJ 07030
FANTASIES
FREE SAMPLES
312-578-5400 Must be over 18.
No Credit Card -- No Premium Charges. Just a phone call away!
INTROSERVICE, 1153 N Dearborn, Suite 430, Chicago, IL 30310
FIRM FIT FEMALES GET SWEATY WITH YOU
1-900-407-5311 Must be over 18. $2.90 a minute.
DISCREET, P.O. Box 5918, #512, Metarie, LA 70009
TALK LIVE WITH A FANTASY CENTERFOLD GIRL
Samantha's girls 1-900-680-1300
Tracy's girls..................1-900-680-1400
Desiree's girls 1-900-680-1500
Suzette's girls...............1-900-680-1600
Strictly for adults over 18. Just $3.95 per minute.
Live All Night, Box 2271, Fort Lee, NJ 07024
1-800-866-8928
Over 18 only. $2.95 a minute. MC/V
PETITE LADIES
Call now for the real names and home phone numbers of petite ladies and beautiful women who want to meet you!
1-900-896-5581
$2.90 per minute. Adults over 18.
TALKNET 3501 Severn Ave., #3C-149, Metairie, LA 70002
Confidential Dating.
Married OK
1-900-407-5287
Just $2.90 per minute. 18/over.
THE BULLETIN BOARD, 3501 Severn Ave. #3C-149, Metairie, LA 70002
Quick Release - 1-800-944-2264
$2.95 a minute. Adults 18+ only. MC/V
New Fantasies
1-900-773-3588
$3.50 a minute. Adults 18 + only.
Fantasy Phone, Box 2018, Hoboken, NJ 07030
I LOVE TO TALK...
NO CREDIT CARD NEEDED
212-319-1190 Over 18 only.
Day & Night Box 856, Grand Central Station, NY, NY 10163
INTROSERVICE, 1153 N. Dearborn, STE 430, Chicago, IL 60610
WOMEN IN JAIL
Introducing America's most exciting dateline–for women who will soon be released from jail–and men who want to meet them!
1-900-884-3786
$2.90 a minute. Adults Only.
Talk live 1 on 1
The Ultimate Live Line!
1-900-454-3786
$4.50 a minute. Adults over 18 only.
Adult Classified Publishing, 2250 East Tropicana, Ste 318, Las Vegas, NV 89119

1997 **Rudy VanderLans & Zuzana Licko** *Hypnopædia: 140 Patterns: designed by Zuzana Licko*. Berkeley, CA: Emigre Fonts, 1997. 28 pp. 21 cm. Designers: Rudy VanderLans; Zuzana Licko (ornaments).

In 1984, the Apple Macintosh was introduced: an affordable personal computer that was a real hit among graphic designers. It did not take long for a good WYSIWYG layout program, Aldus PageMaker, to become available; a 300-dpi laser printer hit the market as well. Now designers didn't have to write layout instructions any more. They could produce text and image layouts themselves, and print their own proofs, while the printer would make the printing plates using their files. Desktop publishing (DTP) had been born.

In Berkeley, California, Rudy VanderLans (b. 1955) and Zuzana Licko (b. 1961) bought a Mac straight away in 1984, still with student discount. VanderLans, who had studied with Gerrit Noordzij in the Netherlands, started to use the Mac to produce layouts for *Emigre* magazine, while Licko used it to design bitmap fonts for the magazine. Because there was a demand for these fonts, Emigre became font publishers as a matter of course. Even though digital layout and font design were still in their early stages, they offered new visual possibilities. However, the 'less is more' modernist Massimo Vignelli (b. 1931) was shocked by these expressions of postmodernism; in an interview, he called Emigre a 'factory of garbage' (1991).

VanderLans was the designer, publisher, and editor of *Emigre* (1984–2005), which became a much-discussed design magazine. Its experimental style had many international followers, but the ornament specimen shown here, designed by VanderLans, with its centred title page in red and black, is virtually classic book typography. It presents Licko's ornament system Hypnopædia: patterns made by concentric rotation of a single letterform. The free brochure is simply stapled. ML

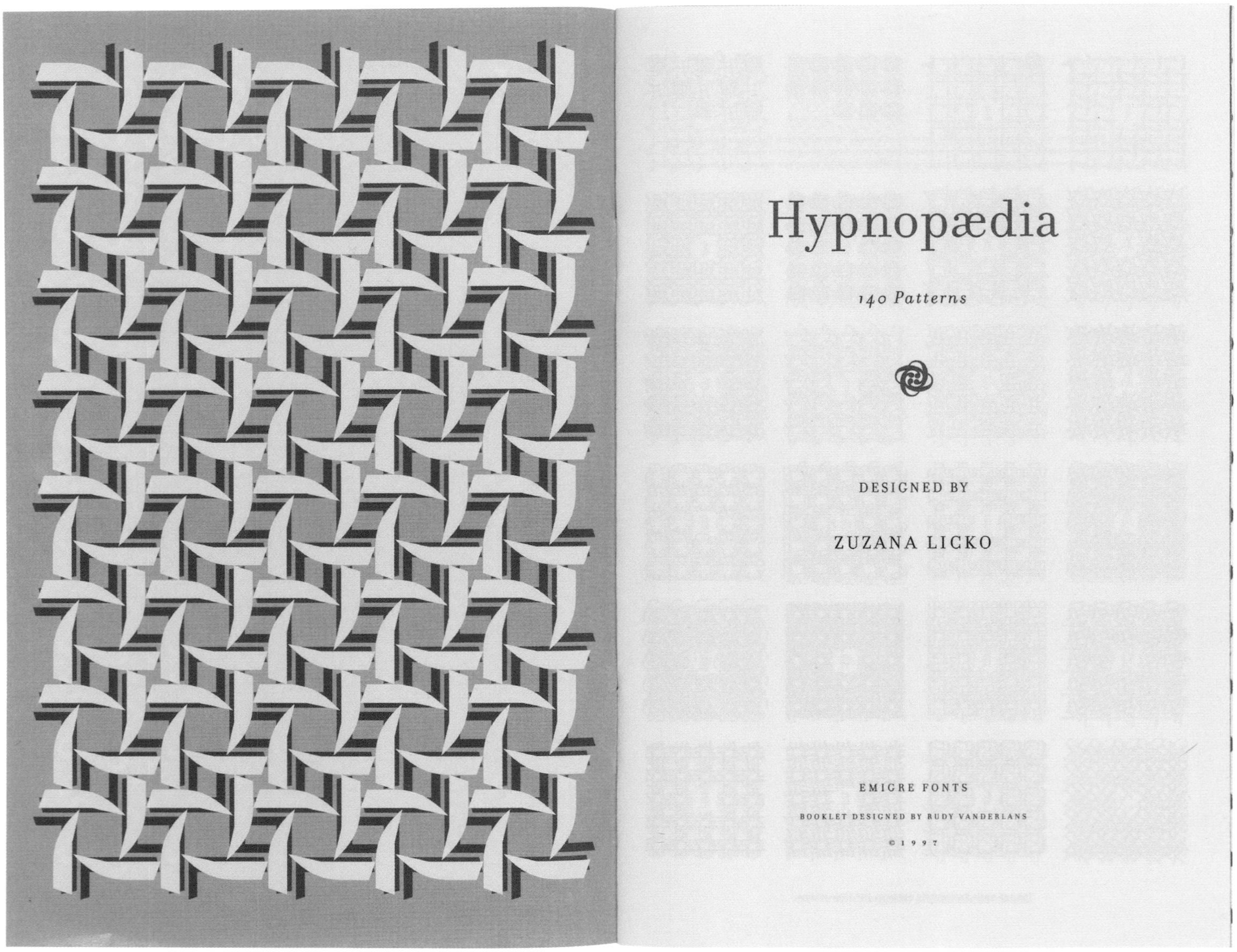

Hypnopædia
140 Patterns
DESIGNED BY
ZUZANA LICKO
EMIGRE FONTS
BOOKLET DESIGNED BY RUDY VANDERLANS
©1997

Filosofia (Emigre Fonts, 1996) was designed by Zuzana Licko and is a free interpretation of the work of Giambattista Bodoni (1740–1813). Licko started to design more classic text fonts in the nineties, because the magazine *Emigre* increasingly focused on text, and because the introduction of new technology enabled the production of fonts with this level of refinement.

Hypnopædia

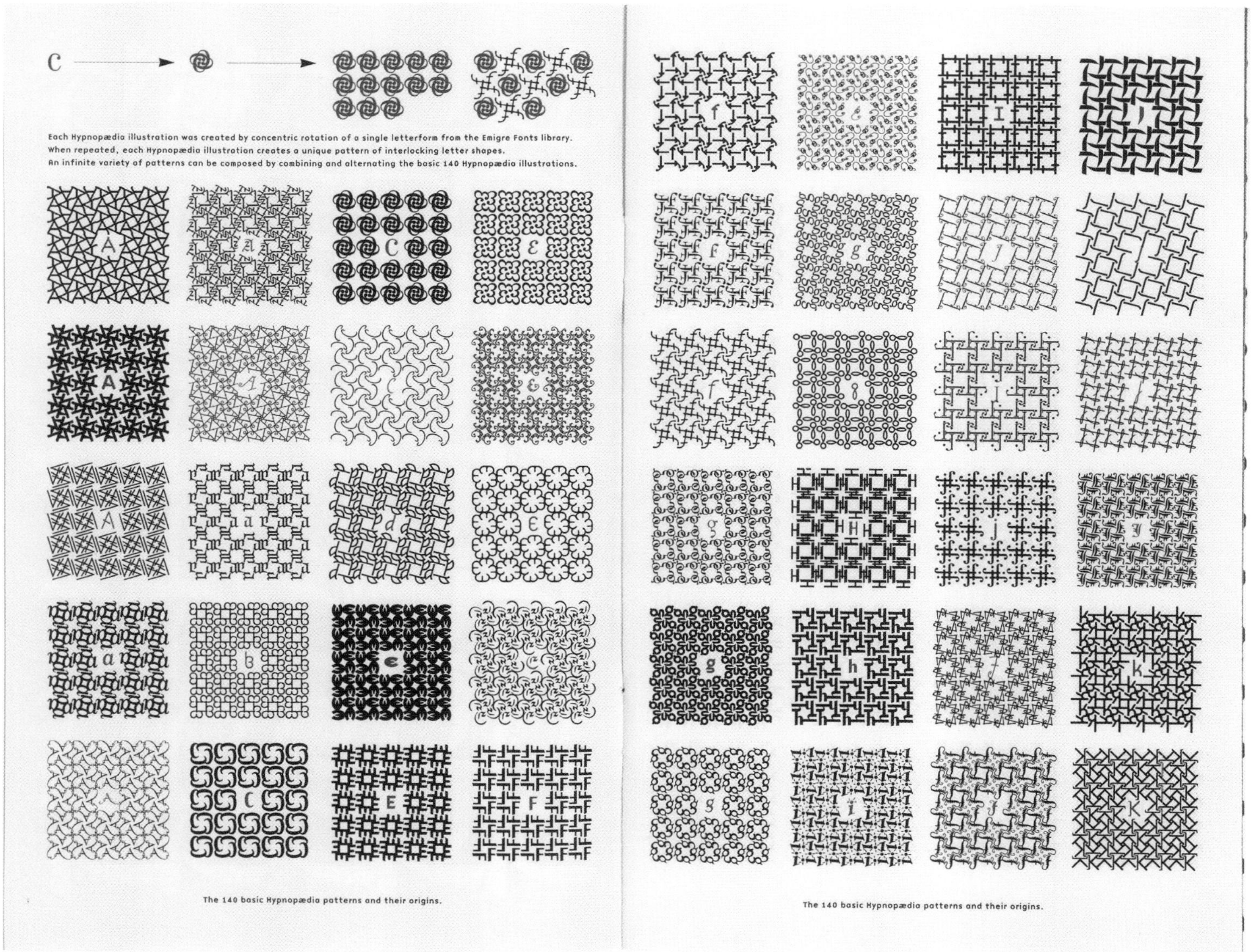

Each Hypnopædia illustration was created by concentric rotation of a single letterform from the Emigre Fonts library.
When repeated, each Hypnopædia illustration creates a unique pattern of interlocking letter shapes.
An infinite variety of patterns can be composed by combining and alternating the basic 140 Hypnopædia illustrations.
The 140 basic Hypnopædia patterns and their origins.
The 140 basic Hypnopædia patterns and their origins.

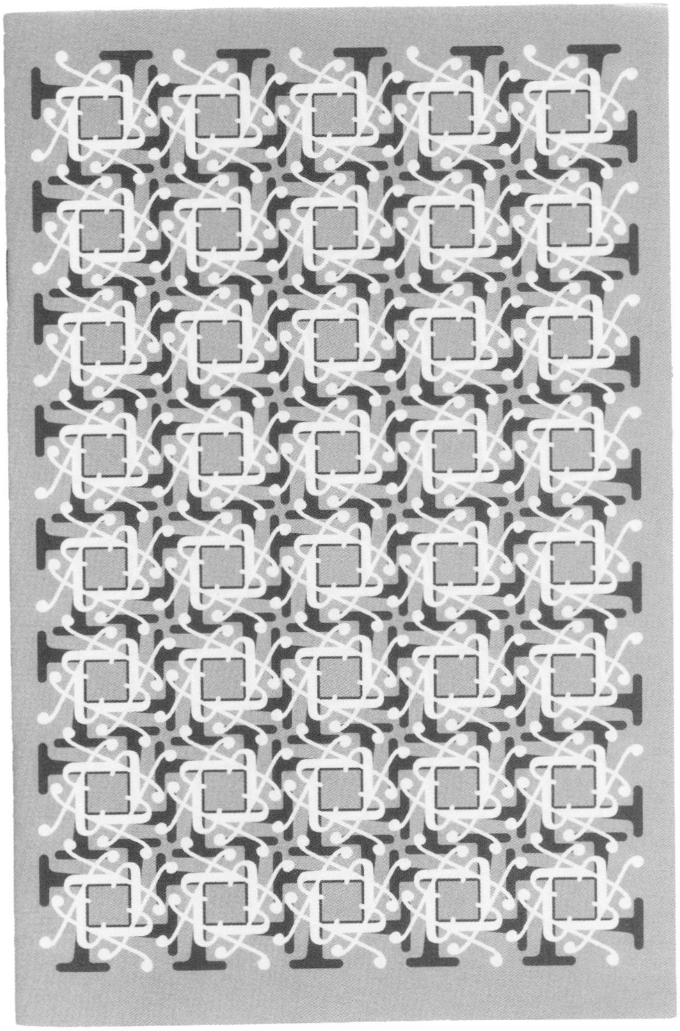

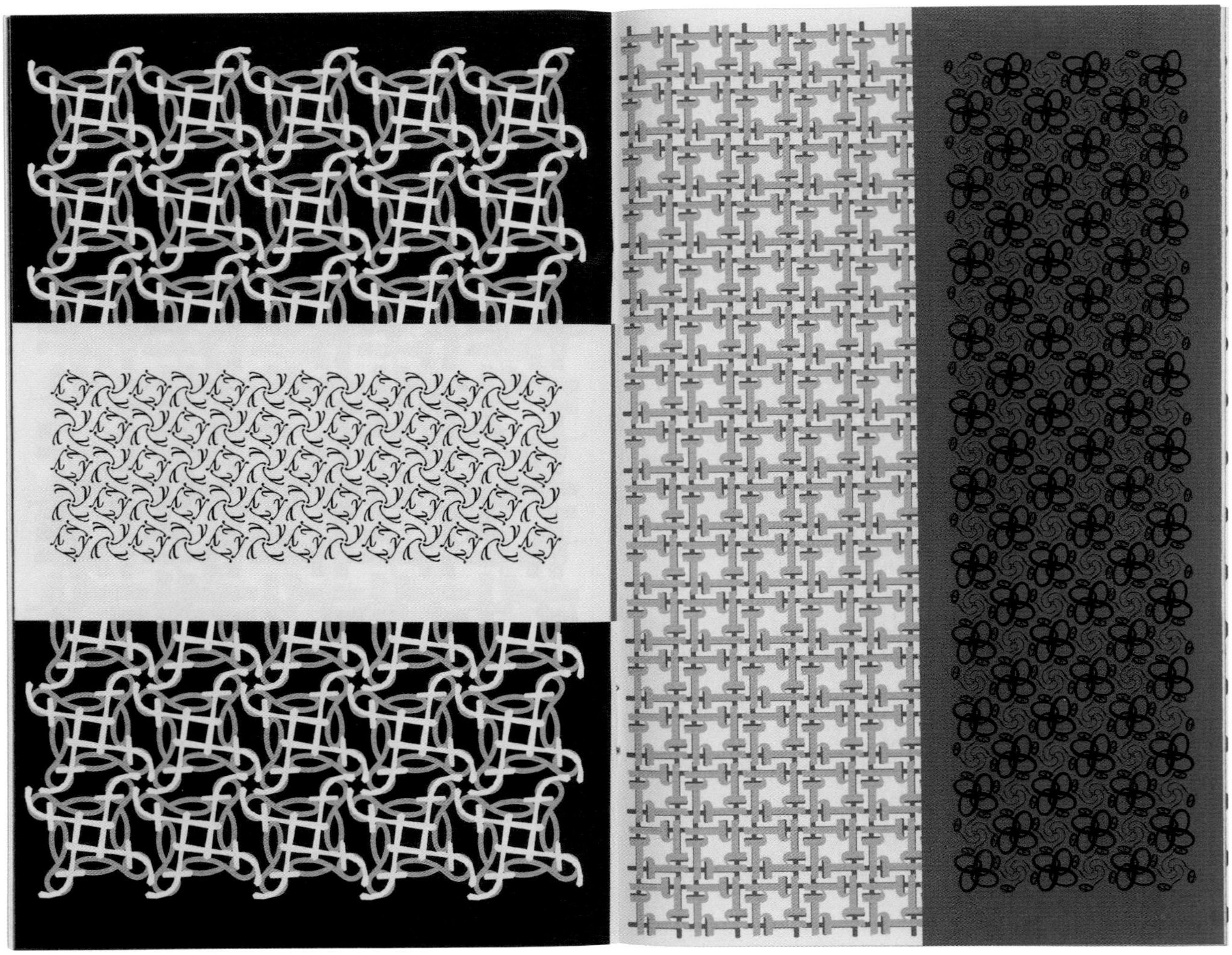

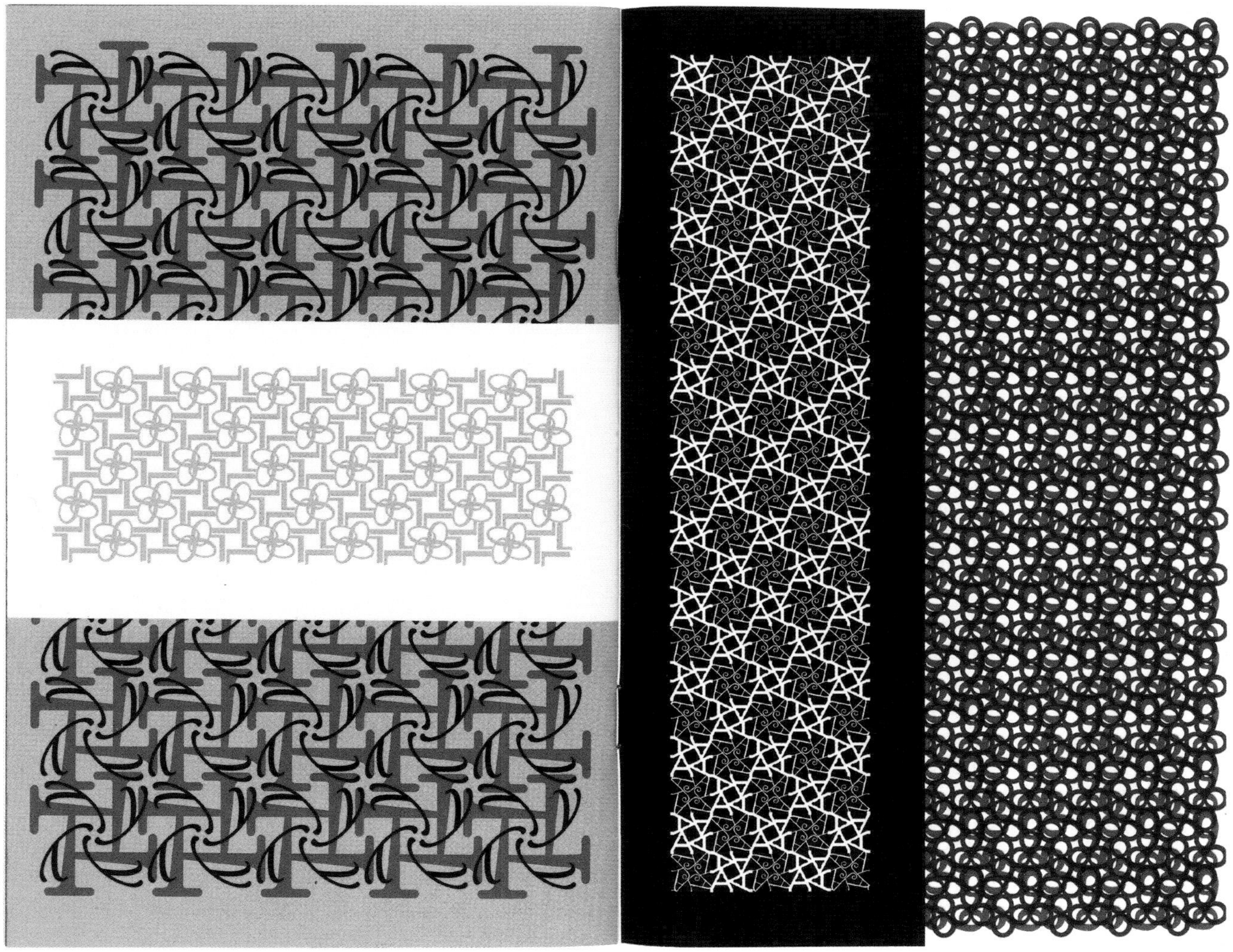

2000 **Derek Birdsall** *Common Worship: Services and Prayers for the Church of England*. London: Church House Publishing, 2000. xi, 850 pp. 21.5 cm. Deluxe edition. Designer: Derek Birdsall. Typesetters: John Morgan & Shirley Thompson (Omnific). In case.

The conveniently sized *Common Worship*, printed on ivory India paper, is the official worship and service book for the Church of England. It had an initial print run of almost a million. *Common Worship* was designed by one of the leading British graphic designers of his generation, Derek Birdsall (b. 1934). He made his name with magazine and book design. He worked for Penguin Books and designed voluminous art catalogues for international museums. In 1983, he was appointed a Royal Designer for Industry (RDI).

Despite his impressive record of service, Birdsall and his London studio Omnific had to pitch for *Common Worship*. He was of course delighted with the assignment and called it 'the job of a lifetime.' Designing this purely typographical church book, Birdsall found that his ample experience designing poetry books served him well. There is an undeniable influence from the modernist Anthony Froshaug, one of Birdsall's teachers at the Central School of Arts and Crafts in London during the fifties.

Birdsall decided to use the ultra-English Gill Sans for the type. This sans serif turned out to be very readable even in dim churches, it was available in all the desired weights, and it had a pleasant italic and clear numerals. In the left-aligned typography, the placement of the subheadings is notable: they are ranged right and in this way clarify the structure. The recurring instruction 'All' is set in the left-hand margins, functioning as a typographical accent. All italic text in red (such as this instruction) was slightly enlarged because otherwise it was optically too small. The cover design is bold in its simplicity: the title forms a cross with the subtitle. ML

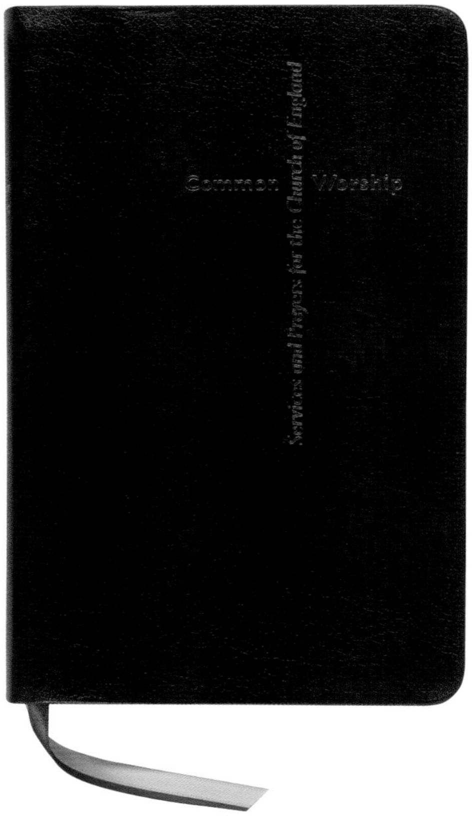

Gill Sans (1928) was one of the typefaces designed by the artist, designer and essayist Eric Gill (1882–1940) for the Monotype Corporation. This sans serif, which was one of Monotype's bestsellers, is virtually omnipresent in the UK, hence its nickname: 'the Helvetica of England'.

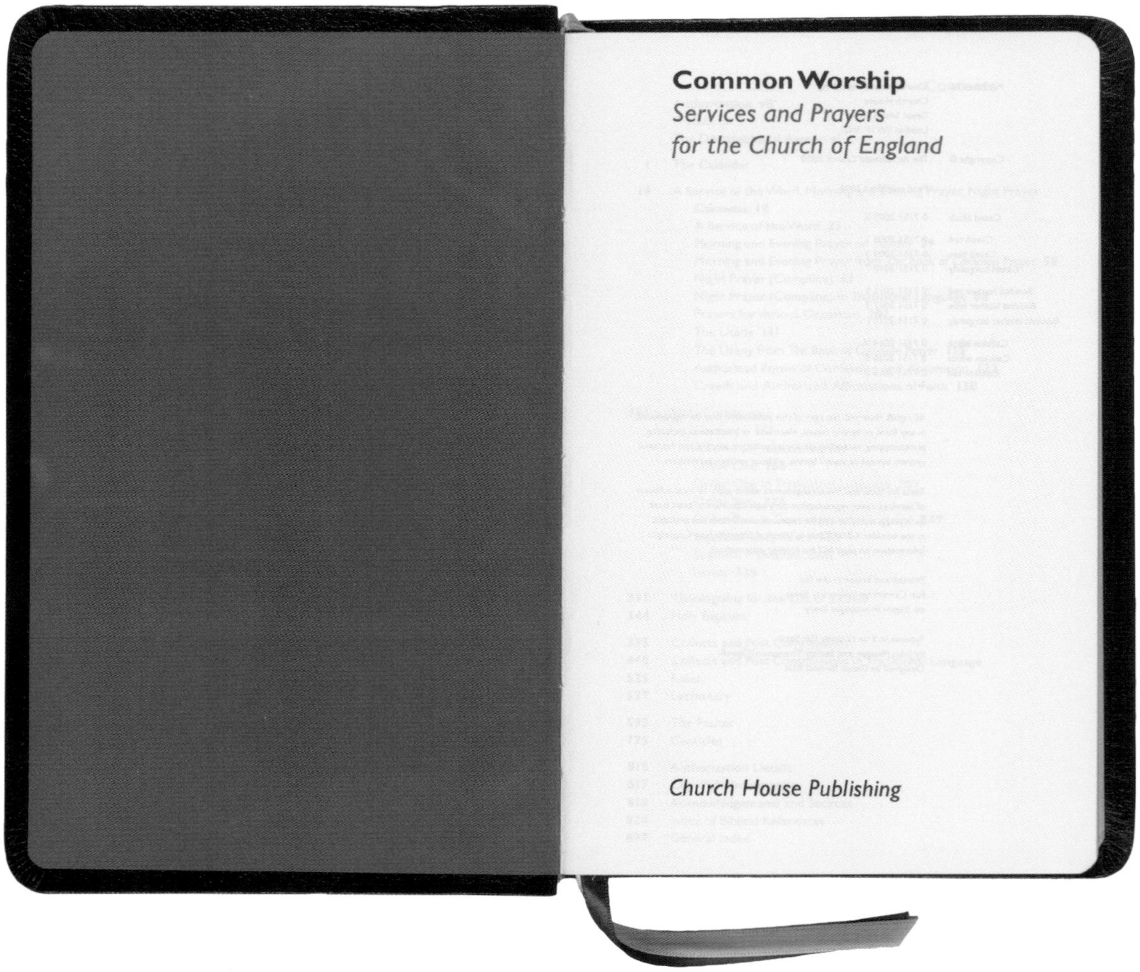

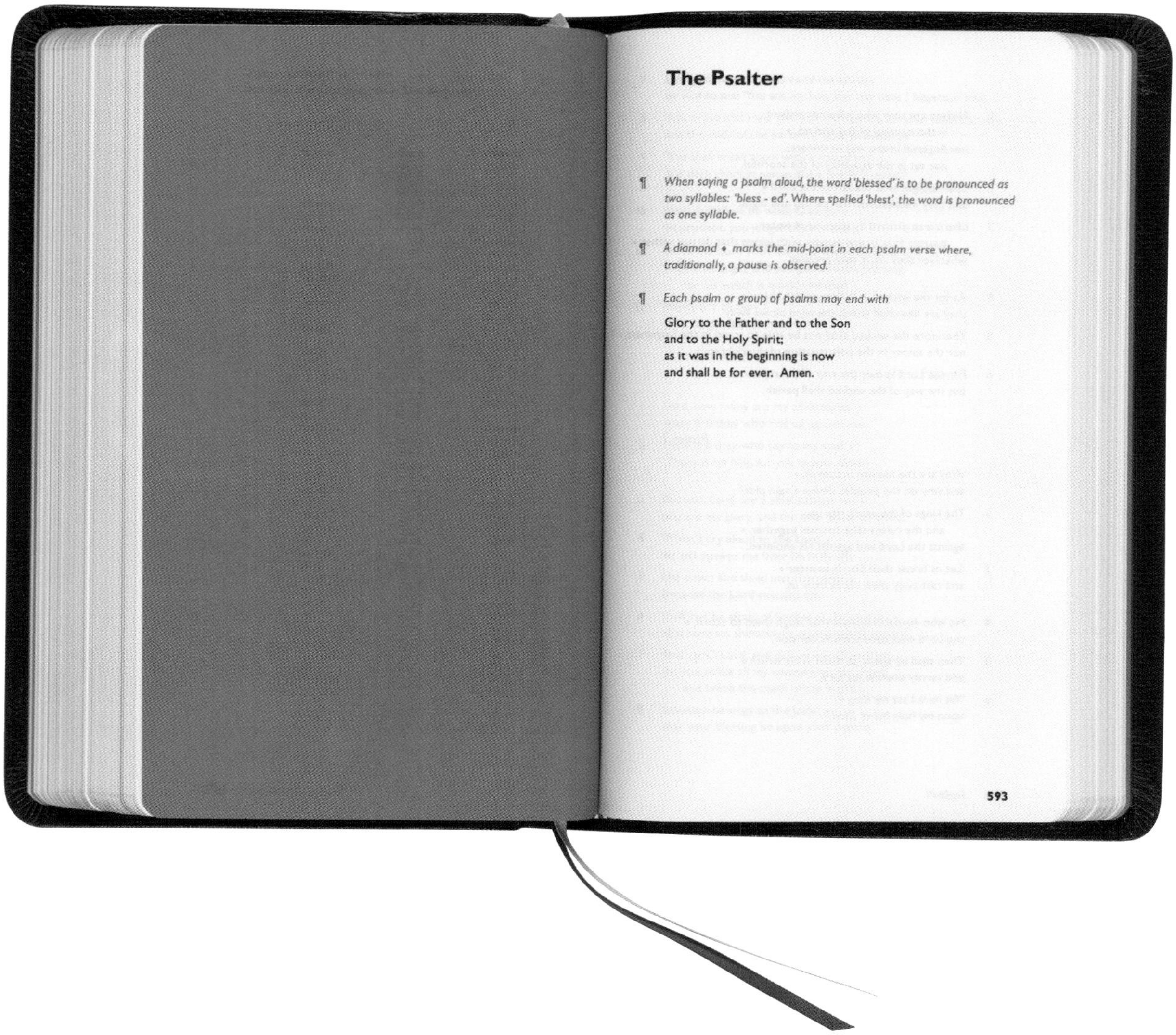
The Psalter
¶ When saying a psalm aloud, the word 'blessed' is to be pronounced as two syllables: 'bless - ed'. Where spelled 'blest', the word is pronounced as one syllable.
¶ A diamond ♦ marks the mid-point in each psalm verse where, traditionally, a pause is observed.
¶ Each psalm or group of psalms may end with
Glory to the Father and to the Son
and to the Holy Spirit;
as it was in the beginning is now
and shall be for ever. Amen.
593

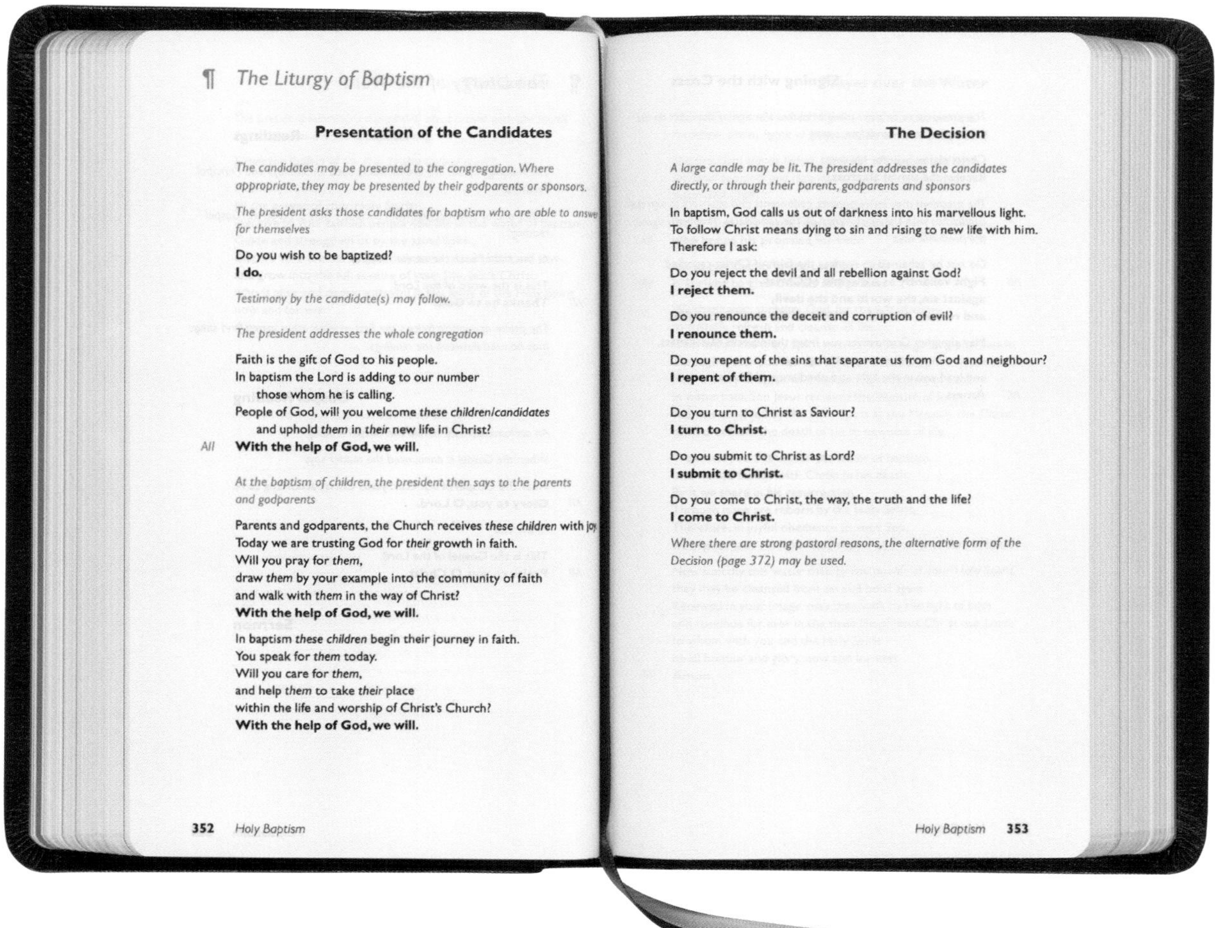
¶ The Liturgy of Baptism
Presentation of the Candidates
The candidates may be presented to the congregation. Where appropriate, they may be presented by their godparents or sponsors.
The president asks those candidates for baptism who are able to answe for themselves
Do you wish to be baptized?
I do.
Testimony by the candidate(s) may follow.
The president addresses the whole congregation
Faith is the gift of God to his people.
In baptism the Lord is adding to our number
those whom he is calling.
People of God, will you welcome these children/candidates
and uphold them in their new life in Christ?
All With the help of God, we will.
At the baptism of children, the president then says to the parents and godparents
Parents and godparents, the Church receives these children with jo
Today we are trusting God for their growth in faith.
Will you pray for them,
draw them by your example into the community of faith
and walk with them in the way of Christ?
With the help of God, we will.
In baptism these children begin their journey in faith.
You speak for them today.
Will you care for them,
and help them to take their place
within the life and worship of Christ's Church?
With the help of God, we will.
352 Holy Baptism
The Decision
A large candle may be lit. The president addresses the candidates directly, or through their parents, godparents and sponsors
In baptism, God calls us out of darkness into his marvellous light.
To follow Christ means dying to sin and rising to new life with him.
Therefore I ask:
Do you reject the devil and all rebellion against God?
I reject them.
Do you renounce the deceit and corruption of evil?
I renounce them.
Do you repent of the sins that separate us from God and neighbour?
I repent of them.
Do you turn to Christ as Saviour?
I turn to Christ.
Do you submit to Christ as Lord?
I submit to Christ.
Do you come to Christ, the way, the truth and the life?
I come to Christ.
Where there are strong pastoral reasons, the alternative form of the Decision (page 372) may be used.
Holy Baptism 353

2001 **Stefan Sagmeister** Peter Hall, *Sagmeister: Made You Look: Another Self-Indulgent Design Monograph (practically everything we have ever designed including the bad stuff).* New York: Booth-Clibborn, 2004. 291 pp. 24 cm. 1st edition 2001. Designer: Stefan Sagmeister. Printed in Hong Kong. In plastic slipcase.

Stefan Sagmeister (b. 1962) is a star designer. He is also a disarming speaker and his lectures draw full houses. He is mentioned in every graphic design survey. His poster for Lou Reed's 1996 album, *Set the Twilight Reeling*, with the lyrics of the title song handwritten on a photographic portrait, has been widely reproduced. He pushed the same idea to its extreme in a poster for a lecture three years later, with an intern cutting all of the lettering into Sagmeister's own torso. It took about eight hours. This poster was a statement in favour of individualism in design and of course became a classic.

Sagmeister: Made You Look is meant to be a 'show and tell' book. Alongside the main text are diary fragments in handwriting and client comments in frames. The order of the book is more or less chronological: his youth and academy years in Austria; his study years at the Pratt Institute in New York; work in Vienna and Hong Kong; back in New York, where he worked for Tibor Kalman for a short time, and then, in 1994, his own studio in Manhattan. His slogan 'Style = Fart' featured on the invitation to the opening of Sagmeister Inc. To Sagmeister, form is less important than concept; which is one of the reasons his work is not limited to printed media.

The fore-edge of *Sagmeister: Made You Look* has two printed 'fore-edge paintings' under metallic silver. On the cover, a benign German shepherd dog is seen through the red transparent slip case. Once removed from the slipcase, the dog, reproduced in red and green, seems to be growling fiercely. ML

In the nineties, industrial, 'non-design' fonts came into fashion. One example is DIN 1451 from 1936, developed for the Deutsches Institut für Normung by Siemens engineer Ludwig Goller (1884–1964). The 1995 FontShop version of DIN, by Dutch type designer Albert-Jan Pool (b. 1960), became a huge commercial success.

> Several ideas in the booklet were explored further in subsequent projects for Reed. The lyrics, for example, are designed in a way that reflects their content (an idea developed typographically in Reed's book of lyrics, pp.234-237). The

The hue and opacity of th
jewel case was particularly
testing the cover with photo
gels beforehand, the studio
that too much opacity would
image beneath. If the color v

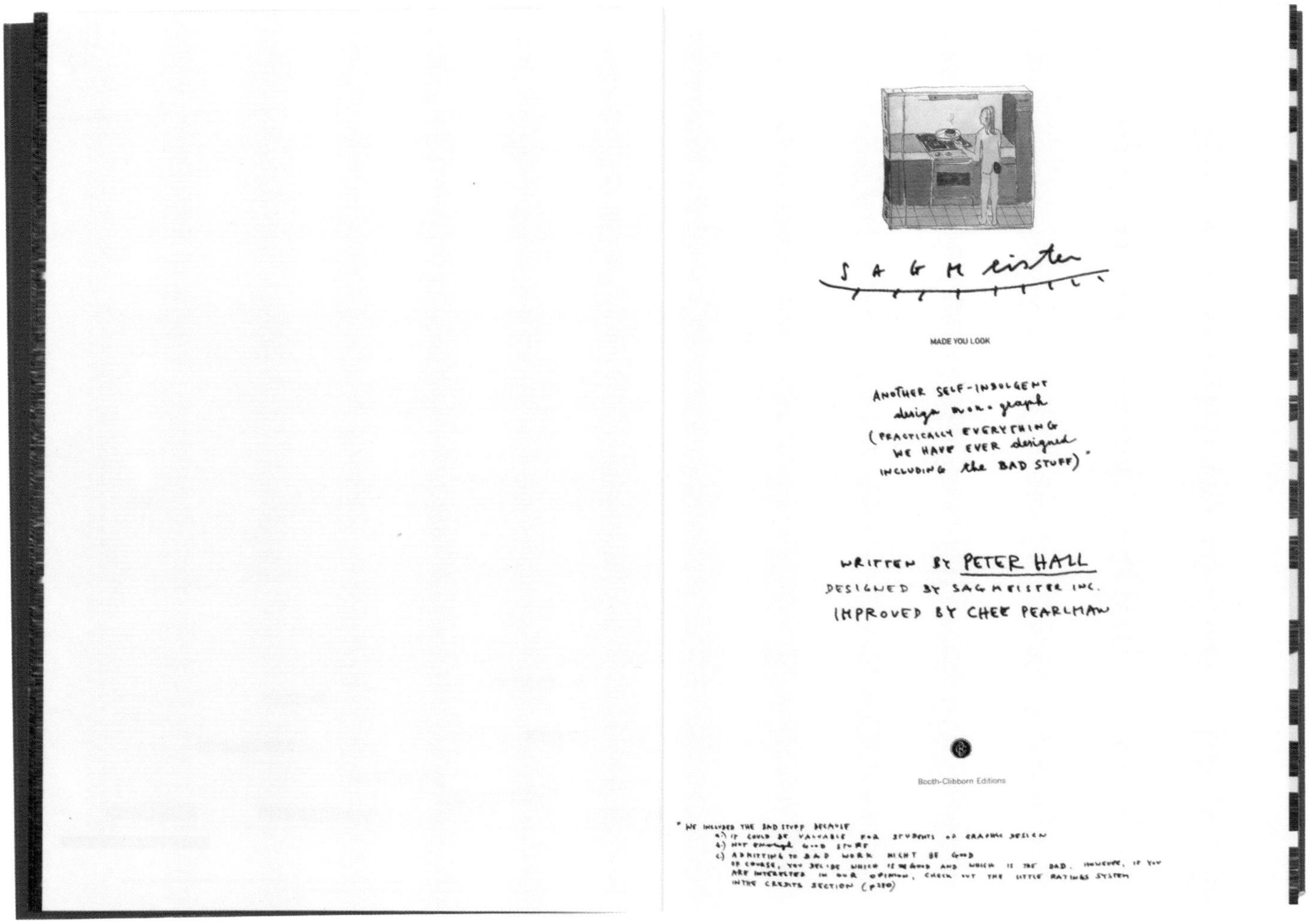
SAGMEISTER
MADE YOU LOOK
ANOTHER SELF-INDULGENT design mono-graph (PRACTICALLY EVERYTHING WE HAVE EVER designed INCLUDING the BAD STUFF)*.
WRITTEN BY PETER HALL
DESIGNED BY SAGMEISTER INC.
IMPROVED BY CHEE PEARLMAN
Booth-Clibborn Editions

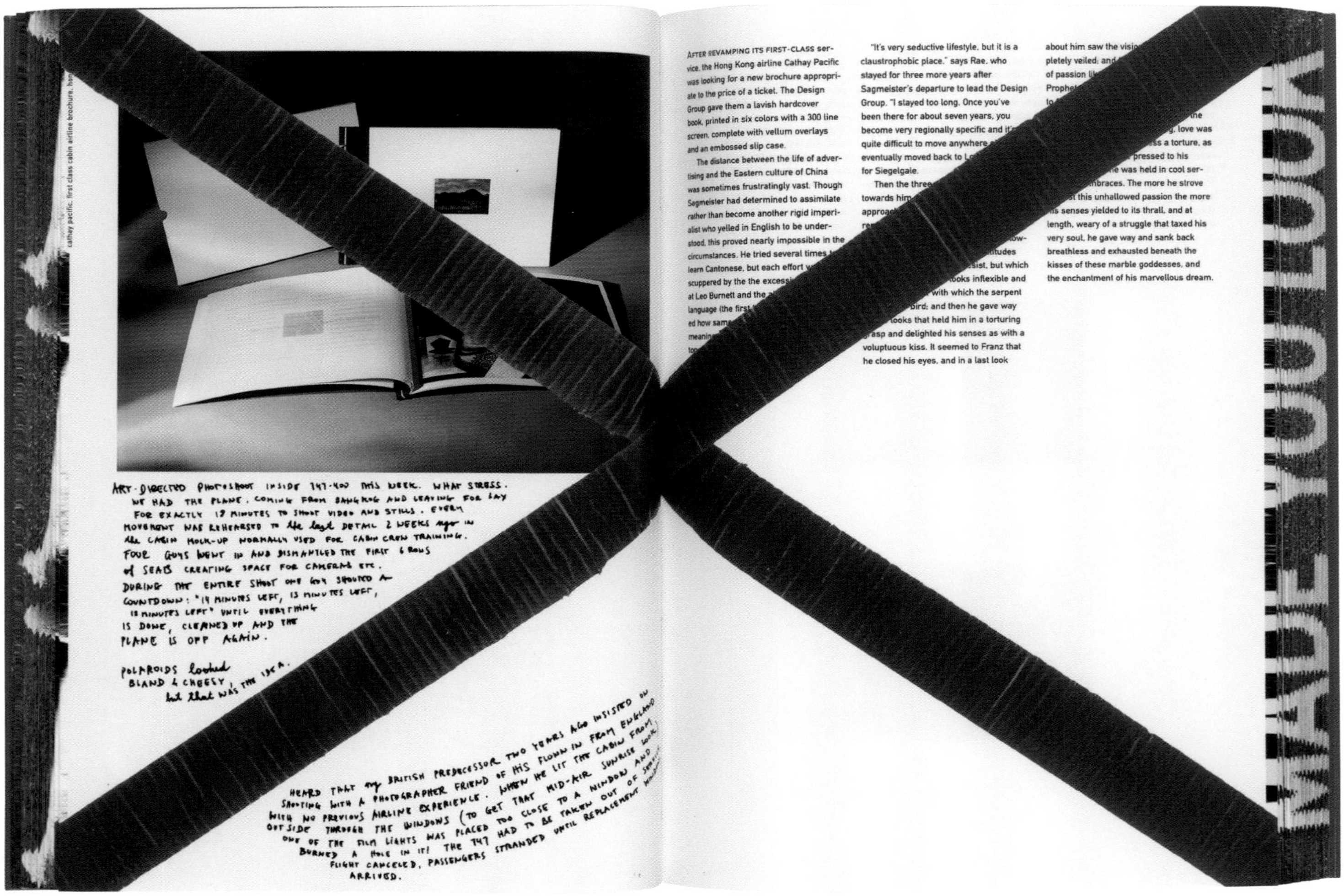
ART-DIRECTED PHOTOSHOOT INSIDE 747-400 THIS WEEK. WHAT STRESS.
WE HAD THE PLANE, COMING FROM BANGKOK AND LEAVING FOR LAX FOR EXACTLY 17 MINUTES TO SHOOT VIDEO AND STILLS. EVERY MOVEMENT WAS REHEARSED TO the last DETAIL 2 WEEKS ago in the CABIN MOCK-UP NORMALLY USED FOR CABIN CREW TRAINING.
FOUR GUYS WENT IN AND DISMANTLED THE FIRST 6 ROWS of SEATS CREATING SPACE FOR CAMERAS ETC.
DURING THE ENTIRE SHOOT ONE GUY SHOUTED A COUNTDOWN: "14 MINUTES LEFT, 13 MINUTES LEFT, 12 MINUTES LEFT" UNTIL EVERYTHING IS DONE, CLEANED UP AND THE PLANE IS OFF AGAIN.
POLAROIDS looked BLAND & CHEESY, but that was THE IDEA.
MADE YOU LOOK

lou reed, set the twilight reeling, poster, new york

> Several ideas in the booklet were explored further in subsequent projects for Reed. The lyrics, for example, are designed in a way that reflects their content (an idea developed typographically in Reed's book of lyrics, pp.234-237). The lyrics to "Egg Cream," Reed's song about a particularly tasty version of the soda drink served at "Becky's" on King's Highway in Brooklyn, are set in the style of an old New York Coffee shop sign (p.227).
The work of Middle Eastern artist Shirin Neshat inspired Sagmeister to hand-write the copy over a photograph of Reed's face. This idea was particularly popular with Reed and became the basis for a poster advertising the CD (right). The lettering effectively conveyed the personal, confessional nature of the songs on the album. It also looked good after eroding from a few days existence on bill-posting sites around New York, torn and buried among other fragments of wheat-pasted images (p.231).

The hue and opacity of the blue-tinted jewel case was particularly difficult. By testing the cover with photographers' light gels beforehand, the studio established that too much opacity would obscure the image beneath. If the color was slightly off, the yellow portrait of Reed would turn under the blue case into an ugly brown rather than black, "thus not transforming a black prince but a brown one," as Sagmeister puts it. >

228

2008 **Joost Grootens** Jelte Boeijenga, Jeroen Mensink, *Vinex Atlas*. Rotterdam: 010 Publishers, 2008. 303 pp. 34.5 cm.

Designer: Studio Joost Grootens (book & maps/map adaptations). Photographer: Kees Hummel. Lithographer: Image Degree Zero, Amsterdam. Printer: Lecturis, Eindhoven. Bookbinder: Abbringh, Groningen.

Joost Grootens (b. 1971) was trained as an architectural designer but became a graphic designer almost by accident. His small studio in Amsterdam receives international attention for its book designs and in particular for its atlases, which stand out for their innovative and intelligent visualization of data. Grootens clearly shares a number of ideals with the modernists of the previous generation and is therefore an outsider in the Dutch design world. For Grootens, designers are neutral problem solvers. His restrained but refined 'less is more' aesthetic is also highly modernist.

In 2008, 010 publishers – one of Grootens's major clients – published the international award-winning *Vinex Atlas*. The book gives an account of the oft-maligned Vinex suburban developments in the Netherlands, which began in 1995 and were meant to strengthen existing urban functions and counteract the urbanization of the countryside. It's an uncluttered book, explaining the projects visually with black-and-white aerial views of their original state, colour maps of the development plan, and black-and-white photos of the completed project. The maps were specially drawn for the atlas and are therefore mutually comparable. The design of the diagrams is perfectly matched.

In the *Vinex Atlas*, the colours are not produced using the standard CMYK (cyan, magenta, yellow, black) model. Grootens likes to choose his own palette, which often includes metallic and fluorescent inks. In subtle ways, the chosen colours reinforce the basic principles of the text. The fact that Grootens appreciates the value of books as objects is exemplified in the *Vinex Atlas* by, among other features, the tactile quality of the cover material and its deep, blind stamp for the title and the development plan. ML

De hoofdstructuur van IJburg best
van blokken van 175 meter lang en
wisselend tussen 45 tot 90 meter. D
samenstelling van een aantal afzor
wen, zijn ingevuld met een mix var
appartementen, bedrijfsruimten en

Neutral (2005) was designed by German typographer Kai Bernau (b. 1978) when he was a student at the Dutch Royal Academy of Art in The Hague. This sans serif is the result of a study of the 'neutrality' concept in graphic design.

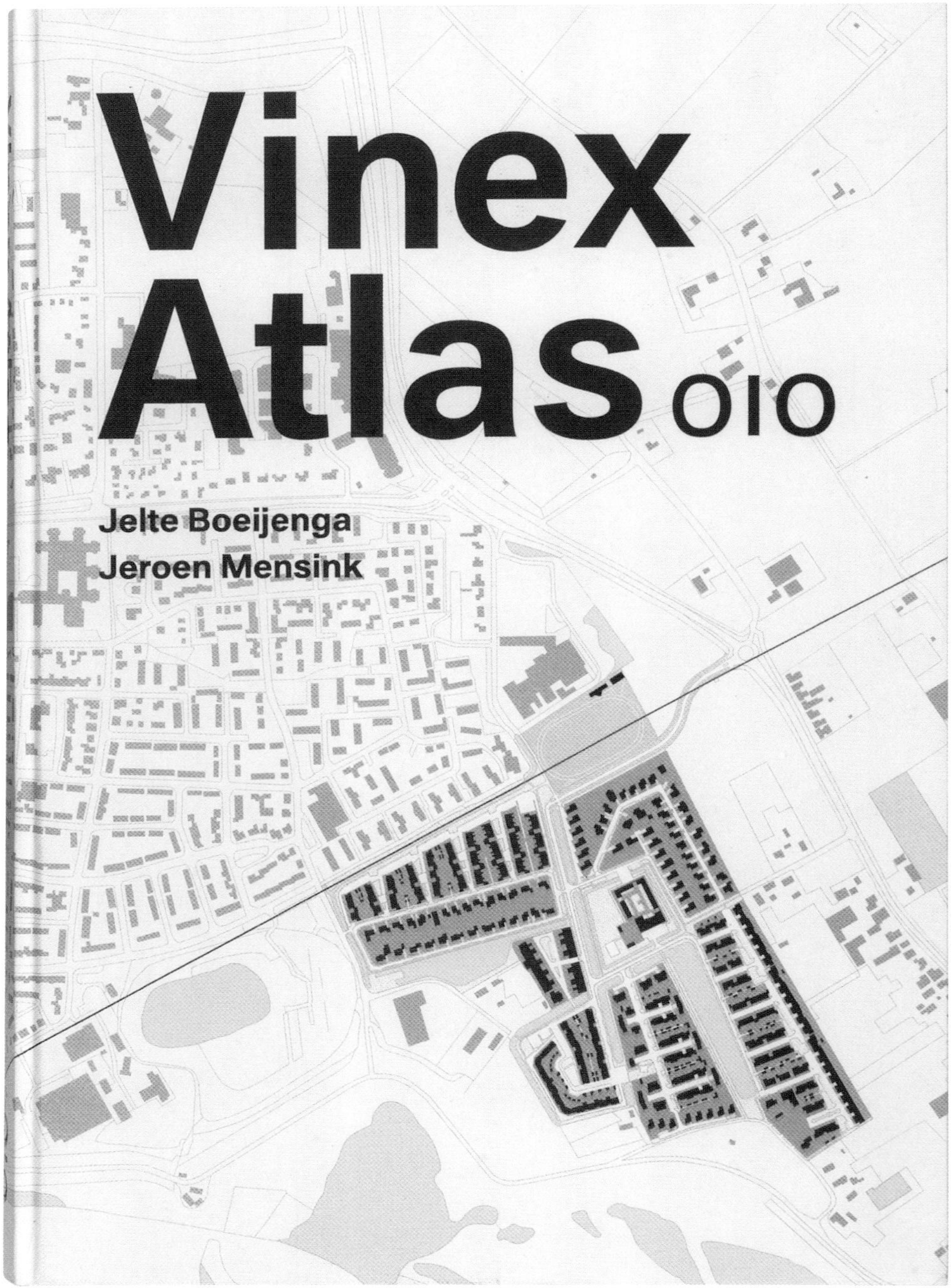

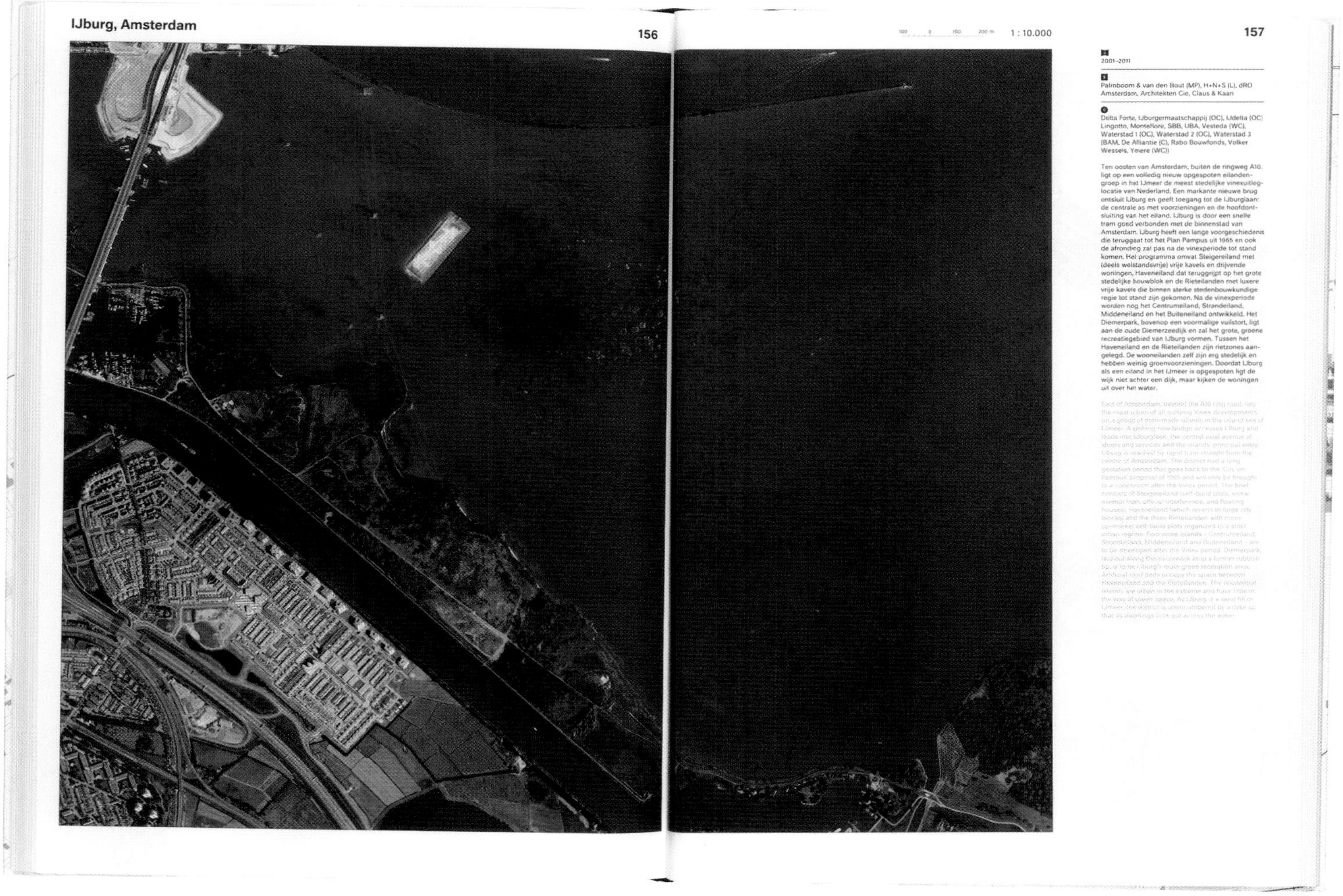

IJburg, Amsterdam

156

1 : 10.000

157

2001–2011

Palmboom & van den Bout (MP), H+N+S (L), dRO Amsterdam, Architekten Cie, Claus & Kaan

Delta Forte, IJburgermaatschappij (OC), IJdelta (OC) Lingotto, Montefiore, SBB, UBA, Vesteda (WC), Waterstad 1 (OC), Waterstad 2 (OC), Waterstad 3 (BAM, De Alliantie (C), Rabo Bouwfonds, Volker Wessels, Ymere (WC))

Ten oosten van Amsterdam, buiten de ringweg A10, ligt op een volledig nieuw opgespoten eilandengroep in het IJmeer de meest stedelijke vinexuitleglocatie van Nederland. Een markante nieuwe brug ontsluit IJburg en geeft toegang tot de IJburglaan: de centrale as met voorzieningen en de hoofdontsluiting van het eiland. IJburg is door een snelle tram goed verbonden met de binnenstad van Amsterdam. IJburg heeft een lange voorgeschiedenis die teruggaat tot het Plan Pampus uit 1965 en ook de afronding zal pas na de vinexperiode tot stand komen. Het programma omvat Steigereiland met (deels welstandsvrije) vrije kavels en drijvende woningen, Haveneiland dat teruggrijpt op het grote stedelijke bouwblok en de Rieteilanden met luxere vrije kavels die binnen sterke stedenbouwkundige regie tot stand zijn gekomen. Na de vinexperiode worden nog het Centrumeiland, Strandeiland, Middeneiland en het Buiteneiland ontwikkeld. Het Diemerpark, bovenop een voormalige vuilstort, ligt aan de oude Diemerzeedijk en zal het grote, groene recreatiegebied van IJburg vormen. Tussen het Haveneiland en de Rieteilanden zijn rietzones aangelegd. De wooneilanden zelf zijn erg stedelijk en hebben weinig groenvoorzieningen. Doordat IJburg als een eiland in het IJmeer is opgespoten ligt de wijk niet achter een dijk, maar kijken de woningen uit over het water.

Haveneiland West, IJburg, Amsterdam

160

161

2001–2011

Architekten Cie, Claus & Kaan, dRO Amsterdam

Tangram, Galis, Van Herk en de Kleijn, Dick van Gameren, Dok architecten, VMX

IJburgermaatschappij (OC), IJdelta (OC), Waterstad 1 (OC), Waterstad 2 (OC), Waterstad 3 (OC)

De hoofdstructuur van IJburg bestaat uit een grid van blokken van 175 meter lang en in breedte wisselend tussen 45 tot 90 meter. Deze blokken, een samenstelling van een aantal afzonderlijke gebouwen, zijn ingevuld met een mix van rijwoningen, appartementen, bedrijfsruimten en voorzieningen. Per blok zijn enkele architectenbureaus uitgenodigd om de verschillende gebouwen te realiseren, wat resulteert in een gevarieerd en levendig straatbeeld. De mix van woningtypen resulteert ook in verschillende soorten buitenruimten, variërend van privétuinen tot openbaar groen en collectieve tuinen tot binnenstraten. Op de grotere schaal van het eiland vormen de uniforme bouwblokken een gridvormig, stedelijk stratenpatroon. Langs de grote doorgaande route, de IJburglaan, is ruimte voor voorzieningen opgenomen op de begane grond. In de straten daarachter zijn juist de woningen gesitueerd aan de straat. Op de kleinere schaal van de voetganger en de fietser, voor wie het gebied vele langzaamverkeerroutes kent over de binnenterreinen van de blokken, is de ervaring van de openbare ruimte veel opener en toegankelijker. De woningen worden dan ook zowel vanaf de straten als vanuit de binnenterreinen ontsloten. Het openbaar groen is geconcentreerd in de verschillende parken en deels in de collectieve binnentuinen. Onder de meeste blokken liggen parkeergarages om te kunnen voorzien in voldoende parkeercapaciteit.

1 : 2.000

Joost Grootens

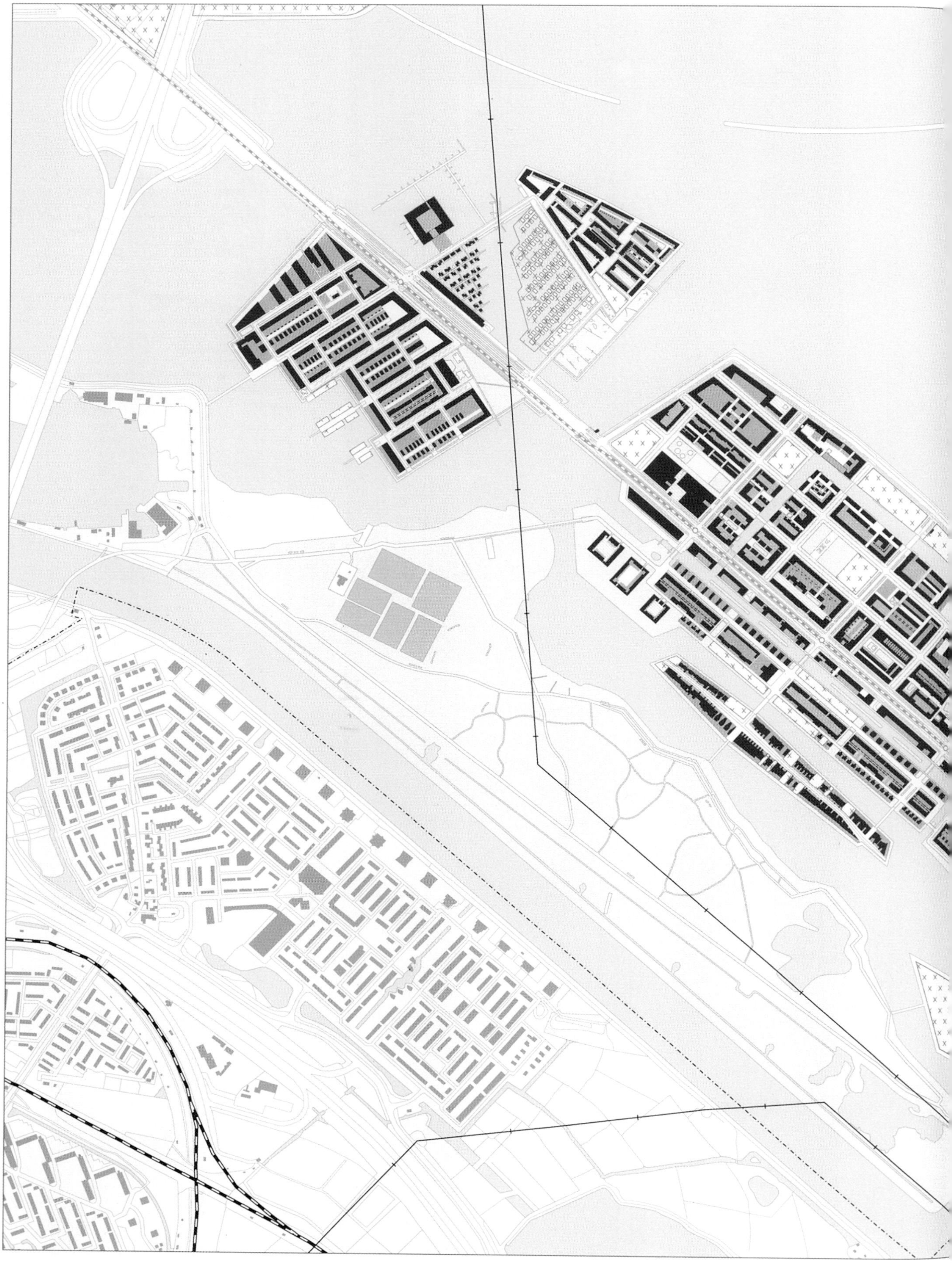

447

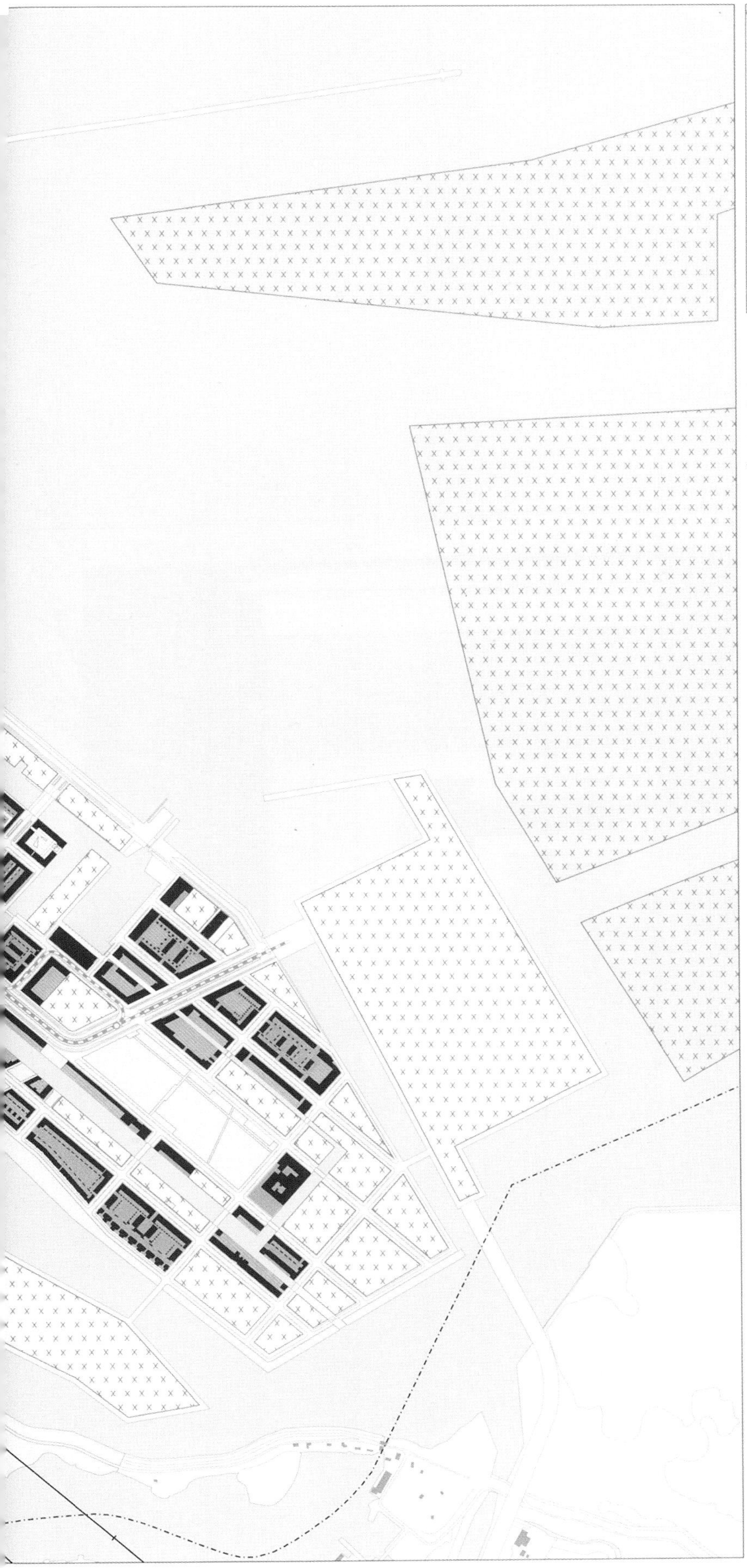

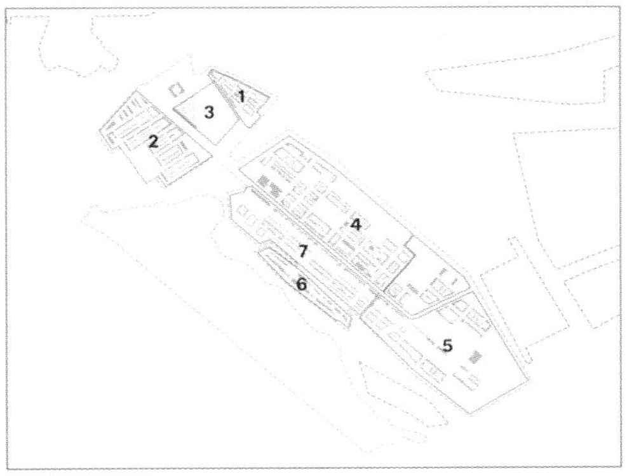

IJburg, Amsterdam 2001–2011	252	170	3178	5101	8701	172,9 / 135,8	308,7	28 wo/ha
1 Steigereiland Noordbuurt 2007–2010	0	0	220	210	430	[illegible] / 2,8 / 2,9	6,2	70 wo/ha
2 Steigereiland Zuidbuurt 2004–2009	80	60	370	420	930	6,4 / 5,6 / 10,6	22,5	41 wo/ha
3 Steigereiland Waterbuurten 2006–2011	127	30	28	76	261	4,6 / 2,7 / 1,6	8,9	29 wo/ha
4 Haveneiland West 2001–2011	0	0	980	2310	3290	9,8 / 17,3 / 19,7	46,8	70 wo/ha
5 Haveneiland Oost 2005–2010	0	10	1090	2070	3170	10,9 / 21,6 / 26,4	58,8	54 wo/ha
6 Kleine Rieteiland 2002–2009	0	0	140	0	140	2,0 / 1,3 / 3,7	6,9	20 wo/ha
7 Grote Rieteiland 2001–2008	45	70	350	15	480	8,9 / 5,5 / 8,5	22,8	21 wo/ha

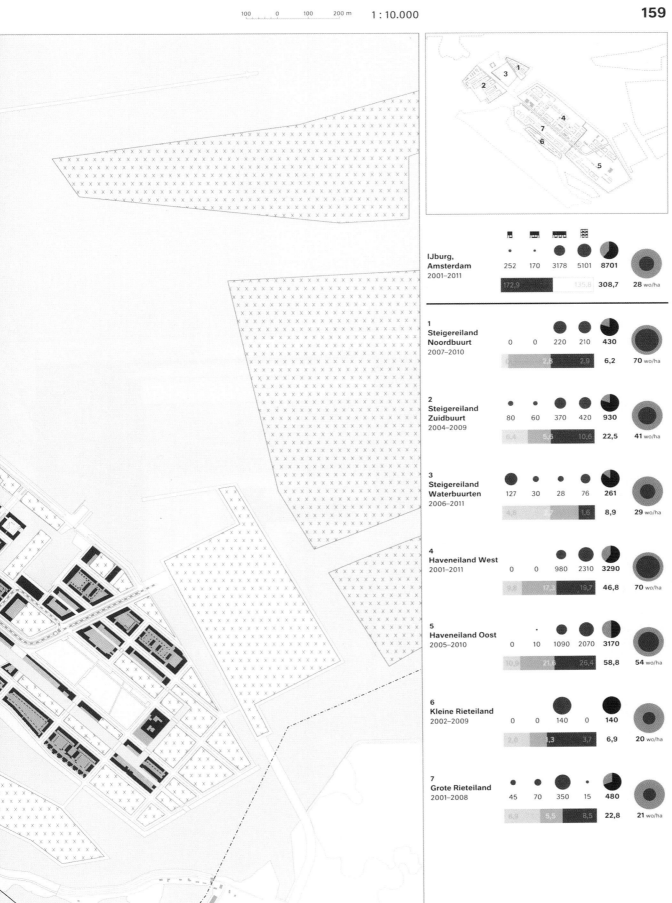

2010 **Irma Boom** Jennifer Butler, *James, Jennifer, Georgina are the Butlers*. London: Erasmus Publishing, 2010. 19.5 cm. 1198 pp. Designer: Irma Boom. Photographer: Erwin Olaf. Printer: Lenoirschuring, Amstelveen. Bookbinder: Van Waarden, Zaandam. In paper box.

Since the beginning of her career, Amsterdam-based designer Irma Boom (b. 1960) has produced scale models: miniature books that she glues together. She says she works from the outside in, and the scale models give an impression of the end result. The miniatures seem extraordinarily bulky; once printed, the books usually turn out slimmer. Still, it is obvious that Boom likes to make bulky books.

Physical exploration of the edge is Boom's trademark. The company book *SHV* (1996), which runs to over 2,000 pages, has a spectacular fore-edge: fanned slightly in one direction it shows a tulip field, in the other a poem. The working title of the thick (almost 900 pages) *Every Thing Design* (2009) is silk-screened over the three edges and the spine. Thus this collection catalogue is automatically perceived as an object.

James, Jennifer, Georgina is voluminous (8 cm thick) and yellow: the silk-screened trimmed edges are yellow, the cloth cover is yellow, and even the binding wire is yellow. A truly innovative touch is the articulated spine, which consists of three strips, giving the book a sculptural quality when it lies open. Similarly, the contents consist of three parts: postcards, conversations, and a photo album. The subject of the book is the problems of the Butler family, and in particular the alcoholism of the father, James. The postcards to their daughter Georgina (both the front and the back are reproduced) form the bulk of the book. The design and production of Boom's work are so unusual that her contribution to the content is easily overlooked. On the colophon page of this bizarre docusoap, which was privately commissioned, she is credited as co-editor. ML

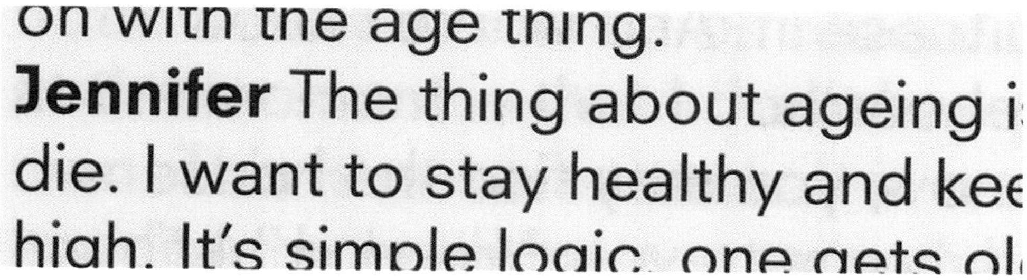
on with the age thing.
Jennifer The thing about ageing i
die. I want to stay healthy and kee
high. It's simple logic, one gets ol

A digital version of Neuzeit-Grotesk. The original metal version of this sans serif by Wilhelm Pischner (1904–89) was issued in 1928 by the Stempel foundry and composing machine manufacturer Linotype. Pischner worked in Stempel's in-house printing office in Frankfurt am Main until 1940.

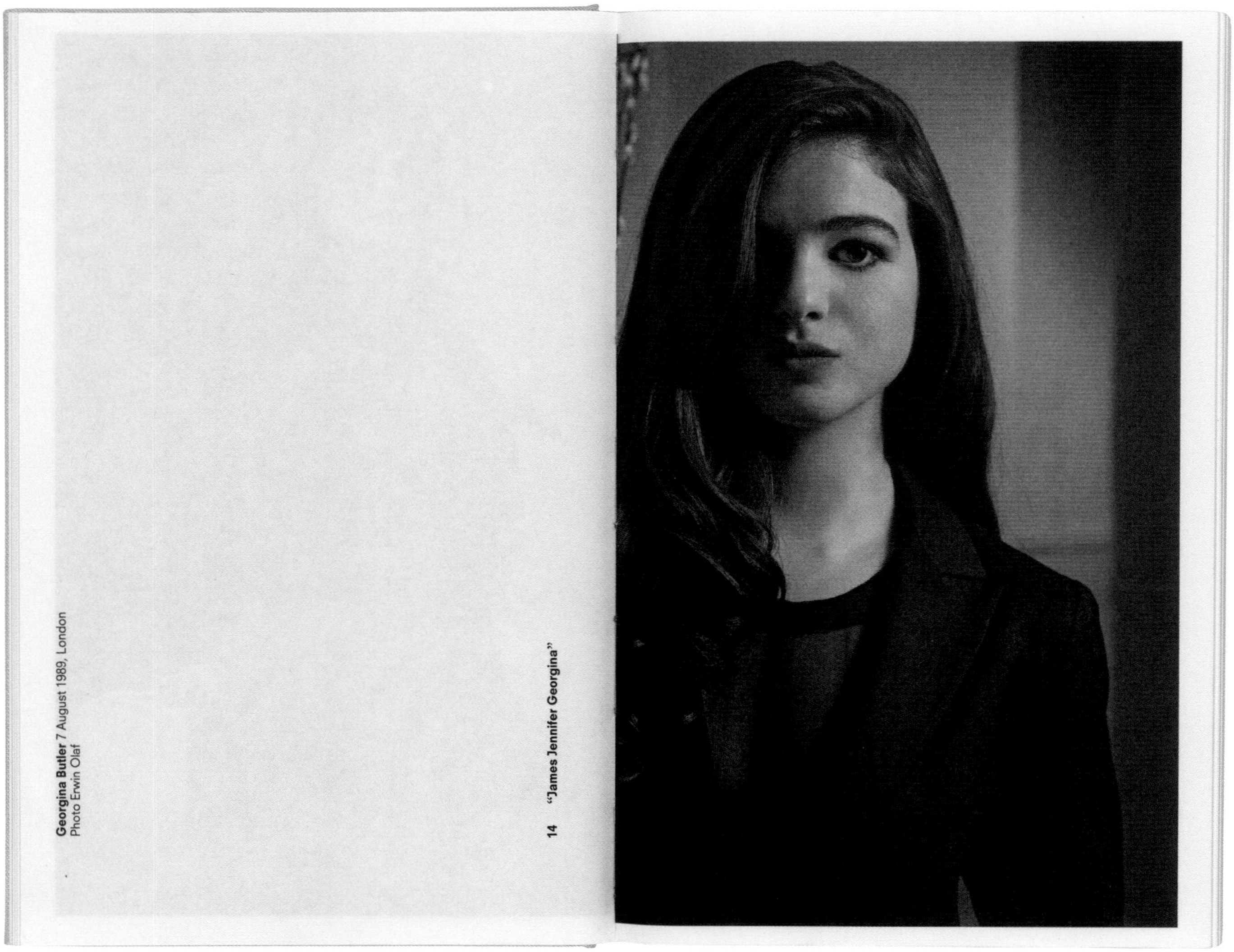
Georgina Butler 7 August 1989, London
Photo Erwin Olaf
14 "James Jennifer Georgina"

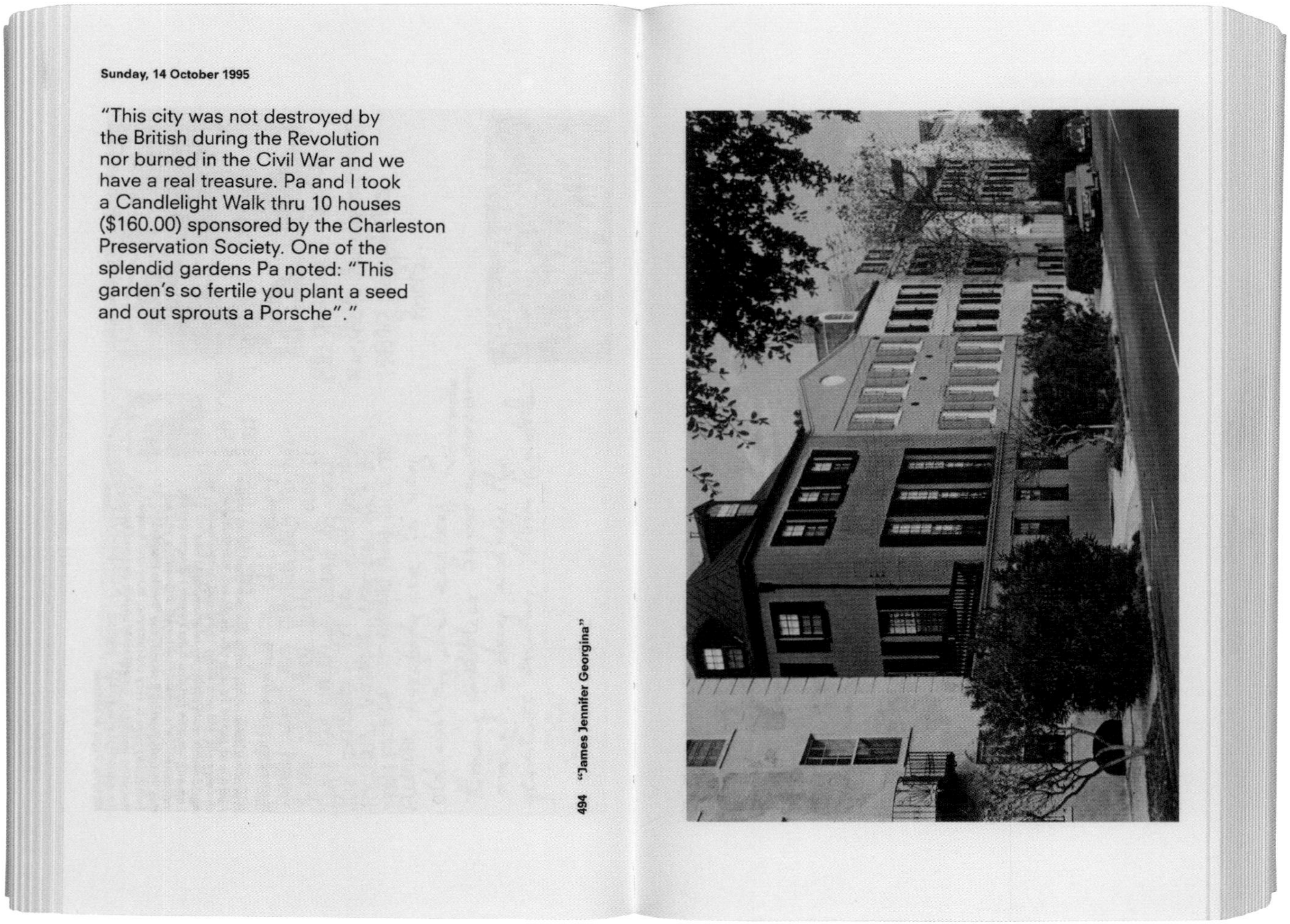
Sunday, 14 October 1995
"This city was not destroyed by the British during the Revolution nor burned in the Civil War and we have a real treasure. Pa and I took a Candlelight Walk thru 10 houses ($160.00) sponsored by the Charleston Preservation Society. One of the splendid gardens Pa noted: "This garden's so fertile you plant a seed and out sprouts a Porsche"."
494 "James Jennifer Georgina"

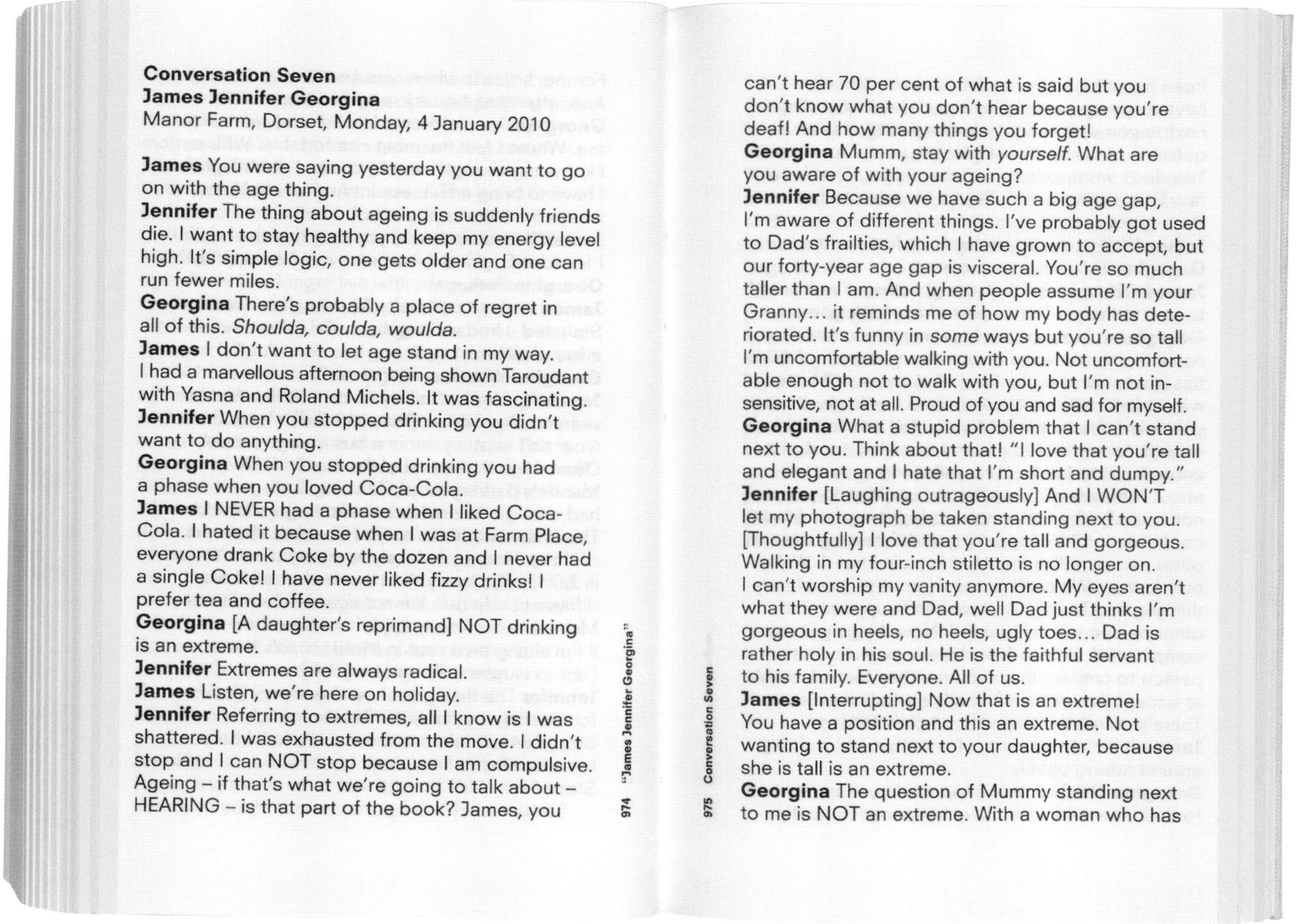

Conversation Seven
James Jennifer Georgina
Manor Farm, Dorset, Monday, 4 January 2010

James You were saying yesterday you want to go on with the age thing.
Jennifer The thing about ageing is suddenly friends die. I want to stay healthy and keep my energy level high. It's simple logic, one gets older and one can run fewer miles.
Georgina There's probably a place of regret in all of this. *Shoulda, coulda, woulda.*
James I don't want to let age stand in my way. I had a marvellous afternoon being shown Taroudant with Yasna and Roland Michels. It was fascinating.
Jennifer When you stopped drinking you didn't want to do anything.
Georgina When you stopped drinking you had a phase when you loved Coca-Cola.
James I NEVER had a phase when I liked Coca-Cola. I hated it because when I was at Farm Place, everyone drank Coke by the dozen and I never had a single Coke! I have never liked fizzy drinks! I prefer tea and coffee.
Georgina [A daughter's reprimand] NOT drinking is an extreme.
Jennifer Extremes are always radical.
James Listen, we're here on holiday.
Jennifer Referring to extremes, all I know is I was shattered. I was exhausted from the move. I didn't stop and I can NOT stop because I am compulsive. Ageing – if that's what we're going to talk about – HEARING – is that part of the book? James, you can't hear 70 per cent of what is said but you don't know what you don't hear because you're deaf! And how many things you forget!
Georgina Mumm, stay with *yourself*. What are you aware of with your ageing?
Jennifer Because we have such a big age gap, I'm aware of different things. I've probably got used to Dad's frailties, which I have grown to accept, but our forty-year age gap is visceral. You're so much taller than I am. And when people assume I'm your Granny… it reminds me of how my body has deteriorated. It's funny in *some* ways but you're so tall I'm uncomfortable walking with you. Not uncomfortable enough not to walk with you, but I'm not insensitive, not at all. Proud of you and sad for myself.
Georgina What a stupid problem that I can't stand next to you. Think about that! "I love that you're tall and elegant and I hate that I'm short and dumpy."
Jennifer [Laughing outrageously] And I WON'T let my photograph be taken standing next to you. [Thoughtfully] I love that you're tall and gorgeous. Walking in my four-inch stiletto is no longer on. I can't worship my vanity anymore. My eyes aren't what they were and Dad, well Dad just thinks I'm gorgeous in heels, no heels, ugly toes… Dad is rather holy in his soul. He is the faithful servant to his family. Everyone. All of us.
James [Interrupting] Now that is an extreme! You have a position and this an extreme. Not wanting to stand next to your daughter, because she is tall is an extreme.
Georgina The question of Mummy standing next to me is NOT an extreme. With a woman who has

974 "James Jennifer Georgina"
975 Conversation Seven

Postscript **Over the centuries, publishers, printers and other book producers have been confronted with rapid changes taking place in their industry. These days, most changes are caused by the internet and its influence on shopping behaviour. Some stores seem to be on the verge of disappearing from towns and cities; changes in the configuration and function of traditional shopping streets are unavoidable. A number of bookshops have closed their doors for good, while publishers' turnovers are either dropping or shifting from printed books to e-books. The industry producing books, newspapers and magazines is undergoing a radical transformation. A single tap on the screen of a tablet PC suffices to order or download a product. Audience-oriented production and publishing are becoming necessary, as the market is subjected to great pressure. Once more, publishers have to push the boundaries. Will instant e-book publishing be the new magic formula? What would the world look like without printed books?**

This book presents special and sometimes iconic books from a period spanning over five hundred years, beginning in 1471 with an edition printed by Nicolas Jenson in Venice – Lorenzo Vallas's *Elegantiae linguae Latinae* – and ending in 2010 with a design by Irma Boom – *James, Jennifer, Georgina are the Butlers*. The compiler of this book, Mathieu Lommen, works as curator of graphic design at the Special Collections of the University of Amsterdam (UvA), the most important scholarly library in the Netherlands. Being a book designer and publisher, I have a particular perspective on the selected books. What is the relationship between form and function? Which fonts were used, what kind of paper, what kind of finishing does the book have? Is the interaction between typography, colour and image effective? Which publishers, designers, photographers, illustrators or printers have contributed the book? And, last but not least, what was the target audience? Always cast a first look at the colophon.

When I first discussed the concept of this book with Mathieu Lommen, it dawned on me that curators and designers tend to favour different approaches to making a book. Books made by designers often seem to be the result of – as Mathieu put it – emptying a bookcase: too personal and lacking in explanation. We have managed to avoid such shortcomings in this visual history of the printed book, thanks to Mathieu's knowledge and responsibility, and have attempted to make this a clear and informative book for a broad and international audience: designers, design historians, bibliophiles and book collectors. Searching the Special Collections of the UvA resulted in a selection of 125 books from different periods and countries. Mathieu, thank you for this enjoyable collaboration.

I also want to express my thanks to Steph Scholten, director of Heritage Collections UvA, and Garrelt Verhoeven, head curator of Special Collections UvA. During our earliest discussions, it was already apparent that we would develop a good interaction in the interest of presenting this world-class treasury of rare and valuable books. I also want to thank Ellen Borger for coordinating the exhibition 'The Printed Book: A Visual History', at the Special Collections in Amsterdam. Finally, Stephan van der Linden (UvA) should be mentioned for his beautiful photographs of the books – exceeding the quantity originally agreed upon – and also book historian John A. Lane for, among other things, his contributions to the notes on type.

Printed books and digital graphic innovations: frontiers are being pushed back again and again.

Cees W. de Jong

About the authors

Paul Dijstelberge is an assistant professor of book history at the University of Amsterdam and a curator of rare books at the UvA Special Collections. He has published several works on the subject of book history.

Frans A. Janssen is a professor emeritus of book and library history at the University of Amsterdam and former director of the Bibliotheca Philosophica Hermetica in Amsterdam. He has published multiple works on the history of typographical design and printing, among other subjects.

Cees W. de Jong is a graphic designer and publisher of international editions on architecture, art and graphic design. He was the author/editor of *Type: A Visual History of Typefaces and Graphic Styles* (2009-10) and the designer of *Meggs' History of Graphic Design* (2011, 5th ed.).

John A. Lane is a book historian, bibliographer, freelance researcher and lecturer at the Plantin Instituut voor Typografie in Antwerp and the Amsterdam University Summer Programmes. He has published multiple works on the history of type design and type specimens, among other subjects.

Mathieu Lommen is a curator of graphic design and typography at the Special Collections of the University of Amsterdam and teaches graphic design history at the UvA. He has published multiple works on book and type design from the nineteenth century onwards and has curated several exhibitions.

Lesley Monfils is a cataloguer of rare books and special collections at the Library of the University of Amsterdam.

Adriaan Plak has worked for many years in the antiquarian book trade. He is currently a curator of church history collections at the Special Collections of the University of Amsterdam.

Jan W. H. Werner is a curator of maps and atlases at the Special Collections of the University of Amsterdam. He has published several works on historical cartography and model cars.

Johan de Zoete is a curator at the Museum Enschedé in Haarlem. He has published multiple works on the history of nineteenth-century graphic techniques, especially illustration techniques.

Further reading

General

Alan Bartram, *Five Hundred Years of Book Design*. London: British Library, 2001

David Bland, *A History of Book Illustration*, 2nd ed. London: Faber & Faber, 1969. First published 1958

Joseph Blumenthal, *Art of the Printed Book, 1455–1955*. New York: Pierpont Morgan Library; Boston: Godine, 1978. First published 1973

Book Typography, 1815–1965, ed. Kenneth Day, London: Ernest Benn, 1966. Translation of *Anderhalve eeuw boektypografie, 1815–1965: in Amerika, Engeland, Frankrijk, Duitsland, Zwitserland, Italië, België en Nederland*, 1965.

Robert Bringhurst, *The Elements of Typographic Style*, 3rd ed. Point Roberts, WA: Hartley & Marks, 2004. First published 1992

John Carter & Percy H. Muir (eds), *Printing and the Mind of Man*, 2nd rev. ed. Munich: Pressler, 1983. First published 1967

Severin Corsten (ed.), *Lexikon des gesamten Buchwesens: LGB 2*, 2nd ed. Stuttgart: Hiersemann, 1985

Patrick Cramsie, *The Story of Graphic Design: from the Invention of Writing to the Birth of Digital Design*. London: British Library, 2010

Robert Darnton, *The Case for Books: Past, Present, and Future*. New York: PublicAffairs, 2009

Johanna Drucker & Emily McVarish, *Graphic Design History: A Critical Guide*. Upper Saddle River, NJ: Pearson/Prentice Hall, 2009

Lucien Febvre & Henri-Jean Martin, *The Coming of the Book: The Impact of Printing 1450–1800*. London: Verso, 2010. Translation of *L'apparition du livre*, 1958

Pascal Fouché, Daniel Péchoin, Philippe Schuwer (eds), *Dictionnaire encyclopédique du livre*. Paris: Éditions du Cercle de la Librairie, 2002–11. 4 vols

Bamber Gascoigne, *Milestones in Colour Printing 1457–1859*. Cambridge: Cambridge University Press, 1997

Philip Gaskell, *A New Introduction to Bibliography*. New Castle, DE: Oak Knoll Press, 2007. First published 1972

E. P. Goldschmidt, *The Printed Book of the Renaissance: Three Lectures on Type, Illustration, Ornament*, 2nd rev. ed. Amsterdam: Van Heusden, 1966. First published 1950

John Harthan, *The History of the Illustrated Book: The Western Tradition*. London: Thames & Hudson, 1997. First published 1981

Wytze Gerbens Hellinga, *Copy and Print in the Netherlands*. Amsterdam: Federatie der werkgeversorganisatiën in het boekdrukkersbedrijf, 1962 (= 1963). 2 vols. Translation of *Kopij en druk in de Nederlanden*, 1962

Jost Hochuli & Robin Kinross, *Designing Books: Practice and Theory*. London: Hyphen Press, 2003. First published 1996

Nicole Howard, *The Book: The Life Story of a Technology*. Baltimore: John Hopkins University Press, 2009. First published 2005

Frans A. Janssen, *Technique and Design in the History of Printing*. 't Goy-Houten: Hes & De Graaf, 2004

Marion Janzin & Joachim Güntner, *Das Buch vom Buch: 5000 Jahre Buchgeschichte*, 3rd rev. ed. Hanover: Schlütersche, 2007. First published 1995

A. F. Johnson, *Selected Essays on Books and Printing*; ed. Percy H. Muir. Amsterdam: Van Gendt & Co.; London: Routledge & Kegan Paul; New York: Abner Schram, 1970

Roxane Jubert, *Typography and Graphic Design: From Antiquity to the Present*. Paris: Flammarion, 2006. Translation of *Graphisme, typographie, histoire*, 2005

Norma Levarie, *The Art & History of Books*. New Castle, DE: Oak Knoll Press; London: British Library, 1995. First published 1968

Mathieu Lommen (ed.), *Bijzondere collecties naar een nieuwe bibliotheek*. Zwolle: Waanders, 2007

Martin Lyons, *Books: A Living History*. London: Thames & Hudson, 2011

D. F. McKenzie, David McKitterick, I. R. Willison (eds), *The Cambridge History of the Book in Britain*. Cambridge: Cambridge University Press, 1999

Henri-Jean Martin, *La naissance du livre moderne, XIVe–XVIIe siècles: mise en page et mise en texte du livre français*. Paris: Éditions du Cercle de la Librairie, 2000

Philip B. Meggs & Alston W. Purvis, *Meggs' History of Graphic Design*, 5th ed. Hoboken, NJ: John Wiley & Sons, 2011. First published 1983

Alain Mercier (ed.), *Les trois révolutions du livre*. Paris: Musée des Arts et Métiers; Paris: Imprimerie Nationale Éditions, 2002. Exhibition catalogue

Stanley Morison, *The Typographic Book, 1450–1935*; with material by Kenneth Day. London: Ernest Benn, 1963. First published as *Four Centuries of Fine Printing*, 1924

Robin Myers & Michael Harris (eds), *A Millennium of the Book: Production, Design & Illustration in Manuscript & Print, 900–1900*. Winchester: St Paul's Bibliographies; New Castle, DE: Oak Knoll Press, 1994. Conference collection

Martin Parr & Gerry Badger, *The Photobook: A History*. London: Phaidon, 2004–6. 2 vols

S. H. Steinberg, *Five Hundred Years of Printing*; ed. John Trevitt, rev. ed. London: British Library; New Castle, DE: Oak Knoll Press, 1996. First published 1955

Michael F. Suarez & H. R. Woudhuysen (eds), *The Oxford Companion to the Book*. Oxford: Oxford University Press, 2010. 2 vols

Michael Twyman, *The British Library Guide to Printing: History and Techniques*. London: British Library, 1998

Michael Twyman, *Printing 1770–1970: An Illustrated History of its Development and Uses in England*. London: British Library; New Castle, DE: Oak Knoll Press, 1998. First published 1970

Hans Peter Willberg & Friedrich Forssman, *Lesetypografie*, 5th ed. Mainz: Hermann Schmidt, 2010. First published 1997

General: type & lettering

David P. Becker, *The Practice of Letters: the Hofer Collection of Writing Manuals, 1514–1800*. Cambridge, MA: Harvard College Library, 1997

Max Caflisch, *Schriftanalysen: Untersuchungen zur Geschichte typographischer Schriften*. St Gallen: Typotron, 2003. 2 vols

Harry Carter, *A View of Early Typography Up to About 1600*; ed. James Mosley. London: Hyphen Press, 2002. First published 1969

A. F. Johnson, *Type Designs: Their History and Development*, 3rd rev. ed. London: André Deutsch, 1966. First published 1934

Cees W. de Jong (ed.), *Type: A Visual History of Typefaces and Graphic Styles*. Cologne: Taschen, 2009–10. 2 vols

John A. Lane, *Early Type Specimens in the Plantin-Moretus Museum*. New Castle, DE: Oak Knoll Press; London: British Library, 2004

Stanley Morison, *Selected Essays on the History of Letter-forms in Manuscript and Print*; ed. David McKitterick. Cambridge: Cambridge University Press, 1980–81. 2 vols

James Sutton & Alan Bartram, *An Atlas of Typeforms*. London: Lund Humphries, 1968

Walter Tracy, *Letters of Credit: A View of Type Design*. London: Gordon Fraser, 1986

Daniel Berkeley Updike, *Printing Types: Their History, Forms, and Use*, 4th ed. New Castle, DE: Oak Knoll Press; London: British Library, 2001. First published 1922

Fifteenth century

Curt F. Bühler, *The Fifteenth-Century Book: The Scribes, the Printers, the Decorators*. Philadelphia: University of Pennsylvania Press, 1960

Martin Davies, *Aldus Manutius: Printer and Publisher of Renaissance Venice*. London: British Library, 1995

Lotte Hellinga, 'Printing Types and the Printed Word: Considerations Around New Insights into the Beginning of Printing', in *Archiv für Geschichte des Buchwesens*, 57 (2003), pp. 249–65

Kristian Jensen (ed.), *Incunabula and Their Readers: Printing, Selling and Using Books in the Fifteenth Century*. London: British Library, 2003. Conference collection

Martin Lowry, *Nicholas Jenson and the Rise of Venetian Publishing in Renaissance Europe*. Oxford: Blackwell, 1991

Martin Lowry, *The World of Aldus Manutius: Business and Scholarship in Renaissance Venice*. Oxford: Blackwell, 1979

Margaret M. Smith, *The Title-Page: Its Early Development, 1460–1510*. London: British Library; New Castle, DE: Oak Knoll Press, 2000

Adrian Wilson, *The Making of the Nuremberg Chronicle*. Amsterdam: Nico Israel, 1976

Sixteenth century

Ruth Mortimer, *French 16th Century Books*. Cambridge, MA: Belknap Press of Harvard University Press, 1964. 2 vols

Ruth Mortimer, *Italian 16th Century Books*. Cambridge, MA: Belknap Press of Harvard University Press, 1974. 2 vols

James Mosley, 'Giovan Francesco Cresci and the Baroque Letter in Rome', in *Typography Papers*, 6 (2005), pp. 115–55

Fred Schreiber, *The Estiennes: An Annotated Catalogue of 300 Highlights of Their Various Presses*. New York: E.K. Schreiber, 1982

Fred Smeijers, *Counterpunch: Making Type in the Sixteenth Century, Designing Typefaces Now*, 2nd rev. ed. London: Hyphen Press, 2011. First published 1996

Hendrik D.L. Vervliet, *The Palaeotypography of the French Renaissance: Selected Papers on Sixteenth-Century Typefaces*. Leiden: Brill, 2008. 2 vols

Hendrik D. L. Vervliet, *Sixteenth-Century Printing Types of the Low Countries*. Amsterdam: Hertzberger & Co., 1968

Leon Voet, *The Golden Compasses: A History and Evaluation of the Printing and Publishing Activities of the Officina Plantiniana at Antwerp*. Amsterdam: Van Gendt & Co.; London: Routledge & Kegan Paul; New York: Abner Schram, 1969–72. 2 vols

Seventeenth century

Jos Biemans et al., *Papieren pracht uit de Amsterdamse Gouden Eeuw*. Amsterdam: Vossiuspers UvA, 2011

Ton Croiset van Uchelen, *Vive la plume: schrijfmeesters en pennekunst in de Republiek*. Amsterdam: De Buitenkant; Amsterdam: Universiteit van Amsterdam, Universiteitsbibliotheek, 2005

John Dreyfus (ed.), *Type Specimen Facsimiles*; introduction by Stanley Morison. London: Bowes & Bowes Putnam, 1963. (I.) *Reproductions of fifteen type specimen sheets issued between the sixteenth and eighteenth centuries*. Facsimiles

György Haiman, *Nicholas Kis: A Hungarian Punch-Cutter and Printer, 1650–1702*. San Francisco: Stauffacher/Greenwood Press; Budapest: Akadémiai Kiadó, 1983

Peter van der Krogt (ed.), *Joan Blaeu, Atlas maior of 1665*. Cologne: Taschen, 2005; text in English, Dutch and French

Herman de la Fontaine Verwey, 'Gerard Thibault and his *Academie de l'espée*', in *Quærendo*, 8 (1978), pp. 283–319

Henri-Jean Martin, *Print, Power, and People in 17th-Century France*. Metuchen, NJ: Scarecrow Press, 1993. Translation of *Livre, pouvoirs et société à Paris au XVIIe siècle*, 1969

Joseph Moxon, *Mechanick Exercises on the Whole Art of Printing, 1683–4*; eds. Herbert Davis & Harry Carter,

2nd ed. New York: Dover Publications, 1978. Photomechanical reprint of 1962 edition

Eighteenth century

Andreu Balius et al., *Imprenta Real: fuentes de la tipografía española; Imprenta Real: Fonts of Spanish Typography*, 2nd ed. Madrid: Ministerio de Asuntos Exteriores y de Cooperación, AECID, 2010. First published 2009. Exhibition catalogue

G. G. Barber (ed.), *Book Making in Diderot's 'Encyclopédie': A Facsimile Reproduction of Articles and Plates*. Farnborough: Gregg, 1973

Giambattista Bodoni, *Manual of Typography; Manuale tipografico 1818*; ed. Stephan Füssel. Cologne: Taschen, 2010. Facsimile of *Manuale tipografico*, 1818

Angelo Ciavarelli et al., *The 'Cimelio' of Bodoni: The Work and its Printer in Essays*. Verona: Edizioni Valdonega; Boston: Godine, 1991. Facsimile of *Cimelio*, 1811

Pierre-Simon Fournier, *The 'Manuel typographique' of Pierre-Simon Fournier le Jeune: together with Fournier on Typefounding*; ed. James Mosley. Darmstadt: Technische Hochschule Darmstadt, 1995. 3 vols. Facsimile

André Jammes, *Les Didot: trois siècles de typographie et de bibliophilie, 1698–1998*. Paris: Agence culturelle de Paris, 1998. Exhibition catalogue

James Mosley et al., *Le Romain du Roi: la typographie au service de l'état, 1702–2002*. Lyon: Musée de l'imprimerie, 2002

F. E. Pardoe, *John Baskerville of Birmingham: Letter-Founder & Printer*. London: Frederick Muller, 1975

Gerard Unger, 'The Types of François-Ambroise Didot and Pierre-Louis Vafflard: A Further Investigation into the Origins of the Didones', in *Quærendo*, 31 (2001), pp. 165–91

Jeanne Veyrin-Forrer, *La lettre et le texte: trente années de recherches sur l'histoire du livre*. Paris: École Normale Supérieure de Jeunes Filles, 1987

Nineteenth century

Doug Clouse & Angela Voulangas, *The Handy Book of Artistic Printing*. New York: Princeton Architectural Press, 2009

Nicolete Gray, *Nineteenth Century Ornamented Typefaces; with a chapter on Ornamented Types in America by Ray Nash*. London: Faber & Faber, 1976. First published 1938

Ruari McLean, *Victorian Book Design and Colour Printing*, 2nd rev. ed. London: Faber & Faber, 1972. First published 1963

William Morris, *The Ideal Book: Essays and Lectures on the Arts of the Book*; ed. William S. Peterson. Berkeley, CA: University of California Press, 1982

James Mosley, *The Nymph and the Grot: The Revival of the Sanserif Letter*. London: Friends of the St Bride Printing Library, 1999. First published 1965

Dag-Ernst Petersen (ed.), *Gebunden in der Dampfbuchbinderei: Buchbinden im Wandel des 19. Jahrhunderts*. Wiesbaden: Harrassowitz, 1994; *Wolfenbütteler Schriften zur Geschichte des Buchwesens*, no. 20

Louis John Pouchée, *Ornamented Types: Twenty-Three Alphabets from the Foundry of Louis John Pouchée*; introduction by James Mosley. London: I.M. Imprimit in association with St Bride Printing Library, 1993. 2 vols

Michael Twyman, *Breaking the Mould: The First Hundred Years of Lithography*. London: British Library, 2001

Walter Wilkes, Frieder Schmidt & Eva-Maria Hanebutt-Benz, *Die Buchkultur im 19. Jahrhundert*. Hamburg: Maximilian-Gesellschaft, 2010. Vol. 1: *Technische Grundlagen*

Twentieth and twenty-first centuries

Jaroslav Andel, *Avant-Garde Page Design, 1900–1950*. New York: Delano Greenidge Editions, 2002; text in English, French and German

Helen Armstrong (ed.), *Graphic Design Theory: Readings from the Field*. New York: Princeton Architectural Press, 2009

Jeremy Aynsley, *Graphic Design in Germany 1890–1945*. London: Thames & Hudson, 2000

Nicolas Barker, *Stanley Morison*. London: Macmillan, 1972

Philipp Bertheau, *Buchdruckschriften im 20. Jahrhundert*. Darmstadt: Technische Hochschule Darmstadt, 1995

Yvonne Brentjens, *Piet Zwart, 1885–1977: vormingenieur*. Zwolle: Waanders; The Hague: Gemeentemuseum Den Haag, 2008

Kees Broos & Paul Hefting, *Dutch Graphic Design*, London: Phaidon, 1993; Translation of *Grafische vormgeving in Nederland: een eeuw*, 1993

Ute Brüning (ed.), *Das A und O des Bauhauses: Bauhauswerbung: Schriftbilder, Drucksachen, Ausstellungsdesign*. Leipzig: Edition Leipzig, 1995

Christopher Burke, *Active Literature: Jan Tschichold and New Typography*. London: Hyphen Press, 2007

Sebastian Carter, *Twentieth Century Type Designers*, new ed. London: Lund Humphries, 1995. First published 1987

Roderick Cave, *The Private Press*, 2nd rev. ed. New York: Bowker, 1983. First published 1971

Theodore Low De Vinne, *The Practice of Typography*. New York: Century Co., 1900–4. 4 vols. (1. *A Treatise on the Processes of Type-Making* etc., 1900; 2. *Correct Composition* etc., 1901; 3. *A Treatise on Title-Pages* etc., 1902. 4. *Modern Methods of Book Composition* etc., 1904)

John Dreyfus, *Into Print: Selected Writings on Printing History, Typography and Book Production*. London: British Library, 1994

Stephen J. Eskilson, *Graphic Design: A New History*. New Haven, CT: Yale University Press, 2007

Roger Fawcett-Tang, *New Book Design*. London: Laurence King, 2004

Friedrich Friedl et al., *Die vollkommene Lesemaschine: von deutscher Buchgestaltung im 20. Jahrhundert*. Frankfurt am Main: Stiftung Buchkunst, 1997

Mildred Friedman & Phil Freshman (eds), *Graphic Design in America: A Visual Language History*. Minneapolis, MN: Walker Art Center; New York: Abrams, 1989

Karl Gerstner & Markus Kutter, *Die neue Graphik; The New Graphic Art; Le nouvel art graphique*. Teufen: Niggli, 1959

Jason Godfrey, *Bibliographic: 100 Classic Graphic Design Books*. London: Laurence King, 2009

Steven Heller & Georgette Balance, *Graphic Design History*. New York: Allworth Press, 2001

Richard Hollis, *Graphic Design: A Concise History*, rev. ed. London: Thames & Hudson, 2001. First published 1994

Richard Hollis, *Swiss Graphic Design: The Origins and Growth of an International Style: 1920–1965*. London: Laurence King, 2006

Jürgen Holstein, *Blickfang: Bucheinbände und Schutzumschläge Berliner Verlage 1919–1933*. Berlin: Jürgen Holstein, 2005

Albert Kapr & Walter Schiller, *Gestalt und Funktion der Typografie*, 2nd ed. Leipzig: Fachbuchverlag, 1980 (= 1981). First published 1977

Robin Kinross, *Modern Typography: An Essay in Critical History*, 2nd ed., London: Hyphen Press, 2010. First published 1992

Ellen Lupton & J. Abbott Miller, *Design, Writing, Research: Writing on Graphic Design*. London: Phaidon, 2004. First published 1996

Vladimir Mayakovsky, *For the Voice*; book constructor El Lissitzky. London: British Library, 2000. 3 vols. Facsimile of *Dlja golosa*, 1923

Rick Poynor, *No More Rules: Graphic Design and Postmodernism*. London: Laurence King, 2003

Margit Rowell & Deborah Wye, *The Russian Avant-Garde Book: 1910–1934*. New York: Museum of Modern Art, 2002

Georg Kurt Schauer, *Deutsche Buchkunst, 1890 bis 1960*. Hamburg: Maximilian-Gesellschaft, 1963. 2 vols

Jan Tschichold, *Die neue Typographie: ein Handbuch für zeitgemäss Schaffende*. Berlin: Verlag des Bildungsverbandes der Deutschen Buchdrucker, 1928. (Facsimiles: *Die neue Typographie*, 1987; *The New Typography*, 1995)

Rudy VanderLans (ed.), *Emigre no. 70: The Look Back Issue: Selections from Emigre Magazine 1–69, 1984–2009*. Berkeley, CA: Gingko Press, 2009

Michel Wlassikoff, *The Story of Graphic Design in France*. Corte Madera, CA: Gingko Press, 2005. Translation of *Histoire du graphisme en France*, 2005

Laetitia Wolff, *Massin*. London: Phaidon, 2007

Index

The index covers punchcutters, typefounders, typefaces, type and book designers, craftsmen, artists, printers, publishers and some related subjects.

Concept
Special Collections, University of Amsterdam, Mathieu Lommen & VK Projects, Cees W. de Jong

Compiling & editing
Mathieu Lommen

Text
Mathieu Lommen, John A. Lane, Frans A. Janssen, Adriaan Plak, Paul Dijstelberge, Johan de Zoete, Jan Werner, Lesley Monfils

Type notes
John A. Lane, Mathieu Lommen

Editorial board
Frans A. Janssen, Cees W. de Jong, John A. Lane, Adriaan Plak

Photography
Stephan van der Linden, Photo Services Special Collections, University of Amsterdam

Design & layout
Cees W. de Jong VK Projects, Naarden Vesting
In collaboration with Asher Hazelaar, Puls, Ermelo

Translation
Textcase, Utrecht; John A. Lane, Leiden
Translation for Textcase: Marianne Kalsbeek

Bookbindings from the hand-press period, which ends in around 1830, are shown in small reproductions. These bindings – not always in good condition – are usually not publishers' bindings, but were made on commission by private owners, often long after the date of printing.

The type details are not reproduced at actual size.

With thanks to:
Constance van den Hil; Ellen Borger; Ton Bruins; Steph Scholten; Garrelt Verhoeven; Falk Eisermann, Staatsbibliothek Berlin; Claus Maywald, Gutenberg Museum Mainz; Stefan Menningh; Sander Pinkse; Suhrkamp Verlag Berlin; Hans Oldewarris, Uitgeverij 010, Rotterdam.

premsela .org/ | The Netherlands Institute for Design and Fashion

Nederlands letterenfonds dutch foundation for literature

VK Projects gratefully acknowledge the support of the Dutch Foundation for Literature.